French Hotels & Restaurants

THE ROUGH GUIDE

Rough Guides and France

In addition to this guide, Rough Guides
publish eight guidebooks on France:

**France • Brittany & Normandy • Corsica
The Dordogne & Lot • Languedoc & Roussillon
Provence & the Côte d'Azur • Paris
The Pyrenees** (French and Spanish)

There is also a
Rough Guide French phrasebook

CREDITS

Rough Guides
Managing editor: Jonathan Buckley
Series editor: Mark Ellingham
Text editors: Vanessa Dowell, Ann-Marie Shaw
Production: Susanne Hillen, Maxine Repath, Julia Bovis, Michelle Draycott,
    Ed Wright, Katie Lloyd-Jones
Design: Henry Iles

Routard
Directeur de collection: Philippe Gloaguen
Rédacteur: Amanda Keraval

Acknowledgements
Thanks to Monique Lantelme, Amanda Keraval, and all those at Lexus who
worked on the first edition: Jane Goldie, Céline Reynaud, Peter Terrell, Sophie
Curien, Alice Grandison, Leslie Harkins, Sarah Cartwright, David Alun Jones,
Anita Leyerzapf

This translation © The Rough Guides Ltd
848pp, includes index
A catalogue record for this book is available from the British Library.
ISBN 1-85828-689-1

Distributed by the Penguin Group:
Penguin Books Ltd, 27 Wrights Lane, London W8 5TZ
Penguin Books USA Inc., 375 Hudson Street, New York 10014, USA
Penguin Books Australia Ltd, 487 Maroondah Highway, PO Box 257, Ringwood, Victoria 3134,
    Australia
Penguin Books Canada Ltd, 10 Alcorn Avenue, Toronto, Ontario, Canada M4V 1E4
Penguin Books (NZ) Ltd, 182–190 Wairau Road, Auckland 10, New Zealand

Printed in England by Clays Ltd, St Ives PLC

French Hotels & Restaurants

THE ROUGH GUIDE
Le guide du ROUTARD

ENGLISH EDITION
2001

LE GUIDE DU ROUTARD
EDITOR: PHILIPPE GLOAGUEN

Translated by
Vanessa Dowell and Lexus

ROUGH
GUIDES

Contents

CONTENTS

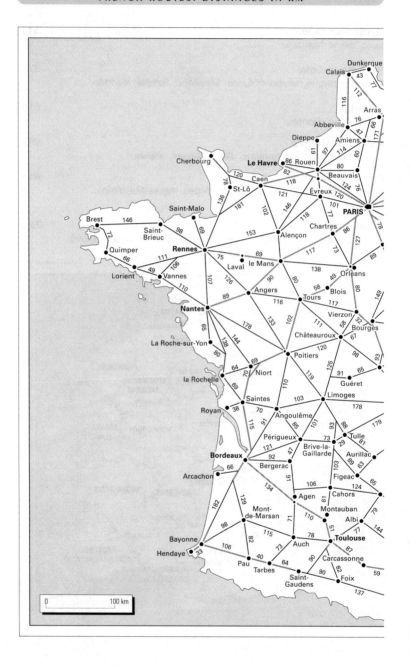

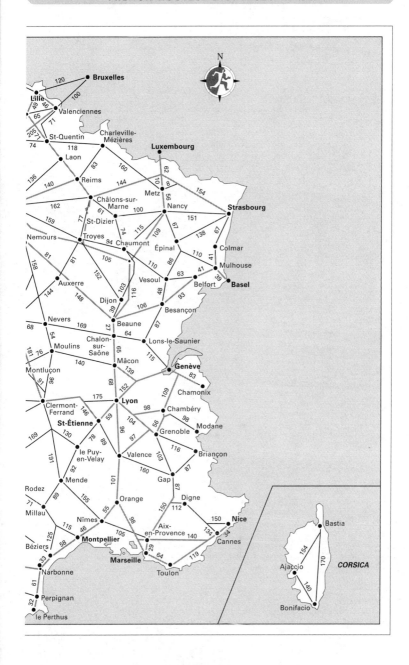

Abouт тHis book

This is the fourth edition of the **Rough Guide to French Hotels & Restaurants**, a translation of the Routard guide, the best-selling French guide to good-value restaurants and accommodation in France. Revised every year, *French Hotels & Restaurants* is up-to-date, comprehensive and opens up the country in a way that no other guide does. Its critical listings include everything from simple hostels and family-run bistros to high-comfort rural retreats and city-centre three-stars. all selected are reviewed by Routard's team of locally based writers, who re-assess the entries for each edition.

The hotels and restaurants selected tend to be small, independent establishments – look out for the Routard stickers on their front doors. There may also be a *Logis de France* sticker, too – a fireplace symbol with one, two or three fires, to indicate the level of facilities provided. This denotes membership to a scheme that promotes family-run hotels, often in rural locations well away from major towns.

The guide's layout
The Routard/Rough Guide is divided into twenty-two **chapter regions**, each with a map identifying the places where a hotel or restaurant is listed. The regions are listed alphabetically and within each chapter the **main towns** are listed in alphabetical order, their names appearing in a dark box that also shows the post code, eg:

QUIBERON   57170

Small towns and villages within a radius of 30km of a larger town are included under the entries for that town; these places are listed in the order of their distance from the main town, and their names are shown in a light box, eg:

LEVERNOIS   21200 (4KM SE)

Within each town entry **hotels** are listed first, followed by **restaurants**, and both are listed in

ascending order of price. Stars indicated are the official ratings of the French hotel industry and not of this guide.

After the address of the establishments, tips are given on how to get there wherever possible, plus phone number, fax number, e-mail address, closing times and a summary of facilities.

Symbols
The following symbols have been used:
♠	hotel
|●|	restaurant
🎄	discount

The **discount symbol** indicates that an establishment offers some sort of benefit to readers of this guide. In the case of hotels, it is usually a discount (generally 10%) on the price of the room. You are usually obliged to stay for a minimum of two nights to qualify. The benefit can be offered during certain periods of the year only. Where possible these conditions have been indicated in the text. In some instances, the concession consists of a free breakfast or free garage space; many restaurants in this guide offer a free coffee, house apéritif or house digestif, but you qualify only when you order a complete meal and, more often than not, the choice of drink will not be up to you. All establishments will insist that you are entitled to the benefit only if you are carrying the current year's edition of this guide book. In all cases, show your copy of this guide book when you check in at the hotel or before you order your meal in a restaurant. French hotels and restaurants are familiar with the Routard guide, but should you have any difficulties claiming the benefits with this translation, point to the front cover where the Routard name is clearly identified.

The Euro
On 1 January 1999, France became one of eleven countries to adopt the **Euro**, the European single currency, identified by the symbol

€. Euro coins and notes are not in circulation yet but will be phased in by the beginning of 2002; until then the Franc remains legal tender. Meanwhile, prices will be quoted in both Francs and Euros. 1€ is the equivalent of 6.56 Francs, or 1 Franc is the equivalent of 0.15. Paper transactions can be completed in Euros using either travellers' cheques or credit cards.

The French way

It pays to know what's what in French hotels and restaurants and your basic rights as a consumer.

• When you're reserving a room, by phone or in writing, it's not unusual for the hotel to ask for a **deposit** by way of guarantee. There's no law to say how much this deposit should be, but don't pay any more than around 25–30% of the total. The French have two words for deposit – *arrhes* and *acompte*. The first is refundable, the second is not. So in the event of cancellation your *arrhes* can be returned in full if you give the hotel reasonable notice. If it's the hotel that cancels the booking, then under Article 1590 of the Civil Code (which dates back to 1804) you're entitled to double the amount of the *arrhes* you paid. So if you do make a deposit, be very specific in your letter as to whether it's *arrhes* or *acompte*.

• Hotels and restaurants are required by law to **display their prices**. You won't get anywhere arguing about extortionate prices if they're clearly marked on a price list. The cheapest set meals are often served at lunchtimes or weekdays only. This should be clearly marked on the board outside.

• Hotels are **not permitted to try to sell you something you haven't requested**; for example they can't force you to book for several nights if you only want to stay for one. Similarly, they can't insist you have breakfast or any other meal at the hotel unless it's clearly stated that **half-board** or **full board** is compulsory. Make sure you find this out before you book into a hotel with a restaurant, and bear in mind that half-board prices often apply to a minimum stay of three nights. This is permitted by law.

• In restaurants the cheapest **set meals** are often served at lunchtimes on weekdays only. This should be clearly marked on the board outside. The same menu may cost more at night.

• **Wine lists** aren't always very clear so be sure that you know precisely what you order. For example, you may order a bottle of Burgundy at 50F and be charged 100F; when you check the list again, you find (maybe in small print) that the price was for a half bottle. A bottle of wine must be opened in front of the customer – otherwise you've no way of knowing that you're getting what you ordered. A jug of tap water is free as long as you're ordering a meal.

• Occasionally restaurants **refuse to serve** customers if they feel they haven't ordered enough. No-one can force you into ordering something you don't want and refusing to serve you is technically against the law.

Alsace

67 Bas-Rhin

68 Haut-Rhin

ALTKIRCH 68130

🕭 ⚑ |●| AUBERGE SUNDGOVIENNE**

1 route de Belfort (West).
☎ 03.89.40.97.18 ➡ 03.89.40.67.73
e aubsu@lemel.fr
Closed Mon, Tues lunchtime, Sun evening in winter and 23 Dec to Jan. **TV. Disabled access. Garden. Lock-up garage.**

A mix of an American motel (it's near the road), a Swiss chalet (Switzerland isn't far away) and a traditional Alsace hotel. All rooms, which cost from 280–330F, are pretty, clean and comfortable, and some have a balcony. The cooking is a pleasant surprise. It's inspired by the fresh produce in the market and shows plenty of imagination: salmon with leeks and Riesling, sole fillet with purple-tipped asparagus and a sauce of Tokay Pinot, and so on. There is a three-course set menu at 70F – not available for Saturday dinner or on Sunday – and others at 160–260F. Half board 240F and full board 360F. The terrace is a great place to sit with a drink, admiring the Sundgau countryside. 10% discount on the room rate.

HIRTZBACH 68118 (4KM S)

🕭 ⚑ |●| OTTIÉ

17 rue de-Lattre-de-Tassigny; it's just as you come into the village, heading towards Ferrette and Hirsingue.
☎ 03.89.40.93.22 ➡ 03.89.08.85.19
e ottierest@aol.com
Closed Mon evening, Tues, a fortnight in June–July, and 25 Dec–6 Jan. **Garden. Car park.**

This lovely little blue inn is set in the heart of Sundgau, though it's by the road. Simple, well-maintained rooms and the ones with garden view are quiet. Doubles with washing facilities 150F, with shower 160F, and with bath 200F. Half board 196–240F. The food is unusual – try the *terrine* of artichokes and *foie gras* or the dandelion salad. There's a weekday lunch menu at 58F, then others 89–215F. The chef has worked in some of Alsace's better kitchens so the cooking has personality: bream with wine and ginger, *fricassée* of kidneys and sweetbreads with caramelised pears. Nice terrace. Free glass of bubbly with your evening meal when you stay overnight.

GOMMERSDORF 68210 (12KM W)

🕭 ⚑ |●| L'AUBERGE DU TISSERAND**

28 rue de Cernay; it's on the D103 as you leave the village.
☎ 03.89.07.21.80/03.89.07.26.26 ➡ 03.89.25.11.34
Closed Mon, Tues, a week at New Year and the second fortnight in Feb. **TV. Car park.**

This is a typical Alsace inn with a long history. Parts date from the 17th century when it was a weaver's house, and other parts are even older. On the first floor, reserved for smokers, the wooden floor has buckled with age. Good cooking and enormous portions at reasonable prices. The weekday lunch menu, 48F, is one of the cheapest around; other menus are 80–180F. They offer Alsace specialities, bake their own bread and serve flambéed tarts every night. A really delightful place with a few rooms for 270–300F with shower/wc. Breakfast 35F. 10% discount on the room rate. Free coffee, or apéritif and *tarte flambée*.

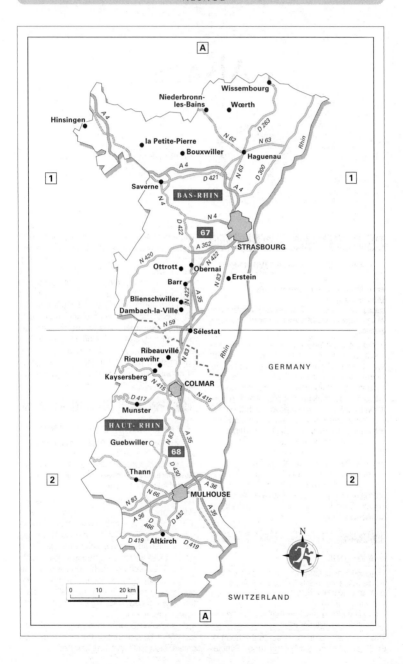

BARR 67140

🕈 🛏 |❂| HÔTEL MAISON ROUGE**

1 av. de la Gare (South); it's near the post office.
☎ 03.88.08.90.40 ➡ 03.88.08.90.85
e maisonrouge@wanadoo.fr
Closed Sun evening, Mon, the Feb school holidays and a fortnight in June/July. **TV**. **Car park**.

This place is far enough away from the centre not to attract too many tourists and the area has been well renovated; there's a square, planted with trees, and a pedestrian area in front of the hotel. In the restaurant, which has been completely refurbished, set menus start at 98F. Alsace specialities include fillet of salmon with *choucroute,* chicken in Riesling sauce and flambéed kidneys. Good choice of beers. Pleasant rooms 250–320F with en-suite bath. Breakfast 45F. Free apéritif if you dine in.

HEILIGENSTEIN 67140 (1.5KM N)

🕈 🛏 |❂| RELAIS DU KLEVENER**

51 rue Principale.
☎ 03.88.08.05.98 ➡ 03.88.08.40.83
Closed Mon, Tues lunchtime and 1 Jan–15 Feb. **TV**. **Disabled access**. **Garden**. **Car park**.

This inn has wonderful views over the vineyards and the Rhine from some of the rooms. Doubles are at 230–270F; number 30 has been specially modified for disabled access. There's a brasserie and a separate restaurant. Generous set menus 98–190F and *à la carte*. Specialities include home-made *foie gras* and *choucroute* made with Klevener wine. The fish is good, too. Half board 250F. Sit out on the terrace and have a glass of Klevener – it's an old grape variety peculiar to Heiligenstein and pretty rare elsewhere in Alsace. Free house apéritif.

ANDLAU 67140 (4KM SW)

🛏 |❂| LE ZINCK HÔTEL

13 rue de la Marne; it's at the bottom of the village.
☎ 03.8808.27.30 ➡ 03.88.08.42.50
Closed Ten days in Feb and ten days in Dec.
TV. **Disabled access**.

Charming hotel in an old restored water-mill. The fourteen comfortable rooms have been tastefully decorated by a designer. They are all different and have names rather than numbers; the Vigneron has a bed with a canopy. Doubles 350–520F. The hall has been beautifully decorated and they have preserved the mill wheel. There's no restau-

rant, but the owner also runs the *Relais de la Poste* which has a good reputation and wine cellar; it's at 1 rue des Forgerons (closed Mon and Tues).

BLIENSCHWLLER 67650

🛏 HÔTEL WINZENBERG**

58 route du Vin; on the N422.
☎ 03.88.92.62.77 ➡ 03.88.92.45.22
Closed 3 Jan–20 Feb. **TV**. **Disabled access**. **Car park nearby**.

The Dresches believe that it's the division of labour that makes their family tick; mother and daughter run the hotel while father and son take charge of the vineyard. They seem to have got it right. The comfortable rooms, with pretty Alsace furniture and brightly coloured bedspreads and curtains, prove good value; doubles cost 265–290F. Mme Dresch is very welcoming; they will show you the family wine cellar, built in 1508, and invite you to taste the wine.

COLMAR 68000

🕈 🛏 HÔTEL COLBERT**

2 rue des Trois-Épis (West); next to the station overlooking the railway tracks.
☎ 03.89.41.31.05 ➡ 03.89.23.66.75
TV. **Pay garage**.

A hotel with no particular charm but the rooms are air-conditioned, comfortable and clean, with double-glazing to keep out the noise. Doubles with bath or shower/wc 220–290F. A small detail that will keep beer drinkers happy: there's a bottle-opener on the wall in the bathroom. The disco-bar, *The Toucan*, is in the hotel basement, so noise levels aren't too bad. 10% discount.

🕈 🛏 |❂| HÔTEL BEAU SÉJOUR**

25 rue du Ladhof (East); it's about 10 minutes from the town centre on foot.
☎ 03.89.41.37.16 ➡ 03.89.41.43.07
Restaurant closed Sat lunchtime and Sun evening out of season. **TV**. **Disabled access**. **Garden**. **Car park**.

This hotel has been run by the Keller family since 1913 and they ran the 18th-century post house that stood here before that. Lots of rooms from 540F and about forty in the annexes, most of which have been renovated with modern facilities, 280–540F. There's a sauna and a gym, a lovely sitting room with blue armchairs, and a little garden with a terrace surrounded by camellias and hydrangeas, with a wisteria clambering over the pergola. Original cooking from an inventive chef. Business lunch on weekdays 75F, with other menus 105–300F. Free parking and 50% reduction on the third night when you stay over the weekend, except on public holidays.

☎ |●| HÔTEL TURENNE

10 route de Bâle (Southeast).
☎ 03.89.41.12.26 ➡ 03.89.41.27.64
TV. Pay car park.

A good little place comprising a collection of buildings with pink, green and cream walls hung with geraniums. The contemporary, functional rooms have been renovated but they're pleasant. The ones over the road are noisier than those at the back. Doubles with bath or shower/wc 340–395F, or there's a winter deal (15 Nov–1 March) for 400–450F for two including breakfast – and the buffet breakfast is generous. Professional, warm welcome. Good value.

|●| LE CAVEAU SAINT-PIERRE

24 rue de la Herse (Centre), Little Venice.
☎ 03.89.41.99.33
Closed Sun evening, Mon, Fri lunchtime, Jan and three weeks in March.

Elegant but affordable, this is undoubtedly the best restaurant in this romantic part of town known as Little Venice. You can only get to it by walking over a wooden footbridge which crosses a charming canal lined with half-timbered houses and beautiful gardens. It's a lovely spot, and when it's sunny, tables are set out by the water. The dining room has lots of alcoves, painted furniture and checked cloths on the tables. The prices are reasonable – set menus 78.50–140F or 140F minimum *à la carte*. Service is polite without being fussy, making you feel relaxed and comfortable. Mouth-watering specialities include oxtail with shallots in Pinot Noir, and beef fillet with a Munster cheese sauce, not to mention the salad *vosgienne*. They make *baeckeoffe*, a stew of beef, mutton and pork marinated in local wine, every Saturday and Sunday in winter.

🎍 |●| RESTAURANT GARBO

15 rue Berthe-Molly; it's in the centre.
☎ 03.89.24.48.55 ➡ 03.89.24.48.55
Closed Sat lunchtime Sun, 1–18 Jan, 5–15 Aug and public holidays.

This restaurant, dedicated to the great Greta Garbo, is in one of the town's old streets

that's lined with private mansions. The huge dining room is part bistro, part gastronomic restaurant and offers good regional cuisine – dishes change with the seasons. Specialities include duck *foie gras* terrine with Gewurztraminer, zander fillet with lavender, and cold beer *sabayon*. The hushed atmosphere makes it ideal for a romantic dinner. Free apéritif.

|●| LE PETIT GOURMAND

9 quai de la Poissonnerie; riverside in Little Venice.
☎ 03.89.41.09.32
Closed Mon evening and Tues out of season, a fortnight in Nov and a fortnight in Jan.

This pretty little restaurant, in the heart of the Little Venice district, only seats fourteen, though there's outdoor seating on the waterside terrace in summer. The decor is low-key, with just a few photos of old Colmar on the white walls. The owner makes a nice fuss of you. Large portions of tasty regional fare, like the extremely tasty *tartiflettes* of Munster cheese with salad and smoked pork, for a modest price (set menus from 105F). If you're struck by the quality of the *baeckeoffe* (a beef, mutton and pork stew), it's because the meat is left to marinate for three days. A real treat.

|●| WINSTUB BRENNER

1 rue de Turenne; it's just beside Little Venice.
☎ 03.89.41.42.33 ➡ 03.89.41.37.99
Closed Tues, Wed, third week in Feb, 13–30 Nov and 23–31 Dec.

Gilbert Brenner, is a real character. He's small, stocky and rosy-cheeked and loves life – and it shows. He does the cooking and the serving, helped by his wife, who always manages to laugh at his jokes. They keep things simple here, with hearty dishes like salad of deep-fried Munster cheese, tripe in Riesling, ham knuckle with potatoes, and *bibalakas* (curd cheese flavoured with horseradish and herbs). Since Gilbert trained as a pastry cook, leave some room for dessert. A meal will cost around 150F. The beer flows well into the small hours and students, regulars, wine-growers and tourists all come to have a good time.

WETTOLSHEIM · 68920 (8KM SW)

☎ |●| HÔTEL AU SOLEIL**

20 rue Sainte-Gertrude; it's on the D17.
☎ 03.89.80.62.66 ➡ 03.89.79.84.45
Closed Thurs, three weeks from mid-June, and 20 Dec–7 Jan. **TV. Garden. Car park.**

Run by a young couple, this is a great little

place just outside Colmar in a tiny, little-known village on the *route des vins*. A good choice if you want to be near but not actually in the town, and, unlike many other hotels in the vineyards, reasonably priced. Reception is in an old, renovated half-timbered building, but you actually stay in a quiet annexe where rooms look out either onto the hotel car park or across acres of vineyards. Double rooms with shower/wc at 245F. There's a short weekday lunch menu at 55F. Half board is compulsory in July, Aug and Sept, at 245F per person. Breakfast 38F.

AMMERSCHWIHR 68770 (7KM NW)

♦ |●| L'ARBRE VERT**

7 rue des Cigognes.
☎ 03.89.47.12.23 ➟ 03.89.78.27.21
Hotel closed Mon to 7pm, mid-Feb to end March and the last fortnight in Nov. **Restaurant closed** Mon evening and Tues except for hotel guests. **TV**.

This is a large, pleasant, post-war building. Both the management and the chef are professionals, and it shows. There are a few good specialities on the menu, like **escalope** of goose liver in Pinot Noir and roast rack of lamb with garlic crust, and the *croustillant* of salmon with leeks is a real treat. Set menus 80–250F. Children's menu 45F. It's a good place if you're looking for gourmet food, and the establishment is quite chic. Rooms are brand new and cost 230F with washing facilities or 330–360F a night for a double bed with bath or shower/wc, telephone and mini-bar. Half board is compulsory in season and starts at 290F in season.

NIEDERMORSCHWIHR 68230 (10KM W)

|●| RESTAURANT CAVEAU MORAKOPF

7 rue des Trois-Épis (South); N415 and the D11.
☎ 03.89.27.05.10 ➟ 03.89.27.08.63
Closed Sun and lunchtimes, a fortnight in Jan, and June. **Disabled access**. **Garden**.

This big green and pink house can be found in a village tucked away in the vineyards. There is a glorious garden in the summer. The restaurant is all wood and comfortable benches and the window panes have been decorated with a "Morakopf" (the same moorish head that adorn T-shirts in Corsica). The food is meticulously prepared and served in generous portions. Excellent home-made *presskopf* (brawn) and *baeckeoffe*, layers of different meats and potatoes marinated for twelve hours (for four people minimum and to order in advance). Specialities include

trout in Riesling, and their duck *confit* on *choucroute* is not to be missed. Good local wines. Attentive, friendly service and unpretentious decor. Expect to pay about 130F for a meal.

TROIS ÉPIS (LES) 68410 (10KM W)

⚘ ♦ |●| HÔTEL-RESTAURANT VILLA ROSA**

4 rue Thierry-Schoéré, on the Turckheim road; it's about 400m from the village.
☎ 03.89.49.81.19 ➟ 03.89.78.90.45
e hotel-restaurant-villa-rosa@wanadoo.fr
Closed Mon, Thurs and 3 Jan–19 March. **Swimming pool**. **Garden**.

A gorgeous house with green shutters run by a lovely couple who really make their guests feel at home. The rooms are delightful – ask for one with a view of the garden and swimming pool. Doubles with shower/wc or bath 300–340F. Half board is compulsory in season at 300F per person. The restaurant serves evening meals only, with a menu at 120F. Produce comes from the garden or local growers, and the cooking has an engaging personal touch. They run all sorts of courses, including cookery and wild food painting. Free apéritif.

ERSTEIN 67150

⚘ ♦ |●| HÔTEL ET L'ESTAMINET DES BORDS DE L'ILL**

94 rue du Général-de-Gaulle (Centre) near the Centre Nautique.
☎ 03.88.98.03.70 ➟ 03.88.98.09.49
TV. **Disabled access**. **Garden**. **Car park**.

You get a lovely welcome in this hotel that's beautifully situated near the banks of the Ill river and has been refurbished in typical Alsace style. Doubles with shower or bath at 310F. The owners make every effort to serve local produce and preserve traditional, local recipes in the restaurant across the road, which has a terrace by the water. Set menus to suit all budgets: 44F (lunchtimes only) and a *menu terroir* at 90F. Wonderful wine from Alsace and elsewhere. 10% discount on the room rate.

HAGUENAU 67500

|●| RESTAURANT AU TIGRE

4 pl. d'Armes (Centre); it's in the pedestrian precinct.
☎ 03.88.93.93.79

The handsome dining room has high ceilings, wood panelling and lots of wrought iron. This is a classic brasserie serving typical fare; seafood platters in winter, kebabs and salad in summer and more exotic things like ostrich and kangaroo steak. Set menus 98F and 135F. When the sun comes out, they open a large terrace where they serve grills.

🎋 |O| S'BUEREHIESEL-CHEZ MONIQUE

13 rue Meyer; it's next to the theatre.
☎ 03.88.93.30.90 ➡ 03.88.06.13.22
Closed Sun, Mon, last week in May, first fortnight in Sept and Christmas to New Year.

A *winstub*, a typical Alsatian wine tavern, serving only wine from the region (as opposed to a *bierstub*, which serves beer). All the stars from the nearby theatre come here, and their photos, with beaming smiles and red eyes from the flash, smother the walls in the main dining room. Weekday lunch menu 47F or around 130F *à la carte*. They concentrate on regional dishes including *choucroute*, of course, braised knuckle of pork in a local Munster cheese sauce, *quenelles* of liver, house *spaetzle* (a type of noodle), and snails *à l'alsacienne* cooked in local wine. Friendly welcome and warm, pleasant surroundings. Free coffee.

SCHWEIGHOUSE-SUR-MODER   67590 (3KM SW)

|O| AUX BERGES DE LA MODER

8 rue de la Gare.
☎ 03.88.72.01.09 ➡ 03.88.72.63.16
Closed Wed evening, a fortnight at All Saints' and three weeks in March.

The view over the industrial park is not beautiful but the two dining rooms are typical Alsace, with a lovely dresser, tiled floor, vermillion walls and decorated beams. Ahmed gives you a warm Mediterranean welcome. The specialities – fish, game and rhubarb strudel – are quite delicious. Lunch menu of the day is 44F, or 100–120F *à la carte* for dinner. A place to enjoy.

KALTENHOUSE   67240 (5KM SE)

🚱 |O| LA CRÉMAILLÈRE (CHEZ KRAE-MER)

32 rue Principale (Centre).
☎ 03.88.63.23.06 ➡ 03.88.63.67.48
Closed Friday evening, Saturday lunchtime and Aug.
TV. Car park.

An inn that's also the village bistro, located only 5km from the frontier. Locals, pensioners

and passing travellers create a convivial atmosphere. It's a family-run place and, at 86, Marthe Kraemer still keeps a watchful eye over proceedings while her grandson cooks up tasty dishes. Dish of the day 40F, menus 65–150F. Doubles at 280F have good facilities, though they're slightly gloomy. Best to avoid the ones overlooking the road.

HINSINGEN   67260

|O| LA GRANGE DU PAYSAN

8 rue Principale.
☎ 03.88.00.91.83
Closed Mon.

This little restaurant, 500m from the border with Lorraine, is something of a local institution – it's the place with the blue French electricity board vans and sales reps' cars parked outside. They always know where to come. Considering the size of the place it probably belonged to a pretty well-off farmer, and today has conventional rustic decor. You'll get an excellent welcome from the professional staff and the service is particularly efficient. They prepare the steak *tartare* in full view of the customer – something of a spectacle. Country-style food served in hearty portions that fill you up – everyone always looks really satisfied, which speaks well for the consistent quality: home-made black pudding with sautéed apples and home-grown horseradish (delicious), chargrilled suckling pig, braised ox cheek, ham cooked in a hay box. Good set menus 68–164F.

KAYSERSBERG   68240

|O| AUBERGE DE LA CIGOGNE

73 route de Lapoutroie.
☎ 03.89.47.30.33
Closed Fri, Sun evening, the first fortnight in July and between Christmas and New Year. **Car park**.

A restaurant popular with long-distance lorry drivers and workers from the Lotus paper factory next door. This is the type of roadside establishment where you get a good, hearty meal without forking out a lot of money. Weekday menu 50F and up to 170F. The food ranges from brasserie classics to a few house specialities like fillet of zander, trout in Riesling and *choucroute*. A good place to stop. It has a terrace for outdoor dining.

🎋 |O| RESTAURANT ST-ALEXIS

Lieu-dit Kaysersberg.

☎ 03.89.73.90.38
Closed Fri.

Service noon–8pm. This pretty, converted farmhouse, covered in ivy and hidden away in the forest, is very popular with locals. Inside, there's an appetising smell of soup and *choucroute*. Set menus 65–100F and they are all very filling; good home-made soup, a large, succulent ham omelette and *crudités* are the appetisers, which set you up for a deliciously cooked free-range chicken which has been simmering in the pan for hours. To round it all off, there's a lovely *tarte Alsacienne* (a kind of jam tart). In nice weather you can eat outside. Free coffee.

LAPOUTROIE   68650 (9KM W)

🕭 ☎ |●| L'ORÉE DU BOIS**

6 rue Faudé (South); it's on the N415.
☎ 03.89.47.50.30 ➡ 03.89.47.24.02
Closed Lunchtimes and mid-Nov to mid-Dec. **TV**. **Disabled access**. **Garden**. **Car park**.

To get to the inn, you take a lovely little winding road up the mountain past fields of cows and pine forests. The view is nothing short of superb. The very modern-looking inn, originally a farmhouse and then a holiday camp, is ideal for outdoor types looking for a nice quiet break with plenty of beautiful countryside to walk in. Each room has its own cooking area and a bucolic name; "*Pâturages*" has the best view. 240–260F for a double room or half board costs 245F per person. The food is mostly traditional but not particularly original. Set menus 95–160F. Free apéritif.

☎ |●| HÔTEL-RESTAURANT DU FAUDÉ

28 rue du Général Dupieux (Centre).
☎ 03.89.47.50.35 ➡ 03.89.47.24.82
e hotel-du-faude@monet.fr
Swimming pool. **TV**.

A traditional hotel that has kept up to date. Besides the extremely comfortable rooms, facilities include a covered and heated swimming pool, Jacuzzi, steam room and gym. Double rooms with shower/wc or bath 320–490F. The quality extends to the restaurant where they serve authentic local dishes with a dash of individuality. Try the *Menu Welsh* at 175F which lists *djalaïe* (a local version of brawn), troutlet salad with bacon and cream sauce, and suckling pig Cordon Bleu with Munster cheese. Other menus start at 58F (weekday lunch), and go up to 400F. They also have a menu of the day served in the bar that's a favourite with local workers. Courteous and friendly welcome.

☎ |●| HÔTEL LES ALISIERS

Lieu-dit Faudé; it's 3km out of the village, follow the signs.
☎ 03.89.47.52.82 ➡ 03.89.47.22.38
e hotel.restaurant-lessalisiers@wanadoo.fr
Closed Tues.

Way out in the wilds at an altitude of about 700m, this friendly and unusual little hotel is classified as a "Hôtel au Naturel" by the National Parks administration. It used to be a farm and the old stone sink and bread oven are still visible. There's a stunning view over the valley and the peaks of the Vosges. The bedrooms and the sitting room, with an open fire where they burn whole logs, are charming and cosy. Double rooms 350–450F. Appetising cooking using updated versions of old family recipes; veal kidneys steamed with leeks, and old-style *choucroute*. Menus 89–169F.

MOLSHEIM   67310 (10KM N)

🕭 |●| RESTAURANT LAUTH & FILS

82 rue Principale; it's 6km south of Wasselonne on the D422 then the D255.
☎ 03.89.50.66.05 ➡ 03.88.50.60.76
Closed Mon and Tues lunchtimes, and Christmas to 15 Jan.

The vast dining room used to be a dance hall and is now a popular, relaxed restaurant. Lauth's son has set up a small brewery, and the beer flows freely. The place has the atmosphere of a tavern and the dishes on offer are in appropriate style: *choucroute*, *pot-au-feu*, horse steak with port. If you've got a sweet tooth, keep some room for the flambéed apple tart – a big draw around here – and the iced kirsch soufflé. *À la carte* is around 80F, and there's a children's menu for 31F. The serving staff wear traditional costume. Across the courtyard in the other part of the building there are two guest rooms. Number 104 is furnished in Alsace style with a canopied bed and a mirror on the ceiling. Double with bath 270F. Free beer.

ORBEY   68370 (10KM W)

☎ |●| HÔTEL DE PAIRIS

Lieu-dit Pairis; it's 2km from Orbey on the way to Lac Blanc.
☎ 03.89.70.20.15 ➡ 03.89.71.39.90
Closed Wed and Nov. **Car park**.

An unusual hotel in a super 1900s house run by a delightful German woman. The entrance hall is modish and minimalist, with designer furniture and white everywhere. Lots of natural materials (wood, latex and sisal) have been used in the rooms. Doubles with shower/wc 290–380, with weekly rates available. Sumptuous buffet breakfast, with freshly squeezed fruit juices, *charcuterie* and cheese. Cakes and cappuccino are served at all times. Half board by arrangement (vegetarian menus available). There's a TV room with a wide choice of books and games. A favourite with German visitors.

LE BONOMME   68650 (18KM W)

🏃 🏚 |O| HÔTEL DE LA POSTE**-RESTAURANT LA BÉHIME

48 rue du 3e-Spahi-Algérien; it's next to the post office.
☎ 03.89.47.51.10 |➡ 03.89.47.23.84
✉ hposte@club.internet.fr
Closed Wed out of season, Wed lunchtime in season.
TV. Disabled access. Swimming pool. Car park.

A good inn with really nice rooms, some with a small sitting room. The ones near the road are noisy. Doubles with shower/wc 300–350F. Six rooms have been especially adapted for the disabled. Regional cooking, as you would expect; *spätzle* (local noodles) and house *foie gras* are specialities. Menus 65–220F. The friendly, very professional woman who runs the place will even let you cancel your skiing holiday if there's no snow. 10% discount on the room rate.

MULHOUSE   68100

🏃 🏚 HÔTEL SCHOENBERG*

14 rue Schoenberg (Southwest); it's at right angles to avenue d'Altkirch, behind the station.
☎ 03.89.44.19.41 |➡ 03.89.44.49.80
TV. Garden. Lock-up garage.

A good little hotel with clean, well-kept rooms where you'll sleep soundly. Prices are modest: 145–160F for a double room with basin and 225F with shower/wc. The toilet and the shower are behind a sliding cupboard door. There's a little garden at the back where you can laze in the sun and eat breakfast. 10% discount for a minimum two-night stay, except July–Aug.

🏃 🏚 HÔTEL SAINT-BERNARD**

3 rue des Fleurs (Centre).
☎ 03.89.45.82.32 |➡ 03.89.45.26.32
✉ stber@ertir.net
TV. Car park 300m from hotel.

The *Saint-Bernard* is probably the nicest hotel in Mulhouse and it's run by a guy who's travelled the world. Haïmos, the St Bernard dog

sprawled across the entrance – the inspiration for the hotel's name – will give you a warm welcome. There's a library, an Internet corner and a white bar, where you can put the world to rights under the gaze of General de Gaulle's portrait. The rooms are all impeccable and have high ceilings; number 16 has a hundred-year-old fresco of the four seasons on the ceiling that you could spend the whole day admiring. Doubles with shower or bath 240–280F, prices varying according to size and which floor they're on. Bicycles available free of charge. 10% discount after the third night.

|O| LE PETIT ZINC

15 rue des Bons-Enfants (Centre).
☎ 03.89.46.36.38
Closed Sun, the first fortnight in Aug, and Christmas to New Year's Day.

A chic but cool bar/restaurant that's a gathering place for artists, musicians, writers and mates. There are loads of photos on the wall and a big bar with a huge old calculating machine. Local dishes with unexpected twists: *choucroute* salad with grilled Cerevelas, lentil soup and regional dishes like *haxala* (pork knuckle) or smoked ox tongue. Weekday lunch starter-main course *formule* for 50F or a meal *à la carte* from around 130F.

|O| WINSTUB HENRIETTE

9 rue Henriette (Centre); it's off pl. de la Réunion.
☎ 03.89.46.27.83
Closed Sun.

This wine tavern is named after Henriette, the first girl in the town officially to become a French citizen in 1798. The interior, decorated in typical Alsace style, has seen many years and many gourmets come and go. Classic regional dishes on the menu include *choucroute* at 90F. The chef's specialities include pan-fried *foie gras* with apples or fillet of beef with Munster cheese. At lunchtime, there's a starter-main course *formule* at 60F. The set dinner menu is 85F, while you'll pay about 130F *à la carte*. There's a terrace open in summer. The welcome, food and surroundings are all attractive, and it's a great refuge when it's cold outside, but the service isn't always up to snuff.

SOULTZ   68360 (21KM NW)

🏃|O| RESTAURANT METZGERSTUWA

69 rue du Maréchal-de-Lattre-de-Tassigny; it's on the main street.
☎ 03.89.74.89.77
Closed weekends, three weeks in July, and Christmas to New Year.

This little restaurant in a green house serves meat, meat and more meat – boned pig's trotters, skirt with shallots, calves' brains with capers, home-made black pudding, veal sweetbreads, and bulls' testicles with cream. The owner is also a butcher. There is an unbeatable *menu du jour* at 43F. Big local following. You can also buy home-made products to take away. Free *digestif*.

MUNSTER   68140

🏂 🏠 |●| HÔTEL-RESTAURANT LE CHALET*

col de la Schlucht (West); from the centre take the D417 to col de la Schlucht on the Alsace-Vosges border.
☎ 03.89.77.38.33 ➡ 03.89.77.15.65
Hotel closed outside skiing season. **Restaurant closed** Wed evening, Thurs out of season and 12 Nov–12 Dec. **TV**. **Garden**. **Pay garage**.

Warm welcome. The rooms, which are only open in the skiing season, are nothing fancy but they're being renovated. Doubles 160F with basin, 195F with shower, and 215F with shower/wc, but prices may go up. They serve good food in the big dining room with a black and white tiled floor which makes it cool in summer. Simple but good regional dishes: *choucroute*, *baeckoeffe* in winter, *schiffele* with potatoes and salad in summer and wild boar stew in the autumn. Half board, 250F with evening meal, is compulsory in peak season. Lunch menu in the brasserie is 60F, with other menus at 110 and 127F. Free apéritif.

🏠 |●| HÔTEL AUX DEUX SAPINS**

49 rue du 9e-Zouaves (Southwest).
☎ 03.89.77.33.96 ➡ 03.89.77.03.90
Closed Sun evening, Mon out of season and 10 Nov–20 Dec. **TV**. **Disabled access**. **Garden**. **Car park**.

You must reserve very early to get in to this excellent place where the emphasis is on quality at reasonable prices. Excellent trout with almonds – you can really taste the Riesling. Set menus 75–200F. The simple rooms are very pleasant and good value. Doubles 250–300F. Windows are double-glazed and soundproofed from the traffic noise, but light sleepers should ask for a room at the back.

|●| RESTAURANT À L'ALSACIENNE

1 rue du Dôme (Southeast); it's behind the Protestant church.
☎ 03.89.77.43.49
Closed Tues lunchtime and Wed.

Locals and tourists alike enjoy sitting at the tables on the pavement alongside the church. The decor is typical of the Alsace region but somewhat lacking in character. They serve individual dishes or set menus 70–155F. A meal *à la carte* will set you back around 150F, Specialities include *choucroute garnie*, stuffed pig's trotters, *escalope* of veal with Munster, game in season, or simply a plate of local Munster cheese served with a glass of Gewürztraminer. At lunch try the fresh pasta and herbs or trout with almonds. Delightful welcome.

SOULTZEREN   68140 (4KM E)

🏂 🏠 |●| VILLA CANAAN-CHEZ LÉOPOLDINE

8 chem. du Buchteren; take the D47 in the direction of col de la Schlucht; after the village it's signposted on the right.
☎ 03.89.77.05.64. ➡ 03.89.77.35.73
Closed lunchtimes, Tues evening, Sun evening and Jan. **Garden**. **Car park**.

This huge yellow house, set high on a rock, dominates the Munster valley and lives up to the "promised land" implied in the name. Prices are reasonable: 260F for a double with basin, 320F with bath, and 285–315F per person half board. The bathrooms are all different, with nice personal touches. You'll get a good night's sleep here, and in the morning you can fling open the shutters to an amazing view. The cooking is organic, and be warned – Léopoldine doesn't stint on the portions. This place is perfect for ramblers: the *col* of the Schlucht is barely an hour's walk away and there's some incredible scenery on the doorstep. Free apéritif and 10% discount on the room rate Nov–April.

STOSSWIHR-AMPFERBACH   68140 (6KM W)

🏂 |●| AUBERGE DES CASCADES

How to get there: leave Stosswihr by the route des Crêtes, turn left before the church at the signpost.
☎ 03.89.77.44.74
Closed Mon and Tues out of season, Tues only 14 July–20 Aug, and Jan.

Service until 10pm, last orders taken about an hour earlier. A very good inn which hasn't yet been spoiled by too many tourists. The pretty house, which has recently been done up, is in a flower garden where you can hear the peaceful sound of a little waterfall nearby. There's a hearty weekday lunch menu at 50F, one at 135F on Sundays or, *à la carte*, there are rather unusual specialities such as flambéed tart of frogs' legs prepared under the attentive gaze of

Madame Decker and her rows of china ducks on the walls. If you fancy something more classic, the *entrecôte* with ceps is excellent. Treat yourself to the house Edelzwicker wine, which isn't expensive but is among the best in the region. The delicious flambéed tart is baked in a wood-fired stove. Free coffee.

STOSSWIHR   68140 (8KM W)

|●| AUBERGE DU SCHUPFEREN

Centre; take the D417 out of Munster to the col de la Schlucht and turn right towards Le Tanet ski resort. About 4km down the road, you'll see a sign to the Auberge on a tree. Take the dirt track (it's OK for cars) for about 3km. Pass the Sarrois refuge on your left and continue along the road on your right (there is a sign).
☎ 03.89.77.31.23
Closed Mon, Tues and Fri.

Service 9am–7pm. Although this place is off the beaten track it's definitely worth the effort to get here. It's popular with skiers in winter and walkers in summer. Christophe Kuhlman, the easy-going owner, will give you a warm welcome. He cooks great dishes like *Fleischsnecke*, pastry filled with mince, or a salad with leaves and vegetables from the garden. The menu is written on a blackboard. It's around 100F *à la carte*. Don't forget to order a small jug of house Edelzwicker, a white wine made from a blend of Alsace grapes. The view over the forest and valleys is amazing.

WIHR-AU-VAL   68239 (9KM E)

|●| LA NOUVELLE AUBERTE

9 route Nationale; it's on the D417 in the direction of Colmar.
☎ 03.89.71.07.70
Closed Mon evening and Tues. **TV**.

The talented chef has worked in some great kitchens but he hasn't let it go to his head. His roadside restaurant packs them in at lunchtime because of the 50F *menu-ouvrier*, which is amazing. You'll be lucky to find a parking space. The other menus, 95–265F, list dishes such as cockerel in Riesling and Tricastin lamb with thyme *jus*, and the dishes are remarkable value given the quality of the produce and the chef's skill. The simple dining room is very pretty, and the welcome is unaffected and kindly. Excellent place.

NIEDERBRONN-LES-BAINS   67110

🏠 |●| HÔTEL-RESTAURANT CULLY**

33–37 rue de la République (West); it's near the station.

☎ 03.88.09.01.42 ➟ 03.88.09.05.80
e hotel-cully@wanadoo.fr
Closed Feb. **TV**. **Disabled access**. **Garden**. **Car park**.

This place gets full around the times when people traditionally come to take the waters, so you should book well in advance. The hotel is low-key and comfortable; most of the big rooms have a balcony. Doubles 330F with shower/wc or bath. Good weekday set menu for 59F or 100F and 120F, or *à la carte*. Classic local dishes. There's a shady arbour where you can sit and have a drink or a quiet meal. The hotel is right beside a park with golfing facilities and games for the kids.

🔌|●| RESTAURANT LES ACACIAS**

35 rue des Acacias (Northwest); it's near the station.
☎ 03.88.09.00.47
Closed Fri and Sat lunchtimes out of season.
Garden. **Car park**.

This is a very classy place on the edge of the forest. There's a terrace for the summer. Stylish service. They do a nice set menu for 70F at weekday lunchtimes; others 95–215F. Traditional Alsace cooking with dishes such as *croustillant* of zander and *onglet* of beef with bone marrow. The pretty view of the valley is sadly marred by the factory. Free coffee.

OBERNAI   67210

🔌🏠 HOSTELLERIE LA DILIGENCE**

23 pl. de la Mairie (Centre).
☎ 03.88.95.55.69 ➟ 03.88.95.42.46
TV. **Pay car park**.

It would be difficult to find anywhere more central – the rooms at the front look out onto pl. de la Mairie in the town centre. With such a great location, you'd think the owners would just sit back and wait for the customers to roll in. In fact, they make a good deal of effort to make you feel welcome. The rooms are of an excellent standard, and there is a lovely breakfast room with bay windows overlooking the square. Rooms with shower/wc 275–440F. 10% discount for a minimum of three nights.

🔌🏠 HÔTEL DU GOUVERNEUR

13 rue de Sélestat.
☎ 03.88.95.63.72 ➟ 03.88.49.91.04
Closed 14 Nov–15 March.

This building dates from 1566, and was the residence of the town's governor. It's generously proportioned and has an interior courtyard, and one wall forms part of the town ramparts. There's a gallery and a Louis XV balustraded staircase. The bright, clean rooms have been refurbished in a sedate, contemporary style and some are very spacious (sleeping 3 or 4 people). Double with shower/wc 320F. The owner makes you feel welcome. Free breakfast.

IOI L'AGNEAU D'OR

99 rue du Général-Gouraud; it's on the main street.
☎ 03.88.95.28.22
Closed Mon, three weeks in Jan and first fortnight of June.

This is an authentic *winstub* serving only wine from the region. The painted ceiling, cuckoo clock, prints and decorated plates all make for a cosy atmosphere. Tasty local dishes are served up in generous portions. Good weekday lunch *menu du jour* at 70F, others 140–210F and a children's menu at 45F. *À la carte* are rack of suckling pig, stuffed pig's trotters and lamb from the Alps.

KLINGENTHAL   67530 (6KM SW)

⌂ IOI HÔTEL-RESTAURANT AU CYGNE

23 route du Mont-Sainte-Odile; take the D426.
☎ 03.88.95.82.94
Hotel closed a fortnight June/July and a fortnight in winter. **Restaurant closed** Tues evening and Wed. **Car park**.

This is a nice little place in a good location on the Mont-Sainte-Odile road. It has a traditional atmosphere with clean simple rooms. Doubles 140–200F. Menus, 90–140F, all include good home-cooking served in enormous portions. The delicious fruit tarts are made in the family bakery next door.

OTTROTT   67530

⌂ IOI À L'AMI FRITZ*

8 rue des Châteaux.
☎ 03.88.95.80.81 ➟ 03.88.95.84.85
✉ hotel@amifritz.com
Closed Wed, a fortnight June/July and the first week in Jan. **TV**. **Disabled access**. **Garden**. **Car park**.

This house, dating from the 17th century, is impressive outside and in, and is one of the least touristy places in town. It's beautifully decorated and very quiet. Bedrooms are pretty, as are the bathrooms, fitted with all mod cons; those in the annexe, *Le Chant des Oiseaux*, 600m away, are cheaper but not so nice. The rooms overlooking the street are air-conditioned. Doubles 440–460F.

Pleasant dining room with rustic decor and efficient, attentive service. Patrick Fritz, the owner, prepares regional dishes in his own fresh style, depending on what is good at the market – black pudding strudel with horseradish, the *choucroute royale*, or the gratinéed tripe braised in Sylvaner. Set menus 125–345F.

PETITE-PIERRE (LA)   67290

⌂ IOI HÔTEL-RESTAURANT AU LION D'OR*

15 rue Principale.
☎ 03.88.70.45.06 ➟ 03.88.70.45.56
Closed Jan and a fortnight June/July. **Swimming pool**. **TV**. **Disabled access**. **Garden**. **Car park**.

A rather chic little village in the Vosges regional park that is popular with German holidaymakers. The *Lion d'Or* qualifies as top of the range and you will receive a warm welcome. In summer, try something from the grill and eat in the garden, or head for the affordable *winstub*. The restaurant prices reflect the quality: set menus 120–330F, and a children's menu at 65F. The hotel has double rooms with shower/wc for 380–450F, but although they're big and comfortable, the 1970s decor grates a bit. Facilities include an indoor swimming pool and a sauna. Wonderful views of the forest.

RIBEAUVILLÉ   68150

⌂ HÔTEL DE LA TOUR*

1 rue de la Mairie (Centre).
☎ 03.89.73.72.73 ➟ 03.89.73.38.74
Closed Jan to mid-March. **TV**. **Garden**. **Pay car park**.

Once a wine-grower's house, this hotel, in the middle of a little medieval town, offers pleasant rooms for 370F with shower/wc, 450F with bath. Guests can use the sauna, Turkish baths and Jacuzzi for free. There is no restaurant but there is a *winstub* where you can try the local wine. Very pleasant, even stylish, place.

IOI L'AUBERGE AU ZAHNACKER

8 rue du Général-de-Gaulle (Centre).
☎ 03.89.73.60.77
Closed Thurs and mid-Jan to mid-Feb.

Service 9am–10pm. This inn, owned by the local wine co-operative, is a little oasis of calm off the main street that's jammed with tourists. Even though it's grey and by a roundabout, in summer, when the sweet-smelling wisteria is in full bloom, you can sit out on the terrace and savour a glass of Pinot Blanc while you wait for your *presskopf* (brawn) or onion tart. In winter the *winstub* has a warm and pleasant atmosphere and is full of locals and tourists. Classic house specialities, like calf's head vinaigrette, tripe in Riesling and *baeckeoffe*. 150F minimum *à la carte*. Good local wines.

ILLHAEUSERN   68970 (11KM E)

🎿 |●| À LA TRUITE

17 rue du 25-Janvier (Centre).
☎ 03.89.71.83.51 ➡ 03.89.71.85.19
Closed Tues evening, Wed, three weeks in Feb and a week at the end of June. **Garden**.

A nice country inn with a terrace which looks onto the river and the weeping willows. The simple, relaxed dining room is full of office workers, factory workers, farmers, long-distance lorry drivers and anyone else on the road looking for an inexpensive meal. The chef's speciality, which has to be ordered in advance, is *matelote Marie-Louise*, a fish stew served with noodles. Alternatively, try the *coq au Riesling*. The bill is always easy on the pocket. Weekday lunch menu 65F then 89–210F, plus dishes *à la carte*. Free coffee.

THANNENKIRCH   68590 (11KM N)

🎿 🛏 |●| AUBERGE LA MEUNIÈRE**

30 rue Sainte-Anne.
☎ 03.89.73.10.47 ➡ 03.89.73.12.31
Closed 20 Dec–25 March. **TV. Garden. Car park**.

From the road it's a typical Alsace inn, festooned with geraniums. From the valley, it's one of a rash of 1970s buildings that sprang up in the Alps. The rooms are rustic but contemporary, done out in a superb combination of natural materials. Most have a balcony or a terrace and splendid views – you can watch the does coming for a drink at day break. Doubles with shower/wc or bath 300–420F. Sauna, Turkish bath and billiards for guests. The fine, inventive cuisine in the restaurant is reasonably priced, with a set weekday lunch menu at 95F and others 100–190F. *À la carte*, you will find tasty dishes like *baeckeoffe* of snails in Riesling, wild boar with juniper berries or ox tongue with a horseradish sauce. The prices are fair, given the quality of the place. Perfect welcome and attentive service. Free house apéritif.

RIQUEWIHR   68340

🎿 🛏 HÔTEL DE LA COURONNE**

5 rue de la Couronne.
☎ 03.89.49.03.03 ➡ 03.89.49.01.01
Car park.

This attractive 16th-century hotel is just right. It has a delightful gateway, and the owners' warm smiles make for a welcoming atmosphere. There are little wooden benches and tables in the porch where you can sit and enjoy a glass of Gewürztraminer before going off to explore the forests. All the rooms have been refurbished and the plain walls have been stencilled with a flower here and a tree there – all in good taste – and some have beams. The prices are pretty decent for where it is – doubles with bath 340–395F. Everything about this hotel is pleasing, making it one of the nicest in Riquewihr. Free house apéritif.

HUNAWIHR   68150 (4KM N)

|●| WINSTUB SUZEL

2 rue de l'Église.
☎ 03.89.73.30.85
Closed Tues and Jan to end-March. **Disabled access**. **Garden**.

The Mittnacht family, who run this wine tavern, make it a warm, welcoming place. There's a view of the pretty church tower and in summer the shady terrace is covered with flowers. The big wooden doors at the back of the restaurant lead to the cellars where you can sample good Alsatian wine. But the main reason to come here is the fine food. Whatever you have it will be good. An onion tart with salad may be enough for some, while the *Katel* menu would satisfy a peckish Obélix; you get onion tart, *roulades farcies* (rolled meat or fish with stuffing), sautéed potatoes, green salad and dessert. Lunch *formule* 89F and other menus 98–140F, some include home-made *choucroute*. *Kougelhopf*, a ring cake with dried fruit and almonds, is a speciality and on Sunday evening they do flambéed tarts.

SAVERNE   67700

🛏 HÔTEL EUROPE**

7 rue de la Gare.
☎ 03.88.71.12.07 ➡ 03.88.71.11.43
TV. Disabled access. Lock-up garage.

Open every day of the year, this is the best hotel in town. Good facilities in the rooms –

some of which have whirlpool baths. 360–490F for a double with shower or bath. Some are more spacious and have cable TV. The ritzy atmosphere, the first-rate service, and the excellent buffet breakfast keep the customers, including a large number of people who work at the European Parliament in Strasbourg, keep coming back. For families there's a flat (700F) in an adjoining house.

|●| TAVERNE KATZ

80 Grand-Rue (Centre).
☎ 03.88.71.16.56
Closed Tues evening, Wed and a fortnight in Jan.

Open every day of the year. This beautiful place was built in 1605 as the residence of a man called Katz, the archbishop's tax collector. The house's history is retold on a board outside just above the menu. Beautiful dining room with wood panelling. The first-rate cooking specialises in traditional dishes and excellent desserts – the menu rarely changes and is most reliable. Weekday lunch menu 89F then 139–169F. Specialities include *timbale* of chicken in pastry served with *spaetzles* (noodles), marinated *baeckeoffe* (which they make with duck), *rognons blancs* (sweetbreads), braised ham hock and *choucroute à l'alsacienne*. The terrace looks out onto the pedestrianised street. Suzie and Jos, the friendly owners, make you feel welcome.

SCHIRMEK   67130
NATZWILLER   67130 (8KM SW)

|●| AUBERGE METZGER

55 rue Principale; take the N420 then the D130.
☎ 03.88.97.02.42 |➡| 03.88.97.93.59
Closed Sun evening and Mon except July–Aug, and three weeks in Jan. **TV**.

A pleasant place to stop in this beautiful valley. Mme Metzger is attentive to all your needs. The rooms are huge and comfortable, particularly the ones that have been renovated. On top of that, prices have stayed fair; 305–365F for a double room. Typical local dishes on the menus which start at 65F for lunch – *salade Vosgienne*, smoked ham with *choucroute* and dessert of the day. There's a terrace overlooking the valley.

SÉLESTAT   67000

🏊 🛏 |●| HÔTEL VAILLANT**

pl. de la République (Centre); it's on the way to the

station from the town centre.
☎ 03.88.92.09.46 |➡| 03.88.82.95.01
Restaurant closed Sat and Sun lunchtimes out of season. **TV**. **Disabled access**. **Car park**.

The rooms in this large, modern hotel, built in 1967, all have their own personality, individually furnished with contemporary pieces that are brightly coloured without being overpowering. Double rooms are 320F with shower/wc, 390F with bath. In the restaurant set menus range from 95 to 225F or you can dine *à la carte*. There is a small gym with sauna and Jacuzzi for the use of residents. Free house apéritif.

🛏 |●| AUBERGE DES ALLIÉS**

39 rue des Chevaliers (Centre).
☎ 03.88.92.09.34
Hotel closed Sun evening, Mon, 15–30 Jan and 27Jun–10 July. **TV**.

The long history of this building starts in 1372; it was a bakery in the first half of the 19th century when Louis-Philippe ruled France, and it's been a restaurant since 1918. In the middle of the dining room is an impressive old, typically Alsace stove, and there's also a beautiful fresco showing the place aux Choux in the first half of the 19th century – the women are not wearing the typical Hansistyle head-dress. The *à la carte* menu is typical of this kind of restaurant, with local dishes such as ham hock with *choucroute* and zander with Riesling. Try the house *foie gras*. Set menus 98–185F. Double rooms with bath 330–360F.

RATHSAMHAUSEN   67600 (3KM E)

🛏 |●| HÔTEL-RESTAURANT À L'ÉTOILE**

Grande-Rue; it's on the D21 in the direction of Muttersholz.
☎ 03.88.92.35.79 |➡| 03.88.92.91.66
Closed Three weeks in Feb. **Swimming pool**. **TV**. **Garden**. **Car park**.

A young couple have cleverly modernised this old house by adding an extension with a bright foyer and a stairway in wood and glass. Pleasant rooms cost 250F for two and 340F for four. The dining room is warm and intimate in the evenings and there's a little Christmas crib in one corner. The *à la carte* menu is limited, but lists good dishes, particularly the fried carp. Expect to pay 110F for a meal or opt for the cheap, limited set menu at 37F. Other menus 70–90F. In summer the terrace is covered with flowers and there's an open-air pool. A really nice little place.

DAMBACH-LA-VILLE 67650 (10KM N)

🏃 🛎 HÔTEL LE VIGNOBLE**

1 rue de l'Église.
☎ 03.88.92.43.75
Closed Sun and Mon evenings out of season, 20 Dec–15 March and ten days in Nov. **TV. Disabled access. Car park**.

Charming hotel, tastefully converted from an 18th-century gabled barn. Stylish, comfortable rooms, with doubles 280–310F and 90F for an extra bed. 5% discount on stays of three to five nights, 10% discount on six nights or more.

STRASBOURG 67200

SEE MAP OVERLEAF

🛎 |❂| HÔTEL SCHUTZENBOCK

81 av. Jean-Jaurès-Neudorf (Southeast). Off map **D4-3**
☎ 03.88.34.04.19
Closed Sat lunchtimes, Sun, Aug, Christmas to 2 Jan.

An inexpensive, clean, friendly hotel. Double rooms from 160F with hand basin. Set lunch menu 50F, then 95–150F, with simple, regional cooking. Half board 180F. Pretty fair.

🛎 HÔTEL PATRICIA

rue du Puits (Centre). **MAP C4-4**
☎03.88.32.14.60 ➡ 03.88.32.19.08
A lovely 16th-century building in a quiet, centrally located side street. A really wonderful place with generously proportioned, clean rooms. TV and smoking are outlawed, so it's a quiet, healthy place. And it's not expensive: 180F for a double with basin, 220F with shower, 240F with shower/wc. Easy-going, gentle welcome.

🛎 HÔTEL DE BRUXELLES

13 rue Kihn (Centre). **MAP A2-6**
☎ 03.88.32.45.31 ➡ 03.88.32.06.22
TV.

A little place near the station. It's decent, clean and friendly. The decoration might not be your taste (the fabrics and carpets are a hotch-potch of different colours), but it's quiet and the bedding is good. Doubles 195–275F, depending on facilities.

🛎 HÔTEL DE L'ILL**

8 rue des Bateliers-Krutenau. **MAP D3-7**
☎ 03.88.36.20.01 ➡ 03.88.35.30.03
Closed a week in Jan. **TV. Disabled access. Public car park opposite**.

A good place in a quiet street, and well-run by the Ehrhardt family. Rooms are not very big

but they're pleasant and clean and prices are reasonable – doubles with shower 250F, with shower/wc or bath 310–380F. Some rooms are set aside for non-smokers and two rooms have direct access onto the lovely terrace on the first floor. From 11am to 5pm you can enjoy the sun and the view of Sainte-Madeleine church. Generous breakfast.

🏃 🛎 HÔTEL COUVENT DU FRANCIS-CAIN**

18 rue du Faubourg-de-Pierre. **MAP B1-5**
☎ 03.88.32.93.93 ➡ 03.88.75.68.46
Closed Christmas to 1 Jan.
TV. Disabled access. Car park.

A centrally located hotel near the covered market. It has been carefully renovated with lots of rooms. Doubles cost 340F with shower/wc, 360F with bath. Buffet breakfast 48F. Warm welcome. 10% discount Jan–Feb.

🛎 HÔTEL GUTENBERG**

31 rue des Serruriers (Centre). **MAP C3-8**
☎ 03.88.32.17.15 ➡ 03.88.75.76.67
Closed first fortnight in Jan. **TV**.

An 18th-century house combining the modern and the traditional with facilities that would expect to find in a three-star hotel. The owner, whose grandfather was an officer in the Grande Armée, is mad about military engravings from the Napoleonic period. His collection is displayed over all the walls. This passion for the Empire carries through into the rooms which have good pieces of old family furniture. The rooms on the fifth floor (three of which have a mezzanine) give delightful views over the rooftops – you'll get more or less the same view on the fourth floor. The breakfast is pretty ordinary, though. Double rooms 340–470F with shower/wc or bath. Warm welcome.

🛎 HÔTEL SAINT-CHRISTOPHE**

2 pl. de la Gare. **MAP A3-9**
☎ 03.88.22.30.30
TV.

This well-run hotel, named after the patron saint of travellers, suits businesspeople arriving by train at the station opposite or holidaymakers travelling by car – it's hard to drive into the centre of town. Rooms – doubles 380–450F – are really comfortable, and you'll get a good night's sleep. The refurbished ones are better and the most expensive look onto a pleasant inner courtyard that is bathed in sunlight nearly all day. It is a nice place for breakfast or a relaxing drink in the late afternoon.

☖ LE GRAND HÔTEL**

12 pl. de la Gare. **MAP A2-9**
☎ 03.88.52.84.84 ➡ 03.88.52.84.00
TV. Disabled access.

You can't miss this huge, concrete 1950s monstrosity on the square. The lines are austere and it's huge, with wide corridors, an awe-inspiring hall, a vast, high-ceilinged sitting room and a superb glass lift that's a prototype and the only one in existence. The interior has been redesigned to suit modern tastes. Good facilities in rooms worthy of a three-star hotel, some with air-conditioning; doubles 410–645F. Service of the same standard. A hotel that lives up to its name.

☖ HÔTEL MAISON ROUGE**

4 rue des Franc-Bourgeois. **MAP B3-12**
☎ 03.88.32.08.60 ➡ 03.88.22.43.73
TV.

The startling red frontage belies the quality of accommodation in this hotel of good standing. Inside, the rooms have all the modern facilities (mini-bar, cable TV and so on) and a very individual decoration of soft pastel walls and matching fabrics. Doubles with shower or bath 490–710F. Very professional staff.

☖ HÔTEL BEAUCOUR***

5 rue des Bouchers. **MAP C4-11**
☎ 03.88.76.72.00 ➡ 03.88.76.72.60
TV. Disabled access. Garage.

This hotel is spread between five half-timbered listed buildings from the 18th century and is in a unique location only five minutes from the cathedral. Considerable refurbishment has somewhat detracted from its authenticity, but it's comfortable and still has a matchless charm. There's certainly no other place like it. All the rooms are individually decorated – attic, Italian-style, regional. Prices 550–780F for a double with bath.

❚❙❙ LA COCCINELLE

22 rue Sainte-Madeleine (South). **MAP D4-27**
☎ 03.88.36.19.27
Closed Sat lunchtime, Sun and Aug.

A pair of sisters run this place; one does the cooking and the other looks after the dining room. The restaurant is crammed with regulars at lunchtime who line up for the reasonably priced dish of the day. It's calmer in the evenings. Good regional specialities include *quenelles* of liver, *pot-au-feu* with rock salt, and *vigneronne* pie. On Saturday winter evenings, order the Alsace classic *baecke-* *offe*, a stew of beef, mutton and pork. Menus 68–120F. Friendly welcome and service.

❚❙❙ AU PONT CORBEAU

21 quai Saint-Nicolas. **MAP C4-21**
☎ 03.88.35.60.68
Closed Sat, Sun lunchtime and Aug.

Firstly, the owner here will always give you a warm, friendly welcome. Secondly, the food is great, and thirdly, it's one of the few *winstubs* in the town centre near the cathedral that's open on Sunday nights. The mineral water is from the Bas-Rhin and the draught beer, from a brewery across the Rhine, is excellent. These little things make all the difference. On the menu there's grilled ham with sautéed potatoes at 72F (a must), salad with a selection of meat and *crudités*, and sautéed potatoes, calves' brains fritters in *rémoulade* sauce served with steamed potatoes and salad. Menus at 72F or *à la carte*. This place sums up everything that's great about Alsace food and drink.

❚❙❙ LE FESTIN DE LUCULLUS

18 rue sainte-Hélène. **MAP B3-23**
☎ 03.88.22.40.78
Closed Sun, Mon lunchtime and 15–30 Aug.

Four years' training under the eagle eye of the famous chef Michel Guérard is character-forming! The chef here was certainly inspired by his time at Eugénie-les-Bains – everything from the well-judged cooking times to the use of fresh herbs and seasonings is put into practice and the results are excellent. The cheerful, friendly welcome, good service and honest prices mean that you will want to come back. Weekday lunch menu 75F or 160F; *à la carte* around 200F. The only slight drawback is that the decor in the long dining room is perhaps a little too formal.

❚❙❙ AU PIGEON

23 rue des Tonneliers. **MAP C4-26**
☎ 03.88.32.31.30
Closed Mon and Tues evening,

In one of the oldest buildings in town, a glorious, half-timbered, gabled residence built in the 16th century, this historic *winstub* has been going for years. Above the door is a wooden frieze featuring a carved pigeon. The faultless dining room is more sobre and classic in style, and serves the likes of *baeckeoffe*, *choucroute* and knuckle of pork. Dish of the day is around 60F, menus 85–145F. A beacon in a galaxy of wine taverns.

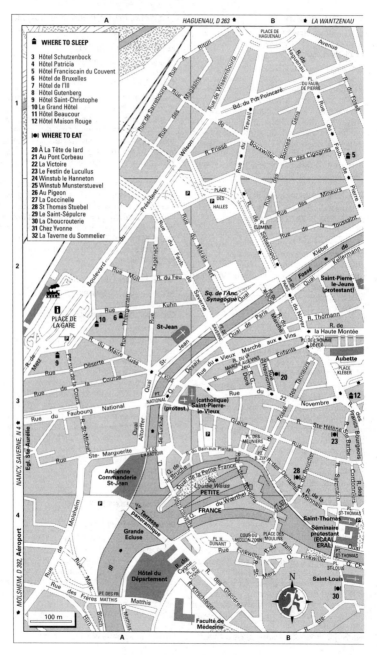

WHERE TO SLEEP

3 Hôtel Schutzenbock
4 Hôtel Patricia
5 Hôtel Franciscain du Couvent
6 Hôtel de Bruxelles
7 Hôtel de l'Ill
8 Hôtel Gutenberg
9 Hôtel Saint-Christophe
10 Le Grand Hôtel
11 Hôtel Beaucour
12 Hôtel Maison Rouge

WHERE TO EAT

20 À La Tête de lard
21 Au Pont Corbeau
22 La Victoire
23 Le Festin de Lucullus
24 Winstub le Hanneton
25 Winstub Munsterstuevel
26 Au Pigeon
27 La Coccinelle
28 St Thomas Stuebel
29 Le Saint-Sépulcre
30 La Choucrouterie
31 Chez Yvonne
32 La Taverne du Sommelier

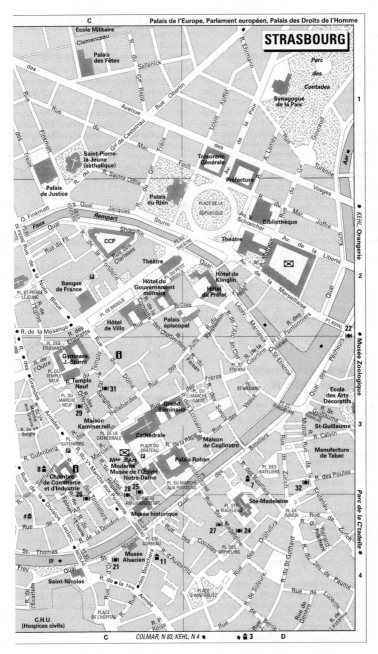

🖈 |●| LA CHOUCROUTERIE

20 rue Saint-Louis. **MAP B4-30**
☎ 03.88.36.52.87
Closed Sun evening, first week in Jan and three weeks in Aug.

Service evenings only, 7pm–1am. Roger Siffer was a folk singer before he went into the restaurant business. The building was a post house in the 18th century and then housed the last *choucroute*-makers in Strasbourg – apparently they made the best in town. You can still get *choucroute* here – seven varieties in fact. Alternatively, try the Munster cheese rissoles with salad. Set menus 85–180F. The owner has decorated the walls of the dining room with a collection of beautiful musical instruments, and when his musician friends drop in they play together. Free coffee.

|●| WINSTUB LE HANNETON

5 rue Sainte-Madeleine **MAP D4-24**
☎ 03.88.36.93.76
Closed Tues and a fortnight at the beginning of Nov.

Open to 11pm. The *winstub* is worlds away from the tourist scramble yet still pretty central. The atmosphere is intimate and pleasant and Monsieur Denis' good humour is refreshing. Very good *tartiflette* with Munster cheese and the *baeckehoffe* is wonderfully moist. With a meal at 80–120F prices are reasonable.

|●| RESTAURANT LA VICTOIRE

2 bd. de la Victoire. **MAP D2/3-22**
☎ 03.88.35.39.35
Closed Sat evening, Sun and three weeks in Aug.

Closes at 1am. This place is always full, so if you can't book you will need to go early. Though it looks anonymous from the outside, it's pretty impressive inside, with a great atmosphere. It's a favourite haunt of students and teachers from the university. Classic regional dishes – menus start at 100F – but you come for the atmosphere more than the food.

|●| ST THOMAS STEUBEL

5 rue du Bouclier. **MAP B3-28**
☎ 03.88.22.34.82
Closed Sun and Mon.

There's nowhere more friendly than this pocket-sized *winstub*. Huge portions of the region's specialities: reasonably priced *choucroute*, veal kidneys with cream and *bibelkäss* (cream cheese with sautéed potatoes). No set menus, but expect to pay 100–120F for a meal. Smiling staff and a relaxed atmosphere. It's a bit of a squeeze so it's best to book.

|●| RESTAURANT À LA TÊTE DE LARD

3 rue Hannomg. **MAP B3-20**
☎ 03.88.32.13.56
Closed Sat lunchtime, Sun and the first fortnight in Aug.

Flambéed tart, grilled knuckle of pork, *choucroute*, Munster cheese, Riesling and a menu with seasonal dishes . . . all the regional specialities are here, served in an unpretentious fashion. Their *flammenküche*, or flambéed tart, is made with bacon, onions and cheese – originally the tart was cooked in a baker's oven beside the bread. Share one among friends and get stuck in with your fingers! This is a very popular place which has stayed special over the years. A meal will cost about 120F *à la carte*.

|●| LA TAVERNE DU SOMMELIER

ruelle de la Bruche. **MAP D3-32**
☎ 03.88.24.14.10
Closed Sun and Mon, New Year's holidays and a week now and then through the year.

The ruelle de la Bruche is very narrow but widens out just by the tavern. It's a nice place with lots of regulars. There is typical *winstub* fare on the menu – *croustillant* of calf's head, grilled tuna or pan-fried *foie gras* escalopes – but the thoughtfully prepared dishes range more widely than the regional classics. Dish of the day 48F at lunch; *à la carte* around 120F. Good little wines by the glass. Down-to-earth, smiling staff.

|●| LE SAINT-SÉPULCRE

15 rue des Orfèvres. **MAP C3-29**
☎ 03.88.32.39.97
Closed Sun, Mon and 7–15 July.

This is one of the most extraordinary places in Alsace and one of the best known in Strasbourg. Robert Lauck, the owner, is a real character whose playful rudeness could sometimes be misunderstood – he'll accost you at the door and demand to know your business. He'll show you to a table while berating one of his regulars for spilling crumbs on theirs, then he'll be away, laughing his head off. He's really a lovely man who thrives on a joke, so come prepared. The food is excellent – there's *confit* of pork tongue, potato salad, ham *choucroute*, goose *foie gras* and a fabulous ham *en croûte* which is sliced in front of you. The typical little bistro glasses, carafes of wine, checked napkins, little curtains, polished floors, and the wooden stove in the middle of the room create the right atmosphere for an unforgettable meal. It'll cost about 130F per person.

|●| WINSTUB MUNSTERSTUEVEL

8 pl. du Marché aux Cochons-de-Lait. **MAP C3-25**
☎ 03.88.32.17.63
Closed Sun and Mon.

Patrick Klipfel and his wife, Marlène, professional to their fingertips, have a solid fan club who gravitate here – and they keep their customers satisfied. The prices are slightly higher –150F *à la carte* – than in a traditional *winstub* but the quality is there. Oxtail *pot-au-feu* with vegetables, marrowbone and *crudités* with horseradish sauce, pork cheek, and *choucroute* are typical of the hearty dishes *à la carte*. Good selection of wines, spirits and draught Météor. The terrace gets crowded on sunny days.

|●| CHEZ YVONNE

10 rue du Sanglier. **MAP C3-31**
☎ 03.88.32.84.15
Closed Sun, Mon lunchtime, mid-July to mid-Aug and Christmas to New Year.

Yvonne Haller's *winstub* is a Strasbourg institution. Politicians and showbiz celebs come here when they're in town and it's also very popular with locals who flock to pay their respects to this great lady's cooking. Calf's head, *choucroute* tart, oxtail *terrine* and stuffed, fresh quails are all first-class. Expect to pay about 200F, which is a bit expensive. The impressive *stammtisch*, or regulars' table, is a tradition. No credit cards.

HANDSCHUHEIM   67117 (13KM W)

|●| L'AUBERGE À L'ESPÉRANCE

5 rue Principale; take the N4 from Strasbourg.
☎ 03.88.69.00.52 ➡ 03.88.69.10.19
Closed Mon, Tues and first fortnight in Jan. **Car park**.

The restaurant in this attractive half-timbered house is open only in the evenings. There's a choice of five pretty dining rooms. *Flammenküche* (flambéed tart) is a particular speciality, cooked here in the old-fashioned way on wood ashes, which gives it its unique flavour and lightness. The place appeals to families and groups of friends, so the atmosphere is warm and friendly. They have some good wines, and they don't push the local vintages too hard. Expect to pay 120F *à la carte*.

THANN   68800

🎿 🏠 |●| HÔTEL-RESTAURANT KLÉBER**

39 rue Kléber (Centre).
☎ 03.89.37.13.66 ➡ 03.89.37.39.67

Hotel closed Feb. **Restaurant closed** Sat lunchtime and Sun.
TV. **Disabled access**. **Car park**.

This hotel is in a residential area away from the hustle and bustle of town. Quite new and stylish, with fair prices. Rooms 24 or 26 in the annexe are really quiet, with balconies overlooking the orchards. Doubles with shower/wc 250–300F. The restaurant, which has a good reputation, offers a weekday lunch menu at 55F and others at 85–130F, with dishes like beef with morels, game, wild boar or kid, and iced *Kugelhopf*. Good value for a two-star. Pleasant welcome. 10% discount on the room rate except July–Aug.

MOOSCH   68690 (7KM NW)

🏠 |●| FERME AUBERGE DU GSANG

How to get there: from Moosch, head for the Mine d'Argent campsite, follow the forest road for 7km, and park in the car park in the Gsang. Then it's a 20-minute walk – there's only one path.
☎ 03.89.38.96.85
Closed Fri and Sun evenings except in July and Aug.

It's worth making the effort to find this delightful farmhouse, where they have yet to discover electricity. You eat very well. They do sandwiches at any time of the day, smoked scrag of mutton, roasts, *fleischschnake*, vegetable stew and the most wonderful soup *fermière*. For 75F per person you get a really good meal. On Sundays the dining rooms are full to bursting and if you want to stay, you should book. Accommodation is in clean, basic dormitories but bring a sleeping bag and a torch. Half board 145F. Great atmosphere and you'll have a memorable stay. The view is fabulous, and you have to walk everywhere.

SAINT-AMARIN   68550 (8KM NW)

🏠 |●| AUBERGE DU MEHRBÄCHEL*

Route de Geishouse. Leave the N66 at Saint-Amarin signposted to Geishouse; about 3km along the main road, before the village, turn off left and keep going (where all the pine trees are) until you come to the inn.
☎ 03.89.82.60.68 ➡ 03.89.82.66.05
Closed Fri and All Saints' school holidays. **Car park**.

The chalet, with woods on one side and pastures on the other, is set on the side of the mountain overhanging the Thur valley. The view of the valley from the bedrooms – which are in a modern annexe – are splendid. Doubles with shower/wc or bath 300–320F. The restaurant is well worth the effort of getting here. Cooking is traditional, but the chef has added his own personal touches. Specialities include trout with almonds, lamb shank, salmon in herbs and Tokay, and superb duck with juniper and ginger. The fried Munster cheese coated with breadcrumbs and served with salad and cumin is also a treat. Menus from 100F (except on Sun) to 200F. The generous breakfast buffet features smoked bacon, ham, cereal, yoghurt and more. And outside there's the soothing sound of cowbells.

TURCKHEIM   68230

🎿 🏨 |●| AUBERGE DU BRAND**

8 Grand-Rue.
☎ 03.89.27.06.10 ➡ 03.89.27.55.51
e Christian.zimmerlin@wanadoo.fr
Hotel closed 15 Jan–25 Feb and 25 June–4 July.
Restaurant closed Tues and Wed except July and Aug.
TV. Garden.

Service noon–1.45pm and 7–10.30pm. This is a superb, traditional half-timbered Alsace building. The forest provides the chef with lots of wild mushrooms for autumn dishes; girolles, chanterelles, ceps, boletus, oyster mushrooms and horns of plenty are fried up with ordinary mushrooms to create a dish full of intense flavour. If you fancy something local try the ham in beer with leeks, or wild boar stew with Pinot Noir. The warm decor of the dining room really complements the food. The menu changes with the seasons. Set menus 85–295F. The stylish and cosy rooms with shower/wc cost 230–500F, breakfast included. Half board, 275–380F per person, is good value if you want to spend a few days in the most beautiful wine-growing region of the Rhine. 10% discount on the room rate for a minimum two-night stay.

🏨 |●| HOSTELLERIE DES DEUX CLEFS**

3 rue du Conseil; it's in pl. de l'Hôtel-de-Ville.
☎ 03.89.27.06.01 ➡ 03.89.27.18.07
TV. Disabled access. Garden. Car park.

This could be an inn or a palace. The wonderful half-timbered house, dating from 1540 and renovated in 1620, has had a number of famous guests, including General de Gaulle and General Leclerc after the liberation of Alsace, Dr. Albert Schweitzer, a friend of the current owners' relatives, and the American actor James Stewart. The huge front door creaks open to reveal superb wood panelling, antique carpets, and a romantic dining room lit like a Rembrandt painting. The light filters through the "stained glass" window panes –

which are actually made up from the bottoms of coloured bottles. There is even a little conservatory full of house plants and a garden at the back. The rooms have been improved so they're better value. Doubles from 380F with shower/wc to 490F with twin beds, bath and TV. The restaurant serves regional food but the cooking is a little unpredictable. Set menus 125–200F and à la carte. A super place with lots of character. 50% discount on breakfast.

WISSEMBOURG   67160

🎿 🏨 |●| HÔTEL-RESTAURANT WALK**

2 rue de la Walk (Northwest); it's next to the hospital.
☎ 03.88.94.06.44 ➡ 03.88.54.38.03
e hotel.moulin.la.walk@wanadoo.fr
Closed Fri lunchtime, Sun evening, Mon, 3–30 Jan and 15–30 June. **TV. Disabled access. Car park**.

This place, outside the town's fortifications and surrounded by lots of greenery, has a relaxing atmosphere. There are ten comfortable, cheery rooms with wood-panelled walls and new bathrooms in an annexe in an old mill, a few with lovely views of the park. They go for 320–360F; half board costs 340F per person. The restaurant is housed in another building. The cooking is pretty upmarket, specialising in *foie gras* and various fish dishes. Menus at 180 or 210F. Free apéritif.

CLIMBACH   67510 (9KM SW)

|●| RESTAURANT AU COL DE PFAFFENSCHLICK

How to get there: Climbach is on the D3, turn left up to the pass.
☎03.88.54.28.84 ➡ 03.88.54.39.17
Closed Mon, Tues, and mid-Jan to mid-Feb. Car park.

The Séraphin family will give you a genuinely warm welcome at their little inn in the heart of the forest. The dining room, with its hefty beams and wood panelling, has a friendly atmosphere, and there's a terrace for summer. They serve ham, snails, salads, cheeses, quiches, onion tarts and regional specialities include free-range chicken in Riesling, wild boar stew or *baeckeoffe* (beef, mutton and pork stew), which has to be ordered in advance. Weekday menu 50F or about 120F à la carte. Madame Séraphin goes out of her way to make your meal as pleasant as possible. A good place, only a few kilometres from Four à Chaux, an important sector of the Maginot Line.

AQUITAINE

AGEN 47000

♠ HÔTEL DES AMBANS*

59 rue des Ambans (Centre); it's near the station.
☎ 05.53.66.28.60 ➡ 05.53.87.94.01
TV.

A simple nine-room hotel in a quiet street in the old part of town. It's well run and clean, though the decor is a bit tired, but the prices are very attractive. Doubles 160F with shower/wc and TV. The owner will welcome you like a friend. Reception closes at 11pm.

♠ HÔTEL DES ISLES

25 rue Baudin (Centre).
☎ 05.53.47.11.33 ➡ 05.53.66.19.25
TV.

Behind the white stone façade, this lovely hotel is arranged around a central skylight. There's every chance the owner himself will check you in, and despite the laid-back ambience everything is well organised. The rooms are clean and well maintained and you'll have peace and quiet in this residential area. Doubles 160–190F with shower/wc and 190–210F with bath. The hotel deserves a star.

犬 ♠ ATLANTIC HÔTEL**

133 av. Jean-Jaurès (Southeast).
☎ 05.53.96.16.56 ➡ 05.53.98.34.80
Closed 24 Dec–3 Jan. **Swimming pool**. **TV**. **Garage**.

Neither the surroundings nor the 70s architecture of this building are particularly attractive, but the rooms are spacious and quiet, and the air-conditioning helps beat the heat. Six rooms overlook the garden. Doubles with shower/wc go for 300F, with bath 330F. Very

warm welcome. Free garage and 10% discount on the room rate.

|●| LES MIGNARDISES

40 rue Camille-Desmoulins (Centre).
☎ and ➡ 05.53.47.18.62
Closed Sun, Mon evening, a fortnight Feb/March and three weeks in Aug.

Though it has no pretentions to being gourmet cuisine, the food here is good value. They do a remarkably cheap menu at 56F, except Saturday evenings, which includes soup, starter, main course and dessert. Settle down on one of the olive-green moleskin benches and get stuck into a seafood platter, the veal stew, a fine trout *meunière* and the smooth *crème caramel*. The place is always packed at lunchtime. Other menus 70–150F.

|●| L'ATELIER

14 rue du Jeu de Paume (Centre).
☎ 05.53.87.89.22
Closed Sat and Mon lunchtimes, Sun, a week in Jan and a week in Aug.

Everyone comes to this lively place in the centre of town, run by a couple of live wires. Monsieur is very skilled in choosing his wines while Madame takes time to serve her guests attentively. There are quite a lot of fish dishes on the menu and, given the region, there's a lot of duck; the plate of carpaccio and *tartare* of duck is amazing. There's a lunch *formule* at 60F and menus 75–125F, with evening menus at 125–150F.

犬|●| LA BOHÊME

14 rue Émile-Sentini (Centre).
☎ 05.53.68.31.00

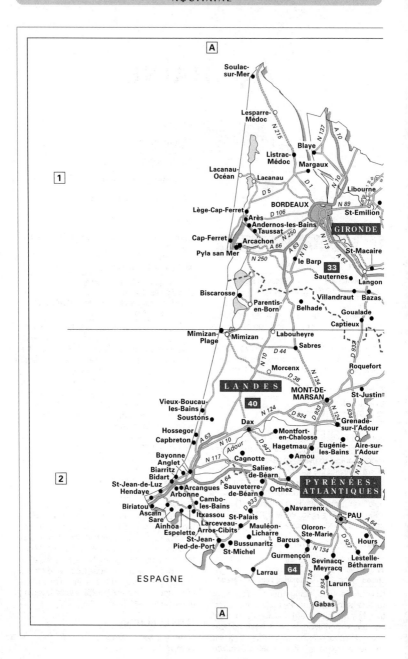

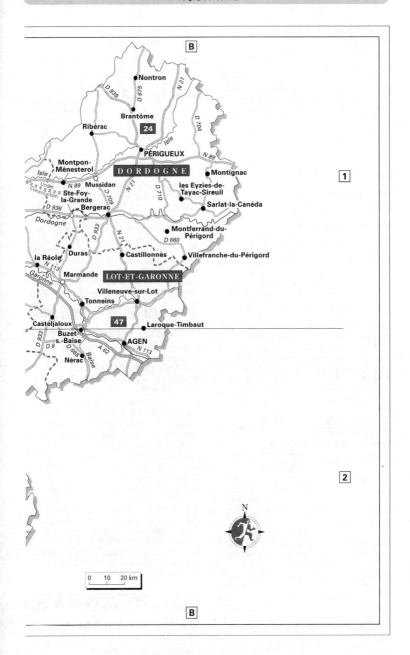

Closed Sat evening, Sun and Wed evenings except July–Aug.

The decor may not be particularly bohemian, but the place definitely seems to belong to a different era. The food is creative and original; dishes include spicy duck breast, leg of lamb with mild garlic and rosemary, shrimps *à la marinière*, pork *colombo* or creole stew followed by either chocolate *fondant* or roast banana with coconut. Weekday lunch menu 69F, with others 99–175F. They host regular theme evenings, concentrating on a country, region or wine. Particularly attentive welcome and service. Free apéritif or coffee.

I●I LES AUCAS

35 rue Voltaire (Centre).
☎ 05.53.48.13.71
Closed Wed evening and Sun.

In the old medieval town, this establishment dedicated to the goose ("aucas" is goose in Provençal) is on a little street that becomes an outdoor café in summer. Inside, the decor is simple but creates a nice atmosphere, with bare brick walls, Basque table cloths, a grandfather clock, and classical music playing in the background. Lunch is a speedy affair but at dinner you can really savour the local gastronomic delicacies – stuffed goose neck with herbs, goose ham fillets and so on – in carefully crafted dishes. Menu at 95F (not Saturday or public holidays), then 135–195F. There's a wide and interesting selection of wines, but the wine by the jug can be unreliable. Very nice welcome.

⚐ I●I RESTAURANT MARIOTTAT

25 rue Louis-Vivent (Centre).
☎ 05.53.77.99.77 ➨ 05.53.77.99.79
Closed Sat lunchtime, Sun evenings, Mon, and one week in Feb. **Disabled access**. **Car park**.

Éric and Christiane Mariottat abandoned their hotel in the suburbs of Agen to set up this restaurant in a very fine master-craftsman mansion surrounded by parkland, just a stone's throw from the Jacobin monastery. The house has a warm atmosphere and a cosy decor with ceiling mouldings, splendid parquet and impressive chandeliers. The chef makes full use of all a duck has to offer, from the liver to the breast – his duck pâté *en croûte* is a real delight. Every morning he re-invents his dishes depending on what he has bought fresh at the market that day. Everything is wonderful, from the potato *millefeuille* with warm *foie gras* and truffle gravy to the suckling lamb medley with basil. To finish, try prune ravioli in wine with orange. Menus 105F, except Sunday and pub-

lic holidays, then 140–295F and a children's menu at 75F. Free coffee.

⚐ I●I RESTAURANT LE NOSTRADAMUS

40 rue des Nitiobriges; it's on the road to Vérone.
☎ 05.53.47.01.02
Closed Sun evening and Mon.

The wife of Nostradamus, medieval seer, is supposed to have come from round here, hence the restaurant's name. This all-wooden house has become a runaway success. It's on the edge of town and you feel as if you've gone to eat in the country. In summer you can have a meal on the terrace in the dappled shade of the trees. Inside the decor is a successful balance between rustic and modern. If you order the 128F *formule*, you start by helping yourself from the twenty starters on the buffet and finish off with a choice from ten desserts. In between, there's a small selction of tasty and original main courses: semi-cooked *foie gras* with quince jelly, quail with grapes, duck with orange, a selection of meats grilled over the open fire, and parsleyed scallops with curry. Youthful and cordial welcome. Free apéritif and house toasts.

SÉRIGNAC-SUR-GARONNE   47310 (8KM W)

⚐ ♠ I●I HÔTEL LE PRINCE NOIR★★★

It's on the D119 in the direction of Nérac, after the bridge over the Garonne.
☎ 05.53.68.74.30 ➨ 05.53.68.71.93
Closed Sun evening. **Swimming pool**. **TV**. **Disabled access**. **Car park**.

A sublime place in an ancient 17th-century convent. The Black Prince was the son of Edward III, the Lieutenant General of Aquitaine who laid waste to the southwest during the 100 Years War. You get to the courtyard through a turreted porch. With high ceilings and period furniture, the rooms, at ground level and upstairs, are all very good, and some are sumptuous. Doubles 300–500F. Menus 105–230F, children's menu 45F or *à la carte*; escalope of duck *foie gras* with grapes, roasted rolled capon stuffed with ceps, suckling pig and so on. Luxury at affordable prices, but it's worth booking because they often host business seminars. Free apéritif and 10% discount on the room rate Oct–May.

AIGUILLON   47190

⚐ ♠ I●I HÔTEL-RESTAURANT LA TER- RASSE DE L'ETOILE★★

It's in a partly-pedestrianised street.

☎ 05.53.79.64.64 ➡ 05.53.79.46.48
Swimming pool. Disabled access. TV. Car park.

A superb little hotel built in white stone. There are seventeen rooms, all different but equally charming, decorated in 1930s style with iron bedsteds and country furniture. Doubles 260F with bath. The dining room is quite elegant (apart from the plastic chairs) and there's a terrace overlooking the swimming pool. The menus start at 78F (except weekends and public holidays), then 98–145F, featuring dishes like scallops in pastry with vegetables, confit of duck with prunes, snail and parsley salad, duck breast with honey, and *foie gras* with apples. Charming welcome. Free apéritif.

CLAIRAC   47320 (8KM NE)

|●| L'ECUELLE D'OR

22 rue Porte Pinte.
☎ 05.53.88.19.78
Closed Sun evening and Mon. **Car park.**

A typical village house in rough brick with oak beams. The dining room is relaxing and there's an open fire where they burn whole logs. Even at lunchtime, the restaurant produces food that's close to gourmet quality but at affordable prices. The fresh produce is turned into imaginative dishes – how about *millefeuille* of courgette flowers? – and the menu changes frequently. They make everything in their own kitchens including the bread. And if you're looking for more traditional fare they list *confit* of duck. Weekday menu 75F, then 95–195F. Excellent welcome.

AMOU   40330

🌴 🛏 |●| HÔTEL-RESTAURANT LES VOYAGEURS**

pl. de Latécoère (Centre).
☎ 05.58.89.02.31 ➡ 05.58.89.25.12
Restaurant closed Fri evening except in summer, and Feb. **TV. Garden. Car park.**

This hotel, its façade covered in Virginia creeper, is set on a plane-tree-lined square. You can cheer on the *pétanque* players from the rooms overlooking the square. Doubles 260–300F with bath. They serve good, unpretentious food, which suits the surroundings; veal sweetbreads with Madeira, fresh *foie gras* with apples, duck *confit*, cep omelette, woodpigeon stew and *omelette norvegienne*. Set menus 70–200F. Free apéritif.

ANDERNOS-LES-BAINS   33510

🛏 HÔTEL DE LA CÔTE D'ARGENT

180 bd. de la République.
☎ 05.56.03.98.58 ➡ 05.56.03.98.68

Probably the best value in the area, with twelve pleasant, well-equipped rooms. 240–300F with shower/wc or bath. There's a small flowery patio with a small fountain – two rooms are at garden level. Breakfast includes fresh fruit and real orange juice. Smiling welcome.

TAUSSAT   33148 (8KM SE)

🌴 |●| RESTAURANT LES FONTAINES

Port de plaisance de Taussat; from Bordeaux take the expressway in the direction of Cap Ferret.
☎ 05.56.82.13.86 ➡ 05.57.70.23.43
Closed Sun evening, Mon and three weeks in Nov. **Car park.**

This modern building near the marina doesn't exactly ooze charm, but it has a really pleasant terrace where you can sit on a warm evening and enjoy the inspired cooking of chef Jean-Pascal Paubert. Try his *tartare* of salmon with chives. Menus 98–235F. As with many of the restaurants in the region, you can bring your own wine. The owner is chairman of the local *sommeliers* association. Free house apéritif.

AUDENGE   33980 (8KM SE)

🛏 |●| LE RELAIS GASCON

24 av. de Certes.
☎ 05.56.26.83.94 ➡ 05.56.26.95.11
Closed Sun evening out of season. **Car park.**

It's hard to find a restaurant offering anything other than oysters in these parts. Though the menus do list oysters, the chef here specialises in authentic Girondin dishes: goose neck stuffed with *foie gras*, goose *rillettes* and Médoc salad but they do serve fish and oysters, too. Menus 63F (not served Sunday or public holidays), 150 and 165F. There are a few simple double rooms with basin and bidet – shower and wc on the landing – which go for 190F.

ARCACHON   33120

🛏 HÔTEL LA PERGOLA

40 cours Lamarque-de-Plaisance.
☎ 05.56.83.07.89 ➡ 05.56.83.14.21
TV. Car park.

A centrally located, delightfully renovated hotel that's quiet, thanks to the double glazing, and well run. Doubles 150–390F with shower, shower/wc or bath. The top-priced ones have a terrace.

⚤ ☎ HÔTEL LES MIMOSAS**

77 [bis] av. de la République (Centre); it's near pl. de Verdun.
☎ 05.56.83.45.86 ➡ 05.56.22.53.40
Closed Jan and Feb. **TV. Car park. Disabled access**.

This hotel is in a fine and large Arcachon house near the ocean. Warm welcome, and clean, neat rooms. Doubles with shower/wc 250–350F, with bath, 280–380F. Some rooms in the annexe are suitable for disabled travellers.

⚤ ☎ |●| VILLA TÉRÉSA HÔTEL-RESTAURANT SÉMIRAMIS***

4 allée Rebsomen (Centre).
☎ 05.56.83.25.87 ➡ 05.57.52.22.41
Closed 10 Jan–28 Feb. **Swimming pool. Garden. TV. Car park**.

A 19th-century villa in a variety of architectural styles – Hispano-Moorish, neo-Gothic, Swiss and colonial – in the part of Arcachon known as the "winter town". Saved from demolition in the 1970s, the house was listed as a historic monument and renovated from top to bottom. The attractive rooms are all very different; some have a balcony. There are others in a little pavilion next to the pleasant swimming pool. Doubles with shower/wc 460–530F, or 550–760F with bath. The restaurant serves fish and seafood such as Biscay sea bream or bass. One set menu at 180F. Half board 445–555F per person. Free breakfast for children under five.

|●| LES GENÊTS

25 bd. du Gl Leclerc (Centre).
☎ 05.56.83.49.28
Closed Sun evening and Mon out of season, 2–18 Jan and the first fortnight in Oct.

The dining room is a classic, serving traditional cuisine and regional dishes. There's a weekday lunch menu at 81F, with others up to 145F. The 99F menu lists nine oysters followed by duck *confit*. Sadly, it's in a poor location with a view of the rail track and a filling station.

⚤ |●| RESTAURANT LE CHIPIRON

69 bd. Chanzy (East); it's near the marina.
☎ 05.57.52.06.33
Closed Tues evening, Wed and Jan.

A Spanish bistro off the tourist track. The decor boasts little more than a few hams hanging from the ceiling for local colour. The cuisine deals in simple, basic dishes: tapas, grilled fish and meat and, unsurprisingly, given the restaurant's name, *chipirons à la plancha* (grilled baby squid). Generous servings of good authentic, tasty little dishes. Reckon on paying 100–120F *à la carte*. Friendly welcome, pleasant service, regular clientele — it's a simple place where you feel at ease and eat well. Free glass of sangria.

PYLA-SUR-MER   33115 (5KM SW)

☎ HÔTEL MAMINOTTE**

allée des Acacias (Northeast); take the D217 or the D218 and it's 200m from the beach.
☎ 05.56.54.05.05 ➡ 05.57.52.06.06
Disabled access. Garden.

This small, twelve-room hotel looks just like all the other houses in this peaceful part of town, lost among the pine trees and 100m from the ocean. Friendly welcome. Comfortable and pleasant rooms which have been decorated in Mediterranean style; some have little balconies. 250F for a double but prices go up to 520F in July and August, which is expensive.

☎ |●| HÔTEL-RESTAURANT CÔTÉ DU SUD**

4 av. du Figuier.
☎ 05.56.83.25.00 ➡ 05.56.83.24.13
Closed mid Nov to early Feb. **TV**.

This unpretentious, single-storey, yellow and blue hotel faces south, as you might guess, and is right by the sea. The whole place has been done up, sound-proofed and double-glazed. Wonderful welcome. Comfortable rooms 350–450F; rates increase to 450–600F in July and August. Highly rated restaurant. Sit on the south-facing shady terrace to try the famous house specialities, such as tuna tartare *Côté du Sud*, shellfish *marinière*, smoked, cured Bayonne ham in a cream sauce, seafood platter, and lobster *fricassée* with vanilla and spices. Set menus 108–165F.

PILAT-PLAGE   33115 (10KM SW)

⚤ ☎ |●| HÔTEL-RESTAURANT LA CORNICHE**

46 bd. Louis-Gaume.
☎ 05.56.22.72.11 ➡ 05.56.22.70.21
Hotel closed 1 Nov to Easter. **Restaurant closed** Wed except July–Aug. **TV. Garden**.

Wonderfully located between pine trees and clumps of flowers at the foot of a large dune with steps down to the beach, so it's close to the water. There's a large communal terrace with deckchairs and hammocks. Very warm welcome. Doubles with basin 150–250F, with shower/wc 350F, and with bath 400–480F. Rooms over the kitchens are noisy; others have balconies overlooking the ocean. The panoramic restaurant offers menus from 95–149F. Fish and seafood predominate: creole-style stuffed crab, Spanish-style sea bream and fresh cod with pickled onions and *piquillos*. It's more expensive *à la carte* – you'll pay an average of 170F, which is a bit pricey for such simple cooking. Dishes include Arcachon-style mussels, *escalope* of meagre (similar to sea bass) with sorrel, and fillet of beef with *gigas*. Half board, compulsory July–Aug, costs 250–500F per person. Free apéritif.

ARÈS　　33740

♠ |●| LE SAINT-ÉLOI

11 bd. de l'Aérium.
☎ 05.56.60.20.46 ➡ 05.56.60.10.37
Closed Sun evening, Mon out of season and Feb school holidays.

Situated among the pines in a quiet location 500m from the beach. Clean, spacious double rooms with good beds; 150F with basin and 175F with shower. The elegant restaurant has a particularly good reputation as all the dishes are perfectly prepared. Menus from 130F. Good wines and competent service.

ASTAFFORT　　47229

☆ ♠ |●| MICHEL LATRILLE

5–7 pl. de la Craste (Centre).
☎ 05.53.47.20.40
Closed Sat lunchtime, Sun evening, Mon and three weeks in Jan. **TV. Disabled access**. **Pay car park**.

Michel Latrille is passionate about cooking local dishes using high-quality produce and he plays around with different flavours. The results are excellent: semi-cooked duck *foie gras*, boned pigeon perfumed with sweet spices and honey, warm monkfish salad with pickled tomato petals and parsley oil, *croustillant* of veal sweetbreads, and his famous *moelleux au chocolat* dessert. Menus 130F (except weekends and public holidays) and 190F or 300F *à la carte*. There are also fourteen comfortable rooms decorated in bright, warm Provençal colours. Doubles 360F. Free coffee.

BARCUS　　64130

♠ |●| CHILO***

Centre.
☎ 05.59.28.90.79 ➡ 05.59.28.93.10
e matiné.club@wanadoo.fr
Closed Sun evening and Mon out of season, and Jan.
Swimming pool. Garden. TV. Pay car park.

A popular place on the borders of the Béarn and the Basque country. It has been enlarged but hasn't lost its soul, and is still family run. Attractive, nicely appointed rooms are 420–450F for a double with shower/wc or 470–500F for bath. Unusual, original cooking: farmers' salad with breaded pigs' ears, and milk-fed lamb chops with ravioli stuffed with sheep's cheese. Keep a space for the speciality desserts; *macaron à l'Izarra* and a *charlotte* made with ewe's milk. 75F menu of the day and 120–240F.

☆ |●| RESTAURANT CHEZ SYLVAIN

pl. du Fronton (Centre).
☎ 05.59.28.92.11 ➡ 05.59.28.94.37
Closed Thurs and 23 May–1 June.

You'll get a charming welcome in this family-run restaurant. It's like a country inn, with a mainly local clientele. The country-style cooking is prepared with a great deal of care and taste. Dishes include lamb in wine, lamb sweetbreads with parsley, delicious omelettes and an excellent home-made *garbure* (Béarnaise vegetable broth). Menus 70F and 80F. Worth going out of your way for. Free coffee.

BARP (LE)　　33114

☆ ♠ |●| LE RÉSINIER

Route de Bayonne (N10); it's 36km south of Bordeaux.
☎ 05.56.88.60.07 ➡ 05.56.88.67.37
Closed Sun evening. **TV. Car park**.

This small hotel and restaurant is a good place to stop on the dusty and often congested N10. They offer a few rooms – doubles 270F with shower/wc or bath – and honest local cooking. Dishes include *foie gras* terrine with Guérende salt, roast monkfish with red pepper *coulis*, *grenier médocain* (sliced cold meats), sturgeon *à la bordelaise*, lamb, and a duck trio of *foie gras*, *confit* and breast. Set menu 89F during the week or 119–220F. Free coffee and 10% discount on the room rate.

BAYONNE   64100

⚥ ⚐ HÔTEL DES BASSES-PYRÉNÉES**

1 pl. des Victoires and 14 rue Tour-de-Sault (Centre); it's in the old town.
☎ 05.59.59.00.29
Restaurant closed Sun and Mon lunchtimes except July–Aug, and 15 Dec–15 Jan. **TV. Pay car park**.

Extremely well-managed family hotel, strategically situated near the ramparts. The rooms overlooking the square are quiet, but if you're not spooked by the creaking floorboards, the one in the executioner's tower is superb. Doubles 180–310F. In the restaurant, menus go for 90–180F. Their specialities are duck breast with peaches and sole stuffed with ceps in a special sauce. 10% discount on the room rate Oct–May.

⚥ ⚐ |●| HÔTEL FRANTOUR-LOUSTAU***

1 pl. de la République (Centre); it's near pont Saint-Esprit on the river bank.
☎ 05.59.55.08.08 ➡ 05.59.55.69.36
ℓ loustan@aol.com
TV. Disabled access. Car park.

On the River Adour, with an uninterrupted view of old Bayonne and the Pyrenees, this 200-year-old hotel offers clean, well-soundproofed rooms which are excellent value. Doubles with bath or shower 390–450F. The restaurant offers specialities such as *favouille* soup or *piperade* with dried duck breast and Serrano ham, roast suckling lamb and Spanish-style cod. Set menus 65–150F. 10% discount on the room rate Oct–July.

|●| LE BISTROT SAINTE-CLUQUE

9 rue Hughes; it's opposite the train station.
☎ 05.59.55.82.43
Closed Mon Oct–July.

The place to eat in Bayonne. David is an excellent English chef who plays with flavours and mixes them inventively, using simple produce. Prices are reasonable. Try the house paella or duck with honey and lemon. There's a basic set menu for 59F, then 85F and 95F in the evening, while *à la carte* you can dine for about 150F. You are strongly advised to book; the place is always full both inside and on the terrace. It's popular with the gay community.

⚥ |●| LE CHISTERA

42 rue Port-Neuf; in the pedestrian area between the town hall and the cathedral.
☎ 05.59.59.25.93

Closed Mon, Tues and Wed evenings except in season, and 1–8 May.

Jean-Pierre Marmouyet has taken over the restaurant originally opened by his father, a former *cestapunta* champion and a great coach. Jean-Pierre manages to combine being a restaurateur and a professional *pelota* player. The food in this local canteen-style place is typical of Bayonne, with fabulous tripe and fish, and daily specials are chalked up on the blackboard. If you see pig's trotters or *louvines* (wild bream), order them. Prices are reasonable – menus 85–120F – and service is friendly. Free sangria.

|●| RESTAURANT LE TRINQUET MODERNE

58 av. Dubrocq (West); follow the Adour, turn left into av. Dubrocq and it's the first on the left after av. de la Légion-Tchèque.
☎ 05.59.59.05.22 ➡ 05.59.25.73.55
Car park.

Despite the drab decor, you get a more genuine feeling of the Basque country here than in the taverns of Petit Bayonne. Jean-Marie Mailharro, a *pelota* fan, attracts all the region's *pelota* and *mus* players to his restaurant, serving them good, solid, simple regional dishes. Hits include the omelette of local ham, *confit* of Béguios sausages, and sweetbreads with ceps. The portions are substantial and there's always a good atmosphere. If they like you they'll seat you at the main table where you can rub shoulders with *pelota* champions and magistrats from the neighbouring law courts. Menus 100–130F.

⚥ |●| RESTAURANT EL ASADOR

pl. Montaut (Centre); it's near the cathedral.
☎ 05.59.59.08.57
Closed Sun evening and Mon, three weeks Christmas–New Year and a fortnight in June.

Set on the Montaut square, with its many antique dealers and junk shops, this small restaurant specialises in grills over the open fire – *asador* is the Spanish word for a grill chef, and the man in question is Maris-Jésus. The line-caught fish is splendid, particularly the cod with garlic or sea bream *à l'espagnole*. Menu 125F, or 170F *à la carte*. Free apéritif or *digestif*.

BAZAS   33430

⚥ ⚐ HOSTELLERIE SAINT-SAUVEUR**

14 rue du Gal-de-Gaulle (Centre).
☎ 05.56.25.12.18

✉ milaty@gironde.com
Closed Sun in winter and 2–15 Oct. **TV**. **Disabled access**. **Pay car park**.

Fifth-generation business that has been handed down from mother to daughter since 1886. The exterior is pretty dull, and it's hard to imagine that it was the residence of the last bishop of Bazas, Grégoire de Saint-Sauveur. The rooms are somewhat cluttered, with a kitsch, 1970s-style decor. They are, nonetheless, pretty good value at 230F for a double with shower/wc or bath. No restaurant, but there's a bistro, the *Saint-Sô*, on the ground floor. Free coffee.

🕊 |●| RESTAURANT DES REMPARTS

Espace Mauvezin (Centre); it's near the cathedral.
☎ and ➡ 05.56.25.95.24
Closed Sun evening and Mon.

Park near the cathedral and walk through the passage to this restaurant. It is next to the Mairie, superbly situated on the *brèche de Bazas*, overlooking the Sultan's garden. You can enjoy these quite exceptional surroundings from the terrace when the weather is fine. The very classic decor is understated, and the cuisine is inspired, using quality produce like Bazas beef or Grignol capon. Set menus 70–220F: sweetbread salad, semi-cooked *foie gras* and cabbage stuffed with duck. À la carte choices include shellfish *millefeuille* in cream and port sauce, and veal sweetbreads in Sauternes with mushrooms. Free coffee.

GOUALADE · · · · 33840 (16.5KM SE)

🕊 |●| RESTAURANT L'AUBERGE GAS-CONNE

How to get there: it's in the centre, on the main road opposite the church.
☎ 05.56.65.81.77
Closed Mon, Sun evening and 26 June–13 July.

This inn is in the middle of nowhere in the Gironde Landaise area. It's deep in the woods across the road from an old village church with a turret. Inside, it is unexpectedly smart and comfortable, and air-conditioned. A group of regulars, including lorry drivers and electricity board employees, flock here for its good cooking and low prices. No one would dream of "reinventing" local dishes here. The simple country cooking comes from good old recipes and is substantial, filling and unpretentious. Large slices of Bayonne ham, wood-pigeon stew, *confit* of turkey, duck, pork, wild boar casserole and *poule-au-pot* all come with as many *frites* as

you can eat. Set menu 60F (including wine and coffee) and around 100F *à la carte* – try grilled quails with sweet herbs, roast guinea fowl or pressed *foie gras* with leeks. Free coffee.

CAPTIEUX · · · · 33840 (17KM S)

⌂ |●| HÔTEL-RESTAURANT CAP DES LANDES

rue Principale; it's on the D932 in the centre of town opposite the church.
☎ 05.56.65.64.93 ➡ 05.56.65.64.75
Closed Sun evening and Mon. **TV**. **Car park**.

This hotel is in the middle of a small market town on a noisy road with lorry traffic at night – try to get one of the simple rooms at the back. Doubles from 230F with bath. Nice family atmosphere. The hotel may be a bit on the noisy side but there are no complaints about the food. Though you can get a meal in the little room by the bar, the dining room next door is more stylish with menus 65–170F. Choose from local duck specialties and various gourmet salads, *escalope* of *foie gras* with apples and fresh grapes.

BELHADE · · · · 40410

|●| RESTAURANT EULOGE-LE CHÊNE PASCAL

☎ 05.58.07.72.01
Closed Sun evening and Mon out of season.
TV. **Car park**.

A charming little inn with kindly staff. The quality of the tasty meat and fish dishes they serve make it worth the detour, the full flavours of the ingredients brought out in the cooking process. There's a very good short menu of the day at 90F then others up to 160F. One of the better restaurants in the Haut-Pays Landais.

BERGERAC · · · · 24100

🕊 ⌂ |●| FAMILY HÔTEL-RESTAURANT LE JARDIN D'EPICURE**

pl. du Marché-Couvert (Centre).
☎ 05.53.57.80.90
Closed Sun except in summer. **TV**. **Car park**.

One of the cheapest hotels in town, in a great location in the old centre. The atmosphere is relaxed and youthful. The rooms are good value, at 180F for a double with basin, 190F with shower/wc, and 245F with bath. If you like a bit of space go for numbers 1, 4, 7 or 10, which have been refurbished and fitted with air-conditioning. The dining room has also been done up, and the bill of fare now includes some good traditional dishes. Menus 85–170F. 10% discount on the room rate Sept–June.

♠ |●| HÔTEL-RESTAURANT LA FLAMBÉE***

153 av. Pasteur; it's 2km north of Bergerac on the N21 towards Périgueux.
☎ 05.53.57.52.33 ➡ 05.53.61.07.57
Restaurant closed Sun evening and Mon out of season. **Swimming pool**. **TV**. **Garden**. **Car park**.

Though not far from the main road this hotel is in substantial gardens with a tennis court and a swimming pool, so it's as quiet as anything behind its thick curtain of trees. The twenty or so standard rooms are split between a large, fine Périgord residence and a summer house. Doubles 350–370F with bath. Some rooms have a small terrace. The restaurant is *the* place to be seen on the Bergerac circuit, thanks to its opulent decor and its reliable cuisine of local dishes and good plain home cooking. It's best to book. Set menus 99–300F. À *la carte* dishes include scallop *marguerite* in champagne, salad of langoustine tails perfumed with raspberries, *escalope* of salmon in Monbazillac wine and strawberries *au gratin* in a Monbazillac *sabayon*. Pleasant terrace for when the weather is fine.

|●| RESTAURANT LA SAUVAGINE

18–20 rue Eugène-Leroy (Centre).
☎ 05.53.57.06.97
Closed Sun and Mon evenings, mid-Jan to Feb, a week in June and ten days in Sept.

Modern, air-conditioned restaurant that serves traditional, well-prepared cuisine at honest prices. Go for fish such as lamprey from the Bordeaux region, seafood, or game in season, and make room for the delicious desserts. Great little menu at 80F and others up to 180F. Classy clientele but a friendly, natural welcome.

⅔ |●| CÔTÉ DORDOGNE

17 rue du Château; it's on the old city walls.
☎ 05.53.57.17.57 ➡ 05.53.57.52.88

This beautiful house is situated above the old port. It has a splendid trellised roof laden with wisteria – but you can still see the Dordogne. Though the terrace is noisy because of the traffic, the dining room is quiet and elegant. They serve high-quality, inventive cui-

sine and offer a good-value 95F menu, with others up to 160F. The range of dishes is vast, and there are lots of local wines. Free apéritif.

|●| RESTAURANT L'ENFANCE DE LARD

rue Pélissière (Centre).
☎ 05.53.57.52.88 ➡ 05.53.57.52.88
Closed Tues, Wed lunchtime and the last fortnight in Sept.

A charming restaurant on the first floor of a 12th-century house on one of Bergerac's finest squares. It's small so it soon fills up, so it's essential to book. It has a warm, intimate atmosphere and a fantastic view of the medieval church. Arias play in the background. The remarkable regional cuisine from the southwest includes quality meats grilled over vines in the superb fireplace, Sarlat-style apples which melt in the mouth, rack of lamb with mint, ceps in parsley *vinaigrette* and a mosaic of pan-fried *foie gras* served with peaches in the summer or lentils in winter. Generous helpings. 150F menu or 200–300F à *la carte*.

SAINT-JULIEN-DE-CREMPSE   24140 (12KM N)

⅔ ♠ |●| LE MANOIR DU GRAND VIGNOBLE***

How to get there: take the N21 then the D107.
☎ 05.53.24.23.18 ➡ 05.53.24.20.89
⊜ grand.vignoble@wanadoo.fr
Closed 15 Nov–30 March. **Swimming pool**. **TV**. **Car park**.

A very fine 17th-century manor house – also an equestrian centre – in beautiful countryside. It's a luxury establishment, with enormous, charming rooms – 380–680F for a double with bath. Facilities include tennis courts, heated swimming pool and fitness centre. The restaurant offers set menus for 150–290F, featuring dishes such as poached *foie gras* with grapes, duck breast with ceps and zander *demi-deuil*. 10% discount on the room rate.

ISSIGEAC   24560 (19KM SE)

|●| CHEZ ALAIN

Tour de Ville; it's on the edge of town, opposite the château.
☎ 05.53.58.77.88
⊜ infor@chez-alain.com
Closed Sun evening and Mon except 1–30 Sept, and 15 Jan–15 Feb. **Disabled access**.

A very elegant residence that has been skillfully restored. There's a huge terrace round a village fountain, and tastefully decorated dining rooms. Dishes change with the season: snail turnovers with crayfish *coulis*, pike *mousseline florentine*, char with basil. The desserts are particularly unusual. Weekday menu 69F, then others 119–195F – the more expensive menus are a little short. The quality is excellent and the aimable owner, who manages front of house, ensures that everything runs smoothly. They do a Sunday brunch.

RAZAC-D'EYMET   24500 (20KM S)

🚶 🛏 🍴 LA PETITE AUBERGE**

It's on the edge of the village.
☎ 05.53.24.69.27 📠 05.53.61.02.63
📧 lparazmet@aol.com
Hotel closed Jan. **Restaurant closed** lunchtimes, Sun and Nov–March.
Swimming pool. Disabled access. Car park.

Peace and quiet is guaranteed in this tiny village where this former farm has been transformed into a charming hotel by an English couple. There are just seven pleasant rooms, some under the eaves, one of them a little suite; 200–300F for a double with shower/wc or bath. The welcoming restaurant has a lunchtime menu for 98F and a children's menu for 50F; in the evening you shouldn't part with more than 100F *à la carte*. Dishes include soup, poached salmon in butter sauce, and walnut tart. You can also rent self-catering houses. The *Poulailler* (henhouse) sleeps four and the *Ferme* (farm) six; rates vary. Delightful swimming pool. 10% discount on the room rate for a stay of two nights minimum.

BIARRITZ   64200

🛏 HÔTEL DE LA MARINE

1 rue des Goélands (Centre).
☎ 05.59.24.34.09

Backpacker-style hotel in a town which is otherwise a bit on the posh side. Very friendly atmosphere and warm welcome. The clean and very well-kept rooms go for 200F with shower or 220F with shower/wc. The bar downstairs, not part of the hotel, is a good place to drink.

🚶 🛏 HÔTEL LA ROMANCE**

6 allée des Acacias (South); from the centre, take the av. du Maréchal, and it's near the racecourse.
☎ 05.59.41.25.65 📠 05.59.44.25.65
Closed 8 Jan–5 March.

A little off the beaten track in a residential area. The wonderful proprietor, for whom nothing is too much trouble, has decorated the ten rooms with a floral theme. Number 10 has a little terrace. Doubles with shower/wc or bath cost 230–410F. Free coffee.

🚶 🛏 HÔTEL LE SAINT-CHARLES**

21 av. Foch (North).
☎ 05.59.24.10.54 📠 05.59.24.56.74
Closed end Nov to the Feb school holidays.
Garden. TV. Pay garage.

A real haven of peace just out of the centre, very prettily done out in pink. *Patronne* Annie goes out of her way to be welcoming. If you like peace and quiet, greenery and flowers, you'll find it hard to leave, especially after breakfasting in the lovely garden. Freshly refurbished rooms with period furniture, singles 240–420F, doubles 270–450F and others sleeping three or four. Well worth going out of your way for. Garage space 30F per night. Free breakfast every three days.

🛏 HÔTEL MAÏTAGARIA**

34 av. Carnot; it's 500m from the sea opposite the public gardens.
☎ 05.59.24.26.65 📠 05.59.24.27.37 **TV. Garden.**

You'd do best to book at this good place, which attracts a host of regulars. It's a charming town house with quiet, comfortable rooms. Doubles 300–360F with shower/wc and 330–360F with bath. There's a very pleasant flowery garden. Warm welcome. 10% discount Oct–May.

🛏 HÔTEL PALYM*

7 rue du Port-Vieux; it's 100m from the sea.
☎ 05.59.24.16.56 📠 05.59.24.96.12
Closed All Saints' holidays. **TV.**

An old-fashioned, well-kept hotel with old-world charm, and decor that strikes a nice balance between past and present. A little winding staircase leads to the rooms, which are neat and tidy. Doubles cost 300F with shower/wc and 320F with bath. The rooms at the rear are quieter than those overlooking the nice but noisy rue du Port-Vieux. Friendly staff. 10% discount 1 April–15 June, 20% discount 15 Oct–31 March.

🛏 LE CHÂTEAU DU CLAIR DE LUNE

48 av. Alan-Seeger (Southeast); it's near the station on the Arbonne road.
☎ 05.59.41.53.20 📠 05.59.41.53.29
📧 hotel-clair-de-lune@wanadoo.fr
TV. Car park.

A secluded 19th-century residence, splendidly decorated in Art Deco style. It's in wonderful, flower-filled grounds with formal and landscaped gardens. Doubles 450–750F. The rooms are enormous and furnished to a high standard. A dream of a place where you can relax away from the hectic life on the coast. Reservations are advisable.

ANGLET   64600 (3KM NE)

🏂|●| LA FLEUR DE SEL

5 av. de la Forêt.
☎ 05.59.63.88.66
Closed Wed and Sun evening, third week in Jan and first fortnight in Nov.

A little restaurant, run by a dynamic young couple, in the midst of the Chiberta forest. It's a quiet contrast to the popular beach resorts and it fills quickly. Modern, inventive, carefully worked cuisine with dishes depending on what's fresh in the market. Weekday lunch *formule* 90F or *menu-carte* at 150F. They open the terrace on sunny days and light a fire when it's cold. Free *digestif*.

ARBONNE   64210 (5KM SE)

🏂 🏠 |●| ESKUALDUNA**

How to get there: take the D255.
☎ 05.59.41.95.41 ➡ 05.59.41.88.16
Closed Sun evening in winter. **Garden. Car park**.

Jolly place with a lively bar. Customers, most of them factory workers, are welcomed into the big dining room. Jacky, the owner, keeps the conversation going between courses, flinging out comments on the latest rugby match or chatting away while cooking up his sauces. He is as robust as the regional cuisine on his set menus at 62–87F and 130F. They also have double rooms with shower for 230F, or 275F with bath. 10% discount on the room rate July–Aug.

BISCARROSSE   40600

🏠 HÔTEL LE SAINT HUBERT

588 av. P. G. Latecoere.
☎ 05.58.78.09.99 ➡ 05.58.78.79.37
📧 lesaint.hubert@wanadoo.fr
Garden. Car park.

It's just outside the village, near the lake, and you feel as if you're way out in the country yet the summer hordes simply don't come here. You can stretch out with a book in the garden

that's full of scented flowers. They put out tables for tea or breakfast. Double rooms 265–340F.

🏂 🏠 |●| HÔTEL LA CARAVELLE**

5314 route des Lacs, quartier ISPE, Lac Nord. On the bank of lac Cazaux on the way to the golf course.
☎ 05.58.09.82.67 ➡ 05.58.09.82.18
Closed Mon lunchtime and mid-Nov to mid-Feb. **TV. Car park**.

A fine, large building in a pleasant setting on the banks of the lake. They've painted the whole place white, and nearly all the rooms have a little balcony that looks out onto the water. Doubles 300F with shower/wc, 400F with bath. There's also a villa to rent in summer, sleeping four. A lovely restful place, though the frogs may disturb some guests on spring nights. The restaurant serves good local food, with dishes such as Landes-style salad with *foie gras, confit* of duck breast, lamb shin in a cream garlic sauce, monkfish kebabs, veal sweetbreads in Jurançon wine, eel *fricassée* and fillet of zander with leek *fondue*. Set menus 90F (not Sunday), and 120–240F. Half board is compulsory in summer, at 320F per person. Free house apéritif, and 10% discount on the room rate in winter.

|●| RESTAURANT CHEZ CAMETTE

532 av. Latécoère (South).
☎ 05.58.78.12.78
Closed Fri evening out of season.

A popular and quaint little inn with white walls and red shutters. There's a short set menu at 65F. Wonderful welcome and generous helpings. The food is simple and unpretentious: a set menu (88–138F) will get you soup, mussels in white wine, and *escalope* in cream sauce. Don't miss out on the house speciality – duck breast grilled over the open fire.

BORDEAUX   33000

SEE MAP OVERLEAF

🏂 🏠 HÔTEL BOULAN

28 rue Boulan. **MAP B3-4**
☎ and ➡ 05.56.52.23.62
TV.

A simple little hotel with no stars, near the cathedral and town hall. The cleanliness of the place, the obliging owners and the peaceful atmosphere (despite its prime location) win you over. Simple, well-maintained rooms with good beds. Doubles with basin 110–120F, with shower (wc on the landing) 140F. Breakfast is served in your room. Good value. 10% discount on the room rate Oct–May.

♠ HÔTEL DAUPHIN*

82 rue du Palais Gallien. **MAP B2-3**
☎ 05.56.52.24.62 ➡ 05.56.01.10.91
Closed last three weeks in Aug. **TV**.

The French star Viviane Romance lived in room 7 during World War II, and even today the hotel is heavily redolent of the 1930s and 1940s. It's right in the city centre, in the quietest part of a street which gets busy in the evening. The comfortable rooms are all different. Rates are a tiny bit higher than for the other one-star hotels in the area, but it's well worth the few extra francs. Rooms with basin (wc on the landing) go for 139F, or you'll pay 159F for rooms with shower, 179F with shower/wc. The rooms around the little patio are the quietest.

♠ HÔTEL DE LYON

31 rue des Remparts. **MAP B3-5**
☎ 05.56.81.34.38 ➡ 05.56.52.92.82
TV.

This small hotel, in a pedestrianised street, doesn't have any stars but it is well run. It's very central, near the cathedral of Saint-André, but even the rooms overlooking the street are quiet. They all have a certain charm and are very reasonably priced. Doubles 145F with shower/wc.

⁂ ♠ HÔTEL GAMBETTA**

66 rue Porte-Dijeaux. **MAP B2-8**
☎ 05.56.51.21.83 ➡ 05.56.81.00.40
e hogambetta@aol.com
TV. Car park.

A hotel with good facilities located in a lively part of the centre of town and it's good value for money. TV and mini-bars in the bright and clean rooms. Doubles 210–295F. The owner is amiable. Free breakfast.

♠ HÔTEL DE L'OPÉRA**

35 rue Esprit-des-Lois. **MAP C2-1**
☎ 05.56.81.41.27 ➡ 05.56.51.78.80
e hotel-opera.bx@wanadoo.fr
TV.

An elegant 18th-century house next to the Grand Théâtre. The splendid stone staircase is original, while the rooms have been decorated in more classical style. Doubles 240–300F with shower/wc, 290F or 320F with bath. The drawback is the location – it's right on one of the busiest streets in the centre of town. It's advisable to ask for a room at the back which will be quieter though not so bright. Warm, friendly and charming welcome.

♠ HÔTEL ACANTHE**

12–14 rue Saint-Rémi. **MAP C2-6**
☎ 05.56.81.66.58 ➡ 05.56.44.74.41
e info@acanthe-hotel-bordeaux.com
TV.

Just 20m from the superb place de la Bourse and the riverside, in the picturesque Saint-Pierre area. The hotel has been taken over and the new owners have refurbished it tastefully, creating personalised rooms and offering good facilities. Doubles 250–340F with shower/wc or 270–350F with bath. The owner greets you warmly and can organise visits to the great wine châteaux of Bordeaux. Parking is fiendishly difficult around here.

⁂ ♠ HÔTEL NOTRE-DAME**

36 rue Notre-Dame. Off map **C1-9**
☎ 05.56.52.88.24 ➡ 05.56.79.12.67
TV. Car park.

At the heart of the Les Chartrons district, which used to be full of wine merchants, this stone-fronted 19th-century house has been beautifully cleaned. It is almost overwhelmed by the monumental Cité Mondiale du Vin where you can find anything and everything related to wine. In contrast to the modern and somewhat neutral decor of the rooms, the rue Notre-Dame overflows with antique dealers and bric-à-brac shops. Doubles with shower/wc 255F, with bath 285F. Pay car park nearby. 10% discount July–Aug.

⁂ ♠ HÔTEL DE LA TOUR INTENDANCE**

16 rue de la Vieille-Tour. **MAP B2-10**
☎ 05.56.81.46.27 ➡ 05.56.81.60.90
TV. Pay car park.

Two sisters take turns on reception in this charming establishment, and guests always encounter the same friendly and obliging service. Here the welcome includes numerous thoughtful touches like freshly squeezed orange juice served at breakfast. Everything is efficient and well organised. In the cellar, you can see a few vestiges of the 3rd-century tower of the hotel's name. The rooms on the pedestrianised street can be noisy in summer due to the many lively restaurant terraces nearby. On the other hand, it's completely quiet at the rear where the cheapest rooms (singles) have a nice view over the rooftops. On the whole the rooms aren't large but they've done their best with the decor. Doubles with show-

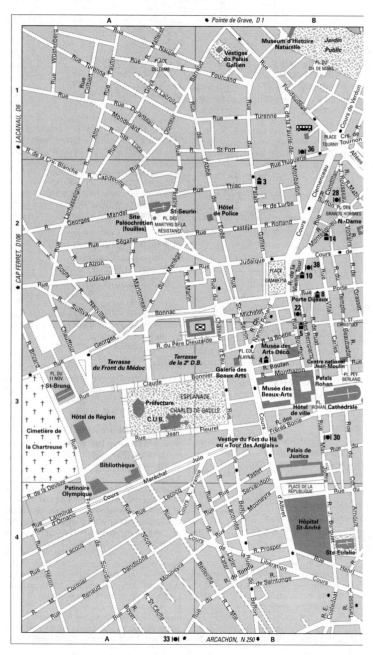

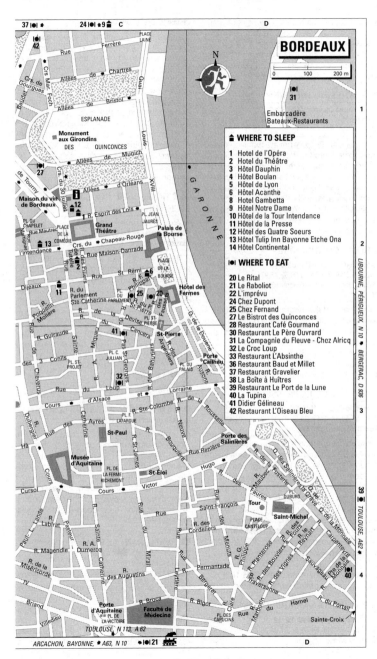

BORDEAUX

0   100   200 m

Embarcadère
Bateaux-Restaurants

🛏 WHERE TO SLEEP

1 Hotel de l'Opéra
2 Hotel du Théâtre
3 Hôtel Dauphin
4 Hôtel Boulan
5 Hôtel de Lyon
6 Hôtel Acanthe
8 Hôtel Gambetta
9 Hôtel Notre Dame
10 Hôtel de la Tour Intendance
11 Hôtel de la Presse
12 Hôtel des Quatre Soeurs
13 Hôtel Tulip Inn Bayonne Etche Ona
14 Hôtel Continental

🍽 WHERE TO EAT

20 Le Rital
21 Le Raboliot
22 L'imprévu
24 Chez Dupont
25 Chez Fernand
27 Le Bistrot des Quinconces
28 Restaurant Café Gourmand
30 Restaurant Le Père Ouvrard
31 La Compagnie du Fleuve - Chez Alricq
32 Le Croc Loup
33 Restaurant L'Absinthe
36 Restaurant Baud et Millet
37 Restaurant Gravelier
38 La Boîte à Huîtres
39 Restaurant Le Port de la Lune
40 La Tupina
41 Didier Gélineau
42 Restaurant L'Oiseau Bleu

er/wc 260F, with bath 280F. Overnight car park 40F, free Sunday and public holidays 7.30pm–9am. Motorcycles free. Free parking for cars Sun and public holidays. 10% discount at weekends and during school holidays.

⅍ ⌂ HÔTEL DU THÉÂTRE**

10 rue Maison-Danrade. **MAP C2-2**
☎ 05.56.79.05.26 ➡ 05.56.81.15.64
TV.

A pair of 18th-century private mansions have been turned into this hotel in the city centre, accessible by car. Animated and friendly welcome. The rooms are rather ordinary but they have good facilities and are kept beautifully clean. Doubles with shower/wc 290F or 320F with bath. There's a small bar on the ground floor that is open during the day. 10% discount July–Aug.

⌂ HÔTEL CONTINENTAL**

10 rue Montesquieu. **MAP B2-14**
☎ 05.56.52.66.00 ➡ 05.56.52.77.97
✉ continental@hotel-le-continental.com
TV.

A very comfortable two-star with lots of facilities, in an attractive bourgeois building close to the place des Grands-Hommes. Bright, spacious rooms with mini-bar go for 360F with shower/wc or 390F with bath, and a few have balconies and air-conditioning. It's well-run and the welcome is courteous.

⅍ ⌂ HÔTEL DE LA PRESSE***

6 rue Porte-Dijeaux. **MAP C2-11**
☎ 05.56.48.53.88 ➡ 05.56.01.05.82
Closed 24 Dec–1 Jan.**TV**.

Close to the junction of rue Sainte-Catherine and rue Porte-Dijeaux in a central area which is pedestrianised during the day; some cars are permitted in the evening. The very comfortable rooms are soundproofed and air-conditioned. If you really can't stand any noise at all, rooms on the courtyard side are the quietest, but if you choose these you'll miss out on the view of the Grand Théâtre, particularly good from rooms 206 and 207, which have balconies. This place offers modest luxury at a reasonable price. Doubles with shower from 400F, with bath 490F. 10% discount for stays of two nights or more.

⅍ ⌂ HÔTEL DES QUATRE SŒURS**

6 cours du 30-Juillet. **MAP C2-12**
☎ 05.57.81.19.20 ➡ 05.56.01.04.28
✉ 4soeurs@mail.city.com

Closed 20 Dec–6 Jan. **TV**.

Built in the 18th century, between allées de Tourny, the Grand Théâtre and place des Quinconces, this hotel is steeped in history. Wagner stayed here in 1850 when he was having an eventful, adulterous affair with a local woman. The staff are really relaxed. Attractive, freshly decorated, classy rooms overlooking either the cours de Tourny or allées de Tourny are more expensive than the quiet rooms above the inner courtyard. All are air-conditioned. Doubles 400F with shower/wc and 400–500F with bath. Buffet breakfast. 10% discount for a two-night stay except June, Sept and Oct.

⅍ ⌂ HÔTEL TULIP INN BAYONNE ETCHE-ONA***

15 cours de l'Intendance. **MAP C2-13**
☎ 05.56.48.00.88 ➡ 05.56.48.41.60 61
Closed last week in Dec and first week in Jan. **TV**.

A 64-room hotel, part of which is housed in an 18th-century building. It belongs to the upmarket *Golden Tulip* group, andis very in keeping with this middle-class area. Courteous staff. Attractive 1930s-style lounge. On the upper floors the rooms have been completely refurbished in an impersonal, contemporary style. Doubles 450F with shower/wc, 610F with bath. Suites 800–900F. 10% discount.

⅍ ⦿ LE RABOLIOT

38 rue Peyronnet. Off map **C4-21**
☎ 05.56.92.27.33
Closed Fri evening, Sat and Sun residents only, a fortnight to three weeks in Aug.

A friendly, lively place, away from the centre. Good quality cooking at very reasonable prices, with a 50F menu of the day. The desserts are particularly good; try the crumble or chocolate cake which is made by the English woman who usually waits at table. Her husband is in charge of the cellar and he has a short selection of good-value vintages. Free coffee.

⦿ RESTAURANT LE RITAL

3 rue des Faussets. **MAP C2-20**
☎ 05.56.48.16.69
Closed Sat and Sun, public holidays and 15–30 August.

In a part of the city where other restaurants come and go every few months, this little Italian place has been around for twenty years. The food is very good and you get a warm welcome. Tables are in a series of linked rooms which each give a view of the kitchen.

The pasta is fresh: fettucine with gorgonzola and basil, tagliatelle with *foie gras*, spaghetti *di baggio* and cannelloni. Also try the *osso-bucco* or aubergine *au gratin*. Good home-made desserts. Lunchtime menu 50F, and others at 58–98F. À la carte you'll spend less than 100F.

|●| RESTAURANT LA COMPAGNIE DU FLEUVE-CHEZ ALRIQ

quai des Queyries. **MAP D1-31**
☎ 05.56.86.58.49
Closed Sun evening and Mon.

Service to midnight. An unusual restaurant in an unusual setting – a kind of alternative self-service restaurant located in the post-war wasteland near the ruined gare d'Orléans. There are plans to redevelop the area. Extremely cool welcome. The restaurant has become rather trendy, and is large enough to host occasional plays and concerts. It has an "unstructured" garden running down to the river, dotted with chairs. Set menus start at 55F but you will most likely eat *à la carte*, around 110F. The dishes available vary according to season: mussels in summer and Béarnaise vegetable broth in winter, with shad, very young eels and lampreys when available.

|●| L'IMPRÉVU

11 rue des Remparts. **B2-22**
☎ 05.56.48.55.43
Closed Tues evenings.

A few bistro tables are set out on the terrace in this pedestrianised street, with a couple of attractive dining rooms inside, one a vaulted cellar decorated with dried flowers and willow baskets. Lots of regulars chatting with the affable owner. Good, quick service and healthy cooking using fresh produce: *pot-au-feu*, beef skirt, pork fillet in mustard and home-made *clafoutis*. Lunch menu 57F, and others from 64–89F. Splendid sweet *crêpes* for dessert. It's a good idea to book.

⚘|●| CHEZ DUPONT

45 rue Notre-Dame. Off map **C1-24**
☎ 05.56.81.49.59 ➡ 05.56.51.35.19
Closed Sun in summer.

About the best value for money you'll get in the Les Chartrons district. Attractive bistro-style surroundings, and traditional dishes, such as *pot-au-feu*, chalked up on the blackboard. The *formule*, 62F, changes every day. There's a more substantial menu with starter, main course and dessert at 129F, and a regularly

updated *à la carte* menu. Friendly welcome and really good atmosphere. Occasional live jazz in the evenings. Free *digestif*.

|●| LE CAFÉ DES ARTS

138 cours Victor-Hugo **MAP C4-23**
☎ 05.56.91.78.46

A really popular brasserie in a busy, buzzy part of town. The terrace is quite wide and the dining room is like an old-style bistro with simple chairs and moleskin benches. Decent, honest traditional dishes in good-sized portions; herrings in oil, *andouillette*, calf's liver with mushroom sauce, and real chips! Lunch menu 68F and brasserie dishes *à la carte*. This place has been going for donkey's years and is a real favourite with the younger crowd.

|●| CHEZ FERNAND

3 pl. du Parlement. **MAP C2-25**
☎ 05.56.52.51.72

They serve only cold food here – a panoply of oysters and three kinds of salmon – and it's very popular with the tourists. And if you can't do without a fix of red meat, try the steak *tartare*. Lunch menu 75F, or 130F in the evening. But the relaxed service is over-casual. Wines are reasonably priced.

|●| LE CROC LOUP

35 rue du Loup. **MAP C3-32**
☎ 05.56.44.21.19
Closed Sun, Mon and Aug.

A lovely, refined little place though it looks like a snack bar from the outside. Warm welcome. The set lunchtime menu at 79F isn't elaborate, but typically it might include duck *pâté* with green peppercorns, grilled beef with shallots and chocolate *millefeuille* with coffee sauce – amazing value for money. Other set menus, 140–170F, include interesting and quite sophisticated dishes like cuttlefish salad *à la provençale*, fresh sea trout *julienne* in saffron sauce, stuffed rabbit with mushrooms, or the house specials – cuttlefish ravioli with coriander, and chicken drumstick with ceps and *foie gras*.

⚘|●| RESTAURANT LE BISTROT DES QUINCONCES

4 pl. des Quinconces. **MAP C1-27**
☎ 05.56.52.84.56 ➡ 05.86.51.61.90
Disabled access.

Service until midnight. This classic brasserie, opposite the famous monument to the Girondins, is Bordeaux's trendiest bistro. If weather permits, sit outside. Efficient service.

You can get all the bistro staples, like steak and roast lamb, along with more unusual offerings such as iced terrine of pickled tomatoes and mozzarella with olive paste, marinaded red peppers, cod steak with hazel nuts, Mexican-style chicken *fajitas* and desserts such as *sabayon* with Lillet vermouth. Prices are reasonable. Weekday *formule* 79F and dinner around 150F *à la carte*. Tapas are also served in the evening. Free apéritif.

🍴 |●| RESTAURANT L'ABSINTHE

137 rue du Tondu. Off map **A4-33**
☎ 05.56.96.72.73 ➡ 05.56.90.14.23
Closed Sat lunchtime, Sun public holidays and 7–21 Aug.

You can almost imagine Toulouse-Lautrec with a glass of absinthe in his hand at this bistro restaurant, with its original, period decor. The food is good, too. Lunchtime *formules* and set menus 92–117F. Extensive choice of dishes, including Landes-style salad, *escalope* of veal with cheese *au gratin*, *fricassée* of scallops with oyster mushrooms, and veal sweetbreads in port. The sweets are home-made. Free apéritif.

🍴 |●| RESTAURANT CAFÉ GOURMAND

3 rue Buffon. **MAP B2-28**
☎ 05.56.79.23.85 ➡ 05.56.52.03.45
Closed Sun.

When the sun makes an appearance sit down at one of the tables they put outside this elegant restaurant and you can admire the covered market. Chef Bruno Olivier comes from a well-known family of chefs, and photos of the lot of them adorn the walls. He produces sound, well-judged dishes at bistro prices, with a lunch menu at 95F, and dinner menus at 125–146F. The brasserie menu includes crunchy salad with mussels and pesto, ham with sage, perfect calf's head and a special version of fried eggs. Free coffee.

|●| LA TUPINA

6–8 rue Porte-de-la-Monnaie. **MAP D4-40**
☎ 05.56.91.56.37

An unmissable place serving gastronomic Bordelais dishes. It's one of the rare restaurants to serve genuine dishes from the southwest: *terrine* of semi-cooked *foie gras*, potted shoulder of lamb with haricot beans, roast chicken with chips cooked in duck fat, and the like. Delicious desserts. The prices reflect the quality of the cooking, with a 100F lunchtime menu and a seasonal menu at 250F. Very good wines. The dining room has

a rustic feel and is quite charming, though the atmosphere is a bit prim.

|●| RESTAURANT LE PORT DE LA LUNE

59 quai de Paludate. Off map **D4-39**
☎ 05.56.49.15.55 ➡ 05.56.49.29.12
Disabled access.

Service until 2am, seven days a week. Opposite the abattoirs in a part of Bordeaux which has recently acquired a nightlife, this is a great place for jazz fans and they have live bands. It's an animated, friendly, "lived in" place, with photos of jazz legends lining the wall. You can eat very well here, with bistro dishes – as well chosen as the music – at reasonable prices. *À la carte* dishes, 58–96F, include harbour salad, mussels and oysters, whole duck breast, and traditional-style veal kidneys. For 106F you can get a *casse croûte* and seasonal dishes including baby eels *à l'espagnole*, shad in green sauce, lamprey, etc, plus dessert, wine and coffee. Wines from 58F. Michel, the boss, creates an easy-going atmosphere with his ready smile and chat.

|●| RESTAURANT GRAVELIER

114 cours de Verdun. Off map **C1-37**
☎ 05.56.48.17.15 ➡ 05.56.51.96.07
Closed Sat lunchtime, Sun, the Feb holidays and 3–23 Aug.

One of the new wave of restaurants in Bordeaux, run by the daughter of one of the famous Troisgros brothers. Her husband, Yves Gravelier, is also a creative chef. The surroundings are modern without being flashy, and prices are reasonable. Lunch menu 110F, with two more at 145F and 195F. The menu changes frequently – look out for mussels and cod in white wine with celery, mullet cooked in a charcoal pan with vine shoots, and saddle of rabbit in cream truffle sauce.

🍴 |●| RESTAURANT BAUD ET MILLET

19 rue Huguerie. **MAP B1-36**
☎ 05.56.79.05.77 ➡ 05.56.81.75.48
Closed Sun.

A specialist cheese restaurant serving 200 kinds of cheese, meticulously selected by M. Baud. He has a great passion for his work and applies strict criteria. The cheeses can be eaten in their natural state but are also used in numerous specialities, which range from *raclette* and *tartiflette* to more daring concoctions. The "cheese and dessert" *formule* is a surprising but tasty combination of sweet and savoury ingredients. There is an impressive and well-chosen selection of nearly a thousand different wines from all over the world, arranged on shelves around the very pleasant, air-conditioned restaurant. Friendly staff. Menus 110–160F. 10% discount on a meal with wine.

🏂 |O| DIDIER GÉLINEAU

26 rue du Pas-Saint-Georges. **MAP C3-41**
☎ 05.56.52.84.25 ➡ 05.56.51.93.25
Closed lunchtime, Sun and a fortnight in Aug.

Its subtle blend of traditional and modern cuisine has led this restaurant to become one of the city's musts in just a few short years. The prices are still unbelievably reasonable. They offer an exemplary menu of the day, 130F, and others 200–300F. Dishes change frequently: cep soup, stuffed turnip with snails followed by *fricassée* of veal kidneys will see you right The desserts are particularly good. Free coffee.

|O| RESTAURANT LE PÈRE OUVRARD

12 rue du Maréchal-Joffre. **MAP B3-30**
☎ 05.56.44.11.58
Closed Sat lunchtime and Sun, one week in winter, and Aug.

This colourful restaurant is a-flurry with judges and lawyers, especially with the first spring sun, when tables are set up outside opposite the École Nationale de la Magistrature. There's a huge blackboard with an appetising selection of bistro dishes: grilled sardines *fleur de sel*, *moules marinières*, and grilled chicken with cayenne pepper, etc. The menu lists more sophisticated dishes, such as salad of caramelised veal sweetbreads with almonds, and excellent couscous with cod spiced with harissa and cumin. Menu 143F, or around 215F *à la carte*.

GRADIGNAN 33170 (6KM SW)

🏠 |O| HÔTEL-RESTAURANT LE CHALET LYRIQUE***

160 cours du Général-de-Gaulle (Centre); take exit 16 off the outer ring road; it's just beyond pl. de l'Église.
☎ 05.56.89.11.59 ➡ 05.56.89.53.37
Restaurant closed Sun in Aug. **TV. Garden. Pay garage.**

Less than fifteen minutes from Bordeaux-Mérignac airport in suburban Gradignan, this resolutely modern building is arranged around a patio planted with ancient olive trees and centring on a fountain. They offer 44 very comfortable rooms, some with balcony. Doubles with bath cost 400–530F. In

the restaurant menus start at 65F (weekday lunchtimes only). All the meat dishes are wonderful – the proprietor used to work at a butcher's – but *à la carte* prices are high.

BRANTÔME 24310

🏂 |O| RESTAURANT AU FIL DE L'EAU

21 quai Bertin (Centre).
☎ 05.53.05.73.65
Closed Mon evening and Tues except July/Aug, and end Dec–1 March.

They don't sell fishing permits behind the bar any more but the decor of this adorable little restaurant still has fishing very much as its theme. There's a boat anchored next to the lovely terrace on the banks of the Dronne. On the *menu-carte* there's a selection of freshwater fish – trout, perch and so on – and local dishes. Menus, from 110F, list uncomplicated but well-presented dishes. Friendly welcome and efficient service. Free *digestif*.

MONSEC 24340 (12KM NW)

🏠 |O| HÔTEL-RESTAURANT BEAUSÉJOUR

rue Principale; take the D939.
☎ 05.53.60.92.45 ➡ 05.53.60.72.38
Closed Fri evenings and Sat in low season, and Christmas to 1 Jan. **TV. Car park.**

Really friendly welcome and quality food served in a pleasant restaurant with a panoramic view of the garden. Fine range of set menus, which celebrate local cuisine: duck sausage, oyster mushroom omelette, *foie gras*, and duck breast kebab. The cheapest menu, 80F, includes a $1/4$ litre of wine and there are others at 120F and 150F. Simple but impeccable rooms cost 150F for a double with basin or 200F with shower/wc.

VIEUX-MAREUIL 24340 (13KM NW)

🏂 🏠 |O| HOSTELLERIE DE L'AUBERGE DE L'ÉTANG BLEU***

How to get there: take the D93, it's 2km before the hamlet and well indicated.
☎ 05.53.60.92.63 ➡ 05.53.56.33.20
@ contact@perigord.hotel.com
Closed Sun evenings in winter. **TV. Car park.**

In a huge park at the edge of a private lake, with a small beach where you can bathe. The spacious, nicely furnished rooms are as quiet as can be. Those overlooking the lake have a covered balcony. Doubles 280–370F, with half board, 300–390F per person, compulsory in July–Aug. Good breakfasts, with boiled eggs. The elegant dining room has a lakeside terrace which is inhabited by noisy ducks. Good, generously flavoured dishes include salmon with cep sauce and slivers of duck breast with morel sauce. 100F weekday menu and then 130–170F. 10% discount on the room rate.

SAINT-JEAN-DE-CÔLE   24800 (20KM NE)

⌂ |●| HÔTEL SAINT-JEAN**

route de Nontron; take the D78.
☎ 05.53.52.23.20
Closed Sat 1 Oct–31 March. **TV**. **Car park**.

Nice little place on a main road that is not too busy at night. Traditional, comfortable and meticulously kept rooms – you'll pay 200F for a double with shower/wc. The proprietor concocts quality regional dishes such as home-made duck *foie gras pâté*, monkfish fritters with parsley and duck breast *à l'orange*. Weekday lunch menu at 70F, two more at 100F and 140F.

BUZET SUR BAÏZE   47160

|●| AUBERGE DU GOUJON QUI FRÉTILLE

rue Gambetta; it's opposite the church.
☎ 05.53.84.26.51
Closed Tues evening and Wed, Nov to 15–30 March.

The village is quiet and pretty – and so is this inn, literally "The Inn of the Wriggling Gudgeon", which stands opposite the church. You sit down to generous helpings of fine food in peaceful surroundings. There is a weekday lunch *formule* at 85F, others 110–150F, and children's menu 50F. Dishes include freshwater crayfish soup with scallops, duck breast in parsley, shin of veal, *choucroute* salad with grilled *cervelas* and bream with lentils in cream. House speciality is pan-fried fresh *foie gras* with a port *jus*.

CAMBO-LES-BAINS   64250

⌂ |●| L'AUBERGE DE TANTE URSULE**

fronton du Bas-Cambo; it's by the *pelota* court.
☎ 05.59.29.78.23 ➡ 05.59.29.28.57
Closed Mon evening,Tues and mid-Feb to mid-March.
TV. **Disabled access**. **Car park**.

This old farm, painted all in white, offers decent rooms for 175F with basin, and

290F with shower. Good food, with a range of set menus from 90–200F. Dishes include gourmet salad, monkfish with green pepper, wood-pigeon stew and duck breast *à l'orange*. Look out for specialities such as braised lamb sweetbreads with ceps, home-made grilled black pudding with pickled garlic, and *tournedos* with morels. The welcome could be warmer but it's good value.

ESPELETTE   64250 (5KM W)

⚹ ⌂ |●| HÔTEL-RESTAURANT EUZKADI**

rue Principale (Centre); take the D918 towards Saint-Jean-de-Luz.
☎ 05.59.93.91.88 ➡ 05.59.93.90.19
Closed Mon and Tues out of season. **Swimming pool**.
Garden. **Car park**.

This is one of the most popular country hotel-restaurants in the Basque country and it's a good idea to book well in advance. Michèle and André Darraïdou, completely mad about Basque cooking, search out old country-style recipes and revamp them for today's tastes. In their enormous restaurant you'll discover dishes you would have very little chance of finding elsewhere: *tripoxa* (black pudding made from veal or mutton and served with a tomato sauce with capsicums), *axoa* (cubed veal browned with onions), *merluza en salsa verde* (poached hake with pea and asparagus sauce), cockles and hard-boiled eggs in a sauce made with Jurançon wine and fish stock, and *elzekaria* (vegetable soup). Set menus 95–180F. The lovely little rooms go for 290F for a double with bath. In the back there's a pleasant garden, tennis court and swimming pool. Free house aperitif.

ITXASSOU   64250 (5KM S)

⌂ |●| HÔTEL-RESTAURANT DU CHÊNE**

How to get there: take the D918 towards Saint-Jean-Pied-de-Port, then the D349 as you enter the Nive valley.
☎ 05.59.29.75.01 ➡ 05.59.29.27.39
Closed Mon, Tues out of season, Jan and Feb. **TV**. **Car park**.

This establishment is superbly situated. Doubles cost 245F with bath, and they serve unpretentious but delicious local cuisine. Set menus from 85–180F. Specialities include chicken with rice and red peppers, risotto of monkfish and chorizo, Biscay-style cod, *escalopes* of *foie gras* in cherry vinegar and tuna with capsicums. Free sangria.

AINHOA   64250 (12KM SW)

♠ |●| ITHURRIA***

rue principale (Centre); it's at the beginning of the village
when you come from Cambo-les-Bains.
☎ 05.59.29.92.11 ➡ 05.59.29.81.28
@ jpte;@ithurria.com
Closed Wed out of season and 2 Nov to Easter. **Garden**.
Swimming pool. **TV**. **Car park**.

A very fine inn in a large 17th-century house
and former coaching inn on the pilgrim route
to Santiago de Compostela. The gorgeously
furnished rooms go for 600–700F. There's an
attractive dining room with hand-made floor
tiles and a vast fireplace. Dishes include pepper stew, Basque *cassoulet* with red kidney
beans, and roast pigeon with plums. Menus
170–260F. Fine garden and swimming pool
to the rear. The welcome is a bit cool.

CAPBRETON   40130

|●| LE BISTRO

pl. des Basques; (Centre).
☎ 05.58.72.21.98
Closed Sun, Mon and Wed evenings. **Car park**.

An innocuous-looking restaurant from the
outside, but delightful within. The owner, his
apron wrapped round his girth, will take your
order and cook your food. The delicious,
carefully prepared dishes are perfect in their
simplicity: pork fillet with mirabelle plums,
grilled ham with honey or hake fillet with red
peppers. Menu of the day 60F or 120F *à la
carte*.

|●| RESTAURANT LA PÊCHERIE DUCAMP

rue du Port-d'Albret.
☎ 05.58.72.11.33 ➡ 05.58.72.26.00
Closed Mon and Tues lunchtimes, then evenings and
Sat lunchtime out of season, and Feb–Oct.

Direct from the fishmonger to the consumer –
the tables are arranged around the fish
counter, and the waitresses wear boots and
plastic aprons. Set menus 90–250F and
include a seafood platter, main course and
dessert. You can get a small fish and seafood
platter for 140F and a gourmet set menu for
220F.

🎋|●| LES COPAINS D'ABORD

Port des Mille Sabords.
☎ 05.58.72.14.14
Closed March.

The decor echoes the colours of the sea, the
green forests of the Landes and the golden

sunshine. The restaurant has a lovely terrace
which is at its best on summer evenings – it
can get too hot at lunchtime. Weekday menu
100F or 155F, listing dishes prepared using
fresh produce straight from the farm or the
ocean; chicken thigh stuffed with *foie gras*,
mussels, and squid with garlic and parsley.
There's a surprise gift at the end of your meal.

CAP-FERRET   33970

♠ LA FRÉGATE**

34 av. de l'Océan.
☎ 05.56.60.41.62 ➡ 05.56.03.76.18
@ info@hotel-la-fregate.com
Swimming pool. **Disabled access**. **TV**. **Pay car
park**.

The hotel is in an ideal location between the
pleasure port and the ocean, 300m from the
place the boat from Arcachon docks. The
grounds are big enough for a swimming
pool which is kept impeccably clean. The
rooms, 220–240F with shower/wc or
260–670F with bath, are spotless, too. The
nicest have a wide balcony and terrace
looking over the pool and three-star facilities. The place is smoothly run by attentive
owners.

🎋 ♠ |●| HÔTEL DES PINS**

23 rue des Fauvettes (Centre).
☎ 05.56.60.60.11 ➡ 05.56.60.67.41
Closed 15 Nov–April.

A delightful house dating from the early part
of the century, with a garden full of flowers.
It's quietly situated between the bassin
d'Arcachon and the ocean. The meticulously planned decor, all classic advertisements
and old billiards tables, creates the impression that time has stood still. Rooms are
290–450F with shower or 330–450F with
bath. You eat on a veranda adjacent to the
garden or on the lawn. There's a single set
menu at 120F, which lists fresh cod steak
with garlic mayonnaise, Bordeaux-style
grilled tuna and Pauillac lamb. Warm welcome. Free apéritif.

🎋|●| PINASSE CAFÉ

2 [bis] av. de l'Océan (Centre); it's on the seafront.
☎ 05.56.03.77.87 ➡ 05.56.60.63.47
Closed Mon and 1 Jan–14 March.

An attractive, turn-of-the-century house
painted blue and white, near the landing
stage. The restaurant is something of a
youthful hang-out, and its young staff offer
wonderfully laid-back yet efficient service.

From the terrace, with its background beat of house and techno music, there's a brilliant view of the ocean, the oyster beds, and the dune du Pyla. They offer a 92F set lunchtime menu and another at 127F – dishes include grilled mullet in green sauce, whelks, winkles and mussels with pine needles, grilled meat, and pork spare ribs. Free *digestif*.

CANON (LE)   33950 (6KM N)

⛵ |○| HÔTEL-RESTAURANT DE LA PLAGE

L'Herbe, 1 rue des Marins.
☎ 05.56.60.50.15
Closed Mon out of season and Jan.

A typical wooden house just by the water with a small grocer's, an old-fashioned telephone and big old mattresses that they hang out to air on the balconies during the day. Thankfully, it has resisted to pressure to modernise. Rooms are simple but nice; eight look out over the water. Doubles with basin 220F; the shower is on the landing. The restaurant is nothing special, but on Sunday they do a great *moules marinières* and grilled sea bream, which they serve on the terrace. Set menus 90–150F.

CASTELJALOUX   47700

🎋 ⛵ |○| LA VIEILLE AUBERGE

11 rue Posterne (Centre).
☎ 05.53.93.01.36
Closed Sun evening and Wed out of season, Feb school holidays, second fortnight in June, and second fortnight in Nov.

In one of the oldest streets in town, this inn has a thoroughly local flavour. Enjoy all the tastes Gascony has to offer with produce skillfully selected according to the season: asparagus in season, monkfish Arles style, bass with chicory, local lamb stew, fillet of beef with morels or duck breast Périgourdine. Set menus 120–240F. Free coffee.

CASTILLONÈS   47330

⛵ |○| HÔTEL-RESTAURANT DES REMPARTS**

26–28 rue de la Paix (Centre).
☎ 05.53.49.55.85 ➡ 05.53.49.55.89
Restaurant closed Sun evenings and Mon out of season. **TV.**

A beautiful, sturdy stone house in the middle of the village. Its conversion into a hotel has been carefully done to respect its original proportions. The rooms are spacious and painted in

pale, soothing colours and the bathrooms are odd shapes; 260–320F for a double. The traditional, regional dishes in the restaurant are predictable but well prepared and the bread is very good. 75F *formule*, 95F *menu terroir* or up to 165F. Attentive, pleasant welcome.

DAX   40100

🎋 ⛵ |○| HÔTEL-RESTAURANT BEAUSOLEIL**

38 rue du Tuc-d'Eauze (Centre).
☎ 05.58.74.18.32 ➡ 05.58.56.03.81
Hotel closed Jan. **Restaurant closed** Mon and Thurs evenings. **Garden. Disabled access. TV. Car park.**

This is the most charming and friendly hotel in town, quietly situated near the centre. It's a pretty white house with a terrace and 32 comfortable rooms with shower/wc. Doubles 250–360F. The food is conventional but good, all of it prepared with quality produce. Menu 70F (except Sun) and others 100–210F. Your bottle is already set on the table next to your napkin ring. Excellent value. Free breakfast

⛵ |○| LES CHAMPS DE L'ADOUR

5 rue Morancy (Centre).
☎ 05.58.56.92.81 ☎ 05.5856.98.61
Restaurant closed evenings in the week.

This little hotel, very close to the covered market, looks more like a private house. The seven refurbished rooms are all quiet because of the double glazing; doubles 250F. The restaurant produces tasty dishes prepared with fresh, natural ingredients. *Formules*, 50–79F, are priced by the main course you choose and start with the *crudité* of the day.

|○| LA GUITOUNE

pl. Roger Ducos.
☎ 05.58.74.37.46
Closed evenings, Sun and Mon.

Ideal if you don't want to spend too much. It's best to come on a Saturday when all local life is on show; the place is teeming with stall-holders from the market and it's a rendezvous for lots of Dax inhabitants. Plates of good food like an omelette with asparagus tips or mushrooms or a dozen oysters with a glass of local white wine. Dishes of the day 35–45F.

🎋 |○| L'AMPHYTRION

38 quai Galliéni.
☎ 05.58.74.58.05
Closed Sun evening, Mon, Sat lunchtime, a fortnight at the beginning of Jan, and 18 Aug–5 Sept.

Eric Pujos will delight you with dishes from the Landes and the Basque country in his bright, modern little restaurant that's one of the gourmet establishments in the area. Dishes include rustic-style *foie gras*, lamb stuffed with axoa (cubed lamb browned with onions) and *pimientos del piquillo* (spicy peppers), hake with squid cooked in the ink and, to finish, a delicious *pastis* from the Landes region. Very reasonable set menus 110–220F. The *à la carte* menu changes every month. Prompt and pleasant service under the watchful eye of Mme Pujos. Free apéritif.

🕇 |●| LA TABLE DE PASCAL

4 rue de la Fontaine Chaude.
☎ 05.58.74.89.00
Closed Sun and Mon lunchtimes.

A genuine little bistro with attractive decor and good food. Dishes include Béarnaise vegetable broth, salmon steak *piquillos* stuffed with hake, calf's liver with parsley, salted belly pork, and beef and duck with potatoes. No set menu; you'll pay around 120–140F *à la carte*. Free apéritif.

|●| EL MESÓN

18 place Camille-Bouvet.
☎ 05.58.74.64.26
Closed Sat lunchtime, Sun, last week in Aug, New Year and a week in April.

You're in Spain here. The decor and the cooking tell you so: panfried squid, grilled whole turbot, eels with parsley, gazpacho and a juicy grilled steak. If all you want is a snack, lean against the bar and order from the range of tapas and wash the delicacies down with a strong Spanish wine or the house sangria. Complete meals from 150F.

DURAS · 47120

🕇 🏠 |●| L'HOSTELLERIE DES DUCS**

bd. Jean-Brisseau; it's near the castle.
☎ 06.63.83.74.58 ➡ 05.53.83.75.03
📧 hostellerie.des.ducx@wanadoo.fr
Closed Sun evenings and Mon except July–Sept.
Swimming pool. TV. Garden. Car park.

Originally a convent, these two fine semi-detached buildings now house the region's most prestigious hotel and restaurant. It's quietly situated, with a pleasant terrace, lovely swimming pool and prize-winning garden. There's a friendly atmosphere in the restaurant, where the food enjoys an excellent reputation. There's a 90F weekday lunch menu and oth-

ers from 128–220F. Specialities include rabbit *terrine* with plums, escalope of duck *foie gras* with white asparagus, beef fillet with morels and a *crème brûlée* with Mandarine Impériale. The chef puts quality regional produce before originality and the result is good, high-quality cooking. The wine list has a fine selection of Duras wines. Comfortable rooms go for 295F for a double with shower/wc, or 350–520F for bath. It's pretty much essential to book in season. 10% discount on the room rate Oct–July.

EUGÉNIE-LES-BAINS · 40320

|●| LA FERME AUX GRIVES

Le bourg (Centre).
☎ 05.58.51.19.08
Closed Mon evening and Tues out of season, and in Jan. **Car park.**

Owned by stellar chef Michel Guérard, who owns several local hotels, a spa and two restaurants. This place is cheaper than some of his others, with *menu-cartes* starting at 195F – well worth it for perfectly simple dishes based on wonderfully fresh produce. Cured hams hang from the ceiling while a suckling pig turns slowly on the spit in the fireplace. You feel good as soon as you sit down. Dishes include boiled beef and pork salad in a herb and shallot dressing, coconut and cod salad with fresh marinated anchovies, smooth *pâté* of calf's head with mayonnaise, Castille-style suckling pig, tripe simmered in Armagnac and Landes-style grilled chicken. For dessert there's Paris-Brest (a large *choux* pastry ring) with praline-flavoured cream, *crème brûlée* with grilled oats and fruit tarts. It's a wonderful celebration of culinary art. You will rarely eat better.

EYZIES-DE-TAYAC (LES) · 24620

🕇 🏠 |●| HÔTEL-RESTAURANT DU CENTRE**

Centre; it's opposite the museum.
☎ 05.53.06.97.13 ➡ 05.53.06.91.63
Closed lunchtimes, Tues lunchtime only July–Aug, and 6 Nov–5 Jan. **TV. Car park.**

On a small, peaceful pedestrian square by the river. The white shutters add a touch of charm to the old ivy-covered walls. Very attractively decorated rooms. Doubles 295F with shower/wc and 350–500F with bath. Beautifully restored rustic restaurant serves well-prepared, reasonably priced traditional dishes. Set menus, 100–225F, are good value and list dishes such as *délice périgourdin* with *foie gras*, chicken breast with walnuts and chicken *confit*, three styles of *foie gras*, veal sweet-breads with morels, pan-fried scallops with ceps, rabbit *confit* in truffle juices, chocolate *rissoles* with pine kernels and almonds, and hot nut *soufflé*. Half board 345F, compulsory Aug–Sept. 10% discount on the room rate Feb–June

☎ |●| HÔTEL DE FRANCE-AUBERGE DU MUSÉE**

rue du Moulin.
☎ 05.53.06.97.23 ➡ 05.53.06.90.97
e hotel-de-france24@wanadoo.fr
Hotel closed Nov. **Restaurant closed** Mon and Sat lunchtimes except for groups and on public holidays.
Swimming pool. **Garden**. **Car park**.

Two establishments standing opposite each other at the foot of a cliff. The inn, which serves traditional and regional food, has two dining rooms – or you can eat outside under the wisteria-covered arbour. Set menus from 100F. There are a few rooms in the main building and others in an annexe on the banks of the Vézève, where there is a garden and a swimming pool. Doubles with bath 300F.

☎ |●| LE MOULIN DE LA BEUNE**- RESTAURANT LE VIEUX MOULIN

Le bourg (Centre).
☎ 05.53.06.94.33 ➡ 05.53.06.98.06
Hotel closed Nov–March. **Restaurant closed** Wed and Sat lunchtimes excluding July–Aug.
Disabled access. **Garden**. **Car park**.

This place, which used to be a mill, is set on the water's edge at the quiet end of the village. The decor of the rooms is understated, a little austere for some tastes, but they're comfortable and good value. Doubles from 300F. Tasty, well-prepared food is served in *Le Vieux Moulin*, which houses the original mill machinery. The 125F menu lists dishes such as country-style Périgord medallion, chicken *ballotine*, and trout supreme with almonds. On the other menus, up to 400F, you'll see things like chicken *pâté* in aspic and duck *confit* with Périgord *mojettes*. In summer you eat in the garden on a delightful terrace, lulled by the murmur of the river.

🎋 ☎ |●| HÔTEL-RESTAURANT LE CENTENAIRE****

rocher de la Penne; it's in the main street.
☎ 05.53.06.68.68 ➡ 05.53.06.92.41
Hotel closed 1 Nov to mid-April. **Restaurant closed** Mon and Tues lunchtimes out of season.
TV. **Car park**.

This exceptional establishment is quite simply the best restaurant in Périgord. Chef Roland

Mazère is a culinary artist and his flavours are subtle, intense and original – try green bean salad with hazelnut oil and *foie gras*, warm cep *terrine* with garlic and parsley, caramelised sturgeon with creamed sweetcorn, and truffle caviar. Weekday lunch menu 180F, with others from 350–650F. Despite its cachet, the dining room is not in the least stuffy. Alain Scholly and his wife offer you a genuine welcome and the service is perfect in its discreet efficiency. Decor is luxurious without being ostentatious, and the rooms are wonderfully furnished. Double rooms from 600F with bath. 10% discount on the room rate except at the weekend.

TURSAC   24620 (6KM N)

🎋 |●| RESTAURANT LA SOURCE

Le bourg; on the D706 between Eyzies and Montignac.
☎ 05.53.06.98.00
e la.source@accesinter.com
Closed Sat in low season and mid-Dec to mid-March.
Garden.

Decent little village inn run by a friendly young couple. It's a rustic-style restaurant, and when the weather is fine you can also eat out on the terrace and admire the spring running through the garden. Modern cuisine with a good selection of local dishes: rabbit *terrine* with hazelnuts, semi-cooked duck *foie gras*, cep mushroom omelette, cod *au gratin* and rack of lamb with mild garlic. Menus, 78–160F, include a vegetarian option. Staff are unobtrusive and pleasant. Free coffee.

TAMNIÈS   24620 (14KM NE)

☎ |●| HÔTEL-RESTAURANT LABORDERIE**

Centre; take the D47 and the D48 – it's equidistant between Sarlat and Montignac.
☎ 05.53.29.68.59 ➡ 05.53.29.65.31
Closed 1 Nov–1 April. **Swimming pool**. **TV**. **Car park**.

Set on a peaceful square in this hillside market town, in exceptional countryside, *Laborderie* started off as a farm, then became a country café and restaurant, and is now a rather chic – though relatively inexpensive – hotel-restaurant. Lovely rooms at reasonable prices. Doubles with shower/wc 150–300F; 180–480F for the more comfortable rooms with bath. Some rooms are in the turreted main house, which has a great deal of charm, while others are in an annexe in the middle of a garden that gives onto open countryside. Those on the ground floor look onto the swimming pool. The large, bright restaurant has become one of the most popular in Périgord. The chef skillfully prepares generous helpings of classics such as Périgord platter, semi-cooked *foie gras* and duck with peaches. Menus 110–260F. There's a terrace.

GRENADE SUR ADOUR   40270

🏃 🛏 |●| PAIN, ADOUR ET FANTAISIE***

14–16 pl. des Tilleuls; it's on the village square.
☎ 05.58.45.18.60 ➡ 05.58.45.16.57
e pain.adour.fantaisie@wanadoo.fr
Closed Sun evening, Mon and Wed lunchtimes and Feb school holidays. **TV**. **Garden**. **Car park**.

This gorgeous old village dwelling stands between the main square and the Adour river. It has eleven comfortable, tastefully decorated rooms with great views. Doubles 380–800F. The food is unforgettable, served in the sophisticated surroundings of the restaurant or on the riverside terrace. Dishes include risotto with glazed prawns, potatoes stuffed with ribbons of pork, pan-fried red mullet in lavender vinegar, braised rabbit with ceps in chestnut *jus*, and lightly grilled duck *foie gras*. The service is unobtrusive and refined without being over-formal. Menus 165–380F. Unbeatable charm and value for money. Free house apéritif.

HAGETMAU   40700

🏃 🛏 |●| LE JAMBON**

27 rue Carnot (Centre); it's opposite the covered market.
☎ 05.58.79.32.02. ➡ 05.58.79.34.78
Closed Sun evening, Mon lunchtime and a fortnight Oct/Nov. **Swimming pool**. **TV**. **Car park**.

Behind the freshly painted pink-and-white exterior is a nice little place that's famous for its good cooking: *foie gras* with spices, hot oysters in champagne sauce, beef with baby vegetables and hot Grand Marnier *soufflé*. Menus 110–180F. The rooms are also recommended; doubles go for 300F with shower/wc or 300F with bath. Free apéritif or *digestif*.

HENDAYE   64700

BIRIATOU   64700 (4KM S)

🏃 🛏 |●| HÔTEL-RESTAURANT BAKEA**

How to get there: take the D258 and follow the signs.
☎ 05.59.20.76.36 ➡ 05.59.20.58.21
e bakea@club-internet.fr
Closed Sun evening and Mon except April–Nov, and 30

Jan–1 March. **TV**. **Disabled access**. **Car park**.

A gorgeous, isolated place where you'll get complete rest and relaxation. They have recently acquired the hotel next door so there is a lot of work in progress. Meantime double rooms cost 260–340F. Excellent restaurant where specialities include warm duck liver *tarte tatin*, joint of monkfish and fresh anchovy lasagne marinated in basil. Set menus from 145F.

HOSSEGOR   40150

🛏 HÔTEL LES HÉLIANTHES**

av. de la Côte-d'Argent (West); 10min on foot from the beaches and 300m from the centre.
☎ 05.58.43.52.19 ➡ 05.58.43.95.19
Closed mid-Oct to end March. **Swimming pool**. **TV**.

This stunning little white building with its red shutters is a family-run establishment where you'll get a warm welcome, peace and quiet, and excellent value. Doubles with shower/wc 190–340F or 220–500F in season including brunch. Evening menu on request out of season. The swimming pool is hidden among the pine trees. 10% discount out of season.

🏃 🛏 |●| HÔTEL-RESTAURANT LES HUÎTRIÈRES DU LAC**

av. du Touring-Club.
☎ 05.58.43.51.48 ➡ 05.58.41.73.11
Closed Mon and Jan. **TV**. **Garden**. **Car park**.

Doubles 300–400F – reserve well in advance to be sure of getting a room overlooking the lake. It's very well kept, if slightly pricey for the area, the food is excellent and there's a nice family atmosphere. Whether or not you spend the night here, it's worth stopping to eat: *foie gras* with peaches, roast pigeon with honey, and bass in a salt crust. Set menus 98–150F. 10% discount on the room rate except public holidays.

LALINDE-EN-PÉRIGORD   24150

🛏 |●| HÔTEL-RESTAURANT LE CHÂTEAU***

rue de la Tour (Centre); off pl. des Martyrs-du-21-Juillet-1944
☎ and ➡ 05.53.61.01.82
Closed Sun evening and Mon in winter, Mon in autumn and spring, Mon lunchtime July–Aug, and 15 Dec–15 Feb. **Swimming pool**. **TV**.

This is a proper little castle with its corbelled turret, pepper-pot towers and balcony overlooking the sleepy Dordogne. Guy Gensou, who has redecorated the entire place, is in charge of the kitchen and gives you a very warm welcome. He adds his own touch to local dishes and uses superb fresh produce. The dining rooms are peaceful and the staff pleasant. The 125F menu includes apéritif, traditional *pâté* with truffle fragments, stuffed trout in white Bergerac or black pudding with apples, and Périgord *milla* (maize flour porridge) or *fromage frais* with melon jam. *À la carte*, an apéritif will set you up for dishes like fillet of smoked goose with onion preserve, knuckle of lamb with vegetables, pig's trotter stew in red wine, or roast Rocamadour cheese with walnut salad. Comfortable double rooms 300–900F. Guy Gensou rides a motorbike himself so fellow bikers are warmly welcomed. The small swimming pool overlooks the Dordogne. Half board is compulsory from May to the end of Sept.

LAROQUE TIMBAUT 47340

|●| LE ROQUENTIN

Centre; it's opposite the church.
☎ 05.53.95.78.78
Closed Thurs, Sun evening, Mon, evenings on public holidays, a week at Easter and a week end of Aug.

Recently built, in the style of a stone Provençal house, with bright decor. The chef has acquired a good reputation for regional cooking, using the finest quality produce and the traditional methods of the southwest. Dishes include duck with honey, sautéed chicken with ceps, zander in a butter sauce, frogs' legs in parsley, and scrambled eggs with truffles. Weekday menu 60F and others 85–210F. There's a fine wine list, with a good Cahors La Coutale 1992 or a Madiran 1991 from Bouscassé.

LARRAU 64560

🏠 |●| HÔTEL-RESTAURANT ETCHEMAÏTE**

☎ 05.59.28.61.45 📠 05.59.28.72.71
Closed Sun evening and Mon out of season.
TV. Car park.

It's easy to fall in love with this contemplative spot, and the welcome and kindness of the Etchemaïte family help to make it a magical experience. Simple, comfortable doubles go for 220F with shower/wc or 280F with bath. Chef Pierre's aim is to combine tradition with originality; he conjures up dishes such as salad *souletine*, peasant soup, cep terrine with *foie gras jus*, grilled hake fillet with herb butter, cutlets of suckling lamb, grilled veal

with a mushroom crust and, for dessert, pear *clafoutis* or apple tart with cinnamon ice cream. Set menus 95–150F or you can eat *à la carte*. The rustic dining room has a view over the mountains. The wine list is full of pleasant surprises at reasonable prices.

LARUNS 64400

|●| L'ARRÉGALET

37 rue du Bourguet (Centre).
☎ 05.59.05.35.47
Closed Sun evening, Mon, 8–24 May and 2–21 Dec.

The Coudouy family cook typical local dishes using the best ingredients the mountain can produce. The owner's brother makes the *charcuterie* and the bread is baked in the kitchens. Their *garbure* and duck *foie gras* with leek *fondue* are both special. But the *poule-au-pot*, with the chicken served whole in a vegetable broth, is the house speciality. Menus 66–125F. *Arrégalet* is the local word for a crust of garlic bread used to wipe the goose grease from the bottom of the dish.

🌳|●| AUBERGE BELLEVUE

55 rue Bourguet (Centre).
☎ 05.59.05.31.58
Closed Tues evening and Wed.

An attractive, friendly place with appetising set menus 80–180F. The chalet is festooned with flowers and there is an uninterrupted view of the mountains. Try the fresh monkfish with scampi or the chicken *fricassée* with freshwater crayfish. Free *digestif*.

LESTELLE-BETHARRAM 64800

🌳 🏠 |●| LE VIEUX LOGIS**

Route des Grottes (Southeast); it's on the outskirts of the village on the D937, towards the caves.
☎ 05.59.71.94.87 📠 05.59.71.96.75
✉ hotel-levieuxlogis@wanadoo.fr
Closed Sun evening and Mon out of season, 25 Jan–2 March and 25 Oct–3 Nov. **Swimming pool. TV. Disabled access. Car park**.

Very large modern, roadside hotel at the foot of the mountains, with a swimming pool and extensive grounds. An ideal place to relax. Excellent value, with impeccable double rooms 210–295F. There are wooden chalets in the grounds and the rooms have balconies. Quality regional cooking, with particularly good desserts. Menus 100–190F. Free apéritif.

LISTRAC-MÉDOC   33480

⬛ |●| L'AUBERGE MÉDOCAINE

13 pl. du Maréchal Juin; it's in the centre on the N215.
☎ 05.56.58.08.86

The patio, set back from the road, is a very pleasant place to eat good local dishes. The set lunch menu, 65F, gets you a selection of starters, a dish of the day, dessert and wine, and there are other menus up to 149F. Rooms are simple and clean, and some have beamed ceilings. Doubles from 220F.

ARCINS   33460 (1KM E)

|●| CAFÉ-RESTAURANT DU LION D'OR

It's in the centre of the village.
☎ 05.56.58.96.79
Closed Sun and Mon.

The owner can be brusque, but the cooking is superb, with game in season and fish from the estuary all prepared to local recipes from the Médoc. The 68F menu offers starter, main course, cheese, dessert and $^1/_2$ litre of country wine. The dishes of the day are always good – try roast lamb, *tournedos*, or a simple omelette. À *la carte*, expect to pay 220F with wine.

MIMIZAN-PLAGE   40200

⬛ |●| HÔTEL-RESTAURANT ATLANTIQUE

38 av. de la Côte-d'Argent; north end of the beach.
☎ 05.58.09.09.42 ➡ 05.58.82.42.63
Closed Sun evening and Mon 1 Nov–31 May, and Jan.
TV. **Disabled access**. **Garden**. **Car park**.

This modest, friendly family establishment stands on the seafront but only enjoys a limited sea view. The façade of the old wooden building is intact and they've built a forty-room modern hotel on the back. Rooms with shower or basin are modestly priced at 140F, while those with shower/wc go for 220–280F. The best rooms are in the main house, and four of them have a sea view. It's also a nice place to eat, with a weekday lunchtime menu at 79F and others up to 159F. Simple, nourishing dishes include *coq au vin*, grilled bass in garlic butter, *vol au vent* with mussels in a rich white sauce, Bordeaux-style lamprey, and pigeon roll stuffed with *foie gras*. Half board available July–Aug.

⚶ ⬛ |●| HÔTEL-RESTAURANT L'ÉMERAUDE DES BOIS**

66–68 av. du Courant; take the D626.

☎ 05.58.09.05.28 ➡ 05.58.09.35.73
Closed Oct to Palm Sunday. **TV**. **Car park**.

This hotel-restaurant is another good family establishment in a charming house surrounded by large trees and decorated in traditional style. Very warm welcome. Double rooms 260–380F with shower/bath. Half board, compulsory in July and August, costs 290–320F per person – well worthwhile given the quality of the cooking. Excellent menus from 99–180F. Try the fish soup or cream of courgette soup, home-made *foie gras*, roast rabbit in mustard sauce, monkfish à *la provençale*, duck breast with honey, and walnut *gâteau*. A great deal of care goes into the preparation and cooking. The verandah and terrace provide welcome shade in summer. Free house apéritif.

⬛ LE PATIO

6 av. de la Côte d'Argent.
☎ 05.58.09.09.10. **Swimming pool**.

It's advisable to book well in advance for this place because its oceanfront location means it gets full. Stunning little rooms that are nicely furnished in Provençal style. Doubles 330–650F. You could choose to stay in the quiet bungalows at the back, near the swimming pool. There's a small *crêperie* next door belonging to the same family.

SAINT-EULALIE-EN-BORN   40200 (12KM NE)

⬛ |●| AUBERGE DU MOULIN DES CYGNES

Quartier Mauras.
☎ 05.58.09.72.63 ➡ 05.58.09.74.35
Restaurant closed weekdays 1 May–15 Sept, Mon lunchtime July–Aug. **Car park**.

A great little surprise. Nice rooms where you sleep quietly – doubles 250F out of season, 390F in season. The restaurant is close by the lake with a view of an odd-looking windmill. The food is delicious; roulade of duck *foie gras* with figs marinated in port or pan-fried with raspberry butter, profiterolles with *foie gras* and apple *clafoutis* – get the picture? Menus138F and 168F.

LÜE   40210 (22KM E)

|●| RESTAURANT L'AUBERGE LANDAISE

In the village; take the D626.
☎ 05.58.07.06.13 ➡ 05.58.07.05.90
Closed Sun evening, Mon and Oct. **Car park**.

A jolly little inn where they serve a string of set menus to suit every pocket, from 58F (excluding Sun in July–Aug), and up to 190F. It's impossible not to find something you fancy – try the wood-pigeon stew, pigeon *confit*, baby squid in ink or monkfish *à l'armoricaine*. The quality of Monsieur Barthet's cooking and the range of prices cut through all social barriers.

MONT-DE-MARSAN   40000

🏂 🏠 |●| HÔTEL-RESTAURANT DES PYRÉNÉES*

4 rue du 34ème R.I.
☎ 05.58.46.49.49 📠 05.58.06.43.57
Closed Fri evening, Sun in July–Aug. **TV**.

You can't miss this wonderful old pink house. At lunchtimes, when there's a 70F menu, it's rather like a canteen for local workers. When it's hot, big bay windows are opened onto a terrace surrounded by trees and flowers. Other menus, up to 195F, list good quality, tasty dishes such as duck breast, *foie gras*, and *confit* of chicken, pork or lamb. The rooms are attractive, particularly those which overlook the garden – the ones on the crossroads side are noisier. Doubles 170F with shower/wc or 250F with bath. Pleasant service. Free coffee.

🏠 |●| HÔTEL-RESTAURANT ZANCHETTIN**

1565 av. de Villeneuve; 2km on the road to Villeneuve de Marsan, next to the campsite in the Saint-Médard district.
☎ 05.58.75.19.52 📠 05.58.85.92.04
Closed Sun evening, Mon and a week in Sept.
TV. **Car park**.

Relatively quiet hotel and restaurant with a bar. Nine good rooms from 200–240F. You can eat on a terrace under the plane trees or in the sweet little restaurant. The weekday menu, 70F, includes wine and coffee, and there are others at 120–160F. It's a little off the beaten track, but it's a well-run place, and well worth the trip.

🏂 🏠 |●| HÔTEL-RESTAURANT RICHELIEU**

rue Wlérick (Centre); it's behind the theatre.
☎ 05.58.06.10.20 📠 05.58.06.00.68
Restaurant closed Sat except for group bookings.
TV. **Car park**.

Central hotel with a crisp, starchy, rather provincial feel. Good-value doubles with shower/wc are 260F, 280F with bath. In the restaurant you get some of the best cooking in town. Set menus, 90–172F, list tasty traditional dishes such as the *panaché* of pan-

fried and semi-cooked liver in shallot *vinaigrette*, medallions of monkfish with Serrano ham and asparagus tips, roast suckling lamb with sweet peppers, and *tarte fine* with *crème brûlée*. This is where the locals come for their business lunches. 10% discount on the room rate except during July.

|●| CHEZ DESPONS

20 rue Plumaçon.
☎ 05.58.06.17.56
Closed evenings, Sun and first three weeks in Aug.

A whole range of *formules* and menus from 42 to 90F, listing good, family dishes, the kind you dream of finding on your travels through France. The stellar dish on the 60F menu is grilled entrecôte steak with sauces or peppered and served with a salad. There's a self-serve *crudité* and *charcuterie* buffet. You pay extra for pudding.

|●| LE BISTROT DE MARCEL

1 rue du Pont du Commerce.
☎ 05.58.75.09.71
Closed Sun and Mon lunchtime.

This is not an old-style bistro but a good restaurant with fine cooking and a rather wonderful setting on an enclosed, heated terrace with a view over the Midouze. The cooking is defiantly of the Landes region and the chef uses excellent local produce. Menus 47–85F.

UCHACQ   40090 (4KM W)

|●| RESTAURANT DIDIER GARBAGE

It's on the RN134, on the way to Sales and Bordeaux.
☎ 05.58.75.33.66

The chef moved to this small village and took all his regular customers with him because of his reputation. The dining room is a pleasant place in which to sit and enjoy his fine cooking; dishes include pan-fried *foie gras* with a *coulis* of figs or *tournedos* of pig's trotter with truffle oil. A 98F menu in the week, then 140–330F. The bistro corner is regularly under seige with friends and regulars. Here, there's a *formule rapide* at 55F or a *menu du jour* for 69F. Otherwise, have a slice of country ham and a glass of wine. Perfect.

MONTFERRAND-DU-PÉRIGORD   24440

🏂 🏠 |●| HÔTEL-RESTAURANT LOU PAYROL

La Barrière; it's on the D26.

☎ 05.53.63.24.45 ➡ 05.53.63.24.45
Closed Wed lunchtime April–June and Sept, and 1 Oct to Easter. **Car park**.

A pretty little country hotel with a restaurant run by Sarah and Thierry, a friendly Anglo-French couple who also run a snack bar across the road. Simple, clean double rooms, some of which have a view of the gorgeous village of Montferrand, go for 210F with basin and up to 260F with bath. Good cooking includes dishes like omelette with ceps, morels or girolles, barbary duck, and chocolate and walnut gâteau. Menus 80–175F. Free apéritif.

MONTFORT EN CHALOSSE   40380

🛎 |●| AUX TAUZINS

It's on the D2, the route to Baigts and Hagetmau.
☎ 05.58.98.60.22 ➡ 05.58.98.45.79
Closed Sun and Mon out of season. **Swimming pool**.

A fine example of a traditional hotel and restaurant, but with some welcome modern facilities, like the pool. The owners have been hotel-keepers for three generations so the establishment has a comfortable, family feel with old-style bedrooms looking over the grounds. It's wonderfully peaceful. Doubles 285F with shower/wc and 305F with bath. The bright restaurant has a view over the valley. Dishes are from the region; *tournedos* Landais, *fricassée* of monkfish and John Dory with ceps. Menus 100F, except weekends, and 135–195F.

MONTIGNAC   24290

🎿 🛎 |●| HÔTEL-RESTAURANT DE LA GROTTE

65 rue du 4-Septembre (Centre); it's opposite the Lascaux road.
☎ 05.53.51.80.48 ➡ 05.53.51.05.96
TV. Disabled access. Pay garage.

A coaching inn which became a hotel around the time that the Lascaux caves were discovered. It's right in the centre, so ask for a room looking out onto the garden. Prices are competitive for the area – 174F for a double with basin, 235F with shower/wc and 285F with bath. Dishes include fillet of veal with truffle *jus*, zander pie with snails in a garlic cream sauce, warm salad of poached goose with light *choucroute*, and escalope of *foie gras* with coriander. There's a limited weekday lunch menu at 65F, and others at 95–215F. Half board is compulsory in Aug, at 295F per

person. Two terraces for when the weather is fine. Free apéritif or coffee and free garage space 1 Oct–14 April.

🛎 |●| RESTAURANT BELLEVUE

Regourdou; it's on the Lascaux road, after the caves at the top of the hill.
☎ 05.53.51.81.29
Closed Sat, evenings and a week each in June, Oct and Jan. **Car park**.

Located close to the Lascaux caves, with superb views from its bay windows and terrace, this place is primarily a restaurant. It serves decent food with a regional flavour at reasonable prices. They do a weekday menu for 60F and other menus 78–138F. You can get chicken *confit* and *enchaud*, baked loin of pork, pig's trotters with garlic and truffles, gizzard salad, and cep mushroom omelette. Rooms 210F with shower/wc or 250F bath.

🛎 |●| HOSTELLERIE LA ROSERAIE***

11 pl. d'Armes (Centre).
☎ 05.53.50.53.92 ➡ 05.53.51.02.23
Closed Nov–March. **Swimmimg pool. TV**.

Solidly built, elegant 19th-century town house. The rose garden referred to in the name is beyond the swimming pool. With its wooden staircase and cosy little lounges, the place really does have a great deal of charm. The fourteen exquisite rooms, all of them different, go for 350–450F. The restaurant, with its delightful terrace, serves sophisticated local cuisine: *foie gras* with strawberries, lobster salad, *tournedos* Rossini with *foie gras*, fillet steak in Périgueux sauce with truffles, and strawberry delight. The Périgueux sauce is made to a secret family recipe and it's been available commercially since 1927. Set menus 145–215F. Half-board costs 320–420F per person. You feel more as if you're in a B&B or a family guest house than in a classy three-star.

SAINT-AMAND-DE-COLY   24290 (8KM E)

🎿 🛎 |●| HÔTEL-RESTAURANT GARDETTE

Le bourg.
☎ and ➡ 05.53.51.68.50
Closed 15 Oct to Easter. **Car park**.

Two pale stone houses overshadowed by a fantastic church. Quiet simple rooms at reasonable prices – 175F with shower and wc along the landing, 215F with bath. There are four new rooms with shower/wc, two of which have a balcony with a view of the abbey. The restaurant, across the lane, has a few small tables in one corner because the owner cooks for the local schoolchildren during term time. Set menus, 70F (except Sunday) and 90–120F, offer salads and dishes from the southwest, such as omelette with cep mushrooms or truffles, duck breast, and *confit*. In summer, it's advisable to book during the classical music festival. 10% discount on the room rate Sept–June.

SERGEAC — 24290 (8.5KM S)

☆ I●I RESTAURANT L'AUBERGE DU PEYROL

How to get there: it's on the D65, between Montignac and Les Eyzies.
☎ 05.53.50.72.91
Closed Mon except July–Aug, and 11 Nov–1 March excluding weekends. **Garden. Car park.**

Traditional stone-built inn standing out on its own just outside a quaint little village. A large bay window looks out over the lovely Vézère valley. The fine rustic restaurant has a large fireplace where they smoke fillets of duck breast. Excellent welcome and tasty food. Jeanine concocts rare country dishes – fresh goose liver, baked loin of pork, pig's trotters with garlic and truffles, duck liver *confit*, duck breast with Périgueux sauce, walnut salad, and Sarlat-style apples. Menus 75–220F. This place has made a name for itself, so it's best to book. Free apéritif.

CHAPELLE-AUBAREIL (LA) 24290 (12KM S)

☆ 🏠 I●I HÔTEL-RESTAURANT LA TABLE DU TERROIR**

From Montignac or Les Eyzies take the road to Lascaux II from where it's signposted.
☎ 05.53.50.72.14 ☛ 05.53.51.16.23
Closed 30 Nov–28 Feb. **Swimming pool. TV. Disabled access. Car park.**

The Gibertie family have developed a tourist complex around their smallholding, deep in the country. The restaurant is on a hill 100m from the hotel; midway between them there's a swimming pool with views over the countryside. The buildings are new, but in traditional Périgord style, and they blend well with their surroundings. Rooms are pleasant, and the rates include breakfast, 220–320F with shower, 240–340F with bath. Half board, compulsory in July and August, costs 250–300F per person per night. Set menus, 75–220F, list sliced duck, duck *confit*, stuffed chicken, country salad, pan-fried *foie gras* and truffles cooked in hot ashes. They can make you a packed lunch and are happy to show you around the farm. Free apéritif. 5% discount on the room rate Sept–June.

MONTPON-MÉNESTÉROL 24700

I●I AUBERGE DE L'ÉCLADE

Take the D708 from Ribérac, turn right at the crossroads before going into town and it's signposted.
☎ and ☛ 05.53.80.28.64
Closed Tues evening, Wed, first fortnight in March, and Oct.

This rustic, flower-filled restaurant is off the beaten track but it has built a large following through word-of-mouth recommendations. Warm welcome and good atmosphere. The food is creative but rooted in tradition: hot liver deglazed with vanilla vinegar, duck breast with truffle shavings, and fillet of lamb in butter and basil. The menus, 80F–240F, are good value.

NAVARRENX 64190

☆ 🏠 I●I HÔTEL-RESTAURANT DU COMMERCE**

pl. des Casernes (Centre).
☎ 05.59.66.50.16 ☛ 05.59.66.52.67
✉ hotel-du-commerce@wanadoo.fr
Closed Jan. **TV.**

One of the oldest houses in Navarrenx. They light a fire in the large fireplace in the foyer at the first sign of cold weather. Pleasant rooms – the nicest are up in the attic – for 250F with shower/wc or 280F with bath. Wonderful Béarn flavours in the restaurant, which has plush surroundings, or there's a cool terrace for the summer. Menus are very reasonably priced at 65–145F. Kindly owner. Free coffee.

NÉRAC 47600

☆ I●I AUX DÉLICES DU ROY

7 rue du Château; on the pl. de la Mairie.
☎ and ☛ 05.53.65.81.12
Closed Wed.

The food is a winning combination of tradition, subtle blends of flavours and high-quality produce. Menus, 98–250F, include unusual fish or meat dishes; canelloni of raw salmon, *foie gras* with baby spinach, cockles in butter with lamb's lettuce, grilled red mullet with olive *pâté*, calf's head *ravigotte*, or braised ox cheek with vegetables. Young and attentive staff. The wine list features regional wines. Free apéritif.

FRANCESCAS 46600 (13KM SE)

I●I LE RELAIS DE LA HIRE

Le bourg; take the D930 for 9km towards Condom, then

left onto the D112.
☎ 05.53.65.41.93 ➡ 05.53.65.86.42
Closed Sun evening and Mon. **Disabled access.**

This restaurant, set in a stunning 18th-century manor house, has a peaceful atmosphere. After working with Roger Verger, with Robuchon, in the kitchens at the *Ritz*, and running the kitchens at the *Carlton*, Jean-Noël Prabonne returned to Gascony. He is particular to buy from local suppliers when creating his masterful dishes: local ceps *en cocotte*, Albret artichokes with a *soufflé* of *foie gras*, red sea bream poached with herbs, farm-bred pigeon with mushrooms, rack of roast lamb with garlic cloves and thyme, and braised leg of maize-fed chicken. Weekday menu 140F, and others from 190–320F. Pleasant reception from Mme Prabonne and attentive service. An unforgettable gastronomic experience.

NONTRON   24300

⚸ ≜ |●| HÔTEL-RESTAURANT
PELISSON**

pl. Alfred-Agard (Centre).
☎ 05.53.56.11.22 ➡ 05.53.56.59.94
Swimming pool. TV. Disabled access. Car park.

This grand hotel right in the centre has an elegant though rather austere exterior and a pleasant garden with a lovely swimming pool. Traditional rooms, particularly quiet at the rear; doubles 255F with shower and up to 305F with bath. Huge, cosy, rustic restaurant with attractive, locally made tableware. The terrace looks onto the garden. They serve traditional local food which has a good reputation: asparagus in flaky pastry, calf's head in a herb and shallot dressing, sliced beef in red wine and casseroled sole with ceps. Set menus 85–270F. Good wine list. 10% discount on the room rate for a two-night stay Oct–June.

OLORON-SAINTE-MARIE   64400

⚸ |●| ≜ RELAIS ASPOIS**

Route du col du Somport; 3km south of Oloron-Sainte-Marie; take the D55 and the N134, in the direction of Zaragoza
☎ 05.59.39.09.50 ➡ 05.59.39.02.33
Closed Mon lunchtime and the second fortnight in Nov.
TV. Children's playground. Garage.

The dining room here is full of character, with slate tiles, bare stone and beams and, in cool weather, a fire crackling in the hearth. Set menus 55–175F – try Béarnaise vegetable

broth, *foie gras* or *confit* of duck leg. They also prepare good regional dishes: ceps with parsley, Basque tripe *pâté*, *foie gras*, trout and duck breast with ceps. Rooms from 250F with bath. Free apéritif.

LUBRE-SAINT-CHRISTAU   64660 (10KM S)

⚸ ≜ |●| AU BON COIN

Route d'Arudy; it's about 1km outside the village.
☎ 05.59.34.40.12 ➡ 05.59.34.46.40
ⓔ valerielassala@worldonline.fr
Closed Sun evening, and Mon from 1 Nov–15 April. **TV.**
Swimming pool. Car park.

A good, comfortable, modern hotel set in quiet countryside in the foothills, 300m from a spa. The swimming pool is across the road. Double rooms 280–430F. In the restaurant they serve unusual dishes at reasonable prices with lots of wild mushrooms: *terrine* with Jurançon wine, cep tart, pigeon with ceps *en croûte*. Menus 90–290F. Free coffee.

ORTHEZ   64300

⚸ ≜ |●| HÔTEL-RESTAURANT AU TEMPS
DE LA REINE JEANNE**

44 rue du Bourg-Vieux (Centre); it's opposite the tourist office.
☎ 05.59.67.00.76 ➡ 05.59.69.09.63
Closed Feb. **TV. Disabled access. Car park.**

The mother of Henri IV, Jeanne d'Albret, bravely professed her Protestantism in this house at a time when it was risky to criticise the Catholic Church. Today it's a peaceful and quiet hotel with lovely rooms. Doubles with shower or bath 285–310F. The restaurant is a pleasant surprise. The decor is modest but the cuisine is opulent: delicate cream of celery soup, *foie gras* terrine with artichokes, joint of monkfish with bacon, duck *cassoulet*, Béarn black pudding on split bread, and suckling pig. A festival of flavours at honest prices. Menus 80–160F. Perfect service. Free apéritif.

|●| AUBERGE SAINT-LOUP

20 rue du Vieux Pont.
☎ 05.59.69.15.40
ⓔ brosse.p@wanadoo.fr
Closed Sun evening and Mon.

A very beautiful house, typical of the region, in a street that's typical of the town. This used to be a coaching stop on the way to Santiago de Compostela; it has a superb half-timbered façade. Patrick Brosse's dishes blend the traditional and the modern: prawns with salt cod mousse with chorizo and chilli, sea bass with lemon and star anis, or roast pigeon with rosemary. Lunch menu 98F, with others from 130–200F. In summer, they open the cool terrace in a peaceful garden. Friendly service.

PAU 64000

☎ HÔTEL D'ALBRET*

11 rue Jeanne-d'Albret (Centre); it's near the château of Henri IV.
☎ 05.59.27.81.58

You get a warm welcome in this 19th-century house. Rooms are quite large and very well kept; 120F with washing facilities and 145F with shower/wc.

☎ HÔTEL BEAU SOLEIL**

81 av. des Lauriers; it's 200m from the supermarket on the Tarbes road.
☎ 05.59.14.20.10 ➡ 05.59.14.20.11
TV. **Garden**. **Car Park**.

In the fashionable part of town, which has long been colonised by the English. It's hard not to like this characterful pebbledash hotel set in a luxuriant garden. The rooms, 220F with shower/wc and TV, are simple and very well kept. Genuine family welcome.

🍴 ☎ HÔTEL LE POSTILLON**

10 cours Camou; it's two minutes from the château.
☎ 05.59.72.83.00 ➡ 05.59.72.83.00
✉ hotel-le-Postillon@wanadoo.fr
TV. **Car park**.

A new-Romantic hotel. There's a little flower garden in the courtyard and a trickling fountain. Doubles with shower/wc 245F or 325F with bath. A good place, particularly given the value for money. 10% discount.

🍴 ☎ IOI HÔTEL-RESTAURANT LE COMMERCE**

9 rue du Maréchal-Joffre (Centre); it's opposite the Préfecture de Police.
☎ 05.59.27.24.40 ➡ 05.59.83.81.74
Restaurant closed Sun and public holidays, except for groups. **TV**. **Car park**.

Traditional hotel in the centre of town, with a certain charm and a warm welcome. Comfortable, soundproofed rooms 250–295F with shower/wc, or 325F with bath. No lift. There's a bar, and a fine restaurant with rustic decor. Menus 90, 100F and a gastronomic menu at 160F; dishes include fresh liver with caramelised apples, sole with ceps and duck breast with prawns. Pleasant

courtyard terrace with good service. 10% discount on the room rate.

🍴 IOI RESTAURANT LA BROCHETTERIE

16 rue Henri-IV (Centre); it's near the château d'Henri IV.
☎ 05.59.27.40.33 ➡ 05.59.27.30.58
Closed Sat lunchtime.

Service until 11pm. Attractive stone-built restaurant where they grill duck breast and meats over the charcoal fire. The lunchtime clientele consists mainly of people who work nearby. Menus 65–115F and a lunch *formule* at 65F. Attentive staff. *À la carte*, try grilled hake flambéed with anis, wild boar cutlets and various fresh salads. A real treat. Best to book. Free apéritif.

IOI AU FIN GOURMET

24 av. Gaston Lacoste (Centre).
☎ 05.59.27.47.71 ➡ 05.59.82.96.77
Closed Sun evening, Mon, and a fortnight in Feb.

This place, a firm favourite with the people of Pau, really lives up to its name. Quality cooking on all the menus, which start at 100F. Dishes are finely prepared – stars include the *foie gras terrine* with pistachios, rabbit and potato pie, and roast pigeon with *foie gras* toast.

IOI LE MAJESTIC

9 pl. Royale (Centre).
☎ 05.59.27.56.83
Closed Sun evening and Mon. **Disabled access.**

Locally born chef Jean-Marie Larrère, who has worked at the *Trou Gascon* and *Le Pressoir* in Paris, is a little ill-served by the dull surroundings – though the shady terrace on the Place Royale makes up for it on sunny days. In any case, Larrère produces remarkable dishes: hot *foie gras* with caramelised pears, salad of *croustillant* of pig's trotters with fresh morels, crayfish tails with spices, saddle of monkfish with a chorizo *jus* and mushrooms, fillet of oxtail with duck *foie gras*. Menus 108–190F. Mme Larrère is very welcoming, and runs the dining room to perfection.

🍴 IOI RESTAURANT LA TABLE D'HÔTE

1 rue du Hedas; it's 5 minutes on foot from the château.
☎ 05.59.27.56.06 ➡ 05.59.21.58.93
Closed Sun, Mon and the All Saints' and Easter school holidays.

In one of the oldest parts of Pau. Pierre will welcome you like a regular to his impressive restaurant which has stained-glass windows and beams. The richly flavoured cuisine is spot on, and uses lots of quality produce: crayfish *fricassée* with *foie gras* and fresh noodles, salad of quail in sherry, duck pie scented with truffle, sole braised in Jurançon wine, and lamb sweetbreads with peppers. If you want just one course from the 118F menu, you'll pay 60F. There's another set menu at 149F, and you can eat *à la carte*. Free coffee.

GAN   64290 (8KM S)

🎿 ⚐ |O| HOSTELLERIE L'HORIZON

Chemin de Mesplet.
☎ 05.59.21.58.93 ➡ 05.59.21.71.80
e eytpierre@aol.com
Closed Sun evening and Mon out of season, and Feb.
TV. Garden. Car park.

A pink house, with a garden full of flowers and a peaceful terrace, in extensive grounds. Attractive, well-equipped rooms for 280F. Sophisticated cuisine – *escalope* of salmon trout with ceps, lambs sweetbreads with girolles and so on – on menus priced 90F, 150F and 300F. Free apéritif.

SÉVIGNACQ-MEYRACQ   64260 (21KM S)

🎿 ⚐ |O| HÔTEL-RESTAURANT LES BAINS DE SECOURS**

How to get there: take the D934 for Laruns, after Rébénacq; as you come into the vallée d'Ossau it's signposted.
☎ 05.59.05.62.11 ➡ 05.59.05.76.56
e jp.paroix@wanadoo.fr
Closed Sun evening, Mon and Jan. **TV. Car park**.

A scenic road leads to this old restored Béarn farm, now an inn, adorned with flower-filled balconies. Well-appointed rooms go from 295F with shower/wc to 360F with bath. Delicious food served by the open fire in winter and on the terrace in summer. Set menus 82F (residents only), and 155F. Try the salad of fillet of sole with ceps, the three fine fillets of beef in three sauces, the squid stuffed with *foie gras* and ceps and the lamb sweetbread *fricassée*. A very good place to eat, close to the very old spa. 10% discount on the room rate Sept–June.

NOURS   64420 (25KM SE)

|O| LE FIGUIER

How to get there: from Pau take the N117 towards Soumoulou then the D940 towards Lourdes; turn right towards Nay and it's the first street on the left after the church.
☎ 05.59.04.67.70
Closed Sun evening and Mon. **Garden. Car park**.

The restaurant is in an old farm way out in the countryside. Thierry is in charge in the kitchen and his wife looks after you in the restaurant. He prepares tasty dishes with great care: fresh duck's liver with apples, veal sweetbreads with ceps, stuffed pig's trotters, Gascon duck and a fantastic chocolate dessert. He bakes the bread with organic flour and uses only fresh local produce. Lunchtime menu 60F, then 90–140F.

PÉRIGUEUX   24000

⚐ |O| HÔTEL-RESTAURANT DU MIDI**

18 rue Denis-Papin; northwest of town opposite the train station.
☎ 05.53.53.41.06 ➡ 05.53.08.19.32
Closed Sat from 20 Oct–15 April, and Christmas to New Year. **TV. Garage**.

A typical station hotel which has been completely renovated by the friendly young couple who run the place. Nice family atmosphere. Very clean, modern rooms, 145F for a double with basin or 245F with bath. Rooms at the back are bigger and quieter. The restaurant is peaceful. Set menus, 62–245F, offer traditional cooking with local dishes such as truffle omelette, steak with ceps and duck breast with *foie gras* cream.

🎿 ⚐ |O| HÔTEL-RESTAURANT PÉRIGORD**

74 rue Victor-Hugo (North).
☎ 05.53.53.33.63 ➡ 05.53.08.19.74
Restaurant closed Sat and Sun evenings 1 Oct–28 Feb, and 15 Oct–5 Nov. **TV. Garden. Pay car park**.

This elegant establishment, boasting a large flower-filled garden, is just out of the centre. They offer double rooms, some in a separate building at the bottom of the garden, for 250–300F. The restaurant enjoys a good reputation. Weekday lunchtime menu 77F, and others from 95–165F. *À la carte* dishes include duck breast with truffles, cep omelette, veal sweetbreads *provençale*, and duck *confit* with potatoes. They prepare a wide range of fish including hake, trout, sole and grilled salmon with anchovy paste. Free apéritif.

🎿 |O| LES BERGES DE L'ISLE

2 rue Pierre Magne.
☎ 05.53.09.51.50
Closed Sun evening and Mon.

This restaurant is in a picturesque spot – on the shore of the island opposite Saint-Front cathedral – and they have the only waterside terrace in town. Unusual cooking such as *soufflé* of *foie gras* with *vigneronne* sauce and lampray with Bordelais sauce. Menus 89–145F. Some wines are served by the glass. Friendly atmosphere. Free coffee.

⚃⦿ RESTAURANT HERCULE POIREAU

2 rue de la Nation (Centre); it's in a small street opposite the main door of the Saint-Front cathedral.
☎ 05.53.08.90.76 ➡ 05.53.04.29.63
Closed 24–27 Dec and 31 Dec–3 Jan.

The name of this restaurant plays on words – Inspector Hercule Poirot was fastidious about what he ate, while *poireau* means leek. Brasserie-style food includes *andouillette*, veal *blanquette*, and, their speciality, a splendid duck dish. The dining room is an impressive 16th-century vaulted cellar. *Formule* 99F for two courses then menus 115–229F. Free coffee.

⦿ RESTAURANT LE 8

8 rue de la Clarté (Centre); it's next to the Saint-Front cathedral.
☎ 05.53.35.15.15
Closed Sun, Mon, Feb school holidays, and a fortnight in July.

Regional and creative dishes served in a sunny dining room – home-made *foie gras* or *croustillant* of duck are the star turns. Set menus 165–400F. They take their cooking seriously here and are happy to serve half portions of any dish on the menu. They have a courtyard and garden, and the cellar has been turned into a sitting room.

CHANCELADE — 24650 (3KM W)

⌂⦿ LE PONT DE LA BEAURONNE**

4 route de Ribérac; it's at the crossroads of the D710 and D939.
☎ 05.53.08.42.91 ➡ 05.53.03.97.69
Closed Sun evening, Mon lunchtime and 20 Sept–15 Oct. **TV**. **Garden**. **Disabled access**.

Service until 9.30pm – last orders half an hour before. The crossroads does nothing for the charm of the place, but the rooms are reasonable and well kept. Doubles with shower 180F or 230F with bath – try to get one at the back, looking out onto the garden. Family atmosphere. The cooking is straightforward, with an accent on the regional. Menus from 72F.

ANNESSE ET BAULIEU — 24430 (12KM)

⌂⦿ CHÂTEAU DE LALANDE-RESTAURANT LE TILLEUL CENDRÉ

How to get there: take the D3 in the direction of Saint-Astier.
☎ 05.53.54.52.30 ➡ 05.53.07.46.67
Closed mid-Nov to mid-March. **Garden**. **Swimming pool**. **Car park**.

Situated in an estate on the banks of the Isle, this is luxury without ostentation. You are welcomed with old-fashioned charm. The rooms are attractively furnished and most of them have a river view. They are all quiet and cosy. Doubles 300–450F. The cuisine is resolutely regional and prepared to the most exacting standards. Menus 150–300F. There's a swimming pool down by the river.

MANZAC-SUR-VERN — 24110 (20KM SW)

⌂⦿ HÔTEL-RESTAURANT LE LION D'OR**

How to get there: take the D43 and the D4 to Manzac-sur-Vern.
☎ 05.53.54.28.09 ➡ 05.53.54.25.50
Closed Sun evening and Mon except July–Aug, and Feb. **Garden**.

In the heart of a region largely bypassed by tourists, in the centre of a small village where nothing happens after 7pm. Doubles with shower or bath 230F – some look onto the garden. The restaurant features modern decor with a few older elements and traditional cooking. Weekday lunch menu 80F, and others 115–210F. The chef's specialities include warm *foie gras*, salmon with mead, veal sweetbreads in Monbazillac, *millas* (maize flour porridge) with apples, and cinnamon ice cream. You can eat outside in summer. Half-board 260F per person.

SORGES — 24420 (23KM NE)

⚃⌂⦿ AUBERGE DE LA TRUFFE***

N21 (Centre).
☎ 05.53.05.02.05 ➡ 05.53.05.39.27
℮ contact@auberge-de-la-truffe.com
Closed Sun evening in winter and Mon lunchtime. **Swimming pool**. **TV**. **Garden**. **Car park**.

Good traditional food in a region famous for truffles: duck with *foie gras*, stuffed carp *à l'ancienne*, cep omelette and beef with *foie gras* or sliced duck. The restaurant is popular with local businesspeople as well as tourists. Friendly service. The limited 80F set menu is well-priced and there's a self-service buffet and fresh dishes daily. Other menus, 110–330F, include a *foie gras* and truffle menu, featuring *marbré* of veal sweetbreads with *foie gras* and truffle vinaigrette, medallions of lamb with truffle, and truffle omelette. Though the inn is right on the road, the rooms look out onto the open countryside, and some have a garden view. Doubles with shower/wc 260F, or bath 280F. Good breakfast buffet. 10% discount on the room rate Sept–June.

PORT-SAINT-FOY 33220

🎿 |●| AU FIL DE L'EAU

3 rue de la Rouquette (North).
☎ 05.53.24.72.60
Closed Mon, the first fortnights in Oct and March.

The restaurant is pleasantly situated on the riverside – it's best to book if you want a table on the terrace. Excellent cooking with a fine menu at 140F – the appetiser, sheep mousse and duck thigh *confit* are finely executed and attractively presented. The desserts are equally good. Weekday lunch menu 85F and others up to 210F. Free coffee.

SAINT-MAURE-DE-PAYRIAC 47170 (17KM SW)

|●| RESTAURANTS DUFFAU-LES 2 GOUR-MANDS

rue Principale; take the D656 from Poudenas in the direction of Sos, then turn left onto the D109.
☎ 05.53.65.61.00
Closed Sat lunchtime and dinner only by reservation and 15 Jan–15 Feb.

At lunchtime during the week, this place is like many others, with a clientele of travelling salesmen, local workers and lost tourists, though the food is slightly better and the dishes are substantial. The menu costs 65F, with soup, *terrine* and omelette typical starters. But Sunday lunch is altogether different; this is a place for gourmets and you have to book well in advance. The chef has worked at the *Ritz* and *Chez Lasserre* (two of the very best kitchens in Paris) and on Sundays he and his associates indulge themselves – and so can you. Really very grand cuisine. They sell prepared meals to go as well. Splendid welcome.

RIBÉRAC 24600

🎿 🛏 |●| HÔTEL-RESTAURANT DE FRANCE**

3 rue Marc-Dufraisse (Centre); it's off the market place.
☎ 05.53.90.00.61 ➡ 05.53.91.06.05
Restaurant closed Mon and Tues lunchtimes except July–Aug, 15 Nov–15 Dec and a fortnight in Jan.
Garden. TV.

Very central, ivy-smothered coaching inn with charming old stonework and a small flower-filled garden. Warm welcome. The rooms have been carefully decorated and are well maintained; 200–3000F for a double with shower or bath. In the restaurant they offer a daily set menu 85F, other menus 100–230F, and dishes *à la carte*. Substantial local dishes are served with flair: duck breast with chanterelles, lamb shank with lavender vinegar, chicken livers and gizzards with baked apples. 10% discount on the room rate 15 Nov–15 April.

🎿 |●| RESTAURANT LE CHEVILLARD

Gayet; 2km from Ribérac, on the D708, Montpon to Bordeaux road.
☎ 05.53.90.16.50
Closed Mon except July–Aug, and 15 Nov–15 Dec.
Garden. Car park.

Restaurant in an old farm surrounded by a huge garden. The owner, who used to be a sales rep, knows how to make you feel welcome, and offers large portions of quality food; fresh farm chicken, oysters from the display and good meats – the name literally means "Restaurant of the Wholesale Butcher" – grilled over an open fire. They do a 69F lunch menu and others from 99–200F. Seafood is also served, at reasonable prices, and they offer a good selection of local wines. Free apéritif.

SABRES 40630

🎿 🛏 |●| L'AUBERGE DES PINS***

rue de la Piscine.
☎ 05.08.30.00 ➡ 05.58.07.56.74
Closed Sun evening and Mon out of season, Mon lunchtime in season, and a fortnight in Jan.
Disabled access. TV. Car park.

A large timber-framed house, typical of the Landes, with a lovely balcony. The Lesclauze family are only happy when you're happy and will pull out all the stops to ensure that you leave with fond memories of the place. The rooms have some fine furniture, pretty ornaments and supremely comfortable beds. Doubles with shower or bath 320–650F. The surroundings are rustic but classy, and the quality of the food is equally high. Tempting dishes include *croustillant* of duck *foie gras*, pan-fried sea bream with salt and aubergine gateau, crayfish ravioli with ceps, and the choice is made more difficult by the tireless inventiveness of the chef. Menu 100F, excluding Sunday, others 150–500F and a children's menu 75F. 10% discount on the room rate out of season.

SAINT-ÉMILION   33330

🏠 L'AUBERGE DE LA COMMANDERIE**

rue des Cordeliers (Centre).
☎ 05.57.24.70.19 ➡ 05.57.74.44.53
Closed 15 Jan–15 Feb. **TV**. **Disabled access**. **Car park**.

A senior officer of the Order of the Knights
Templar used to live here, and during the
French Revolution the disgraced Girondins
used it as a hiding place. Very little of its rich
past is visible today, however. It's now a conventional family hotel with romantic rooms in
the main building and more futuristic ones in
the annexe. Doubles 280F with shower and
up to 550F with bath. There is also an apartment that sleeps four.

🏠 HÔTEL AU LOGIS DES REMPARTS***

rue Guadet.
☎ 05.57.24.70.43 ➡ 05.57.74.44.44
📧 logis-des-Remparts@wanadoo.fr
Closed Jan to 12 Feb. **Swimming pool**. **TV**. **Garden**.
Car park.

A pleasant hotel in a very old building which
has kept the original stone staircase, terrace
and garden bordering the ramparts. Doubles
400–550F with shower/wc or 550–750F bath.
Some rooms can sleep five people. The
owners have recently brought the neighbouring *Maison des Templiers*, doubling the
number of rooms with views over the garden. When the weather's fine breakfast is
served on the elegantly paved terrace or in
the garden. It's substantial and very good –
just try the cake.

🍴 🍽 RESTAURANT FRANCIS GOULLÉE

27 rue Guadet (Centre).
☎ 05.57.24.70.49 ➡ 05.57.74.47.96
Closed Sun evening, Mon, and 2–20 Dec.

Hidden away in a narrow old street, this is the
least touristy restaurant in Saint-Émilion. Francis Goulé, ably assisted by his chatty wife, prepares very good local cooking in the warm,
comfortable dining room. Prices are very fair,
with a 90F *formule* (not served on Sundays),
and menus 150–240F. Choices a pastry case
filled with chicory and gravadlax, breast of
duck *en aiguillettes*, roast potatoes with onion
fondue, marvellous *foie gras*, pigeon *en croûte*
with mild spices and Szechuan pepper, casserole of *brandade de morue* (creamed salt cod)
with morels, dried figs with spices, and pear
dacquoise. Attractively priced wine list. Free
apéritif.

SAINT-JEAN-DE-LUZ   64500

🍴🏠 LE PETIT TRIANON**

56 bd. Victor-Hugo.
☎ 05.59.26.11.90 ➡ 05.59.26.14.10
📧 le petittrianon@wanadoo.fr
Closed Jan. **TV**. **Car park**.

This hotel is charming, simple, clean and
unpretentious. And reasonably priced. The
new owners have retained the family character
of the place, while coming up with a few new
ideas to bring it more up to date, and they're
systematically refurbishing the bedrooms. The
third-floor rooms, 200–260F, have only hand
basins or shower (no wc) but the sloping ceilings make them romantic. Doubles 280–400F.
Pretty private terrace. 10% discount on the
room rate Oct–June.

🍽 LE KAIKU

17 rue de la République (Centre).
☎ 05.59.26.13.20
Closed Mon lunchtime and Wed out of season.

Superb medieval house with elegant mul-
lioned windows and wonderful natural
stonework. They specialise in fish and
seafood, and the cooking is of a very high
standard, though it's a bit touristy. Set menus
from 145F; try the exquisite oysters *gratinée*,
the langoustine ravioli, or milk-fed Pyrenees
lamb. Some recipes, like braised pork
cheeks with Irouléguy, hark back to the past.
.

SAINT-JEAN-PIED-DE-PORT   64220

🍴 🏠 🍽 CENTRAL HÔTEL**

1 pl. du Général-de-Gaulle (Centre).
☎ 05.59.37.00.22 ➡ 05.59.37.27.79
Closed 10 Dec–1 March. **TV**. **Car park**.

Rooms here are simply luxurious and impeccably clean; they cost 340F with shower and
400F with bath. Ask for one with a view of the
Nive and the waterfall. Very high standards in
the restaurant, which offers set menus from
100–250F. The dining room has charm and
the cooking is first-rate: lamb sweetbreads
with *piquillos*, wild salmon, and *soufflé* with
Izarr (a liqueur similar to Chartreuse). Good
welcome and attentive service. Free apéritif.

🏠 🍽 LES PYRÉNÉES***

19 pl. du Général-de-Gaulle (Centre).
☎ 05.59.37.01.01 ➡ 05.59.37.18.97
Closed Mon evening Nov–March, Tues excluding
July–Aug, 5–28 Jan and 20 Nov–22 Dec.

Swimming pool. TV. Car park.

On paper, 580–900F seems a lot to pay for the rooms, but this is a high-class hotel and they're impeccable. There's a very pleasant indoor swimming pool. The restaurant, which has a well-established reputation throughout the Basque country, offers fine cuisine artistically conjured from local produce – delicious *garbure* (vegetable soup served with a piece of goose or duck *confit*), good *foie gras* of duck, roast pigeon with cep-filled ravioli, and freshly caught salmon from the Adour. Remarkable desserts and sorbets. Menus 250–550F.

❙●❙ RESTAURANT ARBILLAGA

8 rue de l'Église; it's inside the fortified part of town.
☎ 05.59.37.06.44
Closed Tues, and Wed out of season.

Grand dining room in a stunning location between the fortified walls and the old houses. The delicious food is served in generous portions, both on the set menus (80–165F) and *à la carte* – try the scrambled eggs with truffle and *foie gras*, scallops with smoked bacon or spit-roast milk-fed lamb. Spirited welcome and service in an intimate atmosphere.

SAINT-MICHEL   64220 (3KM S)

🏃 ≜ ❙●❙ HÔTEL-RESTAURANT XOKO-GOXOA**

How to get there: it's on the D301.
☎ 05.59.37.06.34 ➡ 05.59.37.34.63
Closed Tues out of season and Jan–Feb. **Car park**.

This is a large traditional house surrounded with greenery. Most of the rooms look straight onto the countryside. Comfortable double rooms 200–230F. Atmospheric rustic-style dining room and no-nonsense, good value cooking. Set menus, 70–110F, list specialities such as trout *etxekoa*, steak *à la navarraise* (with sweet peppers, onions and garlic), salad *gourmande* and so on. The *à la carte* prices are very reasonable. Large terrace with a wonderful panoramic view. Free apéritif when you stay three nights.

BUSSUNARITZ   64220 (7KM E)

≜ ❙●❙ HÔTEL-RESTAURANT DU COL DE GAMIA**

col de Gamia; take the D933 then the D120.
☎ 05.59.37.13.48 ➡ 95.59.37.96.96
Closed 31 Dec–15 March. **Car park**.

The little road to this place is one of the loveliest in the region. When you get to the top of the col de Gamia, the view is tremendous.

Clean comfortable rooms, 200F with bath. The excellent Basque cuisine includes delicious wild boar stew in season. Set menus 65–180F. The charming owners are warm and friendly.

BIDARRAY   64780 (14KM NW)

🏃 ≜ ❙●❙ HÔTEL-RESTAURANT BARBERAENEA

pl. de l'Église (Centre).
☎ 05.59.37.74.86 ➡ 05.59.37.77.55
Closed 19 Nov–20 Dec.
Disabled access. TV. Car park.

A very old country inn belonging to the Elissetche family. It has been beautifully renovated after a lengthy closure. Cheery welcome and attractive, charming rooms with white walls, period furniture and shining parquet floors. They look out onto the square and its 12th-century church. Some have a view of the countryside. Doubles 275–340F. In the restaurant you can get appetising dishes including salad of warm cod with garlic sauce, pan-fried lamb chops, and bread and butter pudding. *Menu du randonneur* 95F, *menu du terroir* 135F. Free *digestif*.

SAINT-JUSTIN   40240

≜ ❙●❙ HÔTEL DE FRANCE**

pl. des Tilleuls.
☎ 05.58.44.83.61 ➡ 05.58.44.83.89
Closed Sun evening, Mon, Thurs evening and the last fortnight in Oct. **TV. Disabled access**.

1930s-style decor in this hotel in the middle of a 13th-century fortified town. Peace and quiet reigns here, along with a traditional family atmosphere. Lovely rooms, 240F with shower/wc and up to 300F with bath. The restaurant is at the back. The chef comes up with delicious flavours and prepares everything from fresh produce: salad of duck gizzards and hearts, prawns with diced cep and ginger with green chilli, suckling pig with *ratatouille* or duck breast with mushrooms and *foie gras*. House speciality is goose simmered in red wine. Set menus 70F (except Sun), then 115–150F. Friendly welcome and relaxed atmosphere.

SAINT-MACAIRE   33490

🏃 ≜ ❙●❙ L'ABRICOTIER

2 rue Borgoeing; it's on the N113 between Langon and La Réole.
☎ 05.56.76.83.63 ➡ 05.56.76.28.51

Closed Tues evening, Mon evening from 1 Oct–30 May, and 12 Nov–12 Dec. **Car park**.

This restaurant would be one of the most beautiful in the region were it not on the edge of the N113. At least the little dining room looks out onto the terrace at the back with its apricot tree – lovely when the sun's out. The kitchen turns out imaginative dishes including *gazpacho* of scallops with Jerusalem artichokes, roast sea bass with asparagus, braised shoulder of lamb, *casso-lette* of snails with *confit* of pig's trotters, salad of duck's neck with artichokes, fillet of bream with mixed vegetable *confit*, vegetables with *foie gras*, and, for dessert, roast pineapple with vanilla. Weekday lunch menu 115F, and others 155–230F. Very good wine list – exclusively Bordeaux. A handful of rooms with shower/wc, 300F. 10% discount on the room rate Oct–April.

SAINT-PALAIS   64120

🏄 🏠 |O| HÔTEL-RESTAURANT DE LA PAIX**

33 rue du Jeu-de-Paume (Centre).
☎ 05.59.65.73.15 ➡ 05.59.65.63.83
Closed Fri evening, Sat lunchtime except July–Aug, and Jan. **Disabled access**. **TV**. **Car park**.

You'd never think from the outside that this hotel's been around for 200 years. It's been entirely rebuilt and has all mod cons. Rooms 285–300F with shower/wc or bath. Good regional cooking, with a weekday menu at 65F, and others 115–160F. Dishes include lamb's sweetbreads with ham and ceps, monkfish, marinated salmon and ewe's milk cheese *millefeuille*, *ttoro* (fish stew), and game in season. Charming welcome, but it will be some time before it gets its old character back. 10% discount on the room rate.

SARLAT-LA-CANÉDA   24200

🏄 🏠 HÔTEL LE MAS DE CASTEL**

Sudalissant (South); it's 3km from the town – take the D704 in the direction of Souillac, then La Canéda, and after that it's signposted.
☎ 05.53.59.02.59 ➡ 05.53.28.25.62
Closed 11 Nov to Easter. **Swimming pool**. **Disabled access**. **TV**. **Car park**.

A charming hotel, surrounded by greenery, built in beautiful white stone in the local style. Excellent welcome. The rooms are comfortable, pleasant and restful. Numbers 2, 3, 4, 5 and 14 are larger than the others. Expect to pay

240–260F for a double with shower/wc or bath. Beautiful swimming pool where you can cool off in summer. 10% discount April and Oct.

🏠 HÔTEL LES RÉCOLLETS**

4 rue Jean-Jacques-Rousseau (Centre).
☎ 05.53.31.36.00 ➡ 05.53.30.32.62
e otelrecol@aol.com
Closed Jan. **Car park**. **TV**.

In a quiet, picturesque pedestrian lane away from the cars and the tourist crowds. Sarlat is a historic town so it's good to stay in a hotel with a bit of history – this used to be the cloisters of a 17th-century convent. Today it's managed by a father and son team and you get a convivial welcome. The rooms have been tastefully refurbished; doubles with shower/wc or bath cost 250–300F. A few look out onto a quiet courtyard where you have breakfast. Number 15 is particularly light and has a lovely view over the tiled rooftops in the old town, while number 8 has elegant stone archways.

🏄 🏠 |O| LA MAISON DES PAYRAT**

Le lac de la Plane; pass the police station and follow the signs for 2km.
☎ 05.53.59.00.32 ➡ 05.53.28.56.56
Open weekends only mid-Nov to April. **Swimming pool**. **Disabled access**. **TV**. **Car park**.

A 17th-century hermitage that has been converted and refurbished by the new owners. It's become a charming hotel and is in a delightful place. The thoughtful decor makes the most of the old stonework. Spacious and bright rooms with lovely bathrooms, 250–520F. Very charming welcome. Menus from 100F; tomato *tarte Tatin*, sautéed shrimps. Free coffee.

🏄 🏠 |O| HÔTEL-RESTAURANT SAINT-ALBERT ET HÔTEL MONTAIGNE**

10 pl. Pasteur et 11 rue Émile Faure (South); behind the main post office.
☎ 05.53.31.55.55 ➡ 05.53.59.19.99
Closed Sun evening, and Mon out of season. **Disabled access**.**TV**. **Car park**.

Two hotels and a restaurant on the edge of the old town. Behind the tasteful façade of *Hôtel Montaigne* you'll find pretty rooms which are well equipped and attractively decorated in modern style. The ones on the top floor have ceilings criss-crossed with beams. There's a glassed-in terrace where you have breakfast. On the other side of the street, in *Hôtel Saint-Albert*, the rooms have been refurbished and the ones over the street have double glazing. In both establishments doubles with shower or bath cost 270–330F. In the huge dining room you'll rub shoulders with faithful regulars and local worthies – people who appreciate culinary classics such as calf's head and pig's trotters, and regional food like salad *périgourdine*, omelette with cep mushrooms, and *confit* of duck with walnuts. At lunchtime on weekdays, the bistro serves a dish of the day for 45F, a set 70F menu and others at 120–142F. Free apéritif.

🎭 ≜ HÔTEL DE COMPOSTELLE**

64 av. de Selves; near the centre of town on the road to Montignac/Brives.
☎ 05.53.59.08.53 ➡ 05.53.30.31.65
e hotel.compostel@perigord.com
Closed Sun lunchtime and mid–Nov to Easter. **Disabled access.TV. Garden**.

Friendly welcome. Excellent, large and pleasant rooms; doubles 290–310F with shower/wc, or 310–330F with bath. A few have a glassed-in balcony but they look out onto the street. The quieter rooms at the back overlook a tiny garden. Families can go for the small suites with two bedrooms and bath. 10% discount on the room rate March–April and Oct–Nov.

🎭 ≜ I●I LA HOIRIE

La Giragne; take the Souillac road out of Sarlat, and it's well signposted.
☎ 05.53.59.05.62 ➡ 05.53.31.13.90
e lahoirie@club-internet.fr
Closed 15 Nov–15 March.
Swimming pool. TV. Car park.

Some parts of the original 13th-century house remain, and a recent refurbishment has brought out the brilliance of the pale stone. There are large grounds with a pool so you can sunbathe and cool down afterwards. The rooms are spacious and more like comfortable apartments; 380–680F. The kitchen cooks everything fresh – look out especially for the semi-cooked *foie gras* with fennel *compote*, boned pig's trotter stuffed with goose *foie gras*, duck breast with leeks and an iced fruit *soufflé*. Menus 95–220F. Free apéritif.

I●I RESTAURANT CHEZ MARC

4 rue Tourny (Centre).
☎ and ➡ 05.53.59.02.71
Closed Sun, and Mon evening out of season.

You'll need to book at this minuscule bistro, which has two or three tables set on the terrace on a busy old street. Ideal for lunch. There are menus at 58F, 85F and 135F, or you might pay around 100F *à la carte*: dishes include duck *andouillette* in Cahors wine,

duck breast with red fruit, a choice of fish, and apple *fondant*. Reasonably priced wine.

I●I RESTAURANT LES 4 SAISONS

2 côte de Toulouse (Centre).
☎ 05.53.29.48.59 ➡ 05.53.59.53.74
Closed Wed out of season.

A recently opened restaurant in a steep, narrow street with two dining rooms and plans for a terrace. The set menu at 65F offers some of the best value for money in town. Other menus, 98–250F, list dishes like salad of scrambled eggs and morels, crisp breast of duck with juniper berry sauce, and pig's trotters and ceps in a truffle sauce. Original desserts include *gratin* of seasonal fruit; they also do great chocolate creations and a truffle ice cream with saffron sauce.

I●I LE PRÉSIDIAL

6 rue Landry; it's next to the town hall.
☎ 05.53.28.92.473 ➡ 05.53.59.43.84
Closed Mon and Dec–Jan.

Great gastronomic feats are accomplished in this restaurant run by a charming couple. Madame runs the dining room and Monsieur is a brilliant chef. This jewel is their new enterprise and it's already become *the* place to eat in Sarlat. The building is classified as a historic monument and is a gorgeous house from 1552, in a large, quiet garden in the old town. The dining room is very elegant and the terrace is the loveliest in town. The short menu offers a good choice and value for money. On the others you will find perfect *foie gras*, a nest of tagliatelle with lamb sweetbreads with rosemary, and beautifully cooked pigeon supreme. An extensive wine list with fair prices. Courteous and efficient service.

ROQUE-GAGEAC (LA)   24250 (9KM S)

≜ I●I HÔTEL-RESTAURANT LA BELLE ÉTOILE**

rue Principale (Centre); it's on the D46.
☎ 05.53.29.51.44 ➡ 05.53.29.45.63
Closed Mon out of season and Nov–March. **TV**.

Charming, stylish hotel in a glorious setting in one of the most beautiful villages in France. The rooms are individually decorated and tastefully furnished. A few have a great view of the slow-moving Dordogne. Doubles 320F with shower or bath. The elegant dining room has a vine-smothered terrace overlooking the river. The food is excellent – the kitchen concentrates on the classics but adds the odd unexpected modern touch such as *millefeuille* of *foie gras* with apple and walnut, pigeon, and apple and walnut tart with caramel sauce. Set menus 130–200F.

DOMME   24250 (12KM S)

🏠 |●| NOUVEL HÔTEL*

rue Maleville and Grande-Rue (opposite pl. de la Halle).
☎ 05.53.28.38.67 ➡ 05.53.28.27.13
Closed Mon or Tues, Jan–Feb.

A pretty stone house ideally situated in the centre of the old fortified town. Good prices for the area. Pleasant rooms, 230F for a double with shower/wc or 330F with bath. The restaurant, with set menus 70–240F, offers regional cuisine. Specialities include snails in flaky pastry, *confit* or breast of duck.

MARQUAY   24620 (12KM NW)

🏃 |●| HÔTEL DES BORIES-RESTAURANT L'ESTÉREL**

Le bourg; north of Sarlat take the D47 for Les Eyzies then the D6 signposted for Marquay.
☎ 05.53.29.67.02 ➡ 05.53.29.64.15
Closed Tues lunchtimer and 1 Nov–31 March.
Swimming pool. Disabled access. Garden. TV. Car park.

A delightful hotel in a very good location in a nice village off the beaten track. It has a big garden, a swimming pool and a superb view. Bright clean rooms 180–300F. Thirty-two of them have a corner sitting room, a big fireplace and a view, and some have separate rooms for children. Breakfast served on the two terraces. Friendly welcome. The restaurant next door, now part of this establishment, has a good reputation. They serve dishes such as *aiguillette* of duck with ceps and *foie gras*, scallops and prawns with ceps, and pan-fried *foie gras* with roast pears. Menus 85–195F. 10% discount on the room rate April–June and Oct excluding long weekends and school holidays.

MEYRALS   24220 (12KM NE)

🏃 🏠 HÔTEL DE LA FERME LAMY***

How to get there: take the D47 in the direction of Les Eyzies/Périgueux, then turn left at Benive signposted to Meyrals.
☎ 05.53.29.62.46 ➡ 05.53.59.61.41
✉ fermelamy@aol.com
Swimming pool. Disabled access. TV. Car park.

Charming hotel in an old farmhouse in the depths of the country. Parts of the building date from the 17th century. It's the height of

luxury; ravishing doubles, some with air-conditoning, cost 420–720F with shower/wc or with 550–890F bath. In good weather you can eat breakfast – walnut bread, *brioche* and home-made jam – outside in the garden under the lime trees. A superb swimming pool overlooks the fields and hills. Simple, genuine welcome. 10% discount 16 Sept–14 June.

PAULIN   24590 (24KM NE)

🏃 |●| LA MEYNARDIE

How to get there: from Sarlat, go in the direction of Salignac-Eyvignes, then towards Archignac.
☎ 05.53.28.85.98 ➡ 05.53.28.82.79
Closed Wed, and Dec to mid-Feb. **Car park**.

An old farmhouse deep in the country. The dining room has been carefully restored and has a certain cachet with its paved floor and massive fireplace dating from 1603. Courteous welcome. The atmosphere's a little on the chic side. The 105F weekday lunch menu, and others from 160–250F, are all based on traditional dishes, but include creative variations like *carpaccio* of duck breast and pan-fried duck livers scented with truffles. Good desserts include an iced *soufflé* with walnuts. Sit out on the terrace in summer, or stroll through the chestnut tree forest after your meal. Best to book. Free coffee.

LAVAL-DE-JAYAC   24590 (25KM NE)

🏃 🏠 |●| HÔTEL-RESTAURANT COULIER**

Le bourg; take the D60.
☎ 05.53.28.86.46 ➡ 05.53.28.26.33
✉ hotel.coulier@wanadoo.fr
Closed Sat out of season, and mid Dec to Feb.
Swimming pool. Disabled access. TV. Car park.

You'll find this hamlet in an almost deserted part of darkest Périgord. The pretty converted farm buildings make a U-shape around a courtyard, on a hillock set well away from the road. The fairly small rooms, scattered around the building, go for 210–270F with shower/wc or bath. Friendly welcome. The restaurant serves regional dishes like warm semi-cooked *foie gras*, confit, veal sweetbreads, duck stew with blackcurrants, and breast of duck with violet mustard. Menus 80–240F, and a children's menu at 40F. If you don't want to spend all day by the pool, there are several short trails in the surrounding area. The owners know the area very well so don't hesitate to ask them for advice. 10% discount on the room rate Sept–June.

SAUTERNES 33210

⚹ |●| AUBERGE LES VIGNES

pl. de l'Église.
☎ and ➥ 05.56.76.60.06
Closed Mon and Feb. **Disabled access**.

A gorgeous country inn with log fires and tables laid with checked cloths. Friendly welcome from the American owner, and a warm, homely atmosphere. The authentic local cuisine changes with the seasons – try steak, lamb or duck breast grilled over vine shoots, or smoked ham, or pick a speciality such as rabbit in Sauternes or *foie gras* with apples. The puff pastry fruit tart comes straight from the oven to your plate and the ceps for the mushroom omelette will have been picked that morning. Menus 65–165F. Superb selection of wines in the cellar – many of them are very affordable. Free coffee.

|●| RESTAURANT LE SAPRIEN

11 rue Principale; it's opposite the tourist office.
☎ 05.56.76.60.87
Closed Sun evening, Mon, Wed evening out of season, and Feb and Nov school holidays.

A little house with thick stone walls on the outskirts of the village. It's ever so slightly chic and the elegant interior is a successful blend of old and new. It has a delightful reading room and also a huge terrace that opens out onto the vineyard. They grill food over vine shoots and offer Sauternes by the glass. Primarily, they offer dishes that reflect the changing seasons and what the market has to offer: warm salad of *foie gras*, lamprey in Sauternes or roasted veal sweetbreads in a Sauternes and curry sauce. Various menus, 139–259F, list *foie gras terrine* with Sauternes jelly, lamprey in Sauternes, grilled duck breast or pan-fried *foie gras*.

SAUVETERRE-DE-BÉARN 64390

⚐ |●| L'HOSTELLERIE DU CHÂTEAU*

Centre.
☎ 05.59.38.52.10 ➥ 05.59.38.96.49
Closed 10 Jan–15 Feb. **TV. Garden. Car park**.

A superb house in peaceful surroundings that dates almost as far back as the Revolution, with a magnificent view of the Pyrenees and a large terrace that looks down the valley. Lunch is served in the shade of an ancient copper beech hedge. The restaurant offers menus from 95–150F. Delicious Béarnaise specialities include braised trout in Jurançon, squid *à la basquaise* (tomatoes, peppers and rice), and

oven-baked black pudding and sausage. Good prices, considering the quality. The rooms, some of them more than 20m square, are furnished with antiques. Ask for one with a view of the garden. Doubles 160F with basin, 200–230F with shower and 230F with bath.

CASTAGNÈDE 64270 (10KM NW)

⚐ |●| LA BELLE AUBERGE

It's in the centre of the village.
☎ 05.59.38.15.28 ➥ 05.59.65.03.57
Closed Sun evenings and Dec to end Jan.
Swimming pool. Disabled access.TV.

A good old country inn in a pretty village. Prices for the twelve rooms are very reasonable at 200–250F. There are lots of flowers and a swimming pool and you can sunbathe in the garden. It's popular with travelling businesspeople and pensioners. The restaurant is busy all week. They offer menus from 65–130F, listing dishes such as *pipérade basquaise*, pot-roast pigeon, veal sweetbreads with ceps, and chocolate *fondant*.

SOULAC-SUR-MER 33780

⚹ ⚐ HÔTEL MICHELET**

1 rue Baguenard (Centre); it's on the sea port.
☎ 05.56.09.82.18 ➥ 05.56.73.65.25
Closed Mon and Jan. **Disabled access. TV. Garden**.

A typical seaside villa. The staff are beyond criticism – their thoughtful gestures include giving out little gifts to the kids. The rooms have been redecorated and are pleasant and comfortable; eight have a balcony and three lead out into a sandy garden. Doubles with bath 220–330F, or 260–400F in July and August. It's 50m from the sea and 250m from the town centre. 10% discount for a two-night stay, Oct–May.

SOUSTONS 40140

|●| LA FERME DE BATHURT

route de l'Étang Blanc.
☎ 05.58.41.53.28
Closed Tues evening and Wed out of season, and Nov.
Swimming pool. Garden. TV.

A gorgeous, half-timbered 16th-century house surrounded by oak trees that are rare in the Landes. You can eat on the terrace. Succulent, tasty dishes such as panfried shrimps, grilled squid and lamprey stew. The asparagus or cep omlettes are easily big enough to satisfy. Menus 78–180F.

TARDETS-SORHOLUS   64470

⚐ |●| HÔTEL-RESTAURANT DU PONT D'ABENSE*

Abense-de-Haut; it's 500m outside the town on the banks of the Saison.
☎ 05.59.28.54.60 ➮ 05.59.28.75.91
📧 ÜHALTIA@wanadoo.fr
Closed Wed afternoon and Thurs out of season, and Dec–Jan. **Car park**.

This riverside hotel is a lovely place to stay, with nice quiet rooms. Doubles with shower from 220F or 240F with bath. There's a friendly bar where you can drink the local light ale. The restaurant has a good reputation and the chef, who is also the owner, loves preparing simple dishes using the freshest ingredients. Try warm cep *terrine*, pig's trotter and potato pie, pan-fried hake, or *aiguillettes* of duck with wine. Superb desserts. Menus 98F or *menu-cartes*. You can eat on the terrace.They prefer you stay on a half-board basis in the summer.

TONNEINS   47400

🍴 ⚐ |●| CÔTÉ GARONNE

36 cours de l'Yser.
☎ 05.53.84.34.34 ➮ 05.53.84.31.31
Closed Sun evening, Mon, the first fortnight in Jan, the second fortnight in Aug and the first fortnight in Nov. **Disabled access**. **TV**. **Car park**.

The street doesn't look particularly appealing – neither does the town for that matter – so this beautiful building really stands out. It's like entering a different world when you step inside this tastefully decorated hotel. Jean-Luc Rabanel's combinations of local produce and spices are unexpected but his meticulous preparation and presentation are a triumph. Highlights include duck *foie gras* in a *terrine*, roast or *confit*, lobster with baby vegetables, Tonneins ham in parsley *jus*, and remarkable desserts like the spiked *millefeuille* and a tart with melting almond filling. Weekday lunch menu 165F, others 195–420F. Five luxurious rooms from 850F for a double with wc. 10% discount on the room rate.

VIEUX-BOUCAU-LES-BAINS   40480

⚐ |●| HÔTEL-RESTAURANT DE LA CÔTE D'ARGENT**

4 Grand-Rue; it's in the old village.
☎ 05.58.48.13.17 ➮ 05.58.48.01.15
Restaurant closed Mon from Oct–June.

TV. **Car park**.
Forty well-kept, comfortable rooms, a few of which have a balcony. Doubles 270–330F with shower/wc or bath. Very simple, traditional food in the restaurant, with no surprises. Go for the *confit* of duck, *salmis de palombes* (wood-pigeon in red wine sauce), hake, *blanquette* of scallops, pan-fried prawns with garlic, or sole with ceps. Set menus 95–160F and a children's menu 55F.

VILLANDRAUT   33730

🍴 ⚐ |●| HÔTEL-RESTAURANT DE GOTH**

pl. Principale (Centre).
☎ and ➮ 05.56.25.31.25 ➮ 05.56.25.30.59
📧 📧 evelyne.abadie@online.fr
Closed Sun evening, Mon out of season, and mid-Nov to mid-Jan. **Car park**.

A pretty village inn with stone walls. The rooms are clean and well cared for. Doubles 240F with shower/wc and 260F with bath. Decent traditional local dishes include chicken *confit*, *assiette landaise*, whole breast of duck with peaches, duck *foie gras* with apples, and lamb medallions *persillé*. Set menus 68–149F. In fine weather, sit on the terrace on the square. Free coffee.

VILLEFRANCHE-DU-PÉRIGORD   24550

🍴 ⚐ |●| HÔTEL-RESTAURANT LA PETITE AUBERGE**

How to get there: it's 800m before you reach the village and well signposted.
☎ 05.53.29.91.01 ➮ 05.53.28.88.10
Closed Fri evening, Sat lunch and Sun evening out of season, a fortnight in Nov and a fortnight in Feb. **Garden**. **TV**. **Car park**.

A large house, typical of the region, in the depths of the countryside. It's got an enormous garden and very inviting sun-loungers. The rooms are tastefully decorated. Doubles with shower/wc 240F, or 260F with bath. In the restaurant, there's a weekday menu for 65F and others up to 145F, listing dishes based on regional and seasonal produce. A haven of peace and serenity, with a terrace for the summer. Free apéritif.

VILLENEUVE-SUR-LOT   47300

🍴 ⚐ HÔTEL LA RÉSIDENCE**

17 av. Lazare-Carnot (Centre); it's near the old station.

☎ 05.53.40.17.03 ➡ 05.53.01.57.34
Closed 27 Dec–7 Jan. **TV**. **Garden**. **Car park**.

A pretty little hotel with a pink façade, green shutters and lots of character, in a very quiet neighbourhood near the old station. As soon as you set foot inside, you can see the garden at the end of the corridor. Doubles 135F with washing facilities, 210F with shower/wc and 250F with bath. Ideal if you like things simple and if you're looking for peace and quiet. 10% discount on the room rate for a two-night stay Sept–June.

|●| CHEZ CÂLINE

2 rue Notre-Dame (Centre).
☎ 05.53.70.42.08
Closed Tues.

In a pleasant, cheery place overlooking the Lot river, they serve honest local dishes such as breast of duck stuffed with *foie gras*, fillet of salmon with sorrel, eggs *vignerons* (fried in walnut oil, with white wine, shallot and garlic sauce) and cherry soup with mint. Set menus 75F and 95F, or 120F *à la carte*. Câline is the cocker spaniel.

|●| RESTAURANT AUX BERGES DU LOT

3 rue de l'Hôtel-de-Ville; next door to the Hôtel de Ville.
☎ 05.53.70.84.81 ➡ 05.53.70.43.15
Closed Sun evening, Mon, and a fortnight in Nov.

This nice restaurant, with a shady terrace and a view of the Lot, has become something of an institution in a town that's rather short of good places to eat. The chef sticks to conventional dishes with a serving of imagination: *foie gras* with dried fruit, roast zander with pistachio sausage, duck breast on the bone with red fruit nectar and *foie gras* chips. Set weekday lunch menu 85F, or others 135–210F.

PUJOLS   47300 (5KM S)

⚶ HÔTEL DES CHÊNES***

Lieu-dit Bel-Air.
☎ 05.53.49.04.55 ➡ 05.53.49.22.74
Swimming pool. **TV**. **Car park**.

Keep your eyes open for the restaurant *La Toque Blance* and you'll see the hotel next door. It stands on its own so it's very quiet. Lovely, well equipped rooms looking onto the medieval village, and they're all decorated differently. Doubles from 300F. It's cool down in the pool. Very nice welcome from the owner.

LE TEMPLE-SUR-LOT   47110 (17KM W)

⚓ |●| LES RIVES DU PLANTÏE***

It's on the D13 between Castelmoron and Le Temple-sur-Lot.
☎ 05.53.79.32.06 ➡ 05.53.79.32.05
Swimming pool. **Disabled access**. **TV**.

This was a crumbling wreck of a house before a brave young couple took it on and converted the house and some of the out-buildings into a hotel and restaurant. The grounds are planted with ancient trees and they slope down towards the river. There's space for a swimming pool, tennis courts and games for children. The rooms – 320–390F depending on the size – are spacious and have good facilities but rather ordinary furniture. The view over the park is splendid, however. The cooking has a Mediterranean accent and there are lots of sea fish alongside the duck and typical Aquitaine meat dishes. Weekday *formule* 85F or other menus 130–180F.

MONCLAR   47380 (18KM E)

|●| LE RELAIS

How to get there: take the D911 to Sainte Livrade, follow the D667 for 5km, then turn onto the D113.
☎ 05.53.49.44.74
Closed Sun evening and Mon.

Crowds of locals in here for Sunday lunch and public holidays. Simple dishes and generous portions. The rustic dining room has a beautiful terrace overlooking the valley – lunch could last a while. The cooking has a strong regional biais, with a few fish dishes such as *piccata* of salmon and prawns. Menus around 140F and the service is attentive.

Auvergne

AMBERT   63600

☎ |●| HÔTEL-RESTAURANT LES COPAINS**

42 bd. Henri-IV; it's opposite the town hall.
☎ 04.73.82.01.02 ➡ 04.73.82.67.34
e hotel.rest.les.copains@wanadoo.fr
Closed Sat and Sun, and 15 Sept–15 Oct.

Service noon–1.30pm and 7.30–8.30pm. The dining room is fresh, flowery and air-conditioned and boasts an unusual pianola from 1935. The traditional cuisine, based largely on local produce, is simple, but Thierry Chelle, the fourth generation of his family to be in charge of the kitchen, picked up some tricks from the time he spent in the Robuchon kitchens. Thus the menu has a touch of class:stuffed aubergines with *fourme d'Ambert* (a local cheese), guinea fowl breast with nettle sauce and salmon fillet with creamed mushrooms. Set menus 70–230F. Completely refurbished bedrooms 280F with shower/wc or bath.

⅍ ☎ |●| HÔTEL-RESTAURANT LA CHAUMIÈRE**

41 av. Foch; from the town centre go towards Puy-en-Velay.
☎ 04.73.82.14.94 ➡ 04.73.82.33.52
Closed Sun, Sat Oct–May, and 26 Dec–22 Jan. **TV.**
Disabled access. Garden. Car park.

Service noon–2pm and 7–9pm. A reminder that you can eat well at reasonable prices. Nothing fancy, just good plain cooking and substantial set menus, 95–220F. The restaurant has been enlarged and there's a south-facing terrace overlooking the garden. The dining room is in classical style, with a fire-

place where they do grills over the coals, and the cooking similarly sticks to old faithfuls: *croustillant* of frogs' legs with fennel, snails in *beurre marin*, *coq au vin*, mutton tripe, and casseroled pigeon. The bedrooms are clean, modern and fresh; doubles 310F. Free apéritif.

ARCONSAT   63250

⅍ ☎ |●| L'AUBERGE DE MONTONCEL**

Les Cros d'Arconsat; take the N89 then the D86.
☎ 04.73.94.20.96 ➡ 04.73.94.28.33
e moncatel@aol.com
Closed Mon Oct–May and Jan. **TV. Disabled access.**
Car park.

Service noon–2.30pm and 7.30–9pm. You'll find this old building, housing an old-style restaurant and a simple hotel, in the depths of the forest above Chabreloche. Very substantial 65F *menu du jour* – perfect raw ham, lamb stew, a fine platter of matured cheese and fresh fruit. Other menus, up to 135F, list dishes like frogs' legs, grilled crayfish, sirloin steak with local *bleu d'Auvergne* cheese or fillet of duck with brandy and ceps. The hotel is quiet and clean, occupying a modern annexe, with doubles from 200F with shower/wc or bath. Some rooms have balconies overlooking the pleasant garden. 10% discount on the room rate Sept–June.

ARDES-SUR-COUZE   63420

☎ |●| L'AUBERGE DE LA BARAQUE D'AUBIAT**

How to get there: take the D23 from Ardes in the direction of Anzat and drive for 11km.

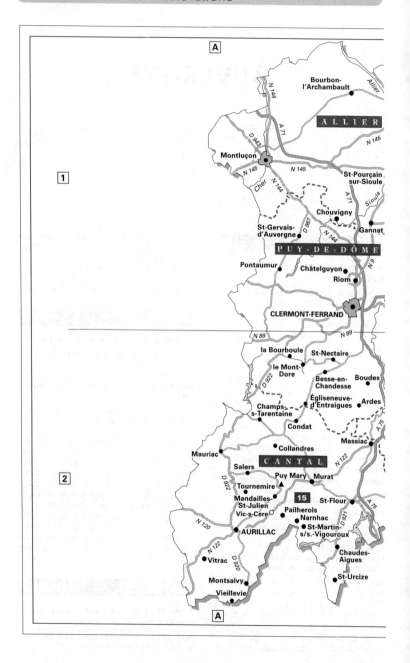

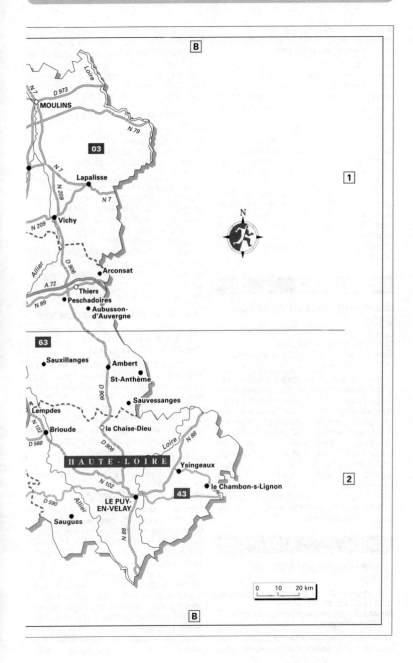

☎ 04.73.71.74.33 ➡ 04.73.71.74.99
Closed Tues evening and Wed except school holidays, and Jan. **Disabled access. Car park.**

Service noon–1.15pm and 7.30–8.30pm. Sheer heaven for hikers and people who love peace and quiet – it's an old farm, now completely refurbished, on the Cézalier plateau south of Puy-de-Dôme. The owners, who have made the most of the restaurant's rustic style, offer generous portions of simple traditional dishes: good house *terrines*, stuffed cabbage, guinea fowl with chanterelle mushrooms and home-made fruit tarts. Menus 75–100F. Comfortable rooms are cosy and practical – some have a mezzanine, ideal if you are travelling with children. Doubles 200F with shower, 210–260F with shower/wc or bath. Or you can sleep in a *gîte* for 50F a night. Good-sized breakfasts including a selection of home-made jams, 35F. You'll receive a very friendly welcome and good advice on day trips.

AUBUSSON-D'AUVERGNE　63120

🎭 🏠 |●| HÔTEL-RESTAURANT AU BON COIN

Centre.
☎ 04.73.53.55.78 ➡ 04.73.53.56.29
Closed Sun evening and Mon out of season, and 22 Dec–22 Jan. **Car park.**

A little inn decorated in pleasant country style. It can get a bit noisy when the big dining room is opened up to accommodate coach parties. The proprietor/chef uses quality ingredients in his cooking and serves generous portions; good house *terrines*, poached trout with crayfish sauce, *entre-deux* of veal with cream sauce, fillets of zander on a bed of cabbage, and delicious pear in flaky pastry with egg custard – and during the crayfish season they have lots of special dishes. Menus 95–350F or 200F *à la carte*. There are a few rooms; 140F with basin, 230F with shower/wc. 10% discount on the room rate.

AURILLAC　15000

🎭 🏠 |●| HÔTEL-RESTAURANT DU PALAIS**

4–6 rue Beauclair (Centre); behind the Palais de Justice.
☎ 04.71.48.24.86 ➡ 04.71.64.97.92
Closed Sun, public holidays and the last fortnight in July. **TV. Pay car park.**

This classic hotel has a striking façade and is quiet with nice rooms, particularly the ones

giving onto the Provençal-style patio. Doubles 260–300F with shower/wc or bath. The restaurant offers a representative taste of Auvergne; stuffed pig's trotter salad, veal sweetbreads with ceps, and calf's head. Menus 75–120F. The owner is welcoming. 10% discount on the room rate.

🎭 🏠 |●| HÔTEL-RESTAURANT LA THOMASSE***

28 rue du Docteur-Mallet.
☎ 04.71.48.26.47 ➡ 04.71.48.83.66
Closed Sun and 20 Dec–5 Jan. **TV. Swimming pool. Car park.**

In a residential area 1km from the centre, this charming hotel overlooks a large park. Pretty rooms in rustic style with proper bathrooms. Doubles 350–420F. Regional dishes and gastronomic cuisine served in the restaurant, which attracts large parties on some evenings. Menus 145–250F. More often than not, the owner will serve you a free glass of champagne as you sit down to eat. He's welcoming and voluble, and the club bar gets lively in the evenings. 10% discount on the room rate.

🎭 🏠 GRAND HÔTEL DE BORDEAUX***

2 av. de la République; it's opposite the public gardens.
☎ 04.71.48.01.84 ➡ 04.71.48.49.93
Closed 20 Dec–7 Jan. **TV. Car park.**

A charming hotel with lots of character, built in 1812 and located in the centre of town. You'll be welcomed with great courtesy and in a very professional manner. Bedrooms are exceptionally comfortable, 420–520F with shower/wc or bath – some have air-conditioning. Stylish bar and lounges and a good breakfast. 10% discount on the room rate, except in Aug.

|●| LE TERROIR

rue du Buis; pl. des Docks; it's near the cheese market.
☎ 04.71.64.31.26
Closed Sun, Mon and public holidays.

Service noon–2.30pm and 7–10pm. A delightful restaurant, specialising in Cantal dishes, in the old part of town known as Saint-Géraud. The area is on the up and the street features a string of cheese shops. The restaurant's decorated in conventional country style and has a good atmosphere and a large choice *à la carte* – *pavé du Cantal* (breaded Cantal cheese with local ham), salad of *cabecou* (goat's cheese) and honey, *pounti* (a mixture of bacon and Swiss chard), a slab of Salers beef with truffles, *bouriol* (a local pancake), stuffed cabbage and a cheese platter. Menus 59–140F. Wine by the glass 10–40F.

|●| LE BOUCHON FROMAGER

rue du Buis; pl. des Docks.
☎ 04.71.48.07.80
Closed Sun, Mon and public holidays.

A cheese and wine bar that's perfect if you're in a hurry or simply want a snack. You get a plate of cheese with a glass of wine bought direct from the vineyards – Auvergne wines 15F. Also try their toasted cheese (in about 24 different varieties) or the platter of *charcuterie* and cheese. They also do a stew of the week or *potée auvergnate* to order. Menu 69F. There's a nice terrace where in good weather you can enjoy an apéritif or take a meal.

衤 |●| L'ARSÈNE

24 rue Arsène-Vermenouze (Centre).
☎ 04.71.48.48.97
Closed lunchtimes, Sun evening, Mon, and a fortnight July/Aug.

Service 7–10.30pm. A warm and cosy dining room, with exposed stonework and modern paintings that go well together. It is very popular with local youngsters, attracted by the cheap hearty food. The restaurant specialises in *fondue*, top rump of beef, *tartiflette*, and either pork fillet or breast of duck, which you cook yourself on a hot stone. If you're on your own, opt for the wonderful onion soup – the genuine article – or the traditional grills, big mixed salads or savoury tarts. Set menus 70F, except Saturday evenings and public holidays, and 120F. Reasonably priced wine. Free coffee.

衤 |●| LA REINE MARGOT

19 rue Guy-de-Veyre (Centre).
☎ 04.71.48.26.46
Closed Mon, Mon evening in season, one week at the end of June and the last fortnight in Feb.

Varnished wood panelling with little paintings creates a traditional setting for this restaurant. Professional welcome. Serious regional cooking served generously. Extensive *à la carte* choice: calf's head, pan-fried turbot, *punti* and good meat dishes. Weekday lunch menu 78F and others up to 220F, or around 200F *à la carte*. Good selection of wines, such as Gaillac, Buzet and Saint-Pourçain for around 70F, and Bordeaux of the month. Free coffee.

SANSAC DE MARMIESSE   15130 (8KM W)

|●| LA BELLE ÉPOQUE

Lesfargues; take the N122 – it's well sign-posted.
☎ 04.71.62.87.87

Closed Sun evening and Mon except July–Aug, and 30 Dec–March.

The restaurant is a restored farmhouse deep in the country near the tiny villages of Haut-Cros and Labattude. The large dining room is decorated in Belle Époque style – a welcome change from the rustic look. Its reputation has grown by word of mouth, so it's almost always full, even on a weekday evening out of season. It has a lively atmosphere, very friendly staff and great local cooking. Prices are very reasonable; menus 98–198F or 225F *à la carte*. They use fresh produce and pick soft fruit and vegetables from the garden. *À la carte*, there are classic dishes; *foie gras* with caramelised apples, mutton tripe and duck breast with orange. The chef is a wild mushroom enthusiast and uses different varieties in his cooking: pig's trotters or veal sweetbreads with morels or a simple omelette with ceps. The terrace is very pleasant in fine weather.

POLMINHAC   15800 (14KM E)

|●| LE BERGANTY

pl. de l'Église; take the N122.
☎ 04.71.47.47.47
Closed Sat and Sun, Sat in summer reservations only, and Christmas and New Year holidays.

The square is superb, with its church and houses with their roofs of *lauzes* (flat stones). And the dining room is absolutely wonderful too. Seating only twenty, it has an old polished sideboard, a massive table positioned in front of the fireplace, and large bouquets of flowers from the garden. The chef prefers to prepare dishes to order and uses only fresh seasonal produce, enhanced with herbs from his vegetable plot; trout with bacon, *truffade* (a potato cake with Cantal cheese) and ham are served at any time; order in advance for the stuffed cabbage, *pounti* (a mixture of bacon and Swiss chard), or *potée auvergnate*, the hearty local soup. Other specialities include rabbit with prunes and carrots, and shoulder of local beef. Menus 70–130F. The young owner has a flair for making people feel welcome.

BESSE-EN-CHANDESSE   63610

衤 🛏 |●| HÔTEL-RESTAURANT LE CLOS**

La Villetour.
☎ 04.73.79.52.77 ➡ 04.73.79.56.67
Restaurant closed Mon–Thurs lunchtimes except school holidays. **TV**. **Swimming pool**. **Car park**.

This modern establishment, just out of the town centre, offers a wide range of facilities – indoor pool, well-equipped gym, Turkish bath and games room. Bedrooms are pleasant and very clean. Doubles from 270–330F with shower/wc or bath and a few family rooms. The owners can provide suggestions for excursions and walks. The food is decent and traditional. Set menus 89–160F. Free apéritif.

🛏 |●| HOSTELLERIE DU BEFFRROY**

26 rue de l'Abbé-Blot.
☎ 04.73.79.50.08 ➡ 04.73.79.57.67
Closed Sun evening and Mon except during school holidays, one week March–April, three weeks in May and Oct to mid-Dec. **TV**. **Car park**.

A 15th-century building, owned and run by Thierry Legros, who has a fine reputation as a chef and a personal way of enlivening local traditional dishes, such as wild salmon, Cantal turnover or *pounti* (a mixture of bacon and Swiss chard). Weekday menu 110F or 130–295F. Rooms are decent but facilities are not all good. Doubles 300F with shower or bath.

SUPER-BESSE   63610 (7KM W)

|●| RESTAURANT LA BERGERIE

Route de Vassivières (West); take the D149.
☎ 04.73.79.61.06
Closed weekdays out of season, and 15 Sept–15 Dec.

It would be a crime to come here without trying the *truffade* (potato cake with Cantal cheese). The young owner serves a hearty portion straight from the frying pan with local ham, 70F. It's cooked to order, and probably the best you'll get in the region; extremely satisfying and well worth the thirty-minute wait. Lots of other local delicacies at 95–155F: soufflé of smoked trout, perch with *aïoli*, snail stew and fantastic cabbage stuffed with trout. You'll really feel at home in this country inn with its delightful decor and atmosphere. Popular in winter and in summer, when you can eat on the terrace overlooking the lake.

BOUDES   63340

🛏 |●| LE BOUDES LA VIGNE**

pl. de la Mairie.
☎ 04.73.96.55.66 ➡ 04.73.96.55.55
Closed Sun evening, Mon, 2–26 Jan, and a fortnight Aug to early Sept. **TV**.

Service noon–2pm and 7.30–10pm. This popular little hotel-restaurant, in a pleasantly renovated building, is in the centre of a small wine-growing village south of Puy-de-Dôme. The cooking is quite delightful: snail ravioli with garlic sauce, *blanquette* of chicken with honey, *croustillant* of scorpion fish with herb butter, and quail wrapped in vine leaves with rosemary. For dessert, it's hard to resist the peach soup with fresh mint. Weekday lunch menu 80F or 125–250F. You're right in the midst of the best vineyards of the Auvergne so the wine list is splendid. Wine is also served by the glass. The hotel was built only recently and is very quiet. Doubles 180F with shower/wc. Free apéritif. 10% discount on the room rate Sept–May.

🛏 |●| GRAND HÔTEL MONTESPAN-TAL-LEYRAND**

1–3 pl. des Thermes (Centre).
☎ 04.70.67.00.24 ➡ 04.70.67.12.00
✉ hotelmontespan@wanadoo.fr
Closed late Oct to early April. **TV**. **Disabled access**. **Car park**.

A superb hotel in a fine building that's full of old-fashioned charm. It's an oasis of peace and quiet – there are reading rooms and card rooms with lots of velvet and tapestries, a bright flower-filled dining room, and a pool among the greenery of the garden. Bedrooms are tastefully and stylishly decorated – some of them are more like suites. Doubles 300F with shower and 400–600F with bath. Very reasonable, given the standard of accommodation. The restaurant sticks to old favourites – calf's head *gribiche*, fillet of *charolais*, rabbit in mustard sauce, and *coq au vin* (the wine in this case being Saint-Pourçain). The cooking is worth the trip. Menus 85–170F. Friendly staff and excellent service.

SAINT-BONNET-TRONÇAIS   03360 (23KM NW)

🛏 🛏 |●| LE TRONÇAIS**

Rond de Tronçais; take the N144, then the D978 in the direction of the forest of Tronçais as far as the Rond de Tronçais, and it's 3km south of Saint-Bonnet-Tronçais.
☎ 04.70.06.11.95 ➡ 04.70.06.16.15
Closed Sun evening, Mon out of season, and mid-Nov to mid-March. **TV**. **Car park**.

Service noon–1.30pm and 7.30–9pm. A peaceful, very comfortable lakeside hotel with lots of charm. The forest of Tronçais, one of the oldest and most beautiful in France, turns every shade of green in spring and every shade of yellow, red and brown in autumn. Spacious bedrooms, doubles 300–380F. The restaurant is strong on traditional local dishes: snails with walnuts, chicken *à la bourbonnaise*, *terrine* of eel with blackberries, pike with Saint-Pourçain, and veal cutlet with ceps. Menus 120–200F. The two dining rooms are very elegantly and tastefully decorated, and the staff are delightful. Pleasant view of the grounds and surrounding countryside. Free coffee.

TRONGET   03240 (23KM S)

♠ I●I HÔTEL DU COMMERCE**

D945; take the D1 towards Montet.
☎ 04.70.47.12.95 ➡ 04.70.47.32.53
TV. Car park.

A hotel that contrasts the new and the traditional. The building is practically brand new and has comfortable, modern, and well-equipped bedrooms, though they're a bit lacking in character. Doubles 260F. Lots of personality in the cooking of the chef, Monsieur Auberger: lamb *au bourbonnais* with thyme, frogs' legs, duck *confit* with ceps and *coq au vin*. Menus 80–150F.

BOURBOULE (LA)   63150

⅔ ♠ I●I HÔTEL-RESTAURANT LE PAVILLON**

av. d'Angleterre.
☎ 04.73.65.50.18 ➡ 04.73.81.00.93
Closed Jan, March, Nov and Dec. **TV.**

Pretty Art Deco façade. The young owners greet you kindly and there's a warm family atmosphere. The rooms are modern and clean, if a little functional. Doubles 230–260F with shower/wc or 250–280F with bath. Simple family cooking using regional ingredients. Menus 85–130F. 10% discount on the room rate, except August.

⅔ ♠ I●I HÔTEL LE CHARLET**

94 bd. Louis-Chousy.
☎ 04.73.81.33.00 ➡ 04.73.65.50.82
e hotel.lecharlet@wanadoo.fr
Closed mid-Oct to mid-Dec. **TV. Car park.**

Service noon–2pm and 7–9pm. An attractive family-run place in a quiet residential area – indeed, the whole town is quiet and residential. The decor in the 38 pleasant bedrooms is a bit bland but they come equipped with modern facilities. Doubles overlooking the street with shower/wc 250–290F, or with

bath and a mountain view 320–360F. There's a very nice pool with a wave machine, a Turkish bath and a gym. The cooking tends to be traditional and local, with dishes like *coq au vin*, stuffed trout and rabbit *terrine* with hazelnuts. Menus 99–169F. 10% discount on the room rate.

BRIOUDE   43100

⅔ ♠ I●I HÔTEL DE LA POSTE ET CHAMPANNE*

1 bd. du Docteur-Devins (West).
☎ 04.71.50.14.62 ➡ 04.71.50.10.55
Closed Sun evening Oct–June, and Feb. **TV. Car park.**

Service noon–2pm and 7.30–9pm. An old country hotel that's been updated to suit modern tastes. There's still a bar on the ground floor. The bedrooms facing the street are rather noisy, while those in the annexe at the back are very quiet. Doubles 260F with shower/wc, or bath, and balcony, and 160F with shower but wc on the landing. The restaurant on the first floor has long had a reputation for good food and does a number of set menus 85–220F and also *à la carte*. Traditional, unpretentious, good food. The star attraction is the owner – a jolly, chubby guy with a ruddy face and a sparkle in his eye. With his team of waitresses, he serves the food himself in the way that innkeepers used to. If you want bigger helpings, just ask. This restaurant still has a soul and doesn't take itself too seriously. Free coffee.

⅔ ♠ I●I HÔTEL LE BAUDIÈRE-RESTAURANT LE VIEUX FOUR**

Saint-Bauzire; it's 8km west of Brioude before Saint-Bauzire, at the D588 and D17 junction.
☎ 04.71.76.81.70 ➡ 04.71.76.80.66
Closed Mon and 20 Dec–20 Jan. **Swimming pool. TV. Disabled access. Car park.**

A pleasant modern hotel with sauna, indoor and outdoor swimming pools, and very comfy bedrooms. Doubles with bath, TV and satellite channels 000F. Right next door is the restaurant, which has a handsome stone oven in the main dining room. The grilled meat is as good as the *escalope* of veal sweetbreads with mushrooms, the seafood *choucroute*, the lentils with morels, the *crépinette* of pig's trotters and the *crème brûlée*. Set menus 90–250F. It's quite well known, and some of the better-off customers arrive by helicopter on the landing strip nearby. Free apéritif.

⅍ 🏠 |●| LA SAPINIÈRE

av. Paul-Chambriard (South); take the N102 through Brioude.
☎ 04.71.50.87.30 📠 04.71.50.10.55
📧 hotel.la.sapiniere@wanadoo.fr
Hotel closed Feb. **Restaurant closed** lunchtimes, Sun evening and Mon. **TV. Disabled access. Car park.**

An appealing new building of wood, brick and glass, between two old farm buildings. The spacious rooms look out over the grounds and are decorated in different styles. They are named rather than numbered – the "Vulcania" has a bedhead carved from lava. Doubles with bath 450F. Friendly welcome. The restaurant serves dishes with interesting flavour combinations, such as bitter dandelion with ham and honey-roast radish, Salers beef with herbs *au gratin*, and vegetable *Pachade*. Menus 92–140F. Free coffee.

VERGONGHEON   43360 (8KM N)

|●| LA PETITE ÉCOLE

Rilhac.
☎ 04.71.76.00.44
📧 petite.ecole@wanadoo.fr
Closed Sun evening, Mon, Tues evening from Oct to Easter, and the last week in June. **Car park**.

The decor takes you straight back to school – blackboards, maps of France, school photos and desks. Françoise and Éric run the place and produce delicious dishes; you choose from an excercise book full of menus from 92–140F with a children's menu at 60F. Good salads, roast pork with apricot sauce, and a fabulous dessert trolley. Best to book.

LAVAUDIEU   43100 (9KM SE)

|●| AUBERGE DE L'ABBAYE

Centre.
☎ 04.71.76.44.44
Closed Sun evening and Mon, Mon only 15 July–31 Aug. **Car park**.

Service noon–1.30pm and 7.30–9pm. A charming village inn in the little street opposite the church. It has a rustic interior, complete with log fires in winter, which has been very nicely renovated and decorated. The carefully prepared traditional dishes, based on local produce, include zander with thyme, *fricassée* of quail with morels or lamb with potatoes *gratinée*. Set menus 80F out of season or 100–180F.

VILLENEUVE-D'ALLIER   43380 (14KM S)

⅍ 🏠 |●| HOSTELLERIE SAINT-VERNY*

Route D585; from Brioude go towards the gorges of Allier and Lavoute-Chilhac.
☎ 04.71.74.73.77 📠 04.71.74.74.20
Closed All Saints' Day to Easter. **Swimming pool. TV. Car park.**

Located a few kilometres from the wonderful village of Lavoute-Chilhac, here's a genuine, simple country inn that's very well run. It's on the south bank of the Allier across from the romantic, ruined château of Saint-Ilpize. Bedrooms look onto the street (250F) or have a superb view of the valley. They're small and well laid out, and there are bunk beds for children. Doubles with shower/wc or bath, 200–250F. The food in the restaurant is perfectly done, with dishes based largely on local produce. Set menus for 100F or around 120F *à la carte*. The house speciality is the *plateau du vigneron* – grilled Cantal cheese, local ham and a salad with walnut oil. There's a bar on the ground floor and a quiet terrace at the back, facing a garden where you can enjoy your meals in summer. Free coffee or *digestif*.

BLESLE   43450 (24KM W)

⅍ 🏠 |●| HÔTEL-RESTAURANT LA BOUGNATE

pl. de Vallat; take the D588.
☎ 04.71.76.29.30 📠 04.71.76.29.39
Closed Tues and Wed except April–Sept, and Jan. **Car park**.

Gérard Klein has been a successful actor, producer and cattle farmer, and now he's an innkeeper. He and his wife, Françoise, started this establishment a couple of years ago. They began by renovating the building. The speciality in the restaurant is their own Salers beef and stuffed cabbage. Menus 90–150F. A few quiet, pretty rooms. Doubles with shower/wc or bath 350–400F. Free apéritif.

CHAVANIAC-LAFAYETTE   43230 (27KM SE)

⅍ 🏠 |●| HÔTEL-RESTAURANT LAFAYETTE*

Centre; take the N102 after Saint-Georges-d'Aurac, turn left onto the D513 then continue ahead for 2km.
☎ 04.71.77.50.38 📠 04.71.77.54.90
Closed Tues Nov–March, and 24 Dec–end Feb. **Garage**.

This very nice family hotel is in the village

where General Lafayette, one of the heroes of the American War of Independence, was born. In the ground-floor bar a sprightly old woman pours drinks for the regulars, and the adjoining restaurant is simple and inviting. The bedrooms are unpretentious and very well maintained. Numbers 10 and 11 overlook the Lafayette château. Doubles 205F with shower/wc or bath. In the restaurant the chef's specialities are veal kidneys and veal sweetbreads with mushrooms. Prices are very reasonable – menus 58–130F and a children's menu at 45F. Very friendly staff. 10% discount on the room rate for two nights Sept–June.

CHAISE-DIEU (LA)   43160

⅍ ☎ |●| HÔTEL DE LA CASADEÏ**

pl. de l'Abbaye (Centre); it's near the steps to the abbey.
☎ 04.71.00.00.58 ➡ 04.71.00.017
Restaurant Closed Sun evening and Mon. **TV.**

Service noon–2.30pm and 7–9pm. You get to the hotel through a flower-filled terrace and an art gallery. The nicest rooms have a view of the abbey and are well furnished. Doubles 260–280F with shower/wc. Friendly staff. In the restaurant they serve *potée auvergnate* (a thick local soup), omelette of chanterelle mushrooms, mutton tripe, and *truffade* (potato cake with Cantal cheese). Set menus 95–140F. The photos are of artists who've stayed at the hotel during the town's festival of sacred music. There's a little terrace at the back. Free apéritif. 10% discount on the room rate May–June and Sept–Oct.

⅍ ☎ |●| HÔTEL-RESTAURANT DE L'ÉCHO ET DE L'ABBAYE**

pl. de l'Écho (Centre).
☎ 04.71.00.00.45 ➡ 04.71.00.00.22
Closed Wed lunchtime out of season, and 15 Nov–10 Feb. **TV. Car park.**

This delightful inn is fully booked during the festival, and all the big names have stayed here at festival time. The very handsome dining room with its antiques and Louis XIII decor is housed in the former monastery kitchens. Eleven bedrooms with doubles 295–380F. Number 7 has a wonderful view of the abbey. In the restaurant they dish up tasty, regional dishes; a timbale of wild mushrooms with cep coulis, rabbit thigh stuffed with hazelnuts on a bed of lentils and a trolley of fresh desserts. Menus 110–320F. 10% discount on the room rate.

CHOMELIX   43500 (15KM SE)

⅍ ☎ |●| AUBERGE DE L'ARZON**

How to get there: take the D906 then the D135.
☎ 04.71.03.62.35 ➡ 04.71.03.61.62
Closed Mon evening and Tues except July–Aug, and All Saints' Day to Easter. **TV. Car park.**

Service noon–1.45pm and 7.30–9.15pm. This is a good village inn and the restaurant is extremely popular. Best to book in summer, especially during the music festival in La Chaise. The bedrooms are impeccable and situated in a quiet modern annexe with shower/wc upstairs and bathroom downstairs; doubles 245–350F. The restaurant uses local produce in carefully prepared local dishes: *foie gras*, duck breasts with blackcurrants, and others that need long slow cooking. It also has excellent fish and a good selection of home-made desserts. Set menus 98F (not Sun) and up to 260F. Decent service. 10% discount on the room rate Sept–June.

PONTEMPEYRAT   43500 (25KM E)

⅍ ☎ |●| HÔTEL-RESTAURANT MISTOU***

How to get there: take the D498.
☎ 04.77.50.62.46 ➡ 04.77.50.66.70
e moulin.de.mistou@wanadoo.fr
Restaurant closed lunchtimes, except weekends, public holidays, and 1 Nov to Easter. **TV. Car park. Disabled access.**

The surroundings, deep in the Ance valley, are as bucolic as you could wish for. The river runs past fir trees at the bottom of the garden. There used to be a watermill here, built around 1730; its old turbine still produces enough electricity to light the hotel. The rooms are enormous, quiet and perfectly decorated; those with a view of the garden are best. Doubles 499–670F with shower/wc or bath. Stylish dining room. Bernard Royx, one of the gurus of regional cuisine, mans the stove, churning out platters of *foie gras* done in four different ways, roast lamb with sea salt, marinated guinea fowl with spiced and roast strawberries with Szechuan pepper. Half board compulsory in high season, 445–590F. Menus 170–320F. Free coffee. 10% discount on the room rate Sept–June, excluding public holidays.

CHAMBON-SUR-LIGNON (LE)   43400

⅍ ☎ |●| HÔTEL-RESTAURANT LA PLAGE*

rue de la Grande-Fontaine (Centre).
☎ 04.71.59.70.56
Closed Oct to end April. **Car park**.

It's peace and quiet you get here rather than a beach. The staff greet you with big smiles and everything's been well thought through. Doubles from 145F to 280F. Although a bit kitschy, it's a very nice place with genuine people. Set menus, 80–120F, offer honest provincial dishes: *mousse* of chicken livers and port, frogs' legs in a saffron sauce, and trout with almonds. Two terraces give you a view of the river. 10% discount on the room rate May, June and Sept.

⅍ ≜ I●I HÔTEL LE BOIS VIALOTTE**

Le Bois Vialotte; from Chambon take the D151 going towards Le Mazet, then turn left onto the route de la Suchère and left again onto a smaller road (there will be a signpost).
☎ 04.71.59.74.03 ➡ 04.71.65.86.32
Closed Oct–May. **Car park**.

The hotel, surrounded by pine woods and meadows, has fifteen acres of beautiful grounds but feels more like a family guest house than a country-house hotel. The attentive but unobtrusive proprietress takes great pride in this new house. The decor of the simple bedrooms is a bit old-fashioned but they're comfortable and very clean. 290–350F for a double; ask for one with a view over the fields and the trees. The restaurant offers home cooking and simple traditional dishes. Menus 80–130F. It's worth going on a half-board basis, since the hotel is rather isolated, but it's not compulsory. Free apéritif.

TENCE   43190 (8.5KM N)

≜ I●I CAFÉ-RESTAURANT BROLLES

Mas-de-Tence.
☎ 04.71.65.42.91

An authentic country inn run by friendly people. The restaurant has been tastefully decorated and the stone floor makes the place feel nice and cool. Sit at the round table beside the fireplace and enjoy home-made *saucisson* and an omelette made from eggs laid by the owner's hens. Good sautéed baby potatoes, lentils and snails, and people come from miles around for the oven-cooked dishes and warm ewe's milk cheese. Set menus 67–180F. Simple but clean rooms with basin, 110F a night for two people; breakfast 20F. Best to book. Credit and debit cards not accepted.

SAINT-BONNET-LE-FROID   43290 (20KM NE)

≜ I●I AUBERGE DES CIMES

rue Principale.
☎ 04.71.59.93.72
Closed Mon–Wed lunchtimes, Tues only July and Aug, and mid-Nov to Easter. **Disabled access**.

One of the pinnacles of cuisine in the area, run by Régis Marcon, who is constantly scaling new gastronomic heights with his inventive, inspirational cuisine. His preparation is meticulous, and everything he buys is of the freshest quality. He is well acquainted with the traditional dishes of the Velay and the Vivarais. Subtle, delicate dishes full of unexpected flavours. Menus, 295–600F, reflect the quality of his art. There are rooms of the same calibre for 800–900F with bath.

CHAMPS-SUR-TARENTAINE   15270

⅍ ≜ I●I L'AUBERGE DU VIEUX CHÊNE**

34 route des Lacs.
☎ 04.71.78.71.64 ➡ 04.71.78.70.88
e danielle.moins@wanadoo.fr
Closed Lunchtimes except Sun, Sun evening and Mon out of season, and 15 Nov–15 March. **TV**. **Garden**. **Car park**.

Service noon–1.30pm and 7–8.30pm. A haven of peace and warmth in an old renovated farm in northern Cantal. Bedrooms have been nicely done up in bright cheerful colours and they all have bathrooms. Doubles 350–380F. There's a wonderful, enormous fireplace on the back wall of the restaurant, and though the dining room's on the large side it is laid out in such a way that it actually feels rather intimate. The menus, 140–190F, feature regional specialities alongside more classical dishes – try the *foie gras* with green peppercorns, veal sweetbreads with morels, entrecôte steak with Roquefort cheese or trout with local ham. Attentive and courteous service. Pleasant garden. 10% discount except July–Aug.

MARCHAL   15270 (5KM NE)

≜ I●I HÔTEL-RESTAURANT L'AUBERGE DE L'EAU VERTE

Centre; take the D679 then the D22.
☎ 04.71.78.71.48
Closed a fortnight in Feb and a fortnight at the end of Sept. **Car park**.

A traditional little inn on a small hill beside the church. Super-friendly welcome. *Menu du jour* 65F. The "taste of Auvergne" menus, 100–180F, which you have to order ahead, offer a delicious plate of cold meat, *truffade* (potato cake with Cantal cheese), salad, cheese and dessert. The 120F regional meal offers substantial portions of well-prepared dishes. There are a few bedrooms from 200F. Half board 180F per person. A good place to appreciate traditional Auvergne cuisine.

CHÂTELGUYON   63140

🎿 🏨 |●| HÔTEL-RESTAURANT CASTEL RÉGINA**

rue de Brocqueville.
☎ 04.73.86.00.15 ➡ 04.73.86.19.44
Closed Oct– April. **TV**. **Car park**.

Service 12.15pm and 7.15pm. A stylish spa hotel. The Belle Époque decor gives it a delightful old-fashioned charm, and it has a relaxed atmosphere. You'll receive a charming welcome with a personal touch. The guests seem to have come out of the same mould as the hotel – no one comes to Châtelguyon for the nightlife. Clean, well-kept bedrooms 175F with shower/wc, 190F with bath. The 75F *menu du jour* features more substantial fare than you would expect from a spa, while the one at 108F includes wine. Free apéritif. 10% discount for two consecutive nights.

🎿 🏨 |●| LES CHÊNES**

15 rue Guy-de-Maupassant; take the D985.
☎ 04.73.86.02.88 ➡ 04.73.86.46.60
✉ leschênes@wanadoo.fr
Closed 2 Jan–10 Feb. **TV**.

Service 12.30–2pm and 7.30–10pm. A good restaurant a bit out of the way in the old village of Châtelguyon. It's lovely in fine weather, when you can eat on the terrace. Refined classic cooking: veal sweetbreads with ceps in pastry, salmon with sorrel sauce or quail salad with *foie gras*. *Menu du jour* 65F and others at 135–165F. The rooms are quiet and pleasant and some have balconies. Doubles 180F with basin/wc, 225–252F with shower/wc. The owner is charming and full of life. 10% discount on the room rate for a two-night stay.

🎿 🏨 |●| LE CANTALOU*

17 rue du Lac-Saint-Hippolyte; on the D985 on the outskirts of Châtelguyon in the Saint-Hippolyte district.
☎ 04.73.86.04.67 ➡ 04.73.86.24.36
Closed Mon lunchtime, except for guests, and 11

Nov–15 March. **Car park**.

A friendly family guesthouse on the edge of town. Good value for money. Bedrooms are clean and well maintained but the decor is a bit old-fashioned. Some rooms have a view of the Monts d'Auvergne and Le Puy de Dôme. Doubles 200F with shower/wc, 200F with bath. The restaurant serves generous helpings of simple food. Set menus 65–130F. The chicken *à l'auvergnate* stewed in white wine is excellent. 10% discount on the room rate for a two-night stay March, April and Oct.

🎿 🏨 |●| HÔTEL BELLEVUE-RESTAURANT LE CÈDRE BLEU**

4 rue Punett.
☎ 04.73.86.07.62 ➡ 04.73.86.02.56
Closed Tues, Wed and Oct–May.

This hotel has been completely renovated and offers rooms with excellent facilities. The soundproofing is particularly effective. Smiling, warm welcome. Doubles with shower/wc 240–270F or 320F with bath. They serve local and regional dishes in the restaurant: Cantal truffles, salmon with lentils, lamb's tripe and soft fruit *au gratin*. Menu of the day 95F, regional menu 125F. Free apéritif. 10% discount on the room rate March–April and Oct–Nov.

|●| RESTAURANT LA POTÉE

34 av. Baraduc.
☎ 04.73.86.06.60
Closed Oct to end March.

The façade of this restaurant is beautifully timbered. The *patronne* is larger than life and scans the dining room from her vantage point behind the bar, to ensure her guests are being looked after. You sit at nice tables with a proper cloth to sample classic dishes: *andouillette* (a type of sausage), mutton tripe, *truffade* (a potato cake with Cantal cheese), pork knuckle and trout with bacon. Menu of the day 65F or 120F *à la carte*.

CHAUDES-AIGUES   15110

🏨 |●| HÔTEL LES BOUILLONS D'OR**

10 quai du Remontalou (Centre).
☎ 04.71.23.51.42
Closed Sun evening and Mon out of season, Jan–March. **TV**. **Car park**.

Service noon–2pm and 7–9.30pm. This is a conventional, well-kept hotel, set back from the main street. It's well managed and you'll get a courteous welcome. Comfortable rooms, 190–250F for a double. Classical cooking that's in keeping with the style of hotel. Menus, 68–140F, list dishes like *briochin* with Cantal cheese, *aligot saucisse* (mashed potatoes and Aligot cheese with sausage), local mutton tripe, *paupiettes* of chicken with cabbage, and *quenelles* of pike with a prawn sauce.

VENTUEJOLS   15110 (5KM N)

🍴 ≜ |●| AU RENDEZ-VOUS DES PÊCHEURS

Pont-de-Lanau; take the D921.
☎ 04.71.23.51.68

An unobtrusive little inn at the side of the road which has been modernised and freshened up. The owner's son is carrying on the long tradition of friendly and unpretentious service. He's a music fan and he's lined the walls with pictures and caricatures of musicians and famous local characters. There's a single menu at 67F (80F at Sun lunch), with good, reliable home cooking: rabbit stew, *potée*, mutton tripe, and home-made ice creams and sorbets. A few basic but clean rooms for 170F and half board at 180F – a bargain. Free coffee.

CLERMONT-FERRAND   63000

SEE MAP OVERLEAF

≜ HÔTEL RAVEL**

8 rue de Maringues. **MAP D2-7**
☎ 04.73.91.51.33 ➡ 04.73.92.28.48
TV. **Car park**.

This little family-run hotel is in a quiet neighbourhood tucked away between the station and the town centre. It has a captivating mosaic façade. The proprietress will give you a warm welcome. She runs the place virtually single-handed and creates a nice relaxed atmosphere – if you want more bread at breakfast, she'll nip across to the baker's. The decor in the bedrooms is simple and charming. Doubles 170–220F, which is good value.

🍴 ≜ HÔTEL DE BORDEAUX**

39 av. Franklin-Roosevelt. **MAP A3-3**
☎ 04.73.37.32.32 ➡ 04.73.31.40.56
TV. **Pay garage**.

This hotel is just outside the centre in an unprepossessing area, but it's quiet, and convenient for the main tourist attractions.

Doubles 180F with basin/wc, 250–290F with shower/wc. Staff are pleasant and unobtrusive. Free garage space at the weekends and July–Aug.

🍴 ≜ HÔTEL ALBERT-ÉLISABETH**

37 av. Albert-Élisabeth. **MAP D2-4**
☎ 04.73.92.47.41 ➡ 04.73.90.78.32
📧 jm.fragne@wanadoo.fr
TV. **Garden**. **Car park**.

Marked by a big red neon sign – so you won't miss it. Well-soundproofed rooms, some overlooking the courtyard, though on the whole they lack character. Doubles 270F with shower/wc and 300F with bath and TV. 10% discount for a two-night stay at weekends Sept–June.

≜ |●| HÔTEL DE LYON***

16 pl. de Jaude. **MAP B3-6**
☎ 04.73.93.32.55 ➡ 04.73.93.54.33
TV. **Garage**.

You can't get more central than pl. de Jaude, in the heart of the town. Comfortable, if conventional, rooms with good facilities, double glazing and telephones. Doubles with shower 370F or 390F with bath. Functional but well maintained. Self-service breakfast in the pub downstairs or brought to your room. Simple menus 60–130F and a *carte brasserie*. Parking fee included in the price of the rooms.

|●| L'OLIVEN

5 rue de la Boucherie. **MAP B2-17**
☎ 04.73.90.38.94
Closed Sat lunchtime, Sun and Mon. **TV**. **Garage**.

Pretty decor in orange hues. Run by a bright, friendly team. Weekday lunch menu 66F and *menus-cartes* 105F or 145F. Specialities include salad with sheep's milk cheese; prawns with lime, coriander and tomato croutons; warm smoked salmon with marinated red peppers and *aïoli*; sea bass with herbs and aubergine stew; coconut cake with ricotta and almond liqueur cream. This is a fresh look at Provençal and Mediterranean cooking and dishes are light and tasty.

|●| RESTAURANT AU BON PINARD-CHEZ MME GRIFFET

7 rue des Petits-Gras. **MAP B2-16**
☎ 04.73.36.40.95
Closed Mon and Aug.

This little bistro dates back to the turn of the century when it was called *Au Bon Pinard*; it was soon renamed *Chez Mme Griffet*.

Though it doesn't look much from the outside, it's definitely worth a visit. You can eat downstairs in the bar's small dining area where there is a never-ending stock of colourful apéritifs. The upstairs dining room is delightfully kitsch, and open late. Everything's made on the premises using only fresh produce – vegetables from the garden or the market: *coq au vin*, pig's trotters and *andouillette*. *Menu du jour* 66F.

🕭 |●| RESTAURANT LE BOUGNAT

29 rue des Chaussetiers. **MAP B2-21**
☎ 04.73.36.36.98
Closed Sun, Mon and Wed lunchtimes, and July.

You might think this is a tourist trap, but it's not. The restaurant has a regional-rustic feel and offers a wonderful selection of regional dishes prepared with confidence – mutton tripe, *pounti* (a mixture of bacon and Swiss chard), pig's trotters with white kidney beans and *potée auvergnate,* the thick local soup. There's a splendid wood-burning stove in the foyer, which the chef uses to prepare Auvergne pancakes. The 78F set menu is very decent. Good wines from the Auvergne. If you're on your own, try to get one of the stools at the counter where the regulars sit. Lots of atmosphere. Free apéritif.

🕭 |●| LES JARDINS D'HISPAHAN

11 ter rue des Chaussetiers. **MAP B2-27**
☎ 04.73.90.23.07.
Closed Sun, Mon and public holidays.

Persian cooking with subtle, flowery, aromatic flavours rather than heavily spiced dishes. The decor's not particularly exciting but not intrusive either. The kebab *bargue*, made with grilled veal marinated in lemon, is delicate and delightful, as are the dishes with sauce. Menus 78–119F or around 100F *à la carte*. If you think you don't like rice, the way they cook basmati here will make you change your mind. Free apéritif.

🕭 |●| RESTAURANT LE CAFÉ DE LA PASSERELLE

22 rue Anatole-France. **MAP D3-23**
☎ 04.73.91.62.12
Closed Sun and 15 July–15 Aug.

With left-wing politicians and ex-ministers among the regulars, this is one of Clermont's liveliest places, thanks mostly to its extrovert owner. Alain Aumaly comes from the south but his cooking is typical of the Auvergne region, with generous portions of pig's trotters, *potée* (a thick soup), stuffed cabbage and satisfyingly thick juicy steaks. There's

one set menu only, 90F, with a starter, main course, cheese and dessert. A good restaurant, but it's small so it's best to book. Free apéritif.

🕭 |●| LE CHARDONNAY

1 pl. Philippe-Marcombes. **MAP C2-26**
☎ 04.73.90.18.28

Service 3pm–1.30am. It's the wine that matters here, as you can see from the shelves of bottles displayed behind the bar. The owner's a trained *sommelier* and will pick out delightful wines for you – some are sold by the glass. On the food front, there are earthy, robust dishes like *andouillette* with green lentils, calf's head *gribiche* with capers, gherkin and herb mayonnaise, or stuffed filleted pig's trotters, and waffles with preserves for dessert. 90–120F *à la carte*. Friendly but unobtrusive staff. There's a piano to add a bit of atmosphere. Free apéritif.

|●| LE 5 CLAIRE

5 rue Saint-Claire. **MAP B2-18**
☎ 04.73.37.10.31.
Closed Sun, Mon, a week in Feb, three weeks in Aug.

A typical Clermont restaurant with retro-chic decor. Welcoming staff who readily give information about the food or advice about the wines. It's not the cheapest place in town, but the dishes are tasty and imaginatively prepared: marinated fresh anchovies on a bed of pickled onions, roast sea bass with squid, shoulder of lamb with pickled lemons or saddle of rabbit with cinnamon served with rigatoni with herby ricotta. Menu of the day 110F then 170–250F depending on the number of dishes, which can get elaborate – creamed peas and asparagus with curried croutons, sea perch with artichokes with a sliver of warm *foie gras* or veal chop in a parmesan crust with an aubergine and thyme *compote*. Sure-handed preparation. Good cheeses and classic desserts.

CHAMALIÈRES   63400 (3KM W)

🕭 🏠 |●| HÔTEL RADIO***

43 av. Pierre-Curie; take the D941b in the direction of Pontgibaud.
☎ 04.73.30.87.83 ➡ 04.76.36.42.44
🅴 hotel.radio@wanadoo.fr
Restaurant closed Sat lunchtime, Sun evening, Mon lunchtime except for public holidays, and Jan. **TV.**
Guarded garage.

Service noon–1.30pm and 7–9.30pm. Built as

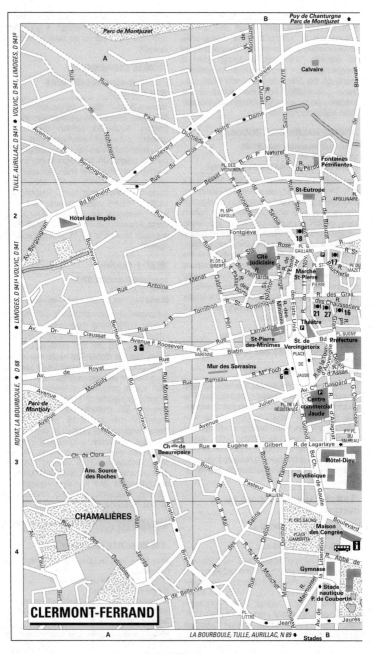

CLERMONT-FERRAND

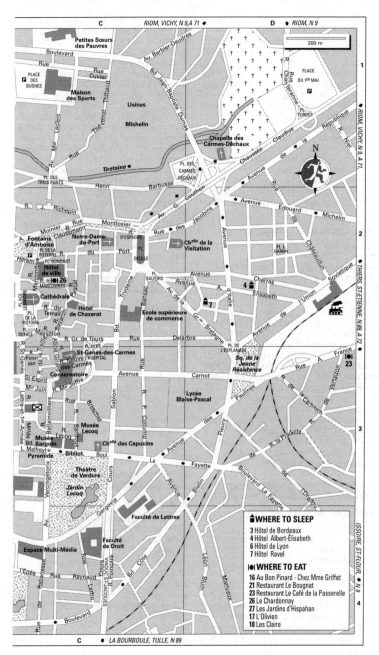

200 m

RIOM, VICHY, N 9,A 71
RIOM, N 9
RIOM, VICHY, N 9 & 71.
THIERS, ST-ETIENNE, N 89 & 72
ISSOIRE, ST-FLOUR, N 9
LA BOURBOULE, TULLE, N 89

Petites Sœurs des Pauvres
Boulevard
Av. Barbier-Daudrée
PLACE DU 1ᵉʳ MAI
Rue
Rue Cuvier
PLACE DES BUGHES
Maison des Sports
Usines
Michelin
Chapelle des Carmes-Déchaux
PL. DES CARMES-DÉCHAUX
PL. TUBBOT
Tiretaine
PL. DES TROIS PONTS
Henri
Barbusse
Chaussée
Claudius
de
la
République
R. Nel
R. J. Richepin
Moinier
Rue
Montlosier
Av. G. Couthon
Avenue
Edouard
Michelin
Clermont
Fontaine d'Amboise
Notre-Dame-du-Port
PL D'ESPAGNE
Rue des Jacobins
Chᵉˡˡᵉ de la Visitation
PL L. GARMY
Châteaudun
PL DE LA POTERNE
Port
du
PL. DELILLE
Avenue
PL SALFORD
Avenue
Charras
Hôtel de ville
PL MARCOMBES
26
Av. de la
Bansac
Trudaine
Av. de la
4
Élisabeth
l'Union
Soviétique
Cathédrale
Hôtel de Chazerat
Ecole supérieure de commerce
7
Gr. Bretagne
d'Italie
R. du Terrail
PL DE LA VICTOIRE
PL ROYALE
Massillon
R. Gr. de Tours
Rue
Delarbre
PL DE L'ESPLANADE
France
23
St-Genès-des-Carmes
PL M DE L'HOSPITAL
Sg. de la Jeune Résistance
R. de la Cartouch
Conservatoire
Avenue
Carnot
M. R M Joffre
Rue
Sablon
R. P. Collonge
Lycée Blaise-Pascal
Fleury
R. la Pradelle
Musée Lecoq
des
Avenue
Boulevard La Fayette
Musée Bargoin
Chᵉˡˡᵉ des Capucins
La
Fayette
Pyramide
Biblict.
Boul.
Théâtre de Verdure
Cours
Biatin
Jardin Lecoq
Faculté de Lettres
Espace Multi-Média
Faculté de Droit
Côte
Léon
Blum
Marcvaux
l'Épée
Rue
Raynaud
Bd.
Boulevard

[79]

🛏 WHERE TO SLEEP

3 Hôtel de Bordeaux
4 Hôtel Albert-Élisabeth
6 Hôtel de Lyon
7 Hôtel Ravel

🍴 WHERE TO EAT

16 Au Bon Pinard - Chez Mme Griffet
21 Restaurant Le Bougnat
23 Restaurant Le Café de la Passerelle
26 Le Chardonnay
27 Les Jardins d'Hispahan
17 L'Olivien
18 Les Claire

a radio station in the 1930s, this hotel-restaurant was run by Michel Mioche for many happy years. Now it's run by his daughter who gave up her career as a journalist in Paris. She, her young chef and a head waiter make up the trio running this successful enterprise. Only top-quality produce is used and dishes are as skilfully prepared as they are imaginative – a revival of real French cooking. There is a fish menu designed around the catch brought in by the fishermen, and another, themed, menu, often inspired by the Orient. Dishes include rabbit *tartare*, casserole-roast pigeon and John Dory with fruit dusted with spices, and hot Caribbean chocolate *soufflé*. Menus 190–460F. Beautiful bedrooms with lots of style. Doubles 450–490F with shower/wc, 410–750F with bath. 10% discount for a two-night stay.

🏃|●| AUBERGE DE LA MORÉNO

Col de la Moréno; it's on the D941A.
☎ 04.73.87.16.46
Closed evenings in the week, lunchtimes at weekends out of season, and from All Saints' Day to Jan. **TV**. **Car park**.

Service non-stop in season. The inn was built in 1905 and it's run by a welcoming couple. The dining room, which has changed hardly at all over the years, has floors polished by time, stone walls and a wide hearth, and you can glimpse the kitchens through the door. Interesting menus with appetising dishes. Weekday lunch *menu du terroir*, 78F, features *tripou*, eggs with truffles and *andouillette*. The menu *Auvergnat*, 135F, is exceptional: pig's trotters stuffed with sweet herbs or char with Cantal and cream sauce with lentils. The 110F menu includes a $^1/_4$ litre of wine to go with *truffade*, local ham, salad and dessert. Of the desserts, don't miss their warm *tarte Tatin*. Free apéritif.

CONDAT-EN-FENIERS   15190

🏠|●| HÔTEL-RESTAURANT CHÉ MARISSOU

Le Veysset, it's 3km from Condat on the D62.
☎ 04.71.78.55.45
✉ marissou@aol.com
Open school holidays and weekends Feb–11 Nov.
Disabled access. **Garden**. **Car park**.

Non-stop service. This hotel, the smallest in the world, was born out of the seemingly genuine passion of a Laval industrialist – a local boy made good – and an elaborate marketing campaign. He had a holiday home in Veyssat, between Condat and Montboudif, birthplace of President Pompidou, and turned it into an inn which is not without charm. You'll be welcomed by the owner himself in a dining room that looks as much like a living museum as it does a restaurant. Marissou's job is to send you away full, no matter how hungry you were when you arrived. You can go back as often as you like to the table of traditional cold meat and *crudités*. That will be followed by the day's special – *potée*, the thick local soup, or mutton tripe – then you serve yourself from the table bearing a selection of perfectly matured regional cheeses, and dessert. With the cheese you'll get a chance to sample, on the house, a glass of rare wine made from late-harvested local grapes. How much you pay depends on how old you are – free for children under 7 and centenarians, 135F if you're aged 10–65, 125F if you're 65–100. The one and only bedroom, 500F including champagne, is traditionally decorated. Perfect for a special night away.

ÉGLISENEUVE-D'ENTRAIGUES   63850

🏠|●| HÔTEL DU NORD*

rue principale.
☎ 04.73.71.90.28.
Closed a week in June and a week in Sept. **Car park**.

After a day's walking in the Cézallier, this pretty little country inn is a lovely place to stop for an Auvergnat snack, 59F, or something a bit more substantial. *Menu ouvrier* 55F then menus 65–130F. Dishes come straight out of a guide to local cooking: salmon with green lentils, warm goat's cheese with hazelnuts and bacon, home-made liver *terrine*, stuffed cabbage or pig's trotters. Doubles 140F with shower/wc. Credit cards not accepted.

GANNAT   03800

🏠|●| HÔTEL DU CHÂTEAU*

9 pl. Rantian; it's opposite the château.
☎ 04.70.90.00.88 ➡ 04.70.90.30.79
Closed Sat out of season, and mid-Dec to 5 Jan. **TV**. **Car park**.

This hotel has the special charm of those 19th-century bourgeois buildings in provincial towns. The kitchen provides the kind of traditional cooking from generations back: *andouillette bonne femme*, sautéed veal and chicken with creamed garlic. They also do a wonderful *pâté bourbonnais*, a potato and bacon pie, and a delicious walnut cake. Set menus 68–140F. Clean simple bedrooms 230F with shower/wc, or 300F for bath.

CHARROUX — 03140 (10KM NW)

|●| LA FERME DE SAINT-SÉBASTIEN

Chemin de Bourion; take the N9, then turn right onto the D42.
☎ 04.70.56.88.83
Closed Mon evening and Tues except July–Aug, and the first fortnight in Jan.
Disabled access. Garden. Car park.

Service noon–1.30pm and 7.30–9pm. This delightful restaurant was opened in 1994 in one of France's most beautiful villages and it has quickly become a local favourite. The building was an old farm which has been well renovated, with an intimate atmosphere in which to enjoy Valérie Saignie's fresh, creative, *bourbonnais* cooking. Menus (95–320F) feature courgette fritters with a cream chive sauce, chicken in Charroux mustard, and Jerusalem artichokes with bacon, local cheeses (Lavor and smoked Lavor), and a good choice of desserts. The staff are warm and attentive. It's very popular, so you'll definitely need to book.

ISSOIRE — 63500

⚹ ▲ |●| AU BON COIN, CHEZ YVES

34–36 rue Aug-Bravard (Centre).
☎ 04.73.89.21.15 ➡ 04.73.89.21.15
Closed Sun evening and a fortnight in Nov. **Car park.**

A place with the warmth of the south about it. The owner is an exile from Nice, who will serve you a drink at the bar before he goes to cook your meal on the stove. The dishes have a *provençal* accent and are liberally served: squid fritters with two sauces, fresh salmon carpaccio, local salt lamb with pesto, fish stew and a mini-*bouillabaisse*. There's a good choice of fish and, from September to the end of April, a bank of oysters and seafood. Lunch *formules*, dish and dessert 57F, or menus 95–139F. A few rooms; doubles 160F with shower and wc on the landing. An unpretentious place with definite personality. Free coffee.

▲ HÔTEL DU TOURISME

3 av. de la Gare.
☎ 04.73.89.23.68 ➡ 04.73.89.65.28
Closed 1–30 Oct **TV.**

A detached house set back from the avenue, next to the station. It's run by a guy who's obsessional about aeroplanes – he's even built one. It's the place the pilots and para-

gliders go. Double rooms with shower/wc or bath, 230F.

SARPOIL — 63500 (9KM SE)

|●| LA BERGERIE DE SARPOIL

From Issoire, take the D996 then the D999 in the direction of Saint-Germain-l'Herm.
☎ 04.73.71.02.54 ➡ 04.73.71.02.99
Closed Sun evening and Mon except July–Aug.
Car park.

The best restaurant in the region. Laurent Jury and Éric Moutard produce marvels using the finest Auvergne produce; free-range pork, Salers beef, suckling lamb and wild ceps and morels from the forest. Menus 130–350F. Dishes include mouthwatering *andouille* pancake with pickled onions, nettle soup with frogs' legs and sweet garlic, and real sweetbreads braised with Boudes wine. On the *Saint Cochon* menu are black-pudding tart with chestnuts and *foie gras* cream, a morsel of pork smoked over rye stalks stuffed with ceps and cooked in a straw crust, and the sublime Caraïbe chocolate tart. There's a little rhyme on the menus – "the art of the cook begins where nature's work ceases". Now you know.

LAPALISSE — 03120

⚹ ▲ |●| HÔTEL-RESTAURANT GALLAND**

20 pl. de la République.
☎ 04.70.99.07.21 ➡ 04.70.99.34.64
Closed Mon and Sun evenings out of season, Feb school holidays, and last week in Nov. **TV. Car park.**

Service noon–2pm and 7–9pm. A delightful place where you can eat green salad with chicken livers and poached egg, pan-fried *escalope* of *foie gras* with gingerbread crumbs, duck breast stew with *foie gras*, slivers of sole and salmon or a sliced Charolais steak in Saint-Pourçain wine. The cooking is fresh and skilfully brings out subtle flavours. *La patronne* is adorable, good-humoured and very stylish, and the staff are keen and attentive. Menus 135–280F. The bedrooms are spick-and-span; 265–295F for a double with shower/wc. Ask for one overlooking the interior courtyerd. A very good establishment. Free apéritif.

LAVOUTE-CHICHAC — 43380

▲ |●| HOSTELLERIE LE PRIEURÉ**

Centre.
☎ 04.71.77.47.93 ☛ 04.71.77.48.00
Closed Tues evening and Wed except July–Aug and mid-Dec to last week in March.

The priory was built in the 18th century. The comfortable rooms have been thoughtfully renovated and all have a startling view of the Allier. The owner is kindly and is emphatic that General Lafayette slept in room 3, which has a view of a humpback bridge. Doubles with washing facilities 200F, or with en-suite bathrooms 240F. Breakfast 30F. Several menus, 78–155F, listing dishes concocted from fresh local produce – the cabbage stuffed with salmon is a *tour-de-force*, as is the summer fruit sorbet. The cheapest menu includes apéritif, dessert, cheese and a $^1/_4$ litre of red wine. Pleasant terrace on the Allier.

SAINT-ARCONS-D'ALLIER 42300 (8KM SE)

🏠 |●| LES DEUX ABBESSES

Le bourg; it's on the D585 in the direction of Prades.
☎ 04.71.74.03.08 ☛ 04.71.74.05.30
Closed 15 Nov–15 March. **Swimming pool**.

The mayoress had the inspired idea of renovating seven houses in her practically deserted village. She has made twelve charming, comfortable and spacious rooms with period furniture. It's a sort of hotel village, gathered around the 12th-century château on an outcrop of rock between the Allier and the Sioule rivers. The garden, where you eat breakfast in summer, has a Romanesque church to one side, built of volcanic rock. The owner is also the cook and she produces simple, tasty dishes – her spiced lamb is splendid, slowly roasted for seven hours and served with potatoes topped with cheese and cinnamon. A single menu at 200F, breakfast 70F, and rooms with en-suite bathrooms, 700–1500F. There's even a swimming pool with a breathtaking view.

MANDAILLES-SAINT-JULIEN 15590

🎿 🏠 |●| HÔTEL-RESTAURANT AU BOUT DU MONDE

Centre.
☎ 04.71.47.92.47 ☛ 04.71.47.95.95

A nice place in the Jordanne valley, which is a starting point for hillwalkers going up the Puy-Mary. The hotel is quiet, simple, and well run. Doubles 200F. The restaurant, with its traditional *cantou*, or inglenook fireplace,

armchairs and gleaming copperware is as cosy as you could wish. The cooking will satisfy the hungriest hiker – portions are generous beyond belief. Everything's delicious, from the selection of *charcuterie* to the vegetable soup and regional specialities like *truffade*, the potato cake with Cantal cheese, and mutton tripe. Menus 80–120F. Stuffed cabbage or *potée*, the local, substantial soup, made to order. You'll get a pleasant smiling welcome. 10% discount on the room rate except in school holidays.

🎿 🏠 |●| HÔTEL-RESTAURANT AUX GENÊTS D'OR*

Centre.
☎ 04.71.47.96.45 ☛ 04.71.47.93.65
Closed 15 Nov–20 Dec. **TV**.

A small hotel with a homely atmosphere in the centre of the village; it's set back from the road 50m down a cul-de-sac, so it's quiet. Good cooking, with set menus at 75–150F. They concentrate on a few specialities: a pie of duck *confit* with ceps, *tournedos* with gentian sauce, scallops on a bed of *fondant* leeks or venison with morels. They offer half board if you like. Doubles 200F with shower/wc. 10% discount on the room rate.

SAINT-CIRGUES-DE-JORDANNE 15590 (8KM SE)

🎿 🏠 |●| HÔTEL-RESTAURANT LES TILLEULS**

Centre; take the D17.
☎ 04.71.47.92.19 ☛ 04.71.47.91.06
Closed except for reservations 31 Oct to Easter.
Swimming pool. **TV**. **Garden**. **Car park**.

Service noon–1.30pm and 7–8.30pm. This is a beautiful building overlooking the road and the valley of the Jordanne. You can relax in the garden, swimming pool or sauna when you come back from a walk on the Puy-Mary. The quiet, pleasant bedrooms all have en-suite bathrooms and some have a terrace. Doubles 250–270F. The dining room is equally pleasant and the open fire is welcome in winter. You'll get a warm reception from Yvette Fritsch who creates her own recipes with wonderful results – snails in flaky pastry, duck breast with mushrooms and red mullet with morels. Menus 75–250F, half board 270F. 10% discount on the room rate.

MASSIAC 15500

🎿 🏠 |●| GRAND HÔTEL DE LA POSTE**

26 av. du Général-de-Gaulle (Centre).
☎ 04.71.23.02.01 ➡ 04.71.23.09.23
Swimming pools. **TV**. **Garden**. **Car park**.

Service noon–2pm and 7.30–9pm. There are 32 bedrooms renovated in trendy, elegant, Neoclassical style. Doubles with all mod cons 260–330F. There's a pleasant restaurant at the back; set menu at 75F, not served on Sunday or public holidays, then 110–160F. À la carte there are a few specialities: Cantal cheese tart, potato in flaky pastry, two types of fish in *beurre blanc*, pig's trotters with lentils, and warm apple tart. 10% discount on the room rate 15 Sept–15 June.

MAURIAC   15200

⊕ |●| HÔTEL DES VOYAGEURS ET LA BONNE AUBERGE

pl. de la Poste.
☎ 04.71.68.01.01 ➡ 04.71.68.01.56
ℯ auberge.des.voyageurs@wanadoo.fr
Closed Sat and Sun evenings, Nov–April and ten days Christmas to New Year. **TV**. **Garden**. **Car park**.

A nice hotel with around twenty rooms that have been prettily redecorated in modern colours. Good bathrooms. Doubles 150F with shower and wc on the landing, 250F with shower/wc or bath. Straightforward, honest menus, 60–170F, listing regional specialities like Salers beef with ceps, and traditional dishes. Very hospitable.

DRUGEAC   15140 (12KM SE)

⊁ |●| L'AUBERGE DES SAVEURS

Centre.
☎ 04.71.69.15.50.
Closed Mon evening and Wed.

A village inn with a simple, inviting dining room and sophisticated cooking. It's run by a husband and wife team – David will welcome you warmly front of house, while Nicole is in charge of the kitchen. She worked in a number of restaurants on the Côte before settling here to develop her own style. The menu features *foie gras terrine*, snails with herbs, fish stew, monk fish with fennel seeds or Mediterranean prawns *provençale*, *tournedos Rossini* and *confit* of duck with cep sauce. She bakes her own bread. Dishes change with the seasons. Weekday lunch menu 60F, or 90–150F. Pleasant sunny terrace. Free apéritif.

MONT-DORE (LE)   63240

⊕ |●| HÔTEL DE LA PAIX**

8 rue Rigny.
☎ 04.73.65.00.17 ➡ 04.73.65.00.31
Closed a fortnight Nov–Dec.

A hotel built in 1880 with a wonderfully old-fashioned decor. It's run by a friendly woman who greets you warmly. Simple, functional rooms; doubles 220–250F with shower/wc. Superb Belle Époque dining room and a charming sitting room. Classic cooking, as is appropriate in such surroundings, using simple, fresh produce. Menus 87–160F.

⊁ ⊕ |●| HÔTEL LE CASTELET**

av. Michel-Bertrand (Northwest); it's near the town centre.
☎ 04.73.65.05.29 ➡ 04.73.65.27.95
ℯ castelet@compuserve.com
Closed 25 March–15 May and 1 Oct–20 Dec.
Swimming pool. **TV**. **Garden**. **Car park**.

Service 12.15–1.30pm and 7.15–8.30pm. They don't emphasise spa cures here as much as they do in the other hotels in town. There's a swimming pool, garden and a terrace, and they have lots of facilities to keep you and the kids amused – ping-pong, snooker, toboggans, video games and outdoor activities – as well as cots and high-chairs, all free of charge. There are 34 rooms, with doubles at 332F with bath. Sophisticated cuisine: smoked duck breast and mango with walnut oil, trout with gentian sauce and salmon *escalope* with green lentils, raspberry *gratin* and *mille fondue* with chocolate. Menus 98–169F. 10% discount on the room rate out of season, excluding school holidays.

|●| RESTAURANT LE BOUGNAT

23 av. Georges-Clémenceau.
☎ 04.73.65.28.19
Closed Tues except during school holidays and 1 Nov–15 Dec. **Garden**. **Car park**.

Traditional cooking with a modern slant – nobody in Mont-Dore does it better. An old stable has been very nicely transformed to make a delightful dining space with little tables and tiny sideboards. The *pounti* (a mixture of bacon and Swiss chard) is one of the best we've ever tasted, and the *truffade* (potato cake with Cantal cheese), is excellent; garlic soup, sautéed rabbit *à la gentiane* and stuffed cabbage are also good. Set menus 82–135F. This is a great place to come on cold winter evenings after a good day's skiing. Best to book – it's very popular.

They've opened a shop, "La Petite Boutique du Bougnat", where you can buy their home-made delicacies.

MONTLUÇON   03100

☎ HÔTEL DE LA GARE**

42 av. Marx-Dormoy (Southwest); it's close to the station.
☎ 04.70.05.44.22 ➡ 04.70.05.90.89
Closed 22 Dec–4 Jan. **TV. Car park**.

This little hotel, the headquarters of the *Contact-hôtel* chain, is typical of traditional, family-run establishments. It's pleasant, quiet, and very handy for the station. Good staff on hand to help. Bedrooms are simple and well maintained, 205F with shower/wc and 235F with bath. Free hearty breakfasts, usually 30F.

⚇ ☎ |●| HÔTEL DES BOURBONS- RESTAURANT AUX DUCS DE BOURBON**

47 av. Marx-Dormoy (Southwest); it's near the station.
☎ 04.70.05.28.93 ➡ 04.70.05.16.92
Closed Sun evening and Mon except public holidays. **TV**.

Service noon–2.30pm and 7–11pm. This beautiful 18th-century town house has been stylishly renovated and has comfortable, bright bedrooms. Doubles 280F with shower/wc and bath. To eat, you might prefer the brasserie (☎04.70.05.22.79) to the restaurant, as it is cosier. Set menus, 78–200F, offer things like home-smoked salmon, sole braised with crayfish, tasty grilled meat and delicious seasonal fruit tarts. Very professionally run. Free apéritif.

|●| LA VIE EN ROSE

7 rue de la Fontaine; it's beside Notre-Dame church.
☎ 04.70.03.88.79
Closed Sun lunchtime.

In the old part of Montluçon. Unwind in the relaxed atmosphere created by the friendly owner. They've decorated the dining room in warm colours and put in new lighting to make for a more cosy feel. The walls are hung with old photos of the town and adverts from the 1950s and 1960s, and the background music is not muzak but a collection of great French songs or standards by American crooners. The cooking is good – various thick and tasty steaks and fresh, big salads. Excellent potato pie. 110F *à la carte*. Menus 50–88F.

|●| LE SAFRAN D'OR

12 pl. des Toiles (Centre); it's in the pedestrian part of the medieval town.
☎ 04.70.05.09.18 ➡ 04.70.05.55.60
Closed Sun evening, Mon, Feb school holidays and three weeks from 16 Aug.

The yellow, marbled façade looks like the front of a Parisian brasserie and the cooking is the kind you'd get in a bistro with a high-class chef. You'll get a warm welcome from the owner, who'll do all she can for you. The service is quick and efficient, but you won't feel rushed – excellent cooking and it won't cost you a fortune. Set menus 98–160F.

NÉRIS-LES-BAINS   03310 (8KM SE)

⚇|●| LE RELAIS DU VIEUX MOULIN

rue des Moulins; take the N144.
☎ 04.70.03.24.88
Closed Tues from 30 Oct–1 March. **Garden. Car park**.

Service noon–2.30pm and 7–11.30pm. A lovely place, especially in summer, when you can sit outside on the delightful terraces below the viaduct. It's really a *crêperie*, but you're in Charolais beef country, and this is the best place for miles around for chargrilled rib of beef, sold by weight. You'll find a wide variety of sweet and savoury pancakes and salads. Free coffee, apéritif or pizza in the evening.

COURÇAIS   03370 (21KM NW)

☎ |●| BAR-HÔTEL-RESTAURANT JOSETTE LAUMONIER

Take the D943; it's on the pl. de l'Eglise.
☎ 04.70.07.11.13
Closed Sun evening, Mon and first three weeks in Sept.

In a peaceful village, this is a simple, pleasant and relaxing place that's ideal for families. There's a cosy atmosphere in the rustic restaurant – the fireplace has a lot to do with that – or you might prefer the terrace on sunny days. Menus 70–130F and you won't go hungry. The free-range poultry from the neighbouring farm is excellent and, if you order in advance, they can provide snails or veal sweetbreads. Four bedrooms, 130F with basin, 150F with shower. Half board is compulsory from April to the end of August. Credit cards not accepted.

MONTSALVY   15120

⚇ ☎ |●| L'AUBERGE FLEURIE

pl. du Barry (Centre).
☎ 04.71.49.20.02
Restaurant closed mid-Sept to mid-Feb.

Service noon–1.30pm and 7.30–9pm. Everything's well maintained and has a rustic feel –
ivy clambering up the front wall, a fireplace,
exposed beams and ancient doors. There's
always a good crowd in the bar and restaurant,
and you'll find the staff very friendly. The menu
of the day, 55F, is not available on Sunday, but
others, 95–185F, are good value. They serve
dishes like *fricassée* of veal knuckle, breast of
duck with Marcillac butter and chestnut charlotte with quince *coulis*. Wines are reasonably
priced. Rooms with basin 120F or 160F with
shower/wc. Half board 290F per person. Free
apéritif.

🏃 🏠 |●| INTER-HÔTEL DU NORD**

Centre.
☎ 04.71.49.20.03 ➡ 04.71.49.29.00
📧 hotel@hotel-du-nord.com
Closed Jan– March. **TV. Garden. Car park**.

Situated in the heart of the Châtaigneraie,
this chic hotel has colourful, comfortable
rooms equipped with telephone, TV and
mini-bar. They cost 270–300F with show-
er/wc or 280–360F with bath. The quiet,
plush restaurant has an excellent reputation
for its traditional local dishes. A husband and
wife team runs the place – he deals with the
dining room while she does the cooking.
Menus (88–250F) include *crépinette* of pig's
trotters, trout *soufflé* with lentil sauce, *falette*
(stuffed breast of mutton), and stew of suckling pig, pan-fried snails with ceps and walnuts, fresh *foie gras* in Sauternes, locally
grown beef, and iced *mousse* flavoured with
gentian liqueur. 10% discount April–June and
Sept–Dec. Free coffee.

CALVINET   15340 (17.5KM W)

🏠 |●| HÔTEL DE LA TERRASSE*

pl. Jean-de-Bonnefon (Centre); take the D19.
☎ 04.71.49.91.59
Closed Nov–May. **Garden. Car park**.

The very chatty lady who's been running
the hotel since 1036 has a talent for taking
care of her guests. She has created a wonderful homely atmosphere, with lovely rustic
decor including copper pans, an old clock
and a sideboard. Her specialities are pear
tart and stuffed pig's trotters and she has
set menus at 65–165F (this last features
two starters). The bedrooms are furnished
with period furniture; doubles 160F with
basin to 225F with bath. Half board 210F
per person.

🏠 |●| HÔTEL BEAUSÉJOUR**

Route de Maurs; get there by the D66, the D45 and the D51.
☎ 04.71.49.91.68 ➡ 04.71.49.98.63
Closed Mon, Sun evening out of season, and mid-Jan
to 1 March. **TV**.

Michelin gave the restaurant a star – the only
one in Cantal to have one – and it's won
regional awards too. In spite of the chef's
success, this place remains down-to-earth
and as friendly, good-natured and simple as
ever, so he hasn't lost the support of his regular customers – travelling executives and
local farmers who come here for family celebrations. Staff are particularly friendly and
offer efficient service in a classic dining
room. Amazingly high-quality cooking and
reasonable prices. Dishes include stuffed
cabbage, black pudding with duck livers,
marbré of *foie gras* with oxtail, guinea fowl
gourmandises, roast crayfish with raw ham,
casserole of milk-fed veal, medallions of
lamb spiked with anchovies, ham hock with
pea *purée*, *fricassée* of Breton lobster, and
farm-raised pigeon. Menus 95–320F. Good
wines at reasonable prices. Comfortable and
pretty bedrooms cost 350F.

MOULINS   03000

🏃 🏠 |●| LE GRAND HÔTEL DU
DAUPHIN**

59 pl. d'Allier (Centre).
☎ 04.70.44.33.05 ➡ 04.70.34.05.75
TV. Disabled access. Garden. Car park.

A 17th-century coaching inn with an air of
romance. The tables are nicely laid and the
refined cooking is classical. Regional specialities include *salmis* of duck in Saint-Pourçain,
frogs' legs with garlic cream, and duck leg
confit. Menus 70–180F. You can order *coq au
vin* using Saint-Pourçain and *cassoulet* with
confit (for four). Delightful comfortable bedrooms, 165F with basin, 275F with bath. 10%
discount on the room rate Jan–March.

🏃 🏠 |●| LE PARC**

31 av. du Général-Leclerc (East); it's near the train station.
☎ 04.70.44.12.25 ➡ 04.70.46.79.35
Restaurant closed Sat, 6–21 July, 28 Sep–6 Oct, 21
Dec–2 Jan. **TV. Car park**.

The Barret family have been running this
hotel since 1956 and the kindly reception
they offer is in the long tradition of good
hotel-keeping. It's a beautiful building, classic in style, and exceptionally well appointed. The bright dining room is relaxing, and

the furniture, fabrics and colours are simple and harmonious. The restaurant serves traditional and local dishes interpreted with imagination: rabbit stew, roast fillet of zander with mustard, medallions of monkfish with shellfish *coulis*, pan-fried fillet of Charolais beef with *fourme d'Ambert* cheese, and duck breast with Sancerre are typical dishes. Set menus 98–220F. Rooms are soundproofed. Doubles 220–280F with shower/wc. Some of the rooms are in an annexe. Free apéritif.

🧍‍♀️|●| LE GRAND CAFÉ

49 pl. d'Allier (Centre).
☎ 04.70.44.00.05
Car park.

Service 11.30am–2pm and 7–11pm. This superb 1900s brasserie is a listed building, and it's the most popular place in the area, where everyone comes for the atmosphere as well as the food. Dishes of the day include grilled pig's trotters, calf's brawn, salad of oxtail or steak. Free coffee.

🧍‍♀️|●| RESTAURANT LA PETITE AUBERGE

7 rue des Bouchers (Centre); it's near the main post office.
☎ 04.70.44.11.68 ➡ 04.70.44.82.04
Closed Sun except public holidays, Mon evening and 22 July–12 Aug.

Service noon–1.30pm and 7.15–9.30pm. The dining room is long and narrow and very traditionally decorated. The chef's expertise with first-rate ingredients produces results that are full of flavour – scallops on a bed of leeks, breast of duck with a lentil *coulis* and mussels with chanterelle mushrooms. Menus 90–200F. Delightful welcome. Free Kir.

COULANDON   03000 (6KM W)

🧍‍♀️ 🏠 |●| HÔTEL LE CHALET-RESTAURANT LE MONTÉGUT★★★

It's on the D945.
☎ 04.70.44.50.08 ➡ 04.70.44.07.09
Closed 16 Dec–31 Jan. **Swimming pool**. **TV**.
Disabled access. **Garden**. **Car park**.

If you're on the lookout for a peaceful relaxing break in a hotel where service always comes with a smile, this late 19th-century chalet nestling in the depths of the countryside is ideal. Bedrooms have been tastefully decorated and they're all different. Doubles 410F with shower/wc, 480F with bath. From the rooms, you'll either have a view of the countryside or of the park with an ornamental lake. The restaurant is in a separate building,

and when summer arrives you can lunch or dine by the swimming pool. The 115F weekday menu is based on fresh market produce; there are others with bigger portions and more elaborate dishes, up to 250F – fillet of lamb *en croûte*, pan-fried crayfish with fresh noodles, and iced mousse with Chivas Regal. The dishes are well thought out and service is good. Free apéritif.

SOUVIGNY   03210 (11KM W)

🧍‍♀️|●| AUBERGE LES TILLEULS

pl. Saint-Éloi.
☎ 04.70.43.60.70 ➡ 04.70.44.85.73
Closed Sun evening except July–Aug, Mon, second week Feb, third week June and 1–10 Oct.

There's a magnificent church and basilica with buildings dating from the 10th to the 15th centuries in this delightful village. The inn is welcoming, fresh and spruce. On the walls there are naive paintings of village life in the 1940s and 1950s. 72F weekday lunch menu and others up to 238F. Specialities include pan-fried duck *foie gras* with fruit purée flavoured with cider, red mullet with fresh noodles, *grenadins* of veal and veal kidneys with Saint-Pourçain, and local venison steak with ceps and sautéed potatoes. The selection of local cheeses, whether from cow's milk or goat's, is perfect. Free apéritif.

CHAPELLE-AUX-CHASSES (LA) 03230 (22KM NE)

🧍‍♀️|●| L'AUBERGE DE LA CHAPELLE-AUX-CHASSES

Centre; take the N79 towards Bourbon-Lancy, then the D30 as far as the village; the restaurant is beside the church.
☎ 04.70.43.44.71
Closed Tues evening, Wed, 14–28 Feb and a fortnight Aug/Sept. **Garden**.

This building looks like a child's picture of a house and you walk through the garden to the sound of bird song, through reception to a pretty little dining room. The cooking is classical, imaginative and bursting with freshness: *terrine* of semi-cooked duck *foie gras*, *fricassée* of farmed rabbit with rosemary and lime, ham braised in a hay box, fisherman's stew with a mandarin and almond sauce, fillet of zander with creamed lettuce, and iced *soufflé* flavoured with verbena liqueur. The prices make it one of the more popular places in the area. *Formule* during the week at 68F and menus 95–190F. There's a shady terrace where they serve in summer. Free coffee.

DOMPIERRE-SUR-BESBRE 03290 (30KM E)

🕮 ≙ |●| AUBERGE DE L'OLIVE**

129 av. de la Gare; take the D12.
☎ 04.70.34.51.87 ➡ 04.70.34.61.68
Closed Fri (except July–Aug), ten days during the Feb school holidays, and a fortnight in Nov. **TV.**

A handsome, well-maintained building covered in Virginia creeper and a delightful place to stop. Care is taken with the cooking and the service is faultless. Set menus 68F, except Sunday and public holidays, to 260F. Doubles with shower/wc 220F or 250F with bath. There are 17 newly renovated rooms and now the by-pass has been built lorries doen't go thundering through the village and disturb your sleep. Half board, 290F, is compulsory July–Aug. Free coffee.

MURAT 15300

≙ AUX GLOBE-TROTTERS**

22 av. du Docteur-Louis-Mallet (South).
☎ 04.71.20.07.22 ➡ 04.71.20.16.88
Closed Sun excluding summer, a week in July and the Nov school holidays. **TV. Garden. Car park.**

There are twenty very clean, modern rooms. Doubles 180–230F. The attic rooms on the second floor are absolutely delightful, though mind your head if you're tall! Very laid-back atmosphere in the downstairs bar which is popular with young people.

🕮 ≙ HÔTEL LES BREUILS**

av. du Docteur-Louis-Mallet (Centre).
☎ 04.71.20.01.25 ➡ 04.71.20.02.43
Closed 1 Nov to Christmas and April except school holidays. **Swimming pool. Garden. Car park.**

A substantial 19th-century private house, which has been turned into a hotel. It has an aristocratic charm and an old-fashioned feel that's a world away from the square-roomed sterility of some modern establishments. They play soft music and there's a restful garden. Charming welcome. Ten cosy, comfortable rooms which have been stylishly redecorated. Doubles 290–460F. 10% discount Sept–June.

|●| RESTAURANT LE JARROUSSET

RN122; it's 4km from Murat heading in the direction of Massiac.
☎ 04.71.20.10.69 ➡ 04.71.20.15.26
Closed Mon–Wed except July–Aug, and Jan.
Swimming pool. Garden. Car park

Service 12.15–1.30pm and 5.15–9.30pm. You can't miss this restaurant at the end of the road; the setting is particularly elegant and the service faultless. Eliane Andrieu runs this place with exceptional know-how and is always courteous and attentive to her guests. Only the best local produce is used in the cooking, and clever combinations of flavours and subtle aromas are created. Perfectly cooked fish and everything's wonderfully fresh. The cheeses are good and the *crème brûlée* and chocolate tart are excellent. They have a brilliant menu at 135F, a veritable feast, but it's not available Saturday evenings or Sunday lunchtimes; others up to 360F. À la carte you can get dishes such as leg of duck *au sel*, braised cabbage with a *coulis* of peppers, or quail stuffed with *foie gras*, *escalope* of *foie gras* with caramelised apples, *blanquette* of veal sweetbreads, cabbage stuffed with truffles, and fillet of sea bass with *fondue* of fennel. Expect to spend 350F. Good choice of wines.

CHALINARGUES 15170 (9KM S)

≙ |●| AUBERGE DE LA PINATELLE

☎ 04.71.20.15.92 ➡ 04.71.20.17.90
Closed Wed evening, and a fortnight Sept–Oct.

A pretty inn popular with people from Allance. The young owners have five comfortable rooms that they have decorated tastefully; doubles 220F. The convivial dining room has been done up in modern style. Menus 70–160F. Alongside trout with bacon, *tripoux* and *coq au vin*, they also do good duck breast, salad with truffles and other Périgord delicacies such as *foie gras* served in a *brioche*. Attentive, smiling service.

DIENNE 15300 (11KM NW)

🕮 |●| RESTAURANT DU LAC SAUVAGE

How to get there: take the D3 from Murat then the D23.
☎ 04.71.20.82.65
Closed Oct–June. **Garden. Car park.**

Paradise for fishermen and walkers, on the banks of a private lake at 1230m. The restaurant is the place to be when summer comes to Dienne – it's a magnificent setting. It is run by the head of the Super-Lioran ski school, and you'll get a nice welcome. The kitchen uses local produce to prepare tasty regional specialities that are served up in generous portions: trout with bacon, *truffade* (potato cake with Cantal cheese), *pounti* (a mixture of bacon and Swiss chard), and mutton tripe are especially good. 75F set menu or à la carte. You can even catch your own trout – no permit needed and there's equipment for hire. Free coffee.

[**87**]

LIORAN (LE)   15300 (12KM SW)

⚥ ⬠ I●I HÔTEL-RESTAURANT LE ROCHER DU CERF**

How to get there: take the N122 from Murat then the D67.
☎ 04.71.49.50.14 ➡ 04.71.49.54.07
Closed 15 April–30 June and 15 Sept–19 Dec. **TV**. **Car park**.

A typical family hotel in a ski resort. Located near the slopes, this is the nicest place in the area and the staff are always friendly and helpful. Bedrooms have been refurbished, and all rooms have views of the mountains. Doubles 160F with basin, 190F with shower/wc, and 230F with bath. The restaurant has the same kind of homely atmosphere and the set menus for full-board guests are planned over a two week period so you don't get the same thing every day. Set menus 49–170F. Specialities include stuffed cabbage, trout with bacon, *truffade* (the local potato cake with Cantal cheese), *pounti* (a mixture of bacon and Swiss chard), *coq au vin*, steak with bleu d'Auvergne, a local blue cheese, *escalope cantalienne* and bilberry fruit tart. A friendly hotel, ideal for skiing in winter and walking in summer. 10% discount on the room rate July–Aug.

LAVIGERIE   15300 (15KM W)

I●I AUBERGE ADRIENNE NIOCEL

Route de Dienne; take the D680 – it's just after Dienne.
☎ 04.71.20.82.25
Closed low season evenings except by reservation, and Dec–Jan.

An authentic Cantal house with a superb dining room. It's got a flagstoned floor, and a vast chimney piece where the old beds in the alcoves have been preserved. Adrienne Niocel is a gifted cook who prepares regional dishes, at their best – good mountain ham, one of the tastiest *truffades* (potato cake with Cantal cheese) in the region, cheese, *poulacre* (lamb's liver with pork belly), and home-made fruit tart. Warm and unpretentious welcome. 80F menu of the day only.

ALLANCHE   15160 (23KM NE)

⬠ I●I HÔTEL-RESTAURANT AU FOIRAIL

Maillargues; take the N122 from Murat, then the D679.
☎ 04.71.20.41.15
Closed evenings except July–Aug, Sept–June and 1–15 Jan. **Car park**.

Service noon–2pm and, in the summer, 7–8pm. On a little hill 1km outside Allanche in the middle of the summer pastures near one of the Auvergne's biggest cattle markets. It's a simple place that serves Salers beef which is particularly full of flavour. Hearty *menu du jour* 70F. On Sun, try the *repas amélioré* for 90F. There are panoramic views from the dining-room windows. Friendly staff. The bedrooms, 120–150F, are simple and well maintained.

NARNHAC   15230

⬠ I●I L'AUBERGE DE PONT LA VIEILLE**

Pont-la-Vieille.
☎ 04.71.73.42.60 ➡ 04.71.73.42.20
Closed 15 Oct–5 Dec. **TV**. **Garden**. **Car park**.

Service noon–2pm and 7–9.30pm. This is a welcoming and relaxing little hotel that has been well restored. It's set back from the main road and has a pretty garden in front. Quiet and pleasant double rooms with shower/wc 230F, or with bath 250F. Half board, from 200F per person, is compulsory in July and August. Set menus, 63–140F, feature regional specialities – choose from dishes like trout with bacon *à l'ancienne*, guinea fowl with ceps, *rissole Saint-Flour* (a sort of fritter with a cabbage and bacon filling), and stuffed cabbage. There are two shady terraces on the river bank.

PAILHEROLS   15800

⚥ ⬠ I●I L'AUBERGE DES MONTAGNES**

Centre; east of Vic-sur-Cère, take the D154 then the D54.
☎ 04.71.47.57.01 ➡ 04.71.49.63.83
Closed 10 Oct–20 Dec, except during the Nov school holidays. **Swimming pool**. **TV**. **Disabled access**. **Garden**. **Car park**.

A pretty little winding road from Vic-sur-Cère will lead you up to this really good family hotel on the outskirts of the village. It's been thoughtfully renovated and there's a new building constructed in the traditional style with a beautiful turret. The pond and the wonderful view complete the setting. There's a terrace, indoor and outdoor swimming pools, a climbing wall, and a games room in the old barn across the road. It also offers horse-drawn carriage rides. The bedrooms are on the small side, but they're cosy and well decorated; the bigger ones are in the new building. Doubles 228–295F. Two very bright dining rooms, one with the traditional *cantou*, or inglenook fireplace. *Menus du jour*, 78F, or others at 98–128F list local dishes such as *pounti* (a mixture of bacon and Swiss chard) and *truffade* (potato cake with Cantal cheese). It's popular, so it would be a good idea to book ahead. 10% discount on the room rate April–June.

PONTGIBAUD   63230

♠ |●| HÔTEL-RESTAURANT DE L'UNIVERS

How to get there: take the D941, it's opposite the station.
☎ 04.73.88.70.09.
Car park.

This family guesthouse looks like a picture postcard. Charlot grows the vegetables and milks the cows. Marie-Antoinette is the highly competent chef – she can feed the local fire brigade on her tripe dish, while at the same time beating up a few eggs for an omelette for another customer. The dining room, with its flowery wallpaper, is clean and bright. You can have a meal here at any time – calf's head, terrific grilled *andouillette* or good pig's trotters. There's no rush to leave, so sit a while and play cards – if you're missing a player, Charlot or Marie-Antoinette will happily make up the numbers. Set menus 60–130F. Double rooms 160F with shower on the landing, or 220F for ones that sleep three or four.

⅍ ♠ |●| HÔTEL DE LA POSTE**

pl. de la République.
☎ 04.73.88.70.02 ╠→ 04.73.88.79.74
Closed Sun evening and Mon except July–Aug, Jan and the first fortnight in Oct.**TV**. **Car park**.

A traditional hotel-restaurant with appealing, old-fashioned rooms. Doubles 180–210F with shower/wc or bath. Delicious local and seasonal dishes: roasted local rabbit with honey, *aiguillette* of duck breast with orange sauce, pig's trotter salad, and chard with *mousserons* (small white or yellow mushrooms). Menus 80–270F. Free apéritif.

MAZAYES-BASSE   63230 (15KM W)

♠ |●| AUBERGE DE MAZAYES

How to get there: take the D578, the D62, then the D52.
☎ 04.73.88.93.90 ╠→ 04.73.88.93.80
Closed Fri lunchtime in summer, Thurs out of season, and Jan. **TV**. **Car park**.

At the end of a winding road, a magnificent stable has been turned into a comfortable inn. It has an authentic rustic air – they've kept the stone drainage gully from the original stable – with an overlay of chic. It's almost

completely silent, and the terrace is a perfect spot for an apéritif while you enjoy the sunset. Proper regional dishes, with an excellent *potée auvergnate* and a tasty *coq au vin*. Weekday menu 80F, or 100–160F. The attractive rooms cost 270F with bath, breakfast included. The ideal place for a weekend in the country.

PUY-EN-VELAY (LE)   43000

♠ DYKE HÔTEL**

37 bd. Maréchal-Fayolle (Centre).
☎ 04.71.09.05.30 ╠→ 04.71.02.58.66
Closed Christmas to 1 Jan. **TV**. **Garage**.

All the advantages of a chain hotel, plus a central location and a lock-up garage. Everything's clean and brand new, the decor is low-key, and the service efficient. Bedrooms are identical and the mattresses very firm. Doubles 230F with shower/wc and 250F with bath. Breakfast, 30F, is served in the bar. "Dyke" refers to the local sugarloaf rock formations which give the area its character.

♠ |●| HÔTEL BRISTOL**

7 and 9 av. Maréchal-Foch (Centre).
☎ 04.71.09.13.38 ╠→ 04.71.09.51.70
Closed Mon out of season and March. **TV**. **Disabled access**. **Garden**. **Car park**.

Service noon–2pm and 7.30–9.30pm. A very English hotel as the name might suggest. It's a tall old building, the kind you might find in a spa town in the Auvergne, with an entirely renovated and modernised interior. There is a brand new building overlooking the garden with impeccable bedrooms that are very bright and very quiet; doubles with shower/wc or bath 250–299F. It may look chic but *Le Bristol* is not at all stuffy, and you'll always get a warm welcome. Try the carefully prepared traditional cooking in the *Taverne Lyonnaise* – the stellar dish is ham hock with lentils. The 59F menu includes wine, and there are other menus at 90–160F.

⅍ ♠ |●| HÔTEL-RESTAURANT LE VAL VERT**

6 av. Baptiste-Marcet; it's at the side of the road near the Puy south exit heading for Aubenas.
☎ 04.71.09.09.30 ╠→ 04.71.09.36.49
Restaurant closed Sat lunchtime15 Nov–30 March, and 22–29 Dec. **TV**. **Car park**.

Service noon–2pm and 7–10pm. They've just finished a complete refurbishment of the hotel and though it looks somewhat like one of a chain from the outside, inside you'll find a friendly, homely atmosphere. Smiling staff always provide excellent service. The comfortable, modern rooms are well maintained and decorated. The ones overlooking the road are soundproofed, but if it's absolute quiet you're after, ask for one at the back overlooking the shopping and residential area. Bedrooms with shower or bath 290–310F. The restaurant serves carefully prepared classics. Weekday lunch menu 73F or menus up to 260F. 10% discount on the room rate Nov–March.

⚲ 🏠 |●| HÔTEL LE RÉGINA***

34 bd. Maréchal-Fayolle (Centre).
☎ 04.71.09.14.71 ▐➔ 04.71.09.18.57
TV. Disabled access. Car park.

Service noon–2.30pm and 7–11pm. This hotel, in a beautiful old building right in the centre of town, is something of an institution in Puy. Prices are very reasonable for a three-star hotel, considering the high standard of the facilities and service. Doubles with shower/wc or bath 350–390F. Staff are courteous and friendly. If you're a light sleeper, ask for a room at the back rather than one overlooking the street. The ground-floor restaurant offers incredible value for money and some of the best cooking in Puy. Menus 85–230F. Free apéritif.

|●| LA PARENTHÈSE

8 av. de la Cathédrale (Centre).
☎ 04.71.02.83.00
Closed Sat and Sun.

A friendly restaurant in a quiet, paved street, at the foot of the imposing cathedral. Regional dishes that are simple and tasty: smoked trout salad with Puy lentils, duck with red wine sauce and *aligot* (potatoes cooked with Tome du Cantal cheese). Desserts include *crème brûlee* with chestnut honey. Menus 86–120F.

|●| RESTAURANT L'OLYMPE

8 rue du Collège (Centre); 200m from the Mairie and the Collegiate church.
☎ and ▐➔ 04.71.05.90.59
Closed Sun evening all year, and Mon excluding Aug.

Service noon–2pm and 7–10pm. A delightful restaurant in a cobbled alleyway in the conservation area. You'll get a jolly welcome. The young chef sticks resolutely to the local specialities but interprets them in his own, sometimes exotic style. He's made this one of the

best eating places in Puy in just a few years. Lentils, trout, game and verbena play star roles in this stylish cuisine. Menus 100–370F and a children's menu 65F.

|●| RESTAURANT TOURNAYRE

12 rue Chênebouterie (Centre); it's behind the town hall.
☎ 04.71.09.58.94 ▐➔ 04.71.02.68.38
Closed Sun and Wed evenings, Mon, and Jan.

The exterior is lovely, but the 16th-century vaulted dining room with stunning murals is magnificent – it's the most beautiful restaurant in Puy. The service is pleasant and unobtrusive and Eric Tournayre is a first-rate chef who creates imaginative dishes of a very high order: knuckle of veal or *croustillant* of pig's trotters, *truffade* (potato cake with Cantal cheese) with a Saint-Agur sauce, *galette* of veal sweetbreads, or pan-fried *foie gras* with ceps. A good range of desserts served in generous helpings. Menus 120–350F include a vegetable menu and a filling children's menu for 70F. Best to book in summer.

SAINT-VINCENT   43800 (18KM N)

|●| RESTAURANT LA RENOUÉE

Cheyrac; take the D103 that follows the gorges of the Loire.
☎ 04.71.08.55.94
Closed Sun evening and Mon except July–Aug, Jan–Feb, and a week in Oct.

The most delightful place in the area; a romantic house in a tiny garden where you'll find a warm welcome and fine, imaginative cooking: zander with crispy onions, morels stuffed with duck *foie gras* or *fricassée* of pike with *velouté* of green lentils. Set menus 98–230F and children's menu 55F. Nice set tea on Sunday afternoons.

SAINT-JULIEN-CHAPTEUIL   43260 (18KM E)

⚲ |●| RESTAURANT VIDAL

pl. du Marché; take the D15.
☎ 04.71.08.70.50 ▐➔ 04.71.08.40.14
Closed Mon evening and Tues out of season and 15 Jan–28 Feb. **Car park**.

Service noon–2pm and 7.30–9pm. Jean-Pierre Vidal is a most brilliant and creative chef and one of the most important in the Haute-Loire, though he modestly describes himself as "a country cook". All the menus, 100–350F, display his exquisite talent, and one of them is reserved for unusual lentil dishes from the starter to the dessert; lentils with vinegar, zander or meat with lentils, Auvergne cheese with lentils and even a lentil tart with iced *nougat*. Courteous, attentive service in the quiet, pleasant dining room next to the bar, where Jean-Pierre's father keeps a quizzical eye on his brilliant son. It's worth making the journey. Free coffee.

MOUDEYRES 43151 (20KM SE)

🏃 🛖 |●| LE PRÉ BOSSU

It's at the beginning of the village on the D361.
☎ 04.71.05.10.21
Closed weekday lunchtimes and Nov to Palm Sunday. **Disabled access. Car park**.

A cosy, characterful cottage in the middle of a field. The air is clean and it's very quiet. There are ten smart, comfortable rooms, some of which overlook the hunched field where lambs gambol from dawn. Other rooms overlook a vegetable garden growing a multitude of herbs. Doubles with shower/wc 395F, or 495F with bath. The red mullet with *ratatouille* and peach soup with coconut are particularly tasty, and there's a vegetable menu. Menus 195–255F. Quick, efficient service. There's a pleasant terrace in summer. 10% discount on the room rate April–June and Sept–Oct.

PONT-D'ALLEYRAS 43580 (29KM S)

🏃 🛖 |●| HÔTEL-RESTAURANT DU HAUT-ALLIER***

How to get there: take the D33.
☎ 04.71.57.57.63 ➦ 04.71.57.57.99
Closed Sun evening and Mon except high season and public holidays, and Dec–Feb. **TV**. **Disabled access**.

Service 12.30–2pm and 7.45–9pm. This delightful hotel-restaurant, in a little village in the valley of Haut-Allier, has been run by the same family for three generations, and you'll get a warm welcome. The building was renovated recently and the large restaurant has a classical decor. The elaborate cuisine is well prepared by Philippe Brun Cacaud, a fine chef specialising in regional dishes full of authentic flavours. There's a wide choice on the set menus, 125–420F; the *civet* of mussels and the young rabbit with herbs are both excellent, or try the pigeon with its juices deglazed with honey vinegar. The simpler yet substantial 65F *menu du jour* is served at speed in the bar and on the terrace. Well-stocked cellar. Doubles 280–380F with bath. 10% discount on the room rate March–April and Sept–Oct.

SAINT-HAON 43340 (29KM SW)

🏃 🛖 |●| AUBERGE DE LA VALLÉE**

Centre; take the N88 in the direction of Pradelles/Langogne, 7km on the D33 to Cayres and then the D31.
☎ 04.71.08.20.73 ➦ 04.71.08.29.21
Closed Mon Oct–May, and Jan to mid-March.

The village is in the wilds, at 970m, and the inn stands in the square dominated by a church with an unusual tower. Just 3km away the Allier cascades down the rocks of a deep valley. The rustic, welcoming inn has ten comfortable rooms, furnished with solid, old furniture, at 190–250F for a double with shower/wc. Nights are quiet. In the restaurant, they serve a series of menus, starting at 82F, featuring the chef's specialities: veal sweetbreads with morels, Auvergnat tripe, duo of local trout, and duck fillets. 10% discount on the room rate Sept–June.

RIOM 63200

🏃 |●| RESTAURANT L'ÂNE GRIS

13 rue Gomot (Centre).
☎ 04.73.38.25.10
Closed Sun, Mon lunchtime and 15–30 Aug.

Whether you think this place is insane, ghastly or heaven on earth will depend on how you feel about the owner, Casimir. He's slightly crazy but ever so nice – he's forever making jokes at his customers' expense, but he's generous with it. He used to just call his chef "baboon" but now he uses the nickname for his favourite customers, too. He'll greet you with a loud, cheerful "What do you want?" To hear him talk, you might think the food wasn't up to much, but the kitchen produces good traditional local dishes: *truffade* (potato cake with Cantal cheese or ham), *aligot* (fried potato cakes with Aligot cheese and sausage), salt pork with lentils, and Charolais steaks. Brilliant list of local wines which Casimir chooses with a genuine passion. No set menus. You'll pay 110–130F *à la carte*. A great place if you're prepared for Casimir's outsized personality. Free apéritif.

TOURNOËL 63530 (1.5KM N)

🏃 🛖 |●| HÔTEL-RESTAURANT LA CHATELLENIE

It's on the D986.
☎ 04.73.33.63.23

Closed Wed out of season and mid-Oct to end March.

Located on the road going up to Tournoël, which dominates Volvic, this hotel is peaceful and the rooms overlook the valley. Doubles 180–220F. The dining room is decorated in rustic style and has a panoramic view. Wholesome local dishes: ceps in pastry, *potée*, *coq au vin*, trout with smoked bacon, duck breast with ceps and a good *blanquette* of veal kidneys and sweetbreads. Menus 90–160F and portions are generous. Children's menu 50F. Friendly service. Free apéritif.

EFFIAT   63260 (27KM NE)

🏕 |●| LE CINQ MARS

Lieu-dit Les Peytoux; it's a hamlet between Chardonnières-les-Vieilles and Blot-l'Eglise.
☎ 04.73.97.44.17
Closed lunchtimes and a week at the end of Aug; reservations only in the evenings.

Behind a deceptively anodyne exterior hides a very good restaurant, formerly owned by the chef's mother-in-law. The man himself has worked with some of the greats, including a Michelin star recipient, and his cooking is excellent. The generous, expertly prepared dishes use the season's best ingredients; highlights include *coq au vin*, trout soufflé, frogs' legs, salmon croquettes, Auvergnat soup, and fillet of cod with creamed lentils. Modestly priced dishes of *charcuterie* are served with Auvergne wine. Wonderful welcome. It's best to book. Free coffee.

SAIGNES   15240

🏕 🛏 |●| HÔTEL RELAIS ARVERNE*

Centre; it's on the main square.
☎ 04.71.40.62.64 ➡ 04.71.40.61.14
Hotel closed Feb school holidays and the first fortnight in Oct. **Restaurant closed** Fri and Sun evenings out of season.
TV. Car park.

This stone building has a huge corner watchtower and the tables on the terrace are made from ancient stone wheels. The bedrooms are comfortable and are reached from the terrace, so you can come and go as you please. Doubles 260–270F with bath. The hotel's full of nooks and crannies and consequently very interesting. The dining room, where they serve dishes from the Dordogne and elsewhere, has a big clock and an even bigger fireplace. Specialities include monkfish with bilberries, *escalope* of *foie gras* with a cider sauce, mutton tripe

bonne femme, veal sweetbreads in flaky pastry with morels, grilled steak *au bleu*, and calf's liver with port caramel. Menus 70–220F. Free apéritif.

SAINT-ANTHÈME   63660

🛏 |●| HÔTEL-RESTAURANT AU PONT DE RAFFINY**

It's 4km along the Saint-Romain road.
☎ 04.73.95.49.10 ➡ 04.73.95.80.21
Closed Sun evening and Mon out of season, and 1 Jan–15 Feb. **TV. Disabled access. Car park.**

Service noon–1.30pm and 7.30–8.30pm (9pm in season). If you're looking for a gourmet meal, head for this place, on the banks of a little river near Saint-Anthème. The main attraction is Alain Beaudoux's light, creative cooking, typified by *andouillette* of fish with shellfish *coulis*, young rabbit *en crépine*, *croustillant* of guinea fowl with morels and verbena *parfait*. 90F weekday menu, and others up to 170F. Excellent wine list and prices are reasonable. The hotel is quiet and comfortable, and rooms with shower/wc or bath cost 220–250F. They've built some single-storey bungalows with facilities for the disabled, available by the week.

LA CHAUME   63660 (10KM S)

🛏 |●| AUBERGE DU CREUX DE L'OULETTE

By the D67 then the 258.
☎ 04.73.95.41.16 ➡ 04.73.95.80.83
📧 auberge.oulette@wanadoo.fr
Closed Tues evening, Wed and 15 Nov–1 March. **Swimming pool. Car park.**

This hotel in a small village has recently been renovated, and is an ideal spot if you want to go hiking in the region. The owners are a dynamic pair who have organised discovery trails that you can follow. Double rooms with shower/wc 220F. The chef is passionate about cooking and his wholesome, family dishes have a good reputation locally; expect to be offered snail stew with mushrooms, fish fillet with Fourme cheese sauce, or *coq au vin*. Menus 63–165F. You can eat on the terrace in summer. 10% discount on the room rate.

SAINT-FLOUR   15100

🛏 |●| HÔTEL-RESTAURANT DES ROCHES**

pl. d'Armes; it's opposite the museum.

☎ 04.71.60.09.70. ➡ 04.71.60.45.21
Closed Sun out of season. **TV**.

Very central place with bright pleasant bedrooms. You'll be warmly greeted. Doubles 220–260F and family rooms 340F. Two styles of cooking in the restaurant – classical and regional: *bavette* steak with blue Auvergne cheese sauce, John Dory with fresh tomato sauce, *potée Auvergnate*, *truffade*, *aligot* and more. Menus 69–180F. They're not clock-watchers; if you turn up at 9pm they'll still be happy to serve you.

🎿 ♟ |O| AUBERGE DE LA PROVIDENCE**

1 rue du Château-d'Alleuze (South).
☎ 04.71.60.12.05 ➡ 04.71.60.33.94
Closed Mon lunchtime in season, Sun evening and Mon out of season, a fortnight in Jan and 15 Oct–15 Nov. **TV**. **Garden. Car park**.

This very old inn has been completely refurbished. The decor is generally low key and the ten rooms are decorated in pastel shades of pink, blue, green and yellow. The bathrooms have been very well laid out. Doubles 280–350F with shower/wc. The set menus, 100–180F, offer some of the best value in town; quail fillet with mushroom sauce, St Nectaire cheese tart, morels in season. Free apéritif.

SAINT-GEORGES   15100 (4KM SE)

🎿 ♟ |O| L'AUBERGE DU BOUT DU MONDE*

Le Bout du Monde.
☎ 04.71.60.15.84 ➡ 04.71.73.05.10
Swimming pool. TV. Disabled access. Garden. Car park.

Service noon–2pm and 7.30–9pm. This place is at the "end of the world", deep in a valley in the countryside outside Saint-Flour. An ideal place for anglers or walkers and the restaurant serves a range of delicious regional specialities. Menus (65–145F) feature *tourte de caillé* (curds), *pounti* (a mixture of bacon and Swiss chard), stuffed rabbit with cabbage, black pudding salad with walnuts, trout with bacon, *coq au vin*, kid *à la cantalienne*, snails in flaky pastry, asparagus with garlic cream, and frogs' legs *à la lozérienne*. Simple, well-maintained rooms, 230F with en-suite bath. Free apéritif.

GARABIT   15320 (12KM SE)

🎿 ♟ |O| HÔTEL-RESTAURANT BEAU SITE**

How to get there: take exits 30 or 31 on the A75.
☎ 04.71.23.41.46 ➡ 04.71.23.46.34

✉ garabitbeausite@wanadoo.fr
Closed Nov–March. **Swimming pool. TV. Disabled access. Garden. Car park**.

The hotel looks down on the the viaduct built by Eiffel, of tower fame, and you get the best views of the lake. It's a huge building with bright, roomy doubles, 210F with shower/wc or 220F with bath. Excellent facilities include a heated swimming pool and tennis courts in wonderful surroundings. An ideal base for fishing, windsurfing and long walks. The restaurant serves classic French dishes and gourmet cuisine. Set menus, 59–210F, list specialities such as *gratinée* of scallops, beef fillet with morels, grilled *confit* of duck with ceps, fried trout with bacon and hazelnuts, *chiffonnade* with warm Cantal cheese and frogs' legs *provençal*. Free apéritif or coffee. 10% discount on the room rate April–June and Sept–Oct.

POMT-DE-LANAU   15260 (18KM SW)

♟ |O| HÔTEL-RESTAURANT L'AUBERGE DU PONT DE LANAU**

How to get there; take the D921.
☎ 04.71.23.57.76 ➡ 04.71.23.53.84
Closed Jan–Feb. **TV**. **Garden**. **Car park**.

This coaching inn has been brilliantly restored and turned into a delightful hotel run by Jean-Michel Cornut and his wife. The restaurant serves fine gourmet dishes drawing inspiration from traditional Auvergne cuisine. There's a weekday lunch *formule* at 70F, while other menus, 115–195F, offer excellent interpretations of local dishes: tripe on a bed of lentils; a *millefeuille* of *bleu d'Auvergne*, a local blue cheese; roast duck with a sauce made from wine lees, and escalope of *foie gras* with an infusion of ceps. The original dishes are full of character – excellent *aligots de canard* (stewed duck wings and giblets with garlic). The wines are of the same high standard, with local wines prominent. The superb dining room has a large stone fireplace and Madame Cornut will give you a warm welcome. Unobtrusive service. The rooms, from 260–360F, all have bath and, since the walls are covered with thick fabric, are quiet and warm. Terrace and large shady garden.

SAINT-GERVAIS-D'AUVERGNE   63390

♟ |O| LE RELAIS D'AUVERGNE**

Route de Châteauneuf-les-Bains (Centre).
☎ 04.73.85.70.10 ➡ 04.73.85.85.66

Closed 25 Dec–1 March. **TV**. **Car park**.

A good stopping place in the middle of the village, with an orange-tinted façade. It's run by an energetic young couple. Bedrooms are regularly decorated and new facilities added – all rooms have feather eiderdowns and hair dryers. Doubles 230F with en-suite bath. The dining room is cosy and there's a huge chimney piece where they light an open fire in winter. Honest, traditional food; *tripoux*, *truffade* (potato cake with Cantal cheese), chicken with Fourme cheese sauce. Menus, 74–160F, are good value. Half board is 225F per person. Friendly service.

🏠 |●| HÔTEL-RESTAURANT CASTEL HÔTEL 1904**

rue du Castel (Centre).
☎ 04.73.85.70.42 ➔ 04.73.85.84.39
Closed 15 Nov to Easter. **TV**. **Car park**.

This house belonged to Monsieur de Maintenon, the husband of Louis XIV's most influential mistress, then to the monks of Cluny, and, more recently, has been in the same family since 1904. If you have a taste for the simple pleasures of days gone by, you'll enjoy the genuine feel of this place. There are two restaurants: the tiny *Comptoir à Moustaches* is open every day and serves traditional cuisine based on local produce. The second, closed on Monday and Tuesday, serves gourmet cuisine delicately prepared by Jean-Luc Mouty, who trained with Robuchon. It's like cooking from a golden age: *pavé* of zander with cider, *fondant* of cabbage with stewed young rabbit, *cromesquis* of veal sweetbreads (fried and battered), and tomato salad with fresh chanterelles. The hotel is spacious and very quiet, and the refurbished rooms are affordable – 370F for a double with shower/wc or bath.

🏠|●| CAFÉ TALLEYRAND-CHEZ MARIE

Lieu-dit Talleyrand-Saint-Gervais; it's 3km on the D531 to Queuille, going towards the dam.
☎ 04.73.85.78.47
Closed Tues and Thurs evenings. **Car park**.

This remote farm on the road leading to the dam is a special place. For lunch or dinner, there's an appetising 65F *menu du jour* (80F on Sun), or you could have a plate of delicious *charcuterie* or an omelette made with eggs from the farm's own chickens. If you want to sample some of Marie's fabulous specialities, though – potato cake, stuffed rabbit or game (in season) – you'll have to give her a call the

night before to place your order. A glass of Auvergne costs only 5F. Free coffee.

SERVANT   63560 (6KM E)

🏠🏠|●| HÔTEL-RESTAURANT LE BEAU SITE

Gorges de la Sioule; take the N144 from Menat then the D915 for Gorges de Chauvigny.
☎ 04.73.85.50.65
Closed Wed and Thurs out of season, Dec and Feb; Jan reservations only.

Located in a really wonderful place that you reach on the road that follows the Sioule,this is a perfect place to stay while you explore the locality and do a bit of fishing. Six double rooms 160–240F. You can have a meal or just a drink on the terrace, overlooking the river. Menus 89–166F. The one at 135F lists nothing but house specialities: Rocquefort *terrine* with chestnuts, *pochouse* (a freshwater fish stew), veal with grain mustard sauce and iced *nougat* with sour cherries. The gastronomic menu includes a meat and a fish course. Free apéritif.

SAINT-MARTIN-SOUS-VIGOUROUX 15230

🏠🏠|●| LE RELAIS DE LA FORGE*

Centre; take the D990; it's west of Pierrefort.
☎ 04.71.23.36.90 ➔ 04.71.23.92.48
Closed Wed out of season. **Car park**.

A simple, welcoming country hotel with a restaurant that has a very substantial *menu du jour* for 70F. It includes a selection of *charcuterie*, and dishes such as farm-bred quail, and *truffade* (potato cake with Cantal cheese). Other menus up to 160F. About ten clean, simple rooms, 160–190F with bath. Half board is 190F. There's a lock-up for bikes and motorcycles. Free apéritif.

SAINT-POURÇAIN-SUR-SIOULE 03500

🏠🏠|●| HÔTEL-RESTAURANT LE CHÊNE VERT**

35 bd. Ledru-Rollin (Centre).
☎ 04.70.45.40.65 ➔ 04.70.45.68.50
Closed Sun evening and Mon out of season, and Jan. **TV**. **Car park**.

Service 12.15–1.30pm and 7.30–9pm. A classic, conventional establishment with excellent facilities. Pleasant rooms with fresh decor, 180F for a double with shower, 320F with bath. Good traditional cooking with lots of game in season, served in an attractive dining room. Menus 95–200F. Free coffee.

SAINT-URCIZE   15110

♠ |●| HÔTEL-RESTAURANT REMISE

East; take the D12 then the D112.
☎ 04.71.23.20.02 ➡ 04.71.23.20.02
Closed Mon evening. **Car park**.

A good, typical country inn that's very popular with anglers, hunters and cyclists. The home cooking is wonderful. Dishes of the day, 50F, may be *aligot*, nettle soup or trout – it depends what's good in the market. Menus 75–99F. Since so many anglers stay here, they make up picnic baskets to see you through a day's fishing, and Madame also makes dandelion jam from an old recipe. The owner can probably tell you anything you want to know about the region, from local history to the best walks and places to visit. Friendly, easy-going atmosphere. Doubles from 180F with shower and from 210F with shower/wc.

SALERS   15140

⅔ ♠ |●| HÔTEL DU BEFFROI**

rue du Beffroi (Centre); it's in the old town.
☎ 04.71.40.70.11 ➡ 04.71.40.70.16
Closed 31 Nov–31 March. **TV**. **Car park**.

This old building, which was renovated not long ago, looks onto a very busy pedestrian street. It has ten bedrooms, 230–260F for a double with shower or bath. There are some small, well laid-out attic rooms with a rooftop view. Substantial regional menus, 65F at lunch, then 80–120F, with *truffade* (potato cake with Cantal cheese), *potée*, *pounti* (a mixture of bacon and Swiss chard) and Salers beef, duck stew with chestnuts. It specialises in looking after independent travellers, being too small for groups. Good friendly atmosphere. 10% discount on the room rate March–Sept.

⅔ |●| LE DRAC

pl. Tyssandiers-d'Escous (Centre).
☎ 04.71.40.72.12

Open 8.30am–2am. In the early 1900s this early 16th-century house was used as a cellar for maturing Salers cheese – now it's a restaurant. It's in the nicest part of this well-preserved medieval town, which swarms with tourists at the height of the season. The house has been in the family for nine genera-

tions, so you'll feel a sense of that history. Good regional dishes on the 70F set menu and a dish of the day plus pizzas, salads and ice cream. They specialise in foreign beers. There's also a tearoom and a *crêperie*. It really buzzes in summer, but the staff are friendly and the service is fast. Free house apéritif.

THEIL (LE)   15140 (3KM W)

⅔ ♠ |●| HOSTELLERIE DE LA MARONNE***

Centre; take the D680 or the D37.
☎ 04.71.69.20.33
📧 hotelmaronne@cfi15.fr
Swimming pool. **Garden**. **TV**. **Car park**.

A substantial, 19th-century Auvergnat residence that has been tastefully renovated by a talented designer. Part of the *Relais du Silence* group, it's set amongst the greenery of a wide park and has a garden, swimming pool, tennis court and a peerless view over the valley. Monsieur Decock keeps thinking up new ideas while Madame, the chef, toils to produce the highest quality cuisine; zander in salted butter, braised and stuffed vegetables, and warm cake with bitter chocolate. Menus 150–280F. A place with class, reflected in the price of the rooms – doubles 520–820F with bath. Free apéritif.

FALGOUX (LE)   15380 (16KM NE)

♠ |●| HÔTEL-RESTAURANT L'ÉTERLOU**

Centre; take the D680 or the D37.
☎ 04.71.69.51.14 ➡ 04.71.69.53.26
Closed 1–22 Dec. **TV**. **Disabled access**. **Garden**.

Halfway between Salers and Puy-Mary, this hotel is beautiful, traditional and very welcoming, and the restaurant serves up hearty portions of tasty dishes. Set menus, 75–160F, give pride of place to Auvergne specialities – the veal sweetbreads with morels are great. Bedrooms are clean and pleasant. Doubles with bath 245–360F. Half board from 230F per person. Nice staff.

SAUGUES   43170

⅔ ♠ |●| LA TERRASSE**

cours Gervais (Centre).
☎ 04.71.77.83.10 ➡ 04.71.77.63.79
Closed Sun evening, Mon out of season, and 15 Dec–15 Jan. **TV**.

Service 12.15–2pm and 7.30–9.30pm. The owner is friendly and particularly attentive to his guests. Rooms have been refurbished, and doubles go for 265–350F with shower/wc or bath. The ones at the back are particularly quiet and have an uninterrupted view of the tour des Anglais. The brasserie serves classic dishes but the restaurant is a bit fancier, with specialities such as *croustillant* of calves' sweetbreads with ceps, apple tart with *foie gras*, lamb noisettes with garlic ,and *délice glacé* with verbena. Set menus 109–165F. Ultra-friendly service. Free apéritif.

THIERS   63300

🏕 🛏 HÔTEL DE LA GARE

30 av. de la Gare.
☎ 04.73.80.01.41 ➡ 04.73.80.01.41
Hotel closed 20–30 Aug. **Restaurant closed** Sun out of season

The cheapest and friendliest hotel in town. It's completely hidden under a covering of wisteria. Simple, clean rooms 90F with basin and 130–150F with shower or bath and wc on the landing. Friendly welcome and a small bar which can get noisy. Free apéritif or *digestif*.

🏕 |●| RESTAURANT LE COUTELIER

4 pl. du Palais; it's in the middle of the old town.
☎ 04.73.80.79.59
Closed Mon evening except July–Sept, Tues, three weeks in June, and 10 days in Oct.

Service noon–2pm and 7–10pm. Thiers is the centre of France's cutlery industry and this restaurant is in a converted cutler's workshop. There's an intriguing collection of old implements and knives displayed on the walls. This is a museum and a restaurant in one, and they're both first rate. Good classic dishes like Puy lentils with smoked bacon, sausage with cabbage, mutton tripe and *coq au vin*. Incredible value given the quality. Menus 75–140F. Free apéritif.

PONT-DE-DORE   63300 (3KM SW)

🛏 |●| HÔTEL-RESTAURANT CHEZ LA MÈRE DÉPAILLE

It's on the N89.
☎ 04.73.80.10.05 ➡ 04.73.80.52.22
Closed Sat lunchtime, Sun evening and Jan. **TV**.

This is a model of hotel-keeping and good cooking. You are always greeted warmly by the hospitable owners, who take every care to make your stay enjoyable. Menus,

75–230F, feature *fricassée* of frogs' legs and snails with leek *fondue* and Sancerre, calf's head with *ravigote* sauce, zander with Anjou wine, kid haunch with spiced bread, and medallion of venison. There's an enormous selection of cheeses, and the *crème brûlée* with kumquats is exceptional. Rooms for 260–390F with shower/wc or bath.

PESCHADOIRES   63920 (4KM SW)

🏕 |●| RESTAURANT LA FERME DES TROIS CANARDS

Lieu-dit Biton; take the N89, then the D212 and head for Maringues – turn left at the sign and you'll find the restaurant 300m further along.
☎ 04.73.51.06.70 ➡ 04.73.51.06.71
Closed Sun evening and a fortnight in early Jan.
Garden. Car park.

Service noon–2pm and 7–9pm. The most delightful place in the area. It's a beautifully renovated, single-storey farmhouse in the heart of the countryside but it's not far from the motorway exit. Dishes on the 128F set menu are perfectly cooked and presented; snails with bacon and stewed oxtail are both superb. Cheeses are matured to perfection and the desserts, like the chestnut mousse with almond milk, are light and delicate. Other menus up to 320F. Friendly, attentive staff. Terrace in summer. Free apéritif.

TOURNEMIRE   15310

🛏 |●| AUBERGE DE TOURNEMIRE

rue principale; take the D60, the D160 and the D260 – you'll find it about 20km north of Aurillac.
☎ 04.71.47.61.28 ➡ 04.71.47.68.76
Closed 10 Jan–10 Feb. **TV**. **Garden**.

Service noon–1.30pm and 7.30–8.30pm. In one of Cantal's prettiest villages, you'll find this delightful inn set on the side of a hill; the views of the valley are gorgeous at sunset. The six simple bedrooms are all very well maintained and one or two have lovely sloping ceilings. Double with shower/wc 200–250F, with bath from 220–270F. Good cooking in the restaurant, with Auvergnat dishes such as black pudding and a *fondue* of onions, and others including *foie gras*, fillet steak with morels, lamb kebabs with red pepper *coulis*, and lobster. Half board from 220–260F per person. By reservation only out of season.

VICHY   03200

⬆ À L'HÔTEL DE NAPLES**

22 rue de Paris (Centre); it's opposite the station.
☎ 04.70.97.91.33 ➡ 04.70.97.91.28
TV. Garden. Car park.

The hotel, in the most famous street in town, isn't luxurious but it's got modern facilities. Doubles 150F with basin/wc, 200F with bath. Ask for a room overlooking the pretty garden, which is full of flowers in summer. The street at the front is rather busy. Cordial welcome. They've done a deal with three nearby restaurants so they can offer a half-board deal at 260F per person.

⬆ |●| HÔTEL DU RHÔNE**

8 rue de Paris (Centre).
☎ 04.70.97.73.00 ➡ 04.70.97.48.25
Closed 1 Nov to Easter. TV. Disabled access. Car park.

The owner is a dynamo and quite a character; he'll cheerfully announce that he deliberately hasn't installed a lift so his guests get a bit of exercise. The decor is cosy and the rooms are clean and simple – go for one overlooking the patio, which is particularly lovely when the hydrangeas are in flower. Doubles 150–450F with shower/wc or bath. Menus range from 69F (weekday lunch) to 250F (gastronomic menu). The cooking is in the hands of the owner's wife, who lovingly prepares simple dishes like Maroilles tart (made with a strong cheese), sea bass with sorrel, ham hock in Saint-Pourçain and veal *escalope* with cream and wild mushrooms. Not a place for anyone on a diet.

🎿 ⬆ ARVERNA HÔTEL**

12 rue Desbrest (Centre).
☎ 04.70.31.31.19 ➡ 04.70.97.86.43
Closed 18–25 Oct and 2 Dec–3 Jan. TV. Garden. Pay garage at 30m.

Robert Pérol spent many years travelling the world staying in a vast number of hotels, and this place is the fruit of his experience. The bedrooms have been attractively decorated; double with shower/wc 220–270F, 240–300F with bath. All rooms are air-conditioned and particularly spacious. Full and half board in conjunction with nearby restaurants. 10% discount for a two-night stay.

🎿 ⬆ |●| LE PAVILLON D'ENGHIEN***

32 rue Callou; it's in the spa area of the town.
☎ 04.70.98.33.30 ➡ 04.70.31.67.82
Hotel closed 22 Dec–1 Feb. Restaurant closed Sun

evening and Mon.
Swimming pool.

Service noon–2pm and 7.30–9.30pm. This hotel-restaurant has been recently renovated and offers some of the best value for money in town. The spacious double rooms, 280–485F, are individualised and soundproofed. Weekday lunch menu 74F, a *menu terroir* at 100F and others up to 180F. They do a good slab of Charolais beef with blue Auvergne cheese sauce, *marbré* of young rabbit with herbs, escalope of salmon in Saint-Pourçain and rather good desserts. Nice swimming pool. 10% discount on the room rate.

⬆ |●| MIDLAND HÔTEL-RESTAURANT LE DERBY'S**

2–4 rue de l'Intendance (North).
☎ 04.70.97.48.48 ➡ 04.70.31.31.89
🅔 hotelmidlandvichy@wanadoo.fr
Closed 15 Oct–15 April. TV. Car park.

Service noon–2pm and 7–9pm. This hotel has retained its warmth and turn-of-the-twentieth-century style. Some rooms are traditionally decorated, others are more modern, but in each case the rooms are quiet and the facilities good. Doubles 295–345F with shower or bath, colour TV and phone. At lunchtime in the restaurant there's a spread of freshly cooked starters where you serve yourself; set menus 160F and two *formules* at 75F with wine included. Specialities include a quiche with Bougnat cheese, fillet of roast zander with shrimp sauce, *croustillant* of duck with bottled apples and honey, and a *bavarois* with bilberries.

|●| L'AUTRE SOURCE

10 rue du Casino (Centre).
☎ 04.70.59.85.68
Closed Sun, Mon and the first week in Sept.

Service noon–2.30pm and 7.30–midnight. Just behind the casino, this is probably the nicest and brightest restaurant in the centre of town – and a change from the "spa" feel you find in some places. The atmosphere is relaxed and cheerful. Inexpensive salads and sandwiches made mostly from local produce, and a cheese platter containing unusual varieties. A meal will cost around 60F. It's also a wine bar, and Patrice chooses the wines himself; he will gladly introduce you to the local vintages, some of which he serves by the glass at very reasonable prices. Opening hours are flexible, to ensure maximum customer satisfaction.

⚲|●| LA BRASSERIE DU CASINO

4 rue du Casino (Centre).
☎ 04.70.98.23.06 ➡ 04.70.98.53.17
Closed Sun evening, Wed and Nov. **Car park**.

Service noon–1.30pm and 7.30–10pm. This restaurant has got more character than any other in Vichy. Big pre-war brasseries have got a certain something, and this one, built in 1920 in a listed building, is no exception. The walls are covered in photos of stars who used to dine here after performing at the opera house. The *à la carte* menu has a long list of classic dishes and balanced set menus are also available, for 89 and 149F; golden roasted goat, calf's liver with onions and killer chocolate dessert. They serve a special dinner after the show has finished in the casino. Free apéritif.

CUSSET   03300 (1KM E)

⚲|●| LE BRAYAUD

64 av. de Vichy; it's on the outskirts coming from Vichy.
☎ 04.70.98.52.43
Closed Wed, Sat lunchtime, and a fortnight Aug/Sept.

Service 11.45am–2.30pm and 8pm–3am. This is where you come if you want to stay out late in Vichy, but more importantly it's the best place to eat meat around here. Exceptional steak – the *entrecôte* of Charolais beef weighs close on 400g and the *onglet* 300g, and you pay by weight and how it's cooked. Lunch menu 55F or at 89F, with a good variety of salads, a meat dish, cheese, and dessert. Enough to satisfy even the biggest appetites. Friendly staff. Free Kir or coffee.

ABREST   03200 (3KM S)

♠ |●| LA COLOMBIÈRE

Route de Thiers; take the D906, it's 2km after Abrest.
☎ 04.70.98.69.15 ➡ 04.70.31.50.89
Closed Sun evening, Mon, and mid-Jan to mid-Feb. **TV**. **Garden**. **Car park**.

Service noon–1.30pm and 7.15–9pm. An old pigeon tower converted into a restaurant high above the Allier. The cooking is imaginative and varied, mixing tradition and modern influences. Menus 96F to 290F. Good regional specialities and delicious home-made desserts. The home-baked bread is excellent and served with an impressive selection of cheeses. Four huge, bright, charming bedrooms. Doubles 265F with shower/wc, 325F with bath. The ones decorated yellow and green have a lovely view of the Allier.

BELLERIVE-SUR-ALLIER   03700 (3KM SW)

⚲ ♠ LA RIGON**

route de Serbannes.
☎ 04.70.59.86.46 ➡ 04.70.59.94.77
Closed Sun out of season, Dec and Jan. **Swimming pool**. **TV**. **Disabled access**. **Garden**. **Car park**.

A little haven of peace and quiet up in the Bellerives hills above Vichy, just five minutes from the town centre. You'll get the best of both worlds here – the excellent service and type of hours you'd expect from a hotel and the intimacy of a good-quality guesthouse. It's a beautiful building, with its own extensive grounds and the bedrooms, decorated in a rustic style, are all special in their own way. Doubles 300–360F with shower/wc. Hearty breakfast 37F. Brilliant swimming pool in a large 1900s glasshouse. Very friendly welcome. 10% discount Sept–June.

MAYET-DE-MONTAGNE (LE)   03250 (23KM SE)

|●| LA VIEILLE AUBERGE

9 pl. de l'Église; take the D62.
☎ 04.70.59.34.01
Closed Mon evening in season, Wed out of season, three weeks in Jan, and the last fortnight in Sept.

Service noon–2pm and 7–9pm. Time seems to have stopped in this old inn near the church in this wonderful little village deep in the Bourbonnais mountains. Decor of stone and wood brighted up by posters. Traditional dishes: hot goat's cheese salad with almonds, duck *confit*, *coq au vin* and wonderful home-made desserts. *Menu campagnard* at 55F with a selection of *charcuterie*, sausage and ham; others 68–140F. À la carte also available.

LAVOINE   03250 (30KM SE)

|●| AUBERGE CHEZ LILOU

Le Fau; take the D49.
☎ 04.70.59.37.49 ➡ 04.70.59.79.95
Closed Nov; reservations the rest of the year. **Garden**. **Car park**.

The dark woods and mountain views are breathtaking at 1000m, where *Chez Lilou* is to be found. It's always crowded on Sunday, and has an extremely good reputation locally. A simple, unpretentious restaurant where they use exclusively local produce in the kitchen. Menus up to 90F, including a *menu ouvrier* at 55F, offering two starters, two main courses and a choice of cheeses or desserts. Try their superb version of *bourbonnais* potato pie, locally farmed trout and delicious fruit tarts, particularly the bilberry one. They're really kind people, and make you feel like one of the family.

VIC-SUR-CÈRE   15800

🏃 🏠 |●| HÔTEL-RESTAURANT BEL HORIZON

rue Paul Doumer.
☎ 04.71.47.50.06 ➡ 04.71.49.63.81
🌐 info@hotel-bel-horizon.com
Closed 20 Nov–20 Dec and 4–25 Jan

A pleasant place on the edge of town where you'll get a warm greeting. It gets full at the weekends because the cooking is totally reliable. Menus 78–140F – the *menu du terroir* lists stuffed cabbage, *pounti* (a mixture of bacon and Swiss chard), trout with bacon and *coq au vin*. The chef rings the changes frequently, but his specialities are dishes such as potted rabbit, kid with girolles and zander with red butter. The home-made ice creams are as delicious as the pear charlotte. The dining room is unprepossessing except for the big bay window. Rooms are comfortable, 210–215F with shower/wc or bath. Free house apéritif.

VIEILLEVIE   15120

🏠 |●| HÔTEL LA TERRASSE**

rue principale; take the D141.
☎ 04.71.49.94.00 ➡ 04.71.49.92.23
Closed 15 Nov–1 April. **Swimming pool. TV. Disabled access. Garden. Car park.**

Service 12.30–2pm and 7.30–9pm. At 200m, this hotel is apparently at a lower altitude than any other in Cantal. It's to be found between an 11th-century château and the river Lot. Comfortable rooms, 250–260F for a double with shower/wc. Good outdoor facilities: a shaded terrace, beautiful swimming pool, garden and tennis courts. You'll enjoy the cooking. Menus 58–190F. Specialities are pig's trotters and veal sweet-

breads *en crépine*, fillets of roast char, and *délice* with walnuts.

VITRAC   15220

🏃 🏠 |●| L'AUBERGE DE LA TOMETTE**

Centre.
☎ 04.71.64.70.94 ➡ 04.71.64.77.11
🌐 latomette@wanadoo.fr
Closed Jan–March. **Swimming pool. TV. Disabled access. Car park.**

This is a delightful village inn set in a large flower-filled garden overlooking the countryside. The hotel is pleasant and has comfortable, ultra-modern double rooms at 295–320F depending on the season. A few duplexes are available for families. There's a new fitness centre. The cosy rustic dining room offers good hearty food and a choice of set menus, 98–200F. Try the chef's specialities: *crépinette* of pig's trotters with chanterelles, Puy lentil terrine and traditional dishes such as stuffed cabbage, *truffade* (potato cake with Cantal cheese) and *potée*. Mme Chausi is friendly and helpful. Free apéritif.

YSSINGEAUX   43200

🏃 🏠 |●| LE BOURBON**

5 pl. de la Victoire (Centre).
☎ 04.71.59.06.54 ➡ 04.71.59.00.70
Closed Sun evening, Mon except in July and Aug. **TV. Car park.**

The hotel has been refurbished and may have lost some of its character in the process. Doubles 290–360F. Handsome dining room decorated in English-garden style. The kitchen serves regional dishes that have been re-thought and made considerably lighter. Set menus from 95F (not available Sun) to 290F, which suit all tastes and pockets. Like the *à la carte* menu, they change every three months. You'll find a list of local suppliers beside the dishes. A reliable and first-rate establishment. Free coffee.

BOURGOGNE

21 Côte-d'Or

58 Nièvre

71 Saône-et-Loire

89 Yonne

ANCY-LE-FRANC   89160

⌂ |●| HOSTELLERIE DU CENTRE**

pl. du Château.
☎ 03.86.75.15.11 ┡➔ 03.86.75.14.13.
Closed 20 Dec–10 Jan. **Disabled access. Swimming pool. TV. Car park.**

In an old, much refurbished building, this hotel looks rather high-class though the atmosphere is easy-going.The cosy, restful bedrooms, decorated in pastel tones, go for 295F with bath. Those with extra facilities – mini-bar, bathroom and so on – are 390F. The restaurant – the larger of the two dining rooms is the prettier – offers traditional local dishes including snails, veal kidneys in a wine sauce, and *andouillette en croûte* in a Chablis sauce. Set menus are as varied as the portions are generous; a weekday lunch menu is 88F and others start from 120F. The terrace is open when the weather's good, and there's a heated indoor swimming pool.

CHASSIGNELLES   89160 (4KM SE)

🌿 ⌂ |●| HÔTEL DE L'ÉCLUSE No. 79

Chemin de Ronde; take the D905 then turn left.
☎ 03.86.75.18.51 ┡➔ 03.86.75.02.04
TV.

A quite delightful, family-run country hotel alongside the banks of the Burgundy canal. Grandmother still runs the bar, which has a terrace by the waterside. Her daughter runs the hotel. The rooms are charming and tastefully decorated at prices that are very reasonable for the region; doubles with shower/wc or bath at 250–280F. The cooking is done by the granddaugher, who specialises in local dishes: *œufs en meurette*, duck *bourguignon*, *terrine* of *andouillete*, and blackcurrant tart. Menus 100–125F. You can hire bikes to ride along the tow-path. Free coffee.

ARNAY-LE-DUC   21230

🌿 ⌂ HÔTEL LE CLAIR DE LUNE

4 rue du Four (Centre).
☎ 03.80.90.15.50 ┡➔ 03.80.90.04.64
TV. Car park.

Pretty hotel owned by the Poinsot family, who also run *Chez Camille* in the neighbouring street (see below). This place is very basic, offering bright, modern and attractive accommodation at 180F for a double with shower/wc. They do an overnight option including dinner and breakfast – you eat in the restaurant's flower-filled conservatory – for 430F for two, and you might also be tempted by the "gourmet half-board" at 680F for two. Children under eleven eat and sleep for free. Free house apéritif or *digestif*.

|●| CHEZ CAMILLE

1 pl. Édouard-Herriot (Centre).
☎ 03.80.90.01.38
TV. Car park.

This authentic, old-fashioned inn with the blue shutters, at the foot of the old town, is straight out of an operetta. Waitresses in flowery dresses enter the lounge, serving apéritifs with cheesy *choux* pastries and home-made ham sprinkled with chopped parsley, before leading you off to the conservatory, which has been converted into a dining room. Here you can sit

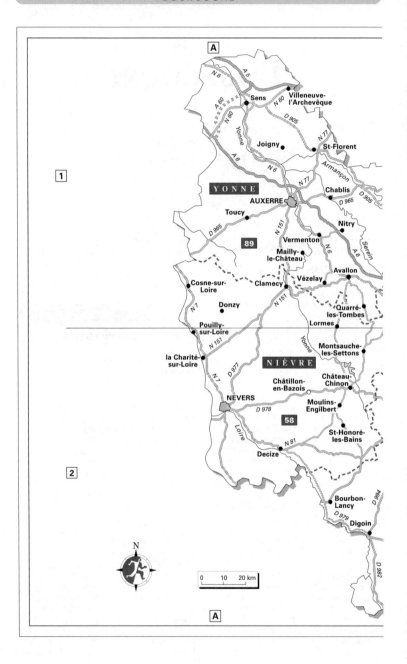

A

N 6
A 5
A 60
Sens
N 60
Villeneuve-
l'Archevêque
N 60
Yonne
D 905
N 77
Joigny
St-Florent
A 6
N 6
Armançon
1
N 77
YONNE
Chablis
D 905
AUXERRE
D 965
Toucy
N 151
Nitry
89
Vermenton
D 965
Mailly-
le-Château
N 6
A 6
Serein
Avallon
Cosne-sur-
Loire
Vézelay
Clamecy
N 151
Quarré-
les-Tombes
N 7
Donzy
Lormes
Pouilly-
sur-Loire
N 151
Yonne
Montsauche-
les-Settons
la Charité-
sur-Loire
N 7
D 977
NIÈVRE
Château-
Chinon
Châtillon-
en-Bazois
NEVERS
D 978
Moulins-
Engilbert
58
St-Honoré-
les-Bains
Loire
N 81
Decize
2
Bourbon-
Lancy
D 984
D 979
Digoin
D 982

N

0   10   20 km

A

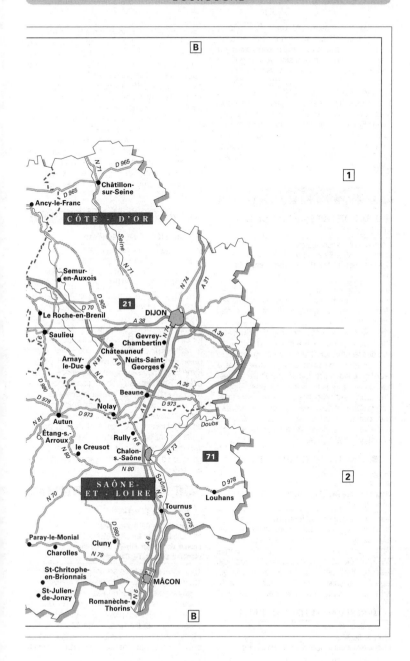

as though in a theatre and watch the amazing ballet of sous-chefs and kitchen staff, which is performed on a kind of stage raised up behind a large window – on one side you've got the pastry kitchen, on the other a tangled web of branches. The whole scene is enacted beneath a glass roof in a room full of pot plants and wicker armchairs. If you choose the cheapest menu at 108F you will find satisfying dishes like *terrine* and *bœuf bourguignon*. The others, 208–298F, will be an experience. The wine list is terrific, and the cellar is worth visiting. There are a few plush bedrooms; doubles with bath 450F. Free apéritif or coffee.

AUTUN 71400

⚐ 🏠 |●| HÔTEL-RESTAURANT DE LA TÊTE NOIRE**

1–3 rue de l'Arquebuse (Centre).
☎ 03.85.86.59.99 ➡ 03.85.86.33.90
Closed 15 Dec–18 Jan. **TV. Disabled access. Car park.**

An imposing frontage to this comfortable hotel which gets prettier every year. The rooms are charming and a good deal of work has repaired the ravages of time. Doubles go for 320F with shower/wc and 340F with bath. The food is good, with a starter, main course and dessert for 70F. There are other menus up to 250F and the dishes change three times a year but always list sound, attractive dishes: hot duck pâté with orange sauce, fillet of Charolais beef with bone marrow, monkfish with green peppercorns, scallops, and bread and butter pudding with apples. Wine is available by the glass and the carafe. Friendly reception. Free coffee.

⚐ |●| RESTAURANT CHATEAUBRIAND

14 rue Jeannin (Centre).
☎ 03.85.52.21.58
Closed Sun evening, Mon, a fortnight in Feb and three weeks in July.

Centrally positioned, just behind the town hall, this reliable establishment offers wonderful, quality cooking year in, year out. Classic dining room and good reception. Set menus 75–225F. Good meat specialities include beef fillet, rack of lamb, *andouillette*, and frogs' legs *Provençale*, fresh *foie gras* and salad with pan-fried prawns. Free coffee or *digestif*.

⚐ |●| RESTAURANT LE CHALET BLEU

3 rue Jeannin (Centre).
☎ 03.85.86.27.30
Closed Mon evening, Tues and a fortnight in Feb.

The outside's nothing to write home about – no way does it look like a chalet – but you can eat here with confidence. Philippe Bouché, who trained in the kitchens of the Elysée Palace, offers five set menus from 90F (weekdays only) to 265F. The cooking is imaginative – frogs' legs with baby onions, pigeon breast, tureen of Burgundy snails with wild mushrooms, Bresse chicken caramelised with ratafia and sour cherry brandy – and the helpings are generous. A wonderful dessert menu (no supplement) offers crystallised oranges pan-fried with saffron and served on chocolate flaky pastry, or a *gratin* of tropical fruit with passion fruit *sabayon*. Not to be missed. Free apéritif.

SAINT-LÉGER-SOUS-BEUVRAY 71990 (20KM W)

⚐ 🏠 |●| HÔTEL DU MORVAN

pl. de la Mairie (Centre); take the D3.
☎ 03.85.82.51.06 ➡ 03.85.82.45.07
Closed Mon and Tues evening out of season, Tues lunchtime in summer, and Dec–Jan.

This little village hotel, in the increasingly depopulated Morvan, survives by keeping its prices reasonable, and by prioritising the comfort and well-being of its guests. A good base for climbing mont Beuvray. Six bedrooms with a wonderful country feel; 180F with hand basin or 250F with shower/wc. The owner, Mme Els O'Sullivan, has a great sense of hospitality. She serves good, regional cooking, a Morvan snack for 55F available every day and set menus 65–150F; chicken *tariettes*, carp with parsley in Aligoté wine, free-range chicken *à la Morvandelle*, *pavé* of beef in pastry, *gratin* of snails, trout with smoked bacon and various salads. Children's menu 40F. 10% discount on the room rate for two nights or more-Sept–June.

ANOST 71550 (22KM NW)

⚐ 🏠 HÔTEL FORTIN**

Centre; take the D978, then the D2.
☎ 03.85.82.71.11 ➡ 03.85.82.79.62
Closed Mon except July–Aug, and Feb.
Disabled access. TV. Car park.

This hotel in the Morvan national park has an interesting history. The owner's a really friendly guy who explored jungles and deserts and oceans round the world before returning to his native land. He then played a vital role in giving a new lease of life to a village which, like so many others in the region, is threatened by decay and depopulation, by setting up this little hotel with its ancillary operations of pub, restaurant and travellers' lodge. It's basic, clean and inexpensive, and no two rooms are alike. Tourists and walkers enjoy meeting for a drink in the friendly ground-floor pub – a little oasis of conviviality in the middle of the Morvan tundra. The result is a kind of link, understanding even, between travellers and villagers. The owner runs *La Galvache* (see below). Doubles with shower or bath 220–260F. 10% discount for a two-night stay except at weekends and July–Aug.

🏃|●| LA GALVACHE

Grand-rue.
☎ 03.85.82.70.88
Open Easter to 11 Nov.

A wonderful little village restaurant, run by the owner of the *Hotel Fortin* (above), offering generous helpings of terrific regional cooking. Their 75F *menu du jour* (not served Sunday lunch) is amazing value for money. Dishes include *terrine*, zander fillet *à la Bourguignonne*, escalope of salmon with a leek *fondue*, delicious crayfish *à l'Américaine*, Charolais steak, or *croustade* of veal sweetbreads with morels, etc. And soft cream cheese to finish, of course. Other menus 88–195F. Free house apéritif.

DETTEY 71190 (28KM S)

🏃🔒|●| RELAIS DE DETTEY

Centre; take the D994, then the D224.
☎ 03.85.54.57.19 ➡ 03.85.54.57.09
Closed Mon evening and Christmas holidays.
Disabled access. TV. Car park.

Situated in one of the smallest villages of the Saône-et-Loire, and at the top of one of its highest "mountains", this inn is a must, but you should book if you want to stay – they have only one bedroom, 250F with bath. The charm of the village and the inn, and the delicious regional cooking are all good reasons to come. You'll get a friendly reception from Daniel and Monique. He's in charge of the dining room – a cosy, low-ceilinged room with two enormous exposed beams and a big fireplace – while she takes care of the cooking. It's popular with families for Sunday lunch. Everything is tasty and served in generous helpings, but the limited choice makes it easier to make up your mind. The cheapest menu at 75F is served every day, including weekends. On fine days you can eat on the terrace in the shade of the church while the horses frolic opposite. The accommodation is in a big studio with its own entrance – almost like a

two-roomed flat with its bedroom and a lounge that sleeps two extra people, a large bathroom and really nice decor. It costs 250F for two, and 90F for each extra guest. 10% discount on the room rate for a two-night stay.

AUXERRE 89000

🏃🔒 HÔTEL NORMANDIE**

41 bd. Vauban (West).
☎ 03.86.52.57.80 ➡ 03.86.51.54.33
Disabled access. TV. Car park. Garden.

Surrounded by a small garden, this fine large bourgeois house dates from the late-19th century. It's named after a famous French liner, and the atmosphere in the elegant, slightly dated hotel with its uniformed night porter is reminiscent of a luxury transatlantic cruise ship. The stylishly furnished rooms are very comfortable and extremely well looked after. Prices range from 300–430F for a double room with shower/wc or bath. A gym, sauna and billiard room are also at your disposal. 10% discount.

🔒 LE PARC DES MARÉCHAUX***

6 av. Foch (West).
☎ 03.86.51.43.77 ➡ 03.86.51.31.72
Disabled access. TV. Car park.

An air of calm, luxury and sheer self-indulgence surrounds this large establishment, which dates from the time of Napoleon III. You'll get an outstanding welcome, and Mme Hervé's legendary good humour is contagious. She's a devotee of Napoleon Bonaparte, and all the bedrooms are named after Marshals of France; all different, they are decorated in the best possible taste. Doubles 495–550F with bath. If it's fine, have breakfast outside beneath the ancient trees. The hotel also sometimes hosts concerts in the grounds. This is the loveliest hotel in Auxerre.

|●| LE JARDIN GOURMAND

56 bd. Vauban; it's in the pedestrian precinct, 50m from the carrefour de Paris.
☎ 03.86.51.53.52
Closed Tues, Wed, a fortnight in March and the first three weeks in Nov. **Disabled access. Car park**.

The chef here is an artist and frequently makes sketches of his dishes. His cooking is very inventive, and sometimes even adventurous. The service is perfection itself – the dining room staff will guide you expertly through the *à la carte* menu that changes according to the whim of the chef and to the season. The set menus, 210–290F, offer an ideal introduction to what is truly imaginative cooking. The *menu "Terre-Mer"*, for example, lists rabbit in sage jelly, Charolais beef steak, whipped egg wells. They have a small selection of Burgundies. The dining room is cosy, and there's a nice terrace for good weather. Best to book.

CHEVANNES   89240 (8KM SW)

🛊 |●| LA CHAMAILLE

La Barbotière – 4 route de Boiloup; from Auxerre, take the Nevers-Bourgnes road, then the D1.
☎ 03.86.41.24.80 📠 03.86.41.34.80
🅔 la/chemaille@wanadoo.fr
Closed Mon evening and Tues 1 March–31 Sept, Mon and Tues 1 Oct–28 Feb, and 2–18 Jan. **Car park**.

An excellent restaurant amid wonderful scenery within minutes of Auxerre. It's in an old, turreted farm smelling reassuringly of polish, with a little stream running through the garden where ducks splash about. There's an open fire when the weather gets cold. The cooking is traditional but shows considerable skill and the ingredients are first rate. There's a weekday menu at 150F then others 180–345F, or give the 300F *formule* a whirl. Wine by the glass at prices that won't make you wince. Two doubles with shower 250F or 300F with shower/wc.

MONTIGNY-LA-RESLE   89230 (12KM NE)

🎿 🛊 |●| HÔTEL-RESTAURANT LE SOLEIL D'OR**

How to get there: on the N77.
☎ 03.86.41.81.21 📠 03.86.41.86.88
Disabled access. TV. Car park.

The hotel and restaurant are housed in old farmhouses that have been thoroughly renovated. The rather pretty bedrooms with shower/wc or bath cost 330F. The kitchen turns out classical dishes that are consistent in quality and sometimes show a touch of imagination. The weekday lunch menu, 79F, includes a $\frac{1}{4}$ litre of wine, then others 98–330F; try the pan-fried *foie gras* with fruit or the calf sweetbreads in Chablis. Wine by the glass is rather expensive. Essential to book in the hotel. Free Kir.

VINCELOTTES   89290 (14KM SE)

🛊 |●| AUBERGE LES TILLEULS

12 quai de l'Yonne.
☎ 03.86.42.22.13 📠 03.86.42.23.51
Closed Wed evening and Thurs fromOct to Easter, and 18 Dec–18 Feb. **TV**.

A lovely place to stop overlooking the Yonne and shaded by lime trees, quiet at night. Doubles with shower/wc at 315F or 370–450F with bath. When the weather is dismal the restaurant, full of flowers and paintings, will cheer you up. If the weather's fine, sit on the shady waterside terrace. The cooking, like the chef, has considerable character and the dishes change constantly. Dishes feature unusual produce like Chinese artichokes, Jerusalem artichokes, swedes or whatever the market in Auxerre has that's freshest and best. The chef particularly likes to use wild rather than farmed fish. The 150F menu is served on weekdays before 1.30pm and 8.30pm, then there are others 228–285F.

AVALLON   89200

🛊 |●| HÔTEL-RESTAURANT DES CAPUCINS

6 av. Paul Doumer; the road leads to the station.
☎ 03.86.34.06.52 📠 03.86.34.58.47
Private car park.

The bright dining room is decorated with a collection of biscuit pots in glass or opaline. The cooking is quite remarkable and prepared by a chef who's a real pro. He makes everything himself, from the *foie gras* to the *nougat* and buys his ingredients and produce from local suppliers that he has sought out himself. There's a weekday menu at 90F then others 127–260F. Wines served by the glass. The rooms are all individual and quiet, even the ones overlooking the road; doubles with all facilities 300F.

🛊 DAK'HÔTEL**

119 rue de Lyon–Étang des Minimes (Southeast); it's on the edge of town, going towards Dijon.
☎ 03.86.31.63.20 📠 03.86.34.25.28
Disabled access. TV. Car park.

Entirely new hotel, with all mod cons. The warmth of the reception makes up for the starkness of the building. Lots of little extras such as tea or coffee, a magazine, a chocolate on your pillow – at no extra cost. No restaurant, but you can have a meal on a tray for 70F. Doubles with bath from 310F.

🎿 |●| RELAIS DES GOURMETS

47 rue de Paris; it's 200m from the main square.
☎ 03.86.34.18.90
🅔 relaisdesgourmets@wanadoo.fr
Closed Sun evening and Mon, 1 Nov–1 May. **Car park**.

This used to be the *Hôtel de Paris* in the days when Avallon was still a staging post and, unlike its contemporaries, which have gone to rack and ruin, has found a new lease of life. It's no longer a hotel but you can have a good meal in a good-humoured, colourful atmosphere. Set menus 85F (served daily except Easter Sun), 152F and 192F. The chef prepares fish with as much skill as he does the meat from neighbouring Charolais herds. There's a terrace in summer. Free coffee.

L'ISLE-SUR-SEREIN   89440 (15KM NE)

🎄 🛏 |●| AUBERGE DU POT D'ÉTAIN

24 rue Bouchardat.
☎ 03.86.33.88.10 ➡ 03.86.33.90.93
Closed Sun evening except July–Aug, and Mon.
TV. Car park.

This charming, tiny country inn is one of the best places in the region to eat. The chef trained with some of the big names and his wonderful cooking is a mixture of the traditional and the modern. There's a *menu du jour* at 108F (not available Sun), and others 146–308F. They have the most fantastic cellar, and a spectacular wine list featuring about 600 vintages. Nine pleasant rooms, from 280F for a double with shower/wc to 420F for a small suite. The ones at the back of the flower-filled courtyard are quieter. Free coffee.

BEAUNE   21200

🎄 🛏 HÔTEL GRILLON

21 route de Seurre (East).
☎ 03.80.22.44.25 ➡ 03.80.24.94.89

Why do people make do with chain hotels, when you can fall into bed after a visit to the wine cellar and wake up to the sound of chirping birds in a place oozing charm? The rooms have style. Doubles 290F with shower and 390F with bath. In the summer, you can eat breakfast in the garden, or on the terrace of this old family house. 10% discount Nov–March.

🎄 🛏 LE HOME**

138 route de Dijon (North); it's at the Beaune-Sud exit of the A31, on the outskirts of Beaune, going towards Dijon.
☎ 03.80.22.16.43 ➡ 03.80.24.90.74
Disabled access. **TV. Garden. Car park**.

Tucked away at the bottom of a garden, this old Burgundian house swathed in Virginia creeper makes a very pleasant place to stop. The decor may raise a few eyebrows or provoke a few winces on occasions but the wel-

come is as charming as the location. Two annexes have bedrooms that lead straight out into the garden. 325–450F for a double with shower/wc or bath. Ideal place for relaxing. Good breakfast 35F. 10% discount Dec–June.

🎄 🛏 |●| HÔTEL CENTRAL***

2 rue Victor-Millot (Centre).
☎ 03.80.24.77.24 ➡ 03.80.22.30.40
e hotel.central.beaune@wanadoo.fr
Closed 22 Nov–18 Dec. **TV**.

An aptly named hotel that everyone, from trendy motorcyclists to fun-loving couples, enjoys. Spacious bedrooms with good facilities at 450F with shower/wc or bath. The cooking (which might look a bit austere, but isn't) also enjoys a good reputation. The owner digs into his books of magic spells, unearthing 17th- and 18th-century dishes that he interprets in his own way. Try the *coq au vin à l'ancienne* or the *oeufs en meurette à l'andouille* . The 98F menu is served all week and there are others 135–220F. 10% discount on the room rate.

|●| AU BON ACCUEIL

La Montagne; take the D970, turn right, and at the Beaune exit go towards La Montagne.
☎ 03.80.22.08.80
Closed 26 Dec–5 Jan and the second fortnight in Aug.
Car park.

The town centre is often more popular with tourists than locals, but this restaurant is more of a local preserve. It's filled with families on Sunday lunchtime, when the menu includes *terrine*, *crudités* and *pâté* (as much as you can manage) and roast beef, followed by a cheese platter and home-made tart. If you like good Burgundian fare, you are well provided for: weekday lunch menu 75F and others 105–140F. Typical local reception and wonderful terrace.

|●| RESTAURANT "LE P'TIT PARADIS"'

25 rue Paradis (Centre).
☎ 03.80.24.91.00
Closed Mon evening, Tues, 19 Nov–3 Dec, last week in Feb, the first week in March and 12–20 Aug.

The road to paradise was a gastronomic purgatory until this gem of a restaurant opened up opposite the Musée du Vin. It's painted in colours as fresh as the cooking, which is very reasonably priced. Jean-Marie Daloz is a fine chef. Sample the snail soup with Aligoté wine, the zander with red wine or the duck breast with honey. Weekday menu at 75F and others 95–165F. Choice of wines at equally good prices. Terrace in summer.

⦿ RESTAURANT LE VERGER

21 route de Seurre (East).
☎ 03.80.24.28.05
Closed Tues, Wed lunchtime and Feb.

Shared entrance with the *Hôtel Grillon*. The architecture of this wonderful restaurant is pretty daring. The smiling, rosy-cheeked owner, with the help of her husband, is slowly building up a local reputation for his regional dishes, such as poached *œufs en meurette bœuf bourguignon*, and adding a few others like tureen of Burgundy snails with bottled tomatoes, a cream soup of baby vegetables, and veal sweetbreads with pistachios and mussels.The cooking is light and well seasoned. Lunch menu 90F or 125–255F. Madame is from a wine family in Gevrey-Chambertin, so she or her husband will help you choose a wine to suit your taste. Enjoy the terrace in summer.

⦿ RESTAURANT LA CIBOULETTE

69 rue de Lorraine (Centre); it's in the old part of town, opposite the theatre.
☎ 03.80.24.70.72
Closed Mon and Tues.

The renovated premises are small and the decor restrained. Two set menus at good prices (99F and 134F), bring in the tourists and also the locals, which is reassuring. Choose from: *émincé* of calves' feet in *vinaigrette*, poached eggs in a red wine sauce, and beef steak with Époisses cheese. An ideal spot to gather your strength for a tour of the Hospices or of the city's numerous wine cellars. Friendly atmosphere.

⚹ ⦿ LE BENATON

25 faubourg Bretonnière; it's five minutes from the town centre, heading towards Autun.
☎ 03.80.22.00.26
Closed Wed, Thurs lunchtime, a week in July and a week in Nov.

Though not ideally located, this restaurant is worth seeking out. The cooking is of the traditional local variety but is by no means dull: pan-fried snails, courgette caviar with tomato sauce, and custard cream. The 130F *menu du marché* is a model of the type, and there are others at 180F and 255F. The wines are good and reasonable. An ideal place to stop before carrying on to Pommard or Santenay. Free Kir.

LEVERNOIS   21200 (4KM SE)

⌂ LE PARC**

rue de Golf: take the D970 in the direction of Verdun-sur-le-Doubs then turn left.

☎ 03.80.22.22.51 ➠ 03.80.24.21.19
Closed 2 Dec–19 Jan. **Disabled access**. **TV**. **Car park**.

An old house that is now a charming hotel. The trees in the grounds are a hundred years old and full of birds. The ideal spot to be lazy or energetic. The nearby tennis court, golf course and pool mean you can exhaust yourself to your heart's content should you feel so inclined. In the evening, you can sit in the bar with a glass in your hand and chat about your day with your fellow guests. The bedrooms are full of character and all different. Doubles 210F with hand basin, 270F with shower/wc or 320F with bath. Lovely – it's best to book.

BOUZE-LÈS-BEAUNE   21200 (7KM NW)

⦿ LA BOUZEROTTE

It's on the side of the D970.
☎ 03.80.26.01.37
Closed Mon evening, Tues, Feb, a week in Sept and the Christmas–New Year holidays. **Car park**.

A real country inn, ten minutes from the centre of Beaune, with real Burgundians, real Burgundy accents, and real Burgundy cooking. Real flowers (so unusual nowadays you have to mention the fact!) decorate the old wooden tables, and there is an old-fashioned sideboard and a fireplace where a fire burns in cold weather. More to the point, they also have good wines from small local vineyards which Christine, who used to be a wine waiter, can recommend. The freshest produce of the highest quality are used in the dishes nd the presentation is lovely. Menus 89–268F.

LADOIX-SERRIGNY   21550 (7KM NE)

⦿ LES COQUINES

N74 – Buisson.
☎ 03.80.26.43.58
Closed Wed, Thurs and a fortnight in Feb. **Car park**.

On one side of this old house there's an old storeroom and on the other large windows offer views of the surrounding countryside. They know all about cooking and looking after guests. Stick to one of the set menus and you will eat without spending a fortune. The one at 165F, which serves *coq au vin* and calf's head salad with a *sauce gribiche*, is quintessentially good Burgundian food. Others up to 245F.

BOURBON-LANCY   71140

⚹ ⌂ ⦿ LE GRAND HÔTEL***

Parc Thermal.

☎ 03.85.89.08.87 ➡ 03.85.89.25.45
Closed end Oct to end March. **Disabled access**. **TV**.
Car park.

This is a place for people with rheumatism or heart problems. There's a covered walkway between the hotel and the hydro. The town looks a bit shabby, but it's quiet and restful and the hotel is typical of a spa town – showy and oversized. Elderly people play *pétanque* in the extensive grounds. The rooms are clean, the bathrooms enormous, and the prices reasonable: doubles 371–482F with shower/wc or bath. The restaurant offers set menus with a range of prices, 69–128F. Classical dishes and a fairly limited choice of wine. 10% reduction on the room rate April, May and Oct. Free coffee.

CHABLIS   89800

🏠 |O| HOSTELLERIE DES CLOS***

rue Jules-Rathier.
☎ 03.86.42.10.63 ➡ 03.86.42.17.11
📧 host.des@wanadoo.fr
Closed 20 Dec–18 Jan.
Disabled access. **TV**. **Car park**.

The waiters wear tails, the tinkling chandeliers gleam luxuriously and Madame sports elaborate, chunky jewellery. In this hostelry, housed in a former hospital and chapel, the illuminated gardens are delightful, the waiters don't take themselves too seriously, and Madame's laugh makes you feel welcome. Her husband uses only the finest ingredients and his best-known dishes are subtly flavoured with Chablis, so take your credit card – menus start at 210F and go all the way up to 450F. If you're eating *à la carte*, choose just a main course and a dessert and they won't object. Double rooms with bath 350–600F.

|O| LE VIEUX MOULIN DE CHABLIS

18 rue des Moulins (Southeast).
☎ 03.86.42.47.30
Closed 25 Dec and 1 Jan. **Car park**.

A lot of water – from the Serein river – has flowed under the bridge since this restaurant started up in a house that used to belong to a wine-growing family. The large dining room has walls of local stone, The cooking is well up to standard and the prices are fair and decent. The best dishes are the local ham in Chablis and the beef fillet in Pinot noir. And the rest isn't bad either. Menus 99–260F.

LIGNY-LE-CHÂTEL   89144 (15KM NW)

🎿 🏠 |O| RELAIS SAINT-VINCENT**

14 Grande-Rue (Centre).
☎ 03.86.47.53.38 ➡ 03.86.47.54.16
Disabled access. **TV**. **Car park**.

The village and the street are from another age, and the ancient half-timbered house dates all the way back to the 12th century. It has been tastefully converted by the welcoming owner and the rooms have all mod cons. Doubles 245–400F with shower/wc or bath. Set menus 78–160F, the cheapest being available every day. Excellent, authentic local dishes are produced by the chef. There's a remarkable cheese selection including a local Époisses. You can sit out in the quiet flowery courtyard. Free Kir.

|O| AUBERGE DU BIEF

2 av. de Chablis; it's next to the church.
☎ 03.86.47.43.42
Closed Sun evening, Mon and Tues evenings in season, evenings out of season.

Very popular locally for lunch on Sunday. There are not many tables so it's advisable to arrive early or book. Otherwise you might find a small space on the terrace. Well presented dishes, *terrines*, *foie gras* and so on, and the cooking is refined. Good value for money with a first menu at 98F and others at 115–260F. Simple, charming, smiling welcome. There's a big public car park nearby.

CHAGNY   71150

🎿 🏠 HÔTEL DE LA FERTÉ**

11 bd. de la Liberté (Centre).
☎ 03.85.87.07.47 ➡ 03.85.87.37.64
Closed Christmas. **TV**.

This substantial house has been attractively refurbished and turned into a welcoming hotel. There are thirteen charming rooms with open fires, flowery wallpaper and antique furniture. And, without detracting from the period style, all the bathrooms are modern. The rooms are also efficiently soundproofed. A country breakfast is served in a room overlooking the garden, or outside in good weather. Doubles 250–300F with en-suite bath. 10% discount weekdays only.

|O| LAMELOISE****

36 pl. d'Armes (Centre).
☎ 03.85.87.08.85

losed Tues and Thurs lunchtimes, and Wed.
TV. **Car park**.

The third generation of the Lameloise family now runs this establishment. The decoration in the five small dining rooms is stylish – stone walls, hefty beams, comfortable chairs, fresh flowers and so on. It attracts a varied clientele from local businessmen and committed foodies to well-heeled couples. The service is discreet, precise and perfect. The cooking has its foundations in local produce: snail ravioli, *gâteau* of liver with crayfish, roast pigeon with truffle fragments, *aiguillettes* of duck with spiced bread, and caramelised pears in a flaky pastry case. In between each course, delicious morsels, both savoury and sweet, appear out of nowhere. The desserts are served in gargantuan portions. Menus 430F and 650F.

CHASSEY-LE-CAMP   71150 (5KM SW)

⚘ ☎ |●| AUBERGE DU CAMP ROMAIN**

How to get there: take the D974 in the direction of Santenay then turn left; it's down the hill from the ruins of a Roman camp.
☎ 03.85.87.09.91 ➡ 03.85.87.11.51
📧 Auberge.du.Camp.Romain@wanadoo.fr
Closed 1 Jan–10 Feb. **Swimming pool. Disabled access**. **TV**. **Car park**.

The inn overlooks a lush green valley and you'd think you were in the mountains. It's a sort of mini *Club-Med* with tennis courts, crazy-golf, a heated pool and even a helipad! The inn has 44 spacious rooms with en-suite bathrooms for 340–410F and there are some for families who spend their whole holidays here. Set menus 135–242F Specialities include lobster ravioli with fresh herbs, prawns with *tabbouleh*, *crème brûlée* with lime, ice creams or spiced bread. Good itineraries for hiking and biking, while the less actively inclined can play billiards. Nice place for a weekend of sport with the family or for lounging around, though not ideal for a romantic weekend *à deux*. Free apéritif.

CORPEAU   21190 (22KM NE)

⚘ |●| L'AUBERGE DU VIEUX VIGNERON

Route de Beaune (Centre); it's opposite the town hall.
☎ 03.80.21.39.00
Closed Mon, the first three weeks in Feb and end of Aug. **Car park**.

The village itself wouldn't merit a special trip, were it not for this inn. In the dining room, there's an atmosphere of a grape harvest supper: old tables, old furniture, a grandfa-

ther clock and a typical, wide fireplace where lamb cutlets and *andouillettes* are cooked. The calling-card dishes include chicken liver salad, omelette cooked over the fire and duck breast served rare. House wines include a Chassagne-Montrachet and a Puligny that are affordable. Menus 85–115F. Simple. Good. Free Kir.

CHALON-SUR-SAÔNE   71100

⚘ ☎ HÔTEL SAINT-JEAN

24 quai Gambetta (South).
☎ 03.85.48.45.65 ➡ 03.85.93.62.69
Disabled access. **TV**.

Booking advisable. If you have to spend a night in Chalon, the *Saint-Jean* is the only hotel on the riverbank and away from the traffic. The mansion has been tastefully decorated by a former restaurateur who gave up cooking in favour of hotel-keeping. Friendly and professional staff. A quiet, clean and welcoming establishment with magnificent views, where everything pleases and the prices are reasonable. Large double rooms decorated in fresh colours go for 300F. You feel there should be a preservation order on the handsome imitation marble staircase that dates from the late-19th century. 10% discount Oct–March.

⚘ ☎ HÔTEL CLARINE

35 pl. de Beaune (Centre).
☎ 03.85.90.08.00 ➡ 03.85.90.08.01
TV. **Car park**.

Large hotel in a renovated old house. Accommodation is in the main building or in two annexes, the more recent of which overlooks an inner courtyard and is quieter. Some rooms have parquet floors, open fireplaces and old furniture. Doubles 305–360F. Breakfast 35F. There's a sauna, a solarium and a gym. 10% discount for a two-night stay, or two for the price of one at the weekend.

☎ |●| LE SAINT-GEORGES

32 av. Jean-Jaurès (Centre); it's opposite the station.
☎ 03.85.90.80.50 ➡ 03.85.90.80.55
Closed Sat lunchtime and 1–10 Aug.

A classic, station hotel. All rooms have been refurbished with good facilities, though they are somewhat lacking in personality. The armchairs will appeal to fans of modern design. All in all, it's value for money with double rooms 400–450F. The gastronomic restaurant has menus 110–160F but the bistro is more friendly and you can have a meal of Burgundian specialities for around 100F. Weekday menu 125F or 170–200F. The food is of good quality in both restaurants.

🎋 |●| RESTAURANT RIPERT

31 rue Saint-Georges (Centre).
☎ 03.85.48.89.20
Closed Sun, Mon, a week in July and a week end Aug.

Alain Ripert has created an institution and offers set daily menus 77–170F. The simple cooking changes constantly, depending on what is available at the market. The dining room is small with a few touches reminiscent of a 1950s bistro (adverts, enamel signs and so on) and fills up rapidly with locals. Main courses include escalope of veal sweetbreads with spices and honey, monkfish stew with saffron, *croustillant* of oxtail, lobster tail *timbale*, and, for dessert, warm *gratin* of raspberries, *nougat* with blackcurrant sauce, and hot apple tart. Unusually for this part of the world, some good wines are available in carafes. Free coffee.

|●| RESTAURANT DU MARCHÉ

7 pl. Saint-Vincent (Southeast); it's in the market square, very close to the cathedral.
☎ 03.85.48.62.00
Closed Sun evening, Mon and a fortnight in late Aug.

This is a rustic-looking restaurant that serves three generous set menus at 88F, 114F and 164F and lots of dishes of the day, which is very common in these parts. Imagination is the extra ingredient in the flavoursome dishes: soufflé of artichokes, goat with cream and garlic sauce, fresh frogs' legs in Aligitoé wine, Paris-Brest with Burgundy snails, and sole *millefeuille* with apples or cider. Wine comes from tiny local vineyards.

|●| RESTAURANT CHEZ JULES

11 rue de Strasbourg (Southeast); it's on île Saint-Laurent.
☎ 03.85.48.08.34
Closed Sat lunchtime, Sun, a fortnight in Feb and 1–15 Aug.

This small restaurant, located in a quiet neighbourhood, is popular with the locals, and the salmon-pink walls, sturdy beams, copper pots, paintings and old sideboard add to the cosy atmosphere. The cooking is inventive. *Menu du jour* at 95F, others up to 175F; mackerel charlotte with new potatoes, boned, sautéd rabbit with pickled tomatoes and at least another eight imaginative dishes, then dessert or fresh, creamy cheese. Good wine list, available by the glass, bottle and carafe. A post-prandial stroll along the embankment will be called for.

🎋 |●| LE GOURMAND

13 rue de Strasbourg (Southeast); it's on île Saint-Laurent.
☎ 03.85.93.64.61
Closed Mon evening and Tues.

Everything in this establishment is yellow, beige or golden, and the owner has a similarly sunny smile. Richly decorated, with tastefully stylish decor and atmosphere, but without being posh or over the top. There are lots of regulars, and everyone seems to know each other. Faultless presentation, refined cooking and combinations of tasty herbs make for very successful sauces, and the fish dishes are cooked to perfection. There are several house classics but try the crayfish tails with lentils, the roast pigeon or the pig's trotter *tournedos* with *foie gras*. Menus 96–195F. Free apéritif.

LUX-SAINT RÉMY   71390 (4KM W)

|●| MA CAMPAGNE

quai Bellevue (Centre).
☎ 03.85.48.93.80 ➡ 03.85.93.33.72
TV. Car park.

A huge country house, standing alone on the banks of the Saône. It's lovely. The rooms have been given the names of precious stones and decorated to match the stone's colour. It's a simple idea and it works. Rooms from 250F and the difference in price depends on the size – the biggest are suites. Sadly, they don't have views of the river. On sunny days, you eat on a wide terrace protected by an awning, accompanied by bird song. The classic cooking is very decent and the chef has a preference for fish dishes. Good quality service and the welcome you get from the female owner is excellent. Menus 99–179F. There are games for the kids and you can walk along the river.

BUXY   71390 (15KM SE)

|●| HÔTEL FONTAINE DE BARANGES

rue de la Fontaine de Baranges (Centre).
☎ 03.85.94.10.70 ➡ 03.85.94.10.79
ℯ Hotel.Fontaine.de.Baranges@wanadoo.fr
TV. Disabled access. Car park.

A substantial, early-19th-century residence in grounds planted with shady trees, right next to a very pretty old stone wash house. The whole place has been completely restored, and the attractively decorated rooms are spacious and peaceful; all come with bath or shower. Three of them and three suites have private terraces overlooking the park. Doubles 290–490F depending on the size; the suites cost 650F. There is no restaurant but there is a charming bar.

CHARITÉ-SUR-LOIRE 58400

☎ HÔTEL LE BON LABOUREUR**
quai Romain-Mollot; it's on the Île de Loire.
☎ 03.86.70.22.85 ➡ 03.86.70.23.64
TV. Garden.

An ancient building where each room is a different size (some sleep three or four people) and each has different facilities. They have all been refurbished. Doubles cost 210–290F with shower/wc or bath. There is an interior garden with a terrace and a bar. Reasonable prices and a warm, smiling welcome.

🎐|●| L'AUBERGE DE SEYR
4 Grande-Rue (Centre).
☎ 03.86.70.03.51
Closed Sun evening, Mon and a fortnight at the end Aug–beginning Sept.

A simple, unpretentious restaurant serving cooking with character. The *menu du jour* at 67F lists very tasty home-made salmon *rillettes*, perch fillet with sorrel, selected cheeses and a respectable home-made dessert. Other menus 95–168F. Free coffee.

|●| AUBERGE DE LA POULE NOIRE
9 pl. des Pêcheurs; it's next to the Saint-Laurent church.
☎ 03.86.70.10.71 ➡ 03.86.57.66.99

Housed in a 12th-century priory, a long, dining room with a grandiose blond wood staircase leading up to a mezzanine. In summer, it's much cooler inside than under a sun shade on the south-facing terrace. Carefully prepared dishes which draws on traditional Burgundian dishes but adds a few new ideas as well. The weekday menu costs 95F then there are others 145–195F. Dishes *à la carte* around 100F. One of the good tables in town. Welcoming greeting.

CHAROLLES 71120

🎐 ☎ |●| HÔTEL-RESTAURANT DE LA POSTE***
2 av. de la Libération (Centre).
☎ 03.85.24.11.32 ➡ 03.85.24.05.74
Closed Sun evening, Mon and 15 Nov–15 Dec. **TV. Car park**.

This is a very important establishment in the Charolais, run by Daniel Doucet, the ambassador of Burgundy gastronomy. His cooking is

as fresh and tasty as ever. The dining room is richly decorated, and the service is faultless and particularly attentive, but this place is definitely not affected. You'll get great advice on wine to suit your taste and choice of dishes – don't miss the Charolais rib steak with Guérande salt, served on a hot plate, *truffe* of potatoes with snails in garlic sauce, *cassolette* of scallops with a leek *fondue*, or *croustillant* of veal sweetbreads with morels and chanterelle mushrooms. Magnificent cheese platter and desserts. Set menus at 130F (during the week), then 160–310F. Eat out under the maple trees in the interior garden on fine days. Comfy bedrooms at 280–360F. Free coffee.

🎐 ☎ |●| HÔTEL-RESTAURANT LE LION D'OR**
6 rue de Champagny (Centre).
☎ 03.85.24.08.28 ➡ 03.85.88.30.96
Closed Sun evening and Mon except July–Aug.
Swimming pool. TV. Car park.

This 17th-century coaching inn is on the banks of a small river. Large double rooms with shower go for 330–350F. Numbers 23 and 25 have a view of the river. The top-notch restaurant serves good regional cooking, with exceptional meat dishes, as you would expect in Charolais country. Set menu 80F except Sunday and public holidays, with others 140–250F. Free apéritif.

BEAUBERY 71220 (12KM SE)

🎐|●| AUBERGE DE BEAUBERY
La Gare; take the N79 from Charolles or Mâcon, then the D79.
☎ 03.85.24.84.74
Closed Wed and Christmas holidays.

Little inns like this, offering a complete meal with wine and coffee for 65F, are few and far between. Basic home cooking, lovingly prepared and served in generous portions, is dished up in a dining room decorated with prints and a kitschy old clock. It's full of regulars and local travelling salesmen. You can get a sandwich filled with local ham, omelette and soft white cheese for 55F. There's a weekday menu, with frogs' legs at 65F, and others, 100–120F, listing Charolais steak, *salmis* of guinea fowl with mushroom sauce, bacon and potatoes, and excellent *coq au vin*. Free coffee.

CHÂTEAU-CHINON 58120

☎ |●| HÔTEL DU PARC-LE RELAIS GOURMAND**

route de Nevers; it's on the left as you leave the village on the Nevers road.
☎ 03.86.79.44.94 ➡ 03.86.79.41.10
Closed Sun evening 15 Nov–15 March, and Feb. **TV**. **Car park**.

This modern, modestly functional hotel looks a little like a rather sombre chain hotel; all the corridors and rooms are identical. The park concerned is the Morvan national park. Double rooms with bath go for 265F. Though the hotel offers little more than a place to sleep, you can enjoy a decent, cheap meal in the restaurant. The 60F menu, not available on Sunday, is particularly good value, and there are others 95–210F.

CHÂTEAUNEUF   21320

🏠 |●| HOSTELLERIE DU CHÂTEAU**

How to get there: take the Pouilly-en-Auxois exit off the A6.
☎ 03.80.49.22.00 ➡ 03.80.49.21.27
Closed Mon and Tues except July–Aug, Dec and Jan. **Disabled access**.

Almost all the 12th- and 14th-century houses in this picturesque hilltop village have been bought by outsiders. Standing in the shadow of a 12th-century castle, the hotel may look medieval but it's modern and comfortable. It would be nice if the welcome were a bit warmer and the *à la carte* menu a bit more imaginative. Set menus 140–220F with traditional local dishes. Doubles 270–380F with shower, 430F with bath; some look out over the countryside. 10% discount on the room rate for stays of two nights except July–Aug and weekends.

🍴 |●| LE GRILL DU CASTEL

☎ 03.80.49.26.82
Closed Mon out of season, Tues in winter, and mid-Dec to mid-Jan.

Facing the *hostellerie* and the château, this is a lovely old stone building in one of France's prettiest villages. In summer, don't bother about the two parasols on the lawn – the real terrace is in the courtyard. Set menus at 92F and 130F: various meats simply grilled over a wood fire, *jambon persillé*, *bœuf bourguignon*, salads, cream cheese, home-made tart and local wine. Congenial welcome. Free coffee after your meal.

VANDENESSE-EN-AUXOIS   21320 (5KM W)

🍴 |●| RESTAURANT DE L'AUXOIS

How to get there: it's very close to Châteauneuf-en-Auxois on the banks of the canal.
☎ 03.80.49.22.36

Closed Sun evening and Mon Oct–June, and 20 Dec–28 Jan. **Car park**.

The entire village, which has the Burgundy canal running through the middle, has benefitted from the re-opening of the grocer's and this restaurant, run by the Walloons. Food served here spices up the local style of cooking. There's a weekday menu at 80F then others 105–190F. The garden is superb in summer, and there's an old-fashioned dining room for those grey days. Free apéritif.

CHÂTILLON-EN-BAZOIS   58110

BRINAY   58110 (11KM NW)

🍴 🏠 L'ANCIEN CAFÉ

In the village (Centre); take the D10 signposted Cergy-La-Tour and turn left at Biches.
☎ 03.86.84.90.79
Closed Sun evening. **TV**. **Car park**.

A modest bar-restaurant-cum-grocery-cum-bread store-cum-gas depot. Cheap, robust dishes include Morvan ham, calf's head, Charolais steaks and local cheeses. The menus cost 55–120F. Run by the owners and their daughter. There's a shaded terrace.

SAINTE-PÉREUSE   58110 (13KM E)

|●| AUBERGE DE LA MADONETTE

Centre; from Châtillon-en-Bazois, take the D978 and follow the signs for Château-Chinon, turning left 8km beyond Châtillon-en-Bazois.
☎ 03.86.84.45.37
Closed Tues and Wed evenings except July–Aug, and 15 Dec–5 Feb. **Car park**.

Marie-Madeleine Grobost used to look after disabled children before making a career change and going into the restaurant business. She transformed this big house which is now decorated in gingham throughout and has a magnificent terraced garden with a stunning view of the Morvan hills. She offers tasty country cooking and dishes like calf's head *à l'ancienne*, pan-fried lamb with parsley and garlic, and pan-fried sweetbreads on *rosés* mushrooms. Set weekday menus 69F and others up to 268F.

CHÂTILLON-SUR-SEINE   21400

🍴 🏠 |●| SYLVIA HÔTEL**

9 av. de la Gare.
☎ 03.80.91.02.44 ➡ 03.80.91.47.77
Disabled access. **TV**. **Car park**.

The previous owners turned this enormous old middle-class family home set in parkland into a delightful hotel, and named it after their daughter. Then Sylvia grew up and the family moved on. The present owners kept the name and they do their utmost to make you enjoy your time with them, offering cosy rooms, *table d'hôte* dinners, and wonderful breakfasts. Simple doubles 140F and up to 280F with bath. Set menus 60F and 80F. 10% discount on the room rate Oct–April.

●I LE BOURG-À-MONT-CHEZ JULIE

27 rue du Bourg-à-Mont; it's in the old town, opposite the old courthouse.
☎ 03.80.91.04.33
Closed Sun evening and Mon out of season.

This is a pleasant surprise in a quiet little town known for the remarkable 5th-century BC Vix burial vessel on view in the museum. The house, decorated with old adverts, original paintings and bright colours, belonged to a grandmother who apparently had a bit of money. There's a youthful spirit about the place nowadays. There are log fires in winter, while in summer the windows, overlooking a little flower garden, are thrown wide open and you can have lunch or dinner there. Lunch menu 65F with others 95–190F. The best dishes are *terrine* of local trout, roast rabbit with prune stuffing, and *bœuf Bourg à Mont*, a spicy version of beef *bourguignon*.

MONTLIOT-ET-COURCELLES   21400 (3.5KM N)

●I CHEZ FLORENTIN

It's on the N71, on the outskirts of the village.
☎ 03.80.91.09.70
Closed Sun evening and Mon except public holidays.

You can go in through the bar, where the lorry drivers eat, to a large dining room used for banquets and christenings. The crowds you'd expect only on high days and holidays are an everyday occurrence, the local accents and laughter of the evening contrasting with the business atmosphere at lunchtime. The reception is friendly and the prices are unbeatable; the 69F menu consists of three courses, with dishes such as fresh mushrooms with cream, *blanquette de veau* and tart. Other menus cost 88–178F.

CLAMECY   58500

⚲ 🏠 ●I HOSTELLERIE DE LA POSTE**

9 pl. Émile-Zola (Centre).

☎ 03.86.27.01.55 ➡ 03.86.27.05.99
TV.

A substantial building looking like a post house that's been there for ever. The rooms are clean and comfortable – it's clear that the hotel is well run. Doubles 265–295F. The menu of the day is pricey at 105F, though the cooking is of good quality; other menus 168–198F. The beef is local Charolais and there are fresh river fish. Free coffee.

⚲ ●I LA CRÊPERIE DU VIEUX CANAL

18 av. de la République (Centre); it's opposite the museum.
☎ 03.86.24.47.93
Closed Mon.

One of Clamecy's friendliest places to eat, where you can have a good, quick lunch. The decor is Breton and they serve savoury and sweet pancakes, as well as pasta dishes and bruschetta. Menus 65–130F. Welcoming owner. Free coffee.

⚲ ●I RESTAURANT AU BON ACCUEIL

3 route d'Auxerre.
☎ 03.86.27.91.67
Closed evenings Oct–May, Sat, Sun and Wed evenings in summer, the Feb school holidays, and the first ten days in July and Dec.

A welcoming restaurant with a peaceful dining room that has views of the Yonne and the collegiate church. François Langlois cooks with flair and passion – dishes change as the mood takes him and there are many regional options on the menu. Attentive service and a delightful welcome from Madame Langlois. Weekday menu 90F, with others 140F and 180F. It's not a very big place, so it's best to book. Free coffee.

TANNAY   58190 (13KM S)

⚲ 🏠 ●I HÔTEL DU RELAIS FLEURI

rue de Bèze (Centre); take the D34 from Clamecy.
☎ 03.86.29.33.88
Closed Sun evening, Mon, and Feb.
Swimming pool. Disabled access. Car park.

A comfortable hotel in a period house. The interior has been attractively refurbished and you will be greeted with a smile. Doubles with shower/wc 240F. The cooking has a good reputation with the emphasis on the regional; *œufs en meurette*, and beef and potato pie. Weekday lunch menu at 60F or 88–150F. Free coffee.

CLUNY 71250

☆ ☎ HÔTEL DU COMMERCE*

8 pl. du Commerce (Centre).
☎ 03.85.59.03.09 ➠ 03.85.59.00.87

In this expensive town, this is a small, well-maintained, central hotel that offers basic, clean accommodation at reasonable prices. Wonderfully friendly reception to boot. Doubles with basin 145F, with shower 205F and bath 240F. Free coffee and a discount on breakfast Sept–June.

☎ HÔTEL SAINT-ODILON**

rue Belle-Croix; it's beside the racecourse.
☎ 03.85.59.25.00 ➠ 03.85.59.06.18
Closed 15 Dec–15 Jan.
Disabled access. TV. Car park.

Surrounded by fields full of grazing Charolais cattle, this is a modern establishment but one that's in sympathy with its surroundings. It's low and squat, and the two wings create a square courtyard reminiscent of the local farms. A nice place to stay – it has modern facilities, the colour schemes are pleasant, and you'll get a friendly welcome from Monsieur and Madame Berry. Rooms with phone, TV and satellite channels are 295F, breakfast costs extra.

BOURGVILAIN 71420 (9KM S)

☆ |●| AUBERGE LAROCHETTE

Le bourg.
☎ 03.85.50.81.73
Closed Sun evening, Mon and 15 Feb–15 March.

A welcoming provincial dining room in this large, traditional village. There are reproductions of Millet paintings on the wall and a country clock in the corner. The excellent cooking carries on the best French traditions. Dishes are finely judged by Monsieur Bonin and served generously. Weekday menu at 80F, with others 105–210F. À la carte you can get warm foie gras with apple and cinnamon sauce, frogs' legs and trompette mushrooms in flaky pastry, zander millefeuille, salmon and bacon paupiette, duck breast with seasonal fruits, and a tasty Charolais steak. Free apéritif.

☆ |●| LA PIERRE SAUVAGE

Col des Enceints.
☎ 03.85.35.70.03
Closed Tues evening and Wed except July–Aug, weekdays 1 Oct to Easter and Jan.
Disabled access. Car park.

This place is on a hilltop 500m up. It was a ruin some fifteen years ago and has since been wonderfully restored and is now an appealing place to stop. You can start off with a hunk of bread and strong cheese or house terrine before getting onto the main courses: game or some Charollais lamb chops. Specialities include cassolette of snails forestière, guinea fowl with vanilla and fresh figs, chicken with seasonal fruits, and pigeon with pêche de vigne. Menus 98–128F. They also do good plates of country ham or terrines at 78F. The terrace is superb in summer. Best to book. Free digestif.

BERZÉ-LA-VILLE 71960 (10KM SE)

☎ |●| RELAIS DU MÂCONNAIS

La Croix-Blanche (Northwest); take the D17.
☎ 03.85.36.60.72 ➠ 03.85.36.65.47
Closed Sun evening, Mon in low season, and Jan. **TV**.

The hushed atmosphere will be to many people's liking and the well-spaced table arrangement means that you won't overhear your neighbour. Christian Lannue's cooking has a very personal touch. The small tartare of beetroot is so original that it deserves to be upgraded from an appetiser to a starter. Dishes, based on local produce, are finely flavoured: try milk-fed veal cutlets with vegetables au gratin or roast pigeon with garlic purée and sautéd mushrooms. Good dessert trolley. Menus 150–300F. About ten comfy double rooms with shower or bath, 370F.

BLANOT 71250 (10KM NE)

☆ ☎ |●| AUBERGE DU MONT SAINT-ROMAIN

Mont St-Romain.
☎ 03.85.33.28.93
Closed Tues out of season and 11 Nov–1 April.

An inn, right up on one of the peaks of the Saône-et-Loire, with a beautiful panoramic terrace. Great reception from the very nice young couple who have to cope with scorching winds in summer and snowdrifts in winter. Dishes are prepared with professional care for a clientele of walkers, horseriders and nature lovers who drop in for a meal. Hearty portions of regional dishes, cooked using fresh produce. The set menus, 90–120F, are good value: supreme of chicken with liver which is very fine and chicken aiguillette with wild mushrooms. Horse rides are on offer to help the digestion, and there's a travel lodge for those who want to stay. Free apéritif or coffee.

COSNE-SUR-LOIRE 58200

🎄 🛏 |●| HÔTEL-RESTAURANT LE SAINT-CHRISTOPHE**

pl. de la Gare; it's opposite the train station.
☎ 03.86.28.02.01 ☞ 03.86.26.94.28
Closed Sun evening, Fri, 24 July–22 Aug and Christmas/New Year holidays.

Delightfully refurbished comfortable rooms with good facilities. Doubles with shower/wc or bath 235–260F. The owner will welcome you with a smile and she seems to be doing something right in the restaurant, which is popular with the locals. The *formule* of main course with a choice of starter or dessert costs 78F, and there are menus 112–210F and options *à la carte*. Straightforward, unfussy cooking. Free *digestif*.

🎄 |●| RESTAURANT LE SÉVIGNÉ

30 rue des Quatre Fils Doumier (Centre).
☎ 03.86.28.27.50
Closed evenings Sun, Mon and Wed, and three weeks in Nov.

Cosne-sur-Loire's gastronomic restaurant, with orthodox service and skillfully cooked regional dishes prepared using market-fresh produce. The produce is very "*terroir*" but the dishes are frankly fashionable. A good establishment. Weekday lunch menu 95F and others 160–300F. Free house apéritif.

|●| LE VIEUX RELAIS

11 rue Saint-Agnan; it's near the Eden Cinema.
☎ 03.86.28.27.50
TV. **Car park**.

A coaching inn straight out of the 19th century. The double rooms are cosy and spacious, as you would expect for 420–480F, and the cooking is one of the establishment's great strengths. There's a father and son team in the kitchen, while mother and daughter-in-law run the dining room with bright smiles. It's a popular place. The cheapest menu is 102F, with others 115–290F. There's a dream of a little courtyard with a balcony that's overgrown with Virginia creeper and a puzzle of higgledy-piggledy roofs.

CREUSOT (LE) 71200

|●| LE RESTAURANT

rue des Abattoirs (South); it's in a cul-de-sac.
☎ 03.85.56.32.33
Closed Sun evening and 1–20 Aug.

Bizarrely located among the abattoirs in an area that's dark and deserted in the evenings. But it's the only beacon of gastronomy in the area for wayward and lost souls. You get a warm reception, and the bright dining room is painted in fresh colours. It feels lofty on account of its mezzanine, and elegantly bare with the zinc counter providing a smooth transition between tradition and innovation. The well-designed cooking aims to preserve the taste of good produce by cleverly combining herbs and other flavours. Set menus 70F and 100–180F. Dishes such as parsleyed eels with pickled onions, roast lamb with fresh mint, calves' kidneys with liquorice *jus*. Excellent selection of wines at reasonable prices and some high-quality, affordable Burgundy wines. It's advisable to book for dinner. This little establishment is going places.

🎄 |●| LE BISTROT DE LA GRIMPETTE

16 rue de la Chaise (Centre).
☎ 03.85.80.42.00
Closed Sun.

Exactly halfway up the stairway connecting the lower and upper town, this is an inexpensive restaurant serving genuine Lyons specialities. The decor is wine red, and the place wafts with the aromas of hot sausage, guineafowl with mushrooms and salt pork with lentils. Attentive service and friendly welcome. There's a basic set menu at 79F and others up to 120F; they include salad with warm calves' feet, flank of beef *Lyonnaise*, and *andouillette* tied with string. Free apéritif.

TORCY 71210 (3KM S)

|●| LE VIEUX SAULE

Route du Creusot (South).
☎ 03.85.55.09.53
Closed Sun evening and Mon.

One of the best restaurants in the region, located in a very old country inn at Torcy, on the outskirts of Le Creusot. Excellent welcome and brilliant decor. Good 100F weekday menu, one at 140F with local dishes, and others up to 240F. The cooking is particularly tasty, and nicely presented to boot – *foie gras* escalope with rhubarb, *millefeuille* of lamb and apples, stew of lobster covered in pastry, and delicious *souris* of lamb. Desserts along the same lines. Excellent choice of local wines.

UCHON 71190 (18KM W)

🎄 🛏 |●| AUBERGE LA CROIX MESSIRE JEAN

La Croix Messire Jean; head for Montcenis, then take the D228.
☎ 03.85.54.42.06 ➡ 03.85.54.32.23
Closed Tues, Wed in winter, and Christmas–New Year.
Car park.

Ideal base for walkers and mountain bikers planning to tackle one of the splendid routes on one of the highest mountains in the département (684m). It's a friendly inn, offering basic but perfectly adequate bedrooms at 180F for a double with basin. Tasteful, rustic decor and prices to suit all pockets. It's best to book in high season, and if you yearn for peace and quiet, this won't be your scene. There's a large, shaded terrace where you can enjoy the 55F four o'clock Morvan snack or the exceptionally reasonably priced little set menus. They do a 60F *menu du jour* and others up to 125F. Mountain bikes for hire. Free coffee, and 10% discount on full board if you stay a minimum of three days.

DECIZE   58300

|●| SNACK DU STADE NAUTIQUE

Promenade des Halles; take the street past the tourist office and it's at the end, next to the camp site.
☎03.86.25.06.54
Open May–Sept.

This is a waterside café in one of the most charming parts of Decize, especially when it's sunny. Sit at a table in the shade of the plane trees with a plate of country ham, an omelette with salad or some fresh cream cheese. They do chips to take away. A couple of menus at 55F, with dessert extra. You can play volley ball or have a pony ride. Some evenings they have live music. Really smiley, friendly welcome.

💃|●| RESTAURANT LA GRIGNOTTE

57 av. du 14-Juillet (North).
☎ 03.86.25.26.20
Closed Sun, and Mon evening.

An unpretentious restaurant unfortunately situated on a busy road. The dining room is lovely and bright but the welcome dull. You can eat decently and cheaply, the lunch menu (not Sun) costs 62F or there others 67–165F. Fondue is a speciality. Free apéritif if you have a meal costing more than 110F.

|●| LE CHAROLAIS**

33 [bis], route de Moulins.
☎ 03.86.25.22.27
Closed Sun evening and Mon.

An attractive dining room with quiet service and classic, well-judged cuisine. The cheap-

est menu, 97F, will allow you to judge, or there's a dish of the day at 85F. The other set menus are less good value for money. The terrace at the back is well sheltered.

|●| AUBERGE DES FEUILLATS

Hameau Les Feuillats; at the tourist office go along the bd. Voltaire, afer the bridge over the RI152, take the road to Moulind. 1km further on turn left onto the route des Fuillats and it's 1km on the left.
☎ 03.86.25.05.19
Closed Wed evening.

This is the place for a slab of Charolais beef – it's all got a Red Label which means its origins can be confirmed. The terrace at the back is right on the bank of a canal that's busy with pleasure boats wherever you look. There's a holiday-like feel to the place. Menus 100–180F. Dish of the day 85F.

DIGOIN   71160

💃 🏠 |●| LES DILIGENCES**

14 rue Nationale (Centre); it's in a pedestrian street in the town centre.
☎ 03.85.53.06.31 ➡ 03.85.88.92.43
e hotel.les.diligences@wanadoo.fr
Closed Mon evening and Tues except July–Aug, 19 Nov–11 Dec. **TV**. **Car park**.

In the 17th century, travellers arriving in the town by mail coach or boat stayed at this inn. It has recently been restored and the exposed stonework, beams, polished furniture and gleaming coppers give it a chic look. But that doesn't mean the prices in the restaurant are insane; the two cheapest set menus cost 98F and 145F and there are others up to 330F, but dining *à carte* is a different story: lobster and crayfish tail salad with raspberry vinegar, Charolais fillet steak with five peppers, *fricassée* of ceps Bordeaux-style and John Dory fillet with watercress sauce are all a bit pricey. Six tastefully furnished and decorated rooms, 270F with shower or 320F with bath, overlook the quiet banks of the Loire. There's a duplex with a private spa in the immense bathroom. Reservations advisable. Free apéritif.

NEUZY   71160 (3KM NE)

🏠 |●| LE MERLE BLANC***

36 route de Gueugnon-Autun; take the D994 going towards Autun.
☎ 03.85.53.17.13 ➡ 03.85.88.91.71
Closed Sun evening and Mon lunchtime Oct to end April. **Disabled access**. **TV**. **Car park**.

The hotel is set back from the road. Doubles with shower/wc for 195F, with bath 260F. Substantial set menus at 85F (not available Sun) and 110–225F offer dishes such as pan-fried duck *foie gras* with spices, pan-fried crayfish with olive oil and avocado cream, *croustillant* of scallops with Noilly vermouth, and apple and walnut crumble. Friendly, efficient staff.

DIJON   21000

SEE MAP OVERLEAF

⚘ ⚑ HÔTEL LE CHAMBELLAN**

92 rue Vannerie. **MAP C2-1**
☎ 03.80.67.12.67 ➡ 03.80.38.00.39
TV. Car park.

The splendours of yesteryear combined with the convenience of all mod cons. It's an old building and a delightfully old-fashioned establishment with extremely reasonable prices. Doubles with basin at 140F; with shower or bath up to 285F. They've all got character, but go for one overlooking the 17th-century courtyard. No charge for animals. 10% discount.

⚘ ⚑ HÔTEL LE JACQUEMART**

32 rue Verrerie. **MAP B1-3**
☎ 03.80.73.39.74 ➡ 03.80.73.20.99
TV.

Book to avoid disappointment. A lovely hotel, with lots of regulars including opera singers during the season. The rooms are quiet and comfortable and all have cable TV. An ideal spot for a well-earned rest after touring the old part of Dijon. Doubles 175–299F. 10% discount Dec–March.

⚘ ⚑ HÔTEL DU PALAIS

23 rue du Palais. **MAP B2-2**
☎ 03.80.67.16.26 ➡ 03.80.65.12.16
Disabled access. TV.

Ideally situated right in the centre of the old town, opposite the public library – which is worth a visit in itself – but totally quiet. The clean, welcoming double bedrooms are soundproofed, 220–280F. Beautiful breakfast room. 10% discount Dec–Feb.

⚏ HÔTEL VICTOR HUGO**

23 rue des Fleurs. **MAP A1-5**
☎ 03.80.43.63.45 ➡ 03.80.42.13.01
TV. Lock-up car park.

Located in Dijon's middle-class neighbourhood, this isn't the kind of place you come to to let your hair down. Spotless and silent, with

an atmosphere that is ever so slightly staid. There are twenty or so comfortable and welcoming rooms; doubles with shower/wc or bath 230–280F. There's a free car park.

⚑ HÔTEL DES ALLÉES**

27 cours Général-de-Gaulle. Off map **C3-6**
☎ 03.80.66.57.50 ➡ 03.80.36.24.81
Disabled access. TV. Car park.

Small, modern hotel on a posh tree-lined avenue leading to the parc de la Colombière. It used to be a maternity hospital. The garden is full of birds and you can be sure of peace and quiet. Doubles with shower/wc 280F or 350F with bath. They lock the doors at 11pm, so remember to ask for the entry code so you can let yourself in. Pets and children are welcome at no extra charge.

⦿ LE PASSÉ SIMPLE

18 rue Pasteur. **MAP B2-13**
☎ 03.80.67.22.00
Closed Sat lunchtime and Sun.

An authentic bistro decorated in old-fashioned style with cosy decor and informal service – the owner is on first-name terms with his customers. It's a place where friends come to have a glass of wine together at the bar or relax in the sun on the terrace for lunch. The 59F lunch menu gives you the opportunity to try the most traditional of dishes, also available on the other menus at 79–120F.

⦿ LE CHABROT

36 rue Monge. **MAP A2-16**
☎ 03.80.30.69.61
Closed Sun.

Service until 10.30pm. Plates of Burgundian specialities available all day long – although there's a new owner, the tried and tested approach of this place hasn't changed. You can eat in the bistro or the restaurant upstairs, and there's a tiny terrace. The cooking style is emphatically local with a few unusual discoveries: pressed goat and smoked salmon, or salmon *unilatérale* (cooked on one side) which is a signature dish. There's a 69F weekday lunch menu and others at 115–160F. You go through the wine cellar to get to the dining areas so you can choose your bottle on the way in. Wines are also served by the glass: Coteaux de l'Auxois at 12F or Epineuil red at 15F.

⦿ LE BOUCHON DU PALAIS

4 rue Bouhier. **MAP B2-12**
☎ 03.80.30.19.98
Closed Sat lunchtime and Sun.

An old favourite that's re-opened under new ownership but the decor hasn't changed one bit. Guests are asked to decorate the paper tablecloths which are then put up on the walls. The cooking is still straightforward and of the same quality and the helpings are still ample: gratinéed marrow bone, *andouillette* terrine, veal escalope with St Marcellin cheese sauce, and tasty lamb chops, followed by *clafoutis* or *crème brûlée*. There's a *formule* based around the dish of the day at 75F and a menu at 99F. Knock back a glass of wine at the bar with the chef. Service is efficient, attentive and kindly.

●I SIMPLE SIMON

4 rue de la Chouette. **MAP B2-14**
☎ 03.80.50.03.52
Closed Mon.

This is an ideal spot for a snack in the oldest part of town, round the corner from the carving of the good-luck owl. Cheese and onion pie, cheese scones, cold meat and desserts are on offer in this little corner of Britain on Burgundian soil. Ideal for a break, or breakfast, any time between 10am and 7pm. Also one of the few places in Dijon where you can get breakfast on Sunday. Reckon on about 80F a head. Very pleasant staff.

●I LE BISTROT DES HALLES

10 rue Bannelier. **MAP B1-19**
☎ 03.80.49.94.15
Closed Sun evening.

This is the place everyone in Dijon goes to eat. It's an old-style bistro with large mirrors and checked napkins. The man responsible for the cooking is Jean-Pierre Billoux, a wonderful chef and one of Burgundy's six great masters. Every dish – home-made *pâté en croûte à l'ancienne*, *jambon persillé*, pig's trotters, or *terrine* of lamb and leeks – bears his mark. Add to that some good country dishes, superb grills and reasonably priced wines (even though the wine by the jug isn't great), and you'll understand why it's such a success. Set lunch menu 97F or 130F *à la carte*. There's a very nice terrace that looks onto the covered market.

🎄●I LE CÉZANNE

40 rue Amiral-Roussin. **MAP B2-20**
☎ 03.80.58.91.92
Closed Sun, Mon lunchtime.

Located in an old street, the restaurant has old stonework and beams and an intimate, even impressionistic, atmosphere. The chef's

cooking has become a gastronomic yardstick in the town. You won't be disappointed by the quality even on the cheapest menu, 99F: red mullet and scallops with saffron and basil, saddle of rabbit stuffed with liver and prunes, and chocolate with pistachio ice cream. Other menus 150–250F. Pleasant little terrace. Free coffee.

🎄●I RESTAURANT LE BISTINGO

13 passage Darcy. **MAP A1-11**
☎ 03.80.30.61.38
Closed Sun, Mon and Aug.

Half-pub, half-restaurant, serving substantial portions of inexpensive dishes 45–60F; salmon with lemon butter, skate with capers, and *andouillette*. You'll pay 120–160F *à la carte*. It's a friendly place where it's easy to get into conversation with the regulars. The owner is a colourful character reminiscent of Figaro of the opera fame, while the friendly waiter uses the familiar *tu* with everybody. In the evening, you'll be served the delicious steak *tartare* almost automatically. Free house apéritif.

HAUTEVILLE-LES-DIJON   21121 (8KM NW)

🎄 🏠 ●I LA MUSARDE**

7 rue des Riottes; it's on the N71 road to Troyes.
☎ 03.80.56.22.82 ➡ 03.80.56.64.40
Closed Mon and 15 Dec–15 Jan. **TV**. **Car park**.

A place with a risqué past that used to be a discreet rendezvous for intimate dalliances, in the years gone by. Nowadays, it's also a restaurant and it's best to book, especially at the weekend, to be sure of a table. The informal, relaxed atmosphere is at the same time sophisticated and professional. It's run by Marc Ogé, a true Breton with his feet planted firmly on the ground. He serves mainly fish and seafood dishes. Sample *terrine* of shellfish with *foie gras* and *confit* of aubergines, or roasted sea trout with *coulis* of mussels. Set menus 165–285F and there's a weekday menu at 115F including wine and coffee. Nice terrace for fine days. Attractive bedrooms 265–335F. Free coffee.

PRENOIS   21370 (12KM NE)

🎄●I AUBERGE DE LA CHARME

It's a turning off the road that goes to Darois aerodrome.
☎ 03.80.35.32.84
Closed Sun evening, Mon lunch, 2–12 Jan and 1–12 Aug.

Prenois used to be famous for its racing circuit. Nowadays the culinary creations of

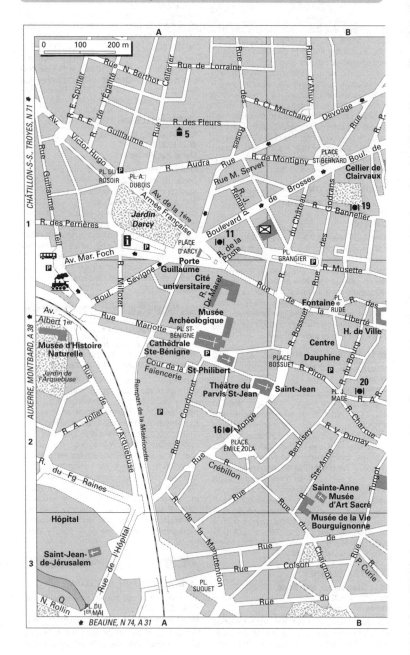

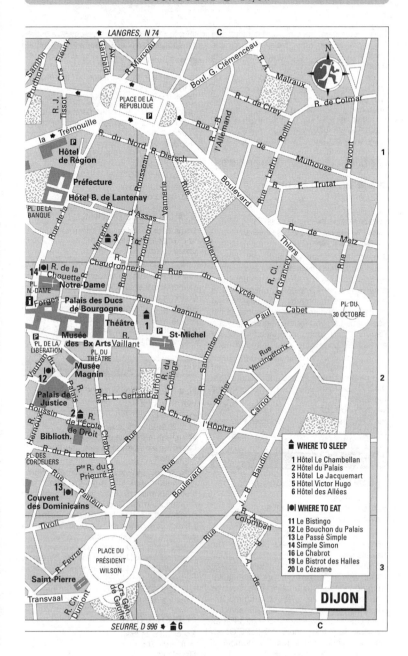

LANGRES, N 74

C

N

PLACE DE LA
RÉPUBLIQUE

Sambin
Prudhon
Crs Fleury
Av. Garibaldi
R. Marceau

Boul. G. Clémenceau
R. A. Matraux
R. de Colmar

R. J. de Cirey

R. J. Tissot

la Trémouille

Hôtel
de Région

Préfecture

Hôtel B. de Lantenay

PL. DE LA
BANQUE

R. du Nord
R. Diersch
Rousseau
Vannerie
Rue

R. J.-B. l'Allemand
de Rollin
Ledru
Mulhouse
Rue
F. Trutat
Davout

1

R. de la
Banque
Rue d'Assas
Verrerie

3

R. Proudhon
Didero
Boulevard

R. de Metz
Thiers

14

R. de la
Chouette
Notre-Dame

R. Chaudronnerie
Rue du
Lycée
R. Cl. de Grancey

PL.
N-DAME

Forges

Palais des Ducs
de Bourgogne

Rue
Jeannin
R. Paul
Cabet

PL. DU
30 OCTOBRE

Théâtre

1

Musée
des Bx Arts

St-Michel

R. Vaillant

PL. DE LA
LIBÉRATION

PL. DU
THÉÂTRE

Vauban

Musée
Magnin

12

Palais de
Justice

R. R. L. Gerland

R. Palais
Buffon
R. du Vx Collège
R. Saulnaise
Rue
Vercingétorix

R. Ch. de l'Hôpital
Barbier
Carnot

2

Roussin
Hernoux

2

R. de l'École
de Droit

Chabot

Biblioth.

PL. DES
CORDELIERS

R. du Pt Potet
Pte R. du Prieuré
R. du Charny
Rue

13

Rue
Pasteur

Couvent
des Dominicains

Boulevard
Baudin
R. A. Colomban

Tivoli

PLACE DU
PRÉSIDENT
WILSON

Saint-Pierre

R. Fevret
Transvaal
R. Ch. Dumont
Crs Gén. de Gaulle

Rue
A. de

3

SEURRE, D 996

6

C

WHERE TO SLEEP

1 Hôtel Le Chambellan
2 Hôtel du Palais
3 Hôtel Le Jacquemart
5 Hôtel Victor Hugo
6 Hôtel des Allées

WHERE TO EAT

11 Le Bistingo
12 Le Bouchon du Palais
13 Le Passé Simple
14 Simple Simon
16 Le Chabrot
19 Le Bistrot des Halles
20 Le Cézanne

DIJON

David Zuddas are the draw. The cooking and the prices are very attractive even though the chef's reputation has grown considerably. He uses good-quality local produce from which he concocts interesting dishes: pressed duck and *foie gras* with sage, and chick pea *galette* with sweet onion, for example. All dishes are seasoned and presented with a rare attention to detail. This is the best establishment in these parts. Set menus 98F at weekday lunchtimes, then 135–400F. Free coffee.

VAL SUZON   21121 (15KM NE)

🏠 ☎ |●| HOSTELLERIE DU VAL SUZON***

It's on the N71.
☎ 03.80.35.60.15 ➨ 03.80.35.61.36
Closed Sun evening, Mon and Tues lunchtimes Oct–May. **TV. Car park**.

A peaceful, comfy establishment serving good food. It's a bewitching place just fifteen minutes from Dijon in a valley, surrounded by magnificent parkland and gardens. The owner gives a country-style welcome and still offers some countrified dishes, while at the same time catering for the tastes of passing Parisians and other "foreigners". Peaceful and comfy bedrooms which have all been renovated. Doubles with shower/wc 450F, and 550F with bath. Yves Perreau is the chef and he likes to use spices and flavours from the Far East, though his cooking remains fundamentally true to tradition. Weekday lunch menu 130F and others 165–270F. Ideal for a romantic weekend. Wonderful terrace. Free coffee.

DONZY   58220

🏠 ☎ |●| LE GRAND MONARQUE**

10 rue de l'Étape.
☎ 03.86.39.35.44 ➨ 03.86.39.37.09
Closed Jan. **TV. Car park**.

This is a delightful village, with a number of 15th-century half-timbered buildings. The hotel is the old stone house practically next door to the Romanesque church. Rustic charm with all mod cons and a warm, taste-fully decorated interior. Spacious doubles with shower/wc are 270F, with bath 310F. There's a *formule express* at 52F served at lunchtime in the week, a menu at 89F (not available Sun), then others 120–220F. Good-quality regional cooking with a number of fish dishes. Free house apéritif.

DUN-LES-PLACES   58230

☎ |●| LE CHALET DU MONTAL

How to get there: it's 1.5km northeast of the village.
☎ 03.86.84.62.77
Closed Mon evening and Tues out of season. **Car park**.

Here's a genuine chalet perched above a river in wild surroundings straight out of *Twin Peaks*. It has a bar and an enormous central fireplace, and is popular with campers from round about. The cooking is simple but a lot of care goes into the preparation of the dish-es. Set menus 90–165F. They offer four basic rooms at 130F if you want to spend the night, and half-board costs 185F per person.

☎ |●| L'AUBERGE ENSOLEILLÉE

Centre; it's on the D6 Lormes to Saulieu road.
☎ 03.86.84.62.76 ➨ 03.86.84.64.57
Closed Christmas.

A typical Morvan inn run by three women; one at the bar, one in the restaurant and one in the kitchen. Honest and smiling welcome. Tradi-tional local recipes include ham with cream sauce, calf's head with two sauces, and salmon with leek purée. Substantial weekday menu at 90F with others 125–225F. Simple, country rooms at 135–280F for a double.

GEVREY-CHAMBERTIN   21220

🏠 ☎ |●| AUX VENDANGES DE BOURGOGNE

47 route de Beaune.
☎ 03.80.34.30.24 ➨ 03.80.58.55.44
📧 aux.vendanges.de.bourgogne@wanadoo.fr
Closed Sun and a fortnight Christmas/New Year.
TV. Car park.

Among the pricey restaurants and world-renowned cellars is this old-fashioned hotel restaurant with a stylish and warm decor and an interior terrace. Good local dishes in hearty portions at reasonable prices, all charmingly served. Specialities include snails in a pastry case with garlic, pig's trotters, *coq au vin*, ox cheek, home-made parsleyed ham, and pears poached in blackcurrant liqueur. Weekday menu at 85F, or 125–150F. Wine is available by the glass. Simple rooms with period furni-ture 229–319F. 10% discount on the room rate for a two-night stay.

🏠 |●| CHEZ GUY

3 pl. de l'Hôtel-de-Ville.
☎ 03.80.58.51.51
Closed Tues.

This is the restaurant Gevrey-Chambertin has been waiting for. Up to now life in the famous wine-growing village has been focused on the famous cellars but this restaurant has brought a good deal of animation to the place. There's a jolly terrace in summer and on Thursday evenings there are jazz concerts. When the weather gets cold, there's a rotisserie churning away in the dining room. The cooking is bright and inventive, with a few new twists on traditional Burgundian dishes: *coq au vin* with parsley, poached eggs with mustard and oyster mushrooms, veal chops with Chambertin, and Burgundy bread and butter pudding. The *menu-carte* at 95F where, you make up your own menu to go with a dish of the day, is superb, then there's a Burgundy menu at 150F. An attractive choice of Gevrey wines at appealing prices. Free coffee.

JOIGNY   89300

🕅 🏨 |●| LE PARIS-NICE**

Rond-point de la Résistance; (Centre).
☎ 03.86.62.06.72 ➡ 03.86.62.56.99
Closed Sun evening, Mon and Jan. **TV. Car park**.

The N6 used to be known as the "Route des Anglais" before the motorway to the Côte d'Azur was built. Those were the glory days of this establishment, though it's recently been done up by its new owners. The rooms are simple but they all have double glazing; 250F with shower or bath. You eat in the *Bistrot de Joigny*, a decent place with good-value menus of typical bistro fare and regional dishes; 54F and 68F on weekdays only, then 99F and 120F. Free coffee.

🕅 🏨 |●| LE RIVE GAUCHE***

Chemin du Port-au-Bois; it's on the banks of the Yonne, very close to the old town.
☎ 03.86.91.46.66 ➡ 03.86.91.46.93
Garden. TV. Car park. Swimming pool.

The Lorains realised that things were changing so they built a modern hotel looking like one of a chain – opposite their famous *Côte Saint-Jacques* (not reviewed here).The new establishment is welcoming and has good-looking, comfortable and functional rooms – doubles with bath 360F. There is a pool, tennis court and a garden. You can eat outside on the terraces or in the dining room where the decor and the food both reflect today's tastes. The cooking is bistro-style, with set menus 105F in the week and others 158–210F. 10% discount on the room rate for a two-night stay.

|●| BRASSERIE DU GOLF

pl. du Marché; it's opposite the tourist office.
☎ 03.86.62.14.05
Closed Mon.

An ideal spot with a splendid panoramic view over the Yonne, just away from the centre of town. Very attractive prices – starters, salads or barbecued meats 30–50F for a dish. Various sandwiches from 20F. The terrace is right by the water's edge.

CELLE-SAINT-CYR (LA)   89116 (8KM W)

🕅 🏨 |●| AUBERGE DE LA FONTAINE AUX MUSES**

How to get there: head for Joigny on the D943; after 3km, turn left when you come to the village of La Motte – the inn is 3km further.
☎ 03.86.73.40.22 ➡ 03.86.73.48.66
Closed Mon and Tues until 5pm.
Swimming pool. Disabled access. TV. Car park.

Set in Burgundy's rolling hills, this country house inn is covered in Virginia creeper, and the rooms are as rustic as you like: doubles with shower or bath for 350–385F. The cooking is irredeemably Burgundian; *foie gras*, snails, pigeon and Burgundy beef. Set weekday menu 185F, or *à la carte*. The Langevin family are musicians (father Claude composed the European anthem), so other musicians often turn up at the weekend and a jam session results. Tennis court and heated swimming pool. 10% discount on the room rate Oct–March.

LORMES   58140

🕅 🏨 |●| HÔTEL PERREAU**

8 route d'Avallon (Centre).
☎ 03.86.22.53.21 ➡ 03.86.22.82.15
Closed Sun evening, Mon Oct–end of May and 10 Jan to mid-Feb. **TV. Car park**.

This is an imposing establishment that has been well renovated and could accommodate a regiment of backpackers. The restaurant is very pretty and rustic-looking with a large fireplace and superb ceiling. The cooking is equally refined and there's a superb Burgundian menu, with prices running 75–165F. Rooms are spacious – the ones overlooking the garden have been renovated – and cost 260–279F with shower or bath. 10% discount on the room rate Sept–June.

VAUCLAIX   58140 (8KM S)

🏨 |●| HÔTEL DE LA POSTE**

Centre; it's 8km south of Lormes on the D944.
☎ 03.86.22.71.38 ➥ 03.86.22.76.00
Swimming pool. Garden. Disabled access. TV. Car park.

Located in deepest darkest Morvan, this is a popular, friendly hotel. Five generations of Desbrûères have run the place and they're constantly doing it up and introducing new ideas – there's a swimming pool in the garden, a giant chess game and ping-pong. The rooms are big but cosy – doubles 205F with basin and 335F with shower/wc or bath. It's worth the trip here for the cooking alone. The two-page menu changes regularly and offers traditional dishes like beef fillet with morels and innovative ones like scallops and crayfish tails on leek purée. 60F weekday menu, and others 98–250F.

BAZOCHES-DU-MORVAN 58190 (17KM N)

⚐ |●| LE TIRE-BOUCHON

How to get there; take the D2 from Lormes in the direction of Clamecy, turn right on the D958 and it's at the beginning of the village.
☎ 03.86.22.11.66
Closed Sun evening and Wed out of season. **Car park.**

The café–restaurant has an atractive decor with bacchanalian paintings on the wall. Good, reliable French cuisine that's both substantial and tasty. The 72F menu is served during the week and there's another at 138F. There's a choice of local wines. A good place to stop if you're visiting the château de Bazoches. Free house apéritif.

LOUHANS 71500

🏠 |●| LE MOULIN DE BOURGCHÂTEAU**

Route de Châlon; from the centre of town take the D978 and turn right before the Citroën sign.
☎ 03.85.37.12 ➥ 03.85.75.45.11
e bourgchateay@francemel
Closed Sun Oct–Easter, Mon lunchtime, and 20 Dec–20 Jan. **TV. Car park.**

If you get the urge to do something romantic, try this old mill built in 1778 on the banks of the Seille, a tributary of the Saône. The location is superb and the rooms are very cosy. Those on the second floor have a stunning view of the river. Doubles 250–310F. Very filling breakfast for 48F. The restaurant also overlooks the river and offers refined cooking. Set menus 100–170F and the *à la carte* list changes regularly; *terrine* of duck with onion marmalade, roast pigeon with

chopped liver sauce, caramelised apples, and walnut and currants in a pastry case.The ideal spot for a weekend away with that very special person.

⚐ |●| RESTAURANT LA COTRIADE

4 rue d'Alsace.
☎ 03.85.75.19.91
Closed a week in the Feb school holidays. **Car park.**

Eating here can be agonising if you find it hard to make decisions – there is a shoal of menus to choose from, all at reasonable prices (72–210F). Fresh ingredients are all-important here and the fish and seafood are brought straight from Brittany; monkfish with seaweed, *cotriade* (a white fish stew with mussels, potatoes and cream), fish soup and sole with sorrel. But if you fancy trying the local speciality, which is chicken, here they prepare it with a cream and morel sauce. The service can be vague, so just remind them you're there. Free apéritif.

SAVIGNY-SUR-SEILLE 71440 (11KM W)

⚐ |●| AUBERGE LA RIVIÈRE

Tiellay.
☎ 03.85.74.99.03
Closed Tues evening, Wed in winter and 10 Jan–13 Feb.

This adorable country inn, on the banks of the Seille, was once the ferryman's home. The attractive wood-framed building has charm. You'll get a good reception and the cooking enjoys an excellent reputation. The owner, a fishing fanatic, catches the fish for the restaurant. Set menus 89–176F or *à la carte*; dishes include Bresse chicken with morels or baked in a salt crust and served with a cream sauce, *gâteau de foies de volaille* (pounded chicken livers with *foie gras*), *suprême* of freshwater crayfish, whitebait, snails and salads. If *silurid* "house-style" is on the menu, order it; it's a monster fish from the local rivers and lakes. *Pocheuse*, a freshwater fish stew with garlic and white wine, can be made to order. Attractive desserts. There's a dreamy terrace for fine days, with a lawn going down to the waters. Free coffee.

BEAUREPAIRE-EN-BRESSE 71580 (14KM E)

⚐ 🏠 |●| AUBERGE LA CROIX BLANCHE**

Centre; take the N78 in the direction of Lons-le-Saunier.
☎ 03.85.74.13.22 ➥ 03.85.74.13.25

Closed Sun evening and Mon 30 Sept–15 June, and mid-Nov to mid-Dec.
Disabled access. **TV**. **Car park**.

There is a real country atmosphere in this genuine 17th-century coaching stop, which has been sympathetically renovated. The first-rate free-range *poulet de Bresse* is irresistible, prepared in different ways at different times of the year by chef Gilles Poulet. Dish of the day 71F, weekday menu 90F, then 125–210F. *À la carte* you can get rabbit with a spinach *mille-feuille*, breast of *poulet de Bresse* with *foie gras*, monkfish with garlic, and game in season. All main courses change six times a year to reflect the seasons and what the market has to offer. The hotel is at the back hidden among the trees. It dates from the 1970s but is not unattractive. You'll get a good night's sleep as long as you don't have noisy neighbours (the partitions are a bit thin). A wonderful breakfast, 43F, is served on the veranda. Doubles with shower or bath 250F. Free apéritif and coffee. 10% discount on the room rate.

SAILLENARD   71580 (20KM NW)

🏃 🏠 |◉| AUBERGE LE MOULIN DE SAUVAGETTE

How to get there: take the D87 signposted to Saillenard and Bletterans – it's 3km from Saillenard.
☎ 03.85.74.17.58 ➔ 03.85.74.17.58
Closed Sun evening, Mon and Feb.

For lovers of country retreats or for lovers pure and simple – the ultimate hideaway on the Burgundy borders, with all the delights of deepest darkest Bresse. It's an old mill way out in the country, attractively converted and decorated. Wonderful bedrooms are furnished in old style at 250–290F with shower and bath. The miller's room is particularly fine, but each has its own personal charm. You'll get a very friendly reception and sample excellent regional cooking served in a beautiful, rustic dining room. Dishes are based on the seasons and what the market has to offer; local *terrine*, free-range chicken, fillet of zander with hazelnuts, and frogs' legs *sauce poulette*. Set menus 125–135F or country platter 75F. Worth visiting more than once. 10% discount on the room rate for a minimum three-night stay.

MÂCON   71000

🏃 🏠 HÔTEL D'EUROPE ET D'ANGLETERRE**

92 quai Jean-Jaurès (Northeast); it's near the train station.
☎ 03.85.38.27.94 ➔ 03.85.39.22.54
TV. **Pay garage**.

This riverside hotel is well located, and even though it feels a bit dated it's still got character and some charm, with an original staircase and large public rooms. You'll get a nice welcome from the owner. It's right on the N6, but the rooms are soundproofed. Doubles 170–280F, and there are rooms to sleep four. Breakfast is free for one child under ten per family. Free garage space.

🏃 🏠 |◉| INTER HÔTEL DE BOURGOGNE**

6 rue Victor-Hugo (Centre).
☎ 03.85.38.36.57 ➔ 03.85.21.10.23
Closed Sat lunchtime, Sun, and the first fortnight in Jan.
Disabled access. **TV**. **Car park**.

Lovely hotel on a shady flower-filled square just a step away from the pedestrian area. Delightful interior with a foyer that's straight out of a Chabrol film. Rooms are painted in pastel shades and have recently been refurbished. Lots of twists and turns, half-landings, nooks and crannies. Doubles with shower/wc are 380F, with bath 440F. In the restaurant there's a 60F lunchtime menu and others 80–220F. Specialities include Bresse chicken in cream sauce and fragrant Oriental prawns. 10% discount on the room rate.

🏃 |◉| MAISON MÂCONNAISE DES VINS

484 av. de-Lattre-de-Tassigny (North); it's on the bank of the Saône, as you come into town from Chalon-sur-Saône.
☎ 03.85.22.91.11
Car park.

Open daily 8am–9pm. This establishment represents a considerable number of vineyard owners from the Côtes Chalonnaises, Beaujolais and Mâcon. You can buy wine by the bottle or fill up a plastic container. They also serve a selection of regional specialities – *bœuf bourguignon*, *andouillette Mâconnaise*, salt pork and omelettes, salads, *fromage blanc*, and particularly good house Mâconnais tarts and waffles; 90F *à la carte*. The dishes are the perfect accompaniment to a Saint-Véran, a Pouilly-Fuissé, a Rully or a Givry – many are served by the glass. You will be spoilt for choice, but had better decide who's driving in advance. There's a terrace overlooking the Saône. Free house apéritif or coffee.

|●| L'AMANDIER

74 rue Dufour (Centre); it's near the Saint-Pierre church.
☎ 03.85.39.82.00
Closed Sun evening and Mon.

Salad of pig's trotters *gribiche* is the house speciality, but Florent Segain often rejigs his 98F set menu (not available on public holidays) to use what's best in the market. It's easy to find the restaurant since it's painted blue – the flowers and the plates are also blue, but the fabrics in the cosy, comfortable dining room are yellow. They offer a string of set menus 135–340F and a weekday one at 105F. *À la carte* there are many delights, including snails in a red wine sauce, roast rack of lamb and *gratin* of crayfish tails. Flowers adorn the terrace.

⅍|●| LE POISSON D'OR

Allée du Parc (North); it's on the marina, 1km from the centre of town.
☎ 03.85.38.00.88 ➡ 03.85.35.82.55
Closed Tues evening in winter, Wed and Feb.
Disabled access. Car park.

You can contemplate the glinting lights in the water and the shady river banks from the large picture windows of this plush but informal establishment, which also has a large, shaded terrace. Regional specialities include rabbit with prunes and onion marmalade, pike soufflé with frogs' legs, duck breast roasted with blackcurrants, and fresh-fried river fish. Menus 98–250F. It's a refined place with tables covered with thick white cloths and enormous vases of flowers everywhere. Attentive service. Free coffee.

|●| RESTAURANT LE ROCHER DE CANCALE

393 quai Jean-Jaurès (Centre).
☎ 03.85.38.07.50 ➡ 03.85.38.70.47
Closed Sun evening and Mon except on public holidays.

The 18th-century house on the river is a refined, elegant setting for this restaurant. The excellent 105F menu is not the kind of loss-leader you find very often in slightly upmarket restaurants; the dishes are delicious and satisfying. If you want to eat more lavishly, there are other set menus up to 200F. The house specialities include warm flan of *foie gras*, Burgundy snails with garlic butter, *poulet de Bresse* with a cream and morel sauce, and fillet of beef with red Mâcon wine sauce. *À la carte* is pricey. They care about the little things here – the bread rolls are served warm and fresh from the oven.

|●| LA VIGNE ET LES VINS (SCOUBIDOU)

42 rue Joseph-Dufour (Centre).
☎ 03.85.38.53.72
Closed Sun, Mon and 1–21 Aug.

Service noon–2pm and 7.30–11pm. It's often hard to get a table in this local, rather ordinary-looking little restaurant, because they serve the best meat and the most generous portions in Mâcon. The owner has a real passion for large chunks of tasty tender meat. The sirloin literally melts in your mouth; eat it plain grilled or with mouthwatering sauces and crispy French fries. There's a pretty good choice — fillet, lamb chops, Châteaubriand, oriental kebabs – and on Fridays and Saturdays in winter, they do couscous. Large first-floor dining room for big groups on a night out – and it won't ruin you. 110F *à la carte*.

SANCÉ   71000 (3KM N)

⅍ ♠ |●| LA VIEILLE FERME**

N6 motorway, exit Mâcon North.
☎ 03.85.40.95.15 ➡ 03.85.40.95.16
Swimming pool. Garden. TV. Car park.

An old farm that's been restored with good taste and turned into a hotel complex. Particularly well positioned on the banks of the Saône, surrounded by real cornfields and real cows, patient anglers and peaceful cyclists riding along the tow-path. The modern part is built like a motel and most of the bedrooms, 280F, overlook the Saône or the countryside. They are spacious and pleasant and you hardly notice the high-speed train hurtling past. The lovely dining room has rustic decor and old-fashioned furniture, but on fine days the terrace is everyone's favourite place to be. Dishes, executed with care, are perfectly affordable; young rabbit stew, free-range chicken with cream, veal sweetbreads with morels, sautéed frogs' legs, and breast of guinea fowl stuffed with ceps. Set menus 89–165F, or a fairly standard *à la carte* menu. Beautiful swimming pool in summer and a generous lunchtime buffet. 10% discount on the room rate for a minimum two-night stay.

CRÈCHES-SUR-SAÔNE   71680 (8KM S)

♠ |●| CHÂTEAU DE LA BARGE**

Centre; take the Mâcon sud exit on the A6 and follow the signs to the train station.
☎ 03.85.23.93.93 ➡ 03.85.23.93.39

Closed Sat and Sun from 1 Nov to Easter, All Saints' and the Christmas–New Year holidays. **TV**. **Car park**.

A little luxury at affordable prices. This enormous house, covered in Virginia creeper, dates from 1679; there are ancient trees in the peaceful grounds. Quite a friendly welcome. The sturdy furniture, the wallpaper that's seen better days, the large rooms ringing with bird song – all seem to have come from another age. Doubles 280F with shower, 350F with bath and TV. The restaurant offers tasty, simple cooking that enhances the quality of the ingredients – *terrine* of pike and tarragon, duck leg in a cider sauce, veal sweetbreads and morels in flaky pastry, sautéed Burgundy snails in cream, and medallions of lamb with bacon and gingerbread. Set menus 98F, served daily, and others 150–220F. Really lovely terrace.

MILLY-LAMARTINE   71960 (10KM W)

|●| CHEZ JACK

pl. de l'Église (Centre); take the N79 from Mâcon, and turn off at Milly-La Roche Vineuse.
☎ 03.85.36.63.72
Closed Sun evening, Mon and Tues evening out of season, a fortnight Aug–Sept and a week in Dec.

A lovely little village restaurant in the shadow of a beautiful church and Lamartine's house, boasting good Beaujolais cooking. Tables are set outside by the church on fine days. Weekday lunch menu 55F. À la carte you can get calf's foot *remoulade*, oven-baked *andouillette*, *entrecôte* steak, hot sausage, veal kidneys in cream, and *tablier de sapeur*, which is a slab of ox tripe egged and crumbed and fried. Good wine selection. by the jug or the bottle: Mâcon rouge, Régnié, Pouilly-Fuissé and so on.

SAINT-VÉRAND   71570 (13KM S)

⅍ 🏠 |●| L'AUBERGE DE SAINT-VÉRAN**

How to get there: leave the A6 at exit 29 to Vinzelles, Juliénas and Saint-Vérand.
☎ 03.85.23.90.90 **➡** 03.85.23.90.91
Closed Tues out of season. **Garden**. **TV**. **Car park**.

In an unspoilt village in the hills among the vineyards, near a stream, you come across a lovely stone house with a terrace and garden. It's a clean, simple hotel with good facilities. The restaurant specialises in regional cooking, with menus 138–245F and attractively priced regional wine. À la carte: little casserole of *andouillette* sausage and veal spleen with Saint Véran, monkfish medallions and

tail in Pouilly, *ballotine* (aspic) of free-range chicken stuffed with morels, and *coq au vin*. A few rooms at 270F, and they do half-board arrangements on request. Free apéritif, and free bed for children under two.

MAILLY-LE-CHÂTEAU   89660

⅍ 🏠 |●| LE CASTEL**

pl. de l'Église.
☎ 03.86.81.43.06 **➡** 03.86.81.49.26
Closed Wed and 15 Nov–15 March.
Disabled access. **Garden**. **Car park**.

It's like something from a picture book; a 13th-century church, a town hall, and a solid, turn-of-the-19th-century house in a courtyard, shaded by lime trees. The hotel and restaurant are both good value for money. Rooms are being renovated one by one and the bathrooms are being re-fitted so, if you wish, you can see the rooms and choose the one that suits you. Doubles 150F with wash basin and up to 330F with bath. The 75F menu is served every day and there are others 105–175F. Free coffee.

MONTBARD   21500

⅍ |●| LA MIRABELLE

Saint-Rémy-les-Montbard; as you leave the town, go towards Forges de Buffon and it's 2km along.
☎ 03.80.92.40.69 **➡** 03.80.92.40.69
Closed Wed. **Car park**.

A small village restaurant serving good food at reasonable prices. There's a menu of the day at 108F, written on the blackboard, with dishes like home-made *terrine*, sautéed pork *grand-mère* and a nougat ice. Others up to 158F. You can buy good wine by the glass. The owner is crazy about wine and he's accumulated a collection of at least 400 French or foreign wines to choose from. Genuinely friendly welcome. An excellent place to stop if you're visiting Fontenay Abbey, 10km away. Free Kir.

MOULINS-ENGILBERT   58290

⅍ 🏠 |●| AU BON LABOUREUR**

pl. Boucaumont (Centre).
☎ 03.86.84.20.55 **➡** 03.86.84.35.52
Closed beginning of Jan. **TV**. **Car park**.

One of the most reliable places in the south of the Morvan where you can have a scrumptious meal at an attractive price. The dishes are amply served and carefully prepared. Weekday menu 65F then 105–238F. The rooms run from simple to quite comfortable, 150–280F. Free coffee and 10% discount on the room rate Nov–March.

SÉMELAY   58369 (19KM S)

|●| RESTAURANT GILLES PERRIN

In the village; it's on the D158 in the direction of Saint Honoré-les-Bains.
☎ 03.86.30.91.66
Closed Mon, every evening except Sat except in July and Aug, and mid-Jan to mid-Feb.

A traditional restaurant with a good local reputation. This is the place to go for a meal with friends, or if someone's just dropped in. Weekday lunch menu 75F then 98–165F, with an amazing salmon and bream in Chablis sauce, veal sweetbreads in Noilly or *noisette* of Charolais steak cooked exactly as you order. The dining room has a countrified, provincial feel.

CHIDDES   58360 (27KM SE)

|●| LA BOUILLE À MALYS

In the village; take the D985 in the direction of Saint Honoré-les-Bains, the Luzy; it's signposted off to the left.
☎ 03.86.30.48.90
Closed Wed and Jan.

This place is run by a couple from the Morvand who wanted to stay in their native area and have a good time. They've created a really matey café-restaurant, decorating it in soft, warm colours. Absolutely reliable local cuisine with dishes of the day at 40F for the order of *andouillette* or the *patronne's* homemade stew or Charolais steak with Roquefort cheese. Lunch menu for 55F and others 85–110F. On Saturday they have karaoke or theme evenings with dishes from other places; couscous, paella, *choucroute* and so on. Free coffee or, if there are four of you ordering the 85F menu, a tee-shirt.

MOUX-EN-MORVAN   58230

|●| HÔTEL-RESTAURANT BEAU SITE*

Bellvue-Moux-en-Morvan: it's on the D121.
☎ 03.86.76.11.75 ➡ 03.86.76.15.84
Closed Sun evening and Mon 15 Nov–20 March, and Jan. **Locked car park.**

An ordinary-looking place but the name's appropriate – it's in a fantastic position. Sound home-cooking at good prices, majoring in traditional dishes with lots of sauce. First menu at 69F is very respectable; others 110–190F. In the hotel, a five-minute walk away, there are cheap, simple, spacious rooms; doubles with basin 148F and up to 250F with bath. Free apéritif.

NEVERS   58000

|●| HÔTEL BEAUSÉJOUR*

5 [bis] rue Saint-Gildard; it's opposite the shrine of St Bernadette.
☎ 03.86.61.20.84 ➡ 03.86.59.15.37
Closed Feb school holidays. **TV. Garden.**

Cheap, simple, functional rooms that are spotlessly clean. Just out of the town centre in a quiet, unfrequented street. It's well soundproofed and the garden rooms are very quiet. Doubles with washing facilities 140F, up to 220F with bath. The welcome is really charming and breakfast is available on the veranda from a self-service buffet. 10% discount on the room rate.

|●| HÔTEL DE CLÈVES*

8 rue Saint-Didier (Centre).
☎ 03.86.61.15.87 ➡ 03.86.57.13.80
TV. Garden.

Well placed, not far from the station in a quiet street in the town centre. A small establishment, very well run by an affable woman who's happy to chat while you have breakfast. The entrance has been redecorated and the rooms updated – they now have quality bedding. There's a small, pleasant corner of a garden. Double with shower 239F, 289F with bath. 10% discount at weekends.

|●| HÔTEL MOLIÈRE

25 rue Molière; take the boulevard du Maréchal-Juin, when you get to the BP garage turn right into the rue de Vauzelles and follow the signs.
☎ 03.86.57.29.96
Closed the first fortnight in Aug. **TV. Car park. Garden.**

A small hotel in a quiet spot near the town centre run by a kindly, welcoming lady. The rooms are bright and cheerful and half of them have views over the garden. Excellent beds. Double rooms 265F with shower/wc and 295F with bath. There's a big, closed (and free) car park across the road.

|●| HÔTEL-RESTAURANT LA FOLIE

Route des Saulaies.
☎ 03.86.57.05.31 ➡ 03.86.57.66.69
Restaurant closed Fri and Sun evening Sept–May, and

Fri lunchtime in June. **Swimming pools**. **Garden**. **TV**. **Car park**.

It's well worth choosing this place over lots of others, as its park, tennis court and swimming pools lend the atmosphere of a holiday club. Bedrooms are contemporary in design at 290F with bath – no charge for children under two and cots are available. You eat either in the dining room or on the terrace with a view of the Loire flowing gently by in the distance. Cheapest menu at 99.50F then others 130–160F. No charge for parking. It's advisable to book.

⚤ |●| LE GOÉMON-CRÊPERIE BRETONNE

9 rue du 14-Juillet.
☎ 03.86.59.54.99
Closed Sun and Mon.

Somewhat dreary-looking setting, but the savoury *crêpes* are anything but dull. There is an excellent variety, the tastiest filled with *Guéméné andouillette* sausage, and the sweet ones are good too. At lunchtime there's a 56F menu of starter, savoury *galette* and dessert. Friendly service. Free apéritif.

|●| RESTAURANT AUX CHŒURS DE BACCHUS

25 av. du Général-de-Gaulle (Centre); near the station.
☎ 03.86.36.72.70
Closed Sat lunchtime, Sun, mid-Dec to beginning of Jan, and the first three weeks in Aug.

Very good – very, very good – little restaurant, and not so little at that. Service is slick, fast and friendly. The cuisine has been honed and improved over the years; it's self-confident and delicious, and the dishes strictly follow the seasons. You can readily accompany each course with a glass of different wine that has been carefully chosen to complement each dish so your meal turns into a feast fit for a king. The 85F menu is also served in the evenings and there are others 122–185F.

|●| LA COUR SAINT-ÉTIENNE

33 rue Saint-Étienne (Centre); it's behind the church of Saint-Étienne.
☎ 03.86.36.74.57
Closed Sun, Mon, a fortnight in Jan and the first three weeks in Aug.

Two dining rooms in soft shades, a discreet classical interior and competent service. So far so good. Better still is the good-value 109F menu; delicate salmon stuffed with artichoke and aubergine and supreme of

chicken stuffed with ceps are both very successful dishes. On the dessert menu the *croquant* of pear with chicory is a triumph. Menus 88F (not served Sat), and 114–148F. In summer they set a few tables on the terrace opposite the beautiful church of Saint-Étienne.

|●| RESTAURANT JEAN-MICHEL COURON

21 rue Saint-Étienne (Centre); it's near the church of Saint-Étienne.
☎ 03.86.61.19.28
Closed Sun evening, Mon and Tues lunchtimes, a fortnight in Jan and 20 July–10 Aug.

A Michelin star for the star restaurant of Nevers. Three small, elegant rooms, one in a particularly charming gothic style. Fine, well-balanced cuisine. Realistic prices, too: menus start at 118F, including cheese and dessert, then 165–240F. Particularly good are the tomato and apple tart and the stewed plaice fillet with a red pepper and sage compote. For dessert, the warm spiced chocolate is a delight. Probably worth booking.

MARZY   58000 (5KM W)

⚤ 🏠 |●| LE VAL DE LOIRE*

Corcelles village; take the D131, it's on the edge of the village on the way to Corcelles.
☎ 03.86.38.86.21
Disabled access. **Car park**.

A quiet, cheap place. Doubles 130F with basin to 200F with bath. The rooms are in a new annexe and are very well maintained. There's a nice family feeling here. The only drawback is that it's a bit far from Nevers and there are only two buses a day. Simple cooking, ample portions and menus 60–120F. Free apéritif.

SAVIGNY-LES-BOIS   58160 (10KM E)

⚤ |●| AUBERGE DU MOULIN DE L'ÉTANG

Take the D978 from Nevers–Château–Chinon then right at the D18. It's just outside the village on the D209.
☎ 03.86.37.10.17
Closed Mon, Wed evening and a fortnight in Jan–Feb.

One of the good tables in the area; excellent brawn on the 110F menu served with all the fat, a "slimline" *sauce gribiche* and a tasty *mignon* of pork in a game marinade. The desserts are a little disappointing – the *crème brûlée* is heavy and over-sweet – but on the whole it's a good place. Attentive, friendly service in the large, provincial-feeling dining room. Other menus 140–240F. Free coffee.

MAGNY-COURS   58470 (12KM S)

🏕 🏠 |●| HÔTEL-RESTAURANT LA RENAISSANCE***

In the village; take the N7.
☎ 03.86.58.10.4 📠 03.86.21.22.60
Closed Sun evening, Mon, three weeks in Feb and a fortnight in Aug. **TV. Car park**.

A smart hotel-restaurant with a good local reputation for the cooking. It's about 3km from Magny-Cours car racing circuit, and the guys from the pits are fans of the tasty cooking of the stylish chef. He uses the freshest produce; frogs' legs *à la bourguignonne*, grilled monkfish with an escalope of duck *foie gras* with Saint-Émilion wine sauce, roast veal sweetbreads, and deep-fried Charolais steak. Good Loire wines at affordable prices. Wine is served with the 250F menu and there are others 300–400F. Pleasant dining room and attentive service. Bedrooms with good facilities from 500F for a double. A seriously good place in this category. Free house apéritif.

NITRY   89310

|●| AUBERGE LA BEURSAUDIÈRE

Chemin de Ronde; it's on the Sacy road.
☎ 03.86.33.69.69
Car park.

Superb Morvan building with a medieval pigeon tower. It's mainly an overnight stop for holiday-makers travelling south. There's an emphasis on "local" character here; waitresses in regional costume, quaint menu titles like "*Roulants*" (driving through) or "*Batteuses*" (threshers), and the like. The terrace is great – it can really sizzle in summer. Sturdy local dishes built for big appetites. In the week, there's a 70F *formule* of starter and a main course, but the first real menu costs 97F, and there are others 175–200F. They're building a hotel.

NOYERS-SUR-SEREIN   89310 (10KM NE)

🏕 🏠 |●| HÔTEL DE LA VIEILLE TOUR

pl. du Grenier-à-Sel (Centre).
☎ 03.86.82.87.69 📠 03.86.82.66.04
Closed Oct to end March.

This elegant 17th-century edifice, covered in creepers, was the home of the writer Charles-Louis Pothier, famed throughout France for the song *Les Roses Blanches*. It's become a picture gallery with a few rooms and a simple place to eat. The setting is warm and informal; the place is more a guest house than a hotel-restaurant. Double rooms are 200F with basin and 250–400F with shower/wc or bath. The *patronne* is a Dutch woman. There's a single menu "*table d'hôte*", at 85F served daily, but you have to book. They use lots of fresh vegetables and herbs from the garden. An amazing place – something from another era. Free coffee.

NOLAY   21340

🏕 |●| RESTAURANT LE BURGONDE

35 rue de la République; Nolay lies between Beaune and Autun.
☎ 03.80.21.71.25
Closed Tues evening, Wed and the Feb school holidays.

Service noon–2pm and 7–9pm. They've kept the shop front of this small department store, but today a restaurant occupies the sales floor. The provincial dining room has a strong bourgeois style with green plants everywhere and a beamed wooden ceiling. It's absolutely charming. In the second dining room there's another surprise; a winter garden on a veranda, enclosed by a conservatory. Very pleasant, very plush. There's a regional menu and the chef uses produce bought from the neighbouring farms and local producers. Menus start at 98F with others 128–235F. Kindly service. Wine at reasonable prices. Free coffee.

EVELLE   21340 (5KM N)

🏕 |●| L'AUBERGE DU VIEUX PRESSOIR

How to get there: after La Rochepot, take the route des Coteaux in the direction of Orches and Saint-Romain.
☎ and 📠 3.80.21.82.16
Closed Mon, Tues lunchtime, a fortnight in Jan and the Feb school holidays.

The winding road leads you through the hills and vineyards to this bright cheerful inn. The cuisine of the Hautes Côtes that you will encounter on the menus (100–160F) will enrapture you; traditional *œufs en meurette* or excellent home-made *terrine* followed by pan-fried calf's liver or fillet steak with a shallot cream, with local cheeses and desserts to follow. The cheapest menu is more than adequate. Free coffee.

NUITS-SAINT-GEORGES 21700

⌂ |●| IRIS HÔTEL

1 av. Chamboland (South); it's on the edge of town in the direction of Beaune.
☎ 03.80.61.10.41
TV. Car park.

This used to be a dreary chain hotel which closed and fell into serious disrepair. But it's been taken over and turned into a small, welcoming establishment that's ideal for an overnight stay. It's a place worth supporting, even though it falls short of perfection. Double rooms 230–290F. The restaurant reassuringly serves local dishes: *terrine* with Marc de Bourgogne, skirt with a sauce using Nuits-Saint-Georges red wine, and chicken breast with Époisse cheese sauce. Weekday lunch menu 65F then 85–135F. There's a corner bar where you can try the local vintage, and a terrace.

|●| LE RESTAURANT DE LA TOUR

14 rue Général-de-Gaulle (Southwest); it's on the Beaune road.
☎ 03.80.61.17.20
Closed Sun evening and Mon.

A very well-run family establishment offering attractive prices, a good choice of wines and dishes cooked using fresh ingredients of the highest quality. Regional dishes include the famous chicken Gaston-Gérard, a recipe that was created by the first wife of the former mayor of Dijon. The mayor was entertaining a gastronome and critic when Madame, in her anxiety, dropped a small tin of paprika into a pan of chicken cooking in white wine and Gruyère cheese. It was a triumph. There's a 65F lunch menu in the week and others 77–169F.

VILLARS-FONTAINE 21700 (5KM W)

|●| AUBERGE DU COTEAU

It's in the centre.
☎ 03.80.61.10.50 ➡ 03.80.61.30.32
Closed Tues evening and Wed, a fortnight in Feb and a fortnight at the end of Aug. **Car park**.

This is a real country inn, serving home-made *terrine*, tender meat grilled on an open fire, *coq au vin*, snails and lots of other lovely local dishes. They'll satisfy your hunger after a walk through the vineyards and your thirst will be more than slaked by the local wines from the Hautes Côtes. There's an open fire, checked tablecloths and old-fashioned prices; the weekday lunch menu costs 60F, and there are others at 75–120F. It's a perfect place to come after an afternoon exploring the countryside behind the Côte de Nuits – a region famous for its goats, artisan craftsmen, hilltop chapels and ruined castle museums.

VOUGEOT 21640 (10KM S)

⅍ ⌂ HÔTEL DE VOUGEOT

18 rue du Vieux-Château.
☎ 03.80.62.01.15 ➡ 03.80.62.49.09
Car park.

Vougeot is world famous for the wine festivals organised by the Confrérie du Clos Vougeot, founded to maintain the quality of Burgundy's wines and to promote them across the globe. This odd hotel, with its dreary façade, is not what you'd expect to find here, but the lovely courtyard and the peace and tranquillity make up for that. Rooms, some with a view of the château, are 380–480F. It has a bar where they serve local wine. Everyone is treated well, even tourists clutching guide books. 10% discount Nov–May.

AUVILLARS-SUR-SAÔNE 21250 (15KM E)

⅍ |●| AUBERGE DE L'ABBAYE

Route de Seurre.
☎ 03.80.26.97.37
Closed Sun and Tues evenings, and Wed. **Car park**.

You have to stop here; it's only 1km from Citeaux Abbey, the mother house of the closed Cistercian order. The chef creates succulent dishes with flair and you can try his specialities at almost *prix fixe* prices. You can eat in the bistro corner that's pretty as can be and opt for the menu of the day; chicken liver terrine, pork with apples and bread and butter pudding are typical of the style. The bistro *formule* at lunchtime in the week costs 82F, and there are other menus 120–245F. Their specialities include crayfish with hazelnuts and spiced bread, veal and chicken pie and, in winter, cream of morel soup. There's a pretty terrace. Free coffee.

CURTIL-BERGY 21220 (18KM N)

⌂ HÔTEL LE MANASSES

How to get there; as you leave the village, take the little road going up to the Hautes Côtes de Nuits.

☎ 03.80.61.43.81 ➠ 03.80.61.42.79
Closed Dec–Feb. **TV**. **Car park**.

There's a splendid view over the vineyards and a remarkable silence to this place. The Chaleys and other winegrowers in the area have built up the reputation of the wines from the Hautes Côtes. In his younger days, the grandfather used to deliver his wines himself; his son continues today, but at least he has a car. They have constructed this charming little hotel and turned a barn into a wine museum where you can sample the goods. Breakfast is Burgundy style. Very comfortable doubles 430–580F.

PARAY-LE-MONIAL   71600

🏃 🏠 |●| GRAND HÔTEL DE LA BASILIQUE**

18 rue de la Visitation (Centre); it's 100m from the basilica, opposite the chapel of the Visitation.
☎ 03.85.81.11.13 ➠ 03.85.88.83.70
Closed 1 Nov–15 March. **TV**. **Pay car park**.

Double rooms go for 260–320F, all with new bathrooms. Regional dishes are served in the restaurant – menus 75–220F. Of the specialities, try the turbot fillet with hay, the Charolais beef steak *label rouge*, *œufs en meurette* and ice cream *du vieux quartier*. Delightful hotel but best behaviour is required – it's a favourite place for visiting pilgrims. 10% discount on the room rate Sept–July.

🏃 🏠 |●| HÔTEL TERMINUS

27 av. de la Gare (North); it's opposite the train station.
☎ 03.85.81.59.31 ➠ 03.85.81.38.31
Restaurant closed Sat and Sun. **TV**. **Car park**.

Big, very well restored hotel. Don't let the austere façade put you off; once inside you'll be warmly greeted and you'll see that the owners pay great attention to detail. The spacious rooms have been revamped and decorated in matching floral fabric. The bathrooms are fantastic; the marriage of materials – wood, perspex and the high pressure jets in the shower – is a little futuristic. Rooms from 315F with shower/wc to 380F with bath. A limited number of good dishes in the brasserie, with a lunch menu at 79F and others up to 120F. Free coffee.

POUILLY-SUR-LOIRE   58150

🏃 🏠 |●| LE RELAIS FLEURI-COQ HARDI

42 av. de la Tuillerie; it's 1km southeast of the centre,

opposite the wine cellars.
☎ 03.86.39.12.99 ➠ 03.86.39.14.15
Closed Tues evening and Wed Oct–April, and mid-Dec to mid-Jan. **TV**. **Garden**. **Car park**.

Typical *Logis de France* hotel, with rustic furniture, and flowers and plants everywhere. The rooms are good, particularly those with a view over the Loire. Doubles with shower or bath are 300–460F. The restaurant serves regional cooking worth its salt. Menus start at 110F then 170F and 260F. All in all, a good establishment. Free glass of dessert wine.

QUARRÉ-LES-TOMBES   89630

🏠 |●| HÔTEL-RESTAURANT LE MORVAN

6 rue des Écoles (Centre).
☎ 03.86.32.29.29 ➠ 03.86.32.29.28
Closed Sun evening and Mon.
Disabled access. **Garden**. **TV**. **Car park**.

One of those places where you feel at ease as soon as you walk through the door, largely because of the simple, smiling welcome. All the rooms are individualised – doubles 295–360F. The cooking is sheer Burgundy and dishes show off the freshness of the seasonal market produce. There's a lunch menu at 80F, a weekday menu at 105F and others up to 250F. Things are done simply but well.

🏃 🏠 |●| AUBERGE DE L'ÂTRE

Les Lavaults; take the N6 then the D10, in the direction of lac des Settons.
☎ 03.86.32.20.79 ➠ 03.86.32.28.25
Closed Tues evening and Wed out of season, 25 Nov–10 Dec and 1 Feb–10 March.
Disabled access. **Garden**. **TV**. **Car park**.

This inn is in an isolated spot in the tough country of the Morvan. The bar is like an old-fashioned bistro with warm, rustic decor. The chef plays around with the plants and mushrooms he picks locally to create his delicious dishes; this is probably the most inventive cooking in the area and at realistic prices. Menus from 145F (weekdays) then 220–295F. It's a charming place where you may well be tempted to stay. If so, they have seven pleasant rooms, 400–550F with good facilities. 10% discount on the room rate 1 Oct–15 Dec and 4–28 Jan.

BRIZARDS (LES)   89630 (6KM SE)

🏃 🏠 |●| AUBERGE DES BRIZARDS**

How to get there: take the D55 and follow the arrows.
☎ 03.86.32.20.12 ➠ 03.86.32.27.40
Closed 5 Jan–8 Feb. **Disabled access**. **TV**. **Car park**.

An utterly romantic inn, buried in the depths of the Morvan forest. An isolated fairytale of a place in a bewitching setting. Doubles with shower/wc or bath 280–750F. There's also a magical "poet's house"; in the winter they light a wood fire so you can snuggle up, while in the summer the old stones prove nice and cool. Service with a smile in a bright well-proportioned dining room that looks nothing like it used to when grandma Odette ran the place. Try the zander stewed in red wine, the port pie, or the genuine black pudding with home-grown apples and spiced bread. Menus start at 85F (weekday lunch) then 160–300F. 10% discount on the room rate for a two-night stay Oct–June.

LA ROCHE-EN-BRENIL   21530

🏊 |●| AUX PORTES DU MORVAN

It's on the RN6.
☎ 03.80.64.75.28
Closed Tues evening, Wed, 20 Dec–20 Jan and a fortnight in mid-June. **Swimming pool**. **TV**. **Car park**.

Tasty, healthy food that won't turn your stomach when you see the bill. The chef's specialities include *terrine façon Ginette*, ham with cream, eggs in wine sauce and Morvan tarts at the weekend. Before your meal, get into the swing by having a drink at the bar which is full of local regulars. Menus start at 65F and they also prepare snacks like omelettes at any time of the day. Free apéritif or coffee with a complete meal.

ROMANECHE-THORINS   71720

🏊 🏠 |●| LA MAISON BLANCHE**

N6 (Centre); it's south of Mâcon, on the border of Rhône.
☎ 03.85.35.50.53 ➡ 03.85.35.21.22
Closed Sun evening, Mon and 5 Jan–5 Feb.
Swimming pool. **TV**. **Car park**.

The roadside location of this establishment doesn't make you feel like stopping, but here you get fantastic regional cooking created with great professional skill. The decor is pretty conventional but the service is attentive and they score points where they count most – for the quality of the food. Highlights from the menus include salmon smoked over beech, pan-fried frogs' legs, lobster with spring vegetables and coral sauce, *andouillette au gratin*, and tournedos with morels – and their *coq au vin* is the best you're likely to

eat. Menus start cheaply at 90F and go up to 220F. Half board 290F. They've a few comfy bedrooms, doubles 180–200F; the ones at the front are soundproofed. Free apéritif.

RULLY   71150

🏠 |●| LE VENDANGEROT**

pl. Sainte-Marie (Centre).
☎ 03.85.87.20.09 ➡ 03.85.91.27.18
Closed Tues, Wed, the first fortnight in Jan and the second fortnight in Feb. **Garden**. **TV**. **Car park**.

On the square of this picturesque wine village stands an ample house surrounded by flowers and greenery. As a souvenir of its previous incarnation, the old *Hôtel du Commerce* sign is still hanging up outside. Inside it's all new and run by excellent staff. The chef, Armand, creates wonderful things; signature dishes include flaky pastry with snails, fillet of zander in red butter sauce, and *coq au vin*, exceptionally cooked with white wine. Weekday menu is 98F with others up to 250F; these include things like oxtail stew with vegetables and morels, crayfish tails in a white Rully wine sauce, crayfish in white Rully wine, and grain-fed pigeon with a truffle sauce. Try the wine of the village – a glass of Rully at 18F – perhaps as an apéritif. The rooms have heavy wooden shutters and the village is quiet, so it's an ideal place to escape from the stress of town life. Rooms cost 280F with shower and 300F with bath.

SAINT-CHRISTOPHE-EN-BRIONNAIS 71800

|●| BAR-RESTAURANT DU MIDI

Grand-Rue (Centre); either on the D34 from Paray-le-Monial or from Clayette on the D989.
☎ 03.85.25.87.06 ➡ 03.85.25.90.63
Closed Mon and Jan.

Thursday is market day and for a good number of years Liliane and Bernard Degueurce have opened at 6am to feed and water the horse-dealers and traders. They pile into the big dining room-cum-canteen beyond the bar and kitchen; dishes include tasty brawn, ham hock or delicious *pot-au-feu* which is meat poached with vegetables. All the meat dishes are good. It's quieter the rest of the week. Menus 60–120F. Decent Côtes-du-Rhône, Mâcon Village and Saint-Véran.

SAINT-FLORENTIN   89600

☎ |●| LES TILLEULS**

3 rue Descourtive (Centre).
☎ 03.86.35.09.09 ➡ 03.86.35.36.90
Restaurant closed Sun evening, Mon, a week at the end of Dec, and Feb. **Garden**. **TV**. **Car park**.

Service noon–2pm and 7.30–9pm. In a quiet side street, just outside the centre. You can have a peaceful lunch under the lime trees, on a pretty terrace surrounded by an equally pretty garden far from the stress of daily life. Set menus start at 105F and go up to 250F. Staff are rather reserved. Comfortable rooms with good facilities cost 310–390F with shower/wc or bath.

NEUVY-SAUTOUR   89570 (7KM NE)

|●| RESTAURANT LE DAUPHIN

Route de Troyes; take the N77 in the direction of Troyes.
☎ 03.86.56.30.01 ➡ 03.86.56.40.00
Closed Sun evening and Mon. **Garden**. **Car park**.

The devilishly good chef here creates tempting little dishes which could cause the downfall of a saint. Be tempted by pan-fried scallops with *soufflé rosé* butter and fresh pasta, *surprise* of snails with herbs from the Yonne or a *crème brûlée* with blue poppy seeds. There are more temptations on the set menus at 85F (weekdays only) or 115–240F. Refinement, creativity in the cooking and very kindly staff.

SAINT-JULIEN-DE-JONZY   71110

⅔ ☎ |●| HÔTEL-RESTAURANT-BOUCHERIE PONT BERNARD**

Le bourg; it's 8km south of Saint-Christophe-en-Brionnais – from Paray-le-Monial, take the D34 and the D20.
☎ 03.85.84.01.95 ➡ 03.85.84.14.61
Closed Mon evening and the Feb school holidays. **Car park**.

This is Charolais country, 30km north of Roanne. They don't do things by halves. While they don't attempt to compete with the Troisgros brothers they know what they do and they do it well. Monsieur Pont is both butcher and cook so the meat is of superb quality, cooked up in generous portions; this is simple, tasty home cooking. Dishes on the middle-priced menus include *coq au vin* and fillet of sea bream with champagne sauce; others include home

made *foie gras*, *tournedos* and farm-raised veal escalope in cream sauce. Excellent desserts. There's a weekday lunch menu at 59F and others 89–159F. Simple and comfortable rooms with bath, 220F. Kind, congenial hosts. Free *digestif*.

SAULIEU   21210

⅔ ☎ |●| LA VIEILLE AUBERGE

15 rue Grillot (South).
☎ 03.80.64.13.74
Closed Tues evening and Wed except July–Aug, and 3 Jan–3 Feb. **Garden**. **Car park**.

This inn is tucked away at a bend in the road so you could drive past a dozen times without noticing it. Everyone who drove south to the Côte on the N6 knew Saulieu well. When the motorway opened, the old town and this old inn fell on harder times. But a new generation of restaurateurs have put Saulieu back on the gastronomic and touristic map and a pair took over the place. Menus 75–175F. Try the brilliant mousse of zander *soufflé* with Aligoté, the *terrine* of Charolais, *marbré* of rabbit, or roast zander with red wine. Absolutely delightful dining room and an attractive hidden terrace. Rooms with shower/wc or bath 210F. 10% discount on the room rate.

⅔ ☎ |●| LA BORNE IMPÉRIALE**

14–16 rue d'Argentine (Centre).
☎ 03.80.64.19.76
Garden. **TV**. **Car park**.

Near Pompom's famous sculpture of a bull – a Saulieu landmark – you'll find *La Borne Impériale*, a gastronomic landmark and one of the last old-fashioned inns in Burgundy. Fully restored after a gas explosion a couple of years back, it has seven rooms at 220–310F, the best of which have a view of the attractive garden. The beautiful dining room has a terrace open on fine days. Weekday menu 110F, then up to 160F, listing good, regional dishes. The welcome is variable. Free coffee.

SEMUR-EN-AUXOIS   21140

⅔ ☎ HÔTEL DES CYMAISES**

7 rue du Renaudot (Centre).
☎ 03.80.97.21.44 ➡ 03.80.97.18.23
Closed Feb and All Saints' school holidays.
Disabled access. **TV**. **Car park**.

In the very heart of the medieval city, just

behind Porte Sauvigny, there's a beautiful 18th-century building which has adapted extremely well to life as a 21st-century hotel. It's cool, clean and comfortable, and you can come and go as you please. Breakfast is served under the pergola. Nicely furnished rooms 320–350F. 10% discount Nov–March.

I●I LE CALIBRESSAN**

16 rue Feveret.
☎ 03.80.97.32.40
Closed Sat lunchtime, Sun evening, Mon and Jan.

A twist of California in this kitchen in Bresse – thus *Calibressan*. An attractive little restaurant combining authentic rustic decor – beams, unadorned brick walls, flowers and pretty curtains – with the vitality and exoticism of the New World, represented by Madame at the reception, a Californian born and bred. You'll also detect flavours of the New World in certain sauces and side dishes. Try the roast kangaroo fillet with Grand Veneur sauce or the house chilli con carne. Weekday lunch menu 82F and others up to 135F.

I●I RESTAURANT DES MINIMES

39 rue Vaux; it's 500m from the town centre.
☎ 03.80.97.26.86
Closed Sun evening, Mon and the end of Dec except for New Year's Eve.

Service noon–2pm and 7.30–9.30 or 10pm. This "local" bistro below the ramparts has become an absolute must for tourists in search of the soul, the voice and the cooking of Semur. There's a pastoral feel to the decor and an informal atmosphere. There's a 98F menu and a *menu-carte* at 150F. The *patronne* loves good wine and good banter and she's completely unphased by anyone, from local politicians to people who don't pay their bills. You can have two different wines with *œufs en meurette* in a red wine sauce, salmon *à l'unilatéral* (grilled on just one side), steak with Époisses cheese, boned and caramelised pig's trogger, calf's head *ravigote* (not summer), *clafoutis* with sour cherries and iced nougat.

PONT-ET-MASSÈNE   21141 (3KM S)

🏠 I●I HÔTEL DU LAC**

10 rue du Lac.
☎ 03.80.97.11.11 ➡ 03.80.97.29.25
Closed Sun evening, Mon out of season, and 20 Dec to end Jan. **Garden**. **TV**. **Car park**.

Down from the lake, this huge building just

reeks of the 1950s. Some pleasant rooms and some fairly dreary; 275–315F. Family atmosphere in the restaurant and the kind of regional cooking you'd eat during a traditional family Sunday lunch; dishes like *jambon persillé* made with local ham, ham in cream sauce, chicken *fricassée* with mushrooms, *coq au vin*, and calf's head in a spicy *vinaigrette*. Set menu, 88F, served in the week, then 105–156F. Try the local blanc de l'Auxois, which is a very drinkable wine and deserves to be better known. There's a terrace with an arbour for fine summer days.

ALÉSIA   21150 (20KM NE)

I●I L'AUBERGE DU CHEVAL BLANC

Rue du Miroir (Centre).
☎ 03.80.97.11.11 ➡ 03.80.97.29.25
Closed Sun evening, Mon and 15 Jan–15 Feb.

Repair here after a morning reviewing the excavations at Alesia where Vercingetorix fought his last against the armies of Julius Caesar. The brasserie menu lists parsleyed ham and other decent dishes. Good regional cooking served in the bigger dining room. The chef uses vegetables from the garden and the market: *fricassée* of chicken with cream and mushrooms or grilled steak with shallot butter. Weekday lunch menu 78F or 98–205F. The place has a young feel – the serving staff are energetic. Have a glass of local Chardonnay or Pinot Noir.

SENS   89100

🌿 🏠 I●I HÔTEL L'ESPLANADE*

2 bd. du Mail.
☎ 03.86.83.14.70 ➡ 03.86.83.14.71
Closed Sun out of season, Aug, Christmas and New Year. **TV**.

Lovely hotel in a fancy house in the centre of town. The place is so old that even the owner can't tell you when it was built. Rooms are on the small side but well renovated and refurbished; there's double glazing in those looking over the road, and new beds and linen. Doubles with a basin only at 146F, or 241F with shower/wc. No restaurant, but they do have a really nice bar where you have breakfast. Free breakfast.

I●I RESTAURANT LE SOLEIL LEVANT

51 rue Émile-Zola (Southwest); it's close to the station.
☎ 03.86.65.71.82
Closed Sun and evenings, and Aug.

Here's a restaurant that's very classical in both decor and cuisine which is well known for its fish dishes, particularly the signature dish of salmon with sorrel. They also do good meat dishes like *foie gras*; the calf sweetbread *vol-au-vents* with scallops is a local favourite, along with the heavenly house desserts. The cheapest menu costs 70F (not served on Sun), then others at 92F or 162F and *à la carte*.

VILLEROY   89100 (7KM SW)

🖄 🏠 I●I RELAIS DE VILLEROY**

Route de Nemours.
☎ 03.86.88.81.77 📠 03.86.88.84.04
Closed Sun evening and Mon, Christmas and Feb school holidays, and a week at the beginning of July. **Garden**. **TV**. **Car park**.

This very smart-looking establishment is one of the nicest in the area. With considerable success, the owners are trying to create a homely atmosphere and to offer a warm welcome and good food. The restaurant smells wonderfully of furniture polish and good cooking. There's a lot of fish on the menu and home-made pastries that melt in the mouth. Set menus 120–245F. The prices in the bistro, *Chez Clément*, next door are much more affordable. The bedrooms, with their flowered wallpaper and antique furniture, are in keeping with the rest of the establishment. Double glazing means you don't have to worry about traffic noise. Doubles 210F with shower/wc and 265F with bath. 10% discount on the room rate and a free glass of champagne with dessert.

VAUDEURS   89320 (24KM S)

🏠 I●I HÔTEL-RESTAURANT LA VAUDEURINOISE*

10 route de Grange-Sèche; take the N60 for Troyes then the D905 towards Saint-Florentin.
☎ 03.86.96.28.00 📠 03.86.96.28.03
Closed Tues and Wed evenings except in July–Aug, and 16 Feb–8 March. **Garden**.

Classic country hostelry in the green and pleasant land of the Othe river. It's in quite a new house, just outside the village, and nice and quiet. They offer six basic but bright rooms, some of which overlook the garden, and all of which have en-suite bath. Doubles 175–250F. In the restaurant, set menus range from 85F (weedays only) to 230F. The menus are dominated by regional cuisine;

snail fritters *à la bourguignonne*, a pastry of Chaource cheese with salad and a mousse of *crémant de Bourgogne* with poached fruit. À la carte are *brioche* filled with ox marrow *à la bourguignonne*, *salmis* of quail with Ratafia liquor and Burgundy cherries. Particularly friendly atmosphere.

TOUCY   89130

🖄 🏠 I●I LE LION D'OR

37 rue Lucile-Cormier (Centre).
☎ 03.86.44.00.76
Closed Sun evening, Mon and 1–20 Dec. **Car park**.

An old hotel with a magnificent wooden staircase, this was one of the places in the Yonne that we fell in love with. Everything smells of beeswax, and the rooms are simple but cosy and meticulously clean. Doubles 180F with basin and 290F with shower/wc or bath. The dining room is delightful. Regional specialities include ham cooked in Chablis, fish *en croûte* with sorrel, and (in season) roast wild boar in a peppery sauce. Menus 90–180F. 10% discount on the room rate.

FONTENOY   89420 (10KM S)

🖄 🏠 I●I LE FONTENOY

Centre; from Tournus take the D14 towards Chapaize,
☎ 03.86.44.02.18
Garden.

Cheap, standardised rooms; 170F for a double with all facilities. The Marseillais boss and his wife in her pinny embrace the regulars and create a very friendly, easy-going atmosphere in this café-restaurant-hotel. It seems as if the whole of the village passes through the place in a day. Good, honest, friendly cooking, too: grilled steak, *bœuf bourgignon* and *andouillette*. They even ask you if you've had enough to eat. The 59F weekday menu includes a $\frac{1}{4}$ litre of wine. Other menus 79F and 89F. There's a terrace and a space for the kids to play in the garden. Best to book at the weekend.

TOURNUS   71700

🖄 🏠 I●I HÔTEL DE SAÔNE**

Rive Gauche (Centre).
☎ 03.85.51.20.65 📠 03.85.51.05.45
Closed Mon and Oct–Feb. **Disabled access**. **Car park**.

A lovely, peaceful location on the riverbank

away from traffic noise. Most of the rooms, 260F, are situated in the annexe and have a river view but ask to choose the one you want because they're not all that appealing. The restaurant offers good regional cooking and set menus 90–140F. They lists frogs' legs and main courses like sirloin or free-range chicken with a morel sauce. If you feel like fish, they have *petite friture* like whitebait, fillets of sole in an Aligoté wine sauce, and zander in a cream and white wine sauce. The terrace is very pleasant in summer, overlooking the houses down by the water and the abbey. Have a post-prandial stroll along the velvety green banks of the Saône. Free coffee.

⊁ ⚑ I●I HÔTEL-RESTAURANT AUX TERRASSES**

18 av. du 23 Janvier (South).
☎ 03.85.51.01.74 ➡ 03.85.51.09.99
Closed Sun evening except July–Aug, Mon and Tues lunchtimes, and Jan. **TV. Car park**.

This place is known for the quality of the cooking in the restaurant. It's set in an enormous roadside establishment, probably a former coaching inn. The lounge separates two large, richly decorated dining rooms. Reception's a bit on the chic side but not overly so, and service is attentive. Set menus start at 100F (weekday lunch only), which is good value, and go up to 258F. *À la carte* lists a variety of dishes: zander with oyster mushrooms, Bresse chicken with morel and cream sauce, and *millefeuille* with pears and gingerbread ice cream. They also do an excellent fish soup. Comfortable rooms with shower/wc 300–340F. Free coffee.

⊁ ⚑ I●I HÔTEL LE SAUVAGE***

pl. du Champ de Mars (Centre).
☎ 03.85.51.14.45 ➡ 03.85.32.10.27
TV.

They say you can't miss this Virginia-creeper-smothered house – but then they all say that! It's just a little set back from the main road. This good old establishment has been ticking over quietly for ages. Pleasant rooms with shower/wc, 350F, or bath 430F. They do a good range of set menus 84–250F – one is dedicated to regional dishes, like parsleyed rabbit with pickled onions, chicken liver *gâteau* with shrimps, *coq au vin*, and fillet of duck with pears and Marc de Bourgogne. *À la carte* you can get Burgundy snails, fresh frogs' legs in parsley, Bresse chicken with cream and morel sauce, grilled or fried Charolais steak, and a hot soufflé with Marc

de Bourgogne. Wines at good prices. 10% discount on the room rate Oct–March. Free apéritif.

PRAYES
71460 (20KM W)

⊁ ⚑ I●I AUBERGE DU GRISON

Hameau de Prayes; from Tournus take the D14 towards Chapaize, and it's near Chissey-les-Mâcon.
☎ 03.85.50.18.31 ➡ 03.85.50.18.31
Closed Mon evening, Tues and mid-Nov to Dec.

Set in a tiny village in one of the most delightful parts of Saône-et-Loire, this charming inn has nine bedrooms at 220F with shower/wc; no two are the same but all are colourful, smart and cosy, and some have exposed beams. Excellent regional cooking is served in the lovely dining room with wooden panels and beams. Snacks are available at all hours, and they do salads of cold meats or cheese, thick local *crêpes*, *andouille* in white wine, and Charolais steak with mushrooms. Set lunch menu at 65F then 88–120F. Small shaded terrace. It would be nice to come across an inn like this in every French hamlet. 10% discount on the room rate Nov–Feb.

VERMENTON
89270

⊁ I●I RESTAURANT DU PARC

24 rue du Général-de-Gaulle; it's on the N6, Auxerre road.
☎ 03.86.81.51.51
Closed Sun and Tues evenings, Wed, a fortnight in Feb.

Don't make the mistake of driving past this place; it's on the main road and looks pretty grim. The dining room hasn't even got much rustic charm. But you are made to feel really welcome and the cooking is something else. Forget about the style implied by the elaborately elongated names for dishes on the menus (79–140F), and enjoy the content: *bavette* of beef with shallots, stuffed fillet of trout in Chablis and duck fillet *à l'ancienne*. The desserts here would hold their own in far grander company. These people care about quality produce and good cuisine, and the value for money is impressive for the region. Free coffee.

⊁ I●I AUBERGE L'ESPÉRANCE

3 rue du Général-de-Gaulle (Centre).
☎ 03.86.81.50.42
Closed Sun evening, Mon and Jan.

However glum you're feeling, the mere

mention of this inn's name – *espérance*
means hope – should perk you up. You'll get
a delightful welcome, and the kitchen turns
out wonderful dishes, including the house *foie
gras*, veal *à la morvandelle*, snails and *œufs
en meurette*, and ostrich in red wine vinegar
sauce. Set menus 88–240F. The place has
been redecorated throughout and they've
provided a play area for the kids. Everyone
will find the air conditioning a blessed relief in
summer. Free coffee.

ACCOLAY   89460 (3KM W)

🏃 🏠 |●| HOSTELLERIE DE LA FONTAINE**

16 rue de Reigny.
☎ 03.86.81.54.02 ➡ 03.86.81.52.78
✉ hostellerie.fontaine@wanadoo.fr
Closed Sun evening and Mon mid-Nov to 31 March, and
Dec and Jan. **Car park**.

A beautiful traditional Burgundy house in a
lovely little village in the Cure valley. On fine
evenings you can relax in the garden while
feasting on salad of snails with mustard
dressing, *quenelles* of pike, fried entrecôte
steak with soft creamy Chaource cheese
sauce, a medallion of monkfish with a leek
upside-down tart, and *clafoutis* with fresh
fruit and raspberry *coulis*. Set menus
80–250F. Bedrooms 270F for a double.
Good breakfast 35F. In winter the small cellar
is pressed into service and they serve traditional local dishes for 95F, including cheese
and dessert with jugs of Aligoté or Pinot Noir.
10% discount on the room rate Sept–May.

BAZARNES   89460 (6KM W)

|●| RESTAURANT LA GRIOTTE

3 av. de la Gare; it's opposite the Cravant-Bazarnes
station.
☎ 03.86.42.39.38
Closed Mon–Wed.

A nice little restaurant with a great chef
whose other skill is seeking out local producers who are expert in what they do. With this
fresh produce, his imagination takes him to
culinary heights. The dishes taste of the
country and you just have to try the pork
andouille. Two menus at 69F and the *menu
du marché* at 98F.

VÉZELAY   89450

🏃 🏠 LE COMPOSTELLE**

pl. du Champ-de-Foire.
☎ 03.86.33.28.63 ➡ 03.86.33.34.34
Closed a month from end of first week in Jan–Feb.
Disabled access. **TV**. **Garden**.

Vézelay was one of the assembly points for pilgrimages to Santiago de Compostela in north-
western Spain. That fact is commemorated by
the name of this pretty house, which has
reverted to being an inn as it was at the beginning of the 20th century. The service is first-
rate and the modern, well-equipped bedrooms
have views of the countryside or the garden for
280F or 340F for a family room. 10% discount.

🏃 🏠 |●| HÔTEL DE LA POSTE ET DU LION D'OR***

pl. du Champ-de-Foire.
☎ 03.86.33.21.23 ➡ 03.86.32.30.92
Closed Mon, Tues lunchtime and 2 Nov–23 March.
Disabled access. **TV**. **Car park**.

This former coaching inn, a superb building
covered in ivy, is an extremely pleasant place
to stay. Rooms are well kept and tastefully
decorated; they overlook the basilica on one
side and the valley on the other. Doubles with
shower/wc start at 330F and go up to 650F
with a bath. The restaurant has a beautiful
terrace. Menus at 118F, 200F and 230F,
while the rather expensive *à la carte* menu
features a mixture of classical and regional
dishes such as *œufs en meurette* in red wine,
snails, rack of lamb with sage, roast pigeon,
and *fricassée* of chanterelles and ceps in
season. Free apéritif.

|●| RESTAURANT LE BOUGAINVILLE

26 rue Saint-Étienne.
☎ 03.86.33.27.57 ➡ 03.86.33.35.12
Closed Tues, Wed, and Dec to mid-Feb.

This restaurant, in a beautiful old building
overflowing with flowers, is very reasonably
priced – a pleasant surprise in a town where
low prices are something of a rarity. Traditional local dishes – *œufs en meurette* and
ham knuckle *à la morvandelle*. Menus
79–208F. The dining room, with its magnificent old fireplace, is a pleasant place to sit.

SAINT-PÈRE-SOUS-VÉZELAY   89450 (2KM S)

🏃 🏠 |●| À LA RENOMMÉE**

19–20 Grande Rue; it's on the D957, at the foot of
Vézelay hill.
☎ 03.86.33.21.34 ➡ 03.86.33.34.17
Closed Tues except from Easter to 11 Nov, and 15
Jan–15 Feb. **Disabled access**. **TV**. **Garage**.

The hotel is also a newsagent's and a tobacconist's so there's a relaxed atmosphere. The more expensive rooms are spacious and have a small terrace with a view over the countryside and the Saint-Pierre church. Doubles 190F with basin up to 295F with bath. The small brasserie, open in season, will do if you're stuck for somewhere to eat. 10% discount on the room rate for a two-night stay Oct–June.

PONTAUBERT   89200 (10KM NE)

🏃 🏠 LE MOULIN DES TEMPLIERS**

Vallée du Cousin; coming from Vézelay, turn right as soon as you cross the bridge and follow the arrows.
☎ 03.86.34.10.80 ➡ 03.86.34.03.05
Closed Dec and Jan. **Car park**.

This large ochre-coloured house covered with Virginia creeper is now a waterside hotel deep in the Cousin valley, with oodles of charm. It's an old 12th-century mill that's been wonderfully restored and there's a flowery terrace for when the sun shines. Lovely

walks and mountain-bike rides in the surrounding woods. Double rooms 270–380F, depending on the size, with shower or bath. Free bottle of wine if you stay for several nights.

🏃 🏠 ❘●❘ LES FLEURS**

route de Vézelay; take the D957.
☎ 03.86.34.13.81 ➡ 03.86.34.23.32
Closed Wed, Thurs lunchtime and 15 Dec–28 Feb.
TV. **Car park**.

This beautiful hotel is surrounded by a delightful garden overflowing with flowers. It's been tastefully decorated by the owners, with lovely wood panelling in the dining room. The bedrooms are pretty, and bathrooms have shower or bath; they cost 270–370F. The restaurant gets it absolutely right and the prices are reasonable – the cheapest set menu is 90F (not served on Sun), with others 130–235F – and there's a wealth of specialities like veal kidneys with blackcurrant mustard, cockerel *à la façon des Ducs* and *pavé de Pontaubert*. 10% discount on the room rate Oct–April.

BRETAGNE

22 Côtes-d'Armor

29 Finistère

35 Ille-et-Vilaine

ARZON   56640

⚲ |●| CRÊPERIE LA SORCIÈRE

59 rue des Fontaines; it's near the naval port.
☎ 02.97.53.87.25
Closed Mon in mid-season and Mon–Thurs in winter.

You'll be bewitched by this pretty stone house, where they conjure up devilishly delicious recipes. All the *crêpes* have names: *la Pensardine*, *la Vendéenne*, *la Périgourdine* or *l'Irlandaise* – and you'll only have to cross their palm with a (small) amount of silver. Quality produce and ingredients are used such as the black wheat selected at the Moulin de la Fatique. Around 60F for a meal of good *crêpes* with interesting fillings. Smiling service. There's a terrace. Free coffee.

AUDIERNE   29770

🏠 |●| HÔTEL DE LA PLAGE

21 bd. Emmanuel-Brusq; it's 2km from the ferry terminal to the Île de Sein.
☎ 02.98.70.01.07 ➡ 02.98.75.04.69
Hotel closed Oct–April.
Restaurant closed 1 Sept to mid-June. **TV**. **Car park**.

On the seafront, this hotel smells of summer holidays. Fresh, maritime-influenced decor in the very pleasant rooms, most of which have a sea view. Lots of charm and good value for money for the area. Doubles with bath from 250F, breakfast 40F.

AURAY   56400

⚲ 🏠 |●| HÔTEL DU LOCH**

2 rue Guhur (North).
☎ 02.97.56.48.33 ➡ 02.97.56.63.55
hotelduloch@wanadoo.fr
Restaurant closed Sun evening Oct–Easter. **Car park**.

Comfortable hotel in a quiet part of town. Double rooms 310–450F with bath. Menus, 105–260F, list dishes like pan-fried bream and scallops with lime. Free house apéritif.

|●| RESTAURANT L'ÉGLANTINE

pl. Saint-Sauveur, Saint-Goustan, port d'Auray.
☎ 02.97.56.46.55
Closed Wed except July–Aug.

The Saint-Goustan district is chic but not formal. Carefully prepared, traditional cuisine. Try the fish *choucroute*, roast fillet of bass in an infusion of rosemary, *blanquette* of monkfish with leeks, seafood casserole, or roast pigeon with a sauce of duck *foie gras*. Set menus 80–190F. The pictures on the restaurant walls pay homage to the officers in Jean Chouan's army; he led an uprising in support of the monarchy during the French Revolution.

SAINTE-ANNE-D'AURAY   56400 (6KM N)

⚲ 🏠 |●| HÔTEL DE LA CROIX-BLANCHE**

25 rue de Vannes (East).
☎ 02.97.57.64.44 ➡ 02.97.57.50.60
Closed Sun and Mon out of season, Jan and Feb.
Garden. **Car park**.

The meeting place for pilgrims and fervent followers of Anne, the patron saint of the Bretons. An elegant establishment with comfortable rooms 200–350F with shower/wc or bath, all with telephone; numbers 10–26 are

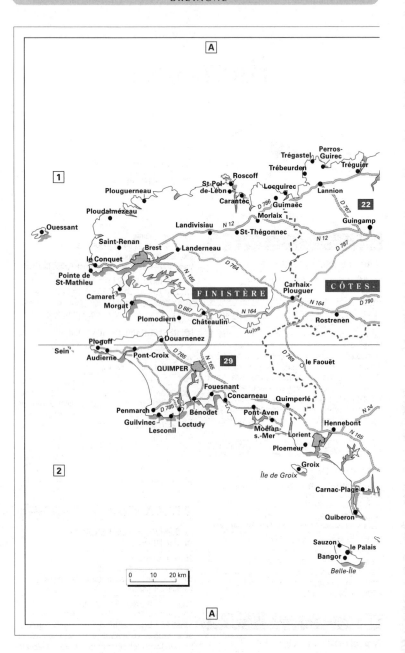

A

1

Ouessant

Plouguerneau

Ploudalmézeau

Saint-Renan

le Conquet

Pointe de
St-Mathieu

Camaret

Morgat

Plomodiern

Plogoff

Sein

Audierne

Pont-Croix

QUIMPER

Penmarch

Guilvinec

Lesconil

Loctudy

Bénodet

Fouesnant

Concarneau

Pont-Aven

Moëlan-
s.-Mer

Brest

Landerneau

Landivisiau

St-Thégonnec

St-Pol-
de-Léon

Roscoff

Carantec

Locquirec

Morlaix

Guimaëc

Trébeurden

Trégastel

Perros-
Guirec

Tréguier

Lannion

Guingamp

FINISTÈRE

Carhaix-
Plouguer

CÔTES-

Châteaulin

Aulne

Rostrenen

Douarnenez

le Faouët

Quimperlé

Hennebont

Lorient

Ploemeur

Groix

Île de Groix

Carnac-Plage

Quiberon

Sauzon

Bangor

le Palais

Belle-Île

N 12

D 786

D 787

D 767

22

N 12

D 764

N 185

D 887

N 164

N 164

D 790

D 769

D 765

N 165

29

D 785

N 24

N 165

2

0   10   20 km

A

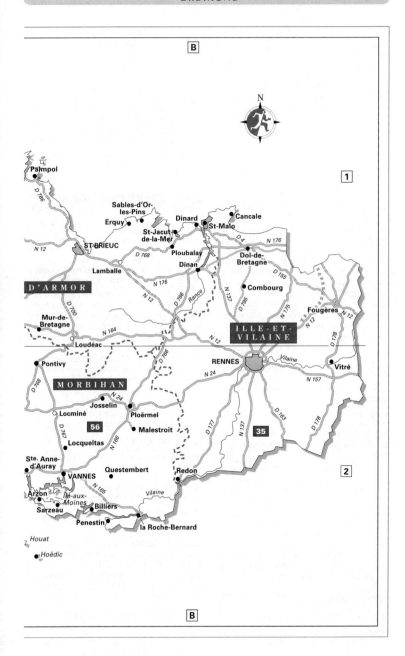

more spacious and have the garden view. Tempting set menus, 95–250F, list traditional dishes prepared with a fine, light touch; salmon medallions with cream and chive sauce or pork *filet mignon* with cider and roast apples. Half board at 325F per person is a good option. Generally excellent shellfish and seafood. 10% discount on the room rate except July–Aug.

⚐ ⌂ |O| L'AUBERGE

56 route de Vannes.
☎ 02.97.57.61.55 ➡ 02.97.57.69.10
Closed Tues except July–Aug, Wed, 5–21 Feb and 12 Nov–5 Dec. **TV**. **Car park**.

One of the best restaurants in the locality; His Holiness John-Paul II dined here when he visited the region in 1996. You can savour the delicacy of Jean-Luc Larvoir's culinary approach from the cheapest menu, 105F (not served Sat evening, Sun lunch or public holidays), or on the other menus 160–300F: try farm-raised guinea-fowl in cider sauce, *gratinée* of seafood flavoured subtly with curry, oysters filled with cider vinegar infused with shallots, veal *blanquette* with shellfish, and the like. The extensive wine list proves excellent value for money. You may find the service and general atmosphere a little cool, but it won't detract from your enjoyment. Rooms 260–290F. Free coffee.

ERDEVEN　　　　　56410 (10KM W)

⚐|O| LA CRÊPERIE DU MANOIR DE KERCADIO

Lieu-dit Kercadio: from Auray, take the road to Ploërmel then Erdeven.
☎ 02.97.24.67.57
Closed Sept to Easter, except on school holidays. **Garden**.

The wood-panelled walls and the original fireplace create an exceptionally lovely setting in the dining room, and there's a wide hearth and the original bread oven in the kitchen. In fine weather tables are laid in the enclosed garden under the huge magnolia. It's an ideal place for kids, who have their own 36F menu. Grown-up menus, 45F and 61F, list scallops *à l'amoricaine* and buttered apples flambéed with Calvados. You can hire a bike or set out from here along the hiking paths. Free apéritif and coffee.

LOCOAL-MENDON　　　56550 (10KM NW)

⚐|O| MANOIR DE PORH KERIO

route d'Auray; take the D120 for 5km, in the direction of Locoal Mendon, then turn right at the sign.
☎ 02.97.24.67.57

Closed Tues evening, Wed, a fortnight in Nov and a fortnight at the end of Jan. **Garden**.

A splendid 15th-century manor, miles out in the country. What a shame it has no rooms! The tables are elegantly laid in a hall with an immense open fireplace. Very fine cooking. A menu of local dishes has a speciality of *gratin* of black wheat with *andouille* from Guéméné, while the seafood menu lists roast monkfish with saffron-suffused cream. Lobster must be ordered in advance. Menus 95–165F. They serve in the garden in summer. Service is efficient and easy-going so it's a pleasure to while away time over the free coffee.

BANGOR　　　　　　　56360

⚐ ⌂ |O| HÔTEL-VILLAGE LA DÉSIRADE

Le Petit Cosquet; it's outside Bangor on the Port-Colon road.
☎ 02.97.31.70.70 ➡ 02.97.31.89.64
Hotel closed 15 Oct–15 March. **Restaurant closed** lunchtimes. **Swimming pool**. **TV**. **Car park**.

A cross between a hotel and a B&B, in a typical architectural style – a series of low buildings with painted walls and shutters. Twenty-six thoughtfully decorated and spacious rooms 390–700F; half board compulsory July–Aug, 480–600F. The owner-chef offers a single menu at 220F, with delicate dishes like roast Dublin Bay prawns with sweet peppers, sea bream with fennel and preserved tomatoes, and small *crêpes* garnished with pears and apples. Brunch is served poolside. They have a lot of regulars in high season, so it's best to book. Free apéritif.

|O| CRÊPERIE DES QUATRE CHEMINS

How to get there: it's at the crossroads of the two main roads on Belle-Île.
☎ 02.97.31.42.13
Closed Wed except July–Aug, and mid-Nov to Christmas. **Disabled access**. **Car park**.

Service noon–2pm and from 7pm. This isolated establishment serves some of the best *crêpes* on the island – hearty, delectable, cooked to perfection and stuffed with unusual fillings. Humorous menus – lots of word-play – and a jovial atmosphere. Brightly decorated, complete with a small children's play area (just like *McDonald's*). Soft jazz or blues in the background. *Crêpe complète* (savoury) 33F.

⚐|O| FERME-AUBERGE DE BOR-DROUHANT

Lieu-dit Bordrouhant; it's about 1km outside Bangor.
☎ 02.97.31.57.06 ➡ 02.97.31.57.06

Closed weekday evenings, except for holidays and July–Aug.

This place, just outside touristy Belle-Île, makes a nice change from the more traditional type of restaurant. It's an old farmhouse and the man in charge makes you feel welcome before going off to the kitchens to prepare your order. Tasty and filling dishes and house *charcuterie*, the *terrine* is splendid, and they stick to old local recipes that are rarely cooked any more – try the chicken *aux Krassens*. Single menu at 105F. It's worth calling to reserve. Free house apéritif.

BÉNODET   29950

☎ HÔTEL L'HERMITAGE

11 rue Laënnec (Centre); it's 300m from the beach, part way up the hill overlooking the town centre.
☎ 02.98.57.00.37
Closed Oct–May. **Garden. Car park**.

Mme Nader Le Moigne pays great attention to detail in running her hotel, a white house with blue shutters set in a garden full of hydrangeas; there's lots of blue and white inside too. It's a really lovely place with a 1950s feel and very reasonable prices. The plain but pleasant rooms cost 180F with basin, 230–250F with shower and 240–290F with bath. Breakfast is 30F. There are studio apartments in a neighbouring building which can be rented by the week.

⚒ ☎ |●| HÔTEL LES BAINS DE MER**

11 rue de Kerguelen (Centre); it's up a steep street 100m from the sea.
☎ 02.98.57.03.41 ➡ 02.98.57.11.07
Closed mid-Nov to mid-March.
Swimming pool. Garden. TV. Car park.

This hotel, in a famous, bourgeois seaside resort, has all sorts of facilities. Very friendly welcome. If the weather is cloudy, dive into the swimming pool or try a relaxing sauna. Lovely double rooms with shower/wc from 290F. Excellent cuisine. Choose from two places to eat: the *Domino*, open until 11pm (midnight in summer) offers a speedy *formule* every lunchtime (grilled meat or pizza, dessert and coffee), as well as salads, pasta, pizzas and grilled dishes. A meal will cost about 120F and there's a children's menu at 40F. Alternatively, the restaurant has set menus 75–148F. Half board 280F is good value. Free apéritif.

|●| FERME DU LETTY

Quartier du Letty; it's 1km from the town centre, well signposted.

☎ 02.98.57.01.27
Closed Wed, Thurs lunchtime and 15 Nov to end Feb.

A restaurant with one Michelin star. The superbly restored building is full of Breton delights: exposed beams, wide fireplace, stone walls, sumptuous furniture and an army of waiters in bow ties, rushing about in all directions, with little effect on the speed of the service! There's no requirement to wear a tie, especially in summer, but the customers are only a tad less smartly dressed than the staff. This is the best table in Finistère, offering wonderful cuisine and some genuinely inspired dishes: Sizun lamb, asparagus flan with prawns and some more exotic dishes such as curried monkfish or chicken *confit* with peanuts. Incredible desserts. Menus start at 193F.

CLOHARS-FOUESNANT   29950 (3KM NW)

|●| RESTAURANT LA FORGE D'ANTAN

It's on the road to Quimper.
☎ 02.98.54.84.00 ➡ 02.98.54.89.11
Closed Mon, Sun evening out of season, Tues lunchtime July–Aug, and the Feb school holidays. **Garden. Car park**.

Way out in the country. Friendly welcome. Superb rustic decor, with a stylish atmosphere and clientele to match. The imaginative seasonal cuisine doesn't come cheap. Set weekday lunch menu 130F, then up to 350F. *À la carte* you get turbot *à la Fouesnantoise*, oyster and prawn *tartare*, pan-fried prawns with champagne sauce, gratinéed rabbit with morels, veal kidneys in spices,and sole fillets with vanilla. Children's menu 75F.

COMBRIT   29121 (5.5KM W)

⚒ ☎ |●| HÔTEL-RESTAURANT SAINTE-MARINE*

19 rue Bac; it's in the port of Sainte-Marine.
☎ 02.98.56.34.79 ➡ 02.98.51.94.09
Closed Wed from Oct to Easter. **TV**.

A favourite with ocean-racing seafarers, novelists and film-makers. The wonderful dining room is decorated in a nautical style and has a magnificent view of the River Odet and pont de Cornouaille; there's also a terrace. Double rooms with shower/wc 320F or 350F with bath. Menus 98–240F. *À la carte* you get marinated scallops with seaweed, pan-fried sole with aubergine caviar, fresh braised cod, pork fillet with leeks, and seafood *tartare* with smoked salmon. Half board, obligatory 10 July–25 Aug, 305F per person. Excellent place. 10% discount on the room rate.

BILLIERS   56190

☎ |●| HÔTEL-RESTAURANT LES GLYCINES

17 pl. de l'Église.
☎ 02.97.41.64.63
Closed Sun evening and Mon out of season.

The façade of this enchanting country hotel is hung with scented wisteria. The straight-forward bar will appeal to adventurers, and food-lovers will enthuse over the beautifully presented cuisine. Menus from 56F up to 190F. Faultless service. Decent rooms with basin at 150F or with shower 185F.

BINIC   22520

⅔ ☎ HÔTEL BENHUYC***

1 quai Jean-Bart.
☎ 02.96.73.39.00 ➡ 02.96.73.77.04
✉ mprovoos@fr.packardbell.org
Closed Jan. **TV. Pay car park**.

Overlooking the boats moored in the pleasure port, this modern hotel is easy to recommend. The freshly decorated, comfortable rooms are well maintained, and most have a view of the harbour or the Banche beach. Doubles with shower 225–365F; the smaller ones are the cheapest but they're still pleasant. Competent welcome. There's also a restaurant serving seafood – *waterzooï* or seafood stew and pan-fried scallops – and a few Belgian specialities from the owners' homeland. Lunch menu 68F and others 95–220F. Free apéritif before your meal if you book half board.

BREST   29200

⅔ ☎ HOTEL ABALIS**

7 av. Georges-Clémenceau: it's 100m from the tourist office and the train station.
☎ 02.98.44.21.86 ➡ 02.98.43.68.32
Disabled access. **TV**. **Car park**.

Very central, with double rooms from 140F with hand basin and from 240F with shower/wc. They all have double glazing, though they're a bit small. Breakfast, 40F, is served till noon. The reception's open round the clock. 10% discount Nov–Feb and in July, 20% discount at weekends except in Aug, town festivals and congresses.

⅔ ☎ HÔTEL ASTORIA**

9 rue Traverse (Centre); it's between the station and the château, close to the rue de Siam.

☎ 02.98.80.19.10 ➡ 02.98.80.52.41
Closed 22 Dec–7 Jan. **TV. Pay car park**.

A hotel that looks like so many others in Brest, but offering good value for the town, considering its excellent position in the middle of things. Bright, cheerful rooms. The six with balconies overlooking the quiet street are double-glazed, but if you need absolute quiet to sleep ask for one at the back. Doubles with basin 145F up to 240–290F with shower/wc or bath. Warm welcome. In July and Aug the Brest *jeudis* are just seven minutes' walk away. This hotel really does the profession proud. 10% discount Sept–June.

⅔ ☎ HÔTEL PASTEUR*

29 rue Louis-Pasteur; it's between the rue de Siam and the covered market.
☎ 02.98.46.08.73 ➡ 02.98.43.46.80
TV.

An establishment that holds its own in its category. It's clean and the welcome is pleasant, and though the soundproofing between the rooms is not great, the beds are OK and at least the windows are double-glazed. Doubles with shower/wc at 190F. Breakfast 27F. 10% discount 30 June–31 July.

☎ HÔTEL DE LA GARE**

4 av. Gambetta (Centre); it's opposite the station.
☎ 02.98.44.47.01 ➡ 02.98.43.37.07
Disabled access. **TV**.

Practical and friendly place with lovely views of the harbour from the rooms on the third floor (but no lift). They're enlarging the hotel, adding a conference room, adapting rooms for the disabled, and creating more rooms with sea view. Doubles with shower/wc 285F or bath 305F. Breakfast 35F.

☎ RELAIS MERCURE-LES VOYAGEURS***

2 rue Yves-Collet (Centre); it's on the corner of av. Clémenceau and rue Yves-Collet.
☎ and ➡ 02.98.80.31.80
TV.

It's rare for a chain hotel to be included in these pages but this brilliant three-star is one of the best of its category in Brest. The hotel has retained its superb 1940s entrance hall. Well-equipped double rooms 405–485F with shower/wc or 485–545F with bath. Pleasant, competent staff. The breakfast room is rather gloomy; breakfast 45F.

⅔ |●| CRÊPERIE MODERNE

34 rue d'Algésiras (Centre).

☎ 02.98.44.44.36 ➡ 02.98.80.58.32
Closed Sun lunchtime. **Disabled access**.

Service 11.30am–10pm. The façade is an arresting lemon yellow and the 90-seat dining room is very classical. The *crêpes*, 14–50F, are delicious, served simply with butter or more elaborately with scallops in vermouth. This establishment was founded in 1922, so they know what they're doing. 20% discount between 2–6pm, except 14 July–15 Aug or during Brest 2000.

⅍ |●| RESTAURANT LA PENSÉE SAUVAGE

13 rue d'Aboville and rue de Gasté; behind Saint-Michel church.
☎ 02.98.46.36.65
Closed Sat lunchtime, Sun, Mon and Aug.

Service noon–1.30pm and 7.30–10pm. You have to hunt a little for this restaurant that's way off the beaten track. But it has two simple little dining rooms that generate a great atmosphere so it's worth the effort. The cooking is tasty: try the home-made *cassoulet* and duck *confit*, or the crayfish Ouessant-style. It's excellent value with a menu at 50F or you can eat for about 110F *à la carte*. Portions are huge and they'll give you a doggy bag to take away what you can't manage. Free apéritif.

|●| LE VOYAGE DE BRENDAN

23 rue Danton: 300m from Saint-Martin church.
☎ 02.98.80.52.84
📧 Dominique-Perrin@wanadoo.fr
Closed Sun, and July–Aug.

You have to search out this tiny place – they can only seat 22. Super-friendly owner offers traditional, quality French cooking using only fresh produce: huge salads like the one with warm Plougastel goat's cheese, duck breast in cider, sole *meunière*, scallop kebabs and the house speciality, fish *choucroute*. Menus start cheaply at 58F and go up to 120F. Every couple of months they have an exhibition of local artists' work.

⅍ |●| AMOUR DE POMME DE TERRE

23 rue des Halles (Centre); it's behind the Saint-Louis covered market.
☎ 02.98.43.48.51 📧 amourPDT@wanadoo.fr
Disabled access. Car park.

Open at lunchtime and in the evening until 11pm. This restaurant is unique in Brest and indeed in the whole of Finistère; they serve only potatoes, and only the "samba" variety, which was developed recently for its baking qualities. A multitude of preparations; with parsley, stuffed with different cheeses – Roquefort,

goat's cheese, Beaufort – gratinéed, puréed or served with *charcuterie*, salads, or grilled meats, fish or shellfish. Menus 59–120F. The lunchtime the dishes of the day change daily, 39F, or 54F with one of the excellent (potato-free!) desserts. The walls and the menus give you glimpses of the owner's sense of humour. The setting is pretty nice, sort of re-visited rustic. And since the tables are crammed in, you may well make new friends. Free house apéritif.

⅍ |●| RESTAURANT LE MARRAKECH

14 rue de la Traverse.
☎ 02.98.46.45.14
Closed Sun, Wed lunchtime and mid-July to mid-Aug.

Service noon–2.30pm and 7–11pm. This restaurant offers an attractive, restrained decor and good-quality cooking. Excellent lamb *tajines* with onions and raisins, chicken, lamb or mixed meat couscous, generously served for the price. Menus 61F and 65F. The delicate and aromatic dishes are expertly spiced, according to secret recipes that have been passed down from mother to daughter for generations. The mint tea is divine, and they serve a good Guerrouane Gris wine. A good place to know. Free apéritif.

⅍ |●| RESTAURANT LA PASTA

12 [bis] rue Turenne (Centre); it's behind Saint-Martin church, 20m from *Le Club* multi-screen in rue J. Jaurès.
☎ 02.98.43.37.30
Closed Sat and Mon lunchtimes, Sun.

Service noon–2pm and 7.30–10.30pm. Real Italian *trattoria*, serving fresh pasta cooked by the chef or his mother. Traditional *antipasti* or polenta, and *pasta mista*, a selection of different types of pasta. Among the specialities, try the excellent tagliatelli with scallops or cannelloni with two different stuffings. There's a menu at 68F, a children's menu at 36F, and you'll pay about 110F for a full meal. Pleasant decor and a very Italian welcome. A fun restaurant supported by the locals. Free apéritif.

⅍ |●| RESTAURANT L'ABRI DES FLOTS

port de Commerce; on the quayside.
☎ 02.98.44.07.31
Closed Sun, Mon evening, 15–30 Sept and the Feb school holidays.

The really nice owner is a livewire and he has created a welcoming restaurant with a personal touch – nothing of the chain here. It's on the merchant port, but the dining room's cosy and in summer there's a pretty veran-dah and pleasant terrace. Various menus, 90–110F, with lots of fish. Their speciality is a seafood couscous and they do *crêpes* as well. Popular locally and for good reason. Free Kir or Celtique apéritif.

🅰️ |●| MA PETITE FOLIE

plage du Moulin-Blanc (Southwest); it's on the marina or coming from Quimper, turn left after the Elorn bridge.
☎ 02.98.42.44.42 ➡ 02.98.41.43.68
Closed Sun, 10–2 Aug and a fortnight Dec/Jan.

Service noon to 2pm and 7–10pm. One of the best fish restaurants in Brest, in a superb, sturdy old Mauritanian fishing boat which landed hundreds of tons of crayfish on the coast of Mauritania between 1952 and 1992. It dropped anchor in well-earned retirement and took on a second lease of life as a restaurant, retaining all the charm of a valiant seafaring vessel. The owner and his wife welcome you warmly and serve up an unmissable culinary experience. Looking around to check she's not being overheard, the hostess will whisper conspiratorially in your ear, offering a fish which isn't on the menu. Accept without hesitation. Your faith will be more than repaid. Very fine cuisine. There's one menu only at 110F, or about 210F *à la carte*. There are some real gems, including scallop and veal *terrine*, crab *rillettes*, excellent oysters, fillet of turbot in a butter sauce, grilled fish *cotriade* (soup), and fillet of sea bream with fennel *choucroute*. Booking is very strongly advised, and virtually essential at the weekend. The food is freshly cooked and there's only one sitting in the evening, so you'll have time to enjoy your meal. The bill won't rock the boat, either! Free apéritif.

GUILERS — 29820 (5KM NW)

|●| CRÊPERIE BLÉ NOIR

bois de Keroual; from Brest head towards Penfeld – the restaurant is near the Parc des Expositions.
☎ 02.98.07.57.40 ➡ 02.98.07.47.83

Almost hidden by trees and bushes next to a small lake, in an ancient mill, this *crêperie* is a dream of a place to stop. Friendly service, delicious *crêpes* served in a modern setting, and plenty of opportunity for wonderful country walks after the meal. A meal will cost 60–80F. Specialities are buckwheat pancakes with medallions of monkfish *armoricaine*, with scallops or smoked salmon, then *crêpe suzette* with lime.

GOUESNOU — 29850 (10KM N)

|●| CRÊPERIE LA FINETTE

rue du Bois-Kerallenoc; from Gouesnou it's signposted and 1km along the road to Kerallenoc.
☎ 02.98.07.86.68

Closed Mon and Tues lunchtime out of season, Mon and Tues lunchtimes in July–Aug, a week at the end of June and a fortnight in Nov. **Garden**.

Lydie and Jean-Yves Pirou used to run one of the best *crêperies* in Brest. They then set up in this lovely old house with a beautiful garden. The interior is old stone with a huge fireplace; you get a real sense of Brittany and the sea. Very tasty, traditional *crêpes*. A meal costs about 75F. Best to book.

CAMARET — 29570

🅰️ 🏠 |●| HÔTEL-RESTAURANT DU STYVEL**

quai du Styvel: one of the last restaurants at the end of the quay, opposite the Rocamadour chapel.
☎ 02.98.27.92.74 ➡ 02.98.27.88.37
Closed Jan.

The thirteen well-kept rooms are generally comfortable and have been redecorated. Some have a view of the harbour. Reasonable prices – 180–260F with shower/wc. They've engaged a new chef and serving staff and while the cooking is inevitably inspired by the fish landed in the harbour, there's a new feel to the menus: scallop kebabs with Choron sauce, a duo of yellow ling and John Dory *à la Ouessanne* and platters of seafood. Menus 78–190F, children's menu 45F or about 90F *à la carte*. Free house apéritif and 10% discount on the room rate Sept–June.

|●| LA VOILERIE

7 quai Toudouze; it's on the harbour facing the tower and the chapel.
☎ 02.98.27.99.55
Closed Wed. **Disabled access**. **Car park**.

Considered to be one of Camaret's most serious restaurants, offering consistent quality, a friendly welcome and service late into the evening. It's in a building that used to be the main sailmaker's and lots of tools and implements from those working days hang on the walls, making a very pleasant dining room. Lots of fish dishes and regional dishes at all prices: the *formule express* includes mussels and chips or fish of the day, and the set menus, 98–180F, might include roast sea bream in *sauce Marie-Jeanne*, scallops *aumônière* and baby vegetables, or *far tiède* (warm tart with caramel sauce). Best to book – only twenty covers.

CANCALE — 35260

🅰️ 🏠 HÔTEL LE CHATELLIER**

route de Saint-Malo; it's 1km from Cancale on the Saint-

Malo road (D355).
☎ 02.99.89.81.84 ➡ 02.99.89.61.69
Disabled access. Garden. TV. Car park.

Small, pretty hotel in a converted farmhouse. Cosy rooms 300–330F. Hearty breakfast 40F. The *patronne*, whose parents used to run the farm, is chatty and can give you all sorts of information about the region. 10% discount.

♜ |●| LE QUERRIEN**

7 quay Duguay-Trouin; it's on the port.
☎ 02.99.89.64.56 ➡ 02.99.89.79.35
TV. Car park.

Probably the best rooms in Cancale. They're all brand new, huge, bright and equipped with good bathrooms. Professional, smiling welcome. Doubles with shower/wc 390–560F and a duplex at 960F. The restaurant is decorated in the style of a big, smart brasserie with wood panelling, copper pans on the walls and a large fish tank. Good cooking and highly competent service. Menus 99F (not Sat evening or Sun lunch) and 159–220F: grilled lobster, hot oysters, seafood platters and *crêpes* in orange butter. You can tell they take their work seriously.

♨ |●| LA CANCALAISE

3 rue de la Vallée-Porcon; it's 2 mins from the Musée des Arts et Traditions Populaires.
☎ 02.99.89.66.08 ➡ 02.99.89.89.20
Closed Mon–Thurs out of season, Mon only July–Aug.

A place frequented by locals and tourists alike. The walls are made from dressed stone and adorned with old photographs, and the tables are nicely set. At the back of the dining room, there's a long range with a double line of hot plates to cook the *crêpes* because all the dishes are made to order. The *crêpes* and *galettes* are crispy and delicate. Savoury stuffings include *andouille* while the sweet specialities are curdled milk with superb home-made jam or apple compote flavoured with cinnamon. There's nothing revolutionary about it but the ingredients are of good quality so everything is very tasty. About 80F for a meal or they do a take-away service. There's a range of Breton ciders to choose from. Free house *Cocktail Breton*.

|●| AU PIED D'CHEVAL

10 quai Gambetta.
☎ 02.99.89.76.95
Closed weekdays from mid-Nov to Palm Sunday, except for the Christmas school holidays, and weekend lunchtimes 15 Nov–1 April.

Matchless oysters are the claim of the house,

and the osyter-farming family who run the place certainly deliver. Their claim also holds good for all the other seafood and cooked dishes – the ingredients are ultra-fresh. Try the *écuelle du Père Dédé*, a mixture of shellfish in a creamy, lemony sauce, or the *patouillou* (whelks *à l'armoricaine*). The tables and stools on the ground floor are rustic but the upstairs dining room is more done up. About 100F for a meal. They play sea shanties to create the atmosphere. Energetic service and good wines.

|●| RESTAURANT LE SAINT-CAST

route de la Corniche; it's a 5-min walk from the centre.
☎ 02.99.89.66.08 ➡ 02.99.89.89.20
Closed Sun evening and Tues out of season, Wed, the Feb school holidays, 25–29 June and 15 Nov–18 Dec.

A delicious restaurant in all senses of the word. It's just outside the town in an elegant building overlooking the sea and an ideal place to spend a delightful evening dining on fresh seafood expertly but simply cooked; try fresh cod with shellfish or *tajine* of lobster. The 115F menu served at lunch and dinner during the week is remarkable for quality and balance. Other menus, 165–215F, feature specialities prepared in the same vein.

SAINT-MÉLOIR-DES-ONDES   35350 (5KM S)

|●| RESTAURANT LE COQUILLAGE-BISTROT MARIN

Maison Richeux; it's next to the *Hotel Bricourt*.
☎ 02.99.89.24.24
Closed Mon and Thurs lunchtimes in Jul and Aug.
Disabled access. TV. Car park.

The location, looking down over the Mont-Saint-Michel bay is splendid. Olivier Roellinger, the *enfant-chéri* of Breton cuisine produces the best dishes from what the sea has to offer; Cancale oysters, sea bream *tartare*, lemon sole with butter, and seafood and shellfish. Menus 115–230F.

CARANTEC   29660

|●| LA CAMBUSE-LE CABESTAN

It's on the harbour.
☎ 02.98.67.08.92 ➡ 02.98.67.90.49
Closed Mon except July–Aug, Tues and 1 Nov to the first week in Dec.

Two restaurants in one here: *La Cambuse* and *Le Cabestan*. Choose the one that suits your mood. The chef is the same for both but the serving staff and atmospheres are very different. *La Cambuse* is a mixture of a brasserie, a bar and an inn, with a lively, even raucous atmosphere in summer; it can get overwhelming at the weekends. A popular meeting place for young people, with rock and Irish music at full blast. A mixture of locals and extrovert holiday-makers of all nationalities are drawn by the atmosphere and the reputation of the cuisine. Generous portions of filling food at reasonable prices – pancake of pollack and crab sausage *des monts d'Arrée* with young garlic, lamb curry with coconut milk, *fario de Camaret* with sorrel – a full meal will cost around 120F *à la carte*. Next door at *Le Cabestan* the mood is quieter, even hushed. With its smart decor and softly spoken diners, this is the place for a romantic dinner. The cuisine is more refined, too, featuring the likes of scallops and prawns with thyme and a lightly smoked sea bream with red butter. Menus 90–250F.

CARHAIX-PLOUGUER   29270

|●| CRÊPERIE LES SALINES

23 rue Brizeux; it's near the tourist office.
☎ 02.98.99.11.32
Closed Sun out of season and Christmas, Mon, Tues and Wed evening, and Jan.

They try to create a maritime feel in the dining room. The tasty *crêpes* are made from Breton organic flour and stuffed with unusual fillings. Menus 36–89F – the most expensive will give you salmon in seaweed preserve and a Breton *crêpe* with apple flambéed in Calvados, or you can choose *à la carte*; *Maquarella* (coarse mackerel *rillettes*, served with onion marmalade in white wine), or a black wheat pancake *grand cru* served with *andouille* sausage, grated apples and cider conserve. A quality place for all budgets.

CARNAC   56340

⅗ ⛫ |●| HÔTEL LE RÂTELIER**

4 chemin Douët.
☎ 02.97.52.05.04 ➡ 02.97.52.76.11
Closed Sun evening and Mon end Sept to end March and 10 Jan–10 Feb. **TV**. **Car park**.

A charming little hotel in an attractive house weighed down by ivy, tucked away down an alley in the town centre. Well-kept rooms for 230F with hand basin up to 280–320F with shower/wc; half board, compulsory July–Aug, costs 295–345F per person. The setting in the restaurant is very *vielle France*, both comfort-

able and charming. The 98F menu is unbeatable of its kind; oysters, salmon cooked three ways, and a delicious chocolate and banana tartlet. Other menus 148–238F. Attentive, polite service. Free coffee. 10% discount on the room rate, except in school holidays.

|●| RESTAURANT LA CÔTE

Kermario; it's 1km from the centre of town, take the Auray road and turn left at the first lights, it's near the standing stones of Kermario.
☎ 02.97.52.02.80
Closed Mon except July–Aug, Sun out of season and Jan. **Car park**.

The owners' son, Pierre, a virtuoso chef fresh out of hotel school, has decided to transform the family restaurant into a temple of gastronomic delights. This has not been a hollow ambition; you will taste dishes of rare subtlety here. Starting with the menu at 120F you are in for an uplifting experience: try sea bream *galette à la tomate confite*, or egg casserole with scallops (on the winter menu). Other menus 170–250F.

CARNOËT   22160

⅗ ⛫ |●| LES FOUS

Pen ar Vern; take the D97 in the direction of Carhaix, it's 1km before the village.
☎ 02.96.21.52.32
Closed Wed and Nov.

Lost in the Breton countryside, this is a lovely restaurant in a charming old dwelling. The English couple crazy enough to open it are obviously doing something right because you have to book in high season. Posters of Celtic monuments and art line the walls – they also run an antique business and have created a family atmosphere. Set menus 58–85F, good *à la carte* selections, grills on the open fire, mouthwatering, home-made desserts, and children's menus. Terrace and playground. Three *gîtes* in the manor courtyard rented by the week (☎ 02.96.21.59.75). Free house apéritif or coffee.

CHÂTEAULIN   29150

⅗ ⛫ |●| HÔTEL-RESTAURANT AU BON ACCUEIL

av. Louison-Bobet; 2km from Châteaulin on the D770.
☎ 02.98.86.15.77 ➡ 03.98.86.36.25
Closed Sun evening and Mon out of season and Jan. **Swimming pool**. **Garden**. **TV**. **Car park**.

A group of buildings on the side of the Nantes-Brest canal make up this establishment. It's in a lovely spot in spite of also being on the main road. The hotel's name means "Good welcome" and the owners keep their staff on their toes to live up to it. The rooms are classicly decorated and vary in size but they all have good facilities; 250–372F with shower/wc or 260–390F with bath. The restaurant serves classic dishes that are well executed and good value, with set menus 79–120F. Specialities include flambéed scallops with garlic butter, and *aiguillette* of duck with raspberry. 10% discount on the room rate Oct–April.

🏕️ |●| CRÊPERIE MARC-PHILIPPE

29 quai Cosmao; it's very close to the tourist office.
☎ 02.98.86.38.00

A very small, very central *crêperie*. The *crêpes* are honestly priced and taste great. A meal will cost 50–69F – the buckwheat *crêpe* stuffed with onions and the *crêpe* with a prune cream are both good. It's a cheerful place where they use quality local produce, including Fouesnant cider and local beer; the flour is produced from grain grown 100% in Brittany. The place has recently been enlarged, but they've kept the terrace. Free house apéritif.

PLOMODIERN   29550 (28KM NW)

|●| AUBERGE DES GLAZICS

rue de la Plage.
☎ 02.98.81.52.32
Closed Tues lunchtime, one week in Feb and Nov.
Garden.

This is a place with a history. At the beginning of the 20th century it was a smithy where grandmother made soup for clients waiting their turn. Now the third generation has taken over, following on the culinary tradition. Olivier Bellin left school at fifteen, and became an apprentice in a great kitchen. In ten years he accumulated a sheaf of diplomas and an array of awards. He was voted best young chef in Brittany and went off to work all over France before returning home and turning part of the dining room into a gastronomic restaurant. They changed the decoration and brought in stylish table linen and plates. This young chef, brimming with passion and imagination, could well be compared to some of the culinary geniuses of France. Menus 130–140F in the week or others 185–295F or you can choose à la carte. Specialities vary all the time, but here's a taster: pan-fried lobster with a lemon *noisette*, or soup of *foie gras* with lentil cream, while for dessert choose a *cristalline* of strawberries with soft

sugar, or a *chaud-froid* of sweet chestnuts. Olivier Bellin's mother sometimes helps with the service. This is a splendid place, one of the best in the region. Bellin is a chef to follow. Booking essential.

COMBOURG   35270

🏨 |●| HÔTEL DU LAC**

2 pl. Chateaubriand; it's on the Rennes road.
☎ 02.99.73.05.65 ➡ 02.99.73.23.34
Closed Fri and Sun evening out of season, and Nov.
TV. Car park. Garden.

"It is in Combourg wood that I became what I am," wrote Chateaubriand in his epic *Mémoires d'Outre-tombe*. It's worth reading the book before stopping off at the village where Chateaubriand grew up. This place has a tranquil charm, just a little old-fashioned. On one side there is the château and on the other the lake which was so dear to Chateaubriand. Rooms for 290F or 340F depending on the facilities. The restaurant has two dining rooms – one is air-conditioned or there's a terrace looking over the lake and a garden. Set menus, 95–168F, offer traditional dishes with specialities of hot oysters Chateaubriand, roast sea bream with salt butter, and raspberry dessert swathed in dark chocolate.

|●| RESTAURANT L'ÉCRIVAIN

pl. Saint-Gilduin (Centre); it's opposite the church.
☎ 02.99.73.01.61
Closed Wed and Sun evenings except 14 July–16 Aug, Thurs, 5 Feb–2 March and 29 Sept–11 Oct.
Disabled access. Garden. Car park.

This restaurant has a reputation, built up over a number of years. The prices are astonishingly low considering the inventive flavours presented to you; try the home-smoked fish or *millefeuille* of *foie gras* and artichokes. Excellent value for money with set menus 85–165F. The restaurant name means "The Writer" and they sell illustrated books here too.

HÉDÉ   35630 (15KM SW)

🏕️ |●| RESTAURANT LE GENTY HOME

Vallée de Hédé; it's on the N137 in the direction of Tinténiac, 500m outside Hédé.
☎ 02.99.45.46.07
Closed Tues evening, Wed, a fortnight in March and three weeks from 15 Nov.

Service noon–2pm and 7–9pm. It's hard not to fall for this charming, flower-bedecked hostelry, with natural stone walls and a huge fireplace. It's run by a highly talented young chef who has already attracted a following of food lovers. He constantly strives to embellish and improve his art. His cooking is excellent and even the most demanding of foodies will be intrigued by the selection of dishes he puts on his menus. Delicious weekday lunch menu at 69F, and a long list of others 95–220F. Specialities include asparagus tips with Cancale oysters, escalope of *foie gras* with a scallop kebab, pigeon breast with *foie gras* and sea bass with leeks and balsamic sauce. Free coffee.

CONCARNEAU 29110

⅍ ☎ |●| HÔTEL-RESTAURANT LES OCÉANIDES

3 and 10 rue du Lin (Centre); it's near the harbour.
☎ 02.98.97.08.61 ➡ 02.98.97.09.13
Closed Sun Oct–April, Sun evening only May–June. **TV**.

For generations, this place has been known as *La crêpe d'or*. Yvonne and family have maintained a homely atmosphere and they'll make you welcome at the bar, telling you about the region and its traditions. They may even serenade you – especially during the Filets Bleus festival. Set menus start at 62F. *À la carte* the choice includes *millefeuille* of beef with onion marmalade, monkfish in pepper *coulis*, scallop *brochettes à la crème*, duck *aiguillettes aux baies roses*, and *crépinette* of crab. Equally attractive room prices, with doubles 200–280F depending on facilities; half board is a good deal at 220–255F per person. A good hotel. Free house apéritif.

⅍ ☎ HÔTEL DE FRANCE ET D'EUROPE**

9 av. de la Gare (Centre).
☎ 02.98.97.00.64 ➡ 02.98.50.76.66
Closed Sat evening and 15 Nov–15 March.
TV. Car park.

Well-positioned in the centre of town, this hotel offers the kind of pleasant, comfortable rooms – with telephones, alarm clocks, good-quality linen on the beds and double-glazing – that you would expect from a modern hotel. They're putting in a lift and a new sitting room, and reception is on the ground floor. Enjoy a drink on the terrace. All this plus a cheerful welcome, a professional attitude and excellent information services. Double rooms 300F with shower/wc or 350F with bath. 10% discount Oct–April.

☎ HÔTEL KERMOR**

Les Sables Blancs.
☎ 02.98.97.02.96 ➡ 02.98.97.84.04
e kermorlespiedsdansl'eau.com

The *Kermor* is a characterful turn-of-the-(20th)-century hotel right on the beach. Inside it's been beautifully decorated with lithographs, etchings and photographs from the 1920s. Rooms are bright and fresh, with panelling and, to complete the illusion, portholes for windows. Each one has a sea view. For a double with shower/wc you pay 360F, while rooms on the first floor, 480F, have pretty wooden balconies. The splendid breakfast room has a fantastic view of the sea. Breakfast, 45F, is served until 11.30am.

|●| CRÊPERIE LE GRAND CHEMIN

17 av. de la Gare; it's 300m from the tourist office.
☎ 02.98.97.36.57
Closed Mon except July– Aug.

The touristy atmosphere in town can get a bit much, but this appealing *crêperie*, which has clocked up fifty years of quality service, doesn't rely on the tourist trade to make a living. Some regulars have been coming here for ages so it has a friendly feel. It's not at all chi-chi; the *patronne* simply sees her job as serving generous portions of *crêpes* at reasonable prices. The menu at 45F gets you two buckwheat *galettes*, a sort of girdle cake, and a chocolate *crêpe*. At 65F or 75F choices include *crêpe* with scallops and leek *fondue*, one stuffed *crêpe* and one flambéed.

|●| RESTAURANT CHEZ ARMANDE

15 [bis] av. du Docteur-Nicolas; it's opposite the marina.
☎ 02.98.97.00.76
Closed Tues out of season, Wed in summer, Christmas to New Year and the Feb school holidays.

One of the best seafood restaurants in Concarneau and the prices won't make you feel queasy. Lovely panelling and pleasant furniture in the dining room, which also has a fish tank brimming with crustaceans. Excellent fresh fish and seafood straight from the quay, which is just a stone's throw away. The cheapest set menu costs 108F and is only served during the week. There are others 138F and 198F. The *cotriade*, a Breton five-fish soup, is the signature dish. You would return to this place for that alone – otherwise try the lobster stew or the seafood platters and a dessert from the selection on the trolley.

CONQUET (LE) 29217

⅍ ☎ |●| LE RELAIS DU VIEUX PORT

1 quai Drellach.
☎ 02.98.89.15.91
Closed Jan.

In times gone by this old harbour inn provided simple rooms and a restaurant. After substantial alterations it has been upgraded to the standards of a modern hotel. It's a friendly place, run by a family who know how to make you feel welcome and at home. Stripped wooden floors and white walls gently brightened up with blue stencilling. Very good beds. Five rooms with a view of the estuary go for 220–320F with shower/wc. These are really excellent prices for the quality. Each room bears the name of a Breton island. Avoid *Bannalec*, the cheapest but the smallest, with a cramped shower. A breakfast, 40F, of white or brown bread with a selection of home-made preserves is set out on a large refectory table. The dining room is a relatively new addition to the building and they've put in an open fireplace – it's about 115F for a meal in the restaurant. In the *crêperie*, it's more like 80F for a meal; there's a good selection of *crêpes*, a savoury *complète*, fried mussels and chips. A good wine cellar. There is live music on Wednesday evening in summer. This hotel caters impressively for tourists. Free house apéritif and 10% discount on the room rate except during school holidays and weekends.

CRACH 56400

|●| RESTAURANT CRÊPERIE L'HERMINE

12 rue d'Aboville.
☎ 02.97.30.01.17
Closed Mon–Wed Oct–March, Mon lunchtime and Wed April–June and Sept, and Feb school holidays.

You can't miss this lovely house, festooned with flowers. The dining room is bright and pleasant, and there is also a lovely verandah opening onto the rock garden. Their locally famous *crêpes* come in about twenty varieties; all are equally delicious. There are also numerous fish and seafood dishes, not least the mussels *façon Hermine*. Anyone with a sweet tooth will be spoilt for choice between the tempting desserts. A meal *à la carte* costs upward of 70F. There's a children's play area, too.

DINAN 22100

⅔ ⌂ HÔTEL LES GRANDES TOURS**

6 rue du Château (Centre); it's opposite the château.
☎ 02.96.85.16.20 ➡ 02.96.85.16.04
📧 carregi@wanadoo.fr
Closed a fortnight in Jan and a fortnight in Feb.
TV. Car park.

Victor Hugo and Juliette Drouet stayed here on 25 June 1836 while they were on a five-week tour of the west of France. "They dined, spent a pleasant night and dined there again the following evening. They found the hotel to their taste." Their recommendation still holds good, even more so now that the rooms have been considerably improved with even better bathrooms. Thirty-six rooms, five overlooking the road, go for 200–295F depending on facilities. Thanks to an arrangement with the neighbouring restaurant, they are able to offer half board at 370F per person. You can park in the courtyard, though there's a charge in summer. Free breakfast for one person if there are two of you.

⅔ ⌂ |●| HÔTEL LES ALLEUX**

Route de Ploubalay (North); it's on the D2 in the ZAC.
☎ 02.96.85.16.10 ➡ 02.96.85.11.40
Restaurant closed Sun evening out of season.
Disabled access. Garden. TV. Car park.

A modern hotel surrounded by greenery with Breton charm; it's a good place to stop on the road between Saint-Malo and Dinard. The rooms have been refurbished and there is one for the disabled. Doubles cost 280F. The cheapest menu in the restaurant is 78F, and they serve a 65F *formule* at lunchtime on weekdays. Children's menu 45F. Half board is 250F per person sharing a double room.

⌂ |●| HÔTEL LE CHALLONGE**

29 pl. Duguesclin.
☎ 02.96.87.16.30 ➡ 02.96.87.16.31
Disabled access. TV.

Eleven of the eighteen rooms look over the square but don't worry about noise, as the double glazing is efficient. All the rooms have good bedding and doubles start at 330F. Some doubles communicate with a twin room for the children. There's also a room especially appointed for the disabled. All the bathrooms have heated towel rails. Honest value. Menus in the restaurant start at 75F.

|●| CRÊPERIE DES ARTISANS

6 rue du Petit-Fort (Centre); it's by the Jerzual gate.
☎ 02.96.39.44.10
Closed Mon except July–Aug, and mid-Oct to 1 April.

A beautiful building in a charming street in the old town. It's an ancient residence with a rustic setting, bare stone walls and wooden tables. The relaxed atmosphere is enlivened by the really friendly owners. Excellent traditional *crêpes* and cider from the barrel. There's a 47F lunch menu or others, including a fun children's menu with a cocktail and two pancakes (one savoury and one sweet). They play nice music and, in summer, they set up a large wooden table in the street.

⚘ |●| RESTAURANT LA COURTINE

6 rue de la Croix; it's opposite the town hall
☎ 02.96.39.74.41
Closed Wed lunchtime in summer, Wed and Sun evening out of season, 15–30 Nov and 1–15 Jan.

You'll get a genuinely warm welcome from the hostess and the setting is cosy and convivial. The service is excellent and there's obviously a talented chef in the kitchen. The fish and seafood are prepared with a light touch and have a hint of the exotic (he's travelled widely). The meat is equally good – try the saddle of lamb with creamed garlic. There's a selection of six coffees on a special menu. Weekday menu 70F (except public holidays), then 98–192F. Children's menu at 55F. Best to book in winter. Theme evenings on alternate Fridays in winter. Free coffee.

|●| LE BISTROT DU VIADUC

22 rue du Lion-d'Or; take the road to Rennes, just after the viaduct on the left at the bend.
☎ 02.96.85.95.00
Closed Mon, Sat lunchtime and 20 Dec–10 Jan.

Incredible views of the Rance valley from this restaurant, which is in a splendid setting and has a pleasant interior with pastel colours and a stove in the dining room. They serve delicious local cuisine, including home-made *foie gras*, fish *choucroute*, *croustillant* of pig's trotters or the celebrated oxtail, cod *à la Bretonne* and marrowbone. There is a short weekday lunch menu for 90F, or *à la carte* you'll pay somewhere in the region of 165F including wine (of which they have a good, affordable selection). Booking is essential.

|●| LA FLEUR DE SEL

7 rue Sainte-Claire; it's next to the tourist office.
☎ 02.96.85.15.14 ➡ 02.96.85.16.66
Closed Tues, Wed and end-Nov to mid-Jan.

Nicholas Boyère, who used to run a splendid establishment in Honfleur, has returned to his roots. He offers *menus* at 125F, 155F and 180F, though you can choose one dish only if you wish. The 125F menu gets you three courses with six choices of starter, a main course and dessert. The 155F one lists raviolis of Breton lobster in a juice squeezed from shellfish, and fritters from three fish (red mullet, barbet and sole) with a herb emulsion. Or choose filleted lamb chops, followed by warm

Plancoëtin accompanied with a *vinaigrette* of maple syrup and cumin, and desserts of caramelised *Kouing-aman*, or pan-cooked raspberries with *fromage blanc* and liquorice. Original cuisine with very fresh produce. Nicholas' wife, Agnes, runs the two dining rooms; the west-facing one is in shades of blue while the south-facing one is in rusty tones. The tables are laid with a great deal of taste – good-quality cutlery and crockery. The service is attentive. The wines come from small vineyards and are reasonably priced; it's always worth trying the wine of the month, which is also served by the glass. There's a children's menu at 75F.

PLÉLAN-LE-PETIT   22980 (13KM W)

|●| LE RELAIS DE LA BLANCHE-HERMINE

Lieu-dit Lourmel; take the N176 towards Jugon-les-Lacs. At the roundabout take the road to Plélan-le-Petit along the old road signposted for the *zone artisanal*.
☎ 02.96.27.62.19 ➡ 02.96.27.05.93
Closed Tues and Wed evening except July–Aug.

This restaurant has a good reputation in the region and is housed in a long stone building by the road. Spacious, lively dining room. There's a 79F menu (not served Sun lunch), and others 105–168F. Seafood or shellfish must be ordered in advance. On the first and third Thursday of every month they cook suckling pig on the spit.

DINARD   35800

🏠 |●| HÔTEL-RESTAURANT DU PARC**

20 av. Edouard-VII (Centre).
☎ 02.99.46.11.39 ➡ 02.99.88.10.58
📧 hotel.du.parc@infonie.fr
Closed Sun evening and Mon except for the school holidays. **TV**.

A small family hotel typical of Dinard. Rooms for 160–290F. Value for money. Since the market moved away and the two discos closed, you'll get a quiet night's sleep. Despite the hotel's name, there is no park or garden, but there is a stylish restaurant with set menus 60–125F.

⚘ 🏠 HÔTEL LES MOUETTES

64 av. George-V; it's 50m from the Yacht Club.
☎ 02.99.46.10.64 ➡ 02.99.16.02.49
Closed Jan.

A pleasant family hotel with ten charming, cosy rooms 170–200F with hand basin or 190–230F with shower/wc. Friendly, simple and inexpensive, with a very warm welcome.

Ask at reception for information about parking. 10% discount except for school holidays and long weekends.

❙❘ RESTAURANT L'ESCALE À CORTO

12 av. George-V (East).
☎ 02.99.46.78.57
Closed lunchtimes and Mon evening except for school holidays.

The proximity of the sea, the cut-out of the cartoon character Corto Maltese, and the owner give this lively little restaurant its personality and account for its popularity with the young locals. It is also known as *restaurant des Marins*. Dod is the barman, while Marie runs the kitchen, producing seafood salad, oysters, salmon *tartare* and various other fish dishes. There are no set menus, everything is *à la carte*, but for about 100F you will enjoy a good, healthy meal. Seafood platter available to order. A great nautical ambience. This restaurant is only open in the evening, as Corto likes to take a nap on the beach in the afternoon.

DOL-DE-BRETAGNE   35120

🏃 🛏 GRAND HÔTEL DE LA GARE*

21 av. Aristide-Briand (Southwest).
☎ 02.99.48.00.44 ➡ 02.99.48.13.10
Closed Mon Oct–April. **Private garage**.

A small, plain and unpretentious hotel with double rooms 160–210F. The new owners have planned a substantial programme of refurbishment to update the rooms. Good, spacious restaurant cheerfully decorated in a conventional style in shades of old rose. There is also a lively café on the ground floor. Free coffee and 10% discount out of season except for public holiday weekends.

🛏 ❙❘ HÔTEL DE BRETAGNE**

17 pl. Chateaubriand (Centre).
☎ 02.99.48.02.03 ➡ 02.99.48.25.75
Closed Sat from mid-Nov to end of March, last three weeks in Oct and a week in the Feb school holidays.. **Disabled access. Garden. TV. Car park**.

Since 1923, the same family has been running this well-kept hotel on an uninspiring square with a small car park. Good welcome and a family atmosphere, though it's rather quiet out of season. Bright rooms, some of them refurbished, for 250–320F with shower or bath. The inexpensive restaurant offers menus at 63–165F listing decent traditional food – seafood *cassolette*, sole, seafood platters and the like.

🏃 🛏 ❙❘ RESTAURANT DE LA BRESCHE-ARTHUR

36 bd. Deminiac (Centre).
☎ 02.99.48.01.44 ➡ 02.99.48.16.32
e labresche.arthur@wanadoo.fr
Closed Sun evening and Mon except July–Aug, Feb and Christmas–New Year. **TV. Car park**.

One of the best restaurants in the region, serving excellent food in a lovely dining room. Menus, 78–195F, are astonishing value for money. The chef is a star who makes wonderful sauces and solemnly respects the seasons. Naturally, he uses only fresh produce; grilled sea bream with bacon and cream sauce and a terrine of lamb cooked with herbs for eight hours. Worth the trip. Rooms also available 180–280F. 10% discount on the room rate out of season except public holiday weekends.

🏃 ❙❘ AUBERGE DE LA COUR VERTE

route de Rennes (Centre).
☎ 02.98.48.41.41
Closed Mon and Tues lunchtime July–Aug, Mon and Tues out of season, and Christmas–New Year. **Disabled access. TV**.

This typical, long, low-built farm has been expertly renovated and it's surrounded by greenery. There is a children's playground in the courtyard. The monumental fireplace that dominates the dining room is used for grilling splendid hunks of meat, which the skilful young chef who owns the place carves on a butcher's block. The meat is cooked exactly as ordered. Other dishes, *crêpes* and salads (*medium* or *senior* according to your appetite) and desserts are prepared in the kitchen, which you can see into from the dining room. Expect to pay 110F *à la carte*. The chef is Belgian and includes various specialities from back home on the menu – notably mussels and a remarkable *sirop de Liège*. The wine is served in jugs marked in centimetres up the side, so you pay for what you drink. There's a warm atmosphere and young staff. A small shop across the courtyard sells foodie goodies. House *digestif*.

DOUARNENEZ   29100

🏃 🛏 ❙❘ HÔTEL DE FRANCE-LE DOYEN**

4 rue Jean-Jaurès (Centre).
☎ 02.98.92.00.02 ➡ 02.98.92.27.05
Restaurant closed Sun evening and Mon except July–Aug, and the second week of Jan. **TV**.

A local institution right in the town centre, which feels both chic and homely. The rooms in the annexe are quieter, while those in the main building are being done up in authentic Breton style like the dining room. Rooms 240–320F. The cooking in the restaurant is resolutely from the region (meaning there's lots of seafood and fish) but it has the imprint of the chef's individuality. Menus 98–220F. House apéritif and 10% discount on the room rate Oct–April – but mention this guide when you book.

🏠 🛏 |●| HOSTELLERIE LE CLOS DE VALLOMBREUSE***

7 rue Estienne-d'Orves (Centre); it's near the Sacré-Cœur church.
☎ 02.98.92.63.64 ➡ 02.98.92.84.98
TV. Car park.

An elegant, early 20th-century building very close to the church and overlooking the sea. It's got a name straight out of a 19th-century novel or a TV soap. Inside, wide fire places, wood panelling, tapestries and leather armchairs create a cosy interior. The rooms are charming and bright, some with a sea view; 330–500F. Charming welcome. The food in the restaurant is in harmony with the surroundings: *cotriade* (a local soup made with five types of fish), grilled lobster glazed with coral, and apple tart with a caramel *coulis*. Menus 99–330F. 10% discount on the room rate.

|●| LA CRIÉE

port du Rosmeur (Centre).
☎ 02.96.92.13.55
Closed evenings in winter, Tues evening only out of season.

Glass-fronted dining room with nautical decor in the bistro and splendid views over the vast bay. They serve fish cooked with simplicity and skill: cod *brandade*, stuffed queen scallops, grilled sardines, scallops in *Noilly* sauce and superb platters of shellfish. They also specialise in Breton desserts. Attractively priced wine by the jug and the background music is not the usual soundstream from some FM station. Lunch menu 44F or 100F for a meal *à la carte*.

🏠 |●| CRÊPERIE AU GOÛTER BRETON

36 rue Jean-Jaurès (Centre).
☎ 02.98.92.02.74
Closed Sun and Mon in winter except during school holidays, a fortnight in mid-June, and a fortnight in Nov.
Disabled access.

Service from noon to 10pm in the summer. Lots of character here: the cool proprietor gets

around on a Harley-Davidson or in a Cadillac and inside the decor is very Breton. The Breton bagpipe music is mixed in with plenty of jazz and rock. It's no surprise to find American hamburgers among the list of *crêpes*. House specialities have names such as *Moscovite*, which comes with smoked salmon, sour cream and lemon, or *La Nordique*, with herrings, onions and potatoes. *Crêpe* menu at 46F and others 70F and 87F. They also do a *crêpe* of the day and a children's menu. Flower-filled terrace to the rear. Free coffee.

ERQUY   22430

🛏 |●| HÔTEL BEAUSÉJOUR**

21 rue de la Corniche.
☎ 02.96.72.30.39 ➡ 02.96.72.16.30
Restaurant closed Sun evening and Mon Oct–June, and the first fortnight in Feb.
Disabled access. TV. Car park.

Only 100m from the port. Small, traditional holiday hotel set way up high. Very warm welcome. Well-maintained doubles 270–320F with shower/wc. Breakfast at 39F. Moderately priced restaurant with generously served set menus 78–140F: mussels in cream, cockles with garlic and parsley butter, seafood *choucroute*, scallop kebabs and *tarte Tatin*. Half board, obligatory July–Aug, is good value at 300F per person.

🏠 |●| LA CASSOLETTE

6 rue de la Saline (Centre).
☎ 02.96.72.13.08
Closed Thurs and Fri lunchtime out of season, Dec and Jan.

The locals are lucky enough to have two excellent restaurants in the town (see *L'Escurial*, below). This one is run by a nice woman who was smart enough to hire a young chef who trained in some excellent kitchens. He uses the best seafood, straight from the briny; scallop raviolis, *cassolette* of crayfish with orange, *andouille* with cider butter, veal kidneys with Pommeau sauce and, for dessert, a *Byzantin* with two chocolates. Prices are reasonable – there's a *formule* at 68F, menus 79–235F or 200F *à la carte*. Free glass of champagne.

|●| RESTAURANT L'ESCURIAL

bd. de la Mer; it's next to the tourist office.
☎ 02.96.72.31.56 **e** escurial@wanadoo.fr
Closed Sun evening, Mon and 15 Nov–10 Dec.

The other "best-known" restaurant in the region. View the ocean from the dining room, from comfortable green-and-white leather armchairs. Set menus 110–350F and a children's menu at 80F. Specialities are seafood, of course, like pan-fried John Dory with *foie gras* and tagliatelle. Reliable value.

●I RESTAURANT LE RELAIS SAINT-AUBIN

Saint-Aubin; 3km from Erquy-bourg, it's signposted off the D34.
☎ 02.96.72.13.22 ➡ 02.96.63.52.31
Closed Mon, Tues out of season, and the Feb school holidays. **Car park**. **Garden**.

Situated in a small hamlet, this beautiful 17th-century priory in exceptional surroundings is full of character. It's a romantic, pastoral place in a huge garden, and enjoys complete peace. A ravishing dining room with ancient beams, antique furniture and a monumental granite fireplace. In summer you can eat on the terrace. A variety of set menus: a weekday one at 80F, then 118–195F. There's also a dish of the day written up on a slate. Warm welcome and excellent service. A good selection of wines, including white or red Menetou Salon. Best to book in season or at the weekend.

FOUESNANT 29170

🎿 🛏 HÔTEL À L'ORÉE DU BOIS**

4 rue de Kergoadig.
☎ 02.98.56.00.06 ➡ 02.98.56.14.17
TV. **Pay garage**.

Small, classic family hotel that's been completely renovated. Genuine welcome. Good rooms at good prices: 195F with basin/wc, 260F with shower/wc and 290F with bath. Some have a sea view of the Cap-Coz, or of the forest of Fouesnant. There are also have rooms sleeping three or four. There is a charge for using the garage. Walking trails start just nearby and the beach is three minutes away by car. 10% discount Sept–June.

GLOMEL 22110

🛏 ●I LA CASCADE

5 Grande-Rue; it's on the main street.
☎ 02.96.29.60.44. **Restaurant closed** evenings and weekends except for guests.

A pleasant little country hotel with four pretty rooms – each has a different decor and is clean and neat. Two have hand basins only and share the bathroom, 160F, while for 180F there's one with a shower and another with shower/wc. Breakfast 25F. They serve a *menu ouvrier* at

55F in the restaurant; in the evenings and at weekends it is open to hotel guests only.

GUINGAMP 22200

●I RESTAURANT LA ROSERAIE

parc Styvel; 1km from the town centre on the Tréguier road, and signposted on the right.
☎ 02.96.21.06.35
Closed Mon evening out of season. **Car park**.

Service 7–11pm. This restaurant is in a lovely bourgeois house, delightfully set in the middle of large grounds. Attractive dining rooms serving tasty grills and seafood. You'll pay 100–150F. Booking highly recommended.

HENNEBONT 56700

🛏 ●I HÔTEL-RESTAURANT DU CENTRE

44 rue du Maréchal-Joffre (Centre).
☎ 02.97.36.21.44 ➡ 02.97.36.44.77
Closed Mon except July and Aug.

A likeable young couple have taken over this grand old hotel and brought it up to date without sacrificing its simple provincial appeal. You will appreciate the *patronne*'s charm and the hotel's excellent value. Doubles 150F with basin or 190F with shower (wc on the landing). Set menus, 75–215F, list good, honest dishes, particularly fish and seafood – grilled crayfish with cream and salmon with two sauces. One of the best restaurants in town.

ÎLE DE GROUX 56590

🎿 🛏 HÔTEL DE LA JETÉE**

It's on the port.
☎ 02.97.86.80.82 ✉ laurencetonnerre@freesbee.fr
Hotel 5 Jan–15 Feb.

The very last house on the right before you drive into the sea, this is a picture-postcard of a place, fronted by a jetty with a lighthouse at the end, with anchored boats bobbing, gulls wheeling and squealing, and the sea practically licking the hotel walls. The decor inside is tasteful and the rooms are pretty. Doubles with shower/wc 260F or 420F with bath. Breakfast 40F. A lovely place to find refuge. Free coffee.

ÎLE DE HOËDIC 56170

🛏 ●I LES CARDINAUX

☎ 02.97.52.37.25 ➡ 02.97.52.41.26
✉ lescardinaux@aol.com

Closed Sun evening and Mon out of season, and Feb.

Ten rooms with a sea view, naturally. Half board, at 295F per person. There's also a restaurant with menus 135–195F. Good idea to book – it's the only hotel on the island.

ÎLE D'OUESSANT   29242

|●| CRÊPERIE TI À DREUX

Le bourg.
☎ 02.98.89.00.19 ➡ 02.98.89.15.69
Closed end Sept to Easter, except for school holidays.

Ti à Dreux means crooked, and the leaning stone façade here looks as if was built in a force ten gale. Inside it's painted blue and white. There's a huge choice of *crêpes*, stuffed with a variety of fillings – try scallops and *sauce aurore* or *fario* (sea trout) from Camaret. The best pudding is the *Joséphine*; nothing to do with Napoleon, but a concoction of home-made lemon preserve, pineapple and vanilla ice cream. *Crêpes* from 9F to 39F and around 80F for a meal. Nice family-run feel, and they have a real eye for quality.

JOSSELIN   56120

♠ |●| HÔTEL DE FRANCE**

pl. Notre-Dame (Centre).
☎ 02.97.22.23.06 ➡ 02.97.22.35.78
Closed Sun evening and Mon out of season, Christmas to end of Jan. **TV**.

Superb location opposite the basilica. The lovely rooms are well maintained, with some spacious ones in the roof; 280–290F with shower/wc or bath. Good, traditional, bourgeois cooking: hot oysters with leeks *julienne* or sole braised in red Saumur wine. Menus 85F, 99F and 145F or *à la carte*. Decent value for money. They take their work seriously.

|●| BAR CRÊPERIE DE LA MARINE

8 rue du Canal; it's on the bank of the canal at the lower end of the town centre.
☎ 02.97.22.23.06 ➡ 02.97.22.35.78
Closed Tues evening and Wed out of season. **TV**.

Several little dining rooms with really pleasant maritime decor(blue predominates), and in season they put a few tables out on the flower-festooned terrace. They serve savoury pancakes made with black wheat in a dozen specialities: try black pudding with cooked apple or scallop with leek. There's also a good selection of sweet *crêpes* and desserts. There's a *formule* of the day at 55F (not evenings or weekends) or you can make your own selection.

LANDÉDA   29870

♠ HÔTEL LA BAIE DES ANGES***

350 route des Anges; it's on Aber-Wrac'h port.
☎ 02.98.04.90.04 ➡ 02.98.04.92.27
Closed 3 Jan–15 Feb. **Disabled access. Car park**.

The jolly, very chatty owner is justifiably proud of his establishment. It's a lovely house, dating from the early 1900s, with a yellow façade set just above the beach, overlooking the ocean. The views and sunsets are breathtaking. Attractively decorated rooms with sitting rooms 420–520F with shower/wc or 460–560F with bath. Breakfast 60F with a choice of coffees, home-made jams, and bread from the baker next door – delicious. There's a splendid terrace.

LANDERNEAU   29220

♠ |●| L'AMANDIER**

55 rue de Brest; coming down from the station, turn right at the first set of traffic lights, 500m from the town centre.
☎ 02.98.85.10.89 ➡ 02.98.85.34.14
Restaurant closed Sun evening and Mon. **TV**.

This hotel offers remarkable value. Very elegant interior without being over-fussy, with attractive paintings and refined furniture. The rooms are particularly pleasant and have superior facilities. Doubles 270–300F. The local, traditional cuisine comes with a good reputation and there are some delightful new dishes. There's an 85F *formule*, or menus 140–180F; choose from *roulade* of roasted pig's trotters and pork knuckle, guinea-fowl, stuffed mussels and clams, seafood *mouclade*, or *croustade* of queen scallops in a butter sauce. Excellent desserts such as *gourmandise* with almond milk and red fruit, pear *tulipe* with chocolate, and iced Grand Marnier soufflé.

|●| RESTO DE LA MAIRIE

9 rue de la Tour-d'Auvergne; it's on the quay opposite the town hall.
☎ 08.98.85.01.83 ➡ 08.98.85.37.07
Closed Tues evening.

A long, thin, friendly bar-restaurant. Plush decor with stained glass, red carpet and lush plants. The *patronne* has been running the place for thirty years with infectious *bonhomie*. For the kids, there's a tortoise called Nono which hides in the patio. Among the specialities try the *marmite Neptune*, a seriously good fish stew, made with scallops, monkfish, shrimps and prawns expertly cooked with cream and cognac (you'll have to wait half an hour for this, because it's prepared fresh to order). Otherwise, depending on the season, try the mussels *maison* or scallops, monkfish and spring vegetable stew or, for carnivores, the *fricassée* of veal kidneys. Good-value dishes *à la carte*. The *menu express* costs 59F, and there are others 75–180F. You can get wine by the glass. They make you feel very welcome.

ROCHE-MAURICE (LA) 29800 (4KM NE)

IOI AUBERGE DU VIEUX CHÂTEAU

4 Grand-Place.
☎ 02.98.20.40.52
Closed evenings in the week. **Car park**.

A fine inn set in a peaceful village square near a lovely Breton church and in the shadow of a ruined 11th-century château. It undoubtedly offers the best value for money in the Landerneau region. The first menu, 74F at lunchtime, is really astonishing, attracting swarms of local farmers and people who travel for their job. The others offer *terrine* of scallops with lobster *coulis*, sole Périgourdine, John Dory with a crayfish *coulis* and other seafood dishes. The restaurant appeals to people from all walks of life who know a good place to eat when they find one.

LANDVÉNNEC 29560

🏃 🏠 IOI SAINT-PATRICK

rue Saint-Guénole; it's next to the church.
☎ 02.98.27.70.83
Closed Wed and Sun evening out of season and 17 Oct –17 March.

A charming little hotel in a peaceful village on the Crozon peninsula, with an unspoilt bistro where old wooden chairs scrape noisily on the tiled floor. There's a parade of aged Irish whiskeys on the shelf behind the cramped bar. Good home cooking in the restaurant with a lot of fish dishes. Menus start at 90F and go up in tiny steps to 105F or you'll pay about 120F for a meal *à la carte*. The lovely rooms are like you'd find in a private home: marble chimney pieces and scattered ornaments. Rooms 1, 4 and 7 have windows overlooking the Rade de Brest. Doubles, with basin only, 190–210F. Friendly, easy-going welcome. 10% discount on the room rate after three nights Sept–June.

LANDIVISIAU 29400

🏠 IOI RESTAURANT LE TERMINUS

94 av. Foch (Northeast).
☎ 02.98.68.02.00
Closed Fri evening and Sat. **TV**. **Car park**.

One of the best *Routier* restaurants in Finistère. The impressive 62F *menu-ouvrier* comprises two starters (including seafood), a main course with as many vegetables as you can eat, salad, cheese, dessert, coffee and a litre carafe of red wine! Unbeatable. A dish of the day will cost about 50F. The line-up of lorries parked outside are evidence of its winning formula. They have a few double rooms with shower/wc starting at 160F.

LANNION 22300

IOI LA VILLE BLANCHE

route de Tréguier; it's 6km along on the Tréguier road, by Rospez.
☎ 02.96.37.04.28 ➡ 02.96.46.57.82
Closed Sun evening except July–Aug, Mon, Wed evening, 20 Dec–11 Feb, and 15–24 Oct.

Cooking fit for a king prepared by a pair of brothers who have gone back to their roots. If they offer to show you their aromatic herb garden, don't refuse. Their specialities are seasonal – scallops from November to March, Breton lobster from April to October. Try the monkfish in cider and fresh vegetables, roast Brie with rhubarb and the *millefeuille* with caramelised apples. Weekday menu at 130F or others 210–300F. Children's menu at 85F. You can also buy good wines by the glass, which is rare in a place of this quality.

LESCONIL 29730

🏠 IOI GRAND HÔTEL DES DUNES**

17 rue Laennec.
☎ 02.98.87.83.03 ➡ 02.98.82.23.44
Closed mid-Oct to end March. **TV**.

This huge establishment is in a fabulous location: one side looks out over a sand dune which falls away to the sea 100m beyond. There's a lovely walk from the hotel along the shore. The rooms have been refurbished; doubles from 290F. They're spacious and well appointed – obviously the ones with sea view are the best. The food is pretty good value, and even on the half-board menu there's lots of choice. Menus start at 110F (not served Sun lunch). The friendly, professional *patron* makes you feel welcome.

LOCQUIREC   29241

⚲ ☎ |●| HÔTEL LES SABLES BLANCS

15 rue des Sables-Blancs; it's on the road to Morlaix.
☎ 02.98.67.42.07 ➡ 02.98.79.33.25
Closed Tues and Wed April–June and Sept, Wed in
July–Aug, and Jan to mid-March. **Car park.**

Small hotel and *crêperie*, tucked away in the
dunes facing Lannion Bay. Wild, magnificent
setting. Warm welcome. Decent rooms,
some with superb sea views. Doubles with
basin at 220F or 250F with shower/wc
though refurbishment is planned and prices
may change. *Crêperie* and salad buffet on a
veranda looking out over the sea. Set menus
from 60F. Mussels *au chouchen*, and excellent *crêpes à l'andouille* or filled with feta
cheese. Oysters served at any time. Free
house apéritif.

☎ |●| LE GRAND HÔTEL DES BAINS***

15 [bis] rue de l'Église; it's near the church.
☎ 02.98.67.41.02 ➡ 02.98.67.44.60
e hotel.des.bains@wanadoo.fr
Closed Jan and Feb. **Disabled access. Swimming
pool. Garden. TV. Car park.**

This imposing building is one of the very few in
Finistère that are right on the seashore, and it
has a beautiful garden with ancient lime trees.
It was bought up by a Belgian who turned it
into a luxurious hotel-restaurant with 36
rooms. The panelled rooms have the luxurious feel of an Edwardian seaside hotel, with
painted furniture and bent osier chairs. The
sitting room has bay windows with lovely
views. The rooms with balconies and sea
view are the most expensive; doubles start at
1050F. In the restaurant, menus go for
150–295F, with specialities including Brittany
lobster *à la nage de Sauternes* scented with
ginger and served with baby vegetables, and
seafood stew with a *langoustine* cream. Good
selection of wines. There's a heated, covered
swimming pool, a sauna and a Jacuzzi.

GUIMAËC   29620 (3KM W)

|●| LE CAPLAN AND CO

Lieu-dit Poul-Rodon; take the Plouganou road out of
Guimaëc and turn right at the third crossroads.
☎ 02.98.67.58.98
Closed Sat lunchtime, noon–9pm Sun and public
holidays out of season.

Right at the end of a track, at the mercy of the
howling winds, *Le Caplan* stands defiantly
against the elements. Push open the door and
you'll find a warm friendly café-bookshop that

is almost unique in France – a brilliantly successful combination of reading room and bar
with a spirit of its own. Piles of books are
strewn here and there on the tables, selected
by Lan and Caprini, who used to work in pub-
lishing. The menu is a real surprise in Brittany
– it features a platter of Greek specialities at
58F, served with Greek wine. There's a games
corner for the kids.

LOCTUDY   29750

⚲ ☎ HÔTEL DE BRETAGNE**

19 rue du Port.
☎ 02.98.87.40.21

The renovation work they've done on this old
building is exquisite. The two owners provide
excellent facilities yet have retained the building's character and charm. Lavishly decorated rooms, all with shower/wc and telephone,
250–280F. Breakfast costs 35F per person.
Walkers and cyclists welcome. Some of the
best accommodation in south Finistère. 10%
discount except July–Aug and public holiday
weekends.

⚲|●| RELAIS DE LODONNEC

3 rue des Tulipes, plage de Lodonnec; it's 2km south of
Loctudy.
☎ 02.98.87.55.34
Closed Mon July–Aug, Tues evening and Wed out of
season and 15 Jan–15 Feb.

This old granite fisherman's house, just 20m
from the beach, is home to one of the
region's up-and-coming restaurants. Pleasant ambience, with blond wood and exposed
beams. Depending on the menu, 70–260F,
you get a platter of eight oysters or seafood,
gratinéed sea trout or red mullet fillets in a
sea urchin sauce. *À la carte* dishes include
scallops *rosace* with two sauces, hot *foie
gras* in a pastry case, and grilled bass with
basil. The wine list has some affordable bottles, including Touraine and Côtes-du-Rhône
at well under 100F. Booking advised at
weekends.

LORIENT   56100

⚲ ☎ HÔTEL DU SQUARE*

5 pl. Jules-Ferry (Centre).
☎ 02.97.21.06.36 ➡ 02.97.84.76.23
Closed Sun and public holidays 12.30–4pm. **TV.**

Small hotel whose lack of restaurant means
they bring you breakfast in your room for just
28F! Modest and quiet, next to the Jules-

Ferry gardens. Doubles with washing facilities 130F and 170F, or 190F with shower/wc. 10% discount Oct–June.

♠ ⬤ HÔTEL-RESTAURANT GABRIEL**

45 av. de la Perrière (South); it's on the main road from Keroman fishing port.
☎ 02.97.37.60.76 ➡ 02.97.37.50.45
Restaurant closed Sun from Oct to end June. **TV**.

Small, unfussy hotel with a cheap and friendly restaurant. Modern, very clean doubles for 130–200F. The set menu costs 58F including wine (lunchtime and evening) and there are others 68–155F. There's to be a new management so things may change.

⚲ ♠ HÔTEL VICTOR HUGO**

36 rue Lazare-Carnot (Southeast); it's near the ferry terminal for Île de Groix.
☎ 02.97.21.16.24 ➡ 02.97.84.95.13
TV. Car park.

Warm welcome from the cheery *patronne*. Clean doubles with hand basin go for 180–200F, 260–300F with shower/wc and 310–350F with bath. Buffet-style breakfast 44F. Children under ten get a free breakfast.

⬤ RESTAURANT LE PIC

2 bd. du Maréchal-Franchet-d'Esperey (North); it's near the post office.
☎ 02.97.21.18.29 ➡ 02.97.21.92.64
Closed Sat lunchtime and Sun. **Disabled access**.

A pleasant spot with Parisian bistro decor and a terrace for sunny days. Simple, tasty cooking including crab *croustillant* with a prawn *coulis*, cod with *aïoli*, pig's trotters stuffed with oxtail, and chocolate *fondant* or pears with cream tea sauce. Cheapest set menu at 80F and others 105–220F. The restaurant has just been included in the *Qualité de France* selection, and the owner, Pierre Le Bourhis, is a wine connoisseur who was voted Brittany's best wine waiter in 1986. Have a good look in the cellar.

⬤ RESTAURANT LE JARDIN GOURMAND

46 rue Jules-Simon (Northwest); it's near the train station.
☎ 02.97.64.17.24 ➡ 02.97.64.15.75
Closed Sun, Mon, the Feb school holidays and 1–10 Aug.

Delicious dishes concocted from the freshest local produce are served outside under a pergola or in the airy, elegant dining room. Courteous service from the host, skilful, creative cooking by his wife and well-pitched prices. Weekday lunch menu 95F, otherwise 120F and 165F, or 180F *à la carte* for an excellent meal including wine. There's a selection of coffees or teas on a special menu. One of the best restaurants in Lorient so it's best to book.

PORT-LOUIS   56290 (20KM S)

⚲ ♠ ⬤ HÔTEL-RESTAURANT DU COMMERCE**

1 pl. du Marché (Centre); take the N165 to Port Louis.
☎ 02.97.82.46.05 ➡ 02.97.82.11.02
Closed Sun evening and Mon out of season and 15 Jan–15 Feb. **Disabled access. TV. Garden**.

A quiet, comfortable hotel in the centre of town on a tranquil, tree-lined square with a small orchard behind. Double rooms 190F with hand basin and up to 380F with bath. The cheapest menu in the week is 70F, and there are others 90–220F. 10% discount on the room rate Nov–March, and free apéritif.

MALESTROIT   56140

⬤ RESTAURANT LE CANOTIER

pl. du Docteur-Queinnec.
☎ 02.97.75.08.69 ➡ 02.97.75.13.03
Closed Sun evening and Mon.

Good value and the best cooking in town at this split-level restaurant. Set menus (82–173F) feature the obligatory seafood platter and dishes as different as fillet of zander and Scandinavian smoked fish platter. There's also a daily menu served weekday lunchtimes. Easy parking on the market square.

CHAPELLE-CARO (LA)   56460 (8KM N)

⚲ ♠ ⬤ LE PETIT KERIQUEL**

1 pl. de l'Église (Centre).
☎ and ➡ 02.97.74.82.44
✉ galettebeurre@aol.com
Closed Sun evening and Mon out of season, the Feb school holidays and 1–15 Oct. **Garden. TV. Car park**.

This pretty hotel has been rebuilt and now has eight decent, inexpensive rooms mostly facing the church; double with hand basin 175F or 220–240F with shower/wc or bath. Though part of the often stuffy *Logis de France* chain, there's a relaxed, young feel about the place, created by the friendly husband and wife team who run it. In the restaurant, classic dishes are made from really fresh ingredients and are generously served. There's a *menu du jour* at 65F (not served on Sun), and menus 93–155F listing queen scallops in pastry cases with baby vegetables, zander with shellfish butter, country salad, and pork *confit* with apple and cabbage. Half board, 190F per person, is compulsory in summer. Free coffee.

MOLAC   56230 (13KM S)

ᵃ⛟ |●| HÔTEL-RESTAURANT À LA BONNE TABLE

pl. de l'Église.
☎ 02.97.45.71.88 ➡ 02.97.45.75.26
Closed Sun evening, Fri evening out of season, and 21 Dec–3 Jan.

The old coaching house standing on the church square dates back to 1683. Satisfactory clean and simple rooms with good beds above the restaurant or in a quieter annexe; 110–150F with washing facilities, 155–185F with shower/wc. There's a weekly rota of dishes of the day: fish couscous is Thursday's special, for example, though you can order it in advance on other days. Weekday menu 52F or 105–210F. Cheerful, welcoming, busy atmosphere, well-served traditional dishes and attractively laid tables. You can really do yourself proud here. Free coffee.

MATIGNON   22550

ᵃ |●| CRÊPERIE DE SAINT-GERMAIN

Saint-Germain-de-la-Mer, on the village square; from Matignon, drive 1km on the D786 in the direction of Fréhel, turn right for Saint-Germain and continue 2km.
☎ 02.96.41.08.33
Closed 1 Oct to Easter except for school holidays. **Garden**.

Service from noon until late in July–Aug. It's worth making the trip to this seaside village for the best pancakes and girdle cakes in the area. They're made using local black wheat flour and while the fillings are not unusual, Mme Eudes uses top quality ingredients. And it's not pricey – expect to pay 70–80F for a meal. The old house is lovely and so is the garden terrace in summer. Free coffee.

MOËLAN-SUR-MER   29350

ᵃ⛟ MANOIR DE KERTALG****

Route de Riec: on the D24, 2km outside Moëlan, take right fork to Riec.
☎ 02.98.39.77.77 ➡ 02.98.39.72.07
Closed 15 Nov–15 April. **TV. Car park**.

An impressive building of hewn stone, smothered in ivy and set in grounds in the forest. The rooms are vast and individually decorated – they have huge beams and are carpeted in blue or red. Doubles and duplex rooms 490–990F. You can eat breakfast, 65F (served until 10.30am), on the magnificent terrace, which has a panoramic view over the countryside. They hold exhibitions in the tea room. 10% discount Sept–June. Free house apéritif.

MORGAT   29160

ᵃ⛟ |●| HÔTEL LA VILLE D'YS**

quai Kador.
☎ 02.98.27.06.49 ➡ 02.98.26.21.88
Closed Oct to Easter. **TV. Garden. Car park**.

A substantial house, just outside the tourist bustle, overlooking the port and the beach. Doubles 235–365; nearly half the bright and pleasant rooms look over Morgat Bay and some have balconies or terraces. The attic rooms are cute. Breakfast costs 38F and half board, compulsory July–Aug, is 320F per person. The restaurant is good and they do a lot of fish dishes with sauces – the chef is a master sauce-maker and worked in Paris for a long time. Menus, 90–240F, list fish and scallop *terrine*, house *foie gras*, grilled lobster, grilled turbot with *beurre blanc*, scallops and prawn in flaky pastry with a cream sauce, escalope of braised monkfish with seaweed, and more. A real treat. Free coffee.

⛟ |●| LE GRAND HÔTEL DE MER***

17 rue d'Ys; it's by the beach
☎ 02.98.27.02.09 ➡ 02.98.27.02.39
Closed Mon, Tues lunchtime and Nov–March. **Disabled access. Garden. TV. Pay car park**.

The outside of this large, seaside hotel has retained some of the elegance it had in the 1930s when Armand Peugeot wanted to turn Morgat into a smaller version of Deauville. The inside has been changed around so many times since that it's very ordinary by comparison. There are 78 identical and functional bedrooms, but the ones looking over the sea have a spectacular view. Prices for a double with bath start at 310F. There's a substantial buffet breakfast. The saving grace is the restaurant where the cooking has personality: queen scallops with *anise* butter, zander in a seaweed crust, roast sole with artichokes *barigoule* and so on. The menus, from 110F, give a good choice of fish. The restaurant gets very full in season so if you just want to eat there's a smaller dining room.

MORLAIX — 29600

♠ |O| HÔTEL-RESTAURANT SAINT-MÉLAINE

75 rue Ange-de-Guernisac (Centre); it's close to the viaduct on the harbourside.
☎ 02.98.88.08.79
Closed Sat evening and Sun in winter, and the school holidays.

Small, well-maintained family hotel in a quiet street. Plain rooms in which the furnishings are sometimes mismatched but the wallpaper is fresh. Doubles 150–160F; it's difficult to find cheaper. The very friendly boss serves traditional dishes. The set menu at 65F includes a self-service buffet of starters.

♠ HÔTEL DU PORT**

3 quai de Léon (North); it's 400m from the viaduct on the quayside.
☎ 02.98.88.07.54 ➡ 02.98.88.43.80
TV.

With its harbour view and reasonable prices, this little hotel offers value for money. Fresh, pleasant rooms with shower/wc for 210F, 230F with bath. Very warm welcome. Breakfast 30F.

|O| LE BAINS-DOUCHES

45 allée du Paon-Ben; it's opposite the Palais de Justice on the river bank.
☎ 02.98.63.83.83
Closed Sat lunchtime, Sun and Mon evening.

One of the most original restaurants in town. They've kept the turn-of-the-century feel, with the railings, tiles and etched glass from the old public baths. Decent bistro food at very reasonable prices. Start with a dozen *carantecoises* oysters or fresh anchovies marinated *à l'orientale*, followed by *noisette* of stuffed lamb, peppered duck steak or *fricassée* of rabbit in cider with gingerbread for 69F. Good desserts include coconut and pear *gratin* and caramelised apples in flaky pastry. Lunchtime *formule* for 67F (except Sun), 89F in the evening, 150F *à la carte*. Children's menu at 42F.

🍴|O| LA MARÉE BLEUE

3 rampe Saint-Mélaine (Centre).
☎ 02.98.63.24.21
Closed Sun evening and Mon out of season, and three weeks in Oct.

A good fish and seafood restaurant. Elegant and intimate surroundings on two levels, with lots of wood and stone. Dishes are seasonal – the menus change every three months – and

they're carefully prepared using very fresh ingredients. Set menus 80–235F. Children's menu 48F. Free coffee.

SCRIGNAC — 29600 (25KM SW)

|O| RESTAURANT HÉNAFF

How to get there; take the D9 then the D42 and it's in the main street.
☎ 02.98.78.20.08
Closed evenings.

Lunchtimes only. There's no name painted on the white walls of this large building with blue shutters, just the word "Restaurant" – though this doesn't stop it filling up by 12.30pm! You go up a few steps to the dining room. Lovely welcome and warm atmosphere. There's no menu – they serve freshly cooked, family dishes every day. The soup is flavoursome and robust, then there are a couple of starters, a dish of the day, cheese, dessert and coffee. A bottle of red is planted on the table. The *menu-ouvrier* costs all of 70F. For Sunday lunch the menu is more elaborate and there's a seafood menu as well.

MUR-DE-BRETAGNE — 22530

🍴♠ |O| AUBERGE GRAND-MAISON***

1 rue Léon-le-Cerf (Centre); it's near the church.
☎ 02.96.28.51.10 x02.96.28.52.30
Closed Sun evening, Mon and Tues, a fortnight in Feb and three weeks in Oct.

A smart place that will set you back a bit. Jacques Guillo is one of the best respected chefs in the *département*. You need to be good to make a success of a restaurant out in the country– just read the menus: *foie gras* profiteroles with a truffle *coulis*, pigeon in game sauce, *millefeuille* of spiced bread with Roquefort cheese. This is a serious gastronomic experience as reflected in the prices – 170–360F or around 350F *à la carte*. The magnificent rooms have been confidently redecorated and they're worth the price; doubles 380F with shower/wc, 650F with bath. Breakfast, 90F, is like a complete meal. Half board is a good option, 500–700F per person. This is an exceptional place. Free coffee. 10% discount on the room rate Sept–June.

GOUAREC — 22570 (17KM W)

🍴♠ |O| HÔTEL DU BLAVET**

It's on the RN 164.
☎ 02.96.24.90.03 ➡ 02.96.24.84.85
Hotel closed Christmas and Feb. **Restaurant closed**

Sun evening and Mon out of season. **TV. Car park**.

A sturdy, stone-built house on the banks of the river Blavet with the relaxed atmosphere you find in remote Brittany. Nice, comfortable rooms, 180F with basin/wc, 220–280F with shower/wc and 260–350F with bath. For 45F you can use the sauna. The restaurant offers an interesting range of six menus, 85–300F. Traditional dishes are well worked by the owner/chef. A pleasant dining room with big mahogany cupboards and a lovely view of the river Blavet. 10% discount on the room rate except in Aug.

PAIMPOL   22500

♠ |●| K'LOYS

21 quai Morano (Centre); it's on the harbour.
☎ 02.96.20.93.80 ➡ 02.96.20.72.68
Disabled access. TV.

The owner runs two establishments, side by side on the harbour. The cheaper rooms are over a pub-restaurant, *L'Islandais*, though they have a separate entrance. They're very attractive – real little love nests – and cost 250–395F. The *Hotel K'Loys* is in the 19th-century ship-fitter's house, now an elegant hotel with an intimate atmosphere and a new lift put in to assist disabled access. The eleven superior double rooms, 495–595F, have been tastefully furnished in keeping with the period; some look over the harbour and one has a sitting room with a bow window.

⅍ ♠ |●| LE REPAIRE DE KERROC'H***

29 quai Morand; it's on the marina.
☎ 02.96.20.50.13 ➡ 02.96.22.07.46
Restaurant closed Tues and Wed lunchtime out of season, and 15 Nov–23 Dec. **Disabled access. TV**.

Dating back to 1793, this house, in a style originating in St Malo, was built by a privateer who pillaged the seas for Napoleon. Its thirteen stylish, scrupulously clean and spacious rooms cost 290–650F. In the elegant dining room, done out in shades of green, you can treat yourself to some old recipes reinterpreted by the chef: spiced honeyed roast duck, scallop specialities and delicious desserts. Set menu weekday lunchtimes 140F, others 175–495F. 10% discount on the room rate Sept–June, except public holidays.

♠ |●| RESTAURANT DE L'HÔTEL DE LA MARNE**

30 pl. de la Marne; it's near the train station.

☎ 02.96. 20.82.16 ➡ 02.96.20.92.07
Closed Sun evening and Mon except July–Aug and public holiday weekends, and the Feb school holidays. **Car park**.

This is a favourite with the locals and you can rely on the quality. Dishes in this lovely place include crayfish with tarragon *au gratin* and a tomato sorbet, scallops *vinaigrette* with truffle oil, *croustillant* of pigeon with vanilla pears, and roast brill with wine sauce and dandelions. Whatever your choice, you will relate to Curnonsky's motto, printed on the menu: "True happiness is things that taste the way they should." Menus 120–450F and a children's menu at 65F. An impressive wine list, with at least 300 different wines. They sell their own gourmet dishes: home-made *foie gras*, salmon, *terrines* and so on, with everything cooked to order. There are rooms, too, and they've all been renovated; 335F with shower/wc or bath. Half board is compulsory July–Aug and on public holiday weekends, at 315F per person.

|●| CRÊPERIE-RESTAURANT MOREL

11 pl. du Martray.
☎ 02.96.20.86.34
Closed Sun out of season, and mid-Nov to mid-Dec.

A genuine Breton *crêperie* in a welcoming room that's heaving with a lively regular clientele. Delicious *crêpes*, such as *à l'andouille de Guémené* (a type of sausage). Dish of the day at 45F. Excellent cider. For an apéritif, try the *pommeau des Menhirs*.

PALAIS (LE)   56360

♠ HÔTEL LA FRÉGATE

quai de l'Acadie; it's opposite the ferry terminal.
☎ 02.97.31.54.16
Closed mid-Nov to 31 March, but open during Christmas and Feb holidays.

Nice, cosy little hotel that's pleasantly furnished and excellent value for money. Cheery welcome. Most of the rooms, and the guests' sitting room, look out onto the harbour. They cost 140–190F with basin or 250F with shower/wc. There's a good atmosphere in the ground-floor bar, but the noise doesn't disturb you in the rooms.

SAUZON   56360 (8KM NW)

|●| LE ROZ-AVEL

rue du Lieutenant-Riou.
☎ 02.97.31.61.48
Closed Wed out of season, and 1 Jan–15 March.

An elegant venue that is without doubt the best restaurant on the island. Sophisticated cuisine. The fairly expensive *à la carte* menu, 250–300F, offers a good Belle-Île *cotriade* or fish soup, roast fillet of John Dory with saffron, pan-fried Dublin Bay prawns and monkfish *osso buco* with spices. Lobster to order. Menus from 120F. The setting and service match the excellence of the food.

PERROS-GUIREC   22700

🕊 🏠 |●| LE GULF STREAM

26 rue des Sept-Îles; it's at the start of the road to the plage de Trestraou.
☎ 02.96.23.28.82 ➡ 02.96.49.06.61
Closed Wed and Thurs except July–Aug, and 2 Jan–2 Feb. **TV. Garage for motorbikes**.

There is a pleasant turn-of-the-last-century feel to this charming establishment. Some of the simple, pretty and well-maintained rooms have splendid views of the ocean, while the cheapest, 175–200F, share bathrooms on the landing. 300–350F for a double with shower/wc or bath. The owners enjoy their work, which is obvious from the way they welcome you. Bikers and hikers welcome. In the restaurant there's the same atmosphere. The well-spaced tables are attractively laid and the dining room is brightened up with green plants. The views from here are also spectacular. Menus 98–225F. Fish and seafood are the dishes of choice; scallop stew with leeks, pollack *en papillote* with a pancake stuffed with seasonal vegetables, or the *cotriade*. The local wines are well chosen, too. Free space in the garage for bikes.

🕊 🏠 |●| LA BONNE AUBERGE

pl. de la Chapelle; it's on the hills between Perros-Guirec and Plonmanach.
☎ 02.96.91.46.05 ➡ 02.96.91.62.88
Restaurant closed Sat lunchtime from Oct–May except for public holidays. **TV**.

Warm welcome, charming place. There's a huge wood fire and a piano; they serve very more-ish little *canapés*. Rooms, 155–210F, are small and simple but all have shower/wc. Numbers 1, 2 and 3 have a sea view. Half board, 190–225F per person, is compulsory in July–Aug and on holiday weekends. The restaurant has a terrace. Lunchtime menu 75F during the week, then 105–160F. Children's menu at 40F. The new chef has introduced his own specialities: crayfish and goat's cheese tart with baby vegetables in *vinaigrette*, ear-shell salad, roast ling with walnut and sweet wine sauce, hot apple tart

with honey butter, and roast pineapple with ginger. You can hire bikes. A really reasonable, pleasant place of a type that is getting harder to find. 10% discount on the room rate 15 Sept–15 June for a stay of several nights or on a half-board basis.

|●| CRÊPERIE HAMON

36 rue de la Salle; it's in a steep little street opposite the marina.
☎ 02.96.23.28.82
Closed Mon and Fri except school holidays.

Service from 7.15pm. This place has become an institution since it opened in 1960. It would be a secret little hideaway if its reputation didn't go before it – *Hamon* is known for miles around as much for its rustic setting and good atmosphere as for the spectaclular way the host tosses the *crêpes* to the waitress to catch. And boy, do they taste good! A meal costs about 85F. Booking essential.

PLÉNEUF-VAL-ANDRÉ   22370

|●| AUBERGE DU POIRIER

Rond-point du Poirier at Saint-Alban; it's next to the petrol station.
☎ 02.96.32.96.21 ✉ ternet.olivier@wanadoo.fr
Closed Sun evening and Mon out of season, June and Oct.

Olivier Termet has made such a success of his restaurant that he's had to build a new dining room. The chef trained in some of the most famous kitchens and he's brought his talent home. The first menu, 75F, lists straightforward dishes; there are more original ones on the menus, 95–200F, which change four times a year with the seasons. Each dish is prepared with meticulous care. Maria Véronique, Olivier's wife, is in charge of the dining rooms. If you're in the region the restaurant is definitely worth a trip.

|●| AU BINIOU

121 rue Clémenceau; it's near Val-André beach.
☎ 02.96.72.24.35
Closed Tues evening and Wed out of season and Feb.

This has long been a favourite locally. A traditional, elegant restaurant with excellent cuisine prepared by the owner/chef. Seafood specialities include *fricassée* of crayfish and scallops in *Noilly*, cauliflower with coriander, fillet of sea bass braised in fennel-scented milk, *millefeuille* of broccoli and grilled *andouille*, braised sweetbreads with potatoes and morels and so on. Weekday lunch menu 98F, 130F in the evening. Whet your appetite with a bracing walk on the wind-blown Val André beach or along the customs officers' tracks.

PLŒMEUR 56270

🏠 |●| LE VIVIER**

au fort de Lomener.
☎ 02.97.82.99.60 📧 levivier.lomener@wanadoo.fr
Closed Sun evening except in July–Aug.
Garden. TV. Car park.

One of the really good tables in the region with a view of the Île de Groix and the sea beyond. Specialities from the sea, naturally enough, and other dishes besides – salt-water crayfish, oysters, boned quail with *foie gras vinaigrette* with truffle *jus*, *fricassée* of squid in cider, grilled sea bass with fennel. There's a 105F menu (not served at week-ends or on public holidays), others 165–260F and a children's menu at 65F. Good value. The welcome comes with a smile and the ser-vice is attentive without making you feel crowded. Some of the rooms, 420F with shower/wc or 530F with bath, have terraces with sea view. 10% discount on the room rate weekends Oct–March.

|●| CRÊPERIE LE GRAZU

It's on the harbour near the car park.
☎ 02.97.82.83.47
Closed Tues and Wed in winter except in school holidays, and Nov.

The young owners are making a real suc-cess of this place. They have sorted out a network of local suppliers so they use buck-wheat as well as ordinary wheat and the fill-ings are fresh and very interesting. Prices start at 45F for a savoury pancake with a salad, chocolate pancake and a drink, there are two weekday lunch *formules* 60F, offering steak and chips, salad, a chocolate pancake and a ¼ litre of wine, and a variety of other reasonably priced combinations.

PLOËRMEL 56800

🏃 🏠 |●| HÔTEL LE COBH**

10 rue des Forges (Centre).
☎ 02.97.74.00.49 📠 02.97.74.07.36
📧 le.cobh@wanadoo.fr
TV. Car park.

The reputation of this hotel, with its brilliant yellow façade, is totally justified. You'll appre-ciate the convivial and comfortable Irish atmosphere. Lovely furnishings in the spa-

cious rooms, 200–285F. The meal they bring to your room on a tray is excellent, so you won't have to dress for dinner. Otherwise they do a bar menu for 55F and others 88–200F, with dishes such as veal *mignon*, *fricassée* of chicken with mussels, brill fillet with leek *fon-due*, and caramelised apples with honey ice cream. 10% discount on the room rate, free house apéritif with a meal and 10% discount on meals and drinks in the restaurant.

🏃 🏠 |●| HÔTEL-RESTAURANT SAINT-MARC**

1 pl. Saint-Marc (West).
☎ 02.97.74.00.01 📠 02.97.73.36.81
Closed Sun afternoon in winter and the second fortnight in Sept. **Garden. TV.**

Trains rarely call at the neighbouring station so it's quiet. The well-maintained rooms have been redecorated; a double costs 210–250F. The bar is a popular local watering hole, while the restaurant, which attracts the smarter set, is generally regarded as the best in Ploërmel. They list dishes such as *cas-soulette* of four scallops with light curry sauce, fillet of salmon with a *hollandaise* sauce and cheese or goat's cheese salad. Menus 72F and 95F, *à la carte* around190F and children's menu 95F. 10% discount on the room rate 15 Sept–15 June.

PLOGOFF 29770

🏃 🏠 |●| HÔTEL DE LA BAIE DES TRÉPASSÉS**

On the seafront; it's 3km from pointe du Raz and pointe du Van.
☎ 02.98.70.61.34 📠 02.98.70.35.20
📧 hoteldelabaie@god.com
Closed 15 Nov–7 Feb. **Garden. TV. Car park.**

Service noon–2pm and 7.15–9pm. This large, prosperous hotel stands on a broad beach in an exceptionally wild situation. Doubles 185F with wash basin, 290–380F with shower or bath. Half board, 285–382F, is compulsory 1–25 Aug. Menus in the restaurant are 86–300F; house specialities are scallop *brochettes*, grilled lobster in cream sauce and baked Alaska. Children's menu 46F. Free coffee.

PLOUARET 22420

🏃 |●| CRÊPERIE TY YANN

24 impasse des Vergers (Centre); it's in a cul-de-sac next to the curch.

☎ 02.98.38.93.22 **e** ty_yann@club-internet.fr
Closed Mon–Thurs from Oct to June except in the
evening during the school holidays, Jan and Feb.

Service noon–2pm and 7–11pm July–15
Sept. One of the best *crêperies* of the
legion in the Côtes d'Armor but there are
only a few tables. Pretty decor and an
open, friendly welcome. They use the best
black wheat flour for the savoury pancakes,
and the fillings are varied and interesting,
including *la Bigoudène,* an unusual sweet
and sour one. It won't cost a fortune – 50F
for a meal in a very friendly place. Free
house apéritif.

PLOUBALAY 22650

◐ RESTAURANT DE LA GARE

4 rue des Ormelets.
☎ 02.96.27.25.16 **e** zavier.termet@wanadoo.fr
Closed Tues evening, Wed, the first fortnight in March,
and Oct.

They closed the station long since. On weekdays, Xavier Termet posts up a *menu
guinguette* that features *salade paysanne*
with a poached egg, a fish casserole and a
pudding – the dishes change almost daily.
The other menus, 80–220F, have a selection
of interesting dishes and original combinations where the chef displays the talent that's
earned him his reputation; black pudding *en
Modeste,* made according to a recipe of his
grandmother's, or veal brawn served in a
crab shell. The desserts will bewitch anyone
with a sweet tooth: try *pavé de dame Ferière,*
with bitter chocolate and sour cherries, or
douceur de Lucie, a fresh pear poached in
sirop in a delicate flaky pastry with a chocolate caramel sauce. You can enjoy the
sophisticated cuisine in one of three lovely
dining rooms decorated with splendid vases
of flowers arranged by Madame. Good wine
list, with a particularly good Muscadet-sur-
Lie du Clos du Bois Gautier. As you might
guess, you should book.

PLOUDALMÉZEAU 29830

◐ LA SALAMANDRE

pl. du Général-de-Gaulle (Centre).
☎ 02.98.48.14.00
Closed Wed out of season, weekdays from Oct to Easter
and mid-Nov to mid-Dec.

The art of *crêpe*-making has been passed
down through three generations. Grandma
opened the place. Her grandson is the pre-

sent owner and he must have been dunked in
a vat of *crêpe* mixture when he was chris-
tened. He and his wife are now carrying on
the tradition in this pleasant and bright
crêperie. The *crêpes* are tasty; try one with
scallops and baby vegetables, the
bigoudène which is stuffed with andouille,
fried potatoes and cream, or the *paysanne*
which is bacon, potatoes, cheese and
cream. Children are welcome. Around 75F
for a full meal. Free apéritif.

PLOUGUERNEAU 29880

◐ RESTAURANT TROUZ AR MOR

plage du Corréjou-Saint-Michel; it's north of
Plouguerneau, near Correjou beach, 2km from the town
centre, towards Saint-Michel.
☎ 02.98.04.71.61
Closed Mon and Wed evening out of season except
public holidays and Feb. **Car park**.

From the outside, this looks like a totally typical Finistère building with a terrace for fine
weather. Inside the decor is rustic but cosy
and well tended, and the service is efficient.
Typical dishes from Finistère are of a high
quality and very good value. Seafood and
fish on all the set menus 89–300F; *fricassée*
of ear-shell with tarragon, fish *pot-au-feu,*
brill with a Loire wine stock. The speciality
dessert is apple *au gratin* with almond
cream. Free Kir.

POINTE-SAINT-MATHIEU (LA) 29217

◐ HOSTELLERIE DE LA POINTE SAINT-MATHIEU***

It's in the village, opposite the lighthouse and the ruined
abbey.
☎ 02.98.06.02.58 **▶** 02.98.89.15.68
Closed Sun evening out of season and Feb.
Disabled access. Swimming pool. TV.

They've added a wing with new rooms to the
existing building, which has more traditional
rooms. All are individually decorated with portholes for windows, balconies and fantastic
sea views. Doubles with shower/wc or bath
310–700F. Superb dining room. The gastronomic menus have a good reputation locally.
Brasserie dishes or more elaborate ones on
menus 98–420F: *croustillant* of fresh cod or
fish *pot-au-feu,* clams and calf's foot with
mushrooms, *croustillant* of plaice and red mullet or saddle of rabbit with milk, stuffed with
prunes.

PONT-AVEN   29930

≫ |●| CRÊPERIE LE TALISMAN

4 rue Paul-Sérusier; it's on the way into the town on the Riec road.
☎ 02.98.06.02.58
Closed Sun lunchtime out of season, Mon and a fortnight mid-Oct. **Garden**.

The village is beautiful, if a bit touristy. This place doesn't exactly offer gourmet dining but the *crêpes* and dishes are satisfying and the prices reasonable. Marie-Françoise is in charge, cooking recipes her grandmother taught her. The *crêperie* is in a charmingly renovated old house with a lovely, quiet terrace facing the garden. Three *crêpes* will set you back 50–60F. The house specials include the *Talisman*, with ham, chipolata, spicy *merguez* sausage, smoked sausage, garlic and anchovies, along with seafood specialities. Also flambéed potato *galette*, omelettes, salads and ice cream. Free house apéritif.

≫ |●| RESTAURANT LE TAHITI

21 rue Belle-Angèle; it's on the Bannalec road.
☎ 02.98.06.15.93 ➡ 02.98.71.85.60
Closed Mon and Tues lunchtime, 15–28 Feb and 15–30 Nov.

This is run by a local man and his Tahitian wife whom he met while travelling there. They are kindness itself. The restaurant has been prettily decorated, and the cooking is exotic because Madame is in the kitchen – Tahitian chow mein with chicken, yellow noodles, black mushrooms and vegetables, or Tahitian fish marinated in lemon and blanched with onion. Divine desserts start with a *compote* of banana with vanilla pod cream. There's a weekday lunch menu at 70F and you'll pay about 110F *à la carte*. They also do a take-away service. The table staff don't rush to serve you. Free *digestif*.

|●| CAFÉ DES ARTS

11 rue du Général-de-Gaulle (Centre).
☎ 02.98.06.07.12
Closed Thurs from Oct–May.

A traditional café-brasserie with a convivial atmosphere and excellent music. The supercharged *patronne* greets guests warmly; she's created a lively, though not overpowering, place. Artists and young people (and the not-so-young, too) use this as their local where they put the world to rights. Wine is served by the glass and the beer is good; swig it down with a Lyon sausage served with sautéed

potatoes simmered in white wine. They also serve Mexican dishes like fajitas with chicken or Thai chicken, which is the house speciality. There's a menu for 50F, or expect to pay 80F *à la carte*. They have live concerts from time to time – sea songs, jazz evenings, rock and even local folk music.

RIEC-SUR-BELON   29340 (4.5KM SE)

|●| RESTAURANT CHEZ ANGÈLE

route de Rosbras; it's 5km southwest of Riec and about 1km before you get to Rosbras.
☎ 02.98.06.92.07
Closed Tues except school holidays and in the week from mid-Nov to the end of Jan. **Disabled access**. **Car park**.

Home-made *crêpes* and excellent cider. You enter the restaurant through the *Ty Couz* bar, which is run by Angèle's husband, a retired sailor. Warm interior of wood and stone in a lovely cottage dating back to the Revolution. Take a look at the strange *dolvouettes*, solid wooden tables with a special drawer for holding large loaves of bread. Reckon on something like 70F for a meal.

|●| RESTAURANT CHEZ JACKY

port de Belon; it's 4km south of Riec.
☎ 02.98.06.90.32 ➡ 02.98.06.49.72
Closed Mon and Oct to end March.

Large house situated in a prime spot in an adorable little port in a crook of the River Belon. Excellent seafood, naturally, straight from the crab and shellfish tanks next to the dining room. Talk about fresh! There's nowhere better to try the delights of Breton seafood, though the prices are a little high and the atmosphere inevitably touristy. You can eat cheaply *à la carte* but there are more elaborate dishes to be had on the menus 190–450F; seafood platters, Belon oysters, skate in black butter, fresh salmon, scallops *à la bretonne*, *moules marinière* and so on. It's lovely on a spring or summer evening.

TRÉGUNC   29910 (6KM SW)

≫ 🏠 |●| HÔTEL-RESTAURANT LE MENHIR

17 rue de Concarneau.
☎ 02.98.97.62.35 ➡ 02.98.50.26.68
Closed Wed evening Oct–May and in Jan. **Car park**.

Cathy and Patrice Blomet took over this business a few years ago and quickly built a good reputation. Their welcome is cheerful and sincere. The cuisine is refined, which is hardly surprising considering that Patrice has worked with some top chefs. His creations have a touch of the inspirational – at once tasty, aromatic, traditional and imaginative. Pleasant dining room. Set lunch menu 52F and others 95–175F; scallop stew, suckling pig braised in wine, roast sea bream with fennel, medallions of monkfish with Guémenée *andouille* and pears with liquorice *sabayon*. They've opened a shop, "Au Menhir Gourmand", selling prepared dishes to take away. For an overnight stay, decent rooms, 160–170F with basin, 240–250F with shower/wc, or 260–270F with bath. 10% discount on the room rate Sept–June.

PONT-CROIX   29790

🎿 🏠 I●I HÔTEL-RESTAURANT TY-EVAN**

18 rue du Docteur-Neis (Centre); it's next to the town hall.
☎ 02.98.70.58.58 ➡ 02.98.70.53.38
Closed Feb.

Pont-Croix is a delightful, characterful town, worth visiting for its magnificent cathedral portal. If the crashing waves have got too much, this is an ideal place to come for some gentle charm. This hotel on the quiet main square has good double rooms 230–290F. Warm welcome and honest food with set menus 80–185F. Half board, 240–280F per person, is obligatory 1–15 Aug. 10% discount on the room rate Sept–June.

PONTIVY   56300

🎿 🏠 I●I HÔTEL-RESTAURANT ROBIC*

2 rue Jean-Jaurès.
☎ 02.97.25.11.80 ➡ 02.97.25.74.10
Closed Sun evening 31 Oct to Easter.
Swimming pool. Garden. Lock-up garage.

Simple place with good food and a good cellar. Set menus 60–148F. Pitchers of cider to accompany the dishes created by Louis the chef: trout fillets with perry, slivers of duck with Pommeau, pork leg with mushrooms, and Breton cake. Rooms are also available for 170F with hand basin, 180F with shower and 260F with bath; those at the back are quieter. They've got a boat for guests to take trips on the Blavet river. Free apéritif.

PONT L'ABBÉ   29120

PENMARCH   29760 (11KM SW)

🏠 I●I LE DORIS

port de Kerity, pointe de Penmarch; take the D785 in the

direction of Plomeur.
☎ 02.98.58.60.92 ➡ 02.98.58.58.16
Restaurant open daily from Easter to 31 Oct.

Right on the harbour of this little port, this place is something of an institution, with a reputation for serving good seafood and fresh fish. It's run by a fishing family so the fish are straight from the sea and served in traditional ways: scallops on a skewer, poached turbot with *beurre blanc*, and medallions of monkfish cooked to a Cancale recipe. The meat is good too; sliced leg of lamb with herbs, duck breast with a spiced wine sauce, and so on. Menus 69–360F. There are three attractive bedrooms – more like guest rooms – which cost 200F for a double including breakfast. The bar is always lively, and it's easy to meet people.

PLONÉOUR-LANVERN   28720 (18KM NW)

🎿 🏠 I●I HÔTEL-RESTAURANT DES VOYAGEURS**

How to get there: take the D2 and it's behind the church.
☎ 02.98.87.61.35 ➡ 02.98.82.62.82
Closed Fri evening and Sat lunchtime out of season, Sun evening and 1–15 Nov. **Garden. TV. Car park**.

A reassuringly classic, village hotel. Affable owners, good cooking and moderate prices. The rooms are all pleasant but numbers 4, 5 and 9 are the biggest; 205–270F with shower/wc or 225–295F with bath. Menus offer a range of fish dishes or traditional recipes: seafood platter, house fish soup, skate with sherry vinegar and capers, house *coq au vin*, monkfish kebab *à la diable*, and veal chop with morels. Menus start at 72F and go up to 180F or expect to pay 170F *à la carte*.

QUIBERON   56170

🏠 I●I PARC TEHUEN*

1 rue des Tamaris
☎ 02.97.50.10.26 ➡ 02.97.21.59.37. (winter) or 02.97.30.49.08 (summer)
Closed 30 Sept–3 April. **Car park. Garden**.

A really nice family pension. It's got a huge garden and is only 300m from the beach. Doubles with shower/wc 220F; half-board 240–260F per person, is compulsory May, June and Sept. You can eat cheaply here, with menus 50–92F.

🎿 I●I HÔTEL-RESTAURANT BELLEVUE***

rue de Tiviec, BP 30341, 56173 Quiberon Cedex. It's 1.5km from the centre of town.

☎ 02.97.50.16.28 ➡ 02.97.30.44.34
Closed 30 Sept–1 April.
Swimming pool. **TV**. **Car park**. **Garden**.

This is a big 1970s building set back from the beach by the casino. While not having the appeal of a more traditional building, it is quiet and comfortable, and boasts lots of facilities – heated swimming pool, solarium and gardens. Warm welcome, too. Doubles with shower/wc 350–440F or 350–700F with bath. Half board is compulsory July–Aug at 320–540F. Menus in the restaurant are 100–175F, with a selection of local and other dishes; semi-cooked duck *foie gras* with Beaumes-de-Venise sauce served with home-made bread, or pan-fried scallops with exotic spices and asparagus tips. 10% discount on the room rate April–June.

⚄ |O| CRÊPERIE-RESTAURANT DU VIEUX PORT

42–44 rue Surcouf; the street is above the old port of Port-Haliguen.
☎ 02.97.50.01.56
Closed 4 Nov–17 Feb. **Car park**.

In a street overlooking the harbour you'll find this *crêperie* which, though a tad more expensive than others around, is in a lovely spot. On top of that, the staff are very friendly so it's worth finding the energy to stroll up the street. An all-inclusive menu of *crêpes* and cider at 69F will limit your cash outlay, but you shouldn't spend much more than 90F for a meal *à la carte*. Their speciality *crêpe* is served with salt butter and caramel but they do also do sound seafood at the order of lobster *à l'Armoricaine*. Free coffee.

|O| LA CHAUMINE

36 pl. du Manémeur; it's in the village of Manémeur.
☎ 02.97.50.17.67
Closed Sun evening and Mon, Mon lunchtime July–Aug, 11 Nov–20 Dec and a fortnight in mid-March. **Disabled access**. **Swimming pool**. **Car park**.

The restaurant is in an adorable spot, surrounded by fishermen's cottages. Arrive in time for an apéritif at the bar and join the fishermen and locals sipping a Muscadet – a million miles from the stress and traffic jams of city life. The set menus have no frills, just good, honest ingredients: mussels, prawns, fish. The chef will sometimes make *tête de veau* for aficionados. The menu at 85F is served at lunchtime though not on Sun, or there are others 115–275F.

⚄ |O| RESTAURANT LA CRIÉE

11 quai de l'Océan; it's on the fishing port opposite the fish market.
☎ 02.97.30.53.09
Closed Sun evening except July–Aug, Mon lunchtime in July–Aug, and Jan.

One of the best seafood and fish specialists of the peninsula – *La Criée* means the fish market. Good value for money and service at the double with a smile. There are dishes of the day on the 89F menu. *À la carte* they do *sole meunière*, fish *choucroute*, grilled fish, house smoked fish and seafood platters; expect to pay 180F. Free coffee.

SAINT-PIERRE-QUIBERON   56510 (5KM N)

⚄ ♠ |O| HÔTEL DE BRETAGNE**

37 rue du Général-de-Gaulle.
☎ 02.97.30.91.47 ➡ 02.97.30.89.78
Closed 15 Nov–Easter. **TV**. **Car park**.

Pleasing, traditional hotel only 50m from Saint-Pierre's pretty beach. Bright, well-kept rooms cost 260–290F with shower/wc. Half board is compulsory July–Aug, at 340F per person. Friendly welcome. Decent menus with fish and other local dishes, 80–210F. Free house apéritif. 10% discount on the room rate from Easter to end of June and Sept to mid-Nov.

QUIMPER   29000

♠ |O| LA TOUR D'AUVERGNE***

13 rue des Réguaires (Centre).
☎ 02.98.95.08.70 ➡ 02.98.95.17.31
Restaurant closed Sat lunchtime, Sun out of season until 30 April, and a fortnight in Dec. **Disabled access**. **Garden**. **TV**. **Car park**.

This hotel is located in the town centre and has been well renovated. A traditional, rather plush place with doubles 300–545F. Menus 125F and 138F. Children's menu 72F. Some specialities: sea bass with Chinese spices, *brochette* of scallops, *Cézanne* fruit and seasonal sorbet palette.

⚄ |O| CRÊPERIE AU VIEUX QUIMPER

20 rue Verdelet (Centre).
☎ 02.98.95.31.34
Closed Sun, Tues lunchtime, the first fortnight in June, and mid-Nov to Dec.

A *crêperie* that deserves its reputation. The little dining room has bare stone walls and Breton furniture and it quickly gets full. There's a friendly family atmosphere and everyone tucks into the tasty *crêpes*, swigging down tumblers of cider or milk *ribot*. The pancakes are delicate and crispy. The mushroom and cream filling is unctuous, and the speciality of the house is the scallop filling. It's an excellent place so it's good to book. Free coffee.

CRÊPERIE DU SALLÉ

6 rue du Sallé (Centre).
☎ 02.98.95.95.80
Closed Sun and Mon.

The *crêperie* is in an ancient half-timbered building in the heart of the old town. This is the most touristy area but the welcome is as good as anywhere in the depths of Brittany. In theory it closes around 10pm, but the owner will always greet you with a smile and say, "We're open as long as the lights are on…!". Pleasant, rustic surroundings for delicious *crêpes*. Home-made batter is carefully and skilfully made, and they use only the freshest of ingredients. Attentive service. House special *crêpes* include *paysanne*, warm goat's cheese, scallop *provençale*, *forestière*, candied orange zest etc. Free coffee.

CRÊPERIE LA KRAMPOUZERIE

pl. au Beurre (Centre).
☎ 02.98.95.13.08
Closed Sun and Mon except during school holidays.

Service 11.45am–2pm and from 6.45pm. Good traditional *crêperie* where all the *crêpes* are made from organic buckwheat flour – prices from 8–42F each: *crêpe complète* (savoury) or stuffed with scallops with shredded leek, and *crêpe aux algues d'Ouessant*. Fresh, clean venue. You can sit outside on the terrace overlooking the square.

LA CAMBUSE

11 rue Le Déan (Centre); going towards the train station, it's on the right after the theatre.
☎ 02.98.53.06.06
Closed Sun lunchtime.

A friendly *crêpe* and *tarte* establishment with a small garden. Original, colourful decor evokes the style of a ship's cabin, with varnished wood, portholes and maritime bric-a-brac. Try the delicious homemade *tartes*, which are out of the ordinary, filled with aubergines and Saint-Marcellin cheese or walnuts, asparagus and Brie, or go for *crêpes* with vegetables, cheese and meat. A great selection of wheat and buckwheat *crêpes* and appetising mixed salads. Recent additions to the menu are fried mussels, steaks and *tartiflette*. Prices are reasonable and they do take-aways. Free house apéritif.

LE CLOS DE LA TOURBIE

43 rue Elie-Fréron (Centre); take the road going uphill from the cathedral.
☎ 02.98.95.45.03
Closed Wed and Sat lunchtime.

Chef Didier le Madec started his training in the kitchens of the *Tour d'Argent* in Paris and then with Jacques Cagna; he worked in London, Jersey and Ireland then came home to open this lovely restaurant next to the cathedral. It's elegant, and sober, yet warm in restful shades of orange and mahogany, and full of fresh flowers and leafy plants. A charming welcome. The quiet atmosphere allows you to concentrate on the conscientious yet inspired cuisine. Superb set menus at 95F and 140F and one at 180F for special occasions. The freshest ingredients are used and the menu changes with the seasons. The chef has revived some classics, such as stewed pig's trotters with oysters, braised veal sweetbreads with truffles or oyster mushrooms, spiced duck *fricassée* and fisherman's hot pot. There are also wonderful inventions such as oyster and John Dory with the head on, pigeon with ceps and so on. Very good desserts – a soft-fruit *mille-feuille*, strawberry shortbread and a *fondant* with three chocolates. The wine list is short but has a good choice in each category Free house apéritif or coffee.

LE STEINWAY

20 rue des Gentilshommes; it's in the centre of the old town.
☎ and ➡ 02.98.95.53.70
Closed Sun lunchtime and Mon except July–Aug.

The decor hails from the 1950s, with posters of James Dean and ornaments and memorabilia of the writers Vian and Prévert; there's also an old petrol pump, a trombone, old radios and telephones. The whole place feels warm and welcoming, with solid wooden floorboards and red checked tablecloths. Open since 1987, it's well worn in and full of regulars. They do an excellent slab of steak and servings are ample. Normally they produce good peasant food but occasionally they'll spice it up with Mexican or American dishes. Menus 99.50–149.50F. Wine by the glass. A live band plays in the corner in summer. The boss is very pleasant and he runs a good place which works well.

KERFATY

15 rue Le Dean (Centre).
☎ 02.98.90.36.78
Closed Sat lunchtime, Sun and Mon.

This place has a history. Fatima hails from Grenoble and a few years ago she thought she'd open a restaurant. The banks there frowned on the project and gave her no support, so she decided to take the plunge in Brittany and started up her bar-restaurant. *Kerfaty* means "Faty's place" and everything in the decor pays tribute to the spirit that created it – hundreds of photographs of friends cover the walls and ceiling. Her couscous is excellent but you should also try the Algerian *briks*, including grilled peppers and meat, the Tunisian *briks* of tuna, onion and spices, or her *tajine* of lamb. On the second Friday of each month, she prepares *Kig Ha Farz*, a local dish from north Finistère, but you have to book. Expect to pay about 115F *à la carte*, while individual dishes start at 70F. The desserts, however, are a bit of a let down.

|●| AU P'TIT RAFIOT

7 rue de Pont-l'Abbé; near the quay.
☎ 02.98.53.77.27 ➡ 02.98.52.96.19
Closed Sat and Mon lunchtimes, and Sun.

The outside looks a bit tatty, but inside it's thoughtfully decorated in marine style with portholes. In the middle of the room there's a splendid aquarium full of sea creatures with huge claws – the cook will only work with the freshest ingredients, and all fish and shellfish come from the *patron*'s own tanks. The dishes are well served, very tasty and good value; try the Breton *bouillabaisse*, seafood couscous or lobster of the *P'tit Rafiot*. The waiter gives very clear descriptions of the dishes, and you'll pay about 170F for a complete meal.

ERGUÉ-GABÉRIC   29500 (5KM E)

⚑ 🏠 |●| HÔTEL-RESTAURANT À L'ORÉE DU BOIS*

Odet; from the junction of the N165 and the Coray road, head towards Odet-Lestonan.
☎ 02.98.59.53.81 ➡ 02.98.59.58.83
Restaurant closed Fri, Sat and Sun evenings, Fri only in high season. **TV**. **Garden**. **Car park**.

Small neo-Breton establishment with the benefit of a small quiet garden and a car park. Rooms 230F with basin/wc, 245F with shower/wc, half board 250F per person, depending on the season. There's a new reception area and a bar with a view. The breakfast room has a similar aspect. There's a 62F *formule* and menus at 68–180F. Seafood specialities include medallion of monkfish *au Kig-Sal* and *au médoc*, and scallop *cassolette au riesling*. Seafood and

shellfish platters to order. Children's menus 35 and 50F. 10% discount on the room rate Sept–June.

PLUGUFFAN   29700 (6KM W)

🏠 LA COUDRAIE**

Impasse du Stade; on the 4-lane road from Pont L'Abbé, take the Pluguffan-Pouldreuzic exit. There's a sign.
☎ 02.98.94.03.69 ➡ 02.98.94.08.42
Closed Sun out of season, ten days Oct/Nov and a week in Feb. **TV**. **Car park**.

Superb, granite-built Breton house, surrounded by a well-kept garden. A nice spot to stay and relax when the sun comes out. The eleven rooms are well furnished and you could easily find yourself making new friends in the comfortable, British-style lounge. Choose rooms 1, 3, 4, 6 or 11 which are more spacious. Doubles for 250F with shower/wc and 280F with bath.

QUIMPERLÉ   29300

|●| LE BISTRO DE LA TOUR

2 rue Dom-Morice; it's in the *ville basse*, by the covered market, opposite Sainte-Croix church.
☎ 02.98.39.29.58 ➡ 02.98.39.21.77
Closed Sat lunchtime and Sun evening out of season.

Beautifully furnished – the owners are also in the antique trade. Traditional cuisine prepared by the very friendly host, who is a great wine connoisseur and, appropriately enough, looks rather like Bacchus, the god of wine. There's a new cellar which you can visit. Specialities include fresh fish of the day such as Breton salmon, bass or sole, hot and cold scallops, pan-fried prawns *à la façon de ma grand-mère*, peppers stuffed with cod, tuna tournedos, oxtail *compotée*, lamb *roulade* with aubergine, and cold *escabèche* of Breton sardines. Weekday lunchtime menu at 80F and others 99F, 155F and 220F before a big hike up to 360F.

|●| LA CIGALE ÉGARÉE

5 rue Jacques-Cartier (Centre).
☎ 02.98.39.15.53
Closed Sun, and Mon and Tues evenings out of season.

This place feels as though it comes from much further south than Brittany, with its two delightful dining rooms with colour-washed walls and its trellissed terrace. The chef insists on using fresh produce from the market and while there is a touch of Provence, his dishes combine original flavours; *carpaccio* of salmon with Breton honey, *croustillant* of fresh sardines with ginger and lime, or *fricassée* of scallops with royal jelly and grilled bacon with pesto. Desserts include strawberries with *pastis* and a *coulis* of aromatic herbs. Dishes change every four months. Lunch menu 87F, others 99–195F, children's menu 55F and 120F *à la carte*.

⦿ LE RELAIS DU ROCH

Forêt Domaniale de Toul Foën; 2km out of town following the river on the Pouldu road, it's on the right. ☎ 02.98.96.12.97 ➡ 02.98.39.22.40
Closed Sun evening and Mon, and a fortnight in Jan. **Garden. Car park**.

Well-run restaurant in the heart of the forest. There's a gastronomic dining room with an open fire place, pink tablecloths and abundant floral arrangements. Here, the chef puts his favourite dishes on the menu: grilled lobster with coral butter, *confit* of duck, smoked salmon and a home-made *foie gras* which is so good that it challenges the stuff they produce in the southwest for quality. Lunch menu at 87F and a shoal of others 110–260F.

REDON   35600

⦿ CRÊPERIE L'AKENE

10 rue du Jeu-de-Paume; it's near the old harbour. ☎ 02.99.71.25.15
Closed Tues and Wed evenings out of season.

Good-quality, inexpensive food in a pleasant setting. *Crêpe complète* and other savoury options, good waffles and mixed salads. Around 60F for a complete meal.

RENNES   35000

SEE MAP OVERLEAF

✿ HÔTEL LE RIAVAL*

9 rue Riaval. Off map **B3-1**
☎ 02.99.50.65.58 ➡ 02.99.41.85.30
Closed 14–22 July. **Garden**.

A simple, unpretentious hotel conveniently located behind the station, in a pleasant part of town. The building has been refurbished and is well maintained. Brightly painted, modern rooms, some of which have brown wallpaper with medallions. Doubles 140F with basin, up to 200F with shower/wc. The ones with a garden view look onto a huge lime tree.

✿ HÔTEL DE LA TOUR D'AUVERGNE

20 bd. de la Tour-d'Auvergne. **MAP A2-8**
☎ 02.99.30.84.16
TV.

Plain but spotless rooms 140F with basin, 185F with shower or 220F with shower/wc. A bargain! Ideal family hotel for limited budgets, run by a very kindly woman. Breakfast served in your room – there's no breakfast room. Parking in the street.

✿ HÔTEL D'ANGLETERRE*

19 rue du Maréchal-Joffre. **MAP B2-3**
☎ 02.99.79.38.61 ➡ 02.99.79.43.85
Closed Sun afternoon. **TV**.

A well-kept hotel with friendly owners in an elegant bourgeois building with an impressive staircase and wide corridors. Good value. Traditional, spacious rooms 165F with hand basin, 210–225F with shower/wc or bath. Renovation of a dozen rooms now completed.

🍴 ✿ HÔTEL DE LÉON*

15 rue de Léon; it's near the station. Off map **B2-2**
☎ 02.99.30.55.28 ➡ 02.99.36.59.11

Small, quiet hotel set back from the road. Stylish retro furniture. The rooms, 165F with basin, 200F with shower/wc or bath, are good value. Free coffee.

✿ ⦿ HÔTEL-RESTAURANT AU ROCHER DE CANCALE**

10 rue Saint-Michel. **MAP A1-5**
☎ 02.99.79.20.83
Closed Sat and Sun and a fortnight in Aug. **TV**.

You couldn't ask for a better location. It's in a famous medieval street full of bars – one of the liveliest streets in the town and, consequently one of the noisiest. The hotel has been renovated and the very stylish, comfortable double rooms cost 220F. Good restaurant on the ground floor. Set menus 85–150F and *à la carte*.

🍴 ✿ LE GARDEN**

3 rue Duhamel. **MAP B2-4**
☎ 02.99.65.45.06 ➡ 02.99.65.02.62
Garden. TV. Car park.

Charming, tasteful hotel, between the station and the old town. There's a café, decorated in apple-green, and a small internal garden. Friendly welcome. Very nice, individualised rooms in fresh colours; a double with shower goes for 260F or 340F with bath. 10% discount July–Aug.

🍴 ✿ HÔTEL DE NEMOURS**

5 rue de Nemours; it's near the pl. de la République. **MAP B2-9**

[**173**]

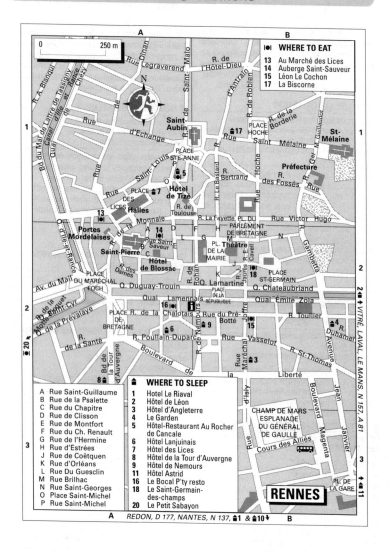

WHERE TO EAT
13 Au Marché des Lices
14 Auberge Saint-Sauveur
15 Léon Le Cochon
17 La Biscorne

WHERE TO SLEEP

A	Rue Saint-Guillaume	1	Hôtel Le Riaval
B	Rue de la Psalette	2	Hôtel de Léon
C	Rue du Chapitre	3	Hôtel d'Angleterre
D	Rue de Clisson	4	Le Garden
E	Rue de Montfort	5	Hôtel-Restaurant Au Rocher de Cancale
F	Rue du Ch. Renault		
G	Rue de l'Hermine	6	Hôtel Lanjuinais
H	Rue d'Estrées	7	Hôtel des Lices
J	Rue de Coëtquen	8	Hôtel de la Tour d'Auvergne
K	Rue d'Orléans	9	Hôtel de Nemours
L	Rue Du Guesclin	11	Hôtel Astrid
M	Rue Brilhac	16	Le Bocal P'ty resto
N	Rue Saint-Georges	18	Le Saint-Germain-des-champs
O	Place Saint-Michel		
P	Rue Saint-Michel	20	Le Petit Sabayon

RENNES

VITRÉ, LAVAL, LE MANS, N 157, A 81

REDON, D 177, NANTES, N 137, ▲1 & ▲10

☎ 02.99.78.26.26 ➡ 02.99.78.25.40
TV. Car park.

This hotel has probably the smallest lift in the world. In reception the walls are covered with autumn leaves, engravings and butterflies. The rooms are undergoing a programme of refurbishment so prices – doubles 265F with shower/wc and 295F with bath – may change. The quieter rooms are on the courtyard. Everyone is made welcome. 10% discount June–Aug.

♠ HÔTEL LANJUINAIS**

11 rue Lanjuinais. **MAP A2-6**
☎ 02.99.79.02.03 ➡ 02.99.79.03.97
TV.

A quiet well-maintained hotel in a small street leading to the quai Lamennais. Most rooms look over the street but some look into the dark courtyard. They have reasonable facilities, doubles 275F with shower/wc or 295F with bath, with special deals for weekends out of season.

♠ HÔTEL DES LICES**

7 pl. des Lices. **MAP A1-7**
☎ 02.99.79.14.81 ➡ 02.99.79.35.44
e hotel.lices@wansadoo.fr
Disabled access. TV. Car park.

On one of the most beautiful squares in the old town. They have completely modernised the hotel. It's full of light and well appointed. The very pleasant rooms have balconies and the ones on the upper floors have good views over the rooftops and the old town. Doubles 290–310F. Bright, efficient welcome.

♠ HÔTEL ASTRID

32 av. Louis Barthou. Off map **B3-11**
☎ 02.99.30.82.38 ➡ 02.99.31.85.55
Closed New Year's Eve and New Year's Day. **Disabled access. TV Garden.**

Well located near the station and only a 10-minute walk from the town centre. A pretty, chic hotel where you will get a friendly welcome. It's spotless and the rooms, modern, large, quiet and well-equipped, cost 340F with shower/wc or 360F with bath. The whole place is quiet and pleasant. The breakfast room looks out onto a small garden. A reliable establishment, run very professionally. 10% discount in school holidays and public holidays.

齐 |●| LA BISCORNE

8 rue Saint-Mélaine. **MAP B1-17**
☎ 02.99.30.18.37
Closed Sun and Mon evening, and the first fortnight in August.

Charm of the warm, rustic variety, harmonising well with the traditional cuisine. The young chef offers a range of set menus at 75–180F, *à la carte* dishes, and a lunchtime menu at 58F. The dishes change every four months, but these are typical: mackerel *terrine* with a chive cream and pickled shallots, pork kebab with apple served with cauliflower and tomato. The home-made lemon tart is sublime and the wine is reasonably priced. Free Kir.

|●| LE BOCAL-P'TY RESTO

6 rue d'Argentré. **MAP A3-16**
☎ 02.99.78.34.10
Closed Sun, Mon and 1–20 Aug.

This friendly restaurant is overflowing with creative ideas. First, the decoration is lovely: glass jars are filled with all sorts of strange things collected here and there and the lids have been used to decorate the walls and even the doors in the toilet. The dishes of the day – like chicken with spices and topped with grilled cheddar, or grilled squid with butter and lemon – are scrawled up on a blackboard. There's a particularly delicious sticky *moelleux au chocolat*. Lunch menu 59F then 65F and 85F. There's a well-chosen, cheaply priced wine list and they're all served by the glass. Trendy, young and appealing.

|●| AU MARCHÉ DES LICES

3 pl. du Bas-des-Lices. **MAP A1-13**
☎ 02.99.30.42.95
Closed Sun, first week in Jan and three weeks in Aug.
Disabled access. Car park.

Relaxed and friendly atmosphere. Dish of the day 40F served at lunchtime, except on Sat. Mixed salads, *galette complète* (savoury), and other *crêpes* made using 100% locally grown buckwheat. Good cider. Reckon on 65F for a meal. Open fire in the winter to warm up the atmosphere.

齐 |●| LÉON LE COCHON

1 rue du Maréchal-Joffre. **MAP B2-15**
☎ 02.99.79.37.54 ➡ 02.99.79.07.35
Closed Sun July–Aug.

A lot of thinking has gone into creating this restaurant, which is at once modern, noble, refined and authentic – not an easy achievement. Dried-out trees, walls hung with chilli peppers and windows full of leaves are the backdrop for unpretentiously prepared local cooking. There's a 69F menu or *à la carte* will set you back around 130F. Try the chef's oxtail or his pig's trotter *du Petit Jesus en culotte de velours* and the *andouillette à la ficelle*. Free house apéritif.

⦿I LE SAINT-GERMAIN-DES-CHAMPS

12 rue Vau Saint-Germain. **MAP B2-18**
☎ 02.99.79.25.52
Closed Sun, and Mon–Wed evenings. **Disabled access**.

When the cows went mad, chickens were steeped in dioxin and vegetables were genetically modified, this had to be the place to come. A genuine organic vegetarian restaurant where you can have a good meal without eating bits of animal. Interesting ingredients like sprouting grains and seaweed in dishes that are full of colour and generously served; vegetable *pâté* with *crudités* and sprouting beans, a grain dish with vegetables that has different ingredients every day, chocolate cakes, crumbles and cheesecakes. Dishes from 50F, a menu at 70F, 90F *à la carte* and a children's menu at 40F. Even the wines and fruit juices are organic. One dining room has a plate-glass window onto the street while the second looks onto the courtyard.

⦿I LE PETIT SABAYON

16 rue des Trente. **MAP A3-20**
☎ 02.99.35.02.04
Closed Sat lunchtime, Sun evening, Mon and 4–21 Aug.

One of the best tables in town, with simple decor and diligent, smiling service. Try the salad with two kinds of *foie gras*, tournedos of sardines with rhubarb sauce or the *marquise* with chocolate and an arabica coffee sauce. Realistic prices: 78–161F. Good wine list at reasonable prices. The restaurant is a smoke-free zone.

⦿I AUBERGE SAINT-SAUVEUR

6 rue Saint-Sauveur. **MAP A2-14**
☎ 02.99.79.32.56
Closed Sat, Sun, Mon lunchtime, the first fortnight in Aug and a week in Sept.

In a lovely 16th-century canon's house behind St-Pierre cathedral, this restaurant has a warm, intimate, sophisticated atmosphere. Set menus, 78–162F, offer quality traditional cuisine in dishes such as roast monkfish with cabbage, grilled lobster and good duck *foie gras*. A place to bring your loved one or an old friend. Free coffee.

ROCHE-BERNARD (LA)   56130

⬠ ⦿I LES DEUX MAGOTS**

3 pl. du Bouffay (West).

☎ 02.99.90.60.75 ➡ 02.99.90.87.87
Closed Sun evening and Tues lunchtime out of season, Mon, a week in June, a week in Oct and 20 Dec–15 Jan. **TV**.

This comfortable hotel has a lovely façade with arched windows, and fifteen pleasantly furnished rooms. Doubles 280F with shower/wc and 300–350F with bath. Seafood dishes predominate – warm crayfish salad, braised sea bream with baby vegetables, roast turbot in cider and onions – but don't miss out on the veal sweetbreads with morels. Menus 85–280F. Lengthy wine list. The bar has an impressive collection of miniature bottles of apéritifs, cognac, whisky and so on. Friendly welcome.

ROCHEFORT-EN-TERRE   56220

⦿I HOSTELLERIE DU LION D'OR

rue du Pélican.
☎ 02.97.43.32.80 ➡ 02.87.43.30.12
Cosed Sun and Tues evenings and Wed, 20 Sept–1 May, 20 Jan–10 Feb and 25 Nov–5 Dec.

The best restaurant in town, in a 16th-century post house. Even the cheapest menu at 85F is just fine while there are others, including a *menu terroir*, up to 185F. *À la carte* will cost about 210F. The dishes are seasonal; try *croustillant* of seafood with a crustacane *coulis* or pan-fried fillet of bream with sorrel cream and saffron potatoes. It's a bit uptight and traditional but it suits the surroundings – this is one of the most beautiful houses in Rochefort.

ROSCOFF   29680

⚘ ⬠ HÔTEL AUX TAMARIS**

49 rue Édouard-Corbière; it's next to the Kerléna clinic.
☎ 02.98.61.22.99 ➡ 02.98.69.74.36
e auxtamaris@dial-olcome.com
Closed mid-Nov to 1 March. **TV**.

A nearly great location because although this welcoming hotel looks out towards the Île de Batz it's separated from the sea by the coast road. Bright, comfortable rooms; doubles with shower/wc 260–320F or 290–350F with bath. Some have views of the Île, and you can watch the sun slip into the ocean. No restaurant, but some of the best hospitality in Finistère. 10% discount Oct, Nov and March.

⚘ ⬠ ⦿I LES CHARDONS BLEUS**

4 rue Amiral-Réveillère; from the bridge, it's towards the church.
☎ 02.98.69.72.03 ➡ 02.98.61.27.86

Closed Thurs except July–Aug, Sun evening in winter, and Feb. **TV**.

Good value for money for this town and a good atmosphere. There's a weekday lunch menu at 65F and others up to 210F. Lots of classic dishes, cooked well; sea trout with warm apples, John Dory with cream, seafood platters, pan-fried scallops with leeks, fillet of sole with mushrooms. Comfortable rooms at reasonable prices: doubles 290–310F for shower/wc, 310–330F with bath. The owner is warm and welcoming so it's a pity the staff are sniffy.

🛏 |●| HÔTEL TALABARDON***

pl. de l'Église.
☎ 02.98.61.24.95 📠 02.98.61.10.54
Closed Sun evening and Thurs lunchtime, and end Oct to end Feb. **TV**. **Pay car park**.

A characterful hotel that is so close to the water it was partly destroyed in a storm back in 1996. They've chosen yellow and blue for some floors, yellow and green for others – Brittany's national colours. Bright clean rooms from 370F in low season or 470F in high season; some have sea view. Three rooms have balconies. Very big buffet breakfast. The dining room is lovely, with lots of extremely fresh fish and shellfish on the menu. The menus, from 100F, change with the seasons and according to what the fishermen land. Interesting wine list. The place has charm and they make you feel very welcome. Only one drawback – they charge 50F for the car park. Even though it's hard to park in the town that seems excessive.

|●| L'ÉCUME DES JOURS

quai d'Auxerre.
☎ and 📠 02.98.61.22.83
✉ Michel.Quévé@wanadoo.fr
Closed Tues evening and Wed out of season.

This fine granite building, which must have been a shipwright's house, is now a restaurant which has quickly gained an excellent reputation. Comfortable, warm, intimate interior with a wide fireplace. Some inspirational dishes by the chef combining produce from land and sea in extraordinary ways: pan-fried queen scallop with smoked duck breast, *foie gras* and scallops with oyster mushrooms and balsamic vinegar, braised emperor fillet, vegetables from the garden etc. Menus 95–215F or around 200F *à la carte*.

ROSTRENEN   22110

|●| COEUR DE BRIEZH

14 rue Abbé Gibert (Centre).

☎ 02.96.29.18.33
Closed Tues evening and Wed.

Service to 10pm in the week, 11pm at the weekend. In the middle of the hamlet, in a substantial yellow house. The owners raised the money to get started through friends and clients who had been trying to persuade them to open a bar and restaurant. It worked. The setting is totally seductive – stone walls and a Breton decor. Roger is a natural front of house and Anne-Laure is a self-taught chef with talent. She cooks local dishes, using fresh, good-quality produce, organic for the most part, that she sources through local farmers and producers. Delicious main courses and an array of seductive sweets. Set menus 98–149F.

SABLES-D'OR-LES-PINS   22240

🧖 🛏 |●| HÔTEL DES PINS**

allée des Acacias (Centre); it's 400m from the beach.
☎ 02.96.41.42.20 📠 02.96.41.59.02
Closed Oct–March.

Very clean rooms with slightly faded charm; doubles 220F with shower or 260F with shower/wc. Half board 220–310F per person, obligatory July–Aug. Set lunch menu 78F and 98–168F. Lots of seafood and fresh fish. Miniature golf in the garden. 10% discount on the room rate 15 Sep–15 June.

PLURIEN-FRÉHEL   22240 (2KM S)

🧖 🛏 MANOIR DE LA SALLE

rue du Lac; it's 1km from Sables-d'Or-les-Pins, just before you get to Fréhel.
☎ 02.96.72.38.29 📠 02.96.72.00.57
✉ Aude.Labruyere@manoir_de_la_Salle.com
Closed Oct–March. **Disabled access**. **TV**. **Car park**.

A noble, stone, 16th-century manor house which you enter through a beautiful gothic portal built a century earlier. Bright, comfortable rooms furnished with modern pieces; doubles 250–350. They've converted another old building to make a couple of apartments with kitchens, sleeping four to six. Lots of things to keep you amused, like the solarium and ping-pong, and there's a golf course nearby. There are even stalls for horses and ponies if you're on a holiday. It's an excellent place, run by a delightful young couple, and is very fashionable in these parts. 10% discount April–June.

FRÉHEL 22240 (5KM E)

☎ HÔTEL LE FANAL**

Lieu-dit Besnard; take the road to Cap-Fréhel and when you get there turn right for Plévenon – the hotel is on the left after 1.5km.
☎ 02.96.41.43.19
Closed Oct–April. **Garden. Car park.**

A tall chalet, the sort of architecture you'd expect to find in Scandinavia – perfect for this barren Breton wasteland that stretches to the ocean. Sparklingly clean with a Bergmanesque frisson and music by Chopin in the lounge. Regulars come to recharge the batteries. Comfortable rooms 250–340F. TV is outlawed. Rooms 6–9 are more spacious than the others. Children under ten get a free breakfast.

SAINT-BRIEUC 22000

♟ ☎ HÔTEL DU CHAMP DE MARS**

13 rue du Général-Leclerc.
☎ 02.96.33.60.99 ➦ 02.96.33.60.05
Closed 20 Dec–5 Jan. **Disabled access. TV.**

This very well-run, pleasant establishment, with all the facilities of a two-star hotel, has the merit of being reasonably priced: 270–300F for a double. Breakfast 38F. Friendly owners. Discount Sept–June.

♟ ☎ |●| HÔTEL-RESTAURANT LE DUGUESCLIN**

2 pl. Duguesclin; it's in the pedestrian area.
☎ 02.96.33.11.58 ➦ 02.96.52.01.18
Disabled access. TV.

Centrally located and completely refurbished with bright, comfortable rooms. Doubles with shower/wc 270F, 275F with bath. Set menus 60–172F or à la carte, specialities include mousseline of scallops, bream with fennel, home-smoked fish and chocolate fondant. 10% discount except in Aug, and from 1 Nov–30 April a special exclusive rate of 200F for a double room.

♟ |●| RESTAURANT LE SYMPATIC

9 bd. Carnot; it's behind the train station.
☎ 02.96.94.04.76
Closed Sat lunchtime and Sun.

Open until 11pm. A happy combination of a good atmosphere and good food grilled over a fire of vine shoots. The ambience is warm, and service is friendly and efficient; dishes using quality ingredients are served on huge plates with a side vegetable, and they're inex-

pensive. Set menus 68–250F or à la carte. Free Kir Breton.

|●| AUX PESKED

59 rue du Légué; it's 1km north of the town centre.
☎ 02.96.33.34.65
Closed Sun evening, Mon, 24 Dec–15 Jan and 28 Aug–12 Sept.

The gastronomic reputation of this restaurant is highly regarded in Saint-Brieuc. It's got everything going for it, a sober, elegant, modern setting and a terrace which gives superb views of the Légué valley. Delightful light, mouth-watering dishes, with a 115F weekday menu and others 145–390F. The extensive cellar contains a modest collection of 13,000 bottles! Some are rare and expensive, lots are Loire wines but many are less prestigious and more affordable.

SAINT-MALO 35400

♟ ☎ HÔTEL DU LOUVRE**

2 rue des Marins (Centre).
☎ 02.99.40.86.62 ➦ 02.99.40.86.93
📧 lelouvre@aol.com
TV. Car park.

Although it has an impressive number of rooms – fifty – this is still a family hotel has appeal. Very comfortable doubles; 240F with shower, 290F with shower/wc and 340–380F with bath. The ones overlooking the pretty courtyard are more spacious. They have rooms sleeping three and one sleeping seven. From Nov to March they offer a 50% (yes, 50%!) discount; at other times it's 10%.

☎ HÔTEL LE NAUTIL

9 rue de la Corne de Cerf (Centre).
☎ 02.99.40.42.27 ➦ 02.99.56.75.43
📧 nautilus-st-malo@wanadoo.fr
TV.

A little hotel inside the old town, just five minutes from the beach. It's newly decorated in bright, young colours. Smallish rooms with good facilities, 250–350F for a double with shower/wc . On the ground floor, there's a lively pub with psychedelic walls – more Yellow Submarine than Nautilus. Better avoid the rooms on the first floor, because of the din in the bar.

♟ ☎ HÔTEL LA RANCE**

15 quai Sébastopol, Port Solidor, Saint-Servan (South).
☎ 02.99.81.78.63 ➦ 02.99.81.44.80
TV. Free car park. Pay garage.

Small hotel with a family atmosphere and eleven rooms, some with splendid views over the port and Baie de la Rance. The decor is sophisticated, from the reception to the rooms which are individually decorated and tastefully appointed – some are under the eaves; doubles 340F with shower/wc or 525F with bath. Very big breakfast. 10% discount except July–Aug and public holiday weekends.

|●| CRÊPERIE LA BRIGANTINE

13 rue de Dinan; it's inside the town walls.
☎ 02.99.56.82.82
Closed Tues evening and Wed except in school holidays, 15 Nov–10 Dec, and 15 Jan–5 Feb.

Snug, welcoming *crêperie* with wonderful photographs of old sailing ships on the walls, straw chairs covered with check cushions and a lot of blond wood everywhere. Good, classic *crêpes* at reasonable prices. Menus from 60F, or make your own selection and you'll pay 55–60F for a meal.

|●| RESTAURANT CHEZ GILLES

2 rue de la Pie-qui-Boit (Centre).
☎ 02.99.40.97.25
Closed Wed, Wed lunch only 15 July–31 Aug, Thurs 15 Nov–Easter except Christmas week, Feb school holidays and 21 Nov–13 Dec.

The seafood here, so fresh that it's still got sea water on it, is cooked with enthusiasm and served in a cosy, comfy, bourgeois dining room with intimate corners. A 78F lunch *formule* (92F in the evening), and other menus 132–182F. The owner/chef cooks fish to perfection, in delicate, aromatic sauces; slivers of John Dory with oysters and bacon pieces, and brill in a chicken stock and *foie gras*.

|●| RESTAURANT BORGNEFESSE

10 rue du Puits-aux-Braies; it's inside the town walls.
☎ 02.99.40.05.05
Closed Sun, Mon, a fortnight June/July and a fortnight Christmas/New Year.

A restaurant with a pirate theme run by a larger-than-life *patron*, a poet and seafarer – a legendary character in Saint-Malo. At the drop of a hat he'll weave tales of pirates and derring-do and how the restaurant got its name. On the food front, the *crêpes* are made with selected, locally grown produce: organic eggs and full-cream milk. The house specialities are the savoury *galette Borgnefesse* which is stuffed with black pudding and served with baked apples, and the sweet *Saint-Patrick* with apple compote flavoured with cinnamon, raisins, whisky and cream. They serve dishes of the

day – lamb chops with creamed garlic and mussels in season. Set menus 85–160F.

|●| LE PETIT CRÊPIER

6 rue Sainte Barbe (Centre).
☎ 02.99.40.93.19 **e** LePcrepeir@aol.com
Closed Wed out of season, a fortnight in Nov and a fortnight in Jan.

The pancakes and girdle cakes are as good as they are surprising. Excellent produce and subtle, often unexpected alliances of flavours. The man who makes the pancakes is a real chef: try his mussel flan, girdle cake with fish *mousse* or pancakes with Breton *andouille* and onion marmalade. He also does monkfish liver and king prawn salad. Equally unusual sweet pancakes; poached pear with orange caramel or another with seaweed marmalade. There's an interesting list of beers and Breton ciders. You'll pay around 85F for a meal.

|●| LA CORDERIE

Chemin de la Corderie; it's next to the Alet camping site.
☎ 02.99.81.62.38
Closed Mon except July–Aug, and mid–Oct to mid-March.

This is off the beaten tourist track and wonderfully lacking in traffic noise. *La Corderie* is an old family house filled with old furniture, books and paintings. From the terrace and dining room, there is a beautiful view of the sea, the Solidor tower, La Rance and Dinard beyond. They serve light, well-presented dishes at reasonable prices, and they change practically every day; a Greek salad, perhaps, or a grilled fish. Menus at 98F or *à la carte* a meal will cost around 150F.

SAINT-POL-DE-LÉON 29250

≜ |●| LE PASSIFLORE-LES ROUTIERS

28 rue Penn-Ar-Pont; it's near the station.
☎ and ☛ 02.99.69.00.52
Closed Sun evening, Christmas and New Year's Day. **TV**.

This really unpretentious little place offers a genuine welcome and pleasantly classic rooms at low prices; from 210F with shower/wc. *Les Routiers* restaurant on the ground floor is absolutely excellent, so don't be surprised if it's packed at lunchtime, when 58F menu is very popular because of the plate of starters. There are others up to 170F. Seafood platters, Breton lobster *à l'Améri-caine* and other fish dishes.

|●| LA POMME D'API

49 rue Verderel; it's in a street at right angles to rue

Général-Leclerc.
☎ 02.98.69.04.36
Closed Sun evening and Mon out of season, the last fortnight in Nov and the Feb school holidays.

A lovely stone building dating from the mid-16th century. This restaurant is full of real Breton charm with its interior of natural stone and wood and its splendid open fireplace. Here you can sample some excellent food, said to be the best in town. There's a 85F set menu weekday lunchtimes, with a top-price menu at 185F, while you'll pay about 200F *à la carte*. Dishes include a *fricassée* of artichoke hearts with scallops, escalope of Breton salmon, pan-fried turbot with verbena, *andouille de Guémédé*, roast Brittany lobster perfumed with sesame and saffron, fillet of sea bream steamed in seaweed, *blanquette* of sole fillet *au chouchen* and roast lamb *pavé*.

CLÉDER   29233 (9KM E)

🖈 I●I ENTRE TERRE-ET-MER

9 rue de l'Armorique.
☎ 02.98.19.53.22
Closed Mon and Tues evening.

You don't come here for the decor, but the service is delightful and someone in the kitchen really knows what they're up to. Dishes change regularly, because they use fresh market produce. Good-value weekday lunch menu – it's best to book for this because it's served in the bar only and there aren't many tables. However, the *menu carte* at 110F offers the main interest: mussel and artichoke risotto, pigs' cheeks with spices, and fresh strawberry tart, prepared by a young chef with a skilfull hand, using locally grown and produced ingredients. Free coffee.

SAINT-RENAN   29290

🖈 I●I LA MAISON D'AUTREFOIS

7 rue de l'Église.
☎ 02.98.84.22.67
Closed Sun, Mon evening, and mid-Jan to mid-Feb.

Superbly attractive, half-timbered house. Inside, the decor, with old furniture and farm implements on the natural stone walls, creates a feeling of lightness. The young owners opted for blue-and-white table linen and they put vases of flowers here and there. Good, traditional *crêpes* – the *Bretonne* is stuffed with scallops, chopped leeks and cream and flambéed with Calvados, while the *Sauvage* drips with wine caramel and honey ice cream. Individual dishes from 53F,

a full meal for 95–105F. Free house apéritif.

SAINT-THÉGONNEC   29410

🏠 I●I AUBERGE DE SAINT-THÉGONNEC***

6 pl. de la Mairie.
☎ 02.98.79.61.18 ➡ 02.98.62.71.10
🅴 auberge@wanadoo.fr
Closed Sat lunchtime, Sun lunchtime and Mon from mid-Sept to mid-June, and 22 Dec–3 Jan.
Disabled access. **TV**. **Car park**.

Seriously good cooking in elegant, sophisticated surroundings. The service is faultless. Seasonal dishes are cooked expertly from fresh produce: fillet of ling with an aubergine *tian* and fresh tomato *coulis*, braised veal *mignon* with morels, a pocket of veal sweetbreads with oyster mushrooms and grain mustard, and orange *terrine* with nutmeg and mint. In short, this is recommended as one of the best restaurants in Finistère. Menus from 130F. Three lovely rooms with good facilities from 390F, with breakfast served in the comfortable lounge. The stuff that dreams are made of.

I●I CRÊPERIE STEREDENN

6 rue de la Gare (Centre).
☎ 02.98.79.43.34 ➡ 02.98.79.40.89
Closed Mon and Tues from Oct to mid-June.
Disabled access.

The owners, Christine and Alain, offer a friendly greeting. Open fire. A choice of 150 good, cheap *crêpes*: the *Picardie*, with leek sauce; the *Indien*, with white sauce, onions, mushrooms and curry; the *Douarnenez*, with sardine butter and green peppercorns; the *Saint Thégonnec*, with onions, tomatoes, cheese, ham and curry, or the sweet *Druide*, with marmalade, almonds and Grand Marnier. Set menus 60–71F. Wash it down with cider brewed on the premises. Disabled access to the dining room.

I●I RESTAURANT DU COMMERCE

1 rue de Paris; it's in the centre of the village.
☎ 02.98.79.61.07
Closed evenings, Sat, Sun and three weeks in Aug.

A roadside restaurant of the *routier* variety, open for breakfast (22F) and lunch. Friendly welcome, good cooking, huge portions and cheap prices. For 59F you get soup, starter, dish of the day, cheese and dessert – the menu states that a drink is included for "workers" but not for people "passing through"! They also have a few specialities ilike *pot-au-feu*, a broth with large chunks of meat and vegetables, *choucroute*, *Kig-ha-Farz* and couscous. Pleasant dining room with dry-stone walls. It's a lively place.

SARZEAU 56370

|●| RESTAURANT L'HORTENSIA

La Grée Penvins.
☎ 02.97.67.42.15 ⊧✦ 02.97.67.42.16
Closed Mon evening and Tues out of season.

The brand-new restaurant is in an old house where you go through one dining room to get to the next. They're all painted hydrangea-blue, a colour that's repeated decoratively and which contrasts with the starkness of the granite walls.

⚘|●| AUBERGE DE KERSTÉPHANIE

Route du Roaliguen; it's on the right at the end of a cul-de-sac.
☎ 02.97.41.72.41 ⊧✦ 02.97.41.99.15
Closed Tues evening and Wed out of season, Mon in season, and Jan to mid-Feb. **Car park**.

In all respects one of the best restaurants in the Morbihan. Elegant setting and service without excess formality. Virtuoso cuisine by the chef/owner Jean-Paul Jego, ably supported by his wife. The menus, 99–215F, change with the seasons: pan-fried squid with potatoes and onions sprinkled with matured wine vinegar, salmon *unilatéral* (cooked only on one side), *granité*, a sorbet, and an exquisite dessert of honey *sabayon* with apples and *nougat* ice cream. Mr Jego found a spit made in 1952, renovated it and set it up in the dining room. It's used to cook the day's special, like leg of ham on the bone served with a *sauce Malaga*. The excellent *à la carte* menu has all the specialities. Absolutely fabulous food at excellent prices. Free coffee.

PENVINS 56370 (7KM E)

⌂ |●| LE MUR DU ROY**

Lieu-dit Le Mur-du-Roy à Penvins.
☎02.97.67.34.08 ⊧✦ 02.97.67.36.23
Closed Wed lunchtime out of season, and Jan.

Well situated with direct access to the beach. The comfortable hotel offers impeccably clean rooms, four of which have views of the sea. Doubles 335–445F with shower/wc or 370F with bath. The excellent restaurant has a good range of fish and seafood. The 98F menu is excellent value and includes starter, main course, cheese and dessert. Other menus, 138–198F, offer dishes such as Breton fish stew, lobster and scallops *au gratin*, grilled lobster flambéed with whisky, or pan-fried scallops with raspberry butter. The most

expensive one give you the "surprise of the *Mur du Roy*", four main dishes (which change daily) and a selection of desserts.

TRÉBEURDEN 22560

⚘ ⌂ |●| HÔTEL-RESTAURANT KER AN NOD**

rue de Pors-Termen (Centre); it's opposite île Millau.
☎ 02.96.23.50.21 ⊧✦ 02.96.23.63.30
e kerannod@infonie.fr
Closed Thurs lunchtime except in school holidays and Jan–March. **TV**.

Peaceful hotel in sight of the Île Millau, almost on the vast beach, run by Catherine and Gildas. Of the twenty rooms, fourteen look out to sea. Doubles 290–370F with shower/wc or 370–420F with bath. Comfortable and bright with great picture windows. The dining room is equally pleasant; you dine here on fresh fish, seafood and local dishes; gratinéed oysters with nutmeg butter, fisherman's soup, Trégor chicken with crayfish, and caramelised apples with duckling. Menus 90–185F. Children's menu 60F. 10% discount on the room rate 15 Sept–31 Dec.

TRÉGASTEL 22730

⚘ ⌂ |●| HÔTEL-RESTAURANT DE LA CORNICHE**

38 rue Charles-Le-Goffic (Centre); it's in the town centre, 300m from the beaches.
☎ 02.96.23.88.15 ⊧✦ 02.96.23.47.89
Closed Sun evening and Mon outside school holidays and mid-Nov to mid-Dec. **TV**. **Garden**. **Car park**.

A bright, place where rooms with basin go for 170F, 200–280F with shower/wc and 250–320F with bath. The cheery decor puts you in a good mood. Menus, 85–190F, list lots of local dishes, and there's a children's menu at 50F. Half board, 200–250F, is obligatory July–Aug. 10% discount on the room rate except July–Aug.

⚘|●| AUBERGE DE LA VIEILLE ÉGLISE

In the old town; it's 2.5km from the beach.
☎ 02.96.23.88.31
Closed Sun evening, Mon out of season and March.

This place used to meet all the local needs: as canteen for the workers, butcher's, fruit and veg shop, mini-market, the lot. It's been completely transformed since Monsieur Lefessant and his family took over the place in 1962. They've turned it into an unmissable restaurant and you *won't* miss it – the outside is smothered in flowers. Weekday lunch menu at 85F and others 120–220F; tagliatelle with scallops, fish *choucroute*, fish *pot-au-feu* and John Dory roast with bacon are house specialities. Exceptionally high-quality cuisine, served by attentive staff, on good dinnerware in delightful surroundings. It's worth booking in the evening during the season and at weekends. Free coffee.

TRÉGUIER 22220

♠ |●| HÔTEL AIGUE MARINE ET RESTAURANT DES TROIS RIVIÈRES***

It's on the marina.
☎ 02.96.92.97.00 ➡ 02.96.92.44.48
Closed Sat lunchtime, Sun evening and Mon out of season, and 8 Jan–11 Feb. **Disabled access. Swimming pool. Garden. TV. Car park.**

A new establishment on the harbour. The 48 rooms are very comfortable, 380–520F with bath. There's a heated swimming pool and a garden, and they've built a sauna and Jacuzzi. The talented young chef shows his skill with local dishes. The menus, 115–220F, go by names – *Jaudy*, the *Armor Passion* and the *menu du Trégor* – and list dishes such as *croustille* of buckwheat with cheeks of monkfish, a *trou breton* sorbe, and *papillonnade* of brill. The prices are good for such high-quality cuisine. Children's menu at 60F. 10% discount on the room rate March–April and Sept–Dec.

♠ |●| KASTELL DINEC'H***

Route de Lannion; take the N786.
☎ 02.96.92.49.39 ➡ 02.96 92.34.03
Restaurant closed Tues evening, Wed out of season, and lunchtimes 31 Dec–20 March. **Disabled access. Swimming pool. TV. Garden. Car park.**

They've kept a good deal of the antique furniture from this elegant Breton manor house, and retained its intimate atmosphere. There's a swimming pool in the garden. Fifteen lovely rooms 460–550F. They like you to go half board from 15 July–15 Aug, which is fine because the cooking is good and the staff attentive. Menus from 135F serving fish specialities including a crab *bisque*, scallop pancake with parsley and salmon with fruit.

|●| LA POISSONNERIE DU TRÉGOR

2 rue Renan (Centre).
☎ 02.96.92.30.27
Tasting rooms open daily July–Sept.

A warm yet unusual establishment run by Mme Moulinet for the last thirty or so years.

Jean-Pierre Moulinet runs the fishmonger's where you can buy fish to cook or you can try fish, seafood and shellfish dishes in the tasting rooms upstairs. Crab mayonnaise, *moules marinières* 35F, and platters of shellfish from 110F. The *formule Petit Mousse* is an inspiration for children, to give them the chance to try seafood on their own plate. Marine frescoes line the walls – you'd think you were at sea. No puddings.

VANNES 56000

♨ ♠ |●| HÔTEL-RESTAURANT LE RELAIS DE LUSCANEN**

Zone commerciale de Luscanen (West); N165, route d'Auray – look for signs to the *zone commerciale*.
☎ 02.97.63.15.77 ➡ 02.97.63.30.45
Closed Sat evening, Sun, Whitsun weekend and a fortnight in August. **TV. Car park.**

A real roadside hotel-restaurant. The set menu, 56F, gives a choice of a hot or cold starter, a choice of main course, cheese, dessert *and* as much wine, bread and butter as you can manage. Children's menu 25F. Twenty-four clean simple rooms; all doubles 170F. Welcome with a smile. Free house apéritif.

♠ HÔTEL LE BRETAGNE**

36 rue du Mené (Centre); it's 50m from the Prison gateway.
☎ 02.97.47.20.21 ➡ 02.97.47.90.78
✉ hotel-le-brtagne@wanadoo.fr
Closed Sat evening, Sun, Ascension day weekend and a fortnight in Aug **TV.**

A little old-fashioned charm. Quiet, smallish rooms, some overlooking the town walls, and a courteous welcome. Doubles 200F with shower/wc or 240F with bath. Good value, and it's often full.

♠ HÔTEL LE MARINA**

pl. Gambetta (Centre).
☎ 02.97.47.22.81 ➡ 02.97.47.27.34
TV.

This hotel is over *L'Océan* bar, among the drinking holes around the square. Pretty rooms, most of them recently refurbished, have views of the harbour and town walls, and good facilities including TV. Ideal if you like to be where the action is. Doubles 200F with basin up to 320F with bath.

♨ |●| LE COMMODORE

3 rue Pasteur; it's behind the post office.
☎ 02.97.46.42.62

Closed Sun and Mon lunchtime.

Despite being poorly located in a quiet district with few passers-by, this restaurant has steadily built a regular trade because of its attractive setting, excellent service and cuisine. The nautical decoration is simple, elegant and warm. And there are plenty of culinary delights from the kitchen, made to carefully prepared recipes using fresh ingredients: *gravlax*, monkfish with dill, stewed crab claws, grilled bream with fennel, pan-fried scallops with saffron or *fricassée* of crayfish – you're in for a treat. They serve a lunchtime *formule* at 63F. Other menus at 98F and 169F or *à la carte*. Good wine list at affordable prices. They've set aside a kid's corner too. Free house apéritif or a shot of rum.

|●| RESTAURANT DE ROSCANVEC

17 rue des Halles (Centre); it's in the pedestrian area.
☎ 02.97.47.15.96 ➡ 02.97.47.86.39
e le-pavé-des-halles@wanadoo.fr
Closed Mon except July–Sept, Sun evening, and 1–23 Jan.

This cosy, traditional restaurant occupies two floors of a characterful 14th-century house. The young owner/chef is full of talent and ambition and he has succeeded in attracting a clientele of informed gourmets. Things get serious right from the first menu at 109F, and menus go up to 350F: turbot in honey crust, asparagus and truffle stew, croustillant of sea bream, roast pigeon with shollots, and coconut milk blancmange with grated walnut. The menus change regularly to reflect what's good in the market. First-rate wine list.

SAINT-AVÉ   **56890 (4KM N)**

|●| RESTAURANT LE TOURNESOL

2 pl. Notre-Dame-du-Loc; Saint-Avé is on the Vannes-Pontivy road.
☎ 02.97.44.50.50
e restaurant.le.Tournesol@wanadoo.fr
Closed Mon, Wed evening and a fortnight in Oct.

A doll's house decorated in sunflower yellow with copies of Van Gogh's pictures on the wall. Seven tables only in the dining room. The *menu traditionel* costs 85F and it's only 110F for the *menu gourmand* – duck *foie gras* or scallop and crayfish tail *brochette*, salmon escalope, *filet mignon* with oyster mushrooms, and roast cod with smoked bacon – and 160F for the *menu coup de cœur* – half a lobster and tournedos *Rossini*. Good cheeses and a difficult choice of desserts. Seafood platters to order. The wine

list is well priced. Service is friendly and efficient. Best to book.

|●| LE PRESSOIR

7 rue de l'Hôpital; it's 1km out of Saint-Avé.
☎ 02.97.60.87.63 ➡ 02.97.44.59.15
Closed Sun evening and Mon except July–Aug, Tues and 1–15 March, 2–10 July and 1–24 Oct. **Car park**.

Exceptional surroundings and facilities, a warm welcome and gastronomic delights in this attractive house just outside the town. Quite simply the best restaurant in these parts, serving *galette* of red mullet with potato and rosemary, *croustillant* of *andouille Guémené* sausage with pan-fried *foie gras* and buckwheat tagliatelle. The cheapest set menu, 190F, is served only on weekday lunchtime, but it's worth going out of your way to try it. Other menus 240–480F.

ARZ (ÎLE D')   **56840 (8KM S)**

|●| RESTAURANT-GRILL LE RIGADO

Grand-rue; it's in the centre of the village.
☎ 02.97.44.30.95 ➡ 02.97.44.33.61
Closed Tues evening, Wed and All Saints' to Easter.

Nadège runs the kitchen, Bruno runs the dining room. Together, this charming couple turned this old grocer's into a convivial meeting place where they serve good dishes from the islands: gratinéed oysters, lobster or meats grilled over the open fire before your eyes. Reading the menu will give you an appetite. Menus 100–160F. It's worth making the trip.

LOCQUELTAS   **56390 (6KM N)**

⚶ ☎ |●| HÔTEL LA VOLTIGE**

8 route de Vannes (North); from Vannes, take the D767 for Pontivy, the turning to Meucon aerodrome, then it's signposted.
☎ 02.97.60.72.06 ➡ 02.97.44.63.01
Restaurant closed Sun evening Sept–Easter, Mon, 10–23 March and a fortnight in Oct.
Garden. **TV**. **Car park**.

A dozen impeccably clean rooms, 225–270F with shower/wc and 235–285F with bath, all of which have been refitted and redecorated. Check out the great split-level rooms for three or four people. Half board, 225–270F, is attractive because of the rather good traditional food to be found even on the cheapest menu (75F). Other menus 105–250F. Efficient, unobtrusive service. There's a garden with an area set aside for games. Free coffee.

ARRADON
56610 (8KM SW)

⌖ 🏠 |❍| HÔTEL-RESTAURANT LE STIVELL***

rue Plessis-d'Arradon; take the D101.
☎ 02.97.44.03.15 ➠ 02.97.44.78.90
Restaurant closed Sun evening and Mon out of
season, and mid-Nov to mid-Dec. **TV**. **Car park**.

A *Logis de France*, located on one of the
prettiest stretches of the coast of the gulf of
Morbihan. It's very well run, with comfortable
double rooms 270–375F. Menus from 58F
(weekday lunchtime) to 250F. The dishes are
inspired by the sea; seafood *choucroute*,
warm oysters in champagne, etc. The
patronne makes you feel welcome. Ideal for
those who like the serenity of the sea without
having to stray too far from Vannes and,
since the owner is a fisherman himself, he'll
tell you where to fish in the sea or the river.
10% discount on the room rate. Free house
apéritif or coffee.

VITRÉ
35500

⌖ 🏠 HÔTEL LE MINOTEL**

47 rue Poterie (Centre).
☎ 02.99.75.11.11 ➠ 02.99.75.81.26

Really pretty hotel in the old town; they've
virtually rebuilt the house but have respected
the local style while providing modern facilities. If you wanted to split hairs you might feel
they were a little unimaginative. The green and
tartan decor is a bit like a golf clubhouse. Fun-
nily enough, they've done a deal with the local
golf club and offer packages if you want to
play a round or two. Doubles 295F with bath.

Good welcome. 10% discount weekends
Oct–March and free breakfast (otherwise 38F).

⌖ |❍| LA GAVOTTE

7 rue des Augustins (Centre).
☎ 02.99.74.47.74
Closed Mon,Tues except in the shool holidays, the first
fortnight in March and the middle fortnight in Sept.
Disabled access.

This restaurant fits in well with the surroundings in this charming village. It's a *crêperie*,
serving excellent girdle cakes and pancakes
with fillings from the traditional to the unusual; *Darley* cheese, *andouille* or various
sausages and an apple variety in which the
fruit filling comes somewhere between *purée*
and chutney. There are two menus at 53F
and 69F; *à la carte* you'll pay around 110F for
a complete meal. Free coffee.

|❍| AUBERGE SAINT-LOUIS

31 rue Notre-Dame (Centre).
☎ 02.99.75.28.28
Closed Sun evening, Mon and Wed evening, 1–15 Sept
and second fortnight in Feb. **Disabled access**.

A 15th-century house transformed into an inn
which has built up a solid reputation. The
wood panelling in the dining room creates a
warm, sophisticated yet family-style atmosphere. The young *patronne* will bring you a
small plate of appetisers to nibble while you
select your meal. You're in for a feast in a cosy
setting. The 66F *formule* is a dish and a
dessert, 74F for the same with a $\frac{1}{4}$ litre of
wine, then set menus 94–142F. There's a
good selection of grilled meats and superb
fish, accompanied by well-crafted sauces.
Proper tablecloths and napkins.

CENTRE

AMBOISE   37400

⬧ |●| HÔTEL LE CHANTELOUP

12 av. Émile Gounin.
☎ 02.47.57.10.90 ➡ 02.47.57.17.52
Closed end Sept to early April. **TV**. **Car park**. **Garden**.

Staying in Amboise tends to be expensive so it's good to find a hotel, open in season only, offering good value for money. This big block of a house, fronted by a private car park, is just outside the centre of town. There's little style – the armchairs are in fake leather, the surfaces are Formica. There are three floors (with lift), and very simple rooms; a double with shower/wc costs 245F or with bath 280F and 310F. The rooms up in the roof have skylights. It's very well maintained but the welcome is impersonal. There's a small garden and a terrace behind the hotel.

|●| RESTAURANT L'ÉPICERIE

46 pl. Michel-Debré (Centre); it's opposite the château car park.
☎ 02.47.57.08.94
Closed Mon evening and Tues except 15 June–30 Sept, and 8 Nov–16 Dec. **Car park**.

A magnificent half-timbered building painted olive green. There are pretty curtains at the windows that screen the dining room from the waves of tourists surging past outside. Good cooking with specialities including *fricassée* of veal sweetbreads and little kidneys, duck with peppercorns preserved in Chinon wine and *filet mignon* of spiced pork. The 68F set menu is not served on Sunday or evenings in season, others 110–220F. The service is efficient yet relaxed which is slightly at odds with the rather classical style of the dining room.

|●| LE MANOIR SAINT-THOMAS

1 Mail Saint-Thomas
☎ 02.47.57.22.52
Closed Mon and Tues lunchtime. **Garden**.

The manor and garden make a harmonious setting for the luxurious dining rooms and well-proportioned salons. The tables are beautifully laid and the waitresses all wear uniforms. The welcome is the ultimate in chic with cooking to match. Even on the cheapest menu, 175F, you are served *amuse-bouches* (a melon cocktail with Muscat de Beaumes de Venise) and *petits-fours* with your coffee. The menu at 205F includes a cheese course and the one at 295F has three main courses. The sweetbread and morel *terrine* is fine and delicate, while the pigeon *confit* is flavoured with juniper and served with green cabbage and a highly concentrated, deep-brown *sauce glace*. The *Gâteau Dame Anne* is a white chocolate dessert served with a kiwi *coulis*. This is gastronomic cooking at affordable prices in a restaurant that's a fine example of the art of good living.

POCÉ-SUR-CISSE   37530 (3KM N)

|●| CAVES DE LA CROIX VERTE

20 route d'Amboise; it's on the D431 from Amboise.
☎ 02.47.57.03.65
Closed Sun evening and Mon, Tues evening Oct to end of April, three weeks in Jan and weeks in Sept. **Disabled access**. **Car park**. **Garden**.

A quality place in a genuine cellar with a few tables where they don't treat tourists like pests. Émmanuel is in charge and will make you feel welcome. He produces absolutely straightforward but excellent cooking. He

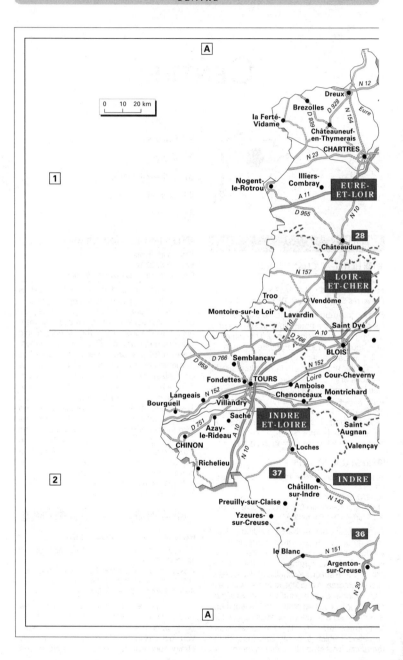

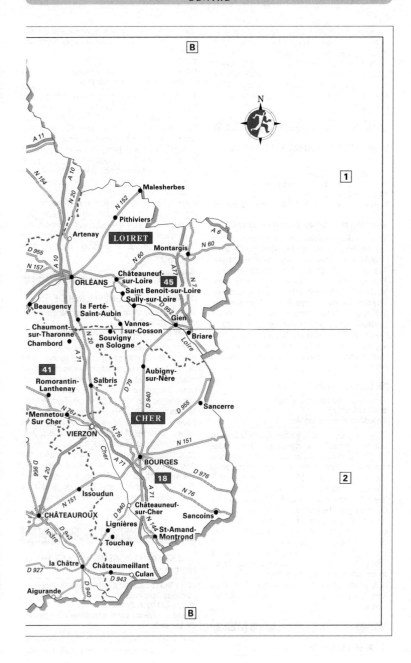

uses only the freshest produce bought at market – and you won't be rushed through your meal. A weekday lunch *formule* at 60F and menus 100–185F. You can take your time over your meal because the kids can play safely in the lovely garden. You can go for a constitutional in the Parc de la Chatellerie after lunch. Best to book.

BLÉRÉ   37150 (10KM S)

🛏 |●| HÔTEL-RESTAURANT LE CHEVAL BLANC**

pl. Charles-Bidault (Centre).
☎ 02.47.30.30.14 ➡ 02.47.23.52.80
e le chevalblancblere.com
Closed Sun evening and Mon except July–Aug, and Jan to mid-Feb.
Swimming pool. Garden. TV. Lock-up garage.

This is a delightful hotel in a 17th-century residence. Prettily arranged rooms at 340F for a double with shower/wc and 360F with bath. The ones looking over the garden are best. The reputation of the place comes from Michel Blériot's fresh, light, inventive cooking. The 98F set menu, (not Sun), offers some of the best value for money in the area. Serious gastronomic cuisine on the menus 215–300F. Good wine list with fine Loire wines and a superb selection of vintage armagnacs. Reservations essential at the weekend and public holidays.

|●| CHARCUTERIE POMMÉ

21 rue Paul-Louis Courier; (Centre).
☎ 02.47.57.91.15
Closed Sun afternoon and Mon.

This is a place of pilgrimage which is sought out by devotees of Touraine *charcuterie*. In the window and on the shelves inside, there's a collection of pottery vessels used to preserve the *confits* and lard. It's more a shop than a restaurant; as you go in, the *charcuterie* on the left is where you find the Pommé couple. On the right, there's the grocer's while at the back there's a small dining room where you can commune with an *andouillette*, their divine *pâtés* or *rillettes*, and wash it all down with a glass of local wine. Their *rillons* are a relic from the past, and prepared as they used to be when families made their own. You will only spend about 60F for a unique meal. They keep shop hours and make you feel very welcome.

CANGEY   37530 (12KM N)

🛏 |●| LE FLEURAY**

Route Dame-Marie; take the N152 Amboise–Blois road, turn left onto the D74 signposted to Cangey, Fleuray and Dame-Marie-les-Bois.
☎ 02.47.56.09.25 ➡ 02.47.56.93.97
Closed during the winter school holidays.
Disabled access. Garden. Car park.

This 19th-century manor house, surrounded by greenery, is a cross between a hotel and a guesthouse. Hazel and Peter Newington have called their eleven prettily decorated rooms after flowers such as *bouton d'or* (buttercup), *cerisier* (cherry blossom) and *clochette* (bluebell) – *capucine* (nasturtium) and *perce-neige* (snowdrop) are larger than the others. Doubles 475–600F with shower/wc or bath. Pricey gourmet cooking, with set menus 165–225F, served in a pleasant dining room or out on the terrace. Nice welcome, and a very international clientele, but you must book. Half board compulsory April–Oct; prices according to room and menu choice.

CHISSEUX   37150 (17KM SE)

|●| AUBERGE DU CHEVAL ROUGE

30 rue Nationale; it's on the road to Montrichard.
☎ 02.47.23.86.67
Closed Mon, and Tues out of season. **Garden**.

A few steps lead out of this lovely, country bistro into a charming dining room that's decorated with taste. Mme Léron serves her husband's tasty cooking with great kindness, though when the restaurant is full, she sometimes has too much to do. Try the *feuillantine* of Sainte-Maure cheese with tart apples, a salmon *bavarois* with cream and chives, saddle of rabbit "Grand-mère Julienne", a good *entrecôte* steak and a fish *choucroute*. The chef takes great care in the preparation of his wine or cream sauces. Menus start at 99F. This is a place where cooking is taken very serously and they don't take short cuts. There's a lovely garden and a terrace.

ARGENTON-SUR-CREUSE   36200

🎢 🛏 |●| HÔTEL-RESTAURANT LE CHEVAL NOIR**

27 rue Auclert-Descottes (Centre); it's on the road to Gargilesse-Dampierre.
☎ 02.54.24.00.06 ➡ 02.54.24.11.22
Closed Sun evening and Mon lunchtime out of season.
TV. Car park.

The restoration work done on this 19th-century post house has been particularly well executed. The rooms are quiet, comfortable and have been freshly decorated. Doubles 240–280F with shower/wc and 280F with bath. The large dining room has a highly polished parquet floor. The elegant, subtle cuisine is prepared by chef Christophe Jeannot, whose skill shows in his specialities: *foie gras* with Guérande sea salt, pigs' trotters *parmentier*, or fillet of zander. Set menus at 60F, not served on public holidays, then 95F and 135F or *à la carte*. Free house apéritif.

⅍ ☎ MANOIR DE BOISVILLERS**

11 rue du Moulin-de-Bord (Centre); beside the N20 in the direction of Limoges.
☎ 02.54.24.13.88 ➡ 02.54.24.27.83
📧 maison.de.boisvilliers@wanadoo.fr
Closed Sun in low season, and Dec.
Swimming pool. Garden. TV. Car park.

The first stone of the riverside residence of the Chevalier de Boisvillers was laid in 1759. This most unusual country manor house is elegantly set on the banks of the Creuse and it deserves more than two stars. The decor is elegant, the carpet has deep pile and there's a friendly little lounge next to the bar. You can have a drink by the pool in the grounds. The rooms are decorated in various styles – those under the eaves are the prettiest. Doubles with shower 240F, or shower/wc or bath 290–395F, which is reasonable considering the facilities. 10% discount on the room rate.

AUBIGNY-SUR-NÈRE   18700

☎ |◉| HÔTEL-RESTAURANT LA CHAUMIÈRE**

1 av. du Parc-des-Sports; it's next to the château, on the Sancerre road.
☎ 02.48.58.04.01 ➡ 02.48.58.10.31
Closed Sun evening except July–Aug, Mon lunchtime and the Feb school holidays.
TV. Pay car park.

A comfortable little thatched cottage. The decoration of the rooms is well up to standard, as is the reception. Doubles, 245F with shower/wc or bath, are on the small side. Traditional dishes served on all menus, which start at 95F, then 140–230F. Specialities include duck *foie gras*, fillet of beef with truffle sauce, and assorted sorbets with fresh fruit.

ARGENT-SUR-SAULDRE   18410 (10KM N)

☎ |◉| LE RELAIS DU COR D'ARGENT

39 rue Nationale; it's set back from the D940, coming from Aubigny-sur-Nère.
☎ 02.48.73.63.49 ➡ 02.48.73.37.55
Closed Tues evening and Wed except July–Aug, and mid-Feb to mid-March. **TV.**

This is a country place with some style: hunting trophies on the walls, stuffed partridges and pheasants, a few copper pots dotted around, and country flowers on the tables. Delicious smells drift out of Laurent Lafon's kitchen, hinting at the gastronomic delights from the Berry to come. The game in season, duck *confit*, and *fricassée* of lobster in Noilly with leeks are all excellently prepared. Menus from 90F. This is a good place to spend the night; the seven tastefully decorated rooms combine the charm of highly polished old-fashioned furniture and the comfort of modern bedding. Doubles 220–250F.

VAILLY-SUR-SAULDRE   18260 (17KM E)

|◉| LE LIÈVRE GOURMAND

14 Grand-Rue; by the D923 in the direction of Sancerre.
☎ 02.48.73.80.23 ➡ 02.48.73.86.13
📧 le.lievre.gourmand@wanadoo.fr
Closed Sun evening, Mon and mid-Jan to mid-Feb.

Service noon–2pm and 7.30–9.30pm. This old Berry house belongs to William Page from Australia. His exceptional cooking makes inspired use of spices; *roulade* of semi-cooked *foie gras* and fig *compote*, boned quail stuffed with roast dates in Maghreb spices, caramelised pineapple kebab with poached dried fruits and *anise* ice cream. The menu changes with the seasons but the inventiveness is constant. Set menus at 100F, 140F, 160F and 220F. Mr Page has some Australian vintages in the cellar. Give it a whirl – it's one of a kind.

AZAY-LE-RIDEAU   37190

⅍ ☎ HÔTEL DE BIENCOURT**

7 rue Balzac (Centre); it's on the pedestrian street leading to the château.
☎ 02.47.45.20.75 ➡ 02.47.45.91.73
Closed 15 Nov–1 March.
Disabled access. TV. Car park.

This is a very beautiful 18th-century house in a typically Tours style. The sixteen comfortable rooms are variously furnished in Directoire or rustic style, and some overlook the flower-filled patio at the back. Charm and tranquility guaranteed. Good value, with doubles at 210F with hand basin/wc, 270F with shower/wc, and 330F with bathand TV. 10% discount in March, Oct and Nov.

⅍ |●| RESTAURANT L'AIGLE D'OR

10 av. Adélaïde-Richer; head for Langeais.
☎ 02.47.45.24.58 ➡ 02.47.45.90.18
Closed Sun evening and Wed, Tues evening out of season, Feb school holidays and the last fortnight in Nov.
Disabled access. Garden.

Service noon–2pm and 7.30–9pm. One of the best gastronomic restaurants in Touraine, with a welcoming and refined setting; even the beams in the dining room are a relaxing soft green. Attentive service. Meals served in the garden in summer. Weekday lunch menu 105F then 155–250F. The *à la carte* menu changes frequently but keeps a few classics: *langoustine* salad with *foie gras*; *blanquette* of zander, and *la griottine* with chocolate. The wine list is most instructive, with maps showing where the numerous wines come from. Free glass of Azay-le-Rideau sweet wine Nov–April.

VILLANDRY   37510 (12.5KM E)

⅍ |●| L'ÉTAPE GOURMANDE

Domaine de la Giraudière; take the D121 from Villandry in the direction of Druye; cross the Loire on the D57, then at Libinières take the D7 for Tourain.
☎ 02.47.50.08.60 ➡ 02.47.50.06.60
Closed 12 Nov–13 March reservations only.
Disabled access. Garden.

This is a splendid 17th-century farm which, despite the complicated-looking directions, is easy to find. The superb dining room has a huge fireplace and you can eat outside on the terrace. The chef gave up life as a diplomat to start the place, so you can expect a courteous welcome and punctillious service. They serve their own goat's cheese and there are plenty of local dishes, complicated salads, omelettes, quiches and lovely Loire wines. Set menus 71–112F or *à la carte*. On the first Saturday of the summer they give concerts with singers and story-tellers. You can buy goat's cheeses and fruits preserved in wine. They will show you the goats and take you round the dairy. A refreshing place. Free coffee.

BEAUGENCY   45190

♠ |●| HOSTELLERIE DE L'ÉCU DE BRETAGNE**

pl. du Martroi (Centre).
☎ 02.38.44.67.60 ➡ 02.38.44.68.07
e ecu-de-bretagne@wanadoo.fr
Closed Sun evening. **TV. Garden. Car park.**

Heraldic shields on the wall, and an atmosphere reminiscent of a Chabrol film, but no connection with Brittany. It gets its name from the Breton family who have owned the place since the 15th century. Ask for a room in the coaching inn rather than in the annexe across the way; they cost 200–285F with shower/wc or 295–490F with bath. The restaurant is pricey but the quality is good, and the house speciality is zander. Menus 98–220F and a children's menu at 55F.

♠ HÔTEL DE LA SOLOGNE**

6 pl. Saint-Firmin (Centre).
☎ 02.38.44.50.27 ➡ 02.38.44.90.19
Closed weekends in Jan and a fortnight from Christmas. **Garden. TV. Car park.**

The medieval rue de l'Evêché leads to this delightful little square dominated by an 11th-century keep. This is the historic heart of the town, and the hotel's handsome stone façade is festooned with geraniums. Quiet, well-equipped rooms. Doubles from 250F with shower/wc or 330F with bath. There's a pretty lounge with ceiling beams and fireplace, a balcony overlooking a flower-filled courtyard, and a conservatory where an enormous philodendron has pride of place. Quite charming. And you won't be able to fault the reception, either.

TAVERS   45190 (3KM SW)

⅍ ♠ |●| LA TONNELLERIE****

12 rue des Eaux Bleues.
☎ 02.38.44.68.15 ➡ 02.38.44.10.01
e tenelri@club-internet.fr
Closed Mon lunchtime, Sat, also Sun evening and Mon Oct–April, and Jan-Feb. **Swiming pool. TV. Car park.**

An austere building in the centre of the village where they used to make barrels – inside it's a different story. By general consent, this is the best place in Beaugency; very chic, with relaxing, comfortable decor. It's so quiet that you can hear the bird song and the chimes of the church bell, and you can stroll through the park that's full of chestnut trees. The cooking is luxurious and fragrant: *mesclun* of chicken, skate wings with pickled onions, *foie gras* soufflé and chocolate *moelleux*. The rooms are super-comfortable. The ones in the eaves are the nicest, and the best value. Doubles cost from 480F in low season, to 1240F for a luxury room in high season. 10% discount on the room rate.

BLANC (LE) 36300

🏃 🛏 |◉| DOMAINE DE L'ÉTAPE***

Route de Bélâbre; drive 5km along the D10 in the direction of Bélâbre.
☎ 02.54.37.18.02 ➡ 02.54.37.75.59
Disabled access. TV. Car park.

Service noon–2pm and 7.30–9.30pm. This magnificent 19th-century estate is a magical place. It's in 500 acres of grounds, with a lake, woods and fields, and the 35 rooms are decorated individually. There are rooms in the château itself, in the more modern lodge, or the rustic farm over by the stables. Doubles 240F with shower/wc or 230F with bath. You can hire a horse for an hour and ride over the whole estate, or fish for carp, zander and pike in the lake; they'll cook your catch for supper. Great place. There's a set menu at 130F or *à la carte*, listing dishes such as zander escalope with cider vinegar sauce, duck *foie gras* escalope with apples and balsamic vinegar, lobster salad with Provençal herbs and chocolate *marquise* with orange marmalade. Free house apéritif.

🛏 HÔTEL DU THÉÂTRE**

2 [bis] av. Gambetta (Centre); it's near the tourist office.
☎ 02.54.37.68.69 ➡ 02.54.28.03.95
TV.

This hotel is bang in the middle of town. The clean, small rooms, all with en-suite bathrooms, are soundproofed. The street is extremely busy in summer – it's an alternative route to Paris – so ask for a room that isn't over the street. Doubles 250F.

|◉| LE CENDRILLE

1 pl. de la Mairie (Centre).
☎ 02.54.28.64.94 ➡ 02.54.28.64.93
Closed Tues evening, Wed and 2 Jan–28 Feb.

This delightful restaurant, in the middle of a village in the Brenne, has been stylishly done up by Florence and Luke Jeanneau with the aid of a grant from the town hall. They have chosen strong yellows and blues to decorate the restaurant and created a warm atmosphere; they'll welcome you warmly, too. The cooking is simple, tasty and traditional; *mousseline* of zander, warm goat's cheese with honey, simmered oxtail or calfs' head. All their cheeses are local. Menus start at 58F, then 80–180F.

|◉| LE CYGNE

8 av. Gambetta (Centre).
☎ 02.54.28.71.63 ➡ 02.54.28.32.13

Closed Mon and Tues except July to 15 Aug, and a week in summer.

A fairly new restaurant with a reputation that's spread beyond the town. The decor is fresh – pinkish walls, blond floor and pale green chairs. The first-floor dining room is more rustic, with big beams and walls painted straw-yellow. The intimate salon is perfect for groups of four to nine. Cordial welcome from the owners, and the chef comes out of the kitchen to chat to his clients. Menus 95–260F; specialities include *cassolette* of snails Berry style and ox kidneys cooked whole and flambéed with Marc.

LINGÉ 36220 (16KM N)

🏃 🛏 |◉| AUBERGE DE LA GABRIÈRE**

La Gabrière; take the D6 at Lingé, follow the signs for La Gabrière; the inn is across from the lake.
☎ 02.54.37.80.97 ➡ 02.54.37.70.66
Restaurant closed Mon evening and Tues except July –Aug. **Disabled access. Garden. TV**.

The inn is beautifully situated on Lake Gabrière. The restaurant is crowded all year because the cuisine is good and you can enjoy the view of the lake while you eat; try the 98F menu with clam and oyster mushroom salad, roast shoulder of lamb spiked with green garlic, or fillet of perch with cream and chives – just the thing to set you up for a walk in the surrounding countryside. There are also menus from 65F, served on weekdays, to 150F. *À la carte* there's fillet of carp *paysanne*, pike with cream and chive sauce and *fricassée* of frogs' legs *provençale*. The inn has a number of rooms, some with a lake view. Doubles with shower/wc or bath 210F. Free coffee.

BLOIS 41000

🛏 HÔTEL SAINT-JACQUES

7 rue Ducoux (West); it's opposite the train station.
☎ 02.54.78.04.15 ➡ 02.54.78.33.05

Large, bright rooms, neither pretty nor ugly, that are particularly well maintained. Doubles range from 225F for a big room with shower/wc down to 140F for a simpler, smaller room with only a hand basin.

🏃 🛏 HÔTEL LE SAVOIE**

6 rue Ducoux (Northwest); it's in the street opposite the train station.
☎ 02.54.74.32.21 ➡ 02.54.74.29.58
Closed 24 Dec–3 Jan. **TV**.

This is a nice little hotel, reminiscent of a guest house, away from the hustle and bustle of the tourist area. Rooms are clean and bright; doubles start at 240F with shower/wc or 290F with bath. You'll get a very nice welcome. Best to book. 10% discount Oct–May.

🏊 🛉 |O| HÔTEL DE FRANCE ET DE GUISE**

3 rue Gallois (Centre); it's opposite the château.
☎ 02.54.78.00.53 ➡ 02.54.78.00.53
Closed Nov–March. **TV**.

Very, very *Vieille France*, from the welcome to the atmosphere – and particularly in the floral wall coverings and sofas in the hall and the dining room. The rooms are in the same style, but brighter and freshly decorated. Some are particularly attractive, with plaster mouldings and big fireplaces, and a few have a view of the castle. They are all wonderfully maintained. Double room with shower/wc 280F or 340F with bath. 10% discount April–May and Sept–Oct. They don't accept American Express or Diner's Club cards.

🛉 HÔTEL ANNE DE BRETAGNE**

31 av. Jean-Laigret; it's 300m from the château and the city centre, near the tourist office.
☎ 02.54.78.05.38 ➡ 02.54.74.37.79
Closed 9 Jan–6 Feb. **TV. Car park**.

A stylish hotel with a welcoming atmosphere and a quiet bar for people who want to talk. It has 29 slightly noisy but pleasant rooms for 315–360F with shower or bath and phone. They don't accept American Express or Diner's Club cards.

|O| RESTAURANT LA GARBURE

36 rue Saint-Lubin (Southwest); it's between the market and the steps leading up to the château.
☎ 02.54.74.32.89
Closed Wed (lunchtime only in season), and Sat and Thurs lunchtimes.

Service noon–2pm and 6.30–10.30pm. This restaurant in a Louis XV building has two dining rooms. The main one has exposed beams while the tiny second one in the cellar is used only for groups. They specialise in dishes from southwestern France: duck *confit* with Sarlad potatoes and truffles and, of course, the hearty traditional *garbure* soup, made with cabbage, swedes, turnips, Toulouse sausage, duck wing and drumsticks. Set menus 79F (weekdays) and 89F.

|O| RESTAURANT LES BANQUETTES ROUGES

16 rue des Trois-Marchands; it's between the château and St Nicholas' church.
☎ 02.54.78.74.92
Closed Sun and a week Christmas to New Year.

Service noon–2.30pm and 7–11pm. A friendly little restaurant that takes its name from its red bench seats. Even tourists who drop in to ask for a glass of water or to use the loos are met with a smile. The food is traditional and beautifully presented: pan-fried calf's liver with sour cherries is the house speciality. The dishes of the day on the cheapest set menu, 89F, change daily. You can also choose from *formules* which allow you to mix and match, menus 119–159F, or *à la carte*. Popular locally.

|O| LE BISTROT DU CUISINIER

20 quai Villebois-Mareuil; 500m along the left bank of the Loire.
☎ 02.54.78.06.70 ➡ 02.54.74.81.75
✉ bistrot.du.cuisinier@wanadoo.fr
Disabled access.

Service noon–3pm and 7–11pm. It's only 50m from the pont Gabriel, also known as the Vieux Pont, and there's a wonderful view of the city from here. Simple, unpretentious dining room with decent, good-value food. There's a *formule* at 98F and a set menu at 136F. The cuisine is really delicious and portions are big. Specialities include *marbré* of rabbit and f*oie gras* with sweet Vouvray, roast salmon with Chinon wine, and *nougatine* with honey and hazelnuts with chocolate sauce. Very interesting list of wines from the Loire. About once a month the chef cooks dishes from other French regions and further afield; Poland, Russia, Italy, Cajun country in the American South, Spain and Provence.

|O| L'EMBARCADÈRE

16 quai Ulysse Besnard (Southwest); it's on the N6, in the direction of Tours.
☎ 02.54.78.31.41
Closed Mon evening 15 Nov–15 Feb.

A splendid country-style drinking and eating haunt decorated as if it were a a boat tied up on the banks of the Loire, with views over the flats and sand dunes. Hail, rain or shine, this is the place for mussels, chips, river fish and seafood and a few tasty meat dishes such as rabbit *terrine* with *trompette* wild mushrooms. Prices are reasonably cheap, there's a fish dish of the day and you can expect to pay 110–120F for a whole meal. They also serve good local wine by the jug. Dance evenings on a Friday.

|●| AU BOUCHON LYONNAIS

25 rue des Violettes (Centre); head for pl. Louis XII.
☎ 02.54.74.12.87
Closed Sun and Mon except in summer and public holidays, and Jan.

Blois has everything, including this genuine traditional Lyon-style bistro. Specialities include calf's head, warm *saucisson*, salad *lyonnaise* with warm lentils, grilled salmon escalope and steak with Beaujolais sauce The prices are really very reasonable given the quality and quantity. Set menus 118–170F. The setting is a superb Louis XII house and there's a terrace for sunny days. Best to book or turn up early.

MOLINEUF 41190 (9KM W)

👬 |●| RESTAURANT DE LA POSTE

11 av. de Blois; take the D766 in the direction of Angers.
☎ 02.54.70.03.25 ➡ 02.54.70.12.46
e thierry@poidras.com
Closed Sun and Tues evening out of season, Wed, and the first fortnight in Nov.

Service noon–2pm and 7.30–9.30pm. This little restaurant on the outskirts of Molineuf is a place to stop and treat yourself to some of the delicious creations of chef Thierry Poidras. Try his duo of hot and cold *foie gras*, crayfish tail stew with morels, fillet steak with morel and cream sauce, or *fondant* of bitter chocolate and iced mousse with nuts. Menus start at 100F and you should expect to pay 280F if you eat *à la carte*. Attentive service. An extremely good restaurant. Free coffee.

CANDÉ-SUR-BEUVRON 41120 (15KM SW)

👬 🏠 |●| LA CAILLÈRE**

36 route des Montils (South); take the D173 along the south bank of the Loire.
☎ 02.54.44.03.08 ➡ 02.54.44.00.95
Closed Wed, Thurs lunchtime, Jan and Feb. **Disabled access**. **TV**. **Car park**.

A delightful hotel with a restaurant in a sympathetically converted 18th-century farmhouse. There are fourteen rooms; doubles with shower/wc 360–390F. Some have been designed for the disabled. The restaurant has a good reputation locally, so it's advisable to book. Weekday menu at 98F or 138–298F. Specialities vary with the season; you might find skate and *foie gras* salad,

pigeon *pot-au-feu* with pine nuts, pickled turnips with sautéed *foie gras*, roast peaches, and *brioche* and butter pudding. In summer, meals are served in the very pleasant garden. Half board, 408F per person, is compulsory June–Aug. Free bottle of wine on the second day of your stay.

CHITENAY 41120 (15KM S)

👬 🏠 |●| L'AUBERGE DU CENTRE**

pl. de l'Église (Centre); take the D956 as far as Cellettes and then the D38.
☎ 02.54.70.42.11 ➡ 02.54.70.35.03
Closed Sun evening, Mon out of season and Feb.
Disabled access. **Garden**. **TV**. **Car park**.

The classical frontage doesn't really give any clue that this hotel has a very handsome interior and a delightfully peaceful garden. The rooms are well equipped and decorated in very sophisticated style. Doubles 288–360F with shower/wc and 320–400F with bath. The restaurant is up to par. Set menus start at 115F (not Sat evening, Sun or public holidays), then 130F, 155F and 210F. Specialities from the Sologne include *ballotine* of rabbit with morels and *foie gras*, pike *brandade* with a shrimp *coulis*, game in season and *feuilleté* of roast pears with an *anise* ice cream. Friendly welcome. Free house apéritif.

CHAUMONT-SUR-LOIRE 41150 (18KM SW)

|●| RESTAURANT LA CHANCELIÈRE

1 rue de Bellevue; it faces the Loire very near the château, on the way out of the village.
☎ 02.54.20.96.95 ➡ 02.54.33.91.71
Closed Wed, Thurs, 16 Jan–5 Feb and three weeks from 10 Nov. **Disabled access**.

Service noon–2pm and 7–9pm. This is a cuisine to savour and its reputation continues to grow. There are two dining rooms: one in a restrained rustic style, the other prettier and more quaint. The cooking is fresh, and the flavours are delicate. The chef comes with a good pedigree, having trained in the kitchens of Barriers and the Troisgros brothers: quail *pâté* in *brioche*, zander with *beurre blanc*, and a house *terrine* of *foie gras*. The meat is tender and the desserts first-rate. Excellent value. The cheapest set menu is 85F and there are others from 125F. You'll be in for a feast. Nothing is too much trouble, and service comes with a smile.

BOURGES 18000

SEE MAP OVERLEAF

⅍ 🏠 HÔTEL LE CHRISTINA**

5 rue de la Halle. **MAP A2-14**
☎ 02.48.70.56.50 ➡ 02.48.70.58.13
e christina-hotel-bourges@wanadoo.fr
TV. Pay car park.

Well-located hotel, on the edge of the historic town, near the pedestrian area. Good facilities. All rooms have effective soundproofing, some have attractive rustic furniture and the toilet is separate from the bathroom. Doubles 249–330F. Nice welcome. 10% discount at the weekend Nov–March.

⅍ 🏠 HÔTEL DE L'AGRICULTURE**

18 bd. de Juranville and 15 rue du Prinal; it's opposite the île d'Or stadium. **MAP A2-3**
☎ 02.48.70.40.84 ➡ 02.48.65.50.58
Closed Christmas and New Year. **TV. Car park.**

You'll get a very warm welcome indeed from Madame Maigret, who likes to talk delightedly about how she realised her dream of having a farm in the Sologne. If you arrive by car, use the door opposite the car park on boulevard de Juranville. Rooms are quiet and pretty, and have been completely refurbished. Doubles 300F with shower/wc or bath. Some are air-conditioned and have exposed beams, but they're on the top floor. Studios are available for rent. 10% discount Nov–March.

⅍ 🏠 |O| INTER HÔTEL-LES TILLEULS**

7 pl. de la Pyrotechnie. Off map **C3-2**
☎ 02.48.20.49.04 ➡ 02.48.50.61.73
e Antoine.Falleur@wanadoo.fr
Closed 24 Dec–2 Jan.
Disabled access. Swimming pool. Garden. TV. Car park.

The hotel is on a little square just out of the centre but will suit very well if you're tired of desperate for peace and quiet. It has a beautiful garden and pretty rooms with bath. The rooms and bathrooms have been refurbished, and there's air-conditioning in 18 of them; doubles cost 345F with shower/wc or bath. The mini-bars are well stocked, but if you wind down best with physical exercise you can work out in the gym, swim in the pool or hire a mountain bike. Meals can be brought to your room on a tray. 10% discount on the room rate.

|O| LE COMPTOIR DE PARIS

1 rue Édouard-Vaillant. **MAP B2-15**
☎ 02.48.24.17.16

Car park.

Service 11.30–2pm and 6.30–10.30pm. It's painted bright red so it stands out from the wonderful medieval houses in the prettiest square in Bourges. Inside the decor is wood, so it's a bit more subdued. There's a friendly atmosphere and lots of animated conversation. This is where the lively and creative people in Bourges congregate. The speciality is *andouillette à l'ancienne*. There's a 75F *formule*, another menu at 98F and a dish for children at 28F. The downstairs dining room is cosier than the one upstairs.

⅍ |O| RESTAURANT LE JARDIN GOURMAND

15 [bis] av. Ernest-Renan; follow the signs for Nevers until you get to carrefour Malus; it's near the National Engineering school – the ENSIB. Off map **C3-20**
☎ 02.48.21.35.91
Closed Sun evening, Mon, and 2–28 Jan.
Disabled access. Garden. Car park.

Service noon–1.45pm and 7.30–9.30pm. This is a very pleasant restaurant, much appreciated by local gourmets who enjoy a good meal in delightful surroundings. Handsome bourgeois building with panelling and beams; the dining room is decorated with flowers and watercolours on the walls. Staff are pleasant, the service is unobtrusive and the cooking shows the same refinement as the decor. Specialities include fish *pot-au-feu*, braised veal, house duck *foie gras*, fillet of beef in Chinon sauce, and chocolate *fondant*. Set menus 95–235F. You can eat in the garden, weather permitting. A good restaurant in Bourges. Free coffee.

⅍ |O| RESTAURANT LA COURCILLIÈRE

rue de Babylone; head for av. Marx-Dormoy and look for a narrow street off to the right. Off map **C1-19**
☎ 02.48.24.41.91
Closed Tues evening, Wed, and the Feb school holidays.
Disabled access. Car park.

This is a magical, mysterious, marshy part of the region, watered by the river Yèvre slinking by. In this restaurant, the regional dishes are lovingly prepared by Denis Julien. Set menus at 98F and 135F with excellent house *terrines*, frogs' legs, *coq au vin* with calf's head and *couilles d'âne* – nothing scarier than eggs in wine sauce. They've renovated the place, and the handsome wooden furniture, small aviary and copious flowers make it very pleasing. Dine on the terrace overlooking the river Yèvre with waterlilies flowering at the water's edge. Everything's genuine here, from Annie's smile to the local accent of the gardeners, and you feel so relaxed that you lose all sense of time. Free house apéritif.

⚗️ |●| RESTAURANT PHILIPPE LARMAT

62 [bis] bd. Gambetta. **MAP A1-21**
☎ 02.48.70.79.00
Closed Sun evening, Mon and 16 Aug–2 Sept.

Gourmet heaven run by Philippe Larmat. As you are gently guided to your place, your feet sink into the deep piled carpet. There's lots of space around the tables and the colours are subtle and calming. Refined cooking produces well-balanced dishes; crispy zander with apples, pigeon *en crépine*, goat's cheese ravioli, lobster salad with fresh mint and red mullet in a sharp curry sauce. This is a well-known, stylish restaurant but it's not stiff and starchy. Menus 110–210F and children's menu 60F.

SAINT-JUST   18340 (6KM SW)

🛏️ |●| HÔTEL-RESTAURANT LE CHEVAL BLANC*

Take the N75.
☎ 02.48.25.62.18 ➡️ 02.48.25.63.41
Closed Mon evening, Tues and the first three weeks in Jan. **Garden. Car park**.

The neon lights that edge the roof can be seen from some distance, making this place look like a motorway stopover. In fact, you find excellent cooking and a proper welcome here. The hotel is comfortable and the rooms are well soundproofed; doubles with shower/wc 185F. The restaurant has a sort of "holiday club" feel: there's a huge buffet of *hors-d'œuvres*, cheeses and desserts and you help yourself to as much as you want. The self-service deal applies for the cheapest menu, at only 59F, and the others at 94F and 120F. The service comes with a smile and great care is taken over the smallest details.

ALLOGNY   18110 (18KM NW)

|●| RESTAURANT LE CHABUR

route de Mehun-sur-Yèvre; take the D944 in the direction of Neuvy-sur-Barangeon.
☎ 02.48.64.00.41 ➡️ 02.48.64.04.87
Closed Wed, 23 Dec–15 Jan and 1–15 Sept. **Garden. Car park**.

Service noon–10pm. The infamous witches of the Berry were supposed to gather in the forest. They must have left some good vibrations behind – this is a pretty good place. Marie-Jo and Gérard serve tasty snacks,

warm goat's cheese salads and cheese dishes including *fromage blanc* with herbs and cream. Generous portions of dishes like *coq au vin* at lunchtime. Set menus 54–110F or around 105F *à la carte*.

BOURGUEIL   37140

🛏️ LE THOUARSAIS

10 pl. Hublin.
☎ 02.47.97.72.05
Closed Sun evening from Oct to Easter and the first fortnight in Oct. **Garden**.

A simple, yet well-maintained hotel centrally located on a quiet square. The rooms in the annexe are the more comfortable and they look out over a garden. Doubles 155F with basin and 230–260F with shower or bath and wc. When the weather is warm, breakfast is served outside in the flower garden that's full of tweeting birds. Other than these, animals are not welcome. Prices go down if you stay for more than three nights.

⚗️ |●| RESTAURANT L'AUBERGE LA LANDE

On the D35, follow the signs for the *cave touristique*.
☎ 02.47.97.92.41 ➡️ 02.47.97.99.91
Closed Sun evening, Mon, and Jan. **Car park**.

The restaurant, in a very pleasant old bourgeois house, stands a little way outside the village. Good honest traditional cooking with no pretentions, using fresh, seasonal, regional produce. Menus 75–145F; dishes include a seafood *mousseline* with a crayfish *coulis*, trout fillet with a *julienne* of vegetables, and lamb shank with Guérande sea salt. Meals are served out on the terrace. Free coffee.

|●| AUBERGE DE TOUVOIS

route de Gizeux; on the Tours-Saumur-Anger road, turn right for Gizeux and you'll find the inn 5km from Bourgueil
☎ 02.47.97.88.81
Closed Sun evening, Mon, and Jan. **Car park**.

A genuine country inn right out in the country run by two dyed-in-the-wool professionals concerned to look after your every wish. When you sit down, they bring you a little plate of *amuse-bouches*, they give advice about the wine you might try and they don't pressurise you to have an apéritif or a bottle of mineral water if you don't want it. The precisely timed cooking is full of personal touches, with delicately judged flavours and subtle seasoning, and you really get the

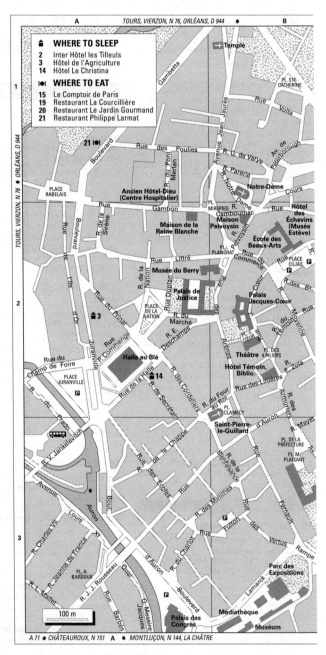

WHERE TO SLEEP
2 Inter Hôtel les Tilleuls
3 Hôtel de l'Agriculture
14 Hôtel Le Christina

WHERE TO EAT
15 Le Comptoir de Paris
19 Restaurant La Courcillière
20 Restaurant Le Jardin Gourmand
21 Restaurant Philippe Larmat

TOURS, VIERZON, N 76, ORLÉANS, D 944

A71 ✦ CHÂTEAUROUX, N 151   A   ✦ MONTLUÇON, N 144, LA CHÂTRE

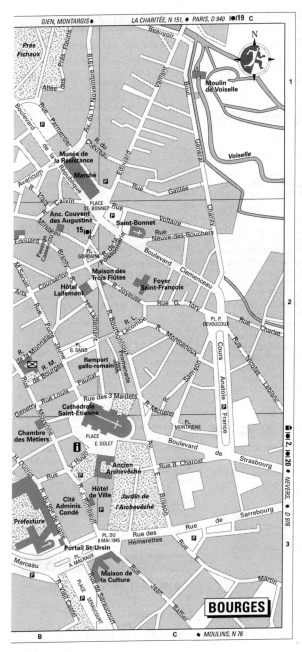

feeling that the chef tastes his dishes critically. These change with the seasons and the produce available in the market, with a few local specialities and some personal inventions. Excellent value for money, with menus starting at 85F. You can eat in the garden when the weather is fine. Best to book.

BREZOLLES   28270

🎿 🏠 I●I LE RELAIS DE BREZOLLES**

4 rue Berg-op Zoom; it's on the outskirts of town, in the direction of Chartres.
☎ 02.37.48.20.84 ➡ 02.37.48.28.46
Closed Fri and Sun evening, the first fortnight in Aug and three weeks in Jan. **TV**. **Garden**. **Car park**.

When you first catch sight of this large pink and brown inn, with its window boxes overflowing with flowers, you might wonder if you've taken a wrong turning somewhere and ended up in Bavaria. But it's really worth stopping here.The proprietors will make you feel welcome. The rooms are comfortable and some have been refurbished; they cost 250F with shower/wc or 300F with bath. The decor in the restaurant and the range of set menus at 75–200F are also an enticement. À la carte, you'll find interesting meat, fish and vegetables to satisfy any gourmet. The specialities change with the seasons – *émincé* of scallops and monkfish with berries, duck thigh with acacia honey, scallop kebab on a bed of vegetables, snails in a Chablis sauce, and warm stewed apples with butterscotch. 10% discount on the room rate 1 Feb–30 May and Oct–Jan.

MONTIGNY-SUR-AVRE   28270 (8KM NW)

🎿 🏠 I●I HÔTEL-RESTAURANT MOULIN DES PLANCHES**

How to get there; it's 10km from Brezolles on the D102.
☎ 02.37.48.25.97 ➡ 02.37.48.35.63
📧 moulin.des.planches@wanadoo.fr
Closed Sun evening, Mon, and Jan.
Disabled access. **TV**. **Car park**.

This is the mill of your dreams, on the banks of the River Avre, surrounded by woods and fields. The old flour mill has been turned into a very handsome inn by an ex-farming couple. There's a friendly simplicity in the welcome, and the light has a special quality. Delightful, comfortable rooms 300–390F. Set menus start at 120F with *terrine* and *fricassée* of chicken in cider, and with others 160–280F. The chef specialises in *foie gras* and veal sweetbreads. Free apéritif.

BRIARE   45250

🎿 I●I RESTAURANT LE BORD'EAU

27 rue de la Liberté; it's on the main street.
☎ 02.38.31.22.29
Closed Wed and Sun Dec–March.

This is a region of rivers and canals, though this isn't a waterside restaurant. The *patronne* treats her guests like family. The chef puts lots of fish on the menu – braised salmon, sea bass with shallots, perch fillets *persillade* and bream in a Sancerre sauce. The food is good and simple, and portions are generous. Set menus cost 95F, 145F, 160F and 195F. The small, pleasant dining room is decorated in pastel shades. Best to book. Free coffee.

BONNY-SUR-LOIRE   45420 (10KM SE)

🏠 I●I LES VOYAGEURS

10 Grande-Rue (Centre).
☎ 02.38.27.01.45 ➡ 02.38.27.01.46
Hotel closed Sun evening, three weeks in the Feb school holidays and a fortnight in Sept. **Restaurant closed** Sun evening, Mon and Tues lunchtime.**TV**. **Car park**.

Given the prices – menus are listed at 85F, 135F, 175F and 220F – you might not realise that this is one of the best gourmet restaurants in the area. Philippe Lechauve is a local, but he was the chief sauce-maker for the Troisgros brothers for years. The prices are really unbelievable, given his pedigree. The cheapest menu lists *émincé* of calf's tongue, fillet of pollack with a *fondue* of chicory, and sour cherry *charlotte*. He manages to provide such interesting dishes by simplifying the ingredients and relying on his talent to produce something wonderful. Take the second menu: *terrine* of monkfish cheeks, *croustillant* of cod joint with spices and celery *purée*, cheeses, and *chocolat fondant* – the chocolate trickles into the pistachio sauce as you cut the cake. There are also some decent wines on the list. Double rooms with shower/wc 205–220F.

CHAMBORD   41250

🎿 🏠 I●I HÔTEL DU GRAND SAINT-MICHEL

Château de Chambord.
☎ 02.54.20.31.31 ➡ 02.54.20.36.40
Closed 15 Nov–20 Dec. **TV**. **Car park**.

This hotel is in an exceptional location opposite the château. Spacious, comfortable and pleasant rooms, even without the view. Doubles 300–450F. The dining room is traditionally decorated to provide an appropriate setting for the bourgeois cuisine, including salmon, zander and good game in season. Menus 105F and 140F. Considerate, attentive service and a friendly welcome, not at all the mechanical toil you might expect in such a touristy place. In summer you can eat on the terrace with the château right in front of you. Book well in advance. 10% discount on the room rate Oct–March.

SAINT-DYÉ   41500 (5KM N)

🍴 🏠 |O| LE MANOIR DE BEL-AIR

1 route d'Orléans.
☎ 02.54.81.60.10 ➡ 02.54.81.65.34
TV. Car park.

This old building, smothered in ivy, is on the banks of the Loire. It has a delightfully provincial feel and there's a smell of good wax polish. Rooms are honestly priced given the facilities and cleanliness; doubles go for 320–380F. The ones with a view of the river are the best. The dining room, which also has the view, is bright and spacious. Specialities include salmon steak in Chinon sauce, *andouillette* braised in Sauvignon, scorpion fish *mousseline*, game and quail *à la Solognote*. Set menus start at 128F. There's a track along the riverbank for a post-prandial walk. 10% discount on the room rate Oct–April.

|O| LE JARDIN DE LA FORGE

pl. de l'Église.
☎ 02.54.81.60.19
Closed Wed, and 1 Sept–18 May.

The chef has revolutionised this ex-pizzeria to create a quality restaurant in a pretty house that's worth the detour. It has a stylish, attractively decorated dining room and a small, cool, shady courtyard looking onto the church. The dishes are inventive and appetising; upside-down vegetable tart or pastry cases with potato and snails, a fan of *boudin blanc* with cep *jus*, and bread and butter pudding with salted butter. *Formules* at 70F and 95F. They serve wines from the Loire, some by the jug, and still do good pizza, in a proper oven.

MONT-PRÈS-CHAMBORD   41250 (10KM SW)

🍴 🏠 |O| HÔTEL-RESTAURANT LE SAINT FLORENT**

Le bourg; take the D33 to Huisseau then the D72.
☎ 02.54.70.81.00 ➡ 02.54.70.78.53
Closed Mon and 8 Jan–8 Feb.
Disabled access. Garden. TV.

A neat hotel in the heart of the Châteaux of the Loire just 8km from Cheverny. Bright, jolly rooms at good prices: 195–325F with shower/wc or 295–365F with bath. They have a sauna. Weekday lunch menu at 85F and others up to 218F. Their specialities are worth trying; pig's trotters *Solognote* (stuffed with *foie gras*), eel casserole with vegetables, or pan-fried *foie gras* with honey vinegar. They make you feel pleased you came. 10% discount on the room rate Nov–March.

CHARTRES   28000

🍴 🏠 |O| HÔTEL-RESTAURANT DE LA POSTE**

3 rue du Général-Kœnig (Centre); it's between the post office and the *Hôtel Grand Monarque*.
☎ 02.37.21.04.27 ➡ 02.37.36.42.17
e hotelposte.chartres@wanadoo.fr
Restaurant closed Fri and Sun evenings.
Disabled access. TV. Pay garage.

A practical place to stay, given its excellent location. It's not exactly a bundle of laughs, but you can sleep well. Clean, comfortable rooms 325F with shower/wc, 360F with bath. Some have a lovely view of the cathedral. Menus 89–170F in the restaurant; dishes include duck with honey and lemon, beef steak *à la Chartres*, and zander fillet with pepper *sabayon*. The breakfast is extra good. There's a charge for the garage. Free apéritif and breakfast (Nov–Feb).

|O| BRASSERIE BRUNEAU

4 rue du Maréchal-de-Lattre-de-Tassigny; it's 30m from the town hall.
☎ 02.37.21.80.99
Closed Sat lunchtime and Sun.

There's a 1940s atmosphere in this brasserie and a French version of British style. There is a zinc bar, bistro tables, benches covered in red velvet and posters advertising operettas on the walls. Traditional food cooked using exclusively fresh produce, speedy yet relaxed service and a forthcoming, youthful welcome. Prices start with the 70F *formule*.

|O| AU P'TIT MORARD

25 rue de la Porte-Morard.
☎ 02.37.34.15.89
Closed Sun evening, Wed, a fortnight in Feb and three weeks in Aug.

No middle-class girl from a good family would have ventured to the lower end of town a quarter of a century ago, but it's become the liveliest, friendliest, greenest, loveliest part of Chartres. It's full of attractive cafés, and everyone loves the old doorways and mill buildings. You'll be as happy inside the *P'tit Morard* as out on the terrace where you'll pick up a buzz from the cheerful crowds in the street. Set lunch menu 80F during the week, others at 99F and 145F. Advisable to book.

🏠◉ LE DIX DE PYTHAGORE

2 rue de la Porte-Cendreuse; it's about 200m from the back of the cathedral.
☎ 02.37.36.02.38
Closed Mon, Tues and 15–31 July.

Good old-fashioned classics – steak with truffles, ox kidneys, salmon *à la Dugléré*, snails flambéed with Sauvignon – are served up in the basement dining room under the watchful eye of the *patronne*. Good service and affordable prices make this place popular. Menus 80F, 82F and 145F or around 200F *à la carte*. Free apéritif.

◉ RESTAURANT LE SAINT-HILAIRE

11 rue du Pont-Saint-Hilaire; it's between pl. Saint-Pierre and pont Saint-Hilaire.
☎ and ➡ 02.37.30.97.57
Closed Sat and Mon lunchtimes, Sun, three weeks mid-July/Aug, and Christmas and New Year holidays.

Service noon–2pm and 7–9.30pm. You can't possibly go to Chartres without eating in this delightful small restaurant – there are only ten tables. Everything's of a piece: the welcome, the service, the cooking and the decor. Benoît Pasquier's family have been in the Beauce for five generations and he makes a point of showing off local produce to its best advantage. The dishes change with the seasons, though favourites such as *petit-gris* snails with a *fondue* of tomato and veal sweetbreads cooked in a haybox are available all year. Set menus 95F, 145F and 190F. Good selection of wines at reasonable prices.

◉ LE MOULIN DE PONCEAU

21–23 rue de la Tannerie; it's below the collegiate church of Saint-André.
☎ 02.37.35.30.05
Closed Sat lunchtime and Sun evening.

Arguably the most attractive table in Chartres. It's in a romantic, charming situation on an arm of the river, just behind the cathedral. There's a terrace at the waterside and another made from an old wash-house, once numerous in these parts. Attentively and laboriously produced dishes that are a bit pricey but the setting adds considerably to the pleasure. Menus 128–250F.

MAINTENON   28130 (18KM NE)

◉ LE BISTROT D'ADELINE

3 rue Collin-d'Harleville; it's in the main street, 100m from the chateau.
☎ 02.37.23.06.67
Closed Sun and Mon.

The rustic style of this little restaurant is evident from the old, iron cooking pot in the entrance. It's one of the best in Maintenon both for its welcome and the family dishes the boss prepares. He's particularly reputed for his calf's head and makes sauces that will never go out of fashion. Essential to book, especially since menus start at 69F.

CHÂTEAUDUN   28200

🛏◉ LE SAINT-LOUIS**

41 rue de la République (East).
☎ 02.37.45.00.01 ➡ 02.37.45.16.09
TV. **Garden**. **Car park**.

Ben Maamar has pulled off quite a double in a very few years, first by turning a ruin into a decent, comfortable hotel and then by adding a restaurant and a brasserie next door. Menus in the traditional restaurant 100F, grills 60–100F and pizzas 35–65F. For an encore, he opened up a brasserie next door which is *the* place to eat in Châteaudun, especially in summer when the piano bar gets going outdoors. It's the loveliest terrace in town. Mussels, salads, grills – dishes to satisfy all tastes from 60–110F. A real success. And the rooms are fairly priced, at 260F for doubles with shower/wc or bath.

◉ LA LICORNE**

6 pl. du 18-Octobre (Centre); it's in the main square.
☎ 02.37.45.32.32
Closed Tues evening, Wed, 20 Dec–15 Jan and a week in June.

The dining room is long and narrow and decorated in salmon pink. Solid bourgeois cooking in big portions; dishes include pan-fried skirt of beef with shallots, chicken in mushroom sauce, oysters and leeks *au gratin*, breast of duck with orange and honey, and if you're famished, a *millefeuille* of *crêpes*. They've only got two people to wait tables so when things get busy they can get pushed.

Nice terrace on sunny days. Set menus 70F on weekdays and then 88–180F.

I●I AUX TROIS PASTOUREAUX**

31 rue André-Gillet (South); it's between pl. du 18-Octobre and espace Malraux.
☎ 02.37.45.74.40
Closed Mon, Thurs evening, the first fortnight in Aug and Christmas–New Year holidays.

This is the oldest inn in Châteaudun and there's a calm atmosphere amid the simply set tables in the green dining room. There's a wide variety of à la carte dishes to choose from, including some unusual ones – petit-gris snails with oyster mushrooms and Szechuan peppercorns, roast pigeon stuffed with wheat and lemon juice, veal kidneys in Chenonceau sauce, and so on – this is sophisticated cooking. 90F weekday lunch menu, then others 119–330F.

CHÂTEAUMEILLANT   18370

♠ I●I HÔTEL-RESTAURANT LE PIET À TERRE**

21 rue du Château; it's next to the Gendarmerie.
☎ 02.48.61.41.74 ➡ 02.48.61.41.88
Closed Sun evening, Mon, Tues lunchtime, and Jan–Feb. **TV**. **Car park**.

A two-star hotel with a three-star restaurant – service noon–1.30pm and 7.30–9pm. Lovely beams and pastel shades in the dining room. Thierry Finet is passionate about cooking and he makes the bread and breakfast rolls on the premises. The cheapest menu, 98F, is designed around the fresh produce from the market and reflects the mood of the chef; it includes a main course, and a selection of cheese or the dessert of the day. There's a menu tradition, specialising in local dishes. Menus 240–390F and children's menu 60F. The vegetables and herbs come from grandfather Piet's kitchen garden. The bedrooms are named after flowers. Doubles 260–280F with shower/wc or 310–390F with bath.

CHÂTEAUNEUF-EN-THYMERAIS   28170

♠ I●I L'ÉCRITOIRE

43 rue Emile Vivier.
☎ 02.37.51.85.80 ➡ 02.37.51.86.87
Closed Sun evening, Mon, and school holidays in Oct and Feb.

This is an old post house and the restaurant is one of the best places to eat in the Eure et Loire. Chef Luc Pasquier travelled all over, to

Asia, Africa and elsewhere, before returning home. His cuisine is excellent in the classical style, which means he uses a lot of local produce: petit-gris snails, rabbit from Thimerais, and honey from the Beauce. Impressive menus and the reasonable prices start at 150F. Expect to pay 240F for a meal à la carte, where you'll find some appetising specialities like salmon tartare with yoghurt, and fillet of roast lamb with a croustille of small snails. If you feel like lingering, there are a few clean simple rooms with balconies, 285F, looking into the interior courtyard. Attentive welcome and perfect service.

SENONCHES   28250 (13KM SW)

♠ I●I AUBERGE LA POMME DE PIN**

15 rue Michel Cauty; take the D928 to Digny then the D24.
☎ 02.37.37.76.62 ➡ 02.37.37.86.61
Closed Sun evening, Mon lunchtime, the last ten days in Oct and first three weeks in Jan. **Garden**. **TV**. **Car park**.

A half-timbered inn that used to be a post house on the edge of the Perche area. Ten comfortable rooms from 300F with shower/wc. They serve good quality, wholesome food with an emphasis on local specialities like Percheronne salad or sweetbreads with girolles, game and wild mushrooms in season. Menus start at 88F, then 105–240F.

CHÂTEAUNEUF-SUR-LOIRE   45110

🎋 ♠ I●I LA CAPITAINERIE**

1 Grande-Rue-du-Port (Centre).
☎ 02.38.5842.161 ➡ 02.38.58.46.81
Closed Mon lunchtime.

An impressive white house that stands proudly in the centre of town. Chic, sober decor and clean, comfortable rooms – even if some are singularly lacking in charm. Doubles 280F with shower, 353F with bath. Breakfast 38F. There are some family rooms at good prices. The restaurant has three stars which explains the prices: menus 125–260F. The terrace looking onto the château grounds is very pleasant. Free coffee.

COMBREUX   45530 (13KM N)

🎋 ♠ I●I L'AUBERGE DE COMBREUX**

35 route du Gâtinais; take the D10 then the D9; it's on the outskirts of the village.
☎ 02.38.46.89.89 ➡ 02.38.59.36.19
Closed Mon, Tues and 15 Dec–20 Jan.
Swimming pool. **TV**. **Car park**.

This magnificent 19th-century coaching inn, swathed in ivy and Virginia creeper, has been thoughtfully refurbished. There's a cosy little sitting room with an open fire and a rustic dining room with a veranda overlooking the flower garden. In fine weather you can sit under the trees. Weekday menu 110F and others up to 210F. Well-prepared dishes include house *terrines*, escalope of *foie gras*, veal kidneys with raspberry vinegar, game in season and warm fruit tarts. The bedrooms are in the main building or in one of the little annexes hidden among the trees. They're delightful, with flower-sprigged wallpaper, beams and large wardrobes. Prices from 325F with shower/wc to 395F with bath. Half board, compulsory at weekends and May–Oct, costs 400F per person. You can hire a bike to explore the Orléans forest nearby and there's a tennis court and a heated swimming pool. One of the best hotels around. 10% discount on the room rate.

CHÂTEAUROUX   36000

☎ HÔTEL LE BOISCHAUT**

135 av. de la Châtre (Southeast).
☎ 02.54.22.22.34 ➡ 02.54.22.64.89
Closed 27 Dec–7 Jan.
Disabled access. TV. Garage.

Boischaut is the area around Châteauroux – it's where Gérard Depardieu comes from. The hotel has large, comfortable double rooms at 198–250F with shower/wc and 230–250F with bath. There are also some family rooms sleeping three or four. There's no restaurant, but they do have a bar, and you can have a meal on a tray for 56F with a hot main dish, cheese and dessert. Since it's a twenty-minute walk to the centre of town this is a good option. Free lock-up parking for two-wheelers.

⚒ ☎ HÔTEL BONNET**

14 rue du Marché; it's not far from the town hall.
☎ 02.54.22.13.54 ➡ 02.54.07.56.78
✉ HOTEL-BONNET@wanadoo.fr
Closed Sun afternoons.
Disabled access. TV. Pay garage.

The rooms are clean, comfortable and well looked after, and the extremely nice managers do a wonderful breakfast. Doubles 200F with basin/wc and 220F with shower/wc. There's a lock-up garage for a small charge. From the beginning of Nov until Easter their *formule Lune* deal will save you 20–50F a room. 10% discount after the second night.

⚒ ☎ ÉLYSÉE HÔTEL***

2 rue de la République (Centre); it's practically opposite the Équinoxe cultural centre.
☎ 02.54.22.33.66 ➡ 02.54.07.34.34
✉ elysee36@aol.com
Closed 24 Dec–2 Jan. **TV. Disabled access**.

An excellent little hotel right in the centre of town, with spotlessly clean, pleasant rooms. Doubles 270–330F. The new owners have opened a salon-bar where they serve a good breakfast, and though there's no restaurant they offer a meal on a tray for 45F. 10% discount at weekends and 1 July–15 Aug.

⚒ |●| RESTAURANT LA CIBOULETTE

42 rue Grande (Centre).
☎ 02.54.27.66.28
Closed Sun, Mon, public holidays, 31 Dec–11 Jan and 22 July–23 Aug.

Service noon–2pm and 7.30–10pm. This is probably the best restaurant in Châteauroux and everybody eats here. It has a pleasant decor and friendly service, and the menus have been thoughtfully put together. There's a weekday menu at 98F and others 113–208F and they often include local specialities like *couilles d'âne* (eggs poached in red wine and shallot sauce) and sautéed chicken with prunes and cinnamon. About a dozen wines available by the glass, and a few organic wines. 10% discount on the price of a meal.

|●| LE BISTRO GOURMAND

10 rue du Marché (Centre).
☎ 02.54.07.86.98
Closed Sun, Mon lunchtime, a fortnight in Feb and three weeks in Aug.

The dining room is bright yellow and soft green and really cheerful. A huge blackboard displays the fresh dishes of the day because they only use fresh produce here; *foie gras* of duck with sea salt, rib of beef for two, duck thigh *confit* on a bed of oyster mushrooms, *tarte tatin* or pear soup with preserved orange. You'll pay around 130F *à la carte*.

DÉOLS   36130 (2KM N)

|●| L'ESCALE VILLAGE

How to get there; it's on the N20.
☎ 02.54.22.03.77 ➡ 02.54.22.56.70

This restaurant attracts people of all ages from the entire region – whole families crowd in. Good traditional dishes include seafood platter, sole *meunière*, beef with shallots and *moules marinière*. Menus start at 64.50F, then 86.50–148.50F. They serve excellent draught beer, white Reuilly and Valençay. Long-distance lorry drivers prefer the brasserie where they can watch TV while they eat. It's open round the clock – you never know who you'll bump into having a drink after midnight. It could be an artist passing through or a sports celebrity – the owner's a cycling fan. A lively, vibrant place.

|●| LE BOURG DIEU

39 rue du Pont-Perin (Centre).
☎ 02.54.27.36.61
Closed Wed evening, Sat lunchtime and Sun.

The restaurant has a very narrow frontage onto a street that runs down to the River Indre. Fine cuisine is served in the rustic, soberly decorated dining room, and there's a terrace leading onto a garden. The menus, 100–158F, change weekly, but Berry tarte, *papillotte* of trout fillet with *beurre blanc*, cheese, and *aumônière* of fresh fruit with orange butter would be typical of the 100F menu. Good value.

COINGS   36130 (8KM N)

☎ |●| LE RELAIS SAINT-JACQUES***

How to get there: take exit 12 off the A20, going in the direction of the airport, then Coings. Turn left before Céré.
☎ 02.54.60.44.44 ☛ 02.54.60.44.00
Restaurant closed Sun evening. **TV**. **Garden**. **Car park**.

Don't let the dreary setting, near the airport, put you off because this modern hotel is pleasant, comfortable and quiet. Each of the 46 rooms is decorated differently and looks onto the garden or over the countryside at the rear. Doubles start at 320F. But the establishment is best known for the gastronomic cuisine of the chef/proprietor, Pierre Jeanrot. The dishes change frequently and the lunchtime menu at 100F is the cheapest. In good weather, there's a more affordable brasserie service with carpaccio, tuna *tartare* and various salads served on the terrace.

LEVROUX   36110 (21KM NW)

⅔ ☎ |●| HÔTEL-RESTAURANT DE LA CLOCHE**

3 rue Nationale; get there by the D956.
☎ 02.54.35.70.43 ☛ 02.54.35.67.43
Closed Sun evening, Mon evening, Tues and 1–27 Feb.
TV. **Car park**.

The same family has run this friendly village inn since 1895, and it has kept its friendly atmosphere. You'll get a really warm welcome, and they've maintained their traditional approach to cooking. They make their own duck terrine with prunes there's a good mixture of fish cooked with tarragon. Set menus 78–240F. Rooms with hand basin 178F, with shower/wc or bath 260F. Free coffee.

⅔ |●| RESTAURANT RELAIS SAINT-JEAN

34 rue Nationale; it's near pl. de la Collégiale-de-Saint-Sylvain.
☎ 02.54.35.81.56 ☛ 02.54.35.36.09
e acceuil.relais.saint.jean@wanadoo.fr
Closed Wed, Sun evening except public holidays, the last week in Feb.

Service noon–2pm and 7.30–10pm. The chef who owns this old coaching inn studied with Vergé, and has made this one of the best restaurants in the Indre département. His skilful use of first-rate ingredients, and the charming welcome you get from his wife, make a winning combination. The dining room is pleasant and from some tables you can see the chef in his spotless kitchen. In summer, you can admire the dramatic sunsets over the Saint-Sylvain collegiate church from the terrace. There's a menu at 90F, not served on Sun or public holidays, others 128–225F, and an impressive children's menu at 65F, which includes a drink. Specialities include scallop ravioli with a cep sauce, fillet of beef with *foie gras*, and *marbré* with two chocolates. The cooking is judged to perfection and sings with flavour. Free coffee.

BUZANÇAIS   36500 (25KM NW)

⅔ ☎ |●| HÔTEL-RESTAURANT L'HERMITAGE**

Route d'Argy–Écueille; take the N143 then follow the signs for Argy.
☎ 02.54.84.03.90 ☛ 02.54.02.13.19
Hotel closed first fortnight of Jan and 9–18 Sept.
Restaurant closed Sun evening and Mon.
Garden. **TV**. **Car park**. **Pay garage**.

Service noon–1.30pm and 7.30–11pm. As tranquil as a hermitage. The hotel is covered in Virginia creeper and overlooks a broad expanse of greenery on the banks of the Indre. There's a big kitchen garden and a really nice terrace. Bedrooms in the main building have been carefully decorated and have a view of the grounds. The ones in the annexe are slightly less attractive, but they too have been redecorated and overlook the courtyard. Comfortable doubles 305–370F. Set menus at 98F (not Sun) and others up to 245F. The cooking is fairly sophisticated, featuring specialities from Berry and the Landes and lots of fish. 10% discount if you stay half board 15 Oct–30 April.

CHÂTILLON-SUR-INDRE   36700

🏃 🏠 |●| L'AUBERGE DE LA TOUR**

2 route du Blanc.
☎ 02.54.38.72.17 ➡ 02.54.38.74.85
TV. Garden. Car park.

A lovely 17th-century house that's been well renovated. There are flowers everywhere. In summer, people eat on the terrace rather than in the rustic dining room, which has a fireplace and exposed beams. The chef's specialities include fillet of beef in Chinon wine sauce, zander with sorrel, gratinéed fish flavoured with curry and veal escalope *forestière*. Set menus 60–220F and a children's menu at 50F. Rooms have been decorated in up-to-date style and have bathrooms; 170F with shower to 260F with bath. Free coffee.

MÉZIÈRES-EN-BRENNE   36290 (20KM S)

🏠 |●| HÔTEL-RESTAURANT AU BŒUF COURONNÉ**

9 pl. Charles-de-Gaulle; it's on the D43.
☎ 02.54.38.04.39 ➡ 02.54.38.02.84
Closed Sun evening and Mon except public holidays, 20 Nov–31 Jan. **TV.**

The Brenne is a mysterious region, full of lakes and marshlands. The gateway that leads you into this former coaching inn dates from the middle of the 16th century. In the restaurant, try the carp with shellfish butter, carp *rillettes* with onion marmalade, frogs' legs, fried smelt, pigeon breasts, game in season and iced nougat with Brenne honey. The dining room is a little old-fashioned and lacking in warmth. Set menus from 80F (not available Sun) to 250F. Children's menu – for under eights – 42F. Doubles with shower/wc 245F. It's best to book at the weekend.

CHÂTRE (LA)   36400

🏃 🏠 HÔTEL NOTRE-DAME**

4 pl. Notre-Dame (South).
☎ 02.54.48.01.14 ➡ 02.54.48.31.14
Disabled access. Garden. TV. Car park.

La Châtre is a very pleasant town to live in, and this hotel is in a 15th-century building with a flower-filled balcony. They've painted the spacious bedrooms cream – some are particularly big and well laid-out. It overlooks a quiet little square that rings with birdsong. Doubles 235F with shower, 250F with shower/wc, 270F with bath. It has a terrace and a private garden. Hotels like this are rare. 10% discount Jan–May.

NOHANT-VIC   36400 (6KM NW)

🏠 |●| L'AUBERGE DE LA PETITE FADETTE**

pl. du Château; it's on the D943.
☎ 02.54.31.01.48 ➡ 02.54.31.10.19
TV. Garden. Car park.

This beautiful building covered in Virginia creeper has been owned by the same family for three generations. The novelist George Sand spent the greater part of her life in Nohant, and her visitors included the poet Théophile Gautier, novelists Flaubert and Balzac, and artist Delacroix. The 19th-century wood panelling has a brilliant shine and is hung with Aubusson tapestry. The bedrooms are very prettily decorated in shades of green. Doubles with shower/wc from 320F and with bath 460F. The dining room walls are lined with hunting trophies and tapestries. Menus 85–240F.

SAINT-CHARTIER   36400 (8.5KM N)

🏃 🏠 |●| HÔTEL-RESTAURANT LA VALLÉE BLEUE***

Route de Verneuil.
☎ 02.54.31.01.91 ➡ 02.54.34.04.48
Hotel closed Tues lunchtime March to end April, and Oct. **Restaurant closed** Mon and Tues lunchtimes and Oct.
Swimming pool. Garden. TV. Car park.

This house, once owned by George Sand's doctor, has been wonderfully converted, retaining many original features. Everything is in keeping – the dining rooms, the lounge and the bedrooms. You'll have a pleasurable stay here and the restaurant is pretty good too. Set menus 100–295F, so there's a lot of choice. *À la carte* lists a dish for vegetarians and the specialities change regularly; try the medallions of crayfish that called "George Sand", poached eggs with creamed lentils, smoked duck breast, *civet* with fresh noodles, chocolate *fondant* with sour cherries in Kirsch, and honey ice cream. Children's menu 75F. There are two terraces and a swimming pool in the nine acres of grounds. Very comfortable rooms 395–645F with shower/wc or 595–845F with bath. Free apéritif.

LYS-SAINT-GEORGES 36230 (23KM NW)

⚒ |●| LA FORGE

How to get there: take the D927 in the direction of Neuvy-Saint-Sépulcre and then the D74. It's opposite the château.
☎ 02.54.30.81.68
Closed Mon, Tues Sept–June, three weeks in Jan and a fortnight in Oct.

Service noon–2pm and 7.30–9.30pm. This rather good inn is the only commercial enterprise in a village of 180 souls. It has handsome beams, pictures by local artists, an open fire in winter and a terrace with a pergola in summer where you can enjoy the peace and quiet and the birdsong. The *patronne* is friendly and very witty, and her husband, the chef, prepares tasty classic dishes with clearly marked flavours. These change regularly with the seasons, though there are a few constants like grilled goat's cheese salad, duck *foie gras*, and braised duckling in honey. The cheapest menu at 98F, served on weekdays, is substantial, and there are others 185–240F. Children's menu 48F. Free apéritif.

CHAUMONT-SUR-THARONNE 41600

|●| RESTAURANT LA GRENOUILLÈRE

Route de La Ferté-Saint-Aubin; take the Chaumont exit, follow the signs for La Ferté-Saint-Aubin.
☎ 02.54.88.50.71
Closed Mon evening and Tues except in July–Aug.
Garden. Car park.

Service noon–2pm and 7.30–9.30pm. An old house deep in the forest that's been converted into a luxurious country inn. It's surrounded by a wildlife park where peacocks and Japanese golden pheasants shimmer in the sunlight. Meals are served in a glassed-in terrace from where you can see the lake, which is full of golden carp, moorhens, swans and forty different species of wild duck. There is a set weekday menu at 100F and others 158–210F. You get a choice: *terrine* of duck *foie gras*, boned quail stuffed with *foie gras* and truffle *jus*, veal fillet with Roquefort cheese, and *pot-au-feu* terrine with creamed chives. Your post-prandial stroll in the garden will take you past the aviaries and their exotic occupants.

CHENONCEAUX 37150

⚒ |●| RESTAURANT AU GÂTEAU BRETON

16 rue du Docteur-Bretonneau (Centre); it's in the main street.
☎ 02.47.23.90.14 📠 02.47.23.92.57
Closed Tues and Wed evenings in season, Tues evening and Wed out of season, and Christmas–New Year's Day.

A large terrace for the summer and a small dining room for the winter. The name and frontage of the restaurant make you think it could have been a baker's. Menus 66F, 76F, 89F (including $1/4$ litre of wine) and for 116F, you get a cold starter, a hot starter and a main course from their specialities: chicken *à la tourangelle* with green beans and haricot beans, *andouillette* with Vouvray wine, rabbit *chasseur* or *coq au vin*, all of which are delicious and served generously. Nice welcome. Free house apéritif or coffee.

CIVRAY-DE-TOURAINE 37150 (1KM W)

🏠 |●| L'HOSTELLERIE DU CHÂTEAU DE L'ISLE**

☎ 02.47.23.63.60 📠 02.47.23.64.62
📧 chateaudelisle@wanadoo.fr
Restaurant closed Sun evening and Mon lunchtime (unless you're a guest) and 15 Nov–26 Dec. **Car park**.

Service noon–2pm and 7.30–9pm. The staff go to a lot of trouble to make you feel welcome in this beautiful 18th-century house. It has ten comfortable rooms with shower/wc or bath ranging in price from 330F to 600F. All the rooms are different so you can ask to see them and choose the one that suits. The chef prepares first-rate dishes with the freshest produce from the market and prices reflect the quality, starting with a *menu-carte* at 170F. There are two dining rooms, both with an open fireplace. You can eat on the terrace and then go for a stroll in the grounds that are planted with huge trees, or you can go on a boat trip on the Cher.

CHINON 37500

⚒ 🏠 LE POINT DU JOUR

102 Quai Jeanne d'Arc; you get there via the Quai de la Vienne.
☎ 02.47.93.07.20
Closed 10 Dec–4 Jan. **TV**.

A simple, quiet hotel with eight rooms, above a bar. It's easy to find a parking space across the road, on the banks of the Vienne. This is a really good place which has appeared in this guide for ten consecutive years, and it won't let you down. The owners have maintained their standards: the rooms are very clean, some have a view of the river, while others, higher up the house, have Velux windows. Doubles 120F with wash basin, 160F with shower, then 170F and 180F with shower/wc or bath respectively. 10% discount out of season.

🕊 🛎 HÔTEL DIDEROT**

4 rue Buffon; it's away from the centre, 100m from pl. Jeanne-d'Arc.
☎ 02.47.93.18.87 ➡ 02.47.93.37.10
Disabled access. TV. Car park.

Through the big gateway at the end of the courtyard you'll see a very handsome 18th-century house covered in ivy and Virginia creeper. Inside there's a 15th-century fireplace and an 18th-century staircase, and beams everywhere. It's very lovely. The 28 very cosy rooms are all decorated differently, and range in price from 310F to 410F. Breakfast comes with wonderful jams. Very professional and welcoming greeting. Note that the car park closes at 10pm. 10% discount Nov–March.

🛎 HÔTEL DE FRANCE-RESTAURANT AU CHAPEAU ROUGE**

47–49 pl. du Général-de-Gaulle; (Centre).
☎ 02.47.93.33.91 ➡ 02.47.98.37.03
Closed Tues, 23 Feb–9 March and the second fortnight in Nov. **TV. Pay car park**.

This beautiful 16th-century building has been well renovated and is now a *Best Western* hotel. The rooms are comfortable – some have views of the château and the rue Voltaire, a pedestrianised medieval street. Doubles with shower or bath 380–500F. The public parts are pleasant, with little seating areas here and there. Banana, orange, lemon and bay trees grow in the Mediterranean garden in the inner courtyard. Traditional dishes in the restaurant, with specialities such as pan-fried prawns with green asparagus, escalope of veal sweetbreads, *croustillant* with hazelnuts and chocolate mousse with sour cherries. Menus start at 120F.

AVOINE   37420 (5KM N)

🕊 🛎 I●I HÔTEL LA GIRAUDIÈRE-RESTAURANT LE PETIT PIGEONNIER**

Beaumont-en-Véron; take the D749 towards Beaumont for about 4km, turn left at Domaine de la Giraudière and the restaurant is 800m further on.

☎ 02.47.58.40.36 ➡ 02.47.58.46.06
📧 giraudiere@hotels-france.com
Disabled access. TV. Car park.

Service 7.30–10pm. Off the beaten track, this delightful country seat of some 17th-century gentleman has been made into an incredibly peaceful hotel. The 16th-century pigeon tower has been turned into a sitting room and library with a piano. The 25 rooms cost 200–350F with shower/wc and 370–590F with bath. Good gourmet cooking at affordable prices is served in the restaurant; menus 120–230F. Half board costs 240F per person. They've also got an Internet club. Free house apéritif or coffee.

COUR-CHEVERNY   41700

🕊 🛎 I●I HÔTEL-RESTAURANT DES TROIS MARCHANDS**

rue Nationale (Centre); it's on the main street next to the church.
☎ 02.54.79.96.44 ➡ 02.54.79.25.60
Closed Mon and 2 Feb–12 March. **Garden. TV. Car park**.

Service noon–2pm and 7.30–9.30pm. This half-timbered village inn has a lot of charm. Thirty-six rooms, some overlooking the garden, from 180F with basin, 270F with shower/wc and 360F with bath. Avoid the rooms in the annexe across the way if you can. The cooking has earned the place a good reputation. In the gourmet dining room specialities include frogs' legs with garlic and herbs, sea bream in a sea-salt crust, roast pigeon with truffle *jus* and game. The other one serves traditional dishes and grills. Menus 127F (not Sun lunch) and 199–260F, with a children's menu at 55F. 10% discount on the room rate.

🕊 I●I RESTAURANT LE POUSSE-RAPIÈRE

rue Nationale (Centre); it's opposite the path leading to the château.
☎ 02.54.79.94.23 ➡ 02.54.79.27.67
Closed Sun evening, Mon, 1 Dec–30 Jan. **Disabled access**.

Service noon–2pm and 7–9.30pm. You'll get a friendly welcome in this comfortable restaurant. The choice of good, original dishes includes goat's cheese quiche, *foie gras* with grapes, *paupiette* of zander in a chard and bacon parcel, pike with smoked bacon and goat's cheese sauce, shin of beef in Cheverny wine, or game in season. Set lunch menu 70F and then 105–210F, with a children's menu at 68F. Free coffee.

DREUX 28100

⬆ HÔTEL LE BEFFROI**

12 pl. Métézeau (Centre).
☎ 02.37.50.02.03 ➡ 02.37.42.07.69
Closed Sun noon–5.30pm and 1–10 Aug. **TV**.

This is a good place to spend the night when you're just passing through, with bright, quiet, comfortable rooms overlooking the river or the square (where there's an underground garage). Doubles with shower/wc 325F; some rooms sleep three.

🍴 I●I AUX QUATRE VENTS

18 pl. Métézeau (Centre).
☎ 02.37.50.03.24
Closed evenings except Sat and during the summer.

They've given this bistro a good retro look. The best options are the menus where you help yourself to as many *hors-d'œuvres* from the buffet as you like: choose from salmon, shellfish, excellent *charcuterie* and *crudités*. Follow that with a main course like rack of veal *à l'ancienne* or roast chicken, then finish with dessert. There's a *formule*. Prices range from 144–144F. Make the most of the terrace when the weather's good. Free apéritif.

VERNOUILLET 28500 (3KM S)

⬆ I●I AUBERGE DE LA VALLÉE VERTE

6 rue Lucien-Dupuis: it's in the centre near the church.
☎ 02.37.46.04.04 ➡ 02.37.42.91.17
Closed Fri and Sun evenings and Mon.
TV. Car park.

This recently refitted hotel offers cosy rooms with all amenities, 350–400F. But the big draw is the cooking. There's a brigade of professionals in the kitchen and they produce classic cuisine using locally farmed produce. Menus start at 145F. You can either dine in the pretty rustic dining room or up on the mezzanine under the eaves. There's an intimate atmosphere with a feeling of space. Convivial, smiling welcome. It's best to book at weekends.

FERTÉ-SAINT-AUBIN (LA) 45240

I●I L'AUBERGE DES CHASSEURS

34 rue des Poulies; it's in a street behind the tourist office.
☎ 02.38.76.66.95
Closed Mon evening and Tues.

This used to be a hunting lodge, and the name stuck, along with some of the culinary traditions. In other words, you'll get a warm welcome and in season you'll be served game in front of the impressive fireplace where they light a fire in autumn and winter. The food is good, simply cooked and served up in generous portions. There's a dish of the day at 58F, a weekday menu at 71F, then prices go on up. One departure from local tradition is the mussel menu which offers mussels, chips and beer for 55F.

MÉNESTREAU-EN-VILLETTE 45240 (7KM E)

🍴 I●I LE RELAIS DE SOLOGNE

63 place du 8-Mai; take the D17 from La Ferté-Saint-Aubin.
☎ 02.38.76.97.40 ➡ 02.3849.60.43
Closed Sun evening, Wed and the first week in Sept.

Thierry Roger runs this place. He's the chef and one of the virtuosos of French gastronomic cooking. The dining room is traditional for the Sologone region: red brick walls, substantial beams, soft, warm lighting and an abundance of fresh flowers and plants. It creates a harmonious setting for the refined local dishes the chef creates. The menus change frequently and make the most of seasonal produce: pressed quail with vintage port, *foie gras* with Muscat, poached white fillet of zander with preserved tomatoes and basil. The desserts are so good they'll make you weep! Try the mandarine chocolate tears or the strawberry soup with Kummel honey. Exquisite wines. Menus start at 98F then 168–208F.

MARCILLY-EN-VILLETTE 45240 (8KM NE)

🍴 ⬆ I●I AUBERGE DE LA CROIX BLANCHE*

118 pl. de l'Église; take the N20 and then the D921.
☎ 02.38.76.10.14 ➡ 02.38.76.10.67
Closed Fri, 13 Feb–5 March and 15–31 Aug.
TV. Garden. Car park.

Service noon–2.30pm and 7.30–9pm. When this inn opened in the 17th century a sign went up; "Tapholot, wigmaker, serves drink and food; soup with vegetables at any time. We also cut hair". The sign's still there. They've stopped cutting hair but they still sell food. A *menu-ouvrier* is served in the bar, where you can also buy a newspaper. It's best to book. In the pleasant dining room, you'll get good-natured service and traditional dishes prepared by a skilled chef. The menus, 104–190F, change almost daily because the chef is uncompromising when it comes to the quality of his raw ingredients. You'd come back here just for the desserts. The pleasant, simple rooms overlook the Place de l'Église, which comes from another era. Rooms 200F with basin and 270F with shower/wc. 10% discount if you stay half board, which costs 290F per person.

FERTÉ-VIDAME (LA)   28340

I●I LA TRIGALLE*

How to get there: coming from Verneuil, as you come into the village it's on the right at a crossroads.
☎ 06.12.97.82.00
Closed Mon and Tues except public holidays, and from the second week in Jan to the third week in Feb. **Garden. Car park**.

It's a pleasure to find a good restaurant like this. Classical music plays in the restaurant but Emmanuel's cooking is far from classical. He invents delicious concoctions like red mullet fillets with lobster butter, duck breast with maple, *fromagée*, a regional speciality, and a supreme of dark chocolate with figs and mandarin sauce. Set weekday lunch menu 65F and others 99–135F, all of them good and generously served. The wine list is exceptional and there are a number of bottles with prices into four figures! They hold themed evenings when the music and the food harmonise. Saint-Simon, the famous 18th-century diarist who chronicled events at the court of Louis XIV, had a château here. It's in ruins now but it's worth a visit – the grounds are enormous.

GIEN   45500

☎ SANOTEL**

21 quai de Sully; it's on the left Loire riverbank, opposite the château.
☎ 02.38.67.61.46 ➡ 02.38.67.13.01
Disabled access. Garden. TV. Car park.

This is a fairly ordinary two-star hotel on the banks of the Loire, but the prices are reasonable: a double with air-conditioning and bath costs 190F and there's a clear view of the town, huddled at the foot of the château. The rooms overlooking the garden are quieter. Nice welcome. The Italian brasserie in the hotel is run by separate management and is rather expensive.

I●I RESTAURANT LE RÉGENCY

6 quai Lenoir; it faces the Loire, near the bridge.
☎ 02.38.67.04.96
Closed Sun evening, Wed, the Feb school holidays and a fortnight June/July.

The restaurant specialises in freshwater fish from the Loire and local dishes that are cooked simply and with care: chicken liver *terrine* with sour cherries, duckling fillet with thyme or haddock with red pepper sauce, snail *fricassée* with oyster mushrooms, zander fillet with sorrel sauce and *foie gras terrine*. Prices are reasonable with menus 90–210F. The terrace is on the banks of the river – but it has a road running in front of it.

ILLIERS-COMBRAY   28120

I●I LE FLORENT

13 pl. du Marché; it's near the church.
☎ 02.37.24.10.43 ➡ 02.37.24.11.78
Closed Sun, Mon and Wed evenings except on public holidays. **Disabled access**.

An elegant, unpretentious restaurant – they don't flog the Proust connection to death. The little dining rooms are delightful, and Hervé Priolet is an excellent and imaginative chef whose speciality is fish. There are tempting set menus, 118F (Mon–Fri except public holidays), and others up to 315F; one's named after Marcel Proust, which will get your flavour-memory going. They do a country platter at 70F.

BROU   28160 (13KM SW)

☆ I●I RESTAURANT DU STADE

1 rue du Mail (Centre).
☎ 02.37.47.01.39
Closed Wed evening, Thurs, the first fortnight in Jan, the last fortnight in June, the first week in July and the last week in Dec.

An unpretentious restaurant; the regulars rave about its family atmosphere and the good, honest cooking. There's a *formule* at 75F. The 96F set menu gets you as many *hors d'œuvres* as you can manage, a choice of five main courses with vegetables, a cheese platter and any house dessert. The other menus, up to 155F, are perfect if you're out with friends or the in-laws. There's a terrace and a small inside patio decorated with the owner's bonsai collection. Free coffee.

ISSOUDUN · 36100

⅍ ♜ |●| HÔTEL DE FRANCE-RESTAURANT LES TROIS ROIS**

3 rue Pierre-Brossolette (Centre).
☎ 02.54.21.00.65 ➡ 02.54.21.50.61
Closed Sun evening, Mon except July–Aug, the first fortnight in Feb and the first three weeks in Sept.
TV. Car park.

Most rooms here are large and spotlessly clean but there are some smaller ones which need to be refurbished. All the doubles have en-suite bath and cost 290F. The dining room is comfortable and stylish, with superb mirrors, *fleur-de-lys* wallpaper, and wood-work that shows the patina of age – but it gets unpleasantly smoky when it's full. You'll get an exuberant welcome from the owner, a very efficient woman who keeps an eye on everything. The cooking is conventional but you won't be disappointed. Weekday menu is 90F and there are others 120–140F. Specialities include calf's head *à l'ancienne*, duck breast with Berry honey, house *foie gras* cooked in a cloth, and a tureen of crayfish. In fine weather, there is a flower-filled terrace overlooking the courtyard. Free house apéritif.

⅍ ♜ |●| HÔTEL-RESTAURANT LA COGNETTE***

2 bd. Stalingrad; take the N151, go into the town centre and it's near the big marketplace.
☎ 02.54.21.21.83 ➡ 02.54.03.13.03
🄴 alain.nonnet@wanadoo.com
Closed Sun evening and Mon except public holidays and during summer, and Jan. **TV. Disabled access**.

Service noon–2pm and 7.30–10pm. Balzac gives a very accurate description of this 19th-century hotel in his novel *La Rabouilleuse*. Then, it was run by a pair called Cognet and a widow from Houssaye, who had a reputation as a fine cook. The dining room decor is a mixture of Empire, Restoration and Louis-Philippe, which would have delighted Balzac. He'd also have liked the way the ornaments, wall-hangings and pictures look as if they've just been put there, though in fact they've been carefully arranged. The restaurant is reputed to be one of the best in the *département*; the kitchens are in the hands of Alain Nonnet and his son-in-law, Jean-Jacques Daumy. Set menus 135–250F. The formality may feel a bit awkward if you're dining alone. The hotel rooms are comfortable and perfect in every particular; they supply a dressing gown and

hairdryer. Doubles 490F with bath. Each room has its own terrace where you can have breakfast in fine weather and enjoy the scent of roses. It thoroughly deserves the three stars. Free apéritif.

⅍|●| LE PILE OU FACE

rue Danielle-Casanova (Centre).
☎ 02.54.03.14.91
Closed Sun evening, Mon, and 15 Aug–6 Sept.

Service 1.15–9.15pm. Whether you choose to eat in the conventional dining room or out on the more pleasant covered terrace, the menus are the same. Weekday lunch menu 80F, then 120–290F. Children have their own menu for 45F. Specialities include *cassolette berrichonne*, lobster *croquant*, veal kidneys with Pinot Gris, and zander with herbs. Free coffee with all menus over 80F.

DIOU · 36260 (12KM N)

|●| L'AUBERGEADE

Route d'Issoudun; by the D918, heading for Vierzon.
☎ 02.54.49.22.28
Closed Wed and Sun evenings.

A warm welcome, a pretty terrace, a pleasant, comfortable dining room and beautifully simple cooking. The tables are closer together inside than out. Menus run from 100F and there are two for children at 50F and 70F. On the cheapest menu, starters could be quail *terrine*, then Thai fish curry with coconut milk or pan-fried farmhouse chicken with rosemary *jus*, followed by well ripened cheeses and the house dessert of the day. Their specialities include slivers of farm-raised chicken with green cabbage and truffles, veal cutlets roasted with fresh rosemary and a melting chocolate *moelleux*, served warm with a mint ice cream.

BRIVES · 36100 (13KM S)

|●| RESTAURANT LE CÉSAR-CHEZ NICOLE

Centre; take the D918; it's beside the church.
☎ 02.54.49.04.43
Closed Mon.

The church is almost invisible behind the trees and there are vestiges of the old dyke built by Caesar's legions. The restaurant is in the heart of the village. The ceiling of the large dining room is supported by enormous beams. Weekday menu at 60F and others 65–90F or around 130F *à la carte*. Try the house *terrine*

César, calf's head with lentils, or *coq au vin* with potatoes.

LANGEAIS 37130

⚘ ⌂ |●| HÔTEL-RESTAURANT ERRARD-HOSTEN

2 rue Gambetta.
☎ 02.47.96.82.12 ⬥ 02.47.96.56.72
Closed Sun evening, Mon and Wed lunchtime except in July–Aug, and mid-Feb to March. **TV**. **Car park**.

An old inn right in the centre of the town with eleven cosy rooms boasting lots of facilities. Double with shower/wc 280F, 360–450F with bath. The ones overlooking the courtyard are the quietest. There's a warm dining room on the ground floor with a small bar off it. High-quality gastronomic cooking with dishes precisely cooked and seasonings finely judged: eel *rillettes*, pigeon with honey and ginger, and a classic zander with *beurre blanc*. Delicious. Menus start at 145F. Exemplary service and welcome. Free coffee.

LOCHES 37600

⌂ |●| HÔTEL-RESTAURANT DE FRANCE**

6 rue Picois (Centre).
☎ 02.47.59.00.32
Closed Sun evening, Mon and Tues lunchtime except July–Aug, and 8 Jan–15 Feb. **TV**. **Garden**. **Car park**.

This is an old post house with a wide courtyard and flower garden where you can have lunch in the summer. Lovely rooms range from 300–370F with shower/wc or bath. Some are split-level, and they're all very cosily furnished. They serve inventive and refined cooking prepared with great care and attention. The dishes are served under domed covers, the plates are hot and the tablecloths and napkins are not made of paper! After some *amuse-bouches* to get your appetite going, the 88F weekday menu includes dishes such as coddled eggs *basquaise*, Norwegian salad with smoked salmon, perfect haddock with a *julienne* of baby vegetables with lemon butter, and roast pork with prunes and carrot purée and wild mushrooms. On the 120–260F menus, specialities include eel stewed in wine, Géline chicken (a local breed) and prune ice cream with Touraine Marc. The desserts are prepared on the premises. Apparently Lodovigo Sforza, the duke of Milan, was imprisoned by Louis XI in the dungeons in Loche and had his meals brought in from the hotel.

BEAULIEU-LÈS-LOCHES 37600 (1KM E)

⚘ ⌂ HÔTEL DE BEAULIEU**

3 rue Foulques-Nerra; take the D760 in the direction of Valençay; it's opposite the church.
☎ 02.47.91.60.80
Closed Oct to end-March.

This very handsome 16th-century building, originally belonging to the abbey opposite, is typical of the Touraine. It offers nine bedrooms round a beautiful inner courtyard, decorated in an appropriately rustic style. Doubles with shower/wc from 200F. 10% discount April, May and Sept.

⚘ |●| RESTAURANT L'ESTAMINET

14 rue de l'Abbaye (Centre).
☎ 02.47.59.35.47
Closed Sun evening, Mon, and the last week in Aug

The kind of café-restaurant that every French village should have. It's in a 16th-century building in the middle of the town, next to the abbey and its 60m bell tower. There's a 1900s coffee percolator behind the brass bar. Fresh cooking and local specialities are the watchwords here. The dishes of the day, 40F, are prepared with care by Madame, while Monsieur serves in the dining room. He also catches the fish and picks wild mushrooms for his wife to cook. Dishes include goat's cheese salad, rabbit in mustard sauce, *coq au vin*, and squid *à l'Espagnole*. Other menus 60–105F and inexpensive *à la carte*. Free apéritif or coffee.

MALESHERBES 45330

⌂ |●| L'ECU DE FRANCE**

10 pl. du Martroy (Centre).
☎ 02.38.34.87.25 ⬥ 02.38.34.68.99
Restaurant closed Thurs and Sun evenings. **TV**.

The courtyard, where the stagecoaches used to turn in, has been transformed into the reception hall. Comfortable, well-maintained double rooms with shower/wc for 285F or 360F with bath. The restaurant won't shake the world, but the *formule brasserie* served in the bistro is tasty and good value. They offer decent dishes of the day and a particularly good dessert with cream and cream cheese beaten together – it's even better with strawberries. A good place to stop if you're driving on the A13, which is just 13km away, and Fontainbleau is nearby.

MENNETOU-SUR-CHER   41320

♠ IØI LE LION D'OR

2 rue Marcel-Bailly (Centre); it's on the edge of the N76.
☎ 02.54.98.06.10 ➡ 02.59.98.06.13

Delicious cooking like *cassolette* of snails with girolle mushrooms and Mennetou *andouillette*. The dining room is attractively rustic and there is a brasserie area with a more ordinary short menu at 58F. They have sixteen rooms at 150F with basin or 190F with shower/wc, which are adequate for an overnight stay. The ones overlooking the courtyard give you a view of the medieval walls rather than the main road.

MONTARGIS   45200

♠ HÔTEL LE BON GÎTE*

21 bd. du Chinchon (Centre).
☎ 02.38.85.31.01 ➡ 02.38.93.28.06
Disabled access. TV. Car park.

Good place for a decent night's sleep at a reasonable price. It's not much from the outside, but inside it's clean and quiet. A few simple rooms on the upper floors look over the inner courtyard and you could imagine you were near the Mediterranean in summer. Doubles cost 150F with basin and bidet, and up to 239F with shower/wc or bath. The very nice Spanish owners have been here for more than thirty years. Let them know if you'll be arriving after 8pm.

IØI RESTAURANT LES PETITS OIGNONS

81 [bis] av. du Général-de-Gaulle; it's near the train station.
☎ 02.38.93.97.49
Closed Sun evening, Mon, a fortnight in the Feb school holidays and the first three weeks in Aug. **Disabled access. Garden.**

The bright decor is uncluttered and a bit modern, but it's the garden and terrace that really make the place. You can be sure of peace and quiet and you're away from the gaze of the passers-by and the noise of the street. Sneak a look at what's going on in the kitchen, something they encourage you to do. They set to work in great style using first-rate ingredients to produce very refined cooking. Try their home-smoked salmon, *confit* of duck, lamb's brains *meunière*, roast salmon with garlic and the fillet of zander in cream and saffron, which is still produced hereabouts. All very good. You'll get a cheerful welcome and impeccable service

and the menus are realistically priced at 75–185F.

AMILLY   45200 (2KM SE)

IØI L'AUBERGE DE L'ECLUSE

74 rue des Ponts.
☎ 02.38.85.44.24
Closed Sun evening, Mon and Thurs evening.

From the dining room, you can watch while the lock-keeper manually opens the lock. The classical decor contrasts with the modern, extraordinarily inventive cooking. Try zander with shredded leek and wild *mousseron* mushrooms, turbot with samphire, or the delicious home-made desserts and ice creams. Prices are a little high – 130F menu in the week, 185F on Sunday – but the dishes are in no way disappointing. There is also a terrace on the waterside.

DORDIVES   45680 (15KM N)

IØI RESTAURANT LA TRUITE

chemin du Puits; it's on the N7
☎ 02.38.92.77.17
Closed Mon except in season and public holidays.

Situated on the edge of a small lake, fed by a river that rises in the property, out in the countryside. The huge dining room has a bay window and a wide fireplace and there's a lovely terrace in summer. It's popular with fishermen – there's a stretch of water where you can go fly-fishing – and people who like fish. The trout is caught fresh every morning and is the house speciality. They also serve zander, plates of oysters and home-made *bouillabaisse*. Menus start at 80F.

MONTRICHARD   41400

♠ HÔTEL DE LA CROIX BLANCHE**

64 rue Nationale.
☎ 02.54.32.30.87 ➡ 02.54.32.91.00
Closed Nov to end March.

The hotel has been completely renovated and is wonderfully clean but it started life as a coaching inn in the 16th century and it's right next to the dungeons. The rooms are a bit dark but well appointed, with en-suite bathrooms and phones; doubles around 250F. Some have a view over the River Cher.

♣ IØI BISTROT DE LA TOUR

34 rue du Sully, (Centre); it's near the tourist office.
☎ 02.54.32.07.34

Closed Sun.

A lovely house with a pretty terrace on the town square. The stone and wood decor inside is warm and attractive. Weekday lunch menu 65F, others 78F and 119F, or à la carte around 120F, with classic, carefully prepared dishes like poached eggs in Gamay sauce, ox kidneys with basil, zander fillet and a particularly good dish of snails, bacon and oyster mushrooms. There's a selection of substantial salads. A nice place for a tasty, reasonably priced meal.

CHISSAY   41400 (4KM W)

🛏 |●| CHÂTEAU DE CHISSEY

Centre; it's on the right bank of the Cher, on the D176, in the direction of Tours.
☎ 02.54.32.32.01 **e** chateau-chissay@wanadoo.fr
Swimming pool. Garden. TV. Car park.

Stay in a château in château country. This one was immortalised in the famous "Riches Heures du Duc de Berry" and was built by Charles VIII. It's a sublime, meticulously restored château, in the heart of the Cher valley. The terrace is under the arcades, while the splendid dining room is luxuriously decorated with exquisite taste and period furniture. Menus start at 195F and double rooms at 495F, or there's an off-season weekend deal that includes dinner and breakfast for two nights.

PONTLEVOY   41400 (7KM N)

🛏 |●| HÔTEL-RESTAURANT DE L'ÉCOLE**

12 route de Montrichard (Centre); it's on the main road coming from Montrichard.
☎ 02.54.32.50.30 **➡** 02.54.32.33.58
Closed Sun evening and Mon except public holidays, 19 Nov–12 Dec and 16 Feb–14 March.
Garden. TV. Car park.

This is a pleasant place to stop after you've visited the 10th-century abbey. It's a charming little hotel with eleven comfortable rooms with shower/wc at 260F or bath at 280F. The cooking is very traditional but sophisticated and nicely presented. They do several set menus starting at 103F and going up to 270F. Try their pike and prawn fish balls, salmon with crayfish tails, duck ham or zander fillet. In fine weather, you can eat under the pergola in the garden. Excellent service.

OISLY   41700 (18KM NE)

⚒|●| RESTAURANT LE SAINT-VINCENT

Centre; take the D764 as far as Pontlevoy then turn right

onto the D30.
☎ 02.54.79.50.04
Closed Tues, Wed and 20 Dec–3 Feb.

Service noon–1.30pm and 7–9pm. This is quite an exceptional restaurant. It doesn't look like much – the sign is very ordinary and you might mistake it for just another restaurant in just another village square. But step inside: the decor is fresh and well presented, there's space between the tables, and the linen and cutlery have been chosen to match the rustic ambience. The menu is varied, full of tempting and original dishes: crab cake with onion chutney and fruits served with *tabbouleh* and green curry, venison *civet* with cocoa beans, and desserts such as pears poached in Oisly wine and blackcurrant sorbet. The creative chef will probably have invented even more culinary delights by the time you read this. Set menus 125F (weekdays) and 170–240F. Best to book. Free coffee.

NOGENT-LE-ROTROU   28400

🛏 |●| LE LION D'OR**

28 pl. Saint Pol (Centre).
☎ 02.37.52.01.60 **➡** 02.37.52.23.82
Closed the first three weeks in Aug and Christmas–New Year. **TV. Car park**.

Once you're over the shock of the 1970s wallpaper in the corridor, you'll find the rooms mostly spacious and comfortable. The hotel is in a brilliant location right on the main square but try to avoid the rooms overlooking it on a Friday night because there's a market held there on Saturday and setting up starts really early. Lovely welcome. Doubles with shower/wc 260–320F depending on size.

🛏 |●| INTER HÔTEL SULLY***

12 rue des Viennes (North).
☎ 02.37.52.15.14 **➡** 02.37.52.15.20
Closed Fri evening, Sat and 15 Nov–15 March.
Disabled access. TV.

Sure, it's a chain hotel but you get a genuine, smiling welcome that inspires confidence. The prices are affordable given that it's a three-star establishment; doubles with en-suite bathrooms start at 349F. It's quietly locted just away from the centre of town in an area that's recently been built. A problem-free place.

|●| LA PAPOTIÈRE

3 rue Bourg le Comte.
☎ 02.37.52.18.41
Closed Sun evening and Mon.

A really odd name for this superb, 16th-century stone house. One of the windows on the façade has been beautifully carved. Inside it's warm, and the pleasant service helps you relax very quickly. There's a bistro *formule* menu at 75F which is a big hit and more complete ones 150–210F with excellent traditional, bourgeois cuisine. They do guinea fowl with figs and a good *noisette* of lamb – and don't miss the house dessert, *kanougat* with chocolate.

ORLÉANS 45000

🛏 |●| HÔTEL DE PARIS

29 faubourg Bannier (North).
☎ 02.38.53.39.58
Closed Sat lunchtime and Sun except by reservation.
Garage.

You'll get a nice, very laid-back welcome; something the boss learned from his years in the US. The rooms are simple but pleasant and a lick of paint and new wallpaper have smartened them up. The beds are good, too. Doubles with basin go for 160F, or there are some with bath. Guests here range from American students to workmen travelling to some job or other. The bistro on the ground floor, where they serve a dish of the day every lunchtime at 43F, is popular with locals. There's a garage where you can park a bike, and dogs are welcome. They don't accept credit cards.

🍴 🛏 HÔTEL MARGUERITE**

14 pl. du Vieux-Marché (Centre); it's 50m from rue Royale, near the main post office.
☎ 02.38.53.74.32 ➡ 02.38.53.31.56
Closed Sun noon–4.30pm.
Disabled access. **TV**. **Car park**.

A handsome, delightfully old-fashioned building – the rooms are comfortable, the prices are reasonable and it's run like a three-star hotel. The jovial owner will greet you at reception on the first floor; he's helpful and friendly. They offer 25 large, comfortable, well-maintained rooms; you'll pay 160F for a room with a basin but no TV, up to 250F for bath and TV. The rooms over the street have double-glazing to cut down the noise. Breakfast includes as much hot coffee as you can drink, fruit juice and honey for only 30F – they bring it to your room for no extra charge. 20% discount for weekends and in July–Aug.

🛏 HÔTEL DE L'ABEILLE**

64 rue d'Alsace-Lorraine (North); it's in a street that flanks the Palais de Justice.
☎ 02.38.53.54.87 ➡ 02.38.62.65.84
e hotel-de-labeille@wanadoo.fr
TV.

There's something very special about this hotel. It was opened by the family that still runs it way back in 1919, after World War I, which makes it one of the oldest hotels in town. There's a creaky old sign and they've put green shrubs and flowers out all over the pavement. The old wooden staircase shines from years of polishing and the rooms, all decorated differently, have a discreet, antiquated charm. Prices are fair, 170F for a room with wash basin, 290F with shower/wc and 310F with bath. Pleasant staff.

🍴 🛏 HÔTEL SAINT-MARTIN**

52 bd. Alexandre-Martin (Centre); turn left as you come out of the train station and make for the theatre.
☎ 02.3862.47.47 ➡ 02.38.81.13.28
Closed Sunday 11am–5.30pm and Christmas–New Year. **Garden**. **TV**. **Pay car park**.

A little, old-fashioned hotel in a detached building with some rooms that look onto a tiny flower-filled courtyard. Prices start at 170F for a double with washing facilities but no TV, and 260–270F with shower/wc and TV. 10% discount July–Sept or free use of shower if you're in a room with basin only.

🛏 JACKOTEL**

18 cloître Saint-Aignan (Southeast); follow quai du Châtelet in the direction of Montargis and turn before you get to the bridge.
☎ 02.38.54.48.48 ➡ 02.38.77.17.59
Disabled access. **Garden**. **TV**. **Car park**.

A nice hotel, recently built, with a flower-filled courtyard. There are 61 comfortable, neat rooms that are worthy of a three-star establishment. Doubles 300F with bath, TV and phone. There is a display of carved parrots in the reception; the real birds are outside, twittering in the lovely little square in the shadow of the church of Saint-Aignan. A good hotel.

🍴 |●| RESTAURANT LES FAGOTS

32 rue du Poirier (Centre); it's near the Châtelet covered market.
☎ 02.38.62.22.79 ➡ 02.38.77.99.87
Closed Sun, Mon, the first week in Jan, and the second fortnight in Aug. **Disabled access**. **Pay car park**.

There's an unexpected atmosphere as you walk through the door. The big fireplace in the middle of the dining room draws all sorts of people, from actors to romancing couples as well as a host of regulars. Decor includes old posters on the wall, enamel and china coffee pots here and there, and a few photographs of actors. You also come here for the grills, which they do over the open fire; their speciality is thick steaks of donkey meat, though you have to order this a day in advance. The lunchtime set menu costs 65F, another at 85F, *à la carte* around 110F, and a children's menu at 55F. Friendly welcome and service. It's better in the evening but on a sunny day, the terrace makes it a nice place for lunch. Free Kir.

⚶ |O| RESTAURANT DON QUICHOTTE

165 rue de Bourgogne (Centre).
☎ 02.38.62.36.57
Closed Mon, Tues lunchtime, a fortnight in Feb, and three weeks in July.

Service noon–2.15pm and 7pm–12.30am. A really popular Spanish restaurant with cured hams hanging from the ceiling and the benign figures of Don Quixote and his faithful companion, Sancho Panza. They serve paella, lots of dishes with lashings of garlic, and sangria by the jug. There are no set menus but you can eat till very late, just like in Spain. Free house apéritif.

⚶ |O| L'ARCHANGE

66 faubourg Madeleine (West); starting from la pl. Croix Morin, take the rue Porte Madeleine; it's on the right after bd. Jean-Jaurès.
☎ 02.38.88.64.20 ➡ 02.38.45.08.81
Closed Sun evening, Tues, Wed, Thurs evening, a week in the Easter school holidays, three weeks in Aug and Christmas–New Year's Day.

The chef, Monsieur Schnitt, won the *grand prix d'honneur* at France's national academy of cuisine so prepare yourself: duck *foie gras*, veal sweetbreads with cream, sole *paupiettes* with crayfish *jus*, and a white chocolate dessert with apricot *coulis*. This is serious cooking prepared with great art. Menus 85–215F. There's an eclectic wine list with some excellent vintages – such as a red or white Cheverny – at affordable prices. The dining room is elegantly decorated and there are engravings of the local countryside on the walls. Free coffee.

|O| LA DARIOLE

26 rue Étienne Dolet (Centre).
☎ 02.38.77.26.67
Closed Wed and Sat lunchtimes, Sun and three weeks in Aug.

Wood panelling, old-rose tones and refined cuisine in this lovely restaurant. The specialities change frequently; pressed sardines with pickled tomatoes and creamed olives, steamed turbot and vegetables, and rhubarb

and strawberry tart. Menus 110–150F. In summer you eat outside on a pedestrian square. Charming welcome but the service is tentative and nervy. Maybe it will relax with time.

⚶ |O| LA PETITE MARMITE

178 rue de Bourgogne (Centre); it's near the préfecture.
☎ 02.38.54.23.83 ➡ 02.38.54.41.81
Closed Sat lunchtime, Sun and public holidays.

The best place in a street full of restaurants. It's open seven nights a week 7–11pm. They stick to traditional local dishes served in a pretty, rustic dining room, with a choice of three menus 118–188F or *à la carte*. Dishes include *foie gras à l'ancienne* or with truffles, *coq au vin*, rabbit *à l'Orléanaise*, game in season and *crème brûlée* with pears. Nice proprietress who spoils her customers. Free *digestif*.

CONBLEUX   45800 (7KM E)

|O| LA MARINE

How to get there: take the N460
☎ 02.38.55.12.69

The house is smothered in wisteria and there's a terrace on the canal bank. The Loire flows through the village, revealing sandy beaches on the banks. Just in front, the water flowing through the old lock sounds like a waterfall. Time seems to have stood still here. The restaurant specialities are freshwater fish from the Loire – eel, lampray and zander – in dishes which complement each other expertly, and sumptuous desserts. Menus 120–160F. A dish for children at 35F. The superb dining room is built from stone and pale wood. Warm welcome.

PITHIVIERS   45300

⚶ |O| LE RELAIS DE LA POSTE**

10 Mail-Ouest (Centre).
☎ 02.38.30.40.30. ➡ 02.38.30.47.79
Restaurant closed Sun evening. **TV. Pay car park.**

A good provincial hotel dominating a square, with a reliable restaurant serving classic dishes. Menus 99–149F; the cheapest one lists dishes such as brawn, steak with shallots, cheese and a choice of desserts including the famous local delicacy, the Pithiviers with puff pastry and almond paste. The dining room is rather dull but very well soundproofed. The rooms have wooden wainscoting and the ones up in the eaves boast beamed ceilings. Doubles 300F with shower/wc or bath. A good place to stop. Free house apéritif.

PREUILLY-SUR-CLAISE 37290

♠ |●| AUBERGE SAINT-NICOLAS
6 Grande-Rue (Centre).
☎ 02.47.94.50.80. ➡ 02.47.94.41.77
Closed Sun evening and Mon except July–Aug, and mid-Sept to 3 Oct. **TV. Lock-up car park**.

Service 11.30am–2pm and 7.15–9pm. This hotel near the abbey has nine rooms with bathrooms which have been completely refurbished and are cheerfully decorated in shades of yellow. Doubles with shower/wc or bath at 240F. Pleasant welcome and good value for money. The dining room is a brightly coloured and they serve good, regional cooking, with menus from 120F.

PETIT-PRESSIGNY (LE) 37350 (9KM N)

|●| RESTAURANT LA PROMENADE
11 rue du Savoureulx; take the D41 in the direction of Loches, then the D50.
☎ 02.47.94.93.52 ➡ 02.47.91.06.03
Closed Sun evening, Mon and Tues lunchtime, three weeks in Jan and a fortnight Sept/Oct.

Some of the most ordinary villages hide real treasures and this is one. A feast awaits you here. Jacky Dallais was a pupil of Robuchon. He converted his father's old smithy into a splendid restaurant with two pretty, contemporary-looking dining rooms reached through a sitting-room reception area where Madam receives you. Monsieur is a genuinely creative chef of integrity and imagination and he creates dishes of great distinction. The menu changes constantly and the prices are wisely pitched to accommodate lots of pockets. The *menu du marché*, served on weekdays, is excellent value at 140F while the one at 400F would suit appetites verging on the Rabelaisian – five dishes plus cheeses plus dessert. The specialities are an absolute must, including free-range pork chop with beans, and black pudding *parmentier* with mashed potatoes. They bake their own bread and the wine list is sumptuous. Efficient service. Best to book at weekends.

RICHELIEU 37120

♣ ♠ |●| LES MOUSQUETAIRES
4 av. du Colonel-Goulier (Centre).
☎ 02.47.58.15.17

Closed Tues until 6pm. **Disabled access. TV. Garden**.

An unpretentious but comfortable little hotel outside the old ramparts. It has five double rooms leading straight out into the garden. Prices start at 160F for shower/wc rising to 230F for a room that sleeps four. For a small charge, you can have a TV. Nice welcome, and the bill will come as a pleasant surprise. There's a small bar and you can order a meal – there's a menu at 58F. 10% discount on the room rate if you stay a week, out of season.

ROMORANTIN-LANTHENAY 41200

♣ ♠ |●| HÔTEL-RESTAURANT LE COLOMBIER**
18 pl. du Vieux-Marché; it's 150m from the town hall.
☎ 02.54.76.12.76 ➡ 02.54.76.39.40
Closed Sun evening and mid-Feb to mid-March.
Garden. TV. Car park.

Service noon–2pm and 7–9pm. Rooms are comfortable though nothing more; those overlooking the courtyard are quieter. Doubles 240F with shower/wc or 270F with bath. Pleasant garden. The spacious, cosy restaurant specialises in cooking from the Sologne and the carefully prepared dishes change with the seasons – *papillote* of zander with lime flowers, ox kidneys with shallot marmalade, duck *foie gras* with horn of plenty mushrooms and raspberry shortcake. Menus 100–175F. A place with a good reputation. 10% discount on the room rate

SACHÉ 37190

|●| AUBERGE DU XIIIÈME SIÈCLE
It's in the main street.
☎ 02.47.26.88.77
Closed Sun evening and Mon.

This village is enough to make many a restaurateur green with envy. It's a place of pilgrimage for devotees of Balzac and the splendid restaurant is one of the best in the region. The old beams and wide fireplace can't have changed in centuries. Xavier Aubrun and Thierry Jimenez are the two excellent chefs. They have put together a Balzac menu and the dessert is loaded with caffeine! Other delights include dishes with contemporary combinations of flavour such as pigeon salad, zander with rhubarb and Géline chicken (a local breed) with capers. The prices, starting with the 110F menu, are very fair. Exciting to anticipate and a delight to look back on.

SAINT-AIGNAN   41110

🛏 |O| GRAND HÔTEL SAINT-AIGNAN**

79 quai J. J. Delorme (Centre).
☎ 02.54.75.18.04 ➡ 02.54.75.12.59

An old coaching inn, covered in ivy, standing on the banks of the Cher. Warm greeting, friendly setting and chic environs – the walls are hung with medieval tapestries. Pretty rooms at a range of prices from 144F with shower on the landing to 330F with en-suite bathroom, and some have a view of the river. Specialities in the restaurant include smoked salmon with onion rings, braised ox kidneys with ceps and *assiette de trois provinces*. Delicious but portions are a little small. Menus 90–205F. 10% discount on the room rate Nov–March.

CHABRIS   36210 (25KM E)

🛏 |O| HÔTEL DE LA PLAGE**

42 rue du Pont; it's on the Valençay to Romorantin road, in the direction of the Sologne.
☎ 02.54.40.02.24 ➡ 02.54.40.08.59
Closed Sun evening, Mon except mid-July to end Aug, and Jan. **Garden**. **TV**. **Car park**.

Service noon–2pm and 7.30–9pm. A nice little stop to eat and sleep. Mme d'Agostino cooks traditional dishes while her husband extends a genuine Berry welcome. The dishes on the menu change every three months and the fresh fish depends on the catches at the ports. There's a 90F *formule* and other menus 95–180F. In summer, they serve meals in the garden where there's a fountain. The rooms are comfortable; the ones on the first floor are older and more spacious, while the ones on the second floor have been modernised. Doubles 245F with shower/wc or bath. Free house apéritif or coffee.

SAINT-AMAND-MONTROND   18200

🛏 |O| HÔTEL-RESTAURANT LE NOIRLAC**

215 route de Bourges; it's 5km from the A71 motorway exit on the N144 in the direction of Bourges and 2.5 km from the 12th-century Cistersian abbey of Noirlac.
☎ 02.48.82.22.00 ➡ 02.48.82.22.01
Hotel closed 22 Dec–1 Jan. **Restaurant closed** Fri evening, Sat lunchtime and Sun evening Nov–Easter. **Swimming pool**. **Disabled access**. **TV**. **Car park**.

A perfect overnight stop if you're driving through, even though it looks like an unattractive chain hotel at first. It's ultra-modern, with a pool, tennis courts and putting green. Have a look around the back! The super-comfortable, practical rooms cost 355F with bath; two have been specially adapted for the disabled. Staff in both the hotel and the restaurant are efficient. The cheapest set menu at 78F is substantial and is served daily; other menus 128–150F. Specialities are *fricassée* of snails, *cassollette* of ox kidneys, calf's head in balsamic vinegar and *crème brûlée* with Bourbon vanilla. In summer they hold theme evenings. 10% discount on the room rate.

|O| RESTAURANT LE SAINT-JEAN

1 rue de l'Hôtel-Dieu; it's near the Saint-Vic museum.
☎ 02.48.96.39.82 📧 lesaintjean@wanadoo.fr
Closed Sun evening, Mon, a week in the Feb school holidays and a fortnight Aug/Sept.

A restaurant that's worth a visit. It has a rustic dining room complete with flowers, beams and a wonderful old parquet floor. Chef Philippe Perrichon prepares a quite incredible set menu for 95F that includes cheese and dessert. That's the best value for money you'll find in town, so you hardly need to venture into the realms of the other menus, 100–185F, though the specialities are worth a try: smoked zander with blinis and seaweed and salmon stuffed with green Berry lentils. Booking essential at weekends. Free coffee.

ORVAL   18200 (4KM W)

🛏 |O| HÔTEL-RESTAURANT DU PONT DU CHER*

2 av. de la Gare; it's on the D925.
☎ 02.48.96.00.51 ➡ 02.48.96.49.26
Closed Sun evening and Mon except on public holidays. **Garden**. **Car park**.

Service noon–2pm and 7.30–9pm. A pleasant country inn with geraniums at the windows. You can sit at a table in the glassed-in terrace and admire the lovely view of the Cher and the countryside. This is serious, traditional cooking and the professional chef does a particularly good duck in orange sauce. Cheapest set menu 70F. The hotel is quiet and comfortable, with doubles from 160–200F.

BRUÈRE-ALLICHAMPS   18200 (9KM NW)

|O| AUBERGE DE L'ABBAYE DE NOIRLAC

How to get there: at Saint-Amand, take the N144 in the direction of Bourges; 4km further on, turn onto the

Noirlac road. It's opposite the abbey.
☎ 02.48.96.22.58
Closed Tues evening and Wed.

They turned one of the old abbey chapels into a restaurant with a bistro where, in summer, you can get cheap snacks – sandwiches, an omelette or a plate of *charcuterie* at reasonable prices. The proper restaurant, which serves more serious food, has red quarry-tiles on the floor, beams and exposed stonework. Chef Pascal Verdier cooks meat and fish with equal skill; try duck breast with pan-fried *foie gras*, or young rabbit with horn of plenty mushrooms. Prices are good – the cheapest set menu at 98F includes cheese and dessert, with others at 135F and 170F.

SAINT-BENOÎT-SUR-LOIRE   45730

🏠 HÔTEL DU LABRADOR**

7 pl. de l'Abbaye; it's opposite the basilica.
☎ 02.38.35.74.38 ➽ 02.38.35.72.99
ℰ oteldulabrador@wanadoo.fr
Closed Jan. **Disabled access. Garden. TV.**
Car park.

The hotel is in a little square that's so peaceful you can sit quietly and meditate – maybe it picks up good vibrations from the abbey. It's a charming place. The rooms in the main building are a little old-fashioned, while those in the newer annexe are more comfortable and tastefully decorated. Some have beams, others a view of the abbey or the countryside. Doubles with hand basin 175F, with shower or bath 335F. There's no restaurant but there is a tea room with a very pleasant terrace, and half-board can be arranged in conjunction with the *Grand Saint-Benoît* (see below).

🍴|◉| LE GRAND SAINT-BENOÎT

7 pl. Saint-André.
☎ 02.38.35.11.92 ➽ 02.38.35.13.79
ℰ oteldulabrador@wanadoo.fr
Closed Sun evening, Mon, Sat lunchtime and 27 Aug–3 Sept and 24 Dec–23 Jan.

Even after it had just opened, this establishment quickly earned a reputation as one of the best tables in the region, and it's not one of the most expensive, either. The heavenly cuisine is simple, unusual and stamped with the personality of the chef. The weekday menu is less interesting, though perfectly adequate, but the 140F menu is splendid; snail pancake, roast zander with Chinon wine, veal chop in coriander *jus* and a caramel and hazelnut soufflé. Other menus up to 270F. Free coffee.

SALBRIS   41300

🍴 🏠 |◉| DOMAINE DE VALAUDRAN***

Route de Romorentin; it's at the Salbris exit from the mortorway, on the right as you head for Romorentin.
☎ 02.54.97.20.00 ➽ 02.54.97.12.22
ℰ info@valaudran.com
Closed 22 Jan–26 Feb.
Swimming pool. Disabled access. Garden. TV. Car park.

Service noon–2pm and 7–10pm. The magnificent 19th-century mansion stands proudly at the end of an avenue of trees. The interior has been brightly decorated with taste and sophistication and would readily deserve a place in a glossy magazine. The dining room extends to a terrace, cool in the mottled shade of the trees and the shimmering reflections of the swimming pool. The rooms are superb and ultra-comfortable, 595–650F. Tantalising smells come from the kitchens of chef Christophe Cosme, who trained under Bernard Loiseau in Saulieu, and he has forgotten none of the great man's teaching: just try the semi-cooked *foie gras* with the fig and Bourbon compote, the Sologne pigeon and the excellent *tarte tatin*. You can dine here for remarkably little. The weekday set menu changes daily and costs a mere 98F with others 160–240F, and there's an extensive *à la carte* menu. Very pleasant, welcoming staff. Free apéritif.

NOUAN-LE-FUZELIER   41600 (12KM N)

🍴|◉| LE DAHU

14 rue Henri-Chapron; take the N20 in the direction of La Ferté-Saint-Aubin.
☎ 02.54.88.72.88 ➽ 02.54.88.21.28
Closed Tues except in July–Aug and 16 Feb–20 March.
Car park.

Service noon–2pm and 7.15–9.15pm. Marie-Thérèse and Jean-Luc Germain have created an incredible garden around their restaurant dedicated to the mythical "dahu". In an otherwise drab suburb their wonderful half-timbered farmhouse is surrounded by greenery. The cosy interior manages to be both rustic and elegant. The menus start at 100F (not available Sat evening or Sun), then 130–255F, and list all sorts of delights; snails with pigeon with ginger and honey, crayfish tails with coriander, warm apricot tart and pear *fondant*. Free apéritif.

|◉| LE RABOLIOT

1 av. de la Mairie (Centre).

☎ 02.54.94.40.00
Closed Wed and mid-Jan to mid-Feb. **Car park**.

The chef is a local personality, with a reputation that goes before him. He's very welcoming and really passionate about what he does. This is an excellent restaurant with honest prices. Try the specialities; fresh *fois gras*, snail ravioli, beef with marrow bone or *foie gras*, veal kidneys, zander with sliced Belles de Rontenay potatoes, rabbit leg stuffed with girolle mushrooms, and pan-fried eel. There is plenty of game in season. The desserts are tempting, particularly the apricot tart with thyme granita and the rhubarb *mousseline*. *Menu touristique* 100F, weekdays only, and others up to 220F. At lunchtime, they serve simpler dishes – like free-range chicken with sage, potatoes *gratinée* with Sauvignon – for 40–50F.

SAINT-VIÂTRE   41210 (20KM NW)

🎿 🏠 |●| AUBERGE DE LA CHICHONE**
pl. de l'Église; by the N20 and then the D93.
☎ 02.54.88.91.33 ➡ 02.54.96.18.66
Closed Wed and a fortnight in March. **TV**.

Service noon–2.30pm and 7.30–10pm. In summer, you'll have to book a table in the garden which is popular with the regulars. The interior is typical of a Sologne farmhouse, decorated in a bourgeois rustic style with hunting trophies on the walls and beams that show the patina of age. The subtle cooking is inspired by the immediate region; dishes like *petit-salé* made with duck or stuffed carp. Set menus from 85F – not available Sun – to 185F; they are all pretty substantial. Doubles 290F with shower/wc, 320F with bath. There's a 14th-century church just across from the inn which bears witness to pilgrimages of former centuries. The *route des étangs* starts here, so you'll need a fresh film in your camera. Free coffee.

SANCERRE   18300

|●| RESTAURANT LA POMME D'OR
pl. de la Mairie (Centre). If you're coming from Sancerre, follow the signs for the town hall.
☎ 02.48.54.13.30
Closed Tues in high season, Wed, and a week at Christmas.

An elegant restaurant in a narrow street in the old part of town. The cooking uses fresh, seasonal produce and it's traditional without being too heavy to suit modern tastes. Dishes have some original rustic touches; roast

zander in Sancerre, veal kidneys in thyme-flavoured juices, or young pigeon with spices. The 92F menu is excellent value and there are others 132–235F. The proprietor, Didier Turpin, is the master of his cellar and offers a wonderful selection of wines, including some venerable Pouilly-Fumés, at very attractive prices.

SAINT-SATUR   18300 (3KM NE)

🎿 🏠 |●| HÔTEL-RESTAURANT LE LAURIER**
29 rue du Commerce; by the D955.
☎ 02.48.54.17.20 ➡ 02.48.54.04.54
Closed Sun evening and Mon except in July–Aug, Thurs out of season, the first fortnight in March and the last three weeks in Nov. **TV**.

After buying a few good bottles in Sancerre, carry on to Saint-Satur. You'll find this place swathed in Virginia creeper, 100m from a handsome abbey. The dining room, with its copperware, exposed beams and old wooden furniture, has clearly been decorated by someone with a taste for authenticity. You'll pay 120F for a double with basin and 250F for a larger room with bath – prices that are truly reasonable for this very touristy area. The restaurant offers good regional cooking with set menus at 80F (weekdays only) and 100–250F. Its specialities are poached eggs in wine *à l'ancienne*, calf's head and tongue with two different sauces, zander with chive butter, and game in season. Free coffee. 10% discount on the room rate Dec–March.

CHAVIGNOL   18300 (5KM W)

|●| RESTAURANT LA CÔTE DES MONTS DAMNÉS
Le bourg; from Sancerre, take the D955 in the direction of Cosne/Gien and then the D183.
☎ 02.48.54.01.72 ➡ 02.48.54.14.24
Closed Sun evening, Mon, and Feb.

Service 12.15–1.30pm and 7.30–9.30pm. The "damned mountains" give their name both to a highly reputed vineyard in Sancerre and to this inn, a rustic place with beams, patterned curtains and a cosy, almost romantic atmosphere. Local produce plays the central role in robust dishes with a very distinct character; try tagliatelle with *crottin*, a fairly strong goat's cheese made in the village, saddle of lamb stuffed with veal kidneys, or the very good salmon with a sauce made from wine lees. Menus start at 118F. The wine list is full of bargains from all parts of France. Nice staff.

SANCOINS 18600

☗ HÔTEL DU PARC**

8 rue Marguerite-Audoux.
☎ 02.48.74.56.60 ➡ 02.48.74.61.30
Closed 1–15 Jan. **Garden. Car park**.

This classy place looks like a château and is set in extensive grounds. The rooms are lovely, with Baroque mirrors and red or blue velvet bedspreads, and they are quiet. Pleasant welcome. Doubles with shower or bath 230F, or rooms sleeping three or four 290F.

SELLES-SUR-CHER 41130

⅍ ☗ |●| LE LION D'OR

14 pl. de la Paix (Centre); it's behind the church.
☎ 02.54.97.40.83

The smaller dining room is really nice, done out with fishing motifs – an ideal place for lunch or a plate of something tasty. There's a larger dining room which is good for more elaborate festivities. The chef also runs a food shop where you can buy dishes to take home. Menus 85F and 129F and a range of simpler dishes and regional specialities; grilled goat's cheese with smoked salmon, pike steak with truffles and vegetable soufflé, medallions of lamb and potato cakes, and a marvellous dark chocolate gâteau. The wines are reasonably priced, too. Rooms are decent, 258F for a double with shower/wc or bath. Free Kir.

SOUVIGNY-EN-SOLOGNE 41600

⅍ |●| LA PERDRIX ROUGE

22 rue du Gattuces.
☎ 02.38.54.88.41.05.
Closed Mon, Tues, 16 Feb–3 March, 27 June–5 July and 26 Aug–3 Sept.

The dining room manages to be at once sophisticated and rustic, with tasteful furniture and good table linen. Warm greeting and efficient service. They offer *amuse-bouches* while you peruse the menu. The food is light and tasty; *foie gras* with Muscat de Beaume-de-Venise, *aiguillette* of roast pigeon with honey and baby cabbage, rack of lamb with garden herbs, and zander with *beurre blanc*. Many dishes are based on local recipes and use only fresh produce. Weekday menu 85F then 145–300F. Good value. Free *digestif*.

SULLY-SUR-LOIRE 45600

⅍ ☗ |●| HÔTEL-RESTAURANT DE LA POSTE**

11 rue du Faubourg-Saint-Germain (Centre).
☎ 02.38.36.26.22 ➡ 02.38.36.39.35
TV. Car park.

Service noon–2pm and 7–9pm. Some of the rooms in this old coaching inn have a view of the Loire. In others, you'll have to make do with the TV. Doubles 200F with washing facilities and 300F with shower/wc or bath. Menus 96–210F or *à la carte* feature lots of fish dishes, with crab cakes with sorrel or fillet of perch as a main course. This place is a bit of an institution in Sully and the large cage full of parrots is equally famous. 10% discount on the room rate.

TOURS 37000

SEE MAP OVERLEAF

☗ HÔTEL SAINT-ÉLOI*

79 bd. Béranger. **MAP A2-2**
☎ 02.47.37.67.34 ➡ 02.47.39.34.67
TV. Garden.

There's a superb magnolia tree in the garden, and the hotel is set back from the boulevard in a courtyard. This is a small place, run by a young couple, and it's clean, quiet, simple and friendly. Rooms come with washing facilities or shower/wc. Doubles 140–190F. Street parking in the boulevard or behind the hotel in rue Jules-Charpentier.

☗ HÔTEL RÉGINA

2 rue Pimbert. **MAP C1-4**
☎ 02.47.05.25.36 ➡ 02.47.66.08.72
Closed Christmas to 1 Jan.

A cheap, cheerful, simple and clean hotel with window-boxes full of flowers. It's really pretty and you feel so welcome that you wouldn't think it out of place to go down to breakfast in your slippers. Annie and Gérard Lachaize ran a hotel in Lyons for ten years so they know their job. The soundproofing is good and the cleanliness is evidenced by the smell of polish A double room with hand basin is 150F, or 195F with shower/wc. 5% discount.

⅍ ☗ |●| HÔTEL-RESTAURANT MODERNE**

1–3 rue Victor-Laloux. **MAP C2-3**
☎ 02.47.05.32.81 ➡ 02.47.05.71.50
Restaurant closed Sat and Mon lunchtimes and Sun.
TV.

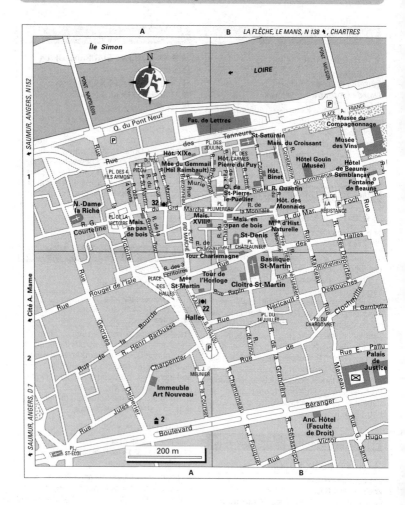

A   B   *LA FLÈCHE, LE MANS, N 138 ↖, CHARTRES*

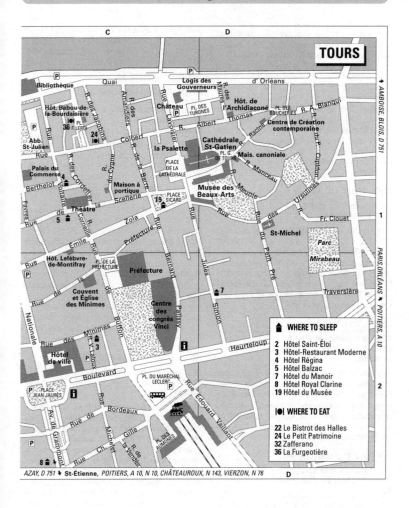

TOURS

AMBOISE, BLOIS, D 751

PARIS, ORLÉANS ← POITIERS, A 10

Bibliothèque
Quai
Logis des
Gouverneurs
d' Orléans

Hôt. Babou-de-
la-Bourdaisière
PL. F. LEROI
Château
PL. DES
TURONES
Hôt. de
l'Archidiaconé
PL. DES
BOUCHERIES
R. A. Blanqui

R. des Jacobins
R. des Amandiers
R. Lavoisier
Albert
Thomas
Racine
Centre de Création
contemporaine

Abb.
St-Julien
Colbert
la Psalette
Cathédrale
St-Gatien
PL. G.
DE TOURS
Mais. canoniale

R. du Cygne
R. de la Barre
PLACE
DE LA
CATHÉDRALE
R. Manceau

Palais du
Commerce
R. des Cordeliers
Berthelot
Voltaire
Maison à
portique
Scellerie
PLACE
SICARD
19
Musée des
Beaux-Arts
Meunier
R. des Ursulines

Favre
Rue
de la
Corneille
Théâtre
Zola
Rue
Rue du Petit Pré
Fr. Clouet

Émile
Préfecture
St-Michel
Parc
Mirabeau

Hôt. Lefèbvre-
de-Montifray
PL. DE LA
PRÉFECTURE
Préfecture
Bernard
Jules
Simon
7
Traversière

Rue
de
la
Couvent
et Église
des Minimes
Buffon
Centre
des
congrès
Vinci
Parissy
8

Rue
Nationale
des Minimes
3
Hôtel
de ville
Heurteloup

PLACE
JEAN JAURÈS
Boulevard
PL. DU MARÉCHAL
LECLERC
Rue Édouard Vaillant

Av. de Grammont
Rue de Bordeaux
Rue Ch. Gille
R. de Vendée
PL. DES
AUMÔNES

8

▲	**WHERE TO SLEEP**
2	Hôtel Saint-Éloi
3	Hôtel-Restaurant Moderne
4	Hôtel Régina
5	Hôtel Balzac
7	Hôtel du Manoir
8	Hôtel Royal Clarine
19	Hôtel du Musée

|●|	**WHERE TO EAT**
22	Le Bistrot des Halles
24	Le Petit Patrimoine
32	Zafferano
36	La Furgeotière

AZAY, D 751 ↓ **St-Étienne**, *POITIERS, A 10, N 10, CHÂTEAUROUX, N 143, VIERZON, N 76*

This hotel, a fine building in traditional Touraine style, is located in a quiet neighbourhood. There are 23 rooms in all, 190F with basin, 215F with shower, and twelve have bathrooms 290–340F; the ones in the attic have sloping ceilings. There's almost a hushed atmosphere but nothing will stop you enjoying the excellent tasty cooking. Set menus, 78F and 98F, feature things like salad with hot *rillons* and *andouillette*, salad with goat's cheese, apple flambéed with rum or pears in Chinon. 15 Oct–31 March. There's a pay car park nearby. 10% discount on the room rate.

☎ |●| HÔTEL DU MUSÉE

3 pl. François Sicard. **MAP C1-19**
☎ 02.47.66.63.81 ➡ 02.47.20.10.42

Though this establishment needs to be refurbished it would lose its charm with every coat of paint. The façade is worn but all the rooms are decorated differently, with lovely wood panelling, and either a terrace or a fireplace. The furniture is old but not rickety. Double rooms start at 210F. They have a lovely dining room, too, and menus start at 65F.

⅍ ☎ HÔTEL BALZAC**

47 rue de la Scellerie. **MAP C1-5**
☎ 02.47.05.40.87 ➡ 02.47.05.67.93
TV. Garden.

Right in the middle of town, this friendly, rather plush establishment has twenty rooms, fifteen with shower or bath (310F) and five with basin only (225F). Some are particularly quiet and spacious. In fine weather, eat your breakfast on the terrace or sit quietly over a drink. 10% discount after two nights.

☎ HÔTEL DU MANOIR**

2 rue Traversière. **MAP D2-7**
☎ 02.47.05.37.37 ➡ 02.47.05.16.00
TV.

This hotel, located in a quiet street, is a town house dating from the 19th century. There are twenty tastefully refurbished rooms in pastel colours and with English-style furniture. Doubles 260–290F with shower/wc. The attic rooms are very pleasant. Nice welcome, and very good value.

⅍ ☎ HÔTEL ROYAL CLARINE***

65 av. de Grammont. **MAP C2-8**
☎ 02.47.64.71.78 ➡ 02.47.05.84.62
Disabled access. TV. Pay lock-up garage.

This is a modern hotel with no great charm but a calm feeling. The bedrooms and the dining room are tastefully furnished in Louis XV and Louis XVI or contemporary style and they're very comfortable. All fifty rooms have bath, satellite TV and phone. Doubles from 380F. 10% discount.

|●| LE PETIT PATRIMOINE

58 rue Colbert. **MAP C1-24**
☎ 02.47.66.05.81
Closed Sun evening.

Service noon–2pm and 7–10pm. A regional restaurant of quality with a dining room decorated in salmon and orangey colours. The owner has a real interest in preserving the gastronomy of the Touraine though he's always keen to take it gently forwards. So the specialities are quite delicious: Touraine tart with *rillons* and goat's cheese, pike Bourgueil-style, entrecôte steak with Saint-Maure sauce, salmon envelope stuffed with Saint-Maure cheese, *andouillette à la Vouvrillonne* (sausage in Vouvray, a white Loire wine), *matelote* of veal with red wine, onions and mushrooms, and a superb selection of cheeses. If you've got room for dessert, try the pears in wine or the goat's cheese with blackberry jelly. Menus 70–155F and good Touraine wines from 60F. Best to book.

|●| LE BISTROT DES HALLES

31 pl. Gaston-Paillhou. **MAP A2-22**
☎ 02.47.61.54.93
Closes at 11pm.

Outside this old-fashioned brasserie there's an eye-catching red and green frontage, while inside the walls are covered with pictures from the turn of the (last) century. It attracts everyone from the great and the good to the ordinary folk. The service is faultless but that doesn't stop the place being relaxed and informal. Regional specialities – *pot-au-feu* with three meats, *rillons* (a local dish of diced pork), pork *rillettes*, *bouillabaisse* fish soup from the south and so on – have pride of place in here. Try their *tarte tatin*, the upside-down apple tart with caramelised fruit. *Formule* at 75F and a menu at 135F, while from Sept–May there are two seafood *formules* at 165F and 200F. Reckon on 110F *à la carte*. Good selection of Loire wines.

|●| LA FURGEOTIÈRE

19 pl. Foire-le-Roi. **MAP C1-36**
☎ 02.47.66.94.75

Furgeot is the family name of Marie-Hélène, who runs this place with her husband Michel.

The walls are in tufa, and there are wooden beams and French-style ceilings. If you feel like a traditional dish, opt for the oxtail *parmentier* (with mashed potato) or the saddle of rabbit with tarragon; the less conventional might go for the *croustillant* of pig's trotters in cider with sautéed potatoes and celeriac *purée*. Four menus 99–249F and a business lunch menu at 152F which includes apéritif, wine and coffee. The service is efficient, and the wines reasonably priced. In summer they put tables out on the square. Essential to book in the evening.

|O| ZAFFERANO

47 rue du Grand Marché. **MAP A1-32**
☎ 02.47.38.90.77
Closed Sun, Mon, the second fortnight in Aug and a week around Easter.

A pizzeria serving all sorts of Italian dishes from different regions and using fresh, home-made pasta. Forget about *bolognese* and tomato sauce and let them surprise you. Their meat dishes are amazing – the *saltinbocca*, *piccata* and *osso-bucco* are prepared with precision. Menus 100F and 152F or around 140F *à la carte*. But the success of the place is down to the atmosphere; there's always opera playing and you really feel you're in Italy and enjoying the best the country has to offer. They also have a small grocery counter selling Italian specialities. Credit cards accepted only for bills over 140F.

FONDETTES   37230 (5KM E)

⅍|O| AUBERGE DE PORC-VALLIÈRES

Vallières; it's on the N152 in the direction of Langeais.
☎ 02.47.42.24.04 ➡ 02.47.49.98.83
Closed Mon and Tues evenings, Wed, ten days in winter and a fortnight at the end of June.

Because the inn is right on the edge of the N152, you might hesitate to stop. But it's worth it. There are lovely tiles on the floor, armfuls of wild flowers from the fields in huge vases and a relaxed, pleasant atmosphere. You hardly hear the traffic at all. The welcome is friendly and straightforward and the cuisine brilliantly judged. There's only one menu, 90F, which changes all the time and that's what attracts the locals. Original dishes and their own specialities: lots of fried fish from the Loire, eel or pike. Free coffee.

VOUVRAY   37210 (8KM NE)

⌂|O| LE GRAND VATEL

8 av. Léon Brulé.
☎ 02.47.52.70.32 ➡ 02.47.52.74.52
Closed Sun evening and Mon.

Everything here is made on the premises and the results are brilliant: *terrine* of *foie gras*, warm oyster ravioli with a light cream and herb sauce, or a moist joint of rabbit stuffed with onion preserve. Waitress service, and informed advice on the dishes from the chef's delightful wife, who clearly has a fine palate. Menus 118–352F. There's an impressive list of Vouvray wines and some are served by the glass. Upstairs, there are a few, well maintained rooms. A double with shower/wc or bath costs 220–270F.

SEMBLANÇAY   37360 (12KM NW)

⅍ ⌂ |O| HOSTELLERIE DE LA MÈRE HAMARD**

pl. de l'église (Centre); take the N138 in the direction of Le Mans.
☎ 02.47.56.62.04 ➡ 02.47.56.53.61
Closed Sun evening, Mon, and mid-Feb to mid-March.
TV. Car park.

You'll dine on delicious regional dishes and gourmet cuisine that has a reputation hereabouts. The dining room is comfortable and welcoming. Menus from 100F (not served on Sun),up to 270F. Specialities include duck *foie gras* with morels, pigeon with truffles and potato cakes with *foie gras*. There are nine lovely double rooms in a delightful annexe from 240F with shower/wc. Free coffee.

MONNAIE   37380 (14KM NE)

|O| RESTAURANT AU SOLEIL LEVANT**

53 rue Nationale (Centre); it's on the N10 north of Tours.
☎ 02.47.56.10.34 ➡ 02.47.56.45.22
Closed Sun and Wed evenings, Mon, the first fortnight in Jan and the first fortnight in Aug.

This is among the best gourmet restaurants in the area, with a stylish interior decorated in bright, luminous colours. They produce exceptional dishes that bear no resemblance to the usual things that pass for regional specialities. The best ingredients of the season are imaginatively combined to create wonderful results. However hungry you are and whatever you have to spend, there's a set menu to suit you: fillet steak in Chinon, roast zander with truffle fragments and Vouvray sauce or veal sweetbreads with morel mushrooms – all delicious. Menus 99F (except Sun), 145F and 190F.

VANNES-SUR-COSSON 45510

|●| RESTAURANT LE VIEUX RELAIS

route d'Isdes.
☎ 02.38.58.04.14
Garden. Car park.

It's easy to see that this superb, Solognote manor house is pretty old but you wouldn't guess that the original buildings go back to 1462 and that the beams come from a building in the 800s. It's been an inn of some kind since 1515 and is one of the six oldest inns in France.Who made the gash in the staircase with a sword? If only the walls could talk! It's an absolutely sumptuous place and the cooking doesn't let the surroundings down. You should certainly go for the chef's *foie gras* if it's on the menu. He uses seasonal produce for all his dishes so it's hard to list his specialities but the game is superb, as are the calf's sweetbreads with whisky and don't miss out on the *crème brûlée*. Menus start at 98F. Essential to book.

VENDÔME 41100

☗ |●| HÔTEL-RESTAURANT L'AUBERGE DE LA MADELEINE

pl. de la Madeleine (Centre); head in the direction of Blois.
☎ 02.54.77.20.79 ✦ 02.54.80.00.02
Hotel closed Feb. Restaurant closed Wed. TV. Car park.

Service noon–1.45pm and 7.30–9pm. An unpretentious place with attractive enough rooms. Doubles 210F with shower/wc, 240–290F with bath. Numbers 7 and 8 are the largest. Good plain cooking with set menus 85–220F. The one at 140F is realy worth a try given the choice of dishes like calf's head and a main course choice of zander with vanilla or rabbit with mushrooms. You can eat out in the garden. Friendly welcome.

⚆|●| RESTAURANT LE PARIS

1 rue Darreau (North); go up faubourg Chartrain and it's after the train station.
☎ 02.54.77.02.71 ✦ 02.54.73.17.71
Closed Sun and Tues evenings, Mon, and 20 July–13 Aug.

This is an excellent gourmet restaurant. It's run by a charming woman, the service is faultless and the chef, who has a particular talent for sauces, is inspired. Try the calf's head *ravigote* in a spicy *vinaigrette*, ox kid-

neys with Rougier, turbot *millefeuille* with *mousseline* sauce, or the cep pancakes. Delicious dishes, all of which go well with a good local wine like the Bourgueil Domaine Lalande. Set menus 90–180F. Free coffee.

SAINT-OUEN 41100 (2KM N)

|●| LA VALLÉE

34 rue Barré-de-Saint-Venant; from Vendôme, take the D92 and head for Paris and the centre of Saint-Ouen.
☎ 02.54.77.29.93 ✦ 02.54.73.16.96
Closed Sun evening and Mon except public holidays, Wed evening Oct–May, and 15 Jan–15 Feb.

Don't let the uninspiring exterior put you off – go straight in and take a look at the menu. You won't regret it. Even the cheapest set menu at 95F (not served Sun), has a selection of delights. The specialities change with the seasons, the cooking is sophisticated and the dishes are beautifully presented. Courteous welcome. Other menus 130–230F.

VEUIL 36600 (6KM SW)

⚆|●| AUBERGE SAINT-FIACRE

Le bourg (Centre).
☎ 02.54.40.32.78
Closed Tues evening and Wed except public holidays and Feb school holidays. **Disabled access.**

A 17th-century inn in a flower-filled village with a stream babbling through it. In summer you dine under the ancient chestnut trees to the accompaniment of the trickling fountain and in winter around the giant fireplace. The chef changes his menus frequently, inspired by fresh, changing seasonal produce. Light, tasty dishes include snails and veal sweetbread salad or Dublin Bay prawns *croustiallant*, panfried escalope of *foie gras* with figs, and moist fig and almond cake with vanilla ice cream. Menus 130F (not Sun), 185F and 225F. Free *digestif*.

PEZOU 41100 (15KM N)

|●| AUBERGE DE LA SELLERIE

Fontaine; it's on the RN10.
☎ 02.54.23.41.43
Closed Mon, Tues and three weeks in Jan.

Rustic but chic decor. It's a good inn set back from the main road from Chartres to Vendôme. There's an attractive menu at 99F, which changes nearly every day and includes half a bottle of wine and coffee. Dishes are of the order of warm *andouille* salad, *brandade* of salt cod, farmhouse cheeses and strawberry *au gratin*. The cuisine is rich, inventive and of good quality. Other menus 150–280F. They serve until late, and even if you show up towards the end of a service they still give you a smile.

LAVARDIN   41800 (18KM W)

⚑ IOI LE RELAIS D'ANTAN

6 pl. du Capitaine du Vignau (Centre); take the D917, when you get to Saint-Rimay, turn left on the road to Montoire.
☎ 02.54.86.61.33
Closed Tues, Mon in winter.

You're in for a real feast and at a reasonable price. The choice is deliberately limited so the chef can ensure only the freshest ingredients are used to create his refined, inventive dishes such as prawn lasagna with parmesan cheese and grilled zander with *beurre blanc*. Two menus at 145F and 190F. The service is friendly and the dining room is pretty. They only have a few tables so you need to book. Free coffee.

NANÇAY   18330 (18KM NE)

IOI LE RELAIS DE SOLOGNE

2 rue Salbris.
☎ 02.48.51.82.26 ➡ 02.48.51.10.70
Closed Tues evening, Wed, a fortnight in Feb and a fortnight in Sept. **Disabled access**.

Alain-Fournier, who wrote the bewitching tale *Le Grand Meaulnes*, spent his childhood in this little village. The house is almost hidden under all the flowers and it's hard to resist

going up and pushing open the door. Alain Bonnot is the owner and chef, and his forte is his sauces. He is unbeatable when it comes to preparing game and other regional dishes. His specialities are *poulet en Barbouille – coq au vin*, in other words – salmon with sorrel sauce and *meringue Relais*. You can eat in the elegant dining room, decorated mainly in royal blue, or on the terrace. Set menus at 105F and 160F or there's a weekday lunch menu at 77F.

YZEURES-SUR-CREUSE   37290

⚓ IOI HÔTEL-RESTAURANT LA PROMENADE***

1 pl. du 11-Novembre (Centre); it's on the D104.
☎ 02.47.91.49.00 ➡ 02.47.94.46.12
Closed Tues and Jan. **TV**. **Car park**.

This hotel is in a handsome 18th-century building that used to be a coaching inn. The fifteen rooms are decorated in restrained rustic style in delicate pale green, grey and dark red. Doubles with bath 320F. There's a small sitting room with a piano on the mezzanine. Mme Bussereau creates delicious dishes that bear her own inventive imprint, from the best produce she can find on the market – game in season, free-range poultry and good fish. She also makes the house *terrines* and bakes the bread. Set menus 99–315F. The cheapest one is not served after 8.30pm or on Sunday. A good restaurant.

CHAMPAGNE-ARDENNES

08 Ardennes

10 Aube

51 Marne

52 Haute-Marne

AIX-EN-OTHE 10160

🎿 🏠 |●| AUBERGE DE LA SCIERIE***

3 route de Druisy, lieu-dit La Vove; it's 1.5km from Aix-en-Othe on the D374.
☎ 03.25.46.71.26 📠 03.25.46.65.69
Closed Mon and Tues 1 Sept–30 April. **Swimming pool. Garden. TV. Car park**.

The stream winding through the peaceful grounds of this hotel used to power the sawmill. Much of the original charm of the 17th-century building has been retained. About fifteen stylish rooms, all 407F with shower/wc or bath. In summer they set tables out in the garden for lunch or dinner. There's an 88F lunch menu (not Sun or public holidays), and others 148–260F. Specialities include trout stuffed with mushrooms, Troyes *andouillette* in pastry, house *foie gras terrine* and *crème brûlée* with cider Ratafia. 10% discount on the room rate 1 Sept–15 May.

BAR-SUR-AUBE 10200

🎿 🏠 HÔTEL SAINT-PIERRE

5 rue Saint Pierre (Centre)
☎ 03.25.27.13.58
Closed Sun and public holidays. **Car park**.

A simple, well-run family-style hotel just opposite Saint-Pierre church which is worth a visit for its wooden gallery and tombstones. Rooms 8, 9 and 10 have a view of the church but the bells start ringing at 7am. Doubles with basin 130F, shower (wc along the landing) 140F, or shower/wc 180F. There's no restaurant, but there is a lively bar. A nice place at very reasonable prices. Free coffee.

|●| UN P'TIT CREUX

pl. du Corps-de-Garde (Centre); entrance 24 rue Nationale.
☎ 03.25.27.37.75
Closed Sun and Mon except in Aug.

This bright, friendly *crêperie* is in a modern shopping centre in the old centre of Bar. It's ideal if you fancy a quick bite. The specials menu features pancakes and pizzas in a curious alliance between Brittany and Italy. There are several other menus, based mostly on *galettes*. Menus 58–140F. Great in summer, when you can sit outside on the terrace.

|●| LA TOQUE BARALBINE

18 rue Nationale.
☎ 03.25.27.20.34
Closed Sun evening and Mon except public holidays, and three weeks in Jan.

After years working in different restaurants on the Côte d'Azur, the owner returned to his roots and opened his own gourmet restaurant. He won a loyal local following within months of opening. Sophisticated cooking in very pleasant surroundings. Menus 70–295F. Friendly, unaffected staff. Service noon–2pm and 7–9.30pm. Free coffee.

🎿 |●| LE CELLIER AUX MOINES

rue du Général-Vouillemont; it's behind St-Pierre church.
☎ 03.25.27.08.01
Closed Sun, Mon, and Tues evening.

The cellar is magnificent. It was built in the 12th century and in 1912, when the local sparkling wine lost the right to be called champagne, the local winegrowers held angry meetings here. Scrawled inscriptions on the walls, some in verse, recount the suffering of

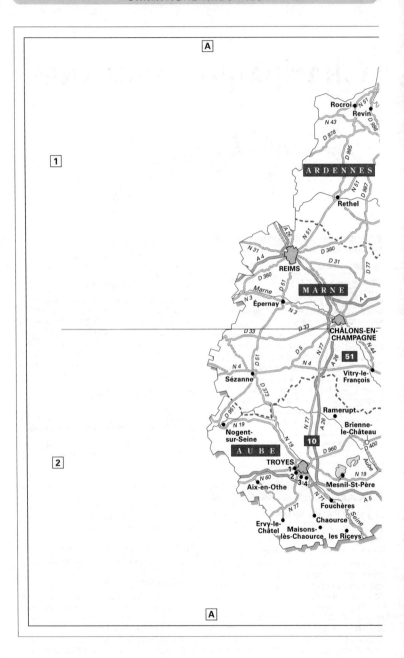

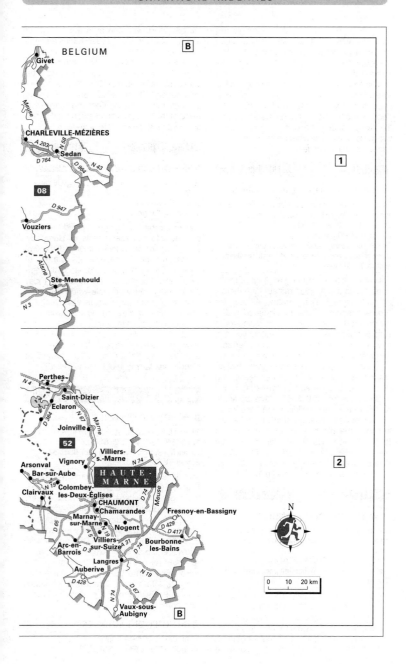

the wine-growing villages. After a struggle, the wine was reclassified as champagne and you will find it on the pricey end of the wine list. Make the most of the confident cooking; *lentillons* salad with Champagne, smoked salmon and haddock, stuffed boneless chicken with a sweet and sour onion marmalade, and grilled Chaource cheese. Menus 80–175F. The decor is a bit spartan, though the candles on the tables soften the general appearance. Service is on the brisk side of efficient, but it will relax in time. Free coffee.

ARSONVAL   10200 (6KM NW)

🏕 🏠 |●| HOSTELLERIE LA CHAUMIÈRE**

How to get there: take the N19 in the direction of Troyes and it's on the left on the way out of Arsonval.
☎ 03.25.27.91.02 ➡ 03.25.27.90.26
📧 lachaumiere@pem.net
Closed Sun evening and Mon except in summer and public holidays, and mid-Feb to mid-March. **Disabled access. TV. Car park.**

This old village inn, run by an Anglo-French couple, has a very good restaurant – there's an old, red English telephone box for "*couleur locale*". Carefully prepared meals are generously served in a lovely dining room with wooden beams. In fine weather you can have lunch or dinner on the shady terrace, and they have opened a new dining room as well. Dishes include house *foie gras*, chicken supreme with melting Chaource cheese, and fish in champagne sauce. Weekday menu 100F with others 150–300F. There are some rooms in the main building and others in a starkly modern structure that's out of keeping with the old half-timbered house, but they all have views of the grounds and the river. Doubles with shower/wc 320F or 340F with bath. Good, friendly welcome. 10% discount on the room rate Oct–April

DOLANCOURT   10200 (9KM NW)

🏕|●| LE MOULIN DU LANDION

How to get there; going towards Troyes on the N19, take the left fork 2km after Arsonval and follow the signs in the village.
☎ 03.25.27.92.17 ➡ 03.25.27.94.44
Closed 1 Dec–15 Feb. **Swimming pool. Garden. TV. Car park.**

This place is ultra-classy. The shady garden has a swimming pool; inside, the decor is smart and the bright, spacious rooms have small balconies. They are modern in contrast to the rustic dining room, which is in the old mill. The restaurant overlooks the river, while

the bay windows open onto the mill wheel which is still in working order. Tables are also set at the waterside. Prices reflect the quality of the surroundings. Double rooms run 425–470F; breakfast costs 50F extra. The cheapest set menu at 110F is not served on the weekend. Other menus 165–340F. This is a tranquil spot not far from the mad, mad world of the Nigoland amusement park. 10% discount on the room rate Nov–April.

CLAIRVAUX-SUR-AUBE   10310 (14KM SE)

🏠 |●| HÔTEL-RESTAURANT DE L'ABBAYE*

18–19 route de Dijon; where the D12 and D396 cross.
☎ 03.25.27.80.12 ➡ 03.25.27.75.79
Closed 20 Dec–10 Jan.
Garden. TV. Car park.

You've left the Champagne behind here and crossed into the vast forests of Burgundy. Saint Bernard of Clairvaux founded the first Cistercian abbey in these woods in the 12th century. The monks of the order shut themselves away from the outside world, and today the building houses people who have been sent away from the outside world – it's a prison, with high walls and watchtowers. The hotel is just opposite, which some may find sinister, especially in room 17, which has a view of that eerie building. Doubles from 150F with basin to 230F with bath. It's very quiet at night. Weekday menu 66F, then 77–125F.

BOURBONNE-LES-BAINS   52400

🏠 |●| HÔTEL D'ORFEUIL**

29 rue d'Orfeuil (Southwest); 80m from the spa.
☎ 03.25.90.05.71 ➡ 03.25.84.46.25
Closed Nov–March. **Swimming pool. Disabled access. TV. Car park.**

This lovely 18th-century house has aged beautifully. It's on a hillside surrounded by a leafy garden where they've built a very pleasant pool. Very tasteful inside, with antique family furniture, rugs and fireplaces. It's a welcoming hotel where you get good value for money: 240–300F for a double with shower in the new annexe — the old part is reserved for people taking the waters. Ask for a room with a balcony and a view over the park. Informal restaurant with set menus 60–160F. Healthy buffet breakfasts for the diet-conscious.

🏠 |●| HÔTEL DES SOURCES**

12 rue de l'Amiral Pierre (Centre).
☎ 03.25.87.86.00 ➡ 03.25.87.86.33

Closed Nov–March.
TV. **Garden**. **Car park**.

A dynamic, young couple run this establishment offering modern, functional and pleasant rooms. Ask to see one or two, because their size varies considerably – number 34 is big and has a corner sitting room and a garden view. All rooms have en-suite facilities and some have a separate wc; doubles with shower/wc and corner kitchen, 240F. Half board from 300F per person. Unlike others in town, the restaurant does not limit itself to diet cuisine; specialities include duck breast with sherry vinegar and honey, *timbale* of scallops with chicory and an excellent chocolate *trufflon*. Menus 75–200F. Professional yet personal welcome.

🔆 🛏 |○| LES ARMOISES-HÔTEL LE JEANNE D'ARC***

12 rue de l'Amiral Pierre (Centre).
☎ 03.25.90.46.00 ➡ 03.25.88.78.71
Closed Sun evening and Nov to mid-March. **Swimming pool**. **Garden**. **TV**. **Car park**.

Not surprisingly, this is the only gourmet restaurant in this old spa town where people come for their health. The standard is good: *fricassée* of snails in Coiffy wine and pan-fried salmon with smoked bacon, or, for dessert, *biscuit fraîcheur* with chocolate, pecan and chestnuts with white chocolate, no less. Set menus 98–198F. Service in the garden in fine weather. The rooms are simple rather than charming and a double with shower or bath is 270–350F. Most people come here to take the waters and the town is quiet after 8pm; last orders here are at 9pm. 10% discount or free apéritif with dinner.

FRESNOY-EN-BASSIGNY   52400 (12.5KM NW)

🔆 |○| RESTAURANT DU LAC DE MORIMOND

How to get there: on the D139, 2.5km after Fresnoy-en-Bassigny, take the right turn for lac de Morimond.
☎ 03.25.90.80.86
Closed evenings except June–Sept, and Nov–March. **Disabled access**. **Garden**. **Car park**.

In the depths of the country, close to the ruined Cistercian abbey, a little lake encircled by forest. In the dark of the night fishermen come to tickle for carp. This is the ideal spot to enjoy some freshly caught fish or a nice fillet steak with wild girolle mushrooms, which you can eat on the terrace overlooking the water. The dining room is also lovely, with an attractive, welcoming fireplace. You get a good selection of dishes on the lengthy menu – set price 130F or 150F *à la carte*. Free apéritif.

MOUZON   08210 (18KM E)

|○| LES ECHEVINS

33 rue Charles-de-Gaulle.
☎ 03.24.26.10.90

The dining room is on the first floor of a glorious, 17th-century Spanish house. The excellent cuisine combines a traditional style with a modern approach and the dishes are meticulously prepared. While you order, a profusion of *amuse-bouches* and other delicacies are served by the smiling, professional waiting staff. The menus, 100–190F, list dishes such as asparagus and leeks with *ravigote* sauce and fish *paupiettes*. One of the best restaurants in the area.

CHÂLONS-EN-CHAMPAGNE   51000

🛏 HÔTEL PASTEUR**

46 rue Pasteur (East); it's about 600m from the church of Notre-Dame-en-Vaux.
☎ 03.26.68.10.00 ➡ 03.26.21.51.09
Disabled access. **Garden**. **TV**. **Car park**.

Part of this hotel used to be a convent which explains the superb, grand staircase. The quiet rooms over the courtyard at the back get the sun. Doubles 180F with shower but no TV, 240F with shower/wc and telephone, or 280F with bath.

🔆 🛏 |○| RESTAURANT JEAN-PAUL SOUPLY

8 faubourg Saint-Antoine; it's 500m from the town centre opposite the young workers' hostel.
☎ 03.26.68.18.91 ➡ 03.26.21.76.47
✉ Restaurant.souply@wanadoo.fr
Closed Sun except Easter Day and Whitsun for communion celebrations, and Aug. **Car park**.

A family business where everyone has a role. Grandmother runs the bar, the daughter-in-law manages the restaurant and the son is the owner and chef. He specialises in traditional dishes served in portions to satisfy a hungry trooper. Menus 70–145F and a weekday *formule* at 60F. They have a few modest rooms where you can stay half-board at 195F per person. Free coffee.

🔆 🛏 HÔTEL DE LA CITÉ**

12 rue de la Charrière (Northeast); take rue J-J Rousseau, turn right after pl. des Ursulines and follow the signs to the Cité Administrative.
☎ 03.26.64.31.20 ➡ 03.26.70.96.22

Disabled access. Garden. TV.

This is a peaceful, provincial place, very much like a family guesthouse, with a regular clientele of businessmen, sales reps and students. Everyone is warmly greeted by the owners who spare no effort in keeping their hotel nice – it's clean though not luxurious. A few rooms look onto the garden where you can enjoy breakfast (30F) in fine weather or just relax with a book. 200F for a room with a shower, and 220F with a bath. Room 1 is bright and spacious, with an enormous bathroom. There's a pool table and TV room. 10% discount.

🏄 ≜ HÔTEL DU POT D'ÉTAIN**

18 pl. de la République (Centre).
☎ 03.26.68.09.09 ➡ 03.26.68.58.18
TV. Car park.

This impressive 15th-century house has been beautifully renovated by the family who owns it. Double rooms with shower/wc and telephone 300F, with bath 310F. There's also a pleasant single room and six family-size rooms which sleep four. Number 102 has a view of the square which is lively day and night. Monsieur Georges, who used to be a baker, prepares the croissants for breakfast and all the tarts and puddings – he'll bake different things as the mood takes him. You can leave your car parked outside the hotel and explore Châlons on foot. Weekend deal; stay Fri, Sat and Sun and you get the third night free – Jan–March only.

≜ I●I HÔTEL LE RENARD***

24 pl. de la République (Centre).
☎ 03.26.68.03.78 ➡ 03.26.64.50.07
Closed Sat lunchtime, Sun evening and Christmas–New Year. **TV. Car park.**

The futuristic decor in the 35 rooms of this establishment has stood the test of time and still looks good – though some may not like the bed being positioned in the middle of the room. On the other hand, the party walls are thin and the hotel's noisy. Doubles 360F with bath. The brasserie terrace is very popular because it opens out onto the square and serves pretty decent food. There is also a gourmet restaurant which offers a balance between modern tastes and traditional dishes. Menus 98F, 118F and 190F. Credit cards not accepted.

🏄 I●I LE PRÉ SAINT-ALPIN

2 [bis] rue de l'Abbé Lambert (Centre).
☎ 03.26.70.20.26 ➡ 03.26.68.52.20

This magnificent establishment dates back to 1850 and still has its resplendent stained-glass windows and moulded ceilings. It is a fine example of 19th-century architecture, displaying both nobility and elegance. But when you're sitting on the terrace on a beautiful summer evening, in a wonderfully serene atmosphere, you could be sitting down to dinner in your own home. Inventive cuisine: *parfait* of crab with turmeric, marinated salmon with four spices, pan-fried sea bream with fresh tomatoes and *reblochon* cheese, *fricassée* of quail *en rustique*, gazpacho of fresh fruit with mint, and fresh peach crumble. The chef, who trained in some of the best kitchens, achieves the perfect balance between tradition and innovation. Menus from 130–230F, *menu-carte* 160F. The separate bistro serves a *formule* with cold starters, main course and dessert. Free coffee.

CHEPY   51240 (7KM SE)

🏄 I●I COMME CHEZ SOI

49 route Nationale; from Châlons, take the N44 in the direction of Vitry-le-François.
☎ and ➡ 03.26.67.50.21
Closed Sun and Mon evenings and Tues, a fortnight in Jan and a week in Aug.

Both the setting and the cooking are classically provincial. Weekday menu 70F and others 110–190F. The regional menu gives you a good idea of the local specialities: salad of *andouillette* and apples, braised trout with juniper berries, regional cheeses and sorbet with *marc de Champagne*. You can also get a straightforward menu with a choice ranging from steak and chips to more elaborate dishes like potatoes Maxime and scallops. Friendly welcome. Free house apéritif.

LA CHAUSÉE-SUR-MARNE 51240 (15KM S)

≜ I●I LE CLOS DE MUTIGNY**

17 ave du Docteur-Jolly.
☎ 03.26.72.94.20 ➡ 03.26.72.65.76
TV. Car park.

Originally built as the *Auberge de Jolly* in 1785, then a private residence and finally taken over by a local watchmaker and scrupulously renovated as a hotel again. Comfortable, quiet rooms with views over the river or the huge estate surrounding the house – number 3 gets the best of both worlds. Doubles with shower/wc go for 310–365F, with bath 385–480F. Sensitive, charming welcome.

CHAOURCE 10210

🎿 🛏 |●| HÔTEL-RESTAURANT LES FONTAINES

1 rue des Fontaines (Centre); D443.
☎ 03.25.40.00.85 📠 03.25.40.01.80
📧 Alain.Musnier@wanadoo.fr
Closed Mon evening, Tues, 2–23 Jan and the last week in July. **TV. Car park**.

Chaource is located where Champagne borders Burgundy and the restaurant serves authentic regional dishes from both departments. The 79F set menu (not Sat evening, Sun or public holidays), offers a choice of four dishes at each course, there's a *menu surprise* at 99F and a *menu du terroir* at 149F. Specialities include fresh mushroom upside-down tart with farmhouse Chaource cheese, salmon escalope with foaming Champagne sauce, and *croustillant* of Troyes andouillette 5A. Half a dozen rooms with shower/wc, telephone and TV at 180F. Half board, 230F, is compulsory at weekends. 10% discount on the room rate weekdays.

MAISONS-LÈS-CHAOURCE 10210 (6KM S)

🎿 🛏 |●| HÔTEL-RESTAURANT AUX MAISONS***

How to get there: take the D34.
☎ 03.25.70.07.19 📠 03.25.70.07.75
Swimming pool. Disabled access. TV. Car park.

A large, well-kept family hotel in a little village in the south of the Aube, the region famous for Chaource cheese. The hotel has undergone substantial refurbishment and gained a third star. Doubles 295F with shower or bath – some overlook the garden and the swimming pool. The restaurant has been renovated, too, and the main dining room boasts a splendid monumental fireplace. In the kitchen, the owner, Monique Enfert, and her son concoct exquisite regional dishes served in substantial portions. Set menus 110F, 140F and 180F. Service can take time. 10% discount on the room rate Oct– March.

RICEYS (LES) 10340 (22KM SE)

🛏 |●| HÔTEL-RESTAURANT LE MAGNY**

Route de Tonnerre; it's on the D453.
☎ 03.25.29.38.39 📠 03.25.29.11.72
Closed Tues evening, Wed, and Jan–Feb. **Disabled access. Swimming pool. Garden. TV. Car park**.

Les Riceys is not satisfied with having three churches. It's also the only village in France to produce three AOC wines – one of them a famous rosé that was one of Louis XIV's favourite tipples. The chef uses the wine in the sauces of a number of dishes and he also uses Chaource cheese and Troyes *andouillette*. Set menus 70–210F. Peaceful rooms; 270F for a double with shower/wc and telephone. There's a small garden with a heated swimming pool in summer, or you can visit the park nearby, designed by Le Nôtre.

GYÉ-SUR-SEINE 10250 (28KM E)

🎿 🛏 |●| HÔTEL LES VOYAGEURS

It's on the D70, on the edge of the village.
☎ 03.25.38.20.09 📠 03.25.38.25.37
Closed Wed, Sun evening and the Feb school holidays. **Car park**.

It's the reputation of the restaurant that attracts the clientele. It's hard to choose from the good range of menus 80–190F. They serve *amuse-bouches*, *olivettes* or cheese *gougères*, to fill the gap between taking your order and serving the starter – their *hors-d'œuvres variés* come in a selection of individual glass dishes. The dish of the day is often fish, or you could opt for a speciality such as kidneys with wholegrain mustard or grilled zander with herb butter – all totally reliable dishes. Unobtrusive service. There are a few rooms with shower at 150–180F – the wc is along the landing. Free coffee.

CHARLEVILLE-MÉZIÈRES 08000

🎿 🛏 HÔTEL DE PARIS**

24 av. G-Corneau (Southeast); it's opposite the station.
☎ 03.24.33.34.38 📠 03.24.59.11.21
📧 hotel-de-paris-08@wanadoo.fr
Closed 24 Dec–4 Jan. **TV**.

Rimbaud was born here, and although he cursed the arrival of the railway, his statue stands proudly in the station square. The hotel owner and her cat provide a friendly welcome, and the rooms are classically decorated. Those on the street side are soundproofed, while those overlooking the inner courtyard couldn't be quieter. Doubles with shower 285, 295F with bath, and three family rooms. 10% discount Sept–June.

|●| RESTAURANT LE DAMIER

7 rue Bayard (South); coming from Charleville, take the avenue d'Arches and take the second on the right after the bridge over the Meuse.
☎ 03.24.37.76.89
Closed Mon–Thurs evenings, Fri, Sat lunchtime and

Aug.

This is a unique restaurant run by an association set up to give the young and disadvantaged a chance and some training, so be patient if the service is sometimes a bit below par. The 39F dish of the day and the 55F menu make this place good value for money; the food is simple but tasty. The restaurant is bright with a chequered floor. Prices go up a notch on Fri and Sat evening, when menus go for 75F, 79F and 105F and the cooking is slightly more sophisticated: *feuilleté du Carolo*, beef *à l'Ardennaise*, trout soufflé with a scallop sauce, and game in season. The menus change every week. An initiative that deserves support.

❙●❙ BALARD RESTO

10 rue de Tivoli (South); from place Ducale walk along the pedestrian rue de la République as far as the cours Aristide-Briand then it's the first on the right.
☎ 03.24.33.60.06
Closed Sun, public holidays and 10–31 Aug.

This restaurant is named after a station on the Paris métro and they've done it out to look like a station, with tiled walls, wooden benches, and old train doors. It's very unusual and it works. The food is perfect for lunch or a meal with friends. Nice little bistro dishes in keeping with the Parisian style: tripe, marrowbone, calf's head, *œufs en meurette* in red wine sauce, and, in summer, a selection of abundant salads. Wine by the jug and beers from local small breweries. Madame greets you with a smile, Monsieur creates in the kitchen. Dish of the day, 48F and a full meal costs about 130F *à la carte*. A pretty good place.

CHAUMONT   52000

⚥ 🏠 ❙●❙ HÔTEL-RESTAURANT LE RELAIS

20 faubourg de la Maladière (Northeast); it's 1km from the centre of Chaumont, on the N74 to Nancy.
☎ 03.25.03.02.84
Closed Sun evening, Mon, a fortnight in Jan and a fortnight in July. **TV**.

A former coaching inn on the outskirts of Chaumont, this is an unpretentious place by the roadside and on the banks of the canal linking the Marne and the Saône. Seven, fairly peaceful rooms which have been renovated – numbers 6 and 7 are particularly quiet – and prices are reasonable; 200–240F for a double with shower or bath. Carefully prepared, sophisticated cuisine where seafood is a speciality – prawn kebab, scallops with whisky,

salmon escalope *with mustard*. Menus 85–140F. Friendly welcome. Free coffee.

⚥ 🏠 ❙●❙ HÔTEL-RESTAURANT DES REMPARTS**

72 rue de Verdun (Centre).
☎ 03.25.32.64.40 ➟ 03.25.32.51.70
Closed 25 Dec and 31 Dec.
Disabled access. **TV**. **Public car park** opposite hotel.

This place offers the best value for money in Chaumont. The rooms, decorated with posters from the Chaumont Arts Festival, are clean and well soundproofed. Doubles with shower/wc or bath 270–310F. Newer, more spacious rooms in the annexe. Classic setting in the slightly classy restaurant. First-rate, imaginative cooking; pan-fried *foie gras* with tart apples, scallops with tagliatelle, salmon in Pinot Noir sauce and veal sweetbreads in flaky pastry with morels. Set menus 72–280F. The *Lucifer* grill provides a more relaxed atmosphere and brasserie dishes or a selection of pizzas at modest prices. 50% discount on the room rate for a two-night stay between 15 Nov and 15 April, if you stay over a weekend and have two meals in the restaurant each day.

🏠 ❙●❙ GRAND HOTEL TERMINUS REINE***

pl. Charles-de-Gaulle (Centre); it's opposite the train station.
☎ 03.25.03.01.11 ➟ 03.25.32.35.80
TV. **Car park**.

The former residence of the Counts of Champagne. It was rebuilt in the middle of the 20th century and its turreted, yellow façade and blue shutters give it a modern air. All the facilities you'd expect in a three-star hotel are provided in this establishment. Nearly all the 63 rooms have been refurbished; they're spruce and spacious with modern bathrooms. Doubles with shower 305F, 410F with bath. The restaurant serves classic dishes at rather high prices, but there's a more modestly priced pizzeria and grill. Appropriately professional service.

CHAMARANDES   52000 (2KM SE)

⚥ 🏠 ❙●❙ AU RENDEZ-VOUS DES AMIS**

4 pl. du Tilleul (Southeast).
☎ 03.25.32.20.20 ➟ 03.25.02.60.90
Hotel closed 1–20 Aug. **Restaurant closed** Fri and Sun evenings, Sat. **Disabled access**. **TV**. **Car park**.

The River Marne runs through this unspoilt little village where the old church and school stand near the shady banks. You can glimpse the manor house through the trees of the estate. This is a genuine, quiet country inn with charm where you get a friendly welcome – all in all, a great place to stop. Rooms have been tastefully renovated and doubles cost 250F with shower, or 330–370F with shower/wc or bath – one room has been fitted out for disabled access. The restaurant is full of hunters, fishermen, businessmen and people travelling through. In summer they serve outside on a lovely terrace shaded by an ancient lime tree. Creative, gourmet cooking – the chef, Pascal Nicard, invented the duck *foie gras* with monkfish liver dish and he's patented it, or try the salmon cooked in leaves or the roast duck back with a *foie gras fondant*. The wine list has 320 different vintages. Weekday menu 95F and 135–230F. Free house apéritif.

MARNAY-SUR-MARNE 52000 (18KM SE)

♠ |●| HÔTEL-RESTAURANT LA VALLÉE

It's on the N19, in the direction of Langres.
☎ 03.25.31.10.11 ➡ 03.25.03.83.86
Closed Sun evening except July–Aug, Mon, a fortnight Sept/Oct and a fortnight at the beginning of March. **TV**. **Car park**.

Monsieur Farina produces such good food that it's easy to forget the noise of the main road outside. His place has a good reputation, and rightly so, because his local dishes are skilfully prepared. Try his *cassolette* of snails with Marc de Bourgogne or his chicken supreme with oyster mushrooms, and finish with a *gratin* of soft fruit. The small, rustic dining rooms are crammed with diners – the overflow goes onto the terrace when the weather is good. Menu of the day 68F or 95–190F. The half-dozen rooms, decorated in provincial style, are fresh and pleasant but quite noisy because of the main road. Doubles with shower/wc 250F. Really warm welcome and a family atmosphere.

VIGNORY   52320 (20KM N)

♠ |●| LE RELAIS VERDOYANT**

rue de la Gare; take the N67 inn the direction of Saint-Dizier then signs to Vignory gare.
☎ 03.25.02.44.49 ➡ 03.25.01.96.89
Closed Sun evening, Mon lunchtime, Mon evening Oct–April, Nov, and 22 Dec–15 March. **TV**. **Garden**. **Disabled access. Car park**.

This house was built in the early 1900s to provide accommodation for travellers getting off the train at Vignory station. There aren't so many trains nowadays, but the hotel and garden are as elegant as ever The small, stylish rooms are named after flowers, 215–250F for a double with shower/wc or bath, and as charming now as they look in the sepia photos of the hotel in the reception area. Traditional cuisine at reasonable prices, offering duck breast with shallots, chicken liver *terrine* with port and iced nougat with a fruit *coulis*. Set menus 82–145F.

VILLIERS-SUR-SUZE 52210 (20KM S)

♠ |●| AUBERGE DE LA FONTAINE

1 pl. Moreau; take the N19 in the direction of Langres, then the D143 to Villiers-sur-Suze.
☎ 03.25.31.22.22 ➡ 03.25.03.15.76
Closed evenings except by reservation.
Disabled access. TV.

A very nice small inn with red shutters smothered in creeper, in a village surrounded by woods and fields. It's a fun place to stop for a drink, buy your papers or have a bite to eat. Settle down like the locals in the bar with its shiny ceiling, in the corner sitting room in front of the open fire, in the restaurant with its has ancient stone walls, or, in sunny weather, on the terrace. Dish of the day, 45F, and one set menu, 70F, with good, simple, flavoursome dishes that change frequently; try steak with shallots, *bœuf bourguignon*, rabbit with mustard, or *civet* of wild boar in season. Seven or so newly decorated, comfortable rooms, in a separate building just a step away, 230F for a double with shower/wc or 270F with bath. And if you've forgotten your toothpaste, no worries – the village grocer's is in the hotel. Genuine, warm welcome extended by the young owner. This place has brought life back to the village.

ARC-EN-BARROIS   52210 (25KM SW)

⚘ ♠ |●| HÔTEL DU PARC**

1 pl. Moreau.
☎ 03.25.02.53.07 ➡ 03.25.02.42.84
Closed Tues evening and Wed 15 Sept–31 Jan, Sun evening and Mon March–May, and Feb. **Open** daily 1 June–15 Sept.
TV.

This hotel used to be a hunting lodge. It's in a tiny Burgundy-style village opposite the castle, surrounded by forests where they shoot game. Doubles 300–350F with bath. The rooms are quiet and comfortable and they were done up in 1998 because the Jamaican football team lodged here during the World Cup. Hearty regional cuisine; set menus from 100F–250F feature venison and wild boar in season, and there are tables on a terrace.

Fishing, hunting, golf and mountain-bike hire all available. Free apéritif.

COLOMBEY-LES-DEUX-ÉGLISES 52330

⌂ |●| L'AUBERGE DE LA MONTAGNE**

17 rue de la Montagne.
☎ 03.25.01.51.69 ➡ 03.25.01.53.20
Closed Mon evening and Tues out of season, mid-Jan to mid-Feb. **TV. Car park.**

Small inn, little village, great man – this was Géneral de Gaulle's home, the man who was the leader of the Free French in World War II and the first President of the Fifth Republic. The owner, Gérard Natali, was one of the twelve young pall-bearers at the general's funeral in 1970. Today people from all over the world come to stay here, from the ex-King of Yemen to the Japanese ambassador, Breton quarry-owners to French colonials from Pondicherry. Gourmet dining in a chic, rustic setting, and the seasonal dishes feature fresh, local produce. First-class, extensive menus at 130F on weekdays or 190–450F. The charming rooms are really peaceful; 280–330F with shower/wc or bath. Breakfast is pricey.

ÉPERNAY 51200

⌂ HÔTEL DE CHAMPAGNE***

30 rue Eugène-Mercier (Centre).
☎ 03.26.53.10.60 ➡ 03.26.51.94.63
e infos@loc-hotel-champagne.com
Closed first fortnight in Jan. **TV. Car park.**

The best hotel in the town centre. It's modern and comfortable, and has double glazing. Room prices depend on facilities; 450F with shower to 550F with bath. About ten rooms are due to be fitted with air conditioning. Unlimited self-service buffet breakfast 60F.

🖈|●| LA GRILLADE

16 rue de Reims; it's near the station.
☎ 03.26.55.44.22
Closed Sat lunchtime and Sun except public holidays and a fortnight in Sept. **Garden.**

This place is more commonly known as *Chez Blanche*, after the owner. Their speciality is their grill, over an open fire: sardines, bass with fennel, T-bone steak, and *andouillettes* cooked to perfection. The surprise is the dessert; banana grilled over the open fire then flambéed. There's usually a full house. The pretty flower-filled garden and shady terrace are at their best in summer. Set menus

88–179F. Free apéritif.

ÉPERNAY-GAMBETTA 51200 (1KM)

|●| CHEZ MAX

13 av. A. Thevenet; it's 1km from the town centre on the Dizy road.
☎ 03.26.55.23.59
Closed Sun and Wed evenings, Mon, a fortnight in Jan and three weeks in Aug.

This is a popular restaurant that has been going for about 50 years and has always maintained its good reputation. Weekday set menu 71F with a choice of five starters, three main courses – braised ham, scorpion fish *bouillabaisse* or veal stew – salads or cheese and dessert. Other menus, 95–200F and dishes change frequently. There's also a celebration menu to order at the weekend.

ERVY-LE-CHATEL 10130

🖈|●| AUBERGE DE LA VALLÉE DE L'ARMANCE

It's opposite the station.
☎ 03.25.70.66.36
Closed Sun evening, Mon and 16–31 Aug. **Car park.**

You don't go through the bar to get to the restaurant, it has its own entrance round the back. The dining room has been converted from an old cow shed and part of an old wooden manger has been left in its place. It's decorated with old implements – hay forks and wooden bread paddles hang on the wall. Good regional food includes *gratin d'andouillette*, house *foie gras* or veal sweetbreads with oyster mushrooms. Set menus 68F and 115F. Free coffee.

GIVET 08600

🖈 ⌂ |●| HÔTEL-RESTAURANT DU NORD*

27 rue Thiers (North).
☎ 03.24.42.01.78 ➡ 03.24.40.46.79
Closed Sun evening and last three weeks in Dec.
Disabled access. TV. Car park.

This is a little place with low prices. The street's quiet despite being in the middle of town. Rooms are basic and situated above the restaurant or opposite, in an annexe – you've got to like psychedelic wallpaper. Doubles with washing facilities 140F, or 210F with shower/wc. Unpretentious bar-restaurant with classic cooking and a slighty old-fashioned atmosphere. Set menus at 65–160F. 10% discount on the room rate.

▲ LES REFLETS JAUNES

2 rue du Général-de-Gaulle.
☎ 03.24.42.85.85 ➡ 03.24.42.85.86
Disabled access. TV. Car park.

A brand new hotel with colourfully painted rooms with particularly good facilities; hair dryer, mini-bar, air conditioning, video-player and Internet access. The rooms are sound-proofed too, which is just as well because the hotel is in the centre of town. Doubles 295–480F. Buffet breakfast.

🏃 ▲ HÔTEL LE VAL SAINT-HILAIRE**

7 quai des Fours; coming from Charleville, it's on the left as you get into the town.
☎ 03.24.42.85.85 ➡ 03.24.42.85.86
Disabled access. TV. Car park.

Givet produces a blue stone and, back in the 18th century, it was used in the construction of this building which was a printer's. The bedrooms are pleasant and subtly decorated in contemporary style. The ones overlooking the road and the river Meuse have double glazing (triple glazing on the ground floor) but if you're very sensitive to noise, ask for a room overlooking the courtyard. Doubles with bath 350F. The restaurant specialises in local dishes – veal sweetbreads in champagne, bronze turkey and trout à l'ardennaise. Menus 110–165F. The bar has a terrace on the waterside where the pleasureboats tie up. You get the best welcome in town and the owners are very information about the walks you can do in the area – you might just as well start off along the superb Meuse valley. Free house apéritif.

AUBRIVES   08320 (5KM SW)

🏃 ▲ |●| HÔTEL-RESTAURANT DEBETTE**

2 pl. Louis-Debette; it's on the N51 in the direction of Charleville.
☎ 03.24.41.64.72 ➡ 03.24.41.10.31
Closed Sun evening except public holidays, Mon lunchtime and mid-Dec to mid-Jan. **Disabled access. TV. Car park.**

This used to be a reliable country place with a bourgeois, somewhat old-fashioned style. Since two young brothers took over it's become much more informal. The rooms, which are either in the house or in an annexe on the other side of a peaceful village square, are really comfortable, and most of them have been refurbished, although the

decor doesn't quite sparkle with originality; 220F for a double with shower/wc or bath. The dining room is a bit fancy but has huge bay windows opening out onto the garden.The young chef produces great dishes, like veal kidneys with scallops, and regional specialities such as Ardennes ham or wild boar in season. Weekday menu 75F or 110–220F. Free coffee or *digestif*.

FUMAY   08170 (20KM S)

|●| HOSTELLERIE DE LA VALLÉE

146 pl. Aristide-Briand; it's on the N51.
☎ 03.24.41.15.61
Closed Sun evening, Mon and the end of Feb.

Just the country inn you were looking for. There are dining rooms and salons to hold receptions which pack people in at lunchtime. The owner is in charge of the dining room and serves the varied local dishes which come in substantial portions; Ardennes *charcuterie*, frogs' legs and white pudding in pastry with port sauce. Weekday menu 65F or 98–225F.

JOINVILLE   52300

▲ |●| HÔTEL-RESTAURANT DE LA POSTE**

pl. de la Grève; it's on the St-Dizier road.
☎ 03.25.94.12.63 ➡ 03.25.94.36.23
Closed Sun evening in winter, and 10 Jan–10 Feb. **TV. Car park.**

They do have rooms here but the draw is the chef's delicious specialities; *emincé* of monkfish with baby vegetables, *poussin* with morels, trout *sire de Joinville*. The weekday set menu for 80F is remarkable value, giving you starter, meat or fish main course, cheese and dessert. Other menus 132–210F. Impeccable service. Comfortable, quiet rooms 200–280F with double glazing and shower/wc or bath.

▲ |●| LE SOLEIL D'OR***

9 rue des Capucins (Centre); it's beside Notre Dame church.
☎ 03.25.94.15.66 ➡ 03.25.94.39.02
Closed Sun evening, Mon, last week in Feb, first week in Aug, and a week in Nov. **TV. Car park.**

If you're a fan of cosy rooms with stone walls this is the hotel for you. It's spacious and light, and offers good value for money. Doubles 230–400F depending on size. The vaulted dining room is neo-gothic with wooden beams, stained glass, stone and wood. It's warm and refined and provides the perfect setting for the chef's specialities: zander turnover with shrips, quail from Dombes with cinnamon, pan-fried scallops with saffron sauce. It doesn't come at give-away prices; 190F or 300F for the two gourmet menus, but there's a more basic weekday menu at 120F.

VILLIERS-SUR-MARNE   52320 (17KM S)

⅔ |●| LA SOURCE BLEUE

Lieu-dit La Source; take the N67 in the direction of Chauon, at Villiers, take the Doulaincourt road and follow the signs.
☎ 03.25.94.70.35 ➡ 03.25.05.02.09
Closed Sun evening, Mon and 24 Dec–20 Jan. **TV**. **Garden**. **Car park**.

An ideal little country retreat in an old forge by a river way out in the country. It's run by a young couple who have decorated it thoughtfully and created a warm atmosphere. Dynamic service and modest prices. Trout *tartare* with red peppercorns, duck fillet with blackberries, zander fillet with cream and goat's cheese sauce, and an array of delicate desserts. A short menu at 65F, another at 95F, a *menu dégustation* at 175F, or around 140F *à la carte*. In summer they serve out on the front lawn. It's a genuinely charming place and you get good value for money. Take a quick look at the spring that feeds the lake where the trout spawn, right next to the house. It's a truly remarkable blue. Free house apéritif.

LANGRES   52200

⅔ ♠ |●| GRAND HÔTEL DE L'EUROPE**

23–25 rue Diderot (Centre).
☎ 03.25.87.10.88 ➡ 03.25.87.60.65
Closed Sun evening in winter. **TV**. **Pay car park**.

This unique hotel hails from some forgotten past, displaying the charm of pre-revolutionary France: 17th-century wood panelling, squeaking floorboards and huge rooms with blue shutters. It has rare provincial style, friendly staff and reasonable prices for the quality. Doubles 300F with shower/wc and 360F with bath. The rooms on the second floor have been refurbished and painted yellow and blue – they're undoubtedly more functional but a good deal more impersonal. Older-style rooms in the annexe in the courtyard and they're quieter. The restaurant is splendid too: weekday set menu at 84F, then others up to 250F. 25F charge for use of the private car park. Free house apéritif.

⅔ ♠ |●| L'AUBERGE DES VOILIERS**

Lac de la Liez (East); it's 4km from Langres, on Vesoul road.
☎ 03.25.87.05.74 ➡ 03.25.87.24.22
Closed Sun evening, Mon except May–Sept, and 1 Feb–15 March. **TV**. **Garden**.

This is about the best place in Langres, close to a peaceful lake. Fair prices, wonderful welcome and great food. Doubles 300F with shower/wc and telephone or 350F with bath. Room 4 has a balcony with a view of the lake and numbers 8 and 11 look over the countryside towards the walled city of Langres. Set menu 80F (100F on Sun), then 100–160F. Children's menu 50F. Their fillet of pike with nettles is a speciality, and you should try the *nougat glacé* with fresh fruit. In summer the shady terrace adds to your enjoyment. 50F discount on the room rate if you dine in the restaurant.

♠ |●| LE CHEVAL BLANC**

4 rue de l'Estres (Centre).
☎ 03.25.87.07.00 ➡ 03.25.87.23.13
e cblangres@aol.com
Restaurant closed Tues evening except July–Aug, Wed lunch time, and 15–30 Nov. **Disabled access**. **TV**. **Car park**.

The *Cheval Blanc* is a converted medieval abbey; gothic arches in some rooms, a terrace overlooking the medieval church, hewn stone walls and exposed beams on every floor. The decor is simple yet refined. All the rooms have been refurbished and are as quiet as a monk's cell. The new rooms in the *Pavillon Diderot*, opposite, are equally well equipped but don't have the same charm. Doubles with shower or bath 320–420F. The cuisine in the restaurant offers a panoply of gastronomic delights which change with the seasons; scallops *vinaigrette* with green apples, morel stew with an egg, pan-fried *foie gras* with spiced honey or, for dessert, a warm soup of soft fruit perfumed with violet. Set menus 140–390F. One of the best tables in the *départmente*.

|●| BANANAS

52 rue Diderot (Centre); it's on the main street.
☎ 03.25.87.42.96
Closed Sun, Sun lunchtime July–Aug, and a week at the end of Nov.

Service noon–1.45pm and 7–10pm. The staff here make a real fuss of you. The decor is sparkling, and the tables are covered with red and white checked cloths. They play country music and there's a buffalo head hanging on the wall – all you need is a cowboy hat and you're in John Wayne country. The atmosphere is great, as is the service and everything on the Tex-Mex menu: tacos, enchiladas, chilli con carne, burgers and steaks. Evenings are usually very busy. A meal will cost about 130F.

VAUX-SOUS-AUBIGNY   52190 (25KM S)

|●| AUBERGE DES TROIS PROVINCES

rue de Verdun; it's on the N74.
☎ 03.25.88.31.98
Closed Sun evening, Mon and 15 Jan–5 Feb. **Car park.**

The wonderful paved stone floor and impressive fireplace are from another era. The decor goes well with the food, which makes good use of local produce with a sparkle of originality. Good set menu at 95F: home-made country *terrine*, salmon-trout *pouchouse* in red wine, selection of cheese. Desserts include pears poached in wine and *moelleux* of bitter chocolate with roasted sesame seeds. Other menus up to 135F. It's not long since the chef was running the kitchen of a top restaurant in Saint-Maxime and it shows. The wine list contains one or two curiosities from the little-known neighbouring vineyard in Montseaugeon.

AUBERIVE   52160 (27KM SW)

☎ |●| HÔTEL-RESTAURANT DU LION D'OR

How to get there; from Langres take the Dijon Road then the D428 to Auberive.
☎ 03.25.84.82.49 ➡ 03.42.79.80.92
Closed Tues and Oct to April.
Disabled access. Car park.

This adorable little, seasonal, country hotel is set right beside a 12th-century Cistercian abbey in a peaceful village in the embrace of the forest. The Aube is nothing more than a big stream here and it runs past the house. The eight rooms are all different and so tastefully decorated they wouldn't look out of place in an interiors magazine; doubles 310–370F. There's also a restaurant with a handful of tables around the fireplace. The cooking is based primarily on fresh, seasonal, local produce: snails, rabbit *à la Dijonnaise* and *profiteroles de Langres*. Set menu 98F or *à la carte*.

MESNIL-SAINT-PÈRE   10140

☎ |●| HÔTEL-RESTAURANT AUBERGE DU LAC***

How to get there: take the N19 from Troyes, it's at the beginning of the village.
☎ 03.25.41.27.16 ➡ 03.25.41.57.59
e Auberge.lac.p.gublin@wanadoo.fr
Closed Sun evening out of season and 12–30 Nov.
Disabled access. TV. Car park.

This is a stylish timber-framed house near to the lake in the forest of Orient – an ideal place for a romantic weekend. There's a suite at 930F or doubles with shower or bath 390–690F, which are extremely quiet. The restaurant, *Au Vieux Pressoir*, is really charming. The chef's cooking is excellent and prices reflect the quality: weekday lunch menu 120F, 175F or 300F *à la carte*.

MENILOT (LE)   10270 (3KM W)

🏃 ☎ |●| LA MANGEOIRE

It's on left of the N19.
☎ 03.25.41.20.72 ➡ 03.25.41.54.67
Swimming pool. TV. Lock-up garage.

The village is like a leisure centre for the lakes of the Orient forest. Although this attractive wooden building is right on the main road, the restaurant is on the other side, away from any noise. The appealing, comfortable rooms, 270F, all have en-suite bathrooms. Prices are reasonable given the amenities. A 70F *menu routier* is served in the bar for both lunch and dinner on weekdays only, or you can get others, 120–250F, in the restaurant. Boat trips on the lake can be arranged from the hotel. 10% discount on the room rate.

NOGENT   52800

🏃 ☎ |●| HÔTEL DU COMMERCE**

pl. Charles-de-Gaulle (Centre).
☎ 03.25.31.81.14 ➡ 03.25.31.74.00
Restaurant closed Sun from Oct to Easter.
TV. Lock-up garage.

This town is famous for its cutlery and this establishment has keen prices. Well-kept and pleasant doubles 175F with basin/wc, 260–280F with shower/wc or bath. The entrance hall is huge and welcoming, as is the restaurant with its exposed beams and 18th-century-style decor. Set menus are generous and well thought out; weekday lunch menu 84F, or 98–158F. Try snail soup with Burgundy butter or spiced fillet of duck with honey. The ideal place to stay if you're visiting the cutlery museum. Free coffee.

NOGENT-SUR-SEINE   10400

⅍ 🏠 |●| HÔTEL-RESTAURANT BEAU RIVAGE**

20 rue Villiers-aux-Choux (North); it's about 1km from pl.de l'Église.
☎ 03.25.39.84.22 ➡ 03.25.39.18.32
Closed Sun evening, Mon and the Feb school holidays. **TV**. **Garden**.

A friendly, peaceful place with a beautiful garden beside the Seine. There are a few pleasant rooms all of which have been renovated. 300F for a double with shower/wc or bath. Rooms 1, 2, 4 and 5 have a view of the Seine, the trees, the countryside and, in the distance, the incongruous outline of a nuclear power station. Breakfast 38F. Cheapest set menu 95F and others 135–205F. The chef uses fresh herbs generously and expertly — and he smokes his own salmon. A lovely spot in Nogent. 10% discount on the room rate Sept–June.

PINEY   10220

⅍ 🏠 |●| LE TADORNE**

1 pl. de la Halle.
☎ 03.25.46.30.35 ➡ 03.25.46.36.49
📧 le.dadorne@wanadoo.fr
Closed Sun evening Oct–March, and the Feb school holidays. **Disabled access**. **Swimming pool**. **TV**. **Car park**.

Near to the Orient forest nature park, this huge, half-timbered building houses a bar, a restaurant and a hotel in a peaceful, relaxing setting. Cosy, stylish, impeccably clean rooms in a recently converted annexe; 260F for doubles with shower/wc, or 290F with bath. Half board, compulsory July–Aug and public holidays, is 300F per person. Prices include use of the very pleasant hotel pool. If you want to spend less, there are basic rooms in the main building. These start at 160F a night with basin, with a shower along the landing. In the restaurant they serve a lunch menu at 59F and others 92–195F. 10% discount on the room rate 15 Oct–31 March.

BREVONNES   10220 (5KM E)

⅍ 🏠 |●| AU VIEUX LOGIS

1 rue de Piney; it's on the D11
☎ 03.25.46.30.17 ➡ 03.25.46.37.20

📧 annick.baudesson@worldonline.fr
Closed Sun evening and Mon from mid-Sept to end-May, Mon lunchtime in season, and March. **Swimming pool**. **TV**. **Car park**.

This old Champenois house has kept its style – exposed beams, antique furniture, flocked wallpaper and a large ceramic cauldron hanging in the fireplace. Appropriately, they serve traditional dishes that are prepared with great care; tasty Bernon snails, home-made *terrines*, chicken *mignardise*. The service is invisibly efficient. The 80F menu (not served Sun) is good value. A couple of other menus 140F and 200F or *à la carte*, which lists dishes like baby cabbage with crayfish *à la vigneronne*, stuffed supreme of chicken in Ratafia sauce, and oxtail salad with vegetable *terrine*. The rooms are warm and cosy – doubles 235F with shower/wc, 255F with bath. Free coffee.

MESNIL-SELLIÈRES   10220 (10KM SW)

⅍ |●| LA CLÉ DES CHAMPS

Grande-Rue.
☎ 03.25.80.65.62
📧 la clefdeschamps@wanadoo.fr
Closed Sun and Wed evenings, Mon, and 1–15 Jan. **Disabled access**. **Car park**.

A little gastronomic stop on the way to the Orient forest national park, with a bright yellow and blue dining room. The chef serves a good selection of colourful, well-balanced dishes to match, made from fresh ingredients that he has bought himself from that morning's market; *craquant* of bacon *confit* with andouillette, queen scallops and mussels with salmon in a pastry case, farmed pigeon with morel *jus* and, for dessert, spiced bread pudding with green *anise* and honey ice cream. Best to book. Free coffee.

RAMERUPT   10240

⅍ |●| RESTAURANT LE VAL D'AUBE

rue Cour-Première.
☎ 03.25.37.39.45
Closed Tues and Aug.

After enjoying great success cooking for the diplomats in the French foreign office at the Quai-d'Orsay, the young chef, Hervé, came back to join his family in their country bar-restaurant. He creates decent traditional food: set weekday menu 62F. They don't take credit cards. Free coffee.

REIMS   51100

SEE MAP OVERLEAF

🎎 🏨 HÔTEL LE SAINT-MAURICE*

90 rue Gambetta. **MAP C3-3**
☎ 03.26.85.09.10 ➡ 03.26.85.83.20
TV.

The hotel frontage is like a shop window. The rooms mostly look out onto the peaceful little courtyard where the guests sit out in the open air as they might in Andalucia – there's a Spanish feel to the place. The atmosphere is warm and friendly, and regulars have their "own" room, as people used to in old guesthouses. There are a number of single rooms which aren't quite as nice as the others, but good for anyone on a budget: doubles with shower (wc along the hall) at 155F, or 220F with bath or shower/wc. 10% discount.

🏨 ❙●❙ AUX BONS AMIS

13 rue Gosset. Off map **B1-17**
☎ 03.26.07.39.76 ➡ 03.26.07.73.06
Restaurant closed Fri evening, Sat and Sun. **TV**.

The popular restaurant is always crammed at lunchtime with businessmen, workers and local pensioners in-the-know about the excellent lunch menu – a steal at 67F. There's a choice of two starters and three main courses, then cheeses, dessert and a drink. The dishes are real classics – ox tongue with rice, *blanquette de veau* (a type of veal stew), veal *sauté* – and you get good-sized portions. Good, quick service guaranteed by the friendly waitresses who work really hard. They wear name badges so service is more personal. *Aux Bons Amis* is also a very basic, clean hotel. All rooms have a TV. Breakfast 25F. Half board, 170F per person, is compulsory.

🏨 AZUR HÔTEL**

7 rue des Écrevées. **MAP B1-6**
☎ 03.26.47.43.39 ➡ 03.26.88.57.19
Closed Sun out of season. **TV**.

In a quiet street in the town centre this unobtrusive, tranquil hotel has a sort of English charm. You are greeted warmly and the rooms are neat and tidy. Doubles 195F with washing facilities, 265F with shower/wc, and 295F with bath. Numbers 17, 27, 37, 12 and 22 are brighter than the others. Very near the *Henry IV* bar and the rather chic *Au Comptoir* bistro. It'll take you ten minutes to walk to the place d'Erlon. They don't take credit cards.

🏨 ❙●❙ HÔTEL LE BARON**

85 rue de Vesle. **MAP B2-9**
☎ 03.26.47.46.24
Closed Sun. **TV**.

Don't let the name mislead you – there's nothing aristocratic about this place; a *baron* is slang for a 50cl glass of beer. *Le Baron* deserves some respect, nonetheless. The hotel has been totally renovated and the rooms have all mod cons. Those looking onto the street have been soundproofed. Doubles 220F with shower, 230F with bath, and a few rooms sleeping three. The restaurant serves lunch only, with a 55F menu.

🎎 🏨 ❙●❙ HÔTEL-RESTAURANT LE BON MOINE**

14 rue des Capucins. **MAP B2-8**
☎ 03.26.47.33.64 ➡ 03.26.40.43.87
Hotel closed Sun Sept–June. **Restaurant closed** Sun lunchtime. **TV**.

The rooms have been freshly painted – choose the one with the colour of your favourite ice cream. Doubles 230–265F. They're all located above the café-restaurant and the establishment is in the centre of town. Weekday menu 59F, and others 85F and 95F. Nice welcome. 10% discount on the room rate June–Sept.

🏨 ARDENN HÔTEL**

6 rue Caqué. **MAP A2-4**
☎ 03.26.47.42.38 ➡ 03.26.86.82.44
TV. **Pay car park**.

A place to stay in the town centre that doesn't cost an arm and a leg. The hotel has been renovated but has a flagrantly kitsch decor which seems to appeal to the artists appearing at the nearby theatres. Doubles with shower 240F and with bath 280F.

🏨 ❙●❙ COTTAGE HÔTEL**

8 av. Georges-Pompidou (South). Off map **C4-7**
☎ 03.26.36.34.34 ➡ 03.26.49.99.77
Restaurant closed Sun evening.
Garden. **TV**. **Car park**.

This place is perfect if you're looking for somewhere quiet out of the town centre. Rooms 260F for a double with shower/wc and telephone. In the restaurant there's a decent menu at 70F, not served at weekends. Other set menus at 110F and 160F, and a children's menu at 45F. Warm, professional welcome.

🏨 HÔTEL CRYSTAL**

86 pl. Drouet-d'Erlon. **MAP A1-5**
☎ 03.26.88.44.44 ➡ 03.26.47.49.28
TV.

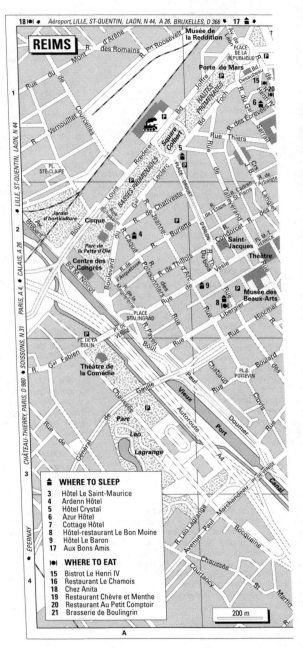

REIMS

Musée de
la Reddition

Porte de Mars

WHERE TO SLEEP

3 Hôtel Le Saint-Maurice
4 Ardenn Hôtel
5 Hôtel Crystal
6 Azur Hôtel
7 Cottage Hôtel
8 Hôtel-restaurant Le Bon Moine
9 Hôtel Le Baron
17 Aux Bons Amis

|●| **WHERE TO EAT**

15 Bistrot Le Henri IV
16 Restaurant Le Chamois
18 Chez Anita
19 Restaurant Chèvre et Menthe
20 Restaurant Au Petit Comptoir
21 Brasserie de Boulingrin

200 m

A

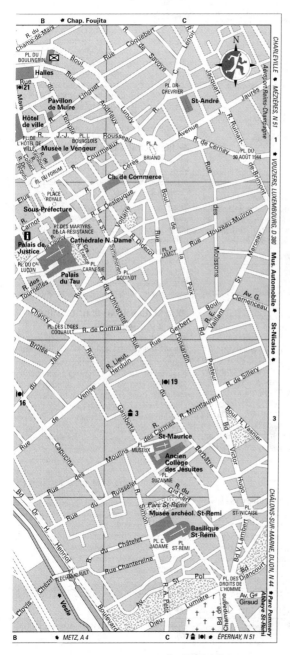

Two good reasons to stay here: its location – near the liveliest square in Reims, and yet it's nice and quiet – and its interior, which looks like hotels used to, with a beautiful old lift. You imagine lots of things must have happened here – if only the walls could speak. The comfortable rooms have modern bathrooms; 310F for a double with shower/wc or 380F with bath. There's also a pretty little courtyard where they serve breakfast in good weather.

◉ RESTAURANT LE CHAMOIS

45 rue des Capucins. **MAP B3-16**
☎ 03.26.88.69.75
Closed Wed, Sun lunchtime, and first fortnight in Aug.

This intimate, relaxing restaurant draws its inspiration from the mountains, with a menu of *fondues savoyardes*, and *raclette valaisanne* or *vaudoise*. Short traditional menu at 59F (weekday lunchtime only), or 75F. The service and food here are tremendous.

◉ BISTROT HENRI IV

29 rue Henri-IV. **MAP B1-15**
☎ 03.26.47.56.22
Closed Sun, Mon and Tues evenings, 20 July–15 Aug and 25 Dec–5 Jan.

As good a local bar/restaurant as you could hope to find. By 7am they are already serving the first customers, who take a shot of coffee and exchange news on their way to work. On the dot of midday the lunchtime rush starts and the place is packed with people grabbing a quick snack. Dishes of the day change regularly; tripe *à la mode de Caen*, *bœuf bourgingon*, lamb *navarin* or, *à la carte*, dishes of the order of *andouillette* with mustard, *entrecôte* steak with red wine sauce, calf's head and so on. The place is packed on market day (Sat). *Formule* at 52F and a weekday menu at 65F.

🥢◉ CHEZ ANITA

37 rue Ernest-Renan. Off map **A1-18**
☎ 03.26.40.16.20
Closed Sat lunchtime, Sun and first three weeks in Aug.

If you like Italian food, *Chez Anita* is for you. Brilliant oven-baked pizza with a choice of toppings and pasta galore. The portions are generous and very filling – so go easy ordering lunch if you want to stay awake to explore the town in the afternoon. A really popular place with a good local reputation. Set menus 68F and 95F at lunchtime, then 140F. Free coffee.

◉ BRASSERIE DU BOULINGRIN

48 rue de Mars **MAP B1-21**
☎ 03.26.40.96.22

Closed Sun

A genuine brasserie that's been running since 1925 and does credit to the breed. The lunchtime din resounds in the vast Art Deco dining room but in the evening, it's warm and convivial. The walls are painted with murals and there's a corps of uniformed waiters. The great 100F *formule* offers a choice of three starters, three main courses, cheese or desert and a $^1/_2$ litre of wine and coffee included. There are other menus at higher prices.

◉ RESTAURANT CHÈVRE ET MENTHE

63 rue du Barbâtre. **MAP C3-19**
☎ 03.26.05.17.03
Closed Sun, Mon, a week in April, three weeks in Aug, Christmas and New Year.

This place has had an excellent reputation for years, so you won't be disappointed. The plate glass windows are decorated with naive pictures and inside there are two small dining rooms. The nicer one is reserved for smokers. The food sounds modest enough but is actually very impressive: try the house tart of goat's cheese with mint, *papillotte* of salmon *à la parisienne*. Menus from 100F.

◉ RESTAURANT AU PETIT COMPTOIR

17 rue de Mars. **MAP B1-20**
☎ 03.26.40.58.58
Closed Sat lunchtime, Sun, 1–11 Jan and 10–26 Aug.

Fabrice Maillot has worked with famous chefs in the past and is having great success with this bistro, which has the kind of big-city feel that you'd find in Lyon or Paris. He's a clever, creative chef who produces first-rate cooking which looks simple but is finely and precisely judged. The place appeals to people who appreciate good food and the quality of his dishes is often amazing: upside-down cream with chicken livers, crayfish and offal stew, *tartiflette* with Val d'Ajol *andouillette* or *millefeuille* of Morteau sausage with cabbage. The desserts are delicious, too; soft caramel with salted butter with a fan of *noutagine* and ice cream with vinegar, and iced *sabayon* with champagne finished with blackcurrant. The menus change with the season, and the impressive wine list features a good selection from the Rhône valley. Expect to pay 220F for a meal.

VAL DE VESLE   51360 (18KM E)

◉ L'ÉTRIER

How to get there: take the N44 to Courmelais, then the D8.

☎ 03.26.03.92.12 ➡ 03.26.03.29.72
Closed Sun–Fri evenings.

Run by a family who make a delightful team. During the week there are two menus: the one at 60F includes *crudités* and *charcuterie*, dish of the day, cheese, dessert and wine. The 140F menu appeals even more – it's a real feast: house apéritif and savouries, followed by *foie gras* of duck with toast, or different *terrines* of chicken liver or venison, then a choice of fish (fillet of zander in butter, salmon *escalope* in champagne), a choice of meat (*gigot* of lamb, steak, veal kidneys in champagne, duck breast), salad, cheese, then dessert. Enough to sort anyone out.

FISMES   51170 (23KM E)

🏠 I●I À LA BOULE D'OR

11 rue Lefèvre.
☎ 03.26.48.11.24 ➡ 03.26.48.17.08
Closed Sun evening and Mon.

Worth a visit for the restaurant – it's a well-known gourmet stop in the region but it's exceptional value for money. Huge care is taken over the cooking. Weekday menu 69F, others up to 140F and *à la carte*, 240F. Very nice welcome. Double rooms 230–290F.

RETHEL   08300

⅍ 🏠 I●I HÔTEL-RESTAURANT LE CHAMPAGNE*

bd. de la 2e-DI (West); it's opposite the Aisne.
☎ 03.24.38.03.28 ➡ 03.24.38.37.70
Restaurant closed Sun evening. **Disabled access.**
TV. Car park.

Originally built as a block of flats over a parade of shops, it got turned into a hotel. Not exactly what you'd call charming, but the rooms are nice and clean and it's good value at 215–220F for a double with shower/wc. Half board is 270F. There are two restaurants: a cafeteria where you come more for the prices than the surroundings (50–60F for a meal) and a more attractive dining room with good traditional cuisine – local white pudding, calf sweetbreads, zander with ginger. Set menus 80F on weekday lunchtime, 105F and 155F. 10% discount on the room rate.

⅍ 🏠 I●I HÔTEL-RESTAURANT LE MODERNE*

pl. de la Gare (South).
☎ 03.24.38.44.54 ➡ 03.24.38.37.84

TV. Pay car park.

For forty years plus, this place, situated across from the station, has been a favourite with travellers passing through. There aren't many trains so the rooms are quiet. When they were renovated, they kept some of the old retro style, which fits in with the overall look of the solid brick and stone building. Well-equipped doubles 230F with shower/wc and 260F with bath. Decent menus 100–160F; *à la carte* you'll get modern classics such as *cassolette* of white pudding and *émincée* of pigeon with *foie gras*. Free house apéritif.

PAUVRES   08310 (15KM SE)

⅍ I●I RESTAURANT AU CHEVAL BLANC

How to get there: take the D946 and it's in the centre of the village.
☎ 03.24.30.38.95
Closed Mon evening and Aug. **Car park**.

Pauvres means poor, but this town is richer for this little gem of a place. There is a sign outside saying they welcome people on foot or on horseback – two famous French poets, Rimbaud and Verlaine, used to hang about this area, so maybe they came here. Today you're more likely to see vans or commercial vehicles at lunchtime when it's full of people who work locally. They generally opt for the 65F *menu du jour*, which includes a litre of red wine. The good, hearty portions of family cooking are served with a smile, though the desserts are a little uninspired. At the weekend families come in for the more regional set menus, 90–135F, which might include *tourte* of white pudding, veal sweetbreads with cream and raspberry vinegar, or saddle of rabbit. Free house apéritif or coffee.

SIGNY-L'ABBAYE   08460 (23KM N)

🏠 I●I AUBERGE DE L'ABBAYE*

pl. Aristide-Briand; it's on the D985.
☎ 03.24.52.81.27 ➡ 03.24.53.71.72
Closed Tues evening and Wed, Jan and Feb.
TV. Car park

This lovely inn has been in the same family since the Revolution. It's in the middle of a small picturesque market town on the edge of a huge forest. You'll get a warm welcome and there's a nice family atmosphere. The stylish rooms, all of them different, are done up regularly. Room 9 has its own little sitting room. Doubles with shower/wc or bath 300F and 350F. In winter, they light a fire which makes a nice atmosphere in the rustic dining room.

Lots of local produce is used in the home cooking. There's a weekday menu at 75F, one at 110F, which lists local specialities, and a gastronomic menu at 220F served on Sunday lunchtime. The Lefebvres are still farmers; the excellent beef comes from their own herd, while the rhubarb for the rhubarb tart is grown in their garden. It's rare to find this sort of place anywhere, let alone in such a wonderful spot – it's in the undulating woodlands of the Ardennes that's full of fortified churches.

REVIN   08500

☎ |●| AUBERGE DU MALGRÉ-TOUT

chemin des Balivaux; from Revin, go along the Hautes-Buttes road for several kms, it's signposted on the left.
☎ 03.24.40.11.20
Closed Sun evening. **Car park**.

The *ferme-auberge* (a farm offering food and lodging) of your dreams way out in the forest. There are sturdy, wooden tables and a stone fireplace. They serve *terrine*, house *foie gras*, *charcuterie* and game – in quantity! Menus 110–150F. The rooms are extremely quiet, as you'd expect, and cost 230F. Lovely, warm welcome but you have to book.

ROCROI   08230

☎ |●| LE COMMERCE

4 pl. d'Armes.
☎ 03.24.54.11.15 ☞ 03.24.54.95.31
Restaurant closed Sun evening and Mon. **TV**.

The star-shaped fortifications in perfect condition are worth a visit. They're close to this typical village hotel that's a little old-fashioned but well run. Small, unoriginal rooms though they're spotless. Doubles 230–250F. Regional dishes in the restaurant and there's lots of choice including local *charcuterie* and white pudding with onion. Weekday lunch menu 60F, or 80–180F.

SAINT-DIZIER   53100

☎ HÔTEL PICARDY**

15 av. de Verdun; it's 200m from the train station.
☎ 03.25.05.09.12 ☞ 03.25.05.36.81
TV. **Garden**. **Car park**.

A small hotel in an old craftsman's house with old-style rooms. They're slightly out-dated but clean and comfortable. Numbers 7 and 10 have a view of the little garden at the back, the others look over the street but have effi-

cient double glazing. It's got the atmosphere of a family guesthouse – it's like visiting relatives you haven't seen for ages. Doubles with washing facilities 156F or shower/wc at 232F. An unpretentious, friendly, relaxed place.

ÉCLARON   52290 (9KM SW)

☎ |●| L'HÔTELLERIE DU MOULIN**

3 rue du Moulin; from Saint-Dizier, take the D384 in the direction of the Lac de Der-Chantecoq
☎ 03.25.04.17.76 ☞ 03.25.55.67.01
e hotellerie.moulin@wanadoo.fr
Closed Sun evening and Mon lunchtime, Mon evening also in winter, a fortnight in Oct and three weeks in Jan.
TV. **Car park**.

One of the few romantic spots near the Lake de Der, in an old, wooden mill that's typical of the region. There are five quiet, clean rooms with no particular charm except for number 3, which has a view of the mill and the woods. Doubles 300F with shower/wc and telephone. Half board "strongly advised", from 290F per person. Simple but tasty cuisine; home-smoked salmon, *noisette* of veal with morels, red mullet fillet with vanilla and poached pear with honey and cinnamon ice cream. *Formule du jour* 72F at lunchtime, 85F in the evening (up to 8.30pm), available from Tuesday to Friday lunch. Other menus 115–165F. Unremarkable welcome. With a little more fun, this could be a really nice place to stay.

PERTHES   52100 (10KM W)

🍴 ☎ |●| HÔTEL-RESTAURANT LA CIGOGNE GOURMANDE

It's on the old Route Nationale, opposite the post office.
☎ 03.25.56.40.29 ☞ 03.25.06.22.81
Closed Sun evening, a week in Feb and the second fortnight in July. **TV**. **Car park**.

This rather chic, cosy restaurant caters for formal business lunches and fancy golden wedding parties, but during the week, they serve an excellent 80F set menu. The subtle and carefully cooked dishes are served meticulously. Try the lobster medallions with shellfish *vinaigrette*, *chausson de foie gras*, or turbot fillet. Other menus 80F (except public holidays), and 120–295F and *à la carte* dishes that change with the seasons. The rooms are in a separate little house near the church 200m away; 185F with shower, or 275F with bath and mini-bar. Free coffee.

🍴 |●| LE PARIS-STRASBOURG

It's on the old Route Nationale.

☎ 03.25.56.40.64 ➡ 03.25.56.40.64
Closed Sun evening, Mon, the last fortnight in Aug and the first week in Jan.

A haunt for gourmets but the prices are accessible to all pockets. Very cosily decorated with faultless welcome and service. Rare dishes are prepared but they're good value. The dining room is full of businessmen in the week, tourists and local residents at the weekend. Delicate dishes such as biscuit of zander *à la bohémienne*, farmhouse chicken fillet stuffed with Munster and cumin sauce, quails' eggs with *foie gras* and morel sauce, duck breast with apples and a sculpted garnish. Menus 98–240F. Free coffee.

MONTIER-EN-DER   52220 (24KM SW)

♠ |●| AUBERGE DE PUISIE

54 av. Victor-Hugo (East).
☎ 03.25.94.22.94
TV. Car park.

There's a 12th-century abbey and the national stud in this town, just five minutes from the Lake de Der. And this simple hotel, which is a nice place to stop, with prices that are far from ruinous; doubles 195F with shower/wc and TV. The six rooms are not very big but they're pretty enough and have good facilities. Numbers 1 and 2 look over the quiet courtyard. Traditional cooking and family dishes served in the yellow and blue dining room or out on the shaded terrace. Menus 70–130F, *à la carte* around 100F. Probably worth booking, because the area is a magnet for bird-watchers who come to watch the autumn migrators on the lake. Kindly welcome.

|●| AU JOLI BOIS

Route de Saint-Dizier; it's 1km out of the village on the left, in the direction of Saint-Dizier.
☎ 03.26.60.80.16 ➡ 03.26.60.97.37
Closed evenings except Sat Oct–April, the Feb school holidays, a week at the beginning of Sept, Christmas and New Year's Day.

This big building is easy to miss even though it's by the road – it's slightly set back and hidden by a tall hedge. Keep your eyes peeled because you eat well here. The dining room is rustic-modern and the terrace on the edge of the wood is very pretty. Try the zander fillet in beer and chervil, the *mignon* of pork with grain mustard or the pan-fried tournedos with girolles. The 59F weekday menu is good value and offers a choice of five starters and six main courses followed by cheese and dessert. Other menus

98–138F or 130F *à la carte*. Unusually, they have a list of 30 beers.

SAINTE-MÉNEHOULD   51800

🏂 ♠ |●| HÔTEL-RESTAURANT DE LA POSTE**

54 av. Victor-Hugo (East).
☎ 03.26.60.80.16 ➡ 03.26.60.97.37
Closed Sun evening and Jan. **TV. Car park.**

An unassuming place run by friendly owners, not far from the station. The rooms are nicely old-fashioned but with decent facilities: doubles with shower/wc and telephone go for 210–240F. Rooms at the back are quieter and number 9 is the largest. The 65F menu lists the local speciality, pig's trotters *à la Sainte-Ménehould*. Other menus 98–130F. Free coffee.

♠ |●| HÔTEL-RESTAURANT LE CHEVAL ROUGE**

1 rue Chanzy (Centre).
☎ 03.26.60.81.04 ➡ 03.26.60.93.11
e rouge.cheval@wanadoo.fr
Closed Mon Oct–April, and 15 Nov–7 Dec. **TV.**

The weekday menu is reason enough to stay here. Judge for yourself: sardine *rillettes* with onion marmalade or cucumber gazpacho, followed by sautéed gizzards *basquaise* or fillet of salmon with dill, and for dessert, rhubarb *clafoutis*. The set menu at 92F is equally imaginative: lamb with pineapple chutney in a curry sauce, pan-fried chicken *à la chinoise*, and rack of lamb *dijonnais*. There are other generous set menus up to 250F. *À la carte* you'll find the local speciality, pig's trotters, and, according to the connoisseurs, these are really quite something. Comfortable double rooms 260–270F with shower or bath. They have one room that sleeps four.

|●| L'AUBERGE DU SOLEIL D'OR*

pl. de l'Hôtel-de-Ville (Centre).
☎ 03.26.60.82.49

The owner of this place, Yvan de Singly, a spry eighty-something, has two passions – his pedalo and pig's trotters. He holds the record for crossing the Channel on a pedalo, and the way in which he prepares the local speciality is worth another award. The trotters are wrapped in a cloth, simmered for forty hours in an aromatic stock, kept in a cold room for six hours, covered in batter and served with apple sauce – a world first. His inn is like an 18th-century museum, filled with saucepans, copperware and old furniture. Louis XVI is supposed to have spent his last night here before fleeing to Varennes in 1792. Expect to pay about 250F for a meal. It's open in the evening only and you must book.

FLORENT-EN-ARGONNE   51800 (7.5KM NE)

⩗ ☎ HÔTEL LE JABLOIRE★★★

How to get there: take the D85.
☎ 03.26.60.82.03 ➡ 03.26.60.85.45
Closed Sun evening Nov–March, and Feb. **Disabled access. Car park. TV.**

The hotel is in a splendid 19th-century bourgeois house on the quiet church square. It was a wedding gift from a cooper to his son. Barrel-making was the livelihood of the village, and there's a sculpture of Bacchus with two barrels over the front door that the owner, Yves Oudet, will gladly tell you all about. The rooms are peaceful and bright, all with shower/wc or bath, and cost 250F. A charming place. 10% discount.

SEDAN   08200

⩗ ☎ I●I LE RELAIS★★

rue Gaston-Sauvage (Southwest).
☎ 03.24.27.04.41 ➡ 03.24.29.71.16
Restaurant closed Sun evening.
Garden. TV. Car park.

A huge brick building of some character that was once a soap factory. Today it's a successful hotel where you will get a friendly welcome. The rooms are quiet, and although you're still in town, there's a real country feel to the place. Doubles with shower/wc 250F, with bath 280F. Rooms 31 and 32 have a more personal decor and look onto the garden. Rooms in the adjoining annexe are also good. In the huge restaurant there is a 70F set menu at lunch and dinner, then others at 98F and 140F or à la carte. Traditional cuisine with a choice of regional dishes, including Ardennes pâté and the cacasse à cul nu, a stew of potatoes, onions, bacon and beef. 10% discount on the room rate or free house apéritif.

☎ I●I LE SAINT-MICHEL★

3 rue Saint-Michel (Centre).
☎ 03.24.29.04.61 ➡ 03.24.29.32.67
Restaurant closed Sun evening. **TV.**

This is in an ideal spot in a quiet little street beside the high castle walls – the castle is said to be the largest in Europe, and the town is a thousand years old. Decent rooms, 255F with

shower and 275–300F with shower/wc or bath. The restaurant is pretty traditional, with menus at 70F (lunchtime and evening except Sun), and others 100–195F. They do a few local specialities, like sautéed wild boar, seafood platters and fish dishes. However, the service could be a bit more attentive.

I●I LE MÉDIÉVAL

51 rue de l'Horloge; (Centre).
☎ 03.24.29.11.52
Closed Monday and evenings except Fri and Sat..

Just by the château in the centre of the old town, you'll find this charming little restaurant hidden away. The rustic, bistro-style dining room has an open fire, beams and stone walls. Excellent value for money on the menus which start at 60F. For 89F, you get house *foie gras*, lamb fillet with herb crust and coffee. Wines are affordably priced. Excellent place and the smiles come for free.

⩗I●I RESTAURANT LA DÉESSE

35 av. du Général-Margueritte (Northwest); it's about 200m from the Dijonval Museum of Industry.
☎ 03.24.29.11.52
Closed Sat, a week in Feb, and Aug.

This little bar-restaurant is always full of regulars so you have to grab a table when you get the chance. The atmosphere is warm, friendly and definitely informal. Good set weekday lunch menu at 70F. They use only fresh ingredients, even in the desserts – and there's not a microwave in sight. It's authentic, simple and classy – they do game in season. The service is relaxed but efficient, and the owner goes round to make sure everyone's all right. The weekend set menu, 98F, caters more for families. This is the best value in town. Free coffee.

BAZEILLES   08140 (4KM SE)

⩗ ☎ I●I AUBERGE DU PORT★★

Route de Rémilly (Southeast); from Bazeilles take the D129 towards Rémilly for about 1km.
☎ 03.24.27.13.89 ➡ 03.24.29.35.58
Closed Sat lunchtime, Sun evening, 17 Dec–3 Jan.
Garden. TV. Car park.

This pretty white house stands at the end of a little port, well, a mooring berth actually, on the River Meuse. There's a kind of colonial atmosphere to the place, and the garden and surrounding meadows make it really charming. The characterful bedrooms are in a separate building; those looking out over the river are brighter. They cost 325F for a double with shower or bath. There's an excellent menu at 99F (not Sun), and others 142–235F. The food is beautifully presented and quite imaginative: try herb-covered veal sweetbreads *en crépinette*, or steamed medallions of pork in a ginger sauce. On the fish front, there are *rillettes* of salmon with spices, and roast monkfish with artichokes and ginger. Game in season. Shaded terrace for summer months. 10% discount on the room rate.

⌂ |●| CHÂTEAU DE BAZEILLES-RESTAURANT L'ORANGERIE

It's on the D129, on the edge of the village.
☎ 03.24.26.75.22 **➡** 03.24.26.75.19
Hotel closed end Feb. **Restaurant closed** Sat and Mon lunchtimes, and Sun evening. **Disabled access.** **TV. Car park.**

Within the precincts of the château, this lovely establishment offers quiet, spacious rooms with modern decor and great views. There's a special one, number 201, in a huge separate pavillion with its own open fireplace. Excellent value with rooms 405–460F. The restaurant is of high quality and is situated in the old orangery in the middle of the grounds. Inventive cooking with menus that change constantly; caramelised scallops with chicory *crème brûlée*, roast venison haunch with hazelnuts and brill with butter and flambéed with *anise*. Menus from 148F.

RÉMILLY-AILLICOURT · 08450 (6KM SE)

⋇ ⌂ |●| HÔTEL-RESTAURANT LA SAPINIÈRE**

How to get there: take the D6 towards Raucourt Vouziers.
☎ 03.24.26.75.22 **➡** 03.24.26.75.19
Hotel closed Jan and the third week in Aug.
Restaurant closed Sun evening and Mon lunchtime.
Disabled access. Garden. TV. Car park.

This is a traditional country hotel-restaurant which used to be a coaching inn. The rooms are clean and spruce with good facilities, and quiet as they look out onto the garden; doubles 290F with shower/wc, 310F with bath. The restaurant has a big room which is often used for wedding parties and the like. Weekday menu 95F, then 138–225F. Cuisine is traditional, using a lot of local produce, sometimes with a nice original touch: try Ardennes ham with fresh fruit or grilled lamb chops with sautéed oyster mushrooms in mixed herbs. Game served in season, and summer salads. Pleasant terrace. Free house apéritif.

CARIGNAN · 08110 (20KM SE)

|●| RESTAURANT LA GOURMANDIÈRE

19 av. de Blagny.
☎ 03.24.22.20.99
Closed Mon, three weeks in Jan, and Feb.
Disabled access. Car park.

The rather fancy dining room is in keeping with the style of this elegant bourgeois residence. There's still a very homely atmosphere about the place. The talented and daring chef mixes local produce with foreign spices; try the *chiffonnade* of Ardennes ham powdered with garam masala. The dishes come from all over, so this is the place to be adventurous: tuna salad *mimosa*, braised fillet of smoked haddock with preserved lemons , saffron and cumin and pastry case of crab with a salmon cushion. The weekday lunch menu at 72F gives you a choice from two starters, two main courses and a dessert; others 120–265F. Lovely terrace in the garden for sunny days. Free coffee.

BUZANCY · 08240 (35KM S)

⌂ |●| LE SAUMON

pl. Chanzy; it's on the D6.
☎ 03.24.30.00.42 **➡** 03.25.30.27.47
❻ h-saumon@wanadoo.fr
Closed Fri evening, Sat lunchtime, a fortnight in Feb and a fortnight in Nov. **TV.**

A charming hotel that would be easy to fall in love with, right in the middle of the small town. The house has been totally refurbished – each of the nine rooms is decorated differently but with the same taste throughout. The rooms are different in size but all have the same facilities; some have a garden view. Doubles from 190F. Two dining rooms, one of them a very pleasant bistro offering a *menu-carte* put together in the light of the fresh produce bought at market. Menus from 95F. Particularly friendly welcome.

SÉZANNE · 51120

⋇ ⌂ |●| HÔTEL-RESTAURANT DE LA CROIX D'OR**

53 rue Notre-Dame (Centre).
☎ 03.26.80.61.10 **➡** 03.26.80.65.20
Closed Tues and 2–17 Jan.
Disabled access. TV. Car park.

Gun dogs and birds of prey watch over the car park of this modestly priced establishment. Simple rooms with basin, 150F, attractive ones with shower or bath, 280–300F. The set menu at 85F is ideal for travellers on a budget, but there are others up to 210F for more of a blow-out. The chef regularly goes to the fruit and vegetable market at Rungis to get fresh, seasonal produce. Free coffee.

☎ |●| HÔTEL-RESTAURANT LE RELAIS CHAMPENOIS**

157 rue Notre-Dame; it's on the Troyes road.
☎ 03.26.80.58.03 ➡ 03.26.81.35.32
e relaischamp@infonie.fr
Closed Fri and Sun evenings out of season, and 15 Nov–6 Jan. **Disabled access. TV. Car park**.

As you come into the village you enter real Champagne country. This is a friendly old inn with ancient walls. The lovely rooms have been delightfully renovated – from 250F with shower/wc to 310F with bath. Monsieur Fourmi is the chef here, and he prepares superb food inspired by local produce — scallop salad in Reims vinegar, medallion of monkfish with wild nettles and cockerel in champagne sauce, to give you an idea. Set menus 95F (in the week) to 250F. Over more than twenty years, Monsieur and Mme Fourmi have built up a well-deserved reputation for offering quality service and a great welcome. Ask to try a glass of Ratafia de Champagne – a discovery.

TROYES 10000

🏃 ☎ HÔTEL DES COMTES DE CHAMPAGNE**

54–56 rue de la Monnaie (Centre); it's in a street in the old town between the town hall and the station.
☎ 03.25.73.11.70 ➡ 03.25.73.06.02
Disabled access. TV. Pay garage.

A 12th-century building, which was the bank of the counts of Champagne when they reigned supreme. The walls are thick and the wood panelling from the time of Louis XIV creates an authentic feeling of the past. There's also a small, quiet conservatory. Good prices for a two-star hotel: doubles from 120F with basin, to 210F with shower/wc and 290F with bath. Some rooms are particularly spacious. There's a charge for the garage. Excellent welcome. A very good place. 10% discount.

🏃 ☎ HÔTEL ARLEQUIN**

50 rue de Turenne (Centre); it's near the church of Saint-Pantaléon.

☎ 03.25.83.12.70 ➡ 03.25.83.12.99
TV.

The *Arlequin* is a brightly coloured hotel just off the pedestrian area, where friendliness seems to be the byword. The staff take real pride in looking after guests. They have about twenty bright, spacious rooms at reasonable prices: doubles with shower 210F, 260F with shower/wc and 290F with bath. They also have a number of family rooms that can sleep three, four or five. If you decide to stay in Troyes, this is the place to be. Another bonus: a loyalty card gets your seventh night free – a good deal for regular visitors or if you are staying slightly longer. 10% discount.

🏃 ☎ HÔTEL DE TROYES**

168 av. du Général-Leclerc (Northwest).
☎ 03.25.71.23.45 ➡ 03.25.79.12.14
e hotel.de.troyes@wanadoo.fr
Disabled access. Garden. TV. Car park.

For those who prefer somewhere outside the town centre. Immaculate rooms 285F with shower/wc, decorated in a contemporary style. You'll get a charming welcome. Buffet breakfast 39F. There's no restaurant but the owners will gladly guide you to good places to eat nearby. 10% discount.

☎ HÔTEL LE CHAMP DES OISEAUX***

20 rue Linard Gonthier (Centre); it's near the cathedral.
☎ 03.25.80.58.50 ➡ 03.25.80.98.34
e menage@champdesoiseaux.com
Disabled access. TV. Pay car park.

In a cobbled street with half-timbered houses, this three-star hotel occupies two 15th-century houses. There are twelve rooms and a private courtyard, which is a lovely spot to eat breakfast in the summer. Most of the rooms range between 490F and 830F for a double, but if you want the very best, the two enormous suites with elegant names – *La suite médiévale* and *Les Bengalis* will set you back 980F. They're both gorgeous, with exposed beams, armchairs, period furniture and so on. A bewitchingly delightful place, ideal for a special occasion or a romantic break, if you're willing to pay the price.

|●| LE COIN DE LA PIERRE

34 rue Viardin (Centre).
☎ 03.25.73.58.44
Closed Sun and a fortnight in Aug.

This is in an old 16th-century, half-timbered house on a street corner. You go in through a little courtyard with a spiral staircase curling upstairs. The huge room is very welcoming with its fireplace; the perfect setting to try their cheese specialities from the mountains; *raclettes*, *pierrades* and so on. Great variety of salads from 40–47F. Summer lunctime menu at 50F with a mega-salad and dessert or 60F in winter for a cheese dish and dessert. A good place if you can't face another *andouillette*. Nice atmosphere and regular customers.

|●| LA GALTOUZE

18 rue Urbain-IV (Centre); it's next to the tourist office.
☎ 03.25.73.22.75

There are three chic dining rooms in this classy 17th-century building, one on the ground floor and two upstairs – the one at the back has a brick fireplace with a wooden chimneypiece. Cuisine is traditional yet simple, and comes in generous portions. The 68F menu, served daily, includes *terrine de campagne*, a main course such as grilled *andouillette* or *bœuf bourguignon*, cheese and dessert. Good going. There's a *formule* at 55F and two other menus at 79 and 98F.

🍴|●| AU JARDIN GOURMAND

31 rue Paillot de Montabert (Centre); it's near the town hall.
☎ 03.25.73.36.13
Closed Sun and Mon lunchtime, three weeks in Aug and a week in Feb.

This stylish and intimate little restaurant is right in the old part of Troyes. It has a pretty courtyard, which is heated and sheltered in winter and which looks out onto a 16th-century timbered wall that the owner restored himself. Excellent welcome. Menus at 70F (lunchtime) or 100F. But what really makes this place stand out is its speciality: home-made *andouillettes* 5A cooked in ten different ways. This is a must if you're a fan. All their other dishes use only fresh ingredients. Wine by the glass. Free coffee.

|●| L'ÉTOILE

9–11 rue Pithou (Centre).
☎ 03.25.73.12.65
Closed every evening, all day Sun, and Aug.

This old local bistro is set back from the cobbled street. The bar has been polished by thousands of elbows over the years; it's a place where regulars come to down a glass of *vin jaune* before lunch or dinner. The house speciality is calf's head, is excellent. At 70F it's a must. The restaurant is so full that you may need to book or come early. The appetising 90F menu includes starter, *andouillette*,

cheese and dessert. There's a lovely terrace open in summer.

🍴|●| LA PANINOTECA

27 rue Paillot-de-Montabert (Centre); near Saint-Jean church in a road at right angles off the rue Champeaux.
☎ 03.25.73.91.34
Closed Sat lunchtime, Sun and 15–30 Aug.

This street is lined with the liveliest restaurants and bars in town but there are also some splendid 16th-century, wood-fronted houses. Bernardo opened this place which quickly became a regular haunt of the Trojan youth. It's packed. There's a warm atmosphere and tasty Italian cooking, including plenty of *panini* – rolls with all manner of fillings. The choice of pasta sauces is extensive and there are some tasty meat dishes. Prices are fair; pasta around 45F, rolls 20–30F, and around 90F for a meal. Free coffee.

|●| RESTAURANT LE CAFÉ DE PARIS

63 rue du Général-de-Gaulle (Centre); it's next to the church of la Madeleine.
☎ 03.25.73.08.30
Closed Sun and Mon evenings, and 20 July–10 Aug.

A good place with average prices that has something for everyone. Set menus 120–235F. The chef takes a straightforward approach to his cooking – house brawn with tomato *fondue*, quail salad, saddle of rabbit with broad beans, *croustillant* of scorpion fish with sorrel, Troyes *andouillette gras* with Chaource cheese – and although it's essentially a lunch spot, it's a warm and friendly choice for a dinner by candlelight.

SAINTE-SAVINE   10300 (2.5KM WEST)

🍴🏠|●| MOTEL SAVINIEN**

87 rue La Fontaine; take the N60, the "Paris par Sens" road, 2km further on turn right
☎ 03.25.79.24.90 ➡ 03.25.78.04.61
Restaurant closed Sun evening and Mon lunchtime.
Disabled access. Swimming pool. TV. Car park.

Numerous signposts ensure that this hotel is not hard to find. Though it looks as if it could be part of a chain, it isn't; it is, however, popular with people on the road for business. There's a swimming pool, a sauna and a gym. The rooms are pretty standard, and lack character, but prices are attractive considering the quality of service: 260F for doubles with shower or twins with shower/wc or bath at 280F. Breakfast costs 40F. Lunch menu 90F, and others 130–195F. Very warm welcome. Free coffee.

BRÉVIANDES   10450 (5KM SE)

☎ |O| HÔTEL-RESTAURANT LE PAN DE BOIS**

35 av. du Général-Leclerc; it's on the N71 to Dijon before the intersection on the southbound bypass.
☎ 03.25.75.02.31 ➡ 03.25.49.67.84
Hotel closed Sun evening. **Restaurant closed** Sun and Mon lunchtime.
Disabled access. Garden. TV. Car park.

A fairly new, well-conceived establishment with all the facilities you would expect from a chain. The modern building is designed to suit the local style. The rooms at the back, looking out onto a row of trees, are the most peaceful. Doubles with bath 310F. The restaurant is just next door in a similar building; the cheapest set menu is 94F (not served on public holidays) and a meal *à la carte* costs about 170F. They specialise in meats and steaks chargrilled over the open fire and serve good local wines. The terrace is especially pleasant in summer.

SAINT-ANDRÉ-LES-VERGERS   10120 (5KM SW)

☎ CITOTEL LES ÉPINGLIERS**

180 route d'Auxerre; take the N77 in the direction of Auxerre, and it's 500m after the Saint-André roundabout.
☎ 03.25.75.05.99 ➡ 03.25.75.32.22
TV. Disabled access. Garden. Car park.

This modern hotel has about fifteen rooms with good facilities – bath, TV, telephone and alarm. Each room looks out onto a bit of the flower garden. Doubles 230–290F, and buffet breakfast costs 40F. The owner is happy to recomment places to eat, though there is a restaurant next door which is under separate management.

⌂ |O| LA GENTILHOMMIÈRE

180 route d'Auxerre.
☎ 03.25.49.35.64 @ gentilhommière@wanadoo.fr
Closed Sun and Tues evenings, Wed and Aug. **Car park.**

A modern building which belies a stylish interior. The atmosphere, service and food are quite refined: witness the slivers of sweetbreads with a concentrated sauce of *Vin de Paille*, the pressed *foie gras* with leeks in Ratafia jelly, the roast quail with spiced bread sauce, roast shark with sea urchin cream sauce, the moist cake with runny chocolate and the banana and ginger sorbet – all served with Mozart playing gently in the background. Delicious food that's a real hit with businessmen and locals. The chef serves *andouillette*

chopped into small pieces and melts Chaource cheese over the top – an absolute must. Set menus 120–330F or 250F *à la carte*. Free coffee.

FOUCHÈRES   10260 (23KM SE)

⌂|O| L'AUBERGE DE LA SEINE

1 faubourg de Bourgogne.; it's on the N71 between Troyes and Bar-sur-Seine.
☎ 03.25.40.71.11
Closed Tues evening, Wed out of season, a fortnight in Oct and a week in Feb. **Car park.**

A charming restaurant on the banks of the Seine that could be straight out of a de Maupassant story. The dining room has been carefully arranged; the bay windows open onto the river so you can enjoy the cool view, and quacking ducks will serenade you as you dine. The cuisine is delicate and inventive, featuring Chaource cheese custard, *croustillant* of *andouillette* with cider, and river fish, the speciality of the house. There's a 65F weekday lunch menu, a *menu du terroir* at 90F and others 130F and 165F. A stylish place where you will be warmly welcomed. Free coffee.

VITRY-LE-FRANÇOIS   51300

⌂ ☎ |O| HÔTEL-RESTAURANT LE BON SÉJOUR*

faubourg Léon-Bourgeois (East); it's about 500m from the centre on the Nancy road.
☎ 03.26.74.02.36 ➡ 03.26.73.44.21
Closed Fri evening, Sat, the second fortnight in Aug, and 24 Dec–3 Jan. **TV. Car park.**

This is a small, basic hotel that's clean and well run. The rooms, in an annexe with a drab corridor, look out onto a quiet tree-lined street. Doubles with shower/wc cost 200F, 240F with bath. Set menus 59–140F. There's a dish of the day and options *à la carte*. It's has the kind of atmosphere you get in a provincial bistro. Free house apéritif.

☎ |O| HÔTEL-RESTAURANT DE LA POSTE***

pl. Royer-Collard (Centre); it's behind the Notre-Dame cathedral.
☎ 03.26.74.02.65 ➡ 03.26.74.54.71
Closed Sun and 23 Dec–3 Jan.
Disabled access. TV. Car park.

The hotel seems better value for money than the restaurant, where the cheapest set menu is 108F. There are others at 130F, 160F and 220F, and you can choose *à la carte*. They do a lot of fish, and smoke their salmon on the premises. You'll pay 310F for a double room with shower/wc and telephone, 340–370F for a double with bath, 380F for a family room sleeping three, or 620F for a suite with bath. There are nine rooms, 480F, with a Jacuzzi or you can relax in the sauna or solarium. The bar has a great choice of beers and whiskies. The hotel looks out onto a quiet street, where you can park quite easily. Warm welcome.

♠ |●| HÔTEL-RESTAURANT DE LA CLOCHE**

34 rue Aristide Briand (Centre).
☎ 03.26.74.03.84 ➡ 03.26.74.15.52
Hotel closed last fortnight in Aug and 20 Dec–2 Jan.
Restaurant closed Sun evening out of season.

A peaceful provincial town that was 95% destroyed in the war. It's not exactly an architectural jewel. Mme Sautet will make you feel welcome. Everything is impeccable, whether it be the napkins in the restaurant, the sheets, the bedspreads or the bathroom towels. The windows have been double glazed so nothing will disturb your sleep. A double room with shower/wc or bath costs 360–390F a night. Jaques Sautet, the chef in charge, was classically trained and knows his onions – he specialises in good traditional French food and has a talent for *pâtisseries*. His skill has won three stars for the restaurant. There's a daily set menu at 130F, a fish menu at 200F, and a more lavish one with truffle specialities from Périgord at 280F. Children's menu 69F.

|●| RESTAURANT L'ASIE

54 rue de la tour (Centre).
☎ 03.26.72.13.87
Closed Mon, Tues lunchtime and 10 Aug–3 Sept.

Service noon–2pm and 7–10pm. This terrifically popular restaurant, opened by Chinese Cambodians in the late 1980s, is full every night. The place is exceptionally clean, you always get a really warm welcome, and the food is consistently good. They specialise in both Chinese and Thai cuisine. Set lunch menu 59F. Evening *à la carte* only, around 90F for a meal. Air-conditioned dining room.

|●| LA PIZZA

17 Grande Rue de Vaux.
☎ 03.26.74.17.63

The pizzas come with a range of sizes to suit all appetites, and with original, tasty toppings.

Great welcome. Around 60F for a meal. The menus and the decor change often.

VITRY-EN-PERTHOIS 51300 (4KM NE)

|●| AUBERGE DE LA PAVOISE

Centre; on the D382, in the direction of Givry-en-Argonne.
☎ 03.26.74.59.00
Open Sat evening, in the week by reservation. **Closed** first fortnight in Jan.

A converted cow shed, which was part of the working farm, done up in rustic style. Menus cost 105F, 120F and 130F. For starters try chicken gizzard salad with snail butter, chicken soufflé or creamed mushroom soup, followed by leg of duck with mirabelle plums or guinea fowl with grapes. And for dessert, *charlotte*, tarts or *bavarois,* which are a hit with everyone. Wines include Aligoté, Morgon, Regnié, all at reasonable prices. They don't accept credit cards.

SAINTE-MARIE-DU-LAC 51290 (20KM SE)

|●| LE CYCLODER

2 rue de l'Église.
☎ 03.26.72.37.05
Closed 15 Oct–April except weekends in March and Nov.

A lovely *crêperie* where you can get great quality *galettes* from 12–30F and *crêpes* from 10–23F along with a friendly welcome. You can hire bikes by the hour for 25F, for a half-day for 50F or a full day for 75F. Visit the nearby model village, which features old Champagne buildings of wattle and daub. Credit cards not accepted.

GIFFAUMONT-CHAMPAUBERT 51290 (26KM SE)

🎄 ♠ |●| HÔTEL-RESTAURANT LE CHEVAL BLANC**

21 rue du Lac; take the D384, then the D153.
☎ 03.26.72.62.65 ➡ 03.26.73.96.97
Restaurant closed Sun evening, Mon, Tues lunchtime, 2–23 Jan and 2–25 Sept. **TV. Car park**.

Set in an adorable village full of half-timbered houses. Thierry Gérardin, the young owner, was spurred into rapid action: all the bathrooms have been renovated and there's a new reception and sitting room. The modern rooms cost 320–360F for a double with shower or bath. Wonderful welcome. The cheapest set menu is 125F – duck *foie gras* or scallops in raspberry wine are typical.

Other menus up to 195F. 10% discount on the room rate except July–Aug.

🎿 |●| RESTAURANT LA GRANGE AUX ABEILLES

4 rue du Grand-Der; it's on the D13 towards Arrigny, 500m from the village of Giffaumont.
☎ 03.26.72.61.97 **e** infos@lgaa.com
Closed Tues except July–Aug, and Dec-Feb.
Disabled access. **Car park**.

This timber-framed inn is typical of the buildings in the Champagne region and many can be found in the Der. It's only a five-minute walk from the lake of Der-Chantecoq. Sadly, you can't see the lake from the dining room, but there's a shady terrace with views of the countryside. Set weekday menu 85F then up to 158F. The *crêperie-brasserie* is good for families, and the kids can go off and find out about bees and the secrets of honey in an exhibition put together by the owner, Michel Fagot. Free coffee and game of mini-golf.

VOUZIERS   08400

🏠 |●| ARGONNE HÔTEL**

route de Reims; it's on the way out of town on the Châlons-Retel road, by the first roundabout.
☎ 03.24.71.42.14 ➡ 03.24.71.83.69
Restaurant closed Sun evening and Christmas– New Year. **TV**. **Car park**.

This modern building in the commercial park is neither characterful nor charming, though the welcoming owners certainly are. It's an ideal place to overnight stop. The rooms are attractively decorated and good value: 230F for a double with shower/wc or bath. Menus at 95F and 150F. Very classic cuisine with occasional exotic touches — try rabbit with cream and thyme, or pork fillet *à l'indienne* – basically a curry.

CORSICA

20 Corse

AJACCIO 20000

🏃 🏠 HÔTEL MARENGO**

2 rue Marengo, BP 244; it's near the casino.
☎ 04.95.21.43.66 📠 04.95.21.51.26
Closed 15 Nov–15 March. **TV. Car park.**

This is a lovely little place at the end of a cul-de-sac. Some rooms look out onto a peaceful courtyard with flowers everywhere. Warm welcome. Double rooms 360F with shower in peak season. It's basic but well run and has good facilities including air-conditioning and double-glazing. 10% discount for a minimum two-night stay except July–Aug.

🏠 HÔTEL IMPERIAL***

6 bd. Albert 1er.
☎ 04.95.21.50.62 📠 04.95.21.15.20

A three-star hotel with a lovely, Napoleonic-style entrance. Take a look at the poster for Abel Gance's film epic, *Napoleon*, in reception. The rooms are cosy and old-feeling, but comfortable and well maintained. Depending on facilities and the season, doubles are 290–480F. It's not cheap, but prices include a parasol and sun bed on the private beach just across the way. There are other rooms in the more modern annexe behind which are smaller and don't have air-conditioning. *Le Baroko* is the restaurant and the cooking is pretty good, which is just as well as half board (275–375F per person) is compulsory July–Aug.

🏃 🏠 HÔTEL FESCH***

7 rue Fesch (Centre).
☎ 04.95.51.62.62 📠 04.95.21.83.36
www.hotel-fesch.com
Closed 15 Dec–2 Jan.

The *Fesch* is very well located in the centre. The rooms are mostly comfortable and the furniture is made of chestnut wood. The price of a room depends on the facilities and the season. Doubles 325F and 455F with shower/wc or bath. If you want a top-floor room with a balcony, it will cost 50F extra. Professional service. Free breakfast.

🍽 A CASA

21 av. Noël-Franchini (North); it's 2km north – go along the coast road towards the airport and turn left at the end of bd. Charles-Bonaparte.
☎ 04.95.22.34.78
Closed Sun except July–Aug, and 20 Dec–10 Jan.

This restaurant is outside the centre, but the originality of the place draws a lot of local people. They've squeezed about ten tables onto the patio/balcony which is surrounded by plants, flowers and parasols. The cooking is uncomplicated but good; the *menu Corse* is particularly tasty. Weekday menus at 76F and others at 125 and 180F. Excellent Sartène or Muscat wine. The real attraction is on a Friday or Saturday night when there's a *menu spectacle* because Frank, the boss, a professional magician, puts on a show. He does all the tricks – cutting people in half, levitation – and even burns his partner alive! You have to book and you'll have a great evening.

🍽 LE 20123

2 rue du Roi-de-Rome; it's in the old town.
☎ 04.95.21.50.05
Closed Mon and Sat lunchtimes, mid-Jan to mid-Feb.

This restaurant used to be in Pila Canale, up in the mountains behind Ajaccio, where the

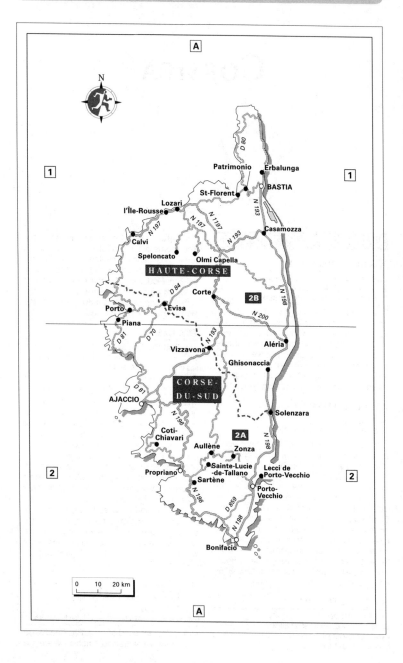

post code was 20123. They moved and set up a good, new place with the same decor as before. Inside it's almost like a Corsican village with a fountain and small houses; they've even got an old Vespa parked there. There's a small terrace as well. Lunch menu 95F, or for 165F there's serious Corsican *charcuterie*, *brocciu* tart made with sheep's-milk cheese, followed by a variety of meats – pork, veal or boar – which are grilled or served as stews. Finish with some genuine local cheese and a simple dessert like flan made with ground chestnuts. Good cooking in a place with character, but they don't accept credit cards.

BASTELICACCIA   20129 (13KM E)

♠ M'HÔTEL L'ORANGERAIE**

It's on the way out of the village coming from Ajaccio.
☎ 04.95.20.00.09 ➡ 04.95.20.09.24
TV. Garden. Car park.

The garden is one of the most beautiful in Corsica with palms, arbutus and orange trees. The bungalows are hidden away in glorious Mediterranean vegetation. You can rent studios for two or four people by the night or the week, 200–400F out of season and 320–500F July–Aug. They're not brand-new but they're well equipped, with good bedding, thermal insulation, hair-drier, kitchen, terrace and barbecue. There's a small swimming pool. Remember to book in advance; it's often full.

AULLÈNE   20116

♠ I●I HÔTEL-RESTAURANT DE LA POSTE*

Centre.
☎ 04.95.78.61.21
Closed Oct–April.

This attractive stone inn was built when people were going round in carriages. It has a lovely view over the mountains. Double rooms 230F with shower/wc on the landing. Half board, 280F per person, is obligatory July–Aug. The cooking in the restaurant is simple – in season, try the wild boar or the house *charcuterie* at any time. The owner, Jeannot Benedetti, knows all the interesting places to visit and writes guide books you can borrow.

QUENZA   20122 (6KM E)

⅔ ♠ I●I AUBERGE SOLE E MONTI**

Centre; take the D420, in the direction of Aullène.
☎ 04.95.78.62.53 ➡ 04.95.78.63.88
Closed Oct to 15 April. **TV. Garden. Car park.**

Félicien Balesi has run this friendly inn for more than 25 years. He's a *bon vivant* who knows how to make his guests feel at home. The regulars tend to gather round the fireplace in the sitting room to while away an evening, a lovely thing to do after a meal of delicious dishes inspired by old Corsican recipes. Set menus 150F (not Sun), 200F and 250F. Pleasant, well-equipped rooms. Half board, compulsory from July to September, costs 350F per person and 450F in season. There are renovations under way so the prices are likely to go up. The perfect place to admire the beauty of the Corsican mountains. Free apéritif.

LEVIE   20170 (15KM E)

♠ I●I FERME-AUBERGE A PIGNATA

Route du Pianu (Northwest); from Levie, drive 3km along the Sainte-Lucie-de-Tallano road, then turn right towards Cucuruzzu; 2km further on, turn left through the second gate, up the rising track.
☎ 04.95.78.41.90 ➡ 04.95.78.46.03
Closed Reservations only. **Car park.**

A very secretive inn you have to be in the know to find – there are no signposts, no arrows, no board, nothing. When you get there, however, the hospitality is tremendous. Half board only, for 330–370F per person. The rooms are spacious. According to the locals the authentic Corsican specialities you get here are the best in the region. These include cannelloni with *brocciu* (a mild sheep's milk cheese), stuffed aubergines, and braised wild boar. There's no *à la carte*, but the 170F set menu is excellent and the portions are large. Wines are extra but there's a good house wine. A great place.

BASTIA   20200

⅔ ♠ HÔTEL CYMÉA

Route du Cap.
☎ 04.95.31.41.71 ➡ 04.95.31.72.65
Closed 15 Dec–15 Jan.
Disabled access. TV. Pay garage.

A long, 1970s building that's very well maintained with air-conditioned rooms and fans. Behind, the big garden slopes down to a little pebbly beach 30m from the hotel. Depending on the season and whether you have a sea or road view, doubles are 340–550F, including breakfast. The sea-view rooms all have a balcony which is ideal for watching the sun rise over breakfast. Free use of the lock-up garage.

☎ L'ALIVI***

Route du Cap; it's 1km from the marina on the right.
☎ 04.95.55.00.00 ➡ 04.95.31.03.95
Swimming pool. Disabled access. Car park.

Seen from the sea, this long, oblong structure, three storeys high, doesn't do the coastline any favours. But inside, you really appreciate the comfort of the rooms and direct access to the pebble beach. All rooms have a sea view and a balcony and all the facilities you'd expect from a three-star hotel. Depending on the season, a double room with shower costs 510–680F, with bath 600–800F.

❚●❚ RESTAURANT A CASARELLA

6 rue Sainte-Croix (South); it's in the citadel near the old Genoese governors' palace.
☎ 04.95.32.02.32
Closed Sat lunchtime, Sun and three weeks in Nov.

The inventive chef here prepares good authentic Corsican dishes scented with herbs from the *maquis*. You have to climb up to the citadel, near the Palais of the Genoese governors, to find the place. Take a seat on the terrace, with views of the old port down below, and enjoy a feast. Try the *casgiate*, a *fromage frais* fritter baked in the oven, the prawns in flaky pastry and the rolled veal with herbs, which is excellent. Desserts include the curious *storzapretti*, a stodgy cake that the people here used to bake for the parish priest on Sundays, and the wonderful *fiadone*, a cheese and orange flan. Set lunch menu 130F or 180F *à la carte*. A good place.

ERBALUNGA   20222 (10KM N)

☎ HÔTEL CASTEL BRANDO

It's in the village.
☎ 04.95.30.10.30 ➡ 04.95.33.98.18
Closed mid-Oct to end March.
TV. Disabled access. Swimming pool. Car park.

This hotel is in an authentic 19th-century Corsican mansion and has great character and charm. It has been tastefully restored and furnished with antiques. The walls are colour-washed in strong pigments and there's an impressive monumental staircase; it all feels somewhat Latin American. The garden is planted with palm trees. The rooms in the annexe have air-conditioning and a corner kitchen; they are quieter than those in the main building. Doubles 380–630F depending on facilities and season. The welcome is second to none.

CASAMOZZA   20200 (20KM S)

♨ ☎ ❚●❚ CHEZ WALTER

It's on the N193, about 2.4km south from the airport crossroads.
☎ 04.95.36.00.09 ➡ 04.95.36.18.92
Restaurant closed Sun out of season.
TV. Disabled access. Swimming pool. Garden. Car park.

A fine, comfortable and reliable establishment that's very professionally run. Very good facilities in the air-conditioned rooms. Doubles with shower or bath 390–500F depending on the season. There's a swimming pool, a tennis court and a lovely garden. It's a place used by crews stopping over or football teams come to play against Bastia. The restaurant has a good reputation and there are good fish dishes (sea bream, crayfish and seafood). Menu at 110F. Free coffee.

BONIFACIO   20169

☎ DOMAINE DE LICETTO

Route du phare de Pertusato.
Hotel ☎ 04.95.73.03.59 ➡ 04.95.73.03.59
Restaurant ☎ 04.95.73.19.48
Closed lunchtimes. **Disabled access. Car park**.

There's an unusual view of Bonifacio from the grounds here and you can make out the upper and lower towns. The *Domaine* is right in the *maquis* and the modern hotel is in a separate building from the restaurant. The rooms are smart; 200–420F with shower/wc or 280–500F with bath. The single set menu, 170F, is gargantuan and includes everything: apéritif, starter, two courses, cheeses, desserts, wine, coffee and *digestif*. Typically Corsican cuisine: stuffed squid, milk-fed lamb in sauce, cabbage stuffed with chestnuts, and iced charlotte with chestnut cream. It is essential to book, and credit cards are not accepted.

♨ ☎ HÔTEL DES ÉTRANGERS*

av. Sylvère-Bohn; it's 300m from the port, hidden beneath a cliff, at the side of the road from Ajaccio.
☎ 04.95.73.01.09 ➡ 04.95.73.16.97
Closed 31 Oct–1 April. **TV. Car park**.

Pretty close to the road but the soundproofing is efficient. Good facilities including shower/wc, telephone and TV. Most rooms have air-conditioning and they're clean. 260–470F for a double depending on the season which is good value for Bonifacio. Lock-up for motorbikes. 10% discount April, May and Oct.

♠ |●| A TRAMA

Cartarana, route de Santa-Marza; it's 1.5km from the town centre.
☎ 04.95.73.17.17 ➡ 04.95.73.17.79
Restaurant closed telephone out of season. **TV**.

In a peaceful, very lovely setting amidst greenery, this new, small complex has been handsomely built and it's well maintained. There are 25 rooms at garden level, each with a private terrace facing the swimming pool – ideal for breakfast. Rooms all have modern facilities like TV, mini-bar and air-conditioning, and the beds are "dorsopedic", apparently. Doubles 395–1010F in Aug depending on season. It's a nice place and the welcome is calm, courteous and professional. The restaurant is called *Le Clos Vatel* and has a good reputation.

♠ |●| HÔTEL-RESTAURANT DU CENTRE NAUTIQUE***

It's on the marina.
☎ 04.95.73.02.11 ➡ 04.95.73.17.47
TV.

This big, beautiful building stands along on its own quay that's quiet compared to the one opposite. It has ten duplex rooms with real class. They're spacious and airy, with contemporary interiors and lots of facilities like a mini-bar and air-conditioning. There's a sofa bed in the sitting room on the first floor and a bedroom and shower upstairs. A room with a sea view costs 550–1050F depending on the season. The price drops for garden-view rooms. There's also a restaurant serving excellent fresh pasta.

CALVI   20260

♠ |●| HÔTEL-RESTAURANT CASA-VECCHIA

Route de Santore; it's 200m from the beach and pine wood.
☎ 04.95.65.09.33 ➡ 04.95.65.37.93
Closed winter but accepts reservations. **Car park**.

The accommodation is in simple, attractively priced bungalows in a garden full of flowers. Rooms are 200F with shower and shared outside wc, 360F with shower/wc. Good, generously served family cooking with menus at 85F and 110F. Half board is obligatory July–Aug, at 480–640F for two people. Meals are served on a shaded terrace. Nice welcome from Madame and her daughters.

♠ HÔTEL LES ARBOUSIERS**

Route de Pietra-Maggiore (South); go about 800m in the direction of Bastia, then turn right at the start of the pine forest, 5 minutes from the beach, and follow the signs.
☎ 04.95.65.04.47 ➡ 04.95.65.26.14
Closed Oct–April. **Garden**. **Car park**.

It's best to stay just outside Calvi, where you get more space. This hotel is in an attractive big house with pink walls. An old wooden staircase leads up to the bedrooms. The decor isn't spectacular but the place is very clean and there are lots of pleasant little terraces overlooking the courtyard. Ask for a south-facing room, for the sun. The prices are reasonable for Calvi. Doubles with bath 235–310F. Good welcome.

♣ ♠ RÉSIDENCE LES ALOÈS**

Quartier Donatéo (East).
☎ 04.95.65.01.46 ➡ 04.95.65.01.67
e info@hotel-les-aloes.com
Closed Oct to mid-April. **TV**. **Garden**. **Car park**.

This hotel was built in the 1960s on a fabulous site above Calvi, so you get a panoramic view of the bay, the citadel and the wild countryside towards Monte Cinto. The surroundings are peaceful with flowers everywhere. The decor in the foyer is a bit kitsch but elegant, while the refurbished rooms have TV, telephone and balcony. Prices range from 250F for a double depending on the season and the view (mountain or sea). Attentive staff. 10% discount for a two-night minimum stay Sept to mid-July.

♣ ♠ LE GRAND HÔTEL**

3 bd. Wilson (Centre).
☎ 04.95.65.09.74 ➡ 04.95.65.25.18
Closed Nov–March. **TV**.

They don't build places like this turn-of-the-(20th)-century grand hotel any more; corridors as wide as a room, a smoking room as large as a ball room and giant bedrooms. The tea room looks a bit dated, and the armchairs need to be re-covered, but they're comfortable; the rooms themselves have been given a lick of paint and the beds are good. Doubles 380–560F depending on the season and facilities. Nice welcome, a good atmosphere and a spectacular view from the breakfast room: it's high up, so you look down on the rooftops of Calvi to the sea beyond. Free breakfast in April, May and Oct.

♣ |●| L'ABRI CÔTIER

quai Landry; it's by the harbour.
☎ 04.95.65.12.76
Closed Oct to mid-April

The restaurant is on the first floor, over a bar and tea room. There's a big dining room that looks over the marina. Excellent spot. The cooking zings with really fresh flavours – try their grilled fish with a drizzle of olive oil, the starters that combine fresh fruit and vegetables or their dishes using *brocciu* (mild sheep's milk cheese). Pleasant, efficient service and one of the most reliable places in Calvi. Menus 110F and 180F. Free coffee.

CORTE   20250

☎ HÔTEL DE LA POSTE*

2 pl. du Duc-de-Padoue (Centre).
☎ 04.95.46.01.37
Closed Dec. **Disabled access**.

An old hotel on a shady square, with simple, reasonably priced rooms which look out at the back. Doubles 200F with basin, 250F with shower/wc. Good if you're on a budget and want somewhere central. They don't take credit cards.

⚜ |●| L'OLIVERAIE

Lieu-dit Perru; head for the university, when you come to the junction with the main road, it's 150m further on the left.
☎ 04.95.46.06.32
Closed Mon evening in winter, and Nov.

This very good restaurant is on the outskirts of town surrounded by greenery. Mme Mattei uses Corsican produce to prepare tasty dishes like *buglidicce*, *fromage frais* fritters, herb tart, squid stuffed with *brocciu* (mild sheep milk's cheese), and for dessert, hazelnut and ground chestnut tart, which is the house speciality. Generous helpings. Popular with students and staff from the neighbouring campus. Set menus 65–150F. Free *digestif*.

|●| U MUSEU

rampe Ribanelle; head for pl. du Poilu near the citadel.
☎ 04.95.61.08.36
Closed Sun in winter, ten days in Feb, ten days after All Saints' Day and a fortnight at Christmas.

An attractive restaurant where you'll get good food without paying a fortune. Very pleasant terrace. Set *formule* at 75F for main course and dessert or an 89F menu – herb tart, wild boar stew, and *délice* of chestnuts – which is truly delicious. The jugs of AOC wine go down a treat. A good place to go, but the serving staff get stressed out in summer, especially when it's full.

COTI-CHIAVARI   20138

⚜ ☎ |●| HÔTEL-RESTAURANT LE BELVÉDÈRE

How to get there: it's on the left of the Acqua Doria road before you get to the village.
☎ 04.95.27.10.32 ☛ 04.95.27.12.99
Hotel closed Nov–Jan. **Restaurant closed** evenings in winter.
Disabled access. **Garden**. **Car park**.

A long, low and fairly modern building on its own overlooking the bay of Ajaccio. From the large circular terrace, you get one of the best views of the island here. Caroline, the *patronne*, really takes care of her guests. Good, generous Corsican dishes. Set menus 140F and 160F. The rooms are lovely and have a view of the sea; 260F for a double with shower/wc. Half board, 500F for two, is obligatory in summer. Very reasonable prices which, unusually for Corsica, are the same year round. This place is reliable and offers personal service – nothing like the rip-off joints you can find on the coast. They don't accept credit cards. Free apéritif.

ÎLE-ROUSSE (L')   20220

☎ L'AMIRAL

bd. Charles-Marie Savelli; it's about 150m from the town centre across from the beach.
☎ 04.95.60.28.05 ☛ 04.95.60.31.21
www.hotel-amiral.com ✉ info@hotel-amiral.com
Closed 10 Oct–1 April.

A seriously appealing place in a brilliant situation across from the beach. Rooms are clean and comfortable, with air-conditioning in high summer. Peaceful, family atmosphere. Doubles 320F or 520F depending on the season or the view (sea or garden).

LOZARI   20226 (10KM E)

☎ |●| AUBERGE A TESA

How to get there: from Lozari beach take the country road to the Codole dam, and it's about 3km further on.
☎ 04.95.60.09.55 ☛ 04.95.60.44.34
Restaurant closed lunchtimes. **Garden**. **Car park**.

This is a fairly new inn with olive-green shutters and seven pretty, cheerful rooms, a pink one, a blue one, a green one – choose the colour you want. They cost 350F year round, with breakfast included in the price. The owner, Marylène, will give you a great welcome. Excellent cuisine in the restaurant, where they serve incredibly tasty Corsican dishes: salad made with lettuce grown in their garden, chicken in honey, salmon and *brocciou terrine*, and chestnut ice cream plus apéritif, wine and coffee, will cost you 180F. Advisable to book; it's one of the best restaurants in Corsica.

SPELONCATO 20226 (18KM SE)

⚥ ♠ A SPELUNCA**

pl. de l'Église; it's south of L'Île-Rousse on a very windy road.
☎ 04.95.61.50.38 ➡ 04.95.61.53.14
e spelunca-hotel@freesbee.fr
Closed Oct–April.

A hotel with charm, in this village with lots of character, stuck up on a rock in the Balagne. This is the real Corsica. The pink house with a little turret and a lovely terrace was built in 1856 as the summer residence of cardinal Savelli, the Secretary of State to Pope Pius IX. You can see his portrait in the grand drawing room – an echo of the island's Napoleonic past. The rooms lead off a superb staircase. Some rooms are in the attic. Doubles 290–350F with shower or bath. Great value for money. Courteous welcome. 10% discount Sept–June.

OLMI-CAPELLA 20259

⚥ |●| LA TORNADIA

How to get there: it's about 2km from Olmi-Capella on the Balagne–Pioggiola road.
☎ 04.95.61.90.93 ➡ 04.95.61.92.15
Closed mid-Nov to mid-March.

You can dine under the chestnut trees or in the beamed dining room and the wonderful dishes just keep on coming. There's roast, milk-fed lamb with herbs from the *maquis*, pasta made from chestnut flour, killer cheeses, and brandy like fire water! Menus 115–160F or *à la carte*. They've got a shop where you can buy local products. Warm, friendly welcome. A very good place that's been going more than thirty years. Free apéritif.

PIANA 20115

♠ HÔTEL CONTINENTAL*

route d'Ajaccio; it's on the outskirts of town.
☎ 04.95.27.89.00
Closed Oct–March. **Garden. Lock-up garage.**

This is an old coaching inn which has aged beautifully – it's a place some great 19th-century novelist could have spent the night. It's a bit retro, but very clean and delightfully old-fashioned. The garden is full of pines and apricot trees; the rooms have natural wooden floors, big old-fashioned shutters and thick walls, though the ones over the street are pretty noisy. Doubles 200F with no pri-

vate facilities, 280F with shower/wc in the annexe. No credit cards.

PORTO 20150

♠ |●| HÔTEL-RESTAURANT LE PORTO*

route de Calvi.
☎ 04.95.26.11.20 ➡ 04.95.26.13.92
Closed mid-Oct to mid-April. **Car park**.

A good restaurant in Porto, the tourist centre in Corsica. Menus at 100F and 130F list a fine selection of tasty dishes like duck fillet with orange, veal fillet with mustard and delicious fish – all served with a smile. Good local wine at fair prices. Similar standard in the hotel, with simple spacious rooms and real bathrooms. 240F or 350F depending on the season. Half board, 560–700F for two, is obligatory in Aug.

EVISA 20126 (10KM E)

⚥ ♠ |●| HÔTEL RESTAURANT DU CENTRE

It's in the centre of the village.
☎ 04.95.26.20.92
Closed end Oct–1 March. **Car park**.

This village house contains a genuine country restaurant. The dining room is very simple and the service rudimentary, but the cooking is sublime. Only fresh produce is used in the dishes that are skillfully prepared (try the swordfish with basil), slowly cooked (try the soup or tripe) or creatively concocted (try the wild boar with orange and bitter chocolate). Portions are colossal – you get a whole shoal of prawns, for example. And the desserts are equally tasty, particularly the chestnut *parfait*. Lunch menu 89F then 120F. It's wise to book, especially if you want a table on the terrace. The same is true for the four simple, clean rooms, which have varying toilet facilities; doubles from 220F. Free apéritif and 10% discount on the room rate March–May.

PORTU-VECCHIO 20137

♠ HÔTEL LE MISTRAL**

5 rue Toussaint-Culioli.
☎ 04.95.70.08.53 ➡ 04.95.70.51.60
Closed Nov–March. **Car park**.

In the old town this attractive and comfortable two-star has doubles with shower/wc or bath for 250–680F, depending on the season. The rooms are meticulously kept. Good welcome. The high-season prices seem steep, but they tend to be in this town. You can also rent studios by the week.

▥ HÔTEL LE GOËLAND

La Marine.
☎ 04.95.70.14.15 ➡ 04.95.72.05.18
Closed end Oct to Easter. **TV**. **Car park**.

The best located hotel in Porto-Vecchio overlooking the gulf and with its own private beach. It's very simple but it's the only establishment in town to enjoy such a splendid situation. The rooms are variously sized, though most have been refurbished. Doubles with shower or basin 290–430F, with shower/wc 390–540F, or with bath 490–540F. Nice welcome. There's a bar and a terrace with a sea view. They prepare simple meals: tapas, pasta, soups and so on.

⥮ |●| LE TOURISME

12 cours Napoléon; it's in the old town near the church.
☎ 04.95.70.39.33
Closed Sun lunchtime.

You eat well at *Le Tourisme*, where the cuisine is light and very unusual. They do an excellent dish of spicy mussels *à la porto-vecchiaise*, and great dishes of the day like tagliatelle with asparagus and, for dessert, a soup of strawberries and bilberries. Menus from 78–138F and a *formule express* with salad, a pasta dish or *moules marinières*, and carpaccio of melon; if you're really in a hurry, try the short menu with a dish and a dessert. A little pricey for what it is but the quality is good and the service is speedy. Free apéritif.

LECCI-DE-PORTO-VECCHIO   20137 (7KM N)

▥ |●| HÔTEL ET RÉSIDENCE CARANELLA VILLAGE

route de Cala-Rossa; 3km along the road to Bastia, at La Trinité, turn right at the Cala-Rossa signpost, turn left at the next roundabout and go straight on for 4km.
☎ 04.95.71.60.94 ➡ 04.95.71.60.80
Swimming pool. **Garden**. **Car park**.

Set in flower-filled grounds, just 300m from the Cala Rossa beach, are about forty self-catering studios and apartments (some with oven, microwave, TV, telephone and dishwasher). Most have a terrace and are set around the heated swimming pool. Facilities include a fitness centre, bike hire, a bar, linen hire, a cleaning service and a washing room. Given the prices in Porto-Vecchio this is a very good option. Studios with shower and corner kitchen cost 270–535F, depending on season; you pay more for a bathroom. The villas or apartments

sleep four to six people and cost 560–1390F, depending on the type and the season.

PROPRIANO   20110

▥ LOFT HOTEL

3 rue Jean-Paul-Pandolfi.
☎ 04.95.76.17.48 ➡ 04.95.76.22.04
Disabled access. **TV**.

An old wine warehouse that's been converted into a hotel with clean rooms with a modern look – pale tiles and blond wood. Doubles 280–350F. Nice welcome.

▥ MOTEL ARIA MARINA**

Lieu-dit la Cuparchiata; it's in the hills above Propriano, from Viggiarello follow the signs to the motel.
☎ 04.95.76.04.32 ➡ 04.95.76.25.01
Closed Nov–April. **Swimming pool**. **Garden**. **Car park**.

This is a good motel, some distance from the brouhaha in Propriano and, better still, with a great view of the Gulf of Valinco. The studios or two-roomed apartments are spacious and have good facilities, from 300–550F in low and mid season. In July and August they rent the studios by the week only, 3500–4000F; the two- and three-roomed apartments are more so you'll need to check. They're really nice people and the pool is lovely.

⥮ |●| RESTAURANT L'HIPPOCAMPE

rue Jean-Paul-Pandolfi (South).
☎ 04.95.76.11.01
Closed Sun out of season, and end Sept to Easter.

Antoine, aka the American, runs this place. He loves the sea and really fresh fish. What you eat in the evening is what the American has caught that morning in the Gulf of Valinco. Good cuisine and good value for money too, served in warm, simple surroundings or out on the terrace. Set menu 100F *à la carte*. Efficient and friendly service. Free coffee.

SAINT-FLORENT   20217

▥ HÔTEL MAXIME**

Centre; it's in a quiet little street off place des Portes.
☎ 04.95.37.05.30 ➡ 04.95.37.13.07
TV. **Garage**.

A recent, very clean hotel that's good value for money for the resort. Each room has a mini-bar and balcony; some of them overlook the Poggio river, where you can arrange to moor your boat. Doubles from 260–380F with shower or bath;

prices also vary with the season. There's a lock-up for motorbikes.

⚓ MOTEL TREPERI**

route de Bastia (East); it's 1km out of town; take the Bastia road, which goes along the beach, then turn right where you see the sign to the motel.
☎ 04.95.37.40.20 ➡ 04.95.37.04.61
Closed 15 Nov–15 March. **Swimming pool**. **Garden**. **TV**. **Car park**.

All the rooms are airy, spacious and well kept, with shower and wc; each has a small terrace leading onto the flower-filled garden. A double room costs 280F out of season, 480F in high season. The surroundings are peaceful and there are splendid views over the gulf. Swimming pool and tennis courts. This is a nice place.

PATRIMONIO　　　　20253 (5KM NE)

⚓ HÔTEL U CASONE

In the village (Centre); take the D81 out of Saint-Florent, and continue past the church on the D81.
☎ 04.95.37.14.46 ➡ 04.95.37.17.15
Garage.

This is a large house faced with grey rough-cast in the upper village with a pretty garden where you can have breakfast or take the sun. Huge, well-maintained bedrooms with views over the countryside or the sea. Doubles 200–400F depending on facilities and season. There's a family atmosphere, and a friendly welcome from Mme Montemagni who runs this unpretentious place. No restaurant. Try a bottle or two of the Clos Montemagni with your meal. Credit cards not accepted. It's a good place for bikers because there's a lock-up.

SARTÈNE　　　　20100

⚓ HÔTEL VILLA PIANA**

route de Propriano; it's 1km before Sartène.
☎ 04.95.77.07.04 ➡ 04.95.73.45.65
Closed Oct–April. **Swimming pool**. **Garage**.

A pretty ochre house amid trees and flowers with a delightful entrance. Charming welcome. The rooms have been carefully decorated, and most have a view over Sartène. Doubles 290–390F. Facilities include tennis court and games room, bar and swimming pool with a super panoramic view. Good place. Lock-up for motorbikes.

SAINT-LUCIE-DE-TALLANO　　20112(14KM NE)

🎿 |●| LA SANTA LUCIA

Centre; take the Sartène/Ajaccio road and turn right for the village.
☎ 04.95.78.81.28
Closed Sun out of season.
Swimming pool. **TV**. **Disabled access**. **Car park**.

Excellent Corsican food. The first menu, 85F, is decent enough if rather ordinary, but the second, 135, really showcases the talents of the two chefs, both lads from the village. The dishes are very attractively presented, the food is tasty and accurately seasoned, and the cooking is judged to perfection. The roast pork with honey and rabbit with myrtle are triumphs. Very natural, smiling welcome from the boss. There's a pleasant terrace with a view of the fountain. Free house apéritif.

SOLENZARA　　　　20145

⚓ HÔTEL LA SOLENZARA**

Centre; it's on the Bastia road on the edge of town.
☎ 04.95.57.42.18 ➡ 04.95.57.46.84
Closed out of season (except by reservation).
Swimming pool. **TV**. **Disabled access**. **Car park**.

This ancient house was built 200 years ago by the squire of Solenzara. It has been simply and tastefully decorated and is now a charming hotel. The rooms are vast, with high ceilings; they're cool in summer and have newly equipped bathrooms. There are more conventional rooms in a new building. Tall palm trees in the garden, and a magnificent swimming pool. Direct access to the beach or the port. Reasonable prices for a place of such character. Doubles 280–480F.

ZONZA　　　　20124

🎿 ⚓ |●| HÔTEL-RESTAURANT LA TERRASSE

Centre; it's set back from the main road.
☎ 04.95.78.67.69 ➡ 04.95.78.73.50
Closed Nov–March. **Car park**.

The best thing about this place is the terrace where you can eat. It's the best placed in the village with a view over the roofs and the impressive mountains, so it's fantastic at sunset. Good Corsican food. The house *charcuterie* is particularly tasty and their regional dishes are the genuine article and generously served; standouts include the wild boar with noodles, cannelloni and chestnut desserts. Menus 88–180F. The owners, the Mondolini-Pietris, welcome you with warmth and good humour. The rooms are decent and well maintained. Some have a terrace over the valley. Though there isn't a fixed half-board rate, you are encouraged to have lunch or dinner. But since the cooking is good and prices are reasonable, there's no problem. 10% discount on the room rate April–June and Oct.

FRANCHE-COMTÉ

25 Doubs

39 Jura

70 Haute-Saône

90 Territoire de Belfort

ARBOIS   39600

☖ HÔTEL LE MÉPHISTO

33 pl. Faramand (Centre).
☎ 03.84.66.06.49
Closed Mon, except July–Aug.

Friendly and good value. All the rooms are different and the decor about as far as you can get from run-of-the-mill. Room number 7 is very bright, with a splendid view over Arbois. Doubles with basin at 145F, 190F with shower/wc.

🏃 ☖ HÔTEL DES MESSAGERIES**

2 rue de Courcelles (Centre).
☎ 03.84.66.13.43 ➡ 03.84.37.41.09
Closed Wed 11am–5pm out of season, Dec and Jan.
TV. Garage.

You get a warm reception in this comfy hotel which has a pleasant, family atmosphere. It's a popular stopping point for foreign travellers passing through, so there's an international feel. Room prices vary according to facilities – 195F with basin, with wc down the landing, 330F with bath. 10% discount March–June and Nov, and free use of garage.

|○| RESTAURANT LA CUISANCE

62 pl. Faramand (South).
☎ 03.84.37.40.74
Closed Tues and Wed evenings, and Jan.

La Cuisance is the little river that runs through Arbois; you can enjoy it from the cool terrace that looks over the water. This lively village restaurant is run by particularly welcoming proprietors. The cheapest menu at 40F includes a starter, main course,

cheese and dessert. Other menus 55–110F including chicken with *vin jaune* sauce, mushrooms in a pastry case, and game in season.

|○| LA BALANCE-METS ET VINS

47 rue de Courcelles.
☎ 03.84.37.45.00
Closed 3 Nov–30 April. **Garden. Car park.**

For ages, this was a popular restaurant with gourmets, then it closed down. Since it re-opened it, it's re-established its reputation. Thierry is an enormously talented chef and he launched himself on this mad adventure not long ago but he's got a winning formula; the atmosphere is young and genuinely friendly and there's a lovely terrace. The menus are varied, the dishes pure local with a modern treatment, and the prices are modest. The lunch menu, 84F, includes a glass of wine, the 101F menu lists a casserole of the day, and a there's a *menu-carte* at 151F. The *sommelier* helps you through the extensive wine list – the owners have a lot of wine-growing friends – and most are served by the glass.

POLIGNY   39800 (9KM SW)

🏃 ☖ |○| DOMAINE DE LA VALLÉE HEUREUSE

Route de Genève; it's on the RN5.
☎ 03.84.12.13 ➡ 03.84.37.08.75
Closed 3 Nov–30 April. **Garden. TV.**

The river meanders past this 18th-century mill converted into a hotel-restaurant. It's absolutely charming. Original cooking with

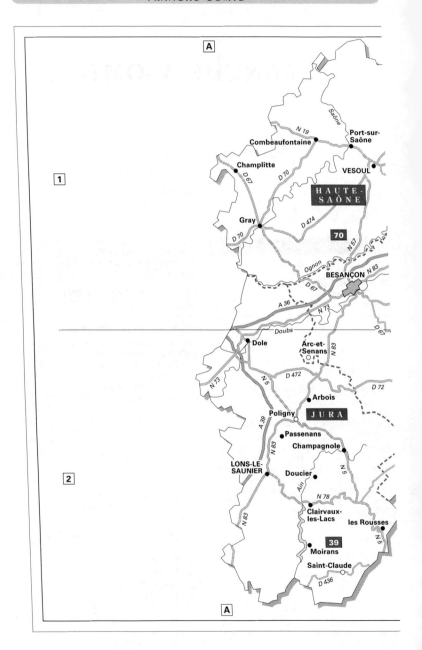

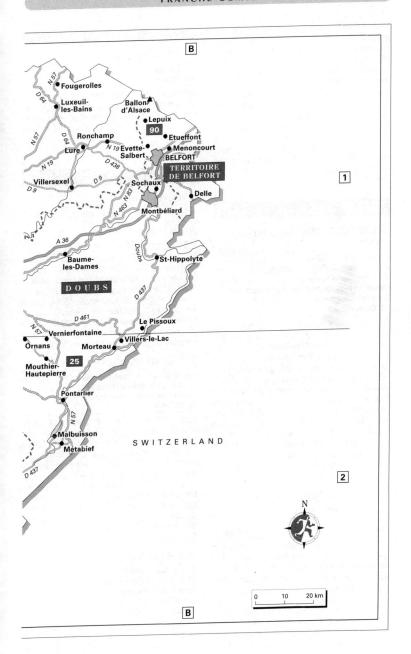

light, flavourful dishes created by Danièle using flowers and herbs grown in the garden. Fair prices with a weekday lunch menu at 95F and others from 135F. Half board is compulsory over public holiday weekends and in summer. The hotel is sheer luxury and you pay for it. The recently redecorated rooms are amongst the most beautiful to be found in the Jura, confidently mixing pale wood, rope and linen. Doubles with shower/wc or bath 450–700F. There's also a swimming pool, sauna, Jacuzzi and fitness room. Free coffee and 10% discount on the room rate except on public holidays and 14 July–15 Aug.

BAUME-LES-DAMES 25110

🏂 🛏 |○| HOSTELLERIE DU CHÂTEAU D'AS**

22 rue du Château-Gaillard.
☎ 03.81.84.00.66 ⟶ 03.81.84.59.67
e chateau.das@wanadoo.fr
Closed the last fortnight in Nov, the first week in Dec, and a fortnight Jan–Feb.
TV. Car park.

A pair of brothers, both gifted cooks, set up here. The dining room is big and round and somewhat sombre in atmosphere. The 135F menu comprises two starters, two main courses, two desserts, two glasses of wine and coffee. Local dishes with a twist of individuality; chunky snail kebabs with peasant bacon, pike force-meat balls with crab *coulis*, and pastry cases with soft fruit. Good wine list. Half the rooms are attractively (and newly) decorated and have good facilities, the others are still dreary. Prices start at 270F. Breakfast is served with home made preserves and farmhouse yoghurt. 10% discount on the room rate Nov–March

|○| RESTAURANT LE CHARLESTON

10 rue des Armuriers (Centre).
☎ 03.81.84.24.07
Closed Sun evening, Mon, 15–30 March, 15–30 Nov.

The decor is less cluttered than you might expect from the genuine Belle Époque but is attractive nonetheless. The cooking sticks to strictly orthodox regional dishes; small Conté cheese tart with snails and garlic, a duo of trout and salmon on a thin cauliflower pancake, and a pastry case with a ham bone with green cabbage *compote*. Menus start at 64F but for a few francs extra there are more creative dishes. Friendly reception and impeccable service.

LOMONT-SUR-CRÊTE 25110 (9KM E)

🛏 CHEZ LA MARTHE

23 Grande Rue.
☎ 03.81.84.01.50

A friendly, simple village café-restaurant. Nice family dishes prepared using good produce. If you want fish, whitebait or trout, you have to order because the cook uses fresh (not frozen) fish. Around 70F for a meal. A surprise of a place.

BELFORT 90000

🛏 NOUVEL HÔTEL*

56 faubourg de France (Centre); 300m from the train station.
☎ 03.84.28.28.78
Closed 15–20 Aug. **TV**.

A practical hotel in a pedestrianised street in the town centre, 300m from the train station. Double rooms with basin are good value at 135F, 150F with shower, 220F with shower/wc and 250F with bath/wc. All the rooms are spotless and the proprietor is always ready to be of service. Breakfast 34F, or free for under 12s. At the weekend, if you take two rooms, you can have a third for free.

🏂 🛏 AU RELAIS D'ALSACE**

5 av. de la Laurencie (Northeast); 500m from the centre.
☎ 03.84.22.15.55 ⟶ 03.84.28.70.48
Closed three weeks at New Year.
TV. Car park.

About ten years ago, a dynamic Franco-Algerian couple, Kim and Georges, were looking for work and they decided to take a risk and re-open this hotel. They renovated it from top to bottom. Their hard work has created a most welcoming hotel where you are greeted by Kim's infectious cheerfulness. It's the kind of place that is becoming increasingly rare nowadays. The bedrooms are simple and clean, 210–235F for a double. Breakfast 28F with real orange juice. 10% discount Sept–June.

🏂 🛏 HÔTEL VAUBAN**

4 rue du Magasin (Centre).
☎ 03.84.21.59.37 ⟶ 03.84.21.41.67
e hotel.vauban@wanadoo.fr
Closed Sun Nov–March, Christmas and New Year.
Garden. TV. Pay garage.

The hotel is in a peaceful district just a few steps from the old town. The owner has covered all the walls with his paintings, adding freshness and almost a party atmosphere to the place. Pleasant bedrooms, some opening onto the lovely garden. Doubles with shower or bath 300F. On fine days, you can breakfast beside the lily pond and enjoy the birdsong. Good welcome. Garage 30F. 10% discount.

⅔ 🏠 I●I HÔTEL-RESTAURANT LE SAINT-CHRISTOPHE**

pl. d'Armes (Centre).
☎ 03.84.55.88.88 ➡ 03.84.54.08.77
Hotel closed 25 Dec–2 Jan. **Restaurant closed** Sun and New Year's holidays. **TV**.

The dynamic owners of this establishment are always looking to improve it. The main building has comfortable and spacious double rooms at 335F with shower/wc and a view of the famous lion. The nearby annexe is very quiet, with impeccable doubles with shower/wc or bath 300–345F. A reasonable set menu for 65F is served Mon–Thurs in the restaurant. In summer they open the terrace in the square, where they serve salads. Lunch menu Tues–Thurs 67F, or 110–190F. 10% discount on the room rate.

⅔ 🏠 GRAND HÔTEL DU TONNEAU D'OR***

1 rue Reiset (Centre); 100m from the police station.
☎ 03.84.58.57.56 ➡ 03.84.58.57.50
Disabled access. TV. Car park.

The foyer is like the hall of a palace, with an elaborately decorated ceiling, grand staircase and elegant, turn-of-the-century charm. The magnificent stained glass was created by Gruber, a local master craftsman, and over the drawing room there's a magnificent listed dome. This small luxury establishment is full of character. Spacious, exceptionally comfortable rooms, at 600F with bath. The decor is modern and tasteful, and the piano bar lends a final touch of sophistication. Free breakfast.

I●I AUX CRÊPES D'ANTAN

13 rue du Quai; it's in the old town.
☎ 03.84.22.82.54

Fresh and attractive interior, decorated in shades of blue, grey and yellow. This good little establishment not only serves excellent *crêpes*, but also is open daily until midnight. Lots of choice, including sweet or black-wheat *crêpes* with morels, and a *complète forestière* of mushrooms, bacon and potatoes combined as they are in Vosges. Pancakes from 15–60F They also do salads, flank of beef and calf's head; there's always a dish of the day and a 49F menu. Prices are reasonable and the welcome friendly.

I●I L'AUBERGE DES TROIS CHÊNES

29 rue de Soissons (Northwest).
☎ 03.84.22.19.45
Closed Mon–Thurs evenings, the first fortnight in Aug and 25 Dec–2 Jan. **Car park**.

The comfortable, cosy inn, just outside town, specialises in modern cuisine that's anchored in tradition. There's a decent lunch menu for 65F on weekdays or set menus 120–170F listing fillet of beef with morels, pan-fried sole with saffron sauce, monkfish with fresh noodles, and mountain ham in Madeira and cream.

I●I LA GRANDE FONTAINE

pl. de la Grande-Fontaine; it's in the old town.
☎ 03.84.22.45.38
Closed Sun evening and Mon.

In this pleasant restaurant they create inspirational dishes using only the freshest produce, and combining herbs in original and intriguing ways. The lamb shank braised in a hay box is of remarkably high quality, as is the baked fish with fennel, the *foie gras* risotto, the *châteaubriand en croûte* with spiced salt, and all the desserts. Lunch menu 90F, others up to 220F, or *à la carte*. Best to book in the evening. In fine weather they put a few tables outside on the pavement. Half-bottles of wine start at 60F but none sold by the glass.

⅔ I●I LE MOLIÈRE

6 rue de l'Étuve (Centre).
☎ 03.84.21.86.38 ➡ 03.84.58.01.22
Closed Tues evening, Wed, a fortnight in Feb and three weeks Aug/Sept.

This establishment is in an attractive tree-lined square, surrounded by smart façades in local sandstone. Ignore the plastic chairs, if you can, and enjoy the charm of the place and the excellence of the cuisine. Only fresh produce is used here and the owner makes a trip to Mulhouse every morning to get his fish. The dishes are delightfully flavoured and change as different meats, vegetables or salads and herbs come into season. The *à la carte* choice is almost too extensive, and there's a dazzling selection of menus too, starting at 100F (not served Sun or public holidays) and going up to 250F. Here's a taster: *pannequet* of snails flambéed with aniseed, lamb cutlet and *foie gras* with port and shallots, veal sweetbreads with sorrel cream and sautéed morels, fillet of zander with snails and diced bacon, large prawns in a stew, and veal sweetbreads with garlic cream. Delicious desserts. The wine list is also impressive, and you should be able to pick out a good little vintage for around 80F. The custom of drinking a *digestif* at the end of the meal may be going out of fashion, but they have a large selection of fruit liqueurs. Free coffee.

PHAFFANS   90150 (7KM NE)

|●| L'AUBERGE DE PHAFFANS

10 rue de la Mairie; take the N83, turn right onto the D46 in the direction of Denney and it's on that road.
☎ 03.84.29.80.97
Closed Mon, Wed and Sat lunchtime, 1–20 Jan, and 25 June–20 July. **Car park**.

The influence of neighbouring Alsace is evident in this quaint little village inn. They serve dishes you haven't eaten for years and their specialitiy is frogs' legs, guaranteed fresh year-round thanks to regular arrivals from the Vendée. The same goes for the farmed eels served April–Dec. They also serve unmissable morel mushrooms *en croûte*, pigeon *paysanne* with prunes, quails with red and white grapes and Arbois wine, marinated leg of venison in season, and raw boar ham. Weekday menu 68F or 103–125F. Children's menu 45F.

CHAUX   90330 (10KM N)

|●| RESTAURANT L'AUBERGE DE LA VAIVRE

36 Grande-Rue; take the D465, the Ballon d'Alsace road.
☎ 03.84.27.10.61
Closed evenings, Sat, and 15 July–15 Aug. **Car park**

This inn, on the road to the Vosges, is run by a mother and daughter who have decorated it most attractively. It's an old barn with a mezzanine. They really make you feel welcome. A lot of care goes into preparing traditional dishes, such as sausage in *brioche*, monkfish *au gratin*, *confit* of duck in cider, *émincé* of liver and some delicious homemade puddings like fresh fruit tarts or biscuit with chocolate and hazelnut dessert. Lunch menu 55F then 95–200F. A nicely presented fine wine list, served by the glass or jug.

BESANÇON   25000

SEE MAP OPPOSITE

♠ |●| AUBERGE DE LA MALATE*

Chemin de la Malate; it's 4km out of the centre in the direction of Lausanne; after the Porte Taillée, take the Calèze-Arcier road. Off map **B2-1**
☎ 03.81.82.15.16 or 06.08.60.36.20
Closed Jan–Feb. **TV**. **Car park**.

A picturesque country inn just out of town in the forest facing the Doubs where peace and quiet are assured. Fairly comfortable, modernised rooms; doubles from 180F with shower/wc. The restaurant is lovely in summer when you can sit in the shade near the water's edge. Regional dishes with fish as the speciality – small fry or fillets of perch or zander. Menus from 70F.

♠ HÔTEL DU NORD**

8–10 rue Moncey. **MAP B1-2**
☎ 03.81.81.34.56 ➡ 03.81.81.85.96
Disabled access. **TV**. **Car park**.

A pleasant city-centre hotel run by real professionals who are always ready to be of service. The 44 rooms are functionally designed but comfortable, impeccably maintained and with good facilities – several have two double beds. Reasonable prices; doubles from 230F. Double glazing and room service.

♠ HÔTEL REGINA**

91 Grande-Rue. **MAP B2-4**
☎ 03.81.81.50.22 ➡ 03.81.81.60.20
Closed 24 Dec–2 Jan.
TV. **Car park and lock-up garage**.

Charming, quiet and comfortable hotel with a pleasant inner courtyard – a haven of peace and tranquility in the city centre. The rooms are regularly redecorated – some have balconies or a terrace hung with wisteria; doubles with shower/wc or bath 240F. There's also a small, independent studio for two. Nice welcome.

♠ LE GRANVELLE**

13 rue du Général-Lecourbe. **MAP B2-3**
☎ 03.81.81.33.92 ➡ 03.81.81.31.77
TV. **Car park**.

In a quiet part of the city, not far from the citadel. An elegant, stone-built hotel in a wealthy street with many private mansions. It's quiet, comfortable and characterful, and the owners have created a relaxing atmosphere. All the rooms look out onto an attractive paved courtyard. Doubles with wc/shower 260F, and some are organised for families.

♠ HÔTEL CASTAN

6 square Castan. **MAP B2-5**
☎ 03.81.65.02.00 ➡ 03.81.83.01.02
TV. **Car park**.

Chic and charming hotel established in a pri-

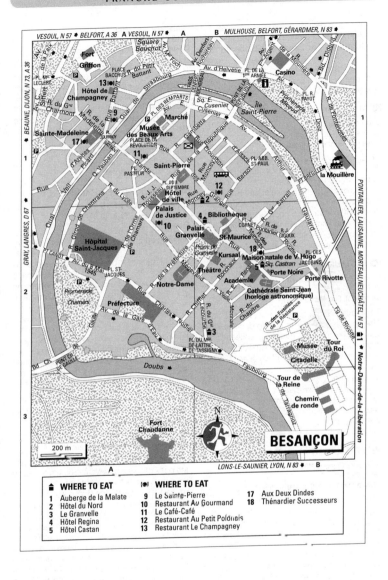

vate mansion dating back to the 17th century. Wide fireplaces, wood panelling, period furniture and a luxurious atmosphere. You can choose your room – Versailles, Pompadour, Pompei (which has a Grecian-style bathroom), Trianon, Regence and so on. Doubles 580–980F. Breakfast costs 60F.

I●I AUX DEUX DINDES

30 rue de l'École.
☎ 03.81.83.15.56
Closed Sat lunchtime and Sun.

Great cooking served in a sweet, unpretentious dining room. Dishes change daily depending on the inspiration of the owner and the produce she has selected. No frozen stuff here and you won't be disappointed; fresh calf's head on a Friday, *pot-au-feu* on Thursday in winter. Dish of the day 39F, *formule* for 49F, dessert at 18F. It's convivial, friendly and inexpensive.

I●I RESTAURANT AU GOURMAND

5 rue Mégevand. **MAP A2-10**
☎ 03.81.81.40.56
Closed Sat, Sun, Mon, and Aug.

The place is small so get here early or book. They always take the trouble to decorate the window, and inside there's a collection of pretty jugs. The huge menu could almost fill a book: curried *émincé* of chicken breast, savoury *clafoutis*, an egg custard with sausage and potatoes, salads with fantasy names like *la Javanaise* or *Metro Goldwyn*, and desserts. Uncomplicated home cooking using fresh produce. For a quick lunch, try the 62F lunch menu, though there are more substantial ones or you can eat *à la carte*.

I●I RESTAURANT AU PETIT POLONAIS

81 rue des Granges. **MAP B1-12**
☎ 03.81.81.23.67
Closed Sat evening, Sun, and 14 July–15 Aug.

The dining room is very formal and the waitresses wear black and white uniforms. It's a deeply traditional restaurant, a real institution. The *patronne* is charming and keeps an experienced eye on everything. There's a range of menus from 64F with a choice of dishes on each one. Very classic cuisine with a strong regional bias including the renowned *boîte chaude*, melted Edel de Cléron cheese with Morteau sausage and boiled potatoes served in a birch bark box. Excellent value for money for a popular restaurant of its type.

I●I THÉNARDIER SUCCESSEURS

11 rue Victor Hugo. **MAP B2-18**
☎ 03.81.82.06.18
Closed Sat lunchtime, Sun and Mon.

Victor Hugo was born in a house in the square next door and the owners named this establishment after one of his works. Fresh, well-judged cooking in dishes which veer away from the local classics, nicely shown off on pretty plates. *Formule* 65F, *à la carte* starters 32–46F and main courses 75–95F. The tables are elegantly laid, the decor is brightly coloured and the atmosphere is relaxed. Put it all together and that's how it's built a regular clientele.

I●I RESTAURANT LE CHAMPAGNEY

37 rue Battant. **MAP A1-13**
☎ 03.81.81.05.71 ➡ 03.81.82.19.76
Closed Sun.

This restaurant is in a splendid 16th-century town house that's been sensitively renovated; they move tables out into the old courtyard in summer. Inside they have retained the old fireplace and all the beams of the original ceiling. The decor is a mixture of modern and baroque with lots of style but no stuffiness, and the welcome and the service are efficient and cool. The cuisine is a combination of classic favourites and contemporary inspiration. Dishes change frequently, but the regular specialities include salmon with *vin jaune* and duck breast with Fougerolles sour cherries. Menus start at 68F. Wines seem pricey.

I●I RESTAURANT LE CAFÉ-CAFÉ

5 bis rue Luc Breton. **MAP A1-11**
☎ 03.81.81.15.24
Closed Sun, Mon–Wed evenings, and 15–30 Aug.

A discreet, almost anonymous place, hidden at the back of a little courtyard. You have to keep your eyes open for the slate at the entrance where they chalk up the dishes and menus of the day. Dishes, around the 59F mark, are never short on imagination or exotic touches. You'll get platters or *assiettes* with names like *jurassienne*, *de la ferme*, *comtoise* and so on, with selections of different things that are a complete meal in themselves. An ideal place for lunch. Charming welcome. Reservations are essential in this pocket-sized dining room that's crammed with bric-à-brac.

I●I LE SAINT-PIERRE

104 rue Battant. **MAP A1-11**
☎ 03.81.81.20.20.99
Closed Sat lunchtime and Sun.

There's a contrast of styles in this elegant setting – ancient beams, bare stone walls and contemporary pictures. Very good, sensitively prepared dishes, with lots of fish. The 190F menu is satisfying in all respects and the home-made bread is excellent. The atmosphere is welcoming and very relaxed even though this is one of the smart places in town. Nice terrace in warm weather.

CHALEZEULE   25220 (2.5KM E)

🏠 HÔTEL DES 3 ILES**

rue des Vergers; it's on the Belfort road.
☎ 03.81.61.00.66 ➥ 03.81.61.73.09
Closed 20 Dec–5 Jan. **TV. Garden. Car park.**

Amazing to find such a quiet village only a few minutes' drive from the town centre. It's a recently built hotel with a few nods to local architecture, in a lovely garden enclosed by high walls. The garden and sitting room are for guests' use. It's part of the *Relais du Silence* group so the peace and quiet are guaranteed. Double rooms with shower/wc or bath from 280F.

CHAMPLITTE   70600

🏠 I●I HÔTEL-RESTAURANT DU DONJON**

46 rue de la République (Centre).
☎ 03.84.67.66.95 ➥ 03.84.67.81.06
Restaurant closed Fri evening out of season, Sun and Mon. **TV. Car park.**

The only medieval element here is the vaulted cellar which is used as the dining room. The cuisine is honest and traditional; fillet of red mullet with basil, veal chop in Pinot Noir or pan-fried snails *forestière*. Set weekday menu 68F and others 110–210F. The rooms are clean and comfortable though not dazzling; doubles with shower 180F, 230F with shower/wc or bath.

CHAUX-NEUVE   25240

🏠 I●I AUBERGE DU GRAND-GÎT**

rue des Chaumelles; take the Mouthe road out of the village and then turn right 400m on.
☎ 03.81.69.25.75 ➥ 03.81.69.15.44
Closed Sun evening and Mon except public holidays, April and 15 Oct–15 Dec. **Disabled access. Car park.**

Quiet place on the outskirts of the village. Recently built, but in keeping with local architecture, with a sloping roof and wooden façade. Excellent welcome. Only eight bed-

rooms which are wood-panelled and cosy – from 246F for a double with shower/wc and telephone. Some have a lovely view of the surrounding countryside; number 5 has a mezzanine and can sleep five. There's also stop-over *gîte* for hikers: two rooms with six beds. Classic regional dishes in the restaurant. There's a weekday *menu du jour* for 73F, while the 85F regional set menu offers ham Arbois-style or pink trout sautéed in butter and served with parsley and lemon juice. The ideal place for sporty types and nature lovers. The owner is a skiing instructor and uplands guide so he knows all the local long-distance footpaths and cross-country skiing routes like the back of his hand.

CLAIRVAUX-LES-LACS   39130

BONLIEU 39130 (12KM SW)

🏠 I●I LE POUTRE

25 Grande rue; take the D67.
☎ 03.84.25.57.77 ➥ 03.84.25.51.61

An excellent establishment – not in the first flush of youth but the table is high quality. The decor in the rooms, 120–350F, and dining room has faded a bit and it has a provincial, bourgeois feel. Servings in the restaurant are as huge as they used to be in times past. There's almost more than you can manage on the 120F menu and there are others up to 350F. House specialities include chicken and mushroom *vol-au -vent*, trout fillet with hazelnuts and pan-fried foie gras in Macvin. Excellent welcome and punctilious service.

DELLE   90100

🏠 I●I RESTAURANT LE GALOPIN

29 Grand-Rue (Centre); it's opposite the old town hall.
☎ 03.84.36.17.52 ➥ 03.84.36.17.52
Closed Sun and Mon.

This is where local lovers of good food meet, including many Swiss customers who pop over the border. Diners make for the restaurant cellar, which is more than a hundred years old, to celebrate the potato, the main component of many dishes. Chic choices include potatoes with smoked salmon and shallot sauce, though there are other, more local dishes such as *roësti* with Morteau sausage or *à la cancoillotte* – they also do *raclette*, mountain ham, spaghetti and a range of salads.Link there are sometimes italics where there shouldn't be (here, mountain ham onwards should be plain text), although it doesn't recognise them as such: what to do? I have put them in outline shading so you can find them No set menus so expect to pay 70–150F. Good, inexpensive and friendly. Free apéritif or coffee.

DOLE   39100

♠ HÔTEL DE LA CLOCHE

1 pl. Grévy.
☎ 03.84.82.06.06 ➡ 03.84.72.73.82
TV.

A somnolent provincial hotel that started life as a coaching inn. It's conventional, with classical, rather bland decor, and the welcome just about goes through the motions. Nonetheless, the rooms are clean and well maintained, the façade is pretty, there's a sauna upstairs, and it's in the middle of town – a big plus in a place where central hotels are a rare commodity. Inevitably, it's often full. Doubles with en-suite facilities from 280F up to 390F with whirlpool bath.

♠ |●| LA CHAUMIÈRE

346 av. du Maréchal Juin.
☎ 03.84.70.72.40 ➡ 03.84.79.25.60
Garden. Swimming pool.

Behind the Virginia creeper is a huge, faux cottage. It's cosy, bourgeois and ordinarily decorated but it gains charm with its grounds, flowerbeds, terraces, swimming pool and secret places. The rooms are particularly comfortable though they're oldfashioned and, at 380F up for a double, overpriced. It owes its reputation to the quality of the cooking in the restaurant. The youthful chef is the latest in a long line and produces delicious dishes at reasonable prices; menus from 130F. He has a personal, sensitive approach and doesn't overload the plates.

🍴 |●| CHEZ COCO

34 rue des Vieilles Boucheries (Centre).
☎ 03.84.79.10.78
Closed Sun and evenings except May–Sept, and Jan.

"Home cooking by the *patronne*" it says at the top of the menu in this popular local restaurant. In a corner, there are rows of sporting cups and photos of the town's junior teams. Coco, the manager, holds the fort behind the zinc counter, emerging to take orders and serve the food. Weekday menu at 60F and others 70–125F: *crudités*, pork chop *à la Provençale*, or fillet of fish cooked in white wine, and dishes are

served with three different vegetables, followed by cheese and dessert. Coco is a good-humoured, chatty guy who provides unrushed service. Free *digestif*.

|●| LE BEC FIN

67 rue Pasteur (Centre); it's near the marina.
☎ 03.84.82.43.43
Closed Mon, Tues except July–Aug, and the first fortnight in Jan.

When you walk in the door you're greeted by the delightful *patronne*'s kind smile and effusive welcome. The bright dining room has a romantic view over the canal des Tanneurs while the other one is in the medieval cellars. In good weather you can sit outside on the terrace where you have a view of the canal as well. Weekday menu 80F, the one at 95F changes often and is very popular – salad of *Comté* cheese *croquettes*, chicken sausage with bacon, and peach dessert flavoured with tarragon. Other menus up to 220F. Service is a bit awkward, but attentive. Grownups have comfortable chairs and there are high chairs for the little ones.

SAMPANS   39100 (3KM NW)

♠ |●| LE CHALET DU MONT-ROLAND**

North; take the N5; before Monnières turn right towards mont Roland.
☎ 03.84.72.04.55 ➡ 03.84.82.14.97
Disabled access. TV. Car park.

The series of crosses along the road up to this chalet puts you in mind of Golgotha. A slightly distrubing experience. From the top of Mont Roland there's a superb view over Chaux Forest and on a clear day you can see Mont Blanc. It's particularly delightful in the spring and the place to spend a relaxing Sunday in the country. Double rooms with shower/wc or bath cost 270F. The restaurant has a glassed-in terrace so you can really enjoy the view. There's a weekday lunch menu at 85F and others 115–200F – all of them are highly caloric. Good regional fare.

CHAUSSIN   39120 (20KM S)

🍴 ♠ |●| HÔTEL-RESTAURANT CHEZ BACH**

4 pl. de l'Ancienne-Gare; take the N73, then turn onto the D468 at La Borde.
☎ 03.84.81.80.38 ➡ 03.84.81.83.80
Closed Fri except July– Aug, Sun evening, Mon lunchtime and 20 Dec–3 Jan. **Disabled access. TV. Car park**.

Make a little gastronomic detour to enjoy this fine cuisine. The big modern building doesn't look at all promising from the outside but the reputation has been established for a generation or two. Several menus of regional specialities with sauces using the local *vin jaune*, frogs' legs or tournedos with marrow. Weekday menu 80F and others 130–300F. Half-board is compulsory July–Aug. The rooms are comfortable but impersonal like the welcome; 200–320F for a double with bath. Free coffee and 10% discount on the room rate Oct–March.

DOUCIER   39130

🏃 🛏 |●| HÔTEL LOGIS DE FRANCE-RESTAURANT LE COMTOIS

It's in the village opposite the post office.
☎ 03.84.25.71.21
Closed Tues evening and Wed except 15 June–15 Sept, Sun, and 15 Nov–15 Feb. **TV. Car park**.

Wine from the best wine-growers in the region on the splendid wine list, carefully selected by the young *sommelier* who's also the owner. Each entry has a short description. The dining room is bright and fresh, a lovely combination of stone and beams illuminated by well-placed lights. There's also a solid brick chimney breast and the old Franche-Comté dresser adds a country touch. The cooking is in the brasserie-bistro tradition and served in huge portions. There's a wine-tasting room and a bistro menu. The rooms are functional and could do with brightening up though the ones on the first floor have been refurbished. Free coffe of *digestif*, and 10% discount on the room rate out of season.

CHATILLON   39130 (5KM W)

🛏 |●| CHEZ YVONNE

It's on the road to Lons-le-Saulnier.
☎ 03.84.25.70-82
Closed Tues and Wed. **Swimming pool**.

There's a river running by this big old house that's been taken over by a friendly young couple and turned into a charming hotel. There's a terrace at the water's edge, green banks and a swimming pool. You can almost feel the silence - it's an ideal place to stop. Good food on menus 92–168F – try the Morteau salad or trout in Savagnin wine sauce. Lovely salads, about 60F, are served at the waterside. Eight modest rooms, 240–270F in summer, 195–240F out of season. The drawback is that there's one show-

er to share between four rooms. That apart, the beds are good and the decoration is adorable. Two of the rooms have a river view.

ILLAY   39150 (12KM SE)

🏃 🛏 |●| L'AUBERGE DU HÉRISSON

5 route des Lacs.
☎ 03.84.25.58.18 ➡ 03.84.25.51.11
Closed Nov–beginning of Feb. **TV**.

A good base for local excursions and visiting the waterfalls in the area. Three of the rooms have been perfectly refurbished and they're pretty and comfortable. The others are due to go through the same process. Doubles with shower/wc or bath, 240–300F. Straightforward, honest dishes in the restaurant. Nothing too complicated but the ingredients are fresh and the results are good. Menus 65–22F. The cheese selection is exceptional (as many as you like plus a salad and dessert on the 83F menu). There are also a few Jura specialities and *fondues*. There's a well-priced children's menu offering six snails or smoked salmon, chicken breast with cream sauce and *tagliatelle* followed by chocolate *profiteroles*. Free house apéritif.

ERRUES-MENONCOURT (LES)   90150

🏃 🛏 |●| LA POMME D'ARGENT

13 rue de la Noye.
☎ and ➡ 03.84.27.63.69
Closed Wed and a fortnight in Nov.

This lovely place, well off the beaten track, is a real find. It's the welcoming restaurant that's the draw, where the commitment to service has been honed over twenty years. Fine, delicate cooking on menus priced 98–185F – highlights include home-smoked salmon, frogs' legs and snail *cassolette*, and the vanilla cream is to die for. The pretty terrace is open in spring and summer. Rooms with shower and wc along the corridor, 160F. Free coffee.

ETUEFFONT   90170

|●| AUBERGE AUX TROIS BONHEURS

Centre; north of Belfort take the D23 from Valdoie.
☎ 03.84.54.71.31
Closed Sun and Tues evenings, and Mon.

If this is the *Inn of the Three Happinesses* then the fourth is the journey through flower-filled villages to get to this elegant town house. It's built in brick and natural stone and is in a delightful rustic setting. The restaurant is very popular because of the hearty, tasty cooking served in generous portions – it's a place for family gatherings and groups of pensioners out on a spree. They come for the fantastic home-made brawn, fried carp or zander, chanterelle mushrooms with parsley, the special *planchette des Trois Bonheurs* and *tartiflette*, and good home-made desserts and fruit tarts. Lunch menu 52F, or 95F. Seafood stew available *à la carte*. Friendly reception and efficient service.

EVETTE-SALBERT 90350

⚘ |●| AUBERGE DU LAC

Lac de Malsaucy; take the D24.
☎ 03.84.29.14.10 ➡ 03.84.29.14.10
Closed Mon and Tues evening in season, 2–16 Jan and 16–30 Oct.

This is a big pink house where you'll get a typical Franche-Comté welcome and good regional food. There's a large, pleasant dining room with well-spaced tables and a terrace with a view of the lake. The choice of dishes is considerable; *parmentier au Morteau* (a kind of shepherd's pie made with *Jésus de Morteau*, a local sausage), cream of lentil soup, *terrine* of oysters and mussels with coriander seeds, prawn kebabs, pan-fried fillet of red mullet with basil, trout with morels, honey-glazed breast of duck, and more. Weekday menu 80F, others 125–160F or around 150F *à la carte*. Good wines at affordable prices or wine by the pitcher. Even when it's raining you can still appreciate the view of the lake from the comfort of the dining room. Free coffee.

FOUGEROLLES 70220

|●| RESTAURANT LE PÈRE ROTA

8 Grande-Rue.
☎ 03.84.49.12.11
Closed Sun evening, Mon and 3–25 Jan. **Car park**.

Jean-Pierre Kuentz is probably the beacon for the cuisine of the Haute-Saône. He uses local produce of the highest quality and brings a touch of modern influence to the regional cuisine but inspiration from way beyond local boundaries: duck *terrine* with sour cherries, poached John Dory, lobster with *vin jaune*, zander with powdered mustard, and fillet of beef with red Jura wine sauce. The service is thoughtful and the table settings and modern, bright decor have been put together with care.

Weekday menu 98F and 175–350F. The atmosphere is just a tad uptight.

FOURNET-BLANCHEROCHE 25140

⌂ |●| HÔTEL-RESTAURANT LA MARAUDE**

How to get there: follow the signposts off the D464 between Fournet-Blancheroche and Charquemont.
☎ 03.81.44.09.60 ➡ 03.81.44.09.13
Closed 24–25 Dec. **TV**. **Car park**.

An old 18th-century farm in a remote, peaceful part of the Haut-Doubs. A nice young couple fell in love with the place and moved in. The interior was completely transmogrified a few years ago but it has retained much original charm. There are seven pretty rooms with wooden panels and beams from 280F for a double with shower/wc – some are non-smoking rooms. In the little sitting room there is an old fireplace where they used to smoke the salted meat. Relax in the sauna after a game of tennis or billiards. In the cosy dining room, they serve principally regional cuisine: *foie gras* and smoked salmon with morels, *cassolette* of snails, duo of Morteau and Montbéliard sausage. They also serve dishes from outside the region. Menus start at 70F.

GRAY 70100

⌂ |●| HÔTEL-RESTAURANT LE BELLEVUE**

1 av. Carnot (Centre)
☎ 03.84.64.53.50 ➡ 03.84.64.53.69
Closed Sat and Sun out of season. **TV**. **Garden**. **Car park**.

This hotel near the Saône is aging gracefully. The rooms are still good and the ones looking onto the public gardens are quiet. Doubles 180F with hand basin, to 210F with shower/wc or bath. Two approaches in the restaurant: the brasserie does simple but substantial dishes of the day, like *coq au vin* with mashed potato, while the other dining room has menus from 69F and 100–160F with a good, standard choice, or *à la carte*.

|●| RESTAURANT DU CRATÔ

65 Grande-Rue (Centre).
☎ 03.84.65.11.75
Closed Mon.

A small restaurant in a sloping lane in the old part of Gray. There aren't many restaurants in the area providing such value for money. The dining room is simple and pleasant. Weekday menu 78F, others 95–145F. The chef offers a dazzling choice of starters and main courses, with cheese and dessert on all menus. Relaxing atmosphere, friendly service and the owner likes to play the odd joke on her guests.

LEPUIX   90200

|●| LE SAUT DE LA TRUITE**

Malvaux; take the D465.
☎ 03.84.29.32.64 ➡ 03.84.29.57.42
Closed Fri, and Dec–Jan.
Garden. **TV**. **Car park**.

A superb setting on a hairpin bend on the road leading up to the Ballon d'Alsace, in a forest clearing. In summer you can hear the gushing waterfall. It's a mountain refuge that's been open since 1902 and run by the same family for forty years. There are some rooms but they're not an ideal place to stay. It's a better place to eat, with trout freshly caught from the pond and a fine selection of regional specialities such as cockerel in Riesling, pigeon with chanterelles or bilberry tart. Weekday menu 90F or 110–180F.

LONS-LE-SAUNIER   39000

⅔ ☎ |●| HÔTEL-RESTAURANT TERMINUS**

37 av. Aristide Briand (Centre).
☎ 03.84.24.41.83 ➡ 03.84.26.68.07
Hotel closed Sun. **Restaurant closed** 20 Dec–5 Jan.
TV. **Pay car park**.

A solid building that was gradually fading as the years passed. Luckily, a change of ownership – although it stayed within the same family – put a stop to the process of decay, as they began a massive renovation programme. The relatively large rooms have all been modernised and painted white so they look a lot brighter, if a little sparse. Doubles with shower or bath 300–380F. The ones at the back are quieter. Simple fare is served in the restaurant, where you can get a set menu at 100F or choose *à la carte*. 10% discount on the room rate.

|●| LA COMÉDIE

pl. de la Comédie (Centre).
☎ 03.84.24.20.66
Closed Sun, Mon evening, Easter and 3 weeks in Aug.

A stylish restaurant, though it would be dreary were it not for the flowery terrace. Modern and traditional cuisine on menus 98–155F and around 230F *à la carte*. Choose from

cassolette of snails with morels, garlic and croutons, duck breast lacquered with sesame honey and sour cherry, and the like.

|●| LE BAMBOCHE

23 rue Perrin (Centre).
☎ 03.84.24.49.30

Young, friendly atmosphere and good, original cooking. The best place in town. About five types of carpaccio available: fillet steak, veal, goose and rabbit. If raw meat turns your stomach, there are plenty of salads or grills cooked on the old-fashioned spit – try lamb shank, kebabs or veal kidneys. The meat is decent and the cooking perfectly judged. Enough choice to satisfy all appetites and suit all pockets. Around 100F *à la carte*.

CHILLE   39570 (3KM E)

⅔ ☎ |●| HÔTEL-RESTAURANT PARENTHÈSE***

How to get there: head for Besançon on the bypass, then go 1km on the D157 and look for the signs.
☎ 03.84.47.55.44 ➡ 03.84.24.92.13
Restaurant closed Mon lunchtime, Sun evening, and a fortnight in Feb during the school holidays.
Disabled access. **Garden**. **TV**. **Car park**.

In a small village just off the major roads, this beautiful 18th-century residence in the middle of an extensive park has been converted into a comfortable hotel and restaurant by its very friendly, welcoming proprietor. The hotel has thirty rooms, all of which are tastefully decorated and named after painters; 270–720F for a double with shower/wc or bath. The restaurant offers a weekday menu at 95F with others 118–265F. Classic cuisine with a local bias: *chiffonade* of scallops roasted with honey and grapefruit, *croûtes* with morels and *vin jaune*, *fricassée* of lobster with ginger cream sauce or *pavé glacé* with Marc. Free apéritif.

CHÂTEAU-CHALON   39210 (12KM N)

|●| LES 16 QUARTIERS

rue de l'Église.
☎ 03.84.44.68.23
Closed Wed and Sun except July–Aug and Nov to mid-March. **Car park**.

After a morning spent wandering around the rich, historic town, settle down at one of the tables on the garden terrace of this restaurant just next to the church. Go for the *formule* at 55F; cheese flan, tomato salad and a glass of Jura wine. Menus from 78F, including a "medieval" menu with mushrooms sautéed with spices, lamb and *tarte blanche*. The wine list is worthy of the region. Free coffee.

|●| LA TAVERNE DU ROC

rue de la Roche.
☎ 03.84.85.24.17

A tiny restaurant with white walls, in a timeless house, right in the middle of Château-Chalon. The chef has been here for years concocting delicious dishes – try her Bresse chicken with *vin jaune*, the best for miles around. Any of her Jura dishes are worth a try and on a Sunday, there's a menu with trout and chicken. Menus from 140F.

BAUME-LES-MESSIEURS   39210 (20KM NE)

🎄|●| RESTAURANT DES GROTTES

How to get there: take the D471 to Roches-de-Beaume, then the D70.
☎ 03.84.44.61.59
Closed evenings and Wed 15 Oct–15 April. **Garden. Car park**.

The restaurant is opposite a marvellous, foaming waterfall cascading down from the high rocks of the Baumes-les-Messieurs natural amphitheatre. Its tranquility is in sharp contrast to the racket of tourists at the nearby caves. Open for lunch only with menus 85–150F listing mainly Franche-Comté specialities. The terrace is open in summer where you can enjoy platters of *charcuterie* or cheese washed down with a glass of Jura wine. Free coffee.

LUXEUIL-LES-BAINS   70300

🎄 🏠 |●| HÔTEL-RESTAURANT DE FRANCE**

6 rue Georges-Clémenceau; it's opposite the hospital.
☎ 03.84.40.13.90 ➡ 03.84.40.33.12
Restaurant closed Sun evening, and Fri evening in winter. **TV. Garden. Car park**.

The white building surrounded by greenery is behind the parc des Termes. There are twenty or so rooms – doubles with basin 200F and from 230–300F with shower/wc or bath. The chef prepares good, traditional, filling dishes: stuffed ham with wild mushroom sauce, *noisette* of beef, *panaché* of fish with cream and mushroom sauce, etc. Menus 70–195F, so you can eat well without punching a hole in your bank account. Free apéritif.

🎄 🏠 |●| HÔTEL-RESTAURANT BEAU SITE***

18 rue Georges-Moulimard; it's close to the casino.

☎ 03.84.40.14.67 ➡ 03.84.40.50.25
Closed Fri evening, Sat, Sun evening mid-Nov to mid-March, and Christmas–New Year. **Swimming pool. Garden. TV. Car park**.

This is a large, very pleasing place, surrounded by a green park with a swimming pool. The rooms are comfortable and charming and the prices are attractive: doubles with shower/wc 340–380F in both the main building and the annexe. Luxeuil ham is a must in the restaurant and, in season, the game dishes are classics – boar *civet à l'ancienne*, venison *Grand Veneur*. Weekday menu 85F or up to 160F. They do special weekend rates in conjunction with the spa. 10% discount on the room rate.

MALBUISSON   25160

🏠 |●| LE BON ACCUEIL

It's in the centre of the village.
☎ 03.81.69.30.58 ➡ 03.81.69.37.60
Closed Sun, Mon and Tues lunchtime Oct–April, mid-Dec to mid-Jan, and a week in April. **Car park**.

The reputation of this establishment is being made by the restaurant which gets better and better. Traditional cooking with a modern touch. The chef-owner, Marc Faivre, is committed to using only fresh, quality, local produce. A few specialities; fine tart with Morteau, braised leeks with poached egg, tomatoes stuffed with snails and herbs with a parsley sauce and, for dessert, a gentian sorbet or macaroons with grapefruit. Menus from 135F. A few rooms at 270–400F.

CHAUDRON 25160   (3KM N)

🏠 |●| LE BROCHET D'OR

8 rue Edgar-Faure; it's 3 km north of Malbuisson, on the banks of the lake.
☎ 03.81.69.31.94
Closed Mon evening out of season.

The owners' careful renovation of an establishment which had snoozed quietly for a while has given it a shot in the arm. There are shower cubicles in the six rooms and a shared wc along the landing; doubles from 210F. Monsieur does a sterling job in the kitchen and produces good regional dishes and a few innovations besides. There's a 59F weekday lunch menu and others 79–120F. It's a friendly place run by kindly people who've even thought to set aside a children's corner.

MÉTABIEF — 25370

⌂ |●| HÔTEL-RESTAURANT L'ÉTOILE DES NEIGES**

4 rue du Village (North).
☎ 03.81.49.11.21 ➡ 03.81.49.26.91
Hotel closed 30 May–15 June and 15 Nov–15 Dec.
Restaurant closed lunchtime in winter. **TV**.

A modern building a little way away from the ski resort, above a small river. The renovated rooms are cosy and comfortable. All have balconies with views of the Mont d'Or or the countryside. Double with shower/wc or bath from 235F. In the restaurant there's a welcoming, family atmosphere. They serve exclusively local specialities and use organic produce. A meal *à la carte* costs 80–90F.

LES HÔPITAUX-VIEUX — (4KM NE)

⌂ |●| HOTEL LAKE PLACID

48 rue de la Seigne.
☎ 03.81.49.00.72 ➡ 03.81.49.00.42
Car park.

It's outside the village, near the departure points for the cross-country skiing and hiking trails. There are only five rooms in this small hotel that's run by Denis Sandona – he competed in the cross-country skiing at the Lake Placid Winter Olympics in 1980 – and his delightful wife. Flawless, pretty rooms from 220F for a double. Mountain dishes and good, honest country cooking; *pot-au-feu* and home-made tarts. Dishes from 45F, specialities 45–90F. There's a jovial atmosphere and a warm setting. Excellent welcome.

LONGEVILLES MONT D'OR (LES) — (4KM SE)

⌂ |●| HÔTEL-RESTAURANT LES SAPINS**

58 rue des Bief-Blanc; take the D45.
☎ 03.81.49.90.90 ➡ 03.81.49.94.43
Closed Oct–Nov. **Car park**.

In the centre of a little village which hasn't lost any of its authentic character even though it is part of the Métabief resort. Pleasant rooms that are the best value for money in the area; the ones on the second floor are big and have sloping ceilings. Doubles 156F with shower/wc and 178F with bath. The menu of the day at 66F is served at lunch and dinner during the week and is worth a try. Home-made regional cooking: *franc-comtoise* salad, cheese flan, *entrecôte* of beef and *gratin dauphinois*. A genuinely friendly welcome.

JOUGNE — 25370 (5KM E)

⌂ |●| HÔTEL-RESTAURANT DE LA COURONNE*

pl. de l'Église (Centre); take the D9 and the N57 then head for the Swiss border.
☎ 03.81.49.10.50 ➡ 03.81.49.19.77
Closed Sun and Mon evenings out of season and Nov.
Disabled access. Garden. Car park.

Service noon–1.30pm and 7–10.30pm. Set on a real village square with a church and fountain, this small country hotel is fortunately far enough away from the main road to be nice and quiet. Pleasant rooms which have been renovated and have shower/wc from 195F for a double. Numbers 11, 12, 14 and 16 have a nice view over the Jougnenaz valley and you also get a lovely view from the garden. Classic cuisine with lots of local dishes from the Franche-Comté: duck fillet with wild mushrooms, morels and *petit-gris* snails in flaky pastry, trout fillet in Savagnin. Cheapest menu at 100F, served daily, and others up to 220F.

MOIRANS-EN-MONTAGNE — 39260

⌂ |●| HOSTELLERIE DE LA CUZON***

19 rue Pasteur.
☎ 03.84.42.33.22 ➡ 03.84.42.38.34
TV.

The house was built in 1722 and is now the only three-star hotel in the Haut-Jura. The eleven spacious rooms with modern facilities are faultless; 300–380F. It's an ideal place if you travelling through – whatever time you arrive, there's always a ready smile. The gourmet restaurant is frequented by local suits while the brasserie and terrace are more relaxed. Both serve the same menus, decently priced at 80–230F.

|●| LE REGARDOIR

It's at the Belvédère; take the north exit to Moirans.
☎ 03.84.42.01.15
Closed Mon evening and Tue except 15 June–30 Aug.

Stop for a snack here just so you can enjoy the panoramic view which takes in the Lac de Vouglans way below. There's something special about the light at sunset, a moment to linger over with an apéritif. Nice, smiling welcome and a straightforward menu though the cook is serious about his work. The fried small fry and the pizzas cooked in a wood-fuelled oven are tasty. *À la carte*, there's hot goat's cheese, trout with almonds, cockerel with Burgundy wine sauce, *andouillette* with mustard sauce and iced soufflé with pear schnaps. Weekday menu 65F and others 80–98F. It's always full.

CUTTURA 39170 (20KM E)

✱ L'AUBERGE DU VIEUX MOULIN

Take the D470 and it's between Moirans and St-Claude.
☎ 03.84.42.84.28

The apparent simplicy of this place is misleading. The short 65F menu – starter, steak or trout – draws in everyone who knows, but that's only the half of it. This is a lovely old water mill and you eat down by the waterside, overlooking a small dam that squawks with ducks and moorhens. Then you discover the menus and the *à la carte* listings; fried baby trout, frogs' legs, *Morteau* with Gex blue cheese, perch and parsley, guinea-fowl with bilberries and escalope of *foie gras* with sour cherries. The home-made fruit tarts are as delicious as the ice creams. Handsome portions and fairly priced menus from 98F.

MONTBÉLIARD 25200

✱ ✱ HÔTEL DE LA BALANCE✱✱✱

40 rue de Belfort (Centre); it's in the old town.
☎ 03.81.96.77.41 ➡ 03.81.91.47.16
Restaurant closed Sat lunchtime. **Disabled access.**
TV. Car park.

Like a lot of the other buildings in the old town, the façade of this 16th-century house has been painted and is now a dusky pink. Inside, the elegant, yellow-ochre dining room, the antique furniture and a solid wooden staircase add to the charm of the place, which definitely belies the rather sad image people tend to have of the town. The rooms are stylish, all with shower/wc or bath from 410F, depending on the season. If you're interested in history, ask for the room where Field Marshal de Lattre de Tassigny stayed in 1944. Buffet breakfast 40F. Very classic menus, 69–195F. Cosy piano bar.

✱ RESTAURANT DU CHÂTEAU

4 rue du Château; it's on the edge of the old town, on the way to the château.
☎ 03.81.94.93.06

A small establishment which is often full. Very classical cuisine using fresh produce: you may come across the owner buying his ingredients fresh in the local markets. The proprietor is rightly proud of his filleted fried carp at 80F. Frogs and crayfish are served in

season. The 85F menu is served at lunchtime and sometimes in the evening, other menus 120–200F which are fairly priced given the quality of the produce used. Good wine list.

AUDINCOURT 25400 (16KM S)

✱ HÔTEL DES TILLEULS✱✱

51 av. Foch.
☎ 03.81.30.77.00 ➡ 03.81.30.57.20
Disabled access. Garden. Swimming pool. TV.
Lock-up garage.

In a quiet street – make sure you go to the *avenue*, not the *rue* Foch. Excellent welcome. The rooms are very well equipped with fridge, power shower and hair dryer, and the decor is modern but warm. They're dotted about the main building or in annexes around the garden where there's also a lovely heated swimming pool. Doubles from 290F. There's no restaurant but they'll get meals brought in for you in the evening.

MORTEAU 25500

✱ HÔTEL DES MONTAGNARDS✱✱

7 [bis] pl. Carnot (Centre).
☎ 03.81.67.08.86 ➡ 03.81.67.14.57
Disabled access. TV. Pay car park.

This is a small, friendly hotel in the centre of the village looking out onto the surrounding countryside where you're warmly greeted. Attractive panelled rooms, some of which have been redecorated in pastel shades. Doubles 190F with washing facilities, 245F with shower/wc and 286F with bath.

✱ RESTAURANT L'ÉPOQUE

18 rue de la Louhière (North); it's on the Besançon road.
☎ 03.81.67.33.44
Closed Wed evening and Sun except public holidays and 25 July–15 Aug. **Car park.**

They know what they're about in this restaurant – the welcome is natural and the service friendly. There are a couple of bistro-like dining rooms where you instantly feel at home. The tasty food is inventive enough without ignoring its regional origins: sausage *de Morteau*, which the owner really loves, in red Arbois wine, Bresse chicken with *vin jaune* and morels. Set menus 75–185F; flaky pastry with *filet mignon forestière* or stuffed lemon sole fillet *à la dieppoise* (poached in white wine with mussels, shrimps, mushrooms and cream). There's an impressive selection of whiskies and the owner, who has a huge moustache and is a bit of a local character, has set up a club for whisky-lovers.

MONTLEBON   25500 (2KM SE)

⚑ IOI HÔTEL-RESTAURANT BELLEVUE*

2 rue de Bellevue; it's on the D48.
☎ 03.81.67.00.05 ➡ 03.81.67.04.74
Closed Sun evening, Fri evening in winter, and 15
Dec–15 Jan. **TV**. **Car park**.

This Comptois farmhouse dominates the
whole of the Morteau valley, a truly *belle vue*.
The 55F lunchtime menu is a magnet for local
people who travel in the course of their work –
plumbers, wood-cutters, gas employees and
so on – and the regional dishes are generously served and well prepared. Try trout *meunière*, *filet mignon* with morels, or hot mountain
ham, for example. A range of menus 80–150F.
Rooms are plain but reasonably priced at
170F for a double with washing facilities or
235F for a shower/wc.

GRAND'COMBE CHÂTELEU   25500 (4KM S)

IOI RESTAURANT FAIVRE

It's on the main road.
☎ 03.81.68.84.63
Closed Sun evening, Mon and the first three weeks in
Aug. **TV**. **Pay car park**.

A huge chalet with a cosy, very pleasant dining
room. The classic, regional dishes betray no
threat of inventiveness but are decent and
carefully prepared. A good place to stop.
Lunch menu 108F and others 130–300F.

ORNANS   25290

⚑ IOI HÔTEL DE FRANCE***

51 rue Pierre-Vernier (Centre).
☎ 03.81.62.24.44 ➡ 03.81.62.12.03
Closed Sun evening and Mon depending on reservations
and 20 Dec–1 Jan.
TV. **Garden**. **Pay car park**.

A good example of traditional hotel-keeping in
a place that really lives up to its name but with
extra comfort. There's a 100F brasserie menu
with dishes like a flan with *comté* cheese and
raw ham, and trout *au bleu* with a lemon
sauce. Other menus 150–310F. The rooms
have an upmarket, rustic feel, and some look
out onto the famous Grand Pont (which actually isn't that big). The road outside is noisy, but
you'll get peace and quiet in the rooms at the
back. Doubles 380–400F with shower/wc or
400–450F with bath, TV and mini-bar. Half
board is compulsory at the weekend in season. There's a big terrace and a garden behind
the hotel. Private fishing.

VERNIERFONTAINE   25580 (17KM E)

⚑ IOI L'AUBERGE PAYSANNE

18 rue du Stade; take the D492 in the direction of
Saules, then the D392 to Guyans-Durnes then
Vernierfontaine.
☎ and ➡ 03.81.60.05.21
Closed Wed,Thurs, and Nov–March except for the
Christmas holidays. **Garden**. **Car park**.

An old farmhouse in a remote village way out
in the country. The decor is cluttered but the
cuisine is traditional and full of flavour, using
the panoply of wonderful local produce:
smoked meats from the Haut-Doubs, *roësti*
(grated potatoes fried in a heavy pan), flaky
pastry cases with morels in rich sauce, *fondue*
using *comté* cheese, *poêlée paysanne* (big
pans of potatoes, smoked bacon, onions,
sausage and eggs), and a wonderful apple
strudel prepared by the boss who originates
from Germany. Menus start at 66F, and go up
to 135F. There are four rooms with wood-panelled walls; 230F for a double with shower/wc.
The gigantic breakfast includes sausage,
cheese and yoghurt.

AMONDANS 25330   (14KM W)

IOI LE CHÂTEAU D'AMONDANS

9 rue Louise-Pommery.
☎ 03.81.86.53.14
Closed Tues, Wed and Sun evening.

One of the culinary hits of the region and with
good reason – the cooking is quite simply
remarkable. There may be more inventive
cuisine, but chef-owner Frédéric Médique
brings a personal interpretation to traditional
dishes, especially his speciality dessert, *l'A-
mondanais*. Menus from 195F. The setting is
sumptuous, the welcome friendly and the service faultless. The only drawback is that the
wine list concentrates on the great growths of
Burgundy, Bordeaux and Jura, missing out on
less prestigious offerings.

PONTARLIER   25300

🎿 ⚑ IOI HÔTEL-RESTAURANT LE SAINT-PIERRE*

3 pl. Saint-Pierre (Centre).
☎ 03.81.46.50.80 ➡ 03.81.46.87.80
Closed Mon out of season. **TV**.

This place sits on a square in an area that feels
villagey. Nearly all the rooms look out on to the
porte Saint-Pierre, the rather elaborate
triumphal arch that has become the symbol of
the town. The double rooms with shower/wc

aren't exactly huge, but they are stylish and good value with prices starting at 180F. The restaurant serves decent traditional food on menus from 68F. They have the sunniest terrace in town, the perfect spot to sip your free aperitif.

☎ |●| HÔTEL-RESTAURANT DE MORTEAU**

26 rue Jeanne-d'Arc (Centre).
☎ 03.81.39.14.83 ➡ 03.81.39.75.07
Closed daily 3–6pm, Sun and a week in March, June, Sept and Oct. **TV**.

This place looks vaguely like an old farmhouse, and although it's in the middle of the village, it's in a quiet spot. The rooms have been completely renovated and are good value for money – doubles from 220F with shower/wc or 230F with bath. Good traditional cooking using only fresh produce with menus from 68F.

GRANGETTES (LES)　　　25160 (12KM S)

☎ |●| HÔTEL-RESTAURANT BON REPOS**

How to get there: it's on the lac de Saint-Point on the D129.
☎ 03.81.69.62.95 ➡ 03.81.69.66.62
Closed Sun and Mon out of season, and 20 Oct–20 Dec. **Garden. TV. Car park**.

On the edge of a little village on the lakeside. An old-fashioned inn – the tablecloths are white and the welcome is inviting. Substantial platters of home-made *charcuterie* and fine fish specialities like fillet of perch with mushrooms and noodles. Menus from 73F. Comfortable, well-maintained rooms – some have been renovated. Doubles from 185F.

OUHANS　　　25520 (17KM NW)

☎ |●| HÔTEL-RESTAURANT DES SOURCES DE LA LOUE**

13 Grande-Rue (Centre); take the N57, at Saint-Gorgon-Main, turn left onto the D41.
☎ 03.81.69.90.06 ➡ 03.81.69.93.17
Closed Wed and Sun evenings out of season, All Saints' holidays and 20 Dec–31 Jan. **TV. Car park**.

A lovely inn in an unspoilt village in wonderful countryside. The cooking produces local dishes, as you would expect, like steak with morels, trout *meunière* or in *vin jaune*, smoked ham, Morteau sausage with potatoes *au gratin*, and house smoked salmon. Weekday lunch menu 72F and others up to 200F. Pleasant, simple rooms, some in the roof, which are reasonably priced for the area: 200F with shower/wc and 250F with bath.

RENÉDALE　　　25520 (24KM N)

|●| AUBERGE DU MOINE

Grange-Carrée; take the N57 to Saint-Gorgon-Main then the D41 in the direction of Ouhans and it's 400m from the Belvédère du Moine.
☎ 03.81.69.91.22
Closed Mon evening and 15 Dec–1 March.

A lovely old farm in the country, where the stable has been converted into a dining room with pine panelling. On Sunday it's full of local people who have known of this fine establishment for ages. Danielle runs the place and does the cooking. She uses a lot of family recipes mixed in with regional dishes: trout in *vin jaune* or pastry cases with morels. Set menu at 68F (not served Sun), then others 112–142F. There are lovely walks over the *belvédère du Moine* and the source of the Loue river.

PORT-SUR-SAÔNE　　　70170

☎ |●| HÔTEL-RESTAURANT DE LA PAIX

3 rue Jean-Bogé (Centre); it's opposite the church.
☎ 03.84.91.52.80 ➡ 03.84.91.61.21
Closed Sun evening and Jan. **Car park**.

The hotel is in a 16th-century priory They've recently refurbished it and the decoration is in keeping with the building. Doubles 150F with basin, 190F with shower/wc. Unpretentious cooking and traditional dishes: morels in pastry cases, duck breast *Montmorency*, salmon *pâté* in pastry and *coq au vin jaune*. Weekday menu 58F and others 75–150F.

⅍|●| RESTAURANT LA POMME D'OR

1 rue Saint-Valère.
☎ 03.84.91.52.66
Closed Sun evening, Mon, and the last fortnight in Aug. **Car park**.

You can eat in a smart little dining room right on the banks of the Saône. The cuisine is good: *œufs en meurette* in red wine, *fricassée* of kidneys in mustard, warm duck tart, fillet of red mullet on the lees and for desserts, don't miss out on the golden apples in leaves, the house speciality. Menus 60–155F. In summer, you might find a table on the tiny terrace overlooking the water, where they serve only cold meals. Free coffee.

|●| RESTAURANT LA MARINE

15 rue de la Fontaine.
☎ 03.84.91.51.00
Closed Wed and Feb.

This is a genuine *guinguette*, the old type of café where they used to have dancing outside, on the banks of the Saône. The people in their boats have only to tie up to eat in this pleasant establishment, where the owner really treats his clients to excellent cuisine. The 80F weekday menu and others at 120F and 170F are changed regularly, but they always list fish specialities like fillet of plaice *grenobloise*, or game in season like a boar stew, then *aiguillettes* of duck in cognac and rabbit *sauté dijonnaise*. Best to book whether you come by boat or not.

COMBEAUFONTAINE   70120 (12KM W)

♠ |●| HÔTEL-RESTAURANT LE BALCON**

Centre; take the N19.
☎ 03.84.92.11.13 ➡ 03.84.92.15.89
Closed Sun evening, Mon, 25 June–5 July, and 26 Dec–1 Jan. **Garden. TV**.

A former coaching inn smothered with ivy and with a flower garden. It's a magnificent house with a really warm atmosphere. Pleasant, simple rooms 250–380F with shower/wc or bath – given the hotel's situation on the main road, the ones at the back are quieter. Delicious dishes like chicken in *vin jaune* and morels, Montbéliard sausage with lentils, pigeon in flaky pastry *à la bourguignonne* and some more innovative dishes – scallops in herb vinaigrette and slivers of duck with a cherry infusion. 70F weekday lunch menu and others 145–340F.

RONCHAMP   70200

⅍ ♠ |●| HÔTEL-RESTAURANT CARRER**

Le Rhien; it's 2km outside Ronchamp on the N19.
☎ 03.84.20.62.32 ➡ 03.84.63.57.08
e carrer@ronchant.com
Disabled access. TV. Car park.

People come from far and wide to eat in this restaurant in a forest hamlet. The family cooking is very orthodox and they use the best quality fresh produce. The results are delicious: duck *terrine*, trout in *vin jaune*, fried carp and game in season. Weekday lunch menu at 60F and others 110–220F. There are twenty rooms, 200–240F for a double, depending on facilities. Mountain bike hire. 10% discount on the room rate Oct–March.

CHAMPAGNEY   70290 (5KM E)

♠ |●| HÔTEL DU COMMERCE**

4 av. du Général-Brosset.

☎ 03.84.23.13.24 ➡ 03.84.23.24.33
e hotel-du-commerce@70.fr
Closed 23 Dec–14 Jan. **Garden. TV. Car park**.

This old house has been transformed from cellar to roof, but the family that own it have taken care to retain the original character. There are four dining rooms which are all different; one has a wide fireplace where they serve country dishes, another is more like a sitting room-cum-library. The rooms are either starkly modern or have period furniture. Doubles with shower/wc or bath 200F. The waitresses still wear white aprons and the chef hasn't changed so you still get good quality regional and traditional dishes that are soundly prepared; casserole of lacquered pork with Champlitte wine, zander fillet with oyster mushrooms, and brawn. Weekday menu 58F and a range from 65F to 250F. There's a fitness room, a sauna and a turkish bath.

FROIDETERRE   70200 (10KM W)

|●| HOSTELLERIE DES SOURCES

4 rue du Grand Bois; take the N19 in the direction of Lure, when you get to La Verrerie, take the road that goes north.
☎ 03.84.30.13.91
Closed Sun evening and Mon except public holidays, and a fortnight in Jan. **Car park**.

The house looks like a classic rustic farm inn but is completely different inside. The decor is very plush, almost luxurious, and almost too big a contrast. However, the main event is the cuisine, which is creative and intelligently conceived. The menus change with the seasons but all the dishes look and taste good; Jura snails with marrowbone and mushrooms in wine sauce, veal kidneys with pickled tomatoes, perch fillets with a watercress *fondant* and sliced pineapple with sour cherry *sorbet*. Menus 105–295F. It's a pity they don't have rooms.

MELISEY   70220 (10KM N)

⅍|●| RESTAURANT LA BERGERAINE

27 route des Vosges; take the N10 towards Lure, then the D73.
☎ 03.84.20.82.52
Closed Tues evening and Wed except public holidays, Feb school holidays and 28 June–10 July. **TV. Lock-up garage**.

It's such a small place that, unless you want to go away hungry, it's advisable to book. Appetising, classic dishes prepared with care and really well cooked. The chef has created a place which brings people into the country to eat but it's not ruinously expensive. House smoked salmon, seasonal leaves with cray-fish, veal sweetbreads with morel,s or morels in a pastry case with *vin jaune* sauce. Week-day lunch menu 65F then 85–280F. Free aperitif.

ROYE 70200   (15KM SW)

|●| LE SAISONNIER

56 rue de la Verrierie; it's at the beginning of the village, on the N19.
☎ 03.84.30.46.80
Closed Wed.

In the Haute-Saône, you can stumble on some quite surprising places – such as this one. It used to be a farm and it shows with its thick stone walls which keep it warm in win-ter and cool in summer, and its low ceilings (tall people have to duck). Very sober decor but pleasant nonetheless. Friendly service. Excellent seasonal cooking with a lot of up-to-date dishes, offering good value for money. Weekday menu 85F then 140–270F. There's a quiet terrace at the back.

ROUSSES (LES)   39220

♠ HÔTEL DU VILLAGE**

344 rue Pasteur (Centre).
☎ 03.84.34.12.75 ➡ 03.84.34.12.76
Closed Sun evening out of season, last week in June, and 15 Nov–8 Dec. **TV**. **Pay garage**.

This ten-room hotel in the middle of the resort has been completely renovated. Large double rooms, all with shower/wc or bath 270–330F. There's a small suite sleeping four to five on the second floor.

♠ |●| HÔTEL ARBEZ FRANCO-SUISSE

La Cure; it's 2km out of town on the D5.
☎ 03.84.60.02.20 ➡ 03.84.60.08.59
Closed Mon and Tues.

With a foot in France and another over the Swiss border, this is an odd place – depend-ing where your room is in the hotel, you could be sleeping in either country. The rooms are lovely and comfortable with blond wood panels on the walls. Doubles 300F with shower, 340F with bath. They serve good local fare with a brasserie option, where the cooking is more filling, and a more gourmet one. Menus 120–210F. Charming welcome and a very good place.

SAINT-CLAUDE   39200

MOLUNES (LES) 39310   (13KM SE)

♠ LE COLLÈGE

How to get there: take the D436 in the direction of Septmoncel then the D25 in the direction of Moussières; it's in the middle of the village.
☎ 03.84.45.52.34

The hamlet is 1250m up and is so small it does-n't even have a church. This place used to be a bakers' and grocer's shop and its reputation has spread through the Haut-Jura. It can seat 64 but there's often a fight to get in at the week-end. The food is not only good, it's beautifully presented. First-class weekday menu at 58F with *charcuterie*, the dish of the day – such as sautéed veal with rice, braised chicory and spinach – then cheese and dessert. The others, 98–148F, are just as good. Attractively priced wine list. The decor has a genuine country feel.

SAINT-HIPPOLYTE   25190

🌿 ♠ |●| AUBERGE DE MORICEMAISON

Route du Dessoubre – Valoreille (Southwest); head for the Dessoubre valley on the D39 for about 11km.
☎ 03.81.64.01.72/04.30
Closed Tues evening and Wed mid-Sept to mid-May. **Car park**.

Very picturesque old farm with a nice view over the river. Warm, natural welcome. Anglers gather here and if you catch anything, the pro-prietor will be happy to cook your catch. Oth-erwise there's trout on the menu, cooked in *vin jaune* or fried. Good menus of the day at 58F during the week and other menus 95–190F. Six modest, recently redecorated rooms – basins only; showers and wc are down the corridor – cost 160F for a double and there's one that sleeps five. 10% discount on the room rate except July–Aug.

GOUMOIS   25470 (20KM SE)

♠ |●| AUBERGE LE MOULIN DU PLAIN**

Lieu-dit Le Moulin du Plain; at Goumois on the D437b follow the road along the Doubs and look for the signs.
☎ 03.81.44.41.99 ➡ 03.81.44.45.70
Closed 1 Nov–24 Feb. **TV**. **Car park**.

This fairly modern house, built in the local style, is on the banks of the Doubs, which cuts through a fabulous, wild valley. It's a rendezvous for anglers. The inn was started a few years ago by a family of farmers and it's become a thriving business. Twenty-two very comfortable double rooms – all with shower/wc or bath from 295F. Some have balconies. In the restaurant there are lots of trout dishes in *vin jaune* with shallots, and a *timbale* of pike, alongside other local dishes like tournedos with morels and hot ham. Set menus 95F (not Sun), then 115–200F.

VESOUL   70000

⌂ HÔTEL DU LION**

4 pl. de la République (Centre).
☎ 03.84.76.54.44 ☛ 03.84.75.23.31
Closed Sat evening in Jan, 5–17 Aug, and 26 Dec–6 Jan. **TV. Car park**.

Family-run, very traditional hotel in the centre of town. Lovely welcome, and the staff know what good service is. The comfortable rooms have modern furnishings and are spacious; doubles with shower/wc cost 256F or 276F with bath.

FROTEY-LES-VESOUL   70000 (3KM E)

⌂ |●| EUROTEL-RESTAURANT LE SAINT JACQUES

Route de Luxeuil.
☎ 03.84.75.49.49 ☛ 03.84.75.55.78
Closed Sat lunchtime, and Sun evening except July–Aug. **TV. Car park and lock up garage**.

The outside is very off-putting – it looks exactly like lots of chains throughout France – and the motorway exit is hardly the most joyous view, but you leave all that behind once inside. The rooms are pleasant and contemporary; doubles with bath 360F. The dining room is equally modern but the bar and dining room are truly elegant. Very professional yet warm welcome. The cuisine is splendid and has lots of personal touches – as you would hope, it changes with the season. Check out the cheapest *menu du marché*, 100F, and you'll see. Other menus 165–350F.

VILLERSEXEL   70110

🖫 ⌂ |●| HÔTEL DE LA TERRASSE**

Route de Lure; it's on the banks of the Ogno.
☎ 03.84.20.52.11 ☛ 03.84.20.56.90
Closed Sun evening and Mon lunchtime out of season, and 15 Dec–3 Jan. **Garden**. **TV**. **Car park**.

Gérard Ème established the hotel, but it's now run by his daughter. It's quiet and cosy and very relaxing. The rooms are prettily decorated and furnished with taste. You'll have a very good night here because it's really peaceful. Doubles 220–240F with shower/wc and 280–300F with bath. The restaurant has a rustic decor warmed by a fire in the open hearth in winter. In summer, there's a terrace amid the greenery, so whatever the season, you will be able to enjoy your meal in an attractive setting: try hare stew *à l'ancienne*, small casserole of morels in cream or fillet of zander in *vin jaune*. Traditional menu at 69F, and others 90–180F. Free house apéritif.

⌂ |●| HÔTEL-RESTAURANT DU COMMERCE**

1 pl. du 13-Septembre; it's near the chateau-museum.
☎ 03.84.20.50.50 ☛ 03.84.20.59.57
🖄 commviller@aol.com
Closed Sun evening and a week in Oct. **TV**. **Car park and lock-up garage**.

Huge, absolutely classic, provincial inn. Sadly the rooms feel like those in a chain hotel, though they're simple, clean and reasonably priced. Doubles 240F with shower/wc or bath. The owner prepares good regional dishes; home-smoked ham cooked on the bone, frogs' legs, poached trout with morels, or grilled meats and flambéed tarts. A range of set menus 54–215F should satisfy any appetite. There's a huge fireplace where they light a fire on cold nights.

Île-de-France

75 Paris

77 Seine-et-Marne

78 Yvelines

91 Essonne

92 Hauts-de-Seine

93 Seine-Saint-Denis

94 Val-de-Marne

95 Val-d'Oise

ANGERVILLE   91670

🏂 🏠 |●| HÔTEL DE FRANCE***

2 pl. du Marché (Centre).
☎ 01.69.95.11.30 ➡ 01.64.95.39.59
TV. Car park.

This beautiful old inn, built in 1715, has been restored at various times without losing its elegance or character. The old beams, fireplace, conservatory and drawing room exude an air of gracious living. There's a sitting room where you can relax over an apéritif before proceeding to the dining room. The cuisine is reassuringly traditional and reliable: cream of watercress soup – this is the region for watercress – and *salade mérévilloise*. Expect to pay 220F *à la carte*. There is a pair of ravishing rooms with canopied beds with shower or bath for 430F. Free house aperitif.

ARPAJON   91290

SAINT-SULPICE-DE-FAVIÈRES 91910 (7KM SE)

|●| AUBERGE DE CAMPAGNE LA FERRONNIÈRE

10 pl. de l'Église; take the N20 towards Orléans, after Arpajon take the Mauchamps exit onto the D99.
☎ 01.64.58.42.07
Closed Wed.

A jewel of a village with a country inn that looks like a Wild West saloon. It must have been an old coaching inn, with the smithy next door. You won't find a better welcome or service; there's even a shower available for use by walkers. Huge plates of wonderful traditional food with a few authentic regional dishes besides: house *pâté* under a layer of parsley, snails, duck breast, rack of lamb, steak with shallots. Weekday menu at 65F. Terrace in summer. Don't miss it if you're in the area.

ASNIÈRES   92600

🏂 |●| LE PETIT VATEL

30 bd. Voltaire; it's near the dog cemetery; M° Asnières-Gabriel-Péri.
☎ 01.47.91.13.30
Closed evenings, weekends and Aug.

Though you'd be likely to walk past this very ordinary, Formica-table lunch place with without a second look, you'd be wrong to do so. Firstly, the welcome they extend is genuinely warm; secondly, the quality of the cuisine is remarkable – and you almost get more than you can eat. They take tremendous care in preparing traditional family dishes like ham hock or *provençal* beef stew, and the salads are huge. Menu at 65F and reasonably priced wine. Free coffee.

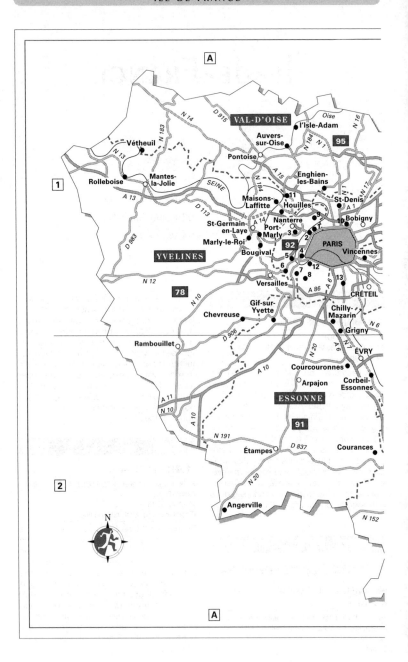

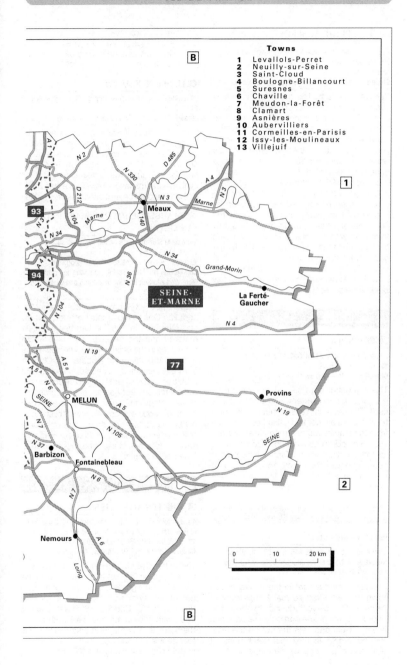

Towns

1 Levallols-Perret
2 Neuilly-sur-Seine
3 Saint-Cloud
4 Boulogne-Billancourt
5 Suresnes
6 Chaville
7 Meudon-la-Forêt
8 Clamart
9 Asnières
10 Aubervilliers
11 Cormeilles-en-Parisis
12 Issy-les-Moulineaux
13 Villejuif

涟|●| LA PETITE AUBERGE

118 rue de Colombes; take the overground train from
Saint-Lazare to Asnières or Bois-Colombes.
☎ 01.47.93.33.94
Closed Sun and Wed evenings, Mon and a week in Aug.

Service until 9pm. The decor is completely
over the top, like the set of a Grande Époque
operetta – wood panelling and pictures
everywhere. You are scooped up by the
patronne or her daughter and conducted to
your table; dad, in the kitchen, produces
wonderful food. For 150F you are served a
superb meal, with dishes that change with
the seasons. Of the starters, the *andouillette*
in Chablis in a pastry case is meltingly delicious, the *émincé* of veal kidneys is tender
and served in plenty of sauce, while the
supreme of chicken *à l'indienne* is subtly
flavoured with paprika and other delicate
spices. The fish is as fresh as can be. Try the
gratin of fresh fruit or the succulent soft fruit
in pastry. The only reservation is that the wine
is a little expensive. You should definitely
book. Free coffee.

AUBERVILLIERS   93300

涟|●| L'ISOLA

33 bd. Édouard-Vaillant; M°Fort-d'Auberviliers
☎ 01.48.34.88.76
Closed Sun, Mon–Wed evenings and Aug.

This is a genuine Italian restaurant run by a
pair of charming sisters who are kindness
itself. The decor is pleasant but not ostentatious. Dishes are cooked using fresh produce
from the market with a strong Italian accent:
veal escalope, *osso bucco*, ricotta ravioli,
lasagne, and a delicious Sardinian dish called
coulourgionisi. You'll pay 150–180F for a
meal. Free apéritif on the first visit, coffee
from then on.

AUVERS-SUR-OISE   95430

|●| LE CORDEVILLE

18 rue du Rajon; leave the A15 at exit 7 onto the N184,
then take the N322 in the direction of Méry-sur-Oise.
☎ 01.30.36.81.66

The restaurant is right in the centre of this
town that attracted so many Impressionist
painters. They serve traditional, family cuisine
and don't stint on the portions. The *patronne*
is very sweet and sets the pot on the table
for you to help yourself, just like at home. It
appeals to a range of people, from local

workers to holiday-makers, and has a
brigade of regulars. Weekday menu at 60F,
otherwise 85F. Limited choice of wines. No
credit cards.

|●| LE VERRE PLACIDE

20 rue du Général-de-Gaulle; opposite the train station.
☎ 01.34.48.02.11
Closed Mon, Wed and Sun evenings, and Aug.

One of the oldest restaurants in Auvers, with
a spacious and bright dining room. At 135F
you get a starter, main course and a dessert,
or it's around 150F *à la carte*. Try the salad of
quail *confit*, turbot with a fennel compote, or
lamb in a pastry case. The wine's a little prici-
er than it should be, but service is very polite.

涟|●| AUBERGE RAVOUX-MAISON DE VAN GOGH

8 rue de la Sansonne; it's on the town hall square.
☎ 01.30.36.60.60
📧 auberge-Ravoux@maison-de-van-gogh.com
Closed Sun and Mon evening sin spring and summer,
Mon–Wed and Sun evening in autumn and winter, and
25 Dec–25 Jan.

Service noon–3.30pm and 7.30–11pm. Vincent van Gogh lived in this hotel for a while,
and died here in 1890. It has been entirely
restored and the decor is just as it would
have been in the painter's day. The cooking is
good, and helpings are substantial. Choose
from old-fashioned dishes such as pressed
rabbit on a bed of lentils and pickled onions,
roast lamb *de sept heures*, and, for dessert,
mousse Tagliana, which is named after one
of the previous owners of the establishment.
A *formule* at 155F gets you a main course
plus starter or dessert; all three courses cost
195F – not particularly cheap, but worth it.
Free house apéritif.

BARBIZON   77630

涟 🏠 |●| LES ALOUETTES**

4 rue Antoine-Barye; at the tobacconist's on the corner
of Rue Grande, turn up the street and it's 500m along.
☎ 01.60.66.41.98 📠 01.60.66.20.69
Closed Sun evening. **TV. Garden. Car park**.

This rather chic 19th-century house has been
turned into an inn, set in its own substantial
grounds with a garden and trees. It is the only
hotel that's away from the main street. The
decor is rustic. Doubles 180F with shower,
280F with shower/wc and 390F with bath –
there are also two apartments which sleep
four people at 530F and 600F. In the restaurant there's a set menu at 170F, while eating

à la carte will cost around 250F. Specialities include pan-fried fresh *foie gras* of Landes duck served with golden fruit, and roast rabbit *aux saveurs provençales*. Free apéritif.

🏃|●| L'ERMITAGE ST ANTOINE

51 Grande-Rue (Centre).
☎ 01.64.81.96.96
Closed Mon, Tues, and a fortnight Dec/Jan.

It's an unexpected pleasure to come upon this wine bar run by some young people who wanted to put a bit of a spark into this conventional tourist town. More unusual still is that this is a 19th-century farm house that's been brilliantly re-arranged and decorated with *trompe-l'œil* paintings. 100F will buy you a decent meal. They scribble the dishes of the day on the blackboard – such as gazpacho, rabbit salad with green lentils, black pudding with apples and curried spare ribs – or you can get a plate of *charcuterie* or cheeses served with a glass of wine. If the owner offers advice about which wine to order, take it – he really knows what he's talking about. Most of the wines are served by the glass – and even if this is all you order, you'll still get a smile. Free coffee.

BOUGIVAL   78380

🏠|●| LE CAMÉLIA

7 quai Georges-Clémenceau
☎ 01.39.18.36.06
Closed Sat lunchtime, Sun evening, Mon and the first fortnight in Aug. **TV**.

A welcoming, refined setting. The cuisine is prettily prepared and manages to be both solid and delicate. All the produce used is fresh and the cooking shows off the flavours extremely well. The fixed-price menus list the more elaborate dishes, which change regularly. Menu at 140F and a *formule* with wine at 185F. Swift, efficient service.

|●| RESTAURANT CHEZ CLÉMENT

It's on the RN13.
☎ 01.30.78.20.00

Service from early morning to 1am. A huge English-style park surrounds this superb house with green shutters. You go through the smoking room – when it's cold, they light a fire – to the main room, which used to be the orangery. The simple cooking uses fresh, seasonal produce. The oysters and shellfish are kept cool under a running waterfall. A meal will cost you around 170F. This is a very pleasant place.

BRAY-ET-LÛ   95710

🏃🏠|●| LE FAISAN DORÉ

12 route de Vernon.
☎ 01.34.67.71.68
Closed Sun evening, Mon, mid-Aug to early Sept and three weeks in winter. **TV**.

The balconies are festooned with an abundance of geraniums and petunias and there's a family atmosphere with a touch of class. In the summer, it's more pleasant to sit on the terrace than under the flowery parasols. The set menu, 128F, offers starter, main course, cheese and dessert. There's a wider selection on the 160F menu, with pepper steak, Burgundy snails and a light fruit *charlotte*. Dish of the day or a main course *à la carte* will cost about 80F: try *fricassée* of veal sweetbreads with morels or veal chops Normandy-style. Good value for money, with attentive service. The rooms are plain; doubles with basin 150F, or 190F with shower. Free coffee.

CHAVILLE   92370

🏃|●| RESTAURANT LE MAGLOIRE

2049 av. Roger-Salengro (Northeast); it's on the N10, near pl. du Général Leclerc.
☎ 01.47.50.40.32
Closed Sun evening, Mon, and mid-July to mid-Aug. **Garden**.

A charming provincial house with a rustic dining room looking onto a pleasant garden. For quality and quantity the 85F set menu is good value, and there are others at 180F and 230F. There's an interesting variety of dishes *à la carte*, like snails in flaky pastry, monkfish liver, *symphonie périgourdine*, and *croustillant* of John Dory and scallops with apples and Calvados. A complete meal should cost about 200F. Free apéritif.

CHEVREUSE   78460

|●| AUBERGE LA BRUNOISE

2 rue de la Division Leclerc.
☎ 01.30.52.33.87
Closed Mon and Tues evenings, Wed, three weeks from 14 July and a week in Feb.

The village is charming and the walk over the bridges of the Yvette river and the canal is incredibly picturesque. Unpretentious cuisine is on offer here – it's honest and good on all the menus, even the 65F weekday lunch menu. There are others 85–225F. Natural, friendly service, and the young owners' eagerness to keep the clients satisfied has earned them a good number of regulars. The dining room has a rustic aspect, though the glorious terrace looks onto the main road.

CHILLY-MAZARIN   91380

⅍ ⏐●⏐ THYM ET BASILIC

97 rue de Gravigny; take the Longjumeau exit off the A6 and continue along the right of the motorway.
☎ 01.69.10.92.75
Closed Sun evening, Mon and Aug.

Service noon–2pm and 7.30–10pm. There's a hint of Provence in the yellow and blue dining room, and a taste of Provence in the dishes: pasta with lobster, king prawns, crayfish, *bouillabaisse* (to order), stuffed queen scallops and cod fillet. The 78F lunch *formule* offers a traditional main dish like *blanquette de veau*. The higher-priced menus are expensive for what you get. Free coffee.

CLAMART   92140

⏐●⏐ RESTAURANT LA COSSE DES PETITS POIS

158 av. Victor-Hugo (Northeast); it's a little bit outside the centre of town, 300m from the train station.
☎ 01.46.38.97.60
Closed Sat lunchtime, Sun evening, a fortnight in Aug.

Service noon–2pm and 7.30–9.30pm. They've cleverly arranged the round tables so that the fireplace remains the centrepiece of this small, pleasant dining room. Service is attentive and somebody in the kitchen has considerable flair. A good set menu at 160F including wine. The chef produces a single *formule* with dishes that change with the season. Prices are a little high, but not unreasonable given the quality of the food and the work that goes into preparing it.

CORBEIL-ESSONNES   91100

🏠 ⏐●⏐ AUX ARMES DE FRANCE

1 bd. Jean-Jaurès; it's on the N7.
☎ 01.64.96.24.04 ➡ 01.60.88.04.00
Closed Aug.

One of the oldest hotels in the *département* – it's starting to show its age but provides unbeatable value for money. The rooms over the courtyard will give you a quiet night's sleep. Doubles 170–210F. Winning cuisine and dish-

es that change with the seasons; wild boar haunch, fresh fish of the day brought straight from the market, truffle risotto, and a fish soup with garlicked croutons worth running the gauntlet of the N7 for. Menus 120–235F. Friendly, unobtrusive service.

⏐●⏐ L'ÉPICURE

pl. de l'Hôtel de Ville/5-7 rue du Grand Pignon; it's opposite the town hall.
☎ 01.60.88.28.38
Closed Sat lunchtime and Sun.

Epicurean pleasures of the table *par excellence* in this charming, aptly named restaurant. Soft music plays in the background and the setting is refined-rustic. The chef produces fine, traditional cooking: *croustillant* of duck (a must!), game terrine, and the famous "*Délice Épicurien*" – calf's head with calf's liver and kidney. Good value on the set menus, which start at 130F, while dishes *à la carte* are almost the same price. Stylish, friendly service.

COUDRAY-MONTCEAUX (LE)   91830 (3KM S)

⏐●⏐ RESTAURANT LA RENOMMÉE

110 berges de la Seine; it's opposite the train station.
☎ 01.64.93.81.09
Closed Tues evening, Wed and the Nov school holidays.

A pleasurable place whatever the weather. In summer, you'll feel tranquil on the terrace, watching the fishermen glide along the Seine. In winter, you'll hunker down in a dining room that's warm and quietly cosy with a roaring fire. The 95F weekday menu lists hot sausage in flaky pastry with port sauce and roast salmon with olive butter. Other menus 145F and 190F. The wine is pricey.

CORMEILLES-EN-PARISIS   95240

⏐●⏐ LA MONTAGNE

route Stratégique; it's in the woods above Cormeilles.
☎ 01.34.50.74.04
Closed Tues and 10–25 Aug.

This is the place for robust, straightforward cooking which seems to go down well locally; the restaurant is full every lunchtime. A typical *menu du jour* at 60F will list egg mayonnaise, seafood salad, steak and *andouillette*, sausages with lentils, and *crème caramel*; for 100F you can have goose *rillettes*, lamb tripe and *crème brûlée*. There's another menu at 160F, or you'll pay the same price *à la carte*. There's a small terrace in summer.

COURANCES   91490

🏃🍴 AUBERGE ARC-EN-CIEL

6 pl. de la République (Centre).
☎ 01.64.98.41.66
Closed Sun evening and Mon. **Garden.**

This is what you want from a French village: a magnificent château with lovely grounds, and a charming leafy main square where you can stop for lunch or dinner. The *crêperie* is a recent innovation and has the added attractions of a small terrace and a garden which are lovely in summer. Good-humoured service. Pancakes from 32–42F. Free house apéritif.

COURCOURONNES   91080

🏃🍴 LE CANAL

31 rue du Pont-Amar; 5km south of Ris-Orangis and it's in the Quartier du Canal, near the hospital.
☎ 01.60.78.34.72
Closed Sun.

Courcouronnes is concrete city and this restaurant is a spark of life in an otherwise desolate wasteland. It's an oddball place with an attractive bar and friendly service, and a smoochy piano bar open at the weekend. The owner cooks robust, colourful dishes – try the duo of bream and salmon with chives –and his pig's trotters are up to the standard set by many of the great-name chefs. Menus 85–169F. Free house apéritif.

DOURDAN   91410

VAL SAINT-GERMAIN (LE)   91530 (5KM NE)

🍴 AUBERGE DU MARAIS

Lieu-dit Marais; from Dourdan, take the D116 in the direction of St Cheron; at Sermaise, turn left onto a windy road through the forest.
☎ 01.64.58.82.97
Closed Sun and Mon evenings.

A large, rustic house on the edge of the forest, with a terrace that's open in summer. Traditional dishes made with fresh, quality produce. The *terrines* and the *foie gras* are particularly fine and it's definitely worth following the chef's suggestions. Weekday menus start at 68F, then others 110–225F.

ENGHIEN-LES-BAINS   95880

🏃🏠🍴 VILLA MARIE-LOUISE**

49 rue de Malleville; it's behind the spa, near the lake.
☎ 01.39.64.82.21 ➡ 01.39.34.87.76
Garden. TV.

This is a fine turn-of-the-century house with a big garden in the centre of town near the spa. The 22 simply furnished, comfortable rooms have been nicely decorated. Doubles with shower/wc 255F, with bath 295F. Probably the cheapest hotel in town. If you're looking for a meal, you have a choice of savoury and sweet pancakes on a 65F menu or *à la carte* for about 80F. They take a lot of care of you here. Free house apéritif.

DEUIL-LA-BARRE   94170 (1KM NE)

🏃🍴 VERRE CHEZ MOI

75 av. de la Division-Leclerc.
☎ 01.39.64.04.34
Closed Mon and Sat lunchtimes, Sun, 30 June–25 Aug and 24 Dec–1 Jan.

This restaurant feels like a Lyonnais tavern; it occupies the ground floor of a villa which has been converted into flats. They serve good, well-prepared traditional dishes. There are no set menus, only a daily list on which you'll find *coq au vin*, *miroton* of beef – a typical Lyonnais dish with slices of boiled beef in a rich sauce with onions – or top-quality *andouillette A5*. Simple starters include herrings and warm steamed potatoes or *charcuterie*, and they offer a limited range of cheeses (the farmhouse Camembert is excellent), and basic but brilliant desserts like *crème brûlée*. The place is lovely and cosy, with a friendly feel plus very fair prices. You should pay about 130F for a meal with a jug of wine. Free coffee.

SAINT-GRATIEN   95210 (2KM E)

🍴 LE PHARE DU FORUM

14 pl. du Forum; it's in the Forum district in the middle of town.
☎ 01.34.28.23.07

Deliveries of fresh fish from the market at Rungis arrive three times a week. All the produce is brilliantly fresh and cooked to order: lots of shellfish and crustaceans, oysters, stuffed mussels, *bouillabaisse*, lemon sole, Dover sole, skate or you can fill up on pasta or home-cooked pizzas. The restaurant has a maritime decor – model ships, starfish and fishing nets. Weekday menu 49F, then 79–129F. Musical entertainment on Saturday and Sunday evenings. Smiling, brisk service.

🏂 |●| CHEZ BABER

71 bd. Pasteur; it's on the N14, on the edge of Sannois.
☎ 01.39.89.64.72
Disabled access.

You are welcomed by the gentle music of the sitar and the tabla. The perfumed air and Indian decor transport you far from the noise of the road outside. Lunchtime menu at 59F and two dinner ones at 99F and 129F. Their tandoori specialities feature delicious sauces – including one using bananas – while other dishes, like lamb tikka or fish magala, are good. You'll pay around 160F *à la carte*, including wine. Free coffee or *digestif*, and, if you can prove it's your birthday, a free glass of champagne.

SOISY-SOUS-MONTMORENCY 95230 (2KM NW)

🏂 |●| LE TABAC DES COURSES

34 av. Kellerman; it's 100m from the racecourse, opposite the railway line.
☎ 01.34.17.25.09
Closed Sun, evenings and 17 Aug–5 Sept. **Car park**.

This place looks like nothing special, but they serve decent, honest food which is well cooked and generously served. Menus from 75F: *œufs en meurette* in red wine sauce, herring fillets, duck with pears, fillet of sole with sorrel, steak with the house sauce. They also do a huge steak *tartare* with a serious serving of chips. There's a shady terrace which is on a rather busy avenue. Free coffee.

ÉTAMPES 91150

♠ HÔTEL DE L'EUROPE À L'ESCARGOT**

71 rue Saint-Jacques (North); it's near the motorway entrance for the leisure complex.
☎ 01.64.94.02.96
Closed 20 June–30 July. **TV**. **Car park**.

A small, very well-run hotel offering, a smiling welcome, comfortable rooms and good value for money. It's in the middle of town yet quiet. Doubles 175F with shower/wc, 200F with bath.

|●| LE SAINT-CHRISTOPHE

28 rue de la République (Centre); it's next to the church Notre Dame-du-Fort.
☎ 01.64.94.69.99
Closed Wed evening, every other Sun (phone to check) and Aug.

You come here for good traditional Portuguese cooking. Ask the owner if he's changed his speciality dish – cod – and he'll

tell you "Why? Change a winning formula?". It's the national dish, after all. The decor's pretty trashy, with plastic flowers and tiles on the walls, but you can eat well for less than 100F. There's a set menu for 60F.

|●| RESTAURANT LES PILIERS**

2 pl. Saint-Gilles (Centre).
☎ 01.64.94.04.52
Closed Sun evening, Mon and a fortnight July/Aug.

The restaurant is in the oldest house in town, dating from the 12th century. Go through the paved arcade to find the entrance. Good, home cooking with a fair splash of creativity – *crépinette* of pig's trotters, house *confit* and the like. The 95F *formule* gives you a couple of courses, the one at 135F gives three but be sure to order the dishes you want. There's a 60F menu for children. A few *appellation* wines under 100F. A place with some class.

|●| AUBERGE DE LA TOUR SAINT-MARTIN

97 rue Saint-Martin.
☎ 01.69.78.26.19
Closed Mon, Tues Wed and Sun evenings, and Sat lunchtime.

Right next to the leaning tower of Saint-Martin's. Light, inventive cooking delicately flavoured with herbs and spices in dishes which change with the seasonal produce. Just choose from the chef's suggestions: *colombos*, curries, duck breast with spiced caramel. You can eat quickly if you opt for the weekday lunch menu, 150F, which includes canapés, main course and either starter or dessert. Booking essential.

FERTÉ-GAUCHER (LA) 77320

🏂 ♠ |●| HÔTEL DU SAUVAGE**

27 rue de Paris (Centre); it's by the main square
☎ 01.64.04.00.19 ➡ 01.64.20.32.95
e info@hotel-du-sauvage.com
Closed the second week in Jan. **Restaurant closed** Wed. **TV**.

This 16th-century inn was once a brothel that entertained Good King Henry. Its name is said to come from the wild game once abundant in the marshland that used to surround it. The Teinturier family have been innkeepers here for six generations. They've had the courage to refurbish the place to provide attractively modern and comfortable rooms while keeping the squeaky floors and the character of the place. Doubles with shower 260F, shower/wc 300F. Delicious regional dishes made with local produce on set menus 105–220F. Try the *fricassée* of oyster mushrooms, the black pudding with apples, the braised veal sweetbreads or the ham hock in cider. Good fish. Perfect service and smiling welcome. Free house apéritif.

FONTAINEBLEAU   77300

♠ |●| HÔTEL VICTORIA**

112 rue de France (Centre).
☎ 01.60.74.90.00 **e** hotelvictoria@iname.com
TV. Garden. Pay car park.

Georges Sand and Alfred de Musset frequented this place in the 1830s, which gives you an idea of its quality – they had excellent taste. Here and there you'll discern the vestiges of this lovely master-craftsman's house even though all nineteen rooms have been renovated. They're clean and pleasant, particularly the ones overlooking the large garden. It's a real pleasure to be woken by the billing and cooing of the birds. Paul and Isabelle will welcome you like friends. Double rooms with bath cost 365F.

⅍ |●| RESTAURANT BAR-LE WOODEN HORSE

10–12 rue Montebello (Centre); it's between the pl. du Jet d'Eau et the pl. d'Armes.
☎ and **F▶** 01.60.72.04.05
Closed Mon and Tues lunchtime. **Disabled access.**

Slap-bang in the middle of the most touristy part of Fontainebleau, close to the château, and the wooden statue of a horse. As you walk in, there's a large bar and a bright conservatory. There's a 79F *formule* (not available Fri evening or Sat), and menus 130F and 160F. Expect to pay around 155F *à la carte*. The cooking is exactly what you would expect in this traditional, ex-royal town: *sauté* of veal kidney with two-mustard sauce, perch fillet with red pepper butter, lobster *fricassée* with mussels, amd rack of lamb with garlic cream – not very original, perhaps, but the dishes are good value for money, attentively prepared and unobtrusively served. Free apéritif.

⅍ |●| RESTAURANT CHEZ ARRIGHI

53 rue d'Alsace (Centre).
☎ 01.64.22.29.43
Closed Mon.

This is just the sort of place for a family Sunday lunch or to celebrate first communions. It's got an old-fashioned feel about it, with its sturdy, stone façade and luxurious curtains. Menus 98F, 145F and 195F in a

variety of combinations which include dishes like frogs' legs in parsley, boned quail in flaky pastry stuffed with *foie gras*, *goujons* of salmon with creamed spinach, and lamb's tongues in sorrel sauce. They're all well prepared and will surprise and delight any fan of good traditional cooking, though some portions are a bit skimpy. Delicious bread. The decor and the ambience are more charming than you might expect in a suburban restaurant. Free house apéritif.

⅍ |●| LE CAVEAU DES DUCS

24 rue de Ferrare (Centre); it's near the château.
☎ and **F▶** 01.64.22.05.05
Closed a week in Jan and the first fortnight in Aug.
Disabled access.

This may not be Versailles but you'll know you're in Fontainebleau in this 17th-century vaulted cellar with its period decor and chandeliers. Classical cooking, faultlessly served. Set menu 125F (except Sat evening), then 185F and 250F. The chef uses excellent ingredients to produce dishes with southern influences and sometimes a touch of the exotic – something of a surprise in this most conventional of towns: snails in pastry, fillets of red snapper with vanilla, stewed monkfish *provençale*, veal sweetbreads or kidneys in madeira sauce. Free *digestif*.

BOIS-LE-ROI   77590 (4KM NE)

♠ LE PAVILLON ROYAL***

40 av. du Général-Galliéni; it's near the train station.
☎ 01.64.10.41.00 **F▶** 01.64.10.41.10
TV. Disabled access. Swimming pool. Car park.

A new building in very Neoclassical style, which is plain and aesthetically pleasing. Quiet, spacious and impeccably clean rooms for 295F with shower/wc or 350F with bath. Lovely swimming pool and relaxation centre. They charge two-star prices for three-star service. A good place even though it's a little lacking in character. 10% discount Oct–May
.

VULAINES-SUR-SEINE   77870 (7KM E)

⅍ |●| ÎLE AUX TRUITES

6 chemin de Basse-Varenne; cross the Valvins bridge, on the D210, turn left and it's 1km along the river bank.
☎ 01.64.23.71.87
Closed Wed, Thurs lunchtime, and 20 Dec–25 Jan.
Disabled access. Car park.

You're right on the Seine here, in a thatched cottage surrounded by huge willow trees and trout ponds where the children can fish (40F a kilo) for their lunch – and as the tables are right by the water's edge, you can keep an eye on them. Very decent cuisine and perfect service make this restaurant one of the most attractive in the region. It's quite charming without being too expensive. Try grilled fish served with baked potatoes or the *assiette de l'Île aux Truites* which includes smoked trout, marinated fillet of trout and fish *terrine*. Menus at 120F and 170F, and a children's menu at 80F. They also have an interesting selection of wines, like a red Mennetou-Salon. You must reserve in summer to have any hope of getting a table. Free apéritif.

BOURRON-MARLOTTE   77780 (8KM S)

I●I RESTAURANT LES PRÉMICES

12 [bis] rue Blaise-de-Montesquiou; take the N7 in the direction of Nemours-Montargis, at the Bourron-Marlott ZI exit, follow the signs to the village.
☎ 01.64.78.33.00
Closed Sun evening, Mon, a week in the Feb school holidays, 1–15 Aug and a week at Christmas. **TV. Car park.**

The restaurant is in the outbuildings of the superb château Bourron-Marlotte where they've built a conservatory so you can appreciate the glory of the countryside. Véronique will greet you charmingly; her husband, in charge in the kitchens, is a first-rate chef. Weekday *formule* at 150F or 195F, a gourmet menu at 380F: pan-fried *foie gras* with royal jelly, lamb with herbs, lamb shank *confit* with potatoes, grilled crayfish with beetroot *coulis*, and bitter chocolate and ice cream scented with lily of the valley The wine list is unusually good.

MONTIGNY-SUR-LOING   77690 (10KM S)

▲ I●I HÔTEL-RESTAURANT DE LA VANNE ROUGE**

rue de l'Abreuvoir; take the D148 along the banks of the Loing river.
☎ 01.64.78.52.49 📠 01.64.78.52.49
Closed Sun evening and Mon except on public holidays, Tues lunchtime from end-Sept to Easter, and ten days in winter. **TV. Car park.**

Charming, super-quiet hotel with six lovely rooms with views over the River Loing. Doubles 350F with shower/wc. There's a large sunny terrace where you are lulled by the sound of the waterfalls near an old mill and you can practically trail your feet in the water while you eat. Chef Serge Granger's speciality is fish – lobster salad with fresh herbs and

balsamic vinegar, cod with green peppercorns or John Dory with *beurre blanc* – but that doesn't mean you shouldn't try his *foie gras* topped with mashed potato. There's a weekday *menu-carte* at 175F rising to 220F at the weekend. There's an exceptional wine list. Altogether one of the best places in the locality so it's essential to book.

CHARTRETTES   77590 (11KM)

I●I RESTAURANT LE CHALET

37 rue Foch; take the D39 and it's on the right by the marina.
☎ 01.60.69.65.34
Closed Mon, Tues and Wed evenings, Feb, and a fortnight in Sept. **Garden. Car park.**

This place buzzes with energy and laughter. It's a friendly, popular restaurant in a private mansion that looks like all the rest in the street. The large rustic dining room decorated in Louis XIII style extends onto an elevated terrace with a pergola. The cuisine consists of traditional dishes with good sauces: home-made goat's cheese tart, brawn with *vinaigrette*, *coq au vin* or rabbit *chasseur*. A substantial set menu at 75F (not served Sat evening or Sun), then 122F and 165F.

GIF-SUR-YVETTE   91190

I●I LE BŒUF À SIX PATTES

D-128 Chemin du Moulon; take the Centre universitaire exit off the N118.
☎ 01.60.19.29.60
Disabled access. Car park.

Service 11.30am–2.30pm and 7–10pm (10.30pm Fri and Sat). You could well get a crick in the neck as you crane round to look at the cow Slavik has hung up in this restaurant. Unsurprisingly, they specialise in meat dishes, which are first-rate and served with chips – so good you'd ask for a second helping if you weren't so full. They also do lamb chops with rosemary, *confit* of duck thigh and grilled salmon steak – for dessert they offer a great caramelised rice pudding. Good menus at 59F, 79F and 128F. There's a terrace.

HAUTE-ISLE   95780

▲ I●I LE LAPIN SAVANT***

36 route de la Vallée; it's near La Roche-Guyon.
☎ 01.34.78.13.43
Closed Wed evening, Thurs and Nov.
Garden. Car park.

You can't fail to notice this delightful half-timbered house that's almost groaning under the weight of geraniums and other lovely flowers. It's very close to Normandy here, and the house is typical of the area, with exposed beams and a rustic decor. There are twelve double rooms; 270F with shower or shower/wc and 310–330F with bath. The cuisine will satisfy a gourmet. Two set menus at 135F and 165F. The *cassolette* of young rabbit, the crayfish in flaky pastry and the scallops are delicious.

ISLE-ADAM (L')   95290

⚜ 🏠 |●| LE CABOUILLET**

5 quai de l'Oise; it's after Cabouillet bridge, on the right as you come from the station.
☎ 01.34.69.00.90 ➡ 01.34.69.33.88
Closed Sun evening and Mon. **Disabled access**. **TV**.

This big, beautiful bourgeois country house is covered with ivy. Inside, Old Masters hang on the walls and there's a beautiful, polished wooden staircase. Five prettily decorated rooms 320–440F. The restaurant is the best in L'Isle-Adam. Set menus 175F and 265F, or around 175F *à la carte*. The cooking is refined and tasty and the dishes change with the seasons; trilogy of *foie gras*, fried eel with a herb salad, *gratin* of sole with morels and pigeon with ceps. From the terrace you get a view of the Oise river. Free coffee.

|●| AU RELAIS FLEURI

61 rue Saint-Lazare; it's 300m from St Martin's church.
☎ 01.34.69.01.85
Closed Mon evening, Tues and 5–24 Aug. **Garden**.

The decor is absolutely classic, with blue fabric stretched on the walls and matching curtains. The Roland brothers will give you a courteous welcome and their delicate, sophisticated cooking offers good value for this town. Dishes change with the seasons. Set menu 155F or about 250F *à la carte*: mussels *rémoulade*, snail casserole, roast fillet of Dover sole with a lobster *coulis*, queen scallops with *beurre blanc* and fresh pasta, roast duck with spiced wine, *bouillabaisse* with fish and lobster, and superb desserts. There's an enormous shady terrace where you can enjoy a *digestif* after your meal.

ISSY-LES-MOULINEAUX   92130

|●| LES QUARTAUTS

19 rue Georges-Marie (North); M° Porte-de-Versailles or

Corentin-Celton.
☎ 01.46.42.29.38
Closed weekends and Aug.

It's hard to believe that you could find such a good establishment in such a nowhere place. The street's so quiet that the restaurant can only have made its reputation by word of mouth. Simplicity and quality are the watchwords in this bistro, with a welcoming warmth generated by the owners, Régine and Christophe. Succulent home cooking is served in substantial helpings, and they do superb meat dishes. There's a huge choice of wines from small vineyards at very reasonable prices. The cheese selection is impressive and the desserts are all made on the premises. Expect to pay 140F *à la carte*.

|●| LA MANUFACTURE

20 esplanade de la Manufacture; M° Corentin-Celton.
☎ 01.40.93.08.98
Closed Sat lunchtime, Sun and a fortnight in Aug.
Disabled access.

The restaurant takes up the ground floor of an old tobacco factory. It's a huge room with a high ceiling painted cream and beige. A few modern pictures and green plants brighten it up. At lunchtime it's full of media execs and exhibitors from the exhibition centre. The huge space makes this a perfect place for private conversations or tricky negotiations because you can hear each other without being overheard. The cooking is particularly fine, revelling in subtle flavours. Try the pigs' ears and lamb shank braised in cider, which literally melts in the mouth. It's the best kind of home cooking re-thought and served to suit the styles and tastes of today. The menu changes frequently, but there are some staples: roast cod with a pepper stew, calves' brains and tongue *ravigotte*, braised beef cheek, lacquered belly of veal, crab with mashed potato and so on. Excellent desserts, and the bill won't be a shock. *Menus-cartes* at 155F and 180F, or 250F *à la carte*. The only tiny quibbles are that the welcome is a bit snooty (they're not too keen on men wearing earrings), and that it can be a problem booking a table for one person. The wines are attractively priced, though pricey by the glass at 35F.

|●| ISSY-GUINGUETTE

113 bis av. de Verdun; M° Mairie-d'Issy, then by bus 123 to the Chemin des Vignes stop.
☎ 01.46.62.04.27
Closed Sat lunchtime, Sun and Mon evening.

Yves Legrand, the boss of this place, is the force behind the resuscitation of the vineyard in

Issy. On sunny days, sit out on the terrace among the vines with a view of lovely old houses out of sight of the RER line. It's hard to believe you're in the suburbs of the capital. If it gets too hot, Yves puts up the parasols. Bistro dishes are carefully cooked and served in generous portions. There's not an extensive choice but the dishes change all the time; salmon *unilatérale* (it's cooked on one side), rolled lamb with fresh herbs, pork with cabbage, roast rabbit fillet with sage, stuffed breast of veal, cod with cream sauce, duck *fricassée* and pineapple preserved in red wine and ginger. There's an excellent wine list, as you would expect from such a buff. The service is perfect and the atmosphere relaxed and often quite festive. Lunchtime sees lots of businessmen from the area. In winter, they serve in the bright dining room where they light a fire in the hearth. Around 200F *à la carte*.

MAISONS-LAFITTE 78600

⅍ ≜ |●| HÔTEL-RESTAURANT AU PUR-SANG*

2 av. de la Pelouse; go over the Maisons-Lafitte bridge, turn right, and skirt the racecourse until the roundabout, then turn right into av. de la Pelouse.
☎ 01.39.62.03.21 ➡ 01.34.93.48.69
Closed Sun, three weeks in Aug, and a fortnight at the end of the year. **TV**. **Car park**.

Just by the entrance to the racecourse, at the bottom end of a cul-de-sac, you'll find this thoroughly provincial-looking hotel-restaurant. Simple rooms with shower 250F. Take a seat in the rustic dining room or on the terrace, and opt for the 72F set menu – it will offer something along the lines of herring fillets, steak and chips and *crème caramel*; à la carte, served only on race days, will set you back around 150F for a meal. 10% discount on the room rate, or a free coffee with a meal.

|●| LA VIEILLE FONTAINE

8 av. Grétry (Centre).
☎ 01.39.62.01.78
Closed Sun evening and Mon. **Garden**.

The building is a fine example of Second Empire architecture and there's been a restaurant here since 1926. Over the years it's built up a solid reputation. The dining room and interior decoration are very attractive and there's a lovely terrace in the garden. Tasty dishes are produces with great skill; kebabs of veal kidneys served with *gratin dauphinois* and blackcurrant sauce, and their chocolate tart with a raspberry *coulis* is exquisite. The

service is beyond reproach. The *menu-carte* at 177F means you can get a good meal for a fair price. Affordable wines. The place has a certain atmosphere. It was used as a movie set for a couple of forgettable movies and was a haunt of some of the Nazi high-command during the occupation.

MARLY-LE-ROI 78160

⅍ ≜ |●| LES CHEVAUX DE MARLY-RESTAURANT LA TEMPÊTE***

pl. de l'Abreuvoir (Centre).
☎ 01.39.58.47.61 ➡ 01.39.16.65.56
Swimming pool. **TV**. **Car park**.

Ten faultlessly presented rooms at 420F a double with bath, which is good value for a three-star hotel in this area. Some of them have a view over the imposing Abreuvoir (the drinking fountain for horses) and the Marly horses. There's a very high standard in the restaurant, maintained by the *sommelier*, master pastry chef, and the chef, who has won a string of medals. There's a menu at 200F, but watch out if you order *à la carte*, which should cost around 300F, because lots of dishes attract supplements. Excellent fish specialities. 10% discount on the room rate, or free *digestif* after your meal.

⅍ |●| LE FOU DU ROI

6 [bis] Grande-Rue.
☎ 01.39.58.80.20
Closed Sat lunchtime, Sun and three weeks in Aug.

A bright, simple little restaurant where you go for the quality of the cuisine. There are two set menus; at lunchtime, 98F gets you a meal, a $\frac{1}{4}$ litre of wine, and coffee. The evening menu, 169F, offers gourmet dishes: pan-fried duck *foie gras*, snail in pastry, turbot in butter and white rum soufflé. Wine and drinks are extra. The classic, well-balanced dishes are chalked up on the slate and change according to the whim of the chef or what's best at the market. Courteous service, decent prices and a satisfying meal make it a good establishment. The dining room is tiny, so it's best to book. Free coffee.

PORT-MARLY 78560 (2KM E)

≜ L'AUBERGE DU RELAIS DE MARLY

13 rue de Paris.
☎ 01.39.58.44.54
Closed Sun and Tues evenings, Wed and Aug. **Garden**.

The fact that the owners have been successfully running this charming country inn for over a quarter of a century suggests they're doing something seriously right. Madame produces delicious Normandy dishes but adds a few from other regions as well. Monsieur is debonair and smiling and greets passers-by with a hearty "Bonjour", creating a lovely, relaxed atmosphere. Most people opt for a single dish at around 70F each, or there's a menu at 149F. The garden is gorgeous in summer and, if you fancy fishing, you can wander across the road and drop your hook in the Seine.

♨ L'AUBERGE DU RELAIS BRETON

27 rue de Paris.
☎ 01.39.58.64.33
Closed Sun evening, Mon and Aug.

The cuisine is deliciously prepared and served in substantial portions: try stuffed sole or chocolate tart to get the picture. Menus 159F or 229F or choose à la carte. Sometimes they get you to sit outside when it's a bit too cold, even though there's room in the dining room. Good service, nonetheless.

MEAUX   77100

⅔ ♨ ACOSTEL**

336 av. de la Victoire; take the N3 in the direction of Châlons-en-Champagne, it's on the right just after the Total garage; if you get to Trilport, you've gone too far.
☎ 01.64.33.28.58 ➡ 01.64.33.28.25
TV. Garden. Car park.

The unadorned concrete building is forbidding, but don't let that put you off – it's the back of the hotel. The front is much more appealing, with a lawn leading from the front door to the banks of the Marne, which is quite beautiful here. Clean rooms at garden level, 285–299F with shower/wc or bath. 10% discount.

⅔ |●| LA MARÉE-BLEUE

8 rue Jean-Jaurès.
☎ 01.64.34.08.46
Closed Sun evening. **Garden.**

This inn, surrounded by a lovely garden, is the good restaurant that this town lacked. The dining rooms are huge and have a rustic decor. They specialise in seafood and Alsatian cooking, with fish *choucroute* their stellar dish. On weekdays, the 98F *formule* is more than ample, giving you starter, main course and dessert. There's a menu at 145F and a gourmet one for 175F. Free apéritif, coffee or *digestif*.

MEUDON-LA-FORÊT   92360

⅔ |●| RESTAURANT LA MARE AUX CANARDS

carrefour de la Mare-Adam (Northwest); at the Meudon-Chaville exit on the N118, take the first left at the radio mast then head in the direction of Mare Adam.
☎ 01.46.32.07.16
Closed Sun evening and Mon.

This restaurant, miles from anywhere, is a little isolated – the perfect place for lunch after a long walk in the Meudon woods on a sunny or misty day. The big family dining room is convivial; they roast ducks on a spit in the handsome fireplace. You are made to feel welcome and the service is fast. The terrace is very pleasant in fine weather. There's a 72F *formule* of starter plus a quarter of chicken; otherwise à la carte is about 140F a head. Free apéritif.

|●| LE CENTRAL

26 rue Marcel-Allégot.
☎ 01.46.26.15.83
Closed Sun and 10–23 Aug. **Disabled access**.

Whether you've got a raging hunger or an appetite like a bird, you will find just what you want here. Try a few Cancale oysters at the bar with a glass or two of Pouilly or sit down in the dining room for plates of *coq au vin*. The aim of the owners is to send their customers away with a smile on their face. They serve delicious calves' feet, herrings in oil with potatoes, *andouillette* (lamb's tripe) as good as you'll find in the Aveyron, and peppered steak. The boss will give you advice about the wines so you can be sure to get something good. Reasonably priced menus from 140F.

|●| LE BRIMBORION

8 rue de Vélizy; it's next to Bellevue station.
☎ 01.45.34.12.03
Closed Sun.

This is not a modern house – on the contrary, you'll notice the faded sign of the old hotel-restaurant *Billard* where the railway workers on the Versailles line used to come for a glass or two. One dining room is reserved for non-smokers. The family cooking is as creative and delicious as the owner is convivial and friendly. They offer a classic tomato, Cantal cheese and mustard tart, salad of *andouille* with potatoes, saddle of rabbit or scallops with finely sliced chicory. Appetising, satisfying, honest cooking. Whatever you do, leave space for the crumble, which is a firm favourite. Menus start at 160F. There's the tiniest irritation about the service – the staff start packing up as soon as they stop taking orders – but you can still enjoy the terrace.

🔭|●| LES TERRASSES DE L'ÉTANG

Route des Étangs, Étang de Villebon.
☎ 01.46.26.09.57
Closed Sun evening, Mon and Aug.

This is a really romantic spot for a quiet lunch *à deux*. Trees grow right down to the edge of the lake, a few lonely seagulls wheel and squeal overhead, a clutch of ducks swim around, and a thatched cottage completes the view. As soon as spring arrives they open the terrace. It's only ten minutes from Paris but it feels like a lifetime away. The chef is very skilful so you'll enjoy your meal: pan-fried escalope of *foie gras* with caramelised apples, *cassolette* of snails, *crépinette* of sweetbreads and calves' feet, or sautéed beef fillet with mustard. In season they serve good game: wild boar, venison or partridge. Menus 170Fand 190F and about 250F *à la carte*. Not too much to pay for lunch with that special person. Free coffee.

|●| MILLY-LA-FORÊT   91490

|●| RESTAURANT AU COLOMBIER

26 av. de Gamay; it's in the main street.
☎ 01.64.98.80.74
Closed Fri evening and a week at Christmas. **Car park opposite.**

Simple and cheap. The small, rustic dining room with sturdy beams adjoins the bar. It's where local workers come for lunch in the week and it's full of families on a Sunday. There's a huge array of *hors d'œuvres* set out on the buffet and the 49F *menu-express* (weekdays), is unbeatable value – dish of the day, coffee and a chocolate. Their regional dishes are impressive, especially the *coq au vin*. Sweet welcome.

MONTFORT-L'AMAURY   78490

|●| CHEZ NOUS

22 rue de Paris, (Centre).
☎ 01.34.86.01.62
Closed Sun evening and Mon.

The best place to eat in this town. The dining room is long and decorated in bourgeois style and warm colours. The cooking is good value and sophisticated – *foie gras* salad with a honey vinaigrette, *aiguillettes* of duck with soft fruit sauce. Monsieur creates, while

Madame organises the service. A successul family affair which attracts gourmets in the know. There's a weekday *formule* at 90F and menus 140 and 180F.

|●| L'HOSTELLERIE DES TOURS

pl. de l'Église.
☎ and ☛ 01.34.86.00.43
Closed Tues evening, Wed and mid-July to 10 Aug.

They hold the market on the pretty church square where this restaurant serves sound, traditional cuisine. The clientele of regulars come here because they know the dishes are well prepared. Menus 90F, 125F and 185F; the herrings in cream are splendid and the lamb shank cooked to perfection.

MONTMORENCY   95160

|●| LA PAIMPOLAISE

30 rue Galliéni; it's on the hill on the way to Champeaux, and signposted off to the left.
☎ 01.34.28.12.05
Closed Sun, Mon and Aug.

It's almost like being in Brittany, but without the sea, and there is a regional feel to the fresh decor: Breton pictures, Breton furniture and Breton cuisine produced by a woman from Paimpol. Her *galettes* are the genuine article, around 90F for a meal. Try the good *trégoroise* (*andouillette* and mustard), a fantastic *galette* with Maroilles cheese, and the creamy flan with pears and whipped cream. Good dry cider too. There's a quiet terrace.

PARIS   75000

SEE MAP OVERLEAF

1st arrondissement
🔭 🏠 HÔTEL DU PALAIS*

2 quai de la Mégisserie; M° Châtelet.
☎ 01.42.36.98.25 ☛ 01.42.21.41.67

The rooms have a superb view of the Seine, the Conciergerie and Notre Dame cathedral. The higher up you are the quieter it gets, but all windows are double-glazed. On the fifth floor all you can see is sky, but if you stand on a chair you can get a glimpse of the Châtelet. People come here because of the view and the location. Doubles 236–386F, depending on facilities. Professional welcome. There's a new carpet and the public areas and some of the rooms have been redecorated. On the whole it's fairly clean. 10% discount 15 Jan–28 Feb.

✿ HÔTEL DE LILLE**

8 rue du Pélican; M° Palais-Royal, Louvre or Pyramides.
☎ 01.42.33.33.42

This hotel is in a quiet street with a notorious past. In the 14th century it was called *rue du Poil-au-Con* because of its brothels. The more respectable residents ended up calling it rue Pélican, which caused much less of a sensation on their address cards. It's small, with just fourteen rooms, romantic and slightly old-fashioned, but it's well looked after by a nice family. Room numbers 1, 4, 7 and 10 are gloomy but quiet. Doubles 260F with basin, 320F with shower. They don't serve breakfast, but they do have a drinks machine. Ideal if you're on a budget.

✿ HÔTEL DE LA VALLÉE*

84 rue Saint-Denis; M° Les Halles, Rambuteau or Châtelet.
☎ 01.42.36.46.99 ➡ 01.42.36.16.66
✉ hvallée@cybercable.fr

In the middle of Les Halles – you couldn't find a more central location if you tried. It's pretty decent and the price is reasonable, though the sex shops along the street may not be to everyone's taste. Rooms are double-glazed but if you want to be sure of a quiet night, ask for one with a view of the courtyard or on one of the higher floors. Doubles 260F with basin (shower along the corridor, though you have to pay) and 320F with shower/wc. It would be difficult to find cheaper accommodation in the area. They take credit cards but not cheques and rooms must be paid for in advance.

✵ ✿ HÔTEL LONDRES SAINT-HONORÉ**

13 rue Saint-Roch; M° Tuileries.
☎ 01.42.60.15.62 ➡ 01.42.60.16.00
✉ hotel.londres.st.honore@gofornet.com
TV.

Here's a delightful hotel with a warm family atmosphere in an area that is not exactly alluring. The rooms are spacious and comfortable with double glazing, satellite TV and mini-bar. Some are air conditioned. Doubles 560F with shower or 600F with bath. There are a number of pay car parks round about the hotel. 10% discount.

✵ ✿ HÔTEL AGORA**

7 rue de la Cossonnerie; M° Les Halles or Châtelet.
☎ 01.42.33.46.02 ➡ 01.42.33.80.99
TV.

The street dates back to the 12th century and owes its name to the "*cossons*" or second-hand dealers who traded here. The hotel has been well renovated in modern colours, and has a small and tastefully laid-out reception. Rooms are pleasant and unfussy, and some are furnished with antiques. Doubles with shower or bath 640–730F. It's a really great little hotel, and pretty quiet for such a lively neighbourhood. 10% discount except Sept–Oct.

▐●▌ RESTAURANT À LA CLOCHE DES HALLES

28 rue Coquillière; M° Louvre or Les Halles.
☎ 01.42.36.93.89
Closed Sat evening, Sun, public holidays and a fortnight in Aug.

Service until about 9pm. No fake beams or farm tools hanging on the walls, just a bell over the entrance, which used to sound the opening and closing of the old market. When the bell, or *cloche*, rang, people could gather up what was left – hence the word *clochard*, meaning tramp. Serge Lesage bottles the wine from his own vineyard and serves it in the restaurant. There are plates of *charcuterie*, ham on the bone and farm cheese. A very pleasant place with good prices. Reckon on 60F for a plate of something and a glass of wine.

▐●▌ HIGUMA

32 [bis] rue Sainte-Anne; M° Pyramides.
☎ 01.47.03.38.59
Closed Christmas and New Year's Day.

Service 11.30am–10pm. This is a good little Japanese restaurant, a sort of upmarket works canteen where crowds of people working for the Japanese companies in the neighbourhood throng for a quick but substantial meal. Various clear soups, which won't leave you feeling hungry, large helpings of sautéed noodles, and a few goodies such as excellent fried ravioli. Perfect set menu at 63F. If you sit at the counter you can admire the doftness of the Japanese chefs kneading the noodles or setting the vegetables skidding around the enormous woks. Don't count on getting a smile or even a look from them – at these prices that would be extra.

▐●▌ RESTAURANT FOUJITA

41 rue Saint-Roch; M° Pyramides or Tuileries.
☎ 01.42.61.42.93

Service noon–2.15pm and 9–10.15pm. One of the best sushi bars in Paris and prices are

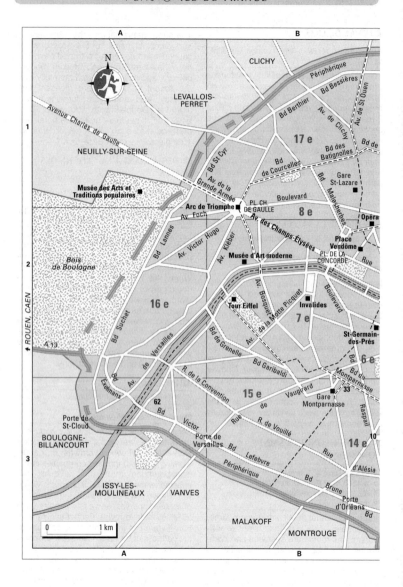

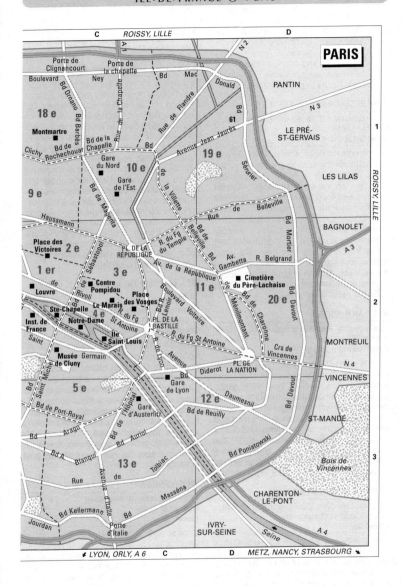

ROISSY, LILLE

C

D

PARIS

ROISSY, LILLE

Porte de
Clignancourt
Porte de
la chapelle
Boulevard   Ney   Bd   Mac
Bd Ornano
Bd Barbès
Bd de la
Chapelle
Rue de Flandre
Donald
PANTIN
N 3
Bd
61
18 e
Montmartre
LE PRÉ-
ST-GERVAIS
1
Avenue Jean Jaurès
Clichy
Bd de
Rochechouart
Gare
du Nord
10 e
19 e
LES LILAS
Gare
de l'Est
de la Villette
Sentier
9 e
Bd de Magenta
de   Belleville
Haussmann
Rue
BAGNOLET
Bd Mortier
Place des
Victoires
2 e
Bd de Sébastopol
PL. DE LA
RÉPUBLIQUE
R. du Fg
du Temple
Belleville
Bd de
Bd
A 3
Av.
Gambetta
R. Belgrand
3 e
Av. de la République
1 er
Centre
Pompidou
Rivoli
de
Louvre
11 e
Cimetière
du Père-Lachaise
de Ménilmontant
20 e
Bd Davout
2
Place
des Vosges
Boulevard   Voltaire
Bd de Charonne
Ste-Chapelle
Le Marais
4 e
R. du Fg
St Antoine
PL. DE LA
BASTILLE
Inst. de
France
Notre-Dame
Île
Saint-Louis
R. du Fg St Antoine
MONTREUIL
Saint
Avenue
Crs de
Vincennes
N 4
Musée
de Cluny
Germain
Bd Saint Michel
PL. DE
LA NATION
VINCENNES
5 e
Bd
Diderot
Bd
Gare
de Lyon
Daumesnil
Bd Davout
ST-MANDÉ
Bd de Port-Royal
Bd de l'Hôpital
Gare
d'Austerlitz
12 e
Bd de Reuilly
Arago
Bd A
Blanqui
Bd Auriol
Bd Poniatowski
3
Rue
13 e
Avenue d'Italie
de
Tolbiac
Bois de
Vincennes
Masséna
CHARENTON-
LE-PONT
Bd Kellermann
Bd
Jourdan
Porte
d'Italie
IVRY-
SUR-SEINE
Seine
A 4

reasonable. They do very substantial set menus at lunchtime for 68F and 72F, or 110F and 120F in the evening. There's sushi, sashimi (raw fish) and natto, a bowl of rice topped with raw fish. It's always full which is a good sign, so try to get there early.

🎍 |●| RESTAURANT LA FRESQUE

100 rue Rambuteau; M° Étienne-Marcel or Les Halles.
☎ 01.42.33.17.56
Closed Sun lunchtime.

Service until midnight. This is a nice friendly little restaurant in a shop that used to sell snails. The interior is lovely, with very old white tiles on the walls, brilliantly coloured frescoes and long wooden tables. It's very friendly, relaxed and cosmopolitan – you're jammed right up against your neighbour. The lunchtime *formule* offers starter, carefully prepared main course, $1/4$ litre of wine and coffee for 68F. Every day there are good starters, three or four traditional main course dishes, each with an original touch, and a vegetarian dish (a rarity in this town). About 120F *à la carte*. Free coffee.

|●| LA MOUSSON

9 rue Thérèse; M° Pyramides or Palais-Royal.
☎ 01.42.60.59.46
Closed Sun and 1–25 Aug.

Service noon–2.30pm and 7.30–10.30pm. Lucile is the Chinese-Khmer chef here. Her specialities are sautéed beef with garlic, steamed fish amok (in a Cambodian sauce), minced pork with lemongrass, and spare ribs. All the food is delicately perfumed and very tasty. Dishes of the day around 50F, a lunch menu at 69F, and another at 92F. She also does a weekday lunch *formule* with a main course and dessert – chicken or beef curry, squid with basil or beef satay.

🎍 |●| LA ROBE ET LE PALAIS

13 rue des Lavandières-Saint-Opportune; M° Châtelet.
☎ 01.45.08.07.41 📧 paris@venue.fr
Closed Sun.

This is really a wine bar with a good restaurant menu attached – the owners are amateurs of fine wine so you will have an excellent choice. Food is good and soundly prepared: *cassolette* of avocado and warm goat's cheese, monkfish and bacon kebab with curry sauce, beef on the bone with marrowbone and desserts like orange flower *crème brûlée*. The 75F lunch *formule* gets you a main course and a glass of wine, or expect to pay around 180F *à la carte*. Free glass of wine.

🎍 |●| CA D'ORO

54 rue de l'Arbre-Sec; M° Louvre.
☎ 01.40.20.97.79
Closed Sun and 5–17 Aug. **Disabled access**.

Service until 11pm. This welcoming, unobtrusive little Italian restaurant knows exactly what it's doing and sticks to what it does best. Go through a tiny room and down a narrow corridor and you'll come to another room where the decoration is gently evocative of Venice, the chef's home town. Before moving on to the pasta, treat yourself to grilled peppers with basil, or bruschetta, a slice of toast fried in olive oil and rubbed with garlic, basil and tomato. Main dishes include penne *disperata*, with a sauce including garlic, anchovies, capers and olive oil, home-made ravioli, or, for two, an excellent risotto with ceps or seafood. Reckon on 140–160F with a little wine. The lunchtime *menu complet*, 85F, is not complete enough to include wine but it's very good. Free house apéritif.

|●| À LA TOUR DE MONTLHÉRY, CHEZ DENISE

5 rue des Prouvaires; M° Louvre, Châtelet or Les Halles.
☎ 01.42.36.21.82
Closed Sat, Sun and mid-July to mid-Aug.

Open 24 hours.This is one of the oldest all-night restaurants in Paris. It's kept the atmosphere of an old Halles bistro, but the prices are definitely up to date – or even ahead of their time. The welcome is off-hand but the place is lively. There are artificial leather banquettes, checked tablecloths, and hams hanging from the ceiling. Big-hearted cooking includes *andouillette*, tripe, roast lamb with beans, beef *gros sel*, brains and other such traditional fare. No set menu; dishes cost 90–130F.

|●| JUVÉNILES

47 rue de Richelieu; M° Palais-Royal.
☎ 01.42.97.46.49
Closed Sun.

Service until 11pm. This is a very Parisian wine bar run by a joyful Scot with a sense of humour. The place is frequented by groups who come to share a bottle of wine and tapas: squid rings, spicy chicken wings or slices of sausage. Inventive main dishes include pan-fried pollack fillet with spiced skin, sausage and mash, and sautéed hare with fresh noodles. Menus 98F, 135F and 155F or *à la carte* around 220F. They sell a good selection of wine and sherries by the glass, and offer an impressive array of malt whiskies. Best to book.

|●| LE RUBIS

10 fur du Marché-Saint-Honoré; M° Pyramides or Tuileries.
☎ 01.42.61.03.34
Closed Sun, public holidays, three weeks in Aug and a fortnight over Christmas and New Year.

Open to 10pm (4pm on Sat). The kind of typical Parisian bistro/wine bar that's on the verge of extinction – great little dishes and wines direct from producers in Beaujolais. You can have a sandwich at the bar with a glass of red. Wines by the glass at really decent prices. They do excellent horse *charcuterie* and dishes of the day from 50F. In summer, they set up a couple of barrels on the pavement where you can prop yourself up and enjoy a cool glass of wine.

|●| RESTAURANT LESCURE

7 rue de Mondovi; M° Concorde.
☎ 01.42.60.18.91
Closed Sat, Sun, three weeks in Aug and a week at Christmas.

A very good restaurant for the financial district. It's quite surprising to find *poule-au-pot* or beef *bourguignon* for around 50F in this part of Paris. The cooking is bourgeois, and the prices are popular. On the 110F menu you get a starter such as mackerel, a generous portion of the main dish, a choice of cheese or dessert, and a ½ bottle of wine. You'll pay around 150F *à la carte*. In the evening, they sit people at the big communal table at the back of the room, which creates a relaxed atmosphere. In summer people jostle for tables on the terrace.

|●| WILLI'S WINE BAR

13 rue des Petits-Champs; M° Pyramides, Bourse or Palais-Royal.
☎ 01.42.61.05.09
Closed Sun.

Service noon–11pm, with the bar open until midnight. This is a chic wine bar which has been tastefully decorated. The wood gives it a cosy feel, there are pretty posters on the walls, the lighting's perfect, and there are big round tables for large groups of friends. *Willi's* is a magnet for wine-lovers among the British executives working in Paris, stock market traders and the ladies of the place des Victoires. They do a few elaborate dishes, such as roast cod with caramelised aubergine or roast salmon with bacon, pickled onions and sherry, and some original salads – potato salad with melted Fourme

cheese, bacon and grilled walnuts. The food's primary purpose is to be a foil for the tremendous Côtes du Rhône, of which the owner is a great connoisseur, though you'll also find Spanish, Californian and Italian wines listed too – a lot of wines are available by the glass. Excellent cheeses. Menus at 153F (lunch) and 195F (dinner).

⅔|●| RESTAURANT LA POULE-AU-POT

9 rue Vauviliers; M° Louvre or Les Halles.
☎ 01.42.36.32.96
Closed Mon.

Service 7pm–5am. If you're around les Halles at 2am and you suddenly feel peckish, head for this place that's been around for more than a quarter of a century. The long room, decorated with posters and copper pots, has retro lighting, which gives the place a certain intimacy, and a pleasant brasserie atmosphere. Service is courteous, which is not always the case in this part of town, and the menu lists solid traditional dishes such as *pot-au-feu*, *entrecôte* with marrowbone and, of course, the *poule-au-pot* from which the restaurant takes its name. Set menu 160F or about 220F *à la carte*. Free *digestif*.

⅔|●| L'ARDOISE

28 rue du Mont-Thabor; M° Tuileries.
☎ 01.42.96.28.18
Closed Mon, Sat lunchtime, a week in Jan, a week in May, and Aug.

Service noon–2.30pm and 7.15–11.30pm. Pierre Jay may be young, but he trained as a chef at the restaurant *Chez l'Ami Jean*. He's now spreading his wings and his flights of fancy appear on the 175F menu, which is bursting with ideas: marinated fresh anchovies, *tournedos* of lamb with herbs, *foie gras* cooked in a cloth, free-range chicken in a sea-salt crust (for two) and caramelised strawberries – not bad for a list chalked up afresh each day on the blackboard. The wines are really well priced, too; expect to pay about 175F for a meal with a glass or two of wine. Free *crème de cassis*.

|●| DAVÉ

39 rue Saint-Roch; M° Pyramides.
☎ 01.42.61.49.48
Closed Sat and Sun lunchtimes and 10–20 Aug.

Davé, the owner of this Chinese restaurant, has his picture plastered all over the walls – here with Deneuve, there with Bowie, and so on. The walls are covered in red velvet, the carpet is red, the hangings are . . . red. The steamed dumplings are worth a try, as are the prawn fritters and coconut balls. The dishes are modest though the prices aren't – expect to pay 200F *à la carte*.

|●| MACÉO

15 rue des petits-Champs; M° Pyramides, Bourse or Palais Royal.
☎ 01.42.97.53.85
Closed Sun.

Service noon–1pm. This restaurant opened in 1880 and has had an elegant following ever since. It was recently taken over by Mark Williamson, the owner of *Willi's* wine bar next door, who changed its name from *Le Mercure Gallant* to *Macéo*, after Macéo Parker, one of James Brown's Famous Flames. The decor has a modern British flavour, and the menu is a delight to read: smoked haddock with spinach and hazelnuts, joint of yellow pollack with a small dish of clams and asparagus, shepherd's pie with morel mushrooms, risotto with vanilla and a small orange salad, and pineapple with sweet spices. Menu 220F, or 180F for the vegetarian one. The wine list is very impressive and the *fino* they serve at the bar while you're waiting for your table is excellent.

2nd arrondissement
⅍ 🛊 HÔTEL SAINTE-MARIE*

6 rue de la Ville-Neuve; M° Bonne-Nouvelle.
☎ 01.42.33.21.61 ➡ 01.42.33.29.24
TV. Pay car park.

This is a pretty little hotel in a quiet street, very close to the shopping area of the Grands Boulevards. It has about twenty rooms, all of which are very well maintained. Some have beamed ceilings, but if you're tall and have a room in the attic mind your head because they are low. Doubles with basin 250F, with shower 340F; triples with shower/wc 450F. Breakfast 25F. The car park costs 50F per day. Free breakfast for children. 10% discount Nov and Jan–Feb, and 10% discount rest of year for a minimum seven-night stay.

🛊 TIQUETONNE HÔTEL*

6 rue Tiquetonne; M° Étienne-Marcel or Réaumur-Sébastopol.
☎ 01.42.36.94.58 ➡ 01.42.36.02.94
Closed Aug and one week Christmas–New Year.

The pedestrian streets leading to this one-star hotel are calm and beautiful. The rooms, which vary in size, are very well maintained, though the decor is faintly old-fashioned and the bathrooms are pretty ordinary. The ones

on the first two floors have double glazing and are quieter. Double with shower/wc 256F. Breakfast 25F. By the way – no good trying to book here for friends; the *patronne* will insist on meeting them first herself.

🛊 HÔTEL BONNE NOUVELLE**

17 rue Beauregard; M° Bonne Nouvelle or Strasbourg-Saint-Denis.
☎ 01.45.08.42.42 ➡ 01.40.26.05.81
e info@hotel-bonne-nouvelle.com
TV.

Check out the lovely screen with a *trompe-l'oeil* picture of a moonlit apartment block. Doubles with bath from 370F; they're equipped with TV, direct phone and hair drier. Number 25 is rather dark and you have to open the skylight in the bathroom with a system of counterweights. There's a suite which is ideal for four and has a splendid view of the Pompidou Centre, the Montparnasse tower and the rooftops of Paris. Breakfast 30F. Really warm welcome.

🛊 HÔTEL VIVIENNE**

40 rue Vivienne; M° Rue-Montmartre, Richelieu-Drouot or Bourse.
☎ 01.42.33.13.26 ➡ 01.40.41.98.19.
e paris@hotel-vivienne.com
TV.

This hotel is in a neighbourhood with lots of tiny streets and lanes where the shops specialize in coins and medals. It's very close to the *Hard Rock Café*, the Musée Grévin, the wax museum, and the Théâtre des Variétés. Warm and informal welcome. The rooms have been refurbished and are bright, clean, comfortable and quiet. Number 14 is particularly attractive, and there's a communicating door through to number 15, which makes it good for a family. On the fifth or sixth floors you get a lovely view of Paris, and a few rooms have balcony. Doubles 400F with shower, 480F with shower/wc, or 500–540F with bath.

⅍ 🛊 HÔTEL FRANCE D'ANTIN***

22 rue d'Antin; M° 4-Septembre or Opéra; RER Auber.
☎ 01.47.42.19.12 ➡ 01.47 42.11.55

This very pleasant three-star hotel is just 100m from the Opéra Garnier and the Louvre. It is classy yet congenial. It's been completely overhauled and re-decorated. Many of the public rooms have exposed stonework and vaulted ceilings. The thirty pretty rooms all have mini-bar and satellite TV, and they're all air-conditioned to give you respite from the Paris summer heat. Double with shower/wc or bath 880F. Free coffee and breakfast, usually 40F.

|O| RESTAURANT CHEZ DANIE

5 rue de Louvois; M° Bourse or Quatre-Septembre.
☎ 01.42.96.64.05
Closed evenings, Sat and Sun.

This tiny restaurant right next to the Bibliothèque Nationale is an absolute delight. It serves good traditional dishes that change daily – *bœuf ficelle*, rabbit *en gibelotte*, beef with carrots or tarragon – and all the desserts are home-made. Great value in an area that's full of expensive, mediocre sandwich shops. The 52F *formule* offers a main course with a choice of starter or a dessert.

|O| LE TAMBOUR

41 rue Montmartre; M° Châtelet, Les Halles or Sentier,
☎ 01.42.33.06.90

Open 24 hours. The owner, André Camboulas, will make you feel welcome. He has built up a group of authentic Parisian bistros similar to this one. The dining room is decorated with urban detritus – cobblestones, drain covers and road signs. The cooking is very French. There is a lunch *formule* at 55F; expect to pay 100F for lunch or 150F for dinner *à la carte*.

|O| BAR-RESTAURANT LES VARIÉTÉS

12 passage des Panoramas; M° Rue-Montmartre.
☎ 01.42.36.98.09
Closed Sat, Sun, and Aug.

Service lunchtime and evening until 10pm or 11pm, depending on how busy they are. Walk past the fast-food outlets of the Grands Boulevards until you get to the passageway where you'll find this old-fashioned Paris café. It's popular with people who work nearby, who come for the owner's good cooking rather than his bad jokes. You'll pay around 100F at lunchtime and not much more in the evening. You can eat before or after the theatre – simple starters like egg mayonnaise, leeks vinaigrette, home-made *terrine* or savoury tart with salad, and good dishes of the day like fillet of beef or duck *confit*. A glimpse of what Paris used to be like.

🎋|O| LA GRILLE MONTORGUEIL

50 rue Montorgueill; M° Les Halles or Étienne-Marcel.
☎ 01.42.33.21.21
Closed Sat and Sun evenings, and Aug.

Closes at midnight in the week, 5pm on Sat and Sun. This establishment, which has been around a good hundred years, has been attractively renovated – as has the pedestrian street it stands on. The authentic zinc bar dates from 1904. The menu is full of traditional Parisian bistro fare: oxtail with Guérande salt, snails in red wine sauce, calf's head *ravigotte*, beef with shallots, duck with orange, and grills and fish dishes. Straightforward, honest cooking with no frills. There are no set menus but there are always some reasonably priced dishes of the day and a meal will set you back about 130F. There's a terrace in summer. Free house apéritif or coffee.

🎋|O| LE PETIT VENDÔME

8 rue des Capucines; M° Opéra or Madeleine.
☎ 01.42.61.05.88
Closed Sat evening and Sun.

Service 7am to 8pm. This is an Auvergne establishment with a display of local cheeses set out on the bar counter, and Auvergne sausage used for their filling sandwiches. There's a scramble for places at lunchtime, when a dish of the day costs 65–75F or a complete meal around 150F *à la carte*. Reliable, substantial offerings: pork stewed in Bergerac wine, grilled pig's trotters and the like. Efficient, attractive service. Free house apéritif.

|O| LE GRAND COLBERT

4 rue Vivienne; M°Bourse or Palais-Royal.
☎ 01.42.86.87.88

Service daily noon–1am. This unusual brasserie acts practically like the canteen of the Bibliothèque Nationale, which you can enter from here. The whole place has been freshly redecorated – the friezes, copper bar and lamps have been restored to their 1830s glory. Typical brasserie fare – fresh cod with olive oil, curried lamb and steak *tartare* – on menus starting at 160F.

3rd arrondissement
🎋 🏠 HÔTEL DU VIEUX SAULE**

6 rue de Picardie; M° République or Temple.
☎ 01.42.72.01.14 ⊨ 01.40.27.88.21
TV. Garden. Pay car park.

The window boxes and tiny flower garden brighten up this lovely hotel; inside the decor feels somewhat high-tech, though there are a few antiques on sale. Modern, very comfortable doubles with shower/wc or bath 590–690F. Prices increase during trade fairs. All rooms are air-conditioned and equipped with hair drier, trouser press and iron, telephone, safe and cable TV (thirty channels), and there's free use of the sauna. Pleasant staff. Buffet breakfast, 60F, is served in a 16th-century vaulted cellar. One free breakfast per day.

🍴 |●| HÔTEL DU MONT-BLANC

17 rue Debelleyme; M° Filles-du-Calvaire.
☎ 01.42.72.23.68
Closed evenings, Sun and Aug.

It's like walking back in time. The tables have waxed cotton table cloths and there's a Formica bar with Madame Morvan enthroned behind it – she's run the place since 1959 but the establishment has been going for over a century. It's where the local artists, artisans and office workers have lunch: plates of *crudités*, egg mayonnaise, steak and chips, paella or salt cod. The prices are pretty pre-historic, too – meals 55–120F. Pop in after you've been to the nearby Picasso museum and sink a cup of decent Italian coffee.

|●| CHEZ OMAR

47 rue de Bretagne; M° Temole.
☎ 01.42.72.36.26.
Closed Sun lunchtime.

Service until around 11pm. Omar has been here for a good twenty years. He serves an eclectic mix of locals, transients and visitors from all over the world in his restaurant where Paris meets North Africa. The ceilings are high, the mirrors have bevelled edges, there's a superb bar counter and the tables are snugly spaced. Waiting staff are smiling and attentive. The couscous is excellent, 60–100F, as are the pastries, but their meat dishes are particularly tender. Expect to pay 150F *à la carte*.

4th arrondissement
🏠 GRAND HÔTEL DU LOIRET*

8 rue des Mauvais-Garçons; M° Hôtel-de-Ville.
☎ 01.48.87.77.00 ➡ 01.48.04.96.56

The whole building has been refurbished and the rooms are redecorated every two years – wooden staircase, marbled walls. Rooms from the first to the fourth floors are in warm colours and have en-suite shower/wc, 310F, or bath, 410F. There is a room sleeping four on the seventh floor; it has a panoramic view over Paris, the Panthéon and the Sacré Coeur.

🍴 🏠 HÔTEL DU 7E ART**

20 rue Saint-Paul; M° Saint-Paul or Sully-Morland.

☎ 01.44.54.85.00 ➡ 01.42.77.69.10
TV.

A fairly friendly hotel that's well managed and original. The staircase is black, the walls are white, and the rooms are decorated with photomontages and posters of films from the 1940s, 1950s and 1960s. Rooms 430–690F with shower or bath and 25-channel TV. The top prices are for suites in the attic, which have sloping ceilings. Breakfast 45F. There's a bar on the ground floor, and an unusual display case with plaster figures of Ray Charles, Mickey Mouse, Donald Duck, Laurel and Hardy and so on. Free house apéritif.

🏠 GRAND HÔTEL JEANNE D'ARC**

3 rue de Jarente; M° Saint-Paul, Chemin-Vert or Bastille; RER Châtelet.
☎ 01.48.87.62.11 ➡ 01.48.87.37.31
TV

You couldn't find a better location than this quiet neighbourhood near place Sainte-Catherine. The hotel is classy and well run, and has been stylishly decorated. There's an enormous mirror in the foyer made by a local artist. All of the rooms have been refurbished and have shower/wc or bath, phone and cable TV. Doubles 440F and rooms that sleep four 660F. Extra bed 75F; cots provided on request. Breakfast 38F. It's essential to book. Pets welcome.

🏠 HÔTEL DE NICE**

42 bis rue de Rivoli; M° Hôtel-de-Ville.
☎ 01.42.78.55.29 ➡ 01.42.78.36.07
TV.

A very elegant and refined hotel with a small entrance. Multi-lingual welcome at reception. The owners used to run an antique business and they have kept a large number of attractive pieces to furnish the hotel. Breakfast is served in the television lounge, which has soft-coloured furnishings, 18th-century engravings and a portrait of an elegant woman with her pets. The sound-proofed rooms are decorated with sumptuous wallpapers and have good bathrooms. Doubles with bath or shower cost 580F, which is not bad value for money. In summer the rooms overlooking place du Bourg-Tibourg are particularly good.

🏠 HÔTEL DE LA PLACE DES VOSGES**

12 rue de Birague; M° Saint-Paul or Bastille.
☎ 01.42.72.60.46 ➡ 01.42.72.02.64
✉ hotel.place.des.vosges@gofornet.com
TV.

This is in a grand street leading from place des Vosges to the Pavillon du Roi. The entrance is delightful but you get a rather impersonal welcome. There are sixteen rooms which, though not spacious and with pretty ordinary furniture, are quiet, comfortable and impeccably clean. Doubles with bath from 660F.

|●| RESTAURANT PICCOLO TEATRO

6 rue des Écouffes; M° Saint-Paul.
☎ 01.42.72.17.79 **e** liang@cybercable.fr
Closed Mon and Aug.

Service noon–3pm and 7–11pm. Excellent vegetarian food in pleasant surroundings. There are wooden tables, soft lights, a few exposed beams and a friendly atmosphere. The menu lists dishes such as *douceur pour une dame blanche* (a "caviar" of carrots, baby onions and coriander), *pour qui chantent les oiseaux* (warm goat's cheese), and, for dessert, the poetically named *poussière de sable dans un Sahara d'étoiles*. They use imagination in the way they cook, as well as on naming the dishes. They do good *gratins* and a very substantial vegetarian plate. The only reservation is that the service can be a bit slow. Lunchtime menu 52F, others 63–115F, or about 110F *à la carte*.

|●| RESTAURANT LE TEMPS DES CERISES

31 rue de la Cerisaie; M° Bastille or Sully-Morland.
☎ 01.42.72.08.63
Closed evenings (but you can get a drink until 8pm), Sat, Sun, public holidays and Aug.

This picturesque low-ceilinged late-18th-century building used to house the office of the Celestine convent's bursar but it's been a bistro since 1900. The decor looks familiar right away – zinc-topped bar where you can just have a drink, marble-topped tables and imitation leather banquettes – and the day's menu is written up on a blackboard. That, plus the photos of old Paris, the cheerful atmosphere and the good-natured customers are reminders of what a Paris bistro used to be. They do a good set menu, unbeatable value at 68F with egg mayonnaise, grilled *andouillette* with mashed potato, *pot-au-feu*, and lasagne. There's a three-course menu at 63F, *à la carte* dishes at 65–68F, and an eclectic selection of wines. Credit cards not accepted.

|●| RESTAURANT L'ENOTECA

25 rue Charles-V; M° Saint-Paul.
☎ 01.42.78.91.44 ➡ 01.44.59.31/72
Closed one week in mid-Aug and Christmas lunchtime.

Open daily till 2am. This wine bar, which spe-

cialises in Italian wines, is a must. It gets really full and appeals to a very Parisian clientele – it's not unusual to spot the odd TV star. The decor is typical of the Marais, with exposed beams and old stonework. The famous, the not so famous and the downright obscure come here to sample some of the 450 different Italian wines – the ones available by the glass change every week. You can travel north to south, tasting the whites of Trentino and Sicily or the reds of Piedmont and Basilicata to wash down a few *antipasti misti* or *crostini* with Parma ham and mozzarella, fresh pasta with beef stew or chicken livers and tomatoes. Reckon on paying 55F for a dish at lunchtime or there's a 75F lunch *formule* of starter plus pasta and a glass of wine.

|●| RESTAURANT LES FOUS DE L'ÎLE

33 rue des Deux-Ponts; M° Pont-Marie.
☎ 01.43.25.76.67
Closed Sat lunchtime, Sun evening, Mon and a fortnight in Aug.

Service noon–11pm. This is primarily a restaurant, but it is also a tea room. There's a nice 78F set menu at lunchtime, while in the evening you'll pay 150–180F *à la carte*. There are three *formules* for Sunday brunch. Live jazz, blues or accordion music every second Tuesday from 10pm, when there's a single menu at around 100F.

|●| AMADEO

19 rue François-Miron; M° Saint-Paul or Pont-Marie.
☎ 01.42.87.01.02
Closed Sun, Mon lunchtime and a week at the beginning of Aug.

As you might expect from such a name, you're bathed in an operatic ambience with quality service, even though the dining room is hardly bigger than a diva's dressing room. Fairly bold dishes on the menu that change regularly every three months: fish *rillettes*, shellfish with paprika, and *crème caramel* flavoured with orange. There's a lunch *formule* at 75F for a starter and main course, a lunch menu at 95F and a gourmet *menu-carte* at 185F in the evening. Once a month there's a concert as well.

|●| VINS DES PYRÉNÉES

25 rue Beautreillis; M° Bastille or Saint-Paul.
☎ 01.42.72.64.94
Closed Sun evening.

A warm, chummy cellar-bar-restaurant with a retinue of regulars – though new faces are warmly welcomed. It's a nice mix of formal city and easy-going provincial town and it's reassuring that a place like this has managed to survive. Great little meat dishes, a few others with sauce and a fish dish or two, all chalked up on the slate. The recipe is simple: select excellent quality meat, grill it and serve with good side dishes and a decent glass of wine in a wood-panelled dining room with engraved mirrors and moleskin seats. Finish by issuing a reasonable bill – 80–140F for a full meal. A selection of wines by the month.

🕎 |●| LE SOLEIL EN COIN

21 rue Rambuteau; M° Rambuteau.
☎ 0142.72.26.25
Closed Sat lunchtime, Sun and a week mid-Aug.

Open until 10.30pm, 11pm on Fri and Sat. The façade of this building is sunshine-gold and the interior has a provençal warmth enlivened by brightly coloured table cloths. The 116F menu is good: starter of warm Roquefort mousse or courgette *terrine* with a tomato *coulis*, for example, and main course of lamb with *provençal* herbs or a *blanquette* of veal. The desserts are good, and made on the premises. Dish of the day, around 70F, might be a veal chop *normande* with cream (74F in the evening, if there is any left) and a full meal costs about 126F. Wines by the glass. There's a notice board where people can write information about local concerts and things they want to sell or exchange. It's really full at lunchtime and quieter in the evening – except on Saturday. Free coffee.

|●| LE CAFÉ DE LA POSTE

13 rue Castex; M° Bastille.
☎ 01.42.72.95.35
Closed Sat and Sun.

The café is opposite the post office, a brick building from the 1930s. It's a stylish place, with mosaic walls, wide banquettes, a huge mirror and a splendid wooden bar. There's always a pasta dish on the blackboard and a few meat dishes – beef Strogonoff or *mas-salé* of lamb – and large salads. Expect to pay around 120F for a meal – dishes 55–70F.

🕎 |●| RESTAURANT LE GRIZZLI

7 rue Saint-Martin; M° Hôtel de Ville or Châtelet.
☎ 01.48.87.77.56
Closed Sun.

Service noon–2.30pm and 7.30–11pm. The bear of an owner comes from the Ariège and he serves dishes from back home in a lovely old-fashioned bistro setting: *ratatouille* with poached eggs, slices of country ham, *daube*

of duck, rabbit with raisins, squid in its own ink, *cassoulet*, calf's liver with dried ceps and duck *confit*. There's a lunch menu at 120F and an evening one at 160F, or about 185F *à la carte*. Free Kir.

|●| RESTAURANT BARACANE

38 rue des Tournelles; M° Bastille.
☎ 01.42.71.43.33
Closed Sat lunchtime and Sun.

Service noon–2.15pm and 7pm–midnight. Cooking from Gascony predominates at this pocket-sized bistro, with dishes like home-made *cassoulet* with duck or goose *confit*, good roast lamb from Lozère, grilled duck breast, and a *croustillant* of apples in aged plum brandy. Menus from 148F and the *menu-carte* at 238F includes apéritif, three courses, a $1/2$ bottle from the wine list, and coffee. Faultless cooking.

|●| RESTAURANT À L'ESCALE

1 rue des Deux-Ponts; M° Pont-Marie.
2 quai d'Orléans.
☎ 01.43.54.94.23
Closed evenings, Mon, and Aug.

Lunch noon–3pm. This rather pleasant restaurant gets the sun on the side overlooking the Seine. It's a perfect place to restore your spirits after you've trailed round Notre Dame or the Île Saint-Louis. There's no set menu, so opt for the dish of the day, 70–80F, lovingly prepared by Mme Tardieu: the *pot-au-feu*, roast farm-bred veal, *coq au vin* and grills are all good. All wines are selected by Monsieur Tardieu who is quite a connoisseur. Expect to pay 150F *à la carte*.

|●| BRASSERIE DE l'ÎLE-SAINT-LOUIS

55 quai de Bourbon; M° Pont-Marie.
☎ 01.43.54.02.59
Closed Wed, Thurs lunchtime, a week in Feb, and Aug.

Service noon–1am, 6pm–1am Thurs. Nothing's changed at this place for ages – the waiters have worked here for 25 years on average, and are still enthusiastic and good humoured. A stuffed stork lords it over the bar, and there's an old clock from the Vosges. Rugby fans gather here in the evening if there's a match on. Star turns include the *choucroute*, *cassoulet* and Welsh rarebit. If you choose a decent Alsace wine to accompany your meal you will pay about 160F.

5th arrondissement
🛏 HÔTEL ESMERALDA*

4 rue Saint-Julien-le-Pauvre; M° Saint-Michel or

Muabert-Mutualité.
☎ 01.43.54.19.20 📠 01.40.51.00.68

This small, 17th-century hotel is a listed monument with a listed staircase. The nineteen rooms are fussily decorated with lots of attention to detail but you should cast a blind eye over the furniture, which is a bit dated. The whole place is really due a thorough redecoration, but because of its location, it's always full – some rooms have a glancing view of Notre-Dame or Square Viviani. Doubles 350F with shower or 480–520F with bath, though the basins are old and not always clean. Breakfast 40F.

⅗ ♠ FAMILIA HÔTEL

11 rue des Écoles; M° Jussieu, Maubert-Mutualité or Cardinal-Lemoine.
☎ 01.43.54.55.27 📠 01.43.29.61.77
TV.

A comfortable hotel run by the welcoming Gaudreron family who will go out of their way to help you. Doubles 460F with shower/wc, 515–595F with bath. The bathrooms are being modernised one by one. Breakfast 32F. The rooms on the fifth or sixth floors have views of Notre Dame and the Paris rooftops. The artist Gérald Pritchard, of the Beaux-Arts art school, has personalised some of the rooms by painting Notre Dame, Île de la Cité and Pont-Neuf on the walls in burnt sienna. The flowery fitted carpet is soft and there's a genuine late 18th- or early 19th-century bookcase in the refurbished foyer. 10% discount 15 Jan–28 Feb and Aug.

♠ HÔTEL DE LA SORBONNE**

6 rue Victor-Cousin; M° Saint-Michel or Cluny-Sorbonne.
☎ 01.43.54.58.08 📠 01.40.51.05.18
TV.

You go through a gateway to find this small pleasant hotel, which is in the student quarter and at the centre of things. All rooms have a phone, TV and hair drier. Doubles with shower/wc or bath 480–550F – very reasonable considering the place is well run and the reception is pleasant. Some rooms could do with improved soundproofing. The highest prices are for the largest rooms with marble bathrooms.

♠ HÔTEL DES GRANDES ÉCOLES***

75 rue du Cardinal-Lemoine; M° Cardinal-Lemoine or Monge.
☎ 01.43.26.79.23 📠 01.43.25.28.15
📧 Hotel.Grandes.Ecoles@wanadoo.fr
Disabled access. Garden. Pay car park.

The hotel is in a private lane just round the corner from pl. de la Contrescarpe. It's a house of charm and character, with a small paved courtyard and a leafy garden – you could almost imagine yourself out in the countryside. The owner and her daughter have long been welcoming tourists from all around the world. Book well in advance, since this is a favourite with Americans in Paris. There are 51 rooms on either side of the lane which are carefully looked after and tastefully arranged. They all have shower/wc or bath, 570–750F. In fine weather you can have tea in the garden, even if you're not staying here.

|⊙| RESTAURANT TASHI-DELEK

4 rue des Fossés-Saint-Jacques; RER Luxembourg.
☎ 01.43.26.55.55
Closed Sun and Aug.

Service lunchtime and evenings until 11pm. This was the first Tibetan restaurant in Paris, run by Tibetans who fled their country after the Chinese invasion. The Tibetan decor is restrained and the menu consists of regional dishes from U-Tsang, Kham and Amdo – this is a good place to familiarise yourself with Tibetan cuisine. Try *momok* (beef ravioli), *chabale* (stuffed pancakes) or *baktsa markou* (pasta dumplings with melted butter and goat's cheese) – and, if you're feeling brave, drink your tea with salted butter. Menus 56–105F or about 90F *à la carte*.

|⊙| FOYER DU VIETNAM

80 rue Monge; M° Monge.
☎ 01.45.35.32.54
Closed Sun, public holidays and Aug.

Service until 10pm. This restaurant, which seems to have some connection with the Union of Vietnamese Workers in France, is very plain indeed. It is brightened up only by a poster of Ho Chi Minh and a TV – supposedly for the regulars' amusement but actually of more interest to the waiter. The genuine Vietnamese cooking makes no concessions to Western tastes and remains resolutely authentic. They do an excellent and wonderfully tasty pork soup – the small serving is very substantial – and delicious steamed ravioli. The other dishes, like fish simmered in a spicy sauce, pork kebabs and Hanoi soup, are of the same calibre. There are a few interesting specialities at the weekend, such as rice soup with tripe, duck soup or grilled prawns with vermicelli. The cheapest set menu costs 58F.

|⊙| RESTAURANT LE VOLCAN

10 rue Thouin; M° Monge or Cardinal-Lemoine.
☎ 01.46.33.38.33

Closed Mon.

Service noon–2.30pm and 6.30–11pm. This reliable restaurant has been around for years and has kept its natural, popular character. Menus 59F, 95F and 145F, or 110F *à la carte*. Wine is included only at lunchtime. The cooking is French with a few nods in the direction of Greece, as in their good *moussaka*.

🎋 I●I RESTAURANT PERRAUDIN

157 rue Saint-Jacques; RER Luxembourg, it's next to the Luxembourg Gardens.
☎ 01.46.33.15.75
Closed Sat and Mon lunchtimes, Sun, and the last fortnight in Aug.

Service until 10.15pm. Around the corner from the Panthéon and the Luxembourg Gardens, here's a little bistro which is a favourite with local publishers and students from the Sorbonne. It's unpretentious and unshowy, with a lot of traditional dishes on the menu. Try the onion tart, *quiche lorraine*, leg of lamb with potatoes *dauphinoise*, duck *confit*, beef *bourguignon* or rack of lamb with herbs. The 63F lunch menu gives a choice of three starters, two main courses and three desserts, there's a gourmet menu at 150F, or it's about 120F *à la carte*. In summer you can eat in a small interior courtyard. Free apéritif.

I●I RESTAURANT LE PORT DU SALUT

163 [bis] rue Saint-Jacques; M° or RER Luxembourg.
☎ 01.46.33.63.21
Closed Sun evening, Mon and 1–22 Aug.

Service noon–2.30pm and 7–10.30pm. If *Perraudin* is full, this is the next best thing. Lovely setting with heavy beams, a tiny staircase, a piano and paintings of pastoral scenes. The famous French singers who have passed through here are too numerous to list. There's a daily 67F menu, and an extremely good 94F *formule* of main course plus starter or dessert; you'll get a small casserole of mussels or warm goat's cheese salad, followed by either veal stew or roast salmon with *beurre blanc*. All in all, a very pleasant restaurant with an intimate atmosphere, cloth napkins and attentive service. There's a large cellar for groups.

I●I RESTAURANT HAN LIM

6 rue Blainville; M° Monge.
☎ 01.43.54.62.74
Closed Mon and Aug.

This part of town is full of pleasant surprises. Right in the heart of Paris and surrounded by kebab joints, this excellent Korean restaurant does a lunchtime menu for 73F. They also offer a Korean barbecue for 100F, which is ridiculously cheap for the exotic thrill of tasting a style of cooking that may be totally new to you. Very good char-grilled meat and delectable garlic chicken. 120–140F for a complete meal *à la carte*. After your meal knock back a pint at *Connolly's Corner*, the latest Irish pub in Paris.

I●I RESTAURANT AU BISTROT DE LA SORBONNE

4 rue Thoullier; M° Saint-Michel; RER Luxembourg.
☎ 01.43.54.41.40
Closed Sun and Aug.

Service until 11pm. A friendly little place where you can eat well and affordably – ideal for the local students. It's an agreeable place with two dining rooms, one with a wall that recalls how the Sorbonne looked in the 14th century. The 75F lunchtime menu gives you a starter, dish of the day, such as chicken in a cream sauce, and cheese or dessert.

🎋 I●I RESTAURANT PEMA THANG

13 rue de la Montagne-Sainte-Geneviève; M° Maubert-Mutualité.
☎ 01.43.54.34.34 📧 pemathang@aol.com
Closed Sun, Mon lunchtime, and Aug.

Service noon–2.30pm and 7–11pm. The Latin Quarter is still a magnet for the various ethnic groups in the French capital. Take this restaurant, for example, which feels as though you might have stepped into an inn on the high plateaux of Tibet. The cooking, which involves a lot of steaming, is full of delicate, subtle flavours and deserves to be better known. While the dishes couldn't be anything but Tibetan, the flavours might remind you of India, China or Japan and the cuisine is just as good. The lunchtime crowd consists of students from the Sorbonne and white-collar workers; they are here to savour *sha momok* (which might remind you of dim sum), *thouk* (home-made noodles in clear soup) and *pemathan* (meat balls in a sweet and sour sauce with sautéed vegetables). Weekday lunch menu 79F, others 85–97F. Free coffee.

I●I RESTAURANT SAVANNAH CAFÉ

27 rue Descartes; M° Cardinal-Lemoine.
☎ 01.43.29.45.77
Closed Sun, Mon lunchtime and 17 Dec–3 Jan.

If you absolutely must have dinner in the Contrescarpe-Mouffetard area, try this place.

Richard, the owner, is Lebanese, and he'll welcome you with that very particular politeness that it would be nice to come across more often in French restaurants. He offers tabbouleh and hummus, naturally, but also dishes such as *ceviche*, pumpkin with nutmeg, chicken with toasted almonds, aubergines with basil, milk-fed lamb with pistachio and pine nuts, fruit and vegetable curry with cardamom – the list is endless. Try the *crème de lait* for dessert. Set menus 85F at lunchtime, and 137F. If you'd rather go *à la carte*, reckon on paying 150–180F.

|●| RESTAURANT LE BUISSON ARDENT

25 rue de Jussieu; M° Jussieu.
☎ 01.43.54.93.02
Closed Sat, Sun, Aug and a week at Christmas.

This is a very French place, the kind of restaurant you'd miss if ever it closed. The decor is as comforting as the cooking, but while they use a lot of good regional produce, the approach is modern and the results tasty and full of colour. They do a lunch menu at 90F and an excellent dinner menu at 160F.

|●| RESTAURANT L'ATLAS

10–12 bd. Saint-Germain; M° Maubert-Mutualité.
☎ 01.46.33.86.98
Closed Mon.

If you've been looking round the Institut du Monde Arabe, you can prolong the experience by eating here. The food is prepared by a man whom many people believe to be one of Arabic cooking's best ambassadors in Paris. Benjamin El Jaziri, who has worked with some of the big names, has remained faithful to the cooking of his native Morocco but goes easier on the fat and sugar. Try his incredibly light couscous served with meat and vegetables that is beyond reproach, or one of sixteen superb *tajines*. Apart from these classics, you can feast on grilled *gambas*, large prawns with paprika, lamb with mallow plant leaves, baked bream Moroccan style or, in season, partridge with mint and lemon. Warm welcome and attentive service. A menu at 98F, or 150F *à la carte*.

|●| LE MAUZAC

7 rue de l'Abbé-de-l'Épée; RER Luxembourg.
☎ 01.46.33.75.22
Closed Sat, Sun, a week at Easter, three weeks in Aug and a week at Christmas.

Service 6.30am–9pm, 11pm on Thurs and Fri. This place is endlessly interesting with its rare 1950s tables and zinc bar, and the odd curiosity like a pilaster from a temple and a

pillar disguised as a sturdy tree. The wines are rich and fruity and offer a choice of 35 vintages. Laurent, the young chef, prepares a selection of particularly good dishes of the day which are always worth ordering; lamb stew with baby vegetables, free-range chicken in tarragon vinegar, *spelt* – a kind of wheat – with mushrooms, and grilled scorpion fish with mashed potatoes flavoured with garlic and olive oil. What's on the menu depends on what proprietor Jean-Michel brings back from the market at Rungis. Plates of *charcuterie* and cheese are available until 10pm. Prices average 100F at lunchtime and 160F in the evening. Prompt service from Christine, the lady of the house, and her smiling waitress.

⅔ |●| RESTAURANT AU JARDIN DES PÂTES

4 rue Lacépède; M° Jussieu or Monge.
☎ 01.43.31.50.71 ➡ 01.46.35.42.12
Closed Mon.

Service noon–2.30pm and 7–11pm. They serve nothing but home-made pasta made from organic flour, and it has quite a reputation. You'll get real value for money, since you can have a substantial, satisfying meal for 100F *à la carte*. Try the buckwheat pasta with chicken livers, sesame butter and prunes, or the rice pasta with sautéed vegetables, ginger and tofu. All the beers and wines are organic, too. Free coffee.

|●| RESTAURANT LE LANGUEDOC

64 bd. de Port-Royal; M° Gobelins; RER Port-Royal.
☎ 01.47.07.24.47
Closed Tues, Wed, 20 July–20 Aug and 23 Dec–7 Jan.

Service noon–2pm and 7–10pm (last orders). They specialise in dishes of the southwest, and the cooking is excellent. The service is reminiscent of the kind you'd get in a country restaurant, even if the *patronne* can be stern. If you order herring, for example, they'll bring the entire dish to your table so you can help yourself. The duck *confit* with Sarlade potatoes and truffles is the star turn, but the meat dishes are well worth a try and the Rouergue wine washes it all down superbly. The white and red Gaillac from the proprietor's own vineyard aren't bad either. Set menu 115F; 120F *à la carte*.

|●| RESTAURANT LE BALZAR

49 rue des Écoles; M° Cluny-la-Sorbonne or Odéon.
☎ 01.43.54.13.67 ➡ 01.44.07.14.91
Closed Aug.

Service noon–midnight. This fairly plush brasserie has been taken over by the *Flo* group. It is a very pleasant place for supper after the theatre or the cinema, with artificial leather banquettes, large mirrors, and waiters in white aprons. There's a very pleasant, long, narrow glassed-in terrace where in winter you can people-watch in the warmth. The house specialities are rabbit *terrine* at 46F, skate in melted butter at 114F and *choucroute* at 87F. Good food of the classic variety. A meal *à la carte* will set you back about 200F.

6th arrondissement
ᕯ ☎ DELHY'S HÔTEL*

22 rue de l'Hirondelle; M° Saint-Michel.
☎ 01.43.26.58.25 ➡ 01.43.26.51.06
TV.

This small typical Parisian hotel is in one of the capital's least-known streets – which means peace and quiet. It's part of the 16th-century town house, with exposed stone work and ancient beams, that François I gave to his favourite, Anne de Pisseleu, the Duchess of Étampes. The rooms are newly and attractively furnished; 300F with basin, 390F with shower. That's pretty standard for hotels in the neighbourhood but this is definitely the most central. 10% discount after the third night.

ᕯ ☎ HÔTEL DES ACADÉMIES*

15 rue de la Grande-Chaumière; M° Vavin.
☎ 01.43.26.66.44 ➡ 01.43.26.03.72

Small family hotel in a quiet street. It has been going since the 1920s, but the atmosphere is more reminiscent of the 1950s. Doubles 330F with shower, or 375–400F with shower/wc. 10% discount after the third night.

☎ HÔTEL DE NESLE

7 rue de Nesle; M° Odéon.
☎ 01.43.54.62.41 ➡ 01.43.54.31.88
Garden.

This hotel, in a quiet street, is a throw-back to the great hippy era. Anglo-Saxon and American accents mingle with Madame's North African one. She and her son shower affection on her guests and reign over their little kingdom with infinite good humour. "Free-wheeling" rather than "organized" best describes things here – but there's a definite sense of people enjoying themselves. There's a small interior garden where you can have a quiet read, and when it's not open there's a pretty terrace overlooking the garden. The twenty rooms are simple, clean, well maintained and individually decorated. Doubles overlooking the street range from 350–400F with basin to

450–600F with shower/wc and a garden view. There are wcs on each floor. Each room has its own personality; number 2 has old paintings, slightly faded wallpaper and antique furniture, while number 9 has been decorated in an Egyptian style. Breakfast 25F. The shower is rather awe-inspiring and there's even a little hammam, or steam bath, in room number 4! They don't take reservations, so to be sure of a room turn up before 10am.

ᕯ ☎ HÔTEL DES CANETTES**

17 rue des Canettes; M° Saint-Germain-des Prés or Mabillon.
☎ 01.46.33.12.67 ➡ 01.44.07.07.37
TV.

This establishment, in a very busy street with lots of pubs and Americanised shops, looks old, but the decor is coloured and very hi-tech. The rooms overlooking the street have more light but no double glazing; overlooking the courtyard it's quieter but darker. Doubles with shower/wc 470F. If you book – and it's advisable – you need to guarantee the room with a credit card at least three days before arrival. 10% discount.

☎ HÔTEL DU LYS**

23 rue Serpente; M° Saint-Michel or Odéon.
☎ 01.43.26.97.57 ➡ 01.44.07.34.90
TV.

A pleasant hotel on a quiet street, with a nice family atmosphere. You'll get a great welcome. Rooms all have cable TV, individual safes and a hair drier; those at the front are the best, others look onto the courtyard and are brightly decorated. Doubles with shower/wc or bath 580F, breakfast included.

☎ GRAND HÔTEL DES BALCONS**

3 rue Casimir-Delavigne; M° Odéon; RER Luxembourg.
☎ 01.46.34.78.50 ➡ 01.46.34.06.27
email: RESA@www.balcons.com
TV.

You'd be hard pressed to find another place in the Latin Quarter, just 100m from the Odéon theatre, that offers such value for money. Doubles 600F with shower/wc or bath. All-you-can-eat buffet breakfast for 60F – it's free if it's your birthday! The reception and common parts of the hotel are Art Deco style, though sadly the rooms are merely functional. Everyone gets a warm welcome.

|●| RESTAURANT NOUVELLE COURONNE THAÏ

17 rue Jules-Chaplain; M° Vavin.
☎ 01.43.54.29.88

Closed Sun and Mon lunchtimes.

Service until 11pm. An excellent Thai restaurant in a secluded street. Someone has taken a lot of trouble over the setting, with its soft colours, subdued tones and well-spaced tables. Fish soup delicately flavoured with coconut milk, casserole of seafood, lacquered chicken with lemongrass, spicy duck sautéed with bamboo shoots and pork spare ribs are among the wonderful things listed on a very tempting menu, which also includes lots of Chinese dishes and some steamed specialities. The wine prices are very reasonable and they serve Thai and Chinese beer. Remarkable value. The service is efficient, the welcome charming and the food delicious. Set menus 45F and 52F at lunchtime, 69F and 98F in the evening; à la carte you'll pay 110F or so.

🕏 |●| RESTAURANT INDONESIA

12 rue de Vaugirard; M° Odéon; RER Luxembourg.
☎ 01.43.39.43.72
Closed Sat lunchtime.

Service until 10.30pm, 11pm on Fri and Sat. Best to reserve in the evening. This is the only Indonesian restaurant in Paris to be set up as a workers' co-operative. The food is good and service comes with a smile. Weekday lunch menu 59F, then 89–129F. The rice tables, or *rijsttafel*, consist of a series of dishes from Java, Sumatra, Bali and Celebes; *rendang* is meat in coconut milk, and *balado ikan* is fish in spicy tomato sauce. Great curries and mutton satay. Free apéritif.

🕏 |●| RESTAURANT L'ASSIGNAT

7 rue Guénégaud; M° Odéon.
☎ 01.43.54.87.68
Closed Sun and July.

Service at the bar 7.30am–9.30pm, in the restaurant noon–3.30pm. Who would have thought you'd find a quiet little neighbourhood restaurant in this crowded narrow street? It's popular with local art dealers, people who work at the Mint and art students – many people eat what they want, write down in a book what they've had, and settle up at the end of the month. The restaurant is crammed and you enjoy good, simple cooking in a lively atmosphere. The owner's mother, who's been doing the cooking for a very long time, clearly revels in her job. Set lunch menu 60F or around 75F à la carte. Free coffee.

|●| RESTAURANT AUX TROIS CANETTES

18 rue des Canettes; M° Saint-Germain-des-Prés or Mabillon.
☎ 01.43.26.29.62
Closed Sat lunchtime, Sun and Aug.

Service noon–2.30pm and 7.30–11pm. Antonio is a Neapolitan who's run this place since the 1960s, and the restaurant has probably changed very little since then. It's a historic house which, in the 19th century, had a famous reading room frequented by Balzac. The ocean-and-volcano decor on the ground floor evokes Antonio's home town. As for the food, try the sardines *Antonio*, the onions *à la sicilienne* or the aubergines in olive oil. There's a good selection of pasta: linguini with clams, penne *à la sicilienne* or lamb Toscana. All the dishes are influenced by the changing seasons. Lunch menu 62F or another at 82F. In June there is a poetry festival in pl. Saint-Sulpice, and the restaurant awards an international literary prize.

🕏 |●| LE PETIT VATEL

5 rue Lobineau; M° Mabillon.
☎ 01.43.54.28.49
Closed Sun, Mon and Feb.

Service noon–3pm and 7–11pm. After a period in the doldrums, this place has been revamped, re-opened and is back on track. The 70F *formule* gets you main course plus starter or dessert and coffee; if you opt for individual dishes, a meal will cost about 100F. Try the home-made *terrine* or the cheese *tourte*, or, if you go for dishes that require more preparation, kidneys in white wine, sautéed lamb or beef *miroton*. The wines complement the cooking perfectly; they do quite a few by the glass. Free apéritif.

|●| BOUILLON RACINE

3 rue Racine; M° Cluny-Sorbonne or Odéon.
☎ 01.44.32.15.60

Service 11.45am–2.45pm and 7pm–midnight. Just when the Latin Quarter seemed set to be overrun by fast-food joints and clothes shops, this restaurant came on the scene – or, to be more accurate, made a comeback, since it first appeared at the beginning of the twentieth century as the *Bouillon Camille Chartier*. After lots of ups and downs it ended up as a civil service canteen. Luckily the building was listed, so the original interior remained, albeit in a rather dilapidated state. Today this magnificent Art Nouveau establishment has taken on a new lease of life, and has been restored to its earlier elegance. It's all there – bevelled mirrors, etched glass, stained glass, marble mosaics, and gold-leaf lettering. Beer plays a large part in the cooking, and there are lots of beers to drink, including famous Trappist names like Rochefort, Chimay and Orval. Set *"bouillon"* menus 79F at lunchtime, drink included, and others up to 189F. Brown sugar tart and spiced buns are served at teatime (3–6pm), and you can get a *café liégeois* at any time of the day.

IOI NOURA

121 bd. du Montparnasse; M° Vavin.
☎ 01.43.20.19.19 ➡ 01.43.20.05.40
Garden.

Service noon–midnight. This place is less sophisticated than its counterpart on the Right Bank but has something its sister restaurant lacks – a small garden so you can eat outside in summer. Lebanese specialities are much in evidence on the menu, and you're spoiled for choice. Cleverly constructed *formules assiettes* with photos to help you make up your mind – choose from a large or small service of *hors d'œuvres*, mixed *charwarma*, and meat and chickpea *charwarma*. Lunch menu 97F, or 149F. Be adventurous and try the *jellab*, dates in syrup with pine nuts, and the Lebanese beer. This is primarily a brasserie where you can have a very quick meal.

⚘ IOI LA RÔTISSERIE D'EN FACE

2 rue Christine; M° Odéon.
☎ 01.43.26.40.98 **e** rotisface@aol.fr
Closed Sat lunchtime and Sun.

Service noon–2.30pm and 7–11pm, 11.30pm Fri and Sat. Top chef Jacques Cagna, whose flagship restaurant is across the way, has every reason to be pleased. In just a few years he's made this enterprise one of the Left Bank's institutions. Try the barbecued Barbary duck, guinea-fowl with aubergines and onions, lamb moussaka, roast free-range chicken, or duck breast with honey and spices served with tomatoes and new potatoes. There are lots of things cooked on the *rotisserie*, all served with old-fashioned mashed potatoes. It's very good on the whole, though there have been a few hiccups – probably because of the large staff turnover. The wine list isn't very tempting and the noise from other tables is irritating. Lunch menu 100F, others up to 230F. Free house apéritif.

IOI L'ÉPI DUPIN

11 rue Dupin; M° Sèvres-Babylone.
☎ 01.42.22.64.56 ➡ 01.42.22.30.42
Closed Sat and Sun.

Service noon–2.30pm and 7.30–10.30pm.

François Pasteau, who trained under Kérever and Faugeron, is a happy man, as you can tell from his beaming smile – his restaurant is full at lunchtime and his customers leave nothing on their plates but the pattern. You'll also get pretty good value for money – there's a a lunchtime *formule* for 115F and a *menu-carte* for 175F without wine. The menu reflects what's been available at the Rungis market that day. You get a daily choice of six starters, eight main courses and six desserts; these might include rabbit turnovers with aubergines, scallops with lemons, and pears and warm apples in flaky pastry with a mascarpone sorbet. Sheer delight from start to finish. Pleasant and efficient service.

IOI RESTAURANT AUX CHARPENTIERS

10 rue Mabillon; M° Mabillon or Saint-Germain-des-Prés.
☎ 01.43.26.30.05 ➡ 01.46.33.07.98
Closed Christmas Eve, Christmas Day and 1 May.

Service noon–3pm and 7–11.30pm. This restaurant used to be the headquarters of the guild of master carpenters; scale models, souvenirs and old photos fill the place. The restaurant owner, who's an expert on the guild's history, has taken a vow of secrecy; you'll find out more from the guild museum next door. They serve good traditional cuisine, with great specials: veal Marengo with tomatoes, garlic and mushrooms on Monday, beef *à la mode* (simmered in wine, vegetables and herbs) on Tuesday, salt pork and lentils on Wednesday, *pot-au-feu* and vegetables on Thursday, etc. By comparison, the starters are expensive. They do a *formule* at lunchtime for 120F, which includes $\frac{1}{4}$ litre of wine. The equivalent costs 158F in the evening, or expect to pay 180–210F for a meal *à la carte*.

⚘ IOI RESTAURANT LE PROCOPE

13 rue de l'Ancienne-Comédie; M° Odéon.
☎ 01.40.46.79.00.

Service 11am–1am. This is the oldest café in Paris. In 1686, an Italian called Francesco Procopio dei Cotelli came to the city and opened a café that served the then unknown beverage of coffee. His establishment, close to the Comédie Française, soon gathered a clientele of writers and artists. In the 18th century it was a meeting place for the Enlightenment philosophers – the idea for Diderot's famous Encyclopaedia was spawned here during a conversation between him and d'Alembert. During the French Revolution, Danton, Marat and Camille Desmoulins met here, and it was also a haunt of Musset, Sand, Balzac, Huysmans, Verlaine and many others. It's still a meeting place for intellectuals and, incredibly, its prices are still reasonable. The cooking is unabashedly French – you haven't been to Paris if you haven't eaten at *Procope*. Set menus 130–178F or 200F *à la carte*. Reasonably priced wine list. Free house apéritif.

🏃 |●| RESTAURANT LE MACHON D'HENRI

8 rue Guisarde; M° Saint-Germain-des-Prés.
☎ 01.43.29.08.70

Service till 11.30pm. This is a good wine bar with stone walls and hefty beams. They serve a rich selection of carefully prepared classical dishes; slow-roast lamb cooked for seven hours with *gratin dauphinois*, courgette terrine, calf's liver with onion *compote*. 130F or thereabouts for a full meal. Free house apéritif.

🏃 |●| L'O À LA BOUCHE

157 bd. du Montparnasse; M° Vavin; RER Port-Royal.
☎ 01.56.54.01.55 ➡ 01.43.21.07.87
Closed. Sun, Mon, a week in Jan, the second week in April and the first week in Aug.

Service noon–2.30pm and 7.30–midnight. Franck Paquier is a dynamic young master chef with genuine talent, and he's put together a brilliantly constructed three-course *menu-carte* at 195F. You can mix and match with some of the dishes of the day chalked up on the board, around 260F *à la carte*. There's also a two-course menu (main course and starter or dessert) at 140F. All the ingredients are fresh and the dishes freshly cooked. His creations include duck *foie gras* pan-fried with soft fruit, lobster ravioli with *Beaumes de Venise* sauce, broad beans and celery, roast rack of lamb with thyme and crispy vegetable fritters, fillet of John Dory with pickled aubergines, Grand Marnier soufflé and vanilla ice cream, and lime, orange and grapefruit *sabayon* with a pepper sorbet – irresistible. The wines are affordable but service is slack.

🏃 |●| LA BAUTA

129 bd. du Montparnasse; M° Vavin.
☎ 01.43.22.52.35
Closed Sat lunchtime, Sun, and Aug.

Service noon to 2pm and 7.30–10.45pm. The decor is inspired by Venice – there's a superb collection of masks on the walls – but the menu draws inspiration from the whole of Italy. The beautiful people who eat here are on to a good thing; everything is remarkably fresh and cooked with finesse. The pasta will satisfy everyone, and the chef cooks it perfectly *al dente* with all manner of sauces and accompaniments like langoustine and rosemary, cinnamon, squid ink or clams. The *menu affaire* costs 300F, or you'll pay around 350F for a meal *à la carte*. Free *digestif*.

7th arrondissement

🏃 ≜ HÔTEL-EIFFEL RIVE GAUCHE**

6 rue du Gros-Caillou; M° École-Militaire.
☎ 01.45.51.24.56 ➡ 01.45.51.11.77
TV.

This hotel, in a peaceful street, quietly exudes that discreet charm of the bourgeoisie. You reach the four floors by an elegant staircase encircling a pretty patio that leads onto a small interior courtyard with a sliding glass roof. Subtle shades of old rose and ochre predominate, almost as if you were in Andalucia. From the top floor you will catch a glimpse of the Eiffel Tower, while others look onto the patio. A double with basin/wc costs 305F, 495F with bath. Buffet breakfast 40F. Friendly welcome and it's best to book. 10% discount except over New Year, Easter and Whitsun.

🏃 ≜ HÔTEL DU QUAI VOLTAIRE**

19 quai Voltaire; M° Rue du Bac.
☎ 01.42.61.50.91 ➡ 01.42.61.62.26

A two-star hotel in a magnificent location on the banks of the Seine, opposite the second-hand booksellers' stalls and the Louvre, and near the Musée d'Orsay. It was built in the 19th century and has welcomed a number of famous people including Wagner, Baudelaire, Oscar Wilde and Pissarro. Doubles with basin 400F, 720F with shower, 770F with bath and shower. Free Kir.

≜ HÔTEL DU PALAIS BOURBON**

49 rue de Bourgogne; M° Varenne, Assemblée-Nationale or Invalides.
☎ 01.44.11.30.70 ➡ 01.45.55.20.21
e htlbourbon@aol.com
TV.

Pleasant reception with lofty, beamed ceilings. Some of the rooms are vast, the benefit of an old building; all have double glazing, mini-bar, TV, renovated bathroom, and sockets for connnecting a fax or modem. Doubles with shower/wc or bath from 420F. Good prices for the district.

♨ ♨ GRAND HÔTEL LÉVÊQUE*

29 rue Cler; M° École-Militaire or Latour-Maubourg.
☎ 01.47.05.49.15 ➡ 01.45.50.49.36
e info@hotelleveque.com
TV.

The Eiffel Tower is very close by but you may find the picturesque street market in rue Cler, outside the hotel, even more appealing – rooms over the street get taken first! This is an authentic part of the district and the hotel with its fifty renovated rooms is reasonably priced. Doubles with shower/wc 450F. The decor doesn't leave a lasting impression but the rooms are clean and they have safes and a hair drier. It's a well-known place, so you may have to book. On a good day, you'll get a jovial reception. Free breakfast (usually 49F).

♨ ♨ HÔTEL LE PAVILLON**

54 rue Saint-Dominique; M° Invalides.
☎ 01.45.51.42.87 ➡ 01.45.51.32.79
TV.

This place started out as a convent, and despite becoming a hotel, it has retained a provincial charm. The pretty façade really stands out. There are just eighteen rooms, all of them soberly decorated and comfortable. The Mother Superior's old chamber is in great demand. Double rooms with shower/wc 460F, 575F with bath. Try numbers 10 and 14, which have two double beds and a sizeable bathroom. On the other hand, avoid the ones in the basement, which are deeply depressing. Breakfast 41F. 10% discount Jan–Feb.

♨ HÔTEL MUGUET**

11 rue Chevert; M° École Militaire or Latour-Maubourg.
☎ 01.47.05.05.93 ➡ 01.45.50.25.37
e muguet@wanadoo.fr
TV. Disabled access.

This hotel has been completely refurbished from top to bottom, and it stands out in this quiet little road that's away from the traffic noise. The rooms are air-conditioned; doubles with shower 580F, twin with bath 620F. Three rooms on the sixth floor have a view of the Eiffel Tower, others overlook the Invalides.

♨ HÔTEL D'ORSAY**

93 rue de Lille; M° Solférino or Assemblée Nationale.
☎ 01.47.05.85.54 ➡ 01.45.55.51.16
e hotel.orsay@wanadoo.fr

A quiet, comfortable hotel in the buildings of the old *Hotel Solférino* and the *Résidence d'Orsay*. Attractive reception. Double rooms 600F with shower/wc or 700–1500F with en-

suite bath. That's about what you'd expect to pay in this district. Probably wise to book.

♨ ♨ HÔTEL BERSOLY'S SAINT-GERMAIN***

28 rue de Lille; M° Rue-du-Bac.
☎ 01.42.60.73.79 ➡ 01.49.27.05.55
e bersolys@wanadoo.fr
Closed Aug. **Disabled access. TV. Pay car park.**

Gorgeous hotel in a proud mansion that was built in the 18th century, in the middle of this historic part of Paris near the antique shops. The rooms may be small but they're absolutely lovely and perfectly clean. Each one bears the name of a painter, and there's a reproduction of one of the artist's pictures on the wall; "Gauguin" and "Turner" are particularly attractive. The hushed atmosphere, period furniture and exposed beams create a nostalgic ambience. Rooms overlooking the courtyard with shower cost 750F. The telephones have Internet points. There's a small bar near the reception area. Breakfast, normally 50F per person, is free 1 Nov–28 Feb.

♨ I●I THOUMIEUX***

79 rue Saint-Dominique; M° Latour-Maubourg.
☎ 01.47.05.49.75 ➡ 01.47.05.36.96
TV. Disabled access.

Service noon–3.30pm and 6.30–midnight; on Sunday it's open noon–midnight. This large, attractive brasserie, founded in 1923, was taken over in 1976 by Françoise Thoumieux and Jean Bassalert. If you're looking for a lively place with good food at reasonable prices, this is the place of your dreams. The home-made *cassoulet* with duck *confit*, the cep omelette and the duck breast with blackcurrants are delicious. Menus start at 100F and there's one with specialities from the Corrèze at 180F: grilled duck breast salad, maize flour dumplings, *cabécou* (goat's cheese), and $1/4$ litre of Corrèze wine. This is also a hotel; all double rooms have bathrooms and cost 750F.

I●I CHEZ GERMAINE

30 rue Pierre-Leroux; M° Duroc.
☎ 01.42.73.28.34
Closed Sat evening, Sun, and Aug.

A simple, clean little dining room with a slightly provincial feel and a truly warm welcome. Lots of people who work in the area come here for lunch, as do local pensioners and people in love. There's a 69F menu, which is good value for the Left Bank. Try the excellent creamed salt cod and the ox tripe.

They have a lot of classic dishes, such as sautéed rabbit *chasseur*, *coq au vin*, fillet of cod with *aïoli*, and pork *colombo*; try also their *clafoutis*, an egg custard with cherries or pear. A carafe of unassuming Bordeaux costs 18F. A full meal will cost about 110F.

𝕏 |●| RESTAURANT LE ROUPEYRAC

62 rue de Bellechasse; M° Solférino.
☎ 01.45.51.33.42
Closed Sat evening, Sun and Aug.

Service noon–2.45pm and 7–9.30pm. This is the kind of neighbourhood restaurant you used to find everywhere in Paris. There's none of the flim-flam or the intrusive fancy decor that distracts you in places where the kitchen is full of microwave ovens. Monsieur and Mme Fau have been running this place for over a quarter of a century, and it's named after the hamlet near Durenque in the Aveyron where they come from. Wonderful country home cooking, with three or four fresh dishes every day – duck with orange, *haricot de mouton* (leg of lamb with haricot beans), or oxtail in a *pot-au-feu*. A weekday lunch menu at 80F, others at 115F and 155F. Efficient, attentive service. Free apéritif.

𝕏 |●| L'ŒILLADE

10 rue Saint-Simon; M° Rue-du-Bac.
☎ 01.42.22.01.60
Closed Sat lunchtime, Sun, the second fortnight in Aug and over New Year.

Service at lunch and then 7.30–11pm. Jean-Louis Huclin, the chef here, is a *bon vivant*; he eats enough for four and likes his clients to do so, too. Both dining rooms are always crowded, because he serves excellent, robust dishes: stuffed cabbage, salad with *foie gras* and lobster, *fricassée* of chicken with *foie gras* and cloves of garlic, beef cheek stew, and braised sweetbreads with morels. There's a 98F menu or about 220F *à la carte*. Free apéritif.

|●| RESTAURANT LE BABYLONE

13 rue de Babylone; M° Sèvres-Babylone.
☎ 01.45.48.72.13
Closed evenings, Sun and Aug.

The large dining room is delightfully old-fashioned; the pictures on the walls have yellowed with age and the imitation leather banquettes are comfortable. The cooking is good. The 110F lunch menu includes three courses and wine. Dishes of the day cost around 60F; you'll pay about 120F for a full meal. They don't accept credit cards.

|●| LE POCH'TRON

25 rue de Bellechasse; M° Solférino; RER Musée.
☎ 01.45.51.27.11
Closed Sat and Sun.

The restaurant has an outlandish name but the delightfully warm *patronne* has a popular touch and her chef-husband prepares the dishes with great care. Try the calf's head with *sauce gribiche*, *andouillette de Troyes* or *baeckofe* and all the traditional fare you would expect in a good bistro. You'll spend about 120F *à la carte*. They won the Bouteille d'Or "best bistro" award in 1996, so you can rely on the wine list which has particularly good bottles from Alsace.

𝕏 |●| LES OLIVADES

41 ave de Ségur. M° École-Militaire.
☎ 01.47.83.70.09

Walk through the door and you could almost believe you were in Provence. Flora, the chef, is from Avignon and her cooking is full of flavours from the south. The 135F menu leads with a *croustillant* of red mullet and sardines with balsamic vinegar, fresh crab mayonnaise, quails preserved in olive oil and russet apples, or scallops, pan-fried in their shells. Desserts are of the order of *millefeuille* scented with orange blossom. There are other menus up to 250F. The wine list is compiled by Raphaël, Flora's husband who knows what he's about – if he offers advice, take it. Free house apéritif.

|●| AU BON ACCUEIL

14 rue de Monttessuy; M° Alma-Marceau.
☎ 01.47.05.16.11
Closed Sat, Sun, 24 Dec–2 Jan.

The name evokes a quiet country restaurant somewhere out in the country – which might raise a smile when you're in the classiest part of the 7th *arrondissement*, but is actually rather appropriate. The staff are delightful and the cuisine is equally good. Jacques Lacipière is as professional a restaurateur as he is a passionate epicurean and he treks to the food market at Rungis practically every day to choose seafood, poultry and vegetables. The menus reflects what he has selected and the dishes change constantly. In the evening, seated at your table on the terrace, you have a superb view of the Eiffel Tower. Lunch menu 145F or 165F in the evening.

𝕏 |●| LA MAISON DE COSIMA

20 rue de l'Exposition; M° École-Militaire.
☎ 01.45.51.37.71

Closed lunchtimes, Sun, a week in Feb and three weeks in Aug.

Open evenings only until 10.30pm. The street is full of restaurants. Here, Jean-Michel Reverdy and his wife Hélène create a lovely atmosphere with cooking to match. *Pâté en croute* with duck and *foie gras*, *terrine* of veal with onion jelly, ox cheek *bourguignon*, and a splendid pumpkin and cinnamon pie. All dishes are subtly flavoured and seasoned. Menu at 168F for a three-course meal. They have a small private dining room you can book for a celebration lunch. Free coffee.

❙●❙ RESTAURANT LE BASILIC

2 rue Casimir-Périer; M° Solferino or Invalides.
☎ 01.44.18.94.64

Service noon–2.30pm and 7.30–10.30pm. Everyone in the 7th *arrondissement* comes to this comfortable brasserie with its welcoming terrace looking across at Sainte-Clothilde church. Try the roast lamb in salt, the sole *meunière* or the other classics that appeal to regulars who tend to be a little conservative in their eating habits. A complete meal comes to 250F including wine. It's a bit chintzy, but a relaxing place to come after a walk around the area admiring the splendid architecture.

8th arrondissement
⌂ HÔTEL WILSON*

10 rue de Stockholm; M° Saint-Lazare.
☎ 01.45.22.10.85

A reasonably priced one-star hotel that is conveniently near St Lazare station. It is simple, functional, clean and well run. There's no lift, so you have to climb all the way up to the fifth floor to get to the rooms with a fantastic view over the city. Doubles with basin cost 220F, 260F with shower/wc, 280F with bath. Some rooms sleeping three. Breakfast is included, which makes it even better value.

⌂ HÔTEL DES CHAMPS-ÉLYSÉES**

2 rue d'Artois; M° Saint-Philippe-du-Roule or Franklin-Roosevelt.
☎ 01.43.59.11.42 ➡ 01.45.61.00.61
TV.

A clean, comfortable two-star hotel away from the racket on the Champs Élysées. The 36 spacious rooms are soundproofed and air-conditioned, and they're each decorated differently. Doubles with shower/wc 495F, twins with bath 580F; there's a TV, mini-bar, room safe, hair drier and direct dial telephone. Breakfast, 44F, is served in a pretty vaulted room. Think about booking, as it's

often full. They offer a dry cleaning service.

❙●❙ RESTAURANT CHEZ LÉON

5 rue de l'Isly; M° Saint-Lazare.
☎ 01.43.87.42.77
Closed Sun and Aug.

Service noon–3pm and 7–10pm. There's a "Relais Routier" sign outside which is a real poser because this place, right in the centre of town, is near a station, not a main road. But it is the real thing: the set menus, the waitresses in their white aprons, the transparent plastic table covers to protect the tablecloths, the hole-in-the-ground loos and the huge 1950s fridges in black and canary yellow prove it. On the food front there are main courses like beef with tomato sauce and noodles, or roast beef with mashed potato and cauliflower. The wine comes in $\frac{1}{4}$litre jugs. Expect to pay 80–100F for a meal. The only "Routier" in Paris earned its sign because the Federation of Road Hauliers is across the street.

⌘ ❙●❙ LE BOUCLÉON

10 rue de Constantinople; M° Europe.
☎ 01.42.93.73.33
Closed Sat and Sun.

Dinner served until 11pm. An easy-going local restaurant named after one of the gates of Constantinople. When it's hot they don't expect men to wear ties or jackets. The decor is simple but colourful – green checked tablecloths – and they only have room for thirty, though they put a few extra tables on the pavement in summer. All the dishes chalked up on the blackboard are good – salmon *tartare*, duck *foie gras*, calves' liver pan-fried with juniper berries, *entrecôte béarnaise* or a duck *pot-au-feu* with celery. All are thoughtfully prepared and well judged. From the desserts, go for the *financier au chocolat* served hot with pistachio cream. Around 120F for a meal. The owner serves wines by the glass and you can buy a bottle to take away. Free coffee.

❙●❙ SPOON

14 rue de Marignan; M° Franklin-Roosevelt.
☎ 01.40.76.34.44
Closed Sat and Sun.

Service at lunchtime and until 11pm in the evening. Minimalist, sober interior design creating a peaceful, Zen atmosphere. Nothing interrupts your studious enjoyment of the flavours produced by Alain Ducasse, one of the high priests of modern cooking. It's new-concept world food: a fusion of flavours, spices and fragrances without a hint of fat. The "vegetable garden" is divine, as is the roast lamb. As well as a wine list, there's a list of waters by the bottle. A meal will set you back about 300F. It's very fashionable: you have to book at least a fortnight in advance and the well-heeled regulars greet each other across the dining room. It's also pretentious, which may be its downfall.

9th arrondissement
🏨 HÔTEL DES ARTS**

7 cité Bergère; M° Rue-Montmartre or Cadet.
☎ 01.42.46.73.30 ➤ 01.48.00.94.42
TV. Disabled access. Car park.

A two-star hotel with a pretty, pastel pink façade in a lovely passageway. There is a confusing number of hotels to choose from around here – this one is the cheapest. Friendly welcome. It's far enough from the faubourg to be peaceful, and the rooms are clean and freshly refurbished. The ones on the fifth floor are tiny but cheaper at 380F; other doubles with shower/wc cost 400F, or 420F with bath. The stairway is decorated with old showbills – this is the *Hôtel des Arts*, after all. Try engaging the handsome grey parrot in conversation – he may well reply. Breakfast 33F.

🏨 HÔTEL CHOPIN**

46 passage Jouffroy; M° Grands Boulevards or Bourse.
☎ 01.47.70.58.10 ➤ 01.42.47.00.70
TV.

This 19th-century town house is in a picturesque setting at the end of a narrow street – a quiet backwater round the corner from the Grands Boulevards. The handsome façade dates from 1850 and features elegant old woodwork. The rooms are quite pretty, their walls covered in Japanese cloth. The view over the rooftops is reminiscent of an Impressionist painting, particularly if you're lucky enough to have a room where you can see the setting sun. Doubles with shower/wc or bath 450–520F. See if you can get a room on the fourth floor, as they are the brightest. It's best to avoid the ones looking onto the courtyard – all you'll get to see from those is a massive wall. Free breakfast, usually 40F.

🏨 HÔTEL DES CROISÉS**

63 rue Saint-Lazare; M° Trinité.
☎ 01.48.74.78.24 ➤ 01.49.95.04.43
TV.

This place attracts a host of regulars, so you really ought to book. It's in a marvellous location, and looks wonderful. The superb reception area has old wood panelling and you just sink into the carpet. The wood-panelled lift with wrought iron gates takes you up to the

rooms, which are sheer magic. They're absolutely huge and each has an individual style with period furniture and marble fireplaces; some have Art Deco wood panelling. Number 25 has an alcove which doubles as a little sitting room. Some of the bathrooms are enormous. Doubles with shower/wc or bath 490F. Breakfast costs 40F, and they'll bring it to you in your room. A superb two-star hotel at reasonable prices.

🏨 HÔTEL DE LA TOUR D'AUVERGNE***

10 rue de la Tour d'Auvergne; M° Cadet.
☎ 01.48.78.61.60 ➤ 01.49.95.99.00
TV.

A pretty three-star hotel in a quiet street near the Sacré-Cœur. The spacious, elegantly decorated rooms have beds with canopies, bath or shower, and hair driers. There is a bar, and 24-hour room service. Doubles with bath 600–750F. The fifth floor is exclusively for non-smokers. Breakfast, 55F, is appetising, with lots to choose from like yoghurt, cornflakes, *pain au chocolat* or *pain aux raisins*.

◐ LE BISTROT DU CURÉ

21 bd. Clichy; M° Pigalle.
☎ 01.48.74.65.84
Closed Sun, public holidays and Aug.

This eating place, in an old church, is something of a sanctuary in a street that's full of sex shops.There's a stone statue of the Virgin Mary in front of the counter, and a priest who goes from table to table, almost as if he's blessing your food. Even the waiters minister to your needs with great kindness. They offer several menus, 45–95F, of simple, good dishes: dishes include *crudités,* soup or egg or prawn mayonnaise, roast beef with *purée* of peppers, turkey *blanquette* with white sauce and saffron rice, steak with green peppercorns, pan-fried saddle of lamb and veal escalope. You can opt for a dish of the day if you're not very hungry. If you wish to go to confession see the priest upstairs.

◐ LYCÉE 43

43 av. Trudaine; M° Anvers or Gare-du-Nord.
☎ 01.48.78.43.25
Closed Sat evening, Sun and Aug.

Monsieur Tachot, who used to be a butcher at the old market, Les Halles, bought this old place in 1969; he's the chef now and his wife looks after the customers. The tourists going up to or down from the Butte Montmartre get the same friendly welcome as the local "villagers" who inhabit the place. The 70F menu is extremely substantial, and there's another at 100F. The cat purrs on top of the radiator and the genuine family atmosphere makes it easy to ignore the unadorned decor.

🍴 RESTAURANT CHARTIER

7 rue du Faubourg-Montmartre; M° Grands-Boulevards.
☎ 01.47.70.86.29

Last orders 10pm, no reservations. You come in through a huge revolving door and find yourself in an immense, turn-of-the-(19th)-century restaurant with its original decor completely intact – in fact they've made it a listed building. Get there quickly before someone has the bright idea to refurbish it. There are only two or three places like this left and they're not half as wonderful as this one. It's always packed with regulars, pensioners from the area, students, poverty-stricken artists and tourists – 80–100F à la carte including a drink The food is passable, though not always as hot as it could be. There are 350 covers, 16 waiters and they serve 1200 meals a day.

🍴 RESTAURANT AU PETIT RICHE

25 rue Le Pelletier; M° Richelieu-Drouot.
☎ 01.47.70.68.68
Closed Sun, Sat and Sun in July, and Aug.

Closes at 12.15am. The restaurant was founded in 1880, and you could be dining in an Impressionist painting. With its labyrinth of intimate salons and Belle Epoque decor, you're back in the time of sumptuous suppers. They serve dishes like poached haddock scented with a sweet-and-sour sauce, beef with sea-salt and tuna with green peppercorns – specialities are from the Val de Loire. Menus at 140F, 165F and 180F, or à la carte around 180F. The restaurant buzzes with atmosphere and it works with the local theatres, to offer special price "theatre-dinner" promotions. Free apéritif.

🍴 CHEZ CATHERINE

65 rue de Provence; M° Chaussée-d'Antin.
☎ 01.45.26.72.88
Closed Sat, Sun, Mon, public holidays, the first week in Jan, and Aug.

Service noon–2pm and 7.30–11pm. Under new management for a couple of years, this respected, pretty bristro, previously the *Poitou*, has undergone a revolution. Out with the dull cooking and indifferent wines, in with inventive dishes cooked to perfection and a stunning wine list. Catherine, the chef, must have inher-

ited her cooking gene from her father who's a chef with a great reputation; her fillet of prawn with spices is splendid and her Gers duck breast is faithful to the traditions of southwest France. Her husband, Frédéric, loves his wine and manages his cellar with passion and intelligence. A selection of decent wines served by the glass or carafe – Côte de Brouilly or Coteaux-de-l'Ardèche du Domaine du Colombier – and the wine list proper offers real delights. Try the Comas de Robert Michel, the Côteaux d'Aix-les-Baux-de-Provence Clos Milan, or a superb Saumur Champigny Clos Rougeard; prices are very reasonable. À la carte a meal costs 250–300F. Excellent cuisine, excellent cellar and friendly, efficient service.

10th arrondissement
🏨 HÔTEL VICQ D'AZIR

21 rue Vicq d'Azir; M° Colonel-Fabien.
☎ 01.42.08.06.70 📠 01.42.08.06.80
📧 vicqazir@club.internet.fr

Service 8am–10pm. A simple hotel with seventy low-priced rooms which look out onto a charming interior courtyard planted with bushes. You have to pay when you check in and you're given a key. Rooms 120–195F depending on size and facilities. At these prices you can't expect luxury but it's good value.

🏨 HÔTEL MODERNE DU TEMPLE

3 rue d'Aix; M° République or Goncourt.
☎ 01.42.08.09.04 📠 01.42.41.72.17
📧 vlado.fundarek@libertysurf.fr

This is a genuine, pleasant surprise and you'll find it between the lock on the Saint-Martin canal and the steep section of the faubourg du Temple. It's in a narrow, busy street, where the crumbling façades are tinted with bright colours that have faded in the sun like the houses in some southern fishing port. The place is owned by a friendly Slovak who, after rather modest beginnings in 1989, now has 43 rooms with facilities that compare favourably with the nearby youth hostel. Some rooms have been improved. Doubles 180F with washing facilities up to 250F with shower/wc. Direct dial telephone in each room. Breakfast 25F, and there's a bar.

🏨 NORD-EST HÔTEL**

12 rue des Petits-Hôtels; M° Gare-du-Nord or Gare-de-l'Est.
☎ 01.47.70.07.18 📠 01.42.46.73.50
📧 hotel.nord.est@wanadoo.fr
TV. Garden. Pay car park.

This hotel has a delightful provincial charm which is fitting in a street with such a name. It's actually in a little garden where you can really relax in good weather. Pleasant welcome. The place has recently been completely renovated using a good deal of oak for the sitting room, dining room and reception. Clean, functional rooms with pink-tiled bathrooms. Doubles 400–460F with shower/wc or bath. Book well in advance. There's a car park at 90F per day. 10% discount Nov–Feb, except for public holidays.

⚥ 🏠 HÔTEL GILDEN MAGENTA**

35 rue Yves-Toudic; M° République or Jacques-Bonsergent.
☎ 01.42.40.17.72 ➡ 01.42.02.59.66
📧 hotel.gilden.magenta@multi-micro.com
TV. Pay garage.

This place is a real bargain, so it's advisable to book a week in advance. It's in a quiet street between the pl. de la République and the Saint-Martin canal. Rooms 61 and 62 on the sixth floor are the most appealing, with their panelled ceilings and exposed beams. Number 3 looks out onto a pretty patio where they serve breakfast. All rooms have TV and direct dial telephone. The owners are friendly, smiling and accommodating. Doubles with shower/wc 410F, 465F for three people or 550F for four. Best to book a week in advance. Breakfast 40F. They have a lock-up garage at 65F a day. 10% discount.

⚥ 🏠 NEW HÔTEL**

40 rue Saint-Quentin; M° Gare-de-l'Est.
☎ 01.48.78.04.83 ➡ 01.40.82.91.22
📧 info@newhotelparis.com
TV. Pay car park.

Areas around train stations are notoriously grim, and it would be wrong to pretend that this place is anything other than a cheap hotel – but it does have the advantage of being quiet. The rooms are functional, and most of them have the facilities you'd expect from a two-star – multi-channel TV, hair dryer, etc. The vaulted basement has been transformed into a cellar with three dining rooms, each decorated in medieval style with rough stone walls; here you can have a full breakfast, 30F, of *croissants*, *brioches*, cornflakes, orange juice and so on. If you turn right when you leave the hotel, you'll come to a terrace at the end of a short street that gives a rare view over Paris. Double rooms 435F with shower, 545F with bath. Free breakfast.

🍴 RESTAURANT DE BOURGOGNE-CHEZ

MAURICE

26 rue des Vinaigriers; M° Jacques-Bonsergent or République.
☎ 01.46.07.07.91
Closed Sat evening, Sun, public holidays, the last week in July and the first fortnight in Aug.

Service at lunchtime and in the evening until 11pm. This little neighbourhood restaurant, not far from the *Hôtel du Nord* and the romantic Saint-Martin canal with its Venetian bridge, hasn't changed for years; it's got a provincial feel and serves local people. Very inexpensive set menus at 55F and 60F for lunch or 60F and 65F for dinner. The house wine is reasonably priced.

⚥ 🍴 RESTAURANT BAALBECK

16 rue de Mazagran; M° Bonne-Nouvelle.
☎ 01.47.70.70.02
Closed Sun.

Service 11.30am–3pm and 7.30pm–midnight, 1am Fri and Sat. A couple of pointers on how to have a successful time here: one, you absolutely positively *must* book, and two, come in the evening. This Lebanese restaurant has some of the best Middle Eastern cooking in Paris. If there are four of you, have the special *mezze* and you'll get eighteen different dishes. Or there's a 59F lunch menu or a 99F dinner menu. Things really begin to hot up after 10pm, when the belly dancers make their appearance – they're the genuine article and could rival those in Istanbul or Cairo. Don't forget the tip for the dancers. Free coffee and Lebanese pastry.

🍴 LA VIGNE SAINT-LAURENT

2 rue Saint-Laurent; M° Gare-de-l'Est.
☎ 01.42.05.98.20
Closed Sat, Sun, three weeks in Aug, and one week at the end of the year.

Service noon–2.30pm and 7–10pm. If you've got a train to catch or you're seeing someone off, don't just dive into the nearest brasserie, take a couple of minutes to find this pleasant wine bar instead. Inside there's a long, narrow room with a beautiful spiral staircase. At the far end, the pair of polite chaps who run the place prepare delicious little dishes with great care; rabbit with house *tapenade*, calf's head *sauce ravigote*, etc. Menus from 75F or a meal will cost 130–150F. If you want just a snack, try the plate of *charcuterie* or perfectly ripened cheeses like the Saint-Marcellin matured in the Lyonnais style or Arôme de Lyon matured in Marc with a salad and a glass of wine. By the way they have a good selection – Viognier d'Ardèche, Côteaux-du-Lyonnais, Mondeuse-de-Savoie or Saint-Joseph.

⚐ |O| RESTAURANT FLO

7 cour des Petites-Écuries; M° Château-d'Eau.
☎ 01.47.70.13.59
Closed Christmas.

Open daily till 1.30am. This is *the* place to go for *choucroute*. Herr Floederer's old brasserie dates from 1886 and is as sparkling as a new pin. Sarah Bernhardt used to have her meals delivered from here when she was at the Renaissance – others followed suit. Superb 1900 decor with stained-glass windows separating the rooms, richly decorated ceilings, leather banquettes, brass hat-stands and period lighting. Platters of shellfish and seafood, sensational *choucroute*, escalope of *foie gras* with apples and grapes, and *sole meunière*. Given the wonderful surroundings, prices are reasonable; menus 138F or 189F or around 240F *à la carte*. The place is always buzzing with locals and lots of tourists. Free apéritif.

|O| RESTAURANT JULIEN

16 rue du Faubourg-Saint-Denis; M° Strasbourg-Saint-Denis.
☎ 01.47.70.12.06
Closed Christmas.

Service noon–3pm and 7pm–1.30am. Another restaurant – one of the oldest in Paris – given a makeover by the talented Monsieur Bücher. The same old ingredients continue to work their magic: the dazzling Art Nouveau interior, service that's as fast as it is efficient and a reasonable bill. Skilfully prepared specialities include salad of duck *foie gras* and morels, warm *foie gras* with lentils, goose *cassoulet*, grilled sole and sole *meunière*. Customers are mainly showbiz types. You'll spend 180–220F *à la carte*; lunch menu at 138F and a *menu brasserie* at 189F.

|O| CHEZ MICHEL

10 rue de Belzunce; M° Gare-du-Nord.
☎ 01.44.53.06.20
Closed Sun, Mon, Christmas and 1–15 Aug.

Service noon–2pm and 7pm–midnight. The countless people who choose to stay in one of the many hotels near the station will be delighted to know that they can now eat in the area as well as sleep there. Thierry Breton trained at two luxury hotels, the *Ritz* and the *Crillon*; his skill, and the fact that his restaurant resembles a little farm, draw attention to this place, which is in a part of the city where greasy spoons abound. He offers a set menu for 180F, and what you get for your money is sheer magic –

first-rate cooking and first-rate ingredients. The *terrine* of *andouille* with peppercorns and shortbread biscuits is out of this world, while the guinea-fowl ravioli with a sauce of ceps and crushed walnuts is so incredibly good that you'll have to loosen your belt to make room for the *kig ha farz* of pig cheeks and pork fat, not to mention the desserts which include warm *kouign aman* (traditional Breton yeast cake) – it's worth every calorie. There's also a *table d'hôte* menu at 130F.

11th arrondissement
⚐ ⬫ HÔTEL MONDIA**

22 rue du Grand-Prieuré; M° République or Oberkampf.
☎ 01.47.00.93.44 ☞ 01.43.38.66.14
@ info@hotel-mondia.com
TV.

This well-run hotel in a quiet little street is a good base if you're doing the sights on foot – Belleville, Ménilmontant and the Bastille are not too far away and the Marais-Les Halles area is very close. The comfortable rooms have shower or bath, hair drier, safe and direct telephone – some even have marble fireplaces and the three on the top floor have sloping ceilings. Doubles 340–390F. Prices negotiable if you're planning a long stay. Breakfast 35F. 10% discount out of season.

⬫ HÔTEL BEAUSÉJOUR**

71 av. Parmentier; M° Parmentier or Oberkampf.
☎ 01.47.00.38.16 ☞ 01.43.55.47.89
TV. Pay car park.

A hotel with 31 rooms on six floors – with a lift. They all have bath or shower, double-glazing, TV and direct telephone, and cost 380–480F – some rooms sleep three or four. The little bar in the reception area is open 24 hours a day, and they offer room service.

⚐ ⬫ HÔTEL NOTRE-DAME**

51 rue de Malte; M° République or Oberkampf.
☎ 01.47.00.78.76 ☞ 01.43.55.32.31
@ hotelnotredame@wanadoo.fr
TV.

A well-run two-star hotel in a good location. Everything is grey, down to the business cards and the cat. The tastefully redecorated rooms have direct-dial phones, clock-radios and colour TV. The ones on the street are brighter. Singles with basin or shower 200–320F, doubles with shower/wc or bath 380F. Breakfast (38F) is served until 9.30am. They don't take cheques and it's best to book. 10% discount.

𝄞 ≜ HÔTEL DAVAL**

21 rue Daval; M° Bastille.
☎ 01.47.00.51.23 ➡ 01.40.21.80.26
e hoteldaval@wanadoo.fr
TV.

A nice two-star hotel in the heart of the lively Bastille neighbourhood, near the bars of rue de Lappe and rue de la Roquette. It has modern decor and facilities – TV, double glazing and mini-safe. Doubles with shower 415F. Free breakfast, usually 50F and better than the average.

≜ |●| HÔTEL BEAUMARCHAIS***

3 rue Oberkampf; M°Filles du Calvaire.
☎ 01.53.36.86.86 e hotel.beaumarchais@libertysurf.fr
TV.

An ideal situation in a lively street full of bars, close to the Bastille, the République and the Marais. It's a modern hotel, decorated in bright sunshine colours. Double rooms 490F, all with en-suite shower or bathrooms.

|●| NEW NIOULLAVILLE

32 rue de l'Orillon; M° Belleville.
☎ 01.40.21.96.18

Service until 1am. This immense restaurant, which can seat five hundred, has a whole new look. The kitchen has been renovated throughout, the ceiling and lighting in the dining rooms have been renewed, and they've put in air conditioning. The dim sum trolley does its rounds from table to table until 11pm. Other delights include Cantonese or Szechuan specialities like duck smoked over jasmine – then there are tofu dishes, noodles, soups, roasts and Cambodian dishes, not to mention the ones from Vietnam and Thailand. The lacquered duck is memorable, its skin is served with rice pancakes, while the meat is stir-fried with vegetables or noodles and clear soup; it's the kind of thing that's good to share. There are a dozen or so high chairs available for the kids. Great atmosphere. Several set menus 38–78F or 150F à la carte. The one at 38F, described as being "for women", consists of plain salad, an assortment of dim sum and boiled rice.

𝄞|●| LES CINQ POINTS CARDINAUX

14 rue Jean-Macé; M° Faidherbe-Chaligny or Charonne.
☎ 01.43.71.47.22
Closed Sat, Sun, and Aug.

Service until 10pm. You can eat here, as Madame says "with no worries and without being ripped off, whoever you are". Old tools belonging to local artisans of yesteryear hang from the ceiling and the benches are crammed at lunchtime. The atmosphere is relaxed and the cooking unpretentious: herring fillets, sausage and lentils, avocado with melted Roquefort cheese or duck *confit*. Lunch menu 62F then 65F and 106F. Free coffee.

|●| LOULOU DE BASTILLE

11 rue Richard-Lenoir; M° Voltaire.
☎ 01.40.09.03.31

The cooking may not rival what you get in a top-notch establishment but it's uncomplicated and unadorned. Best of all is the atmosphere created by the two young owners – it's like a genuine *restaurant du quartier*. A lunch menu at 69F or à la carte about 150F. There are lots of local regulars who drop in to finish their evening off here.

|●| SUDS

55 rue de Charonne; M° Ledru-Rollin.
☎ 01.43.14.06.36
Closed Sat lunchtime.

"*Suds*" refers to the south of all sorts of different countries, so your choice of food will take you on a culinary tour of France, Spain, Portugal and South America. If you have a wandering spirit and a fascination with unusual cooking, you will enjoy this place. The owner has a farm in the Gers where they raise ducks: try the *foie gras* with sweet potato. The signature dish is a banana mousse with white and dark chocolate – just a dream. Weekday lunch menu 75F, 160F à la carte.

|●| CEFALÙ

43 av. Philippe-Auge; M° Nation.
☎ 01.43.71.29.34
Closed Sat lunchtime, Sun, and a fortnight in Aug.

Service noon–1.30pm and 7.30–10pm. Mr Cala comes from Mussomeli, famous for its impregnable fortress. His skill does his homeland proud, and his Sicilian restaurant is one of the best ambassadors for regional Italian cooking in Paris: Sicilian *antipasti*, spaghetti *à la Sicilienne* (with garlic, tomato, aubergine, capers, anchovies, olives and basil), tagliatelli with four flavours (cream, gorgonzola, smoked bacon, mint and basil). Try the *cannolo*, a Sicilian dessert traditionally served on Sunday, something like a brandy snap filled with fresh ricotta, candied fruit and chocolate; it's usually accompanied by a glass of Marsala. Pretty decor in the naïf style and very, very clean. Menus start at 89F with a *menu dégustation* at 180F.

弐|●| RESTAURANT L'AMI PIERRE

5 rue de la Main-d'Or; M° Ledru-Rollin.
☎ 01.47.00.17.35
Closed Sun, Mon and 14 July–15 Aug.

Service until 2am. Marie-Jo's been in the Bastille area for more than thirty years, the last ten of them in this restaurant. She's very easy-going and treats her clients like friends. The atmosphere can get a bit heated some evenings if the rugby fans tangle with the regulars – arty types like film-makers and designers. You can have a glass or two of Pouilly, Cahors or Quincy, and fill up on a plate of *charcuterie*. Dish of the day might be beef *bourguignon*, *pot-au-feu*, oxtail or creamed salt cod. Portions are substantial, which will help prepare you for the long night ahead – things can keep going around here until dawn. 100F *à la carte*. Free *digestif*.

|●| LE VILLARET

13 rue Ternaux; M° Parmentier.
☎ 01.43.57.75.56
Closed Sat lunchtime, Sun, a week in May, a week in Aug, and a week for Christmas and New Year.

Service until 1am. Joël, who used to run the dining room under the previous owner, and the young chef Olivier Gaslain are in charge. Olivier goes to Rungis market for the produce and devises his menus according to what he selects. The prices haven't changed much over the years and the wide-ranging wine list includes great vintages at reasonable rates. Starters include dishes such as scallops and thyme *en papillote* (baked in a paper sack), *fricassée* of ceps with garlic and flat-leaf parsley, or great fat stalks of green asparagus; for a main course try medallions of monkfish with a sauce made from small crabs, calves' liver in Banyuls vinegar, a terrific sirloin steak with shallots, or a *gratin* of Jerusalem artichokes. One of the best restaurants in Paris for dinner. *Formules* at 120F (2 courses) or 150F (3 courses), or 200F for a meal *à la carte*.

12th arrondissement
≙ HÔTEL DES TROIS GARES**

1 rue Jules-César; M° Gare-de-Lyon.
☎ 01.43.43.01.70 ➡ 01.43.41.36.58
TV.

The façade is smart and the reception is decidedly modern as are the functional, minimally decorated rooms. Doubles with basin 240F, 360–380F with shower/wc or bath, TV and direct dial telephone. This is a well-located two-star in a quiet street between the Gare de Lyon, the Gare d'Austerlitz and Bastille-Plaisance. Very nice owner.

≙ HÔTEL MARCEAU**

13 rue Jules-César; M° Gare-de-Lyon or Bastille.
☎ 01.43.43.11.65 ➡ 01.43.41.67.70
Closed 20 July–20 Aug. **TV**. **Pay car park in hotel**.

It's anyone's guess as to whether General Marceau really slept here. He led the troops in 1793 who put down the insurrections in the Vendée against the revolutionary government. But the fact that the hotel and the general share a name gave the proprietor a good excuse to display in reception a page in the general's handwriting that he bought at auction. The rooms aren't bad, and some are quite well decorated, with co-ordinating fabric, wall lights and wood panelling. Those overlooking the courtyard don't have a great view. Some have Swedish showers. Doubles 400F with shower or bath.

≙ NOUVEL HÔTEL**

24 av. Bel Air; M° Nation.
☎ 01.43.43.01.81 ➡ 01.43.44.64.13
e nouvelhotel@wanadoo.fr
TV. **Garden**.

A stone's throw from pl. de la Nation where you can hook up with any number of buses, the metro or the RER. The street couldn't be quieter and all the rooms have double glazing. It's as clean as a whistle, and most rooms overlook a delightful garden where you can sit and relax in the shade of a tree. Laura Ashley-style decor, new flooring in all the common areas and excellent facilities. Doubles with shower 410F, with bath, 450F. There are connecting rooms for families sleeping three or four. Breakfast 43F.

弐 ≙ HÔTEL SAPHIR**

35 rue de Cîteaux; M° Faidherbe-Chaligny, Reuilly-Diderot or Gare de Lyon.
☎ 01.43.07.77.28 ➡ 01.43.46.67.45
e saphir.hotel@wanadoo.fr
TV.

Well-equipped, modern rooms decorated in a riot of colour – pink, blue, green or beige, take your pick. Doubles with shower/wc or bath, TV, mini-bar and direct telephone 470F. Rooms that sleep three, 565F, or four, 615F. Breakfast, 35F, is served in a wonderful vaulted cellar. 10% discount and free breakfast.

|●| AU PAYS DE VANNES

34 [bis] rue de Wattignies; M° Michel-Bizot.
☎ 01.43.07.87.42
Closed evenings, Sun and Aug.

A good, local eatery with a large Breton flag on the wall; the proprietors are proud of their roots in the Armor in Brittany. The 60F menu includes wine and offers a choice of main courses: sautéed pork with salsify, roast guinea-fowl with shredded leeks, chicken with rice, or breast of veal stuffed with braised celery hearts. Starters are along the lines of egg mayonnaise, and dessert, like home-made *crème caramel*, is also included. You'll get a good simple traditional French meal that's the best value for money in the *arrondissement*. There are other set menus at 75F and 120F. Whole families turn up on Saturday lunchtime for a feast of oysters brought direct from Brittany. Friendly reception and service.

|●| CAPPADOCE

12 rue de Capri; M° Michel-Bizot or Daumesnil.
☎ 01.43.46.17.20
Closed Sat lunchtime, Sun and last three weeks in Aug.

Service noon–2.30pm and 7–11.30pm. Turkish hospitality, kindness and unobtrusiveness are the hallmarks of this establishment and, together with fairly elaborate cooking, they have helped spread its reputation far beyond the neighbourhood. The cheese roll and the aubergine caviar are exquisite, while the *pides* (Turkish pizzas), the grilled chicken with aubergines and yoghurt, the stuffed leg of lamb with spices and the kebabs will give your tastebuds a real treat. It's obvious why the restaurant is a success and it's best to book for dinner. Three well-planned set menus at 76F, 85F and 130F. Don't turn down the home-made desserts – the pumpkin in syrup is extraordinary, a bit like quince paste.

⅍ |●| LES ZYGOMATES

7 rue de Capri; M° Michel-Bizot or Daumesnil.
☎ 01.40.19.93.04 ➡ 01.44.73.46.63
Closed Sat lunchtime, Sun, and Aug.

Service noon–2pm and 7.30–10.30pm. Virtually nothing has changed here since the turn of the 20th century – the *trompe l'œil* decor, varnished wood, marble and hunting scenes were all here when this was a butcher's shop. Best of all, the prices are reasonable – there's a set lunch menu for 80F, and an incredibly good one at 140F with quite elaborate dishes: cannelloni with goat's cheese and lambs lettuce, pig's tail stuffed with morels, cheese and dessert. Considering the quality of the cooking and what they charge, this is more like a philanthropic undertaking than a restaurant, so it's best to book. Free coffee.

|●| RESTAURANT SQUARE TROUSSEAU

1 rue Antoine-Vollon; M° Ledru-Rollin.
☎ 01.43.43.06.00
Closed ten days in Feb and three weeks in Aug.

Service until 11.30pm. Two layers of curtains – lace and red velvet – shield you from prying eyes here. In style and atmosphere the restaurant resembles an elegant 1900s bistro; there's a superb antique zinc bar, a mosaic tiled floor, red artificial leather banquettes, and mouldings on the ceiling. It's a refined place where you can relax. The day's specials are chalked up on big blackboards along with the 115F set lunch menu: starter, main course, dessert and coffee. Dinner menu 135F. Good home cooking. The *à la carte* dishes change according to the season and what's fresh at the market. The presentation is pretty and the wine list has been well researched. Customers are elegant but relaxed. Reckon on 200F *à la carte*. A very good restaurant with lots of regulars. Terrace in summer.

|●| RESTAURANT À LA BICHE AU BOIS

45 av. Ledru-Rollin; M° Gare-de-Lyon or Ledru-Rollin.
☎ 01.43.43.34.38
Closed Sat, Sun, mid-July to mid-Aug, and Christmas week.

Service at lunchtime and in the evening until 10pm. If you like the old style of restaurant that does traditional dishes then this is the place for you. Even the decor, which is delightfully old-fashioned, is appealing, with prints and paintings on the walls, a Louis XIV style clock, artificial flowers, and artificial leather banquettes. This little restaurant gives good value on its 118F and 130F set menus. Dishes such as *foie gras* with salad, fillet of beef with a cep sauce, fillet of salmon with wild mushrooms, *coq au vin*, or game in season — haunch of venison, say, or venison *terrine* — pheasant casserole, or wild duck with fruits of the forest. Home-made pastries and reasonably priced wines. An excellent restaurant, where you can eat well for under 150F.

13th arrondissement
⅍ 🛏 HÔTEL STHRAU*

1 rue Sthrau; M° Nationale, Tolbiac, Porte-d'Ivry or Bibliotèque.
☎ 01.45.83.20.35 ➡ 01.44.24.91.21
TV.

A modest but clean little hotel five minutes from the Bibliothèque François Mitterrand – it's ideal if you're on a tight budget. Doubles with basin170F, 215F with shower or 270F with shower/wc – there are some quiet ones overlooking the courtyard. Free breakfast Jan–Feb.

♠ HÔTEL TOLBIAC

122 rue Tolbiac; M° Tolbiac or Place-d'Italie.
☎ 01.44.24.25.54 ➡ 01.45.85.43.47
TV.

An enormous hotel with 47 rooms just five minutes from pl. d'Italie. Doubles with basin 175F, 220F with shower/wc; all have TV. 21F for breakfast with *croissants*, *brioches*, cereals and coffee or tea, served in a bright, new breakfast room. Pleasant reception, and the rooms are clean. Rue de Tolbiac is quite noisy but a number of the rooms are fitted with double glazing.

♣ ♠ RÉSIDENCE LES GOBELINS**

9 rue des Gobelins; M° Gobelins; buses 27, 47, 83, 91.
☎ 01.47.07.26.90 ➡ 01.43.31.44.05
✉ goblins@cybercable.fr
TV. Garden.

The rue des Gobelins follows the same route it did in the Middle Ages. The château that belonged to Blanche de Castile, wife of Louis VIII and mother of Louis IX, is just round the corner. The hotel is peaceful and great value for money. Lovely double rooms 435–455F with bath and they all have satellite TV. Breakfast 38F. You can sit outside in the little garden on warm evenings. 10% discount after two nights.

♣ ♠ HÔTEL LA MANUFACTURE**

8 rue Philippe-de-Champaigne; M° Place d'Italie.
☎ 01.43.35.45.25 ➡ 01.43.35.45.40
✉ lamanufact@aol.com
TV.

A very new, elegant hotel, just next to the local town hall and the old Gobelins tapestry workshop. It's managed by a trio of women who run things like clockwork. The decor is in browns and beiges with splashes of red. The entrance hall has a wooden floor and a corner bar where you can have a drink next to the open fire in winter. Rooms are not huge; 450–640F for a double with shower/wc or bath. 10% discount and free buffet breakfast.

♣ ♠ RÉSIDENCE HÔTELIÈRE LE VERT GALANT***

41–43 rue Croulebarbe; M° Gobelins or Corvisart.
☎ 01.44.08.83.50 ➡ 01.44.08.83.69
Disabled access. Garden. TV. Pay car park.

A corner of the Basque country in the middle of the 13th arrondissement, just across from

the Gobelins gardens. It's next to the *Auberge Etchegorry* restaurant (reviewed below) belonging to the same owners. It's set back from the road with a garden and lawn so it's quiet and has a certain charm. There are ten superb rooms, doubles 450F with shower or bath, and some studios, 500F, with a corner kitchen, fridge and direct-dial telephone. Free breakfast (on day one), served in a room overlooking the garden.

●❙ RESTAURANT BIDA SAIGON

44 av. d'Ivry; M° Porte-d'Ivry.
☎ 01.45.84.04.85

Service 10am–10pm. A huge Vietnamese canteen at the top of an escalator at the entrance to the Terrasse des Olympiades and Paris-Store. Friendly welcome. The menu consists of the standard twenty or so savoury dishes. The soups, *phô* and Saigon soup, come in large or small bowls, and helpings are generous. The spring rolls are crisp and the steamed rice cake is . . . steamed rice cake. Pork spare ribs, grilled chicken with lemongrass, and rice with pork and stuffed crab. For dessert, try the white beans with sticky rice or the lotus seeds with seaweed and *longans* – weird, but not unpleasant. A meal costs 45–55F. It's not licensed except for beer, but naturally they also have fizzy drinks, fresh fruit juice and tea.

●❙ PARIS-VIETNAM

98 av. de Choisy; M° Tolbiac.
☎ 01.44.23.73.97
Closed Sept.

Service 8am–11pm. The outside of this place is rather grotty but inside there are two decent-sized, welcoming dining rooms and you're greeted with smiles. Put the (lengthy) menu to one side and order the Vietnamese fondue. Plates with slivers of beef, squid, and chicken dusted with coriander are set down, another with king prawns, a third with noodles and tofu. Chopsticks are placed by your plate. Picking your chosen morsel up with the chopsticks, plunge it into a pot of steaming broth until it's cooked as you wish. When there's nothing left, crack an egg into the broth and drink it down. All delicious. Menus 55–85F, dishes around 45F each.

●❙ VIRGULE

9 rue Véronèse; M° Place d'Italie.
☎ 01.43.37.01.14
Closed Sun and Mon lunchtimes and Christmas.

Service until 10.30pm. Mr Dao is a young chef, originally from Cambodia, and his restaurant has a lot to recommend it. The 58F lunch menu shows how Mr Dao has fused the flavours of the Orient and the cuisine of the West. It changes regularly but may well list cream of cauliflower soup followed by lacquered roast pork or *choucroute* with ham hock and a fruit tart or cream caramel for dessert. The other menus, 64–145F, feature some astonishing dishes – sautéed scallops with oyster sauce with celeriac in a mustard mayonnaise, pan-fried scallops with chicken broth and perfumed mushrooms, and *cassoulet* like you find in the southwest of France. It's engaging food served very generously and, on top of all that, Monsieur and Mme Dao are charming.

🏂|◉| À LA BOUILLABAISSE, CHEZ KERYADO

32 rue Regnault; M° Bibliotèque or Porte-d'Ivry.
☎ 01.45.83.87.58
Closed Sun, Mon evening and last fortnight in Aug.

Service noon–2.30pm and 7.30–10.30pm. Located on the fringes of the 13th *arrondissement* and Bercy, this is a wonderful fish restaurant run by a young couple. Bistro-type decor. The *bouillabaisse*, 140F, is excellent, and Lord knows how hard it is to find a decent *bouillabaisse* in Paris. Dishes are cooked to order and prices are not too bad considering – weekday lunch menu 59F, or 150F *à la carte*. If you don't want fish, there's a choice of grilled dishes and the meat is very tender. Free house apéritif.

|◉| L'AVANT GOÛT

26 rue Bobillot; M° Place-d'Italie.
☎ 01.53.80.24.00 ℮ rufine@club.internet.fr
Closed Sun lunchtime, Mon and the first three weeks of Aug.

Christophe Baugront was the chef at *La Courtille* up in Belleville for ages, then he decided to open a place of his own, and set up in Touraine before returning to the Butte-aux-Cailles to open a restaurant here. You can tell that he has spent a lot of thought and energy on this place, from the dishes on the menus to the vintages on the wine list. He offers a triumphant combination of peasant food and elegant preparation. Try the fantastic pork *pot-au-feu*. There's a lunch *formule* at 63F which includes dish of the day, salad, a glass of wine and coffee; you might get roast free-range chicken with macaroni cheese or leg of lamb with flageolet beans. Another option is the *menu-carte* at 150F, which lists a choice of four starters, five main dishes and four desserts. Push the boat out with the

190F *menu dégustation*. The wine list includes a sparkling Vouvray from Champalou, a Touraine Sauvignon du Père Aug and a red Beaume-de-Venise domaine de la Fermette-Saint-Martin. *À la carte,* a complete meal will cost about 150F.

|◉| NOUVEAU VILLAGE TAOTAO

159 bd. Vincent-Auriol; M° Nationale.
☎ 01.45.86.40.08.

Service until 11.30pm. This vast establishment – practically a village on its own – has dining rooms on two floors. Menus – 70F and 75F or 156F for two – as long as a novel, with evocatively named Chinese and Thai dishes, and pictures of the dishes next to the text. as Starters include spicy duck soup with bamboo shoots and coconut milk or stuffed Thai crab, while among the main dishes are spicy chicken with honey, sautéed prawns, Peking duck, frogs' legs with dumplings or scallop fritters. There's a long dessert menu as well. Sometimes the waiters flambée something, dramatically, in the midst of the diners.

🏂|◉| ETCHEGORRY

41 rue Croulebarbel; M° Place-d'Italie or Corvisart.
☎ 01.44.08.83.51
Closed Sun, Mon and three weeks in Aug.

On the façade of this building you can still make out the old inscription "Cabaret de Madame Grégoire". Some two hundred years ago, Victor Hugo, Châteaubriand and various poets wined and dined here. The old charm still remains; the decor is rustic and warm and the windows look onto the square. The local clientele enjoy Basque and Béarnaise cuisine: *piperade*, stuffed squid and cod with red peppers, duck and pork *confit* with garlic potatoes, sheep's cheeses and delicious desserts. Everything is cooked fresh on the premises, even the bread. A lunch *formule* at 100F which includes wine, and others 155–180F. Free coffee.

🏂|◉| LE BISTRO DU VIADUC

12 rue Tolbiac; M° Meteor and Biblioteque.
☎ 01.45.83.74.66
Closed evenings, Sun, public holidays and three weeks in Aug.

This bistro used to be a workman's café known as *Chez Mammy*. The blue collars have been replaced by white collars and the cooking has become more elaborate. The 103F menu, including drink, is good value, while the one at 165F lists some noble dishes – langoustines with poached egg and tarragon vinegar, or sole *meunière*. Good classical cooking. Free apéritif.

|●| L'ANACRÉON

53 bd. Saint-Marcel; M° Les Gobelins.
☎ 01.43.31.71.18
Closed Sun, Mon and Aug.

Service noon–2.30pm and 7.30–11pm. Situated in a rather dreary street, this restaurant offers gourmet food. The chef trained at *Prunier* and *La Tour d'Argent*. Try the splendid 190F *menu-carte*, which lists well-devised, well-prepared dishes using country produce: rabbit *terrine* with *foie gras* and vegetables, *fricassée* of snails with tomatoes, veal kidneys in a mustard sauce, cod with chicory, *parfait* with egg custard. Extremely good service and a wine list that matches the cooking. Set lunch menu 120F.

⅔ |●| CHEZ PAUL

22 rue de la Butte-aux-Cailles; M° Place-d'Italie or Corvisart.
☎ 01.45.89.22.11
Closed Sun evening, Christmas–New Year.

Service at lunchtime and in the evening until midnight. New-style bistro that has been successfully grafted onto the Butte. Pleasant, low-key setting decorated with fleshy-leaved plants. Excellent bistro cooking and friendly welcome. The proprietor has a sly sense of humour and has had some fun ideas – including digging up apéritifs from the Neanderthal age. The menu is quite extensive, offering dishes such as oxtail *terrine*, *coq au vin*, stewed beef in a wine sauce, roast suckling pig with sage, and home-made braised tripe. Wine is reasonably priced – you can have a jug of Lyonnais at 60F or a Château de la Bonnelière at 95F. Desserts are delicious. There are always one or two dishes of the day on the slate. Expect to pay 150–200F. Free house apéritif.

14th arrondissement
☎ HÔTEL DU PARC MONTSOURIS**

4 rue du Parc-Montsouris; M° Porte-d'Orléans; RER Cité-Universitaire.
☎ 01.45.89.09.72 ➟ 01.45.80.92.72
e hotel-parc-montsouris@wanadoo.fr
TV.

Great location if you like an early run – Parc Montsouris is nearby. Everyone can appreciate the peace and quiet of this delightful street. The hotel has been renovated and is resolutely modern and functional. Doubles from 350F with shower/wc – other rooms with bath, some sleeping three and others sleeping four. Breakfast 30F.

⅔ ☎ HÔTEL DES BAINS*

33 rue Delambre; M° Vavin or Edgar-Quinet.
☎ 01.43.20.85.27 ➟ 01.42.79.82.78
TV. Pay car park nearby.

This one-star hotel has real character and an elegantly restrained façade. The rooms have been tastefully decorated and even the bedspreads and lampshades for the wall lights have been carefully chosen to complement the colour scheme. Doubles with shower/wc and TV with eleven channels, 420F. One particularly nice thing about the hotel is that it brings luxury within everyone's reach. Suites in a separate building in the courtyard cost 560F for a couple with a child and 675F with two children – ideal, since they have two bedrooms and a bathroom. They're also very quiet and comfortable. It's really not expensive considering what you get. 10% discount mid-July to end Aug and weekends.

⅔ ☎ HÔTEL DELAMBRE***

35 rue Delambre; M° Edgar-Quinet or Vavin.
☎ 01.43.20.66.31 ➟ 01.45.38.91.76
Disabled access. TV.

This hotel has changed a good deal since André Breton, the founder of surrealism, stayed here. There have been big renovation works. Doubles 490F with shower/wc or bath in low season and 550F in high season. Buffet breakfast 48F. Very reasonable prices for a hotel in this category. In summer you can sleep with the window open without being disturbed by noise. 10% discount Feb and Aug.

⅔ ☎ HÔTEL DAGUERRE**

94 rue Daguerre; M° Gaité.
☎ 01.43.22.43.54 ➟ 01.43.20.66.84
e hotel.daguerre.paris.14@gofornet.com
Disabled access. TV.

If you have a taste for luxury but not the means, then this is for you! It may be only a two-star but it's treated itself to a facelift of the kind usually reserved for the great hotels of the world. The marble, the statue, the *trompe l'oeil* painting, the co-ordinated fabrics, the exposed beams in the dining room, and the romantic patio all combine to create the illusion of a much more glamorous era. And all the rooms have been done, too; everything is clean and shiny, and they've got a safe, mini-bar, and cable TV. There are even one or two rooms specially equipped for the disabled. The warm friendly welcome comes at no extra charge. And talking of money, the rates really are incredibly reasonable considering the level of service. Doubles with shower or bath 500–650F or some suites sleeping four. Buffet breakfast or breakfast served in your room at 48F. 10% discount Dec–Jan and July–Aug.

|●| AUX PRODUITS DU SUD-OUEST

21–23 rue d'Odessa; M° Edgar-Quinet.
☎ 01.43.20.34.07
Closed Sun, Mon, public holidays and a month end-July/Aug.

Service noon–2.30pm and 7–10pm, 11pm Fri and Sat. This restaurant-cum-shop sells home-made preserves and conserves from the southwest and the prices are unbeatable. It's not gourmet cooking, but decent country fare like *charcuterie*, *terrine* of rabbit or wild boar, *cassoulet* with goose *confit*, pigeon in a red wine sauce, duck *confit* served with baked sliced potatoes and truffles, and a terrific apple and Armagnac tart. The lunch *formule* at 35F includes dish of the day, a glass of wine and a coffee. Around 130F *à la carte*.

|●| RESTAURANT AU RENDEZ-VOUS DES CAMIONNEURS

34 rue des Plantes; M° Alésia.
☎ 01.45.40.43.36
Closed Sat, Sun, public holidays, and Aug.

Service at lunchtime and in the evening until 9.30pm. There aren't many tables, so you need to book. Despite the name, there are very, very few cloth caps or overalls to be seen – lunchtime customers tend to be people who work in the area, and there are a few artists in the evening. Set menu 76F, day's special around 50F – rib of beef with marrowbone or house *canard confit*. Rarely more than 120F *à la carte* and children's portions are half price. It would be hard to do better.

|●| RESTAURANT LE CHÂTEAU POIVRE

145 rue du Château; M° Pernety.
☎ 01.43.22.03.68
Closed Sun, 8–20 Aug, mid-Aug and Christmas week.

Service until 11pm. A quiet neighbourhood restaurant that's popular with the locals but the planned refurbishment could affect the prices quoted. Dishes like *andouillette*, *cassoulet*, tripe, Hungarian goulash and steak *tartare* are prepared by the proprietor. The service is extremely pleasant. Excellent menu 89F, *à la carte* about 180F.

⅍ |●| LE RESTAURANT BLEU

46 rue Didot; M° Plaisance or Pernety.
☎ 01.45.43.70.56

Closed Sun, Mon public holidays and Aug.

A quiet old bistro in a working-class district of Paris. It's worth a visit for its wonderfully old-fashioned decor alone. It's been taken over by Christian Simon, an excellent chef who used to work at *Bertie's*. The 165F *menu-carte* changes with the seasons and is full of good ingredients from the Aveyron. Depending on what month it is, you'll be served game, mushrooms or soft fruit. The basket of Rouergue *cochonailles*, a selection of delicacies made from pork, is a very good place to start, as is the *terrine* of mushrooms, leeks and *foie gras*. Then move on to the *truffade*, a sort of Auvergnat pancake made with cheese and potatoes, stuffed tripe, or grilled fresh scallops with a parsley sauce. For dessert, try the mascarpone with raspberries and lime, vanilla rice pudding with apricots and *feuillantine* with bitter chocolate. Christian Simon doesn't ignore the other regions of France – or indeed other parts of the world – if there's something particularly good available at Rungis. On Friday, fish is the big star on the menu, as both a starter and main course. Interesting lunchtime set menu 98F. Free house apéritif.

|●| RESTAURANT LE VIN DES RUES

21 rue Boulard; M° Denfert-Rochereau or Mouton-Duvernet.
☎ 01.43.22.19.78
Closed Sun, Mon, a week in Feb, and Aug.

Service from 1pm; Wed, Fri and Sat evenings from 9pm with reservations only; bar 10am–8pm. The premises used to house an old Auvergne café and the new proprietor hasn't touched the decor. Now the excellent cooking is principally in the Lyons style, with two or three very substantial dishes that change every day. For starters there's marinated sprats with red peppers or lamb's foot *ravigotte*; main dishes include things like calves' liver *à l'étouffée* or braised sweetbreads. Regional cheeses and home-made desserts. Wines and the day's menu are chalked up on a blackboard which also tells you what saint's day it is, and gives you a thought for the day. You will take your time over your meal here whether you like it or not. The only thing that makes the proprietor lose his temper is when somebody asks if they could be in and out in twenty minutes. 100F for lunch or 130F for dinner *à la carte*.

|●| RESTAURANT LA COUPOLE

102 bd. du Montparnasse; M° Vavin.

☎ 01.43.20.14.20

Breakfast served 8.30–10.30am, brasserie noon–1am. This aircraft hangar of a restaurant is the largest in France in terms of square feet, and can accommodate 450 diners. Artists have been coming here since it opened in 1927 – people like Chagall, Man Ray, and Josephine Baker, complete with lion cub. The bar has been restored to its original location in the middle of the room and the pillars repainted the green they used to be. The dance hall has been preserved, too, and you can trip the light fantastic at one of the early afternoon tea dances or in the evening at weekends. Set lunch menus 102F (not served Sun), then up to 138F, or from 180F *à la carte*. It looks better than it used to, but it's also more expensive.

|●| BISTROT MONTSOURIS

27 av. Reille; M° Porte d'Orléans; RER Cité-Universitaire.
☎ 01.45.89.17.05
Closed Sun, Mon and three weeks in Aug.

This was once a coaching inn called the *Relais de l'Argouët*. The name changed and so did the style, but the high quality remains the same. The decor is more country inn than city bistro, and the cuisine less trendy than traditional, prepared with attentive care. The dishes change regularly with the seasons and what is available at the market: seafood *cassoulet*, free-range chicken with shrimps, *andouillette* braised in Mâcon with *dauphinoise* potatoes, pan-fried cod with parsley potatoes, or authentic veal *blanquette*. The 108F *formule* includes a main course with a choice of starter or dessert; *à la carte* a meal will cost 160–200F.

|●| L'AMUSE-BOUCHE

186 rue du Château; M° Mouton-Duvernet.
☎ 01.43.35.31.61
Closed Sun and Mon lunchtime, and Aug. **Disabled access.**

Service noon–2pm and 7.30–10.30pm. Gilles Lambert, formerly of *Cagna* and the *Miraville*, is a consummate artist in the kitchen. If you want proof, try his *menu-carte* at 168F. Starters might be langoustine ravioli with tarragon, or *mousseline* of pike with saffron mussels, while for a main course you can choose between dishes such as peppered tuna steak with a honey and soya sauce, cod risotto, or *croustillant* of rabbit. The dessert of *croustillant* with lime mousse is to die for. Lunch menu 145F, another at 178F or about the same *à la carte*.

|●| LA RÉGALADE

49 av. Jean-Moulin; M° Alésia or Porte-d'Orléans.
☎ 01.45.45.68.58
Closed Sat lunchtime, Sun, Mon, Aug and Christmas–New Year.

Service noon to 2pm and evenings until midnight. This is a gem of a place, with a decor that's both low-key and refined and a chef who is quite simply inspired. Monsieur Camdeborde, the man in question, puts as much enthusiasm into his recipes and his choice of vegetables as he does into chatting to his customers. Service is efficient and unobtrusive. The *menu-carte* at 195F, with wine extra, offers as a starter a basket of *charcutailles* supplied by Camdeborde senior, who owns a *charcuterie* in Pau. Try the silky smooth pumpkin soup, the delicate kidneys with pickled shallots, the roast pigeon with bacon, the scallops with shredded celery, the braised cheek of suckling pig with caramelised cabbage, the fillet of sea bass with fennel – the list of wonderful things just goes on and on. The wine list is astonishing, too, and all at giveaway prices. So far, success hasn't changed this very special restaurant. It's essential to book at least five days ahead.

15th arrondissement
♨ 🏠 HÔTEL AMIRAL

90 rue de l'Amiral-Roussin; M° Vaugirard.
☎ 01.48.28.53.89 ➡ 01.45.33.26.94
TV.

This small, discreet hotel is at the back of the 15th arrondissement's town hall but has much to recommend it: punctillious welcome, decent rooms and honest prices. Numbers 7, 25, 26 and 31 each has a balcony and a very Parisian view of the Eiffel Tower in the distance. Doubles with basin 255F, with shower/wc 390F or with bath 420F. 10% discount 15 July–31 Aug.

♨ 🏠 PACIFIC HÔTEL**

11 rue Fondary; M° Émile-Zola or Dupleix.
☎ 01.45.75.20.49 ➡ 01.45.77.70.73
e acifichotel@wanadoo.fr
TV.

A quiet, charming hotel and the receptionist has a ready smile. The entrance hall is brightly decorated and the rooms are simple, entirely functional and double-glazed. They are in all the different wings of the building – one of which has been completely restored. It's clean and well managed. Doubles with basin 260F, with shower 319F, with shower/wc or bath 375F. 10% discount Fri–Sun.

☎ LE NAINVILLE HÔTEL

53 rue de l'Église; M° Félix-Faure or Charles-Michels.
☎ 01.45.57.35.80 ☛ 01.45.54.83.00
Closed Sat 1–7pm, Sun, and 17 July–27 Aug. **TV**.

An unobtrusive little hotel with a retro café on the ground floor, a genial proprietor, and bedrooms that are old-fashioned in the nicest possible way. It's incredible to find a place like this in a neighbourhood where they're throwing up blocks of flats everywhere. Clean and cheerful inside. Go for a room, like 10, 20, 30 and 40, which has a view over Square Violet. Doubles 310F with shower, 375F with shower/wc. A very good hotel for the 15th *arrondissement*.

☎ DUPLEIX HÔTEL**

4 rue de Lourmel; M° Dupleix.
☎ 01.45.79.30.12 ☛ 01.40.59.84.90
TV.

When you come from the calm of the 7th *arrondissement* and the Eiffel Tower the hustle and bustle of this very busy, shopping street makes a huge contrast. Ask for a room on the top floor. Number 19 is blue throughout and number 18 is red. Doubles all have shower/wc and double glazing and cost 320F. Breakfast, 35F, can be served in your room if you wish. Clean, family-owned and handy if you're stuck for accommodation. Mini-bar and satellite TV.

⅔ ☎ HÔTEL LE FONDARY**

30 rue Fondary; M° Émile-Zola.
☎ 01.45.75.14.75 ☛ 01.45.75.84.42
TV. **Garden**.

Good location in a quiet street in one of the liveliest parts of the 15th *arrondissement*. Modern decor. Pretty patio with a well completely filled with plants. Prices are quite high but not excessively so for a two-star – doubles with direct phone, cable TV and mini-bar cost 400F with shower, 435F with bath. Breakfast, 38F, is served in a tiny courtyard in summer. Quiet at night. 10% discount July–Aug.

⅔ ☎ HÔTEL CARLADEZ CAMBRONNE**

3 pl. du Général-Beuret; M° Vaugirard.
☎ 01.47.34.07.12 ☛ 01.40.65.95.68
TV.

Carladez is a region in Auvergne where the original owners came from. It's a charming hotel in a little square with a pretty fountain in a busy shopping area. All the rooms are soundproofed and come with mini-bar, satellite TV, hair drier and direct-dial telephone.

Doubles with shower 420F, with bath 450F. Breakfast costs 37F. 10% discount during the school holidays and at weekends when there aren't trade fairs at the exhibition centre.

⅔ ☎ HÔTEL DE L'AVRE**

21 rue de l'Avre; M° La Motte-Picquet-Grenelle.
☎ 01.45.75.31.03 ☛ 01.45.75.63.26
Disabled access. **Garden**. **TV**.

The hotel is located in a quiet narrow street. In summer the amiable owner sets out deckchairs in the pleasant garden where breakfast is served. The prices are fairly reasonable for Paris, with doubles 420F with shower/wc or 440–470F with bath. The renovated rooms are decorated in blue or yellow; numbers 22 and 28 overlook the garden. It's difficult to park in the street but there are two car parks just minutes away. 10% discount at weekends.

●| RESTAURANT AUX ARTISTES

63 rue Falguière; M° Falguière or Pasteur.
☎ 01.43.22.05.39
Closed Sat evening, Sun and three weeks in Aug.

Service until 12.30am. This restaurant is really something. The price of the set menu has hardly increased in twelve years and the atmosphere and the decor haven't changed much either; the coloured frescoes are still everywhere. The customers are a mixed bunch – students, teenagers from the housing estates, professionals, a few artists (Modigliani came here in his time), and older people – who all enjoy their meals in a noisy, lively atmosphere. You'll have to wait for a table on weekend evenings, but the bar serves a mean Kir. Two-course lunch *formule* 58F, and a three-course menu 80F. *Hors d'œuvres* are substantial and they can prepare you a steak in many different ways. The surprise of the house is the dessert poetically entitled "young girl's dream".

⅔ ●| BANANI

148 rue de la Croix-Nivert; M° Félix-Faure.
☎ 01.48.28.73.92
Closed Sun lunchtime.

Open until 11pm. The dining room here is so large that it's divided into two by a low wall and has tables hidden away in bays. There is a wall painting of a Hindu temple, warm wood panelling and low lighting. The Indian dishes come from different corners of the continent and the spicing is skilfully judged: fresh tender tandoori dishes, mutton korma, butter chicken, prawn biryani, and so on. The naan breads come fresh and hot, and the lassi comes salty or sweet. Portions are generous and the smiling service is somewhat slow. Lunchtime *formule* at 59F, menu 99F, and a substantial evening set dinner at 159F. Free house apéritif and 10% discount on take-away meals.

|●| RESTAURANT CHEZ FOONG

32 rue de Frémicourt; M° Cambronne.
☎ 01.45.67.36.99
Closed Sun and 15–31 Aug.

Perfumed, spicy Malaysian cuisine, skilfully prepared by Mr Foong, a Malay Chinese from Kuala Lumpur – he's a master in the art of using spices. The meal might begin with a salad of shrimp and fresh mango in a subtle, delicate sauce or with beef curry using the restaurant's own blend of spices, continuing with mixed satay, the house speciality, or fish wrapped in a banana leaf and grilled, and end with sweet potato balls or a Malaysian pancake stuffed with coconut. About 100F *à la carte*. Set menus 60F, 85F and 90F.

⅍ |●| LE BISTROT D'ANDRÉ

232 rue Saint-Charles; M° Balard.
☎ 01.45.57.89.14
Closed Sun, 1 May, Christmas and 1 Jan.

This is one of the few survivors from the (André) Citroën era. It's been updated to cater for today's tastes by the people from the *Perraudin* (in the 5th *arrondissement*) and given a shot in the arm. "Pre-war" prices for appealing family dishes such as leg of lamb with *gratin dauphinois*, beef *bourguignon*, *andouillette* in a mustard sauce and *canard confit*. It's great to have discovered such a decent restaurant in an area where there's little else to see. Set menu 65F at lunchtime, except Sunday. It's *à la carte* in the evening, when you should reckon on a bit more than 130F for starter, main course, dessert and drinks. There's a children's menu at 43F with a surprise. Wine-lovers take note: there's a tasting of wines from very small vineyards every month. Free apéritif.

⅍ |●| RESTAURANT TY BREIZ

52 bd. de Vaugirard; M° Montparnasse-Bienvenue or Pasteur.
☎ and 📠 01.43.20.83.72
Closed Sun and Aug.

Service noon–3pm and 7–10.45pm. A little off the track in comparison to other restaurants which fill with theatre audiences dining after the show; that's probably why this pancake place has retained its pleasant family atmosphere. In 2000, it was voted "Best Crêperie in Paris" by a national paper. Very good *galettes*,

especially the *savoyarde* with cheese and potato. Even the simple double butter one is great, as long as you're not worried about cholesterol. The dessert *galettes* cost about 40F – try the chocolate and orange, *martiquinaise* or *Normande*. Excellent value for money – you'll pay about 70F for a meal – and the place is as clean as a whistle. Free Kir.

⅍ |●| LE GARIBALDI

58 bd. Garibaldi; M° Sèvres-Lecourbe.
☎ 01.45.67.15.61
Closed evenings, Sat, Sun, and Aug.

This used to be a working-man's caff though nowadays white-collar workers are much more in evidence. It's almost compulsory to have the *museau vinaigrette* or *crudités* as a starter. The 72F set menu features sautéed lamb with flageolet beans, beef *bourguignon* or *blanquette de veau*. Service is friendly and there are still traces of the old decor, such as the beautiful counter at the door and a 1900 ceiling in an otherwise plain dining room. Every weekend the proprietress goes back to her native Pas-de-Calais for vegetables, salt pork, smoked sausage and other delicacies to cook for her customers. Free coffee.

|●| RESTAURANT L'AGAPE

281 rue Lecourbe; M° Convention or Boucicaut.
☎ 01.45.58.19.29
Closed Sat lunchtime, Sun and 5–26 Aug.

Service until 10.30pm. More interesting outside than in – the dining room is very plain and lacks any originality. But you can still eat well and diners squeeze onto the outdated imitation leather benches. You can scratch this off the list of restaurants for a romantic dinner for two. They scrawl the menu up on the blackboard outside; *osso bucco* with ginger, lamb with baby vegetables, spare ribs with honey and mushy peas, cassoulet made with broad beans, and *confit* of duck. Menus 95F and 120F.

|●| LE BÉLISAIRE

2 rue Marmontel; M° Convention.
☎ 01.48.28.62.24
Closed Sat, Sun and Aug.

The restaurant is named after a 5th-century Byzantine general who vanquished the Vandals and the Ostrogoths; he was an inspiration to Marmontel after whom the street is named. There is a splendid old zinc bar, a pretty country dresser in the corner, homely furnishings and ornaments, and a few Art Deco touches. Very French cuisine, with a modern twist – the sauces, in particular, are something special. All the standards, from snails in garlic to chicken casseroles and green salads with good dressing. There's a menu at 98F or you will pay 160F *à la carte*.

|●| RESTAURANT LA PETITE AUBERGE

13 rue du Hameau; M° Porte-de-Versailles.
☎ 01.45.32.75.71
Closed Sun, Sat in summer, public holidays, 1–26 Aug and Christmas–New Year.

Service until 10pm. This is the "HQ" of supporters of the local rugby team and consequently sees lots of emotional highs and lows. If you prefer *après-ski* to *après-match*, avoid this place like the plague on match days. Good plain cooking, nonetheless, with daily specials 53–85F: salt pork *à la potée*, sautéed lamb with haricot beans, *blanquette de veau*, pork spare ribs with lentils, roast chicken with herbs, and steak with proper chips.The bill will come to 110–145F.

|●| RESTAURANT LE CLOS MORILLONS

50 rue des Morillons; M° Porte-de-Vanves.
☎ 01.48.28.04.37
Closed Sat and Mon lunchtimes, and Mon.

Service till 11pm. Chef Philippe Delacourcelle has spent a long time in Asia, where he developed a taste for spices and sweet and sour combinations. East meets West here in a perfectly orchestrated and sometimes brilliant performance. The 175F set menu might feature warm calf's brains with cabbage and roast peanut *vinaigrette*, *parmentier* of smoked duck in China tea, and baked pear with dried fruit and Marsala. Sheer bliss. The *menu-dégustation* at 295F is equally inspiring. The wines are chosen by a knowledgeable *sommelier*; Vouvray by Champalou and an Anjou by Richou, both of them excellent winemakers. Colonial decor.

16th arrondissement
🎍 🛏 HÔTEL VILLA D'AUTEUIL**

28 rue Poussin; M° Porte-d'Auteuil.
☎ 01.42.88.97.69 ➡ 01.45.20.74.70
e villaaut@aol.com
TV.

Its location in the classy part of the 16th *arrondissement* says everything you need to know. In an area where hotels try to collect stars, this two-star has spotless rooms, each with private bathroom, and all at very reasonable prices. The staff are particularly attentive and can't do enough for you.

There's efficient double glazing in the rooms overlooking the road, 360F, but the ones at the back, 370F, have a prettier view over the greenery of the courtyard. When you book, confirm you're using this guide; the prices quoted are a special deal.

🎍 🛏 HÔTEL LE HAMEAU DE PASSY**

48 rue de Passy; M° Passy, La Muette or RER Muette-Boulainvilliers.
☎ 01.42.88.47.55 ➡ 01.42.30.83.72
e hameau.passy@wanadoo.fr
Disabled access. **TV**.

The entrance is between a handbag shop and a baldness treatment centre. You come out into a small courtyard full of flowers and ringing with birdsong – a far cry from the luxury designer shops nearby. The hotel is run by an energetic team. Doubles with shower/wc or bath, 500–560F. Free breakfast and 10% discount Jan–Feb and 15 July–31 Aug.

🎍 🛏 AU PALAIS DE CHAILLOT**

35 av. Raymond-Poincaré; M° Trocadéro.
☎ 01.53.70.09.09 ➡ 01.53.70.09.08
TV.

This is a delightful 28-room hotel which is fresh and clean-looking. The rooms are decorated in yellow with curtains in red or blue. All have satellite TV, phone and hair drier. Doubles with shower/wc 580F, with bath 650F. Buffet breakfast is served in a bright little room on the ground floor or they'll bring it to your room. A two-star hotel that easily deserves three – book well ahead. 5% discount, or 15% 15 July–31 Aug.

|●| LES CHAUFFEURS

8 chaussée de la Muette; M° La Muette.
☎ 01.42.88.50.05
Closed 1 May, a fortnight in Aug, Christmas Day and New Year's Day.

Service at lunchtime and dinner to 10pm. A classic restaurant if ever there was one. The menus are roneo-typed with purple ink and list all those great traditional dishes: vegetable soup, herring fillets, leeks *vinaigrette*, *andouillette*, veal *blanquette*, roast chicken and puréed potatoes, and desserts like *crème caramel*. There are a few echoes of Alsace – where the owners come from – so pickled turnips or *choucroute* turn up on the menu at regular intervals. Menu 68F, 95F on Sunday.

🎍|●| RESTAURANT LA FERME DES GOURMETS

82 rue Boileau; M° Exelmans.

☎ 01.46.47.87.19
Closed Sun.

Service noon–2pm and 7–10pm. The deli, which sells produce from the southwest, is on one side of the street and this restaurant is opposite. The produce you buy in one ends up, beautifully prepared, on your plate in the other: try *cassoulet* with duck *confit* or chicken with rice. Menus start from 82F and expect to spend about 130F *à la carte*. Terrace in the summer. It's advisable to book. Free coffee.

|●| RESTAURANT LE PETIT RÉTRO

5 rue Mesnil; M° Victor-Hugo.
☎ 01.44.05.06.05
Closed Sat lunchtime, Sun and Aug.

Service until 11pm. Superb decor with a retro theme – coloured tiles and ceiling-light fixtures dating from around the turn of the 20th century. The bistro-style cooking is simple and tasty: poached eggs with chorizo cream, *terrine* of oxtail with shallots, crunchy black pudding with apples, rack of lamb with herbs from Provence. For dessert try the *brioche* covered in honey, roasted in the oven and served with gingerbread ice cream at 44F, or the *nougat glacé* with dried fruit served with vanilla-flavoured *crème brûlée*. No set menus but *formules* at 98F and 125F, or 185–200F *à la carte*. The wine list isn't very long but it offers several *crus* by the glass, Morgon, Touraine and Côtes du Rhône.

🎄|●| RESTAURANT DU MUSÉE DU VIN-CAVEAU DES ÉCHANSONS

5–7 square Charles-Dickens-rue des Eaux; M° Passy.
☎ 01.45.25.63.26
Closed Mon and the Christmas/New Year holidays.

Service noon–3pm. The restaurant is in the wine museum and the dining room is in a 14th-century vaulted cellar – they were dug out of the Chaillot clay by the monks who used to cultivate the vines. Many of the dishes use wine in their preparation: *coq au vin*, say, or perch fillets in Muscadet sauce. Menus, 99F, 139F and 169F, change regularly You sit down at a hefty wooden table and a waiter proffers you a glass of wine which you are invited to identify. The wine list is twelve pages long and lists 200–250 vintages, from a Château d'Yquem 1908 at 13,000F a bottle, rare *grand crus* from Bordeaux, Burgundy, Alsace, Jura and wines from lesser regions in France. Every day there is a selection of fifteen wines sold by the glass. Free coffee.

17th arrondissement
🎄🏠 HÔTEL CHAMPERRET-HELIOPOLIS**

13 rue d'Heliopolis; M° Porte de Champerret.
☎ 01.47.64.92.56 ➡ 01.47.64.50.44
Disabled access. TV.

A very quiet hotel with pretty wooden balconies. Most rooms overlook a delightful patio where you can have breakfast when the weather's nice. The place is spotless, and you'll get a very friendly welcome. Rooms have everything you might need – TV, telephone, hair drier. Doubles with bath or shower 495–540F, breakfast 45F. 10% discount.

🏠 HÔTEL PALMA**

46 rue Brunel; M° Porte-Maillot or Argentine.
☎ 01.45.74.74.51 ➡ 01.45.74.40.90
TV.

This hotel is a stone's throw from the convention centre and the Air France terminal. It has an attractive frontage and foyer, and offers a degree of comfort at reasonable prices. Service is polite and efficient. The rooms, single 520F, double 560F, triple 630F, have been redecorated in Provençal style, to create a warm, bright feel. Breakfast can be served in your room. The sixth-floor rooms are extremely popular, so it's best to book.

🏠 HÔTEL PRONY**

103 [bis] av. de Villiers; M° Pereire.
☎ 01.42.27.55.55 ➡ 01.43.80.06.97
TV.

Although this hotel is part of a chain, it's still got character; doubles 560–790F with bath or shower. No charge for children under twelve sharing with parents. Facilities include room service, satellite TV and double glazing. Room number 32 is huge, and ideal for families with one or two kids. An excellent hotel close to pl. Pereire and five minutes from Porte Maillot. Breakfast served until midday.

🎄|●| RESTAURANT SHAH JAHAN

4 rue Gauthey; M° Brochant.
☎ 01.42.63.44.06

Pakistani restaurant decked out with draperies, glittering paste mirrors and soft background music. *À la carte*, you could have shish kebab, lamb rogan josh or kara lamb (a very spicy curry). Also the classics; chicken or lamb tikka. Accompany your main course with cheese naan and basmati rice with saffron. Delicious lassi flavoured with cumin and cardamom. Service couldn't be nicer. Lunchtime set menus 49F and 79F, others 115 and 130F including drink.

|●| L'ÉTOILE VERTE

13 rue Brey; M° Charles-de-Gaulle-Étoile.
☎ 01.43.80.69.34

Service until 11pm. The restaurant took its name not from the square, which is just five minutes away, but from the green star that Esperanto speakers use as their emblem; the society used to hold its meetings on the first floor. It was redecorated to celebrate its half century – it was founded in 1947 – and still looks fresh and pleasant without losing the patina of age. Set menus 74F (lunchtime only), 110F and 155F. Among the star dishes, you shouldn't miss the scallops *à l'Antillaise*; other specialities are calves' sweetbreads and duck *confit*.

|●| RESTAURANT LE VERRE BOUTEILLE

85 av. des Ternes; M° Porte-Maillot.
☎ 01.45.74.01.02
Closed Christmas Eve and Christmas Day.

Service noon–3pm and 7pm–5am. Excellent wine bar, open until dawn. Night owls can fill up on robust main dishes like steak *tartare* made with chopped – not minced – steak, or very, very large salads. There's one called *nain jaune*, "the yellow dwarf" (also the name of an old card game), which includes Comté cheese, chicken, raisins and curry sauce . Wines come from around the world and about thirty are available by the glass. Things can get lively on weekends by the time 4am strikes. Menus 110F and 170F and a lunchtime menu at 90F. There's a second *Verre Bouteille* at 5 bd. Gouvion-Saint Cy in the 17th *arrondissement* – but that one closes at midnight (☎ 01.47.39.99).

|●| L'IMPATIENT

14 passage Geoffroy-Didelot; M° Villiers.
☎ 01.43.87.28.10
Closed Sat lunchtime, Sun, Mon evening, and a fortnight in Aug.

This restaurant is appropriately named; some evenings the wait for a table is so long you have to be really patient. The menus, 102F at lunchtime, 120F and 162F in the evening, are excellent value for money: squid *escabèche* salad, stew of ox cheek with baby vegetables, endive *sabayon* with cocoa sorbet. Chef Paul Blouet also prepares delicate vegetarian options like *papillotte* of lightly spiced fresh sweetcorn. He really pushes

himself to produce unusual dishes that the customers appreciate. The passage is between 92 bd. de Batignolles and 117 rue des Dames.

⏃ |●| GRAINDORGE

15 rue de l'Arc-de-Triomphe; M° Charles-de-Gaulle-Étoile.
☎ 01.47.54.00.28
Closed Sat lunchtime and Sun.

Service until 11pm. Bernard Broux is an inspired chef who uses his expertise to the greater glory of his native Flanders, re-interpreting his culinary heritage. The 188F set menu gives you a wide choice, offering things like deer *terrine* with *foie gras*, shellfish with lambs lettuce *vinaigrette*, pan-fried calves' tongue, vegetable *pot-au-feu* or roast cod with juniper. For dessert go for jam *baba* in Gueuze chantilly or dark cocolate *fondant* with coffee bean sauce. If you go *à la carte*, you can still enjoy a taste of Flanders – try the *potjevfleisch*, smoked eel in aspic with creamed lamb and white beer, *carbonade* of ox cheek, and red cabbage *à la flamande*. All the produce is fresh, and dishes are cooked to order. Forget the wine list and stick to beer – any one of the many varieties goes perfectly with the food. There's a lunchtime menu at 168F and others 138–260F. Free *digestif*.

⏃ |●| LE BISTROT DU XVIIÈ

108 av. de Villiers; M° Pereire.
☎ 01.47.63.32.77

Lunch noon–2.30pm and dinner 7–11pm. If business is booming here it's all down to the 179F *formule* that gives you the lot – apéritif, starter, main course, dessert, wine and coffee. Seventh heaven for people who think life's complicated enough without having to make decisions about what to eat. The menus change with the seasons, but you will always find a selection of old favourites: duck breast with *foie gras*, rump steak with *hollandaise* sauce, roast rack of lamb with thyme, grilled sea bass with chicory, and, for dessert, a chocolate mousse or rum *baba*. Free glass of champagne with dessert.

18th arrondissement
⏃ 🏠 HÔTEL BOUQUET DE MONTMARTRE**

1 rue Durantin; M° Abbesses.
☎ 01.46.06.87.54 📠 01.46.06.09.09

A conventional hotel that has been taken over by a young couple and refurbished throughout. The rooms are decent, if small, and they are all different. Doubles, 400F, all have their own wc and shower or bath, and doubleglazing. Excellent location, good reception and a wonderful view over Paris from room 43. 10% discount.

🏃 🛏 HÔTEL PRIMA LEPIC**

29 rue Lepic; M° Blanche.
☎ 01.46.06.44.64 ➡ 01.46.06.66.11
TV.

This is the ideal place to start off for a stroll through the neighbourhood. The impasse Marie-Blanche is close by, and definitely worth a look. The reception is bright and fresh and there's a *trompe l'oeil* of an English garden which they've followed through by choosing garden furniture. Rooms, which look like something out of *Homes and Gardens*, are unfussy and well maintained. Doubles 410F with shower or bath. Avoid room numbers 14 and 17, which are very dark. Reduced rate for breakfast, usually 40F.

🏃 🛏 TIM HÔTEL**

11 rue Ravignan (pl. Émile-Goudeau); M° Abbesses or Blanche.
☎ 01.42.55.74.79 ➡ 01.42.55.71.01
📧 Montmartre@timhotel.fr
TV.

This beautiful hotel, which has been recently renovated, is located in a wonderfully romantic square. Doubles with shower or bath 680–780F. Each floor is dedicated to a painter: going from the ground floor to the fifth you have a choice of Toulouse-Lautrec, Utrillo, Dali, Picasso, Renoir and Matisse. All rooms have direct-dial phone and TV. Rooms on the fourth floor and above have a view of the square or the city. Number 412 is especially nice. Great place for a romantic weekend as long as you're not short of a bob or two. 10% discount Nov–Feb and July–Aug.

🍽 RESTAURANT SONIA

8 rue Letort; M° Jules-Joffrin.
☎ 01.42.57.23.17
Closed Sun lunchtime.

Service noon–2.30pm and 7.30–11.30pm. A small Indian restaurant with a pink and purple dining room seating only 25 people, so it's often full. Friendly reception. *Formules* 49F and 79F or a 99F menu. Everything is delicately spiced, beautifully presented and cooked to perfection, from the naan to the chicken Madras and vindaloo, not to mention the lamb korma and the aubergine bhartha.

🏃🍽 LE RENDEZ-VOUS DES CHAUFFEURS

11 rue des Portes-Blanches; M° Marcadet-Poissoniers.
☎ 01.42.64.04.17
Closed Wed, and Thurs in Aug.

This old place has a long history. When Jeannot took it over he had been living inthe States for twenty years. There's a diploma on the wall from Seattle which he was awarded by *Wine Spectator* magazine. Jeannot was wise enough to change things as little as possible; the old wood counter and mirrors are still there, the tightly packed tables are covered by glazed cotton checked tablecloths and the banquettes are imitation leather – he's even kept the brownish paint so typical of old restaurants. The menu at 65F includes wine; it's served at lunchtime and in the evening up to 8.30pm. You might start with celeriac *rémoulade* or egg mayonnaise, follow it with rabbit *forestière* with noodles or lamb with flageolets, and finish with *crème caramel* or pear tart. For 68F you can't beat it. À *la carte*, there's Trouville *sole meunière* or calves' liver in raspberry vinegar; on the wine front, try the Picrate de Négoce. Efficient, friendly service. Free Kir.

🏃🍽 LA MAZURKA

3 rue André-del-Sarte; M° Château-Rouge or Anvers.
☎ 01.42.62.32.95
Closed Wed.

Reservations only at lunchtime, dinner until 11.45pm. Marek comes from Poland originally, though this corner of Montmartre has been his home for more than ten years. He produces great dishes like flambéed sausages, home-made ravioli, pork spare ribs gipsy-style, *bigos* (Poland's answer to *choucroute*), beef Strogonoff, *borscht*, and *blinis* (small pancakes) topped with tarama or smoked salmon. Set menu 115F (not served on Sat) or about 150F à *la carte*, though it all depends on your liquid intake; 25cl, half a pint or so, of vodka will cost you 130F. If Marek is in good form, he'll get out his guitar and sing. Free *digestif*.

🍽 TAKA

1 rue Véron; M° Pigalle or Abbesses.
☎ 01.42.23.74.16
Closed Sun, public holidays, and last fortnight in July.

Service 7.30–10pm. Tiny little Japanese restaurant dumped in a narrow, dingy street at the foot of the Butte with a decor straight out of a Japanese tea house. It's often absolutely crammed so it's best to book. Mr Taka is a lovely chap and attentive to your needs. Authentic Japanese cooking that is perfectly executed and the quality never wavers. You'll find all the Japanese classics – sushi, sashimi, miso soup and so on. Reckon on about 160F a head with a large Japanese beer. Set menus 120F and 150F. When it's time to tot up the bill, Mr Taka prefers an abacus to a calculator.

IOI RESTAURANT MARIE-LOUISE

52 rue Championnet; M° Simplon.
☎ 01.46.06.86.55
Closed Sun, Mon, public holidays, and three weeks in Aug.

Service noon–2pm and last orders for dinner 10.30pm. You'd do well to book – this is a terrific restaurant. When you walk through the door it's as if you've stepped into a *Vieille France* family dining room with brass and copper so highly polished you can see your face in it. The cooking is traditional and the portions are enormous: *foie gras*, hare *Royale*, *coq au vin*, veal chops *grand-mère* and *bœuf ficelle*. The quality of the cooking hasn't changed in years. Prices are reasonable: there's a three-course set menu for 130F or you'll pay about 150F *à la carte*.

🍴 IOI RESTAURANT LE MOULIN À VINS

6 rue Burq; M° Abbesses.
☎ 01.42.52.81.27
Closed lunchtimes, Sun, Mon and three weeks in Aug.

Service 6pm–2am. An authentic wine bar at the foot of the Butte, where the carefully prepared bistro dishes don't sell you short: they do parlseyed ham Morvan-style, *andouillette*, *daube de boeuf à la Provençale*, *coq au vin* and *civet de porc vigneronne*, and heavenly plates of *charcuterie* or cheese. Wine is Dany Bertin-Denis' first love. With meticulous attention he selects the best from the small wine growers in the Rhône, Touraine, Corsica and elsewhere. He has been known to belt out the odd Piaf torch song while you eat. Around 160F for a meal, with wines by the glass or the bottle. They accept only Visa cards. Free house apéritif.

19th arrondissement
🍴 🛉 HÔTEL DE CRIMÉE**

188 rue de Crimée; M° Crimée.
☎ 01.40.36.75.29 ➡ 01.40.36.29.57
e hotel.crimee@free.fr
TV.

A simple, comfortable hotel where thorough renovations have provided air conditioning and new soundproofing in the rooms, and new bathrooms. There's new carpetting everywhere. Doubles 330F with shower/wc or 360F with bath. There are also rooms for three or four. Warm welcome. 10% discount at weekends and July –Aug.

IOI AUX ARTS ET SCIENCES RÉUNIS

161 av. Jean-Jaurès; M° Ourcq.
☎ 01.42.40.53.18 ➡ 01.48.03.10.68
Closed Sat night, Christmas Day and New Year's Day.

Lunch 11.30am–2pm and dinner 7–9pm. You'll see compasses and a set square on the façade of this "canteen" for people who work at the headquarters of the carpenters' guild who maintain artisans' standards for stonemasons and carpenters. Go past the bar to an extremely attractive dining room with a parquet floor, ceiling mouldings and lots of photos of guild members on the walls. The food, like the atmosphere, is provincial in style – things like escalopes, trout and grilled meats. The 60F menu is good, the helpings are generous and wine is included. Dishes of the day 40F and 45F.

IOI LE RENDEZ-VOUS DES QUAIS

10 quai de la Seine; M° Stalingrad.
☎ 01.40.37.02.81 ➡ 01.40.37.03.18

Service to midnight. Monsieur Legendre, from the legendary *Taillevent* restaurant, supervises what goes on here. Regulars are journalists and printers from *Le Monde*, *Le Nouvel Observateur*, *Libération* and *Nova Mag*. The wide terrace, facing south, is right on the water, overlooking the pool of la Villette. When the sun shines the place heaves. Lots of wines served by the glass; they're selected with great care – by the film director Claude Chabrol! The bistro belongs to Marin Karmitz, who also owns the cinemas next door, so if you want to go to the movies, opt for the *formule menu ciné*, 149F, which gets you a dish, glass of wine, coffee and seat at the cinema. Eat *à la carte* for around 150F.

IOI AU RENDEZ-VOUS DE LA MARINE

14 quai de la Loire; M° Jaurès.
☎ 01.42.49.33.40
Closed Sun and Mon.

Service lunchtime and in the evening until 9.45pm. Reservations highly advisable – it's often full. A delightful bistro with flowers on the tables, a few nautical souvenirs scattered around and photos of film stars. It's the in place to be. Noisy, especially at lunchtime and on every other Saturday evening in the winter when a talented female singer out-Piafs Piaf. In summer, tables are set on the terrace and you'll have a view of the canal. Food is reasonably priced and helpings are generous, though the cooking is pretty ordinary. Regular dishes include the house chicken liver *terrine*, mushrooms *à la provençale*, the chef's special prawns, scallops *à la provençale* and duck breast with green peppercorns. If you want paella, you have to order it the night before. Very good apple tart flambéed with Calvados. *À la carte* only – reckon on 150F.

🍴 |●| LE PAVILLON PUEBLA

Parc des Buttes-Chaumont; M° Buttes-Chaumont.
☎ 01.42.08.92.62
Closed Sun and Mon.

It's your wedding anniversary, you've just won a mint on *Who Wants to be a Millionnaire?* and you've decided to celebrate in style? This is the place to do it. Standing in the middle of Paris' most beautiful park, it has a bourgeois setting, with peach the predominant colour and fresh flowers everywhere. The terrace is out of this world, the kind of place you dream about when the weather starts to improve. You'll be received with style, but no bowing or scraping. The cooking is first-rate and chef Christian Verges changes them regularly so they reflect the seasons: delights like squid *à la catalane*, lobster stew with Banyuls wine, *pinata* (braised fish), and oyster ravioli with a curry sauce. The desserts are quite simply to die for. It's expensive – in fact it's very expensive if you go *à la carte* and have wine too – but the 190F set menu lists, for example, anchovies in a flaky pastry case, *bouillinade* (an upmarket sort of *bouillabaisse)* and chocolate *tuiles*. It's absolutely terrific and comes complete with *canapés*, home-made rolls and so on. There's also a 260F set menu. Free apéritif.

20th arrondissement
☗ TAMARIS HÔTEL*

14 rue des Maraîchers; M° Porte-de-Vincennes or Maraîchers.
☎ 01.43.72.85.48 ➡ 01.43.56.81.75
TV.

Reservations advisable. An extremely well-run little hotel with prices of the kind you might be charged in the depths of the country. Doubles with basin 180F, with shower 219F, with shower/wc 255F, and rooms for three 220–280F. Number 16 has a double and a single bed at 190F for three.

The rooms are small and pretty and have flowered wallpaper. Breakfast is 27F. It's a bit old-fashioned, a bit "Paris the way it used to be", and altogether delightful – you'll get a warm welcome too. Best to book.

🍴 ☗ HÔTEL PYRÉNÉES GAMBETTA**

12 av. du Père-Lachaise; M° Gambetta.
☎ 01.47.97.76.57 ➡ 01.47.97.17.61
TV.

A pleasant two-star hotel in a quiet street leading to the Père-Lachaise cemetery. The rooms are perfectly adequate, with large beds pushed into alcoves, and they all have TV and mini-bar. Doubles with shower/wc 300–380F, with bath 420–480F. Breakfast is 35F, which they will serve in your room. Delightful welcome. A good hotel which is quiet and cosy and in a non-touristy neighbourhood that's worth discovering. 10% discount 10 Jan–20 Feb and 14 July–15 Aug. One breakfast free if there are two of you.

🍴 |●| RESTAURANT ARISTOTE

4 rue de la Réunion; M° Maraîchers or Buzenval.
☎ 01.43.70.42.91
Closed Sun and a fortnight in Aug.

Service at lunchtime and till 11.30pm in the evening. This restaurant may not be much to look at but you won't have to go to the cashpoint before eating here. It offers generous helpings of Greek and Turkish specialities served with a smile. Starters include *firinda pastirma* or *firinda sucuk* (Turkish meat or sausage turnovers), and there are lots of kebabs and grills. Try the *hunkar beyendi* (rack of lamb with aubergines and potatoes in a sauce), the *guvec* (veal with vegetables in sauce), or the yoghurt dishes with minced steak or lamb. There are also good fish dishes for non-carnivores. The weekday lunch menu, 52F, has a main dish that changes every day. In the evening, *à la carte* costs 90–110F. Local clientele, background music, pleasant setting and a good atmosphere. Free coffee or *digestif*.

|●| RESTAURANT CHEZ JEAN

38 rue Boyer; M° Gambetta or Ménilmontant.
☎ 01.47.97.44.58
Closed Sun, Mon and the week after 15 Aug.

Service until about 11pm. Jean says his is the best restaurant in the street and he's right – it's the *only* restaurant in the street. He used to be a journalist but then a few years ago he thought he'd rather own a restaurant. Today he is master of all he surveys from his post behind the bar. He provides home cooking in the best French tradition with a few added touches of his own. The atmosphere is that mixture of working-class and trendy so typical of the neighbourhood. It's always good fun, with an accordion player and singer at weekends. Lunch menu 66F, evening menu 98F, and 130–150F *à la carte* depending on what wine you drink.

🏃 |●| RESTAURANT PASCALINE

49 rue Pixérécourt; M° Place-des-Fêtes.
☎ 01.44.62.22.80
Closed Sun, Tues and Aug.

This restaurant has a very pretty name and you'll enjoy a delightful meal of good homemade dishes which are generously served: ham hock with lentils, complicated salads, and pastries. Pleasant dining room with a large fresco and a sunny terrace where you can just chill in the afternoon. Set menu 71F at lunchtime. Reckon on 125F in the evening and try some of the interesting wines they sell by the glass. Free house apéritif.

|●| LE CAFÉ NOIR

15 rue Saint-Blaise; M° Porte-de-Bagnolet or Alexandre-Dumas.
☎ 01.40.09.75.80
Closed lunchtimes Mon–Sat.

Service 7pm–midnight, noon to midnight on Sunday. This was a dispensary at the beginning of the 20th century, but there's little sign of its medical past – the owners collect coffee pots, hats, enamel signs and posters rather than medicine bottles.The owners serve generous portions of good food – dishes such as *millefeuille* of artichokes and *foie gras*, *terrine* of monkfish liver, veal with violet mustard and fillet of beef with *foie gras* and spiced bread. And you can indulge in a cigar afterwards – the bar sells single Havanas. A place like this is just what was needed to breathe life into the area. You'll pay about 150F for a meal.

NEUILLY-SUR-SEINE   92200 (0.5KM NW)

🏃 🏠 HÔTEL CHARLEMAGNE**

1 rue Charcot (West); M° Pont-de-Neuilly; it's 50m from the metro station.
☎ 01.46.24.27.63 ➡ 01.46.37.11.56
TV. Disabled access.

Pleasant reception at this hotel. Comfortable, modern double rooms with mini-bar, direct phone and shower or bath from 445F – these are reasonable prices for Neuilly. The street is quiet in the evening and throughout the night.

An ideal location for anyone with an appointment at La Défense the next day but who doesn't want to spend the night there. The Bois de Boulogne is not far away for a morning jog. 10% discount for a weekend stay.

|●| LE CHALET

14 rue du Commandant-Pilot (Southeast); M° les Sablons; it's near the market square.
☎ 01.46.24.03.11
Closed Sun.

A Swiss chalet for those who didn't get away on a skiing holiday last year. There are snowscape photos on the wall to help the illusion, wainscotting and skis scattered here, there and everywhere. At lunchtime there's a super-fast *formule* at 65F and a set menu at around 80F. Specialities include Canadian lobster, *raclette savoyarde* and fresh pastas. Really pleasant. It's a popular place.

🏃 |●| RESTAURANT FOC LY

79 av. Charles-de-Gaulle (Southeast); M° Sablons.
☎ 01.46.24.43.36
Closed the first fortnight in Aug. **Disabled access. Pay car park.**

You can't miss it – it's got a pagoda roof and a pair of lions guarding the entrance. This is undoubtedly one of the greatest Asian restaurants in the area, as the signatures of the great and the good in the foyer testify. A very refined and varied style of cooking. Exemplary service. Weekday lunchtime *formule* 99F, children's menu 75F and about 180F *à la carte*. Free apéritif.

🏃 |●| LES PIEDS DANS L'EAU

39 bd. du Parc; it's on the Île de Jatte.
☎ 01.47.47.64.07
Closed Sat lunchtime and Sun from Oct–April.

There's an unending feeling of times gone by in this riverside restaurant. The furniture is English-style and there are old engravings on the wall – a sort of club atmosphere. The terraces go right down to the edge of the River Seine, under the poplars, fig trees and weeping willows. The chef landed in town recently and provides touches of distant parts in his dishes that also change with the seasons; grilled fish and meats, monkfish *pot-au-feu aïoli*, trout *carpaccio*, raw marinated salmon salad with whipped cream, tuna *aumônière*, or chicken breasts with figs. Set menus from 140F or 200F *à la carte*. Free apéritif.

BOULOGNE-BILLANCOURT   92100 (1KM SW)

🏃 🏠 LE QUERCY

251 bd. Jean-Jaurès (Southeast); M° Marcel-Sembat.
☎ 01.46.21.33.46 ➡ 01.46.21.72.21
TV.

Freshly renovated and a practical place, something like a chain hotel. One of the least expensive places in Boulogne. Doubles from 190F. Reassuring welcome. Free breakfast.

|●| CAFÉ LE CENTRE

120 route de la Reine; M° Marcel-Sembat.
☎ 01.46.05.47.86
Closed Sun.

A popular, genuine old bistro that feels somewhat out of place in this suburban no-man's land; it's completely refused to move with the times. The walls are hung with old advertising plates and they're yellowed by kilos of nicotine. Food is simple and inexpensive. Dishes of the day include a tasty monkfish *à la provençale*, and they offer a complete menu at 59F.

|●| RESTAURANT PRINCE SULTAN

38–40 rue des-Peupliers; M° Porte-de-Saint-Cloud.
☎ 01.46.10.92.80
Closed Sun.

As the name might suggest, this restaurant, in the Point du Jour area, is a place for couscous rather than traditional French cuisine. They prepare nine different types of couscous from 60–110F, along with *tajines*, which are cooking pots used for preparing slowly cooked, delicately spiced meat dishes and many other Moroccan and Tunisian specialities. Very pleasant decor and genuinely friendly service. Blink and you could be there.

🕭|●| RESTAURANT LA TONNELLE DE BACCHUS

120 av. Jean-Baptiste-Clément (Northwest); M° Boulogne-Pont-de-Saint-Cloud; it's 20m from the métro.
☎ 01.46.04.43.98
Closed Sat, Sun and Christmas to 1 Jan.

The white lacquered piano in the reception sets the tone here – sometimes the *patronne* will sit down and tinkle a tune. There's also an eye-catching copper percolator. The chef prepares good specialities from Lyons like hot sausage and potatoes *vinaigrette*, but there's also *confit* of duck, *profiteroles* from les Landes or steak with shallots, which are all very tasty. Alsace is also represented by their decent *choucroute*. All in all, traditional cuisine of good quality. Menus 115F and 145F. There are some reasonably priced wines on the

list if you look carefully. You can eat on the terrace when it's warm enough. Free coffee.

🕭|●| RESTAURANT LA MARMITE

54 av. Édouard-Vaillant (East); M° Porte-de-Saint-Cloud or Marcel-Sembat; it's 300m from porte de Saint-Cloud.
☎ 01.46.08.06.12
Closed Sat evening, Sun, public holidays and Aug.

The decor is run of the mill, with square pillars and large mirror tiles. Simple brasserie-style cooking: kebabs, poached or grilled salmon, *entrecôte béarnaise*, and lots of fresh fish. Set menus from 120F. Free house apéritif.

🕭|●| CAFÉ PANCRACE

38 rue d'Aguesseau; M° Boulogne-Jean-Jaurès.
☎ and ➡ 01.46.05.01.93
Closed Sun.

You have to fight through the undergrowth and the bamboo to find the door of this place. Inside the place is bright and young, and the yellow decor takes you south to the Med or Andalusia. The tables are rickety, but what makes the atmosphere is the range of the clientele and the quality of the simple, classic cuisine – creamed smoked cod, hot sausage, *potée auvergnate* (soup crammed with meat and vegetables), or steak with shallot sauce. They write the dishes up on a big slate; in the evening there's a 130F menu with some delicious choices. Better still, they serve wines from small vineyards by the glass or in a small jug. This is, without doubt, one of Boulogne's best places to have a convivial meal. Free coffee.

🕭|●| CHEZ MICHEL

4 rue Henri-Martin; M° Porte-de-Saint-Cloud.
☎ 01.46.09.08.10
Closed Sat lunchtime. Sun, Aug and Christmas–New Year's Day.

This is where people come on a lunch break, when it's got the atmosphere of a noisy canteen. In the evening, when friends come and talk more intimately, the voice levels drop. The dishes are chalked up on a blackboard so you can choose your own menu. Try the *aumônière* of warm goat's cheese, ravioli from Royans with cream and chives, monkfish tails with green peppers, veal fillet with shallots or lamb *sauté à l'ancienne*. The prices are also reasonable, with starters and desserts at 29F and main dishes 58F, so it's not ruinous, even if you decide to have a glass of wine. Weekday menu 130F. Free house apéritif.

IVRY-SUR-SEINE   94200 (1KM SE)

|●| L'EUROPE

92 bd. Paul-Vaillant-Couturier.
☎ 01.46.72.04.64.

At lunchtime, the two dining rooms are full of din and overflowing with a cross-section of humanity. The welcome is warm and the service is efficient. They dish up excellent couscous, 50–70F, and also do good grills. On Friday they also offer *choucroute* or paella. The place really buzzes.

LEVALLOIS-PERRET   92300 (1KM NW)

🛏 HÔTEL DU GLOBE

36 rue Louis Rouquier; M° Louise Michel.
☎ 01.47.57.29.39

This is a clean and unpretentious little family hotel in a quiet street. The rooms are small and have double glazing but no wc. Doubles with washing facilities 170F, 250F with shower. Amiable welcome.

|●| LE PETIT POUCET

4 rond-point Claude-Monet (West); it's at the eastern end of the île de la Jatte.
☎ 01.47.38.61.85

Service noon–2.15pm and 7.45–11.15pm. There's been a restaurant here for almost a hundred years. At the beginning of the last century, working-class men used to bring their sweethearts here to have a good time in what was then a tavern out in the country. In the 1980s it became a really fashionable place then, ten years ago, it was transformed into a cosy place that was beautifully decorated with lots of wood panelling and a warm atmosphere. It has three lovely terraces and one is on the bank of the Seine where elegant ladies and fashionable young men come to relax as soon as the sun comes out. Good, classic French cooking with menus from 110F. Fast, efficient service. Best to book.

MONTREUIL 93100   (1KM E)

|●| LE GAILLARD

71 rue Hoche; M° Mairie-de-Montreuil.
☎ 01.48.58.17.37
Closed Sun and Mon evenings.**Garden.**

Atop the Guillands hill, right in the middle of nowhere in particular, this bourgeois residence is a haven of culinary taste and *savoir-vivre*. The starters are delicate, and the dishes have

panache: duck *parmentier* with salad, ox kidneys with puréed potato and simple but delicious desserts. Menus 150F and 220F, but *à la carte* the bill can race away with you, not least because the wines are expensive even though the list offers a fine selection. Faultless service and particularly gracious welcome. There's an appealing open fire in winter and an amazing garden/terrace that comes into its own in the summer. Worth braving the boulevard Périphérique to get here.

NANTERRE   92000 (1KM NW)

🦌 🛏 HÔTEL SAINT-JEAN

24/26/33 av. de Rueil (West); RER Nanterre-Ville.
☎ 01.47.24.19.20 ➡ 01.47.24.17.65

The hotel is a away from the main street, in a very quiet neighbourhood. No two rooms are alike, but they are all clean and more than adequate. Doubles from 150F with basin/wc and 240F with shower/wc. Friendly welcome. The place has been run by three generations of the same family for over sixty years. Free coffee.

🦌 🛏 |●| RESTAURANT LE COIN TRANQUILLE

8–10 rue du Docteur-Foucault (Centre); RER Nanterre-Ville.
☎ 01.47.21.11.80
Restaurant closed Sun, Christmas and 1 Jan.

Service noon–3pm and 7–9pm. Large dining room where they serve traditional cooking at very good prices – scallops with oyster mushrooms, fisherman's stew, for example. Or you can have mussels and chips with a glass of white wine. Menus from 65F. Best to book. Basic rooms with shower/wc or bath180–250F. Free coffee or *digestif* or 10% discount on the room rate.

SAINT-CLOUD   92210 (1KM W)

🦌 🛏 HÔTEL MAGENTA*

1 pl. Magenta (North); it's closer to the park than it is to the centre of town.
☎ 01.46.02.90.18 ➡ 01.46.02.90.17
TV.

In Saint-Cloud you can count the hotels on the fingers of one hand – this one is by far the cheapest, so it's probably best to book. Pleasant, cordial reception. Rooms are small but all have direct phone and mini-bar. Doubles with shower 245F, shower/wc at 275F. Breakfast is free when you reserve quoting this guide.

|●| LA BOÎTE À SEL

2 rue de l'Église (West).
☎ 01.47.71.11.37
Closed Sun and Mon evening.

A nice little place with a chic provincial atmosphere and a touch of suburban, bourgeois refinement which is just right for Saint-Cloud. It's bright, cosy and comfortable. This is a dream of a place for an intimate dinner for two. The cuisine is good, and though it's not complicated cooking, it's carefully prepared; grilled salmon, pork *filet mignon* in cider, duck breast in honey, *andouillette* from Troyes or fish *tartare*. Menus from 75F.

SAINT-MANDÉ   94160 (1KM E)

|●| AUX CAPUCINS

44 rue Charles-de-Gaulle; M° Saint-Mandé Tourelle.
☎ 01.43.28.23.93
Closed Sat lunchtime, Sun and Aug.

This is a serious establishment but they don't take themselves too seriously. As a consequence the chef's cooking is gifted, inventive and successful, the service is efficient without being over-formal and the setting is convivial. Just relax. Gérard Foucné served his apprenticeship with a few great chefs. His menu has a shoal of tasty fish dishes, earthy dishes from the southwest and delicate desserts – chocolate mousse *terrine* with spiced bread, *créme Eerigourdine* with crystalised fruits and apple tart with hazlenut ice cream. Menus from 128F.

|●| LE BISTROT LUCAS

8 rue Janne d'Arc; M° Saint-Mandé Tourelle
☎ 01.48.08.74.81
Closed Sun, Mon evening and Aug.

On the outskirts of Paris and within striking distance of the Vincennes woods. They treat you very well here and you can treat yourself to some really reliable bourgeois dishes in this typical bistro – wooden tables, simple decor and enlarged postcards on the walls. Central-casting dishes on the menu: lentils *rémoulade* with hot Lyons sausage, brains with black butter and pike forcemeat balls. Pudding is prune and grapefruit cocktail or cream cheese with fruit *coulis*. Menu at 130F, main courses 70F and 90F and wines around 100F a bottle. Kindly, attentive welcome.

|●| LES ROUTIERS, MAISON SOL ET RUECH

70 rue de Lagny; M° Saint-Mandé Tourelle.
☎ and ➡ 01.48.51.54.41
Closed Sun and Aug.

Two small, squashed dining rooms, full of regulars from the locality – it's essential to book for lunch and dinner. The walls are panelled with wood and hung with copper pots, hunting trophies and improving mottoes. The atmosphere is convivial and warm. The owners have been running the place successfully for a number of years. Delicous home-cooked dishes and fine meats; fresh scallops or house *foie gras*. Around 160F for a meal.

VINCENNES   94300 (2KM SE)

🎋|●| RISTORANTE ALESSANDRO

51 rue de Fontenay; M° Château-de-Vincennes; RER Vincennes; it's beside the town hall.
☎ and ➡ 01.49.57.05.30
Closed Sun and Aug.

The chef and his wife prepare a vast number of dishes with skill and care. Italian specialities like spaghetti with king prawns, tagliatelle with scallops, and *saltimbocca alla romana*, a wonderful combination of veal, Parma ham and sage which is delicate and delicious. The chef adds something extra to his dishes – a herb here, a spice there or a totally unexpected flavour that comes from whatever it was he deglazed the pan with. The antipasti – artichokes, sun-dried tomatoes, olives, pickled onions and *charcuterie* – are fantastic. And the pizzas are the real thing. Set weekday lunch menu 68F, then 139F and 199F. Reservations essential. Free house apéritif or coffee.

COURBEVOIE-LA-DÉFENSE   92400 (3KM W)

|●| PASTA, AMORE E FANTASIA

80 av. Marceau; train Saint-Lazare to Courbevoie station or RER line A, La Défense.
☎ 01.43.33.68.30
Closed Sun and Mon evening.

In these surreal suburban wastes of Alphaville you are in for a Fellini-esque shock when you walk in the door onto what looks like a Cinecittà set. Anna Magnani lolls at the door, Delon grins seductively and there's a fleeting embrace from Anita Ekberg and Marcello Mastroianni – pity they're only posters. Inside you'll be blown away by the exuberant colours of Naples and they've even hung the washing up across the room, just as they do down south. The dining room is vast but manages to feel intimate. The cuisine is equally exuberant and colourful: delicious antipasti, a huge choice of pizzas, *osso bucco à la piémontaise*, Sicilian ravioli, *piccata parmigiana* and so on. Menu at 85F or around 150F *à la carte*. Live music after 10.30pm on Friday and Saturday.

SAINT-DENIS   93200 (3.5KM N)

⚘ |●| LE RAIL D'OUESSANT-LE WAGON

14 [bis] rue Jean-Moulin (Centre); M° Porte de Paris; it's near the Baleine swimming pool.
☎ 01.48.23.23.41
Closed evenings and 14 July to end of Aug.

This is an amazing restaurant in a railway carriage. It's run by a training school for the restaurant profession so the waiters and kitchen staff apply themselves to their tasks with great concentration. You eat cheaply but well; house specialities are fish and seafood. The *formules* and menus go for 55F or 75F: pan-fried scallops with leeks, *terrine* with red onion marmalade, salmon fillet with grain mustard and excellent house desserts – try the duo of chocolate with bitter cocoa. It's worth booking. Free apéritif.

⚘ |●| LE BŒUF EST AU 20

20 rue Gabriel-Péri (Centre); M° Porte de Paris.
☎ 01.48.20.64.74
Closed Sat lunchtime, Sun and Aug.

No-frills cooking from southwestern France. The service is accommodating. There's a 65F lunch menu in the week or others at 95F and 185F. The menus consist of a good salad followed by a dish of the day cooked with fresh produce bought that morning at the market. You won't be disappointed. Specialities include *foie gras* cooked in a cloth, duck breast with oyster mushrooms and a seafood *méli-mélo*. Free apéritif.

⚘ |●| LES VERDIOTS

26 bd. Marcel-Sembat (North); M° Porte-de-Paris; it's 400m from the Stade de France.
☎ 01.42.43.24.33 ➡ 01.42.43.43.44
Closed Sun, Mon evening and Aug.

Service noon–3pm and 7–9.30pm. Patrick Perney specialises in cuisine from les Landes on the Atlantic coast in the southwest: ham from the Aldudes, duck or gizzard *confit*, pan-fried duck breast or *foie gras* with yellow peaches. Good wines that are not ruinously expensive. The service is friendly and charming, the dining room classic and clean, and the prices honest. A very substantial lunch menu at 75F, otherwise 105F

or a *menu-carte* at 195F. A good place. Free apéritif.

⚘ |●| LE MÉLODY

15 rue Gabriel-Péri (Centre); M° Porte de Paris.
☎ 01.48.20.87.73
Closed Sun, Mon, Tues evenings, and school holidays.

There's a garish blue neon sign outside this pocket-sized restaurant with ordinary decor, warm welcome and good food. The *menu-carte*, 130F, lists dishes drenched in southern sun; duo of *cabécou*, a goat's cheese, roast rabbit *provençale* and *dacquoise*. The chef uses excellent ingredients. A modest number of well-chosen wines. Free coffee.

SAINT-MAUR-DES-FOSSÉS   94100 (10KM E)

⚘ |●| LE BISTROT DE LA MER

15 rue Saint-Hilaire; it's a turning off the A4 autoroute.
☎ 01.48.83.01.11
Closed Sun evening, Mon and Aug.

Service till 11pm. The dining room is decorated in tones of blue and white, which creates just the right atmosphere for a seafood restaurant. Dishes are prepared with style. There's lots of originality and skill in the cooking and the quality is really reliable so the place has earned itself a regular following. Tues–Fri lunchtimes there's an excellent 98F menu with a salad to start, fish of the day generously served and quite delicious, a dessert, wine and coffee. The one at 155F is a feast, with an even better choice like skate, scallops and smoked salmon, and they do a blissful fish soup. They even do fried fish to take away. Free house apéritif.

⚘ |●| LE GOURMET

150 bd. du Général-Giraud (Centre).
☎ 01.48.86.86.96
Closed Sun evening, Mon, and Aug to mid-Sept.
Garden.

There are decent places to eat, there are good restaurants and then there's *Le Gourmet*. This is high-class cuisine at its best. Everything is wonderfully orchestrated; the dining room is discreet Art Deco with armfuls of flowers in big vases, and there's a wide bay window looking out onto a lovely terraced garden where you dine in the summer. The proprietor learned his profession in some of the greatest kitchens in the capital and is absolutely on top of his subject. The food is succulent, delicious and prepared with meticulous care – flavours are delicately balanced and each dish is cooked to perfection. Everything is original and amazing. Lunch menu 130F, others 160F and 230F; *à la carte* you pay for the quality and should expect a bill between 250F and 300F. They also have a take-away service. Free *digestif*.

🕍 |●| CHEZ NOUS COMME CHEZ VOUS

110 av. du Mesnil; RER Varenne-Chennevrière.
☎ 01.48.85.41.61
Closed Sun evening, Mon, 1 May, a week in Feb or March, and Aug.

There's a reassuring, old provincial feel about this place. They've got a battery of copper pots on the walls. It would take more than an earthquake to disrupt the solid traditions in the kitchen, which are rooted deeply in regional cuisine. Here you have no doubt that you're in the hands of real professionals who focus on providing quality rather than originality. Madame has been running front of house for a good quarter of a century and the service is first rate; her husband, the chef, keeps his standards high, too. Dishes of the day include ham hock with lentils, beef and carrots or *choucroute*. There's a very full menu at 200F, which includes cheese and a 1/4 litre of wine, then 220F and a children's menu at 120F which includes a drink. Free coffee.

PONTOISE   95300

🕍 |●| LE PAVÉ DE LA ROCHE

30 rue de la Roche; it's a turning off the pl. de l'Hôtel-de-Ville.
☎ 01.34.43.14.05
Closed Sun evening, Mon and three weeks in Aug.

You'll find this establishment on a bend of a road that climbs above the Oise. The decor is rustic but comfortable.Try the 72F menu, with wine included: you start by choosing from the *crudités* buffet, which has at least twenty dishes, and follow with a good main dish and home-made dessert. There are two other menus at 106F and 148F and *à la carte*: steak Rossini with *foie gras*, medallions of sole, home-made chocolate *fondant*, *crêpes Suzette*. The *patron* and *patronne* welcome you with a broad smile. Free coffee.

CERGY   95300 (5KM W)

🕍 🏠 HÔTEL ASTRÉE***

3 rue des Chênes Émeraude; from the tourist office, go straight down rue de Visors and av. Rédouane Bougara to the roundabout and turn left to Cergy-Centre.

☎ 01.34.24.94.94 ➡ 01.34.24.95.15
e astree95@club-internet.fr
Disabled access. **TV**. **Lock-up garage**.

This hotel gives you the best value for money in the Pontoise area. It's full of businessmen during the week but weekenders come to find peace and quiet in a refined, comfortable place. Double rooms with shower/wc at 600F and breakfast costs 65F. Warm welcome. 10% discount Fri and Sat nights.

PROVINS   77160

🕍 |●| LA BOUDINIÈRE DES MARAIS

17 rue Hugues-le-Grand (Centre); it's at the lower end of town.
☎ 01.60.67.64.89
Closed Tues evening, Wed, Feb school holidays and last fortnight in Aug.

Incredible but true: they make everything on the premises and they even smoke their own salmon. The locals and well-informed sales reps know that for 72F you can get a well-cooked, substantial lunch with 1/4 litre of wine included on a weekday. There are other quality menus at 98F and 149F. Traditional French cooking: rabbit *fondant* with onion marmalade, shrimps with spinach *gratiné*, grilled lamb chops with a garlic crust. The decor is neo-medieval and very heavy, but it suits the place well. Chef Prigent wants to kick fast food out of France and he's going the right way about it. Free coffee.

GURCY-LE-CHÂTEL   77250 (21KM SW)

🕍 |●| RESTAURANT LOISEAU

21 rue Ampère; take the D412 from Provins for 10km, at Jutigny turn onto the D403 for Montereau for 9km. After Donnemarie Dontilly, turn right onto the D95 towards Gurcy.
☎ 01.60.67.34.00
Closed Sun evening, Mon, first week in Jan and three weeks in Aug.

Happiness is a dream of a place in a quiet little village that has no claim to fame. The place looks banal from the outside and the dining room is totally simple. But the name makes you think of the great Loiseau, the Saulieu giant of a chef – he's no relation, but there is evidently more than one Loiseau who knows his way around a kitchen. Specialities are fish dishes – the roast zander with duck *brunoise* is mouthwateringly succulent and the blends of delicate flavours in the scallop *fricassée* with *foie gras* are a sheer delight. Set menus 70–140F and a *menu ouvrier* at 60F – at this price and quality you would come for lunch every day. Madame is kindness itself. At the weekend, it's essential to book. Free house apéritif.

RAMBOUILLET 78120

☎ HÔTEL SAINT-CHARLES**

15 rue de Groussay (Northwest); from the town hall, follow the road that runs along the park for about 1km.
☎ 01.34.83.06.34 ➡ 01.30.46.26.84
Disabled access. **TV**. **Car park**.

A functional hotel not far from the centre. Most of the rooms are fairly spacious and they're all kept scrupulously clean. Rooms 300F with shower/wc or bath.

|●| RESTAURANT LA POSTE

101 rue du Général-de-Gaulle (Centre).
☎ 01.34.83.03.01
Closed Mon, Thurs and Sun evenings and the Christmas and New Year holidays.

If you want to eat here, one of the best restaurants in town, it's best to book. The two dining rooms are extremely pretty, and service is efficient and friendly. The cooking is light and refined, with dishes like salmon escalope with sorrel, chicken *fricassée* with prawns, medallions of lamb cooked like venison and house raspberry soufflé. Set menus 120F and 160F.

|●| LE LOUVETIER

19 rue de l'Étang de la Tour; take the Chevreuse/Cernay exit from the N10 then it's on the D906.
☎ 01.34.85.61.00
Closed Sun evening and Mon.

This is a fish restaurant in a brilliant white house with azure-blue shutters – you feel as if you're by the Med; *bouillabaisse*, *bourride* or fish stew, salad of skate and pesto, scallops with dill or basil. A tasty reminder of the owner's origins – he used to run a garage in Marseilles before he became a chef in Rambouillet. There's a two-course *formule* at 150F or a *menu-carte* at 190F.

ROCHE-GUYON (LA) 95780

⅍ ☎ |●| HÔTEL-RESTAURANT LES BORDS DE SEINE**

21 rue du Docteur-Duval; it's near the tourist office.
☎ 01.39.98.32.52 ➡ 01.30.98.32.42
TV.

You can watch the Seine flowing by from this restaurant. The cheapest menu, 85,F is served at weekday lunchtime – with a

choice of starter or dessert with your main course. There's another menu at 125F or about the same *à la carte*. It's well cooked, served attractively, and you won't go hungry. The fillet of fresh cod is perfectly judged, there's a *nage* of fish, or calf's liver which might be the dish of the day. They serve the wine of the month by the glass. There's a lovely terrace with parasols for the summer which they close in and heat in winter. The hotel is well run, and although the rooms are small they have all got en-suite bathrooms and phones.Doubles with shower/wc 280–420F, 350–420F with bath – some have a river view. Relaxed, smiling service. Free coffee.

ROLLEBOISE 78270

☎ |●| LE CHÂTEAU DE LA CORNICHE

5 route de la Corniche; 10km northwest of Mantes-la-Jolie, when you get to the hilltops of Rolleboise it's at the end of a lane.
☎ 01.30.93.20.00 ➡ 01.30.42.27.44
Closed Sun evening, Mon, and a fortnight end Dec. **TV**.

In 1895 the walls of this folly were painted with frescoes of the amorous adventures of Leopold II of Belgium. It has a view over the Seine valley and it's surrounded by green countryside. The rooms have every modern comfort; prices for doubles start at 490F. The restaurant is elegant and there's a panoramic view from the terrace. Refined, yet somewhat daring gourmet cuisine. Lunch menu 160F Tuesday to Saturday. Other menus 230–360F. Not cheap but definitely worth it in the category. There are lots of country walks to do and you can visit Claude Monet's house and ravishing garden.

ROMAINVILLE 93230

⅍ |●| CHEZ GERMAIN

39 rue de Paris; M° Mairie des Lilas, then by 105 bus to the Mairie de Romainville stop.
☎ 01.48.45.00.20
Closed evenings, Sun and Aug.

You'll find this restaurant close to the Mairie; it's a big old bistro that's very well known. The owners come from the Aveyron but the photograph in the antiquated dining room is of the Alps. A dish of the day will set you back all of 39.50F, or for 49.50F you can really satisfy your appetite: horse steak *tartare*, the rarest of rare beef steak, the best lamb's tripe in the world, *blanquette* of veal *à*

l'ancienne, *bœuf bourguignon* and so on.
There's a menu at 70F. Wash it down with a
slug of Saint-Pourçain and finish off with a
good cheese. Free apéritif.

RUEIL-MALMAISON   92500

🎋 |●| LE JARDIN CLOS

17 rue Eugène-Labiche; RER Rueil-Malmaison (ligne A).
☎ 01.47.08.03.11
Closed Sun evening and Mon from June to mid-Sept;
Sun, Mon and Tues–Thurs evenings from mid-Sept to
end of May. **Garden**.

The countryside is a breath away from the
centre of the town. The exterior doesn't really
give you a clue about what you'll find inside.
There's a lovely, peaceful garden with a well,
and you can eat on the terrace which is a real
pleasure. The cooking is seriously tasty and
generously served. You'll get a good-natured
welcome, too. The 95F menu includes a self-
service buffet of *hors d'œuvres* and $1/4$ litre of
wine, which makes it good value. Other
menus 148F and 174F. *À la carte* try the
salade gourmande scattered with pine nuts,
the rack of lamb, the braised duck fillet, the
beef steak or the poached turbot. Main dishes are often accompanied by rissoled potatoes. Free Kir.

SAINT-GENEVIÈVE-DES-BOIS   91700

🏠 LA TABLE D'ANTAN

38 av. de la Grande Charmille du Parc; facing the town
hall, it's the third road on the left.
☎ 01.60.15.71.53
Closed Sun, Tues and Wed evenings, and Mon.

In a quiet part of the town in a spruce
house. The restaurant has walls with
stretched fabric and is made charming by
touches of lace. In the evenings, they light
candles on the tables. The chef is a duck
specialist – duck *foie gras* in particular – but
menus also include tasty fish and meat
dishes. He uses only fresh produce and
whatever he cooks he's got a real gift.
Menus start at 155F. The mistress of the
house extends a charming welcome.
Essential to book.

SAINT-GERMAIN-EN-LAYE   78100

🎋 🏠 LE HAVRE*

92 rue Léon-Désoyer (Northwest); it's on the old
Chambourcy road.

☎ and ➡ 01.34.51.41.05
TV.

Clean, well-run little hotel in the middle of
town, where a double with shower/wc will
cost 280F. Some of the rooms overlook the
cemetery, so there are no extraneous noises
to wake you. All the rooms are double
glazed, so the rooms over the street are
quiet too. Pleasant, friendly welcome. A
good place in this town. 10% discount
July–Aug.

🎋 🏠 |●| L'ERMITAGE DES LOGES-LE SAINT-EXUPÉRY***

11 av. des Loges (Centre).
☎ 01.39.21.50.90 ➡ 01.39.21.50.91
TV.

A lovely, typical place for Saint-Germain-en-
Laye. It's really smart. There's a wide view of
the avenues of trees that lead through the forest to the château. Rooms are extremely comfortable and service is faultless. Doubles from
700F. Fine, classic cuisine is served in the Art-
Deco-style dining room. The lunchtime *menu
du jour* costs 98F and includes a small bottle of
water and wine. There's another menu at 175F.
Free breakfast when you stay the night or a
house apéritif before your meal.

|●| RESTAURANT LA FEUILLANTINE

10 rue des Louviers (Centre); it's in the pedestrian area.
☎ 01.34.51.04.24
Closed Sun and public holidays.

Very warm welcome, speedy service and a
tasteful dining room so small you're stuffed in
like sardines – but that doesn't stop you
enjoying your meal. You eat very well here –
excellent *foie gras* and omelette with
smoked salmon. *Formules* for under 100F at
lunchtime and a menu at 148F.

|●| LE TABL'O GOURMAND

18 pl. Saint-Pierre.
☎ 01.34.51.66.33
Closed Mon lunchtime.

Set on a quiet little square, a relaxing
restaurant with beams and dressed stone,
decorated in relaxing colours with a
Provençal look. The owner is an art lover
and fills the dining room with pictures by
local artists. He's also a fan of recipes from
centuries past and he treats them appropriately for modern tastes – try his *pantoufle
de cardinal* stuffed with duck and *foie gras*,
but don't miss out on his *crêpes Suzette* .
Menus start at 135F. Unfortunately the wine
list has only a limited number of half-bottles.

SAINT-PIERRE-LES-NEMOURS   77140

♿ 🏠 |●| HÔTEL-RESTAURANT LES ROCHES**

1–3 av. Léopold-Pelletier; it's opposite the church and not far from the Rochers Gréau.
☎ 01.64.28.01.43 ➡ 01.64.28.04.27
Restaurant closed Sun evening, Mon lunchtime and 15 Nov–15 March. **TV**. **Disabled access**. **Car park**.

It's a real pity that this establishment is located at a noisy crossroads but the rooms are quiet nonetheless, and comfortable. Doubles with bath 180–270F; ask for the more modern, spacious ones in the annexe – they're also more expensive, of course. In the restaurant you get remarkable value for money – delicious food from starter to dessert, lovely setting and punctillious service. Great house *terrine* and sole fillet with morels, and a cheese platter and some exquisite pastries to tackle after that. Weekday *menu du jour* 95F and four others 120–270F. One of the best places to eat in the whole region. 10% discount.

SÈVRES   92360

♿|●| LA SALLE À MANGER

12 av. de la Division-Leclerc.
☎ 01.46.26.66.64
Closed Sat lunchtime, Sun evening, Mon and Aug.

It's hard to find a parking spot around here, but it's worth persisting because you mustn't miss this place. The decor is bright and fresh and you immediately feel you're in the country, surrounded by that lovely green smell you get after the rain. On the menu you'll find *œufs en meurette* in red wine sauce, tomato tart with Cantal cheese and mustard, *fricassée* of rabbit with herbs, calves' cheek with orange and cumin or duck breast in honey – a cornucopia of flavours and perfumes. Take your time to enjoy it. The place is a hive of activity and the service is quiet, quick and efficient. It's often full because prices are reasonable for the quality. Menus start at 82F. Free Kir.

SURESNES   92150

♿|●| LES JARDINS DE CAMILLE

70 av. Franklin Roosevelt; from porte Maillot, take bus number 244 to Pont de Suresnes stop.
☎ 01.45.06.22.66
Closed Sun evening.

This big house stands on the hillsides of the Suresnes vineyards, way up high with a fabulous view of Paris below. They serve Burgundy rather than Suresnes wine here, and the cuisine is good too. They do country dishes like *rillettes* of rabbit with Armagnac, snails, *bœuf bourguignon*, game in season and fresh goat from the Morvan – you'll find food like this on their *menu-carte* at 175F. The family Poinsot know what they're about, greet you well and really take care of you. Free coffee.

VERSAILLES   78000

🏠 HOME SAINT-LOUIS**

28 rue Saint-Louis (Centre).
☎ 01.39.50.23.55 ➡ 01.30.21.62.45
TV.

This is a quiet, comfortable, well-looked after hotel not far from the pretty Saint-Louis neighbourhood. Doubles with shower/wc or bath 220–310F. Very good value for money.

♿ 🏠 HÔTEL RICHAUD***

16 rue Richaud (Centre).
☎ 01.39.50.10.42 ➡ 01.39.53.43.36
TV. **Car park**.

This must be the most peaceful and the most central hotel in town. It has forty very clean rooms with TV and direct-dial telephone – ask for one looking over the buildings of the Hôpital Richaud opposite. The furnishings and decoration are very 1970s – they didn't stint on the carpeting. Make sure you see the bar, which is a monument to kitsch. It doesn't deserve three stars but it has two-star prices; double with shower/wc 290F or with bath from 340F. 10% discount.

♿ 🏠 HÔTEL DU CHEVAL ROUGE**

18 rue André-Chénier (Centre); it's on the market square.
☎ 01.39.50.03.03 ➡ 01.39.50.61.27
TV. **Car park**.

A well-located, comfortable hotel. Doubles 310–420F depending on the facilities which is not bad for a town where prices rocket, especially near the château. The hotel is also a tea room. The private car park is an asset in this part of town. 10% discount Nov–March.

♿ 🏠 PARIS HÔTEL**

14 av. de Paris; RER Versailles. it's 400m from the pl. d'Armes.
☎ 01.39.50.56.00 ➡ 01.39.50.21.83
Disabled access. **TV**.

You will get a very warm welcome in this hotel and the proprietor will give you a friendly handshake when you come down for breakfast. Spacious, clean rooms, the nicest overlooking the courtyard; doubles with shower/wc 350F, 400F with bath. 10% discount.

|●| LE BALADIN SAINT-LOUIS

2 rue de l'Occident (Centre).
☎ 01.39.50.06.54
Closed Sun.

Not the greatest setting of all time but you can easily ignore it if you sit on the terrace where you can appreciate the view of the Saint-Louis district. Expressive, daring cuisine that's often imaginative and always of high quality. This is what the chef has striven to achieve over the last ten years. The 115F menu includes wine and coffee or there's another at 189F.

|●| L'ANNEXE

20 rue au Pain.
☎ 01.39.50.33.00
Closed Sun and Mon lunchtime.

This is the offspring of the mother restaurant *La Marée*, in the little street that goes right round the main central market. The decor is pale teak wood with seascapes on the wall and the floor came from a cabin cruiser. You guessed – this is a fish and seafood restaurant. Their watchword is freshness, freshness, freshness. So the fish is really excellent and so are the oysters – the Gillardeau Number Threes are available year round and have a faint taste of hazelnuts. They also serve a couple of meat dishes. *Formule* 118F and a menu at 148F. Terrace in summer.

⚘|●| LA CUISINE BOURGEOISE

10 bd. du roi (Centre).
☎ 01.39.53.11.38
Closed Sat lunchtime, Sun and three weeks in Aug.

This place is perfectly named with its very cosy dining room decorated in shades of green. They serve tasty cuisine with some gourmet dishes in a setting that's more bistro than classic restaurant. Lunch menus 128F and 195F, 180F and 255F in the evening. There's an excellent list of wines by the glass and they have theme evenings, based round wines. Free house apéritif.

MONTIGNY-LE-BRETONNEUX 78180 (10KM SW)

☗|●| L'AUBERGE DU MANET***

61 av. du Manet; coming from Paris on the A12, take the St-Quentin-en-Yvelines exit.
☎ 01.30.64.89.00 ➡ 01.30.64.55.10

The huge farm used to be part of the domaine of the Abbaye de Port-Royal-des-Champs which is about 2km away. They've converted it into a hotel-restaurant in a perfect pastoral setting and they've done it very well. The terrace looks over a pretty pond. The rooms are faultless and definitely worth the price (550F); all have mini-bar, satellite TV and en-suite bathroom with bath or shower/wc. In the restaurant the cooking is deftly prepared and reasonably priced. The first menu includes starter, main course, salad, cheese, dessert and coffee. The braised lamb shank with rosemary is delectable and the *croustillant* of strawberries and almonds delectable. Undeniably, they're classic dishes, but they're cooked with confidence. Menus 140F and 160F. 10% discount on the room rate.

Languedoc-Roussillon

11 Aude

30 Gard

34 Hérault

48 Lozère

66 Pyrénées-Orientales

AGDE 34300

🕈 🛉 HÔTEL BON REPOS*

15 rue Rabelais; it's 200m from the centre in the direction of Béziers.
☎ 04.67.94.16.26
Closed second and third week in Jan. **TV**. **Pay garage**.

In previous incarnations this place was the town brothel, and later, the police station. Nowadays it's a delightful, simple hotel run by a cheerful couple. Large, flower-filled terraces where you can laze around. Rooms 155–195F with shower and 190–235F with bath. 10% discount Sept–June.

🛉 HÔTEL LE DONJON**

pl. Jean-Jaurès (Centre).
☎ 04.67.94.12.32 ➡ 04.67.94.34.54
TV. **Car park**.

An old stone building practically next door to the ancient cathedral of Saint-Étienne on a pleasant square that buzzes with life in summer. The fresh-looking bedrooms are comfy, exceptionally well maintained and good value for money. Doubles 250–320F with shower/wc or 420F with bath. Easy-going atmosphere.

🕈 🛉 |●| HÔTEL-RESTAURANT LA TAMARISSIÈRE***

Lieu-dit La Tamarissière (Southwest); go along quai Commandant-Réveille, then follow the D32 for 5km.
☎ 04.67.94.20.87 ➡ 04.67.21.38.40
e hotel-la-Tama@wanadoo.fr
Hotel closed 5 Nov–1 March. **Restaurant closed** Mon out of season, Mon evenings in season.
Swimming pool. **TV**.

This hotel, on the banks of the Hérault, is the most famous in the region. It's in a lovely rose garden in a pine wood. Stylish, modernised bedrooms cost around 420–580F with shower/wc or 440–725F with bath. The wonderful cooking at the old-fashioned bistro is full of the flavours of the south and successfully combines tradition with style. Choose from dishes such as cuttlefish with parsley, tomato and basil, *bourride* or fish stew, *bouillabaisse*, and fillet of beef with Banyuls wine sauce. Set menus 175–390F. Nicolas Albano is a top-class chef. Easy-going atmosphere. 10% discount on the room rate 16 Sept–14 June when you book in advance.

|●| CHEZ BÉBERT, LOU PESCADOU

18 rue Chassefière (Centre).
☎ 04.67.21.17.10
Closed lunchtimes mid-July to Aug, and Dec–Feb except school holidays.

Simplicity is the key word in this bare room with long tables and wooden benches. There is only one menu, 82F, and dishes are richly flavoured and hearty: to start, fish soup full of mussels, tomato and big slices of courgette, *pâté*, then lemon sole and an enormous dessert if you can manage it. A great place. No credit cards.

LE GRAU D'AGDE 34300 (5KM S)

🕈 🛉 L'ÉPHÈBE*

12 quai du Commandant-Méric; it's on the north bank of the Hérault.
☎ and ➡ 04.67.21.49.88
Closed 15 Nov–15 March. **TV**.

A little hotel 100m from the beach, overlooking the Hérault and the pretty port of Grau-

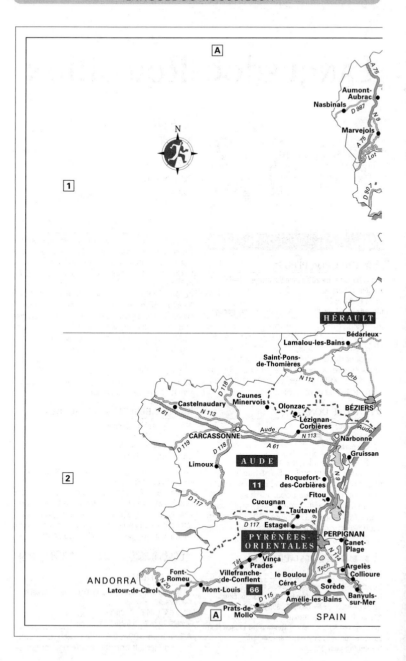

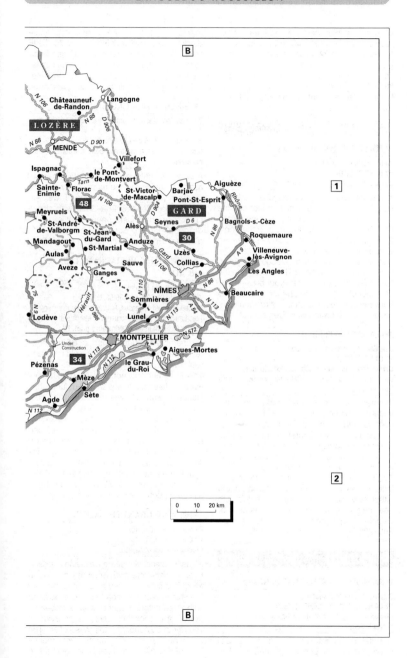

d'Agde. Simple, perfectly adequate bedrooms with TV cost 140–160F with basin, 170–290F with shower or 240–330F with bath. They do an interesting deal out of season – doubles 850F for a five-night stay, including breakfast. The owner's very laid-back. 10% discount for a two-night stay Sept–July.

MARSEILLAN   34340 (7KM NE)

⚘|●| LE JARDIN DU NARIS

24 bd. Pasteur; take the D51.
☎ 04.67.77.30.07
Closed Mon evening and Tues out of season, and Feb.

A pair of young and exceptionally friendly people run this place, which is just outside the centre of town. The walled garden means you dine amongst the flowers and the trees. Simple, traditional dishes include sea bream with a red pepper *coulis*, scallop *millefeuille*, pork cheek curry and a selection of grilled fish. Set menus 60–140F. The crayons on the tables are used to calculate your bill, and you can scribble on the paper tablecloths between courses. The efforts of previous diners are pinned on the wall. Free apéritif.

|●| LA TABLE D'ÉMILIE

8 pl. Carnot (Centre); take the D51.
☎ 04.67.77.63.59
Closed Mon lunchtime in season, Wed and Sun eveningout of season, three weeks mid-Nov/Dec, and 15 Feb–8 March.

Located near the covered market, this little restaurant has a dining room with a magnificent vaulted ceiling and a patio garden for the summer. It's a strange combination of rustic and sophisticated, all of a piece with the traditional yet creative cooking that you find in this good gourmet restaurant. The 100F *menu terroir*, served at lunchtime, includes dishes like *carpaccio* of salmon and either scallops and prawns or whiting with sea salt, tomato and basil, cheese or dessert. Super-fresh fish. Other menus 150–230F or *à la carte* around 180F.

AIGUES-MORTES   30220

⚘ |●| HÔTEL-RESTAURANT L'ESCALE

3 av. de la Tour-de-Constance.
☎ 04.66.53.71.14 ➡ 04.66.53.76.74
Closed a fortnight at both the All Saints' and Christmas school holidays.

A hotel-restaurant with a friendly atmosphere, situated opposite the ramparts. The

regulars linger over a *pastis* or lunch. Weekday lunch *menu du jour* 55F, others 70–130F. Simple but spotless rooms 160F with basin to 250F with bath. The ones over the bar are a bit noisy but air-conditioned, while the ones in the annexe are quieter. Relaxed welcome.

⚘ ⚑ HÔTEL DES CROISADES**

2 rue du Port (West); it's outside the ramparts, near the canal.
☎ 04.66.53.67.85 ➡ 04.66.53.72.95
Closed 1–20 Dec. **Disabled access**. **Garden**. **TV**. **Pay car park**.

A fairly new hotel with an attractive, tranquil atmosphere. Some rooms have a view over the town walls and the Constance Tower. Air-conditioned doubles 280–285F with shower/wc or bath. Most appealing of all is the delightful garden. Best value in town. 10% discount 15 Jan–15 Feb and 15 Nov–1 Dec.

⚘ ⚑ |●| HÔTEL-RESTAURANT LES ARCADES***

23 bd. Gambetta (Centre).
☎ 04.66.5381.13 ➡ 04.66.53.75.46
Closed Mon out of season, Mon lunchtime in season, Tues lunchtime, the first fortnight in March and the second fortnight in Nov. **Swimming pool**. **TV**.

A characterful hotel with a gastronomic restaurant of great charm, in the old town and well away from the hurly-burly of the centre. This is an ancient, noble building with thick walls and spacious, stylish, beautiful rooms. Doubles with shower/wc or bath cost 500–560F including breakfast. The dining room is elegant and the tables have starched white cloths. There's also a small secluded terrace. The classic, regional cuisine is beautifully prepared and perfectly served. Specialities include warm oysters, steak with juniper sauce or medallions of monkfish with saffron. Weekday lunch menu 135F, and around 250F *à la carte*, both good value. Free apéritif.

⚘|●| RESTAURANT LE GALION

24 rue Pasteur (Centre).
☎ 04.66.53.86.41
Closed Mon out of season.

Pleasant place with stone walls and exposed beams. Very attentive welcome and good food. The fish is cooked on a hot stone – try the fillet of bream or sea bass accompanied with three different sauces and potatoes *au gratin*, or opt for their beef *à la gardiane*. If you're not so hungry try the mussel flan. The bill won't come to much. Set menus 79–165F or *à la carte*. Free coffee or *digestif*.

⚘ |O| RESTAURANT ABACA

424 route d'Arles; it's 2km from the castle walls.
☎ 04.66.53.77.96.
Closed Nov.

The owner has his own way of explaining how the restaurant got its name, but the gist is: A is for amicable, B for beautiful, CA for Camargue. He'll make you feel like long-lost friends. The dining room is cosy and there's a pretty, shaded terrace where you can really feel at home. The cuisine has also got that home-made touch, and the dishes are generously served and beautifully cooked. Try the *poêlon* of fish (a kind of stew), the fresh, stuffed mushrooms, *bouillabiasse* or the flambéed beef fillet with pepper. Menus 82–165F. You can eat for much less by ordering the *crêpe-repas*, a full meal of pancakes. Free *digestif*.

SAINT-LAURENT-D'AIGOUZE   30220 (7KM N)

⚘ 🏠 |O| HÔTEL LOU GARBIN**

30 av. des Jardins; the village is on the Nîmes road from Aigues-Mortes and the hotel is on the right.
☎ 04.66.88.12.74 ➡ 04.66.88.91.12
Closed Nov–March (but phone to check) **Disabled access. Swimming pool. TV. Car park.**

A really pleasant place to stop between Nîmes and Aigues-Mortes in a typical village for this little corner of the Camargue. It's at the heart of the village, surrounded by a string of cafés with terraces and with the church to one side. The rooms are in the main building or in bungalows around the pool; they all have TV and en-suite bathrooms. Doubles 220F with basin, 250–290F with shower/wc or bath. They offer a half-board option from Easter to the end of October, 250F per person, and dishes are reassuringly local with lots of beef on the menu. Sadly, you can see and hear the main road, which is about 200m away, but pretty soon the bushes will have grown big enough to form a screen. You can play *boules* and they do barbecues. Free coffee.

ALÈS   30100

⚘ 🏠 HÔTEL DURAND**

3 bd. Anatole-France; it's in a quiet street that starts opposite pl. de la Gare.
☎ 04.66.86.28.94
Disabled access. TV. Car park.

A peaceful little establishment offering good value for money. The rooms are not huge but when they were refurbished, they did a thorough job. Doubles 200F with shower/wc.

There's a small interior courtyard. Friendly, attentive reception and many of the customers are regulars. 10% discount.

☆ |O| HÔTEL-RESTAURANT LE RICHE**

42 pl. Pierre-Sémard (Centre); it's opposite the station.
☎ 04.66.86.00.33 ➡ 04.66.30.02.63
e riche.reception@leriche.fr
Closed Aug. **TV. Pay car park.**

This place, something of an institution, is one of the best restaurants in town. The dining room is enormous and has Belle Epoque mouldings on the high ceiling. Polite, efficient service and carefully and creatively prepared dishes in true classic style that show off the flavours of the fresh produce to best advantage: shellfish salad with fresh basil, fillet of sea bass with a delicate shrimp *bisque*, good Saint-Nectaire cheese and apricot tart. Menus 100F, 150F and 195F. The hotel is run with great professionalism and has all the comforts you need. Impersonal, modern rooms with good facilities. Doubles with shower/wc or bath 250F.

⚘ |O| LE MANDAJORS

17 rue Mandajors.
☎ 04.66.52.62.98 **e** frederic-beguin@wanadoo.fr
Closed Sun and the first fortnight in Aug.

The decor doesn't seem to have changed since the Second World War when the female owner helped members of the Resistance disappear out of the back door. The place is now in the hands of a young man and his wife helps him at lunchtime. In the evening, he's on his own to run the kitchen and the dining room. To make it work, he keeps to strict opening hours and there aren't many covers. Delectable, appetizing cuisine for more than reasonable prices: cep omelette, flavourful Cévenole *fricassée* which is sautéed pork with chestnuts, and good house tarts. 59F lunch menu or 68F and 135F. Free aperitif.

|O| LE JARDIN D'ALÈS

92 av. d'Alsace (North); it's on the Aubenas road.
☎ 04.66.86.38.82 **e** lejardinales.resto@libertysurf.fr
Closed Sun evening, Mon, 25 Jan–12 Feb and 25 June–18 July. **Garden. Car park.**

Located just outside the centre on the edge of a sector with a number of looming high-rises and the terrace is almost too close to the roundabout for comfort. But the dining room has been decorated with great taste by the owners and they serve refined cuisine with dishes from different regions of France: *pâté en croûte cévenol*, veal stew *à la lyonnaise*, stuffed mussels *à la sétoise* (with brandy, tomato and garlic), mullet *à la Mar-*

seillaise (baked with cheese, tomato and saffron), and chicken breast *à la Périgourdine* (cooked with truffles). Weekday lunch menu 72F and others 105–172F. Warm welcome.

SEYNES   30580 (18KM E)

🎿 🏠 I●I LA FARIGOULETTE**

Le bourg; take the D6 from Alès.
☎ 04.66.83.70.56 ➡ 04.66.83.72.80
Swimming pool. Garden. TV. Car park.

A lovely, unfussy country establishment with a garden and swimming pool. Eleven decent double rooms at 230F. Customers from far afield come to enjoy the powerfully flavoured local dishes that the owner and his family prepare – *pâtés*, *terrines*, sausage, casseroles and *confits*. They run the local *charcuterie* shop, and many of the dishes are home-made. Prices are reasonable – set menus 70–180F. Service is in the beautifully simple, rustic dining room. You might fancy following the footpaths to Mont Bouquet (631m) after your meal. Free house apéritif.

SAINT-VICTOR-DE-MACALP   30500 (23KM NE)

🏠 I●I LA BASTIDE DES SENTEURS***

It's in the centre of the village; from Alès, take the D904 then the D51 to Saint-Victor.
☎ 04.66.24.45. ➡ 04.66.60.26.10
📧 senteurs@chateauxhotels.com
Hotel closed Three weeks in Jan. **Restaurant closed** Wed, Wed, Mon and Wed lunchtimes in season, Sun evening out of season, Jan and ten days in Nov. **Disabled access. Swimming pool. TV**.

A charming hotel in a hill village that's not over-run by tourists, set in beautiful countryside right on the edge of the Cévennes. Double rooms 350–430F with bath. The building is a collection of houses that have been soberly and tastefully renovated. Charming rooms with bare stone walls. Outside there's a glorious swimming pool overlooking the Cèze valley – you get the same view from the terrace. The superb restaurant is named after the chef, Franck Subileau, who produces dishes of jubilant invention: stuffed lobster with a mint salad, roast, boned pigeon with truffles, chocolate mousse and banana with rum. Weekday menu 115F, or 170–420F.

AMÉLIE-LES-BAINS   66110

🏠 I●I LE CASTEL-ÉMERAUDE**

Petite Provence, route de la Corniche; follow the signs to the centre sportif Espace Méditerranée.

☎ 04.68.39.02.83 ➡ 04.68.39.03.09
Closed Dec–Feb. **Disabled access. TV. Car park**.

A quiet, tranquil inn on the banks of the river, surrounded by greenery. It's a big castle-like building with two turrets, but inside the decoration is modern. Double rooms at 290F with shower/wc; those with bath (380F) also have a terrace. Set menus 99F, 140F and 198F. The Catalan menu includes scrumptious dishes: Collioure anchovies, duck *confit forestière* and *crème catalane*.

ANDUZE   30140

🎿 🏠 I●I LA RÉGALIÈRE**

1435 route de Saint-Jean-du-Gard (North).
☎ 04.66.61.81.93 ➡ 04.66.61.85.94
Closed Wed and Wed, and 1 Jan–15 March and 25 Nov–31 Dec. **Swimming pool. Garden. TV. Car park**.

La Régalière is a very old, master craftman's house in a vast estate, a little green haven of peace and quiet. The twelve bedrooms have very modern facilities. Doubles are 280–320F; half board, 275–295F per person, is compulsory June–Sept. You can eat on the shaded terrace in summer. House specialities include *aiguillettes* of duck with honey and gentian liqueur, creamed salt cod *gratiné* with *croûtons* with olive paste, and pan-fried duck *foie gras* with white chestnuts and grapes. Menus 100–240F. On Fridays in high season, there are jazz evenings in the restaurant. 10% discount on the room rate.

🎿 🏠 I●I LA PORTE DES CÉVENNES**

Route de Saint-Jean-du-Gard; it's on the D907, 3km out of Anduze.
☎ 04.66.61.99. 44 ➡ 04.66.61.73.65
Closed lunchtimes and Nov–March. **Swimming pool. TV. Car park**.

Just outside the village of Anduze, past the bamboo fields, this modern hotel has spacious, clean and comfortable rooms. Doubles with shower 310F, or 340–400F with bath, TV and a small balcony. The breathtakingly ostentatious swimming pool is covered and heated. The restaurant, open for dinner only, serves traditional dishes. Menus 100–160F. Half board, available for a minimum of three days, costs 300–320F per person. This is a reliable place. Free apéritif.

🎿 🏠 I●I LE MOULIN DE CORBÈS**

Corbès; take the route de Saint-Jean du Gard.
☎ 04.66.61.61.83
Closed Sun evening and Mon out of season, and Jan–Feb. **Disabled access. Car park**.

This isn't just any old restaurant. The grandly sweeping staircase and the crunch of the gravel under your feet as you enter help to create a special atmosphere. The dining room is painted yellow and flooded with sunlight; the flower arrangements on the tables add a touch of class. The choice of dishes changes with the season but they're always simple and full of cleverly combined, delicate flavours – *fromage frais* ravioli in herb stock, *aiguillettes* of duckling with lavender honey and preserved ginger, beef *pot-au-feu*, or fillet of pan-fried beef with spiced wine. Set menus 155–340F. Double rooms with shower/wc or bath 380–400F. 10% discount on the room rate March–April and Sept–Dec.

ARGELÈS-SUR-MER   66700

🕺 🏠 |O| LA CHAUMIÈRE MATIGNON**

30 av. du Tech; it's next to the tourist office.
☎ 04.68.81.09.84 ➡ 04.68.81.33.62
Closed Tues lunchtime, Thurs out of season, Thurs lunchtime in season, and Oct to Easter. **TV. Pay car park**.

Friendly welcome in a seaside hotel that's more a villa than a cottage, just 300m from the beach. Pretty, well-maintained bedrooms with shower or bath and wc. One of the rooms can sleep four. Doubles 240–330F. Honest local dishes in the restaurant: Collioure anchovies, prawns with pine nuts, duck *foie gras* with prunes, duck breast with green peppercorns and cream, or meat and fish grilled over coals. Menus 78–140F. Half board compulsory July–Aug. 5% discount for a minimum three-night stay on a half-board basis 10 Sept–20 June.

AUMONT-AUBRAC   48130

🕺 🏠 |O| GRAND HÔTEL PROUHÈZE***

2 rue du Languedoc; it's opposite the train station.
☎ 04.66.42.80.07 ➡ 04.66.42.87.78
📧 prouheze@prouheze.com
Closed Sun evening and Mon except July–Aug, and Nov–March. **Garden. TV. Car park**.

Guy Prouhèze's cooking is wonderfully imaginative. His subtle dishes bring out the full flavour of salmon, asparagus, mushrooms and other fresh ingredients in an almost magical way. There's an enormous, flowery dining room decorated in country style. Weekday lunch menu 180F, others 220–570F, and good *à la carte* choices. Excellent cellar full of vintage wines and fantastic *vins de table*.

Comfy, attractive rooms of varying size – the bigger ones have the better facilities; doubles 400–600F. 10% discount on the room rate.

FAU-DE-PEYRE   48130 (10KM NW)

🕺 🏠 |O| HÔTEL-RESTAURANT BOUCHAR-INC-TICHIT DEL FAÔU**

How to get there: take the D50 from Aumont-Aubral.
☎ 04.66.31.11.00 ➡ 04.66.31.30.00
Closed Sun evening out of season and ten days at Christmas. **TV. Car park**.

"Faôu" is the local word for "tree"; the inn in this old Aubrac village is surrounded by them. The owners will give you a warm welcome and serve terrific home cooking at modest prices. Ample menus at 65F and 120F: frogs' legs, trout with bacon and *manouls* (lamb breast with tripe). Just next door there's a modern building where you'll find spotless bedrooms with TV and all mod cons. Doubles with shower/wc or bath 250F. Free apéritif.

BANYULS-SUR-MER   66650

🕺 🏠 VILLA MIRAMAR

rue Lacaze-Outhiens; it's 200m from the beach.
☎ 04.68.88.33.85 ➡ 04.68.66.90.08
📧 ange.st@wanadoo.fr
Closed 15 Oct–30 March. **Garden. Swimming pool. TV. Car park**.

Set on the hillside just outside the village, the hotel is surrounded by a garden that's full of trees and flowers. The place is decorated with Far Eastern souvenirs, many from Thailand. The rooms are comfortable with modern facilities – mini-bar, telephones, TV – and cost 260–385F for a double. There are also some basic bungalows in the grounds for slightly less. A well-priced place just 200m from the beach. 10% discount April and Oct.

🕺 |O| HÔTEL DES ELMES-RESTAURANT LA LITTORINE**

plage des Elmes; go towards Port-Vendres.
☎ 04.68.88.03.12 ➡ 04.68.88.53.03
Closed Sun evening and Mon Nov–Feb. **Disabled access. Garden. TV. Car park**.

This seafront establishment is one of Roussillon's best gourmet restaurants. After working in Portugal for a long time, Jean-Marie Patrouix brought back a ton of recipes that he's skilfully adapted to his own style. Superb fish and seafood, sometimes cooked together: fisherman's stew and pigeon with shellfish. Terrific desserts too.

Set menus 130–240F and about 240F *à la carte*. They have a wonderful list of regional wines. About thirty rooms, decorated in an uncompromisingly modern style, and they can't be faulted. Two have facilities for the disabled. Doubles 290–470F. 10% discount Oct–June.

BARJAC   30430

🏊 🏠 |●| HÔTEL-RESTAURANT LE MAS DU TERME***

Route de Bagnols-sur-Cèze; it's 3km from the village, out in the vineyards.
☎ 04.66.24.56.31 ➡ 04.66.24.58.54
Closed Jan–Feb. **Swimming pool. TV. Disabled access. Car park.**

This 18th-century silkworm breeding house has been tastefully converted in the local style by the owners. There's a vaulted sitting room and dining room and a pretty courtyard. The hotel has 23 quiet, attractive bedrooms with modern facilities at 350–420F. the restaurant is pretty good too: lunch menu at 98F and others 128–280F. The local specialities, *escabèche* of red mullet fillets with garlic, cod steaks with black olive paste, stuffed rack of lamb with sea salt and so on, are carefully prepared and not at all bad. 10% discount on the room rate.

BEAUCAIRE   30300

🏊 🏠 |●| HÔTEL-RESTAURANT LE ROBINSON**

Route de Remoulins; it's signposted on the road to Remoulins.
☎ 04.66.59.21.32 ➡ 04.66.59.00.03
📧 contact@hotel-robinson.fr
Closed Feb. **Disabled access. Swimming pool. TV. Car park.**

A good place just on the edge of Beaucaire. On the *menu du terroir* you'll find beef *gardiane*, the local speciality – they make it like nobody else – served with locally grown rice. It goes well with a wine like a Costières de Nîmes. Try donkey and pork sausage as a starter, and a *crème catalane* to finish. Menus at 78–200F. The bright dining room has huge bay windows overlooking the trees in the garden, and it's run by diligent waiting staff. Rooms are pretty, comfortable and really clean; doubles 320–450F. Smiling welcome and a family atmosphere. They have tennis courts as well as a pool. Free apéritif.

BÉZIERS   34500

🏊 🏠 LE CHAMP-DE-MARS**

17 rue de Metz (Centre); it's near the pl. du 14-Juillet.
☎ 04.67.28.35.53 ➡ 04.67.28.61.42
Garden. TV. Car park.

You'll find this little hotel, with a façade smothered in geraniums, in a quiet side street. It's been renovated from top to bottom and the meticulously designed bedrooms overlook the garden. Double rooms 180–250F with shower/wc or bath, breakfast 30F. It's the best value for money in Béziers. The cheerful owner will tell you all about the town. 10% discount Oct–April; children get breakfast free.

🏊 |●| LE BISTROT DES HALLES

pl. de la Madeleine (Centre); it's in the district of les Halles.
☎ 04.67.28.30.46 ➡ 04.67.28.19.11
Closed Sun and Mon.
Disabled access. Pay car park.

Lively place, reminiscent of a Parisian bistro. Set menus 88–139F with a good variety of authentic dishes including a self-service buffet of *crudités* and *charcuterie*, lots of seafood and shellfish, grilled fish, *carpaccio*, pig's trotters, and even *pot-au-feu* and *choucroute* in winter. In summer you can sit out on the delightful terrace in the square. Free apéritif.

🏊 |●| LE CAFÉ DES LOUIS

pl. Saint-Nazaire; it's opposite St-Nazaire cathedral.
☎ 04.67.49.93.13 ➡ 04.67.49.29.92
Closed Sun. **Garden.**

Service noon–2pm and 7–11pm, until midnight at the weekend. *Le Café des Louis* has a lovely patio garden and a pleasant vaulted dining room where they serve hearty traditional dishes. The helpings are large and some specialities are particularly good, including *pot-au-feu*, cuttlefish *à la plancha* (which you cook yourself on a hot stone), and *anchoïade*. Lunch menu 89F, *formule* at 90F, or around 100F *à la carte*. Friendly and efficient service. A good selection of regional wines. Free apéritif or coffee.

|●| LES ANTIQUAIRES

4 rue Bagatelle (Centre); it's near allées Paul-Riquet.
☎ 04.67.49.31.10
Closed lunchtimes except Sun, and Aug.

If you're looking for a gentle, intimate little place this tiny restaurant is just the thing – it's popular, so you should book. It's decorated with cherubs, old adverts and movie posters, and the cooking is wonderful. There's a large and very tasty salad of strawberries, thinly sliced apple and Pélardon (soft white goat's cheese with a nutty flavour), fillet of sea bass cooked to perfection, a big cheese platter and magnificent *crème brûlée* – all for 95F. Another set menu at 140F. Good wines at reasonable prices and courteous service.

🏊 |●| LE JARDIN

37 av. Jean-Moulin (North); it's near the sous-préfecture.
☎ 04.67.36.41.31
In summer also at: Domaine de Pradines-le-Haut, on the old Bédarieux road.
☎ 04.67.30.46.54
Closed Sun evening, Wed, first week in Jan.

The *Jardin* has a solid reputation. They serve tasty dishes using fresh market produce and the chef's skill is obvious in every tasty dish: hot oysters from Bouziques, roast sea bass with crispy skin or pan-fried *foie gras* with caramelised seasonal fruit in a sweet sauce. The menus change frequently. Francis's wife has unearthed some particularly good wines and will advise you as to which are available by the glass. Set weekday lunch menu 100F, others up to 310F. Good local wines, and excellent guidance when choosing. Free coffee or *digestif*.

|●| L'AMBASSADE

22 bd. de Verdun (Centre); it's opposite the railway station.
☎ 04.67.76.06.24 ➡ 04.67.76.74.05
Closed Sun and Mon.

A nicely old-fashioned restaurant with retro lamps and faded *trompe l'œil* paintings. Patrick Olry is a good chef. Try his *découverte* menu – sweetbread salad with *foie gras*, *aiguillettes* (or slivers) of Charolas beef with oxtail and roundels of bone marrow, or salmon steak with creamy shellfish risotto with saffron. The cheese is out of this world and so are the desserts. Menus 145–370F; dishes change regularly depending on what the market has to offer. Even though the atmosphere isn't excessively formal, the waiters wear black double-breasted suits.

NISSAN-LEZ-ENSERUNE   34440 (11KM SW)

🛏 |●| HÔTEL RÉSIDENCE**

35 av. de la Cave; on the A9, take the Béziers Ouest exit; it's in the centre of the village.
☎ 04.67.37.00.63 ➡ 04.67.37.68.63
Closed Dec–Jan. **Garden. TV. Car park**.

A beautiful, typically provincial building with

bags of old-fashioned charm in a big village behind Béziers. It's a good place for either a night or a whole week. There's a relaxed, informal, peaceful atmosphere and flowers everywhere. Several bedrooms have been added in the annexe in the garden. Doubles 295–310F with shower/wc or bath. They'll give you a winning welcome. The restaurant, open only to hotel guests, serves a 100F set dinner.

MAGALAS   34480 (22KM N)

|●| LA BOUCHERIE

pl. de l'Église.
☎ 04.67.36.20.82 ℮ theboucherie@aol.com
Closed Sun, Mon, and the Nov and Feb school holidays.

This butcher's shop doubles as a restaurant, and a good one at that. It has two dining rooms which look as if they've been decorated with oddments bought in a second-hand shop. The attractive terrace spills out onto the typical village square. There's a weekday lunchtime *menu du jour* for 58F, and two others at 95F and 130F: fresh tapas, a selection of cold meats, stews, steak *tartare* that's made in front of you, and delicious *carpaccio*. If you like tripe, you'll love the way they do it here. Blues or jazz plays gently in the background and, to set it all off, there are some good wines. It's advisable to book.

CARCASSONNE   11000

🛏 HÔTEL TERMINUS**

2 av. du Maréchal-Joffre (North); it's near the station.
☎ 04.68.25.25.00 ➡ 04.68.72.53.09
Closed Dec–Feb. **TV. Pay lock-up car park**.

Enormous, modernist, luxury hotel with a winter garden – it has been used many times as a movie set. The foyer is fabulous, with a 1930s revolving door, mouldings on the ceilings, a double staircase, old tiling and a gleaming bar. It has one hundred rooms at what are amazing prices considering the luxury, but sadly, some of them have lost their charm through over-zealous renovation. Doubles 360F with shower/wc or bath. The bridal suite is absolutely magnificent – stylishly furnished and vast, with a glamorous bathroom.Smiling staff welcome you to this grand provincial hotel. Buffet breakfast 40F.

🏊 🛏 HÔTEL DU DONJON***

2 rue du Comte-Roger (South); it's in the heart of the medieval city.

☎ 04.68.71.08.80 ➡ 04.68.25.06.60
Disabled access. Garden. TV. Pay garage.

This place has everything; it's a medieval building with magnificent beams and an unusual staircase, and it offers modern facilities – double glazing, air conditioning, bar, lounges, a garden, and so on. There's good reason for the owner to be proud of the establishment. Doubles 420F with shower and 570F with bath and air conditioning. Very popular with American visitors. The garage means you can bring your car into the middle of the town; it is free to readers of this guide.

⚘ |●| RESTAURANT CHEZ FRED

86 rue Albert-Tomey and 31 bd. Omer-Sarrant (Centre); it's opposite the botanic gardens.
☎ 04.68.72.02.23
Closed Sat lunchtime, Mon and the Feb school holidays.

This is an adorable restaurant with a tasteful, plush decor with plum-coloured walls and rattan armchairs. Frédéric Coste's cooking is modern and full of integrity. He changes his menus three times a year but produces dishes such as *foie gras*, *fricassée* of lamb with thyme, or breast of duck with caramelized pears and, for dessert, two kinds of chocolate *charlotte* or *croustillant* of apples with Armagnac and sorbet. Lunch *formule* 75F, (not served weekends and public holidays), then others 110–140F. Free coffee.

⚘ |●| L'AUBERGE DE DAME CARCAS

3 pl. du Château (Southeast); it's in the medieval city.
☎ 04.68.71.23.23.
Closed Mon, and Jan–Feb.

There's plenty of room on the terrace, in the upstairs dining room or down in the vaulted cellar. Carefully designed rustic decor. The kitchen opens onto the dining room. Given that the quality is so high and that this is a very touristy district, the set menus and dishes are cheap. The menu of regional dishes lists an absolutely terrific suckling pig with honey, *crépinette* of pork in orange sauce, and house *cassoulet*. Menus 85F, 100F and 145F. They even bake their own bread. Good regional wines at very reasonable prices. Remarkable to find this place among the tourist traps in the old town. Free apéritif.

⚘ |●| RESTAURANT GIL-LE STEAK HOUSE

32 route Minervoise; it's in the Ville Basse.
☎ 04.68.47.85.23

Closed Sun, Mon and three weeks in Aug.

You go down a few steps to the smallish dining room of this surprising restaurant. Oddly enough, when you consider its name, this is a fish restaurant. The sea bass, red mullet, sole and salmon are all brilliantly fresh, as are the oysters, mussels and other shellfish. Some good deserts, too, including *crème catalane*. Menus 100–160F. Hospitable service by Madame. Free apéritif.

⚘ |●| LE COMTE ROGER

14 rue Saint-Louis; it's in the old town.
☎ 04.68.11.93.40
Closed Sun, the second fortnight in Nov and the first fortnight in Jan.

Pierre Mesa, who had a fine reputation at the *Château*, took over this restaurant formerly run by his father. Although he changed premises he brought his team and style of cooking with him. The warmth and sincerity of the welcome hasn't changed either. The menus lean heavily in the direction of local recipes using local produce and Corbières wines – better a good Corbière than a poor Bordeaux. Uncomplicated, flavourful, well-seasoned dishes. Menus 118–218F – good value. The setting is very "now" and really pleasant, though the dining room is rather noisy. In summer, head for the terrace which is lovely. Free *digestif*.

|●| LE SAINT-JEAN

1 pl. Saint-Jean; it's in the old town.
☎ 04.68.47.42.43
Closed Tues–Sat lunchtimes and Sun evening Oct–June, and Jan.

A find of a place. It's right next to the castle in a lovely house on a pretty square. The terrace is on the city walls, though a few cars do go past. Exquisite, light cuisine showing off all the delights of local ingredients: *sabayon* of puréed salt cod, red mullet fillets with baby vegetables on olive-paste toast and *cassoulet*. The menu, at 120F, offers very good value for money.

CAVANAC   11570 (4KM S)

⌂ |●| CHÂTEAU DE CAVANAC

How to get there: take the D104, in the direction of St. Hilaire.
☎04.68.79.61.04 ➡ 04.68.79.79.76
Closed mid-Jan to mid-Feb. **Garden. Swimming pool. Car park.**

An overgrown, bourgeois farmhouse in a very pretty garden, in a quiet village. Fifteen lovely rooms (all different) with period furniture, lustrous fabrics, canopied beds and elegantly contemporary decor. Some rooms can sleep five. Doubles 360–585F. The restaurant, in a converted stable, is the bigger draw. There's a genuine country feel – they've kept the mangers and hung some old implements on the walls. There's a single menu, 198F, of delicious local dishes which change regularly: snails, duck *aiguillettes*, char-grilled lamb, goat's cheese with honey and pastries. The bread and wine (their own) are included. And they give you a complimentary cup of coffee and an apéritif as well. There's a tennis court, swimming pool, fitness centre and sauna – a great place.

ROQUEFÈRE 11380 (22KM N)

❘●❘ LE SIRE DE CABART

How to get there: take the Mazamet road, turn onto the Conques road then right onto the D101 to Roquefère.
☎ 04.68.26.31.89
Closed Wed and Sun evening out of season.

A magnificent house in an attractive village in the middle of the Montagne Noire and the Cabardès. There's an imposing fireplace in the stone and wood dining room, used to char-grill meat. When you order *charcuterie*, a huge platter appears laden with sausage, *terrines* and hams, and you can help yourself to more. They also plonk down a bottle of wine. The cheese platter is equally gargantuan – don't miss the goat's cheeses that are eaten smothered with honey around here. It's all handsomely served and fairly priced at 80F for *charcuterie* and cheese, wine and coffee included. Menus 65F (not Sun), 100F and 145F.

CASTELNAUDARY 11400

🏃 🏠 ❘●❘ HÔTEL DU CENTRE ET DU LAURAGAIS**

31 cours de la République.
☎ 04.68.23.25.95 ➡ 04.68.94.01.66
Closed 10 Jan–10 Feb. **TV**.

The rooms are in a huge, bourgeois house on the main square in the town. They're well maintained, comfortable and cost 220F with shower/wc and 280F with bath. Plush restaurant and probably the best cuisine in town, famous for *foie gras* and *cassoulet*. The menus list all the local specialities – *cassoulet*, *foie gras*, duck breast with morels and pigeon with ceps. Menus 92–280F. Slightly impersonal welcome but the service is faultless. Free coffee.

🏃 🏠 HÔTEL DU CANAL**

2 av. Arnant-Vidal.
☎ 04.68.94.05.05 ➡ 04.68.94.05.06
TV. Car park.

A recently built hotel on the edge of the Canal du Midi. There's a tow path you can walk along. The rooms are modern, spacious and well maintained. 280F for a double with bath. Smiling staff. Free breakfast.

❘●❘ LE TIROU

9 av. Monseigneur-de-Langle; it's out of the centre, on the N113 to Carcassonne.
☎ 04.68.94.15.95
Car park.

You go past the gas station and come upon a large, unprepossessing modern house. Inside the dining room has big bay windows and is most attractive and there's a charming garden. You have to go past the kitchen from the car park and you can catch a glimpse of the efficient team. The *cassoulet* ranks with the best you'll get in Castelnaudary and they offer other local dishes that are robustly flavoured but freshly cooked. Weekday menu 95F and others 125–260F. The service is invisible but efficient and the welcome a delight.

CAUNES-MINERVOIS 11160

🏃 🏠 ❘●❘ HÔTEL-RESTAURANT D'ALIB-ERT**

pl. de la Mairie; take the D11 for 6km then turn right for Cannes onto the D620 and it's 2.5km further on.
☎ 04.68.78.00.54
Closed Sun evening out of season, Mon and Dec–Feb.
Car park.

This house, thoroughly lost in the narrow lanes of this Minervois village, looks as if it's straight out of the 16th century. The owners, Monsieur and Mme Guiraud, have run this peach of a place for ages with love and care. There are only seven rooms but they're well maintained and pleasant. Doubles 200F with basin, 350F with bath. The elegant country-manor style restaurant is totally in keeping with the rest of the house, and the open fire adds to the warmth of the atmosphere in cold weather. Good, authentic local dishes produced with great skill. Weekday menu 75F, or 120–170F. The owner will give you good advise about the wines – he's a great connaisseur about the local crus and his pleasure is infectious. Free apéritif.

CHÂTEAUNEUF-DE-RANDON   48170

🏃 🛎 |❍| HÔTEL DE LA POSTE**

L'Habitarelle: take the N88 and it's beside the Mausolée du Guesclin.
☎ 04.66.47.90.05 ➡ 04.66.47.91.41
Closed Fri evening, Sat lunchtime, All Saints' holidays and Christmas to New Year's Day.
Disabled access. TV. Car park.

Though this establishment is on the main road the traffic noise won't bother you because most bedrooms overlook the countryside. They've been modernised and are absolutely spotless; doubles at 270F with shower/wc or 300F with bath. The restaurant is in an old converted barn that's lost none of its rustic charm. José Laurens does the cooking and prepares tasty traditional dishes like ham hock in jelly, chicken liver salad, braised shoulder of beef, fillet of zander with *beurre blanc* and roast shoulder of lamb. Set menus 88–180F. There's an attractively priced wine list. 10% discount on the room rate out of season.

COLLIOURE   66190

🛎 LES CARANQUES**

Route de Port-Vendres; it's 300m from the town centre and the beach.
☎ 04.68.82.06.68 ➡ 04.68.82.00.92
e les-caranques@little-france.com
Closed 15 Oct–1 April.

This warm family-run hotel is right on the sea and has a wonderful view of Collioure and the port of Avall. The 22 peaceful rooms all come with a sea view and a small balcony. Doubles with basin 240F, 300–380F with shower/wc or 350–420F with bath. Breakfast 40F. There's a terrace where you can sunbathe and private access to the rocky beach.

🏃 🛎 LE MAS DES CITRONNIERS**

22 av. de la République (Centre).
☎ 04.68.04.82 ➡ 04.68.82.52.10
Closed 12 Nov to end March. **Garden. TV.**

A generously proportioned 1930s villa with an Art Deco staircase. Well-maintained rooms with good facilities, bathrooms and air conditioning. Doubles 250–480F with bath. The rooms in the annexe have either balconies or terraces onto the garden, surrounded by cypress hedges. There are some triple and family rooms, too. Set menus 125F and 145F, and half board is available in summer at 325–375F per person. 10% discount April, Oct

and Nov, except public holidays.

🛎 |❍| HOSTELLERIE DES TEMPLIERS**

quai de l'Amirauté (Centre); it's opposite the château.
☎ 04.68.98.31.10 ➡ 04.68.98.01.24
Hotel closed Jan. **Restaurant closed** Mon, weekdays Feb–March, and beginning of Nov. **TV.**

"*Chez Jojo Pous*", as it's known, is the place to stay in Collioure. The owner's father, René Pous, used to give artists free board and lodging and they paid him with pictures they'd painted . . . Matisse, Maillol, Dali, Picasso and Dufy were among them. He accumulated 2000 original works of art which are on display all over the hotel, including in the bedrooms. Unfortunately, some of the most precious ones, including a number of Picassos, were stolen a few years ago. The welcome is still friendly, nonetheless, and they've kept the prices reasonable too. Doubles with shower/wc or bath cost 335–395F depending on the season and 250F in the annexe, the *Villa Miranda*. Every room has a unique charm and most are absolutely superb; they feature painted wooden beds, quirky rustic chairs and, of course, the paintings. The hotel is often full, so you need to book well in advance. Be sure to ask for a room in the main building – you should avoid the annexe. The restaurant, specialises in fish dishes. *Formule brasserie* 68F, a menu at 120F or *à la carte*.

🏃 🛎 HÔTEL CASA PAÏRAL***

Impasse des Palmiers (Centre); it's beside pl. du 8 Mai.
☎ 04.68.82.05.81 ➡ 04.68.82.52.10
Closed Nov to end March. **TV. Swimming pool.**

A dream of a place, with a fountain on a patio with masses of greenery, a Hollywood-style swimming pool, a cosy lounge and absolute peace and quiet. High-class luxury in a little corner of paradise. Comfy spacious bedrooms with period furniture; doubles with shower/wc 390–440F, 510–990F in summer. Reservations taken well in advance, especially for summer holidays. A reliable establishment run by professional staff. 10% discount April and Oct, except public holidays.

🏃 🛎 |❍| L'ARPÈDE-RESTAURANT LA FARIGOLE***

Route de Port-Vendres; it's 2km from the centre of town.
☎ 04.68.98.09.59 ➡ 04.68.98.30.90
Hotel closed Dec–Feb. **Restaurant closed** Tues and Wed lunchtime. **Swimming pool. TV. Car park.**

Sturdily built on the rocks above the Mediterranean, so the view is wonderful. Attractive rooms decorated in warm colours; most of them have terraces overlooking the sea. Doubles 460–600F, breakfast 50F. You walk down the hill to a lovely swimming pool. The restaurant has a spacious, bright dining room and some tables are set round the pool. Good, tasty local cooking on menus 95–260F; grilled sea bass, sea bream or monkfish with garlic and cream sauce. Very professional welcome and service. Free coffee.

|●| CAN PLA

7 rue Voltaire; it's 50m from the port d'Avall.
☎ 04.68.82.10.00
Closed Mon out of season, 15 Nov–15 Dec.

A large, very simple dining room with a shaded terrace on the street. The speciality is fish and seafood, served as tapas or grilled. The boss is a solid young man who pays a lot of attention to service. He gets his fish locally or goes over the border to get it in Spain – he's a stickler for it being the freshest possible. Menus 75–150F menu and *à la carte*. around 150F Cod *aïolli*, fish paella, grilled prawns and shellfish, all even better when accompanied by a jug of clear, white local wine.

🏄|●| LE TRÉMAIL

1 rue Arago; it's in the old town.
☎ 04.68.82.16.10
Closed Sun evening and Mon out of season, and Jan.

Located in a lively part of town, with a few tables on a streetside terrace or in the warmly decorated dining room. They serve Catalan specialities: shellfish stews and grilled fish which are caught daily; *boquerones* (fresh, marinated anchovies with garlic), grilled fish, shellfish stew and, for dessert, *crème catalane* or home-made pastries. Wine by the bottle only, a pity when there are so many good local vintages to try. It's best to book. Menu 130F, *à la carte* 160F. Free glass of Banyuls wine.

CUCUGNAN   11350

☎|●| L'AUBERGE DU VIGNERON

2 rue Achille-Air; it's opposite the theatre.
☎ 04.68.45.03.00 ➡ 04.68.45.03.08
Closed Sun evening and Mon out of season, and mid-Dec to mid-Feb. **Car park**.

The inn offers a lovely overnight stop in rustic rooms with rough-hewn stone walls. Double rooms with shower/wc 260F. Make your way below to the old wine store which has been turned into a lovely restaurant. They've decorated it using some of the hogsheads and

there's an open fire. Regional dishes and menus start at 100F. Fantastic welcome.

BUGARACH   11190 (29KM W)

🏄|●| L'OUSTAL D'AL PECH

It's on the D14.
☎ 04.68.69.87.59
Closed Jan.

An isolated country inn in a totally unspoilt village. The rustic decor creates a lovely setting for a gourmet meal. Classic, flavourful dishes using good, local produce – goose gizzard *confits*, shrimps *à la Bugarach*, wild boar stew – and everything is made in the kitchens. The young team running the place are to be congratulated. Four menus 97–180F. Essential to book in winter. Free coffee and glass of Muscat when you order dessert with your meal.

FITOU   11510

🏄|●| LA CAVE D'AGNÈS

How to get there: it's at the top end of the village.
☎ 04.68.45.75.91
Closed Wed and Oct–March. **Car park**.

Tasteful, simple, rustic decor in this very popular place, which used to be a wine cellar. You'll receive a delightful welcome from the owner, who is originally from Scotland. The cooking's good and the portions are generous. Set menus 118–154F. Great buffet of starters and local *charcuterie*, lobster, haddock soufflé, a fan of fish and some very good local wines. For dessert, there's a scrumptious mousse flavoured with rosemary honey. Free apéritif.

FLORAC   48400

☎|●| GRAND HÔTEL DU PARC***

47 av. Jean-Monestier (Centre).
☎ 04.66.45.03.05 ➡ 04.66.45.11.81
Restaurant closed Mon out of season.
Disabled access. **Swimming pool**. **TV**. **Car park**.

Set in very pleasant parkland, this is the oldest and biggest hotel in the region. In atmosphere, though, it's more like a delightful family guesthouse. They offer sixty bedrooms with good facilities, 200–340F with shower/wc or bath. The cuisine has become rather ordinary, though, and the welcome could be more inviting. Set menus 92–185F.

|O| LA SOURCE DU PÊCHER

1 rue de Rémuët; it's behind the town hall on the
water's edge.
☎ 04.66.45.03.01
Closed Wed and Nov to Easter.

Ideally situated in the old town on the banks
of the Vibron and the well spring. From the
terrace, there's a picture-postcard view of
sloping gables, intricate roof patterns and old
architecture set against the tall green mountains, while in front there are some beautiful
trees, an ivy-covered façade and the gentle
sound of flowing water. Dishes include good
nettle soup, warm Pélardon goat's cheese
with Cévennes honey, and tripe made to an
old recipe. Selection of mature house
cheese. Lunch *menu du jour* at 89F, other
menus 120–180F.

SALLE-PRUNET (LA)   48400 (2KM S)

⅍ 🏠 |O| L'AUBERGE CÉVENOLE-CHEZ ANNIE

How to get there: take the Alès road.
☎ 04.66.45.11.80
Closed Sun evening, Mon out of season except public
holidays and mid-Nov to early Feb. **TV. Car park.**

An old building made of local stone deep in
the Mimente valley. Take your meals on the
terrace in summer or, in winter, huddle
round the fire. You feel as if you're eating in
the family dining room. Set menus 78–128F.
Good local *charcuterie*, *Pélardon* (hot goat's
cheese salad), and the house speciality,
noisette of veal with a cep sauce. Simple,
pleasant, very well-maintained rooms; doubles 250F with shower/wc. It's advisable to
book as it's very popular. 10% discount on
the room rate Sept–March.

COCURÈS   48400 (5KM N)

🏠 |O| LA LOZERETTE**

How to get there: take the D998.
☎ 04.66.45.06.04 ➡ 04.66.45.12.93
Closed Tues and Wed lunchtime, Tues lunchtime
July–Aug. **TV. Disabled access. Car park.**

Service noon–1.30pm and 7.30–9.15pm.
This family establishment, in a quiet little village on the picturesque road up to Mont
Lozère, is run primarily by the women.
Granny Eugénie once owned an inn herself,
but nowadays Pierrette Agulhon's in charge.
There's a weekday menu at 90F with local
specialities, and others 120–250F. All the
dishes complement the local Languedoc
wines. Take Pierrette's advice on the best

wine to accompany *panade* of cod with mild
garlic or snail ravioli with nettles. A successful combination of imagination, good taste
and magnificent flavours. The bedrooms are
as stylish as the dining room – floral, pastel-
painted and decorated with a keen eye for
detail. Expect to pay 295F with shower/wc
and 375F with bath. Breakfast is good.

FONT-ROMEU   66120

⅍ 🏠 |O| HÔTEL CARLIT-RESTAURANT LA CERDAGNE***

rue du Docteur-Capelle (Centre).
☎ 04.68.30.80.30 ➡ 04.68.30.80.68
e carlit-hotel@wanadoo.fr
Closed 15 Oct–15 Dec.

Though the modern building looks boring,
this three-star is more than adequate and
prices are fair. Reception is professional and
the rooms have good facilities, though the
decoration is over-bright. Double rooms with
shower/wc or bath 305–470F. Classic dishes
served in the restaurant, where the service is
friendly and warm. The chef uses good-quality fresh produce. Menus 85–180F. If you're
planning to stay a day or two, half board is
reasonably priced at 310–425F per person.
Free coffee or *digestif* and 10% discount on
the room rate.

⅍ |O| RESTAURANT LA CHAUMIÈRE

av. Emmanuel-Brousse.
☎ 04.68.30.04.40 **e** resto.chaumiere@free.fr
Closed Sun evening, Mon out of season, and a fortnight
end of June.

A friendly, gourmet restaurant. The setting is
welcoming, with wood-panelled walls and a
lovely terrace. It's a popular place locally and
it's even busy out of season. The cuisine is
mainly local and regional: peppers stuffed
with hake, aubergines stuffed with pigs' trotters and *crème catalane* for dessert. There
are simpler dishes – you could order a salad
and a grilled steak with real chips. Menus
85–160F. Free coffee.

BOLQUÈRE   66210 (3KM E)

⅍ 🏠 HÔTEL LASSUS*

pl. de la Mairie.
☎ 04.68.30.09.75 ➡ 04.68.30.38.11
Closed All Saints' and Whitsun holidays. **TV.**

If they gave an award for the "best welcome"
Jacqueline and Gérard would win. They chat
to their guests in the bar, and are always solici-

tious. The rooms are clean and quiet and equipped with shower/wc or bath. Doubles 220F. 10% discount if you stay three nights, outside school holidays.

LATOUR-DE-CAROL   66760 (17KM W)

🏠 |O| L'AUBERGE CATALANE

10 av. de Puymorens.
☎ 04.68.94.80.66 ➡ 04.68.04.95.25
📧 carolee@club.internet.fr
Closed Mon, Sun evening except in school holidays, 9–23 May and 18 Nov–20 Dec. **TV. Car park**.

A good place to stop on the road up to the Puymorens pass. When the inn was taken over by new owners they did up all the rooms, so they're attractively decorated in warm colours and well soundproofed. The simplest ones have shower/wc, 290F, while others have balconies and TV. There's a shady terrace and a dining room where they serve honest regional dishes: chicken *à la catalane*, *boles de picoulat* and *crème catalane*. Lunch *formule* 60F and menus 89–160F.

GARDE (LA)   48200

🏃 🏠 |O| LE ROCHER BLANC**

Centre; it's 1km from exit 32 on the A75, which is the first in Lozère coming from the north.
☎ 04.66.31.90.90 ➡ 04.66.31.93.67.
Closed Mon and Nov to end March. **Swimming pool. Garden. TV. Car park**.

The rooms are fairly spacious and they're clean and quiet. Expect to pay 280–300F with shower/wc. Set menus 90–220F; the one at 98F has regional specialities. Margeride is a wild and beautiful part of the country and the hotel is just 3km from France's smallest museum at Albaret-Sainte-Marie. Free apéritif.

CHAULHAC   48140 (10KM N)

🏃 |O| LA MAISON D'ELISA

How to get there: it's on the D8.
☎ 04.66.31.93.32

It's really pretty here, in this isolated village, with flowers planted all over the place. Originally from Lille, the owners run a cosy, unassuming inn. Decent, nicely presented menus which change daily. The one at 80F includes wine and coffee, and there are others up to 145F. Madame has a good touch in the kitchen and Monsieur serves you with a smile. *Truffade* and terrific *aligot* are made to order. Free coffee.

GRAU-DU-ROI (LE)   30240

🏠 HÔTEL BELLEVUE ET D'ANGLETERRE**

quai Colbert (Centre).
☎ 04.66.51.40.75 ➡ 04.66.51.43.78
Closed Dec. **TV**.

There are quite a few rooms with a grandstand view over Grau-du-Roi. They're pretty and well maintained, and prices are competitive. Doubles 180F with basin and 250–295F with shower/wc.

|O| LE GAFÉTOU

6 [bis] rue Frédéric Mistral.
☎ 04.66.51.60.99

Fronted by an awning, the large dining room is decorated in aquatic shades, which sets the scene for the fish, seafood and shellfish you'll enjoy here. The menus, 98–168F, offer good value, and the fish is as fresh as can be. Friendly welcome, perfect service and an ideal spot by the seaside.

GRUISSAN   11430

|O| LE LAMPARO

l4 rue Amiral-Courbet; it's in the village beside the pond.
☎ 04.66.49.93.65
Closed Sun evening, Mon and mid-Dec to end Jan.

This is a good restaurant specialising in fish and seafood at reasonable prices. The dining room is clean and the tables are laid with salmon-pink cloths; there are more tables on the terrace, which has a view of the pond. Excellent menus 100–145F – try the cheapest one which offers roast oysters with duck breast, fillet of sea bream with olive paste, cheese and chocolate *truffé*.

LAMALOU-LES-BAINS   34240

🏠 |O| LE COMMERCE*

av. Charcot (Centre).
☎ 04.67.95.63.14
Closed mid-Dec to early Feb. **Disabled access**.

The owner makes you feel most welcome in this old, almost passé, family-run establishment. The interior is spick-and-span, if a touch dated. Doubles 110–165F with basin, shower or bath. The restaurant is open exclusively to guests in the evening. There's a 53F set menu and a dish of the day; try the stuffed quail or red mullet with *sauce Normande*. It's pleasant out on the terrace.

🎿 🏠 |O| HÔTEL-RESTAURANT BELLEVILLE**

1 av. Charcot (Centre).
☎ 04.67.95.57.00 ➡ 04.67.95.64.18
Disabled access. Garden. TV. Car park.

This is a substantial provincial hotel, typical of a spa town; the house has character and has been entirely refurbished. It's spacious and has good facilities – doubles with basin 150F, with shower/wc 195F and with bath 230F. Many bedrooms overlook the garden. Rustic decor in the restaurant where they serve a series of set menus 70–198F. They specialise in local dishes such as seafood stew, thin slivers of duck in Muscatel and monkfish stew with brandy, garlic and tomatoes. For those in a hurry, the 70F *menu-express* is served on the veranda. An excellent place. 10% discount on the room rate and free house apéritif.

BÉDARIEUX   34600 (8KM NE)

🏠 |O| LE CENTRAL*

3 pl. aux Herbes (Centre); take the D908.
☎ 04.67.95.06.76
Closed Sat out of season, Sat lunchtime in season, a week in June and three weeks in Oct. **TV**.

Here's a country house with an attractive ivy-covered façade, overlooking the Orb. The dining room is rather dark and old-fashioned but the menus list good regional dishes and home cooking. Set menus, 60–110F, list goat's cheese salad, duck and gizzard salad, and shoulder of lamb braised with olives. Decent accommodation – doubles with basin 160F, 180F with shower, 198F with bath. Some have TV.

🏠 HÔTEL DELTA

1 rue de Clairac; it's on the street that runs at right angles to av. Jean-Jaurès.
☎ 04.67.23.21.19
TV.

A lovely young couple have converted this small clinic into a hotel. It may have no stars, but the bedrooms are clean and spacious. Fresh, unusual decor, with Egyptian symbols and Chinese fans here and there. Prices are reasonable, with doubles with shower 160–190F, 180–210F with shower/wc and TV. This is a nice little place.

LÉZIGNAN-CORBIÈRES   11200

🏠 |O| HÔTEL LE TASSIGNY-RESTAURANT LE TOURNEDOS**

Rond-point de-Lattre-de-Tassigny; take av. des Corbières towards the A9.
☎ 04.68.27.11.51 ➡ 04.68.27.67.31
Hotel closed Sun evening, a week in Feb and a week in Oct. **Restaurant closed** Sun evening and Mon.
Disabled access. TV. Car park.

A great place for an overnight stay if you don't want to spend a fortune. Freshly refurbished and modernised, with doubles 210–240F with bath. The cheaper ones are the noisiest. The restaurant is popular locally. Weekday lunch *formule* 68F and menus 76–150F. Hearty specialities include *cassoulet* and meats grilled over a wood fire.

ESCALES   11200 (7KM NW)

|O| LES DINEDOURELLES

Impasse des Pins; it's at the top of the village.
☎ 04.67.44.07.46 ➡ 04.67.44.30.47
Closed Sat and Mon lunchtime May–Sept, Mon and Tues Oct–April, and Nov–Feb.

A good atmosphere and a pleasant, unusual setting. The cuisine is original and there are some sweet and sour dishes. Have you ever eaten a saddle of lamb in pastry with red sugar and lemon zests while sitting in a barrel? You do here. If you've come for a quiet, amorous dinner, you may be seated in a wagon. Select your main dish from the 95F menu, and you will start with a salad of melon and watermelon and finish with a *carbonade flamande*, local cheese and dessert. There's a lovely terrace under the pine trees with a view of the Montagne Noire. Weekday lunch menu 70F then 98–198F. Out of season on two or three Friday nights a month, they feature entertainment such as singers, jazz, storytelling or even short plays.

FABREZAN   11200 (9KM SW)

🎿 🏠 |O| LE CLOS DES SOUQUETS

av. de Lagrasse; take the D611 towards Lagrasse.
☎ 04.68.43.52.61 ➡ 04.68.43.56.76
Closed Sun evening and Nov–March. **Swimming pools. Garden. TV. Car park.**

This is a little jewel of a place on the route of the Cathar chateaux and the Corbières caves. It only has five bedrooms. The Julien family spend the winter in the Caribbean, as you can see from the exotic touches in the bedrooms and in the dishes served around one of the two swimming pools. Simple, tasty dishes – salad *méridionale*, good home-made pizza, and cream cheese with honey – and more unusual ones like *colombo* of lamb and very good *carpaccio* of fish and meat. Best of all is the grilled fish of the day. Menus 100–185F. Half board, 485F per person, is compulsory in summer. Doubles 290–380F. Free apéritif.

HOMPS 11200 (10KM N)

☆ ✿ |O| AUBERGE DE L'ARBOUSIER

Route de Carcassonne.
☎ 04.68.91.11.24 ➡ 04.68.91.12.61
Closed Mon July–Aug, Wed and Sun evening Sept–June, three weeks in Feb and three weeks in Nov. **TV**. **Car park**.

The Canal du Midi flows alongside. It's a lovely spot, with a shaded terrace in summer and quiet comfy bedrooms. Doubles 230–250F with bath. The old stonework, exposed beams and decor contrast well with the modern art. The kitchen prepares classic dishes: breast of duck with honey and pine nuts, fillets of mullet with olive oil, and rabbit salad with artichokes. Set weekday menu 85F, others up to 205F. Free apéritif.

|O| RESTAURANT LES TONNELIERS

Port du Canal du Midi.
☎ 04.68.91.14.04
Closed mid-Dec to mid-Feb.
Disabled access. **Garden**. **Car park**.

The Canal du Midi runs nearby, but though this place offers good food in rustic surroundings it doesn't have much of a view. *Formule* 80F and menus 98–190F, listing specialities like *cassoulet* with *confit* of duck, marinated salmon with two kinds of lemon, and *tarte Tatin*. Tourists come to see the canal in the evening. In summer, sit out in the attractive garden or on the shaded terrace.

LIMOUX 11300

☆ ✿ |O| GRAND HÔTEL MODERNE ET PIGEON***

pl. du Général-Leclerc (Centre); it's by the post office.
☎ 04.68.31.00.25 ➡ 04.68.31.12.43
Restaurant closed Mon, Sat lunchtime and mid-Nov to mid-Jan. **TV**. **Car park**.

This magnificent building had many lives before being converted into a hotel in the early 1900s; originally a convent, it was then a grand town house and later a bank. Take a good look at the 17th-century frescoes on the wall above the splendid staircase. This place is comfy and very well run, without being too formal. Lovely doubles 360F with shower/wc, luxury rooms 540F with bath. Sophisticated decor and quiet atmosphere in the dining room. The cheapest set menu is

160F with others 180–235F, listing some delicious dishes: *terrine* of langoustine with *coulis* of lobster, braised duck in sparkling white wine (the house speciality – a must), followed by cheese and dessert. You can h ave a glass of sparkling wine in the cellar where the pool players hang out. 10% discount on the room rate.

LODÈVE 34700

☆ ✿ |O| LA CROIX BLANCHE**

6 av. de Funel.
☎ 04.67.44.10.87 ➡ 04.67.44.38.33
℮ hotelcroixblanche.com
Restaurant closed Fri lunchtime and Dec–March. **TV**. **Car park**.

An impressive collection of copper pots, pans and basins ornament this place and create a welcoming atmosphere. Generations of sales reps and businessmen have stopped by to enjoy the local hospitality. Simple accommodation, with doubles 170F with basin, 200F with shower/wc, 240F with bath. Unfussy cooking and generous portions in the dining room, with specialities such as local snails, duck *ballotine* and duck with morels. Set menus 70–170F. Free coffee.

✿ |O| HÔTEL-RESTAURANT DE LA PAIX**

11 bd. Montalanque; it's near the old watch tower.
☎ 04.67.44.07.46 ➡ 04.67.44.30.47
℮ hotel-de-laville@wanadoo.fr
Closed Sun evening and Mon May–Aug, and 1 Jan–3 March. **Swimming pool**. **TV**. **Car park**.

The same family have been running this place since 1887. They've refurbished it recently, so it's clean and comfortable and has views of the mountains and the Lergue river. Doubles with bath 250–320F; half board is compulsory in summer, 280–300F per person. The hearty cooking majors on regional dishes and uses fresh produce. The house speciality is an unusual Roquefort flan with figs, and in summer they offer chargrilled meat served outside around the swimming pool. Set menus 85–200F, with a children's menu at 50F.

|O| LE PETIT SOMMELIER

3 pl. de la République; it's beside the tourist office.
☎ and ➡ 04.67.44.05.39
Closed Mon and Wed evening except July–Sept, the last week in June and the All Saints' holidays.

An informal, unpretentious little place with simple bistro decor. Tasty cooking in dishes like breast of duck with apples and honey and warm mussels in a cream sauce with Banyuls wine. Set menus 80–185F. You'll get a warm, friendly welcome in this convivial place. Not surprisingly, it's popular with the locals. There's a pleasant terrace.

LUNEL 34400

☆ |●| AUBERGE DES HALLES

26 cours Gabriel-Péri (Centre); it's next to the covered market.
☎ 04.67.83.85.80
Closed Sun evening, Mon, Feb and a week in Oct.

A well-known restaurant serving honest, traditional cuisine that respects the changing seasons. The 140F Sunday menu depends on what is good at the market, but might include *millefeuille* with mussels, *foie gras* with *Muscat de Lunel* wine, and good home-made desserts. Weekday menu 60F and then 95F. There are tables on the terrace outside and the service is charming. Free coffee.

MENDE 48000

☎ |●| HÔTEL GTM-RESTAURANT LA CAILLE**

2 rue d'Aigues-Passes; it's in the old town.
☎ 04.66.65.01.39

Monsieur Saleil has made a large sign for his establishment, so you won't miss it – it is definitely not a tourist trap. Decent, well-maintained bedrooms at 230F with shower and 320F with bath. Popular with sales reps who have learned to live with the owner's slightly curt manner. Brasserie-style cooking, with a 70F *menu du jour*, and others up to 160F.

☆ ☎ |●| HÔTEL-RESTAURANT DU PONT-ROUPT***

2 av. du 11-Novembre (East).
☎ 04.66.65.01.43 ➡ 04.66.65.22.96
e hotel-pont-roupt@wanadoo.fr
Closed Sun evening out of season and March.
Swimming pool. TV. Car park.

A delightful hotel, in a large house on the banks of the Lot on the edge of town. The decor is contemporary and plain but the bedrooms are comfortable. Doubles with shower/wc at 280F, 380F with bath. There's a pretty indoor swimming pool. The chef draws on a long tradition of cuisine while also creating some modern dishes. The *aligot* and quail with *foie gras* are

wonderful. Menus 120–265F. 10% discount on the room rate.

|●| LE MAZEL

25 rue du Collège (Centre).
☎ and ➡ 04.66.65.05.33
Closed Mon evening, Tues, three weeks Feb/March and ten days at the end of Nov.

This is one of the few modern buildings in the town centre and although the setting's not ideal, the dining room has been tastefully arranged. Jean-Paul Brun uses first-rate ingredients to create fine, flavoursome dishes such as *terrine de campagne* and truffle omelette, fresh fish and duck with wind mushrooms. Menus 80–150F. It's a popular place for business lunches and the best value for money in town.

CHABRITS 48000 (5KM W)

☆ |●| LA SAFRANIÈRE

How to get there: take the N88, cross the Roupt bridge, then straight ahead on the D42.
☎ 04.66.49.31.54
Closed Sun evening, Mon, March and a week in Sept.

This is the gourmet restaurant that the Mende area has been begging for. The dining room is bright and elegant, and it's in a very old building that's been attractively refurbished. The light, delicate cooking makes clever use of herbs, spices and seasonings like basil, tarragon, cumin, saffron and coconut. The choices on the various menus, 105–280F, include snail ravioli, fillet of duckling with a sweet-and-sour sauce and pine nuts, a decent selection of cheeses and a perfect *crème brûlée*, perfumed with jasmine tea. Free coffee.

PALHERS 48100 (28.5KM W)

|●| LE MOULIN DE CHAZE

Route de Mende; take the N88, then the 108 towards Marvejols.
☎ 04.66.32.36.07
Closed Mon except on public holidays. **Garden. Car park.**

Seated at a wrought-iron table out on the terrace of this white stone establishment on a summer's day you could easily imagine yourself in Italy. Inside, the stonework, beams and wall-hangings make for a comfortable setting. The attractive cooking brings out the freshness in the flavours, but it's not particularly innovative. Set menus 110–220F. The service can't be faulted.

MEYRUEIS   48150

☕ ♨ |●| HÔTEL DE LA JONTE**

How to get there: follow the D996 and the gorges of La Jonte.
☎ 05.65.62.60.52 ➡ 05.65.62.61.62
Closed Dec–Feb. **Swimming pool. TV. Disabled access.**

A large establishment, run by Monsieur Vergely, that's well known for its good cooking and the warmth of its welcome. It is cheap and very good. There are two dining rooms, one more touristy than the other. Opt for the one used by workers and travelling salesmen – the cooking is better and the prices are reasonable, with set menus 62–145F. The rooms are very well maintained and are either above the restaurant or in an annexe overlooking the river Jonte. Doubles cost 180F with shower/wc and 200F with bath. The ones with TV and a view of the river are the most expensive. Free *digestif*.

☕ ♨ |●| HÔTEL FAMILY**

rue de la Barrière (Centre).
☎ 04.66.45.60.02 ➡ 04.66.45.66.54
Closed All Saints' to Palm Sunday. **Disabled access. Garden. Swimming pool. TV. Car park.**

A large building standing by the fast-flowing stream that runs through the village. They'll give you a friendly reception. Simple, well maintained rooms; doubles 230–265F with shower/wc, 260F with bath. Those on the top floor are the best. The cuisine majors on local dishes and is reasonably priced; menus 80–200F. There's a pleasant garden with a swimming pool opposite the hotel that you get to by crossing a little wooden bridge. 10% discount April, May and Oct.

☕ ♨ |●| HÔTEL DU MONT AIGOUAL**

rue de la Barrière.
☎ 04.66.45.65.61 ➡ 04.66.45.64.25
Closed Nov to end March.
Swimming pool. TV. Car park.

From the outside this place looks ordinary enough, but appearances can be deceptive. Stella Robert is energetic and lively and she'll give you a charming welcome. There's a beautiful swimming pool at the back of the hotel in an enormous garden. The rooms have been tastefully refurbished; 280F–460F with shower or bath. Daniel Lagrange uses authentic, tasty local produce to create appetizing local dishes: *confidou* (beef stewed in red wine), leg of lamb, and apple *galette* with Roquefort. Menus 98F, 158F and 200F. One of the best restaurants in

these parts, offering consistent quality at reasonable prices. 10% discount on the room rate April and Oct.

MÈZE   34140

☕ |●| LE PESCADOU

33 bd. du Port; go towards the harbour.
☎ 04.67.43.81.72
Closed Tues evening, Wed and Jan.

Le Pescadou has a pretty terrace on the harbour and a spacious dining room attractively decorated with engravings of ships and lots of green plants. It's a fresh, relaxing place that's very popular with the locals. Weekday menu 76F then others up to 186F – lots of fish soup with toasted croutons, squid with *rouille*, mussels with garlic butter, and snails from the Thau pond. Free coffee.

MONT-LOUIS   66210

☕ ♨ |●| HÔTEL-RESTAURANT LOU ROUBALLOU

rue des Écoles-Laïques (Centre); it's on the ramparts, opposite the local primary school.
☎ 04.68.04.23.26 ➡ 04.68.04.14.09
Restaurant closed Wed out of season, May, Oct and Nov. **TV. Car park.**

A family guesthouse with lots of rustic character; it's comfy, delightful and full of charm. You'll be greeted warmly by the entire Duval family, primarily by Christiane, who is Catalan. You can practically feel the warmth of the sun in her voice when she talks about the Pyrenees. You'll feel perfectly at home in one of the attractive little rooms, 160F with basin, 250F with shower/wc and 340F with bath. The restaurant is tastefully decorated. Pierre's crazy about the mountains and his fresh, authentic cooking is up there with the best in the region. Set menus, 125–195F, display his specialities: *aiguillettes* of game with ceps that he picks himself, boar stew, duck with fruit and honey sauce, and *boles de Picolat* (Catalan meatballs). In winter, don't miss the *ollada* (a substantial country soup), or the *hachis* (which is a bit like a shepherd's pie). All year round there are delicious mushrooms. The *rouballou* is a mushroom that grows locally in the moss under little fir trees. Cheap, good and friendly. Free coffee and 10% discount on the room rate Oct–April.

MONTPELLIER 34000

SEE MAP OVERLEAF

⌂ HÔTEL LES FAUVETTES*

8 rue Bonnard. **MAP A1-2**
It's on the route of bus no. 3.
☎ 04.67.63.17.60 ➡ 04.67.64.09.09nard.

Probably the best and cheapest hotel in its class in Montpellier. It's a small establishment in a quiet street, run by a friendly couple. The bedrooms may be basic but they're quiet and clean. Most look onto the interior courtyard. They serve breakfast on the veranda, which is popular in summer. Doubles with basin 140F, comfier ones with shower 170F, 190F with shower/wc and 230F with bath.

⌂ HÔTEL DES ÉTUVES

24 rue des Étuves. **MAP B3-4**
☎ 04.67.60.78.19 ➡ 04.67.60.78.19
e hoteldesetuves@wanadoo.fr
Closed Sun noon–6.30pm. **TV**. **Car park**.

This hotel is clean and friendly; and though not offering luxury, it's a very good for a hotel with no star-rating. 170F with shower/wc and 200F with bath.

⌂ HÔTEL VERDUN-COLISÉE**

33 rue de Verdun. **MAP C3-6**
☎ 04.67.58.42.63 ➡ 04.67.58.98.27
TV.

This place overlooks a lively though not noisy street. Decent, recently refurbished bedrooms in all price ranges – 170F with basin, 225–260F with shower or shower/wc and 285F with bath. Good reception.

⌂ HÔTEL FLORIDE**

1 rue François-Perrier. **MAP D3-5**
☎ 04.67.65.73.30 ➡ 04.67.22.10.83
e hotel.floride@gofornet.com
TV.

Situated in a quiet street near the district of Antigone. You'll receive a warm welcome. Doubles 199F with basin to 269F with bath; the best ones overlook the terrace, which is a riot of flowers. Good breakfast. 10% discount Oct–April.

⌂ HÔTEL LE PARC**

8 rue Achille-Bège; it's on the other side of Verdanson, 300m from the cathedral. Off map **B1-10**
☎ 04.67.41.16.49 ➡ 04.67.54.10.05
Disabled access. **Garden**. **TV**. **Car park**.

This is a typical 18th-century Languedoc building. They give you a friendly welcome.

There is a quiet, attractive garden with pots of flowers on the terrace. The bedrooms are clean, comfy and air-conditioned, and all have mini-bar and telephone. Doubles with basin 290–310F, 310–360F with shower, 290–340F with shower/wc and 340–360F with bath. It is a pity that the garden doubles as a car park.

⌂ HÔTEL DE LA COMÉDIE**

1 [bis] rue Baudin. **MAP C2-8**
☎ 04.67.58.43.64 ➡ 04.67.58.58.43
TV.

You'd be hard pushed to find a more central hotel. It's good and quiet, and run by a nice man. The rooms have been refurbished and they're clean and welcoming. Doubles 305–395F with shower/wc, satellite TV and air conditioning.

⌂ HÔTEL LES ARCEAUX**

33–35 bd. des Arceaux; it's behind promenade du Peyrou. Off map **A2-7**
☎ 04.67.92.03.03 ➡ 04.67.92.05.09
Garden. **TV**. **Pay car park**.

This is an attractive house with an outside staircase leading from the garden to reception. On the other side you have a view of the 17th-century aqueduct near the Peyrou gardens. Homely atmosphere and comfortable bedrooms which have all been refurbished and painted in fresh, pretty colours. Doubles 310–340F with wc, shower or bath. Some rooms have a private balcony and others can sleep three. Breakfast 35F. Excellent value for money. 10% discount.

⌂ HÔTEL DU PALAIS**

3 rue du Palais-des-Guilhem. **MAP A2/B2-12**
☎ 04.67.60.47.38 ➡ 04.67.60.40.23
TV.

This handsome 19th-century building with its splendid marbled entrance is near a quiet little square just five minutes from the centre. The bright, attractive bedrooms are furnished with reproductions, creating a cosy country atmosphere. They're all air-conditioned and have double glazing. Doubles 350F with shower/wc and 380–420F with bath and mini-bar. Excellent breakfast, 52F. A very good hotel with a homely atmosphere.

⌂ LE GUILHEM***

18 rue Jean-Jacques-Rousseau. **MAP A1-13**
☎ 04.67.52.90.90 ➡ 04.67.60.67.67
e hotel-le-guilhem@mnet.fr
TV. **Garden**.

This establishment is tucked away in a delightful little street. The bedrooms overlook a mysterious-looking garden with the cathedral beyond. The place has been tastefully refurbished and the bedrooms are superb – they redecorate a number of them every year. Doubles 360F with shower/wc, 400–700F with bath. Delightful reception from Monsieur and Mme Charpentier.

🎿 🛎 CITADINES ANTIGONE***

588 bd. d'Antigone (and pl. du Millénaire). **MAP D2-9**
☎ 08.25.01.03.52 ➡ 04.67.64.54.65
📧 antigone@citadines.com
TV. Car park.

Reception open 7.30am–8pm in the week, 8am–noon and 5–8pm at weekends and public holidays. Spacious and clean studios and apartments offering a range of hotel services (fresh linen, cleaning, breakfast, etc); 385F for two, with bath. Each has an equipped kitchen which will ease the strain on your restaurant bill. There's an entryphone system and direct-dial telephones. 10% discount.

🎿 🛎 |O| LA MAISON BLANCHE***

1796 av. de la Pompignane; it's on the corner of 46 rue des Salaisons. Off map **D1-14**
☎ 04.67.79.60.25 ➡ 04.67.79.53.39
Restaurant closed Sat lunchtime, Sun and 23 Dec–2 Jan. **Disabled access. Swimming pool. Garden. TV. Car park**.

They planted the trees in this park centuries ago, and there's a preservation order on it. The building looks like a antebellum mansion from the Deep South, with spacious bedrooms decorated in shades of grey and a carpet so thick your toes sink into it. Lots of famous people have stayed here, including Rostropovich, Alain Delon and Johnny Halliday. It's quiet, and the ideal place for the stars to escape from their adoring fans. You'll pay 450–520F a night. In the restaurant, there is a set menu at 120F; à la carte reckon on 220F. Free breakfast.

🎿 |O| CRÊPERIE DES DEUX PROVINCES

7 rue Jacques-Cœur. **MAP B2-22**
☎ 04.67.60.68.10 ➡ 04.67.60.33.98
Closed Sun and mid-June to mid-July

Friendly, watchful service in this restaurant with the noisy atmosphere of a canteen. Filling salads 16–60F (try the one with scallops) and a choice of 160 crêpes 14–56F. Together, they make a good meal. Free apéritif.

|O| LA POSADA

20 rue du Petit Saint-Jean. **MAP B2-20**
☎ 04.67.66.21.25

This establishment has quickly become a roaring success, with a reputation for using quality seasonal ingredients in uncompromisingly good home cooking. The portions are substantial, too. Three-course menu express 50F, others at 69F and 115F, and a children's menu 36F. There are tables on a pretty terrace on the little square, or in the small crowded dining room. Best to book.

|O| LA TOMATE

6 rue du Four-des-Flammes. **MAP B2-25**
☎ 04.67.60.49.38
Closed Sun and Mon.

There are three wood-panelled dining rooms in this attractive restaurant that has been well-known locally for ages. There are two 50F menus du jour (62F evening); one offers the likes of charcuterie, chicken à la diable (in a spicy sauce) and strawberry tart, the other offers a mega-salad and dessert. The specialities include cassoulet with duck confit, foie gras, veal Lolo, and chocolate gâteau. Other menus 62–117F. Generously flavoured dishes prepared with obvious skill.

|O| LA BONNE BOUILLE

6 bd. des Arceaux. Off map **A2-28**
☎ 04.67.52.94.27
Closed Sat lunchtime and Sun.

Fish, fish and more fish. The decor recreates the kind of fishing port atmosphere you find in Sète. You can choose between two lunch menus; the quick formule TGV at 55F, which offers a fish main course, dessert and a $\frac{1}{4}$ litre of wine, or the formule grill at 70F. Expect to pay 130F for dinner. Dishes à la carte change with the seasons; fillet of sea bream with cep sauce, fisherman's stew, zarzuela (another type of fish stew) and parillada which is a selection of different fish, nicely grilled. In summer, eat on the shady terrace.

|O| LE BOUCHON SAINT-ROCH

rue du Pan-d'Agde. **MAP B2-23**
☎ 04.67.60.94.18
Closed Sun lunchtime.

Really tasty, simple dishes prepared by Madame – pan-fried fish and civet of suckling pig in pastry – and served by her smiling daughter. You eat on a pleasant terrace in a quiet street. Three menus 55–100F.

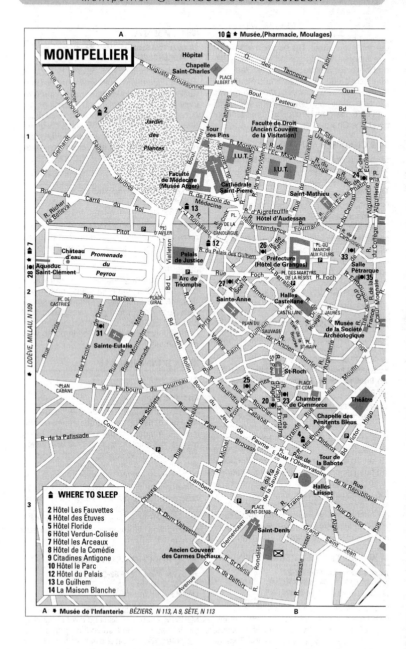

MONTPELLIER

10 🏠 ✦ Musée,(Pharmacie, Moulages)

Hôpital
Chapelle Saint-Charles
PLACE ALBERT 1er
Jardin des Plantes
Tour des Pins
Faculté de Droit (Ancien Couvent de la Visitation)
I.U.T.
I.U.T.
Faculté de Médecine (Musée Atger)
Cathédrale Saint-Pierre
Saint-Mathieu
🏠 2
🏠 13
Hôtel d'Audessan
🏠 7
Château d'eau
Promenade du Peyrou
🏠 12
26
Palais de Justice
Préfecture (Hôtel de Grandes)
Salle Pétrarque
🏠 33
Aqueduc Saint-Clément
28
Arc de Triomphe
27
35
31
Sainte-Anne
Sainte-Eulalie
Halles Castellane
Musée de la Société Archéologique
St-Roch
25
20
23
Chambre de Commerce
Théâtre
Chapelle des Pénitents Bleus
4
Tour de la Baboté
Halles Laissac
Saint-Denis
Ancien Couvent des Carmes Déchaux

🏠 WHERE TO SLEEP

2 Hôtel Les Fauvettes
4 Hôtel des Étuves
5 Hôtel Floride
6 Hôtel Verdun-Colisée
7 Hôtel les Arceaux
8 Hôtel de la Comédie
9 Citadines Antigone
10 Hôtel le Parc
12 Hôtel du Palais
13 Le Guilhem
14 La Maison Blanche

A   ✦ Musée de l'Infanterie   BÉZIERS, N 113, A 9, SÈTE, N 113   B

A   ✦ LODÈVE, MILLAU, N 109

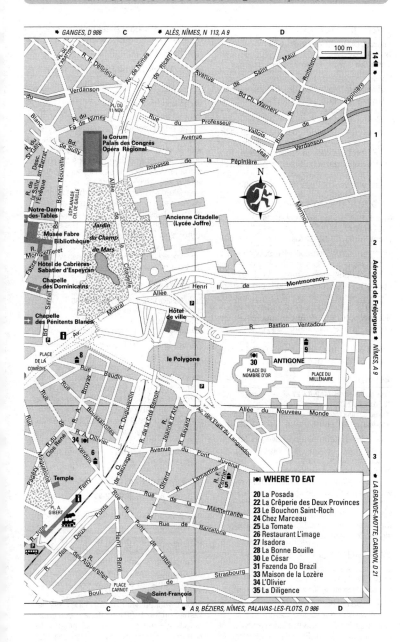

100 m

le Corum
Palais des Congrès
Opéra Régional

Notre-Dame-des-Tables

Ancienne Citadelle
(Lycée Joffre)

Musée Fabre
Bibliothèque

Jardin
du Champ
de Mars

Hôtel de Cabrières-Sabatier d'Espeyran

Chapelle
des Dominicains

Chapelle
des Pénitents Blancs

Hôtel
de ville

PLACE
DE LA
COMÉDIE

le Polygone

ANTIGONE

30

PLACE DU
NOMBRE D'OR

PLACE DU
MILLÉNAIRE

Temple

34

6

5

9

⊨◉⊩ WHERE TO EAT

20 La Posada
22 La Crêperie des Deux Provinces
23 Le Bouchon Saint-Roch
24 Chez Marceau
25 La Tomate
26 Restaurant L'image
27 Isadora
28 La Bonne Bouille
30 Le César
31 Fazenda Do Brazil
33 Maison de la Lozère
34 L'Olivier
35 La Diligence

Saint-François

𝄞|●| CHEZ MARCEAU

7 pl. de la Chapelle-Neuve. **MAP B1-24**
☎ 04.67.66.08.09
Closed Sun in winter and Sun lunchtime in summer.

Service noon–2pm and 7–11pm. Part bistro, part restaurant, on a beautiful little square shaded by plane trees – the perfect place for a spot of lunch outdoors. Good simple cooking and generous portions. It's cheap, but the standards can vary. The 62F set lunch menu is good value, and in the evening they offer menus at 74F or 109F. You'll pay around 100F *à la carte*. They do a lovely breast of duck *à l'orange*, vegetable soup with *pesto*, red mullet with peppers, and bream with vermouth sauce. Free apéritif.

𝄞|●| RESTAURANT L'IMAGE

6 rue du Puits-des-Esquilles. **MAP B2-26**
☎ 04.67.60.47.79
Closed Sun and 15 July–23 Aug.

This typical old stone-built Montpellier house is something of a local hang-out. They've put lots of beautiful posters everywhere. If you're claustrophobic, head for the dining room upstairs. The simple dishes are suffused with Mediterranean flavours and the portions are generous. Set menus 67–129F. A few specialities: fish *parillada* (a selection of fish, tastily grilled), char-grilled meat, *croustillant* of duck and pressed fresh salmon. They do musical evenings. Free glass of Calvados or rum.

|●| ISADORA

6 rue du Petit-Scel. **MAP B2-27**
☎ 04.67.66.25.23
Closed Sat lunchtime and Sun, Sun and Mon lunchtime July–Aug and All Saints' holidays.

A wonderful 13th-century vaulted cellar decorated in Art Deco style. Fine cooking and delicious seafood; hot oysters with braised chicory, pan-fried scallops *à la Provençale* and *tournedos Rossini* which is fillet of beef with *foie gras*. You'll be served by the owner, who knows how to look after his customers. Set menus 85F and 140–170F. In summer, the terrace on the pl. Sainte Anne, overlooking the fountain, is very popular.

|●| LA DILIGENCE

2 pl. Pétrarque. **MAP B2-35**
☎ 04.67.66.12.21
Closed Sat lunchtime, Sun and lunchtimes in Aug.

The restaurant has a splendid dining room with stone walls and a vaulted ceiling. Straightforward classical cuisine with a lunch menu at 90F and others 160–310F: calf's head *ravigote*, calf's liver with honey sauce, monkfish with

shrimps, very good cheeses and desserts. Efficient service. Probably best to book at the weekend.

|●| FAZENDA DO BRASIL

5 rue de l'École-de-Droit. **MAP A2-31**
☎ 04.67.92.90.91
Closed lunchtimes and Sun.

They've managed to create a real feel of Brazil in this bright, colourful restaurant. Their speciality is *churrascos* – char-grilled meat served with as much cassava, *feijaos* (Brazilian black beans), onions and fried plantains as you can manage. Whatever the size of your appetite or your wallet, there's a *formule* to suit you – they have five in all. For 90F you can have pork marinated in lime juice, for 93F rump steak, for 95F four meat dishes, for 115F six meat dishes, and for 165F nine meat dishes. The service is rather slow and since the meat is cooked to order, side dishes tend to go cold. They have some good Argentinian and Chilean wines and the best *piña colada* ever.

|●| LE CÉSAR

pl. du Nombre d'Or, Antigone. **MAP D2-30**
☎ 04.67.64.87.87 ➡ 04.67.22.20.39
📧 le.cesar@wanadoo.fr
Closed Sat, Sun evening and Christmas to New Year.

Service until 10.30pm. A good brasserie with an enormous terrace overlooking the square. There's a satisfying 128F regional menu with, for example, *fondants* of chicken or capon as a starter, followed by fresh cod with *aïoli* or *gardiane de toro* (stewed marinated beef), and home-made dessert. The 95F menu is simpler and the 195F one more extensive. The first Friday of every month (except July–Aug), there's a meeting of the Marie Sara club, the queens of the *rejeneadora*, or horse race festival.

𝄞|●| MAISON DE LA LOZÈRE

27 rue de l'Aiguillerie. **MAP B2-33**
☎ 04.67.66.46.36
Closed Sun and Mon lunchtimes, Wed and a week at the beginning of Jan.

Service 12.15–2pm and 8–10pm. This restaurant and its little sister in Paris are both showcases for Lozère specialities – you can almost hear the mushrooms growing, the torrents gushing and the wolves howling. . . Top-of-the-range cooking served in the superb vaulted dining room in the basement. Dishes on the 140F lunchtime menu change constantly but there's always *aligot* and a platter of appetizing, mature cheeses. Other menus 250–200F. The place doubles as a first-rate grocer's and there is plenty of produce to take home. Good choice of thoughtfully selected Languedoc wines. Free coffee.

🏃|◉| L'OLIVIER

12 rue Aristide-Ollivier. **MAP C3-34**
☎ 04.67.92.86.28
Closed Sun, Mon, public holidays, and Jul-Aug.

Modern decor, a tad *nouveau*, and fine cooking that is popular with local gourmets. Fish is prepared as skilfully as meat: warm lobster salad with baby vegetables, turbot with purple artichokes and clams, braised veal with macaroni and sweetbreads stirred into the sauce, and chocolate *moelleux* with toasted hazelnuts – all as delicious as they sound. Delicate sauces, good presentation and efficient service. Set menus 198F or 218F *à la carte*. Free apéritif.

MAUGUIO   34130 (10KM E)

|◉| LE PATIO

Impasse Molière (Centre); take the D24; it's in a cul-de-sac off Grand-Rue.
☎ 04.67.29.63.90 ➡ 04.67.29.57.75
Closed Sat and Sun lunchtime Oct–March, and Mon.

This little restaurant used to be a wine cellar, so it's got lots of atmosphere. The decor is a bit kitsch – the furniture in the dining room looks as if it came from a second-hand shop. The grill, where they cook duck breast, Mediterranean prawns and so on, takes centre stage. They do an excellent *gardiane* (marinated beef stewed in onions, tomatoes, garlic, olives and red wine). Sit out on the courtyard terrace in summer. Set lunch 69F and 100–180F in the evening, or around 130F *à la carte*.

LAURET   34270 (30KM N)

🏃🛏|◉| L'AUBERGE DU CÈDRE

Domaine de Cazeneuve; take the D17 towards Quissac.
☎ 04.67.59.02.02 ➡ 04.67.59.03.44
🅔 welcome@auberge-du-cedre.com
Hotel closed Jan–21 March. **Restaurant open** Fri evening–Sun evening, lunchtimes on public holidays and daily for residents only. **Swimming pool. Car park**.

This old house used to belong to a winegrower; it has since been converted into a very attractive hotel and restaurant with self-catering cottages, a campsite and a swimming pool. There's a menu at 75F for residents only. For 135F you can have what they call the hiker's platter – sausage, *terrine* with juniper berries, *coppa* and *chorizo* – or a succulent *croustillant* of salmon with figs and honey. There's a wide range of good Mediterranean wines, many of which are available by the glass. Simple but perfectly adequate bedrooms, which sleep two, three or four, cost 160F per person, including breakfast, with prices going up to 210F during school holidays. Bathrooms are on the landing. The campsite has no facilities. Courteous owners and quality food. 10% discount on the room rate out of season, and free tapas in the restaurant when you order a meal.

NARBONNE   11100

🛏 HÔTEL DE FRANCE**

6 rue Rossini (Centre).
☎ 04.68.32.09.75 ➡ 04.68.65.50.30
TV. Pay car park.

A lovely, turn-of-the-20th-century house near the covered market. It offers a number of clean, comfortable rooms; doubles with washing facilities 150F and 230–250F with shower/wc and TV. Straightforward, warm-hearted welcome.

🏃🛏 WILL'S HÔTEL**

23 av. Pierre-Sémard (Centre); it's in the street opposite the station.
☎ 04.68.90.44.50 ➡ 04.68.32.26.28
Closed 25 Dec–2 Jan. **TV. Pay car park**.

There's something solid about the beautiful façade of this bourgeois house that fills you with confidence, an impression reinforced by the hotel owner's friendly reception. The bedrooms are clean and they've been updated, though not very originally, and decorated in pastel shades. Doubles at reasonable prices; 180F with shower/wc to 250F with bath. 10% discount Sept–June.

🛏 LE GRAND HÔTEL DU LANGUEDOC

22 bd. Gambetta
☎ 04.68.65.14.74 ➡ 04.68.65.81.45
TV. Private garage.

A turn-of-the-century mansion with a certain air about it. It's extremely well maintained though the corridors are a little dark and gloomy. The recently refurbished bedrooms are bright and have excellent beds and double glazing. Some rooms have a view of the cathedral. Doubles with shower/wc 290F, 350–450F with bath. There's a lift.

🏃|◉| L'ESPAGNOL

5 [bis] cours Mirabeau.
☎ 04.68.65.09.27
Closed Sun, Mon evening, a week end Nov and a week beginning Feb.

A matey brasserie with a Parisian atmosphere but local cuisine. Reasonable prices: lunch *formule* 62F and a 130F menu. A place to eat quickly and simply. The terrace is open to the sunshine in summer and heated in winter. A popular after-show hang-out for actors from the theatre. Free coffee.

|● LE PETIT COMPTOIR

4 bd. du Maréchal-Joffre (Centre).
☎ 04.68.42.30.35 ➡ 04.68.41.52.71
Closed Sun, the second fortnight in March and the first fortnight in June.

It's probably a good idea to book at this fashionable restaurant-bistro. It has an attractive decor and its enthusiastic owner is meticulous about choosing the produce for his kitchen. Set menus 98F, 148F and 178F – choose one of these and you might be offered fillet of sea bream with vegetable lasagne, tomato tart or souffléd lemon crêpes. The chef is keen on improvising, and he varies his menus regularly.

|● LA TABLE SAINT-CRESCENT

av. du Général Leclerc, it's on the Perpignan road.
☎ 04.68.41.37.37
Closed Mon, Sat lunchtime and Sun evening.

The Palais du Vin was set up to help market the local wines and is ideally located just off the motorway. But it also serves a second purpose as the site for this gourmet restaurant. The decor is extraordinary – it's a mixture of ancient, rough-hewn stone and modern metal sheeting – and places you in a bizarre time-warp. The dining room is in an ancient chapel which adds to the feeling of displacement. The chef, Claude Giraud, brings you back to this world with his thoughtful cuisine. The lunch *formule*, 100F, comprises savouries, dish of the day, cheese, dessert, a glass of wine and coffee. All the dishes show off the quality of the produce he uses and they change frequently – there's a menu at 158F and one at 189F which includes three glasses of wine.

VINASSAN   11110 (6KM E)

|● AUBERGE LA POTINIÈRE

1 rue des Arts (Centre); on the Narbonne-Plage road, turn left onto the D68, then turn onto the D31.
☎ 04.68.45.32.33
Closed lunchtimes and Sun evening out of season and three weeks Jan/Feb.

A pretty inn in a lovely setting where the chef concocts tasty regional dishes. Four menus 90–250F – the cheapest will include fish soup or Narbonnaise salad, free-range chicken or salmon followed by cheese or chocolate mousse; the 139F menu includes the likes of sea bream in *beurre blanc* or rolled duckling with Montagne Noire sauce. The service is courteous, and the food is good and well priced. They have just thirty seats so you may want to book.

BAGES   11100 (8KM S)

⚐ |● LE PORTANEL

It's in the village: take the N9 towards Perpignan and turn left for l'étang de Bages.
☎ 04.68.42.81.66
Closed Sun and Mon Sept–June, and a fortnight in Feb.

In the heart of a fishing village, this unassuming restaurant has two bright, elegant dining rooms with windows overlooking the lake at Bages. Owner Didier Marty is a fisherman, and he takes his nets out early to bring back the freshest catch. The fish is creatively prepared by his wife, Rosemarie. The *autour de l'étang* menu includes a crab mousse, fish broth, slivers of fish in a coriander *jus* with chicory, and a perfect home-made dessert. They do an extraordinary eel dish. Menus 95–220F; the 220F one includes wine and gives you seven courses rounded off with a *dessert des garrigues*. Attentive, amiable service and an exceptional selection of regional wines. Free apéritif.

|● LA TABLE DU PÊCHEUR

21 rue de l'Ancien-Puits.
☎ 04.68.41.15.11
Closed Tues evening, Wed and Jan.

The decor is a charming assembly of *bric-à-brac* and there's a view of the pond, too. Lots of fish and shellfish on the menu, straight from the sea onto your plate, passing briefly through the cooking process. The speciality is prawns in lemon sauce. Menus 110–210F, with a choice of prawns or a seafood platter, followed by dessert and a Kir. Some tapas are included. It's charmingly run by Madame and her daughter, Marine.

ABAYE DE FONTFROIDE   11100 (15KM SW)

⚐ |● LA BERGERIE-LES CUISINIERS VIGNERONS

How to get there: turn off the A9 at the Narbonne-Sud exit onto the N13 in the direction of Carcassonne and then the D6.
☎ 04.68.41.86.06
Closed Dec–Feb.

This is the simplicity of perfection. The building is in the abbey's old sheep-fold and dates from the Middle Ages. Three lunch menus, 84F, 98F and 140F but you'll pay 200–380F for dinner. Although the prices can get high, there's wonderful food on all the menus. The dishes are drenched in the bold flavours of the Languedoc and the Mediterranean and the menus change with the seasons: duck breast *carpaccio*, fresh cod or quail with red peppers, Roquefort in pastry, coconut and pineapple cake. In the evening, the dishes are personally prepared by the chef and he's a serious player. One of the best tables in the *département*. Free coffee.

NASBINALS   48260

☎ |●| HÔTEL-RESTAURANT LA ROUTE D'ARGENT**

Route d'Argent; it's the big building beside the church and the village car park.
☎ 04.66.32.50.03 ➡ 04.66.32.56.77
Disabled access. TV. Car park.

This place is something of an institution – everybody in Nasbinals drops in. It's owned by Pierre Bastide, who's a mine of information about the area, but you'll more than likely be greeted at reception, which is in a corner of the bar, by one of his sons. Guests always get a warm and friendly welcome. The chef's portions are some of the most generous you'll see. He does trout with almonds, stuffed cabbage, *truffade* (potato cake with cheese), and, of course, *aligot* made to Bastide senior's special recipe. Set menus 65–165F. Doubles with shower 200F and 260F with shower/wc or bath. Breakfast is served at the bar. If you prefer a more stylish establishment, they've opened a three-star hotel just outside the town called *Le Bastide* – the prices are roughly the same.

NÎMES   30000

SEE MAP OVERLEAF

⌘ ☎ |●| CAT HÔTEL*

22 bd. Amiral-Courbet. **MAP C1-3**
☎ 04.66.67.22.85 ➡ 04.66.21.57.51
📧 cat.hotel@free.fr
TV. Pay garage.

The owners came from the cold, wet north to open a hotel, and they've made a success of it. The *Cat* is pleasant and cheap. They've done everything up, and have put in double glazing, good ventilation and satellite TV. Everything is judged just right. Double rooms

with shower/wc 189F, 260F with bath. Ordinary restaurant serving simple dishes like steak with sauce. Menus 58–88F. 10% discount on the room rate Oct–April.

☎ |●| HÔTEL ROYAL***

3 bd. Alphonse-Daudet. **MAP B1-4**
☎ 04.66.67.28.36 ➡ 04.66.21.68.97
Restaurant closed Sun and Mon. TV. Car park.

Most rooms look onto the fountain on the quiet pedestrian place d'Assas. The hotel is popular with actors and artists passing through and bullfighters' assistants. The welcome is hospitable and the atmosphere seductive. The rooms are individually decorated and are attractive and charming; they don't all have the same facilities, but prices are fair for this town. Doubles 280F with shower/wc or 350–480F with bath. *La Bodeguita*, which is newish, serves tapas and Mediterranean specialities. Lunch menu 60F or around 150F *à la carte*.

⌘ ☎ HÔTEL DE L'AMPHITHÉATRE**

4 rue des Arènes. **MAP B2-7**
☎ 04.66.67.28.51 ➡ 04.66.67.07.79
📧 hotel.amphitheatre@wanadoo.fr
Closed 20 Dec–21 Jan.

This is a quiet hotel in a generously proportioned 18th-century house, just 30m from the Roman arena. The decor needs to be spruced up a bit, but the place is clean and the beds are comfortable. Doubles with shower/wc or bath for 290F. Good breakfast with home-made jams. Free coffee.

☎ |●| L'ORANGERIE***

755 Tour l'Évêque. Off map **A3-9**
Take the A9 signposted to the airport, then left at the Kurokawa roundabout onto the N86.
☎ 04.66.84.50.57 ➡ 04.66.29.44.55
📧 hrorang@aol.com
Garden. Swimming pool. TV. Car park.

An unusually attractive modern hotel in a big garden with a swimming pool, though the surrounds of the commercial district and the noise from the traffic don't immediately draw you to the area. Professional staff at reception and well-maintained rooms. The prices are reasonable, 350–490F for a double with bath. This is a reliable place. The restaurant has already established a decent reputation; rack of lamb with wild herbs, scallop *tartare* and salmon with asparagus. Weekday lunch menu 100F, or 160F.

⌘ ☎ HÔTEL CLARINE-PLAZZA**

10 rue Roussy. **MAP C2-5**
☎ 04.66.76.16.20 ➡ 04.66.67.65.99

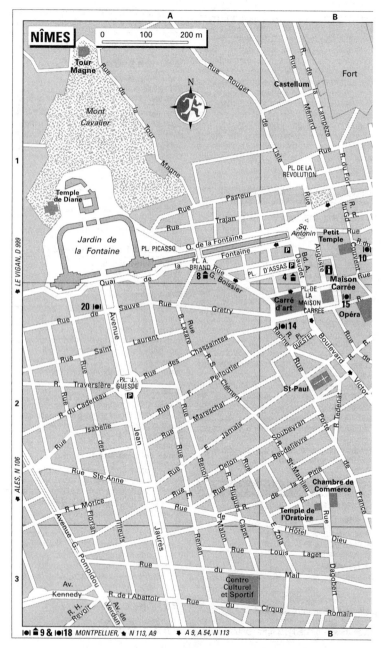

NÎMES

0   100   200 m

Tour Magne

Mont Cavalier

Rue Rouget

Castellum

Fort

Rue de la Tour Magne

Temple de Diane

N

Rue

de

Liste

PL. DE LA RÉVOLUTION

R. de la Lampèze

R. Ménard

Rue

R. du Fort

1

Jardin de la Fontaine

Rue Pasteur

Rue Trajan

Rue

Sq. Antonin

PL. PICASSO

Q. de la Fontaine

Fontaine

Petit Temple

Rue Auguste

Rue du Gd R. du Convent

PL. A. BRIAND

Rue G. Boissier

PL. D'ASSAS

Bd. A. Daudet

10

8

4

Maison Carrée

LE VIGAN, D 999

Rue de la

Quai de

Sauve

Avenue

Rue

Gretry

Carré d'art

PL. DE LA MAISON CARRÉE

Opéra

15

20

Rue Saint

Laurent

R. B. Lazare

Rue des Chassaintes

Rue Racine

14

Bd. QUESTEL

Boulevard

Rue

Rue R.

ALES, N 106

Rue

Traversière

PL. J. GUESDE

R. du Cadereau

Rue Jean

Rue des

Rue F.

R. S. Clément

Rue Pelloutier

Rue Mareschal

Rue Jamais

St-Paul

Porte

Rue Tedenat

Rue Victor

2

Isabelle

Rue Ste-Anne

Rue Benoit

Rue Delon

Soubeyran

Becdelièvre

St-Mathieu

Rue de la Pitié

Chambre de Commerce

R. L. Morice

Avenue G. Pompidou

Rue Florian

Rue Tilleurs

Rue Jaurès

Rue Hugues Capet

Rue de Maton

Temple de l'Oratoire

Rue de France

3

Av. Kennedy

R. de l'Abattoir

Av. de Verdun

R. H. Revoil

Renan

du

Rue E. Zola

l'Hôtel

Louis Laget

Dagobert

Centre Culturel et Sportif

Rue du Cirque

Mail

Romain

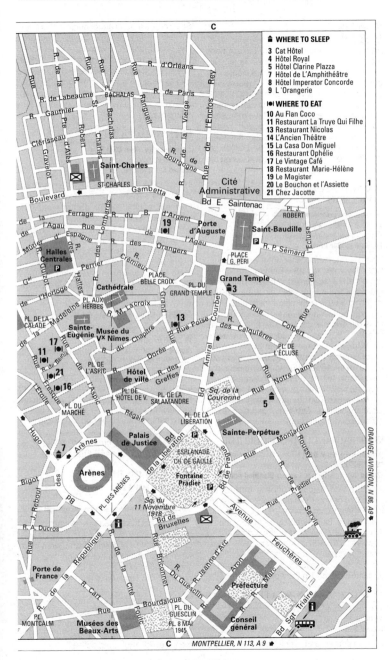

⌂ WHERE TO SLEEP

3 Cat Hôtel
4 Hôtel Royal
5 Hôtel Clarine Plazza
7 Hôtel de L'Amphithéâtre
8 Hôtel Imperator Concorde
9 L 'Orangerie

I○I WHERE TO EAT

10 Au Flan Coco
11 Restaurant La Truye Qui Filhe
13 Restaurant Nicolas
14 L'Ancien Théâtre
15 La Casa Don Miguel
16 Restaurant Ophélie
17 Le Vintage Café
18 Restaurant Marie-Hélène
19 Le Magister
20 Le Bouchon et l'Assiette
21 Chez Jacotte

e viallet@aconet.fr
TV. **Car park**.

Part of the *Clarine* hotel chain, though none their properties looks like a chain hotel. This one is charming, in an old Nîmes house in a quiet street. Its 28 air-conditioned rooms have shower or bath and telephone, 360–380F. Each floor has a different colour scheme and the corridors are decorated with posters advertising bullfights and opera perform-ances. Rooms on the fourth floor have very attractive little terraces and a view of the old tiled rooftops. 10% discount except during the *ferias,* or local festivals.

🏄 🛋 I●I HÔTEL IMPERATOR CONCORDE****

15 rue Gaston-Boissier. **MAP A1-8**
☎ 04.66.21.90.30 **F+** 04.66.67.70.25
e hotel-imperator@wanadoo.fr
TV. **Garden**. **Car park**.

This is a quality four-star hotel with a some-what ordinary façade. Behind the house there's an idyllic garden with an ornamental fountain, and an outside bar on the terrace which is a wonderful place for a drink. The superb rooms are beautifully fitted out. The lift is remarkable; it's a classic Otis that was fitted in 1929 and is guaranteed never to break down. You can stay at the *Imperator* for 550–690F in winter but the price shoots up to near 1000F during the *ferias*. The restaurant serves a modest three-course *formule*, with a glass of wine, for 155F. They have a reputation for producing excellent local specialities. Other menus up to 365F. 10% discount Oct–Aug.

I●I RESTAURANT LA TRUYE QUI FILHE

9 rue Fresque. **MAP B2-11**
☎ 04.66.21.76.33
Closed evenings, Sun, and in Aug. **Disabled access**.

A self-service restaurant under a 14th-centu-ry vaulted ceiling – this place has been an inn since then. Warm service and a lovely patio. Jean-Pierre Hermenegilde puts together a 47F *formule* consisting of main course and dessert, 52F with a starter as well. Local dishes such as *rouille du pêcheur* (fish soup with a spicy mayonnaise) and *brandade* (creamed salt cod in flaky pastry).

🏄 I●I LA CASA DON MIGUEL

18 rue de l'Horloge. **MAP B2-15**
☎ 04.66.76.07.09
Closed Sun.

Service until around midnight, or 3am Fri and Sat. There's a good atmosphere in this *bode-ga* – and a huge range of tapas. There are a few cheap *formules*, which get you three or five dishes of tapas plus coffee or a drink. They do a good *piña colada*, and the sangria and the *fino* are good too, though they don't serve drinks on their own. Lots of theme evenings, with jazz, flamenco or salsa. Free Margarita.

I●I LE VINTAGE CAFÉ

7 rue de Bernis. **MAP B2-17**
☎ 04.66.21.04.45
Closed Sat lunchtime, Sun and Mon.

Tiny place with a vintage bistro-style dining room and a fountain in the middle. It hosts frequent exhibitions of photographs and paintings. Attractive cooking, delicately perfumed to complement the fresh produce from the market – the dishes really do change daily. Try the Serrano ham, sautéed ravioli with pesto and mixed salad, washed down with one of the interesting southern wines served by the glass. Lunchtime *for-mules* 65F and 78F, a *menu-carte* at 138F.

🏄 I●I RESTAURANT NICOLAS

1 rue Poise. **MAP C2-13**
☎ 04.66.67.50.47
Closed Sat lunchtime, Mon except public holidays, 1–15 July, 24–26 Dec and 31 Dec–2 Jan.

The large, stone-walled dining room has been tastefully decorated. The locals flock here to savour the *anchoïade provençale*, monkfish *bourride* (a fish stew with saffron and garlic), creamed salt cod in flaky pastry or beef *gardiane*, and house desserts such as *clafoutis*. This is uncomplicated home cook-ing. Set menus 72–145F. Free coffee.

🏄 I●I L'ANCIEN THÉATRE

4 rue Racine. **MAP B2-14**
☎ 04.66.21.30.75
Closed Sat lunchtime, Sun, and the first fortnight in July.

They say that there used to be a theatre on the place du Carré, just nearby, which was burned to the ground by a singer who went crazy when they didn't hire her to sing. You won't find that kind of behaviour in this place. The hospitality and the well-crafted Mediterranean dishes served by smiling waiters create an altogether more tranquil atmosphere. Try the mussels *au gratin* or the cod fritters, though the menus change every two months. There's an intimate, rustic feel. A lovely place with menus at 78–130F. Free coffee.

⅍ |●| CHEZ JACOTTE

15 rue Fresque. MAP B2-21
☎ 04.66.21.64.59
Closed Sat lunchtime, Sun, Mon, a week in Feb, a week in June and a fortnight in Aug.

Inventive, well-prepared Nîmeois specialities, full of flavour and really satisfying. The lunch *menu du jour*, 80F, lists three starters, main dishes and desserts, or you can choose *à la carte*. The smooth duck liver *parfait* with peppers is particularly good, while the duck breast with peaches is subtly spiced and generously served. They bake wonderful pastries. A meal *à la carte* will cost around 200F which is good value for the quality. Good wines. There are three or four tables outside in the street. Attentive service. Free coffee.

⅍ |●| AU FLAN COCO

31 rue Mûrier-d'Espagne. MAP B1-10
☎ 04.66.21.84.81
Closed evenings except Sat and by reservation, Sun, 15–28 Feb and 15–30 Aug.

A delightful, unusual little restaurant. The two attractive dining rooms are decorated in shades of green and the tables have granite tops; you can sit out on the beautiful terrace in summer. The imaginative dishes vary daily; potato pie, creamed salt cod, chicken leg stuffed with prawn, and apple crumble with *crème fraîche*. Menus 89F and 105F, or around 125F *à la carte*. Free coffee.

⅍ |●| LE BOUCHON ET L'ASSIETTE

5 rue de Sauve. MAP A2-20
☎ 04.66.62.02.93
Closed Tues evening, Wed, the first fortnight in Jan and the first three weeks in Aug.

A gastronomic class act. The cooking has personality and finesse: semi-cooked *foie gras* with Jamaican pepper, nutmeg caramel and white grape jelly, pan-fried zander with herb biscuits and saffron-flavoured carrot *jus*, and honey ice cream. The dining room is full of light and the renovations make a feature of the beams in the ceiling. The efficient waiting staff could afford to relax a little. Lunch menu 95F, and others 125–240F. Free apéritif.

⅍ |●| RESTAURANT MARIE-HÉLÈNE

733 av. Maréchal-Juin; it's beside the Chambre des Métiers on the Montpellier road. Off map A3-18
☎ 04.66.84.13.02 ➠ 04.66.88.11.17.
Closed Sat lunchtime, Sun, Mon–Wed evenings and the first fortnight in Aug.

An ode to Provence, decorated in warm bright colours with huge vases of flowers and attractive table settings. It's a happy kind of place, enhanced by the smile of the owner and the robust cooking. They specialise in char-grilled meat and fish cooked in front of you. There are several menus 95–145F with choices such as chicken tikka with coriander and mint, creamed salt cod and home-made *crème catalane*. Free apéritif or coffee.

⅍ |●| LE MAGISTER

5 rue Nationale (or de l'Agau). MAP C1-19
☎ 04.66.76.11.00
Closed Sat lunchtime, Sun, a week in Feb, and Aug.
Disabled access.

An excellent gastronomic restaurant run by chef Martial Hocquart, who has worked in the most famous kitchens in France – the *Ritz* and the *Tour d'Argent* in Paris. Just reading the menu makes you hungry: roast veal kidneys with house raspberry vinegar, sweet apples roast with cinnamon and served with an almond sorbet – totally exquisite. Weekday lunch menu 130F then 185–220F; even the cheaper ones are a feast. Free coffee.

⅍ |●| RESTAURANT OPHÉLIE

35 rue Fresque. MAP B2-16
☎ 04.66.21.00.19
Closed lunchtimes, Mon, Sun, the last fortnight in Aug.

The tiny courtyard is delightful at dusk, and when Patricia Talbot lights the candles it's quite magical. Authentic and fresh-tasting cooking. Choose from *gratin* of curried mussels, pan-fried *foie gras* with Muscat, roast lamb shank and red peppers, or scallops with basil. *Menu-carte* 140F. Free apéritif.

SAINT-GILLES   30800 (19KM SE)

⅍ ♜ |●| LE COURS**

10 av. François-Griffeuille (Centre); take the D42.
☎ 04.66.87.31.93 ➠ 04.66.87.31.83
Closed 15 Dec to end Feb. **Disabled access. TV.** Car park.

This beautiful white house, shaded by an avenue of tall plane trees, has 34 rooms, thirteen of them air-conditioned; doubles with shower 255–285F or 330–380F with bath. It's clean and fresh. Set menus, 67–160F, list dishes like scallop *terrine* and warm seafood salad, beef *gardiane* (beef stew), cuttlefish with *rouille* (spicy, garlicky mayonnaise) and lots of grilled fish. 10% discount on the room rate weekdays March–June, and Oct–Dec.

🕭 ✿ HÔTEL HÉRACLÉE***

quai du Canal, port de plaisance (South); take the D42.
☎ 04.66.87.44.10 📠 04.66.87.13.65
Closed Jan–March. **Disabled access**. **Garden**.
TV. **Car park**.

This mythical Greek name graces a friendly, pretty hotel housed in a bright building. It looks onto the canal so you can watch the launches, the horse-drawn barges and the houseboats gliding by, though the view is marred by the metal monstrosity on the other bank. Twenty-one tastefully decorated bedrooms; some have a terrace overlooking the canal or the peaceful garden. At 290–350F, they're worth every franc. 10% discount April–June and Sept–Dec.

OLONZAC   34210

I●I RESTAURANT DU MINERVOIS BEL

av. d'Homps; it's opposite the schools.
☎ 04.64.91.20.73
Closed Sat and Sun evening except July–Aug, and evenings mid-Oct to mid-April.

The chef/proprietor's know-how and his skilful use of seasonings is evident even in the cheapest, simplest 63F set menu – house *terrine* and a perfect *omelette aux fines herbes*. Other menus 115–250F – the last is spectacular. The wine list has a particularly rich choice of regional vintages at good prices. A consistently good restaurant that deserves its popularity.

SIRAN   34210 (10KM NW)

🕭 ✿ I●I LA VILLA D'ÉLÉIS***

av. du Château; it's in the village.
☎ 04.68.91.55.98 📠 04.68.91.48.34
✉ villadeleis@wanadoo.fr
Closed Tues evening, Wed and Sat lunchtime Oct–May, and Feb–March. **Disabled access**. **TV**. **Car park**.

An ancient country house that has been carefully restored. The twelve stylish, personalised rooms are quiet and spacious. Doubles 350–480F with shower/wc or 400–780F with bath. Marie-Hélène will greet you, and Bernard Lafuente's cooking is full of southern sunshine. He is a talented young chef who has won critical acclaim. Set menus 160–410F. Opt for the starter of vegetables from the *poule-au-pot* topped with grilled goat's cheese, or Bernard's prize-winning cod with saffron. The owners organise musical evening in summer, including piano and flute recitals, and lead walks to help you learn

about the wildlife and history of the area. 10% discount on the room rate Nov–March.

PERPIGNAN   66000

✿ AVENIR HÔTEL*

11 rue de l'Avenir.
☎ 04.68.34.20.30 ✉ avenirhotel@aol.com.
Pay garage.

Reception closed Sunday afternoons. A pleasant hotel in a quiet street not far from the station. The rooms are simple but well maintained and the prices are reasonable. Vacationing American students stay here, as do trainees on work placements. It has a homely atmosphere and there's a sunny terrace on the first floor where you eat your breakfast, which is cheap at 23F. It's a place to enjoy the sun and the peace and quiet. Single rooms 90F with basin and shower on the landing. Doubles 110–120F with basin, 160F and 190F with shower or with two double beds from 190F. Use of a garage in the next street for 25F per night.

🕭 ✿ I●I HÔTEL DE LA POSTE ET DE LA PERDRIX**

6 rue Fabriques-Nabot (Centre); it's between pl. du Castillet and the quai Sadi-Carnot.
☎ 04.68.34.42.53 📠 04.68.34.58.20
Closed Sun evening, Mon and 28 Feb–5 March. **TV**.

A beautiful, characterful hotel dating from 1832. The sign bears the patina of age, the marble foyer and the gleaming old staircase are delightful and the period stained-glass windows are lovely. The pleasantly old-fashioned bedrooms are well maintained and reasonably priced. Doubles with basin 180F, shower/wc 255F, and bath 275F. Simple food served in the stunning dining room. Menus 65–115F. 10% discount on the room rate Sept–June and free coffee.

🕭 ✿ HÔTEL DE LA LOGE**

pl. de la Loge, 1 rue des Fabriques-Nabot (Centre).
☎ 04.68.34.41.02 📠 04.68.34.25.13
✉ hoteldelaloge@wanadoo.fr
TV.

A 16th-century mansion built round a patio with a cool fountain – welcome on scorching days. The decor is a mixture of Catalan and Andalusian. Comfortable, natty rooms, though they could do with a bit of updating. Most have airconditioning and all have TV. Doubles 250–285F with shower/wc and 330–290F with bath. 10% discount.

🏠 |●| PARK HÔTEL-RESTAURANT LE CHAPON FIN***

18 bd. Jean-Bourrat (Northeast); it's opposite the tourist office in square Bir-Hakeim.
☎ 04.68.35.14.14. ➡ 04.68.35.48.18
📧 acceuil@parkhotel.fr
Restaurant closed Sun and three weeks in Jan. **TV**.
Disabled access.

Amazing luxury at a reasonable price in a hotel with a dull, modern frontage. The bedrooms are decorated in Spanish Renaissance style and have every facility including air conditioning. Double rooms with shower from 350F. The restaurant is one of the best in town. Lunch menu 130F then 200–350F. Dishes include rock fish soup and fillets of scorpion fish with shellfish sauce. There's a wonderful selection of wines. À la carte, dishes are pricey but perfect.

🏠 |●| HÔTEL-RESTAURANT VILLA DUFLOT****

Rond-point Albert-Donnezan (South); make for the Perpignan south motorway exit then go towards Argelès and it's two minutes from the toll both.
☎ 04.68.56.67.67 ➡ 04.68.56.54.05
📧 villa.duflot@little-france.com
Swimming pool. Disabled access. TV. Car park.

If you're planning to stay in Perpignan for a few days, there are better places in town, but if you're heading for Spain on the A9 and want a night of luxury, it's worth stopping here. The rooms have been furnished with enchanting taste – ask for one overlooking the swimming pool rather than the dreary industrial park; doubles 740–1100F. The restaurant tends towards the modern style of cooking but also has traditional local dishes; try the fresh duck-liver *lasagne*. There's a nice selection of Roussillon wines and they've added a wine bar with a panoply of wines from the Pyrenees. À la carte only during the week, about 200F. At weekends there's a single menu at 200F, including wine.

🏕 |●| CASA SANSA

3 rue Fabrique-Couverte (Centre).
☎ 04.68.34.21.84
Closed Sun.

This is a young place full of students and travellers. It's decorated with lots of bits and pieces, garish paintings and posters of the *corrida*. The cooking is Catalan with a few original touches – guinea-fowl with figs, *foie gras* smoked over thyme, or fillet of beef with liquorice – and generously served. There's a lunch *formule* at 49F, a meal-sized selection of tapas at 140F, or you'll pay about 120F *à la carte*. Free coffee or house *digestif*.

|●| AL TRÈS

3 rue de la Poissonnerie (Centre).
☎ 04.68.34.88.39
Closed Sun, Mon, Mon lunchtime 15 June–15 Sept, last week of Dec and three weeks Feb/March.

The decor is a brilliant alliance of Provence and Catalonia and the cuisine is full of sun-drenched flavours served on colourful Spanish plates. Start by sharing a few tapas: grilled red peppers, calamari with garlic, vegetable fritters or anchovies. Follow with a dish of shellfish, a turbot with morels or a *zarzuela* (fish stew). There are also Catalan specialities: veal kidneys in Banyuls and excellent desserts. Good value generally, with a 65F lunch menu, another at 150F or around 200F à la carte. The wine list features 150 wines from the region.

|●| LES TROIS SŒURS

2 rue Fontfroide (Centre); it's opposite the Saint-Jean cathedral.
☎ 04.68.51.22.33

The terrace, which overlooks place Gambetta, is strangely quiet and un-touristy. The dining rooms are bright and air-conditioned and decorated in a cool, modern style. The lunch *formule*, 80F, gives you main course, starter or dessert, and coffee. The dishes are made with fresh produce; they're simple, tasty and well balanced. Specialities include scallops in Banyuls wine and bitter chocolate, *parillada* of fish, Catalan black pudding with apples, and almond mousse. There's a set menu at 150F. Quick service in a relaxed atmosphere.

🏕 |●| LE SUD

12 rue Louis-Bausil (Centre); take rue Élie-Delcros from the Palais des Congrès then rue Rabelais on the left. Rue Louis-Bausil is a continuation of rue Rabelais.
☎ and ➡ 04.68.34.55.71
Closed Oct–March.

This place is in Perpignan's gipsy quarter. The delicacies are a delight, combining the best from Provence, the Orient, Mexico, Greece and Catalonia. The patio is planted with scented bushes and jasmine flowers. Everything they cook on the grill is recommended: little squid with a salad, a skewer of chicken marinated in ginger, lemon and chilli, grilled duck breast. À la carte only, and you'll pay around 160F. The atmosphere is calming, discreet and comfortable. Free apéritif.

CANET-PLAGE 66140 (12KM E)

🎴 🏠 |●| LE CLOS DES PINS-LE BISTRO GOURMAND

34 av. du Roussillon.
☎ 04.68.80.32.63 ➡ 04.68.80.49.19
e masfleuri@wanadoo.fr
Open daily Easter to All Saints' Day. **Garden. TV**.

Henri Delcros, the chef, trained in the kitchens of the great Paul Bocuse. He was a good student. His cuisine is light, creative and skilful: *tuile* and parmesan sorbet, fish mousse, *fois gras crème caramel*, duckling in Banyuls wine and tuna with red pepper *mille-feuilles*. The desserts of similar inventiveness and quality. Menus 145F and 195F. They serve regional wines only but they're a little overpriced and though the staff are very friendly, the service could be slicker. In fine weather you eat in the gorgeous garden. Quality air-conditioned rooms; doubles 480–680F. Free house apéritif.

|●| LA RASCASSE

38 bd. Tixador; it's parallel to the seafront.
☎ 04.68.80.20.79
Closed Mon April–June, and the last Sun in Sept to the first Fri in April.

This is a very well-known fish restaurant. The dining room is a super-traditional example of Vieille France. All the fish, shellfish and seafood are brilliantly fresh and the dishes are delicately prepared: *bouillabaisse*, skate with caper sauce, fish *parillada* and sea bass with *sauce Rascasse*. Try the *crème catalane* for dessert. Reasonably priced menus 105–175F, and affordable wines. Service is friendly and efficient.

VINÇA 66320 (33KM W)

🎴 🏠 |●| LA PETITE AUBERGE

74 av. du Général-de-Gaulle; it's on the N116 in the direction of Prades.
☎ 04.68.05.81.47 ➡ 04.68.05.85.80
Closed Wed and Sun evening except July–Aug.

A little inn, as the name suggests. The chef is chatty, and his cuisine is as straightforward and generous as he is himself. Excellent 88F menu: to start, you help yourself to the *hors d'oeuvre* buffet or have a plate of cooked ham, then for a main course you might get fried Catalan sausage with tomatoes, mullet Roman style, or a dish of the day like stuffed quail with fresh peas. Finally, there's a home-made custard the like of which you won't have tasted in years. Other menus

148–180F, all full of tasty, characterful dishes. There are a few simple rooms – 150F with basin, 180F with shower/wc. Free apéritif.

PÉZENAS 34120

|●| LA POMME D'AMOUR

2 [bis] rue Albert-Paul-Allies (Centre); it's near the tourist office.
☎ 04.67.98.08.40
Closed Mon, Tues evening except in summer, Jan, Feb.

This is a very pleasant little restaurant in an old stone building in the picturesque old part of town. Good, simple cooking and traditional local dishes. They have a few specialities, such as mussels in cream, salmon with saffron, *tiramisù* and salad of orange *Royale* with crystallized zest of orange. Set menus 86F and 116F. You'll get a friendly welcome.

PONT-DE-MONTVERT (LE) 48220

🎴 🏠 |●| LA TRUITE ENCHANTÉE

Centre.
☎ 04.66.45.80.03
Closed mid-Dec to mid-March. **Garden. Car park**.

The hotel, run by Corinne and Edgard, has eight basic rooms that are bright, clean and spacious – they cost 155F with shower (wc on the landing). Good, hearty, regional cooking is served in the dining room next to the kitchen. Set menus 85–145F and a gourmet one for 155F: salmon trout with sorrel, trout *meunière*, lambs' sweetbreads with morels and rabbit *Royale* are among the specialities. Booking advised for both hotel and restaurant. Free *digestif*.

MASMÉJEAN 48220 (7KM E)

🎴 |●| CHEZ DÉDET

How to get there: take the D998 Pont de Montvert-Saint-Maurice-de-Ventalon road then turn left for Masméjean.
☎ 04.66.45.81.51
Closed Wed and weekday evenings out of season.

The food here is out of this world. It's a real country restaurant in an old farm building with enormous beams, walls made out of great slabs of stone and a hearth you could roast an ox in. They use pigs, sheep and poultry from the family farm and get their snails, trout and mushrooms from local suppliers. In season, the wild boar and hare are shot locally. Portions are enormous and you probably won't be able to finish any of the courses: *charcuterie*, stuffed duck's neck in salad, snails with herbs, and a *digestif* of *trou cévenol*, a local brandy. The meat of the day could be delicious fillet of pork plus vegetables, along with as much as you can manage from the platter of local cheese and a perfect dessert like *crème caramel*. Set menus 65–125F. The service is perfect. Credit cards aren't accepted and booking is advisable, especially in winter. Free coffee.

VIALAS   48220 (18KM E)

♨ ☎ |●| HOSTELLERIE CHANTOISEAU***

Centre.
☎ 04.66.41.00.02 ➡ 04.66.41.04.34
Closed Tues evening, Wed and 30 Sept–30 April.
TV. Swimming pool. Car park.

A pleasant combination of chic and rustic decor in this former coaching inn which offers authentic local cuisine of high quality. Patrick Pagès knows and loves this part of the world, its wild valleys, mushrooms, chestnut trees, its fish and its game. Try the *moche* (pork sausage with cabbage, potatoes and prunes), the *saucisse d'herbes*, the *pompétou* of trout, or the *coupétade*. Menus start at 140F, then 200–495F. Double rooms with shower/wc 400F, or with bath 450F. This gourmet restaurant is a must, and has one of the region's best wine cellars. Free coffee.

PONT-SAINT-ESPRIT   30130

☎ |●| AUBERGE PROVENÇALE**

Route de Bagnols-sur-Cèze (South); take the N86 as you leave the village.
☎ 04.66.39.08.79 ➡ 04.66.39.14.28
Closed Sun evening Oct–March, and the Christmas and New Year holidays. **Car park**.

This inn looks far better inside than out. The same family has run it for more than thirty years, cheerfully welcoming travellers, long-distance lorry drivers, families and local worthies alike. They serve large portions of honest traditional food in the two large air-conditioned dining rooms. The cheapest set menu, 70F, sets the tone: *charcuterie*, *crudités*, a dish of the day, seasonal vegetables, cheese platter and fresh fruit or ice cream. Other menus up to 120F. Gigondas and Tavel are served by the glass and reasonably priced. The bedrooms, 200F, have shower/wc or bath. The ones that overlook the courtyard are the more peaceful.

♨|●| LOU RÉCATI

rue Jean-Jacques (Centre).

☎ 04.66.90.73.01
Closed Sat lunchtime and Mon.

"*Lou Récati*" is a local term to describe those little mounds of furniture or clothing that are thrown together to save them from the floodwaters of the Rhône. It's a poetic name for a restaurant run by a talented young chef who produces delicate, skillfully cooked dishes. The prices are fair for cooking by such a pro: snail ravioli, slivers of duck with artichokes and peas and, for dessert, an unrivalled *crème brûlée* perfumed with lavender. It's a real treat to dine here. Weekday lunch menu 75F and others 130 and 195F. Free apéritif.

AIGUÈZE   30760 (10KM NW)

♨ ☎ LE CASTELAS**

It's in the village: from Pont-Saint-Esprit, take the 86 for Montélimar, then left onto the D901 to Aiguèze.
☎ 04.66.82.18.76 ➡ 04.66.82.14.98
Swimming pools. Car park.

Le Castelas is in a remarkable location, in a picturesque hillside village over the Ardèche. It also has some remarkable qualities: the rooms and apartments are charmingly decorated and fitted with a small corner kitchen. They're all within the ancient castle walls. You can stay in the main residence by the first swimming pool where the rooms have terraces and views over the gorges of l'Ardèche; the annexe, just two streets away, has another pool. The owner is polite and attentive and looks after his clients very well. Double rooms with shower/wc or bath 350–450F; studios for two people 550–650F and apartments for four, 850–950F. Rates for long stays on request. Good, self-service buffet breakfast. They'll lend you a bicycle and tell you where to go, or advise on hiring a canoe. Free apéritif.

BAGNOLS-SUR-CÈZE   30200 (15KM S)

♨ ☎ HÔTEL BAR DES SPORTS**

3 pl. Jean-Jaurès (Centre); take the R86 from Pont-Saint-Esprit in the direction of Nîmes.
☎ 04.68.89.61.68 ➡ 04.66.89.92.97
TV. Pay garage.

This is a serious place which deserves its two stars; delightful, clean, comfortable double rooms with bath and double glazing go for 250F. The owner is very kind, and it's really quiet at night because the bar doesn't open late. Free use of the garage at weekends, except July–Aug.

PRADES   66500

🎿 |●| LE JARDIN D'EYMERICH

3 av. du Général-de-Gaulle; it's opposite the lorry park.
☎ 04.68.96.53.38
Closed Sun evening, Mon, the Feb school holidays, and a fortnight June/July. **TV**. **Car park**.

A small restaurant with a warm dining room where excellent dishes are served. It's often full, so consider booking. The generously flavoured regional cooking uses fresh produce, so the menus change regularly: roast saddle of lamb with thyme and cappuccino of white beans. Dish of the day 55F and menus 98–170F. They serve regional wines – the house wine is as good as some on the wine list. Speedy, energetic service from smiling, chatty waiting staff. Free apéritif.

PRATS-DE-MOLLO   11500

🎿 🏠 |●| HÔTEL DES TOURISTES**

av. du Haut Vallespir; it's on the right as you arrive in the village on the road from Amélie-les-Bains.
☎ 04.68.39.72.12 ➡ 04.68.39.79.22
Closed Nov–March. **TV**. **Car park**.

This solidly built stone hotel is an ideal spot from which to explore the wild, mountainous Vallespir region. The rooms are well maintained; doubles cost 210F with basin/wc or 280–300F with shower/wc or bath. Some have balconies, others have little terraces. The ones at the back have a view of the river. In the huge dining room they serve family cooking – duck stewed in Banyuls wine, almond mousse and so on. Menus 100–130F. Free apéritif.

QUILLAN   11500

🎿 🏠 |●| HOSTELLERIE DU GRAND DUC

2 route de Boucheville; it's 4km from Château de Puilaurens.
☎ 04.68.20.55.02 ➡ 04.68.20.61.22
Closed Wed lunchtime out of season, and 11 Nov–1 April. **Garden**. **TV**.

An old craftsman's house with huge charm in a very pretty garden made even lovelier by its pond. The rooms are a combination of bourgeois and country-style with slightly old-fashioned wallpaper. Doubles 320F with bath. Good classic cooking on menus from 130F. Free house apéritif.

ROQUEFORT-DES-CORBIÈRES   11540

🎿 |●| LE LÉZARD BLEU

It's in the centre of town.
☎ 04.68.48.51.11
Closed Oct–July.

The signs with the lizard lead you to this restaurant with the blue door. Inside, the walls are white and hung with modern paintings. The food is lovingly prepared by the owner, a friendly woman who's full of life. There's lots of duck on the menu: *foie gras*, *tajine* (a Moroccan stew), breast of duck, and duck *à l'orange*. Set menus 100F and 130F. The desserts are a bit small for the price. Advisable to book. Free coffee.

SAINT-ANDRÉ-DE-VALBORGNE   30940

🏠 |●| HÔTEL-RESTAURANT BOURGADE**

pl. de l'Église.
☎ 04.66.60.30.72 ➡ 04.66.60.35.56
📧 picoboo@compuserve.com
Closed Mon–Wed evening except mid-June to mid-Sept, and 11 Nov to mid-April. **TV**.

A village at the end of the world, in the hollow of one of the prettiest valleys of the Cévennes. It started as a post house in the 17th century and has been in the family for generations. The latest lot have shaken out all the cobwebs and offer an enthusiastic welcome. Simply charming rooms overlooking the church square or the stream. Doubles 285F with shower/wc or bath. Flavourful and inspirational cuisine by a chef who did part of his apprenticeship with the great Ducasse. He makes lots of regional dishes using fresh produce, and has kept his grandmother's famous crayfish dish on the menus, 100F and up. A lovely place.

SAINT-CHÉLY-DU-TARN   48210

🎿 🏠 |●| L'AUBERGE DE LA CASCADE

How to get there: it's in the Gorges du Tarn, in the direction of Millau.
☎ 04.66.77.06.72
Closed Sun evening and Mon. **Disabled access**. **Swimming pool**. **TV**.

The inn offers good value for money. Reception is in the restaurant and the rooms are in a separate building – they're all brand new and very comfortable; doubles 205F with shower/wc and 280F with bath. The swimming pool is on a terrace overlooking the river Tarn. The restaurant offers regional cuisine but it's not wonderful and the service is slap-dash. Half-board 205–249F, compulsory July–Aug. Free coffee.

SAUVE   30610

📬 |●| CHEZ LA MARTHE

20 rue Mazan (Centre); it's near the town hall.
☎ 04.66.77.06.72
Closed Sun evening, Mon, June and Nov.

Marthe is named after an eccentric woman who ran the local grocery more than twenty years ago. The restaurant has been delightfully decorated in local style. Weekday lunch menu 70F, then 110F and 130F. Dishes include *pieds et paquets* (lamb tripe and trotters), duck sausage with *foie gras* or Cévenole salad. They can close unexpectedly in winter, so check in advance. Free coffee.

|●| RESTAURANT LE MICOCOULIER

3 pl. Jean-Astruc (Centre).
☎ 04.66.77.57.61 ✉ gail.wagman@wanadoo.fr
Closed lunchtimes July–Aug except Sun and public holidays, and Nov–March.

An unusual, pleasant little restaurant is perched on a clifftop in the medieval village. There's a soothing atmosphere in the pretty dining room and the terrace is the kind of place where you can happily sit over a bottle putting the world to rights. The owner has gathered a collection of recipes during his travels, and has adapted them here: goulash, *tajine* (Moroccan stew), curries and a number of Turkish and Mexican dishes. His American wife cooks the pastries and her chocolate cake, lemon tart and *crème caramel* are irresistible. Set menus 92F and 135F.

SÈTE   34200

🏠 |●| LE P'TIT MOUSSE*

rue de Provence (West); it's in the Corniche area 100m from the beach.
☎ 04.67.53.10.66 ➡ 04.67.53.10.66
Closed Oct–March. **Garden**.

Lunch 12.30pm and dinner from 7.30pm. A small, bright ochre building in a quiet little street that's very close to the sea. The rooms are clean but quite small. Doubles 155–195F, and there are rooms for four with two double beds. Simple cooking and homely atmosphere, with set menus at 77F and 99F.

🏠 |●| HÔTEL LA CONGA**

plage de la Corniche (Southwest).
☎ 04.67.53.02.57 ➡ 04.67.51.40.01
TV. **Car park**.

Ideally situated just a few yards from the blue of the Mediterranean and the beach, this is another concrete box in an area that's full of them. Here the bedrooms are clean and rather pleasant and prices are fairly good. Doubles with shower or bath 160–335F. The restaurant is worth a visit for the Mediterranean cooking, and it has a sprinkling of good local specialities: shellfish, fresh fish, grills, a wonderful *bouillabaisse* that you have to order in advance, and *foie gras* raviolis with a morel cream sauce. Set weekday menu at 68–190F.

🏠 LE GRAND HÔTEL***

17 quai de Lattre-de-Tassigny (Centre).
☎ 04.67.74.71.77 ➡ 04.67.74.29.27
✉ hotel-sete.com
Closed 22 Dec–2 Jan. **TV**. **Pay car park**.

This magnificent grand hotel was built in the 1880s, since when it hasn't lost a trace of character. It's spacious and furnished with period furniture, and there's a magnificent patio with a metal-framed glass roof to keep out the bad weather. Rooms 310–330F with shower/wc or 450–620F with bath. Expect to pay extra for an apartment or a suite. Faultless service such as you find in a grand hotel.

📬 🏠 |●| LES TERRASSES DU LIDO***

Rond-point de l'Europe–La Corniche (West).
☎ 04.67.51.39.60 ➡ 04.67.51.28.90
Closed Sun evening and Mon out of season, and Feb.
Disabled access. **Swimming pool**. **Garden**. **TV**. **Garage**.

Owners Michel and Colette Guironnet run this place with considerable skill and taste. Everything's just right, from the decor in the rooms to the friendly welcome and the creative cooking. And there's a swimming pool. It's one of the best places in its category, so it's advisable to book, as there are only nine bedrooms. Colette runs the kitchen and prepares dishes with artistry and style. She particularly likes to cook fish, shellfish and *bouillabaisse*, and her poached oysters on a purée of saffron-flavoured courgettes and lobster lasagne with ceps are excellent. Doubles with bath 380–480F. Menus from 150F. Free coffee. 10% discount on the room rate mid-Sept to mid-June.

📬 |●| LA GOGUETTE

30 rue Révolution (Centre); it's near the flea market.
☎ 04.99.04.07.84

Closed Sun evening and Mon.

A good-humoured local restaurant that's full of personality, in a street where the tourists don't bother to go. It has naïve, colourful, Art Nouveau decor, a tiny terrace, a tiny dining room and a tiny mezzanine. Large portions of simple, home cooking with a range of cheap dishes. Menus 60F or 90F. Efficient service. It's popular, so book ahead. Free coffee.

|●| RESTAURANT THE MARCEL

5 rue Lazare-Carnot (Centre); it overlooks the canal.
☎ 04.67.74.20.89
Closed Sat lunchtime and Sun.

Service until 11pm, or midnight Fri and Sat. *The Marcel* is above all a venue for cultural debate, with classical music or jazz playing in the background. Lovely setting in a huge workshop/studio with contemporary works of art lining the walls. There's plenty of space and no pressure, so you can savour the good, elegantly prepared food. Menus 75F and 120F or 150F *à la carte*. The excellent grilled cuttlefish with *aïoli* is even better when washed down with white Picpoul wine.

⅓ |●| LA MARINE

29 quai Général-Durand (Centre); it's near the fishing harbour.
☎ 04.67.74.30.03 ➡ 04.67.74.38.18
Closed Tues out of season, Tues lunchtime July–Aug.
Disabled access.

You can eat on the terrace, which has a view of the harbour and the trawler fleet, or in the pretty dining room. In both places you'll feast on authentic, traditional, local cooking. They do an 89F *menu du jour* served until 1pm at lunchtime and until 8pm in the evening, and other menus 120–135F. Dishes such as *bouillabaisse*. monkfish in white sauce with shellfish and turbot with sea salt. The desserts are excellent. You'll pay a bit more *à la carte*, which lists their speciality, *bourride*, a sort of fish stew with saffron and bitter orange peel. Free coffee.

|●| LA CORNICHE

pl. Édouard-Herriot; it's opposite the casino.
☎ 04.67.53.03.30
Closed Sun evening and Mon out of season, Mon lunchtime July–Aug and mid-Nov to mid-Feb.

A huge blue neon sign yells '"tourist trap", but actually it's not – this is a good establishment where they serve well-balanced Sète specialities prepared just the way they ought to be. You can get fish soup to die for on the 100F menu, then authentic monkfish *sétoise*

with brandy, tomato and garlic and a decent *crème brûlée* – delicious and not too expensive. For 160F there is a shellfish platter, chef's fish stew, cheese and dessert.

BOUZIGUES   34140 (15KM N)

|●| CHEZ LA TCHÈPE

av. Louis-Tudesq; it's on the bank of the étang de Tau.
☎ 04.67.78.33.19

The little terrace set with plastic tables and chairs is often chock-a-block and it's pretty hard to miss. There are lots of places where everything comes straight from the sea to the table, but this one offers the best value for money. You can get two dozen oysters, a dozen mussels, one *violet* (a small sea creature from the Mediterranean which is eaten raw and looks like scrambled eggs), two warm *tielles* (a small squid soufflé with tomato sauce), a local speciality and a bottle of white wine for 120F – and that's for two people. Excellent value. There are no set menus – you just choose what you want from the display. Eat in or take away, and service at all hours of the day. No credit cards.

⅓ |●| LES JARDINS DE LA MER

av. Louis-Tudesq.
☎ 04.67.78.33.23 ➡ 04.67.78.93.57
Closed Thurs, the last few days in Sept, a fortnight in early Oct and Jan.

This pretty restaurant is in an oyster farm. The shady terrace is decorated with vast white sails and hung with a torrent of shells. Try the *gratin* of mussels with leeks, the seafood platters or meat or fish grilled over the open fire where they use old vinestock as fuel. Menus 110F and 160F. Free apéritif.

SOMMIÈRES   30250

🏠 |●| AUBERGE DU PONT ROMAIN***

2 rue Émile-Jamais; it's 300m from the Roman bridge.
☎ 04.66.80.00.58 ➡ 04.66.80.31.52
Closed 15 Jan–15 March and Nov.
Disabled access. Swimming pool. TV. Car park.

The size of this gigantic place is very impressive, and there's a huge industrial chimney sticking out of the roof. It's been a wool mill, a carpet mill, a silk farm, a distillery and a dye factory in its time and there's a huge industrial chimney piercing the blue sky. Today, it's a chic three-star hotel with affordable prices. Doubles with shower/wc or bath 360–500F – some are designed for the disabled. Half board is compulsory in summer at 400F per person. The restaurant is pricy with menus 185–320F but the food is some of the best in the area. The shaded, flowery terrace and swimming pool are enough to make you feel like lazing about all afternoon.

🏂 |●| L'OLIVETTE

11 rue Abbé-Fabre.
☎ 04.66.80.97.71
Closed Tues in season, Tues evening and Wed out of season, and Jan.

They know how to make you feel welcome here. The dining room has stone walls and wooden beams and is air-conditioned. There's a two-course lunch menu at 75F, then others 100–185F. The cuisine is staunchly local – snails, salt cod stew with olive paste – but with a few flavours from further afield: scallop *mousseline* with ginger, and pork with pineapple and green peppercorns. They use a great deal of butter in preference to olive oil. Free *tapenade* (home-made olive paste).

SORÈDE   66690

|●| LA SALAMANDRE

3 route de Larroque.
☎ 04.68.89.26.67
Closed Sun evening and Mon, Mon lunchtime in summer, 15 Jan–15 March and 15 Nov–1 Dec.

The dining room is on the small side and, curiously, lacks intimacy, but the cuisine should be tried. It's full of originality and combines regional gastronomic recipes with lesser-known ones. The results are delicate and flavourful: sea bream with lime served with a chickpea pancake, leg of lamb with aïoli, for example. Menus, 95F and 135F, change regularly to make the most of seasonal produce. This is a really good place. Just so you know: a "*salamandre*" is the upper arch of the oven where you place dishes to caramelise or brown the top.

TAUTAVEL   66720

🏚 |●| CHEZ DANIEL

3 rue de la République.
☎ 04.68.29.03.23
Closed Mon out of season and three weeks in Jan. **TV**.

This is primarily a village bar-restaurant that's really friendly and popular. It's where locals drop in for an apéritif or a tasty, cheap meal. The single menu at 65F includes a self-ser-

vice *charcuterie* buffet, a choice of grilled lamb chops, Catalan sausages, steak, duck breast, pork belly or fish kebabs. Ice cream to finish – and wine is included. The rooms are clean and functional (pine furniture, white walls) and, at 180F, they offer good value for money for such a touristy place. There are also apartments to rent by the week.

UZÈS   30700

🏂 🏚 HÔTEL SAINT-GÉNIÈS**

Quartier Saint-Géniès, (Southwest); it's 1.5 km from the town centre in the direction of Saint-Ambroix
☎ 04.66.22.29.99 ➽ 04.66.03.14.89
📧 saintgeniesz@wanadoo.fr
Closed 15 Dec–15 Feb.
Swimming pool. **Garden**. **TV**. **Car park**.

This district is a kind of housing estate that's very quiet in the evening. The hotel is new and there are twenty tastefully decorated bedrooms. The ones up in the roof have sloping ceilings, which makes them more intimate. Doubles with shower/wc or bath 260–350F. They offer a set meal, 80F, if you don't want to venture back into town. Free coffee.

🏚 |●| HÔTEL D'ENTRAIGUES- RESTAURANT LES JARDINS DE CASTILLE***

8 rue de la Calade (East); it's opposite the historic bishop's palace and the cathedral of Saint-Théodorit.
☎ 04.66.22.32.68 ➽ 04.66.22.57.01
📧 hôtels.entraigues.agoult@wanadoo.fr
Disabled access. **Swimming pool**. **TV**. **Car park**.

This stylish, charming establishment is organised in a group of town houses from the 15th, 16th and 17th centuries. The 29 air-conditioned bedrooms and apartments are furnished in classic style, and some have a private terrace. Doubles with shower/wc or bath 235–700F. The restaurant has a panoramic terrace and an elegant dining room. Menus 135–220F. Inspired Provençal cuisine.

🏚 |●| HÔTEL-RESTAURANT LA TAVERNE**

4–9 rue Xavier-Sigalon (Centre); it's near the cinema.
☎ 04.66.22.47.08 ➽ 04.66.22.45.90
📧 lataverne.uzes@wanadoo.fr
Garden. **TV**.

The pleasant garden in the small courtyard provides a quiet setting for your meal, though sometimes it's overrun by groups. The owner knows the town like the back of his hand, so he's a good source of information. Good tasty cooking. Weekday lunch menu at 85F (not on Sun) and others 120–150F. They do *confit*, breast of duck and *cassoulet*, and excellent scrambled eggs with truffles. The hotel is a few metres further on and provides quiet rooms – particularly the ones at the back. They all have good facilities and are good value: doubles with shower/wc or bath 320–380F. They're all different and some have beamed ceilings and stone walls from the original house.

🎄|●| LE BISTROT DU GRÉZAL

pl. Belle-Croix.
☎ 04.66.03.42.09
Closed Tues evening and Wed, a fortnight in Feb and a fortnight in Oct.

Just next to the Saint-Étienne church is this brand-new, old-style bistro that's been brilliantly done up. When it's aged a little it will be perfect. The simple, delicious cuisine is Provençal in style. Lunch menu 70F and 100F. Easy-going, efficient service. Sadly, the terrace is just too close to the road for comfort. Free apéritif.

🎄|●| LE SAN DIEGO

10 bd. Charles-Gide; it's next to the town hall.
☎ 04.66.22.20.78
Closed Sun evening, Mon and a fortnight in Feb.

The frontage is unusually dull for Uzès but the restaurant is very good. There are two fresh dining rooms with vaulted ceilings, painted in grey and pink, and there are vases of roses on the table. A great deal of care goes into preparing dishes like veal kidneys with ceps and sea bream with rosemary, and they are famous for their chocolate *fondant* with cherry *coulis*. Menus 83–165F. Friendly, unobtrusive service. Free house apéritif.

SAINT-VICTOR-DES-OULES   30700 (6KM NW)

|●| RESTAURANT DU MAS DES OULES

Route de Saint-Hyppolyte.
☎ 04.66.63.17.15
Closed Sun evening, Mon and Tues.

The restaurant is in one wing of a farm in the grounds of a 17th-century castle. It's a small but typical Provençal house, and the atmosphere is so relaxed it's like being at home with friends. The owner comes over and goes through the menu with you, communicating her enthusiasm with ease. The cuisine is the result of inspirational treatment of fresh, seasonal produce that would hold its own against many a starred establishment. Menus from 150F.

VERS-PONT-DU-GARD   30210 (10KM SE)

🎄🏠|●| LA BÉGUDE SAINT-PIERRE

Les Coudoulières; it's on the D981 between Remoulins and Uzès.
☎ 04.66.63.63.63 ➡ 04.66.22.72.72
📧 begudessaintpierrre@wanadoo.fr
Disabled access. Swimming pool. TV. Car park.

"*Bégude*" is a Provençal word for a farm that doubled as a post house way back when letters were carried on horseback. Times may have changed but fortunately the road that goes past is not busy. The beautiful 17th-century building has been carefully restored and decorated with Provençal prints. The rooms look onto the coach yard or the swimming pool; they're air-conditioned and individually decorated. Doubles with bath 350–750F. The chic restaurant serves cuisine of Provençal inspiration and has menus 190–320F. The staff make you feel welcome. 10% discount on the room rate Sept–June.

VALCEBOLLIÈRE   66340

🎄🏠|●| AUBERGE LES ÉCUREUILS***

How to get there: take the N116 and the D30 from bourg Madame.
☎ 04.68.04.52.03 ➡ 04.68.04.52.34
Closed 15 Oct–10 Dec and a fortnight in May.
Swimming pool. TV. Car park.

This cosy inn, built of solid wood and stone, lies deep in the heart of Cerdagne near the Spanish border. Étienne Laffitte's creativity blossoms in the kitchen, where he creates dishes based on local produce and serves them up in hearty portions. Set menus 122F at lunchtime then 152–252F – or you can eat in the *crêperie* for 95F. Dishes include hot duck *foie gras* with apples and honey, duck breast with ceps and braised lamb fillet. Comfortable bedrooms with marble bathrooms 350–550F. Half-board 350–420F. There's a gym, a sauna and pool tables. You can go on beautiful walks up the mountain which is 2500m high and towers over the hotel. In the winter there's downhill skiing or snow-shoe hikes. 5% discount if you stay half board.

VIGAN (LE)   30120

🏠|●| HÔTEL DU COMMERCE*

26 rue des Barris (Centre).
☎ 04.67.81.03.28 ➡ 04.67.81.86.79
Garden. Car park.

This quiet, cheap hotel is in the middle of the village. Bright, simple, spacious, super-clean double rooms cost 130F with basin or 180F with shower/wc or bath. There are also single rooms at 90F.

|●| LE JARDIN

8 rue du Four (Centre); it's 50m from the tourist office.
☎ 04.67.81.28.96
Closed Mon lunchtime and Feb.

This place is a wine shop as well as a restaurant. It's in a quiet street. The dining room is as pleasant as the small terrace. Naturally enough, you will find lots of local wines and regional AOC wines that you can try by the glass, the jug or the bottle. Start off with a *rinquinquin*, a local peach apéritif while you meander through the menu. Dishes are seasonally inspired and the produce is fresh and local – the beef and veal come from the Aubrac. There's also a fish menu. Weekday lunch menu 85F and others 115–155F. The service is amiable and kind.

AVÈZE   30120 (2KM S)

⅍ ☎ |●| L'AUBERGE COCAGNE**

pl. du Château.
☎ 04.67.81.02.70 ➡ 04.67.81.07.67
Closed 20 Dec–7 Feb. **Disabled access. Car park**.

In the south of France "*cocagne*" means "luck", and this typical country inn, shielded by a clump of trees, couldn't have been more aptly named. It's a 400-year-old building with massive stone walls, red shutters and simple yet comfortable bedrooms. Doubles 170F with basin, 260F with bath. You get a warm welcome – strains of jazz or world music emerge from the dining room. The place has personality and so does the home cooking. It's very typically Mediterranean with lots of olive oil: *terrine* with sweet onion chutney, lamb from the Causse and vegetarian dishes. The vegetables are organic and the cheeses bought direct from the farmer. The wines and apéritifs come from local winegrowers. Set menus 70–195F. Half board costs 210–255F and is compulsory mid-July to mid-Aug and over long bank-holiday weekends. Free coffee or herbal tea.

MANDAGOUT   30120 (10KM N)

⅍ ☎ |●| AUBERGE DE LA BORIE*

How to get there: take the D170; 9km along, turn right towards Mandagout, pass the village, continue towards Saint-André-de-Majencoules, then follow a sloping

street on the left for 250m.
☎ 04.67.81.06.03 ➡ 04.67.81.86.79
Disabled access. Swimming pool. Garden. Car park.

An old Cévennes *mas* on a sunny mountainside, with a swimming pool and reasonable prices. The views over the mountains, the chestnut forests and fig groves are breathtaking. The owners make you feel most welcome. There are about ten nicely appointed rooms with old stone walls. Doubles with basin 165F or 270–295F with shower/wc. Numbers 8, 9 and 10, in the ancient vaulted cellars, are wonderfully cool in summer. They serve home cooking based exclusively on local produce: specialities include *foie gras* with fig preserves and frogs' legs with parsley. Set menus 74–145F. Free apéritif.

SAINT-MARTIAL   30440 (24KM NE)

⅍ ☎ |●| HÔTEL-RESTAURANT LA TERRASSE

Le bourg; take the D999 across Le Vigan, then the D11 and the D20.
☎ 04.67.81.33.11 ➡ 04.67.81.33.87
Closed Wed and end Feb to early March

Good living and good food go hand in hand at this mountainside inn. Dominique, the owner, boasts about the beauty spots in "her" beautiful Cévennes, including the 12th-century Romanesque church in the village. They offer perfectly adequate bedrooms at 190F for a double with shower, but people come here primarily for the local cooking: tart *forestière* with mushrooms, bacon and potatoes, roast guinea-fowl with cider and apples, *millefeuille* of onions with an olive oil *sabayon*, home-made peach tart. Menus 85–171F – you get an extra course on the most expensive menu. A brilliant find. Free apéritif or coffee.

VILLEFORT   48800

⅍ ☎ |●| HÔTEL-RESTAURANT BALME**

pl. du Portalet (Centre).
☎ 04.66.46.80.14 ➡ 04.66.46.85.26
Closed Sun evening and Mon out of season, a few days in Sept and mid-Nov to mid-Feb. **TV. Car park**.

A well-known hotel that's aged elegantly. It's reminiscent of a spa hotel – same type of comfort, same English atmosphere. The cuisine is excellent, combining local dishes and specialities from the East, especially Thailand, where chef Michel Gomy spends part of every year. There is a weekday menu at 115F and others 175–200F. Dishes *à la carte* change regularly so it's hard to know what you'll find, but they do excellent farm-bred lamb with pesto and superb *nems* (small spring rolls stuffed with pig's head). The kitchen opens onto the dining room, so you can see what's going on. Since Micheline is a qualified *sommelier*, they've got a magnificent cellar. The meals are the best value for money in the region. Doubles with basin for 225F, 300F with shower/wc, 320F with bath. 10% discount on the room rate.

🎄 ☎ |●| HÔTEL-RESTAURANT DU LAC**

Lac de Villefort (Nord); take the D906 for 1.5km and it's a white building all by itself on the left by the lake.
☎ 04.66.46.81.20 ➡ 04.66.46.90.95
Closed Wed out of season, 1 Dec–15 March. **Car park**.

The bedrooms and the dining room all have a view of the lake where you can swim in summer. The rooms are reasonably priced considering the excellent location; doubles with shower/wc go for 260F or 380F with bath. The 88F set menu features regional specialities like cep tart followed by stew of suckling pig or veal. It's very popular in high season, so it can get noisy. Free coffee.

VILLEFRANCHE-DE-CONFLENT   66500

|●| AUBERGE SAINT-PAUL

7 pl. de l'Église; it's in the centre of town.
☎ and ➡ 04.68.96.30.95
Closed Mon Easter–Oct, Mon and Tues Oct–Easter, three weeks in Jan, five days in June, ten days end Nov.

Patricia Gomez has a remarkable imagination. She combines unexpected flavours and cooks top-quality ingredients with deft skill to produce memorable dishes such as ravioli with goat's cheese stuffing, roast local lamb and pig's trotters and a perfect vanilla cream. Set menus for 135–400F; you'll pay around 250F *à la carte*. Brilliant wines selected by Charly Gomez. One of the best restaurants in the district, and it has a beautiful terrace.

OLETTE   66360 (10KM W)

☎ |●| HÔTEL-RESTAURANT LA FONTAINE

5 rue de la Fusterie.
☎ 04.68.97.03.67 ➡ 04.68.97.09.18
Closed Tues evening and Wed except during school holidays and Jan. **TV**.

A substantial building painted brilliant salmon-pink. The rooms are attractive and have good facilities, including en-suite bathrooms. Good-value doubles with shower/wc

at 190F. There are three or four tables on the terrace and a pretty dining room on the first floor. Try local goat's cheese in a pastry case or *tournedos* with cream of black pudding. Menus 70–120F. Warm, family welcome.

VILLENEUVE-LÈS-AVIGNON   30400

🎄 ☎ HÔTEL DE L'ATELIER**

5 rue de la Foire (Centre).
☎ 04.90.25.01.84 ➡ 04.90.25.80.06
@ hotel.atelier@wanadoo.fr
Closed beginning Nov to beginning Dec.
Garden. **TV**. **Car park**.

This is a quite delightful 16th-century building with nineteen bedrooms furnished with antiques. Rooms are all different and doubles with shower or bath go for 275–460F. Breakfast is served in the dining room or on the patio where pot plants and flowers proliferate. There's also a rooftop terrace. It's good value for money, and it's advisable to book in season. 10% discount Sept–June.

|●| RESTAURANT LA CALÈCHE

35 rue de la République; it's between the Chartreuse and the village square.
☎ 04.90.25.02.54
Closed Thurs evening and Sun.

The terrace and the patio are very pleasant during the summer months. The restaurant also has two pretty dining rooms decorated in warm colours and the walls are covered in posters and reproductions of Toulouse-Lautrec paintings. Simple cooking, decent food and specialities from Lyon and Provence; *pieds et paquets* (lamb tripe and trotters), beef *daube* and lamb *confit*. Set menus 69–118F. Friendly service.

|●| RESTAURANT LA MAISON

1 rue Montée-du-Fort-Saint-André (Centre); it's behind the town hall, overlooking pl. Jean-Jaurès.
☎ 04.90.25.20.81
Closed Tues evening, Wed, Sat lunchtime. **Car park**.

This good restaurant is attractive, with lace curtains, ceiling fans and a good-looking pottery collection. Simple cooking is served in generous portions. You get a good meal on the 120F menu. Absolutely delightful service.

ANGLES (LES)   30133 (4KM S)

☎ |●| LE PETIT MANOIR-RESTAURANT LA TONNELLE**

15 av. Jules-Ferry; it's on the Nîmes road.

☎ 04.90.25.03.36 ➡ 04.90.25.49.13
Disabled access. **Swimming pool**. **Garden**. **TV**. **Car park**.

This group of modern buildings set around a swimming pool is hardly what you'd call a manor. But the place is not without character or comfort, all the same – most of the quiet, clean rooms have a private terrace. Doubles 270–360F with shower/wc or bath. The restaurant serves traditional, regional cuisine with menus 100–260F. Half board costs 405F and is compulsory in July.

ROQUEMAURE 30150 (11KM N)

⚲ ▲ |●| LE CLÉMENT V**

route de Nîmes (Southwest); take the D980.
☎ 04.66.82.67.58 ➡ 04.66.82.84.66

e hotel.clementv@wanadoo.fr
Closed Sat and Sun out of season except for reservations, and 25 Oct–15 March.
Swimming pool. **TV**. **Garden**. **Lock-up garage**.

A very nice place in a medieval village in the Côtes du Rhône that's not on the tourist track. It's in a 1970s apartment building that looks like many that were built along the coast at that time. The rooms are very conventional but as they've been renovated, a touch of Provence has crept in. The ones overlooking the swimming have balconies but the ones at the back are larger and quieter. Doubles 320–340F with shower/wc. Half board, 275–295F, is obligatory in summer. The menus, 98F and 125F, are available only to hotel residents. Typical, local dishes and the cooking has bags of personality. Free apéritif and 10% discount on the room rate Sept–June.

LIMOUSIN

19 Corrèze

23 Creuse

87 Haute-Vienne

ARGENTAT   19400

🦌 🏠 |●| HÔTEL-RESTAURANT FOUILLADE**

11 pl. Gambetta.
☎ 05.55.28.10.17 ➡ 05.55.28.90.52
Closed Mon out of season, Nov. **TV. Car park**.

A beautiful house that's been running as a hotel-restaurant for two centuries. Scrumptious dishes include duck *confit* with chestnuts, ceps with sorrel butter, and *croustade* with girolle mushrooms. Menus 70–195F. The rooms with their 1970s aspect are less attractive than the building itself. Doubles with shower/wc 220–245F, 235F with bath. Free coffee.

ARNAC-POMPADOUR   19230

🦌 🏠 |●| AUBERGE DE LA MANDRIE**

Route de Périgueux; 5km from Pompadour on the D7 going towards Payzac and Périgueux.
☎ 05.55.73.37.14 ➡ 05.55.73.67.13
e auberge.mandrie@laposte.fr
Swimming pool. TV. Garden.

This place, near the Cité du Cheval and the medieval village of Ségur-le-Château, is like a holiday club with little chalets dotted around in a park. There is a fabulous heated pool and a play area for children. Bedrooms all have a tiny terrace, and either a shower or bath. Doubles 250F. It's an excellent establishment, where the owners take pride in their work and you'll get a warm welcome. The regional dishes are particularly tasty – salad of ceps with flambéed chestnuts, poached eggs with violet mustard, snail *profiteroles* with cream of parsley and warm *cabécou*

cheese with apples, Limousin-style. Set menu 70F (except Sun lunchtime), and 100–180F. You can eat in the dining room or on the enormous terrace. Free apéritif.

AUBUSSON   23200

🦌 🏠 HÔTEL LE CHAPITRE**

53–55 Grande-Rue (Centre).
☎ 05.55.66.18.54 ➡ 05.55.67.79.63
TV.

Run by a friendly man who also owns the downstairs bar. All the rooms have good facilities, with tiled bathrooms and double-glazed windows. Doubles 170F with shower/wc and 190F with bath. A nice little place that's good value. Free coffee.

🏠 |●| LE LION D'OR**

pl. du Général-d'Espagne (Centre).
☎ 05.55.66.13.88 ➡ 05.55.66.84.73
Closed Sun evening and Mon out of season. **TV. Car park**.

A provincial inn without great charm. The bedrooms are comfortable and well maintained; double with shower/wc 270F, or with bath 300F. Courteous reception. The classical cooking uses fresh ingredients. Menus 90–165F.

🏠 |●| HÔTEL DE FRANCE**-RESTAURANT AU RENDEZ-VOUS DES GOURMETS

6 rue des Déportés (Centre).
☎ 05.55.66.10.22 ➡ 05.55.66.88.64
TV. Car park.

This is Aubusson's most delightful establishment. The double rooms, 300–600F, are

[**395**]

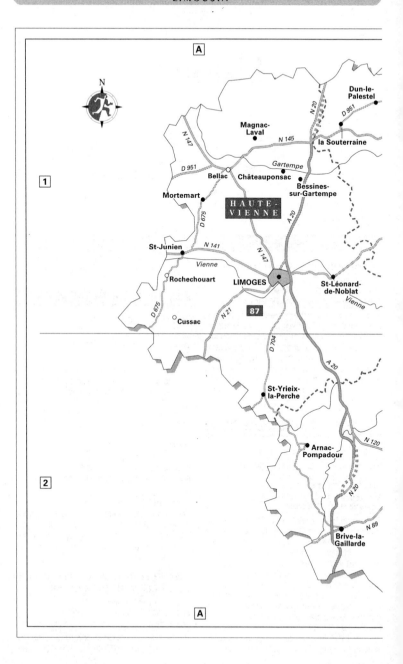

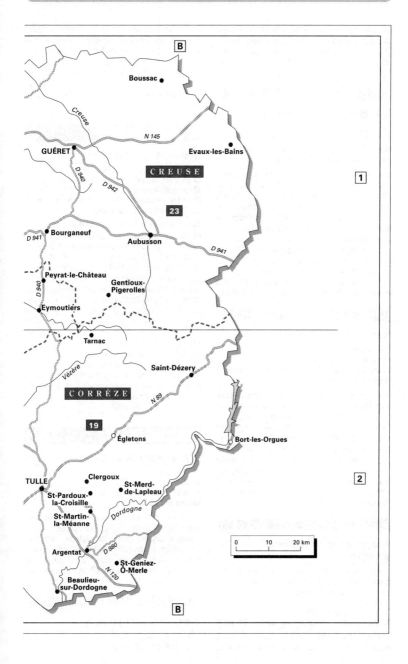

attractive and very well equipped, though avoid the ones overlooking the busy street. The chef is inspired and the cooking high class. Menus 80–280F. In the summer breakfast is served in the conservatory.

BLESSAC   23200 (4KM NW)

⅍ ☎ |●| LE RELAIS DES FORÊTS*

route d'Aubusson.
☎ 05.55.66.15.10 ➡ 05.55.83.87.91
Closed Fri evening, Sun evening out of season, and mid-Feb to mid-March. **TV**. **Car park**.

The only reasonably priced establishment around Aubusson. If you like generous portions of simple home cooking, this is the place to come. Menus from 62F – the one at 100F offers a balanced selection of regional dishes with a decent potato pie and a very tasty ribsteak of Limousin beef. Other menus up to 195F. The decor is rather kitsch but the bedrooms are clean and have been refurbished. Doubles 155F with basin/wc (the shower is along the corridor), 250F with shower/wc, or 285F with bath. Free coffee.

VILLENEUVE (LA)   23260 (23KM E)

⅍|●| LR RELAIS MARCHOIS

It's on the N141.
☎ and ➡ 05.55.67.35.78
Closed Tues evening, Wed, the last week in June and Christmas to New Year.

A real, very charming country inn; the setting, with its interesting collection of fans and old coffee pots, creates the right atmosphere for the cooking. Dishes include grilled rib of beef with potato cake, *fricassée* of chicken with crayfish, pastry case of scallops with whisky, and an irresistible *nougat glacé* with coconut milk and *petits fours*. Menus, 68–215F, are good value. The food is generously served, well presented and the service is charming. Free house apéritif or coffee.

SAINT-MARC-À-LOUBAUD 23460 (24KM SW)

⅍|●| RESTAURANT LES MILLE SOURCES

Le bourg; take the N141 towards Limoges, then the D7 towards Royère, turn left at Vallières in the direction of Saint-Yrieix, and follow the signs for Saint-Marc-à-Loubaud.
☎ and ➡ 05.55.66.09.69
Closed Mon Jan–April, Dec and Jan. **Garden**. **Car park**.

Way up in the north of the Millevaches plateau, this place is very popular, so it's advisable to

book. The quality of the cooking is quite astonishing. Philippe Coutisson's duck *à la ficelle* is a triumph, as are his specialities, chargrilled duck and leg of lamb. Set menus 140–215F. The decor is delightful and the lovingly tended garden is always full of flowers. You'll get a warm welcome. Free coffee and apéritif.

BEAULIEU-SUR-DORDOGNE   19120

☎ |●| HÔTEL LE TURENNE**

1 bd. Saint-Rodolphe-de-Turenne (Centre).
☎ 05.55.91.10.16 ➡ 05.55.91.22.42
@ turenne02@infonie.fr
Closed Sun evening and Mon out of season, and mid-Nov to mid-March. **TV**. **Car park**.

This turreted 12th-century building, covered in creepers, has been elegantly converted into a delightful hotel and restaurant. Arches lead from the dining room onto a terrace and shady garden. You find your way to the spacious bedrooms up a stone staircase. Each room is different. They've all been tastefully renovated and furnished and have en-suite bathroom, satellite TV and phone – a few even have period fireplaces. Doubles cost 290F with shower or 310F with bath. And the restaurant is no disappointment. The cooking is inventive – try duck *foie gras* with ceps, *crépinette* of pig's trotters with violet mustard, and any of the excellent desserts, particularly the *crème brûlées* flavoured with vanilla, walnuts and liquorice. Weekday *formule* 75F or 110–370F.

BOURGANEUF   23400

⅍ ☎ |●| AUBERGE DE L'ÂTRE

17 av. Turgot.
☎ 05.55.64.10.10 ➡ 05.55.64.08.99
Closed Sun evening and ten days before Easter. **TV**. **Garden**. **Car park**.

A conventional inn with a menu consisting of predictable steak and chips but also more unusual dishes, such as *salade fermière*, duck thigh confit or roast bream with fennel seeds. Set menus 62–135F. You'll be received courteously and with a smile. Rooms are very basic, from 120–170F. Free apéritif.

SAINT-HILAIRE-LE-CHÂTEAU 23250 (15KM NE)

☎ |●| HÔTEL DU THAURION**

10 Grand-Rue; take the D941.
☎ 05.55.64.50.12 ➡ 05.55.64.90.92

Closed Wed and Thurs lunchtimes except July–Aug, Sun evening and 30 Nov–28 Feb. **TV**. **Car park**.

An attractively restored coaching inn, owned by Gérard Fanton, who is the chef by whom all other chefs in the Creuse are judged. The 99F *menu du jour* is constructed around fresh produce from the market – although it's reasonably priced, it might not satisfy the biggest appetites. There are other menus from 120F up to 300F. Specialities include braised pork, oxtail pancake with mustard sauce and crayfish tail ravioli. The service is a bit slow and not very efficient.

BOUSSAC   23600

⚘ ☗ |●| CENTRAL HÔTEL*

rue du 11-Novembre; it's near the Grand-Place.
☎ 05.55.65.00.11 ➡ 05.55.65.84.15
Restaurant closed Fri evening and Sat in winter, and 25 Dec–15 Jan. **TV**. **Garden**. **Car park**.

Quiet and conventional hotel with doubles with shower/wc for 180F – some rooms have beds like hammocks. The restaurant offers generous portions of traditional cuisine; menus 78–190F. 10% discount on the room rate or free coffee.

|●| CAFÉ DE LA PLACE

4 pl. de l'Hôtel-de-Ville (Centre).
☎ 05.55.65.02.70
Closed Sun in June, Christmas Day, 1 Jan and Easter Mon. **Car park**.

Paulette Roger is a warm and welcoming figure. She offers just one set menu at 60F (70F on Sun), which gets you a starter, two dishes and a dessert. You choose from five or six different options, but a typical meal might consist of melon, shellfish, meat *en paupiette* and potatoes, with pear tart to finish. Good value.

|●| LE RELAIS CREUSOIS

Route de la Châtre (Nord).
☎ 05.55.65.02.20
Closed Tues evening and Wed out of season, 17 Oct–1 Nov dinner by reservation only, Jan, Feb and ten days in June. **Car park**.

You can't miss the striking green columns of this place. You don't get a choice on the cheapest *formules*, but the cooking is good. The chef prepares lots of local dishes and he also dreams up his own specialities, such as artichoke stew with marrowbone, lacquered duck thigh and cream beaten with spices. Menus 120–350F.

GRENOUILLAC   23350 (20KM W)

⚘ ☗ |●| LA PETITE MARIE

Lieu-dit Montfargeaud.
☎ 05.55.80.85.60
Disabled access. **TV**.

A most welcoming country inn with five rooms. The dining room is warm and has sturdy beams and stone walls. You can eat in the garden in summer. It's a place to take your time while you savour the food and enjoy the view of the valleys and mountains. Honestly prepared dishes include house *foie gras*, duck *confit*, and beef steak with pickled nettle cream. *Formule* 58F and menus 98–148F. The selection of wines is wide-ranging. Martial is something of a virtuoso on the accordion. A convivial place. Free house apéritif.

BRIVE-LA-GAILLARDE   19100

⚘ ☗ |●| HÔTEL-RESTAURANT LA CRÉMAILLIÈRE**

53 av. de Paris; it's 100m from the market.
☎ 05.55.74.32.47 ➡ 05.55.74.00.15
Closed Sun evening, Mon, a fortnight in Feb and a week in July.

Pascal Jacquinot, the new owner, had a hard act to follow after Charlou Raynal left, but he picked up the baton and ran with it. Although the decor is a bit garish, the cooking is splendid and dishes change regularly: roast *andouille* with grain mustard, pot-roast pigeon with girolles, summer truffles with scrambled eggs or char with a *fricassée* of fresh green beans. The milk-fed veal cutlet is simple and perfect. Menus 100–250F. There are a few decent rooms at 200F. Free coffee.

|●| LA TOUPINE

11 rue Jean Labrunie.
☎ and ➡ 05.55.23.71.58
Closed Sun, Wed evening, the Feb school holidays and 15–30 Aug.

This place is on the up. The dining room is almost dull, the welcome is a tad brisk but the cooking makes up for everything: *foie gras* salad with sea salt and fresh walnut bread, fish stew, and pig's trotters served on a *gallette*. It's very, very good and prices are honest. Menu of the day 60F, 98–140F or *à la carte*. Best to book.

|●| CHEZ FRANCIS

61 av. de Paris.
☎ 05.55.74.41.72
Closed Sun, ten days in Feb and a fortnight in Aug.

Lunch until 1.30pm, dinner until 10pm. As the flattering remarks scribbled on the walls of this delightful brasserie reveal, this is a popular place – it's best to book. It's full of objects collected from pre-war bistros. Francis gives free rein to his imagination; his approach to cooking is thoughtful and he produces wonderfully executed dishes that are prettily presented. Try the pot-roast beef, pan-fried cod with baby vegetables or trout with oyster mushrooms. All the chicken dishes are good. Dish of the day 48F and menus from 90F.

MALEMORT-SUR-CORRÈZE 19360 (3KM NE)

🌿 🏠 I●I AUBERGE DES VIEUX CHÊNES**

31 av. Honoré-de-Balzac.
☎ 05.55.24.13.55 ➡ 05.55.24.56.82
Closed Sun. **TV. Car park**.

This establishment isn't much to look at from the outside, but take a look at the menus. It's a good place to experience inventive country-style cooking with a hint of the exotic: creamy risotto with pan-fried *foie gras* and parmesan *tuiles*, ling fillet with Brive violet mustard, upside-down tart with sweetbreads, capers and chestnuts, leaves of bitter chocolate *croustillant* with raspberry and *crème chantilly* or fresh fruit tarts. You'll enjoy the food and the atmosphere in the bright dining room. The rooms have modern facilities – they're similar to the ones you'd find in a chain hotel but cheaper; doubles 230 or 300F with shower or bath/wc. Very good welcome. Free coffee.

DONZENAC 19270 (10KM N)

🏠 I●I RESTAURANT LE PÉRIGORD-HÔTEL LA GAMADE**

Le bourg; take the D920.
☎ 05.55.85.72.34 ➡ 05.55.85.65–83

It's more fun to eat in the bar here even though there's a rather elegant dining room and a tiny terrace. Mme Salesse keeps a stern but benevolent eye on the regulars who drop in for a drink and a bite. There's a *menu du jour* at 85F and others from 120–380F: black pudding salad with caramelised apples, calf's head *ravigote* or duck *confit Périgourdine*. The hotel building, swathed in Virginia creeper, has nine bedrooms, each of them different. Doubles 240–260F with shower/wc, or 290F for a big bathroom and a terrace with a view of the village.

SAINT-VIANCE 19240 (10KM N)

🌿 🏠 I●I L'AUBERGE DES PRÉS DE LA VÉZÈRE**

Le bourg; take the D901 then the D148.
☎ 05.55.84.00.50 ➡ 05.55.84.25.36
Closed Sun evening, Mon lunchtime except July–Aug, and Dec to mid-April. **TV. Car park**.

Lunch noon–2pm, dinner 7.30–9pm. This hotel, shaded by maple and chestnut trees, stands in a meadow that leads down to the Vézère. Eleven spacious, pretty bedrooms, all with bathrooms, 280–395F. The restaurant has a good reputation; it offers a 90F lunch menu and *menus-cartes* at 110–195F. Tempting dishes include Limousine salad with duck and bacon, lamb shank *confit* with pan-fried vegetables and garlic, and fine apple tart with vanilla ice cream. Free apéritif.

TURENNE 19500 (14KM W)

🏠 I●I LA MAISON DES CHANOINES

Route de l'église; take the D38 then the D150.
☎ 05.55.85.93.43 ➡ 05.55.85.93.43
Closed Tues lunchtime, Wed and Thurs lunchtimes except July–Sept, and 6 Nov–1 April.

Turenne is a beautiful old town and this hotel is quite delightful. You'll find it at the start of the lane that leads up to the church and the château. The dining room has a vaulted ceiling, or you can eat under the trees on the lovely terrace. The *menu-carte*, 160–200F, allows you to enjoy imaginative cooking and nicely presented dishes: *foie gras* marinated in truffle vinegar served with home-made walnut bread, mussels with green walnuts, and chargrilled veal with morels. For 300F you enjoy the delights of the truffle menu – to order. There are six comfortable, stylish bedrooms, 350–370F. You'll get a lovely welcome.

AUBAZINE 19190 (15KM NE)

🏠 I●I HÔTEL-CAFÉ-RESTAURANT DE LA TOUR**

pl.de l'Église; take the N89.
☎ 05.55.25.71.17 ➡ 05.55.84.61.83
Closed Mon lunchtime out of season, Sun evening, and the first fortnight in Jan. **TV**.

In a splendid location at the heart of the village, just across from the abbey church. Attractive rooms – 200F with shower/wc, 300F with bath or 400F for a most impressive split-level suite in the tower. The chef has worked in several major Parisian establishments, where he learned to prepare simple, uncomplicated dishes – try the *foie gras* with cabbage. There are gorgeous fireplaces in the two dining rooms. *Formules* from 65F and menus 120–230F. Friendly welcome.

MEYSSAC   19500 (23KM SE)

👫 🏠 |●| LE RELAIS DU QUERCY**

av. du Quercy (Centre).
☎ 05.55.25.40.31 ➡ 05.55.25.36.22
Closed 15 Nov–7 Dec. **Swimming pool**. **TV**. **Garden**. **Car park**.

Lunch noon–3.30pm, dinner 5–11pm. This village is built from red sandstone. The hotel is in a large building with a stylish dining room and a terrace above the pool. Menus 70–220F. Duck figures highly, and alongside classical dishes (*cassoulet* with duck *confit*), you'll find more inventive ones like chilli *à l'aiguillette*, which are slivers of duck. The friendly, easy-going team know that the little things count. They have rooms with good facilities, 200–320F. The most expensive one overlooks the pool. Free coffee.

CHÂTEAUPONSAC   87290

👫 🏠 |●| HÔTEL-RESTAURANT DU CENTRE*

pl. Mazurier; take the D1 and it's opposite the tourist office.
☎ 05.55.76.50.19
Closed Wed evening and Aug.

This popular, modest hotel with a bar/restaurant has clean, cheap rooms. Doubles 130F with basin (wc in the corridor), 190F with shower/wc. A 60F *menu du jour*, and a menu at 80F which includes cheese and dessert. Good value. Free coffee.

ROUSSAC   87140 (11KM SW)

|●| LA FONTAINE SAINT-MARTIAL

Le bourg; by the D771.
☎ 05.55.60.27.42
Closed Wed evening.

A very attractive, brand-new bar-restaurant which also serves as a grocer's and tobacconist's. Marc Foussat, the modest young proprietor/chef does a marvellous job. You can eat in the spick-and-span dining room beside the bar or on the terrace. The 60F *menu du jour* is served on weekday

lunchtimes, and it includes cheese, dessert, wine and coffee. Other menus, 75–115F, list wholesome dishes: carp mousse with sorrel, *roulade* of plaice, ling with *hollandaise* sauce, hare stew, and home-made raspberry *charlotte*. You'll find decent and inexpensive bottles on the short wine list. Classical cooking and friendly professional service. The bar is the meeting place for local football fans, so things really heat up on match nights. It's a convivial, relaxed place.

CHÉNÉRAILLES   23130

🏠 |●| LE COQ D'OR

7 pl. du Champ de Foire (Centre).
☎ 05.55.62.30.83
Closed Sun evening, Mon, a fortnight in Jan, a fortnight in June and a week in Sept.
TV. **Pay car park**.

Located between Château Villemonteix and Châteaux Mazeau, this place has a reputation for quality cuisine. The chef's style is to take local dishes and to update them for today's tastes – go for the trio of smoked fish, beef skirt and potato pie with a *croustillant* of trumpet mushrooms, or rabbit with *fondue provençale*. Weekday lunch menu 65F, and others 105–210F. They have a few double rooms, for 180F with shower, and up to 240F with shower/wc.

CLERGOUX   19320

🏠 HÔTEL CHAMMARD*

Le bourg; at Roche-Canillac get onto the D18 then take the D978 in the direction of Tulle.
☎ 05.55.27.76.04
Closed Nov–March. **Garden**. **Car park**.

Old-style place that wafts with a lovely aroma of beeswax and home-made jam. Georgette is a delightful woman who'll welcome you into her home where the *cantou*, the inglenook fireplace, dominates the place. Doubles with shower, at 160F, are very well maintained and most look onto the garden at the back.

DUN-LE-PALESTEL   23800

🏠 |●| HÔTEL-RESTAURANT JOLY**

square Fernand-Riollet; it's opposite the church.
☎ 05.55.89.00.23 ➡ 05.55.89.15.89
Closed Sun evening, Mon lunchtime, three weeks in March and three weeks in Oct. **TV**. **Disabled access**.

In this very typically French country hotel you'll find quiet, well-maintained rooms for 230–260F with bath or shower. Opt for the ones in the recently built annexe which are spick-and-span and more comfortable. In the huge rustic dining room they serve faultless, traditional cooking: duck *rillettes*, terrine of veal sweetbreads, and free-range chicken *à la Marchoise*. The service is superb. The 86F menu is satisfying, as are those at 115–200F. The owners also organise bike trips.

CROZANT   23160 (11.5KM N)

♠ |●| RESTAURANT DU LAC

Lieu-dit Pont de Crozant; it's on the banks of the Creuse.
☎ 05.55.89.81.96
Closed Mon and Feb.

Exceptionally situated on the water's edge, with a splendid view of the cathedral and the bridge that links the two departments – though it's on the Indre bank of the river, it's actually in the Creuse department. Well-executed cooking that is often inventive: quail salad with Berry lentils and *fricassée* of lamb's sweetbreads with pickled shallots. *Formule* at 95F and a fish menu at 135F. It's building a solid reputation, so it's best to book. There are a few rooms, 210F with shower or 270–300F with shower/wc or bath.

ÉVAUX-LES-BAINS   23110

⅍ ♠ |●| GRAND HÔTEL**

Les thermes: it's down the hill from the town centre beside the spa.
☎ 05.55.65.50.01 ➡ 05.55.65.59.16
Closed Nov–March. **TV. Car park**.

This is a grand hotel with old-fashioned charm which has been going since 1900. It has high ceilings and wide red-carpeted corridors and is full of people who come to take the waters. The guests may not be as young as they used to be but they enjoy the comfort they find here: large, well-heated rooms, all equipped with a bell to call the helpful staff. It's totally peaceful. Doubles 190–235F with basin/wc, 255–315F with shower/wc or 290–325F with bath. The ones that've been done up recently are impeccable. There's also a restaurant with menus 78–155F. Free apéritif.

FONTANIÈRES   23110 (8KM S)

|●| LE DAMIER

Le bourg; go along the D996 towards Auzances and it's

on the left hand side of the road.
☎ 05.55.82.35.91
Closed Mon evening, Tues, a fortnight in Feb/March and three weeks in Sept/Oct.

Lunch noon–2pm and dinner 7.30–9pm. It's not often that you find a pretty little inn like this around here. It has a quiet, stylish atmosphere, with background music and quality regional cuisine. Lunch menu 65F, or others 98–158F: *terrine* of duck with *foie gras*, grilled beef, local cheeses and *nougat* ice with raspberry *coulis*. Or choose *à la carte*.

GENTIOUX-PIGEROLLES   23340

♠ |●| LA FERME DE NAUTAS

Pigerolles; get onto the D982, then the D35, and then the D26.
☎ 05.55.67.90.68 ➡ 05.55.67.93.12
e les_nautas@wanadoo.fr
Closed weekdays out of season.

This place, a working farm run by the hospitable François Chatoux, is a winner. His wife does genuine local cuisine, using first-rate ingredients and serving generous helpings of tasty regional dishes – potato pie, cep tarts, prime quality meat and exceptional veal. The duck and lamb are reared on the farm and are of the same high quality. There are two menus at 85F and 110F. Double rooms 260F with shower/wc.

GUÉRET   23000

⅍ ♠ |●| HÔTEL DE POMMEIL

75 rue de Pommeil.
☎ and ➡ 05.55.52.38.54
Closed Sun and 12 June–1 July. **Car park**.

A very simple, clean hotel with good prices. Doubles 155F with shower or 200F with shower/wc. They have two *menus du jour*, 63F and 97F, which list veal *escalope* with a mushroom and cream sauce and scallops with saffron. There are just nine rooms, so it's best to book. Friendly welcome and atmosphere. 10% discount on the room rate for a two-night stay Sept–June.

♠ |●| HÔTEL AUCLAIR

19 av. de la Sénatorerie; (Centre); it's near pl. Bonnyaud.
☎ 05.55.41.22.00 ➡ 05.55.52.86.89
Swimming pool. Pay car park.

About thirty rooms with good facilities and all furnished with rattan. Doubles with shower 200F with wc on the landing or 290F with bath. There's a luxurious swimming pool.

You must reserve your parking space in advance. Small restaurant with brasserie *formules* or a menu at 130F.

SAINTE-FEYRE — 23000 (7KM SE)

|●| RESTAURANT LES TOURISTES

pl. de la Mairie; take the D942 in the direction of Aubusson
☎ 05.55.80.00.07 ➡ 05.55.81.11.04
Closed Tues evening and Wed out of season. **Disabled access. Car park.**

Service noon–2pm and 7.30–9pm. Tasty, classic local cooking prepared by Michel Roux and served in generous portions. There's a quiet atmosphere and the surroundings are decorative. You will get the measure of this excellent cooking from the menus, 88–220F, which list salmon braised with cucumber, cream and paprika, spiced duck thigh with grapes, or fillet of veal with cream and ceps. The chef's specialities are oxtail *terrine* and calf's foot vinaigrette. Good local meat dishes and skilfully prepared fish.

JOUILLAT — 23220 (17KM NE)

|●| L'AUBERGE DU CHÂTEAU

How to get there: follow Route de la Châtre, turn right when you get to Villevaleix and it's beside the church.
☎ 05.55.41.88.43 ➡ 05.55.41.88.44
Closed Sun evening and Mon.

Don't expect one of the usual olde-worlde inns done up for the tourists that you often find in the neighbourhood of a château; *L'Auberge du Château* fulfills a more important role in holding the local community together – it serves as a grocer's and tobaconist's as well as a restaurant. There's a rustic dining room and a terrific paved garden at the back. Menus, 89–130F, list starter, main course, cheese and dessert. The locals take a glass of red wine at the bar and discuss farming matters in their local dialect. Think about booking in advance.

LIMOGES — 87000

SEE MAP OVERLEAF

🎿 🛎 HÔTEL FAMILIA

18 rue du Gal-du-Bessol (North). **MAP C1-1**
☎ 05.55.77.51.40 ➡ 05.55.10.27.69
TV.

Just a step away from the train station in a quiet street. Though the district has no great appeal, this modest establishment is a find. The owner welcomes you with a smile. You get to the rooms across a pretty, shaded courtyard. They are simple, spacious and perfectly maintained. Doubles with shower/wc 240F. 10% discount.

🛎 |●| HÔTEL-RESTAURANT L'ALBATROS**

av. du Golf (South); follow the N20. Off map **D3-4**
☎ 05.55.06.00.00 ➡ 05.55.06.23.49
Restaurant closed Sun evening and Christmas to New Year. **TV. Disabled access. Car park.**

About half of the bedrooms look onto the fairways of the local golf course, the rest look over the car park. It's a well-run and comfortable hotel where you'll get a friendly welcome, though prices are a little high; doubles are 360F. Try out the bright, flower-filled restaurant, which also has a view of the golf course. Set menus 74–122F.

🛎 LE RICHELIEU***

40 av. Baudin. **MAP B3-3**
☎ 05.55.34.22.82 ➡ 05.55.34.34.363
TV. Car park. Pay garage.

Rooms in this great place are sizeable and comfortable, with large bathrooms; doubles with shower/wc 380–530F. Those at the top end of the price range are particularly good. There's a substantial brekafast menu. Super-attentive staff and 24-hour service.

|●| RESTAURANT CHEZ COLETTE

pl. de la Motte **MAP B2/3-10**
☎ 05.55.33.73.85
Closed evenings, Sun, Mon and July.

Lunch only. This little place in the lively area by the covered market serves traditional food. The cooking is simple, and naturally enough the dishes are inspired by the fresh produce from the market. Portions are generous. Colette will give you a lovely welcome and it's easy to get into conversation with your fellow diners. Set menu 50F. They also serve snacks 8–10am. This place is a must.

🎿 |●| RESTAURANT LE SANCERRE

18 rue Montmailler. **MAP A1-12**
☎ 05.55.77.71.95
Closed Sat lunchtime and Sun.

Service noon–2pm and 7–10.30pm. This restaurant has long been popular, as it has something to suit every appetite. Set lunch menu 56F and others from 78–128F. The decor's a bit of a mixture but the atmosphere

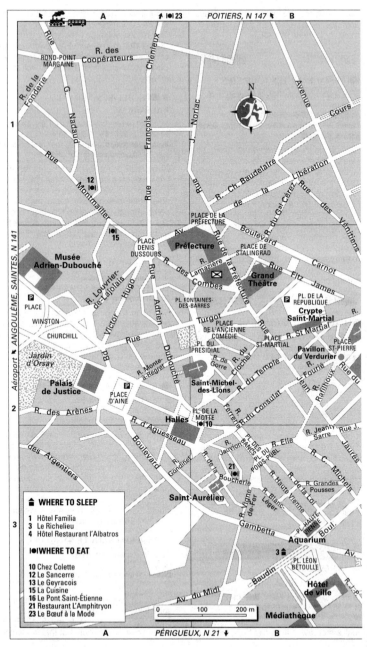

POITIERS, N 147

ROND-POINT
MARGAINE

R. des
Coopérateurs

R. de la
Fonderie

N

Avenue

Cours

R. Ch. Baudelaire

de la
Libération

R. du Gᵃˡ Cerez

des
Vénitiens

PLACE DE LA
PRÉFECTURE

Boulevard

PLACE
DENIS
DUSSOUBS

Préfecture

PLACE DE
STALINGRAD

Carnot

Musée
Adrien-Dubouché

R. des Lamazière

Combes

Grand
Théâtre

Rue Fitz
James

PLACE

WINSTON

CHURCHILL

PL. FONTAINES-
DES-BARRES

PL. DE LA
RÉPUBLIQUE

Crypte
Saint-Martial

Jardin
d'Orsay

Turgot

PLACE
DE L'ANCIENNE
COMÉDIE

R. St Martial

PLACE
ST-MARTIAL

PLACE
ST-PIERRE

Pavillon
du Verdurier

Palais
de Justice

PL. DU
PRESIDIAL

R. de
Gorre

Saint-Michel-
des-Lions

R. du
Clocher

R. du Temple

R. Fourié

R. Jean

R. Raffinloux

Rue du

PLACE
D'AINE

R. Monte-
à-Régret

R. Ferrerie

R. du Consulat

PL. DE LA
MOTTE

R. des Arènes

Halles

10

R. Jeanty
Sarre

Rue J.

Jaurès

Boulevard

R. d'Aguesseau

PL. DES
JAUVION

R. Elie

R. C. Michels

des Argentiers

R. Gondinet

R. de la

PL. DU
POIDS-PUBL

R. Haute Vienne

R. de la Loi

R. Grandes
Pousses

21

R.
Boucherie

R. Haute
Léger

R. Blanc.

Saint-Aurélien

R. Vigne
de-fer

Gambetta

PL. HAUTE
VIENNE

Boul.

Aquarium

3

PL. LÉON
BÉTOULLE

Av.

R. J.-P.

Hôtel
de ville

Médiathèque

PÉRIGUEUX, N 21

🏨 WHERE TO SLEEP

1 Hôtel Familia
3 Le Richelieu
4 Hôtel Restaurant l'Albatros

🍴 WHERE TO EAT

10 Chez Colette
12 Le Sancerre
13 Le Geyracois
15 La Cuisine
16 Le Pont Saint-Étienne
21 Restaurant L'Amphitryon
23 Le Bœuf à la Mode

0   100   200 m

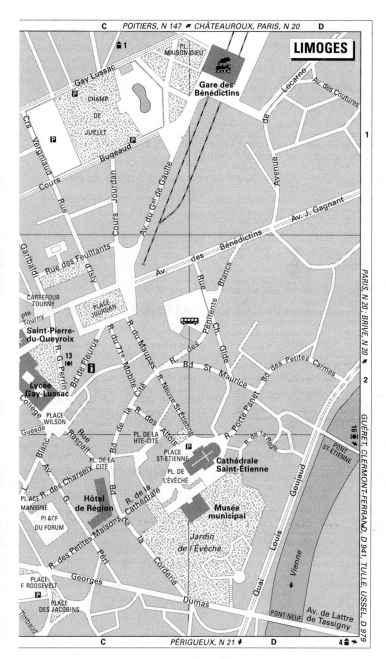

LIMOGES

Gare des Bénédictins

Gay-Lussac

CHAMP DE JUILLET

Bugeaud

Cours

Av. du Gal de Gaulle

Av. des Bénédictins

Av. J. Gagnant

Av. des Coutures

Rue des Feuillants

CARREFOUR TOURNY

Pte Tourny

PLACE JOURDAN

Saint-Pierre-du-Queyroix

13

Lycée Gay-Lussac

Bd de Fleurus

R. du 71e Mobile Cité

Bd St Maurice

Bd des Petites Carmes

PLACE WILSON

Guesde

R. des Allois

PL. DE LA HTE-CITÉ

PLACE ST-ETIENNE

Cathédrale Saint-Étienne

PL. DE LA CITÉ

PLACE MANIGNE

PLACE DU FORUM

Hôtel de Région

PL. DE L'ÉVÊCHÉ

Musée municipal

Jardin de l'Évêché

PLACE F. ROOSEVELT

PLACE DES JACOBINS

Georges

Dumas

PONT-NEUF

Av. de Lattre de Tassigny

Vienne

PONT ST-ÉTIENNE

is lively. They do *boudineaux* with chestnuts and their *foie gras* is excellent, especially with a drop of Sancerre. Free coffee.

🎄 |●| LE GEYRACOIS

15 bd. Georges-Perrin. **MAP C2-13**
☎ 05.55.32.58.51
Closed Sun, public holidays, Sat evening Whitsun to 15 Sept, and 24 Dec–2 Jan.

Service 11.45am–2pm and 6.45–10.30pm. The garish cafeteria-style decor might not appeal, but you eat well here and prices are good. Surprisingly, this is one of the few restaurants to serve local Limousin meat – *tournedos*, rib steaks and fillets that are succulent and juicy. You help yourself to starters and desserts from the buffet where you'll find a wonderful *terrine* made by the owner and pastries by his wife. Set menus 58–93F. Free coffee.

🎄 |●| LA CUISINE

21 rue Montmailler. **MAP A2-15**
☎ 05.55.10.28.29
Closed Sun, Mon and 15 Aug–8 Sept.

Original, highly personal cooking from a chef who uses only the very freshest ingredients: try pigeon in a spiced crust, rolled calf's liver with spinach, or monkfish in a coconut and coriander broth. Dishes are generously served and the waiting staff are efficient and kindly. Lunch *formule* 75F, or reckon on paying 150–200F *à la carte*. Free coffee.

|●| LE PONT SAINT-ÉTIENNE

8 pl. de Compostelle. Off map **D2/3-16**
☎ 05.55.30.52.54 ▶ 05.55.30.56.07

Lunch noon–2pm and 7–10pm, or 11pm at the weekend. Beautifully situated on the banks of the Vienne, this restaurant is also a bar, tobacconist's, newspaper shop and betting shop. There is a stylish upstairs dining room and a terrace for sunny days. The cooking is refined and the dishes change with the season. Portions are generous, the menus are well-balanced and the ingredients are always fresh. Try goat's cheese with beetroot *coulis* followed by chicken breasts with lemon and potato *pallison*, or a Colombo of meats – ribs, cheek and shoulder of pork cooked with a mix of zinging West Indian spices. Menus 76–185F. Wine is a bit pricey. Service is casual.

🎄 |●| RESTAURANT L'AMPHITRYON

26 rue de la Boucherie. **MAP B3-21**
☎ 05.55.33.36.39 ▶ 05.55.32.98.50

Closed Sun, Mon and Sat lunchtimes, 15–30 Aug.

You'll find this reliable restaurant across from the delightful chapel of Saint-Aurélien, the patron saint of butchers. Consistently good service, food served on genuine Limoges china and well-chosen wine. Try *foie gras*, the *tajine* of pigeon with dates or the *roulé* of langoustine and fresh tomatoes – they are all nicely cooked and original without being eccentric. Good-value menus; 100F weekday lunch, 130–198F or 250F *à la carte*. Free coffee.

|●| LE BŒUF À LA MODE

60 rue François-Chénieux. Off map **A1-23**
☎ 05.55.77.73.95
Closed Sat lunchtime, Sun and a fortnight in Aug.

Service noon–2pm and 7–10.30pm. A restaurant in a butcher's shop, run by master butcher Claude Lebraud. Dishes include sirloin of beef in cider, *épigramme* of lamb (cooked on one side only) with honey and spices, and Chateaubriand with bone marrow. Pleasant decor. *À la carte* only; you'll spend 130–200F.

AIXE-SUR-VIENNE   87700 (13KM SW)

|●| AUBERGE DES DEUX PONTS

2 av. du Général-de-Gaulle; take the N21.
☎ 05.55.70.10.22 ▶ 05.55.70.24.74
Closed Sun evening, and Mon evening except June–Sept.

First-rate, reasonably priced restaurant on the banks of the Vienne. The decor is cheery, with lots of yellow and navy blue, and there are flowers everywhere. They do lots of seafood, along with good charcoal-grilled steaks, duck breast with Roquefort sauce and grilled sea bream. Set menus 65–165F and *à la carte*.

SAINT-GENCE   87510 (13KM NW)

🎄 |●| LE MOULIN DE CHEVILLOU

How to get there: take the route de Bellac (N147), turn left towards Nieul and Saint-Gence is only 3km away. Go through the village and turn right 300m further on. It's signposted.
☎ and ▶ 05.55.75.86.13
Closed Mon–Thurs Oct–March.

Service noon–1.30pm and 7–9.30pm. Lovely place hidden in a secluded valley beside the Glane, in a park filled with donkeys, goats, ponies and birds. Children can play on the swings and the chute while dad can fish for trout. Enjoy a pancake and some cider as you are lulled by the splashing sound of the watermill. In the restaurant, go for trout with country ham and ceps, or saddle of rabbit with girolles. Menus 98–146F (the last only on Sun). Service is efficient and staff are delightful. Best to book. Free apéritif.

SAINT-PRIEST-TAURION   87480 (13KM NE)

⚗ ☎ |●| LE RELAIS DU TAURION**

2 chemin des Contamines.
☎ and ➡ 05.55.39.70.14
Closed Sun evening, Mon and 15 Dec–15 Jan.
TV. **Car park**.

Service noon–1.30pm and 7.30–9pm. This is a beautiful, ivy-covered old house set on the edge of a park. The place is memorable for its charm and excellent location rather than for the rooms, 260F with shower/wc or 310F with bath, though they're comfortable enough and well-maintained. There's a restaurant, but it's a bit pricey for what you get. Menus 100–200F. 10% discount on the room rate for a two-night stay.

PEYRILHAC   87510 (15KM NW)

⚗ |●| AUBERGE DE LA QUEUE DE VACHE

It's on the N147.
☎ 05.55.53.38.11
Closed evenings Sun–Thurs except June–Sept. **TV**.

Sadly, this attractive farm is beside the main road, but inside it is pretty and welcoming and the noise is not too intrusive. Typical local cooking using many ingredients from the farm. The beef is unusual for this area because they have their own Highland herd, so Scotch beef appears on the menu. Everything is as fresh as can be: chicken with herbs, warm goat's cheese on green salad, Périgord salad with truffles, oxtail *confit*, pepper steak or pan-fried liver. Good home-made chips. The dessert list is equally appetising, with fruit tarts or melon preserved in honey, and vanilla ice cream. Menus 65–150F. There's a small terrace at the back, away from the road, that's open in summer. Reasonably priced wines. Free coffee.

SOLIGNAC   87110 (15KM N)

⚗ ☎ |●| LE SAINT-ÉLOI

66 av. Saint-Éloi.
☎ 05.55.00.44.52 ➡ 05.55.00.55.56
Closed Sun evening, Mon lunchtime and Jan. **TV**.

A handsome hotel in a peaceful village, run by a young couple. The attractive rooms have very fine linen and they've been tastefully decorated. Some have a terrace and a whirlpool bath. Doubles 280–290F. The elegant dining room has a splendid fireplace and leaded lights. Service is diligent. The cooking is modern and generously served – meat and fish dishes come with well-balanced sauces and the desserts are beautifully presented. Menus 78–210F. Free apéritif.

AMBAZAC   87240 (17KM N)

☎ |●| HÔTEL DE FRANCE*

pl. de l'Église (Centre); take the N20 then the D914 – it's at the main roundabout.
☎ and ➡ 05.55.56.61.51
Hotel closed 20 Dec–15 Jan. **Restaurant closed** Sun Nov–March. **TV**.

You'll receive a hospitable welcome in this cheap, pleasant hotel-restaurant. Clean doubles, furnished with old furniture with no two pieces the same, 150F with shower/wc or 150–160F with bath. The dining room is done up and fresh. Menus 59–140F. There's a bar.

ROYÈRES   87400 (18KM E)

⚗ ☎ |●| HÔTEL BEAU SITE**

How to get there: take the N141 towards Saint-Léonard-de-Noblat, then turn left onto the D124.
☎ 05.55.56.00.56 ➡ 05.55.56.31.17
Restaurant closed a week in Nov and Jan. **Swimming pool**. **TV**. **Car park**.

You can rely on good facilities in this hotel, set in peaceful country surroundings. The comfortable bedrooms are decorated with Madame's ornamental hand-painted designs and they're all different. Doubles 290–328F. There's a nice garden with a wonderful heated pool. The restaurant offers a number of regional specialities, such as *fricassée* of snails with ceps, Limousin beef, fillet of zander with chestnuts and a marvellous chestnut *charlotte*. Menus 90–248F. Attentive service. Free coffee.

THOURON   87140 (22KM NW)

⚗ ☎ |●| LA POMME DE PIN

How to get there; take the N147, then turn onto the D7.
☎ 05.55.53.43.43 ➡ 05.55.53.35.33
Closed Mon, Tues lunchtime, Feb and Sept.
TV. **Disabled access**. **Car park**.

One of the best places in Haute-Vienne, in an old mill in the forest near a small lake. Appealing dishes and delicious charcoal grills cooked over the fire. Weekday lunch menu 89F, with others 140–200F. Specialities are sweetbread and *foie gras* salad, and chargrilled Limousin beef. There's a remarkable list of excellent wines. Double rooms 300F with shower, 350F with bath. Free house apéritif.

MAGNAC-LAVAL 87190

⅍ I●I LA FERME DU LOGIS

How to get there: go as far as Magnac-Laval,in the centre turn right in the direction of Bellac; the restaurant's 2km along on the left-hand side.
☎ 05.55.68.57.23 ➡ 05.55.68.52.80
Closed Sun evening, Mon, and Jan to mid-Feb. **Garden. Car park**.

Service noon–2pm and 7–9pm. This inn is in a converted building, near a small lake. It's always full of flowers, as is the terrace, which looks beautiful in summer. Generous portions of tasty local dishes are served by accommodating staff. They specialise in beef and venison, which come from the family farm. Three appetising and satisfying menus at 75F, 120F and 160F; dishes include pan-fried *foie gras* with apples, smoked duck breast with lemon and honey sauce, and roast leg of lamb with herbs. Wines are also very good. There are spaces for eight tents and room for two in a caravan that's equipped with a shower. Free apéritif.

MORTEMART 87330

⅍ ⋔ I●I HÔTEL LE RELAIS*

1 pl. Royale.
☎ and ➡ 05.55.68.12.09
Closed Tues evening except from 14 July–31 Aug, Wed and the Feb school holidays. **TV**.

Service noon–2pm and 7.30–9pm. A pleasant and very attractive country inn located in one of the most beautiful villages in France. There are a few pretty rooms, 300F with shower/wc, and a stylish stone-walled dining room. Attentive service and a festival of flavours in dishes such as artichoke salad with pan-fried *foie gras* with morel turnovers, duck breast with caramelised pears and *gratin* of wild strawberries. Set menus 98F (except Sun), and 132–205F. You can also choose *à la carte*. Free Kir.

CIEUX 87520 (13KM SE)

⋔ I●I AUBERGE LA SOURCE**

av. du Lac; take the D5 as far as Blond, then turn right in the direction of Cieux.
☎ 05.55.03.33.23 ➡ 05.55.03.26.88
e awaldbauer@aol.com
Closed Sun evening and Mon out of season, and 15 Jan–15 Feb. **TV**. **Car park**.

A renovated former post house which commands a marvellous view of the Cieux lake, the valleys and the Blond mountains. The highly experienced owners have refurbished the bedrooms marvellously. Doubles 350–450F with shower/wc or bath. The restaurant's 80F weekday lunch menu consists of starter, main course, cheese and dessert, and there are other menus from 120–240F. They cook local dishes and serve them efficiently in airy surroundings.

NEUVIC 19160

⅍ ⋔ I●I CHÂTEAU DU MIALARET

It's on the D991 in the direction of Égletons.
☎ 05.55.46.02.50 ➡ 05.55.46.02.65
Closed Jan to Easter. **TV**. **Car park**.

This 19th-century château, set in a gorgeous park, has been turned into a modestly luxurious hotel. It has maintained many original features. Some bedrooms are in the towers; the largest ones, which are superb, have monumental fireplaces. Their conference centre brings in the bulk of the income, so they are able to charge modest prices in the hotel. Doubles 350F with shower/wc or 450F with bath. The dining is impressive and they serve good regional dishes at fair prices; warm fish salad, zander with *beurre rouge* and onion chutney, and fillet of beef with green peppercorns. Weekday lunch menu 80F or others 120–195F. 10% discount on the room rate Oct–March.

PEYRAT-LE-CHÂTEAU 87470

⅍ ⋔ I●I LE BELLERIVE**

29 av. de la Tour; take the D940 in the direction of Bourganeuf.
☎ 05.55.69.40.67 ➡ 05.55.69.47.96
Closed Sun evening, Mon and out of season. **TV**. **Car park**.

The establishment owes its name to its location on the shores of Lake Peyrat. The friendly owner will go to any lengths to please his customers. Delightful bedrooms with balconies and terraces cost 240F with shower/wc or 280F with bath. There are some big ones that sleep four or five. They serve good regional cooking in the restaurant – don't miss the potato cake, local meats and chestnut tart. Set menus 75–150F. Free apéritif.

♨ ☎ |●| AUBERGE DU BOIS DE L'É-TANG**

38 av. de la Tour; take the D940 in the direction of Bourganeuf.
☎ 05.55.69.40.19 ➡ 05.55.69.42.93
Closed Sun evening and Mon from Nov–March, and 15 Dec–20 Jan. **TV. Garden. Car park.**

Set in a magnificent, peaceful area a few kilometres from Lake Vassivière. You'll get a very warm welcome. Decent doubles 250–290F; those in the annexe have been recently done up and are the quietest. The restaurant is very nice indeed, and offers dishes like escalope of *foie gras* with sherry and apples, warm blinis and raspberry caviar, and red mullet with garlic. 75F menu (except Sun lunchtime), then others 95–200F. Half board, compulsory in July–Aug, costs 170–235F per person. 10% discount on the room rate May–Sept.

AUPHELLE   87470 (8KM E)

♨ ☎ |●| LE GOLF DU LIMOUSIN**

How to get there: take the D13 towards Vassivière then the D222 as far as the lake.
☎ 05.55.69.41.34 ➡ 05.55.69.49.16
Closed Nov–March. **TV. Car park.**

This is one of the few hotels that almost overlooks Lake Vassivière. The building is constructed out of hewn stone and is just 200m from the beach. The bedrooms are clean and very comfy with doubles 243–298F. The traditional dining room can get crowded with fans of country cooking; choose from house *terrine*, fillet of beef with ceps, zander with *beurre blanc*, sweetbreads with morels, mutton tripe and the like. Set menus 88–168F. Half board, 246–278F per person, is compulsory July–Aug. There are tennis courts and a crazy golf course across the way. Free house apéritif.

NEDDE   87120 (10KM E)

☎ |●| LE VERROU

Lieu-dit de bourg-Nedde
☎ 05.55.69.98.04

A warm, atmospheric establishment with sever-al dining rooms. One has a beautiful old counter where you can prop yourself up while you have an apéritif. Another has a pancake corner. In summer they open up a charming little terrace. It's very popular locally. The short menu offers dishes cooked with fresh market produce, good Limousin meat dishes, a choice of salads and sweet or savoury pancakes. Expect to pay 80–150F for a meal. There are a few pleasant rooms, 198–231F, which have been very well decorated. Friendly welcome.

AUGNE   87120 (12KM SW)

☎ |●| LE RANCH DES LACS

Lieu-dit Vervialle: take the D14 towards Bujaleuf, go through Chassat. At the next junction go left towards Négrignas; just before the small group of houses take the little road to the left to Vervialle.
☎ 05.55.69.15.66 ➡ 05.55.69.59.52
Closed telephone out of season.

An attractive establishment run by a Belgian couple. It used to be a riding school, and the walls and beams are decorated with old saddles. Nowadays, it's a cross between a hotel and a hostel with a bar and restaurant. They serve a choice of about thirty Belgian beers and in the menus (95–195F) feature a selection of special Belgian dishes such as the *coffret du boulanger* (a loaf filled with scrambled eggs flavoured with herbs), *coucou de Malines* (chicken breast stuffed with a mixture of chicory, mustard and cream), veal cutlet with Gouda, or, if you order in advance, as many helpings of mussels and chips as you like. There's a 65F *formule* that includes wine and coffee. From the veranda you'll get a view of the unspoiled Vienne valley. If you want accommodation, they have two doubles with bath (200F), and four very basic hostel rooms with three or four beds in each and communal washing facilities (70F a head). Children, who are particularly welcome in this truly fabulous place, have a special games area.

SAINT-JUNIEN   87200

☎ |●| LE RELAIS DE COMODOLIAC**

22 av. Sadi-Carnot.
☎ 05.55.02.27.26 ➡ 05.55.02.68.79
Closed Sun evening from Nov–Feb.
TV. Car park. Garden.

A very good restaurant. They've created a modern look in the dining room, but it manages to retain some charm. Prices are fair, with menus 95–195F. The dishes are well prepared, using the freshest ingredients:

salmon, sea bass, local meat and chicken and wild mushrooms. The chef makes excellent sauces. Rooms are comfortable and modern; 270–360F, overlooking the street or the garden.

⚐|●| LE LANDAIS

6 bd. de la République (Centre); take the outer boulevard.
☎ 05.55.02.12.07 ➡ 05.55.02.90.95
Closed Tues and 15–30 Sept.

Service noon–2pm and 7.30–9pm. As soon as you cross the threshold, you sense you're going to eat well here. The restaurant adjoins the bar and it's easy to get comfortable. Honestly prepared dishes include rib of beef Bordelaise, duck stew, *terrine* of quail with juniper berries, scallops with ceps, *salmis* of wood-pigeon and *cassoulet*. Lunch menu 60F then 90–220F. Engaging welcome. Free coffee.

SAINT-AUVENT   87310 (14KM S)

⚐|●| AUBERGE DE LA VALLÉE DE LA GORRE**

pl. de l'Église; it's on the D58.
☎ and ➡ 05.55.00.01.27
Closed Sun and Mon evenings.

A lovely little inn in a lovely little village. The dishes are devised and prepared by Hervé Sutre, the creative young chef. Try *foie gras* with Guérande salt, stuffed ceps, medallions of veal with crayfish and fresh fruit *croustillant*. Menus 76–250F. There's a pleasant covered terrace for sunny days and it's best to book at the weekend. Free coffee.

SAINT-LÉONARD-DE-NOBLAT   87400

⚐|●| LE GAY-LUSSAC

18 bd. Victor-Hugo; it's in the old town, about 30m from Place de la République.
☎ 05.55.56.98.45
Closed Sun evening, Mon, and a fortnight from end Sept to beginning Oct.

Service noon–2pm and 7–10pm, or 11pm in season. Newish restaurant offering traditional home cooking that reflects the changing seasons. The weekday menu, 65F, includes coffee and $1/4$ litre of wine, and there are others 90–140F. Specialities include *marbrée* of *foie gras*, trout with crayfish and watercress sauce, veal sweetbreads with ceps and snails. The menu changes every three

months. À *la carte*, reckon on paying 150F for a good dinner, including wine. It can be difficult to get a table as prices are so reasonable. Staff are attentive and friendly. Free coffee.

CHÂTENET-EN-DOGNON (LE)   87400 (10KM N)

⚐ 🏠 |●| LE CHALET DU LAC**

Pont-du-Dognon; it's on the D5.
☎ 05.55.57.10.53 ➡ 05.55.57.11.46
Restaurant closed Sun evening and Jan. **Garden**. **Car park**.

A touch of luxury without breaking the bank. This impressive chalet overlooks a lake where you can enjoy all sorts of water sports. Comfortable bedrooms 280–350F – the ones with lake view are the most expensive. Very pleasant, traditional food. Set menus 95–230F list dishes like *pavé* of Limousin beef, *cassolette* of beef *du Chalet*, *foie gras* omelette, and salad with salmon cooked with Guéraude salt. There's also a gym and sauna. Half board costs 325F per person. Free apéritif.

SAINT-MARTIN-LA-MÉANNE   19320

⚐ 🏠 |●| HÔTEL LES VOYAGEURS**

pl. de la Mairie; it's in the middle of the village.
☎ 05.55.29.11.53 ➡ 05.55.29.27.70
Closed Sun evening and Mon out of season, Nov to mid-Feb. **TV**. **Car park**.

This typical Corrèze village house, with a garden, has been turned into a family inn with lots of character where you'll feel at ease. Local produce is much in evidence in the cooking, which includes *fricassée* of frogs' legs and snails with parsley, zander with *beurre blanc*, veal sweetbreads with ceps, hot *escalope* of *foie gras*, fillet of char, veal *escalope* with morels and *crêpe soufflé* with orange. Set menus 90–200F. The rooms are attractive and affordable. Doubles with shower 235–255F; some have a view over the countryside. Free apéritif.

SAINT-MERD-DE-LAPLEAU   19320

⚐ 🏠 |●| HÔTEL-RESTAURANT FABRY**

pont du Chambon; it's 8km from Saint-Merd-De-Lapleau via the CD13.
☎ 05.55.27.88.39 ➡ 05.55.27.83.19
📧 faby@medianet.fr
Closed Fri evening and Sat lunchtime 1 Oct–30 April, and 12 Nov–13 Feb.

A substantial building in a magnificent setting on the banks of the Dordogne – many rooms have a view of the river. Lots of fish on the menus, including salmon trout marinated in lime or zander in *beurre blanc*, along with tasty meat dishes such as venison with bilberries and rolled pork fillet stuffed with prunes. The choloclate *fondant* with mint ice cream is the stellar dessert. Menus start at 82F during the week, and there are others from 100–210F. The eight rooms are all smart and prettily decorated. Doubles 240–270F. Half board 265F per person, and twins with shower/wc 270F – a good deal in high season. Warm greeting. Free apéritif.

SAINT-PARDOUX-LA-CROISILLE 19320

☎ |●| HÔTEL-RESTAURANT BEAU SITE***

How to get there: take the D131.
☎ 05.55.27.79.44 ➠ 05.55.27.69.52
Closed Oct–April. **Swimming pool. Garden. Car park.**

Hotel and leisure complex in a delightful spot with a large garden, fishing pond, swimming pool, tennis courts and mountain bikes for hire. The country cooking is fine: *foie gras*, smoked char, veal sweetbreads in pastry with truffle *jus* and raspbery *soufflé*. Menus 85–260F. Doubles 340F. The establishment is roomy enough to accommodate a lot of groups, especially out of season, without them taking over the place. It's a place for people who like sporty holidays, good food and comfortable surroundings.

SAINT-YRIEIX-LA-PERCHE 87500

🎄 ☎ |●| HOSTEL DE LA TOUR BLANCHE**

74 bd. de l'Hôtel-de-Ville.
☎ 05.55.75.18.17 ➠ 05.55.08.23.11
Restaurant closed Sun from 1 Oct to 15 April, excluding public holidays.**TV. Car park.**

The bedrooms are pleasant enough, and although those in the attic are a bit cramped they're comfortable. Doubles 230F with shower/wc, 250F with bath. You won't be disappointed by the restaurant. The first of the two dining rooms is the most classical, serving fresh sweetbreads and ceps, young wild boar stew with horn of plenty mushrooms, house Limousin tripe, duck *foie gras*, veal sweetbreads, or snails stuffed with *lardons* of goose. Weekday menu 85F or 103–188F. The other dining room is more like a snack bar. The cooking is simpler but still pleasant and you'll get big helpings. They do great salads and a reasonably priced dish of

the day with vegetables. Free coffee and 10% discount on the room rate 15 Oct–15 May.

🎄|●| À LA BONNE CAVE

7 pl. de la Pierre-de-l'Homme (Centre); it's near the church.
☎ and ➠ 05.55.75.02.12
Closed Mon except July–Aug.

This is an old white stone building with a pleasant, pale-painted restaurant. The cooking is simple and good, prices are reasonable, and service comes with a smile. Weekday lunch menu 64F, and others 75–138F. Dishes include snail *profiteroles*, veal *tourtière* with ceps, and apple *croustade* with caramel sauce. They have some good bottles of wine, too. Free coffee.

|●| RESTAURANT LE PLAN D'EAU

Le Plan d'Eau-d'Arfeuille; it's on the outskirts of town, head for the campsite.
☎ 05.55.75.96.84
Closed Tues evening, Wed and Jan. **Car park.**

This is a very nice restaurant with a view of Lake Arfeuille. Proprietor Jean Maitraud always has time for a chat with his guests and prepares special menus for important dates like Mother's Day. On less festive occasions there's a dish of the day and menus 68–130F, with others at 68 and 85F. Traditional cooking and local dishes, including Limousin beef, zander fillet, and strawberries flambéed with Grand Marnier. Free apéritif.

COUSSAC-BONNEVAL 87500 (11 KM E)

☎ |●| LES VOYAGEURS **

21 av. du 11 Novembre.
☎ 05.55.72.34.74
Closed Sun evening and Mon out of season, and Jan. **Car park.**

The façade is smothered in ivy. Five of the nine superb rooms look over the garden, and they're all clean and comfortable. Doubles with bath 250–290F. Traditional cuisine – *foie gras*, veal sweetbreads, morels, ceps and duck *confit* – nothing but the best. Weekday menu 70F then others 110–250F. À la carte can get pricey. It's one of the best places in the area.

SERRE-DE-MESTES (LA) 19200

|●| BAR-RESTAURANT LA CRÉMAILLÈRE

Le bourg; take the D982.
☎ 05.55.72.34.74
Closed Mon evening and a fortnight in Sept. **Car park.**

Go through the bar to get to the restaurant – where you'll be welcomed by the friendly smile of the owner. The cooking is simple and generously served, with regional specialities and dishes such as rabbit stew, calf's head, *coq au vin*, *confits* and *foie gras*, and locally raised meat. There are terrific home-made fruit tarts for dessert. Weekday menu 60F, then others 90–140F. This is a simple-looking place from the outside but you'll certainly get your money's worth. Attentive service.

VALIERGUES   19200 (3KM S)

I●I LES MOULINS DE VALIERGUES

Betines; take the D982 then the D125.
☎ 05.55.72.81.31
Closed Mon and Tues lunchtime out of season, three weeks in Jan and three in Sept. **Garden. Car park**.

Philippe studied at hotel school in Dijon, then spent several years as a *sommelier* in an establishment on the shores of Lake Geneva before returning home. Today he and his partner Nadine can be proud of the success they've made of this delightful country restaurant. You're given a very professional welcome. Everything is prepared by Philippe himself; he is an inventive chef who makes good use of locally grown ingredients and mushrooms that he picks himself. His menus are sensitively created to show off the fresh ingredients: semi-cooked *foie gras* with plum brandy, free-range lamb with fruit butter, Limousin beef with sea salt, caramelised pork with spices and iced walnut *soufflé*. Set menus 120–190F. The stylish dining room is almost dwarfed by the huge fireplace. They sell their own *foie gras* and a selection of quality wine.

MEYMAC   19250 (17KM W)

♠ I●I CHEZ FRANÇOISE

rue Fontaine-du-Rat (Centre); it's 100m from the town hall.
☎ 05.55.95.10.63 ➡ 05.55.95.40.22
Closed 14 Nov–15 Dec. **TV**.

Service noon–2pm and from 7.30pm. This delightful old grocer's shop is run by Mme Françoise Bleu. The grocery itself sells a fantastic range of tempting regional products, some of which are prepared on the premises. In the adjoining restaurant the menus feature regional dishes, such as *mounassous* (grated potato cake), pig's trotters with violet mustard, fillet of beef with ceps and *farcedures* (*gratin* of Swiss chard). Lunch menu 85F, and others up to 380F. Lengthy wine list. The three exceptionally comfortable rooms are

reached via a magnificent stone spiral staircase. Doubles 350–450F. You'll receive a wonderful welcome. Highly recommended.

SOUTERRAINE (LA)   23300

♠ I●I HÔTEL MODERNE

11 pl. de la Gare (Centre).
☎ 05.55.63.02.33
Closed Sat lunchtime, Sun and a fortnight in Aug.

This old-fashioned place is a perfect example of a 1970s hotel-restaurant. The convivial hotel bar well deserves its name, *le Pot de l'Amitié*, which roughly translated means "A drink among friends". The prices are old-fashioned, too – rooms 120F with shower wc and menu of the day 55F.

♠ I●I HÔTEL-RESTAURANT JINJAUD

4 route de Limoges (Centre).
☎ and ➡ 05.55.63.02.53

A very well run hotel with gleaming parquet floors and rooms decorated in pale colours or floral wallpaper. Doubles 150–200F. The restaurant, the cheeriest in the area, dishes up quality family cooking prepared from fresh produce – good potato cake (to order the day before) or Limousin beef. Menu of the day 60F or 75F. Friendly welcome.

SAINT-ÉTIENNE-DE-FURSAC   23290 (12KM S)

♠ I●I HÔTEL NOUGIER**

2 pl. de l'Église.
☎ 05.55.63.60.56 ➡ 05.55.63.65.47
Closed Sun and Mon evenings, Mon lunchtime in season, and Dec–Feb. **TV. Garden. Car park**.

A very appealing, typical Limousin country inn with twelve bedrooms, some looking onto the garden. Doubles with bath 300–360F. The elegant dining room serves local dishes updated for modern tastes: fillet of duck with mushrooms, gizzards with pickled artichokes and *croustillant* of pig's trotters. Weekday lunch menu 72F, with others from 105–220F and *à la carte* options. There's also a pretty terrace.

BÉNÉVENT L'ABBAYE   23210 (2KM S)

♠ I●I HÔTEL DU CÈDRE**

rue l'Oiseau (East).
☎ 05.55.81.59.99 ➡ 05.55.81.59.98
Swimming pool. TV. Disabled access.

A magnificent 18th-century building that has been carefully restored. The bright rooms are each different and decorated with infinite taste. The most pleasant have a view of the grounds and a majestic cedar tree. Doubles 250–550F with good facilities. In summer, food is served on an attractive terrace. Weekday menu 68F, with others from 98–140F, and dishes change with the seasons.

TARNAC   19170

⅔ ☎ |O| HÔTEL DES VOYAGEURS

Le bourg.
☎ 05.55.95.53.12 ➡ 05.55.95.40.07
Closed Sun evening, Mon out of season, 20 Dec–10 Jan, and the Feb school holidays.

A huge stone house, in the heart of the village near the church. It's wonderfully maintained by the Deschamps. Madame runs the restaurant with an easy charm while her husband practises his culinary arts in the kitchen. The freshest produce only here – fish, Limousin beef, and mushrooms picked in the woods in season. Try char with chive butter and veal with girolles. Set menus 85–165F and *à la carte* dishes at reasonable prices. The large bright bedrooms upstairs are very pleasant, 255F with shower/wc or 265F with bath. Excellent value all round. 10% discount on the room rate except July–Aug.

TULLE   19000

⅔ ☎ |O| HÔTEL DU BON ACCUEIL*

8–10 rue Canton.
☎ 05.55.26.70.57
Closed Sat evening and Sun except July–Aug, and 25 Dec–3 Jan. **TV**.

A very good, welcoming hotel-restaurant in a quiet street. There are several cosy dining rooms where you can eat excellent duck or chicken *confits*, potato pies and, in season, cep omelettes. Set menus 78–115F; the one at 105F offers two starters that will satisfy even the most ravenous appetites. The bedrooms are quite large and very well maintained – this place deserves more than one star. Doubles 175F with shower, 195F with bath. Free apéritif.

⅔ ☎ |O| LA TOQUE BLANCHE**

28 rue Jean-Jaurès, pl. Martial-Brigouleix (Centre).
☎ 05.55.26.75.41 ➡ 05.55.20.93.95
Closed Sun evening, Mon, three weeks in Jan–Feb and ten days in July. **TV**.

Service noon–2pm and 7–9.30pm. The dining room has a starchy feel but the welcome is informal and relaxed, and you can eat extremely well. Menus 135–250F with regional dishes. Generous portions of very well prepared classical dishes: *millefeuille* of foie gras with apples, rack of lamb with garlic cream ravioli, *mignon* of veal with potatoes and walnuts, pan-fried sole with mushrooms, warm apple tart with almond cream and home-made sorbets. Spacious, pretty double rooms with en-suite bathroom, TV and phone for 230–260F a night. Free coffee.

⅔ ☎ |O| HÔTEL-RESTAURANT DE LA GARE**

25 av. Winston-Churchill; it's opposite the station.
☎ 05.55.20.04.04 ➡ 05.55.20.15.87
Closed a week in Feb, and 1–15 Sept. **TV**. **Car park**.

The classic hotel has very comfortable, soundproofed rooms; doubles 280F with shower/wc and 300F with bath. The popular restaurant has a reputation for lavish cuisine. Menus, 65–140F, list succulent rabbit with mushrooms, *coq au vin*, and excellent fillet of duck stuffed with morels. Breakfast 39F. Free coffee.

|O| LE PASSÉ SIMPLE

6 rue François Bonnelye.
☎ 05.55.26.00.75
Closed Sun evening, Mon and a week in Sept.

A cosy establishment serving delicious dishes: mosaic of artichokes with tomato *coulis*, warm *terrine* of beef cheek pickled in red wine, zander with watercress sauce, grilled duck breast with a sweet and sour sauce, and a deliciously sticky rum baba. Weekday lunch menu 99F including drink or *menu-carte* at 135F for a full meal. Slick service and friendly welcome.

SAINTE-FORTUNADE   19490 (10KM S)

|O| LE MOULIN DE LACHAUD

How to get there: take the D940 to Ste-Fortunade then the D1 for Cornil; 4km further turn onto the D94 towards Chastang, Beynat and Aubazin. It's 2km from there.
☎ 05.55.27.30.95
Closed Mon and Tues excluding public holidays and July–Aug, and 20 Dec–end Jan.

Service noon–1.30pm and 7–9pm. This old mill is way out in the country. The owners are a delightful young couple from Burgundy. Monsieur works wonders in the kitchen, producing inventive dishes from local produce and local recipes, which he redefines in his own way. Menus 85F–265F. Try the *émincés*, braised veal spare ribs with rosemary, duck breast or truffled *foie gras chausson*. The apricot tart with redcurrant and almond jelly is the best. There's a terrace with a lovely view of the lake.

LAGARDE-ENVAL   19150 (11KM S)

🏃 🏠 |●| LE CENTRAL**

Le bourg; it's opposite the church.
☎ 05.55.27.16.12 ➔ 05.55.27.13.79
Closed Mon out of season and Sept. **TV**. **Disabled access**. **Car park**.

This large house, smothered in Virginia creeper, has been in the same family for four generations. It's across from the church and the pretty manor, which are sadly overshadowed by modern buildings. Regional and gourmet dishes – cep omelette, *confit* and *farcidur* (vegetable dumplings) – are served in a rustic dining room. 70F weekday lunch menu or 100F. Very clean, comfortable rooms, 140F with washing facilities, 220F with bath. It's an unassuming establishment and the staff make sure you enjoy your stay. Free apéritif.

GIMEL-LES-CASCADES   19800 (12M NE)

🏠 |●| L'HOSTELLERIE DE LA VALLÉE**

Le bourg.
☎ 05.55.21.40.60 ➔ 05.55.21.38.74
Closed Oct–March. **TV**.

A charming hotel. Crowds of people come to see the Gimel waterfalls, and since the sunny dining room has a fine view of them and the cool terrace is idyllic for dinner in warm weather, you need to book in summer. Doubles 220F with shower, 260F with shower/wc or bath. Some rooms have views of the valley. Good local cuisine in the restaurant – Limousin beef, duck thighs with ceps, zander with leeks, or *grenadins* of veal. Menus 85–150F.

SEILHAC   19700 (15.5KM NW)

🏠 |●| HÔTEL-RESTAURANT LA DÉSIRADE

Le bourg; take the N120.
☎ 05.55.27.04.17
Closed Sun out of season.

This unassuming roadside hotel-restaurant is made more attractive by the friendliness of the owner, who will give you a warm welcome. The dining room has a particularly lovely, unadorned parquet floor. Simple, uncomplicated dishes; Limousin steaks or pizzas, complicated mixed salads and meat grilled over the open fire at night. Weekday lunch menu 60F then 75–95F. The old-fashioned bedrooms have an undeniable charm. Doubles 110F with wash basin or 150F with shower (wc on the landing). A good place for travellers on a budget.

QUATRE-ROUTES-D'ALBUSSAC (LES)   19380 (16KM S)

🏃 🏠 |●| HÔTEL ROCHE DE VIC**

Les Quatre-Routes; it's at the junction of the N121 and the D940, 26km from Brive.
☎ 05.55.28.15.87 ➔ 05.55.28.01.09
📧 roche.vic@wanadoo.fr
Closed Mon out of season, public holidays and Jan to 15 March. **Swimming pool**. **TV**. **Disabled access**. **Garden**. **Car park**.

Service noon–2pm and 7–9pm. The large stone building is a 1950s-style manor with towers. Most of the bedrooms are at the back, overlooking the extensive grounds, the play area and the swimming pool. Doubles 170F with washing facilities and up to 230F with bath. They could be prettier but they're good value. The restaurant offers a large choice of regional dishes, such as *foie gras* with ceps, duck with morels, zander with *beurre blanc*, and pancake *gâteau* with orange. *Formule* at 68F, dish of the day 45F or menus 85–175F. Free apéritif.

CORRÈZE   19800 (22KM NE)

|●| LE PÉCHEUR DE LUNE

pl. de la Mairie.
☎ 05.55.21.44.93
Closed reservations only outside summer.

An unusual restaurant where local dishes are served with a twist – the duck thigh is cooked with bilberries, the skate salad served with asparagus, and the cucumber salad with goat's cheese. The veal escalope with girolles and pigeon braised with horn of plenty mushrooms are delicious. 60F *menu du jour*, or 98–185F.

CHAMBOULIVE   19450 (24KM N)

🏃 🏠 |●| L'AUBERGE DE LA VÉZÈRE

pont de Vernéjoux (East); take the D26.
☎ 05.55.73.06.94 ➔ 05.55.73.07.05
Garden. **Car park**.

A charming riverside inn popular with fishermen. It's a good idea to book in high season as there are only seven bedrooms under the eaves; 200F for a double with shower/wc. On the ground floor there's a friendly, dimly lit bar with a *cantou*, or enormous fireplace, as its focal point; there's also a bright, sunny dining room overlooking the river. Duck features quite prominently (*civet*, *confit* or *foie gras*), and they do an extremely good *confit* of pigeon and scallops with morels. There's a 60F weekday lunch menu or two others at 90F and 130F. You'll get a cheery welcome from the proprietress, and after your meal you can go for a quiet stroll along the banks of the beautiful River Vézère. Free apéritif.

LORRAINE

54 Meurthe-et-Moselle

55 Meuse

57 Moselle

88 Vosges

ABRESCHVILLER   57560

🏃 🏠 |●| HÔTEL-RESTAURANT LE DONON

57 rue Pierre-Marie (Centre).
☎ 03.87.03.74.902 ➡ 03.87.03,78,64
Closed Mon and Tues evening. **TV**. **Car park**.

A small family hotel for walking enthusiasts within easy reach of the forest trails and mountain tracks. Six bedrooms like you might find at home. Simple, substantial, filling local dishes in the restaurant; sea trout with anise, wild boar haunch with girolles, trout fillet with Riesling. Flambéed tarts on Saturday and Sunday evenings. Varied menus 60–160F. Free coffee.

SAINT-QUIRIN   57560 (5KM SW)

🏠 |●| L'HOSTELLERIE DU PRIEURÉ

163 rue du Général-de-Gaulle; take the D96.
☎ 03.87.08.66.52 ➡ 03.87.08.66.49
Closed Wed and Feb school holidays. **TV**. **Disabled access**. **Car park**.

In the 18th century, the Church did not have a reputation for modesty – witness the imposing sandstone priory which now houses this restaurant. Cooking is rich and inventive and has won the restaurant a "Moselle Gourmande" award – try fillet of beef poached in Brouilly, pressed chicken livers with onion chutney, zander fillet in Pinot Noir, game stew and roast pineable with almonds and pears. Weekday lunch menu 70F then 100–250F. You could do worse than stay the night here, too. The new rooms, in an annexe, have modern bathrooms but lack the charm of the restaurant. 240F for a dou-

ble with shower, or 260F with bath. Number 5 is very spacious and has a pretty balcony where you can eat breakfast. Free coffee.

LUTZELBOURG   57820 (22KM NE)

🏃 🏠 |●| LES VOSGES**

149 rue Ackermann (Centre); take the RN4, the A4 and then the CD38.
☎ 03.87.25.30.09 ➡ 03.87.25.42.22
Closed Thurs evening, Fri, 15 Jan–17 Feb, and 12 Nov–8 Dec. **TV**. **Pay car park**.

This is a delightful village in a beautiful part of the world, which is home to several craftspeople. The long-established family hotel has lost none of its charm over the years. All the bedrooms are furnished with antiques, and the beds have lace eiderdowns. Large doubles with basin/wc from 200F, with shower/wc 270F and with bath 320F. Tables are laid with silver cutlery and the setting suits the traditional cooking. During the hunting season, try the sautéed deer with prunes, pheasant with mirabelle plums, or young wild boar with berries. Menus 100–200F. Free parking.

BACCARAT   54120

🏠 |●| HÔTEL-RESTAURANT DE L'AGRICULTURE

54 rue des Trois-Frères-Clément (Northwest).
☎ 03.83.75.10.44
Closed Sat and Sun evenings.

You'll see colourful window boxes and bright flowers tumbling down the façade of this irresistible country hotel. It's just outside the cen-

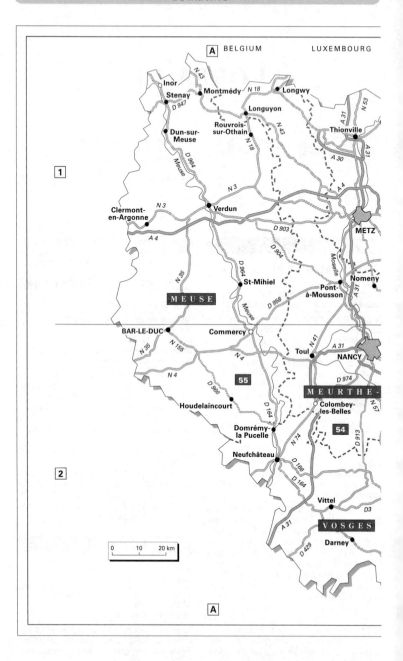

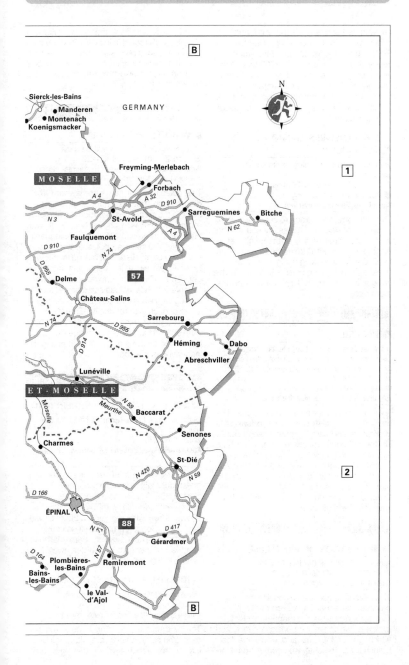

tre, with its famous glass museum, and is a perfect place to stop on a long hike through the Santois or the Mortagne valley. Simple but freshly decorated rooms from 220F, though the wc is along the landing. The convivial family atmosphere in the restaurant attracts a lot of local custom. The cooking is good and the welcome warm. Menus from 70F or about 120F *à la carte*.

⚛ 🍴 HÔTEL-RESTAURANT LA RENAISSANCE**

31 rue des Cristalleries (Centre); it's opposite the glassworks.
☎ 03.83.75.11.31 ➡ 03.83.75.21.09
e renaissance.la@wanadoo.fr
Closed Tues, Fri and Sun evenings.

This is a convenient place to stay if you want to visit the Baccarat glass museum. The rooms have been simply but tastefully refurbished; doubles with shower/wc or bath from 295F. Classical cooking using fresh farm produce; a weekday lunch menu at 65F and others going up to 150F. 10% discount on the room rate

BERTRICHAMPS   54120 (5KM E)

🍴 L'ÉCURIE

Les Noires-Terres take the N59 in the direction of Saint-Dié; as you leave Bertrichamps turn right, don't cross the railway line but follow the signs on the left.
☎ 03.83.71.43.14.
Closed Sun evening, Mon, Feb and the second week in July. **Disabled access**. **Garden**. **Car park**.

A very fine restaurant run by a classy chef. The menus list many tasty specialities, including the *charcuterie* and ham the chef makes himself. Try the delicious *croustillant* of smoked ham with cider and honey, the stuffed saddle of rabbit with mirabelle conserve, or the veal sweetbreads with balsamic salad and shrimp. Old farm implements line the white walls of the beautiful dining room. Menus at 65F (weekday lunch only) and 95–230F.

MAGNIÈRES   54129 (15KM W)

⚛ 🍴 LE WAGON DU PRÉ FLEURY

Ancienne gare: take the D47 from Baccarat.
☎ 03.83.72.32.58 ➡ 03.83.72.32.77
Closed Sun evening, Mon and early Jan.

This restaurant occupies a genuine old railway carriage, parked at the station of Magnières. The station is also the departure point for *draisines*, which are like pedalos on rails, and which go for trips up and down the local branch lines. The chef, who comes from Nor-

mandy, uses only fresh market produce and his dishes are rooted in local traditions, but he gives them an exotic twist. The chef has won over the local inhabitants with his unusual cooking and he also holds theme evenings. Menus from 87F. Free coffee.

BAINS-LES-BAINS   88240

🏠 🍴 HÔTEL DE LA POSTE**

11 rue de Verdun (Centre); it's next to the spa.
☎ 03.29.36.31.01 ➡ 03.29.30.44.22
Hotel closed mid-Oct to March. **Restaurant closed** evenings except Mon and Sat. **TV**.

This establishment has a somewhat forbidding façade, but it's undoubtedly the best place in the area. There are fourteen attractive rooms at 255F with shower/wc, 250F with bath, and some at 178F with washing facilities only. You have a choice of two restaurants: the *Carré Bleu*, which is quite intimate, or the *Relais*, which is plusher and much bigger. The cuisine is innovative and subtly flavoured: dishes include salad of veal sweetbreads with walnut oil *vinaigrette*, and *aiguillettes* of duck with *ratatouille*. The 71F menu is served on weekdays and there are others 99–198F. The dishes change regularly depending on the produce at market and the inspiration of the chef.

BAR-LE-DUC   55000

⚛ 🏠 🍴 HÔTEL-RESTAURANT BERTRAND*

19 rue de l'Étoile (Centre-North); it's behind the train station.
☎ 03.29.79.02.97
Restaurant closed Sun evening. **Garden**. **TV**. **Car park**.

A friendly, warm and welcoming, no-frills guesthouse with a family atmosphere. Menus start at 60F. The rooms are ordinary but well maintained; double with basin 130F, with shower 150F, with shower/wc 200F, or with bath 220F. Some rooms have a balcony over the garden. The gorgeous Parc Marbeaumont is just a couple of minutes away. Free Mirabelle *digestif*.

⚛ 🍴 GRILL RESTAURANT DE LA TOUR

15 rue du Baile (East); it's in the upper town.
☎ 03.29.76.14.08
Closed Sat lunchtime, Sun and public holidays.

This 16th-century building is quite magnificent. You eat in a tiny room with a fire burning in the hearth, where they grill great *andouillettes* and black puddings. The cooking, like the setting, is simple and authentic. Specialities include: rabbit terrine, meat grilled over the open fire and *tarte Tatin*. Lunch menu 65F, then 90–120F. Dinner is served only until 8pm. Free apéritif.

|●| PATATI ET PATATA

9 rue Brandfer (Centre).
☎ 08.00.50.90.31
Closed Sat lunchtime and Sun, except evenings of public holidays.

Lots of garnished and gratinéed dishes, many of them potato-based, and salads served in this young, cool place where you can eat quickly, cheaply and late into the night. Around 100F for a meal.

REVIGNY-SUR-ORNAIN   55800 (15KM W)

☎ |●| LES AGAPES-LA MAISON FORTE***

6 pl. Henriot du Coudray; take the D994 in the direction of Reims.
☎ 03.29.70.56.00 ➡ 03.29.70.59.30
Closed Sun evening on public holidays, Mon lunchtime, a week in Feb and a fortnight in Aug. **TV**. **Garden**. **Car park**.

The owners of the Agapes made such a success of their restaurant that they bought the rooms in *La Maison Forte* and transformed this ancient 14th-century building into a charming hotel-restaurant. It's quite splendid and is the only starred place in the *département*, but all in all, prices are reasonable. The main building, housing the restaurant, is at the end of a tree-lined avenue. It has been thoughtfully decorated and has bare stone walls, old floor tiles and a fireplace. The cuisine is fresh and inventive, using unusual incredients like dandelions and molasses. Menus 165–320F or 280F *à la carte*. Perfect service. The rooms are in the wings to the left and right of the main building, all very comfortable with old-style furnishings. Doubles with bath 370–700F. Some of those in the towers have beds on a mezzanine floor and the suites can sleep three.

CHAUMUNI-SUR-AIRE   55280 (20KM N)

☎ |●| AUBERGE DU MOULIN HAUT

How to get there: take the N35 then the D902.
☎ 03.29.70.66.46 ➡ 03.29.70.66.46
Closed Sun evening, Mon and 15 Jan–15 Feb.

The wheel of this old 18th-century mill turns gently to supply electricity to the restaurant and the noise is masked by the tinkling of a 1910 pianola. This is a peaceful and delightful place run by a welcoming couple who have travelled widely in Africa. The cuisine is balanced and full of flavour. The weekday lunch menu costs 90F and there are others at 140–250F, variously featuring duck specialities, regional dishes and a gastronomic menu. Keep some space for dessert, especially the *croustillant flambé* of mirabelle plums The owners are very welcoming. There are two double rooms in an annexe, costing 300F.

BITCHE   57230

☎ |●| HÔTEL-PENSION DE LA GARE

2 av. Trumelet-Faber; it's near the station.
☎ and ➡ 03.87.96.00.14
Closed Sat, Sun and Christmas holidays. **Car park**.

Service noon–2pm and 7–8.30pm. This is the only cheap hotel in town, and though the rooms are modest they're very clean. Doubles with basin from 110F, or 140F with shower (wc along the corridor). The *patronne* is so kind that you won't notice the slightly fading decor; sometimes the guests even lend a hand behind the bar. Unpretentious country cooking with a weekday set menu at 50F. Half board is 130F. It's advisable to book early.

☎ |●| L'AUBERGE DE STRASBOURG**

24 rue Teyssier (Centre); it's opposite the Protestant church.
☎ 03.87.96.00.44 ➡ 03.87.06.10.60
Closed Sun evening, Mon, a fortnight in Jan and a fortnight in Sept. **TV**. **Car park**.

This lovely place has coffered ceilings in the dining room and naive paintings on the walls. Stylish gourmet cooking: goose *foie gras* served with a spoon, lightly smoked salmon trout fillet, pan-fried bream with hazelnuts, and shoulder of milk-fed lamb. The menu changes every three months. It's all spot on and although the prices are a little high, the quality is worth it. Set menus 130F on weekdays, then 180–380F, with a carefully selected wine list. There are a few comfortable rooms with shower/wc, 290F.

|●| L'AUBERGE DE LA TOUR

3 rue de la Gare; it's close to the Vauban citadel.
☎ 03.87.96.29.25
Closed Mon evening, Tues and Feb. **Car park**.

The Belle Époque decor is atmospheric and cosy. In the brasserie, the local paper, the *Républicain Lorrain*, lies about on the tables – it's a place people come to talk politics. The weekday lunch menu is 70F, and there are others from 130–250F. Interesting food combinations include prawns *marinières* with a vegetable broth, or zander and salmon *terrine*. Try the home-made sorbets. The welcome is a little reserved but not off-putting.

BAERENTHAL   57239 (20KM SE)

⊟ LE KIRCHBERG**

8 rue de la Fôret; it's opposite the post office.
☎ 03.87.98.97.70 ➡ 03.87.98.97.91
Closed Jan. **TV**. **Disabled access**. **Car park**.

This is a modern building and the hotel is absolutely silent, so you'll get a good night's sleep. Double rooms 300–360F with shower or 390F with bath. Even the small rooms are spacious and comfortable. Studios sleeping two or four are let by the week or weekend. Family welcome, and no pretentions.

I●I RESTAURANT L'ARNSBOURG

18 Untermuhlthal (North).
☎ 03.87.06.50.85
Closed Tues, Wed and Jan.

This lofty yellow building towers over a torrent; inside the atmosphere is charming. The service is attentive, and the cuisine is delectable – try the John Dory infused with bay leaf in a salt crust, grilled duck *foie gras* with pickled lemons or the frogs' legs in herbs and coriander. Dishes are served beautifully and there are vases of flowers on the tables. The wine waiter offers you wines to taste and tries to make you identify them. There's a vast bay window looking onto a huge park. Menus 210–455F or 400–500F *à la carte*.

CHARMES   88130

⊟ I●I HÔTEL-RESTAURANT VAUDOIS**

4 rue des Capucins (Centre); it's near the town square.
☎ 03.29.38.02.40 ➡ 03.29.38.01.58
Closed Sun evening, Mon, end Feb and middle fortnight in July. **Disabled access**. **TV**. **Car park**.

This is a charming place. The rooms are rather chic, and all have en-suite bathrooms. A double over the street will cost 205F, while quieter ones overlooking the courtyard cost 285F. Even the most demanding palate will be satisfied with the cooking which is prepared using fresh, seasonal market produce – go for the *turban* of trout with leeks and Pinot Noir, zander with special mashed potatoes, or shellfish in season. There's a weekday lunch menu at 115F and others from 138–320F, with a children's menu at 65F. Attentive service in the pretty dining room that is full of happy families on Sunday.

CLERMONT-EN-ARGONNE   55120

⅔ ⊟ I●I HÔTEL-RESTAURANT BELLEVUE**

14 rue de la Libération (Centre).
☎ 03.29.87.41.02 ➡ 03.29.88.46.01
Closed Sun evening out of season and Wed. **TV**.
Garden. **Car park**.

Service noon–3pm and 7–9pm. The hotel has been totally refurbished. The rooms are functional and anonymous but the façade and the dining room are ravishing. The dining room retains all its original Art Deco features from 1923. It leads onto a balcony overlooking the garden and the countryside. The cooking is simple, and portions are generous: game in season, *navarin* of wild boar with *fricassée* of wild mushrooms. The menu at 85F is served daily except for Sunday, and there are others 130–200F. There are seven rooms, ranging from 260F with shower/wc to 290F with bath. Peace and quiet are guaranteed, especially in the rooms at the back. Free apéritif or coffee.

FUTEAU   55120 (10KM SW)

⊟ I●I HÔTEL-RESTAURANT L'ORÉE DU BOIS**

How to get there: take the N3; at Islettes, turn right onto the D2 and it's on the left, 500m beyond Futeau.
☎ 03.29.88.28.41 ➡ 03.29.88.24.52
📧 oreedubois@free.fr
Closed Mon and Tues lunchtimes in season, Sun evening, Mon and Tues from Nov–March. **TV**. **Disabled access**. **Car park**.

This place is quietly set on the edge of a wood, so you'll sleep well. The fifteen large bedrooms all have en-suite bathrooms; doubles 400–500F. They serve a weekday menu at 125F and others 165–370F. The local pigeon with coriander is particularly good. The *patronne* has two passions: cheese and wine. Staff are friendly and enthusiastic.

CONTREXÉVILLE   88140

⊟ I●I HÔTEL DE LORRAINE*

122 av. du Roi-Stanislas (Centre); it's near the train station.
☎ 03.29.08.04.24
Closed Nov–March. **Car park**.

A big, pleasant old place with a bit of style. Wonderful welcome. The cooking is traditional, though special diets can be catered for. Set menus 75–125F – the last features Lorraine specialities. Try the roast fillet of perch, the snail ravioli with smoked bacon, frogs' legs with parsley, or snails in pastry. Double rooms from 150–180F with washing facilities or 200F with shower/wc. Half board 210–310F, and full board 550F for two. The trains don't run at night, so it isn't too noisy.

⛵ 🛏 |●| HÔTEL-RESTAURANT DU PARC**

334 rue du Shah-de-Perse (Centre).
☎ 03.29.08.52.41 ➡ 03.29.08.54.75
e hotel.duparc@free.fr
Closed Sun evening, and Mon out of season.
TV.

Two twenty-something couples decided to breathe new life into this old establishment in the centre of town. The dining room itself still looks pretty traditional, but you soon see they've put their efforts into the cooking, with dishes like pork sauté with sweet and sour sauce, and *croustillant* of camembert with bilberries. Weekday lunch menu 75F, 115F at weekends. A good choice of wines, with bottles starting at just under 90F. Rooms in the hotel are modest; doubles with basin or shower 150–170F, with shower/wc or bath 250F. Half or full board if you stay three days or more, from 260F per person. Free coffee.

⛵ 🛏 |●| HÔTEL DES SOURCES**

rue Ziwer-Pacha; it's opposite the town hall.
☎ 03.29.08.04.48 ➡ 03.29.08.63.01
e hsources@club-internet.fr
Closed Oct–April. **TV**. **Disabled access**.

An elegant building very close to the esplanade with its colourful fountains. The atmosphere is what you might expect in a spa and guests play scrabble or cards together. The rooms are comfortable and have been decorated with care. On the third floor are a few attic rooms with basin for 185F, doubles with shower for 315F, and with bath for 340F. The restaurant isn't bad at all, with set menus at 100–155F. Free breakfast.

🛏 HÔTEL DE LA SOUVERAINE***

Parc thermal (Centre).
☎ 03.29.08.09.59 ➡ 03.29.08.16.39
Closed two days at Christmas. **TV**. **Car park**.

This elegant building, which used to be the residence of the Shah of Persia, looks onto the spa's park. It's a little formal, with beautifully renovated rooms, but they've kept the prices reasonable. Comfortable rooms with shower/wc 350F or 365F with bath.

DABO   57850

|●| RESTAURANT ZOLLSTOCK

11 route Zollstock, La Hoube; it's 6km from Dabo on the D45.
☎ 03.87.08.80.65 ➡ 03.87.08.86.41
Closed Mon and Christmas to New Year.

Service noon–2.30pm and 7–9.30pm. The restaurant, which looks across a forested valley, doesn't get much passing trade, and most of the customers are regulars. There's a 57F lunchtime menu and others up to 130F. They prepare simple but tasty specialities, including terrific venison in season, frogs' legs, salmon in champagne sauce, and *mignon* of veal with morels. It's small, extremely pleasant and has an appealing family atmosphere.

DARNEY   88260

🛏 |●| HÔTEL-RESTAURANT DE LA GARE

It's near the old station; 1.5km from the centre on the road to Bains-les-Bains.
☎ 03.29.09.41.43
Car park.

This lovely little hotel is on a narrow lane where the old station used to be. It's set in the forest, which is dotted with contemporary sculptures, and is absolutely quiet. Clean, simple, comfortable rooms cost 170F with shower, 210F with bath. Delicious home cooking includes dishes from different traditions: *choucroute*, couscous, paella, *aïoli*, *tartiflette* and grilled Munster cheese with potato salad. Nor for those on a diet. Weekday menu 60F then 70–150F.

DELME   57590

🛏 |●| HÔTEL-RESTAURANT À LA XIIÈ BORNE*

6 pl. de la République (Centre).
☎ 03.87.01.30.18 ➡ 03.87.01.38.39
Disabled access. **TV**. **Garden**. **Pay car park**.

Lunch served till 2pm and dinner till 9.45pm. Delme was once a Roman encampment at the twelfth marker or "*borne*" on the road from Metz to Strasbourg – hence the name. The rooms have been refurbished and cost 250F with bath or shower. There's also a sauna, free for all guests. Menus in the "Roman" dining room are 98–158F, while in the other, gastronomic dining room they feature pork sausages with *foie gras*, zander in *beurre blanc*, and perch fillets in *vin gris*. There's a good list of local wines. Child's bed available for free.

DOMRÉMY-LA-PUCELLE   88630

☎ HÔTEL JEANNE D'ARC

1 rue Principale (Centre); it's next to the church.
☎ 03.29.06.96.06
Closed mid-Nov to March. **Car park**.

A little hotel with seven rooms, very near St Joan's house. Little has changed over the years, and that includes the prices: you'll pay 150F for a quiet, clean double room with shower/wc. Breakfast, 25F, is brought to your room. Very pleasant welcome.

AUTREVILLE   88300 (14KM NE)

☎ |●| HÔTEL RELAIS ROSE**

24 rue de Neufchâteau (Southeast); take the D19 then the N74.
☎ 03.83.52.04.98 ➡ 03.83.52.06.03
TV. **Disabled access**. **Garden**. **Car park**.

The hotel, right on the main road, is not an obvious place to stop, but it's worth it. Inside it's a charming old family house. The rooms are all quite lovely; some have balconies or views over the garden and the countryside beyond. Rooms with basin go for 160F, with bath or shower 350–400F. The weekday lunch menu costs 70F followed by others at 115–250F. They offer excellent rabbit with *vin gris* from Toul, veal sweetbreads with morels, and a number of dishes from the southwest – where Madame comes from – including *foie gras*, *cassoulet* and duck *confit*. Excellent wines in the ancient cellar.

ÉPINAL   88000

☎ AZUR HÔTEL**

54 quai des Bons-Enfants (Centre).
☎ 03.29.64.05.25 ➡ 03.29.64.00.40
e vosgeshotels.com/azurhotel/index.ntm
Closed 25 Dec–1 Jan. **TV**.

Excellent, soundproofed rooms; 190F with shower, 260F with shower/wc and 285F with bath. Number 16 is split-level, with a small sitting room. Some rooms have a view of the canal so you can watch the canoes and the kayaks go by. You will be hospitably received and the staff take good care of guests. Child's bed available for free.

⚞ ☎ CLARINE HÔTEL**

12 av. du Général-de-Gaulle (West); it's opposite the train station.
☎ 03.29.82.10.74 ➡ 03.29.35.35.14
e hotel-clarine-epinal@libertysurf.fr
Closed 23 Dec–2 Jan. **TV**. **Lock-up garage**.

This is part of a chain but you'd never guess so from its appearance. It has the charm of a family-run station hotel where they make you feel very welcome. The whole place has been gutted and renovated and they've put in soundproofing, which is essential because of the noisy road and the trains. Doubles with shower/wc at 320F or with bath 350F. There are three junior suites and a new bar. 10% discount at weekends.

|●| RESTAURANT LES FINES HERBES

15 rue La Maix (Centre); it's near place des Vosges.
☎ 03.29.31.46.70 ➡ 03.29.34.82.98
Closed Sun evening, Mon and the third week in Aug.

Unusual cooking served with care and attention. The decor is streamlined and modern yet inviting. Menus change every month and are reasonably priced; the lunchtime menu costs 70F, with others at 98F and 150F. They do quite a lot of fish dishes, including a fish stew with shellfish, monkfish *tournedos* with morels and skewers of fish with *nantais* butter. They close at 10pm.

|●| RESTAURANT LA TOUPINE

18 rue du Gal-Leclerc (Centre).
☎ 03.29.34.60.11
Closed Sun.

The establishment has gone back to serving well-crafted traditional dishes; aubergine caviar in salmon parcels, sheperd's pie with duck *confit*, *grenadin* of milk-fed veal with girolles, and mirabelle *croustillant* with salted butter. The dining room is tiny, bordering on the cramped, with paintings by local artists on the walls. Charming welcome and service. There's an attractive *menu-carte* with main course, dessert and coffee at 75F, and full menus at 110F and 170F. They serve oysters and seafood in season, and there are lots of Bordeaux on the excellent wine list. Others wines served by the glass.

|●| RESTAURANT LE PINAUDRÉ

10 av. du Général-de-Gaulle (West); it's opposite the train station.
☎ 03.29.82.45.29
Closed Sat lunchtime, Sun and Aug.

The green frontage of this restaurant is rather discreet and easy to miss. The attractive dining room has been done up to look like a modern bistro. Cooking is traditional with a few modern touches. The weekday lunchtime menu at 75F is excellent, and there are others at 88–165F. There's a lot of fish and seafood, both on the menu and *à la carte*: roast salmon fillet with bilberries, John Dory in parsley, and fillet of sea bass with morels. Local dishes include a salad with warm *andouillette* salad or pan-fried escalope of *foie gras* with mirabelle plums.

CHAUMOUSEY 88390 (10KM W)

|●| LE CALMOSIEN

37 rue d'Épinal; take the N460 in the direction of Darney.
☎ 03.29.66.80.77
Closed Sun evening. **Car park**.

From the outside you might mistake this place for a country station, but inside the dining room is more Belle Époque than waiting room. In the summer they set a few tables out in the garden. Classic cuisine and a few local dishes from the imaginative chef: marbré of quail fillets and *foie gras*, scallops and crayfish, pigeon breast with gingerbread sauce, duck thigh *confit* served with salad in a hazelnut oil dressing, pan-fried *foie gras* in balsamic vinegar, *cassolette* of mussels with spinach and plum sauce, fillet of sole with truffles from the Meuse, and so on. Menus 115–290F. There's a great wine list, with a few pleasant surprises. Since it has such an excellent reputation locally, it's best to book.

FAULQUEMONT 57380

🛏 ♦ HÔTEL LE CHÂTELAIN**

pl. Monroë (Centre); it's next to the church.
☎ 03.87.90.70.80 ➡ 03.87.90.74.78
TV. **Disabled access**. **Car park**.

This place looks less than appealing from the outside, but inside you'll find 25 comfortable rooms around a wonderful winter garden dotted with pot plants and troughs. Doubles 290F with shower/wc. It's all very new and lacks that lived-in feeling, but the boss is friendly and very enthusiastic. Best to book. Free coffee.

FORBACH 57600

♦ HÔTEL LE PIGEON BLANC

42 rue Nationale (Centre).
☎ 03.87.85.23.05
Closed Sun. **Disabled access**. **Car park**.

For some inexplicable reason, there's no mention of this hotel anywhere, not even in the tourist office listings – odd for a place that's the best value around. The rooms in the annexe are very spacious and quiet. Doubles range from 100F with basin to 170F for very big, quiet rooms with large bathrooms. The only drawback is that you have to be out of your room by 10am.

🛏 ♦ HÔTEL DE LA POSTE**

57 rue Nationale (Centre).
☎ 03.87.85.08.80 ➡ 03.87.85.91.91
Car park. **TV**.

This is the oldest hotel in Forbach and it's been providing decent accommodation for a hundred years. Rooms have been fully renovated and decorated in blue, yellow or pink depending which floor they're on. Doubles with basin 150F, with shower/wc or bath 270F. It's set back from the street so you won't be disturbed by noise. Staff are friendly and unobtrusive. 10% discount July–Aug.

|●| RESTAURANT DU SCHLOSSBERG

13 rue du Parc (Centre).
☎ 03.87.87.88.26
Closed Tues evening, Wed and a fortnight in Aug. **Garden**.

When Forbach was handed to the Germans in 1870, a rich local industrialist built the substantial summer residence which became this restaurant. He opened the grounds on Sundays so his employees could enjoy a walk on their day off. The service is excellent, the decor is classic, and dishes draw upon local culinary traditions: goose *foie gras*, quail with *foie gras* or *aiguillette* of duck with lemon. But it's quite pricey, with a weekday lunch menu at 140F and others 175–320F.

OETING 57600 (2KM S)

🛏 |●| RESTAURANT À L'ÉTANG

386 rue de Forbach; it's near the church.
☎ 03.87.87.33.85.
Closed Tues evening, Wed, and mid-Aug to early Sept. **Car park**.

Service noon–2pm and 7–10pm. A restaurant in a big, pleasant house with country-style decor and a little pond in front. The cheapest menu costs just 58F in the week, but it's a bit uninspiring. The others run from 80–195F; not surprisingly, the top-priced one is the gastronomic choice, with dishes like carp fillet with sorrel, zander in Pinot Noir and game in season. Free coffee.

FREYMING-MERLEBACH 57800

🏠 |O| HÔTEL-RESTAURANT AU CAVEAU DE LA BIÈRE

2 rue du 5-Décembre; it's opposite the music conservatory.
☎ 03.87.81.33.45 ➡ 03.87.04.95.95
Closed Sat and Sun evenings. **Car park.**

Freyming used to be at the industrial heartland of the Moselle, but today the blast furnaces are cold and things have changed. A few regulars sip beer at the bar but this is mainly a business hotel. Rooms are clean and functional at 130F with basin, 180F with shower, and 250F with bath. They prepare simple traditional dishes like *quiche lorraine*, grilled *andouillette* or tripe in Riesling. Wash it all down with a glass of Amos, one of the few beers that are still brewed locally. Weekday menu 58F and then 80–195F.

GÉRARDMER 88400

🏠 🏠 HÔTEL DE PARIS*

3 rue de la Gare (Centre).
☎ 03.29.63.10.66 ➡ 03.29.63.16.47
TV. Car park.

A very simple little hotel with reasonable prices located in the ski resort's busiest street. It's not a luxurious place, but the rooms have recently been redecorated. Doubles from 170F with basin, 230F with shower or bath/wc. The ones overlooking the interior courtyard are the quieter ones. There's a brasserie on the ground floor. The hotel fills up at the weekend so you should secure your room by sending a deposit. There's a lively bar at street level with a selection of ninety beers, ten of which are on draught. 10% discount.

🏠 🏠 |O| HÔTEL VIRY*-RESTAURANT L'AUBERGADE**

pl. des Déportés (Centre); 200m from the lake.
☎ 03.29.6302.41 ➡ 03.29.63.14.03
e hotel-viry-aubergade@yahoo.fr
Closed Fri evening. **TV. Car park.**

The hotel has been going a good forty years; the common areas, landings and bathrooms have all been renovated. Double rooms 230–250F with shower/wc, or 280–330F with bath. The rustic-looking dining room offers particularly good value. In summer there's a covered terrace on the square. Sound regional cuisine – the 98F *randonneur* menu gives you *vigneronne* salad or brawn with *ravigotte* sauce, fried freshwater fish with *sauce tartare*, chicken *fricassée* with Riesling or tripe

in Sylvaner *à l'ancienne*, followed by dessert. There's a decent *menu du marché* at 78F, others up to 210F and a 48F children's menu. Friendly welcome and courteous service. 10% discount on the room rate excluding school holidays and public holiday weekends.

🏠 🏠 HÔTEL GÉRARD D'ALSACE*

14 rue du 152è R.I.
☎ 03.29.63.02.38 ➡ 03.29.60.85.21
e gerard.dalsace.hotel@liberty-surf.fr
Restaurant closed a fortnight in Nov. **Swimming pool. TV. Car park.**

This substantial Vosges house is only 150m from the lake on a small track. There's little traffic, and all the rooms look over the garden. It's got a retro feel – the hotel opened in the early 50s – but it's not unattractive. The rooms are modest but most of them have been renovated and have double glazing. You'll pay 250–280F for a double with shower/wc or 335F with bath/wc. Guests can hire mountain bikes at a special rate. 10% discount except in Feb.

🏠 |O| HÔTEL-RESTAURANT CHÂLET DU LAC*

97 chemin de la droite du lac (West); it's beside the lake, 1km from the town centre on the D147 in the direction of Épinal.
☎ 03.29.63.38.76 ➡ 03.29.60.91.63
Closed Oct. **TV. Garden. Car park.**

A historic wooden chalet overlooking the lake and the road, which is far enough away not to be distracting. Friendly welcome. Though the rooms have been renovated, they've kept their antique furniture and have a really nice retro feel. All of them have bath or shower and a balcony overlooking the lake, and they each cost 330F. There's an annexe in another chalet a few metres away on the edge of the forest. As for the restaurant, the food is traditional with regional influences. Seven set menus 100–350F. Lovely garden.

🏠|O| LE BISTROT DE LA PERLE

32 rue Charles-de-Gaulle (Centre).
☎ 03.29.60.86.24
Closed Wed out of season, and last three weeks in Oct.

This place, which used to be a butcher's shop, retains its original, picturesque façade. Excellent snail *cassolette*, grilled bacon salad, pork chicken in *civet*, fillet of zander in Côte de Tout or grilled *andouillette* A5. *À la carte*, go for mussels with chips, salmon *tartare* or *cassoulet*. Light, pleasant dining room with friendly service and no-fuss food. Expect to pay 115F *à la carte* or choose the 58F *for-*

mule of starter, main course and coffee. Other menus 87F and 115F. Free apéritif.

𝍐 |●| LES RIVES DU LAC

Centre; it's near the landing stage on the lake.
☎ 03.29.63.04.29
Closed lunchtimes and Sept–June. **Disabled access**.
Car park.

Open on high season evenings only, this restaurant, on the shores of the most famous lake in the Vosges, is inevitably full of tourists. But the food is good and simple, and prices are extremely reasonable given the location and the gorgeous terrace. The drawback is that the service is often slow. Menus 82–92F. Do the done thing and go for the great *fumé vosgien* (salted pork with potatoes and *fromage frais*). Free coffee.

XONRUPT-LONGEMER   88400 (7KM NE)

♠ |●| HÔTEL LE COLLET-RESTAURANT LAPÔTRE***

9937 route de Colmar (Southeast); it's beyond Xonrupt on the D417 in the direction of col de la Schlucht Munster.
☎ 03.29.60.09.57 ➡ 03.29.60.08.77
ℯ hotcollet@aol.com
Restaurant closed Wed outside school holidays, 25 March–8 April and 4–30 Nov. **TV**. **Car park**.

This is a big traditional chalet, set at 1100m in the heart of the Vosges nature reserve; it's near the cross-country ski trails and the ski lifts. The welcome is simple yet special and there's a luxurious feel to the place. Lots of local style in the pretty bedrooms; doubles with shower/wc or bath go for 410F. The nicest ones have a balcony with a view of the forest. Elaborate buffet breakfast for 50F. Very good regional cuisine revamped by a young chef bursting with ideas and enthusiasm. Try the leg of duck *confit* with a light *choucroute*, or the pork fillet coated with spices and served with potato *galettes*. The 68F *plat rapide*, served on weekday lunchtimes, is a main course plus a glass of wine or beer. Other menus, 88–158F, include *bibelaskas* (fresh cheese flavoured with horseradish and herbs), *lewerknepfla* (*quenelles* of liver), and poached trout. The wine list features a lot of Alsace wines and a few gems from other regions.

THOLY (LE)   88530 (11KM W)

𝍐 ♠ |●| L'AUBERGE AU PIED DE LA CASCADE*

12 chemin des Cascades; take the D11 to Tholy, and continue for 5km until you get to the Tendon waterfall.

☎ 03.29.33.21.18 ➡ 03.29.33.29.42
Closed Wed except during school holidays. **TV**.
Disabled access. **Car park**.

A typical old Vosges inn buried in the countryside, right by the forest and the famous Tendon waterfall. Its attractions extend beyond the setting, the terrace and the ancient dining room. For years they've been serving the best trout in the area, caught fresh in the nearby pool. The quiet hotel is tiny, so it's often full. Doubles 160F with basin, 180F with shower and 220–310F with bath. Menus 100–230F or 100F *à la carte*. It's best to book. 10% discount on the room rate for stays of two nights.

BRESSE (LA)   88250 (13KM SE)

♠ |●| HÔTEL-RESTAURANT LE CHEVREUIL BLANC**

3 rue Paul-Claudel (Northwest); as you arrive in the resort coming from Gérardmer on the D486.
☎ 03.29.25.41.08 ➡ 03.29.25.65.34
Restaurant closed Sun evening outside school holidays, 23–31Oct, and the middle fortnight in April. **TV**.
Car park.

The exterior of the building has been freshly decorated, Maria Pia will greet you with a friendly smile and once you try the food, you'll be hooked. It's sophisticated without being pretentious, with lots of local dishes and a great fish stew. There's a weekday menu at 82F and others 99–205F. The hotel is small with just nine rooms, all with shower or bath, wc and telephone. They cost 270F for doubles. Half board from 250F per day per person; there are special rates for children. The owner is a 1950s rock 'n' roll fan, as the photos of Gene Vincent and Buddy Holly testify.

VALTIN (LE)   88230 (13KM NE)

♠ |●| AUBERGE DU VAL JOLI**

12 bis le Village (Centre); follow the signs to Saint-Dié out of Gérardmer, turn right onto the D23 in the direction of Colmar, then left at Zonrupt over the mountain road to Le Valtin.
☎ 03.29.60.91.37 ➡ 03.29.60.81.73
Closed Sun evening, Mon except for public holidays, 8–16 Jan, 19–27 March and 3–16 June. **TV**. **Car park**.

A superb place in one of the region's prettiest villages near pine forests and the mountains. This is a real old-fashioned inn, with a warm and friendly atmosphere. The original, very simple rooms cost 100F with basin or 280F with shower/wc. Numbers 17–20 are modern and smart and have balconies that look onto the mountains. Half board, compulsory during the school holidays, costs 150–350F per person. One of the dining rooms is wonderfully rustic with a superb ceiling, while the other is on the first floor, huge and modern with enormous windows and a wonderful ceiling. Good cooking and traditional local dishes. Weekday menu at 80F, then 110–190F. There's *pâté lorrain* (a sort of pie filled with pork mince), trout *au bleu* with butter sauce, smoked trout with a sorrel sauce, *blanc de sautret* (chicken in cream and Riesling sauce), *choucroute garnie*, and a fairly strong Munster cheese and bilberry tart. On Sunday, set menus cost 70F and 99F.

HOUDELAINCOURT   55130

⌂ ☎ |●| L'AUBERGE DU PÈRE LOUIS**

☎ 03.29.89.64.14 ☛ 03.29.89.78.84
Closed Sun evening, Mon and three weeks in Sept.
TV. **Car park**.

Service till 2pm and 9pm. For anyone who likes good food, this is one of *the* places to eat in the region. The cooking is innovative and exciting, with dishes like roast zander with *beurre rouge*, calf's head with spices, *millefeuille* of snails, calves' feet stew or *escalope* of calves' sweetbreads, and Meuse truffles and sour cherries with claret. The menus start at 115F, with the truffle menu priciest at 320F. There are six quiet, pleasant rooms with shower/wc 250–300F. The welcome is not always tip-top. 10% discount on the room rate.

LONGUYON   54260

☎ |●| HÔTEL DE LA GARE-RESTAURANT LA TABLE DE NAPO*

2 rue de la Gare.
☎ 03.82.26.50.85 ☛ 03.82.39.21.33
Closed Fri evening except July–Aug, first fortnight in March and three weeks in Sept. **Car park**.

The good-natured owner creates a family atmosphere in her establishment which feels like an old guest house. There are a few pretty pieces of furniture in the corridors. The rooms are bright and comfortable; a double will cost 260F with shower/wc. The entrance to the hotel is on the station platforms but you won't be disturbed by the trains because they've put in efficient double glazing. If you're worried about not sleeping well, ask for a room looking onto the street. The restaurant serves dishes cooked with fresh market produce.

☎ |●| HÔTEL DE LORRAINE-RESTAURANT LE MAS**

pl. de la Gare.

☎ 03.82.26.50.07 ☛ 03.82.39.26.09
e mas.lorraine@wanadoo.fr
Closed Mon, Oct–June. **TV**. **Pay garage**.

This Belle Époque hotel has a lot of class and great charm. The façade is attractive and there are beams and ceiling mouldings in the lounge. The bright, spacious rooms have been redecorated; those over the courtyard look into the restaurant's vegetable garden. Doubles with shower/wc or bath, 330F. In the winter there's a blaze in the open fireplace and in summer they open up the terrace and plant troughs of flowers. The restaurant, with menus at 120F (weekdays) and 190F, has a good reputation. Unfortunately, the welcome is frosty.

LONGWY   54400

☎ |●| HÔTEL DU NORD**

pl. Darche.
☎ 03.82.23.40.81 ☛ 03.82.23.17.73
Restaurant closed Sun. **TV**. **Car park**.

Many towns in France have a bar-hotel like this, but this one has particular charm because of its unique location on the impressive square. The modern rooms are clean and quiet; they cost 250F with shower/wc or bath. They've recently opened a small restaurant, which offers traditional dishes. Set menus start at 48F.

COSNES ET ROMAIN   54400 (5KM W)

|●| LE TRAIN BLEU

How to get there: from Longwy-Haut, take the N18 in the direction of Longuyon for 4km, turn right at the sign.
☎ 03.82.23.98.09
Closed Sun evening, Mon and Sat lunchtimes.

They've joined two railway carriages together and you have to push a button to open the door. The decor is plush and the place is very popular at weekends because of the quality of the cooking: try the *cassolette* of calf sweetbreads and girolles, or sole fillets stuffed with smoked salmon. There's something here for every budget, starting with the lunchtime menu at 78F and others to 98F.

|●| AUBERGE DES TROIS CANARDS

69 rue de la Lorraine-Romain; take the D43 in the direction of Cosnes-et-Romain.
☎ 03.82.24.35.36 ☛ 03.82.25.66.40
Closed Mon, Thurs and Sun evenings, the Feb school holidays and 16 Aug–6 Sept. **Car park**.

Service from noon. The Virginia creeper has

smothered this house – it's so dense that you can't even see the walls let alone the sign, so don't drive past. There's a genuine country feel to the place and good country food like calf's head *à l'ancienne*, *foie gras*, house *confit*, roast leg of duck *Henri IV* and quails with mirabelle plums. Menus from 116F. On public holidays there's no choice of menu and the price is hard to justify.

LUNÉVILLE   54300

☎ HÔTEL DES PAGES***

5 quai des Petits-Bosquets; it's across the river from the château.
☎ 03.83.74.11.42 ➔ 03.83.73.46.63
TV. Car park.

This quiet hotel is enclosed by a large court-yard, not far from the river. It has modern facilities, though the 1970s decor may not be to everyone's taste. Double rooms 280–320F. Just next door you can eat at *Au Petit Comptoir*; they will serve late if you book. Menus at 98F and 120F. It's difficult otherwise to find a place to eat after 9.15pm in Lunéville, but the management has now opened another place you could try, *L'Oasis*, on the other side of town.

|❍| MARIE LESZCZYNSKA

30 rue de Lorraine (Centre); it's behind the château.
☎ 03.83.73.11.85
Closed Sun evening and Mon.

This restaurant, named after the wife of King Louis XV, offers a friendly welcome and elegant cuisine: try prawns in whisky, half a pigeon in pepper sauce, or snails in pastry with smoked bacon and *vin gris*. The pretty dining room provides an intimate setting. Menus 87–215F. There's a pleasant terrace in a pedestrianised street – lovely when the sun shines.

MANDEREN   57480

☎ |❍| LE RELAIS DU CHÂTEAU MENSBERG**

15 rue du Château; it's on the D64.
☎ 03.82.83.73.16 ➔ 03.82.83.23.37
Closed 1–5 Jan. **TV. Disabled access. Garden. Lock-up garage**.

The château of Mensberg was built in the 7th century and, according to legend, rebuilt in the 15th with the help of the devil. The impressive building dominates the village. The inn has fif-

teen comfortable, pretty double rooms with shower/wc, 330F. There's an extremely handsome dining room where you can enjoy a number of carefully prepared specialities that change with the seasons; menus 85–280F.

METZ   57000

SEE MAP OVERLEAF

☆ ☎ HÔTEL MODERNE**

1 rue Lafayette. Off map **B3-4**
☎ 03.87.66.57.33 ➔ 03.87.55.98.59
TV. Private car park.

Rooms are modern and functional but not impersonal; the ones at the back are the quietest, while those with two double beds, like number 7, are terrific value. You'll pay 165F for a room with washing facilities and up to 260F for a room with bath. The owner is a charming woman with a ready smile. 25% discount and breakfast at the weekend.

☆ ☎ HÔTEL LA PERGOLA**

13 route de Plappeville. Off map **A1-2**
☎ 03.87.32.52.94 ➔ 03.87.31.41.60
TV. Garden. Car park.

It's easy to miss this hotel, because the sign is not very obvious. You are woken by the birds singing in the wonderful garden. There are brass beds and period furniture in the rooms, which are all furnished differently. Rooms up in the eaves have sloping ceilings, and some of the bathrooms are as big as the rooms. Doubles 195–200F. Ask for one overlooking the garden, where afternoon tea is served under the trees. 10% discount.

☆ ☎ CECIL HÔTEL**

14 rue Pasteur. **MAP B3-3**
☎ 03.87.66.66.13 ➔ 03.87.56.96.02
e cecil-hotel@wanadoo.fr
Closed 26 Dec–2 Jan. **TV. Disabled access. Pay garage**.

The hotel is in a handsome late-19th-century building near the station. Prices for the modern and well-equipped – if slightly soulless – rooms are 290F for a double with shower/wc or 320F with bath. You'll get a good deal if there are four of you willing to share – a room with two double beds costs 320F. Free garage space.

☆ ☎ |❍| HÔTEL ALBION-RESTAURANT DU PÈRE POTOT**

8 rue du Père-Potot. **MAP B3-5**
☎ 03.87.36.55.56 ➔ 03.87.36.39.80
TV. Disabled access. Pay car park.

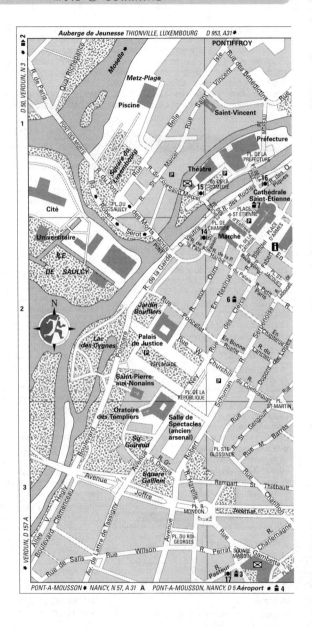

Auberge de Jeunesse THIONVILLE, LUXEMBOURG   D 953, A31

PONTIFFROY

Moselle

Metz-Plage

Piscine

Saint-Vincent

Préfecture

PL. DE LA PRÉFECTURE

Théâtre

15   PL. DE LA COMÉDIE

16

Cathédrale Saint-Étienne

7

PLACE ST ÉTIENNE

Cité

PL. DU SAULCY

PL. DE CHAMBRE

14   Marché

PLACE D'ARMES

Universitaire

ÎLE DE SAULCY

Jardin Boufflers

6

Lac des Cygnes

Palais de Justice

ESPLANADE

Saint-Pierre-aux-Nonains

PL. DE LA RÉPUBLIQUE

Oratoire des Templiers

Salle de Spectacles (ancien arsenal)

Sq. Guiraud

PL. STE-GLOSSINDE

Square Gallieni

PL. ST-MARTIN

Joffre

PL. B. MONDON

PL. DU ROI-GEORGES

SQUARE MANGIN

17   3

PONT-A-MOUSSON   NANCY, N 57, A 31   A   PONT-A-MOUSSON, NANCY, D 5   Aéroport   4

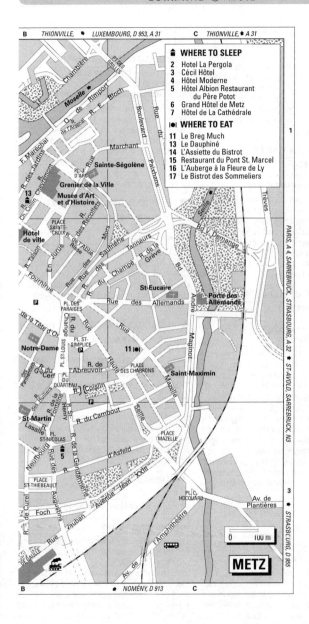

🛏 **WHERE TO SLEEP**

2 Hôtel La Pergola
3 Cécil Hôtel
4 Hôtel Moderne
5 Hôtel Albion Restaurant
    du Père Potot
6 Grand Hôtel de Metz
7 Hôtel de La Cathédrale

🍽 **WHERE TO EAT**

11 Le Breg Much
13 Le Dauphiné
14 L'Assiette du Bistrot
15 Restaurant du Pont St. Marcel
16 L'Auberge à la Fleure de Ly
17 Le Bistrot des Sommeliers

PARIS, A 4, SARREBRUCK, STRASBOURG, A 32 ● ST-AVOLD SARREBRUCK, N3

STRASBOURG, D 955

0   100 m

METZ

Service noon–2pm and 7–10pm. It's centrally located but looks a bit out of place in this particular neighbourhood; the clientele is primarily reps and tourists. The rooms are all alike but not unpleasant, each with a phone and a mini-bar. Doubles cost 325F, with buffet breakfast extra at 35F. The odd-numbered ones look onto the courtyard of an old abbey. Weekday menu 80F then 100–240F. Free apéritif.

🍴 🛏 GRAND HÔTEL DE METZ**

3 rue des Clercs. **MAP B2-6**
☎ 03.87.36.16.33 📠 03.87.74.17.04
TV. **Disabled access**. **Lock-up car park**.

This hotel is in a pedestrianised street in the old part of town; the entrance is ultra-modern and has a superb staircase. The clean, comfortable rooms are decorated in pastels and flower-patterned fabrics, and overlook the inner courtyard; doubles 350F with shower/wc or 450F bath. A parking space costs 40F. 10% discount Fri–Sun.

🛏 HÔTEL DE LA CATHÉDRALE***

25 pl. de la Chambre. **MAP B1-7**
☎ 03.87.30.27.25
✉ hotel-cathedrale-metz@wanadoo.fr
TV. **Disabled access**. **Garden**.

Chateaubriand and Madame de Staël stayed in this coaching inn, which was built in 1627, and various other famous people have stayed here since. Monsieur Hocine restored the building himself and Madame undertook to decorate it – they've done it beautifully. The period beams, the iron work, the casements and the interior courtyard are amazing. The rooms are full of character and charm; they're all bright with elegant fittings, but each is decorated differently and some have a view of the cathedral. Doubles with bath or shower 360–380F. Booking strongly advised.

🍴 🍽 RESTAURANT LE BREG MUCH

51 rue Mazelle. **MAP C2-11**
☎ 03.87.74.39.79
Closed Sun evening, Mon, a fortnight in summer and a fortnight in Nov. **Disabled access**.

Many people in Metz eat here regularly. The dining room and sunny terrace are lovely, the welcome is friendly and, last but not least, the cooking is good. There's a weekday lunch menu at 60F, others at 120 and 160F or à la carte around 200F. The chef produces simple yet imaginative dishes which change with the seasons, using the freshest ingredients. A great place for lovers of good food. Free apéritif.

🍴 🍽 RESTAURANT LE DAUPHINÉ

8 rue du Chanoine-Collin. **MAP B1-13**
☎ 03.87.36.03.04
Closed evenings except Fri–Sat, Sun, and Aug.

An unpretentious restaurant and tearoom with exposed beams. The service is a bit casual. They serve a dish of the day for about 45F; there's a 77F menu (not Sun), and others up to 125F, including a *menu campagnard*. Simple cooking but generous helpings: paella to order, calf's head and *quiche Lorraine*. Free coffee.

🍽 LE BISTROT DES SOMMELIERS

10 rue Pasteur. **MAP B3-17**
☎ 03.87.63.40.20
Closed Sat lunchtime, Sun.

This is a really fun, young place where they write the dishes of the day up on a slate. There's a single menu at 85F or à la carte, about 130F. You can taste a local wine or choose something from the long wine list. Good value.

🍽 RESTAURANT L'ASSIETTE DU BISTROT

9 rue du Faisan. **MAP A/B2-14**
☎ 03.87.37.06.44
Closed Sun, Mon and the last three weeks in Aug.

Service noon–2pm and 7–9.30pm. A classy 1930s bistro that's very popular with men in suits. The cooking is terrific; try the *pot-au-feu* of calf's head, lamb *navarin* with turnips, guinea fowl with morels, or trout Lorraine style. The prices are reasonable; they do three *menus-carte* at 88F (which includes apéritif, wine and coffee), 128F and 160F. Stylish service to boot.

🍴 🍽 RESTAURANT DU PONT-SAINT-MAR-CEL

1 rue du Pont-Saint-Marcel. **MAP A1-15**
☎ 03.87.30.12.29
Disabled access. **Car park**.

This 17th-century building has a terrific location on the banks of the Moselle, with a breathtaking view of the cathedral and the town; there's no place like it in Metz. The delicious regional dishes are based on recipes from a 19th-century collection and include suckling pig in aspic, *ballotine* of duck with plums, carp with white wine, *potée Lorraine* and eel *en matelote* in Toul wine sauce. Menus start at 98F and you'll pay 168F for the "Taste of Lorraine" menu, which features excellent Moselle or Lorraine wines. The restaurant is decorated with frescoes portraying old city scenes, and the dining room staff are dressed in period costume. There's a lovely terrace too, with pots overflowing with flowers. Free apéritif and coffee.

|●| L'AUBERGE À LA FLEURE DE LY

5 rue des Piques. **MAP B1-16**
☎ 03.87.36.64.51
Closed Sat lunchtime, Sun and a fortnight in Aug.

Suzy welcomes you with her bright smile, listing the dishes of the day as she leads you to your table. You can go into the cellar to select your own wine from the new vintages and buy the odd bottle to take away, too. Try the *foie gras* in a cloth, the snail *matelotte*, monkfish with Riesling, pan-fried prawns, saddle of rabbit with rhubarb, or Bresse chicken with morels and *vin jaune*. Menus 170–230F.

SAINT-JULIEN-LÈS-METZ   57070 (3KM NE)

⅍ |●| RESTAURANT DU FORT SAINT-JULIEN

Route de Thionville; it's in the restored part of the fort right in the middle of the wood.
☎ 03.87.75.71.16
Closed Wed, Sun evening, 1–10 Jan and 24 Jul–10 Aug. **Garden. Car park.**

The town has been traded between France and Germany several times since 1870, so it has a sort of dual nationality. You'll be welcomed by Coco, the owner's mynah bird, who might whistle his version of *The Marseillaise* or *Bridge over the River Kwai*. The place is impressively decorated to resemble a cellar and has the kind of relaxed atmosphere that makes you want to get your friends together for a blow-out. They serve substantial dishes like black pudding, *quiche lorraine* or *choucroute* with Riesling. Menus 75–135F and individual dishes 68–92F. Free apéritif.

WOIPPY   57140 (4KM N)

⅍ |●| L'AUBERGE BELLES FONTAINES

51 route de Thionville; take the Woippy exit on the A31.
☎ and ➦ 03.87.31.99.46
Closed Sun, Mon and Tues evenings, the last week in July and the first fortnight in Aug. **Garden. Car park.**

A restful inn just minutes from the centre of Metz. It's decorated in classical fashion in the same shades of green as the trees in the park, and there's a terrace. Customers are mainly regulars. Substantial menus 105–210F. Attentive service. Free coffee.

GORZE   57680 (20KM SW)

⅍ ♙ |●| HOSTELLERIE DU LION D'OR**

105 rue du Commerce (Centre); take the Fey exit on the A31.
☎ 03.87.52.00.90 ➦ 03.87.52.09.62
Closed Sun evening and Mon.
Disabled access. TV. Garden.

There are hand-baked tiles on the floor, timbered walls, a small interior pond, and a huge bay window that lets lots of light into the restaurant. They have a "Moselle Gourmande" award for the quality of their cooking. Although the place is stylish and the tables are set with silver, male diners don't have to wear a tie. There's a 100F menu (weekdays only) and others 140–360F listing rabbit *terrine* with mirabelles and fillet of guinea fowl cooked in Burgundy. The peace is sometimes shattered by the low-flying military jets, but the soundproofing does a pretty good job of cutting down the noise. Free coffee.

MONTENACH   57480

♙ |●| HÔTEL-RESTAURANT AU VAL SIERCKOIS

3 pl. de la Mairie.
☎ 03.82.83.85.20 ➦ 03.82.83.61.91
Closed Mon evening, Tues and 17 July–5 Aug.
TV. Car park.

Service noon–2pm and 7–9.30pm. Among the valleys and woods of northern Moselle where France meets Luxembourg and Germany, this delightful, friendly inn is the ideal place to recharge your batteries. You'll be woken by birdsong and you can go for long walks in the forest. The cooking is unpretentious and there are menus of Lorraine specialities at 85 or 180F. This is hunting country, so try the haunch of venison *Grand Veneur*. They have seven pretty rooms, 190F with shower or 260F with bath.

|●| L'AUBERGE DE LA KLAUSS

1 rue de Kirschnaumen; take the D956.
☎ 03.82.83.72.38
Closed Mon and 24 Dec–7 Jan. **Disabled access.**
Garden. Car park.

This is a "Moselle Gourmande" restaurant, which guarantees quality cooking prepared on the spot using fresh ingredients. You can eat in one of four dining rooms; one is decorated with clocks and old time pieces and another looks like a hunting lodge in warm tones. There's an excellent wine cellar. Lunch menu at 120F with Lorraine specialities, though the ones up to 280F are considerably more substantial. The owner has a farm where he raises pigs and ducks, and the game comes from the nearby forest. You can visit the farm and buy home-made treats. Very friendly welcome.

MONTMÉDY   55600

≜ I●I HÔTEL-RESTAURANT LE MÂDY**

8 pl. Raymond-Poincaré; it's in the main square.
☎ 03.29.80.10.87 ➡ 03.29.80.02.40
Closed Sun evening, Mon except on public holidays and in summer, Christmas, and mid-Jan to mid-Feb. **TV. Car park**.

Functional, characterless double rooms, with en-suite bathrooms, cost 250–290F a night. The restaurant serves generous helpings of good regional dishes, with a few specialities such as knuckle of pork with mirabelle plums and trout from the tank, calf's head vinaigrette, poached eggs *en meurette* with red Toul wine sauce. Weekday menu 85F and others 135–210F. Everything is done in the classic style, from the welcome and the decor to the background music and the cuisine.

NANCY   54000

SEE MAP OVERLEAF

⅔ ≜ HÔTEL CARNOT**

2 cours Léopold. **MAP A2-2**
☎ 03.83.36.59.58 ➡ 03.83.37.00.19
TV.

The façade of this hotel had to be rebuilt after the war. The rooms are decent and the prices attractive. A double with washing facilities costs 160F, 190–260F with a bath. Numbers 25 and 34 have baths and are bigger, brighter and quieter. You'll need to book these rooms in April, when there is a country fair in the square. Free welcome drink.

≜ GRAND HÔTEL DE LA POSTE**

56 pl. Monseigneur-Ruch. **MAP B2-5**
☎ 03.83.32.11.52 ➡ 03.83.37.58.74
TV.

This aged building, once a convent, has been renovated. The 44 rooms are freshly redecorated, and some have pretty wardrobes made locally by Majorelle. They've chosen rather garish colours for the bedspreads. Doubles with shower 185F, with shower/wc 215F and with bath 245F. Extremely good value for money

when you consider that Place Stanislas is so close and you'll be wakened by the cathedral bells. Wonderful welcome. 10% discount July–Aug.

≜ HÔTEL POINCARÉ**

81 rue Raymond-Poincaré. **MAP A3-6**
☎ 03.83.40.25.99 ➡ 03.83.27.22.43
TV. Pay car park.

This hotel is a bit tatty now, but don't be mistaken into thinking that because the rooms are cheap you'll have to sacrifice a degree of comfort. Double rooms with shower/wc 200F, 250F with bath. They offer a good weekend deal: stay Friday and Saturday night and you'll get Sunday night free.

⅔ ≜ HÔTEL LE JEAN-JAURÈS**

14 bd. Jean-Jaurès. Off map **A3-4**
☎ 03.83.27.74.14 ➡ 03.83.90.20.94
e jjaures.hotel@wanadoo.fr
TV. Garden. Pay garage.

This place was built as a craftsman's house and has retained a pleasant old-fashioned atmosphere enhanced by the mouldings and tapestries. The rooms over the boulevard have been soundproofed but you may still prefer the quieter ones over the garden. Double rooms with shower/wc cost 250F and you'll get a hospitable welcome from the young, energetic owner. 10% discount.

≜ HÔTEL LA RÉSIDENCE***

30 bd. Jean-Jaurès. Off map **A3-8**
☎ 03.83.40.33.56 ➡ 03.83.90.16.28
e hotel.la.residence.nancy@wanadoo.fr
Closed 31 Dec and 1 Jan. **TV. Pay car park**.

The fact that you're greeted by someone in a station master's uniform gives you a clue about the owner's obsession. The hotel has been cleverly decorated to continue the theme – magazines on trains are scattered about all over the place and even the bedrooms haven't escaped. Doubles with shower/wc or bath from 300F. You can order a meal on a tray. Parking in the "station car park" costs 25F.

≜ HÔTEL DE GUISE**

18 rue de Guise. **MAP A1-3**
☎ 03.83.32.24.68 ➡ 03.83.35.75.63
Closed 9–24 Aug and 20 Dec–2 Jan. **TV. Pay car park**.

The Countess of Bressey used to live in this mansion in the heart of the old Nancy, and it has a romantic atmosphere reminiscent of a Dumas novel. There's a magnificent monu-

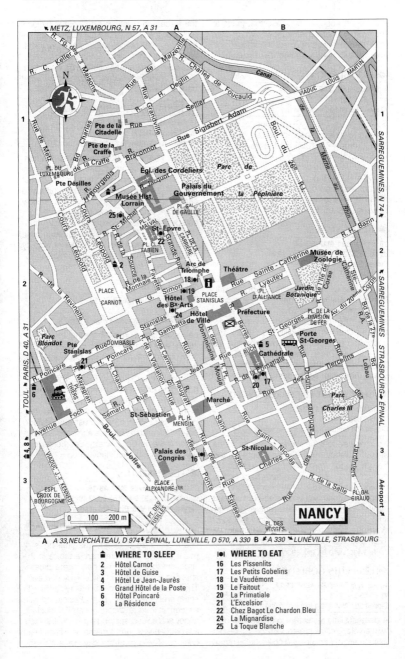

mental 18th-century staircase that leads to the rooms. Doubles with shower/wc or bath 305F. Some have monumental fireplaces and impressive beamed ceilings. Great value.

|●| LE VAUDÉMONT

4 pl. Vaudémont. **MAP A2-18**
☎ 03.83.37.05.70
Closed Mon and a fortnight in Oct.

Service noon–1pm. Good value for money here, and simple, tasty, generous cooking. Menus from 80–130F and a four-course lunch *formule* at 55F during the week, which gets you a starter, main course, such as chicken in Riesling or ham with *choucroute*, then cheese and dessert. They have one of the best terraces in town on a pretty square near place Stanislas.

|●| LA MIGNARDISE

28 rue Stanislas. **MAP A2-24**
☎ 03.83.32.20.22 ➡ 03.83.32.19.20
Closed Sun evening, Mon, Wed evening, 17–31 July and 30 Oct–5 Nov.

This place, which has quite a reputation in Nancy, is finally undergoing some much-needed refurbishment. The 78F lunch menu and the 135F menu are good value and show there's a chef with real skill in the kitchen. The *andouille* of zander and frogs' legs is quite exceptional. Other menus up to 255F and they change with the season. There's a shady terrace for sunny days.

|●| CHEZ BAGOT-LE CHARDON BLEU

45 Grande-Rue. **MAP A2-22**
☎ 03.83.37.42.43
Closed Sun evening, Mon and three weeks in Aug.

It's a fair way from the shores of Brittany to the streets of Nancy, but that doesn't deter Breton Patrick Bagot from offering his customers authentic fish and shellfish from back home. He also serves quail in white pudding, unusual lamb *charcuterie* and *andouillette* of sole and crayfish. The elegant restaurant is brilliantly light and the decor has a maritime feel to it. Weekday lunch menu at 82F and others at 132F and 195F. Around 200F for a meal *à la carte* which is a bit expensive.

|●| LES PETITS GOBELINS

18 rue de la Primatiale. **MAP B3-17**
☎ 03.83.35.49.03
Closed Sun, Mon and a fortnight in Aug.

A delightful little restaurant in a lovely building with an old, gleaming parquet floor. There's an assortment of furniture and collectables about the place and paintings and photos by local artists on the walls, all of which are for sale. Try the crisp *millefeuille* of smoked salmon, the fillet of turbot with orange, or the baked Alaska with sour cherries. At lunchtime on weekdays, there's an 88F *retour du marché* menu and others 108–220F.

|●| RESTAURANT LA PRIMATIALE

14 rue de la Primatiale. **MAP B3-20**
☎ 03.83.30.44.03.
Closed Sat lunchtime, Sun and Christmas.

Service 11.45am–1.30pm and 7.15–9.30pm, or 10.30pm in summer. The rue Primatiale is pedestrianised and the restaurant is just opposite *L'Échanson*, a wine bar where you can stop for an apéritif. This is a friendly restaurant and the cooking is original, light and delicate. They've designed a really attractive wine list with descriptions of each wine and a huge selection of half bottles or wine by the glass. There's an agreeable terrace on the street. Menus from 97F.

|●| LE FAITOUT

7 rue Gustave-Simon. **MAP A2-19**
☎ 03.83.35.36.52
Closed a week in Jan and a week in Sept.

Le Faitout is in a pretty street that the tourists ignore, even though it's just a couple of streets from place Stanislas. The red, black and white decor looks rather sombre but the proprietress gives you a jovial welcome. The cooking is simple, portions are generous and there are always a few unexpected dishes on the menus. Try the *terrine* of trout with cucumber, the leg of lamb in a herb crust, the seafood *pot-au-feu* and the banana and chocolate tart which is the house speciality. Set menus from 99F including a vegetarian menu.

|●| LES PISSENLITS

25 [bis] rue des Ponts. **MAP A3-16**
☎ 03.83.37.43.97 ➡ 03.83.35.72.49
Closed Sun and Mon. **Disabled access**.

Service 11.45am–2.15pm and 7.15–10.30pm. *Les Pissenlits* is the younger sibling of *La Table des Mengi* next door and the cooking is of equal quality. There are marble tables in the large dining room and a handsome dresser showing off a collection of Longwy porcelain. They do the most wonderful pastry cases with snails and mushrooms, pancakes stuffed with salmon in *beurre blanc,* slivers of duck in honey and spices, suckling pig in jelly, fish fillets *à la bouillabaisse,* and a memorable calf's head *gribiche.* The dish of the day costs 49F and menus run from 99–129F. Danièle Mengin, one of France's best *sommeliers*, is responsible for the quite exceptional cellar and there is always a specially chosen selection of splendid wines available by the glass at 10–12F. Extremely popular and often full.

|●| LA TOQUE BLANCHE

1 rue Monsieur Trouille. **MAP A2-25**
☎ 03.83.30.17.20 ➡ 03.83.32.60.24
Closed Sun evening, Mon, the first week in Jan, Feb school holidays and a fortnight July/Aug.

The *Toque Blanche* is a refined place with a fresh-feeling dining room and some of the best cooking in Nancy. They are well-known locally for the interesting and well-priced lunch menu at 100F. There are others from 130–320F – try the ravioli with frogs' legs and cheese. À la carte there are some delicious specialities like a pancake of pig's trotters with potatoes. And the excellent wine list offers a carefully chosen selection at fair prices. The service is punctiliously attentive. This is just the place for a celebration.

|●| RESTAURANT L'EXCELSIOR

50 rue Henri-Poincaré. **MAP A2/3-21**
☎ 03.83.35.24.57
Closed Christmas Eve dinner.

Service 8am–00.30am (11pm on Sun). This has become such an institution in Nancy that it's known as the "*Excel*". You must see this historic monument with its Art Nouveau decor; all the greatest names of the Nancy School are represented, with mahogany furniture by Majorelle and stained glass by Gruber. Cooking and service here are in the best brasserie style. Menus prices start at 128F. Don't miss the pigeon pie or the *choucroute paysanne*. After 10pm they do a late-night set menu for 105F, wine included.

NEUFCHÂTEAU   88300

🏃 🏠 |●| LE RIALTO**

67 rue de France (Centre).
☎ 03.29.06.09.40 ➡ 03.29.94.38.51
Closed Sun except July–Aug. **TV**. **Car park**.

You'll get a pleasant welcome from the young proprietors of this long-standing hotel on the edge of the historic old town. It's been fully renovated and rooms are clean. Those overlooking the river are particularly nice. Doubles cost 220F with shower/wc. Good cooking in the restaurant – nothing fancy – with a 58F lunch menu and others at 90F and 130F. There's a nice terrace open on sunny days. Free coffee.

🏃 |●| RESTAURANT LE ROMAIN

74 av. Kennedy (West); it's on the Chaumont road, as you leave town.
☎ 03.29.06.18.80 ➡ 03.29.06.18.80
Closed Sun evening, Mon, last fortnight in Feb and first fortnight in Sept. **Car park**.

It's the decor rather than the food which recalls ancient Rome. The young chef shows considerable flair in his approach to traditional dishes. Cooking times are judged perfectly and he has an intuition for balancing flavours – you'll feel that you're tasting standard dishes for the first time. Try pig's trotters with potatoes and mushrooms, pan-fried zander with garlic cream, and saddle of rabbit with mirabelle plums. Weekday lunch menu 80F then 125–200F listing dishes such as such as *terrine* of guinea fowl with onion marmalade, fillet of *rascasse* (scorpion fish) with fennel seeds, and beef skirt with shallots. Charming welcome and service. Terrace in the summer. Great wine list with a few wines by the glass. Free coffee.

PLOMBIÈRES-LES-BAINS   88370

🏃 🏠 |●| HÔTEL DE LA FONTAINE STANISLAS**

Fontaine Stanislas – Granges de Plombières; it's 4km north of Plombières on the route d'Épinal via Xertigny.
☎ 03.29.66.01.53 ➡ 03.29.30.04.31
Closed 15 Oct–1 April. **TV**. **Garden**. **Car park**.

The same family has owned this hotel for four generations. It's miles out in the forest overlooking the valley. There are footpaths through the woods and a lovely terraced garden. Bedrooms are regularly decorated and have an old-style charm. Doubles 180F with basin and up to 310F with bath. Numbers 2, 3 and 11 have their own terrace while 18 and 19 have a corner sitting area. Half board from 270F. There's a fantastic view from the restaurant, where they're strong on traditional cuisine and regional dishes like *chiffonade* of smoked salmon with poached egg, burbot with leek fondue, duck fillet with bitter cherries, *andouille* from Val d'Ajol, braised trout with sorrel, kirsch soufflé, and home-made ice creams. Menu of the day at 95F then others up to 220F, and a children's menu at 58F. 5% discount on the room rate.

PONT-À-MOUSSON   54700

🏠 HÔTEL BAGATELLE***

47–49 rue Gambetta; you'll find it as you enter the town

from the east.
☎ 03.83.81.03.64 ➡ 03.83.81.12.63
Closed Christmas to New Year. **TV**. **Car park**.

This modern hotel is brilliantly located near the abbey and the banks of the Moselle. It's a bit mournful, but the rooms are fine; a double with en-suite bathroom will cost 340–380F.

BLÉNOD-LÈS-PONT-À-MOUSSON
54700 (3KM SW)

l●l AUBERGE DES THOMAS

100 av. Victor-Claude; it's on the N57.
☎ 03.83.81.07.72
Closed Sun evening, Mon, Wed evening, the Feb school holidays and three weeks in Aug.

Service noon–1.30pm and 7–9pm. This is an adorable house, smothered in Virginia creeper, standing defiantly against the monstrous factories all around. You'll be greeted warmly and shown into a country-style dining room that's decorated in blue. They prepare delicate dishes for a classy clientele: snails with young nettle shoots, veal sweetbreads with candied orange and green cabbage, *andouillette campagnarde*, small tarts served warm with a caramel ice cream. Menus 105–250F. In summer, you can eat in a courtyard conservatory that's stuffed with greenery. A delightful place.

REMIREMONT
88200

🎿 🏠 HÔTEL DU CHEVAL DE BRONZE**

59 rue Charles-de-Gaulle (Centre).
☎ 03.29.62.52.24 ➡ 03.29.62.34.90
TV. **Pay car park**.

This used to be a coaching inn and has retained a lot of its charm. You enter under the arcade in the centre of town. The staff will make you feel welcome. The clean rooms are quiet and the ones overlooking the road have all been soundproofed. The others look over the flowery courtyard. Doubles with basin 165F, then 220F with shower and 340F with bath. 10% discount for a three-night stay. Free parking space.

l●l RESTAURANT LE CLOS HEURTEBISE

13 chemin des Capucins (South); from the town centre go down rue Charles-de-Gaulle; after the big crossroads turn right into the street that goes up and follow the signs.
☎ 03.29.62.08.04
Closed Wed and Sun evenings and 8–22 Jan. **Garden**. **Car park**.

This rather stylish restaurant stands at the edge of a wood in the hills that circle the town. The decor is chic and classically provincial and the service is impeccable. Excellent cuisine using fresh ingredients. Among the good fish dishes they serve twice-cooked bream and frogs' legs in season. Try the house specialities such as duck *foie gras* or pigeon. There's a trolley of wicked desserts. The weekday menu costs 95F and others 148–265F. The wine list will delight the connoisseur. This is one of the best places in the area and in summer you can eat outdoors.

ROUVROIS-SUR-OTHAIN
55230

l●l LA MARMITE

☎ 03.28.85.90.79
Closed Sun evening, Mon and a week in Aug.

This is one of the gastronomic restaurants in the department. The setting is bourgois and typical of its type though not in perfect taste; good quality ingredients are accurately cooked and servings are very generous. There's an excellent welcome and you get good value for money. 120F weekly menu then others up to 240F.

SAINT-AVOLD
57500

🎿 🏠 l●l HÔTEL-RESTAURANT DE PARIS

45 rue Hirschaue (Centre).
☎ 03.87.92.19.52 ➡ 03.87.92.94.32
Hotel closed Mon mornings. **Restaurant closed** Sat and Sun evenings. **TV**.

In the 16th century, this building belonged to the counts of Créhange, who were Protestants. They built a small chapel at the back of the inner courtyard where they could practise their religion without hindrance. That courtyard is now the restaurant's dining room and the chapel, now an art gallery, retains its sculpted keystones and a fine vaulted ceiling. Menus start at 68F in the week and others 110–250F. You'll pay 150F *à la carte*. The restaurant's not that great but the rooms are decent, clean and quiet, if a touch old-fashioned. Doubles with shower 238F or 288F with shower/wc. Free coffee.

SAINT-DIÉ
88100

🏠 HÔTEL DE FRANCE**

1 rue Dauphine (Centre); it's next to the post office.

☎ 03.29.56.32.61 ➡ 03.29.56.01.09
Closed Sun. **TV**.

A well-located hotel with a courtyard, so the rooms that look out onto it – numbers 3, 6 and 9 – are particularly quiet. Double with basin 120F, shower/wc or bath 240F with a double bed or 260F with twin beds. The owner is welcoming and he will give you the door entry code so you can let yourself in if you come back late.

☆ ☎ HÔTEL DES VOSGES ET DU COMMERCE**

53–57 rue Thiers (Centre); it's near the cathedral.
☎ 03.29.56.16.21 ➡ 03.29.55.48.71
TV. Disabled access. Pay garage.

A welcoming, well-managed hotel with thirty rooms with different facilities at various prices. There are doubles with basin at 130F, with shower and basin (wc in the passage) at 160–235F with shower/wc at 280F, or with bath at 240–280F. It's open 24 hours because they have a night porter. No restaurant. 10% discount for a minimum two-night stay. Free use of garage.

|●| LE BAR AMÉRICAIN

pl. du Marché (Centre).
☎ 03.29.56.28.69
Closed Sun, and end July to end Aug. **Disabled access**.

More of a bar than a restaurant, with American decor. The atmosphere on a Saturday afternoon, after the market has closed, is terrific. One set menu at just 55F – good value for a substantial meal.

☆ |●| RESTAURANT EUROPE

41 rue des Trois-Villes (Northwest).
☎ 03.29.56.32.03
Closed Sun evening, Mon and the first three weeks in Aug.

The restaurant is decorated fairly conventionally in shades of salmon and blue. The nice owner offers a selection of dishes from different culinary traditions: pasta, couscous, a steak *tartare* that they shred with a knife rather than a mincer, and a few Balkan specialities including goulash. The food is good and there are prices to suit all pockets.Set weekday lunch menu 70F, then 90–139F. Free coffee.

PETITE FOSSE (LA)   88490 (17KM NE)

☎ |●| AUBERGE DU SPITZEMBERG**

2 av. Spitzemberg; when driving towards Strasbourg,

take the Provenchères-sur-Faure exit, turn left and go through La Petite-Foss up to the Col d'Hermampaire, turn left and go on about 1km to the end of the road.
☎ 03.29.51.20.46 ➡ 03.29.51.10.12
Closed Tues and three weeks in Jan. **TV**. **Garden**. **Car park**.

A lovely inn in an isolated spot in the Vosges forest where you can relax in peace and quiet. Comfortable double rooms cost 270–300F with shower/wc or bath. The dining room is very attractive, and they serve traditional cooking; try the trout in white Alsace wine, the Munster cheese flambéed in *marc* or in cumin-flavoured alcohol, or the bilberry soup. There's a cheap set menu at 85F, not served on a Sunday lunchtimes, then 110F and 135F.

SAINT-MIHIEL   55300

☆ ☎ |●| HÔTEL-RESTAURANT RIVE GAUCHE**

pl. de la Gare; it's near the old station bridge.
☎ 03.29.89.15.83 ➡ 03.29.89.15.35
TV. Disabled access. Garden. Car park.

Service 11.30am–3pm and 6.30–11pm. They've done a wonderful job of restoring the old station house. The en-suite doubles have shower/wc or bath, cable TV and phone for 250F, which is fair given the facilities and the atmosphere. Good traditional cooking in the restaurant and fairly generous portions. The 65F menu is served daily except on Saturday evening and Sunday lunch, then 98–155F. There's a children's play area outside and plans to build a swimming pool. 10% discount on the room rate Sept–May.

BISLÉE   55300 (5KM N)

|●| LA TABLE DES BONS PÈRES-RELAIS DE ROMAINVILLE

Chemin de Pichaumé; take the Bislée turning off the D964 between St. Mihiel and Commercy.
☎ 03.29.89.09.90 ➡ 03.29.89.10.01
Closed a week or two in winter.

This restaurant, in a restored farmhouse, is on a road that is not too busy in summer. You dine in a bright airy room with a huge fireplace. The property overlooks the meandering river and there's a delightful terrace on the bank. The cuisine has a light touch and there are a few regional specialities – it's a sort of gastronomic "Routier" restaurant. Lunchtime menu at 59F. The other menus, 100–300F, use plenty of seasonal produce including wild mushrooms. Hospitable welcome and stylish service.

LACROIX-SUR-MEUSE   55300 (10KM S)

⋔ 🏠 |●| LA PÊCHE À LA TRUITE

Route de Seuzey; take the D964 then the D109 after Lacroix.
☎ 03.29.90.10.97
Closed Tues out of season and the second fortnight in Jan. **Disabled access. Garden. Car park.**

This is more than a hotel-restaurant – it's a concept. You come here to catch the trout and ling that they let out of the fish ponds at 9am and 2pm daily – rods are available for hire. There are lots of facilities including outdoor games for the children so it's a good spot for families. The restaurant is a converted paper mill and they've built a terrace with an arbour. Naturally, they serve a lot of trout dishes. There's a weekday menu at 78F and others 98–258FF. There are a few rooms, which cost 230–300F with shower or bath. They make you feel welcome. Free fishing if you stay for three days.

VIGNEULLES-LÈS-HATTONCHÂTEL
55210 (17KM NE)

|●| L'AUBERGE LORRAINE

50 rue Poincaré; it's on the D901.
☎ 03.29.89.58.00
Closed Mon.

A quiet inn in the Lorraine regional park, north of the Lake de Madiane, in a peaceful village. It was recently taken over by a mother and daughter team who do simple, good, nourishing fare. Weekday lunch menu 70F or pizzas or grills in the evening, but it's best to phone in advance for an evening meal.

SAUNT-MAURICE-SOUS-LES-CÔTES
55210 (22KM NE)

⋔ 🏠 |●| HÔTEL-RESTAURANT DES CÔTES DE MEUSE**

av. du Général Lelorrain; on the D901 turn left for Vigneulles-lès-Hattonchâtel, then take the D908.
☎ 03.29.89.35.61 ➡ 03.29.89.55.50
Closed Sun evenings, Mon and three weeks at the beginning of Nov. **TV.**

This modest hotel is in a village where they produce Côtes de Meuse wines, which have a refreshing flinty flavour. The hotel itself has no real charm but the quiet rooms have good bathrooms; they're well maintained and nicely decorated. Doubles with shower/wc or bath cost 220F. In the restaurant there's a weekday lunch menu for 60F and other up to

220F. The trout and zander dishes are carefully prepared. The owner takes a lot of trouble to look after you. There's a billiard table in the bar. Free breakfast or apéritif.

SARREBOURG   57400

⋔ 🏠 |●| HÔTEL DE FRANCE**

3 av. de France (Centre).
☎ 03.87.03.21.47 ➡ 03.87.23.93.57
TV. Lock-up car park.

This is a big hotel with fifty well-maintained rooms. Though they're somewhat lacking in charm, they are a good size and ideal for families. Single rooms with basin 150F or doubles with shower cost 250F, 275F with shower/wc and 295F with bath. Friendly reception. The restaurant next door is run by the same family. 10% discount on the room rate.

🏠 |●| HÔTEL-RESTAURANT LES CÈDRES**

Zone de Loisirs-chemin d'Imling (West); there are signs on the N4 to the zone de Loisirs.
☎ 03.87.03.55.55 ➡ 03.87.03.66.33
Hotel closed 22 Dec–2 Jan. **Restaurant closed** Sat lunchtime and Sun evening. **TV. Disabled access. Garden. Car park.**

The architecture looks good in this rural setting and the spacious dining rooms are bright and peaceful. There's a piano with a see-through lid for the guests to play after a game of snooker. Chef Monsieur Morin cooks good food; à la carte try frogs' legs, fillet of zander with choucroute or pan-fried foie gras. They do a weekday lunch menu du jour for 66F, and others 119–209F. Expect to pay 358F for a double room with a bath or shower, or 299F a night at weekends.

|●| RESTAURANT L'AMI FRITZ

76 Grande-Rue (Centre).
☎ 03.87.03.10.40
Closed Wed, a fortnight in Feb and a fortnight in Oct.

The façade of this place is brightened up by lots of flowers in window boxes. It's a good restaurant, popular with local worthies, businesspeople and visiting Germans. You get quantity rather than quality but try the house specialities of fillet of zander à l'alsacienne, choucroute, presskopf (a type of brawn), tripe with Riesling, and calf's head with two sauces. Weekday lunchtime menu 65F, then others 85–185F.

|●| L'AUBERGE MAÎTRE PIERRE

24 rue Saint-Martin (Northeast); head in the direction of the motorway, cross the railway bridge at the

Sarrebourg exit towards Morhange then follow the arrows.
☎ 03.87.03.10.16 ➡ 03.87.23.99.44
Closed Mon, Tues, and 20 Dec–10 Jan. **Garden. Car park**.

This place has changed its name for the nth time; its last incarnation, as the *Auberge de Zoo*, was flummoxed when they closed the zoo. A past owner, Marguerite Pierre, invented *flammenküche*, an open bacon and cream tart. Her successors, Daniel and Lucienne Pierre, carry on the tradition as well as serving good ham in pastry and grills on the open fire. Their cooking is absolutely fresh and satisfying and a meal won't break the bank. Menus 82–180F. The Lorraine specialities are very good. The restaurant is classic with a good atmosphere, though it's a little too large to feel intimate. There's a bar where they serve Tex-Mex dishes at night.

SARREGUEMINES   57200

🏊 🏠 |●| HÔTEL-RESTAURANT L'UNION**

28 rue Alexandre-de-Geiger; take rue du Maréchal-Foch and take the second on the left.
☎ 03.87.95.28.42 ➡ 03.87.98.25.21
Closed Sat lunchtime, Sun and 23 Dec–2 Jan. **TV. Car park**.

Sarreguemines is the capital of the pottery industry, and there are some good pieces on display in the dining room. The food is decent too, with set menus from 77–150F. The owners are very obliging, and you'll pay about 300–380F for a comfortable room with shower/wc or bath. Those overlooking the noisy street have been soundproofed. Free breakfast.

|●| RESTAURANT LA BONNE SOURCE

24 av. de la Gare (Southeast).
☎ 03.87.98.03.79
Closed Sun evening, Mon, and mid-July to mid-Aug. **Car park**.

A traditional looking restaurant with wood panelling and a display of Sarreguemines china, proper tablecloths and cloth napkins. Good Alsace and Lorraine specialities here – *flammenküche* (bacon, cream and onion flan), and *lever knepfle* (liverballs with bacon and cream), home-made *charcuterie*, *choucroute* and spare ribs. Good-natured welcome and a pleasant atmosphere. They serve a lunch menu for 69F on weekdays and others at 89–120F. Good value.

🏊 |●| RESTAURANT LAROCHE

3 pl. de la Gare (Southeast).

☎ 03.87.98.03.23
Closed Fri evening, Sat, 5–25 Aug and 23 Dec–5 Jan. **Disabled access**.

There are two dining rooms, one of which offers a speedier service than the other. The decor is rustic and is beginning to feel a bit tired, but it's as clean as can be. There's a weekday menu at 68F and set menus 85–120F. Dishes are nicely presented and good value. You'll get a cordial welcome. Free coffee.

WOELFING-LÈS-SARREGUEMINES 57200 (12KM SE)

|●| PASCAL DIMOFSKI

113 route de Bitche; it's on the N62 going in the direction of Bitche.
☎ 03.87.02.38.21 ➡ 03.87.02.21.36
Closed Mon evening, Tues, two weeks in winter and three weeks in summer.

This may look like an ordinary roadside restaurant from the outside, but owner Pascal Dimofsky has turned a simply run family establishment into a gastronomic restaurant that's been rated by the "Moselle Gourmande". The dining room has a refined, quiet atmosphere and it's full of businesspeople and regulars. Weekday lunch menus 130F and 160F; and there are others 220–420F; they might feature veal terrine with white port, tuna *carpaccio*, fresh panfried cod, iced strawberry soufflé, and lemon and imperial mandarine sorbet. If you're lucky with the weather, eat in the garden.

SENONES   88210

🏠 |●| HÔTEL-RESTAURANT AU BON GÎTE**

3 pl. Vaultrin (Centre).
☎ 03.29.57.92.46 ➡ 03.29.57.93.92
Closed Sun evening, Mon evening on public holidays, the Feb school holidays and a fortnight in Aug. **TV. Car park**.

This lovely old house has been renovated inside and out and the resolutely modern decor complements the texture of the old walls. Monsieur and Madame Thomas, the owners, are very welcoming. There are about ten attractive rooms which are most comfortable. Doubles 280F with shower or 320F with bath. Numbers 2, 5, 6, and 7 are the quietest. Reliable regional cooking with a good helping of imagination: *terrine* with *andouille*, monkfish with thickened shellfish *jus* and a home-made macaroon with bergamot ice cream. There's a weekday menu at 68F then others 95–175F. It gets busy at weekends.

𝒴|●| LA SALLE DES GARDES

7 pl. Clémenceau (Centre).
☎ 03.29.57.60.06
Closed evenings, Thurs, a fortnight in June and a week at Christmas. **Disabled access. Car park**.

A simple, attractive brasserie run by a friendly guy. There's a short lunch menu at 58F and others reasonably priced up to 90F. The house speciality is meat grilled over the open fire. The place is favoured by young people from all around the area. Free coffee.

SIERCK-LES-BAINS   57480

𝒴|●| RESTAURANT LA VIEILLE PORTE

8 pl. Jean-de-Morbach (Centre).
☎ and ➡ 03.82.83.22.61
Closed Tues evening, Wed, Feb school holidays and 24 Jul–8 Aug.

The old gate dates from 1604 and leads to the restaurant courtyard. Sierck was a refuge for Cistercian monks during the religious wars, and there's an underground tunnel leading from the château to the 11th-century tower. The hot trout with almonds is their signature starter, and there's a peppered fillet of Charolais beef flambéed in Cognac which is a little marvel. Weekday menu 90F, then 190–300F. Confident cooking by the chef, Jean-Pierre Mercier who has a good reputation in these parts and further afield. Free apéritif.

GAVISSE   57570 (9KM W)

𝒴|●| RESTAURANT LE MEGACÉROS

19 pl. Jeanne-d'Arc (Centre); it's on the D64.
☎ 03.82.55.45.87
Closed Mon, Tues, 26 Dec–5 Jan. **Disabled access. Car park**.

The *megacéros* is an extinct ancestor of the deer, but there's nothing prehistoric about this restaurant. The cuisine is innovative and the chef creates subtle combinations with local ingredients – try the veal kidneys with dandelion wine, the salmon *unilatérale* that's seared on one side only, or mirabelle plum ice cream. Menus 100–260F. Mme Seiler is a considerate hostess. Free apéritif.

RODEMACK   57570 (13KM W)

|●| RESTAURANT LA MAISON DES BAILLIS

46 pl. des Baillis; take the D64 then the D62.
☎ 03.82.51.24.25

Closed Mon, Tues and the Feb school holidays. **Garden. Car park**.

The first lords of Rodemack settled in this handsome village in the 12th century, and at the end of the 15th century the Austrians confiscated the estate. In the 16th century, the new owner, bored with being so far from the Viennese court, went home and left a bailiff in the house to manage the place. The restaurant is in this magnificent building. They serve good food in the glorious dining rooms. Menus 85–190F or about 120F *à la carte*.

STENAY   55700

🏠|●| HÔTEL-RESTAURANT LE COMMERCE**

9 rue Aristide-Briand (Centre).
☎ 03.29.80.30.62 ➡ 03.29.80.61.77
Closed Fri evening, and Sun evening in winter. **TV**.

The hotel has been completely renovated and they've equipped the comfortable, spacious rooms with a mini-bar and put in new bathrooms with shower or bath and wc. Doubles cost 180–450F. There's a weekday menu at 75F, another at 100F which includes wine, and others up to 250F. They list simple dishes which are generously served and an array of starters. À la carte there are a few specialities cooked with beer.

INOR   55700 (7KM N)

🏠|●| AUBERGE LE FAISAN DORÉ**

rue de l'Écluse; take the D964, going north.
☎ 03.29.80.35.45 ➡ 03.29.80.37.92
Closed Fri. **Swimming pool. TV. Garden. Car park**.

This place, by the river in a village in the Meuse forest, is popular with hunters. You will eat well – try omelette *ardennaise*, fillet of beef with ceps, or local game in season. The weekday menu costs 68F, and there are other themed options, focusing on Lorraine specialities or tradional dishes, from 110–180F. There's a bar, too. The hotel is decent, though the timbers are fake. The rooms have en-suite bathrooms. Doubles cost 200F.

VILOSNES   55100 (20KM S)

𝒴 🏠|●| HÔTEL-RESTAURANT DU VIEUX MOULIN

rue des Petits Ponts; it's on the D123b.
☎ 03.29.85.81.52 ➡ 03.29.85.88.19

Closed Tues lunchtime out of season, Jan and Feb. **TV**. **Car park**.

The hotel is in the very heart of this quietest of quiet villages. The mill wheel stopped turning years ago but you can watch the Meuse flow peacefully by from the lovely terrace and some of the rooms. The owners are very welcoming. Wholesome family cooking in the restaurant, with good traditional dishes. 75F lunch menu including a drink, then 100F, 120F, 160F and 250F. The rooms, fully equipped with shower or bath, go for 240–300F. They are each different, though some of the beams are fake. 10% discount on the room rate Nov–April. Free breakfast.

THIONVILLE 57100

☎ |●| HÔTEL LE PROGRÈS*

18 rue Jemappes (Centre); it's near pl. Claude-Amould.
☎ 03.82.53.85.47
Restaurant closed evenings and Sun. **TV**. **Car park**.

The hotel is in very good condition, and the rooms have been refurbished and have new beds. You'll pay 200F for a double with shower/wc. It is very cheap to eat in the restaurant where they serve various, reasonably priced dishes of the day or you'll pay around 70F *à la carte*. This place is a good choice if you don't want to spend much.

☎ |●| HÔTEL-RESTAURANT DES AMIS**

40 av. de-Bertier; leave the motorway at exit 40 and turn right at the fifth set of lights.
☎ 03.82.53.22.18 ➡ 03.82.54.32.40
Hotel closed Sun until 5pm. **Restaurant closed** Fri. **TV**. **Car park**.

A large establishment covered in Virginia creeper and geraniums. The proprietress will treat you like an old friend. She keeps the hotel extremely clean. Doubles with shower/wc or bath are 260–310F. The 65F *repas campagnard* is a real treat: *crudités*, smoked country ham, house *terrine*, garlic sausage, *fuseau lorrain*, roast potatoes, and cream cheese with herbs. The dining room has been redecorated and redesigned; Monsieur painted the fresco himself and the place is lit by ornamental Alsatian lamps in highly carved wood.

⅔ ☎ |●| HÔTEL L'HORIZON***

50 route du Crève-Coeur (Northwest); take exit 40 on the A31 onto the Thionville ring-road then straight on towards Bel Air hospital.
☎ 03.82.88.53.65 ➡ 03.82.34.55.84
ℯ info@lhorizon.com
Hotel closed Jan and Feb.

Restaurant closed Sat and Mon lunchtimes. **TV**. **Disabled access**. **Car park**.

The striking façade of this luxurious hotel marks the building out from others nearby. In the restaurant, the dishes are finely prepared with a sure hand, but offer no surprises. Weekday menu 185F then 215–315F. The real luxury is in the rooms; take number 3, which has the softest feather bed ever. In the bathroom you are spoilt with perfumes, soaps, shampoos and other extras. Doubles with shower go for 480F, shower/wc 580F and bath 680F. Free apéritif or coffee, and 10% discount on the room rate Oct–March.

HOMBOURG-BUDANGE 57920 (15KM SE)

⅔ |●| L'AUBERGE DU ROI ARTHUR

48 rue Principale; it's on the D918 to Bouzonville.
☎ 03.82.83.97.15 ➡ 03.82.83.54.04
Closed Sun–Tues evenings, and a week at the beginning of July.

Service noon–2.30pm and 6–10pm. Nothing to do with the legend of King Arthur, but the restaurant is pleasant anyway. They have a series of portraits on the walls from the château, and display a splendid porcelain dish made in Sarreguemines. They serve good country cooking. Menus 75–150F which list *croustade* of snails with Moselle wine, fillet of beef with Roquefort cream sauce, frogs' legs and steak *tartare*. It's popular, and attracts lots of regular customers.

TOUL 54200

⅔ ☎ HÔTEL DE L'EUROPE**

35 av. Victor-Hugo (Centre); it's near the station.
☎ 03.83.43.00.10 ➡ 03.83.63.27.67
Closed Christmas and New Year. **TV**. **Pay car park**.

Paradise for fans of the 1930s style; almost everything dates from that period, including the doors, carpets, furniture and the bathrooms. Some rooms have been redecorated but what they may have lost in authenticity they have maintained in charm. Room 35 is particularly splendid. Prices start at 150F for a double room with washing facilities. Free parking.

⅔ ☎ LA VILLA LORRAINE**

15 rue Gambetta (Centre).
☎ 03.83.43.08.95 ➡ 03.83.64.63.64
TV. **Pay car park**.

The style of this building was influenced by the École de Nancy. It's central, clean and inexpensive, and you'll get a warm-hearted welcome. Double rooms with shower 170F, 218F with shower/wc or 230F with bath. 10% discount for two nights.

LUCEY   54200 (9KM NW)

I●I L'AUBERGE DU PRESSOIR

rue des Pachenottes; it's on the D908 known as the route des Vins et de la Mirabelle.
☎ 03.83.63.81.91
Closed Sun evening, Mon and 16 Aug–3 Sept. **Disabled access. Car park.**

Service noon–2pm and 7–9pm. Popular place; it's essential to book at the weekend and in summer. It's in what used to be the village station, and there's a genuine antique winepress in the courtyard. The cooking is regional and eclectic, with a number of specialities, including *profiteroles* with snails, *filet mignon* with mirabelle plum vinegar, and trout cooked in *vin gris* from Toul. Menus 78–170F.

VAL-D'AJOL (LE)   88340

🍴 🛏 I●I HÔTEL-RESTAURANT LA RÉSIDENCE***

5 rue des Mousses (Centre); at the church take the D20 signposted to Hamaunard.
☎ 03.29.30.68.52 ➡ 03.29.66.53.00
Closed Sun evening and Mon Oct–April except for the school holidays. **Swimming pool. TV. Garden. Car park.**

This handsome 19th-century master crafts-man's house has been developed over the years into a very pleasant establishment. The work has been done by two generations of the same family, and there's a third waiting in the wings. Mme Bongeot will receive you in a hospitable, good-natured way. There are lots of nooks and crannies to explore on your way to the comfortable, cosy, quiet rooms. They all have shower or bath, and cost 320–480F. There are two three-star annexes in the green park, where you'll also find the pool and the tennis court. The cooking is of equal quality. The weekday menu at 68F gives you the dish of the day and a dessert, and there are other menus 98–255F. You should definitely try the famous Val d'Ajol *andouille*, which is served in its own dish, and the free-range chicken with Kirsch. Impeccable service. 10% discount on the room rate except weekends and public holidays 13 July–21 Aug and 23 Dec–3 Jan.

VERDUN   55100

🍴 🛏 HÔTEL MONTAULBAIN**

4 rue de la Vieille-Prison (Centre); it's near the Victory monument.
☎ 03.29.86.00.47 ➡ 03.29.84.75.70
TV.

Narrow streets, traffic jams and a one-way system make this place difficult to reach by car. They offer ten quiet, comfortable rooms with phone, from 150–200F depending on the bathroom facilities. Breakfast 25F. The welcome is friendly and the atmosphere is pleasant. 10% discount Oct–March.

🛏 I●I HÔTEL LE SAINT-PAUL**

12 pl. Saint-Paul (North).
☎ 03.29.86.02.16
Restaurant closed Sun evening and Nov–April.

This well-situated hotel offers moderate prices, a good standard of comfort, peace and quiet, and a pleasant family atmosphere. It's often occupied by people coming to visit the war graves from World War I. The restaurant serves good traditional dishes from the Lorraine with a lunch menu at 89F and others up to 179F. Rooms with washing facilities and wc go for 165F, or 235F with bath. There are a couple of rooms for families. For half board, reckon on paying 120F a head on top of the price of the room. Professional staff.

I●I RESTAURANT LE PICOTIN

38 av. Joffre (East).
☎ 03.29.84.53.45
Closed Sun evening. **Disabled access.**

If you prefer to eat in peace, opt for the dining room; the terrace is fairly noisy. The decor is bright and attractive. Good-quality, inventive cooking; try the goat's cheese pancake. There's a 60F weekday lunch menu, and others at 90F and 130F. If you like steak, go for the excellent *tournedos 1900*. This place is popular with theatre people and night-owls, because it stays open late.

I●I LE FORUM

35 rue des Gros-Degrés (Centre).
☎ 03.29.86.46.88
Closed Wed evening, Sun and a fortnight July/Aug. **Disabled access.**

Delicate, tasteful decor with subtle water-colours. The owner is kind and hospitable. The cooking is simple but fresh and light, adapting traditional regional recipes with a modern twist. The dining room is lovely, though the vaulted basement is rather oppressive. Lunch menu at 65F in the week, then 90–150F – it's good value, and has a strong local following.

|●| LE POSTE DE GARDE

47 rue Saint Victor (Centre-East).
☎ 03.29.86.38.49
Closed Mon–Fri lunchtimes, Fri and Sat evenings, public holidays and Aug. **Disabled access**.

This establishment was set up to employ young people coming out of custody as a way of helping them back into the world of work – ironically, it's in an old guard room. It has been brightly restored in pastel shades with green shutters, but, despite their best efforts, it is still a rather cold building. Happily, the atmosphere is excellent and the guests all seem to be satisfied. Simple, straightforward cooking, which doesn't attempt to be subtle, is served in large portions that will satisfy your appetite. Menus 65–110F or à la carte.

DIEUE-SUR-MEUSE 55320 (12KM S)

乃 ᇽ |●| CHÂTEAU DES MON-THAIRONS***

Les Monthairons; take the D34.
☎ and ➡ 03.29.87.78.55
Restaurant closed Mon, Tues lunchtime and 15 March–15 Nov. **Disabled access. TV**.

A 19th-century château in a walled park with the Meuse meandering gently through it. It's a member of the classy *Château-Hôtels-Indépendants* group. The place is stunning to look at, but although the rooms are extremely comfortable they don't have a particular traditional charm. However, for 450–650F for a double room – hardly a king's ransom – you will spend the night in a lovely place where you get lots of little extras such as dressing gowns and toiletries. The restaurant has a good reputation; you'll pay 130F for the weekday lunchtime menu and 185–450F for other set menus. The breakfast at 65F cannot be surpassed. Specialities include *tourte* of rabbit with truffles, pigeon breast, snail *cassolette* with duck's gizzards and redcurrant soufflé. Free coffee, and 10% discount on the room rate 15 Sept–15 Jan excluding weekends.

SOMMEDIEUE 55320 (15.5KM SE)

乃 ᇽ |●| LE RELAIS DES ÉPICHÉES

7 rue du Grand-Pont; take the D964 as far as Dieue then turn left onto the D159; it's near the war memorial.

☎ 03.29.87.61.36 ➡ 03.29.85.76.38
Closed Sun evening and 15 Dec–10 Jan. **TV**. **Car park**.

Service noon–2.30pm and 7.30–10pm. The bar is populated by regulars sipping a glass of something or calling into the tobacconist's to buy their fix. In the restaurant they serve good, simple cooking. The *quiche lorraine* and calf's head are first class and there is a weekday menu at 70F and others 85–160F. The owner is straightfoward and hospitable. Pity about the fake beams. The rooms are clean and have views of the Dieue stream. A double with basin will cost 180F, or 220F with shower/wc or bath. Free coffee.

ÉTAIN 55400 (20KM NE)

乃 ᇽ |●| HÔTEL-RESTAURANT LA SIRÈNE**

22 rue Prud'homme-Navette.
☎ 03.29.87.10.32 ➡ 03.29.87.17.65
Closed Sun evening, Mon out of season and 22–31 Dec. **TV. Garden. Car park**.

Apparently, Napoleon III dined in this handsome house after the battle of Gravelotte in 1870. The interior is very rustic in style and it's filled with antiques – in the bar there's an elegant old French billiard table. You'll get a pleasant welcome, the atmosphere is hushed and the customers are well-to-do. The rooms are quite comfortable; ask for one at the back, as the road can be noisy. Doubles 235–350F with shower/wc or bath. Half board starts at 180F per person for a minimum three-night stay. The cheapest menu, 70F, is served daily except Sunday, and there are others up to 250F. Good, bourgeois cooking with dishes like salmon with tarragon, ham with peaches and *foie gras*. There are two tennis courts and a place to play *boules*. Free coffee.

VILLE-SUR-YRON 54800

|●| LA TOQUE LORRAINE

1 rue de l'Yron; it's on the D132.
☎ 03.82.83.98.13
Closed Sun evening, Wed, Thurs and a fortnight in Aug.

This pretty Lorraine village is undergoing major restoration work. The restaurant is in one of the cottages opposite the carpenter's. There are several dining rooms, one of which has a proud fireplace. It's got a farmhouse atmosphere, which is refined but formal. The stone walls have been cleaned and they're beautifully shown off by the discreet lighting. The cooking is full of flavour, and will set you up for a good walk round the village. Weekday lunch menu at 70F, others 115–200F; tripe with Toul *vin gris*, brawn, frogs' legs, kidneys with morels and Lorraine cake.

VITTEL   88800

🏃 🛏 HÔTEL LES OISEAUX

54 rue de Sugène (Centre); it's near the spa.
☎ 03.29.08.61.93
Closed Three weeks in Jan. **TV**. **Garden**. **Car park**.

This is not so much a hotel as a pretty little house that's been turned into a B&B by an extremely nice woman. Rooms with basin cost 140F, with shower 240F and with bath 260F. It's quiet and pleasant, with a tiny garden. 10% discount.

🛏 |●| HÔTEL-RESTAURANT LA CHAUMIÈRE

196 rue Jeanne-d'Arc (Centre).
☎ 03.29.08.02.87
Closed Sun in winter. **Car park**.

A tiny hotel with a bar and restaurant. It's not much to look at, but the proprietress is delightful, and the chef, who's been in the business for thirty years, cares about what he's doing. They give the impression that they are enjoying themselves, which makes a nice change from the health farm-style strictness that pervades the rest of the town. Rooms, 180F a night, are simple and clean, with washing facilities only. Lunch menu 60F, and others up to 120F with a selection of local, regional or international dishes.

🏃 🛏 |●| HÔTEL DE L'ORÉE DU BOIS**

L'Orée du Bois (West); it's 4km north on the D18 opposite the race course.
☎ 03.29.08.88.88 📠 03.29.08.01.61
📧 oree-du-bois@dial.oleane.com
Closed Sun evening, and Nov to end Jan. **TV**.
Swimming pool. **Disabled access**. **Garden**. **Car park**.

A modern hotel in a quiet spot, which specialises in getting its guests back into shape. Sports facilities include a gym, tennis courts, indoor heated swimming pool and a sauna. Many guests are executives here for seminars. The rooms are comfortable, and you'll get a friendly welcome. Reckon on paying 325F for a double with bath. The restaurant does menus from 72–195F and the dishes change regularly. There are a few constants like salmon *à l'unilatérale*, grilled on one side only, trout and frogs' legs in red Toul wine, fillet of beef and *chaud-froid* of mirabelles. Free coffee.

Midi-Pyrénées

AIGNAN · 32290

🏃 🏠 |●| LE VIEUX LOGIS

rue des Arts; it's behind the town hall.
☎ and ➡ 05.62.09.23.55
Closed Sun evening. **TV**.

An unobtrusive establishment near the town square, offering good food and a cheery decor. Several cheap menus 55–120F, listing, for example, soup, salad, shrimps *à la provençale*, lamb kebab and dessert. The specialities, produced only when the ingredients are available at market, are fresh *foie gras* salad, zander with *beurre blanc,* ceps with parsley and prawns flambéed with Armagnac. There's a terrace. Rather stern welcome. Rooms with shower/wc or bath 220F. Free apéritif, coffee or *digestif*.

ALBAN · 81250

🏃 |●| RESTAURANT DU MIDI**

9 pl. des Tilleuls (Centre).
☎ 05.63.55.82.24
Closed Tues evening and the last week in Aug.

This unassuming little restaurant on the village square serves surprisingly high-quality food. Five menus 69–140F offering good value for money. Quality ingredients and fresh produce go into dishes such as veal tripe with potato, grilled steak with chips, *aiguillettes* of duck or, in winter, beef *daube*. Dishes of the day change daily, and the standard menu changes at least twice-yealyr. The desserts are made in-house – try the iced *vacherin*. Warm and genuine welcome. Free coffee, apéritif or *digestif*.

ALBI · 81000

🏃 🏠 LA RÉGENCE**

27 av. Maréchal-Joffre (South); it's 150m from the train station.
☎ 05.63.54.01.42 ➡ 05.63.54.80.48
TV. Garden. Pay garage.

This quiet hotel feels like a friendly, family guesthouse. There's a nice garden at the back where they serve breakfast in good weather. Bedrooms are decorated in Laura Ashley style with friezes and coordinated prints. Doubles with basin 140F, 160–190F with shower/wc, 200–210F with bath. Good value for money. There's a 30F charge for the garage. 10% discount for the second night.

🏠 HÔTEL SAINT-CLAIR**

8 rue Saint-Clair (Centre); it's near the cathedral.
☎ 05.63.54.25.66 ➡ 05.63.47.27.58
Closed a month Dec/Jan. **Garden**. **TV. Pay garage**.

A pretty, recently renovated two-star hotel in the old part of town that's maintained with care. Doubles with shower/wc 225F or 315F with bath. Breakfast 38F. Nice owner.

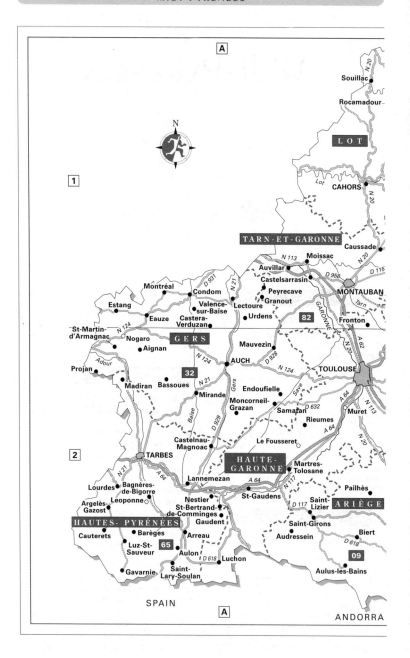

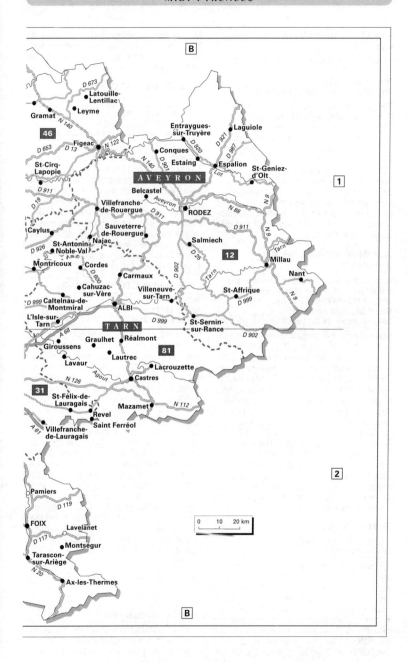

☎ |●| HÔTEL-RESTAURANT DU VIEIL-ALBY**

25 rue Henri-de-Toulouse-Lautrec (Centre); it's 200m from the cathedral
☎ 05.63.54.14.69 📠 05.63.54.96.75
Closed Sun evening and Mon. **TV**. **Car park**.

This simple, well-run hotel is one of the most reasonably priced in this part of town. Double rooms with shower/wc 260F, or 320F with bath. The owner is very congenial, but he doesn't allow smoking anywhere in the hotel. Weekday lunch menu 80F, with others 100–250F. There's a children's *menu découverte* at 60F. The cooking is excellent, with house specialities such as veal sweetbreads in pastry, salt pork liver salad, tripe *à l'Albigeoise* and *fricassée* of monkfish with fruit. Half board is compulsory July–Aug.

🍴 ☎ |●| HÔTEL MERCURE ALBI BASTIDES***

41 rue Porta (Centre); it's on the left after the bridge over the Tarn in the direction of Paris-Carmaux.
☎ 05.63.47.66.66 📠 05.63.46.18.40
Closed Sat and Sun lunchtimes.
Disabled access. **TV**. **Car park**.

Luxury hotel, converted from an 18th-century riverside mill, opposite the cathedral. You pay for the comfort, of course, and the well-equipped rooms are a bit impersonal, as you'd expect from a chain. You also pay for the view, which is probably the finest in Albi. Doubles 460–530F with bath. The fine classical cooking is wonderful – and if you eat on the terrace you get views of the river and the old town. Set menus 100F, 140F and 160F. À la carte you'll pay about 220F. The specialities include *marbré* of *foie gras* with duck *aiguillette*, house *cassoulet* and fillet of zander. Wonderful wine list at rock-bottom prices; try the restaurant's own réserve Mercure. The service is amiable and efficient. 10% discount on the room rate.

|●| LE GÉOPOLY

13 [bis] pl. de l'Archevêché (Centre).
☎ 05.63.49.74.67

A restaurant offering the world on a plate – dishes from Peru, France, Italy, the West Indies, Greece, the United States, China, the Seychelles and Mexico. In fact, the styles of cooking are all rather similar, but it's an original idea, which allows you to try something a bit different. The Peruvian *ceviche*, a mixture of scallops, shrimps and halibut flavoured with coriander is good, as is the *guacamole*.

Menus 49–90F, with a children's menu at 39F. It's in a busy square, popular with tourists and locals, so you can wait a long time to be served.

🍴 |●| RESTAURANT LE PETIT-BOUCHON

77 rue de la Croix-Verte.
☎ 05.63.54.11.75
Closed Sat evening, Sun, public holidays, 1–20 Aug.

There's a warm atmosphere in this clean, Parisian-style brasserie that's decorated with the works of great photographers. The 58F weekday menu consists of a starter, a choice from the dishes of the day which vary depending on what was available at the market – duck *confit*, stuffed mutton tripe, *cassoulet*, sirloin, *coq au vin*, gizzard stew *en daube* etc, and dessert. Other menus 68–128F. Fast, rather brusque service. They specialise in cocktails and have a good regional wine list. Free coffee.

🍴 |●| AUBERGE DU PONT-VIEUX

98 rue du Porta.
☎ 05.63.77.61.73
Closed Tues in winter.

You cross the Pont-Vieux to get to this less touristy part of town. The inn is really great, and you'll have a memorable meal in elegant surroundings. The traditional, generously flavoured cooking is always reliable and good. Dish of the day 39F, *menu du jour* 65F (weekday lunchtimes) and others up to 150F. The meat dishes are excellent and grilled meat comes cooked exactly as you ordered. There are a few dishes from the Aveyron area – some of the particularly successful ones are taken from old recipes. Try broad beans stewed with diced smoked bacon and *andouillette*. Other good choices include crayfish with parsley, duck thigh stuffed with ceps, and supreme of duck breast with *foie gras*. The *assiette Tarnaise* gives you a good selection. The chef comes out to chat to his guests and you'll feel really welcome. The terrace has a superb view of the Tarn. Free glass of red Gavrois or walnut liqueur.

|●| LE LAUTREC

13 rue Henri-de-Toulouse-Lautrec (Centre).
☎ 05.63.54.86.55
Closed Sun evening and Mon.

This restaurant, in the most touristy part of town, is in converted stables that used to belong to Henri de Toulouse-Lautrec.

Some tables are up on a gallery while others are more spaced out. The regional dishes are cooked exceedingly well. Try the pan-fried *foie gras*, scallops with garlic zander with truffle *jus*, duck *confit*, duck breast flambéed with Calvados and the excellent meat dishes. 70F lunch menu and then 90–220F.

|●| LE TOURNESOL

rue de l'Ort-en-Salvy; it's in a side street leading to pl. du Vigan.
☎ 05.63.38.38.14
Closed Sat evening, Sun, Mon, and all week except Friday evening 1–15 May.

This is the best vegetarian restaurant in the region, serving good food at realistic prices. The airy dining room is simply decorated and air-conditioned. The cooking is uncomplicated and very tasty: vegetable *pâté*, courgette flan or falafel. The *assiette Tournesol* gives you lots of variety and wonderful desserts like apple crumble or cheesecake with vanilla and honey. They serve apple juice and organic beer at 15F. A meal will cost about 75F.

MARSSAC   81150 (8KM SW)

|●| LA TAVERNE

rue Abijoux, Castelnau-de-Lévis; from Albi, take the D600, after 4km turn left onto the D1 – Castelnau is 3km further on.
☎ 05.63.60.90.16 ➡ 05.63.60.96.73
Closed Sun evening in winter, Mon, the Feb school holidays and three weeks at All Saints'.

Heaven on earth for lovers of good food. The "chef's suggestions" include raw marinated salmon salad with herbs, red mullet served with prawn *mousseline*, superlative roast duck stuffed with raspberries, and caramelized calf's sweetbreads with Gaillac. The desserts are out of this world, and the extensive wine list includes a terrific Buzet. Menus from 125F. You eat either in the air-conditioned dining room, with its country-style decor, or on the terrace, which is enclosed against the weather. The service is as good as the food.

ARGELÈS-GAZOST   65400

🍴 🛏 |●| HÔTEL BEAU SITE**

10 rue du Capitaine-Digoy
☎ 05.62.97.08.63 ➡ 05.62.97.06.01
Closed 5 Nov-5 Dec. **Garden.**

A self-possessed hotel that's full of character with an ivy-laden façade, brightened up with flowers. Genuine welcome, cosy atmosphere and period furniture. The rooms are all different and the ones overlooking the huge and luxuriant garden are particularly appealing. Doubles 240F with shower or bath. The menu, 85F, offers two starters, main course, cheese and dessert. Not bad. And you can enjoy your meal seated on the terrace which has a splendid view of the garden. Free house aperitif.

🍴 🛏 |●| LE MIRAMONT***

44 av. des Pyrénées (South); at the first roundabout, take the road to Cauterets and it's opposite the spa.
☎ 05.62.97.01.26 ➡ 05.62.97.56.67
Closed 5 Nov–1 Jan. **TV. Garden.**

A fine Art Deco hotel set in a park planted with rose gardens and hydrangeas. The rooms are spacious, elegant and calming, with up-to-date facilities and en-suite bathrooms. They have balconies with views of the old town or over the Pyrenees. Rooms 114, 121 and 122 are larger than standard. Doubles with shower/wc or bath 350–410F. The restaurant deserves a mention in its own right. The chef, Pierre, is the owner's son, and his wife runs the dining room. Dishes change with the season and include good fish specialities and light, deft versions of regional dishes: *fricassée* of veal sweet-breads, truffle salad with poached eggs, pan-fried monkfish with prawns, half-pigeon with Madiran sauce. He has a particular gift for preparing desserts – try the iced *nougat* with honey and almonds or strawberry and redberry *sabayon*. Menus 100F (not Sun or public holidays) then 150–230F. The service is ultra-professional without being too formal. Lots of regulars. Free coffee.

SAINT-SAVIN   65400 (3KM S)

🍴 🛏 |●| LE VISCOS

☎ 05.62.97.02.28 ➡ 05.62.97.04.95
Closed Sun evening and Mon except in school holidays and 1–26 Dec.

A lovely hotel with attractive rooms. 260–290F. Half board 295–315F per person. The cooking is all based on fresh, local produce and it's pretty creative – fish is the speciality: *mosaïque* of duck with *foie gras*, sweet and sour roast salmon or braised duck. There's a *formule* for 90F (Mon–Sat), and menus 120–269F but *à la carte* comes out expensive. They've already established a good reputation but sometimes the welcome is more off-hand than need be. 10% discount on the room rate in summer.

ARCIZANS-AVANT   65400 (4KM W)

🅰 🏠 |●| AUBERGE LE CABALIROS**

16 rue de l'Église (South).
☎ 05.62.97.04.31 ➡ 05.62.97.91.48
Closed Tues evening, Wed out of season, 20 Jan–5 Feb and 8 Oct–8 Dec. **Garden. TV. Car park.**

This attractive inn has a terrace with views over the valley. You will get a good-hearted welcome. Some of the rooms are under the eaves and are lovely but otherwise they're not that attractive, though they do have decent facilities. Doubles with shower or bath 260–300F. Traditional regional cooking with menus 95–170F. The *à la carte* menu includes an authentic *garbure*, a broth with pickled goose, or stuffed neck of duck. Friendly service and a relaxed place.

SALLES   65400 (4KM N)

🅰 🏠 |●| RESTAURANT ET GÎTE LA CHÂTAIGNERAIE

It's in the centre of the village.
☎ 05.62.97.17.84 ➡ 05.62.97.93.14
Closed Mon, lunchtimes in winter and Jan. **Garden. Car park.**

A very beautiful dining room in a renovated farm. Grills are a speciality, and they are prepared in front of you: Pyrenean lamb, braised pigeon *confit*, pan-fried *foie gras* with grapes and bilberry tart. Menus 145–240F and service comes with a smile. There's a lovely terrace in summer. There are rooms available in the *gîte* – 220–250F for a double – and if you book the *gîte* for a week, half board is available. Free coffee.

ARREAU   65240

🏠 |●| HÔTEL D'ANGLETERRE***

Route de Luchon (South).
☎ 05.62.98.63.30 ➡ 05.62.98.69.66
Closed Mon 15 Sept–30 June, 10 Oct–26 Dec, and 15 April–1 June. **Swimming pool. Garden. TV. Car park.**

A 17th-century coaching inn which has been tastefully restored to create a warm, plush, comfortable hotel with quality furnishings and service. Doubles with shower/wc or bath cost 270–380F. Half board is compulsory July to mid-Sept, 280–320F per person. There's a pretty garden and a pool behind the hotel. Good regional cooking: duck *foie gras* cooked in a cloth, medallions of monkfish with sliced red cabbage, and *sabayon* of fruit *au gratin*. Menus 80–200F.

10% discount on the room rate in June and 15 Sept–10 Oct.

CADÉAC-LES-BAINS   65240 (3KM S)

🅰 🏠 |●| HOSTELLERIE DU VAL-D'AURE

Route de Saint-Lary; it's on the D929.
☎ 05.62.98.60.63 ➡ 05.62.98.68.99
Closed 20 Sept–24 Dec. **Disabled access. Swimming pool. Garden. TV. Car park.**

An attractive riverside establishment in a huge shady park. Rooms 225–300F with shower/wc or bath. Some have a terrace. They like you to stay half board, 230–295F per person, in season. The 65F lunchtime *menu-express* is a classic, but it's not served on Sunday. Other menus 95–120F. Attentive, unobtrusive service from the owners, Christine and Claude, who give good advice about local walks. You can hire mountain bikes, play tennis, and swim in the heated pool or in the sulphur spring where people have been taking the waters since Roman times. Free half-bottle of local wine (after your first whole day) as well as a welcome apéritif.

AUCH   32000

🅰 |●| LA TABLE D'HÔTE

7 rue Lamartine; it's between the cathedral and the Jacobin museum
☎ 05.62.05.55.62
Closed Sun evening, Wed, and Jan. **Disabled access.**

A discreet little place with space for only twenty in the cosy and rustic cosy dining room. The *menu du jour* at 70F is particularly good value, and it's best to book if you're determined to taste their famous speciality – Hamburgers Gascon (lunch or dinner). There's another menu at 100F. Terrific welcome from the young owners. Free house apéritif, coffee or *digestif*.

🅰 |●| RESTAURANT JARDIN DES SAVEURS

2 pl. de la Libération (Centre).
☎ 05.62.61.71.99

This place has a big reputation but you can enjoy the quality of the cooking on the cheapest set menu, 120F, which lists the likes of duck *terrine* with green peppercorns and herbs and farmhouse chicken roasted with bacon. The more you spend, the more luxurious the ingredients. The quality of the welcome and the service are of the standard you'd expect in a posh place like this.

There are three other menus: "*Tradition*" 140F, "*Club*" 240F and "*Découverte de Gascogne*" 390F. *À la carte* prices go off the scale but they don't mind if you order only one dish. There's also a coffee menu. Free coffee or *digestif* (except over public holidays).

MONTAUT-LES-CRÉNEAUX   32810 (10KM E)

I●I LE PAPILLON

How to get there: it's on the N21, 6km from the centre of town, in the direction of Agen.
☎ 05.62.65.51.20.
Closed Mon evening, Tues, the Feb school holidays, and a fortnight Aug/Sept.
Disabled access. Garden. Car park.

Good restaurant in a modern building. Mainly meat dishes here, tradition, though there are also few fish dishes. On the land side of the menu, try the *cassoulet* with Gascon beans, the *aiguillettes* of duck with wild mushrooms and bilberries on the sea side, opt for the smooth oyster soup with scallop shavings, the sole stuffed with *foie gras*, or the *millefeuille* of seafood with sesame seed and sweet pepper *coulis*. Traditional and innovative at the same time. The 78F menu (weekday lunchtime) includes wine, then there are menus 98–225F – the middle-range ones are good value.

AUDRESSEIN   09800

🧗 🛏 I●I L'AUBERGE D'AUDRESSEIN**

Route de Luchon (Centre); it's12km from Saint-Girons, at the mouth of the vallée du Biros.
☎ 05.61.96.11.80 ➡ 05.61.96.82.96
Closed 15 Nov–1 March.

The sturdy walls of this 19th-century forge house one of the area's better restaurants. The terrace overlooks a stream. The cooking is some of the best in Ariège and prices are extremely reasonable – menus 115–195F: duck breast *ravioli*, duck *confit* with onion marmalade, cheese mousse with morel broth, tartlet with root vegetables, gizzards *confit* with warm vinaigrette, *cassoulet*, and sautéed sea bream with fennel and pesto. Pleasant double rooms 110F with basin, up to 260F with bath. 10% discount on the room rate April–June and Oct to 15 Nov.

ARGEIN   09800 (3KM W)

🧗 🛏 I●I HOSTELLERIE DE LA TERRASSE

It's on the Portet-d'Aspet road.
☎ 05.61.96.70.11

Closed 15 Nov–1 Feb.

A nice little mountain hotel offering a lovely welcome and good food. The stellar attractions here are the trout or ham cooked on a heated stone and the absolutely superb terrace. There's a 70F weekday menu, then others at 100F and 180F. A few modest rooms at 260F – ask for one with a view of the mountain. Free apéritif and 10% discount on the room rate.

AULON   65240

I●I AUBERGE DES ARYELETS

How to get there: take the D30.
☎ 05.62.39.95.59
Closed Sun evening–Tues out of season, mid-Nov to mid-Dec and ten days May/June.

A typical mountain dining room with timbers and beams, a mezzanine floor and a fireplace. The decor has been brightened by Provençal tablecloths and napkins and a few watercolours. Cuisine is rooted firmly in the local tradition: *garbure* which is broth with pickled goose, lamb steak with shallots and honey, duck breast with bilberries, *foie gras*, upside-down tomato tart, and *raclette* (melted cheese). Menus 89–145F. The place is impeccably clean and the service is friendly and swift. They put a few tables on the terrace in fine weather. It's probably worth booking in high summer.

AULUS-LES-BAINS   09140

🧗 🛏 I●I HÔTEL DE FRANCE**

rue Principale (Centre).
☎ 05.61.96.00.90 ➡ 05.61.96.03.29
Closed mid-Oct to mid-Dec.
Garden. Lock-up car park.

A quiet, charmingly old-fashioned country hotel where you get a warm welcome. Reasonable rooms 140F with basin, 180F with washing facilities or shower, 200F with bath. Good home cooking with menus 58–90F. *À la carte*, there's grilled duck breast, duck *confit*, trout with almonds and calf's sweetbreads with morels. Half board, 210F per person, is good value. The garden leads down to a mountain stream. Free apéritif or coffee.

AUVILLAR   82340

🛏 I●I HÔTEL-RESTAURANT L'HORLOGE**

pl. de l'Horloge (Centre).
☎ 05.63.39.91.61 ➡ 05.63.39.75.20

Closed the second fortnight in Jan.

The pretty village is one of the pilgrimage stops on the way to Santiago de Compostela. The restaurant caters for all appetites and all pockets. It's a charming place and has a superb terrace under theshady plane trees. For lunch, the *formule* "*bouchon*" is ideal, but, if you can afford it, go for the gourmet option. The young chef has real class – try his south-west specialities *à la carte*. Menus 155–320F. They create a welcoming yet smart atmosphere. It's also an ideal spot to stay, with very clean doubles 260–300F. Free apéritif.

BARDIGUES   82340 (4KM S)

|●| AUBERGE DE BARDIGUES

It's on the D11, a 5-min drive from the motorway.
☎ 05.63.39.05.58

A typical restaurant in a tiny, charming village, run by Camille and Cyril, a very young couple. The dining room on the first floor has a contemporary decor and splendid stone walls. There's a beautiful, shady terrace opening onto the village and the surrounding countryside. The cuisine is intelligently prepared, light, tasty and fresh: *millefeuille* of salmon and artichoke and veal *blanquette* are delicate and tasty. The weekday lunch *menu du jour* for 58F includes wine, there are individual dishes at 48F and *menu-cartes* 98–145F. As you would expect, the dishes change frequently and the wine is not too expensive.

DUNES   82340 (12.5KM W)

|●| RESTAURANT LES TEMPLIERS

1 pl. des Martyrs; it's under the arcades. Take the D12 for Donzac then the D30.
☎ 05.63.39.86.21
Closed Sun evening, Mon, and Sat lunchtime and Tues Nov–April.

A nice, local restaurant prettily set on a lovely village square. The dining room is bright and cosy. The lunch menu (not served weekends and public holidays) offers refined local dishes for very affordable prices: quail salad with sour cherries, sea trout *tartare*, fish *soufflé* with crayfish cream sauce, *crépinette* of stuffed guinea-fowl with cabbage and warm apples in cinnamon *coulis*. Other menus 118–330F.

AX-LES-THERMES   09110

⅔ ☆ |●| L'ORRY LE SAQUET

It's on the N20, 1km from Ax-les-Thermes going

towards Andorra.
☎ 05.61.64.31.30 ➡ 05.61.64.00.31
Closed Tues evening, Wed and Thurs lunchtime except during school holidays. **TV. Car park**.

The stiff climb to the top is well worth the effort. The twenty or so rooms in this hotel have all been refurbished and have names of flowers rather than numbers. Doubles 250F with bath. It's a homely, lived-in kind of place. The 105F weekday menu is very good, listing rabbit in jelly flavoured with ceps, shoulder of lamb with whisky in a potato crust and *clafoutis* (custard baked with fresh fruit). Other menus, 155–195F, have excellent surprises including their speciality, twice-cooked pigeon. Free apéritif.

⅔ ☆ |●| LE GRILLON**

rue Saint-Udaut (Southeast); it's 300m from pl. du Breihl.
☎ 05.61.64.31.64 ➡ 05.61.64.25.48
✉ info@hotel-le-grillon.com
Restaurant closed Tues, Wed except in the school holidays, and mid-Oct to early Dec. **TV. Car park**.

A lovely mountain lodge run by Nanette and Philippe, a nice, energetic young couple who know the area well and can organise hikes or snowshoe expeditions in winter. Comfortable rooms 260–280F for a double with shower/wc or bath. You can have half board or full board, and hiking and skiing packages are available. The cooking is excellent. Several dishes have subtle combinations of sweet and savoury flavours such as the house duck *confit* with a cider-flavoured *caramel*, salmon with vanilla, and *croustillant* of duck with mountain honey. Menus 98–170F, and the restaurant is always open for residents. 10% discount Sept–June.

BAGNÈRES-DE-BIGORRE   65200

☆ |●| HÔTEL D'ALBRET**

26 rue de l'Horloge (Centre).
☎ 05.62.95.00.90
Closed Dec.

The hotel has a pretty Art-Déco façade and it's on a corner in the quiet and attractive place d'Albret. Old-style rooms and they're quite big. They've been repainted in fresh colours and the furniture is pretty. The bathrooms have old-fashioned shoe-box baths. There's no double glazing but the road is not noisy. Rooms with washing facilities 140F (shower along the landing, at a charge of 10F), or bath 200F. The Franco-Belgian couple who run the place make you feel very welcome. Good value for money.

⌂ |●| HÔTEL DE LA PAIX**

9 rue de la République.
☎ 05.62.95.20.60 ➡ 05.62.91.09.88
Closed Dec to mid-Jan. **Garden. TV.**

With sparkling white and pink fabrics in the hall, it's kitsch as you like but the facilities are very good and the welcome can't be faulted. The rooms are all different (ask to see more than one) and offer good value for money. They're set around a patio sun-trap or look onto the garden and numbers 19 and 20 even have small balconies. Doubles from 150F with basin to 350F with bath. There are three dining rooms where traditional dishes are served: trout with girolles, steak with wild mushrooms or duck breast with fruit sauce. Menu at 72F or 150F *à la carte*. The place sometimes hosts business seminars, so it's best to book.

⚹ |●| CRÊPERIE DE L'HORLOGE

12 rue Victor-Hugo.
☎ 05.62.95.37.12
Closed evenings except July–Aug, Sun and Mon.

The decor is very pretty – musical scores, old typewriters, a set of scales, time pieces, pots of preserved fruits and blue hydrangeas – give the place the feel of a Parisian bistro. The dish of the day, which costs around 45F, is sometimes surprisingly original: fish curry with Thai rice, or *tajine* of lamb and chilli, for example. They also offer a wide choice of *crêpes*, for 50–70F each. There's a young, alternative feel about the place and they play Latin American music. Nice terrace in summer. Free coffee.

⚹ |●| LE BIGOURDAN

14 rue Victor-Hugo.
☎ 05.62.95.20.20
Closed Mon out of season.

On the first floor of an old, traditional house in a pedestrian street, so it's not noisy. Hefty beams, rough-cast walls, floral fabrics and still lifes on the walls. Good regional specialities cooked using fresh produce – and the menu's as long as your arm. There's a huge choice but quite a lot of supplements on the first menu (64F), or there are ten other menus up to 300F: ravioli with horn of plenty mushrooms, *terrine* of pig's trotters and *foie gras*, *gâteau* of scallops and ceps, duck breast, and rasperries *au gratin*. Free house apéritif.

LESPONNE   65710 (10KM S)

⚹ ⌂ DOMAINE DE RAMONJUAN**

How to get there; take the D935 from Bagnères to Baudéau, turn right onto the D29; leaving Lesponne in

the direction of Chiroulet, it's on the right.
☎ 05.62.91.75.75 ➡ 05.62.91.74.54
Closed Sun evening and a week in April.

This farm, at 800m, has been turned into a nice hotel without losing its homely feeling. The pleasant rooms are named after flowers. Doubles with shower 260–310F, half board is compulsory in high season at 260–320F per person. They offer a host of activities including tennis, volleyball, rafting, ballooning and archery, and there's a gym with sauna and Jacuzzi in an old riverside barn. They hold a good number of conferences so it's advisable to book. Free apéritif and 10% discount on the room rate Sept–June.

BAGNÈRES-DE-LUCHON   31110

MONTAUBAN-DE-LUCHON   31110 (2KM E)

⌂ |●| LES CASCADES*

How to get there: head for the church of Montauban and then follow the signs for the Herran forest road.
☎ 05.61.79.79.16 ➡ 05.61.79.83.09
Closed mid-Oct to end March. **TV. Garden. Car park.**

It is advisable to book at this exceptional establishment. The house is a listed building and it's in a wonderful location, hanging on to the mountainside in the middle of an enormous park, just 45m from a gushing waterfall. You have to leave your car at the bottom and walk up, but you'll enjoy the scenery and the peace and quiet. In summer you eat outside to enjoy the superb views over the valley, otherwise you eat in the elegant dining room that's black and blue. Wonderful traditional cooking, with *pétéram* (stew of sheep's trotters and tripe) and *pistache* (braised leg of mutton with haricot beans). Their meat specialities include beef with ceps, and duck breast with pickled shallots. Lunch menu 110F and 140–170F on Sunday only. *À la carte* you can expect to pay 200F per person. There are a few double rooms; you'll pay 200F with washing facilities and 230F with shower/wc. Half board if you stay for three nights or more, 250F. There are some lovely walks in the forest and for 5F the owners can take you on a fifteen-minute hike.

BARÈGES   65120

⚹ |●| AUBERGE DU LIENZ, CHEZ LOUISETTE

How to get there: 3km from Barèges, going in the direction of Tourmalet, follow the road to the Plateau de

Lienz.
☎ 05.62.92.67.17
Closed Nov.

One of the nicest spots in the valley, surrounded by trees at the beginning of the route around lakes Gière and Néouvielle. In winter, this is where the ski runs finish. It's a bit like the sort of country inn you might find near a big town, not least because of its glorious summer terrace. The *"Petit Menu Randonner"*, 90F, gives you a starter, a main course such as braised ham, and cream cheese to finish but the more expensive menus, 135–200F, have a wider choise of more interesting dishes: *croustillant* of duck *confit*, sliced duck breast with bilberries, poached trout in Madiran or, *à la carte*, lamb chops. Desserts are on the pricey side. Speedy service. Free Kir (with bilberry liqueur) or *génépi*.

BASSOUES   32320

🏧 🛋 |●| HOSTELLERIE DU DONJON*

Centre; take the D943 through Montesquiou.
☎ 05.62.70.90.04
Hotel closed the first week in Sept, and Jan.
Restaurant closed Sat. **Garden**. **Car park**.

Bassoues is a delightful 12th-century fortified town and this is an attractive, welcoming hotel. The owner checks you in with good humour, while his wife, who runs the kitchens dishes up good family cooking at reasonable prices. The rooms are charming, 150F with basin or 200–215F with shower/wc or bath, there's one with a corner sitting room at 240F. The rooms are decorated with furniture that the owner restores. Some of the beds sag a bit. Country-style dining room and Belgo-Gascon cooking. Menu at 62F (not Sun) then 95–205F. There's a pretty, peaceful terrace in good weather – make the most of it before the owners retire. Free apéritif.

BELCASTEL   12390

🏧 🛋 |●| HÔTEL-RESTAURANT DU VIEUX PONT***

It's near the castle.
☎ 05.65.64.52.29 ➡ 05.65.64.44.32
Closed Sun evening, Mon and Tues lunchtime, and Jan to mid-March. **TV**. **Car park**.

Sisters Michèle and Nicole Fagegaltier have turned their beloved childhood home into a much-admired establishment. They serve some of the best cooking in the area, updating old family recipes and drawing upon wonderful

ingredients. Try artichokes and asparagus with cream and vanilla oil, pigeon breast in ginger breadcrumbs and juniper, ceps with garlic, crispy spinach and parsley, bream stuffed with mussels, roast kid with cress *coulis* or caramel tart with juniper. Some of the dishes come at a price but there's a range of menus 150–400F. You get to the hotel by crossing a 15th-century bridge. The accommodation is as good as the cooking – the rooms are bright and well maintained and full of the little extras that make all the difference. Doubles 430F with shower/wc and 470F with bath. Outstanding welcome and service. Free coffee.

BIERT   09320

🛋 |●| AUBERGE DU GYPAÈTE BARBU

pl. de l'Église (Centre); it's 4km from Massat on the road from St. Girons and Tarascon-sur-Ariège.
☎ 05.65.53.97.02 ➡ 05.65.35.95.92
Closed Sun evening Oct–June except in school holidays and 2 Jan–1 Feb, the last week in June and Sept.

Camille Coutanceau took off from the family hotel in Moarsat to spread his own wings. He and his wife took over this village bistro on the square, refurbished it beautifully and then gave it the name of a rare bird of prey which has been recently re-introduced into the wild round here. The menus, 80–165F, are simple and superb: veal sweetbreads *à la massatoise*, pan-fried *foie gras* with tart apples and goat's cheese *soufflé*. There's a pretty terrace and some very basic rooms at 160F.

CAHORS   46000

🏧 🛋 HÔTEL DE FRANCE***

252 av. Jean-Jaurès (Centre).
☎ 05.65.35.16.76 ➡ 05.65.22.01.08
Closed a fortnight in Dec.
Disabled access. **TV**. **Private garage**.

Modern, functional architecture in this eighty-room hotel. Doubles with shower/wc at 250F and with bath 370F. The ones overlooking the courtyard are quieter. They all have a direct phone and mini-bar and some have air conditioning. 10% discount Nov–Feb.

🏧 🛋 |●| HÔTEL-RESTAURANT À L'ESCARGOT**

5 bd. Gambetta.
☎ 05.65.35.07.66 ➡ 05.65.53.92.38
Closed Sun evening, Mon, a fortnight over Christmas and New Year and a fortnight in May. **TV**.

A banal exterior but an attractive interior; the

rooms, in an annexe away from the main building, are comfortable and have good facilities. There are beautiful views of the church or private gardens. Doubles 290F with shower/wc. Number 9 sleeps three and has a mezzanine and a big bay window. Hearty buffet breakfast 35F. You'll get good value for money in the restaurant, which opens onto the street. Set menus 64–110F: snails, *salade Quercyoise*, good grills and home-made chips. Non-smokers have their own dining room. There are chess games every Friday evening. Informal and very friendly reception. It's advisable to book accommodation. 10% discount on the room rate Sept–June.

🏨 |●| LE GRAND HÔTEL TERMINUS***

5 av. Charles-Freycinet (West); it's 50m from the train station.
☎ 05.65.53.32.00 ➡ 05.65.53.32.26
📧 terminus.balaudre@wanadoo.fr
Restaurant closed Sun, Mon and the second fortnight in Nov. **Disabled access. TV. Car park**.

This delightful hotel was built at the turn of the last century by the current owner's grandfather and has never been out of the family. It has been thoroughly renovated, though they've taken care to preserve its period style. The rooms are large, pleasant and air-conditioned. Double from 370F with shower/wc. There's an award-winning restaurant with menus from 200F, or a cheaper *formule* served in the bar.

|●| RESTAURANT LE TROQUET DES HALLES

55 rue Saint-Maurice (Centre).
☎ 05.65.22.15.81
Closed Sun. **Disabled access**.

Non-stop service. This French version of a greasy spoon has been going for a good half century. It heaves with market porters, stall-holders, blue-collar workers and tourists, all here to fill up on robust home cooking at pre-war prices. For 40F you get soup and the dish of the day, and for 60F you get three courses. Incredible value. Dishes served with a selection of two or three vegetables. On Saturday mornings the place is open from 5.30am so if you've got an early start or had a late night you can have a substantial breakfast.

|●| AU FIL DES DOUCEURS

90 quai de la Verrerie (East).
☎ 05.65.22.13.04
Closed Sun evening, Mon and Jan.

The chef in this riverside restaurant has his produce brought in from outlying farms and cooks everything with precision and artistry. He used to be a pastry cook, so try his *foie gras* upside-down tart. The sauces are special, too, in particular the *magret* or duck *foie gras* cooked with seasonal fruits, and the desserts are delicious. Lunch *formule* at 75F and other menus 105–225F. Efficient, friendly service.

🏃 |●| LE BISTROT DU CAHORS

46 rue Daurade.
☎ 05.65.53.10.55
Closed Mon evening and Tues.

A small restaurant with a terrace on a pretty, shady square. It's not a bar but you can try some good local Cahors wines by the glass or the bottle, with your food. A good tasty meal here won't break the bank – dishes include parmesan salad, risotto with Cahors wine, ham with broad beans, good goat's cheese and desserts that include *clafoutis* or baked apples. A single menu at 80F, *à la carte* around 100F. Dishes are generously served and attractively presented. Free house apéritif.

|●| RESTAURANT LA GARENNE

It's on the N20 in the direction of Souillac, 5km outside Cahors.
☎ 05.65.35.40.67
Closed Tues evening and Wed, except mid-July to end Aug, and Feb–10 March. **Garden. Car park**.

This is a substantial private house built in 1846 and wonderfully decorated in the style of a country inn. Reception is pleasant and courteous. The cooking is full of imagination, originality and flair: scallops with truffle butter, pan-fried escalope of *foie gras*, rack of lamb with unpeeled cloves of garlic, eggs scrambled with truffles, and so on. Menus 95–250F.

|●| RESTAURANT LE RENDEZ-VOUS

49 rue Clément-Marot.
☎ 05.65.22.65.10 ➡ 05.65.35.11.05
Closed Sun and Mon out of season, Sun and Mon lunchtime July–Aug, a fortnight in the Easter school holidays.

A modern dining room with a mezzanine where they show work by local artists. The cuisine is simple but inventive. Try the *foie gras* ravioli, zander with baby vegetables and *marbré* of goat's cheese. Weekday lunch menu at 99F or 125F.

PRADINES   46090 (3KM NW)

🏃 🏨 |●| LE CLOS GRAND**

Laberaudi; take the D8 in the direction of Pradines Luzech.
☎ 05.65.35.04.39 ➡ 05.65.22.56.69
Swimming pool. Garden. TV. Car park.

A lovely, provincial inn with a big lush garden and

a swimming pool. The rooms are very pleasant and comfortable, 265F with shower, 285–325F with shower/wc, 335F with bath. Those in the annexe have views over the fields. The restaurant has a very good reputation and their specialities include *chaud froid* of *foie gras*, duck breast with peaches and steak with ceps. The cheapest set menu costs 87F (not served Sun), then 130F and 180F. Free apéritif.

ALBAS   46140 (25KM W)

|●| IMHOTEP

à Rivière Haute (East).
☎ 05.65.30.70.91
Closed Sun evening, Mon and the first fortnight in Jan.

Wonderfully located on the banks of the Lot, this restaurant is out of the ordinary. It's run by a father and son team. Strains of jazz float through the pretty dining room, which is decorated with some splendid photographs of the region. Father is in charge in the kitchen. Duck is the speciality, cooked simply and skilfully: duck breast kebab with sautéed potatoes and ceps, *foie gras* either semi-cooked or pan-fried, duck brochette with curry, truffle salad and duck *civet*. Menus 80–250F. There's a small terrace. You can also buy *foie gras* to take away.

CAHUZAC-SUR-VERE   81140

|●| LA FALAISE

Route de Cordes; it's 15km north of Gaillac.
☎ 05.63.33.96.31
Closed Sun evening, Mon except public holidays, a fortnight end-Nov/Dec and mid-Jan to mid-Feb.

Refined cuisine from Guillaume Salvan, who has a magical talent for combining unexpected flavours in regional dishes and new inventions. The dining room is bright and pleasant. Weekday menu 120F, then 140–250F. Dishes change with the seasons and the produce on the market: snails with artichokes and ham, red peppers stuffed with salt cod, the tenderest haunch of veal, and so on. They give well-judged advice about the wine; their list is interesting and features good local Plageoles. The desserts are also excellent.

CARMAUX   81400

|●| RESTAURANT LA MOUETTE

4 pl. Jean-Jaurès.
☎ 05.63.36.79.90 ➡ 05.63.76.40.76
Closed Sun, Mon evening and ten days in Oct.

This is the best gastronomic restaurant in Carmaux. Monsieur Régis has devised a series of interesting menus, 82–260F, from a weekday lunch menu at 59F, to a menu "*Jaurès*" and a "*surprise*" menu. Specialities include grilled kid, grilled monkfish fillet with garlic and parsley, grilled *andouillette* salad and *petit-gris* snails in flaky pastry.

CASTELNAU-DE-MONTMIRAL   81140

☆ 🏠 |●| AUBERGE DES ARCADES

It's in the main square.
☎ 05.63.33.20.88

Decent, very simple rooms, 180F with basin, 200F with shower. Some overlook the medieval village square and there are some really nice ones under the eaves. There's a straightforward, hearty *menu du jour* at 62F, or you could opt for the 95F menu and have smoked duck salad, the house speciality of wild boar stew, cheese and dessert. There are other menus 95–200F. Free apéritif.

LARROQUE   81140 (14KM NW)

☆ |●| AU VAL D'ARAN

Centre.
☎ 05.63.33.11.15
Closed evenings out of season, Sat, 24 Dec–18 Jan.

A typical village inn with a comfortable dining room and terrace. The chummy owners mix easily with the customers. The weekday lunch menu, 68F, starts with a lavish plate of *charcuterie*, followed by *crudités*, a main course, cheese and dessert. Other menus, 98–155F, list boar *civet* or stew, snails Spanish-style, grills over the open fire and so on. Free coffee.

CASTELNAU-MAGNOAC   65230

☆ 🏠 |●| HÔTEL DUPONT**

pl. de l'Église; take the D929 from Lannemezan.
☎ 05.62.39.80.02 ➡ 05.62.39.82.20
Swimming pool. Disabled access.

The hotel has celebrated its 150th anniversary and is the standard-bearer of all that's good in traditional hotel-keeping. The spacious rooms, 180–220F, are very welcoming, scrupulously clean and good value. You'll be woken by church bells. The swimming pool is open in July and August only. Generously flavoured local dishes in the large, rustic dining room. Menus 60–120.

Specialities include casserole of duck breast, thigh of duck with orange, fresh liver with three fruits, sautéed chicken *paysanne* and a delicious, and unexpected, mussel soup. Free apéritif.

CASTELSARRASIN 82100

☎ HÔTEL MARCEILLAC**

54 rue de l'Égalité; it's in a road off the pl. de la Liberté.
☎ 05.63.32.30.10 ➡ 05.62.32.39.52
Garden. TV. Garage.

There's a surprise when you walk into this seemingly ordinary hotel, purpose-built in the early 19th century. The rooms overlook a small interior courtyard with a glass roof and the reception area is in a kind of glass cage. The whole place is light and airy. The rooms are delightful and the furniture, though it is as old as the hotel, has been well cared for. Doubles with shower/wc or bath 210–260F. Delightful welcome.

CASTERA-VERDUZAN 32410

⋊ |●| LA FLORIDA

☎ 05.62.68.13.22 ➡ 05.62.68.10.33
Closed Sun evening and Mon except public holidays, and a week in the Feb school holidays.

A very old establishment which used to be run by Angèle, the current owner's grandmother. Try calf's sweetbreads *façon Angèle*, upside-down tart with duck *foie gras* and caramelized sauce, and fresh duck liver with Gascon Floc. An excellent weekday lunch menu for 75F, others 130–230F. Free coffee.

CASTRES 81100

⋊ ☎ HÔTEL RIVIÈRE**

10 quai Tourcaudière (Centre); it's on the banks of the Agout, opposite the old tanners' houses.
☎ 05.63.59.04.53 ➡ 05.63.59.61.97
TV. Garage.

The attractive decor – lots of reproductions of Impressionist paintings – and the congenial staff make this a pleasant hotel. The pretty roooms smell fresh and clean. You'll pay 250F with shower/wc and buffet breakfast costs 35F. The rooms overlooking the embankment can be noisy, and the terrace gets noisy in summer. Free breakfast after the second night.

☎ |●| HÔTEL DE L'EUROPE***

5 rue Victor-Hugo (Centre); 30m from pl. Jean-Jaurès.
☎ 05.63.59.00.33 ➡ 05.63.59.21.38
TV.

This glorious 17th-century house was discovered and restored by a group of young people with a passion for art and architecture; it has the feel of an artist's studio. Each room is better than the last – a subtle balance of glass and warm brick, splendid beams and designer furniture, dressed stone and modern bathrooms. Doubles, 335F, all have bathrooms and phones, and some have a mini-bar. They offer an overnight rate for dinner, bed and breakfast for 350F. In the restaurant, there's a 52F self-service buffet of savoury and sweet dishes and menus 100–120F. Specialities include *cassoulet* cooked in duck fat with sausage and duck *confit,* and huge dessert platters. An extremely good hotel.

⋊ ☎ |●| HÔTEL RENAISSANCE***

17 rue Victor-Hugo (Centre).
☎ 05.63.59.30.42 ➡ 05.63.72.11.57
Restaurant closed Sun and Mon lunchtime. **TV.**

Alain Escaudemaison travelled the world during his career as a TV cameraman, but he's finally put down roots in this hotel in the old part of town. He has renovated this enormous 17th-century building with vaulted ceilings, arches, countless nooks and crannies and ancient beams. You'll get a good night's sleep in the beautifully decorated, large rooms. Double with shower/wc 400F, with bath 400–725F. There are some superb suites with canopied beds and they've all got telephone sockets for Internet access. They offer *table d'hôte* for residents in the evening but you'll need to book. There's a weekday menu at 68F or others 100–250F. Good home cooking, featuring local dishes. If you eat *à la carte* you'll spend about 120F. Try the snail casserole *Renaissance*, the house speciality. They offer golf weekends. Free breakfast.

⋊ |●| RESTAURANT LA MANDRAGORE

1 rue Malpas (Centre); it's near pl. Jean-Jaurès.
☎ 05.63.59.51.27
Closed Sun, Mon lunchtime and Jan

This fairly new, fashionable restaurant is renowned for its futuristic designer decor *à la* Philippe Stark and meticulous cooking. The lunchtime menu, 75F, gets you a starter, main course and dessert, each course accompanied by a glass of selected wine.

Other menus 90–240F, from the "*fantaisie du moment*" menu – warm salad of skate with herbs, duck breast in wine, cheese and *millefeuille* of seasonal fruit – to the five-course "*menu surprise*". *À la carte*, dishes include a delicious crab *parmentier*, veal *piccata* with noodles and asparagus, turbot in red *bisque* and sole fillet with crayfish. The wine list is as thick as a phone directory, which is hardly surprising when you learn that the proprietor used to work at *Le Grand Écuyer* and was chosen as Belgium's best *sommelier*. He'll choose something good just for you and it won't cost a fortune. Free apéritif.

BURLATS   81100 (10KM NE)

⅍ ≜ LE CASTEL DE BURLATS

8 pl. du 9-Mai-1945; take the D89 or the D4 then follow the signs to Burlats.
☎ 05.63.35.29.20 ➡ 05.63.51.14.69
Disabled access. TV. Car park.

A splendid château built between the 14th and 16th centuries. The owners have retained the natural charm of the building and the interior without it feeling chi-chi in any way. The comfortable rooms are romantic, their floors laid with old hand-made tiles. Doubles 350F with shower/wc or 420F with bath. There's a working open fireplace in one room. The tearoom is in the huge salon, which also has a handsome billiard room. The extensive gardens are attractive. A very elegant, chic place. Free aperitif.

ROQUECOURBE   81210 (10KM N)

⅍ IOI LA CHAUMIÈRE

14 allée du Général-de-Gaulle; coming from Castres, go through the village and it's on the right.
☎ 05.63.75.60.88
Closed Sun evening, Mon, three weeks in Jan and the first week in July.

A family-run restaurant on a pretty square. You will be welcomed with kindness and the cuisine is excellent. There's a huge, peaceful dining room at the rear. Menus 100–220F. The *terrine* is served in huge portions, and you can get duck *foie gras*, duck breast with ceps *à la Provençale*, local river trout *façon grand-mère*, tournedos with cream and morels, and a whole host of good local dishes. The *patronne* is sometimes willing to share her otherwise secret recipe for two dishes called *melsa* and *bougnette*. If you're there in raspberry season, ask for the raspberry *gratin*. Free apéritif.

SAINT-SALVY-DE-LA-BALME   81490 (16KM E)

⅍ IOI LE CLOS DU ROC

Centre.
☎ 05.63.50.57.23
Closed Wed and Sun evenings and the first fortnight in Feb. **Disabled access**.

A reliable restaurant in a solid, granite house – it's popular locally, so it may be best to book. The dining room is in a converted barn with enormous beams and the decor is stylish and charming. The cuisine has a good reputation and prices are affordable. They do a weekday lunch menu for 60F, which includes cheese, dessert and wine, and others 90–220F. Specialities include trout gougons, duck thigh in Banyuls wine, knuckle of pork *confit* with peaches and *croustades*. Free aperitif.

DOURGNE   81110 (20KM SW)

⅍ ≜ IOI RESTAURANT DE LA MONTAGNE NOIRE

15 pl. des Promenades.
☎ 05.63.50.31.12
TV.

Take a seat on the pleasant terrace and enjoy the wonderful dishes created by David Gely. The cooking gets away from the predictable duck variations, and reinterprets a few traditional dishes with unusual combinations of flavours – a remarkably light *aumônière* of gizzards *confits* and duck breast, or quail breasts in a potato crust. From June to November you should go for the crayfish in parsley, the pot-roast pigeon or the bass with pickled tomatoes. Excellent desserts include home-made *tiramisù*, strawberry *gratin* and an orange pancake *gâteau*. Menus 69–190F. A few newly opened double rooms from 220F. Free apéritif.

CAUSSADE   82300

⅍ ≜ IOI HÔTEL LARROQUE**

av. de la Gare (Northwest).
☎ 05.63.65.11.77 ➡ 05.63.65.12.04
Closed Sat lunchtime, Sun evening out of season and 21 Dec–15 Jan. **Swimming pool. Garden. TV. Lock-up car park**.

A family business that goes back five generations and has a solid reputation. Guests and atmosphere are both rather elegant and the decor is plush. There's a very pleasant swimming pool and a solarium. Double rooms with en-suite bathrooms 265F – one has a small terrace onto the swimming pool. The restaurant offers regional cuisine with a touch of style in dishes such as zander with three preserves, corn biscuits with *petit-gris* snails flavoured with flat parsley, and iced *nougat* with walnuts. Menus 70–200F. Free apéritif.

MONTEILS   02300 (2KM N)

|●| LE CLOS DE MONTEILS

It's just 2km from the motorway exit.
☎ 05.63.93.30.35

It's minutes from the motorway to this gourmet restaurant, run by chef Bernard Bordaries, who has worked in some of the greatest restaurants in France – and, indeed, the world – before settling in this lovely priory, swathed in Virginia creeper, out in the country meadows. He and his charming wife have created a place of refined charm. *Menu-express* 75F, 95F lunch menu or 145F. Dishes include tart with farm bacon, *charlotte* with goat's cheese and artichokes, jellied oxtail and cheek, sea bream with fennel marmalade and light *anchoïade*, stuffed chicken wing and luscious desserts. There's a terrace for sunny days.

CAUTERETS   65110

🏃 🏠 |●| HÔTEL DU LION D'OR**

12 rue Richelieu (Centre).
☎ 05.62.92.52.87 ➡ 05.62.92.03.67
Closed 1 Oct–20 Dec.

The *Lion d'Or*, run by sisters Bernadette and Rose-Marie, is the oldest hotel in this spa town – the ancient yellow-and-white façade is a bit of a clue. It's gradually been renovated with utmost attention to detail – the lift is camouflaged by a wooden door and there's a wondrous percolator in the bar. The rooms are plush and cosy, with elegant light fittings, old beds and working antique phones; doubles with shower or bath 240–400F. Good home cooking is served in the pleasantly old-fashioned dining room, which is almost the last vestige of the old hotel. Half board from 230F per person. 10% discount on the room rate, except during school holidays.

🏠 |●| LE SACCA

11 bd. Latapie-Flurin.
☎ 05.62.92.50.02 ➡ 05.62.92.64.63
Closed Oct and Nov.

The clientele here mainly come for the

waters. The decor is modern and somewhat stereotypical yet the chef, Jean-Marc, produces excellent cuisine that's the best in Cauterets. He's refined the regional recipes and given pride of place to vegetables – a pretty rare occurance. Try the upside-down tart of *foie gras*, sea bream *à l'Espagnole*, *cassoulet*, duck breast or *confit*. You're served a dish of *amuse-bouches* while you're waiting to order. The plates are hot and the service very professional. Menus 80–165F. Half board, 245F per person, is compulsory July–Aug. The rooms have shower/wc or bath, 250–320F, and some have balconies with a view of the mountains.

🏃 |●| LA FERME BASQUE

It's on the road to Le Cambasque, 4km from Cauterets or 1.2km from the ski resort on the road to Lac d'Ilhéou.
☎ 05.62.92.54.32
Closed Mon–Wed, and Oct–Nov.

Lots of *crêpes* and sandwiches served in this old farm that's been going since 1928. The new owners have added some more elaborate dishes, too, like *garbure* with wild spinach, black pudding with onions, *piperade* (pepper stew), *blanquette* of lamb, lamb chops or lamb stew. Menus 85–115F. In season meals are served on the huge terrace which has a fabulous view down to Cauterets. Léon, a shepherd, likes to talk about his work, while Chantal, who spent twenty years abroad, speaks lots of languages. She's brilliant at managing even the most difficult guests without losing her sense of humour. Free coffee.

CAYLUS   82160

🏠 |●| HÔTEL RENAISSANCE**

av. du Père-Huc.
☎ 05.63.67.06.26 ➡ 05.63.24.03.57
Closed Sun evening, Mon, a fortnight in Jan and ten days in May.

The restaurant is in the main street of this very pretty hamlet. The rooms are modern and comfortable – doubles 220F with shower or 260F with bath. Single rooms 180F. Weekday lunch menu 65F, others 100–200F.

CONDOM   32100

🏃 🏠 HÔTEL LE LOGIS DES CORDELIERS**

rue de la Paix; it's near the bandstand, heading towards Agen.

☎ 05.62.28.03.68 ➡ 05.62.68.29.03
📧 le-logis-des-cordeliers@wanadoo.fr
Closed Jan. **Garden. Swimming pool. TV. Garage.**

A quiet, modern hotel in the centre of town; it's surrounded by greenery and has roses climbing over it. Monsieur and Mme Comte go out of their way to take care of you and can give you information about the locality. Rooms are spacious and very comfortable; the ones over the street cost 270F while those over the garden and the swimming pool cost 370F. Free coffee.

🎋 ❘●❘ L'ORIGAN

4 rue du Cadeo; it's on the way to the church, opposite the church school.
☎ 05.62.68.24.84
Closed Sun, Mon (Mon lunchtime in July), and Sept.

Popular pizzeria in the old quarter. At "Jacques' place" you feel as if you're eating with friends. Congenial welcome, attentive service and tasty cooking. Pizzas, pasta and huge salads, escalope of veal *à la parmigiana* or house steak. Set menus 65F at lunch for a main course and a dessert, 50F only for a main course or 100–130F *à la carte*. The tables outside on the street are always full when the weather's good. Free apéritif.

🎋 ❘●❘ MOULIN DU PETIT GASCON

Route d'Eauze; it's on the outskirts of town, on the river bank opposite the stadium.
☎ 05.62.28.28.42
Closed Mon except July–Aug.

A very special place that is so picturesque you could almost believe it was built as a bucolic film set. The terrace is surrounded by greenery on all sides. The cooking is light and prices are reasonable: duck breast in pastry, semi-cooked *foie gras* and home-made *cassoulet*, *osso bucco*, veal sweetbreads and a delicious bitter chocolate *gâteau*. Weekday lunch menu 90F, others 120–185F. In summer, you dine by candlelight. Ask the *patronne* about river cruises. Free apéritif.

CONQUES   12320

☎ ❘●❘ AUBERGE SAINT-JACQUES**

rue Principale (Centre); it's near the abbey.
☎ 05.65.72.86.36 ➡ 05.65.72.82.47
Closed Mon out of season and Jan. **TV. Disabled access. Car park.**

The one hotel in Conques that everyone can afford – it's very good value. Pleasant staff. Clean rooms, some of them very romantic.

Doubles 200–300F. The restaurant serves local dishes but don't expect miracles. *Formule brasserie* 86F and menus from 105F.

☎ ❘●❘ LE DOMAINE DE CAMBELONG***

It's at the bottom of the village next to the Dourdou.
☎ 05.65.72.84.77 ➡ 05.65.72.83.91
Closed Sun evening and Mon 15 Oct–15 March.
Swimming pool. TV. Car park.

One of the few remaining water mills on the Dourdou, in a magnificent setting. Very comfortable rooms, some with balconies or private terraces overlooking the river. Doubles 490F with shower/wc and 580–780F with bath. You eat as well as you sleep: *foie gras* with fig *compote*, zander with potatoes, duck with mashed potato and *fondant foie gras*, and fine tart with cep caviar. The inspiration extends to the desserts – try *crème brûlée* or meringue *millefeuille* with chestnuts. Lunch menu 200F (except Sun) including apéritif and wine, then 195F and 250F.

GRAND-VABRE   12320 (5.5KM N)

❘●❘ CHEZ MARIE

How to get there: by the D901.
☎ and ➡ 05.65.69.84.55
Closed Mon–Wed and Thurs evening mid-May to mid-Sept, and Jan. **Garden. Car park.**

A delightful little inn in this tiny village in the wilds of the Aveyron. It's decorated simply, with a covered terrace where you can eat outdoors. Staff are amiable and the service is attentive. Quality produce in traditional dishes: sweetbreads with ceps, chicken with chanterelles and roast kid with sorrel, and there's *estofinado* in season. Nothing wildly out of the ordinary because Marie prefers to deliver good-quality, traditional, delicious dishes. Menus 78–130F. It's best to book.

CORDES   81170

🎋 ☎ HÔTEL DE LA CITÉ**

rue Haute; it's in the upper town.
☎ 05.63.56.03.53 ➡ 05.63.56.02.47
Closed 15 Oct–1 April.

Eight charming and characterful rooms in this complex of medieval buildings with high ceilings and stout beams. Some have fantastic views over the countryside, and all have modern facilities. Prices are very affordable for a tourist town – 295F for a double with shower/wc or bath. Free coffee.

⅍ ♠ |●| HOSTELLERIE DU PARC**

Les Cabannes.
☎ 05.63.56.02.59 ➡ 05.63.56.18.03
Closed Sun evening and Mon out of season.
Swimming pool. Garden. TV. Car park.

This substantial stone country house, which overlooks an old park and garden, has a large rustic dining room. Efficient welcome and speedy service. Weekday menu 100F, others 150–220F. Chef Claude Izard is a force to be reckoned with. He chairs an enormous number of associations and has appointed himself the champion of authentic local French cooking. His specialities prove the point – try rabbit with cabbage, *petit-gris* snails *à la tarnaise*, or fresh *foie gras*. Sometimes shellfish dishes appear on the menu. A few simple, quite comfortable rooms, 360F with shower/wc or 380F with bath. Free apéritif and 10% discount on the room rate Nov–March.

EAUZE 32800

⅍ ♠ |●| AUBERGE DU GUINLET*

Route de Castelnau-d'Auzan; take the D43.
☎ 05.62.09.80.84 ➡ 05.62.09.84.50
Closed Fri and Jan. **Disabled access. Swimming pool. Garden. TV. Car park.**

A huge holiday complex in the country offering various options: hotel rooms at 250F, bungalows 1km away on the lakeside at 2000F a week, and camping space. The restaurant produces simple family cooking with one or two regional specialities such as slow-cooked stews, *civets*, *salmis* or baked *croustades*. The 60F weekday menu includes wine, while the other menus up to 160F feature local specialities: duck *confit*, *civets* or *croustade*. There's a Gascon menu at 150F. They offer loads of activities, including tennis, swimming and golf. Free apéritif.

ENDOUFIELLE 32600

|●| LA FERME DE MANON DES HERBES

It's on the D634 between Lombez and Isle-Jourdain.
☎ and ➡ 05.62.07.97.19.
Closed Wed and the New Year's holidays.
Swimming pool. Garden. Car park.

This farm has been lovingly decorated with straw-seated chairs, dried flowers hanging from the beams, flowers and candles on the tables, and a wide open fireplace. There's period furniture and old mirrors on the walls. It has an intimate, warm ambience. Double

rooms have good bathroom facilities, around 380F. Regional dishes, grills on the open fire, fish and seafood appear on the menus 165–275F. Try the house specialities: *foie gras*, pan-fried scallops, salmon *carpaccio* with fresh herbs and tasty desserts.

ENTRAYGUES-SUR-TRUYÈRE 12140

⅍ ♠ |●| LA TRUYÈRE**

60 av. du Pont-de-la-Truyère (Northeast).
☎ 05.65.44.51.10 ➡ 05.65.44.57.78
Closed Mon and 15 Nov–30 March. **Disabled access. Garden. Private car park.**

Service 12.30–1.45pm and 7.30–8.45pm. A nice inn near the Gothic bridge with a pleasant garden. There are 25 double rooms, 200F with shower and 220–285F with bath; some have a view of the river and the valley. The cooking is good, with set menus 70–200F. Try *marbré* of chicken in a chive cream, *cassolette* of snails with a pastry crust, or rabbit *terrine*. À la carte they offer roast monkfish with paprika, lamb tripe *Aveyronnais* and green salad with ham and smoked duck breast. A good little family restaurant. 10% discount on the room rate Sept–June.

♠ |●| HÔTEL DU LION D'OR**

Tour de Ville (Centre); it's in the main street.
☎ 05.65.44.50.01 ➡ 05.65.44.53.43
Disabled access. Swimming pool. Garden. TV. Car park.

Large, solid, stone-built hotel with fifty nice rooms. Doubles 260–420F with shower/wc or bath. The restaurant is separate from the hotel and you can enjoy good traditional dishes, such as stuffed cabbage or trout, and a few more inventive dishes, too. Weekday lunch menu 55F, otherd 70–320F. Some have whirl-pool baths andbalconies overlooking the garden. There's a sauna, a gym, and a pleasant garden where you can swim in the pool or play tennis or crazy golf. Relaxation is the key here.

ESTAING 12190

⅍ ♠ |●| HÔTEL-RESTAURANT AUX ARMES D'ESTAING**

quai du Lot.
☎ 05.65.44.70.02 ➡ 05.65.44.74.54
Closed mid-Nov to beginning of Feb.
TV. Lock-up car park.

A delightful, traditional hotel. The more than

adequate rooms with washing facilities in the main building cost 160F while rooms in the annexe have been nicely renovated and cost 250F with shower/wc or 280F with bath. Very pleasant dining room, though the service can be a bit slow, especially when there are groups in. The cooking is good, tending towards the classical but with one or two unexpected dishes. The chef's repertoire includes salad of lamb's sweetbreads with chanterelle mushrooms, monkfish with star anise and vanilla, duck breast with soft fruit and fillet of veal with *foie gras*. Aligot, which is mashed potatoes with cheese and garlic, has to be ordered ahead of time. Set menus 70–180F. Half board is compulsory in Aug, around 235F per person. Free coffee.

≜ I●I AUBERGE SAINT-FLEURET**

rue François-d'Estaing.
☎ 05.65.44.01.44 ➡ 05.65.44.72.19
Closed Sun evening and Mon out of season.
Garden. TV. Garage.

The outside of this building has been renovated as have the rooms – those overlooking the garden are particularly pleasant. Doubles 200–260F with shower/wc or bath. The chintzy dining room is cosy and decorated in shades of blue. The cooking is traditional – snails with walnut butter, roast pigeon breast with cep *jus*, tomato and snail tart topped with Tomme cheese and roast duck breast with spices. This is no place for frugal eaters. Reasonably priced menus 70–195F and there's a gourmet menu with three main courses for 250F. Best to book in season.

ESTANG   32240

⊁ ≜ I●I HÔTEL-RESTAURANT DU COMMERCE*

It's in the centre of the village, near the arena.
☎ 05.62.09.63.41 ➡ 05.62.09.64.22
Closed Sun, Mon and Wed, the last week in Aug and the last week in Dec.

This venerable establishment has had a facelift. The rooms have been completely renovated and are ideal for an overnight stay; doubles 220–230F. The restaurant has a reputation for fine regional cuisine, serving trout stuffed with ceps, warm *foie gras* with fruit, and leg of fattened duck in Madiran wine. Go for the set menus 80–160F or *à la carte*; the *portefeuille royal* (duck breast stuffed with *foie gras* and ceps) is particularly good. Friendly welcome. Free coffee.

FIGEAC   46100

⊁ ≜ HÔTEL CHAMPOLLION**

3 pl. Champollion (Centre).
☎ 05.65.34.04.37 ➡ 05.65.34.61.69
TV.

Ideally located right in the middle of the town and a bit of a change from traditional establishments. Rooms are bright, spacious and attractive with quality beds and linen, and tastefully decorated bathrooms; doubles 270F, which is fair value for money. There's a beautiful staircase in a small atrium. Really friendly bar and a pleasant terrace. The clientele includes everyone from high school kids to travelling businesspeople. 10% discount.

⊁ I●I RESTAURANT LA CUISINE DU MARCHÉ

15 rue Clermont.
☎ 05.65.50.18.55
Closed Sun.

The open-plan kitchen lets you watch the chefs prepare tasty dishes that are much lighter and more refined than most of the local specialities. The colours, flavours and smells really show off the fresh market produce: pan-fried *foie gras*, wonderfully fresh sea bream fillet and highly refined desserts such as *dôme* of soft fruits. Menus 70–170F and a high-quality wine cellar. Joël Centeno, the man in charge, is an experienced hotelier. He acts more like a teamleader than a manager, and creates a delightfully convivial atmosphere. He personally takes care of reception and service, with his wife and an energetic, attentive waitress at his side. Best to book. Free apéritif.

I●I LA PUCE À L'OREILLE

5 rue Saint-Thomas (Centre); it's in the heart of the old town near the covered market and the Champollion museum.
☎ 05.65.34.33.08
Closed Mon except July–Aug, and a week around All Saints' Day.

Located in a pretty 15th-century house in a narrow, picturesque side street, this split-level restaurant looks out onto a garden surrounded by a wall covered with ivy. The cooking has a great reputation. There's a lunch *formule* for 75F and menus from 95F (the cheapest options aren't served on Sun or public holidays). Dishes, such as zander with vanilla-flavoured hazelnut oil and duck breast with onion marmelade, are attractively presented on hot plates. The service is swift and smiling. It's best to book.

FOIX 09000

☎ |●| HÔTEL LONS***

6 pl. G.-Duthil (Centre); it's in the old town near Pont-Vieux.

☎ 05.61.65.52.44 ☞ 05.61.02.68.18

✉ hotel-lons-foix@wanadoo.fr

Closed Fri evening, Sat lunchtime out of season and 20–31 Dec. **Disabled access. TV**.

This hotel is the epitome of discretion and it's a perfect place for an overnight stay. Comfortable double rooms 280F with en-suite bathroom. Traditional, local dishes – *foie gras*, duck breast, *cassoulet* and tournedos with pepper sauce. À *la carte* costs about 125F. Half board costs 250F per person.

🍴 ☎ HÔTEL PYRÈNE***

"Le Vignoble", rue Serge-Denis (South); it's on the N20 about 2km from the centre of townin the direction of Spain.

☎ 05.61.65.48.66 ☞ 05.61.65.46.69

Closed 20 Dec–20 Jan. **Disabled access. Swiming pool. Garden**.

This hotel is modern compared to the others in this town, and is perfectly placed to catch tourists as they migrate south to the Spanish border. As soon as you take a dip in the pool in the garden you'll forget all about the noise from the main road. Doubles with shower/wc or bath 290F. Free apéritif.

|●| LE SAINT-MARTHE***

21 rue Noël-Peyrévidal (Centre).

☎ 05.61.02.87.87 ☞ 05.61.05.19.00

✉ restaurant@le-saintemarthe.fr

Closed Tues evening, and Wed out of season, and Feb.

Although this is a grand restaurant in a very chic part of town, serving quality cuisine, the three stars are actually part of its name rather than awards for culinary excellence. Classic regional dishes – *cassoulet* with duck *confit*, warm goat's cheese with cumin-flavoured whipped cream, scallops with shellfish *coulis*, and upside-down tart with black pudding and mushrooms. Serious stuff. Menus 145–260F or around 290F à *la carte*.

SAINT-PIERRE-DE-RIVIÈRE 09000 (5KM W)

🍴 ☎ |●| HÔTEL-RESTAURANT LA BARGUILLÈRE**

Centre; take the D17.

☎ 05.61.65.14.02 ☞ 05.61.02.62.16

Closed Wed and Nov–Feb. **Garden**.

Pleasant little village hotel with a nice garden. Doubles with bath 220–230F. The cosy restaurant has built up a reputation for good cooking over the last twenty years, and they serve meals in the bar. The 80F set menu includes cheese, dessert, wine and coffee, and there are others 125–220F. The *menu campagnard* features local produce, and local dishes include trout with chives and shrimp, fresh *foie gras* with apples flambéed with *hypocras* and *fricassé* of kid with morels. The chef comes from Charente, so *mouclade* is a speciality. Free coffee.

BOSC (LE) 09000 (12KM W)

🍴 ☎ |●| AUBERGE LES MYRTILLES**

Col des Marrous; take the D17 from Foix.

☎ and ☞ 05.61.65.16.46

Closed Mon and Tues mid-Oct to end June, and mid-Nov to Jan. **Swimming pool. TV. Car park**.

A lovely chalet 1000m up, and just 4km from the ski runs at the Tour Laffont. In summer it's wonderful for walkers and year round it's good for people who enjoy their food. Double rooms with shower/wc 250–290F or with bath 290–310F. In the dining room delicious dishes include trout, omelette with ceps and blueberry tart. Menus 90–135F. Half board, 240–270F, is compulsory July–Aug. There's an indoor pool, sauna and Jacuzzi where you can relax after a walk. Free apéritif.

FRONTON 31620

☎ |●| LOU GREL

49 rue Jules Bersac.

☎ 05.61.82.03.00 ☞ 05.61.82.12.24

Closed Sun evening and Mon.

Swimming pool. Garden. TV.

The house has been renovated with scrupulous taste. Double rooms 230F with bath. The cuisine has an excellent reputation and you are received warmly. Specialities include *foie gras* in salt, *salmis* of pigeon, duck breast Rossini (that's with *foie gras*), *osso buco* and beef fillet with ceps. The 75F menu is served weekdays apart from public holidays, then others up to 195F. There's an all-duck menu and an all-fish menu, both including apéritif, wine and coffee. The dining room is pretty and there's a very pleasant garden terrace with a view of the park and the swimming pool where they serve salads and grills. It's a local institution, so it's best to book.

GAILLAC 81600

⅍ ☎ |●| LA VERRERIE

1 rue de l'Égalité (West); it's on the road to Montauban and well signposted.
☎ 05.63.57.32.77 ➡ 05.63.57.32.27
✉ verrerie@club.internet.fr
Disabled access. TV. Garden.

This is the prestige establishment that was lacking in these parts. It's a newish place, housed in a splendid 19th-century building that used to be the glass factory. The interior design is remarkably tasteful, retaining the original character of the place while establishing a warm modern style. All the rooms are really pleasant and comfortable and have a personal feel. Some have a view over a huge park. Prices are very reasonable; doubles 260F with shower/wc or 360F with bath. The staff are extremely welcoming. You'll find the best in local cooking in the restaurant, on menus from 80F (if you're staying half board) or 100–170F. Free coffee.

|●| LES SARMENTS

27 rue Cabrol (Centre); it's near the tourist office.
☎ 05.61.57.62.61 ✉ sarments@spray.fr
Closed Sun evening and Mon, Wed evening Oct–April, mid-Dec to mid-Jan and mid-Feb to beginning of March.

Located in a beautiful, narrow medieval street in the old quarter, the restaurant has built a reputation by word of mouth. The setting is splendid – an old cellar with 14th- and 16th-century brick vaults which have retained their original character and style. The tables are well-spaced and the welcome is friendly though the atmosphere's a bit starchy. The cooking is good and takes its inspiration from the local produce, combining tastes and flavours in intriguing ways. Try the *gratin* of prawns and mussels on a bed of spinach, a duo of sole *paupiettes* with crayfish, stuffed guinea-fowl flambéed with Marc, snails in flaky pastry or turbot stuffed with sorrel. Menus 135–240F.

BRENS 81600 (3KM SW)

☎ LES CHALETS DE FIOLLES

Route de Montans; take the D87 towards Montans, Laveur. After 3km turn right; it's well signposted.
☎ 05.63.57.69.67 ➡ 05.63.57.65.22
✉ langues.loisirs81alt@wanadoo.fr
Disbled access. Car park.

This place, way out in the countryside on the banks of the Tarn, used to belong to a wine grower. Accommodation is in two wooden chalets, which each have a couple of rooms, bathroom, kitchen and terrace. There's lots of space and they're well maintained. 300F for a double with shower/wc. The prices are more attractive by the week or the month and it's a perfect place for families or groups of friends. There's a common room and a laundry room. They provide games for the children, and boats that you can use for trips on the Tarn. Dinner is by arrangement. Great welcome. Credit cards not accepted.

GAUDENT 65370

⅍ ☎ |●| LA CHAPELLE D'ALBRET

How to get there: by the D26 and the D925.
☎ 05.62.99.21.13 ➡ 05.62.99.23.69
Closed Mon and the first week in Jan.
Garden. TV. Car park.

Although this modern building is just a few metres from the 12th-century chapel, it's not out of place. Cows graze in the meadows below the balconies of the bedrooms. Doubles with shower or bath 220F. Proprietor Michel Castet, who does the cooking, was born in the valley and skilfully reworks traditional recipes such as *roussolle* (stuffed chicken), *parcellous* (stuffed cabbage in a morels sauce) and casserole of duck breast. Half board is compulsory, 210–250F per person, but, at weekday lunchtimes there's a menu for 88F, or in the evening, a 118F *menu-carte*. Reservations only. Free apéritif.

GAVARNIE 65120

⅍ ☎ COMPOSTELLE HÔTEL**

rue de l'Église (South).
☎ and ➡ 05.62.92.49.43
✉ compostelle@gavarnie.com
Closed 30 Sept–26 Dec and beginning of Jan to beginning of Feb. **Disabled access. Car park.**

Sylvie and Yvan, who are keen hikers, travelled a fair bit before taking over this pleasant little family hotel. Rooms are called after Alpine flowers, and almost all of them overlook the corrie; you get the best view from the room called "lys", which has a balcony. The rooms on the second floor have skylights. Doubles 215–290F with shower or bath – they're imperfectly soundproofed even in the part of the hotel that's been renovated. Yvan knows the area well and can organise walks. 10% discount for a two-night stay, except during school holidays.

GIROUSSENS 81500

齐 ☎ |O| HÔTEL-RESTAURANT L'ÉCHAUGUETTE

Centre.
☎ 05.63.41.63.65 ➡ 05.63.41.63.13
Closed Sun evening, Mon except July–Sept, 1–21 Feb and 15–30 Sept.

An *échauguette* is a corner turret on a house – in this case a 13th-century house in wonderful surroundings. There are five rooms with bath for 280F. The restaurant has a good reputation and the dining room is as delightful as the cooking. There's a good choice of menus, 133–270F, and a splendid list of dishes *à la carte*: *marbré* of chicken livers, duckling with cep *jus*, *blanquette* of lamb, beef *daube* stew in Madiran and so on. Wines start at about 64F and you'll get half a bottle of Gaillac for 28F. Claude Canonica will make you feel welcome and fill you in on the history of the village and the region. Free apéritif or coffee, or 10% discount on the room rate.

SAINT-SULPICE 81370 (9KM W)

齐|O| AUBERGE DE LA POINTE

How to get there: take the N88 or exit 6 on the A68 signposted to Saint-Sulpice.
☎ 05.63.41.80.14 ➡ 05.63.41.90.24
e jrchelot@aol.com
Closed Tues evening and Wed except June–Sept, and 14–28 Oct. **Swimming pool. Garden. Car park**.

One of the stars of the local dining scene. The dining rooms are enormous but convivial and well laid out, and there's a shady terrace overlooking the River Tarn. Menus, 100–200F, list dishes like *croustillant* of pig's trotters, calf's head with *sauce gribiche* and flambéed apple tart. Free apéritif.

GRAMAT 46500

齐 ☎ |O| LE RELAIS DES GOURMANDS**

2 av. de la Gare.
☎ 05.65.38.83.92 ➡ 05.65.38.70.99
Closed Sun evening, Mon lunchtime and the Feb school holidays. **Swimming pool. Garden. TV. Car park**.

An enormous, private house in immaculate condition with a swimming pool, an outside bar and a flower garden. Bright, modern and functional rooms with bathrooms and direct-dial phone 290–360F. You'll get a polite and attentive welcome from Susy, the British proprietess. The restaurant has a good reputa-

tion for light inventive cooking, with dishes such as salmon *tartare*, scorpion fish with shellfish and mushroom sauce with Noilly, duck hearts *en brochette*, and stuffed free-range chicken with a garlic *jus*. Good cheeses and fine desserts, particularly the *couronne* of chocolate with orange mousse. Weekday menu 92F (not served Sun), and others 102–225F. Inexpensive local wines. 10% discount on the room rate Sept–June.

齐 ☎ |O| LE LION D'OR

8 pl. de la République.
☎ 05.65.38.73.18 ➡ 05.65.38.84.50
e lion.d.or@wanadoo.fr
Closed Mon and Tues lunchtimes, and 15 Dec–15 Jan.
TV. Car park.

One of the best restaurants in the region, and rooms in the best tradition of French hotel-keeping. Excellent reception and service. The decor is ultra-classic, with cream walls, chandeliers, oil paintings and the finest table linen. René Moméjac is a superb chef with flair and experience. Try lamb sweetbreads on a small pancake, pig's trotters with asparagus tips, gently braised local veal, apple and quince crumble and vanilla ice cream with liquorice milk. Menus 125–270F. The well-chosen wine list features good-value bottles from the region. Rooms are comfortable and splendidly maintained. Doubles with shower/wc or bath 325–450F. 10% discount on the room rate Oct–March.

RIGNAC 46500 (10KM NW)

|O| RESTAURANT MALET

pl. de Rignac; take the N140 then the D20.
☎ 05.65.33.63.85

There's little to identify this as a restaurant. The sign is practically illegible but the door is always wide open in summer. Diners share tables and eat very cheaply. Dishes are hearty and substantial: thick soup, raw ham, *pot-au-feu*, roast beef with chips and beans, strawberry salad, and so on. The regional menu, 60F, lists soup, *charcuterie*, duck *confit*, ceps, salads and the like. If you want to eat in the evening, you have to order in advance. Madame is the chef and her daughter runs the dining room. Here's a tip – you'd better be hungry when you arrive.

GRAMONT 82120

齐|O| LE PETIT FEUILLANT

It's next to the château.

☎ 05.63.94.00.08
Closed Sun evening and Wed, Mon and Tues in winter, and Feb.

Friendly as you like. No *à la carte* options, but six menus, 90–185F, listing the likes of home-made pasta, pork *confit* with prunes, *cassoulet*, gizzard salad, tart with garlic and cheese, duck *confit*, stuffed chicken, house *foie gras* and duck with sea salt. Everyone gets a complimentary apéritif There's a terrace with a view of the château. The good local cuisine is a big draw in the area, so it's important to book. From the end of April to the end of August, they hold craft exhibitions in the inn's cellars. Free *digestif*.

GRAULHET   81300

⅙ |●| LA RIGAUDIÉ

Route de Saint-Julien-du-Puy (East); it's 2km east of the town centre.
☎ 05.63.34.50.07 ➡ 05.83.34.29.27
Closed Sat lunchtime, Sun evening and Mon, 24 Dec–3 Jan, and Aug.

This restaurant, in a fabulous setting in a nature park, has an enormous air-conditioned dining room with a magnificent beamed ceiling. The cooking is excellent and the service professional. Weekday lunch menu 79F then 120–240F. After an apéritif of sweet white Gaillac, try the fish menu which comes with appetizer, shrimp tart with cress sauce, and sole or cod with *tapenade*. You'd do best to go for the cod, which ranks with the best. Other dishes include roast scallops with braised cabbage, pot-roast pigeon with ceps, duck breast with glazed turnips, and small tarts of fat duck with apples and honey sauce. A wonderful experience. Free apéritif.

LASGRAÏSSES   81300 (8KM NE)

⅙ |●| CHEZ PASCALE

Centre; it's on the D84, in the direction of Albi.
☎ 05.63.33.00.78
Closed Sun–Thurs evenings, the last fortnight in Aug.

This classic village bistro has old photographs on the walls, trophies in the cabinet and old-fashioned glazed-cotton tablecloths. It's a lively place. Weekday menu 75F and 100–150F. The cheapest one, which includes wine, is a revelation: a selection of starters from the buffet, followed by a well-prepared local dish, a cheese course and a dessert. This is one of the rare establishments that know how to cook a steak *bleu* – seared on

the outside, raw in the middle but hot right through. Excellent service. Free coffee.

LACROUZETTE   81210

♒ |●| L'AUBERGE DE CRÉMAUSSEL

How to get there: take the D30. The inn is clearly marked.
☎ 05.63.50.61.33 ➡ 05.63.50.61.33
Closed Wed, Sun evening and Jan. **Rooms closed** Nov–March. **Car park.**

Friendly country restaurant with a solid reputation, and five very clean rooms with wooden floors at 200F. Breakfast 25F. The dining room has stone walls and a fine fireplace. Specialities – cheese soup in winter and crayfish in summer – have to be ordered ahead, but they serve a very good Roquefort salad at any time. Menus 90–130F; reckon on 120F *à la carte*. Finish with the local pastry known as *croustade*, which is sheer heaven, for 10F. This is an extremely good restaurant. It's best to book.

LAGUIOLE   12210

⅙ ♒ |●| HÔTEL RÉGIS***

pl. de la Patte-d'Oie.
☎ 05.65.44.30.05 ➡ 05.65.48.46.44
Closed 20 Nov–25 Dec.
Swimming pool. TV. Car park.

This is one of the oldest hotels in Laguiole, with big reception rooms, sitting rooms, a piano and a lot of atmosphere. The tastefully refurbished rooms are huge, comfortable and modern. Doubles 160–240F with shower/wc, 290–360F with bath. The corridors are enlivened by beautiful art photographs. There's a swimming pool, a terrace and a wind break. Good traditional cooking: *tripou,* rib of beef, duck breast with chestnuts and *aligot*. Menus 65–140F. The welcome can be brusque. 10% discount on the room rate except weekends and school holidays.

⅙ ♒ |●| GRAND HÔTEL AUGUY***

2 allée de l'Amicale.
☎ 05.65.44.31.11 ➡ 05.65.51.50.81
e grand.hotel.auguy@wanadoo.fr
Closed Sun evening and Mon lunchtime except mid-June to mid-Sept and school holidays, and mid-Nov to end March. **Disabled access. Garden. TV. Car park.**

A very good establishment with a solid reputation. Pleasant, well-equipped doubles 270–450F with bath. The large dining room is bright, if a bit garish, and the cooking is first rate. Traditional local dishes hold their own in an extensive repertoire of delights: try the *galette* of pig's trotters in meat stock with ceps and potato cake, stuffed tripe, grilled rib of beef with *aligot*, medallions of hare with juniper berries, and salmon trout in a sauce made from Laguiole cheese. Indulge yourself with one of the wonderful desserts. Menus 155–300F. Half board 320–450F per person July–Aug. The welcome and service are very pleasant. 10% discount on the room rate except over weekends and July–Aug.

CASSUÉJOULS 12210 (10KM NW)

🏊 |●| CHEZ COLETTE

How to get there: take the D900 in the direction of the Sarrans dam.
☎ 05.65.44.33.71
Closed Wed out of season.

Reservations essential at this lovely little country bistro. Colette will ensure that you fall in love with the region, first by talking about it with passion and warmth, and secondly by serving you simple, invigorating meals. The setting couldn't be less pretentious or the atmosphere more relaxed and friendly. Menus for a modest 75F: a flan of oyster mushrooms, sausage with *aligot*, cheese and walnut tart, *truffade* and so on. If you don't have much of an appetite, you can eat extremely well for 55F. Free coffee.

LANNEMEZAN 65300

|●| CHEZ MAURETTE

10 rue des Pyrénés (Centre).
☎ 05.62.98.06.34
Closed Sun.

The inauspicious, pinkish frontage of this restaurant in a dreary town wouldn't make you slam on the brakes to stop but that would be an error. Wednesday is sheep market day and everyone local piles in for lunch. The house speciality is the prize-winning tripe, and there's excellent *daube* of beef and calf's head. The owner and her daughters serve you delightfully. *Formule* (dish and dessert) 51F, or menus 57F and 90F.

LATOUILLE-LENTILLAC 46400

🏠 |●| RESTAURANT GAILLARD**

Le bourg.
☎ 05.65.38.10.25 ➡ 05.65.38.13.13

Closed Nov. **Disabled access**. **TV**. **Car park**.

Service noon–2pm and 7–9pm. This traditional restaurant enjoys an excellent reputation. Local regulars come for the trout and duck *confit*, wild mushrooms, local lamb and terrific desserts. Set menus 80F (not Sun lunch) and up to 160F. You get a particularly warm welcome. There are a few rooms from 250F for a double with shower/wc.

LAUTREC 81440

🏊 🏠 |●| LA PERGOLA

5 rue Saint-Esprit (Centre); it's 100m from the church
☎ 05.63.75.98.77 ➡ 05.63.75.98.85
Closed Oct–March. **Garden**.

This old mill, surrounded by a flower garden, is in one of the prettiest villages in the Tarn at the end of well-trodden country paths. It's a really lovely restaurant, serving generous portions of fine, unpretentious family cooking. The *patronne* runs the kitchen, and uses vegetables from the garden. Menus vary with whatever is good at the market: duck breast, duck thigh *confit*, pigeons with prunes, prawn kebab, roast lamb and excellent pizzas cooked in a wood-fired oven. There's a *formule-pizza* for 62F, and menus from 80F. The home-made *gâteau* is a delight. You can eat outside, with lovely views of the forests and church steeple. The evenings are soft and peaceful. There are five guest rooms in an old dwelling nearby, at 250F for a double. Free breakfast or *digestif*.

🏊 |●| LE CHAMP D'ALLIUM

4 route de Castres (Centre).
☎ 05.63.70.05.24
Closed Sun evening and Mon, Tues lunchtime except July–Aug.

The cooking here is considered to be among the most imaginative in the Tarn. It's not cheap for the area, but it is well worth it. The chef buys his ingredients from local farmers and producers or fresh from the markets, and the dishes are fine and delicate as a result. You'll find it hard to choose between the cocks' combs with little onions and the gazpacho with roast crayfish and smoked bacon. The suckling lamb in a herb crust or the fillet of beef with bone marrow and the pot-roast pigeon are simply delicious, as is the turbot spiked with bay leaves. Menus 130–280F. The dining room is pleasant and comfortable. Free apéritif.

LAVAUR · 81500

♨ |●| HÔTEL LE JARDIN**

8–10 allée Ferréol-Mazas (Centre); it's next to the cathedral.
☎ 05.63.41.40.30 ➡ 05.63.41.47.74
℮ hotel.du.jardin@wanadoo.fr
Disabled access. TV. Garden.

The best hotel in town, a grand, traditional residence with comfortable rooms – 250F for a double. The staff make you feel welcome. The restaurant lists classical dishes using nothing but fresh produce: duck with cherries, pigeon in Gaillac wine, rack of lamb with thyme, and fish stew. They make their own bread. Lunch menu 85F, then others 115–225F.

LECTOURE · 32700

⅍ ♨ |●| HÔTEL DE BASTARD**

rue Lagrange (North).
☎ 05.62.68.82.44 ➡ 05.62.68.76.81
Closed 20 Dec to end Jan.
Swimming pool. TV. Garden. Car park.

This marvellous hotel is a fine example of 18th-century architecture. It's furnished and decorated with taste and is ideal for a romantic weekend. Pleasant welcome and incredible value. Doubles 260–395F. In summer, they serve meals on the terrace, which has a wonderful view over the rooftops, the swimming pool and the cypresses. Superlative chef Jean-Luc Arnaud is in charge in the kitchen. Menus 90–350F. There's a *formule à la carte* which means you can try some of the chef's specialities: iced cream of prawns with chives or asparagus in flaky pastry, wing and thigh of roast pigeon with a salad, and, for dessert, prune soufflé or a *millefeuille* of soft fruit. The exceptional gourmet menu features three special *foie gras* dishes served with three different regional fruit brandies. 10% discount on the room rate for a minimum three-night stay Sept–June.

LEYME · 46120

♨ |●| HÔTEL-RESTAURANT LESCURE**

Route de St-Céré.
☎ 05.65.38.90.07
Closed Sun evening out of season. **TV. Car park.**

This characterful hotel-restaurant, which has been run by the same family for more than fifty years, offers comfy accommodation at

reasonable prices. Doubles 200F with shower/wc. Breakfast costs 30F and half board starts at 240F per person. The large dining room looks over a pond; they serve terrific regional dishes like salted and smoked wild boar with local mushrooms. Weekday menu 70F, then 85–150F. There's a good selection of wines. The decoration is thoughtful and tasteful, with a genuine Picasso print and a number of Matisse reproductions.

LISLE-SUR-TARN · 81310

⅍ ♨ |●| LE PRINCINOR

La Noyère (West); it's on the outskirts of town going towards Rabastens.
☎ 05.63.33.35.44 ➡ 05.63.33.89.84
Closed Mon, Sat lunchtime, and a fortnight in Jan.
Disabled access.

Keep an eye out for this place, which is well set back from the road. The chef, who comes from the north, has brought some of his native dishes to the menu, including *waterzooi*, a fish stew. The sauces are excellent and the fish dishes perfectly judged. Dishes go on and off the menu as ingredients appear in the market – try roast salmon on a bed of cabbage, poached eggs with pink peppercorns in a pastry case, pork knuckle with lentils, fillet of zander with sweet mustard, and so on. Menus 60–160F. The building itself is modern, with little real charm, but the rooms are comfortable and clean; doubles with shower 170F, 190F with shower/wc or bath. Free *digestif*.

LOURDES · 65100

♨ |●| HÔTEL RELAIS DES CRÊTES

72 av. Alexandre-Maqui; it's on the right as you come into Lourdes from Tarbes.
☎ 05.62.42.18.56
Closed mid-Nov to March.

The location of this small family guesthouse, at the end of a side street behind a pretty hedge, protects it from the noise of the nearby main road. There are eleven tasteful, simple rooms looking out onto the courtyard. They're all spotlessly clean. In warm weather, breakfast is served on the terrace planted with hydrangeas. A double with washing facilities costs 90–120F, or 170–205F with shower/wc. Lovely welcome from the charming *patronne*.

⅍ ♨ |●| HÔTEL MAJESTIC**

9 av. Maransin (Centre); it's a ten-minute walk from the

shrines at the corner of the avenue and a cul-de-sac where you can park.
☎ 05.62.94.27.23 ➔ 05.62.94.64.91
Closed 15 Oct–15 April. **Disabled access. TV**.

Service at lunchtime and from 7.30pm. A classy establishment run by the friendly Cazaux family. The rustic rooms are extremely comfortable and have all mod cons including direct-dial phones and en-suite bathrooms with hair driers. Some have balconies. Doubles with basin 160F, with shower or bath up to 290F. Family cooking served in the chic dining room. Try salmon *en papillote*, veal escalope with cream and morels, or stuffed cabbage with Armagnac. The 50F *formule* is served daily and there are others 95–120F. The *patronne* takes a lot of trouble for her guests. The only drawback is the traffic noise. Free apéritif, coffee or *digestif* and 10% discount on the room rate mid-April to 30 June.

⅍ 🏠 🍴 HÔTEL D'ALBRET**

21 pl. du Champs-Commun (Centre).
☎ 05.62.94.75.00 ➔ 05.62.94.78.45
Hotel closed 2 Jan–9 March and 19 Nov–20 Dec.
Restaurant closed Sun evening and Mon out of season. **TV**.

The hotel is opposite the covered market and is in the part of Lourdes which looks more like a normal town. It offers comfortable rooms; those at the back are quiet and have a view of the mountains. Doubles with shower or bath 193–290F. The cuisine in the restaurant is traditional with a regional flavour. Menus 70–145F. Try the *garbure* with duck thigh or the *foie gras* escalope caramelized with apples. The boss is welcoming and generous. 10% discount on the room rate or 5% discount on half board, except in Aug.

🏠 🍴 HÔTEL BEAUSÉJOUR***

16 av. de la Gare.
☎ 05.62.94.38.18 ➔ 05.62.94.96.20
Disabled access. Garden. TV.

A reasonably priced three-star conveniently near the station. Classy rooms all have direct-dial telephones and bathrooms with wc and hair drier. The ones overlooking the station are big but poorly soundproofed. The ones at the back are smaller, but they have a view over the town and to the Pyrenees beyond. Doubles with shower/wc or bath, 318–368 in season, lower the rest of the year. There's a pleasant garden where you can eat in good weather. The brasserie is open for lunch and dinner and offers a *formule brasserie* at 75F and menus 100–145F.

LUCHON   31110

⅍ 🏠 🍴 L'AUBERGE DE CASTEL-VIELH

Route de Superbagnères.
☎ and ➔ 05.61.79.36.79
Closed Mon–Thurs Oct–March, and Wed only during the Feb and Nov school holidays. **Garden. TV. Car park**.

A pretty little house in the style of the region, plonked down on a small, green hill. It's got a big garden and an appealing terrace. The cuisine has a good reputation: prawns with mushrooms, local ptarmigan, *croustillant* of veal sweetbreads with morels and *fripounet* of lamb in the old style. Menus 100F, 160F and 190F. The rooms are spacious and have mountain views; doubles 250–300F. Free house apéritif.

⅍ 🍴 LE PAILHET

12 av. du Maréchal-Foch; it's next to the station.
☎ 05.61.79.09.60
Closed Tues evening, Wed and 15 Nov–1 Dec.
Car park.

There's a *bar-tabac* attached to this little house that's obscured by a trellis. Its dining room is always busy with locals. The regional cuisine is straightforward and tasty: frogs' legs with garlic, escalope of *foie gras* with green apples and duck breast with *foie gras*. Menus 85F, 125F and 165F. Free apéritif.

⅍ 🍴 LE CLOS DU SILÈNE

19 cours des Qhinconces.
☎ 05.61.79.12.00
Closed Sun evening and Mon except July–Aug and mid-Nov to mid-Dec. **Car park**.

An attractive restaurant near the spa, run by a husband and wife team. Everything is done with care, from the service to the cooking and the presentation. Inventive cuisine on menus that change with the seasons: *terrine* of *foie gras* with figs marinated in Muscat, *millefeuille* of lamb with *ratatouille*. Weekday lunch *formule* 70F, menus 90–150F, and around 120F *à la carte*. Free apéritif.

CASTILLION DE LARBOUST   31110 (6KM W)

⅍ 🏠 🍴 HÔTEL L'ESQUÉRADE

How to get there: it's on the road to the Payresourde pass, 1km after Saint-Aventin and the hotel is at the bottom of the road.
☎ 05.61.79.19.64 ➔ 05.61.79.26.29
Closed mid-Nov to mid-Dec.

The village is 954m up in gorgeous green countryside. The hotel itself is comfortable, even a little bourgeois, and the building is typical of the locality – it's built of stone and has wooden balconies. Most of the rooms overlook the valley. Doubles 240–320F, and you can stay half board on request. The decor inside is warm. A young and gifted chef took the place over and he produces excellent dishes. The menu changes with each season, because he uses only fresh, local produce: frogs' legs with parsley, crayfish with tomato *concassée* and so on. Menus 90F, 120F and 150–350F. 10% discount on the room rate Oct–June.

MELLES   31440 (30KM NE)

⋔ I●I AUBERGE DU CRABÈRE

How to get there: take the D618 then the N230.
☎ 05.61.79.21.99 ➡ 05.61.79.74.71
Closed Wed in winter, except in the school holidays..

The imposing house is right in the middle of the village, on the route of the GR10 walking trail. There are a few spacious, country-style rooms, with half board compulsory at 190F per person. Patrick Beauchet toiled long and hard as a chef on transatlantic cruise liners before being "chosen" for this more stable, but glorious post. He's made the mountains his home and his cuisine is bursting with local goodies: wild mushrooms, crayfish, snipe and other game in season. He's become so expert that he's even written a recipe book, *Mes recettes de Comminges et des Pyrénées Centrales*. Menus 120–160F and a short menu "*randonneur*" for 70F – ideal if you're walking the trail. Very welcoming.

LUZ-SAINT-SAUVEUR   65120

⋔ ≜ I●I HÔTEL LES TEMPLIERS

pl. de la Comporte; opposite the church of Saint-André.
☎ 05.62.92.81.52 ➡ 05.62.92.93.05
Closed May and 10 Oct–10 Dec.

Rooms are simple but spacious and not without charm – there's some wonderful, highly polished Pyrrenean furniture. Doubles with shower/wc 210F; numbers 1 and 2 can sleep three people and have shutters opening onto the fortified church and the square. There's a welcoming *crêperie* at street level. The woman who runs the place makes you feel welcome. Monday is market day, when the front of the hotel is transformed into a Spanish-style flower stall. Free apéritif.

⋔ I●I CHEZ CHRISTINE

rue d'Ossun prolongée.
☎ 05.62.92.86.81

Closed lunchtimes, 24 May–10 June and 1 Oct–15 Dec.
The setting is welcoming and the decor most attractive: the bedspreads come from as far afield as Mali and Madagascar, and there are dried flowers, Bedouin keffiyehs and Toureg turbans. Snacks and full meals – mixed salads, noisettes of lamb, duck breasts, pizzas and small portions of pasta, with Pyrrenean specialities to order – on menus 120–150F. It's not exactly cheap for what it is. Free apéritif or coffee.

MADIRAN   65700

⋔ ≜ I●I LE PRIEURÉ**

☎ 05.62.31.92.50 ➡ 05.62.31.90.66
Closed Sun evening and Mon Oct–June. **TV.**

In the 11th century, this Benedictine abbey was built facing the church that still survives today. The building has been converted into a hotel-restaurant where you sleep in the monks' cells. They are very plain but they do have bathrooms with wc, telephone and TV. Doubles 300F. The restaurant reassuringly produces regional dishes, *à la carte* only: whole, boned pigeon with liver, sliced beef with morels, zander with morels and *croustade* Gers-style with Armagnac, for example. You'll pay 150–200F for a complete meal. Smiling, relaxed welcome. Free apéritif.

MARTRES-TOLOSANE   31220

⋔ ≜ I●I HÔTEL-RESTAURANT CASTET**

av. de la Gare
☎ 05.61.98.80.20
Hotel closed Nov school holidays. **Restaurant closed** Sun evening and Mon.

A quiet, lovely house just opposite the station. Double rooms with bath 230–250F. There's a 75F menu (not served Sat evening or Sun lunchtime), others 140F and 160F, and good choices *à la carte*. They do specialities of duck or rib of beef cooked in a salt crust, and other more classic dishes using local produce such as duck *foie gras* with fresh fruits. Dishes change with the seasons – there'll be game in autumn, and good fresh fish in summer. There's a wonderful, shady terrace. Free coffee.

LE FOUSSERET   31430 (15KM NE)

⋔ I●I RESTAURANT DES VOYAGEURS

rue Sicart; take exit 23 off the A64 motorway as far as

Fousseret and it's on the road up to the central square.
☎ 05.61.09.53.06
Closed Sat and Sun evening.

A grey house with green shutters. The welcome is as charming as the interior. Family-style cooking and dishes influenced by the region: *pot Gascon*, beef fillet, ceps or ravioli with *foie gras*. Menus start at 58F and the cheaper ones are excellent value for money. The smiling service is an added bonus. In summer you dine on the terrace behind the house. The place is inhabited by people who come back time after time. Free apéritif.

MAUVEZIN   32120

⚕ |●| LA RAPIÈRE

2 rue des Justices; take the right turning as you leave the village heading for Montauban.
☎ and ☛ 05.62.06.80.08
Closed Tues, Wed, a fortnight June/July and three weeks in Oct.

This is one of the few restaurants where you can get authentic local cuisine prepared by an exacting chef. The food here is delicious and succulent: stuffed duck's neck, suckling pig chops with calf's sweetbreads in truffle *jus*, chicken thigh stuffed with *foie gras*, calf's head *sauce gribiche*, quail with *foie gras* salad and home-made *patisserie*. Menu-express 70F, served at lunchtime during the week, and others 110–260F. There's a lovely list of regional wines that includes a number of Madirans. There's also a terrace that's opened in good weather. Free coffee.

MAZAMET   81200

⚓ |●| HÔTEL JOURDON**

7 av. Albert Rouvière (Centre).
☎ 05.63.61.56.93 ☛ 05.63.61.83.38
Restaurant closed Sun evening and Mon.
TV. Car park.

Robust, tasty food. On the menus, 90–250F, you will find specialities like cep ravioli, rack of lamb lacquered with Armagnac, *cassoulet*, vegetable *gratiné à l'ancienne*, tournedos stuffed with *foie gras*, *millefeuille* of monkfish with shellfish cream, and so on. The restaurant is popular with workers at lunchtime when the atmosphere may be very relaxed but the service is up to scratch – though there's not much elbow room. Some of the rooms are a bit cramped, too, but they're clean and air-conditioned. Doubles 280F with shower or 300–350F with bath.

MILLAU   12100

⚓ |●| INTERNATIONAL HÔTEL-RESTAURANT***

1 pl. de la Tiné (Centre).
☎ 05.65.59.29.00 ☛ 05.65.59.29.01
Disabled access. TV. Private car park.

This place looks for all the world like it's an ageing part of a chain, and it's hard to credit that it has been run by the Pomarède family for three generations. There are 110 rooms in all, so there's a good chance of finding a vacancy in the high season. They're all soundproofed and some have air conditioning. Prices are reasonable: doubles with shower/wc 280F, 480F with bath. If you have the choice, take a room facing south with a splendid view over the countryside. The plush restaurant has an excellent reputation and the dishes are elaborate. Menus from 140F with a decent range of local dishes.

⚕ ⚓ |●| HÔTEL-RESTAURANT LE CÉVENOL**

115 rue du Rajol (South); 500m from the centre of town.
☎ 05.65.60.74.44 ☛ 05.65.60.85.99
Closed Sun, Mon–Wed lunchtimes, except Easter Mon and Whit Mon, Fri lunchtime July to mid-Sept.
Disabled access. Swimming pool. TV. Car park.

A pleasant, modern establishment on the edge of the town. Menus, 105F and 150F, are served in the restaurant or on the extremely pleasant terrace. Good, classical, carefully prepared dishes which include rolled calf's head, braised pork cheek and trout fillet in a caul. En-suite doubles cost 320–340F. The place is quiet in spite of the busy road nearby. Free coffee.

⚕ |●| RESTAURANT CHEZ CAPION

3 rue J.-F. Alméras; it's close to bd. de la République, near the town hall.
☎ 05.65.60.00.91 ☛ 05.65.60.42.13
Closed Wed out of season and early July.

This restaurant is highly respected by the people of Millau who use it for all kinds of celebratory meals. The delicious cooking is principally regional and uses a great deal of local produce. The dining room is bright, with slightly old-fashioned decor. Prices are very reasonable, given the quality of the cooking. There's a 70F weekday lunch menu and others up to 185F. *À la carte*, choose from the likes of home-smoked salmon or lamb sweetbreads *persillade* and help yourself as often as you like from the sweet trolley. Friendly welcome. Free coffee.

I●I AUBERGE OCCITANE

15 rue Peyrollerie (Centre).
☎ 05.65.60.45.54
Closed Sun except July–Aug, and the last fortnight in March.

This restaurant is in an extremely old house. The menus are written in both French and Langue d'Oc or Provençal. Menus 78–115F and dishes include *salade du berger*, *aligot*, duck breast, lamb fillet and Aubrac beef. Excellent regional specialities include cabbage with spelt (a kind of wheat), beef in red wine and trout fillets with a nettle sauce.

MIRANDE   32300

♠ I●I AUBERGE DE LA HALLE

rue des Écoles; (Centre).
☎ 05.62.66.76.81
Closed Sun evening. **Garden**.

A totally simple place where you feel relaxed right away. Traditional cuisine in handsome portions on a range of appetising menus 62–138F. There are also a few rooms in a separate building – some overlooking the road, others overlooking the garden. They're modest and clean: double with basin 165F or with shower/wc 185F. The young owners are cool as you like.

MIREPOIX   09500

🎋 I●I RESTAURANT PORTE D'AVAL

cours Maréchal-de-Mirepoix (South).
☎ 05.61.68.19.19
Closed Sun evening and Mon, Tues lunchtime in spring, and Nov.

It's a real surprise to find such a bright, modern restaurant so close to the medieval town. You'll get a splendid welcome and enjoy good cooking that shows off the local produce and fish to their best advantage: duck breast with apples, *foie gras* with peaches and almonds, and trout with fresh herbs and prawns. Honest prices – the lunch menu costs 89F. Nice terrace. Free coffee.

COUTENS   09500 (6KM W)

🎋 I●I LE CLOS SAINT-MARTIN

How to get there; it's on the D119, between Mirepoix and Perriers.
☎ 05.61.68.11.12
Closed Tues and Wed out of season, and end Dec to 14 Feb. **Disabled access. Garden. Car park**.

A convivial place to have a meal or a snack in the luxuriant greenery of the garden or snuggled round the open fire. The ancient house has been respectfully brought up to date, and has warm yellow colour-washed walls and lavender-blue windows and doors. Traditional cuisine and regularly changing dishes. Lunch menu 50F, others 65–130F – try cutlets cooked over the coals, or duck breast. Lovely welcome. Best to book. Free apéritif.

MOISSAC   82200

🎋 ♠ I●I LE PONT NAPOLÉON

2 allée Montebello; it's just by the bridge.
☎ 05.63.04.01.55 ➡ 05.63.04.34.44
Closed Sun evening, Wed and a fortnight at the beginning of Jan. **TV. Car park**.

The hotel is a dream, with fair prices and amazing retro bathrooms which, like the bedrooms, have been redecorated and insulated against the noise of the road. Doubles 220–350F. Nonetheless, the restaurant is better known. The *formule "34 Bis'trot"* provides for all appetites, with old-fashioned dishes such as veal *blanquette* and *pot-au-feu*. At 49F or 79F, it's pretty good value for money, but the gastronomic cuisine of culinary hero Michel Dussau is what's made the restaurant's repuation, better sampled on menus 149–352. Free apéritif.

🎋 I●I LE BISTROT DU CLOÎTRE

5 pl. Drand-de-Bredon
☎ 05.63.04.37.50
Closed Mon and Tues evenings.

A pink-brick house on a quiet, sunny square. An ideal spot for a delicious meal. Simple little dishes – *blanquette*, *pot-au-feu*, duck breasts and salads – at very fair prices. Dish of the day 49F and menus from 89F. The owner of the *Pont Napoléon* (see above) has recently taken it over, so there are no worries about the quality of the ingredients. It's slightly let down by lax service. Free coffee.

DURFORT-LACAPELETTE   82390 (6KM NE)

🎋 ♠ I●I HÔTEL-RESTAURANT AUBE NOUVELLE

How to get there: take the D16 out of the village in the direction of Cages or the D2 towards Lauzerte.
☎ 05.63.04.50.33 ➡ 05.63.04.57.55
Closed New Year holidays. **Garden. Private car park**.

Owner Marc de Smet's parents moved from Belgium to the Quercy in 1955, and he and his wife Claudine took over their business in the fullness of time. It's an idyllic spot surrounded by fields, which you can admire from the lovely terrace and garden. The clean, well-maintained rooms have been renovated to a high standard; 190F with basin, up to 290F with shower/wc or bath. The cooking is regional in flavour and Belgian in influence – rabbit *à la flamande*, shellfish *waterzooi*, and sea bass in a cream sauce with white Belgian beer. The chef's motto is "just because you don't pay a lot doesn't mean you get small portions". Menus 60–220F. A really nice place. 10% discount on the room rate after the third night Sept–June.

MONCORNEIL-GRAZAN   32260

|●| RESTAURANT L'AUBERGE D'ASTARAC

It's between Masseube and Simorre.
☎ 05.62.65.48.81
Closed Sun evening–Tues lunchtime, and mid-Nov to Jan. **Garden**.

This inn, miles from the busy highways, has been lovingly restored by two exceptional people who fell in love with the area. There's an old bar, a delightful dining room and a glorious terrace. At the bottom of the flower garden you will see Christian Termote's kitchen garden that's full of vegetables and herbs. He taught himself to cook and uses herbs with great subtlety. Try the grilled *foie gras* with a sweet and sour carrot *jus* or the pigeon breast with a reduction of Madiran wine. It's inspired and not messed about – he puts extraordinary flavours together. Set menus 130–250F. There's an excellent choice of wine, with a particularly good selection of quality wines from the south. Lucie is the genial lady of the house who creates its lively atmosphere. She even lets her clients choose their own bottle from the cellar or gives advice about the quality of a vintage.

MONTAUBAN   82000

♠ HÔTEL DU COMMERCE

9 pl. Franklin-Roosevelt; it's on the cathedral square.
☎ 05.63.66.31.82 ➡ 05.63.03.18.46
TV. Garden. Car park nearby.

A pretty hotel with a garden and comfortable, pleasant rooms. Double with shower 175–260F and 330F with bath. A traditional provincial town hotel with a nice old-fashioned feel. The ground floor is charming, with

lovely mahogony and walnut furniture, but the stairwell between the second and third floors is in poor repair. The refurbished rooms are a good deal more attractive than the others. and, if you're at all claustrophobic, avoid the rooms on the third floor because the ceilings are low.

🍴 ♠ |●| HÔTEL MERCURE

12 rue Notre-Dame (Centre).
☎ 05.63.63.17.23
TV. Car park. Pay garage.

As a rule, chain hotels do not appear in this guide but this is an exception. The *Mercure* is simply the best hotel in town, very well managed and with real charm. Inevitably it's also the most expensive – double rooms 550F. The decor is bright and warm and the rooms are spacious and decorated in contemporary style. Splendid bathrooms. In the 18th century, the building was a private mansion. Nice welcome. Free car park and pay garage. They also do meals.

🍴 |●| LE SAMPA

21 and 21 [bis] rue des Carmes (Centre).
☎ 05.63.20.36.46
Closed Sun.

The trendy decor may have been inspired by the American west, but the cooking is 100% French and regional: omelettes, grilled meat, duck breast with ceps and a house *confit*. There's a weekday lunch menu for 64F, *à la carte* costs more and there are dishes of the day. It's all good stuff and helpings are enormous. From May to mid-October they serve grills and salads on the lovely terrace. The welcome and service are congenial, and the warm, friendly atmosphere at the bar spreads to the dining room. Free apéritif.

|●| AUX MILLE SAVEURS

6 rue Saint-Jean (Centre).
☎ 05.63.66.37.51
Closed Sun evening and Mon.

It's hard to find a restaurant offering better value for money and this is the class act in town. Although the setting is a tad impersonal, it's pleasant and relaxing. The chef uses only fresh produce and the dishes he produces demand time and patience. For a quick lunch, opt for the speedy *menu du marché*, 65F, but to make more of an occasion of your meal choose from the menus, 100–185F. The chef has travelled a good dea,l and you'll taste flavours from far-away places in dishes which are otherwise rooted in the cuisine of the southwest. The service, though generally attentive, suffers when the place gets full.

⅍ |●| RESTAURANT LE VENTADOUR

23 quai Villebourbon (West); it's on banks of the Tarn, opposite the Ingres museum.
☎ 05.63.63.34.58
Closed Sun, Mon, and the first fortnight in Aug.

Incredibly popular restaurant with a vaulted brick dining room done up to look like the inside of a castle. The place gets flooded whenever the Tarn bursts its banks, but on the other hand it's always cool whatever the temperature outside. This is cooking at its most refined and the service is first-rate. Prices are reasonable – weekday lunch menu 100F then 140–220F. Dishes include *fricassée* of mushrooms and gizzards *confit* in a pastry case with sesame seeds, canelloni with smoked and fresh salmon, duck breast stuffed with *foie gras*. Desserts include *crèpe Suzette* with banana and liquorice cream. Free coffee.

MONTRÉAL   32500

⚐ |●| CHÂTEAU DE FOURCÈS

It's in the village.
☎ 05.62.29.49.53
Closed Nov–March.
Swimming pool. Garden. TV. Car park.

A smart, charming place in a 12th-century chateau in the middle of the village. It has been magnificently restored and has all the modern facilities you could wish for. The rooms are in soft colours and elegantly coordinated. There's a river running through the garden and a swimming pool. High-season prices for doubles, 730–1000F. Very good cooking to match: fillet of beef with Roquefort, duck breast with morels and monkfish with saffron sauce. Menus from 155F (weekday lunch). Formal, stylish welcome and attentive service.

|●| CHEZ SIMONE

It's in the village.
☎ 05.62.29.29.44.40
Closed Mon and sometimes Sun evening.

There are two entrances – one goes into the old-fashioned bistro (Formica heaven!), the other is via the terrace to the main dining room that has all the attributes of a modish, gourmet restaurant. In the middle there's a display showing off all the bottles on the wine list and an impressive collection of flagons of

Armagnac – more than thirty vintages. Smart yet easy-going welcome. There are three menus, 125–205F. The top-price one starts with goose and duck *foie gras,* sliced in front of you and served without adornment. The cuisine is essentially regional but with quite a lot of sauces and they also do good fish. The owner has a nice bar under the arcades in the square where you can knock back a glass or two of Armagnac for 16F.

MONTRICOUX   82800

⚐ |●| LE RELAIS DU POSTILLON*

☎ 05.63.67.23.58
Closed Fri evening and Sat lunchtime Oct–May, and the last fortnight in Nov. **Garden. Car park.**

A pleasant inn providing good regional cooking. The dining room is cosy and they do some wonderful house specialities. Set menus from 92F (not Sun) up to 200F. *À la carte* try the frogs' legs, *civet* of hare, *foie gras*, salmon with sorrel in flaky pastry, zander with saffron or home-made pastries. There's a pleasant shady terrace and a garden. The rooms aren't particularly attractive but they're very well maintained; doubles with washing facilities 110F, or 130F with shower (wc along the landing).

MONTSÉGUR   09300

⚐ |●| HÔTEL-RESTAURANT COSTES**

52 rue Principale.
☎ 05.61.01.10.24 ➡ 05.61.03.06.28
✉ hotel-costes@post-club-internet.fr
Closed Mon out of season, Sun evening and 15 Nov–1 April. **Garden.**

This is the best place to stay if you're planning an assault on the peak of Montségur. Simple, comfortable rooms 195F with shower, 225F with shower/wc. There's a family feel to the restaurant where they serve home cooking: *civet* of wild boar, duck breast with figs, game *pâtés*, and duck *confit* with chanterelle mushrooms. Menus 80–195F. There's a pleasant terrace and garden.

NAJAC   12270

⅍ ⚐ |●| L'OUSTAL DEL BARRY**

pl. du Bourg.
☎ 05.65.29.74.32 ➡ 05.65.29.75.32
Restaurant closed Mon and Tues lunchtime.
Disabled access. Garden. TV. Car park.

This lovely inn is an appealing place to stop and

you'll be warmly received. The decor is plush and the rooms are very elegant while retaining an authentic rustic feel. Doubles with basin 210F, with bath 310–330F. The restaurant serves largely regional dishes, using fresh, seasonal ingredients so dishes change frequently. Menus 140–260F: chicken with cabbage, ox cheek in red wine, sweetbreads with ceps or *astet najacois* (roast pork stuffed with fillet steak, parsley and garlic). And the desserts are mouthwatering. Catherine Miquel created the wine list, and she'll help you find the perfect complement to your meal. Free apéritif.

🏃 🏠 🍴 LE BELLE RIVE**

le Roc du Pont (Northwest).
☎ 05.65.29.73.90 ➡ 05.65.29.76.88
📧 hotel-bellrive.najac@wanadoo.fr
Closed Sun evening April–Oct, and 1 Nov to early April.
Disabled access. Swimming pool. Garden. TV. Car park.

A pleasant hotel in green, leafy surroundings on a bend in the river. The swimming pool and tennis court make it feel something like a family holiday centre. Rooms are bright and pleasant; doubles with shower/wc or bath 300F. The cooking is good – house specialities include semi-cooked *foie gras, astet najacois* (roast pork stuffed with fillet steak, parsley and garlic), zander with veal *jus* and beef with truffle *jus*. Menus 90–220F, and you can eat outside in good weather. Free coffee.

NANT   12230

🏃 🏠 🍴 HÔTEL DES VOYAGEURS*

pl. Saint-Jacques.
☎ 05.65.62.26.88 ➡ 05.65.62.15.64
Car park.

The lovely little town is an ideal base for hikers and this pleasant hotel right in the centre, provides good bed and board. There's a simple, fresh look to the bedrooms: doubles with washing facilities 140F, 165F with shower, 190F with shower/wc. The restaurant has a pretty terrace hung with wisteria in summer, and serves plain, honest food: trout with Roquefort, stuffed cabbage, *émincé* of rabbit *en papillote*, and a choice of home-made desserts. Menus 85–170F. Pleasant welcome and service. They lend guests mountain bikes. Free apéritif or coffee.

SAINT-JEAN-DU-BRUEL   12230 (7KM E)

🏠 🍴 HÔTEL-RESTAURANT DU MIDI-PAPILLON**

☎ 05.65.62.26.04 ➡ 05.65.62.12.97
Closed 11 Nov to Palm Sunday.
Swimming pool. Garden. Car park.

This hotel in the depths of Aveyron welcomed its first guests in 1850 and has been since run by successive generations of the Papillon family. The rooms are exceptionally pleasant, particularly those overlooking the Dourbie, and they've recently been redecorated. Prices are reasonable; doubles with shower/wc 190F or 205–340F with bath. The dining room is decorated with flowers and overlooks the river and there's a pretty and pleasant terrace which is often full. The owner, Jean-Michel, uses only the freshest produce – he grows his own fruit and vegetables, rears his own chickens, fattens his own pigs and gathers his own mushrooms, so the cuisine is full of authentic flavours: lamb *navarin* with aubergine and garlic, roast goose fillet with morel sauce and an exquisite gentian jelly accompanied with *tuiles* and wild blackberries. Menus from 77F (weekday lunchtimes), up to 214F. Pleasant staff and the service is unobtrusively efficient. Best to book.

NESTIER   65150

🏃 🏠 🍴 LE RELAIS DU CASTERA**

Centre.
☎ 05.62.39.77.37 ➡ 05.62.39.77.29
Closed Sun evening and Mon.

The *Relais* looks pretty dull outside but there's nothing dull about the cooking of Serge Latour. He's one of the best chefs in the Hautes-Pyrénées. He composes and presents dishes with elaborate care and the service is perfect. Lunch menu 100F or others 138–250F. You discover all kinds of new flavours at excellent prices. Regional specialities include melting duck *foie gras, fricassée* of crayfish with artichokes, *garbure* with *confit* of duck. Lots of local wines, too. You can also create your own menu, if you order in advance. There are a few comfortable rooms, starting at 260F. Free coffee.

PEYRECAVE   32340

🏃 🍴 CHEZ ANNIE

How to get there: it's halfway between Lectaure and Castelsarrazin on the Tarn and Garonne border.
☎ 05.62.28.65.40
Closed Sat lunchtime, Sun evening and the second fortnight in Sept.

Annie runs this stunning little inn off the tourist track, set by the side of the road. She also does the cooking: house *cassoulet*, *daube* and chicken *galantine*. She has a real feeling for cooking and eating well. Three menus 77–120F. Free aperitif, coffee or *digestif*.

PROJAN 32400

🐾 🛏 |●| LE CHÂTEAU DE PROJAN**

It's on the road from Saint-Mont to the N134.
☎ 05.62.09.46.21 ➡ 05.62.09.44.08
Closed Jan. **Car park.**

A genuine château standing proud and alone on a hill. The family who've owned it since 1986 have transformed the place, letting in light and colour and filling the rooms with contemporary art. The salon, which has been decorated in a modern style, looks out over the countryside. The reading room, dining room and bar have all been decorated with the same refined taste – you can wander round for hours admiring the pictures on the walls. Prices are about right for such a wonderful place; double rooms with basin 320F, then 530–650F with shower/wc or bath. It's not a fully-fledged restaurant but they offer a *table-dhôte* menu at 120F, to order in advance. There's a baby grand piano if you want some quiet entertainment. Free apéritif and 10% discount on the room rate April–June and Oct–Dec.

RÉALMONT 81120

🐾 |●| LES ROUTIERS-CHEZ RICHARD ET PATRICIA

bd. Armengaud (Centre); it's on the N112 halfway between Castres and Albi.
☎ 05.63.55.65.44
Closed Sun, the week of 15 Aug and 25 Dec–2 Jan. **Car park.**

A *Routier* restaurant with a great reputation. There's a huge dining room with attractive stone walls where they serve typical family dishes. The good 65F menu lists a self-service buffet of *hors-d'oeuvres*, a main course, cheese, dessert and wine. The 100F menu is almost too huge to finish. Honestly priced wines. Free apéritif.

REVEL 31250

🐾 🛏 |●| HÔTEL-RESTAURANT DU MIDI**

34 bd. Gambetta (Northwest).
☎ 05.61.83.50.50 ➡ 05.61.83.34.74

Restaurant closed Sun evening Nov to Easter and mid-Nov to beginning of Dec. **Garden. TV. Car park.**

Elegant early 19th-century coaching inn, now a pleasant hotel with smart rooms 250–400F with bath – the most expensive ones look over the garden. The nice dining room is bright and in summer you can eat outside. Weekday menu 90F, others 120–260F. Dishes include radish salad with chicken livers, *cassoulet* with duck *confit*, pot-roast pigeon breast and pan-fried *foie gras*. Very affordable wines including Corbières, Gaillac and Bordeaux. Free apéritif.

RIEUMES 31370

🛏 |●| HÔTEL LES PALMIERS

13 pl. du Foirail.
☎ 05.61.91.81.01
Closed Sun evening. **Garden. TV.**

Swathed in Virginia creeper and fronted by a lovely plane tree, this old building sits on a vast square. The interior has been totally refurbished, and the spacious rooms have have been tastefully decorated and prettily furnished. Doubles 240–330F with bath; the cheapest look onto the square, the others onto the internal garden which is planted with palm trees – hence the hotel's name. In summer you can eat out there. The 70F lunch menu includes wine, the others, 108–220F, offer more elaborate dishes: *carpaccio* of duck with olive paste, seafood *marinière*, *émincé* of duck breast or duck thigh *confit* with Toulouse *aillade*. On Sunday there's a single menu with includes *foie gras*, or you can eat à la carte. Good regional cooking, but the duck breast is let down by the measly chips. The owner is originally from Cuba and he adds some unusual spices to his dishes. In summer, he sometimes organises jazz concerts.

ROCAMADOUR 46500

🐾 🛏 |●| HÔTEL DU GLOBE*

rue de la Couronnerie; it's by the grand steps leading to the sanctuary.
☎ 05.65.33.67.73 ➡ 05.65.38.79.82
Closed Mon evening and Tues except 15 June–15 Sept, 15 Nov–22 Dec and 5 Jan–5 Feb. **Car park.**

A nice little place serving *crêpes*. Madame trained in Brittany but she also makes delicious local dishes cooked in traditional fashion – the *coq au vin*, using Cahors wine, is particularly succulent. À la carte a meal will cost around 80F. You get a natural, family welcome. The rooms are well maintained – some have an incredible view of the cliffs topped by an imposing abbey. Some rooms sleep three. If you want a quiet night, avoid room 3, which is above the bar. Doubles 190F. Free apéritif.

⅍ ☎ |●| HÔTEL-RESTAURANT LE LION D'OR**

It's in the medieval town.
☎ 05.65.33.62.04 ➡ 05.65.33.72.54
✉ liondor.rocamadour@wanadoo.fr
Closed 5 Nov–1 April.

A traditional hotel-restaurant. The comfy bedrooms are reasonable value – 210–280F for a double with shower/wc or 300F with bath. Recent renovation work has retained the character and the spirit of the place. In the restaurant, menus go for 67–210F. Specialities such as *confit* of duck and truffle omelette deserve a mention. Brilliant desserts – just try to resist the walnut *gâteau* with egg custard. 10% discount on the room rate, except Aug.

⅍ ☎ |●| HÔTEL-RESTAURANT BEAU SITE***

It's in the medieval town.
☎ 05.65.33.63.08 ➡ 05.65.33.65.23
Closed 1 Jan–12 Feb and 12 Nov–31 Dec.
TV. Car park.

The *Beau Site* is very appropriately named – it's in the heart of Rocamadour. Some of the well-maintained, attractively decorated bedrooms have a breathtaking view of the abbey perched on the hill. This hotel-restaurant boasts quality facilities which are reflected in the prices. Doubles 320–4395F with shower/wc, 420–520F with bath. Tasty, refined, aromatic dishes are served in a beautiful, flowery dining room. Menus 115–220F. Specialities include leg of free-range lamb and duck *foie gras*. Smiling, unassuming, competent waiters. The terrace is shaded by lime trees. An excellent establishment in its category. 10% discount on the room rate Feb–April and Oct–Nov.

⅍ ☎ |●| HÔTEL-RESTAURANT LES VIEILLES TOURS**

Lieu-dit Lafage (West); take the D673 2.5km in the direction of Payrac.
☎ 05.65.33.68.01 ➡ 05.65.33.68.59
✉ les.vieillestours@wanadoo.fr
Restaurant closed Mon–Sat lunchtimes, Sun evening and evenings of public holidays. **Disabled access**.
Swimming pool. Garden. TV. Car park.

A splendid 16th-century manor house that has been carefully restored by the proprietor,

with a beautiful garden and a swimming pool. The rooms, all with phone and bathroom, are large and extremely pretty, and each is furnished in a different style; doubles 370–500 with shower/wc or bath. TV available on request. Predominantly regional dishes; duck *foie gras* poached in spiced Cahors wine, veal chop in a cep crust with potato, or ham cake with beef *jus*. Menus 130–330F and half board, compulsory July–Aug, costs 377–462F. It's a good idea to book. In summer, the proprietor organises hikes or bike rides in the wild. 10% discount on the room rate April–May and Oct–Nov.

COUZOU   46500 (5KM S)

|●| LA TERRASSE**

How to get there; it's on the banks of the Alzou – cross the bridge on the D36 and it's 5km further on.
☎ 05.65.33.62.83
Closed Sun evening July–Aug, weeknights out of season, a fortnight in Oct and a week at Christmas.

This charming inn has a pair of rustic dining rooms and there's a terrace in summer. Authentic regional cuisine: wonderful *cassoulet*, peasant soup with smoked bacon, duck *confit* and *charcuteries*. The atmosphere and the cuisine are genuinely at one. Menus 95F and a *menu gastronomique*, which costs a little more. Best to book.

MEYRONNE   46200 (14KM N)

⅍ ☎ |●| HÔTEL-RESTAURANT LA TERRASSE**

How to get there: take the D673 for 4km then turn left onto the D15.
☎ 05.65.32.21.60 ➡ 05.65.32.26.93
✉ terasse.Liebus@wanadoo.fr
Closed Tues out of season, and Dec–Feb.
Swimming pool. Garden.

Meyronne is an adorable little village up in the hills and this establishment was at one time the summer residence of the bishops of Tulle. The building is full of charm and character; the stonework walls are covered in ivy and it has beams and turrets with sloping roofs. Prices are reasonable, with comfortable rooms 300–500F in the hotel or the castle proper. They're deliciously cool in summer, which is a considerable plus in this part of the world. The terrace overlooks the valley, which is heavenly in spring. The restaurant specialises in regional dishes, including veal sweetbreads with morels, lamb cutlet with juniper and zander with tarragon. Menus 100–280F. Half board costs 320–400F. 10%

discount on the room rate for the second night Sept–June. Free coffee.

CARENNAC   46110 (25.5KM NE)

🏊 🏠 |●| AUBERGE DU VIEUX QUERCY**

Centre.
☎ 05.65.10.96.59 ➡ 05.65.10.94.05
e vieuzquercy@medianet.fr
Closed Mon out of season, Jan–March and 15 Nov–31 Dec. **Swimming pool. Garden. TV. Car park.**

Handsome tourist complex – with hotels, gardens and swimming pool – built around an old coaching inn in an idyllic setting. The main building is pretty ancient and has character; you can have a room there or in one of the annexes around the pool. Pleasant doubles 280–350F with shower/wc or bath. Half board, compulsory July–Aug, is 310–350F per person. The dining room has views of the garden and a maze of rooftops. Set menus, 98–215F, list local dishes: *feuillantine* of *foie gras* with apples and honey sauce, pancakes with duck *confit* with cabbage, or lamb stew. Good Cahors wine. 10% discount on the room rate 4 May–9 Oct.

🏊 🏠 |●| HOSTELLERIE FÉNELON**

rue Principale.
☎ 05.65.10.96.46 ➡ 05.65.10.94.86
Closed Fri out of season, Sat lunchtime and 6 Jan–17 March. **Swimming pool. Garden. TV. Car park.**

Service lunchtime, and evening until 9pm. A conventional hotel with very decent rooms furnished in country style. Doubles with shower/wc 280F, 350F with bath. The cooking is good, with menus 105–310F. Half board, compulsory July–Sept, costs 290–360F per person. Try the *foie gras*, the pan-fried veal and prawns, morels and ceps in a flaky pastry case or zander with potatoes. The dining room looks over the garden and swimming pool and some tables have views of the river. Free coffee.

RODEZ   12000

🏠 🏠 HÔTEL DE LA TOUR-MAJE***

bd. Gally (Centre).
☎ 05.65.68.34.68 ➡ 05.65.68.27.56
Disabled access. TV. Car park.

This classic hotel incorporates a 14th-century tower which is a vestige of the old ramparts – there's a room sleeping four in the tower. The rooms are pleasant, modern and attractively decorated; 340F with shower/wc, 390F with bath. Piano bar in the

evening. 10% discount mid-Jan to mid-April and mid-Oct to mid-Dec.

🏊 |●| RESTAURANT LA TAVERNE

23 rue de l'Embergue (Centre); it's near the cathedral.
☎ and ➡ 05.65.42.14.51
Closed Sun and public holidays. **Garden.**

A vaulted basement dining room where you'll be served traditional and regional food – rib steak with Roquefort cheese, duck breast, *aligot*, *choucroute*, *fondue*, *tripoux* and *raclette*, and wonderful home-made tarts. Prices are very reasonable; weekday lunch menu 60F and an extensive *menu-carte* for 92F with a selection of nine starters and main courses. There's a terrace at the back, overlooking the garden. Free apéritif.

|●| RESTAURANT WILLY'S

3 rue de la Viarague; it's near the church of Saint-Amans.
☎ 05.65.68.17.34
Closed Sun and Mon.

The building is painted blue and the dining room is in warm, pleasant colours. It's a friendly restaurant specialising in regional cooking with a touch of originality and exoticism. Good fresh produce is used and the fish is very fresh: salmon and prawn kebab with Combara powder, fillet of beef with Arabica beans and *mignon* of pork braised with ginger, cinnamon and nutmeg. 73F weekday lunch menu and another at 120F. You'll be welcomed without fuss and the atmosphere is young, informal and relaxed.

|●| RESTAURANT GOÛTS ET COULEURS

38 rue de Bonald (Centre); it's in one of the streets leading to pl. de la Cité.
☎ 05.65.42.75.10 ➡ 05.65.78.11.20
Closed Sun and Mon.

Service until 9.30pm. Best to book. The dining room is painted in pastel shades and the chef's pictures hang on the walls to create a modern warm atmosphere – perfect for an intimate dinner. The chef is a culinary artist too, and his cooking from the north and south seaboard of the Mediterranean is truly inspired, with delicate touches of colour and flavours: jellied *tajine* of chicken with pickled lemons and olives, fresh sardine *gâteau* marinated with fennel, a *sushi* of wild strawberries with coconut milk, and orange salad with almond milk and orange-flower water. Weekday lunch menus 99F and 115F, with others 142–360F. Attentive but relaxed service. One of the best places hereabouts.

SAINTE-RADEGONDE   12850 (5KM N)

🥾 🏠 |●| SALOON GUEST RANCH***

Landrevie-Sainte-Radegonde; take the D901 in the direction of Massillac.
☎ 05.65.42.47.46 📠 05.65.78.32.36
Closed Mon–Sat lunchtimes to non-residents, and ten days in Feb.

Alain Tournier has created a corner of the American Wild West, with horses and a saloon. It's authentic down to the smallest detail, with mahogony furniture, red wallpaper and lots of photographs. Not surprisingly, meat figures large on the menu, and it's some of the best in the area: thick ribsteaks, spare ribs and char-grilled rib of beef. Very generous set menus, 110–170F. Rooms are spacious and the decor, of course, is cowboy-style – the luxury version. Doubles 300F with shower/wc and 450F with bath. The staff are friendly and considerate. You can ride or take part in any of the many other activities, but you must reserve. Free apéritif coffee or *digestif*.

SALLES-LA SOURCE   12330 (10KM NW)

|●| RESTAURANT DE LA CASCADE

☎ 05.65.67.29.08
Closed Wed evening out of season, Mon evening in season. **Disabled access**.

The small dining room is in pinkish tones and has a ravishing view of the surrounding valleys. The weekday lunch menu, 60F, changes every day and offers two starters, main course, cheese and dessert. Other menus 85–130F. Free *digestif*.

SAINT-AFFRIQUE   12400

🥾 🏠 |●| HÔTEL MODERNE**

54 rue Alphonse-Pezet; it's beside the disused train station.
☎ 05.65.49.20.44 📠 05.65.49.36.55
Hotel closed 20 Dec–20 Jan. **Restaurant closed** second fornight of Oct. **TV. Car park**.

This is a fairly dull part of the town some way from the centre, but it's quiet. Rooms are clean and decent. In the annexe a double with shower (wc along the landing) costs 150F, or 190–390F with shower/wc or bath. The bar is out of this world. Local dishes feature on the menu, but they've been reworked with a lot of imagination – good cooking like this is a rarity in this town. A fair few local specialities use Roquefort, and

there's *charcuterie* and *foie gras*. Set lunch menu 75F or others 90–280F. 10% discount on the room rate Sept–June.

SAINT-ANTONIN-NOBLE-VAL   82140

🏠 |●| HÔTEL DES THERMES**

1 pl. des Moines; if you're coming from the gorges, it's after the bridge on the left.
☎ 05.63.30.61.08 📠 05.63.68.26.23
Closed Thurs out of season. **TV**.

The prices and the waterside location are the best things about this place. Rooms look like those you would find in a chain, and can only just be described as comfortable – the young owners are considering renovations. Doubles with bath from 190F. Some have a view of the river and the Anglars cliff face. Weekday lunch menu 59F, others from 85F.

|●| LA SOURCE

Route de Marsac (South).
☎ 05.63.30.60.28

A lovely stone house with painted shutters on the banks of the Aveyron and a great place if you love your food. The 70F menu offers duck soup, a choice of starters and main courses, and dessert. They don't put the food on plates but bring you a dish to serve yourself. If you have a huge appetite, opt for the 130F menu which adds a gizzard salad, omelette or trout and cheese. If you just want a snack, no problem – choose a salad *à la carte*. The water on the table comes direct from the spring.

SAINT-BERTRAND-DE-COMMINGES   31510

🥾 🏠 HÔTEL DU COMMINGES**

pl. de la Cathédrale.
☎ 05.61.88.31.43 📠 05.61.94.98.22
Closed Nov–March. **Garden. Car park**.

It's great to spend a night in this fantastic village built on a rocky promontory huddled round the cathedral. The hotel is a quite delightful old family house opposite the cathedral, swathed in ivy and wisteria with a small courtyard garden. The whole place is utterly charming. Large rooms with period furniture. Doubles 180F with shower, 300F with bath. 10% discount April, May and Sept.

🥾 🏠 |●| L'OPPIDUM**

rue de la Poste; near the cathedral.
☎ 05.61.88.33.50 📠 05.61.95.94.04
Closed Wed Oct–May and 6 Jan to end of Feb school

holidays. **TV**. **Disabled access**.

A small, pretty hotel that's been beautifully arranged. The rooms are comfortable but rather small, 265–385F with shower/wc or bath, and there's one family room sleeping four. Menus from 85F (not Sun or public holidays) up to185F. There's a tea room. Welcoming staff. They'll lend you a bike if you want to tour this wonderful area. 10% discount on the room rate mid-Dec to mid-May.

◉I CAFÉ-RESTAURANT CHEZ SIMONE

☎ 05.61.94.91.05
Closed evenings out of season and Nov to Christmas.

It's worth making the effort to get here simply for the view, but the cooking, kindly welcome and friendly dining room add to the appeal. The 85F lunch menu is a really full meal from soup to pudding. There's also a 70F menu and, in the evening, only one at 100F. Their speciality is stuffed chicken but you have to order it. Credit cards not accepted.

VALCABRÈRE   31510 (1.5KM E)

◉I LE LUGDUNUM

How to get there: after Valcabrère, join the N25, turn right and it's 400m further on.
☎ 05.61.94.52.05 ➡ 05.61.94.52.06
Closed Sun and Mon evenings, and Wed out of season. **Car park**.

An unusual restaurant which resembles a Roman villa. It has a terrace overlooking the maize fields and a fantastic view of Saint-Bertrand. Renzo Pedrazzini, whose family comes from Lombardy, serves traditional local dishes, but the real attraction here are the recipes he has taken from the ancient Romans: sea bream with grapes, boar with *sauce bouillante*, salad *à l'hypotrima*, Lucanie sausages. He mixes honey and vinegar and won't use tomatoes or lemons, because they were unknown to the ancient Romans, and gets his spices from a local herbalist. He regards himself as an apprentice of Apicius, who wrote a treatise on cooking about 2000 years ago and takes you on a culinary voyage back in time. The 180F *menu antique* offers a gastronomic archeology of forgotten recipes unearthed by Renzo. Take his wife's advice and have a spiced wine with your meal and try the rose or violet apéritif.

SAINT-CIRQ-LAPOPIE   46330

⌂ ◉I AUBERGE DU SOMBRAL

pl. du Sombral (Centre).
☎ 05.65.31.26.08 ➡ 05.65.30.26.37
Closed Tues evening and Wed out of season, and 15 Nov–1 April.

A charming inn with a high-pitched roof and elegant decor. The rooms are appealingly furnished and decorated in soft, warm colours. Professional welcome and attentive service. Doubles 300–420F with shower/wc. Traditional cooking with a justified reputation; *feuilleté quercinois* with ceps, leek *gratin* with truffles and splendid *foie gras*. Menus 75–220F. A reliable establishment.

◉I RESTAURANT L'ATELIER

Le bourg; it's right next to Saint-Cirq.
☎ and ➡ 05.65.31.22.34
Closed Tues evening and Wed except school holidays, and Jan to mid-Feb.

Right at the top of the hill you'll find this old building that's full of character. There's a warm, cosy atmosphere so you'll quickly feel at home and the hearty cooking will delight gourmets and your average traveller alike. Menus 65–160F list a flow of never-ending courses, with dishes like Toulouse sausage and chips, *cassoulet* and good *foie gras* served with a glass of white wine – excellent value for money.

TOUR DE FAURE   46330 (3KM W)

⌂≡ ⌂ HÔTEL LES GABARRES**

Le bourg; take the D662 towards Figeac.
☎ 05.65.30.24.57 ➡ 05.65.30.25.85
Closed Nov–April. **Disabled access**. **Swimming pool**. **Garden. Car park**.

This is not the most beautiful building but the excellent reception and the bright, clean, spacious bedrooms more than make up for this. Half the rooms overlook the swimming pool and in some parts of the establishment you get great views of the valley. Doubles with shower/wc or bath 250–280F. There's a hearty buffet breakfast. The couple in charge can tell you about the various walks around these parts. 10% discount.

SAINT-FÉLIX-LAURAGAIS   31540

⌂ ◉I AUBERGE DU POIDS PUBLIC***

Faubourg Saint-Roch (West).
☎ 05.61.83.00.20 ➡ 05.61.83.86.21
Closed Sun evening Oct–April, and Jan.
TV. Garden. Car park.

Delightful rooms – some with views of the Lauragais hills. Doubles 280–350F with shower/wc or bath and direct phone. There are several little sitting rooms and a large, rustic dining room with fine exposed stonework and panoramic views. The atmosphere is classy. Set menus 140–350F – there's a simple one, a vegetarian one and the menu "*Auberge*" which includes *foie gras* cooked in a cloth, milk-fed lamb, Aquitaine sturgeon and summer fruit *croustillant*. You'll find comparatively unknown wines as well as the great vintages on the wine list from the affordable to the astronomical. The terrace is extremely pleasant in summer.

SAINT-JULIA   31540 (6KM N)

🏃 |●| L'AUBERGE DES REMPARTS

rue du Vinaigre.
☎ 05.61.83.04.79
Closed Sun and Mon evening.

A village inn with a growing reputation. Appetising menu of the day, 65F, lists soup, *crudités*, *charcuterie*, dish of the day, cheese, dessert, wine and coffee. In the evening, the young chef shows his colours with more elaborate, refined cooking on menus 95–135F. Try raw salmon marinated with dill, *croustillant* of sea bream, or roast duck baked with apples. In good weather they serve meals on the shady terrace. Free apéritif and coffee.

SAINT-FERRÉOL   31350

🏠 |●| HÔTELLERIE DU LAC

av. Pierre-Paul-de-Riquet.
☎ 05.52.18.70.80 ➡ 05.62.18.71.13
Closed Sun evening except July–Aug.
Swimming pool. Garden. Car park.

The hotel has been beautifully renovated since Chabrol used it for shooting most of his film, *L'Enfer*. It's plush but colourful. The rooms, 350F, are comfortable and some have views of the lake. The ground floor, dining rooms, sitting room and bar have also had a facelift. The cuisine is of the same high standard, on menus 90F (not Sun or public holidays) and 120–190F: duck *terrine*, lamb shank or red mullet fillets *à la Provençale*. The swimming pool is heated, there's a sauna and a conservatory with retro charm overlooking the garden. Friendly welcome.

SAINT-GAUDENS   31800

🏃 |●| RESTAURANT DE L'ABATTOIR

bd. Leconte-de-Lisle (South); it's opposite the abattoir.
☎ 05.61.89.70.29

Closed Sun evening–Wed.

One of the best restaurants in the region. Nowhere else will you get meat that's as fresh, tender and downright delicious as at Christian Gillet's place. He's at the abattoirs every morning at dawn, choosing cuts of meat to feed the dealers who have come in from the country to sell their animals at market. The dining room is always packed. Try the sirloin, the flank of beef, the rib of beef with bone marrow, or the grilled Arbas black pudding. Weekday lunch menu 70F or 90–120F *à la carte*. The large dining room is bright and pleasant and the atmosphere is more matey than intimate. Free apéritif.

SAINT-GENIEZ-D'OLT   12130

🏃 🏠 |●| HÔTEL DE LA POSTE**

3 pl. Charles-de-Gaulle.
☎ 05.65.47.43.30 ➡ 05.65.47.42.75
Closed Mon Oct–May and Jan-Feb.
Swimming pool. Garden. TV. Lock-up car park.

A traditional village inn with an old part, *La Réception*, and modern annexe, *Le Golf*. The former, furnished with superb antiques, is comfortable and cosy. The rooms are pleasant: 235F with shower/wc and 295F with bath. The restaurant, across the road in the annexe, is well-known for its quality cooking. You can eat in the dining room, on the veranda surrounded by greenery or in the glassed-in terrace on the first floor. Set menus 68F (except Sun), then 80–120F. The house classics include lamb sweetbreads with ceps, rabbit *terrine* with oyster mushrooms and trout *rillettes*. Half board, compulsory 1–20 Aug, costs 260–330F per person. 10% discount on the room rate Sept–June.

SAINTE-EULALIE-D'OLT   12130 (3KM W)

🏃 🏠 |●| AU MOULIN D'ALEXANDRE**

Centre.
☎ 05.65.47.45.85 ➡ 05.65.52.73.78
Closed Sun evening from All Saints' to Easter, 7–20 May and the first fortnight in Oct. **Garden. Car park.**

A most delightful country inn in a renovated 17th-century water mill. The setting is idyllic and very restful. Pleasant welcome. Pretty rooms 240F with shower/wc and 250F with bath. The cooking's good and prices are reasonable, with a 65F menu (not served Sun or public holidays) and others up to 145F, and good *à la carte* choices. The restaurant specialises in regional dishes like home-made *tripoux*, stuffed ceps, chanterelle omelette and stuffed breast of veal. The strawberry *millefeuille* they do in season is quite something. Half board, 280F a head, is compulsory July–Sept. Boats and mountain bikes are available for hire. Free apéritif or coffee.

SAINT-GIRONS   09200

⚥ 🏠 |●| HÔTEL-RESTAURANT LA CLAIRIÈRE**

av. de la Résistance (Southwest); it's on the outskirts of town in the direction of Seix-Massat.
☎ 05.61.66.66.66 ➡ 05.34.14.30.30
Swimming pool.Disabled access. Garden. TV. Lock-up car park.

A really wonderful place away from the grinding traffic on the roads. Rooms are bright and comfortable and overlook the leafy park. Doubles 250–280F. The restaurant, which glows with Mediterranean colour, has a small boat in the centre of the room. Menus 89F for lunch, then 120–220F, listing delicious shellfish *tartare* with *aioli* zinging with garlic and chilli pepper, and very good monkfish stew. In winter the atmosphere changes when they light a fire in the huge fireplace and create menus full of regional dishes. 10% discount onthe room rate Sept–June.

SAINT-LARY-SOULAN   65170

🏠 |●| HÔTEL-RESTAURANT LA PERGOLA

It's in the main street.
☎ 05.62.39.40.46 ➡ 05.62.40.06.55
Garden. TV. Car park.

A pleasant establishment, opened in 1957, that's set back from the road with a pretty garden and, of course, a pergola. The spacious rooms are comfortable, with wonderful beds, en-suite bathrooms, hair drier and TV. The ones facing southwest have a view of Le Pla-d'Adet. Doubles 280–360F. With regard to the service, they sometimes have to be pressed to let you have a room without your being obliged to take breakfast (an extra 40F). But the talent of the chef makes up for this somewhat and he uses lots of fragrant herbs in his cooking. Menus 100–250F.

SAINT-LIZIER   09190

🏠 |●| HÔTEL DE LA TOUR

Route du Pont; it's at the foot of the old town on the banks of the Salat.
☎ 05.61.66.38.02

The renovation of this historic hotel, the only one in the historic capital of the Couserans,

has been long due. It's got nine sweet rooms 190–250F; some have views of the river and others even have little balconies. The chef iis creative – his *foie gras* and apple tart are special, or you can order simple grills. Weekday menu 58F, and others 85–165F.

SAINT-MARTIN-D'ARMAGNAC   32110

🏠 |●| AUBERGE DU BERGERAYRE

How to get there: take the right turning off the D25.
☎ 05.62.09.08.72 ➡ 05.62.09.09.74
Closed Sun and Tues evenings and Wed. **Disabled access.Swimming pool. Garden. TV. Car park.**

A wonderful inn deep in the countryside, complete with garden and swimming pool – you'll revel in the peace and quiet. The extremely comfortable rooms are all at ground level, and distributed in to different buildings; 300–700F with shower/wc or bath. The top-price ones are in the old granary and have real character and luxurious facilities. Half board, obligatory in high season, costs 255–500F. The restaurant has a very good reputation, and you'll eat in a warm, friendly dining room with rustic decor. Menus 100–200F. Dishes change through the seasons as and when fresh produce becomes available – *cassoulet* or *salade Gasconne*, chicken cooked in a caul, potatoes *au gratin* and, if you can stretch to it, try the *foie gras* cooked over vine cuttings. Best to book.

SAINT-SERNIN-SUR-RANCE   12380

⚥ 🏠 |●| HÔTEL CARAYON**

pl. du Fort; it's on the D999 between Albi and Millau.
☎ 05.65.98.19.19 ➡ 05.65.99.69.26
ℯ carayon.hotel@wanadoo.fr
Closed Fri evening, Sat lunchtime, Sun evening and Mon out of season. **Disabled access. Swimming pool. TV. Lock-up car park.**

The *Carayon* is a quality place and something of an institution. The owners are on first-name terms with all the local worthies. Some of the comfortable rooms have a balcony looking over the grounds and the country beyond; doubles 199–399F with shower/wc or bath. The cuisine has a great reputation and the chef gives you every opportunity to try something wonderful by offering seven menus; 55F, not served Sunday lunchtime, and others 135–300F. *À la carte* you can get pot-roast quail, pigeon in *salmis* sauce, lamb sweetbread with garlic and parsley, goose heart kebabs, cep omelette and tempting desserts. If the weather's good, you can sit on the terrace and enjoy the panoramic views or swim in one of the two pools. You can also play tennis or golf, have a sauna or take a pedal boat on the river – all free of charge for guests. 10% discount on the room rate Oct–May.

SALMIECH　　　　12120

🏃 🛏 |●| HÔTEL DU CÉOR

☎ and ➦ 05.65.46.70.13
Closed Sun evening and Mon out of season.

This 19th-century coaching inn offers terrific value. There are thirty pleasant rooms, 130–184F; reckon on 174–229F a head for half board. Regional dishes dominate in the pretty, rustic dining room: *tripou*, *aligot*, duck breast cooked over a fire of vine shoots, and crayfish with the chef's special sauce. Desserts include walnut tart and chocolate profiteroles. Menus 89–199F. You can sit out on the terrace in good weather and admire the view of the village. Very welcoming owner. Free apéritif.

SAMATAN　　　　32130

|●| AU CANARD GOURMAND

La Rente; It's on the road to Lombez.
☎ 05.62.62.49.81
Closed Mon evening and Tues..

Ingenious interpretations of local cuisine. Lots of different *foie gras* dishes: one with dill, another pan-fried with vanilla sauce, and an amazing one with liquorice. The dishes change with the seasons and the fresh market produce. Menus start at 99F, and there are two *menu-cartes* at 130F and 165F. The dining room is warm and pleasant. While the service is efficient, the welcome is distant.

SAUVETERRE-DE-ROUERGUE　　　　12800

🏃 🛏 |●| LA GRAPPE D'OR

It's a stone's throw from pl. des Arcades.
☎ 05.65.72.00.62.
Closed Wed evening out of season. **Garden**.

A small village hotel that's very well run and has double rooms with shower/wc for 185F. The restaurant offers simple, robust country cooking. *Menu du jour* at 68F, one with regional dishes at 85F, and a "celebration" menu at 95F (served Sun and holidays). Good-quality, simple, local dishes: *tripou*, chicken and duck *confit*, and gizzard salad. The garden is very nice and the setting alone is worth stopping for. Free coffee.

🏃 🛏 |●| LE SÉNÉCHAL***

It's north outside the fortifications.
☎ 05.65.71.29.00
Closed Mon and Tues lunchtime except July–Aug and 1 Jan–15 March. **Swimming pool. Disabled access. TV. Car park.**

Local boy Michel Truchon loves his region – he talks about it with passion and will fill you in on its history or send you off to find wild roses. He also cares about quality produce, and sets about his cooking like an artist, creating wonderful dishes which are sophisticated and subtle. Set menus 150–370F. Try the lentil *terrine* served with pig's ears or braised veal with local potatoes drizzled with olive oil and served with aubergine caviar. For dessert try an iced coffee *parfait* with endive seeds. You also get *amuse-bouches* and a lovely welcome. The rooms are quite magnificent with terracotta floors and designer decor. Doubles with bath around 600F. Service is faultless yet unpretentious and friendly. Free apéritif.

SOUILLAC　　　　46200

🏃 🛏 |●| GRAND HÔTEL***

1 allée Verninac (Centre).
☎ 05.65.32.78.30 ➦ 05.65.32.66.34
Closed Wed April and Oct, and Nov–March. **TV. Car park.**

This hotel is owned by the family of Roger Couderc, a popular rugby commentator. There are lots of comfortable rooms and some overlook an atrium; doubles with shower/wc 205–430F or 325–510F with bath. There's also a solarium and a nice terrace with panoramic views. The restaurant, classical in style and understated in decor, has a good reputation for typical dishes from the Quercy region. The cheapest menu is 80F and there are others up to 250F – house specialities include *Périgourdine* tripe with capers, flash-fried sole with truffle oil and creamy sauce, and roast fillet of zander with ceps. A *trompe l'oeil* mural forms the backdrop for a shady terrace, which is pleasant in summer. 10% discount on the room rate April and Oct.

🏃 🛏 |●| LA VIEILLE AUBERGE***

1 rue de la Recège (Centre).
☎ 05.65.32.79.43 ➦ 05.65.32.65.19
Closed Sun evening and Mon Jan–March and mid-Nov to mid-Dec. **Swimming pool. TV. Car park.**

This "old inn" is a very modern hotel with a gastronomic restaurant. All rooms have satellite TV and video, and there's a gym, sauna, solarium and heated swimming pool. Doubles with shower/wc or bath 280–360F. Chef Robert Véril is a staunch traditionalist who uses only local produce to create delicious dishes from the Quercy and Périgord: pan-fried *escalope* of *foie gras* with walnuts, *estouffade* of potatoes with truffles cooked in the oven, *galette* of cabbage with duck *confit*. He has even unearthed some almost-forgotten recipes such as *vermicelle Quercynois*, a garlic soup with eggs. Menus 120–350F. The wine list leans heavily towards Cahors and other southwestern wines. 10% discount on the room rate Sept–June.

TARASCON-SUR-ARIÈGE 09400

⅍ 🏠 HÔTEL CONFORT**

3 quai Armand-Sylvestre (Centre).
☎ and ➟ 05.61.05.57.79
Closed 8–19 Jan.
TV. Garden. Pay garage.

This welcoming place is right in the centre of town but, being on the banks of the Ariège, it's quiet. The setting is magnificent. There are fourteen rooms, all overlooking the garden – some are particularly roomy and also have a view of the river. Doubles 160F with basin, up to 240F with bath. There's a 30F charge for use of the garage. Breakfast 30F. 10% discount on the room rate and free breakfast, except during school holidays.

TARBES 65000

⅍ 🏠 HÔTEL DE L'AVENUE**

78–80 av. Bertrand Barère; it's 50m from the station.
☎ and ➟ 05.62.93.06.36
Disabled access. TV. Car park.

This is a quiet little hotel, despite being close to the station. The rooms are a bit bland but they're good value for money – doubles 100F with basin, and 160F–190F with shower/wc or bath. The ones overlooking the internal courtyard are the quietest. There's a family atmosphere and the owner's father, who retired a while ago, still welcomes the guests occasionally. 10% discount.

⅍ 🏠 |●| L'ISARD**

70 av. du Maréchal-Joffre (North); it's near the station.
☎ 05.62.93.06.69 ➟ 05.62.93.99.55
Closed Sun evening. **Garden. TV.**

A tiny, likeable hotel on a main road, with eight pleasant rooms; doubles with shower/wc or bath 180–220F. Some look over the garden and are really quiet. The owner is

delightful and very accommodating. In the conventional restaurant there are menus and *formules* to suit all budgets – 65–200F. Dishes include *foie gras*, scrambled eggs with fresh liver, *cassoulet* with white kidney beans and prune ice cream with Armagnac. In fine weather meals are served in the garden under the awning. 10% discount on the room rate for a two-night stay Oct–April.

⅍ |●| CHEZ PATRICK

6 rue Adolphe d'Eichtal; on the corner of rue Saint-Jean.
☎ 05.62.36.36.82
Closed evenings, Sun and a fortnight in Aug. **Car park.**

A wonderful local restaurant, just out of the centre, with a clientèle of regulars who work round the corner or live nearby. It's run by a big family, who keep a cheery atmosphere in the dining room. The cooking is generously flavoured and prices are reasonable – the 58F menu includes soup, starter, dish of the day, wine and dessert. It's best to arrive early at lunchtime as it gets very full. Free coffee.

|●| LE FIL À LA PATTE

30 rue Georges-Lasalle.
☎ 05.62.93.39.23
Closed Sun evening and Mon out of season, the first week in Jan and the last three weeks in Aug.

A tiny, chic little restaurant with yellow wall for all the world like a Parisian bistro. New-style, inventive cuisine with lots of fish and local dishes given fresh interpretations. Weekday lunch menu 75F then 97–145F. Polite, slightly distant service that could relax a little.

JUILLAN 65290 (5KM SW)

🏠 |●| L'ARAGON**

2 ter route de Lourdes; it's on the D921A.
☎ 05.62.32.07.07 ➟ 05.62.32.92.50
Closed Sun evening, a fortnight in the Feb school holidays, the first fortnight in Aug and 26 Dec–4 Jan.
Disabled access. TV. Car park.

Lovely double rooms which have been thematically decorated (the sea, rugby and so on) and have efficient double glazing; 290F with shower/wc and mini-bar, 320F with bath. There's a bistro serving *formules bistrot* at 75F and 98F, and a rather plush dining room where the service is impeccable, and the cooking rightly enjoys quite a reputation. *Menu du marché* 180F, a fish menu 250F and a gourmet one for 300F – *gazpacho* with crayfish, scrambled eggs with caviar, duck and goose *confit* with kidney bean stew and a soufflé of pears and fruit brandy.

ARCIZAC-ADOUR 65360 (11KM S)

|●| LA CHAUDRÉE

10 route des Pyrénées; it's on the D935 in the direction of Bagnères.
☎ 05.62.45.32.00
Closed Sun evening, Mon, a fortnight in Feb and three weeks in Aug.

A classic little establishment that, despite its unassuming appearance, is one of the best places to eat locally. The dining room has a rustic feel with solid beams and a splendid walnut buffet table – very "Vieille France". There's a 65F lunchtime menu (not served Sun), and others 98–170F: veal sweetbreads, duck *foie gras* with apple and bilberry sauce, and *garbure* which is broth with *confit*. The cuisine is refined and dishes are beautifully presented.

TOULOUSE 31000

SEE MAP OVERLEAF

♠ HÔTEL ANATOLE-FRANCE*

46 pl. Anatole-France. **MAP B2-2**
☎ 05.61.23.19.96 ➡ 05.61.21.47.66
TV.

You'll get a wonderful welcome in this good-value hotel. Reception is on the first floor. All rooms have direct-dial phones and are exceptionally clean. The rooms have been freshly refurbished: doubles 120F with basin and 175F with shower/wc or bath.

♠ HÔTEL DES ARTS*

rue des Arts, 1 [bis] rue Cantegril. **MAP C2-4**
☎ 05.61.23.36.21 ➡ 05.61.12.22.37

In a picturesque neighbourhood in the middle of town, this hotel has a maze of corridors leading to pleasant, spacious rooms. Some of them have fireplaces or overlook the courtyard. They're not very well soundproofed, Doubles with washing facilities 155F and up to 190F with shower/wc. You order your breakfast the night before and it's served in your room – there's no breakfast room – or you can have it in one of the numerous cafés nearby. 5% discount.

♠ HÔTEL DU GRAND BALCON*

8 rue Romiguières. **MAP C2-3**
☎ 05.61.21.48.08 ➡ 05.61.21.59.98
Closed three weeks in Aug. **TV**.

The pilots who used to fly the mail planes would spend their last night here before taking off for Alicante, Africa or South America. Saint-Exupéry used to stay in room 32. The hotel has hardly changed since and is filled with photos of the glory days. The Marquès sisters ran the place for place for fifty years, and Monsieur Brousse, who took over from them, was here more than forty, so there's a solid feeling of tradition. It's only just changed hands again and the new owners are gradually updating it. Doubles 180–240F. Breakfast 25F. Rooms overlooking the street are noisy.

♠ HÔTEL CROIX-BARAGNON

17 rue Croix-Baragnon. **MAP C3-1**
☎ 05.61.52.50.10 ➡ 05.61.52.08.60

Right in the centre near the 13th-century Romanesque house and the Saint-Étienne cathedral. The hotel itself is also very charming and has an external staircase entwined with plants. You have to go up to the first floor to find reception where a really warm welcome awaits. The rooms are more comfortable than amazing – some have windows over the courtyard – but the atmosphere pervading is more like an apartment building. Doubles 190F with shower/wc and TV, or twin rooms 200–220F. It's advisable to book.

♠ HÔTEL TRIANON**

7 rue Lafaille. **MAP C1-8**
☎ 05.61.62.74.74 ➡ 05.61.99.15.44
TV. Car park.

A delightful little hotel with pleasant, comfortable rooms; doubles with shower/wc 270F or 320F with bath. The ones at the rear are quieter though some at the front have double-glazing. In summer, you can have breakfast on the patio; in winter you eat in the magnificent vaulted wine cellars where the owner also organises wine tastings. He's so keen on wine that he's named the rooms after great vineyards.

♠ HÔTEL VICTOR HUGO**

26 bd. de Strasbourg. **MAP C1-14**
☎ 05.61.63.40.41 ➡ 05.61.62.66.31
Closed a week Christmas to New Year.
TV. Disabled access.

This is one of the better hotels in this category in Toulouse. It's good value for money, though it's more functional than charming. The spotless rooms, 270F with shower/wc or bigger ones at 320F with bath. Some have air conditioning and the triple glazing is efficient. Warm welcome.

♠ HÔTEL SAINT-SERNIN**

2 rue Saint-Bernard. **MAP C1-11**
☎ 05.61.21.73.08 ➡ 05.61.22.49.61
TV. Car park.

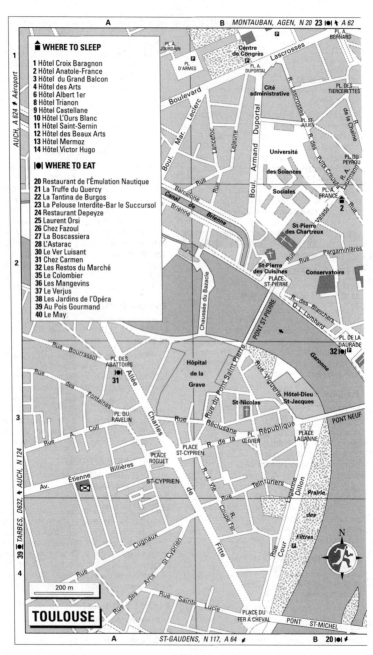

⌂ WHERE TO SLEEP

1 Hôtel Croix Baragnon
2 Hôtel Anatole-France
3 Hôtel du Grand Balcon
4 Hôtel des Arts
6 Hôtel Albert 1er
8 Hôtel Trianon
9 Hôtel Castellane
10 Hôtel L'Ours Blanc
11 Hôtel Saint-Sernin
12 Hôtel des Beaux Arts
13 Hôtel Mermoz
14 Hôtel Victor Hugo

|●| WHERE TO EAT

20 Restaurant de l'Émulation Nautique
21 La Truffe du Quercy
22 La Tantina de Burgos
23 La Pelouse Interdite-Bar le Succursol
24 Restaurant Depeyze
25 Laurent Orsi
26 Chez Fazoul
27 La Boscassiera
28 L'Astarac
30 Le Ver Luisant
31 Chez Carmen
32 Les Restos du Marché
35 Le Colombier
36 Les Mangevins
37 Le Verjus
38 Les Jardins de l'Opéra
39 Au Pois Gourmand
40 Le May

TOULOUSE

200 m

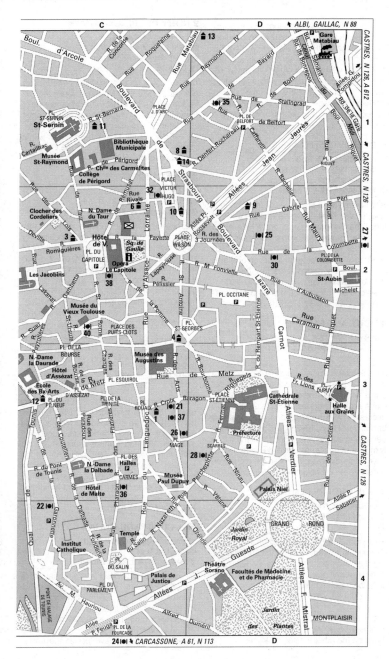

A lovely, comfortable hotel that's been completely renovated. Reception is on the first floor and the staff will welcome you with a smile. Attractive rooms with shower/wc from 290F; 390F with bath, direct phone and mini-bar. There are four rooms with a stunning view of the basilica. The bar on the ground floor isn't fantastic but they serve the best *croque-monsieurs* in town. Very noisy at the weekend because of the local flea market.

⚔ 🏠 HÔTEL CASTELLANE**

17 rue Castellane. **MAP D2-9**
☎ 05.61.62.18.82 ➡ 05.61.62.58.04
e castellanehotel.com
Disabled access. TV. Pay garage.

Very new hotel in an excellent location in a quiet street. Built around a patio, it's full of light. The pleasant rooms are a little small but have modern facilities; doubles with shower or bath cost 300F. There are also family rooms, sleeping up to seven and studios with kitchenettes rented by the night. Nice breakfast room. Pleasant, professional welcome. 10% discount except at weekends and in the school holidays.

🏠 HÔTEL ALBERT-1ER**

8 rue Rivals. **MAP C2-6**
☎ 05.61.21.17.91 ➡ 05.61.21.09.64
TV. Car park.

A small hotel in a quiet street in the commercial centre. Excellent, professional welcome but with a family feel. The owner produces home-made jams for breakfast. The pleasant foyer is decorated with mosaics and pink Toulouse bricks. You'll pay 310–350F for a double room depending on the facilities, and a bit more for a twin room. They're all comfortable and most have air conditioning. They can get you preferential rates in the neighbouring car park.

🏠 HÔTEL L'OURS BLANC**

2 rue Victor-Hugo. **MAP C2-10**
☎ 05.61.21.62.40 ➡ 05.61.23.62.34
TV.

This district is full of mid-range hotels and this one, in a beautiful, rounded 1930s building, has excellent facilities like TV, telephone and air conditioning. Bedrooms all have en-suite bathrooms but the decor is disappointing: doubles 340–380F. Breakfast 40F. They've modernised the foyer but have kept the very old wooden lift cage. There are 75 rooms in total, including those in their other hotel on the other side of the street.

🏠 HÔTEL DES BEAUX-ARTS****

1 pl. du Pont-Neuf. **MAP C3-12**
☎ 05.61.23.40.50 ➡ 05.61.22.02.27
e contact@hoteldesbeauxarts.com
TV. Car park.

This classy hotel is a favourite with visiting politicians and actors staying in Toulouse. The façade is 18th-century but the decor inside is decidedly modern and up to international hotel standards. Doubles with shower/wc 490–1050F. There's one on the top floor with a terrace and a wonderful view of the Garonne. Buffet breakfast 85F.

🏠 HÔTEL MERMOZ***

50 rue Matabiau. **MAP D1-13**
☎ 05.61.63.04.04 ➡ 05.61.63.15.34
Disabled access. TV. Pay garage.

This hotel is protected from the noisy street by an interior courtyard; it's a modern, vaguely Neoclassical building with an elegant flight of steps. The decor makes lots of references to the airmail service, with Art Deco furniture and drawings of aeroplanes on the walls but all given a modern twist. About fifty very well equipped, spacious bedrooms; doubles 530F. Tthey have attractive weekend deals. Buffet breakfast 60F.

⚔ 🍽 LE MAY

4 rue du May. **MAP C2-40**
☎ 05.61.23.98.76
Closed Sun lunchtime.

Right in the heart of the old town you'll find this restaurant with its two small, warm dining rooms. In sumer they add a pleasant terrace. It's often packed because the food is good and cheap. There's a two-course lunch *formule* for 46F and a three-course menu for 56F, and menus at 82F and 95F in the evening. Freshly cooked dishes using local produce: house *confit*, duck breast with *foie gras*, vegetarian platter, marinated fish dishes in summer and casseroles in winter. Free house apéritif or *digestif*.

🍽 LA TRUFFE DU QUERCY

17 rue Croix-Baragnon. **MAP C3-21**
☎ 05.61.53.34.24
Closed Sun, public holidays and Aug.

Renovated country decor and a relaxed family atmosphere in a real local restaurant. Good, traditional dishes from recipes that have been handed down from father to son over seventy years. Menus 55–128F, individual dishes from 40F. À la carte, you can get home-made *cassoulet au confit* and a few Spanish specialities.

🍴 |●| CHEZ FAZOUL

2 rue Tolosane. **MAP C3-26**
☎ 05.61.53.72.09
Closed Sun. Disabled access.

This restaurant has been serving good food for some time in its lovely and rather elegant 17th-century dining room. The weekday lunch menu, 65F, includes wine, service and a self-service buffet of *hors d'oeuvres*. Other menus 105–165F list good regional dishes, particularly the excellent *foie gras* and the rabbit with *aïoli*. Free sangria.

🍴 |●| L'ASTARAC

21 rue Perchepinte. **MAP D3-28**
☎ 05.61.53.11.15
Closed Sat lunchtime, Sun and mid-July to mid-Aug.

Service lunchtime and evening until 10pm. This excellent restaurant is tucked away in a narrow street in the old town; the tall room has sturdy beams and red brick walls hung with attractive paintings. There are discreet booths with comfy banquettes where you can have an intimate dinner for two. Tremendous Gascon cooking, with dishes such as salad of duck legs with *foie gras* or *paupiettes* of chicken with a cep cream sauce. Weekday lunch menu 65F, others 105–165. For 160F you'll get two types of *foie gras*, tournedos of duck with a cep sauce, or *poêlée Gasconne*. Sensibly priced wines like Fronton and Côtes-de-Saint-Mont. Free Pruneau à l'Armagnac.

|●| LA BOSCASSIERA

1 rue Saint-Paul. Off map **D2-27**
☎ 05.61.20.34.11.
Closed Sat, Sun, Mon and mid-July to early Sept.

Nicolas used to run a mountain cabin in the Ariège but came to town to open this restaurant. The dining room is vast – this is where the first French jet plane was designed. It's beautifully furnished and you can see into the kitchen. Nicolas is a big man who cooks dishes from all over the region as they are intended to be cooked. Specialities include *confit* and *fricandeaux* of duck, *garbure*, Baltic herrings and an outstanding cod *cassoulet*. 65F lunch menu, or around 120F *à la carte*.

|●| LES RESTOS DU MARCHÉ

pl. Victor-Hugo. **MAP C2-32**
Closed evenings and Mon.

A real Toulouse special. On market days at lunchtime, go up to the first floor of this concrete shed which has been recently renovated. There you'll find an amazingly lively and colourful scene, with a row of half a dozen small restaurants providing plates of wholesome food cooked using the freshest market produce, for the cheapest prices – menus around 65F including wine. The names give you a clue to the style of cuisine on offer: *Le Méditerranée*, *Le Magret* or *Chez Attila* which specialises in fish and *zarzuela* (a sort of Spanish *bouillabaisse*). *Le Louchébem* offers a broad bean cassoulet on the first Saturday in the month, while at *Samaran*, you can buy your *foie gras* fresh or cooked.

🍴 |●| RESTAURANT DE L'ÉMULATION NAUTIQUE

allée Alfred-Mayssonière. Off map **B4-20**
☎ 05.61.25.34.95
Closed Sun and Mon evenings, evenings if it's raining and Christmas to mid-Jan. **Garden**.

The best of the sailing club restaurants on the island of Ramier, just south of the town centre. It has a beautiful terrace, shaded by plane trees and looking out over the water. Weekday lunch menu 69F; *à la carte* in the evening and at weekends for around 110F. The grills are enormous; try their roast beef or lamb shank, or one of the tasty salads. A wonderful place in summer. Free apéritif.

🍴 |●| LE COLOMBIER

14 rue de Bayard. **MAP D1-35**
☎ 05.61.62.40.05
Closed Sat lunchtime, Sun and Aug.

You're here for the *cassoulet*, with goose *confit* that's been renowned for several generations. The recipe is such a secret that it's been lodged with a notary. *À la carte* it costs 125F, but you can also get it on the 165F and 185F menus along with other regional specialities: salad of *lardons* with *confit* gizzards, medallion of duck *foie gras au torchon*, duck *foie gras* in goose fat and *croustade* of apples in Armagnac. There's a 79F lunch *formule* served in the week and menus 100–185F. Free apéritif.

|●| LE VER LUISANT

41 rue de la Colombette. **MAP D2-30**
☎ 05.61.63.06.73
Closed Sat lunchtime, Sun, and mid-July to mid-Aug.

The restaurant is popular with theatre people and artists – it is smartish and bohemian. The cooking is classical and portions are generous, with excellent, inventive meat and main dishes. In summer, there's grilled duck, salads, kebabs and so on and in winter they produce hearty dishes like *daube*, salt pork with lentils and *confits*. Reckon on 90–120F *à la carte*, with dishes of the day for 35F. Great atmosphere, and a nice bar for an apéritif.

🎋 |●| ORSI-LE BOUCHON LYONNAIS

13 rue de l'Industrie. **MAP D2-25**
☎ 05.61.62.97.43
Closed Sat lunchtime or Sun.

This establishment is named after a famous gourmet chef from Lyons and is run by his brother. He produces specialities from his adopted region and creates very good Lyonnais specialities. The menus list dishes like *tablier de sapeur* (a slab of breaded ox tripe), pig's trotters and sliced *andouillette*, and the one with Gascon specialities features one of the best *cassoulets* in town. Menus 99–195F and a lunch *formule* for 90F. The decor is a classy Belle Époque brasserie. Quality cooking and quick service provided by attractive waiting staff. Free apéritif.

🎋 |●| CHEZ CARMEN-RESTAURANT DES ABATTOIRS

97 allée Charles-de-Fitte. **MAP A3-31**
☎ 05.61.42.04.95
Closed Sun, Mon, public holidays and Aug.

The local abattoirs have gone – they've been turned into a contemporary art centre – but the meat here is as good as ever. The bistro (it's been going 40 years) buzzes with life. Efficient, if brusque service under the watchful eye of the owner, José-Antoine Carmen. Great plates of grilled meat or local dishes *à la carte* – calf's head, pig's trotters, steak *tartare* or steak with garlic. Menu 95F (starter, meat dish and dessert) or about 150F *à la carte*. There are a few tables outside in summer. Free apéritif.

🎋 |●| LA PELOUSE INTERDITE-BAR LE SUCCURSAL

72 av. des États-Unis. Off map **B1-23**
☎ 05.61.47.30.40
Closed Oct–April and when it's raining. **Garden**.

A rare and unusual place – the corners of the extraordinary garden are illuminated by numerous candles, furnished with junk-shop tables, chairs and large armchairs, table football and even hammocks and beds! Inside, in winter, there's a brilliantly coloured bar with a DJ who plays in the week. Delicious, inventive cuisine: goat's cheese and honey turnover, chicken with crayfish, curry, duck breast. It's essential to book. When you get there, ring the bell and wait. There's a *menu-carte*, 100F, and a two-course *formule*. Free aperitif or *digestif*.

🎋 |●| LA TANTINA DE BURGOS

27 av. de la Garonnette. **MAP C4-22**
☎ 05.61.55.59.29
Closed Sun and Mon.

Service 7pm–1am. Very popular, a bit bohemian and decidedly Spanish. The terrace is pleasant in fine weather, while inside there is a large, lively dining room where you can sit at large tables or have a few tapas at the bar that's a long as a barge. They've opened a second, smaller, dining room which serves a mixture of French and Spanish dishes at very reasonable prices, including *chicano* or chicken, *paella*, squid, sea bass *tourte*, prawns and *empanadas*. Expect to pay around 100F *à la carte*. Free aperitif.

|●| RESTAURANT DEPEYRE

77 route de Revel. Off map **C4-24**
☎ 05.61.20.26.56
Closed Sun and Aug.

It's 3km out of town on the edge of the road but both the "Vielle France" decor and the cuisine here are really attractive. Jacques Depeyre is a Maître-Cuisinier de France – so he's no slouch – while his wife used to run a restaurant in Brial. They're real professionals and have only recently come to Toulouse. The menus have names – *"Leger"*, *"Séduisant"*, *"Fameux"* and *"Plantureux"* – and dishes include a *pâté* of three kinds of fish with a sorrel *mousseline*, beef braised in Quercy wine, scallop stew with vegetables, fine fruit tarts and iced Grand Marnier *bombe*. The prices are a tad high – lunch menu 100F, others 170–320F – but not when you consider the quality of the food. A very good restaurant

🎋 |●| AU POIS GOURMAND

3 rue Émile Heybrard (off av. Casselardit). Off map, **near A3-39**
☎ 05.61.31.95.95 ⏩ 05.61.49.52.13
Closed Sat and Mon lunchtimes, Sun, a week in Feb and a fortnight in Aug.

It's not easy to find this place but it's worth the effort. It's a lovely house, built in 1870, which stands on the banks of the Garonne. There is a weekday lunch menu at 130F, and three other menus 200–380F. The cooking certainly deserves its good reputation; just try the brill fillet *à la badiane*. The dining room is magnificent, and there are green plants all round the terrace. Free Kir.

|●| LE VERJUS

7 rue Tolosane. **MAP C3-37**

☎ 05.61.52.06.93
Closed Sun, Mon, and July–Aug.

Service to 11pm. The simple dining room is brightened up by pictures. It's popular for its unpretentious air and good bistro cooking. Nice marble tables. The dishes change frequently with the mood of the chef: lamb sausages, salmon *carpaccio*, ox tongue with *sauce verte* and *andouillette* with Sauvignon. There are also some surprising Thai dishes. Around 160F for three courses. Really nice.

|●| LES MANGEVINS

46 rue Pharaon. **MAP C3-36**
☎ 05.61.52.79.16
Closed Sat, Sun and Aug.

Gérard opened this place mainly to sell and enjoy wines. He's a real connaisseur. To show off the variety he has on sale, he serves excellent *terrines* with very good bread. The dishes include vast salads with *foie gras*, *andouillette*, duck breast and some unadorned specialities, like the *foie gras* with sea salt, roast beef and some of the fish, which is sold by weight. Dishes around 60F or around 170F for a full meal.

🎋|●| LES JARDINS DE L'OPÉRA

1 pl. du Capitole. **MAP C2-38**
☎ 05.61.23.07.76 ➡ 05.61.23.63.00
Closed Sun, Mon lunchtime, public holidays and three weeks in Aug. **Garden**.

The cooking here is refined and inventive, and has long since made a name for itself. *À la carte* is very expensive, but you might want to treat yourself to the 200F menu. Dominique Toulousy, one of the great chefs in town, created it so that his customers don't have to spend a fortune – the other menus cost 295F and 390F. He changes the dishes regularly, but you might find *foie gras* ravioli with truffle *jus*, *cassoulet*, lasagne with vegetables, crayfish and oysters with caviar, pigeon in a spiced crust, or maize flour pancakes with iced apricot mousse. The good wines are reasonably priced, given the quality of the food. Staff are very attentive. The garden has been wonderfully planted and is even more beautiful at night than during the day. Free apéritif.

URDENS   32500

🎋|●| L'AUBERGE PAYSANNE

pl. de l'Église.
☎ 05.62.06.25.57
Closed Mon in summer, Sun evening and Mon in winter, March and Oct. **Disabled access**. **Car park**.

Authentic, rustic inn in converted stables. The terrace is particularly lovely in the summer, and really peaceful. The inn is famous for good local dishes such as stuffed chicken, duck thigh with peaches, Gascon salad, *émincé* of duck with wild mushrooms and *crème brûlée* with prunes. The 65F lunch menu includes wine, and there are others 95–175F. Free apéritif.

VALENCE-SUR-BAÏSE   32310

🎋 🏠 |●| LA FERME DE FLARAN**

route de Condom; it's on the outskirts of the village on the D930.
☎ 05.62.28.58.22 ➡ 05.62.28.56.89
e ferme-de-flaron@mintel.net
Closed Mon except July–Aug, Sun evening, mid-Nov to mid-Dec and Jan.
Swimming pool. **Garden**. **TV**. **Car park**.

This old farm has been successfully converted into a hotel. The small rooms are very comfortable – 295F for a double. Fresh produce from the markets and local producers go to create good regional specialities like *fricassée* of sole with ceps, pan-fried *foie gras*, *carpaccio* of duck breast, veal sweetbreads with morels and a hamburger of monkfish with *foie gras*. Menus 100–190F. 10% discount on the room rate Sept–June.

VILLEFRANCHE-DE-LAURAGAIS   31290

🏠 |●| HÔTEL DE FRANCE**

106 rue de la République (Centre).
☎ 05.61.81.62.17 ➡ 05.61.81.66.04
Closed Sun evening and Mon. **TV**. **Car park**.

This attractive 19th-century inn with years of experience is in Villefranche-de-Lauragais, one of the best places to eat *cassoulet*, the famous local dish made with dried beans and goose and duck *confit*. It's the house speciality. Menus 62F (not Sat, Sun or public holidays), then 97–190F. Rooms, decorated in period style, cost 160–220F for a double with shower/wc or bath. They're quieter at the back. Number 32 has lovely floor tiles and an 18th century fireplace. You'll get a good-hearted welcome.

VILLEFRANCHE-DE-ROUERGUE   12200

🎋 🏠 |●| HÔTEL-RESTAURANT BELLEVUE*

3 av. du Ségala (South); it's just behind the station near the town centre.

☎ 05.65.45.23.17 ➡ 05.65.45.11
Closed Sun, Mon lunchtime except July–Aug. **Garden**.
Car park.

The building won't attract your gaze and the interior decor is pretty dated but you shouldn't pass up the chance to enjoy a culinary moment here. Quality cooking at reasonable prices. Fresh local produce is used exclusively, and the chef decides what he's going to cook depending on which ingredients are at their peak of flavour and freshness. Prices are honest given the quality: menus 85F, 130F, 190F and 280F. You might have *foie gras* in pastry with melting pears, lamb sweetbreads with paprika, prawn ravioli with shellfish sauce, or lobster. The hotel is clean, simple and unpretentious; doubles 100F with shower/wc, 170F with bath. The ones overlooking the street are a bit noisy. 10% discount on the room rate out of season.

♠ |●| HÔTEL DE L'UNIVERS**

pl. de la République (Centre); it's on the north bank of the Aveyron.
☎ 05.65.45.15.63 ➡ 05.65.45.02.21
Restaurant closed Fri evening, Sat out of season except before a public holiday. **Disabled access**. **TV**.
Car park.

A fine-looking conventional building. Rooms are clean and have been recently refurbished. Doubles 185–350F with shower or bath – the nicest ones overlook the Aveyron. The cooking is simple, and includes dishes like *tripou*, calf's head *ravigotte*, duck legs and medallions of lamb in a game sauce. Menus 79–295F.

⅍ ♠ |●| LE RELAIS DE FARROU***

Farrou (North); head for Saint-Rémy, 3km on the Figeac road.
☎ 05.65.45.18.11 ➡ 05.65.45.32.59
Restaurant closed Sun evening and Mon out of season, mid-Feb to the first week in March and mid-Oct to the first week in Nov. **Disabled access**. **Swimming pool**. **Garden**. **TV**. **Car park**.

A small tourist complex with a park, pool, Turkish bath and hot tub. The rooms, comfortable and air-conditioned, cost 290–490F for a double with shower/wc or bath. The decor in the restaurant is a bit showy but the cooking has a good reputation. There's a range of menus: 85F at lunch, except Sun, a *menu terroir* for 130F and a couple of others 172F and 230F. Specialities include *foie gras* cooked with spices, turbot rolled in Italian sausage, and pigeon breast with truffle. Try a glass of plum brandy if you don't fancy a dessert. Free apéritif.

|●| RESTAURANT DE LA HALLE-CHEZ PINTO

pl. de la Halle; (Centre); it's near the cathedral.
☎ 05.65.45.07.74

This workman's restaurant is one of the few remaining examples of that dying breed. You'll get a cordial welcome and be served substantial helpings of home cooking. There's a set menu for 55F.

|●| L'ASSIETTE GOURMANDE

pl. A.-Lescure (Centre); it's beside the cathedral.
☎ 05.65.45.25.95
Closed Sun, Tues and Wed evening out of season. **Car park**.

The decor is fairly clichéd, all wooden beams and copper pots, but the cooking is good. Set menus 80–175F. They grill a lot of things in an open fireplace fuelled with oak from the Causse chalk plateau, which gives the dishes a distinctive flavour. Pan-fried *foie gras* with apples, *aligot* and *tripou*. The terrace is nice in summer.

MONTEILS   12200 (11.5KM S)

|●| RESTAURANT LE CLOS GOURMAND

☎ 05.65.29.63.15 ➡ 05.65.29.64.98
Open all year but by reservation only Oct–March.

This substantial master craftsman's house is good to look at. You'll get a friendly welcome from Anne-Marie Lavergne, who's very well known for the excellent regional specialities she serves her guests. Menus 70–180F, with an extremely good dish of the day. The 120F menu serves exclusively regional dishes, including stuffed duck's neck and walnuts, trout with *lardons*, beef with Roquefort and dessert. The *étape gourmande* lists salad *aveyronnaise*, *terrine* of *foie gras*, and *émincé de confit* with sorrel. Good, traditional cooking without any fussy extras.

VILLENEUVE-SUR-TARN   81250

⅍ ♠ |●| HOSTELLERIE DES LAURIERS**

au bourg (Centre); it's on the D77, 32km east of Albi.
☎ 05.63.55.84.23 ➡ 05.63.55.89.20
Closed Dec to mid-March

An absolutely delightful village hotel right next to the church, with a lawn running all the way down to the riverbank. It's brilliantly run by a lovely young couple. There are eight good rooms, a lovely dining room and a bar which is popular with the villagers. Weekday menu

80F then 110–250F. Several house specialities, including zander fillet with shellfish
coulis, pan-fried *foie gras* with grapes and
apples, slow-cooked veal in its own juices,
fillet of beef with cream and ceps, roast lamb
with cloves of garlic, and so on. They do a
special rate for dinner, bed and breakfast,
and half board starts at 305F per person. The
boss really knows his way around the region
and is a mine of information. There's a lovely
terrace overlooking the grounds. They offer
games for the kids. Free coffee or *digestif*.

Nord-Pas-de-Calais

59 Nord

62 Pas-de-Calais

ARRAS   62000

⚐ 🏠 🍽 CAFÉ-HÔTEL DU BEFFROI

28 pl. de la Vacquerie (Centre); it's behind the bell-tower.
☎ 03.21.23.13.78 ➡ 03.21.23.03.08
Closed Sun.

You'll find this establishment at the end of a cluster of typical, Flemish houses. There's a classic bistro at street-level, jammed with locals. Good, cheap food with a 95F menu or you can even have a complete meal for 80F. The rooms, reached by a steep staircase, are charming and well-maintained, 260F with shower/wc or basin (shower and wc along the landing). Rooms with shower only are cheaper at 210F. Number 10 overlooks the square, so you have a perfect view of the Golden Lion of Artois on the 75m bell-tower. Nice owner. Free house apéritif.

⚐ 🏠 HÔTEL DES TROIS LUPPARS**

49 Grand-Place (Centre).
☎ 03.21.07.41.41 ➡ 03.21.24.24.80
TV. Car park.

This 15th-century listed building, on one of the finest squares in northern France, houses a really charming hotel. The decor may be a touch modern, given the surroundings, but rooms are very comfortable and all have shower/bath. They're good value at 290–330F for a double. The two new owners offer a genuinely warm welcome. One free breakfast per room.

⚐ 🏠 🍽 HÔTEL-RESTAURANT DES GRANDES ARCADES**

8–12 Grand-Place (Centre).

☎ 03.21.23.30.89 ➡ 03.21.71.50.94
TV.

Rooms here are comfortable, modern, clean and well soundproofed following complete renovation of this hotel – and you can't get more central. What a pity they've used electronic keys which are a real nuisance. Double rooms from 320F. The dining room is one of the most beautiful in town, in the style of a 1900s brasserie with a lofty ceiling and gleaming, dark wood panelling – there's a second decorated more traditionally. Decent cooking particularly on the 120F regional menu listing a Maroilles cheese tart, Arras *andouillette* with mustard, and pancakes with brown sugar to finish. 10% discount on the room rate at winter weekends.

⚐ 🍽 RESTAURANT CHEZ ANNIE

14 rue Paul-Doumer (Centre); it's 200m behind the bell-tower.
☎ 03.21.23.13.51
Closed weekday evenings, Sun except for reservations.

This fun little establishment is like a miniature brasserie, with a staircase of almost monumental proportions given the size of the place. Climb the steps to the mezzanine, where you can watch the regulars propping up the bar. Good home cooking. Generous *menu du jour* 60F or around 80F *à la carte*. Free coffee.

⚐ 🍽 LE BOUCHOT

3 rue de Chanzy: it's near the station.
☎ 03.21.51.67.51
Closed Mon.

Open until midnight on Fri and Sat. A bright, freshly decorated restaurant with a marine theme – there's a boat in the middle of the

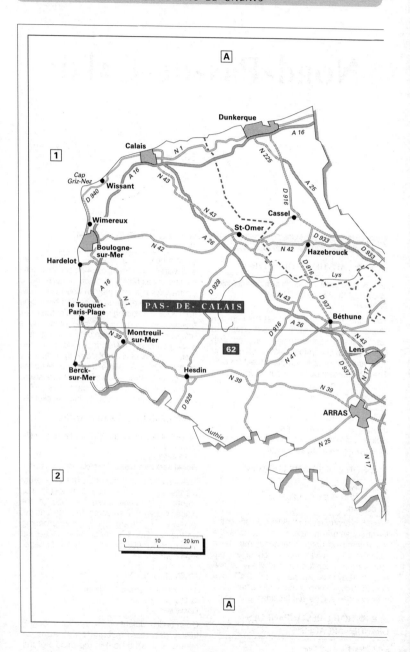

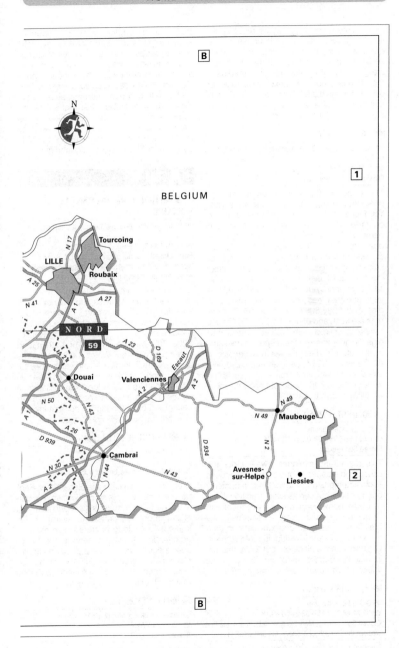

dining room – which specialises in huge portions of good quality mussels prepared in a dozen ways: with Maroilles cheese, *à la Marseillaise* with cream and dill, etc. The chips are good too. They also get good marks for their honestly cooked, inexpensive regional dishes. Menus 62–99F, and around 80F for a complete meal à la carte. Nice service. A good canteen of a place. Free coffee.

|●| LE TROUBADOUR

29 av. du Général-de-Gaulle (Centre); it's opposite the casino.
☎03.21.71.34.50
Closed Sun and Mon evening.

The "bouchon" (Lyonnais restaurant) atmosphere and setting of this place are appealing. You feel as if you're dining with friends in the country. The warm welcome from the *patronne* has something to do with it, as does the cooking. The choices of the day are scrawled up on a blackboard (three lots of starters, main courses and desserts), offering traditional dishes such as calf's head *sauce gribiche*, *pot-au-feu* (boiled beef and veg), and pan-fried scallops with fresh noodles. You'll pay 80F for a meal. The ingredients are fresh and of good quality. The house *terrine* is served with pickled onions and gigantic gherkins and the bread is a peasant-style loaf. The desserts seem expensive in the context – 35F for a fresh fruit salad with strawberries and kiwi fruit – and so is the wine by the jug. It's good but not worth 25F a ¼ litre. Worth booking.

🎋|●| RESTAURANT LA RAPIÈRE

44 Grand-Place (Centre).
☎ 03.21.55.09.92 ➡ 03.21.22.24.29
Closed Sun evening.

This restaurant is hidden away under the sandstone arcades of one of the 155 houses enclosing the Grand-Place. It has a contemporary decor but serves solid, traditional cuisine – salmon *en papillote* or fillet of beef with Roquefort – and local specialities like Maroilles cheese flan or *andouillette* in pastry. Menus 88–200F, including regional wine. Customers are a bit classy but the restaurant is friendly. Expense-account dining in the vaulted 17th-century cellar. Free coffee.

|●| LA FAISANDERIE

45 Grand-Place (Centre).
☎ 03.21.48.20.76 ➡ 03.21.50.89.18
Closed Sun evening, Mon, the first week in Jan, the first week of the Feb school holidays, the first week in Aug.

Michelin took away their star but this is generally acknowledged to be the gourmet restaurant in town. Jean-Pierre Dargent still creates joyous dishes that are full of flavour and exquisitely prepared; fresh cod in a breadcrumb crust with a shellfish *jus*, pan-fried artichokes and *crépiau* of fresh cream cheese with girolle mushrooms, suckling pig roast with sage. Menus 145F (not Sat night), 215F and 385F. The *sommelier* gives informed advice and doesn't push the pricey bottles. At the end of the evening, the chef comes to bid his customers goodnight.

BERCK-SUR-MER   62600

🎋 🏠 |●| HÔTEL-RESTAURANT LE VOLTAIRE

29 av. du Général-de-Gaulle (Centre); it's opposite the casino.
☎ 03.21.84.43.13 ➡ 03.21.84.61.72
Hotel closed Tues out of season, public holiday weekends and 15 Oct–15 Nov. **Restaurant closed** in winter except for hotel guests. **TV**.

Service noon–2pm and 7.30–10pm. The spacious rooms are spotless and have excellent soundproofing and practical, modern decor. Some still have to be renovated. Doubles with hand basin 160F, 190F with shower or 220–270F with shower/wc or bath. Good buffet breakfast 32F. Warm, friendly welcome and a youthful ambience; the same goes for the ground-floor bar, which specialises in beers. Apart from a few local specialities such as *ficelle picarde* (stuffed pancake) and charcoal-grilled beef, the food is not that impressive. Menus 69–119F. Free coffee.

🎋|●| L'AUBERGE DU BOIS

149 av. Quetier.
☎ 03.21.9.03.43
Closed Mon out of season and 4 Jan–4 Feb.

Everyone in town calls this place "Chez Ben" because the owner is so well known. His bar-restaurant has a huge, simple and pleasant dining room decorated in warm tones. Impressive seafood platters which must be ordered in advance. Otherwise the house speciality fish *choucroute* is good and there's plenty of it. Menus 90–200F. Very kindly service. A great place for an evening with your mates. Free apéritif.

🎋|●| LA VERRIÈRE

Casino de Berck-sur-Mer, pl. du 18-Juin.
☎ 03.21.84.27.25
Closed Tues.

There are two entrances to this restaurant –

the one that takes you past the horrific spectacle of ranks of jangling slot machines will give you the wrong impression. This is the spacious, elegant restaurant of the casino where they serve the best cooking in town and, probably, along this stretch of the Opale coast. Perfect service that's efficient without being officious. A weekday business lunch, and others that show off the chef's classic cuisine. He uses only fresh produce, so dishes change all the time. Menus 110–235F. Free coffee.

BÉTHUNE   62400

⽊ 🏠 |●| HÔTEL DU VIEUX BEFFROI**

48 Grand-Place (Centre)
☎ 03.21.68.15.00 ➡ 03.21.56.66.32
Disabled access. TV. Car park.

A solidly built hotel with turrets and gables, standing opposite the 14th-century belltower. In the morning you are woken by the bells, but thankfully they don't ring at night. It's a vast hotel, so don't expect a personalised welcome. Some of the old-fashioned rooms have been renovated and they are not short on charm. Doubles 280F with shower/wc or bath. Meals are served in a lively brasserie. Menus 79–149F. Dishes include duo of fish with basil sauce, house smoked salmon and Périgord salad. Free *digestif*.

⽊ |●| RESTAURANT LA TAVERNE

1 pl. de la République (Centre).
☎ 03.21.56.80.80 ➡ 03.21.65.77.00
Closed Sat lunchtime and Sun evening.

A very traditional, unpretentious brasserie serving regional dishes – it's one of the best places in town. Menus 98–150F and a varied *à la carte* menu where you find the two main specialities – various kinds of *choucroute* and an excellent and substantial fisherman's platter. Customers tend to be locals. Free coffee.

⽊ |●| LA RIPAILLE

20 Grand-Place (Centre).
☎ 03.21.56.22.33
Closed Sat, Sun evening and 24 Dec–8 Jan.

There's not much to this from the outside: it's got a narrow frontage that's very ordinarily decorated. Inside, though, it's crammed with regulars who are very obviously keen on the food. The portions are big, the sauces and broths are appetising and the fish and meat look splendid; this is a good restaurant. The

dish of the day, 59F, is always good and dishes change frequently. The ingredients are really fresh, particularly the fish. Try the pumpkin soup with Maroilles cheese, the *millefeuille* of salmon with cream and herb sauce, *crépinette* of pig's trotters and chicken in cheese sauce. About 140F *à la carte*. Free coffee.

BOULOGNE-SUR-MER   62200

🏠 HÔTEL FAIDHERBE**

12 rue Faidherbe (Centre).
☎ 03.21.31.60.93 ➡ 03.21.87.01.14
Disabled access. TV.

Near the harbour in a charmless part of town rebuilt after the war. Warm welcome. If the weather's fine, Victor, the resident mynah bird, might decide to say a few words. Small, comfy Victorian-style lounge, and individually decorated rooms with good facilities. Doubles with shower 230F, with bath 320F.

🏠 HÔTEL L'ALEXANDRA**

93 rue Thiers (Centre); it's near the port.
☎ 03.21.30.52.22 ➡ 03.21.30.20.03
Closed 28 Dec–31 Jan. **TV. Car park.**

A small, unfussy hotel in a street which manages to escape the worst of the town centre's heavy traffic. Warm, friendly welcome. Rooms are brightly decorated and have good facilities. Doubles with shower/wc 240–280F, or 320F with bath. Best to book in high season and for public holidays.

⽊ |●| L'ESTAMINET DU CHÂTEAU

2 rue du Château (East); it's in the old town opposite the basilica of Notre-Dame.
☎ 03.21.91.49.66 ➡ 03.21.31.92.96
Closed Wed evening, Thurs, and 23 Dec–23 Jan.

A reliable bet in this touristy area in a picturesque street in the fortified 13th-century part of the town. It's a cosy little restaurant where traditions are respected. Accordion music hasn't given way to techno and the bar is still inhabited by regulars. No complaints as far as the food is concerned – menus are reasonably priced at 75–175F. Specialities include monkfish kebabs, skate wings, poached cod and Dublin Bay prawns. Free apéritif.

|●| CHEZ JULES

pl. Dalton (Centre); in the lower town.
☎ 03.21.31.54.12
Closed Sun evening.

This is *the* Bologne brasserie, with a huge terrace on the square. It's been around for eons so the service is efficient and the cooking is tasty and reliable. Good *moules marinière*, beef tripe, ham on the bone, calf's head and sauce *gribiche*. There is a second, more classic dining room and a pizzeria.

PORTEL (LE)   62480 (4.5KM SW)

⫟|●| LE PORTELOIS

42 quai Dugay-Trouin; take the D119 and at Portel follow the signs to the beach.
☎ 03.21.31.44.60 ☛ 03.21.31.34.83
Closed Mon except July–Aug.

A seaside restaurant with a panoramic view of the Channel that's interrupted only by the ruins of a Napoleonic fort. The food's influenced by the sea: there are no fewer than 22 specialities with mussels – *à l'ancienne*, or in Flemish, Pekinese or Hungarian style. There's no shortage of fish dishes, either – the *waterzoï* fish casserole is worth a try. Menus from 69F or around 150F *à la carte*. Free coffee.

WAST (LE)   62142 (15KM E)

⫟ 🛏 |●| HOSTELLERIE DU CHÂTEAU DES TOURELLES**

How to get there: take the N42 towards Saint-Omer then take the D127 to Le Wast.
☎ 03.21.33.34.78 ☛ 03.21.87.59.57
Disabled access. TV. Car park.

As you enter the village you'll see the hotel, which is housed in a very elegant 19th-century mansion, hidden behind the trees in a small park. There's a modern annexe next to the tennis courts. Stay in the superb rooms of the "château" with their Louis-Philippe furniture and small balconies. If your funds won't stretch to that, go for an attic room. Doubles with shower/wc or bath go for 300–320F. If you're staying for a number of days, opt for half board at 280F. Menus 85–250F. Wonderful welcome. Tennis, table tennis and billiards are all free for residents. Free coffee.

CALAIS   62100

⫟ 🛏 HÔTEL WINDSOR**

2 rue du Commandant-Bonningue (Northeast); head for the harbour, it's the extension of the pl. d'Armes.
☎ 03.21.34.59.40 ☛ 03.21.97.68.59
TV. Lock-up car park.

In a quiet part of town, not far from the marina. The atmosphere makes you think you're on the other side of the Channel; it's owned by an Englishman who'll give you a warm, polite welcome. Attractive rooms from 175F. 10% discount for two nights.

⫟ 🛏 HÔTEL PACIFIC**

40 rue du Duc-de-Guise (North); it's near Notre-Dame cathedral.
☎ 03.21.34.50.24 ☛ 03.21.97.58.02
TV. Lock-up car park.

A small family hotel that's centrally located but quiet. The owners are renovating it floor by floor. Good value for money for Calais; doubles with shower from 185F or with bath and telephone from 255F. Like just about every other hotel in town they have family rooms that sleep up to four people. Warm welcome and helpful, chatty service. The lounge and bar have a very retro look. 5% discount.

⫟ 🛏 LE RICHELIEU**

17 rue Richelieu (North); it's opposite Richelieu park.
☎ 03.21.34.61.60 ☛ 03.21.85.89.28
Closed Christmas and New Year's Day. **TV. Lock-up car park.**

Bright, comfortable, pleasant rooms, 250F for a double with shower or 280F with bath. Nine of the rooms have balconies looking over the huge, lush Richelieu park. A soothing contrast to the garish neon signs in the adjacent streets. It's easy to relax here; the welcome is low-key, perhaps too much so, and the street is very quiet. 10% discount.

CAMBRAI   59400

🛏 HÔTEL DE FRANCE*

37 rue de Lille; it's 100m from the train station.
☎ 03.27.81.38.80 ☛ 03.27.78.13.88
Closed Sun. **TV.**

A typical station hotel – neat and tidy and quaintly old-fashioned. Take a look at the vintage postcards on sale at the reception desk. It's surprisingly quiet, even in the rooms overlooking the tracks, since few trains run at night. Doubles with basin 170F, with shower/wc 200F, and with bath 240F. Low-key welcome.

⫟ 🛏 |●| LE MOUTON BLANC***

33 rue d'Alsace-Lorraine; it's about 200m from the train station, in the street opposite.
☎ 03.27.81.30.16 ☛ 03.27.81.83.54
Restaurant closed Sun evening and Mon.
TV. Car park.

Solidly built 19th-century house with a great deal of charm and a genuine family atmosphere. The rooms exude a certain opulence, without going over the top. Doubles with shower/wc 260–300F, or 300–400F with bath. They serve good and interesting dishes in the large dining room. Winners include gnocchi with Maroilles cheese, *fricassée* of scallops and Dublin Bay prawns, baby chicory in lemon, and boned pigeon with acacia honey. Menus 109–195F. Free breakfast.

⅍ |●| LE GRILL DE L'EUROPE

pl. Marcellin-Berthelot (Southwest).
☎ 03.27.81.66.76
Closed Sat lunchtime, Sun evening, and a fortnight July–Aug.

Down in the port district. A popular haunt of truck drivers, sailors and fishermen. It's a simple, warm and lively bar where they serve straightforward home cooking. The 66F menu offers steak, dessert, a $1/4$ litre of wine and coffee; other menus at 110–140F. There's also a self-service *hors d'œuvre* buffet, dishes of the day, and an *à la carte* choice of frogs' legs *provençale*, *fricassée* of sole with port or *andouillette* flambéed with juniper. Free coffee.

⅍ |●| LE RESTO DU BEFFROI

4 rue du 11-Novembre; take the avenue opposite the town hall, and it's the second turning on the right.
☎ 03.27.81.50.10
Closed Sat lunchtime, Sun, the first three weeks in Jan and the first three weeks in Aug.

A rather unusual restaurant tucked away in a little street behind the Grand-Place. The decor is a mixture of traditional bistro and a night club. Some of the cuisine takes its influence from the southwest, where Yves Galan bred ducks before becoming a chef thirty years ago. Today he prepares duck breast and *cassoulet* with duck *confit*, veal sweetbreads *toulousaine*, and chicken with cream and morel mushroom sauce. Friendly atmosphere. Dishes of the day 40F and 50F, and menus 108–150F Free house Kir.

LIGNY-EN-CAMBRÉSIS   59400 (15KM SE)

|●| LE CHÂTEAU DE LIGNY

2 rue Pierre-Curie; take the N43 in the direction of Cateau-Cambrésis, in Beauvois turn off to Ligny.
☎ 03.27.85.25.84 ➡ 03.27.85.79.79
Closed a fortnight in Feb.

A hideaway in countryside inhabited by deer and fawns. The round tower is part of the

original, elegant 12th-century château. It's a stylish, tasteful place. The salons have ornamental ceilings and the rooms have individual personality. The prices reflect the quality: rooms 650–1500F – you could lose yourself in the biggest one. The restaurant has a huge reputation and welcomes people who are not staying overnight. It's a magnificent setting; the library has a splendid parquet floor, wainscotting, elaborate curtains and a vast, carved chimney piece. Top service and cooking that's tasty, light and inspired. Menu 260F. The dishes change frequently, but might be sea bream with veal sweetbread *grillons*, fillet of beef with sautéed duck *foie gras*, or stewed Breton lobster with verbena.

CASSEL   59670

|●| LA TAVERNE FLAMANDE

34 Grand-Place; it's opposite the town hall.
☎ 03.28.42.42.59 ➡ 03.28.40.51.84
Closed Tues evening, Wed, a week in Feb, a week at the end of Aug and a week at the end of Oct.

Lunch from noon, dinner from 7pm. You will get an authentic Flemish meal here. Try Flemish *croustillons*, chicken casserole Ghent style (cooked in a home-made bechamel-type sauce), veal kidneys flambéed with gin, Flemish apple tart sprinkled with brown sugar or *crêpes* flambéed in Houlle. Menus 68–140F. Sit on the veranda, which is perched on the slopes of Mont Cassel, and enjoy the same panorama that so delighted the Romantic poet Lamartine.

⅍ |●| ESTAMINET T'KASTEEL HOF

8 rue Saint-Nicolas; it's opposite the mill.
☎ 03.28.40.59.29 ➡ 03.28.42.43.23
Closed Mon in Aug, Mon and Tues in Sept, weekdays Oct to end March. **Car park**.

This tavern, at the top of Mont Cassel, is at the highest altitude in French Flanders – a mere 175.90m. There's a splendid view from upstairs. It's a wonderful little place with a tiny bar, a few tables, wooden chairs, a fireplace and baskets hanging from the beams. It's stuffed full of spoils from junk shops, and is too typical to be fake. For starters there are various kinds of soup with endives, *cœur casselois* (pork mince with cubes of smoked bacon), *waterzoï* (fish stew) or *potjevfleisch* (a local *pâté* of veal, chicken and rabbit) and apples in flaky pastry. Cheeses include *zermezeelois* or *mont-des-cats*, and even the mineral water is Flemish, hailing from Saint-Amand. This is hop country so there's a list of traditional beers rather than wine. 80–100F for a meal, or you could settle for one of the filling platters of local cheeses or *pâtés*. Free *digestif*.

EECKE   59114 (10KM SE)

|●| BRASSERIE SAINT-GEORGES

5 rue de Castre; take the D933 then the D947 and it's halfway between Cassel and Bailleul.
☎ 03.28.40.13.71
Closed Mon–Thurs lunchtimes, Mon–Thurs evenings except July–Aug and on public holidays, Fri lunchtime, last week in Aug and Christmas Day. **TV**. **Car park**.

This bastion of Flemish culture has its own newsletter. The building started out as a farm in the 16th century, after which it became a mill, and then a post house. The jumbled architecture and decor combine elements from this varied past. They began brewing beer here in the 1970s and now they sell 63 specialist beers – the *des Chênes*, brewed locally, is the most popular. Good traditional Flemish cooking includes *andouillettes*, grilled pork chitterlings with *standevleech* (potatoes cooked in ashes), melted Maroilles cheese with cumin, grilled pork fillet and ham *à la 3 Monts* (ham on the bone, marinated in beer with potatoes with Maroilles cheese *au gratin*). Reasonable prices – menus from 110F or 120F *à la carte*.

BOESCHEPE   59299 (15KM E)

⅔ 🏠 |●| AUBERGE DU VERT MONT**

Route du Mont-Noir; take the D948 towards Steenvoorde then the N348 to the Belgian border, and finally the D10 towards Bailleul; it's signposted from Boeschepe.
☎ 03.28.49.41.26 ➡ 03.28.49.48.58
Closed Mon and Tues lunchtimes. **TV**. **Car park**.

This small tourist complex, next to a hop field, used to be a farm. It retains a rural feel, with ducks splashing about in the pond and goats and sheep bleating in the fields. They offer games for children and there are a couple of tennis courts. Adorable rooms cost 290–360F for a double with shower/wc or bath. The welcome is youthful and friendly. There are flowers everywhere in the restaurant, which offers a range of tried-and-tested, well-prepared regional dishes: fish stew, scallops *à la Hoegarden* and *potjevfleisch* (veal, chicken and rabbit *pâté)*. Menus start at 125F. There's a large selection of Belgian and French beers. Free coffee.

DOUAI   59500

🏠 |●| HÔTEL LE CHAMBORD**

3509 route de Tournai; it's in Frais-Marais, 4km from the centre of Douai on the D917.
☎ 03.27.97.72.77 ➡ 03.27.99.35.14
Hotel closed a week in Feb and a fortnight in Aug.
Restaurant closed Sun evening and Mon.
TV. **Car park**.

Frais-Marais, a suburb of Douai, still feels like a village, though the main road runs past the hotel – don't take a room on that side of the building. Comfortable, attractive rooms at reasonable prices for the area – oddly enough, hotels in Douai cost a lot. Doubles with bath 260F. The restaurant offers a 95F weekday menu and others up to 260F.

⅔ 🏠 |●| HÔTEL-RESTAURANT LA TER-RASSE****

36 terrasse Saint-Pierre.
☎ 03.27.88.70.04
TV. **Car park**.

This is a four-star place and a member of the *Châteaux et Hôtels Indépendants* organisation. It's beautifully situated near the collegiate church in a charming old house that purrs with comfort. It's a serious, traditional place run by very professional staff, but rooms are more than fairly priced at 295F with shower/wc or 380F with bath. The dining room breathes traditional France; it has red brick and white stone walls hung with paintings. Beautifully presented dishes of solid, traditional cuisine on some of the most delicious set menus around – again prices are more than honest; set menus 135F (including wine), 176F and 320F. There's a spectacular wine list of 900 different *appellations* and a stock of 100,000 bottles in the cellar. The proprietor owns vineyards in Burgundy. Free coffee.

🏠 |●| HÔTEL VOLUBILIS***

bd. Bauban; coming from Tournai, it's where the road comes to the Pont de Lille.
☎ 03.27.88.00.11 ➡ 03.27.96.07.41
📧 hotelvolubilis@wanadoo.fr
TV. **Car park**.

At first glance it looks like a chain hotel. On the contrary, it's very pleasant with a fresh, brightly coloured interior. Double rooms from 345F. There is a restaurant (untried), with menus beginning at 99F. The rumour is that it's more than adequate.

|O| RESTAURANT AU TURBOTIN

9 rue de la Massue (Centre); it's near the Scarpe river, opposite the law courts.
☎ 03.27.87.04.16
Closed Sat lunchtime, Sun evening, Mon, the last week in Feb, and Aug.

Au Turbotin is primarily a fish and seafood restaurant, though they also offer other regional dishes. Try the turbot with Maroilles cheese, asparagus *millefeuille*, lobster *brioche*, or specialities like fish *choucroute*, zander stuffed with pike mousse, fish *pot-au-feu*, pike *cannelloni*, or lamb charlotte with cream and garlic. Finely judged cooking. A 95F weekday menu and others 150–258F. With chic yet low-key surroundings, courteous and refined service and customers who don't have to watch the pennies, it's one of the town's classiest establishments.

DUNKERQUE   59240

⅍ ≜ TRIANON HÔTEL**

20 rue de la Colline (Northeast); follow the signs for the beach and the hotel is signposted.
☎ 03.28.63.39.15 ➡ 03.28.63.34.57
TV. Car park.

This place is typical of the picturesque, seaside villas that were built along this coast around 1865. It's primarily a quiet district inhabited by retired people. The hotel is quite charming and the rooms are pleasant, as is the tiny indoor garden next to the breakfast room. Doubles 260F with shower/wc or bath. Helpful owner who knows the area well. One free breakfast per room and free loan of a bike for exploring.

≜ |O| HÔTEL-RESTAURANT L'HIRONDELLE**

46–48 av. Faidherbe (Northeast); from the centre head towards the beach, where it's signposted.
☎ 03.28.63.17.65 ➡ 03.28.66.15.43
Restaurant closed Sun evening, Mon lunchtime, a fortnight end of Feb and three weeks from 20 Aug.
TV. Disabled access. Car park.

Service noon–2.15pm and 7.30–9.45pm. Right next to a lovely little square that's sadly spoilt by the thunder of the traffic, and not far from the sea. It's a faultless establishment with modern decor. The functional rooms all have shower or bath from 344F. The welcome is by the book but friendly. No surprises in the restaurant; poached turbot with Hollandaise sauce, seafood platters and *potjevleesch* (veal, rabbit and chicken in aspic cooked in white wine and vinegar). Weekday menu at 70F and others 98F and 130F, or around 145F *à la carte*.

⅍|O| LE PÉCHÉ MIGNON

11 pl. du Casino; across the square from the casino.
☎ 03.28.66.14.44
Closed Sat lunchtime, Sun evening and Mon. **Garden.**

A cosy little dining room in pastel shades with soft armchairs. If you've lost your shirt in the casino across the square, you will probably still be able to afford the cheapest menu, costing a modest 75F. If you're dining before you make for the tables, there are others 125–175F. Traditional, generously flavoured dishes: house stuffed crab, haddock in buttermilk and garlic, guinea-fowl breast with pine kernels, kangaroo steak with wild mushrooms, sole coral stuffed with scallops, and a mouthwatering dessert trolley. When it's sunny, make for the little terrace in the garden – a consolation for the lack of sea view. The welcome is also excellent. Free apéritif, coffee or *digestif*.

⅍|O| AU PETIT PIERRE

4 rue Dampierre (Centre).
☎ 03.28.66.28.36
Closed Sat lunchtime, Sun and Mon evenings.

This is one of the town's very few 18th-century residences that wasn't shelled. The owners have lovingly renovated it, creating an elegantly sober setting with varnished wooden furniture and salmon-pink walls. The smiling welcome is warm and the cooking is some of the best along the coast, with inspired regional dishes such as *gratin* with Bergues cheese, leek tart, and red mullet marinated in lime and dill. The meat dishes are splendid, particularly the tournedos with spiced bread and ginger, and the veal kidneys flambéed with beer. On the fish list, try the *waterzoï* or stuffed sole, while for dessert you should plump for *crème brûlée* with endive or rhubarb with preserved stawberries. Menus 95–159F. Free coffee.

BERGUES   59380 (10KM SE)

≜ |O| HÔTEL-RESTAURANT AU TONNELIER**

4 rue du Mont-de-Piété.
☎ 03.28.68.70.05 ➡ 03.28.68.21.87
Closed Fri, Sun evening, 1–15 Jan and 15–30 Aug.
TV. Car park.

Attractive, extremely quiet ochre-yellow brick inn at the heart of the medieval village. It's opposite the Mont-de-Pié, a superb 17th-century building which has been converted into a museum. The welcome is very warm. Doubles with basin 190F, or 245–360F with shower/wc. The rooms looking onto the lovely little paved courtyard are quietest, and they get the most light. The good plain home cooking doesn't seem out of place in the opulent surroundings of the Regency dining room. There are a number of regional specialities, including a terrific *potjevleesch* (veal, rabbit and chicken in aspic cooked in white wine and vinegar). Menus at 103F (except Sun lunchtime), then 135 and 175F.

LOOBERGHE   59630 (15KM SW)

⚶ |●| LE CAMPAGNARD

456 rue de Cassel; it's at the D11-D3 crossroads.
☎ 03.28.29.81.97s
Closed evenings and the second fortnight in Nov.

A nice village restaurant run by a young, local couple. Warmhearted welcome. The pretty dining room is decorated with pictures and photographs of old windmills. They serve excllent country cooking. The 78F menu is good value, and there are others at 88F and 98F. Free coffee.

ETROEUNGT   59219

⚶ |●| FERME DE LA CAPELETTE

La Capelette; it's 7km south of Avesnes.
☎ 03.27.59.38.33
Closed Wed.

Naf and Dany Delmée converted their farmhouse into a country inn with splendid results. There's a pleasant dining room, and a vast terrace high above the Helpe valley. Best of all is the superb local cuisine, prepared with passion and professionalism. Nothing but fresh produce is used – the oyster mushrooms are grown on the farm. The *terrines* are tasty, particularly the one with duck and shiitake mushrooms. Other hits include the suckling pig *civet*, prepared with dry cider, duck with sweet and sour sauce and baby onions, roast lamb with caramelised honey, and guineafowl flambéed with apple brandy. The apple tart is made with crisp pastry and fruit picked from the orchard. The dishes change regularly with the fresh produce in season. Menus 95–190F. Booking essential. Free coffee.

GODESWAERSVELDE   59270

⚶ |●| HET BLAUWERSHOF

rue d'Eecke (Centre); it's between Steenvoorde and Bailleul on the D18.
☎ 03.28.49.45.11
Closed Mon and a fortnight in Jan

The most famous tap-room in Flanders, one

of a dying breed. The bar and dining room have enormous charm – old furniture, old pots, and long wooden tables where people sit round with a band of friends. You can also play traditional bar games. There's a big mixture of patrons enjoying the convivial, lively atmosphere. You can also eat well, as they serve herring fillets, leek tart, mustard tart, bacon or *potjevleesh* with chips, and beef *carbonade*. For pudding, there's *clafoutis* with apples, or ice creams.Dishes start at 30F and you'll pay about 90F for a meal. One free 75cl bottle of Blauwersbier per table.

⚶ |●| LE ROI DU POTJE VLEESCH

31 rue du Mont-des-Cats.
☎ 03.28.42.52.56
Closed Mon, Tues in winter, and Jan.

There's a shop selling all sorts of regional delicacies that are made on site – delicious *terrines* with *andouillettes* and the best *potjevleesch*. The dining room is warm and welcoming; odd to think that it used to be the family-run abattoir (you can still see the tethering rings on the walls). It's decorated with old domestic objects, plates, tools and photographs. The cuisine is resolutely Flemish: *pâté* with garlic, *carbonade*, cockerel in beer. Excellent meals at very modest prices; menus 45F and 120F or 80–120F *à la carte*. Best to book at the weekend. Free coffee.

HARDELOT   62150

⚶ ☗ |●| LA RÉGINA

185 av. François 1er; it's 1km from the town centre.
☎ 03.28.41.98.79 ☛ 03.28.43.11.06
Closed Sun evening and Mon except July–Aug, Whitsun and Easter, 1 Jan–15 Feb, and 11 Nov–31 Dec.

A handsome, modern establishment on two floors, in a quiet residential district of the resort. Behind it is wooded countryside. It's quiet and pretty good value, given the facilities; doubles with shower/wc or bath, 360F. The restaurant, *Les Brisants*, has a bright, elegant dining room. The cooking is fresh and skillfully prepared; cream of mussel soup or fish stew with mussel *jus*. Weekday menu 120F only or 185F *à la carte*. Tennis, golf and stables are all close by, and the beach is 1km away. Free house apéritif or coffee.

HAZEBROUCK   59190

☗ HÔTEL LE GAMBRINUS**

2 rue Nationale (Centre); it's between the Grand-Place

and the train station.
☎ 03.28.41.98.79 ➡ 03.28.43.11.06
TV. Car park.

This is Hazebrouck's only hotel, in a substantial 19th-century house, so it's here or in the car. Inside, all is bright and tastefully decorated. Pleasant doubles with shower/wc cost 295–350F. The owners really know how to make you feel welcome.

🏦 |●| RESTAURANT LE CENTRE

48 Grand-Place (Centre); it's opposite the town hall.
☎ 03.28.48.03.62

The regional specialties are the thing to go for here: Welsh rarebit, herring with warm apples, *carbonnade flamande* (beef and onions braised in beer). Alternatively, try their well-prepared classic dishes, such as scallops and fillet of beef with morels or leg of duck with oyster mushrooms. Weekday lunch menu 65F, regional menu 120F and others up to 235F. Warm-hearted welcome and service, and the whole place has been completely refurbished. Free house apéritif.

🏦 |●| RESTAURANT LA TAVERNE

61 Grand-Place (Centre).
☎ 03.28.41.63.09
Closed Sun evening and Mon, a week in Feb and three weeks in Aug. **Car park**.

This convivial restaurant has a warm atmosphere, an elegant decor typical of Flanders, and appropriate cooking: Maroilles cheese and leek quiche, juniper and apple tart, *potjevfleisch* (a veal, rabbit and chicken pâté), veal kidneys flambéed with juniper, and *carbonnade flamande* (beef braised in beer). Generous portions served by good-natured staff. They offer specials on some nights – mussels and chips on Friday, *fondues* in the evening. Menus 98–145F, 120F *à la carte*. Free house apéritif.

MOTTE-AU-BOIS (LA)   59190 (5KM S)

🏠 |●| AUBERGE DE LA FORÊT**

Centre; it's five minutes from Hazebrouck on the D946 heading towards Merville.
☎ 03.28.48.08.78 ➡ 03.28.40.77.76
Closed Sat lunchtime, Sun evening, Mon, 1–21 Jan and 16–23 Aug. **TV. Garden. Car park**.

Service noon–2pm and 7.30–9pm. This 1950s hunting lodge, almost buried under foliage, is situated in the heart of a village deep in the vast Nieppe forest. The panelled rooms are simple but pleasant, particularly those with latticed windows that open onto

lovely little gardens. Doubles with shower or bath 225–320F. The restaurant is rustic in style, naturally enough, and offers regional specialities and some exceptionally inventive cooking which justifies the rather high prices. Weekday menu 140F or 235–285F on Sundays. There's a good wine list, and the cellar is one of the best in the region. Customers are well-heeled, and the welcome can be a bit cool.

SERCUS   59173 (6KM W)

🏦 |●| ESTAMINET-AUBERGE AU SAINT-ÉRASME

18 route de Blaringhem; take the D106 or the N42 and turn off at Wallon-Capel.
☎ 03.28.41.85.43
Closed Mon, Sun–Thurs evenings, a week in Feb, and a fortnight Aug/Sept.

A spruce country inn with a pretty façade. Inside, it's snug and convivial. They serve home cooking in generous portions. All the local dishes appear on the menu, including *flamiches* with Maroilles cheese, a tasty chicken in beer, and chips as crispy as can be. Very reasonable prices: 45F *menu du jour* or 75F. There's a terrace in summer and traditional bar games. Free coffee.

HESDIN   62140

🏦 🏠 |●| HÔTEL DES FLANDRES**

20–22 rue d'Arras (Centre).
☎ 03.21.86.80.21 ➡ 03.21.86.28.01
Closed ten days June/July and ten days Dec/Jan.
TV. Car park.

No-fuss hotel with a family atmosphere in the midst of the "Seven Valleys" area. The rooms are straightforward and comfortable; doubles with shower/wc or bath 300F. It's the same story in the restaurant, which serves traditional local dishes. The specialities are chicken in beer and salmon *flamand*. Weekday *formule*, 95F, includes main course, dessert and a glass of wine or beer. Also menus 101–135F. Free house apéritif.

SAULCHOY   62870 (22.5KM SW)

🏦 |●| LE VAL D'AUTHIE

How to get there: take the D928 towards Abbeville, then turn right onto the D119, which follows the River Authie.
☎ 03.21.90.30.20
Closed Thurs out of season and the first week in Sept.

A good, friendly old country inn with character. The menus say they offer "good plain home cooking prepared by the proprietor". Tried and tested recipes include *vol au vent*, *coq au vin*, duck breast and leg of lamb. Weekday menu 80F, others 130–185F. In season, for 250F, they serve copious quantities of game – hare casserole, wild boar stew, venison in cream sauce, pheasant in port. Attractive guest rooms with shower/wc; 230F for two including breakfast. There's also a *gîte* (sleeping 4–6) to rent. Free coffee.

LENS   62300

▌●▐ RESTAURANT LA DÉCOUVERTE

11 rue des Déportés; it's not far from the train station.
☎ 03.21.42.70.00
Closed Sun and Mon evenings.

A discreet restaurant in a little street without much traffic. They've divided up the huge dining room with partitions decorated with flowers. The clientèle tends to be elderly. Menus, 70–135F, list lots of offal dishes; pig's trotters in *vinaigrette* or coated in breadcrumbs and fried, *rillettes* (potted pork and goose meat), liver *meunier* (coated in flour and fried) or grilled kidneys. No place for vegetarians. If you opt for a bottle of *réserve maison* wine you'll be charged only for what you drink.

BULLY-LES-MINES   62160 (5KM W)

⅔▐ ☎ ▌●▐ L'ENFANT DU PAYS

152 rue de la Gare.
☎ 03.21.29.12.33 ➡ 03.21.29.27.55
e m.verbrugge@nordnet.fr
Closed Sun evening. **TV**.

This place, despite its unprepossessing location at the back of the slag heaps, has got a good reputation for serving generous helpings of straightforward, authentic dishes made with fresh produce. Try *estouffade* of veal sweetbreads in port or sautéed chicken in beer. Menus 62–180F. The large dining room has a pleasant atmosphere with service to match. The bedrooms have all been refurbished. Rock-bottom prices – doubles with basin and TV 85F (the shower and wc are along the corridor), or 140F with shower/wc or bath. 10% discount on the room rate or free house apéritif.

LIESSIES   59740

☎ ▌●▐ LE CHÂTEAU DE LA MOTTE**

How to get there: take the D133 towards the lac du Val-Joly.
☎ 03.27.61.81.94 ➡ 03.27.61.83.57
Closed Sun out of season and mid-Dec to early Feb.
TV. **Car park**.

The grounds of this hotel and restaurant back onto the Bois-l'Abbé national forest. The château was built in 1725 as a place of retreat for the monks of Liessies Abbey. It has unusual pink brick walls with slate along the top which reflect in the waters of the lake nearby. The rooms offer the peace and silence the monks sought. Doubles 330–395F. Menus, from 120F, include pork haunch *pot-au-feu*, fish stew with white wine, lamb's tongue with smoked garlic, and farm-raised chicken *water-zoï*. They also offer a 92F *formule*, and host gastronomic evening and weekends.

⅔▐ ▌●▐ CHEZ LOUIS

25 rue Roger Salengro; it's on the D133 on the road from Avesnes.
☎ 03.27.61.82.38
Closed Mon.

Despite the sign, which calls this place a *friterie*, this is in fact a good restaurant with a pretty dining room. The setting is appealing and you will be welcomed with warmth and kindness. Children are well catered for, with a playground and special pony and buggy rides. The building is an old farmer's house with hefty beams, tiled or stone floors and a wide hearth. The tables are long so you share. They use only the freshest local produce to prepare devilishly good *terrines*, *andouillette*, *carbonade* stews, tripe, white pudding and Maroilles cheese tart. Everything is home-made and tasty – including the wonderful chips. Your wallet won't suffer from a visit here – you can get a snack for around 40F, and only the *entrecôte* steak costs more than 50F. There's a splendid terrace in summer. Free coffee.

▌●▐ LE CARILLON

It's in the centre of the village, opposite the church.
☎ 03.27.61.80.21
Closed Sun evening except July–Aug, Tues evening, Wed, and a fortnight in Nov.

A beautiful Avesnois house which has been tastefully restored. It's run by a couple of young professionals who have enhanced the gastronomic reputation of this region. Real cooking without fuss or show. All the dishes change with the seasons and their desserts are flamboyant. Weekday menu 85F, then others 118–198F. The wine cellar next door sells a selection of *vins de pays* and vintages at all sorts of prices, as well as a good range of whiskies.

LILLE 59000

SEE MAP OVERLEAF

♠ HÔTEL DE FRANCE**

10 rue de Béthune; M° Rihour. **MAP C2-4**
☎ 03.20.57.14.78 ➡ 03.20.57.06.01
Closed a week from Christmas to New Year. **TV**.

Right in the centre of town, close to the Grand-Place, this hotel can get pretty noisy. It lacks charm but there's nothing to find fault with. 180F for a double with basin, 250F with shower/wc or 270F with bath and direct-dial telephone. Very friendly welcome. In the breakfast room there is a gigantic fresco of Nord-Pas-de-Calais painted by a former night porter who was a student at the Fine Arts school.

⅔ ♠ LE BRUEGHEL**

5 parvis Saint-Maurice. **MAP C2-5**
☎ 03.20.06.06.69 ➡ 03.20.63.25.27
TV. Pay car park.

This hotel, in an enormous brick building near the St-Maurice church, has personality and – better still – soul. The decoration shows excellent taste, with trinkets and antique furniture everywhere. Double rooms to suit every pocket: 190F with basin, 265F with shower, 360F with shower/wc, and 400–450F with bath. The rooms at the rear are very pleasant and quiet. The welcome couldn't be better – the staff love their work and the night porter practically has a fan club. It's a favourite meeting place for actors performing in shows in town so it's best to book. 10% discount.

⅔ ♠ HÔTEL FLANDRE-ANGLETERRE**

13 pl. de la Gare. **MAP D2-3**
☎ 03.20.06.04.12 ➡ 03.20.06.37.76
TV. Car park.

The unfussy, well-soundproofed rooms all have nice bathrooms and quite modern decor. Doubles 200F with shower or 390F with bath. It's used mainly by businesspeople, so prices drop at the weekend if you stay at least two nights. It's opposite the station in a pretty dull part of town, but at least it's not noisy, despite being close to Euralille. 10% discount at the weekend.

⅔ ♠ LE GRAND HÔTEL**

51 rue Faidherbe. **MAP C2-6**
☎ 03.20.06.31.57 ➡ 03.20.06.24.44
Closed first three weeks in Aug. **TV**.

A comfortable hotel near the station with attractive rooms, a very nice female owner and efficient staff. Doubles with shower/wc 340F, with bath 380F. They also have a few family rooms sleeping three and four. 10% discount at the weekend.

⅔ ♠ HÔTEL DE LA PAIX**

46 [bis] rue de Paris. **MAP C2-7**
☎ 03.20.54.63.93 ➡ 03.20.63.98.97
TV.

Beyond the grand reception of this hotel there's an 18th-century staircase that's so superb it's a shame to use the lift. The rooms are tastefully furnished and spacious; doubles with shower/wc 380F, or 450F with bath. The proprietor gave up painting when she entered the hotel business, but it has remained a passion. She has devoted each room to paintings by a different contemporary artist and put reproductions on the walls. It adds to the charm of the place. Number 12 has a terrace and a garden! 10% discount at the weekend except in Aug and during the Lille antiques fair.

●❙ RESTAURANT LA PÂTE BRISÉE

65 rue de la Monnaie. **MAP C1-15**
☎ 03.20.74.29.00 ➡ 03.20.13.80.47

Service 11.45am–2.15pm and 7–10.30pm. In the face of stiff competition, this restaurant is still the specialist for sweet and savoury tarts – Roquefort, Maroilles cheese or *tarte Tatin* – and regional baked cheese dishes like *tartiflette* with potatoes, diced bacon, braised onion and melted Maroilles cheese. The various reasonably priced *formules*, 47–98F, include drinks. The food is good and the portions generous. It's packed at lunchtime so it's a good idea to arrive early. Relaxed atmosphere with a mainly student clientèle. After 3pm, it also functions as a tearoom.

⅔ ●❙ RESTAURANT LE SQUARE

52 rue Basse. **MAP C2-17**
☎ 03.20.74.16.17 ➡ 03.20.93.21.49
Closed Sun, Mon evening and 1–22 Aug.

The dining room is pleasant and quite intimate and both the welcome and service are friendly. À la carte they serve warm or cold salads and generous portions of other regional dishes which change with the seasons; *andouillette*, steak *tartare*, duck breast with honey, lasagne with salmon and so on. Menus start from only 50F and there's an attractively priced *formule* at

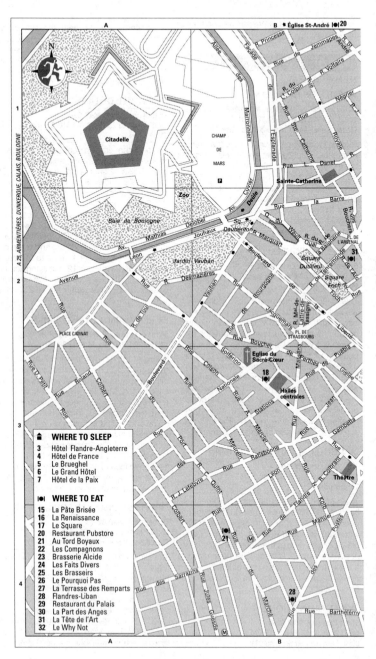

WHERE TO SLEEP

3 Hôtel Flandre-Angleterre
4 Hôtel de France
5 Le Brueghel
6 Le Grand Hôtel
7 Hôtel de la Paix

WHERE TO EAT

15 La Pâte Brisée
16 La Renaissance
17 Le Square
20 Restaurant Pubstore
21 Au Tord Boyaux
22 Les Compagnons
23 Brasserie Alcide
24 Les Faits Divers
25 Les Brasseirs
26 Le Pourquoi Pas
27 La Terrasse des Remparts
28 Flandres-Liban
29 Restaurant du Palais
30 La Part des Anges
31 La Tête de l'Art
32 Le Why Not

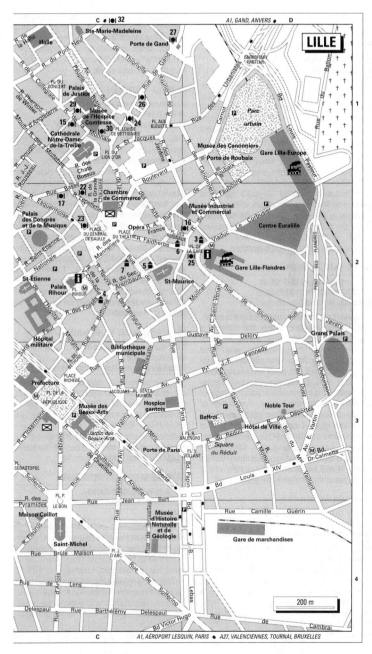

140F with nice wines included. The wine list has decently priced choices. Free coffee.

|●| RESTAURANT LES BRASSEURS

22 pl. de la Gare. MAP D2-25
☎ 03.20.06.46.25 ➡ 03.20.06.46.29

It would be good to find pubs like this one more often. The decor is a real success and makes you feel good and relaxed. The place is noisy, lively and friendly. Several different brews: amber, scotch, Lille white and a pale ale as well, all brewed on the premises using the best barleys and hops – 12–70F for a pitcher containing 1.8 litres. There's an extensive menu of snacks and dishes, from a Munster cheese sandwich to grills and good brasserie dishes – you'll be hard pressed to finish the ham hock *choucroute*. *Formules* at 65F and 69F. If you're famished go for the *formule Choucroute 3 Brasseurs* for 85F, which includes a $^1/_2$ litre of beer. Reliable quality and sizeable portions.

|●| LES FAITS DIVERS

44 rue de Gand (Centre). MAP C1-24
☎ 03.20.21.03.63 ➡ 03.20.31.48.53
Closed Sun, Mon lunchtime, and 1–20 Aug.

A convivial yet dynamic atmosphere is created in this restaurant where the setting is brightly coloured yet subtle and a bit retro. Welcoming and attentive service – you'll have a good evening here. The clientele is cool and youthful, but the food is classic bourgeois fare: scallops in pastry cases with baby vegetables and curry-cream sauce, smoked salmon with scrambled eggs, a selection of fish with a cream and saffron sauce, duck leg *confit* with Salard potatoes, *croustillant* of banana and chocolate fondue, and a dessert selection. Lunch menu at 69F, 105F in the evening. It's a fairly new establishment but it's settled in well because of the quality of the cooking and the professional young staff.

|●| LE POURQUOI PAS

62 rue de Gand (Centre). MAP C1-26
☎ 03.20.42.12.16 ➡ 03.20.55.93.83
Closed Sat lunchtime, Sun and 2–3 weeks in Aug.

Dinner served until 11pm, midnight at weekends. It's in one of the older streets of Lille that's lined with restaurants. The setting is refined, the tables are some distance from each other, and the lighting is low. Courteous welcome. The dishes reveal various influences and the servings are very generous. There's a 70F lunch *formule* and a 110F menu in the evening or you could go *à la*

carte. Good options include medallions of monkfish with smoked bacon, snail *croustade* with puréed leek, duck breast with raspberries, *gratin* of scallops and shellfish and the perfectly cooked steak. The background music is soft and exotic.

⅍ |●| LE WHY NOT

9 rue Maracci. Off-map C1-32
☎ 03.20.74.14.14
Closed Sat lunchtime, Sun reservation only.

This place seems to have been unearthed from the Lille of yesteryear. Affable and attentive welcome that suits the authentic, warm decor in this beautiful, vaulted cellar. There are small tables for two or big ones for many, all arranged higgledy-piggledy round a central bar. Traditional dishes and regional cooking, though inventive enough to satisfy the most exacting of foodies; roast goat's cheese with almonds, *andouillette* with mustard, baked Maroilles cheese flambéed with gin, ostrich fillet with pickled shallots, chocolate mousse with mandarin and beer tart. There's something for all budgets on menus 74–175F. Besides these culinary delights, lots of reasonably priced vinous ones on the wine list. Go for it. Free apéritif.

|●| RESTAURANT LA RENAISSANCE

29 pl. des Reignaux. MAP D2-16
☎ 03.20.06.17.56
Closed Sun, Mon and Tues evenings, and 15 July–15 Aug.

They've completely redecorated inside and out since a fire destroyed the front. It's got the atmosphere of a Parisian bistro, but still serves excellent family cooking and regional specialities. Try chicory Flemish style, *potjevfleisch* (a veal, rabbit and chicken pâté) or Maroilles cheese tart, and any of the homemade desserts. Menus from 79F.

⅍ |●| RESTAURANT PUBSTORE

44 rue de la Halle. MAP C1-20
☎ 03.20.55.10.315 ➡ 03.20.24.48.93
Closed Sun.

A busy restaurant on a busy street in the north of the old town – it's even full in the middle of the week. They been serving the same quality food for the past thirty years. Inside the lights are dimmed, creating a sort of old-fashioned gangster-movie atmosphere, but it's bright enough to read the menus of poetically named dishes and their more prosaic explanations: grilled ham with pineapple, grilled steak with vegetables, veal chop with mushrooms and noodles with grated cheese.

Big helpings. There's a wide range of desserts to finish you off. The lunch menu, at 85F, is the cheapest. Free coffee.

🏃 |O| LA DUCASSE

96 rue Solférino. MAP B3-18
☎ 03.20.57.34.10
Closed Sun and a fortnight in Aug.

An old-style local restaurant with a really warm atmosphere, and the team who have run it for twenty years or more have left well enough alone – the long carved benches, the traditional tables and a truly lovely counter. In a corner there's a mechanical music player dated 1910 that is activated once in a while, but the huge wooden jukebox seems to be there just for show. Authentic bistro cuisine: *cassolette* of seafood, chicken *fricasée*, grilled meats, shrimp *croquettes*, prawn cooked in Gueuze, huge salads and the Flemish platter which is a selection of three specialities. Good desserts. Menus from 90F. Free apéritif.

🏃 |O| LA TERRASSE DES REMPARTS

Logis de la Porte de Gand, rue de Gand (North).
MAP C1-27
☎ 03.20.06.74.74.

Service noon to 11pm (10pm on Sun). This place combines a softly lit seating area with red brick walls and a veranda, on two levels, that opens onto a terrace in good weather. Warm welcome and efficient, attentive service. The menu lists appetising dishes that change with the seasons and plenty of regional specialities: potato pie with crab and horn of plenty mushrooms, brill with pickled chicory, and venison haunch with aubergine. The dessert buffet offers a panoply of pastries and fresh seasonal fruit. Lunchtime menu 98F, then up to 153F. Free coffee.

🏃 |O| RESTAURANT FLANDRES-LIBAN

125–127 rue des Postes. MAP B4-28
☎ 03.20.54.89.92
Closed Sun evening.

A Lebanese restaurant on the edge of Wazemmes, for now, the last working-class part of Lille. The decor, with its delicate panels of carved wood, fountains and hangings, is a far cry from the usual places around here. They do a very good *mezzé*, and the waiters, whose polite demeanour is impeccable, explain the secrets of the twenty or so specialities; hoummus, *shwarma*, *kofte* kebabs, cucumber and yoghurt, chicken kebab with three flavours, and *kebbé* (a

beef rissole with ground wheat). Menus start at 100F; *à la carte* you'll pay around 130F. These are reasonable prices for what is definitely the best Lebanese restaurant in or around Lille. Free *digestif*.

🏃 |O| RESTAURANT LE PALAIS

4 rue du Palais-de-Justice. MAP C1-29
☎ 03.20.74.53.47
Closed Sat lunchtime, Sun evening and 1–20 Aug.

Service noon–2pm and 8–10pm (11pm Thurs–Sat). This grand-looking, friendly restaurant resembles a 1900s bistro; it's a meeting place for trendy young executives, lawyers and the more mature sort of student. Traditional dishes include duck *confit*, *andouillette* and Flemish char-grilled beef, served at reasonable prices. *À la carte* only, around 100F for a full meal. Free coffee.

|O| LA TÊTE DE L'ART

10 rue de l'Arc. MAP B2-31
☎ and ➡ 03.20.54.68.89
Closed Sun, evenings except Fri and Sat, and three weeks in Aug.

Service noon–2pm and 7.30–10.45pm. Quiet little restaurant in a quiet little street but it's still worth booking. They serve a single, excellent *formule-carte*, comprising starter, main course, cheese, dessert and as much wine as you like, all for 112F. There's an unbelievably wide variety of offal and regional dishes: oyster mushrooms and shrimps *à l'armoricaine*, *andouillette* and bacon casserole, fish stew, Maroilles cheese with slivers of chicory, ling *blanquette* with Breton seaweed, mussels *au gratin* with basil, chicken liver stew with apples and Calvados, pig's kidneys with mustard, orange *terrine* with warm chocolate sauce and juniper sorbet with blackcurrant *coulis*.

🏃 |O| LES COMPAGNONS DE LA GRAPPE

22 rue Lepelletier (Centre). MAP C2-22
☎ 03.20.21.02.79
Closed Sun and Mon evening out of season.

Along a narrow passage, you'll find one of the nicest restaurants in Lille. The terrace is crammed in sunny weather while the two dining rooms have lovely wood panelling and designer lighting. Handsome portions of well-cooked bistro classics with a modern twist – don't miss the *pot-au-feu* if it's listed. The bread deserves a special mention, too. Menus start at 120F and children eat free. There's an extensive wine list and a choice by the glass.

The only gripe is the slowish service. Free ginger liqueur.

🕏 |⦾| LA PART DES ANGES

50 rue de la Monnaie (Centre). **MAP C1-30**
☎ 03.20.06.44.01
Closed Sun evening.

A noisy, Parisian-style wine bar – a world away from the local nordic atmosphere – in the busiest street in the middle of the old town. There's a selection of at least twenty wines, some of which come from unusual shippers – Mauza Roux from Plageoles, Mâcon Blanc from Thévenet, and a superb Aubance from the Domaine de Montgilet. There are a few foreign wines as well, even a Pinot Blanc from Egypt. The split-level dining room has sponged walls and big green plants. There's a vibrant atmosphere created by the business-people, yuppies and students, and it's always full. You can have a snack at the bar or eat under the awning or in the small dining room at the back. Decent, straightforward bistro food with a blackboard chalked up with the dishes of the day; these might be chicory *au gratin*, steak, salmon with spinach, or *terrine*. At lunchtime on Sundays, you can have a *charcuterie* or cheese platter. Service can be slap-dash when it gets busy. Expect to pay 120–150F for a meal. Free house apéritif.

|⦾| AU TORD BOYAUX

11 pl. Nouvelle-Aventure. **MAP B4-21**
☎ 03.20.57.73.67
Closed Sat and Sun evenings.

The Wazemmes district, with its famous square, is the heartbeat of the city. Monique runs the place. She's adorable and cooks like a dream – good, family-style dishes that are substantial and tasty – if her pheasant *choucroute* is on the menu, order it. She uses fresh seasonal produce so all the dishes are satisfying. *À la carte* dishes start at 45F. It's popular for Sunday lunch so you may have to book.

|⦾| BRASSERIE ALCIDE

5 rue des Débris-Saint-Étienne **MAP C2-23**.
☎ 03.20.12.06.95
Closed 24 and 25 Dec.

The discreet charm of the bourgeois brasserie; uniformed waiters standing in line, an oak bar, large mirrors – and an equally discreet, Chabrolesque middle-aged clientele. The *formule* offers a choice between *moules marinière*, three regional dishes – including a very good char-grilled steak –

and three beers. Menus from 130F for typical brasserie cuisine. Dishes of the day at 70F; chicken *waterzoï*, *cassoulet* with meat *confit*, salmon and leek *andouillette*, fisherman's stew and so on.

VILLENEUVE-D'ASCQ   59650 (8KM SE)

🕏 |⦾| RESTAURANT LES CHARMILLES

98 av. de Flandre (North).
☎ 03.20.72.40.30
Closed Wed and three weeks in Aug.

A very spacious dining room painted pale and olive green that is ideal for intimate meals for two. Cooking is creative; menus at 75F, 85F and 125F. Local dishes such as Maroilles tart, *carbonade* of rabbit, tournedos flambéed with whisky and prawn sauce, fish of the day, *waterzoï*, and slivers of pear with Rocquefort. Free coffee.

MAROILLES   59550

🕏 |⦾| L'ESTAMINET

83 Grand-Rue (Centre).
☎ 03.27.77.78.80
Closed Sun, Mon and Tues evenings.

A typical village restaurant in the town that produces the famous local cheese. Over the years this place has established a solid reputation for good, reliable local and regional dishes. The 65F weekday menu offers two courses, and there are others up to 148F or *à la carte*. The dishes of the day are listed on a blackboard. You might get steak with Maroilles cheese sauce, mushroom tart, *andouillette* and a good selection of cheeses. Wines are reasonably priced. Warm welcome. It's best to phone for a weekend reservation out of season. Free coffee.

LOCQUIGNOL   59530 (4KM N)

🕏 ⬢ |⦾| AUBERGE DU CROISIL

R oute de Maroilles; from Maroilles or Le Quesnoi, follow the D233, and it's signposted 3km from Maroiles.
☎ 03.27.34.20.14 ↦ 03.27.34.20.15
Closed Sat evening and Mon except public holidays,and 22 Dec–12 Feb.

This inn is way out in the Mormal forest. They serve splendid traditional dishes, prepared by the boss, in a tranquil atmosphere. The *terrines* and goose *cassoulet* are winners, not to mention the frogs' legs, stuffed pig's trotters, home-made *andouillette*, quails with mushroom sauce and cockerel in beer. Tasty cooking with dense flavours. The menus, 68–145F, change every week. In the hunting season, they do a lot of game, including wild boar cutlets with green peppercorns and delicious venison steak with raspberry. They have a couple of simple rooms, 120F, with shared washing facilities. Free apéritif.

MAUBEUGE   59600

⅍ 🛏 |●| LE GRAND HÔTEL-RESTAURANT DE PARIS**

1 porte de Paris; it's near the station.
☎ 03.27.64.63.16 ➡ 03.27.65.05.76
📧 grand.hotel.maubeuge@wanadoo.fr
TV. Disabled access. Lock up car park.

The best restaurant in the area, a place for family celebrations and business lunches. Lots of local produce, fish, seafood and game in season. Menus 80–240F. Renovated rooms; double with shower/wc or bath 260–370F. Free breakfast at the weekend.

MONTREUIL-SUR-MER   62170

🛏 |●| LE DARNÉTAL

pl. Darnétal (Centre).
☎ 03.21.06.04.87 ➡ 03.21.86.64.67
Closed Mon and Tues, Mon evening and Tues July–Aug. **Car park**.

Traditional hotel on a lovely little square in the old town. The restaurant boasts a collection of great antiques. Lots of delicate, delicious fish dishes – brill cooked in a *court-bouillon*, lobster in *pastis* and warm oysters in champagne. Menus at 100F (not Sat evening and Sun), 145F and 190F. The four spacious, rather bare rooms are decorated in late 19th-century style. Ask to see them before handing over your money, because they're all very different. Doubles 220–300F.

🛏 |●| LE CLOS DES CAPUCINS**

46 pl. du Général-de-Gaulle (Centre).
☎ 03.21.06.08.65 ➡ 03.21.81.20.45
Closed Sun evening, Mon, 1–15 Feb and 1–15 Nov. **Car park**.

A neat, pretty dining room and an attentive welcome that puts you at your ease. You just know you're going to have a good meal. Start with the house smoked salmon, then the calf's head *ravigote* or braised shoulder of pork with cabbage. Good, well-matured cheeses to follow. Specialities include Saint-Vaast oysters. Menus 98–210F. Good wines

from 100F a bottle. A very reliable place; it seems to attract English foodies who hop across the Channel for a gastronomic weekend. Above the restaurant, there are a few rooms; 340F with shower/wc.

MADELAINE-SOUS-MONTREUIL (LA)   62170 (5KM W)

🛏 |●| LA GRENOUILLÈRE

It's in the centre of the village.
☎ 03.21.06.07.22 ➡ 03.21.86.36.36
📧 auberge.la.grenouillere@wanadoo.fr
Closed Tues and Wed, Tues only in July, 1–8 Aug and Jan. **Garden. Car park**.

Pretty country inn down in the Canche valley, at the foot of the bastion of Montreuil. You dine in a typical setting – all low beams, copper pots and decorative frogs (have a look at the murals) – or, in summer, in a pretty flower garden. The chef has reinvented local dishes to create delicate, interestingly seasoned dishes: *fricassée* of *petit-gris* snails served with pig's trotters in licorice *jus*, potted chicken with coconut milk, and veal with honey and spices – a real feast. The house speciality is frogs' legs. The chef always wants to know if you enjoyed your meal and asks you for your opinion. Weekday menu 160F, with others up to 400F. Affordably priced wines. There are four perfectly charming rooms with bath on the ground floor, 400F.

|●| AUBERGE DU VIEUX LOGIS

pl. de la Mairie; take the D139 or the D917 and it's at the foot of the walls.
☎ 03.21.06.10.92
Closed Mon, Tues and 1–20 Feb.

Service noon–2.30pm and 7–9.30pm. Country inn serving traditional dishes using quality produce: house *cassoulet* with goose fat, veal kidneys *Vieux Logis* and excellent grilled beef. More original dishes include *carpaccio* of raw fish. Menus 80F, 105F, 145F and 175F or *à la carte*. Rustic decor and nice, unaffected staff. In fine weather you can eat on the terrace.

SAINT-OMER   62500

⅍ 🛏 |●| HÔTEL-RESTAURANT LE VIVIER

22 rue Louis Martel (Centre).
☎ 03.21.95.76.00 ➡ 03.21.95.42.20
Closed Sun evening and Jan. **TV**.

A charming hotel, though you wouldn't guess it from the unusual name, situated in the pedestrianised centre of this attractive town.

Attractive, clean rooms with good facilities; doubles 290F with shower/wc or bath, hair drier, mini-bar, TV and phone. Appetising dishes served in the pleasant dining room: pork fillet with celery cream, fresh fish, numerous shellfish and seafood platters. Menus at 92F (not Sat evening or Sun), then 132–192F. Friendly, efficient service. Free coffee.

⅍ ☎ |●| HÔTEL SAINT-LOUIS**/ RESTAURANT LE FLAUBERT

25 rue d'Arras (Centre).
☎ 03.21.38.35.21 ➡ 03.21.38.57.26
Closed Sat and Sun lunchtimes and 24 Dec–2 Jan.
Disabled access. **TV**. **Car park**.

Service noon–2pm and 7–11pm. The hotel has been around since the 1920s, though it has been attractively renovated since. Calm, comfortable rooms from 305F with shower/wc. Friendly, retro bar. The restaurant has a brasserie menu, plus a 78F weekday one and others 98–157F listing more elaborate and upmarket dishes. Specialities include fish *choucroute*, duck and *cassoulet*. Free apéritif.

|●| AUBERGE DU BACHELIN

12 bd. de Strasbourg (Northeast).
☎ 03.21.38.42.77
Closed Sun evening and Mon, and Thurs evening except for reservations for a minimum of 15.

A classic restaurant with flowery decor and a friendly atmosphere. Menus 79–139F. On Friday they make *couscous*; other specialities include perch fillet with garlic, fish stew, and beef *carbonade* with beer. The service is pleasant and efficient.

BLENDECQUES   62575 (4KM SE)

⅍ ☎ |●| LE SAINT-SÉBASTIEN**

2 Grand-Place (Centre); take exit 4 off the A26.
☎ 03.21.38.13.05 ➡ 03.21.39.77.85
Closed Sat lunchtime and Sun evening. **TV**.

Service noon–2pm and 7.30–10pm. Stone-built inn on a pretty square. Pleasant, comfortable rooms; doubles 260F with shower/wc or bath. The staff are straightforward and friendly. In the nice rustic restaurant you'll find dishes like *andouille* salad, chicken *fricassée* with vinegar, *croustillant* of pigs' ears, pan-fried pigs' tripe, veal kidneys with Houlle juniper, and local ale pie. Menus 79.50F–175F or 220F *à la carte*. Free coffee.

TOUQUET (LE)   62520

⅍ ☎ |●| HÔTEL LE CHALET**

15 rue de la Paix (Centre).
☎ 03.21.05.87.65 ➡ 03.21.05.47.49
Closed Jan. **TV**.

Spick and span rooms at prices that are more than reasonable for Le Touquet – and this place looks nothing like a chalet! Doubles with basin 170F, 250–300F with shower/wc or bath. Some rooms look onto a small patio. You'll pay the top price if you want TV and a view of the sea – it's more of a glimpse at the end of the road as long as you strain to look round the corner to the left. Free breakfast.

⅍ ☎ |●| HÔTEL BLUE COTTAGE**

41 rue Jean-Monnet (Centre); it's behind the market place.
☎ 03.21.05.15.33 ➡ 03.21.05.41.60
Closed 15 Nov–15 Feb. **TV**. **Car park**.

Reasonably priced hotel with pretty blue and yellow rooms. Doubles with washing facilities 260F, 200–400F with shower/wc, and 350–410F with bath. It's one of the few places in pricey Touquet to offer half board, which costs 330F per person and is compulsory July–Aug. Buffet breakfast 42F. In the restaurant a dish of the day costs 59F and there are menus 85–165F. Very welcoming owners. Third night free if you arrive on Sun, Mon or Tues 11 Nov–31 March. Free coffee.

⅍ ☎ HÔTEL LES EMBRUNS**

89 rue de Paris (Centre).
☎ 03.21.05.87.61 ➡ 03.21.05.85.09
Closed 15 Dec–15 Jan.
Disabled access. Garden. TV.

In a quiet situation set back from the road and not far from the sea. The simple, comfortable rooms are clean and attractive. Some look onto the garden, others have terraces. Doubles 260–360F with shower or bath, 350F for a triple or 420F for a room sleeping four. You'll get a warm welcome and you can park bikes or motorbikes in the garden. 10% discount for a two-night stay Sept–June.

⅍ ☎ HÔTEL LE NOUVEAU CADDY**

130 rue de Metz (Centre); it's opposite the covered market and 150m from the beach.
☎ 03.21.05.83.95 ➡ 03.21.05.85.23
Closed Jan. **Disabled access. TV.**

Reception closed 1–3.30pm. Tastefully decorated hotel with four floors (and a lift), each painted a different colour to represent a different season. All the rooms are pleasant and comfortable and have en-suite bathrooms; doubles 265–365F. They also have studios with kitchenettes. Warm welcome. 10% discount, except on public holidays and the Easter and summer school holidays.

🔆 |●| LES DEUX MOINEAUX

12 rue Saint-Jean (Centre).
☎ 03.21.0509.67
Closed Mon and a fortnight in June.

This brick-walled dining room has a warm, intimate atmosphere, with gentle jazz playing in the background. The owner will welcome you pleasantly and the staff are equally kind. Try the snail stew or the cockerel in wine sauce. Since they changed their supplier, their cheese platter offers an array of well-matured regional cheeses. Menus 85–140F. The wine list has a few reasonably priced bottles. Free coffee.

|●| AUBERGE L'ARLEQUIN

91 rue de Paris; it's near rue Saint-Jean and the seafront.
☎ 03.21.05.39.11 ▸ 03.21.06.13.06
Closed Wed from May to end Sept, Wed and Thurs from Oct to end April, and 20 Dec–31 Feb.

A classic, small restaurant where the owner cooks straightforward dishes: monkfish kebab with cabbage, veal *blanquette à l'an-cienne* and skate with olive and raspberries. The cheap weekday menu, 89F, is well balanced, and there are others at 98F and 145F.

|●| RESTAURANT AU DIAMANT ROSE

110 rue de Paris (Centre).
☎ 03.21.05.38.10 ▸ 03.21.05.89.75
Closed Tues evening except July–Aug, Wed and Jan.

Service noon–2.15pm and 7–9.30pm (10pm on Sat). This pastel pink restaurant attracts a clientele of regulars and quiet holidaymakers. Traditional, honest French cuisine – salmon *Béarnaise*, duck thigh *confit* in goose fat, *foie gras* and *fruits de mer* – plus a wide variety of meats and a good wine list. Menus 98F, 135F and *à la carte*.

SAINT-JOSSE   62170 (7KM SE)

|●| LE RELAIS DE SAINT-JOSSE

Grand-Place; follow the D143 for 5km, take the D144 and it's near the church.
☎ and ▸ 03.21.94.61.75
Closed Sun evening, Mon and a fortnight in Oct.

Set on a pretty square in a village that's festooned with flowers, *Le Relais* has window boxes overflowing with geraniums. From first

thing in the morning the proprietor, Étienne Delmer, who's a butcher's son, offers excellent rabbit *pâté*, scrambled eggs, cold meats in aspic, a wonderful *pâté de campagne*, smoked fish and, in winter, a good brawn. Those who prefer more conventional mealtimes can eat in the restaurant where there's an 85F weekday menu and others up to 210F.

🔆 |●| L'AUBERGE DU MOULINEL

116 chaussée de l'Avant Pays, hameau du Moulinel; take the road to Moulinel, go under the motorway and 2km further, there's a sign where you turn left.
☎ 03.21.94.79.03
Closed Mon and Tues except for school holidays, the first three weeks in Jan and the last week in June.

One of the best restaurants along the Opal coast, run by Alain Lévy who produces deftly prepared dishes. He likes to use strong flavours and unusual but intriguing flavour combinations; veal sweetbreads with Maroilles cheese sauce, hare *à la royale* with poached pear which is richly flavoured and spicy. The fish dishes show similar expertise. Menus 147–260F. Affordable wines. The restaurant is in a restored farmhouse way out in the countryside between Le Touquet and Montreuil-sur-Mer. Meticulous service. Book to avoid disappointment. Free coffee.

TOURCOING   59200

🔆 |●| RESTAURANT LE RUSTIQUE

206 rue de l'Yser (North); from the town centre follow rue de Gand for 3km which leads into rue de l'Yser.
☎ 03.20.94.44.62
Closed Mon, evenings except by reservation. **Car park.**

Service noon–3pm and 7.30–9.30pm. The surroundings have a rustic feel – logs burn in the fireplace and copper pans hang from the walls – but the service and food are rather more refined. Dishes include ham on the bone, scallops on the shell, house *foie gras* and rack of lamb with herbs. This is gourmet food at modest prices. Weekday menu 69F, a regional one at 148F and another at 160F – wine is included. You can eat on the terrace when the weather is fine. Free house apéritif.

TRÉLON   59132

🔆 |●| LE FRAMBOISIER

1 rue F. Ansieau (Centre).
☎ 03.27.59.73.34

Closed Sun evening, Mon, a fortnight in early Feb and three weeks early Sept. **Disabled access**.

A rare beacon of quality in a culinary desert, run by a couple who wanted to improve the region's gastronomic reputation. The dining room is fresh and pleasant; sturdy beams, pink paint, pictures on the walls and classical music playing in the background. Service is quietly efficient. The dishes are full of new flavours and often inspired. They change depending on what's available in the markets. Good choices include escalope of char, lobster tails with vanilla essence, *millefeuille* filled with zander, stewed rabbit, spaghetti with leeks and a few classics – calf's head or veal sweetbreads with kidneys. Menus 90–248F. Themed evening twice a month. It's best to book at the weekend. Free coffee.

VALENCIENNES 59300

♠ LE BRISTOL**

2 av. de-Lattre-de-Tassigny (North); it's near the train station.
☎ 03.27.46.58.88 ➡ 03.27.47.34.39
Disabled access. TV.

There's nothing original about this hotel, but it's quiet and clean, and the pleasant staff have ready smiles. The rooms are light and spacious. Some overlook a courtyard and others the street – fortunately you don't hear the trains. Good-value doubles with basin 200F, 250–300F with shower/wc or bath.

♠ HÔTEL LE CLÉMENCEAU**

39 rue du Rempart; 200m from the Grand-Place and 200m from the train station.
☎ 03.27.30.55.55 ➡ 03.27.30.55.56
Closed Jan and Feb. **Disabled access. TV**.

Right near the station, this is a solid red-brick hotel with about twenty rooms, all with double glazing, fully equipped bathrooms, hair drier and safe. Doubles 250–340F, which is good value but doesn't compensate for the slightly off-putting welcome.

⚞ ♠ HÔTEL NOTRE-DAME**

1 pl. de l'Abbé-Thellier-de-Poncheville (Centre); it's opposite the basilica of Notre-Dame.
☎ 03.27.42.30.00 ➡ 03.27.45.12.68
e hotel-notredame@wanadoo.fr
Disabled access. TV. Pay car park.

Charming little hotel in a converted convent. The interior decoration is chic but not flashy. Doubles with shower 250F, with shower/wc or bath 300–360F. Number 36, on the ground floor, looks out onto the indoor gar-

den and is superb. The staff are pleasant. 10% discount.

⚞ ♠ ⎮◉⎮ LE GRAND HÔTEL-RESTAURANT DU GRAND HÔTEL***

8 pl. de la Gare (Centre).
☎ 03.27.46.32.01 ➡ 03.27.29.65.57
Restaurant ☎ and ➡ 03.27.29.65.57
e grandhotel.val@wanadoo.fr
TV.

The hotel is in a superb 1930s building just opposite the station. Thoroughly refurbished, it now boasts an elegant interior and spacious, attractive rooms. Doubles with shower/wc or bath 475F; you'll pay a 55F supplement for a third person. The splendid dining room has a lofty ceiling, a Tiffany stained-glass dome, columns, heavy curtains, old-fashioned lighting and long banquettes – totally beguiling. Great cooking, too. They offer a splendid selection of regional dishes and classic family dishes: home-made *potje vleesh*, pig cheek *confit* in a stew served with lentils, calf's tongue *à la Flamande*, beef *carbonade*, calf's head, shepherd's pie, *choucroute* with pickled meats or smoked pork, and *mousselline* of pike with Riesling. Various salads. Menus 120–250F. Good wines at all prices. Free coffee. 10% discount on the room rate 13 July–15 Sept.

⚞ ♠ ⎮◉⎮ AUBERGE DU BON FERMIER

64 rue de Famars (Centre).
☎ 03.27.46.68.25
TV. Car park.

An old coaching inn in a splendidly preserved listed building. The interior resembles a museum, with ornaments and trinkets displayed in the smallest nooks and crannies. There are some images of the Stations of the Cross, rescued from a church that was destroyed in the war. The corridors are skewed and tilted, and the staircases are narrow. All the rooms are very charming and decorated in medieval or classical style. Doubles 570–640F. The restaurant offers menus 128–285F with a number of local dishes; *millefeuille* with Maroilles cheese, *carbonnade Flamande* and local pear *du Hainaut*. 10% discount on the room rate Sat and Sun. Free house apéritif.

⚞ ⎮◉⎮ L'ORANGERIE

128 rue du Quesnoi (Centre).
☎ 03.27.42.70.70
Closed Sun, Mon, weekday lunchtimes and Aug.

Service 8pm to midnight. Old local restaurant that's been transformed into a popular, lively, modern place. It has an easy-going, relaxed atmosphere with a warm setting and soft lighting. They serve fresh bistro dishes at affordable prices: veal *blanquette à l'ancienne*, grilled lamb cutlets, puréed salt cod, mussels with chips and various salads and *terrines*. On Thurs, Fri and Sat nights they hold dances after dinner and don't close until at 3am. Free *digestif*.

⅍ |●| RESTAURANT AU VIEUX SAINT-NICOLAS

72 rue de Paris (North).
☎ and ➡ 03.27.30.14.93
Closed Sun and Mon evenings and 14 July–15 Aug.

The decor is fresh, clean and modern. A statue of a bishop contemplates the Klee and Kandinsky reproductions. Simple, tasty cooking includes *andouille* with juniper, chicken in beer, duck breast in honey and orange, *paella*, and big salads. Service is charming and the atmosphere is peaceful. Menus 75–135F. Affordable wines. An unpretentious little place. Free coffee.

|●| LE BISTROT D'EN FACE

5 av. d'Amsterdam (Centre).
☎ 03.27.42.25.25
Closed Sun evening.

This is the bistro belonging to the gastronomic restaurant *Rouet* opposite (see below). It's cheaper and more relaxed and the decor is fresh and pleasant. They serve huge bowls of mussels, frogs' legs, fresh scallops, *blanquette de veau à l'ancienne*, *choucroute*, *gratin* of *andouille* with Chablis, duck legs with wine and blackcurrant, beef steak and oysters – there's a huge choice. Menus 79F and 98F.

⅍ |●| LA PLANCHE À PAIN

1 rue d'Oultreman, (Centre); it's 50m from the Place d'Armes.
☎ 03.27.42.25.25
Closed Sun evening, Mon and 5–25 Aug.

A solid establishment in a quiet street. The dining room is homely, and you feel cossetted. Everyone comes here for the quality traditional cooking – they prepare dishes from the region and from the Mediterranean, including squid stew, coddled eggs with Maroilles cheese, joint of monkfish pricked with garlic, cockerel in Jenlain, red mullet fillets with asparagus croquant and creamed parsley, and a divine home-made alliance of *foie gras* and smoked tongue. Menus 80–170F. Free coffee.

⅍ |●| RESTAURANT LA TOURTIÈRE

34 rue E. Macarez (East); it's just out of the town centre, near the tax office.
☎ 03.27.29.42.42
e latourtiere@evropost.org
Closed Mon and Wed evenings, and Sat lunchtime.

The outside is really dreary, but it's much more friendly inside, with a relaxed, lively atmosphere. The food is a mixture of regional dishes and Italian specialities – sometimes they're even combined as in the macaroni with Maroilles cheese. There's an Italian menu, 88F, and a local one, 98F, which lists egg with Maroilles cheese, Avesnois veal and *tarte à la cassonade*. À la carte you'll inevitably find pizzas and pasta dishes, leek and onion quiches and so on. Everything is served in vast portions. Free *digestif*.

|●| ROUET

8 av. d'Amsterdam (Centre).
☎ 03.27.46.44.52
Closed Sun evening and a fortnight in Aug.

Well-established gastronomic restaurant that just keeps going. Only the decor, sort of faded classic, shows its age. The clientele and the atmosphere are conventional – businesspeople, well-off retired folk, local dignitaries and the like. But everyone is treated alike. The service is so friendly that occasionally the waiters spend more time chatting than serving. The seafood is sparklingly fresh and all the dishes are brilliantly prepared. Menus from 100F and seafood platters upwards of 200F.

WIMEREUX   62179

⅍ ☎ |●| HÔTEL DU CENTRE

78 rue Carnot (Centre).
☎ 03.21.32.41.08 ➡ 03.21.33.82.48
Closed Mon, 1–22 Jan and 17–31 Dec. **TV**. **Car park**.

A well-established, seriously run establishment in the centre of the town, just two minutes from the beach. Clean, comfortable rooms (all due to be refurbished and some to be enlarged); doubles with shower/wc 228F, 325F with bath. The bistro has been completely renovated and it's cheery and pleasing. *Formule* at 85F or menus 105–175F, listing good, traditional dishes: rabbit in jelly, fish soup, local mussels and poached skate with *beurre noisette*. Friendly owner. 10% discount on the room rate Sun–Thurs except July–Aug and public holidays.

☎ |●| L'ATLANTIC

Digue de Mer (Centre).

☎ 03.21.32.41.01 ➡ 03.21.87.46.17
📧 alain.delpierre@wanadoo.fr
Closed Sun out of season. **TV**. **Car park**.

An impressive seafront place in one of the prettiest resorts on the Opal coast. There are only ten rooms, five of which look over the esplanade and the sea. They're spacious and bright; doubles from 395F. Just the place for a truly relaxing weekend but it's best to book. There are two restaurants – of which *La Liégoise* is the more stylish, with a good reputation – plus a brasserie with an airy dining room, and a terrace serving good, honest fish dishes like fish soup and seafood platters. Menus from 130F.

WISSANT 62179

🛏 |●| HÔTEL-RESTAURANT LE VIVIER**

pl. de l'Église (Centre).
☎ 03.21.35.93.61 ➡ 03.21.82.10.99
📧 le.vivier@wanadoo.fr
Restaurant closed Tues and Wed. **Disabled access**. **TV**. **Car park**.

Service 11.30am–3.30pm and 6.30–10.30pm. The *flobart*, a local fishing boat in front of this restaurant, is a give-away – they specialise in seafood and fish, on menus 96–198F. The little rooms upstairs are really pretty, but those in the annexe further along the Boulogne road are even better, their balconies affording wonderful sea views over Cap Gris-Nez, the bay of Wissant and, in fine weather, the English coast. Doubles with basin 180F, with shower 220F, and with bath 330F (these last also have sea views).

🥁 🛏 |●| HÔTEL DE LA PLAGE

pl. Édouard-Houssin; it's on the river bank, 300m from the beach.
☎ 03.21.35.91.87 ➡ 03.21.85.48.10
📧 hotelplage.wissant@wanadoo.fr
Lock-up car park.

An old hotel with a good deal of charm and friendly, unaffected staff. There's a long wooden terrace along the pond of a mill that's been converted into a museum. The nicest ones are on that side of the hotel, though the ducks get noisy. There are fifty or so rooms altogether, randomly distributed along the labyrinth of corridors. The rooms are plain but pleasant and they're all no-smoking. Doubles with shower or bath 290–320F; there are also some family rooms sleeping four or five. They offer special prices for windsurfers – Wissant boasts one of the best-known spots for windsurfing on the Côte d'Opale. The cuisine in the huge, ancient restaurant is not totally reliable, but they have a good cellar of Bordeaux wines. Menus 100F and 160F with a children's menu at 60F. 10% discount if you stay half or full board Oct–Sept.

ESCALLES-CAP BLANC-NEZ 62179 (5.5KM NW)

🛏 |●| HÔTEL-RESTAURANT À L'ESCALE**

rue de la Mer; take the D940.
☎ 03.21.85.25.00 ➡ 03.21.35.44.22
📧 hotel-lescale@hotel-lescale.com
Hotel closed 2 Jan–9 Feb and 16–27 Dec. **Restaurant closed** Wed Oct–March. **Disabled access**. **TV**. **Car park**.

Ivy-smothered hotel in a tiny village at the foot of the magnificent chalk cliffs of the cap Blanc-Nez. The rooms are charming; doubles with washing facilities 205F, with shower/wc 280F, with bath 350F. To reach the restaurant you cross the tiny road leading to the fossil-strewn beach. The dining room is big and lively, and the cooking makes skilful use of seafood, with dishes such as fisherman's stew and a seafood platter, but they do regional dishes as well. The good 82F menu offers an excellent Licques chicken. There's a whole range of other menus, 100–160F. Facilities include a tennis court and mountain bikes for hire.

BASSE-NORMANDIE

14 Calvados

50 Manche

61 Orne

AIGLE (L') 61300

●| LA TOQUE ET LE VIN

35 rue Pasteur (Centre).
☎ 02.33.24.05.27
Closed Sun, Mon and Tues evenings, and Feb school holidays.

The cooking is done by an experienced chef who opened this small wine bar with a colleague who takes care of the wine. He serves wholesome dishes at reasonable prices in a bright dining room. Fresh produce is used, chosen when it's in season and full of flavour. *Formule* at 62F – dish of the day and a glass of wine – then menus 95–161F.

SAINT-MICHEL THUBEUF 61300 (3KM E)

🏃|●| AUBERGE SAINT-MICHEL

Take the N26.
☎ 02.33.24.20.12 ➡ 02.33.34.96.62
Closed Tues and Wed evenings, Thurs, the first fortnight in January and the first three weeks in Sept. **Disabled access. Car park.**

Service noon–2pm and 7–9.30pm. A friendly country inn, which is quiet despite being so close to the road. Unassuming, friendly staff provide excellent service in the cosy, characterful little dining rooms. Generously flavoured local dishes: house chicken liver *terrine*, calves' kidneys with Calvados, *granite* with Calvados and fresh cream cheese. The 90F menu is served daily and there are others up to 190F. Free coffee.

CHANDAI 61300 (8KM E)

●| AUBERGE DE L'ÉCUYER NORMAND

It's on the N26.
☎ 02.33.24.08.54
Closed Mon, reservations only in winter.

A flint-stone and brick building with evergreens in big planters. There's an inviting feel in the hushed dining room with its open fire, beams and whitewashed walls. The talented chef adds a personal, modern touch to the traditional dishes he prepares: prawn charlotte, port with Camembert and boned pig's trotters. His fish dishes are well judged. Menus 88–298F. Very warm welcome and attentive service.

FERTÉ-FRÊNEL (LA) 61550 (14KM NW)

🏃 🏠 |●| HÔTEL DU PARADIS**

Grande-Rue.
☎ 02.33.34.81.33 ➡ 02.33.84.97.52
e choplin.le.paradis@wanadoo.fr
Closed Mon, three weeks in Feb, and a fortnight in Oct.
Disabled access. TV.

This attractive little village inn lives up to its name and has a homely, friendly atmosphere. The most romantic room is number 16, which has a delightful bathroom and sweet little windows. Doubles 185–290F with shower/wc or bath. The restaurant serves generous portions of lovingly prepared, traditional, local dishes: mussels in cream sauce, seafood platter, fillet of beef with Roquefort cheese sauce, *tarte Tatin* flambéed with Calvados. 61F weekday menu and others 80–240F. It's a very pleasant place to spend a summer or autumn evening. 10% discount on the room rate Oct–May.

ALENÇON 61000

🏠 HÔTEL DE PARIS*

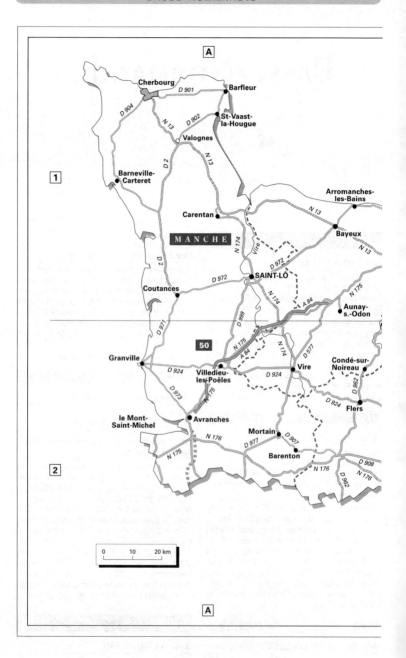

26 rue Denis-Papin; it's opposite the station.
☎ 02.33.29.01.64 ➡ 02.33.29.44.87
TV.

Modest, extremely clean rooms with double glazing at the lowest rates in town – 130–140F for a double with basin and telephone, 160–180F with shower or 180–200F with shower/wc. Easy-going but courteous welcome. The little bar is frequented by lots of regulars.

🍴 🛎 |●| LE GRAND SAINT-MICHEL**

7 rue du Temple; it's near the corn exchange (Halle aux Blés).
☎ 02.33.26.04.77 ➡ 02.33.26.71.82
Closed Sun evening, Mon, the Feb school holidays and July. **TV**. **Car park**.

Service noon–2pm and 7–10pm. A handsome stone building with apple-green shutters situated in a very quiet street in the old part of town. Inside there's a lovely provincial feel and a large friendly dining room with nicely arranged tables. The chef likes to flambé things – veal kidneys with vermouth and mustard, escalope of *foie gras* with port, or fillet of beef *vieille mode*. Decent set menus 95–175F. The comfy rooms have been renovated, though the imitation half-timbering and the garden furniture don't particularly suit the character of the building. Doubles 160F with basin, 180F with shower, 260F with shower/wc and 280F with bath. An ideal place, central yet quiet. Free house apéritif.

🍴 🛎 |●| LE GRAND CERF**

21 rue Saint-Blaise (Centre); it's near the Préfecture.
☎ 02.33.26.00.51 ➡ 02.33.26.63.07
Closed Sat lunchtime, Sun evening and 1–15 Jan. **TV**. **Garden**.

With its splendid 1830 façade this hotel looks like a palace The rooms are spacious and are currently being refurbished. While the work is going on, they offer an overnight rate of 350F per person including dinner. A high standard of cooking at one of the best restaurants in town. There are several dining rooms and a garden where they serve in summer. Menus 100–205F. Free apéritif.

|●| RESTAURANT AU JARDIN GOURMAND

49 rue des Granges; it's in the Saint-Léonard district.
☎ 02.33.32.22.56
Closed Sun and Wed evenings, and Mon. **Disabled access**. **Garden**. **Car park**.

This delightful restaurant has moved to a splendid 15th- and 17th-century house with ancient beams, hand-made floor tiles, wide fireplaces, a garden and a terrace. The cooking is as inventive and imaginative as ever, and the gifted young chef constantly changes the menus. He takes the simplest but the freshest seasonal ingredients and works wonders: sweetbread tart, pollack roasted with smoked bacon and *gâteau* of *andouillette* with potatoes cooked in cider. Menus, 120–270F, include an interesting vegetarian one. Credit cards not accepted.

ARGENTAN   61200

🛎 |●| HÔTEL DU DONJON*

1 rue de l'Hôtel-de-Ville (Centre).
☎ 02.33.67.03.76
Hotel closed ten days in Feb. **Restaurant closed** three weeks in Aug. **TV**. **Car park**.

Simple, clean rooms very reasonably priced for the area. Doubles 120F with basin/bidet but no TV, and 170F with shower/wc and telephone. It has a brasserie-restaurant with set menus from 52F.

🛎 |●| HOSTELLERIE DE LA RENAISSANCE**

20 av. de la Deuxième ED (Southwest); it's on the road to Flers.
☎ 02.33.36.14.20 ➡ 02.33.36.65.50
Closed Sun evening, Mon, a week in Feb and a fortnight in Aug. **TV**. **Car park**.

An excellent contemporary restaurant serving delicious dishes with a novel slant; *foie gras*, braised veal sweetbreads, sea bream cooked on its skin and a *moelleux* of bitter chocolate with coconut ice cream. Menus 95–240F. The hotel has comfortable, well soundproofed rooms; doubles 340F with shower or 355F with bath.

|●| RESTAURANT D'ARGENTAN

22 rue du Beigle (Centre).
☎ 02.33.36.19.38
Closed Sun, Tues evening and a week in Feb.

Service noon–2pm and 7–10pm. The three cosy dining rooms buzz with activity and are frequently crammed, making demands the service can't always meet. Everything is incredibly fresh. They serve wonderful calf's head and sweetbreads in pastry with Pommeau sauce. The 73F menu, available every day, is excellent value. Other menus 88–145F. A good little place.

ARROMANCHES-LES-BAINS   14117

☎ |○| HÔTEL-RESTAURANT DE LA MARINE**

quai du Canada; it's on the sea shore by the harbour wall.
☎ 02.31.22.34.19 ➡ 02.31.22.98.80
📧 mc.verdier@caramail.com
Closed mid-Feb to mid-Nov 2001.
Disabled access. **TV**. **Car park**.

Service noon–2.30pm and 7–9.30pm. The large bay windows overlook the sea and the beach, where you can still see the relics of the pontoons used in the D-Day landings. It's a haunting, arresting view that's reflected in the prices. They serve mainly seafood dishes, seafood platters, grilled or flambéed lobster, and savoury or sweet pancakes, but some dishes could be better. Menus 145–195F. The clean, comfortable bedrooms cost 360F with shower/wc or 390F with bath.

CRÉPON   14480 (7KM SE)

☎ |○| LA FERME DE LA RANÇONNIÈRE**

route d'Arromanches; take the D12 towards Cruelly
–14km on, turn left onto the D65.
☎ 02.31.22.21.73 ➡ 02.31.22.98.39
TV. **Garden**. **Car park**.

The oldest parts of this beautiful and imposing fortified farmhouse date from the 13th century. The place is charming and not at all stuffy, offering a friendly, sincere, family welcome. All the rooms are individually decorated and tastefully furnished in traditional style. Some look onto a large, peaceful garden. Doubles 295–350F with shower/wc or bath. Half board, compulsory in high season, costs 320F per person, which is good value – though it has to be said that the restaurant is not fabulous. The dining room has vaulted ceilings and the cuisine is typical of the region: *parfait* of chicken livers, fish and shellfish stew, *mignon* of pork with lemon, veal sweetbreads with prawns and duck breast. Menus 60–280F.

AUNAY-SUR-ODON   14260

☆ ☎ |○| HÔTEL-RESTAURANT SAINT-MICHEL**

6–8 rue de Caen (Centre).
☎ 02.31.77.63.16 ➡ 02.31.77.05.83
Closed Sun evening, Mon, a fortnight end July–Aug and public holidays, and 15 Jan–15 Feb. **Disabled access**. **TV**. **Car park**.

Service noon–2pm and 7–9.30pm. This large hotel is in a village surrounded by marshes

and it was badly bombed during the war so it doesn't look great from the outside. Inside, though, it's pleasant, with a modern dining room that contrasts nicely with the traditional cooking they serve. The chef uses all the good things that Normandy produces to create his dishes: *civet* of monkfish (a slowly cooked casserole) with fresh noodles, duck *foie gras* with Pommeau sauce and classic dishes like *tournedos Rossini*. Menus 75–220F. They also do a children's menu for 50F. Decent, basic bedrooms 150F with washing facilities and 240F with shower/wc. Half board, 220F, is compulsory at the weekend. 10% discount on the room rate for a two-night stay.

AVRANCHES   50300

☆ ☎ |○| HÔTEL DE LA CROIX D'OR**

83 rue de la Constitution (North).
☎ 02.33.58.04.88 ➡ 02.33.58.06.95
Closed Sun evening from mid-Oct to mid-March, and Jan. **TV**. **Garden**. **Car park**.

This quite delightful 17th-century coaching inn is beside the monument to General Patton. It has a superb garden with a stone urn and an old cider press. Inside, it's like a museum with its stone walls, beams, enormous fireplace, and walls hung with copper, pewter and earthenware pots. Doubles with shower/wc 260–360F and 330–350F with bath. Service is impeccable in the very attractive dining room. Try the fish flan with watercress sauce, the house *terrine* with hazelnuts, or the warm oysters with apples. 80F lunch menu or 125–225F. The chicest restaurant in town. Free coffee.

|○| LE LITTRÉ

pl. de la Mairie.
☎ 02.33.58.01.66 ➡ 02.33.79.35.82
📧 nivard.littre@wanadoo.fr
Closed Sun and Mon except July–Aug, a fortnight end-June/July.

This place doesn't look like much from the outside, but it's one of the nicest restaurants around with a beautiful dining room. No surprises here – you could order the dish of the day with your eyes shut and depend upon it being great. Good traditional cooking – dishes such as eggs *en meurette* and veal chops with artichokes – with menus 60–128F. Good desserts, including apple *clafoutis* (baked apple custard), and *pavé au chocolat*.

DUCEY   50220 (10KM SE)

☎ |○| AUBERGE DE LA SÉLUNE**

2 rue Saint-Germain; take the the Ducey exit off the

N176, and you'll find it on the left just before you get to the bridge.
☎ 02.33.48.53.62 ➡ 02.33.48.90.30
📧 info@selune.com
Restaurant closed Mon from Oct–March, 20 Jan–10 Feb and 20 Nov–15 Dec. **TV**. **Garden**. **Car park**.

Service noon–2pm and 7–9pm. Huge inn on the old road to Mont-Saint-Michel – it was originally a hospice. The attractive bedrooms are individually decorated and you'll pay 280F for a comfortable double with shower/wc or 315F with bath. A lucky few will get a view of the garden that runs down to the slow-moving Sélune, one of the best trout and salmon rivers in France which draws lots of fishermen, so pack your fishing rod. Very carefully planned menus, 84–205F. They serve specialities such as salmon with perry, trout soufflé, stuffed saddle of rabbit with cider vinegar, fillet of sole with Vermouth or crab pie. Friendly staff. 10% discount on the room rate for a two-night stay Sept–June, except weekends.

BAGNOLES-DE-L'ORNE   61140

🏃 🏠 ⏺ LA POTINIÈRE

rue des Casinos.
☎ 02.33.30.65.00
TV. **Car park**.

An ideal place to enjoy the slightly out-dated feel of the spa. It's hard to miss the place because the façade is one of the prettiest and most striking in town. There's a view of the lake from the dining room and most of the bedrooms – the others look onto the main road that's very quiet at night. This is a nice place and prices are modest. Doubles with basin 130F or 250F with shower/wc or bath. The one with the turret is rather special. The cooking is simple, light and tasty and perfectly prepared; hot Camembert, *andouillette de Vire* with mustard, ham in cider or ostrich fillet. Menus 84–175F. Free coffee.

🏃 🏠 ⏺ MANOIR DU LYS***

Route de Juvigny-sous-Andaine; take the D235 and it's 3km from Bagnoles.
☎ 02.33.37.80.69 ➡ 02.33.30.05.80
Closed Sun evening and Mon from Nov to Easter. **Disabled access**. **Garden**. **Swimming pool TV**. **Lock-up car park**.

A delightful manor deep in the Andaines forest, built as a hunting lodge by a fervent royalist. You'll hear cuckoos in the springtime and glimpse a deer straying into the orchard, drawn by the fallen fruit. The rooms are bright and tastefully decorated; some have bal-conies overlooking the garden. Doubles 400–650F with shower/wc or bath. The staff and the cooking are as wonderful as the setting. The restaurant uses fresh local produce and revives traditional flavours. There's *andouille* tart, beech-smoked salmon and divine desserts – *pain perdu* with local honey and cinammon ice cream and *croustillant* of pear. Menus 160–320F. Ideal for a romantic weekend with the special person in your life. Free apéritif. 10% discount on the room rate out of season.

TESSÉ-LA-MADELEINE   61440 (1.5KM SW)

🏃 🏠 ⏺ LE CELTIC**

14 bd. Albert-Christophe; it's on the outskirts of the village coming from Bagnoles.
☎ 02.33.37.92.11 ➡ 02.33.38.90.27
📧 leceltic@club-internet.fr
Closed Tues evening and Wed out of season, 1 Jan–20 Feb. **TV**.

The owners, Michèle and Erick Alirol, make you feel very welcome in this seaside house that's typical of the region. The pleasant bedrooms all have bath and telephone. Doubles with shower/wc 230F or 240F with bath. Menus 88–140F or *à la carte*. It's good, plain cooking using fresh local ingredients and seasonal produce. The rustic dining room is just right and the friendly staff serve with a smile. 10% discount on the room rate and free apéritif.

FERTÉ-MACÉ (LA)   61600 (7KM NE)

🏃 🏠 ⏺ LE CÉLESTE**

6 rue de la Victoire (Centre); it's near the church of Notre-Dame and the tourist office.
☎ 02.33.37.22.33 ➡ 02.33.38.12.25
Closed Sun evening, Mon, ten days in Jan, and ten days in Oct. **TV**. **Car park**.

This hotel is conveniently located in a pedestrianised street so you won't be bothered by traffic noise at night. Most of the bedrooms have been refurbished; doubles with basin 105F, or 220F with shower/wc or bath and TV. The restaurant offers a 68F *formule* (not available Sun) and menus 90–290F; try the *terrine* of duck *foie gras à mode de La Ferté*, the delicious apple tart or *crème brûlée*. In fine weather you can eat out on the terrace. A good place that's very popular locally. Free coffee.

RÂNES   61150 (20KM NE)

🏃 🏠 ⏺ HÔTEL SAINT-PIERRE**

6 rue de la Libération; it's on the D916.

☎ 02.33.39.75.14 ➡ 02.33.35.49.23
Restaurant closed Fri evening out of season.
TV. Lock-up car park.

Service 2–9pm. This place, in a substantial stone building, is run by very friendly staff. You can relax in their deep sofas and the dining room is painted pistachio-green and red. The cooking is excellent and prices are reasonable. The house speciality is the tripe, which has won countless prizes and awards – check out the certificates on the walls. Other winners include the roast chicken, which is perfectly cooked and seasoned, the *bœuf ficelle* (where the meat is tied with string, cooked in stock and served with a Camembert sauce), veal escalope with artichokes and frogs' legs. There's a weekday menu at 78F and others 112–198F. Pleasant bedrooms 245F with shower/wc or 345F with bath. Ask for one overlooking the courtyard; you'll get absolute peace and quiet. Cheerful, helpful owner. 10% discount on the room rate April–Oct.

BARENTON   50720

I●I RESTAURANT LE RELAIS DU PARC

pl. du Général-de-Gaulle (West).
☎ 02.33.59.51.38
Closed Sun and Mon evenings, reservation only in the evening over Christmas and New Year, and the Feb school holidays.

If you get here early, you can overhear the Swedish chef issuing orders in the kitchen in jovial but commanding tones. You're in good hands. He provides a very attractive 70F menu of dishes prepared using local produce with imagination, like the *fricassée* of cockerel with cider vinegar and a range of typical Normandy dishes featuring apples and cream. Other menus 120–170F. The dining room centres on a very attractive fireplace and an antique clock.

BARFLEUR   50760

⅔ ♙ I●I LE MODERNE

1 pl. du Général-de-Gaulle; it's in front of the post office, 50m from the harbour.
☎ 02.33.23.12.44 ➡ 02.33.23.91.58
Closed Tues and Wed from 15 Sept to beginning of Jan, Tues only from March–June.

A colourful, pretty place with lots of flowers. Sadly there's no sea view from the clean, simple bedrooms; 150F with basin, 220F with bath. Half board costs 270F per person.

In the restaurant they serve carefully prepared dishes on a range of menus, 85–189F. There's a good fish *choucroute* with *beurre blanc* and scallop kebabs. The owner smokes his own salmon and duck breast and makes the bread and flaky pastry. Marvellous desserts – warm flambéed apple tarts, raspberry *feuillantine*, and *gratin* of soft fruit. The place has a delightful charm, though the welcome is somewhat cool. 10% discount on the room rate for a two-night stay.

♙ I●I LE CONQUÉRANT**

16–18 rue Saint-Thomas-Becket; it's 50m from the port
☎ 02.33.54.00.82 ➡ 02.33.54.65.25
Hotel closed 15 Nov–15 March. **Restaurant open** evenings, only for residents. **TV. Garden. Car park**.

A handsome 17th-century building with a sizeable formal garden at the back. The rooms run from simple to more comfortable, 330–350F with shower/wc or bath, and the best ones overlook the garden though none has a sea view. Breakfast 30–55F. You'll pay 95–140F for a meal in the stylish dining room, which is also a *crêperie*.

ANNEVILLE-EN-SAIRE   50760 (5KM S)

I●I CAFÉ DU CADRAN GPLM

Le bourg; take the D902 in the direction of Quettehou.
☎ 02.33.54.61.89
Closed evenings, Sun, and 15 Aug–15 Sept.
Car park.

Almost hidden behind the crowd of tractors and juggernauts in the car park, this ordinary café prepares good, honest dishes such as steak and mashed potato and *blanquette* of lamb. Really tasty and very cheap – menu 55F.

BARNEVILLE-CARTERET   50270

⅔ ♙ I●I L'HERMITAGE**

promenade Abbé-Lebouteiller; it overlooks the port.
Hotel ☎ 02.33.04.46.39 ➡ 02.33.04.88.11
Restaurant ☎ 02.33.04.96.29 ➡ 02.33.04.78.87
Closed Sun evening and Mon in winter, end Nov/beginning Dec and the second fortnight in Jan. **TV. Lock-up car park**.

There's a delightful view of the sea and Carteret's little fishing port from the dining room and the terrace. The place specialises in seafood, serving *moules marinière,* skate *à la crème,* monkfish *à l'américaine* and big seafood platters. They also grill meat or fish on the open fire. Menus 95–260F. There are a few pleasant bedrooms, 200F for a double with shower/wc and 380F for ones overlooking the harbour. Free coffee and 10% discount on the room rate out of season, excluding public holiday weekends.

⬧ |●| HÔTEL DE LA MARINE***

11 rue de Paris.
☎ 02.33.53.83.31 ➡ 02.33.53.39.60
Closed Mon lunchtime and 3 Nov–15 Feb.
TV. Car park.

There are breathtaking views from this large white building that overlooks the harbour. Some bedrooms have a balcony, others a tiny terrace, and the decor throughout is fresh and stylish. Doubles 450–620F. The good reputation of this establishment is due mostly to its restaurant, where the cooking is sophisticated, imaginative and very elaborate. The elegant dining room has a rather chic atmosphere. Monsieur and Madame Cesne run the place smoothly, and the service is as it should be. Their son, Laurent, is the chef and he has put together a series of appetising and imaginative menus, 150–420F: oysters *en nage* glazed with gherkins, plaice lacquered with honey and thyme with an onion and apple preserve, fillet of duck with shallots, *terrine* of goat's cheese with pickled aubergines, and iced mousse with orange liqueur.

BAYEUX   14400

⬧ |●| HÔTEL-RESTAURANT NOTRE-DAME*

44 rue des Cuisiniers (Centre); it's near the cathedral.
☎ 02.31.92.87.24 ➡ 02.31.92.67.11
Hotel closed 15 Nov–20 Dec. **Restaurant closed** Sun evening and Mon lunchtime from Nov to Easter. **TV**. **Car park**.

A comfortingly traditional hotel where the decor in the rooms has a timeless quality and, without being opulent, they are comfortable. Prices for double rooms start at 180F with basin, around 280F with bath. Fancy, succulent cooking with mainly local dishes – shellfish *timbale* or *fricassée* of rabbit in cider. Menus start at 75F. Half board, compulsory in July–Aug and weekends in high season.

⬧ ⬧ HÔTEL MOGADOR**

20 rue Alain Chartier-pl. Saint-Patrice (North).
☎ 02.31.92.24.58 ➡ 02.31.92.24.85
Closed Feb school holidays.

A discreet hotel on the edge of the touristy centre of town. The rooms are classic and comfortable, and those around the courtyard are very quiet. Doubles with shower/wc 260F or 290F with bath; there's an extra charge of

80F per person in family rooms. Relaxed, friendly welcome. 10% discount Nov–March.

⬧ ⬧ HÔTEL D'ARGOUGES

21 rue Saint-Patrice (Centre).
☎ 02.31.92.88.86 ➡ 02.31.92.69.16
dargouges@aol.com
Closed Jan. **TV**. **Garden**. **Car park**.

A lovely 18th-century mansion, built for the Argouges family with a delightful, large courtyard. The dining room is majestic but, behind the house, there's a big tree-filled garden and it's one of life's pleasures to have breakfast there when the weather's good. All the rooms have shower/wc or bath, TV and mini-bar, 310–470F. Rooms 1–5 have a view of the garden. 10% discount.

⬧ |●| LA TABLE DU TERROIR

42 rue Saint-Jean (Centre); it's in the pedestrian area.
☎ and ➡ 02.31.92.05.53
Closed Sun evening and Mon from 1 May–15 Oct, and 15 Oct–15 Nov.

Service 11.30–3pm and 6.30–10pm. Louis Bisson brought the notion of the *table d'hôte*, so popular in the country, to the city. He was a butcher by trade then he decided to return to his home town and indulge his passion for cooking. He has set out a few tables in a beautiful room with stone walls. Traditional, local, uncomplicated dishes: house *terrines*, rib of beef for two, grilled flank or skirt, calf's head with *sauce gribiche* or tripe. There are four honest menus 60–165F. This is a good, friendly little place which appeals equally to tourists and locals who want a decent lunch. Free coffee.

|●| LE PETIT BISTROT

2 rue Bienvenue (Centre); it's beside the cathedral.
☎ 02.31.51.85.40
Closed Sun, Mon and Jan.

This is a genuine little bistro, chic yet very pleasant. The cooking is fresh-tasting and flavoursome, emphasising the flavours of the local ingredients; try veal sweetbreads with hazelnut butter or artichoke flan with *foie gras*. Set menus, 98F and 175F, change with the seasons. A very good restaurant. Dogs not admitted.

COLOMBIERS-SUR-SEULLES   14480 (14KM E)

⬧ |●| CHÂTEAU DU BAFFY**

How to get there: exit 7 from the Caen ring-road in the direction of Creully; turn right after Pierpont.
☎ 02.31.08.04.57. ➡ 02.31.08.08.29.
Restaurant closed Dec to mid-March. **Car park**.

Disabled access.

Service from noon and from 7pm. This pretty château, dating from the Age of Enlightenment, is a lovely romantic spot, with a river running through the beautiful garden. The bedrooms are comfortable, though prices are a little high; doubles with shower/wc or bath/wc go for 390–560F including breakfast. In the restaurant there's a 125F weekday menu, with others up to 210F. They do typical home cooking and some more refined dishes – *grenadin* of veal, stuffed duck leg with a Pommeau sauce or prawn *croquants* scented with vanilla. There's a gym and tennis courts, and you can try your hand at mountain biking, archery and horse riding.

BELLÊME   61130

⚓ |●| LE RELAIS SAINT-LOUIS**

1 bd. Bansard-des-Bois (Centre).
☎ 02.33.73.12.21 ➡ 02.33.83.71.19
Closed Sun evening, Mon, and ten days in Oct.
TV. Car park.

This is a good old-fashioned kind of inn. It's a long, white building with pillars constructed on the old fortifications of this tiny village. The large dining room, its waiters sporting bow ties, is terribly old-fashioned but rather pleasant. The chef, Ghislaine, prepares classic dishes which take their inspiration from local recipes. Weekday menu 95F and others up to 290F. Specialities include *foie gras* from Normandy, fresh scallops and the famous black pudding from Perche. The bedrooms are tastefully decorated; some overlook the gardens at the back of the inn. Doubles 300F with shower/wc or bath.

⚓ |●| DOMAINE DU GOLF DE BELLÊME

Les Sablons
☎ 02.33.73.00.07 ➡ 02.33.73.00.17
e bellême@lemel.fr
Disabled access. **TV. Car park**.

Service up to midnight. Despite being part of a golf club, this restaurant is actually located in the old convent of the 16th-century priory of Saint-Val. The excellent menus, starting at 105F, list perfectly cooked fish and inventive desserts. Specialities include guinea fowl *terrine* with smoked bacon and Calvados, trout with smoked bacon and Pommeau butter, and the plum *terrine* with gingerbread and cinnamon ice cream is heavenly. They also serve grills and salads. Attentive service and a relaxed atmosphere. There are a few comfortable rooms in the out-buildings which

have modern facilities. Doubles 420–590F – if you stay for a week in high season, rooms are charged at 519F per night.

⚓ |●| MOULIN DE VILLEGRAY

Villegray; take the D203.
☎ 02.33.73.30.22 ➡ 02.33.73.38.28
e moulin.de.villeray@wanadoo.fr
Swimming pool. **Garden**. **TV**. **Car park**.

A charming establishment with several little mills, the biggest still with its wheel, dotted around the garden, terrace and swimming pool. The rooms are pricey – doubles from 490F – but the place is romantic. And you can enjoy it just as much if you come for a meal. The talented chef offers a *menu du marché* of dishes dependent upon that day's fresh produce: pigeon and artichoke *terrine*, fish *pot-au-feu*, and strawberry soup. All the dishes are delicate and flavourful, with a particularly imaginative selection *à la carte* – try the marrowbone with snails and mushrooms, calf's cheek stew, and any of the divine desserts. Expect to pay 270–350F. The chef's "thing" is mushrooms and in the autumn he arranges special mushroom weekends that include picking, cooking and tastings. The clientele is well-heeled, but everyone is very relaxed. Attentive welcome.

CABOURG   14390

⚓ LE BEAURIVAGE**

allée du Château (West); it's 800m from the centre of Cabourg on the route du Hôme.
☎ 02.31.24.08.08 ➡ 02.31.91.19.46
Closed 15 Nov–15 Dec. **TV**. **Car park**.

A large ochre-coloured building beside the sea. The decor and the clean bedrooms are more than adequate but since this is the seaside you pay a bit extra. Doubles 300F with shower/wc, 350F with bath. Breakfast 40F.

⚓ HÔTEL LE COTTAGE**

24 av. du Général-Leclerc; it's opposite the church.
☎ 02.31.91.65.61 ➡ 02.31.28.78.82
TV. **Garden**. **Car park**.

You easily fall under the spell of this delightful hotel in a charming, traditional Normandy house with a pretty flower garden. The owner will greet you like an old friend, and the bedrooms are cosy and charming with their Laura Ashley-type decor. Doubles from 380F with shower/wc or bath. Although it's beside the road the double glazing is good and the bedrooms are quiet. Facilities include a billiard room, sauna and sunbed – so there's something to do when it rains.

DIVES-SUR-MER   14160 (2KM S)

|●| RESTAURANT CHEZ LE BOUGNAT

29 rue Gaston-Manneville.
☎ 02.31.91.06.13
Closed evenings except Fri and Sat, but Tues and Wed lunchtimes only in season.

When the old owner retired, no-one knew what would become of this restaurant with its established reputation. The new owner wisely decided to change very little, not even the metro signs, 1950s advertising posters, furniture, and trinkets that would turn a junk dealer green with envy. The food is excellent; taking its inspiration principally from the region, it's prepared from fresh produce and first-rate ingredients. Dishes are firmly traditional, very simple and excellent: *pot-au-feu*, lamb with haricot beans, calf's head. There's only one menu at 82F which includes starter, main dish, cheese *and* dessert. You can also choose *à la carte*, which will set you back about 150F. This is the best value for money locally so it's best to book.

AMFREVILLE   14860 (10KM SW)

🛏 |●| AUBERGE DE L'ÉCARDE

19 route de Cabourg; it's on the D514.
☎ and ➡ 02.31.72.47.65
Closed Sun evening and Mon, in season Mon lunchtime only, and Dec–Jan. **Garden. Car park**.

A small, unassuming stone-built house on the side of the road, run by a kind, welcoming couple. The dining room is attractive and the garden terrace is peaceful in summer. Best of all, the simple country cooking is produced using only the freshest ingredients: pollack fillet with sorrel, skate with chive cream, veal kidneys with grain mustard, steak with Camembert and Roquefort sauce or *entrecôte* flambéed with Calvados. Good-value weekday menu 89F, a *formule* at 79F and other menus up to 169F, with a children's menu for 50F. Simple rooms – double with basin 180F, or 210–240F with shower and garden view.

BEUVRON-EN-AUGE   14430 (14KM SE)

🍽|●| AUBERGE DE LA BOULE D'OR

pl. Michel Vermughen.
☎ 02.31.79.78.78 ➡ 02.31.39.61.50
Closed Tues evening and Wed except July–Sept, and Jan.

Right in the middle of one of the lovliest villages in the Auge, this superb half-timbered house was built in the 18th century. The beautiful façade is so typical that it was photographed for a full-page advertisement in *Le Monde* newspaper. The dining room is stylishly rustic, intimate yet friendly. They serve good local cooking, with tasty dishes at honest prices – go for the hot *andouille de Vire* with cider, veal kidneys with grain mustard, and the apple tart to finish. Menus 99F, 133F and 180F. Free coffee.

CAEN   14000

SEE MAP OVERLEAF

🍽 🛏 HÔTEL SAINT-ÉTIENNE*

2 rue de l'Académie. **MAP A2-3**
☎ 02.31.86.35.82 ➡ 02.31.85.57.69
st.etienne.hotel.fnac.net
TV.

Characterful hotel in a peaceful street. It was built before the Revolution and much of the stonework and wood panelling is original. The bedrooms are pretty, and doubles at 150F with basin or 210–230F with shower/wc and telephone make it the cheapest hotel in Caen so it's often full. The staff are very friendly. It doesn't have a restaurant, but there are plenty nearby. 10% discount Oct–April.

🍽 🛏 HÔTEL DES CORDELIERS**

4 rue des Cordeliers. **MAP B2-4**
☎ 02.31.86.37.15 ➡ 02.31.39.56.51
Closed Sun afternoon. **TV**.

A 17th-century town house with great charm in a street that leads to the castle. It's charming and quiet. The bedrooms are decorated in contemporary style with white walls and pale, wooden furniture, and they look out over the pleasant patio or a narrow pedestrianised street. Doubles 170F with basin, 230F and 250F with shower/wc or with bath. Free coffee and 10% discount.

🍽 🛏 CENTRAL HÔTEL*

23 pl. Jean-Letellier. **MAP B2-2**
☎ 02.31.86.18.52 ➡ 02.31.86.88.11
TV.

This 1960s building has no charm at all, but at least the square is quiet and you get a friendly welcome. The rooms are bright and attractive and prices are reasonable; doubles 190F with shower, 230F with shower/wc or 250F with bath. Some have a view of the

William the Conqueror's castle. It's a very good hotel considering it's only got one star. 10% discount Oct–April.

犬 ≜ HÔTEL BERNIÈRES*

50 rue de Bernières. **MAP C2-5**
☎ 02.31.86.01.26 ➡ 02.31.86.51.76
e hotelbernieres@wanadoo.fr
TV.

This hotel is in a gruesome post-war building in a busy street, but the double glazing keeps out all unwelcome noise and inside it's more like a guest house than a traditional hotel. Clean, attractively decorated rooms and a cordial welcome from the proprietress who takes great care of her guests. Memorable 28F breakfast. Doubles 240F with shower/wc and 260F with bath. The rooms under the eaves sleep four or five people and cost 300F. A one-star hotel that thoroughly deserves to be upgraded to two. 10% discount Oct–March.

|●| RESTAURANT MAÎTRE CORBEAU

94 rue de Geôle. **MAP B1-11**
☎ 02.31.86.33.97.
Closed Sat and Mon lunchtimes, and Sun.

The decor is bizarre at this cheese restaurant – there's a cow on the ceiling and a motley collection of cheese adverts and packets dotted around the place. They serve cheese *fondues* using local cheese or goat's cheese, *tartiflette*, coddled eggs with cheese, and *escalopines* of Roquefort flambéed with Calvados. Weekday lunch menu 60F and others up to 120F. Informal and enthusiastic welcome and service. There's nowhere else like it in the region.

|●| LA PETITE AUBERGE

17 rue des Équipes d'Urgence. **MAP C2-17**
☎ and ➡ 02.31.86.43.30.
Closed Sun and Mon, first three weeks in Aug and a fortnight from 24 Dec.

The dining room is small and cosy, with faux-rustic decor; it's extended by a glassed-in terrace. Low-key welcome, peaceful atmosphere and professional service. The good local dishes change with the seasons. Highlights include tripe *à la mode de Caen*, grilled saddle of lamb with butter and fresh thyme, and salmon *rillettes* made from fresh and smoked fish. *Formule du jour* 68F and *menu-carte* 98F.

犬|●| LE BOUCHON DU VAUGUEUX

12 rue du Graindorge. **MAP C2-14**
☎ 02.31.44.26.26

Closed Sun, Mon, the first three weeks in Sept and 23 Dec–9 Jan.

Service noon–2pm and 7–11.30pm. This little place stands out in an area where restaurants do a thriving trade – and where many places don't deserve their good reputation. You choose from a list of tasty dishes chalked up on big blackboards – winners include tripe in Calvados and the salads served at lunchtime, such as the *salade Normande* with *andouille*, potatoes, eggs and Camembert. The salads are huge and quite enough for a whole meal, served in half-portions as a starter and priced accordingly. Set menus 69F or 98F. The staff are genuinely warm and friendly, just like the atmosphere, so it's not surprising that it's always very busy – it's really best to book. Free apéritif.

|●| RESTAURANT ALCIDE

1 pl. Courtonne. **MAP C2-13**
☎ 02.31.44.18.06 ➡ 02.31.94.47.45
Closed Sat and 20–31 Dec.

The outside is painted sky blue and the decor inside isn't exactly earth-shattering, but the warm atmosphere makes up for it. This is not the place to come if you're on a diet – they serve honest, robust local cuisine that's very substantial: ox tongue with a spicy sauce, lamb *sauté*, ham hock with lentils or calf's head and tripe *à la mode de Caen*. Menus 84–138F. One of the town's classics.

|●| L'EMBROCHE

17 rue Porte-au-Berger. **MAP B1-12**
☎ 02.31.93.71.31
Closed Sat and Mon lunchtimes, and Sun.

Pretty little dining room where you can see through into the kitchen – the atmosphere is enlivened by cool jazz and be-bop. Charming, efficient service. Chalked up on the board you will find local dishes cooked with fresh produce and bags of imagination – try *andouilles* with apples and cider vinegar, or tripe with cider and Calvados. Lunch menu 89F, others up to 108F. All the wines on the short but interesting list are the same price.

|●| LE GASTRONOME

43 rue Saint-Sauveur. **MAP A2-18**
☎ 02.31.86.57.75 ➡ 02.31.38.27.78
Closed Sat lunchtime, Sun, and the first fortnight in Aug.

Service noon–2pm and 7.30–10pm. The dining room is sober and quite chic. The chef

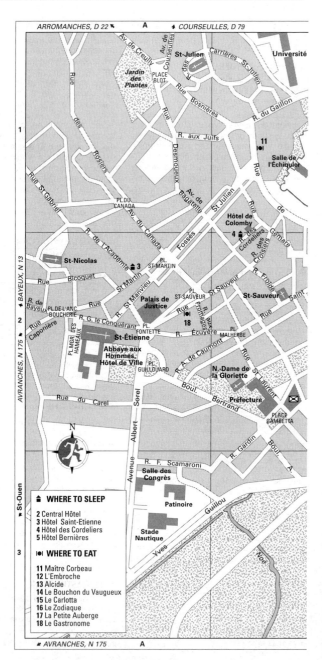

☖ WHERE TO SLEEP

2 Central Hôtel
3 Hôtel Saint-Etienne
4 Hôtel des Cordeliers
5 Hôtel Bernières

⦿ WHERE TO EAT

11 Maître Corbeau
12 L'Embroche
13 Alcide
14 Le Bouchon du Vaugueux
15 Le Carlotta
16 Le Zodiaque
17 La Petite Auberge
18 Le Gastronome

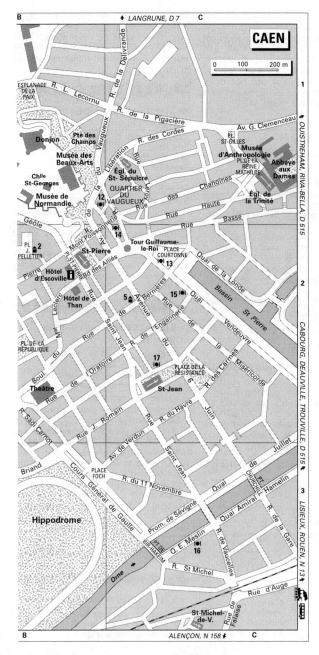

CAEN

0   100   200 m

B ↑ LANGRUNE, D 7 C

ESPLANADE DE LA PAIX
R. L. Lecornu
R. de la Délivrande
R. de la Pigacière
Av. G. Clemenceau

Donjon
Pte des Champs
Musée des Beaux-Arts
Chlle St-Georges
Musée de Normandie
Égl. du St-Sépulcre
QUARTIER DU VAUGUEUX
R. des Cordes
PL. ST-GILLES
Musée d'Anthropologie
PL. DE LA REINE MATHILDE
Abbaye aux Dames
Égl. de la Trinité

Géôle
Rue des Chanoines
Rue Haute
Rue Basse

PL. J. PELLETIER
Mont Poissonnerie
St-Pierre
Tour Guillaume-le-Roi
PLACE COURTONNE
Quai de la Londe
Bassin St-Pierre

Hôtel d'Escoville
Hôtel de Than
Avenue de Bernières
Rue de l'Engannerie
Quai Vendeuvre

PL. DE LA RÉPUBLIQUE
Rue de l'Oratoire
PLACE DE LA RÉSISTANCE
St-Jean
R. des Carmes
Rue de la Miséricorde

Théâtre
R. Sadi Carnot
Rue J. Romain
R. du Havre
Rue Saint Jean
Juin
de
Juillet

Briand
Cours Général de Gaulle
PLACE FOCH
R. du 11 Novembre
Av. de Verdun
Prom. de Sévigné
Quai
Pt. Churchill
Quai Amiral Hamelin
R. de la Gare

Hippodrome
Pte. de BIR-HAKEIM
Q. E. Meslin
R. de Vaucelles
R. St Michel
Rue d'Auge

Orne
St-Michel-de-V.
Rue de Falaise

B ↓ ALENÇON, N 158 C

OUISTREHAM, RIVA-BELLA, D 515 →
CABOURG, DEAUVILLE, TROUVILLE, D 515 ↗
LISIEUX, ROUEN, N 13 →

1

2

3

2
5
12
13
14
15
16
17

adds his own touch to classic and local ingredients to produce dishes like warm oysters on an apple and pear *compôte*, turbot *gratiné* with clams, tripe *croustillant* with cream and Calvados, fillet of duck with artichokes with a sauce thickened with *foie gras* and a *gratin* of fresh fruit with Pommeau. Very decent menus 99–240F. The service is attentive, efficient and unobtrusive.

|●| LE CARLOTTA

16 quai Vendeuvre. **MAP C2-15**
☎ 02.31.86.68.99
Closed Sun and a fortnight in Aug.

Service until 11pm. The name makes it sound like a pizza parlour but the white tablecloths, the waiters in starched aprons and the rather plush, tasteful decor are pure Belle Époque, down to the moleskin banquettes. This is a good, genuine, Parisianstyle *brasserie* with provincial prices. You'll get first-rate cooking here without spending a fortune. Good fish dishes include brill with *vin jaune* sauce and monkfish steamed over seaweed with caramelised chicory, and the meat dishes are tasty – the steak *tartare* is would be hard to beat. Set weekday menu 100F and others up to 180F.

|●| RESTAURANT LE ZODIAQUE

15 quai Eugène-Meslin. **MAP C3-16**
☎ 02.31.84.46.31
Closed Mon–Wed evenings, Sun, public holidays, end of July and three weeks in Aug.

This cosy restaurant, decorated on the theme of the zodiac, has created a reputation for the meats they grill on the open fire – T-bone steak, duck breast or steak fillet. There are terrific home-made pastries for dessert. No set menus; expect to pay about 100F *à la carte*.

BÉNOUVILLE   14970 (10KM NE)

⅔ 🛏 |●| HÔTEL-RESTAURANT LA GLYCINE**

Centre; it's on the Ouistreham road, opposite the church.
☎ 02.31.44.61.94 ➡ 02.31.43.67.30
Closed Sun evening out of season and mid-Feb to mid-March. **TV. Car park**.

This is a beautiful stone building covered in wisteria. Refurbished bedrooms with shower/wc and telephone, 310F. Breakfast 35F. Good food that's imaginatively and carefully prepared. The young chef is in a class of his own, creating dishes such as duck breast with five peppers and baby vegables, turbot perfumed with seasonal herbs, Normandy

foie gras, lobster with a coral sauce, gratinéed shellfish and *crêpes aumonières* with fresh fruit. Menus 95F (not served Sun), then 120–230F. Children's menu 80F. 10% discount in winter and a free *sorbet Normand*.

COLLEVILLE-MONTGOMERY   14880 (10KM N)

|●| RESTAURANT LA FERME SAINT-HUBERT

3 rue de la Mer; take the D515 and turn left 5km before Ouistreham.
☎ 02.31.96.35.41
Closed Sun evening and Mon except in season and on public holidays, and 22 Dec–12 Jan. **Disabled access. Car park**.

Service noon–2.30pm and 7.30–10pm. A large, typical Normandy house where you can lunch in the cosy rustic dining room or in a bright conservatory. Good, traditional food includes monkfish in cider, duck, *fricassée* of kidneys and calf's sweetbreads – enough to satisy the heartiest appetites. Weekday lunch menu 90F and others 120–255F. Free coffee.

NOYERS-BOCAGE   14210 (12KM SW)

⅔ 🛏 |●| HÔTEL-RESTAURANT LE RELAIS NORMAND**

How to get there: take the D675 or the N175.
☎ 02.31.77.97.37 ➡ 02.31.77.94.41
Closed Tues evening, Wed, 28 Jan–10 Feb and 12 Nov–10 Dec. **TV. Lock-up car park**.

The proprietor/chef is a Grand Master of the *Confrérie de fins Goustiers du Pré-Bocage*, an association of defenders of "real" food. He's punctilious over the preparation of local dishes. Set menus 75–280F or *à la carte* – dishes include oysters poached in champagne, *foie gras* in flaky pastry, duck *à l'orange*, *blanquette* of fish with baby vegetables, flambéed *tarte Normande* with aged Calvados and the prize-winning *bonneau Normand* for dessert. The attractive, plush dining room is decorated in a rustic style. Doubles with shower/wc or bath, 235–285F. It's a very peaceful, out-of-the-way place. 10% discount on the room rate late Oct–June.

SAINT-AUBIN-SUR-MER   14750 (16KM NW)

⅔ 🛏 |●| LE CLOS NORMAND**

Digue Guynemer; it's 30m from the casino.
☎ 02.31.97.30.47 ➡ 02.31.96.46.23
℮ closnormand@compuserve.com

Closed Nov–March.
Disabled access. **TV**. **Car park**.

Service noon–2.30pm and 7.30–9.30pm. A lovely L-shaped building with only a path separating it from the beach. It's got a wonderful atmosphere. Clean and very well-maintained bedrooms decorated in ocean tones, the ones with a sea view are the nicest. Doubles 340–390F with shower/wc or 350–410F with bath. Half board is compulsory in July–Aug and on public holidays. There's a vast dining room with a flurry of waitresses in black and white. And the cuisine is no let-down, either. Set menus 72–295F with lots of fish (try the fillets of sole *à la Normande*) and *andouille* tournedos with apples and Calvados. It's not an ideal spot for a romantic weekend out of season because it's often full with groups. Free house apéritif.

VILLERS-BOCAGE   14310 (26KM SW)

⬠ I●I AUBERGE LES TROIS ROIS**

2 pl. Jeanne-d'Arc.
☎ 02.31.77.00.32 ▶ 02.31.77.93.25
Closed Sun evening, Mon, Jan, and 25 June–3 July. **TV**. **Car park**.

A white stone inn on the large village square. The restaurant is elegant, and though the decor is a tad stuffy the cooking is full of lively invention. The chef has run the kitchens for thirty years – his tripe *à la mode de Caen* is award-winning. He uses top-quality ingredients in every dish; try the John Dory with fresh sorrel, *crépinettes* of veal sweetbreads on a lettuce sauce, or the light liqueur soufflé. Menus 120–310F. The rooms are well maintained and regularly refurbished. Doubles 200F with shower and 300–380F with bath. The staff are a bit cool.

CAMEMBERT   61120

I●I LA CAMEMBERTIÈRE

How to get there; go through the village, cross the D246 and it's straight on.
☎ 02.33.39.31.87
Closed Mon. **Car park**.

You have to like Camembert cheese to dine here; it is used in virtually all the sauces, and you can taste varieties made by different cheesemakers. The chef brings a lot of innovation to his recipes. However, some dishes are Camembert-free zones; the avocado and mango salad and the shoulder of lamb with ceps are both good. Various *formules* from 78F, menus 125F and 170F, or around 190F *à*

la carte. The restaurant is in a dreamy setting, in an old granary with a view over the green valley. It's wise to book.

CARENTAN   50500

⬠ I●I HÔTEL DU COMMERCE ET DE LA GARE*

34 rue du Docteur-Caillard; it's opposite the train station.
☎ 02.33.42.02.00 ▶ 02.33.42.20.01
Closed Christmas–New Year. **TV**. **Lock-up car park**.

The hotel has a beautiful, ivy-covered façade. The restaurant is attractive too; it's an intimate place with low lighting, a soothing colour scheme, and a polished parquet floor. There's a piano bar, too. You'll get very good home cooking on the set menus at 79F, 99F and 139F. Meat and fish specialities include kebabs grilled on a wood fire, and they do a fine line in elaborate salads. Children's menu 40F. There's a sign encouraging customers to tell the chef what they thought of the food. Double rooms 185F with shower/wc or 230F with bath.

MOITIERS-EN-BAUPTOIS (LES) 50360 (20KM NW)

I●I AUBERGE DU TERROIR DE L'OUVE

Village Longuérac; it's 16km west of Sainte-Mère-Église.
☎ 02.33.21.16.26 ▶ 02.33.41.83.61
Closed 30 Sept to Easter.

This lovely inn stands on the banks of the Ouve miles from anywhere, surrounded by a cluster of old farms, a few horses frolicking about and a line of trees at the water's edge. Great welcome. The restaurant has an attractive decor and a warm atmosphere. The cuisine is wonderful and the menus, very cheap at 65–120F, feature as much *terrine* as you can eat, potato stew with cream, smoked ham cooked in cider, and duck with potatoes. À la carte, try the eel stew.

CHERBOURG   50100

⅔ ⬠ HÔTEL DE LA RENAISSANCE**

4 rue de l'Église (Centre); it's opposite the church of La Trinité.
☎ 02.33.43.23.90 ▶ 02.33.43.96.10
TV. **Car park**.

The hotel has a great location, in front of the wonderful church of La Trinité. Madame, who used to paint designs on china, has applied her artistic talents to the comfortable bedrooms. Doubles go for 140F with basin and 220F with shower/wc. The smiling owner goes to great lengths to please her guests. Very substantial breakfast, 30F. 10% discount Nov–April.

🏂 🏠 HÔTEL DE LA CROIX DE MALTE**

5 rue des Halles (Centre); it's near the harbour, the theatre and the casino.
☎ 02.33.43.19.16 ➡ 02.33.43.65.66
Closed first week of Jan. **Disabled access**. **TV**. **Car park**.

The quiet rooms have been spruced up and are extremely comfy. You'll get a very warm welcome from the owners. Doubles with shower/wc cost 180F, or 280F with bath, direct telephone and TV. If you book in advance, ask for room numbers 3, 8 or 15 – they're the biggest. Good value for money. 10% discount Sept–June.

I●I LE FAITOUT

25 rue Tour-Carrée; it's 100m from church of La Trinité.
☎ 02.33.04.25.04
Closed Sun, Mon lunchtime, and a fortnight at Christmas.

This is a good local restaurant where the quality is reliable and the prices affordable. The basement dining room is built of wood and stone, and the atmosphere is relaxed. Good traditional cooking: a dozen fresh oysters, duck braised in cider, calf's head *gribiche*, *andouillette* with Calvados, grilled salmon. *Pot-au-feu* is the house speciality, which you should accompany with a bottle of dry cider. The owner has also included some cheaper mussels dishes offering them *marinière*, *à l'escabèche* (marinated and served cold), and in a cream sauce. Menus 115F and 145F or *à la carte* about 140F. It has a faithful, regular clientèle, so it's best to book for dinner and at weekends.

OMONVILLE-LA-PETITE   50440 (20KM NW)

🏂 🏠 LA FOSSARDIÈRE**

hameau de la Fosse.
☎ 02.33.52.19.83 ➡ 02.33.52.73.49
Closed 15 Nov–15 March. **Car park**.

You'll find this lovely hotel straddling a stream in a flower-filled hamlet just 500m from the sea. You'll be treated to a warm welcome from owner Gilles Fossard. The bedrooms are comfortable, and some have a whirlpool bath. Reasonable prices; 260–370F. There is a tiny sauna. 10% discount for a two-night stay Sept–June or free breakfast after the second night of a stay.

AUDERVILLE   50440 (28KM NW)

I●I RESTAURANT L'AUBERGE DE GOURY

Port de Goury; it's on the D901.
☎ 02.33.52.77.01
Closed Mon in the Feb and Christmas holidays. **Car park**.

Service noon–3pm and 7–9pm. A restaurant that feels as if it's at the end of the earth, at the very tip of La Hague. The enormous windows give you a marvellous vista of the sea. There are appreciative comments from movie and theatre actors in the visitors' book. The owner is a big character, and it's hardly surprising that this place gets very busy in high season. The restaurant specialises in fish and meat grilled on an open wood fire, along with some more carefully prepared dishes like monkfish with leeks in flaky pastry, grilled leg of lamb, seafood platters and lobster. Menus 95–305F.

FLAMANVILLE   50340 (28KM SW)

🏂 🏠 HÔTEL BEL AIR**

Le bourg; take the D4 and it's 300m from the château.
☎ 02.33.04.48.00 ➡ 02.33.04.49.56
Closed 20 Dec–1 March. **Disabled access**. **TV**. **Car park**.

A very attractive hotel in the countryside near the magnificent Flamanville headland. The friendly welcome will make you feel at home. Rooms are comfortable and have a certain charm – 295–395F. The larger ones are in the main building, while those in the annexe are small and cosy. They either overlook the fields or the garden. 10% discount mid-Sept to end June.

SAINT-GERMAIN-DES-VAUX   50440 (29KM NW)

I●I RESTAURANT AU MOULIN À VENT

hameau Danneville; it's on the D90 Port-Racine road.
☎ 02.33.52.75.20 ➡ 02.33.52.22.57
Closed Sat and weekday evenings from Dec–March, Sun evening and Mon 11 April–30 Nov. **Car park**.

Service noon–2pm and 7.30–9pm. Booking strongly advised. A gastronomic restaurant high above the bay beside the ruins of an old mill. The large pleasant dining room overlooks a little garden that's full of exotic plants, and beyond to Saint-Martin's cove. Superb cooking, using the freshest produce. The good-value 98F menu, served in the week, includes eight oysters. Other menus up to 170F, or expect to pay 260F *à la carte* for dishes like roast, boned pigeon, grilled red mullet, salmon fillet *à l'unilatérale* (grilled on one side only) and lobster stew with fresh pasta. Children's menu 42F.

CONDÉ-SUR-NOIREAU 14110

沐 龠 |●| HÔTEL-RESTAURANT DU CERF**

18 rue du Chêne; it's 500m from the centre on the Aunay-sur-Odon road.
☎ 02.31.69.40.55 ➡ 02.31.69.78.29
e restcert@wanadoo.fr
Closed Sun evening, Mon, and the Feb school holidays.
TV. Garden. Car park.

Service noon–2pm and 7.30–9.15pm. A traditional country hotel that has moved with the times. You'll be greeted like a friend by Mme Malgrey, a very nice woman who is the vice-president of the local tourist office and knows the Suisse Normande like the back of her hand. Her husband's domain is the kitchen, where he specialises in traditional local cooking. The weekday menu, 69F (not available on public holidays), is decent enough, but there are better dishes on the others, 92–145F. Winners include *boeuf à la ficelle* with Camembert sauce, pan-fried perch with poppyseed butter, sliced *andouille* with cider butter, and honey dessert with Pommeau jelly. Ask for a room overlooking the garden. Doubles 204F with shower/wc and 240F with bath. Free coffee.

COUTANCES 50200

龠 |●| RELAIS DU VIADUC

25 av. de Verdun (South); it's beside the service station on the outskirts of Coutances on the Granville road.
☎ 02.33.45.02.68 ➡ 02.33.45.69.86
Closed Fri evening, Sat out of season. the second fortnight in July and the second fortnight in Dec.
TV. Car park.

Rooms are basic but pleasant – doubles 160F with basin or 180F with basin/wc. Half board costs 190F per person. Numbers 4, 6 and 8 have a pretty view of the upper town and the cathedral towers. The restaurant is really a good *Relais Routier*. Weekday menu at 56F, and others 100–145F. Good dishes include duck *foie gras*, lemon sole fillets in vanilla butter, sea bass steak with star anise and fillet of scabbard fish in ginger sauce. Children's menu 38F.

|●| RESTAURANT NOTRE-DAME

rue d'Harcourt (Centre); it's next to pl. Saint-Nicolas.

☎ 02.33.45.00.67
Closed Sun except in summer and beginning of Jan.

One of the few restaurants in town that's open at Sunday lunchtime in season. It's pretty and cosy. Welcoming staff and quality cooking. Menus 50–90F and children's menu 39F. Specialities include breast of duck with Pommeau and a duo of fish in Sauvignon. The *crêpes* and *gallettes* are cooked in the old-fashioned way, all the vegetables are grown organically, and the owner serves a selection of organic wines.

MONTMARTIN-SUR-MER 50590 (10KM SW)

沐 龠 |●| HÔTELLERIE DU BON VIEUX TEMPS**

7 rue Pierre-des-Touches (Centre); it's opposite the post office.
☎ 02.33.47.54.44 ➡ 02.33.46.27.12
Closed Sun evening and Mon lunchtime out of season, beginning of Jan, and a week Sept/Oct. **TV. Car park.**

Service noon–1.30pm and 7.30–9pm. This inn, barely a couple of kilometres from the sea, is appropriately named. The spacious wood-panelled dining room is hung with paintings. They serve good country cooking with lashings of cream and cider: grilled lobster to order, warm *andouille* with Pommeau sauce, and fillet of salmon stuffed with poached oysters with a Benedictine sauce. Menu at 70F (not available Sat evening, Sun or public holidays), and others 100–200F. Children's menu 45F. Double rooms 150F with basin and 230–250F with shower/wc or bath. Everything is very well run. 10% discount on the room rate Oct–March.

REGNÉVILLE-SUR-MER 50590 (10KM SW)

沐 |●| LE JULES GOMMÈS

Le bourg; take the D20 towards Granville, then 7km further turn onto the D49.
☎ 02.33.45.32.04
Closed Tues and Wed except school holidays and 15 June–15 Sept, and Nov.

The drive here along the D49 gives you splendid views of the sea. Part-restaurant, part-*crêperie* and part-Irish pub, this is one of the cosiest places in the area and it has magnificent sea views. The first-class decor includes beautiful furniture and walls covered in gorgeous watercolours of the region. It's run by a nice young couple. Terrific *crêpes* and *galettes* – try the *crêpe* flambéed with Calvados. Reasonably priced menus at 69F and 95F. The pub is convivial. Free house apéritif.

SAVIGNY   50210 (10KM E)

☎ |●| LA VOISINIÈRE

rue des Hêtres; it's signposted on the Saint-Lô-Coutances road. Take the D52 or the D380.
☎ 02.33.07.60.32 ➡ 02.33.46.25.28
Closed Sun evening, Mon and Tues lunchtime except Easter Sunday and Whitsun, ten days at the beginning of Jan, Feb and All Saints' school holidays. **TV. Car park**.

A big, charming building, right out in the country. They've planted superb Brazilian plants in the large garden. The four bedrooms, 240F for a double, are attractive and traditionally furnished, and the cooking has quite a reputation locally. Menus, 99–229F, list escalope of veal with cream, escalope of salmon with leek fondue, *fricassée* of guinea fowl with mushrooms or grapes and juniper berries, pan-fried prawns flavoured with orange, and skate with creamed capers. They grill meat over the open fire and prepare lots of good seafood. Children's menu 50F. Booking is essential for Sunday lunch.

MESNILBUS (LE)   50490 (12KM NE)

⅔ ☎ |●| AUBERGE DES BONNES GENS

Le bourg; go to Saint-Sauveur-Lendelin and then take the D53.
☎ 02.33.07.66.85
Closed Sun evening and Mon, a fortnight in Oct and a fortnight in Jan. **Car park**.

A good little village inn in beautiful countryside. They have four pleasant bedrooms with shower, 145F, and a rustic dining room where they serve generous portions of traditional Normandy dishes cooked with lashings of cream. Weekday lunch menu 50F, and others 90–160F; they list dishes such as fish soup, local ham with cider or tripe, *méli-mélo* of kidneys, veal sweetbreads with Pommeau, warm oysters *au gratin* with cider, monkfish stew, fillet of bass cooked in red wine, and a Normandy pudding. 10% discount on the room rate Oct–March and free house apéritif with a meal.

TRELLY   50660 (13KM S)

☎ |●| VERTE CAMPAGNE**

Hameau Chevalier; take the D7 or the D971, south of Coutances.
☎ 02.33.47.65.33 ➡ 02.33.47.38.03
Closed Sun evening and Mon out of season, Mon

lunchtime in season, 1–8 Dec and 10–20 Jan.
Car park.

Service 12.30–1.30pm and 7.30–9pm. This magnificent, traditional building is swamped with ivy. It's in a tiny village in wonderful surroundings deep in the country. The lovely interior features enormous beams and stone walls and there are lots of decorative objects dotted around. The staff are a little formal in their welcome but the cooking is some of the very best you'll taste. Menus 140–230F, or a good deal more *à la carte*: roast pigeon with spices, roast langoustine with creamed salt cod, red mullet and artichokes in a warm *vinaigrette*, and, for dessert, *moelleux* of chocolate. The wine list is interesting and prices are reasonable. Very pleasant double rooms 220–380F.

HAMBYE   50450 (20KM SE)

⅔ ☎ |●| AUBERGE DE L'ABBAYE D'HAM-BYE

Route de l'Abbaye
☎ 02.33.61.42.19 ➡ 02.33.61.00.85
Closed Sun evening, Mon, 14 Feb–1 March and 1–15 Oct. **Car park**.

In a beautiful, green country setting you'll find this quiet little hotel with charming and comfortable bedrooms, 300F with shower/wc or 330F with bath. The place is meticulously run and Micheline and Jean Allain welcome you in a friendly, courteous fashion. The menus, 100–200F, list appetising and delicious dishes from different regions: Burgundy or Alsace snails, fish soup, seafood platters, lamb kebabs grilled over the coals and good *crêpes*. 10% discount on the room rate.

DEAUVILLE   14800

⅔ ☎ LE PATIO**

180 av. de la République (Centre); it's near the racecourse.
☎ 02.31.88.25.07 ➡ 02.31.88.00.81
Closed Jan. **Disabled access. TV**.

The bedrooms in this large, white hotel have recovered their old charm since the refurbishment was completed. Some overlook the shaded flower-filled patio. Prices are reasonable for Deauville, with doubles at 200–280F with shower and wc on the landing, and 290–430F with bath, TV and phone. There's a gym. 10% discount on the room rate excluding weekends and school holidays.

🎋 🏠 HÔTEL LE CHANTILLY**

120 av. de la République (Centre); it's 500m from the train station.
☎ 02.31.88.79.75 ➡ 02.31.88.41.29
📧 hchantilly@aol.com
TV.

This hotel has been renovated throughout and has modern facilities. It radiates a certain charm and it's advisable to book. Doubles with shower/wc or bath, 305–345F, which is not too bad for Deauville. And they have some family rooms which will accommodate up to four children. You'll get a nice welcome from the friendly, chatty proprietress. Free breakfast if you stay for three nights.

FALAISE   14700

🎋 🏠 |●| HÔTEL-RESTAURANT DE LA POSTE**

38 rue Georges-Clémenceau.
☎ 02.31.90.13.14 ➡ 02.31.90.01.81
Closed Sun evening, Mon, the third week in Oct and 20 Dec–20 Jan. **TV**. **Lock-up car park**.

Service noon–2pm and 7–9pm. This is a very pleasant inn, the kind of place where you feel at ease. The owners provide good cooking and comfortable, nicely decorated rooms. The chef uses lots of local ingredients and cooks simple traditional dishes such as calf's head *sauce ravigote*, sautéed veal kidneys with morels, tripe kebabs, and monkfish *à la Normande*. Weekday menu 90F and others up to 235F. Bedrooms are well maintained and double glazed; 300F with shower/wc and 360F with bath. Efficient, friendly service. 10% discount on the room rate.

🎋 |●| LA FINE FOURCHETTE

52 rue Georges-Clémenceau.
☎ 02.31.90.08.59
Closed Tues evening, Wed evening out of season, and 25 Jan–12 Feb.

Bright, cheerful restaurant. Every year the chef goes off to work with great chefs in different parts of the country, so his cooking is always innovative and dynamic. His pan-fried zander with orange zest he picked up at the *Ritz*; his crab canelloni with cream comes from his days at the *Grand Véfour*. You get a good idea of the cooking even from the 88F menu and a better one on the others up to 205F. Efficient service by genuinely friendly staff. Free *digestif*.

PONT-D'OUILLY   14690 (18KM W)

🎋 🏠 |●| HÔTEL DU COMMERCE**

rue de Falaise (Centre).
☎ 02.31.69.80.16 ➡ 02.31.69.78.08
Closed Sun evening and Mon except from June–Sept, the first week in Oct and 15 Jan–15 Feb. **TV**. **Car park**.

Service noon–2pm and 7–9pm. Surrounded by pastureland and little farms, this country inn is in a characterless building, though the dining room is large and bright and the staff are genuinely friendly. Good ingredients are used to make mainly local dishes – try prawns flambéed in Calvados with sauce thermidor, steak with Camembert sauce, or the fish duo with cider butter. Menus 70–195F. Quiet comfortable rooms, doubles 200F with washing facilities, 250F with shower/wc or bath. Free apéritif.

🎋 🏠 |●| AUBERGE SAINT-CHRISTOPHE**

How to get there: take the D511 towards Pont-d'Ouilly for 17km then the D23 in the direction of Thury-Harcourt.
☎ 02.31.69.81.23. ➡ 02.31.69.26.58
Closed Sun evening, Mon, and the Feb and Nov school holidays. **TV**. **Garden**. **Car park**.

Lovely inn with a tangle of Virginia creeper all over the façade. The owners make you feel welcome. The pretty decor gives the place its undeniable charm, and when summer comes you can eat out in the lush flowery garden. The chef serves traditional dishes wtih a little something extra that makes all the difference: farm-raised chicken with cider, *bœuf à la ficelle*, poached eggs with mussels, beef with Camembert cream, *fondant* with apples, and caramel ice cream. The menus, 1055–230F, will satisfy any appetite. Staff are welcoming and attentive. The pretty little bedrooms overlook the garden; doubles 280F with shower/wc or bath. Free *digestif* and 10% discount on the room rate Sept–March.

FLERS   61100

🏠 HÔTEL OASIS**

3 [bis] rue de Paris (Centre).
☎ 02.33.64.95.80 ➡ 02.33.65.97.76
TV. **Pay garage**.

This town was destroyed by bombing in World War II and had to be rebuilt. The post-war building doesn't have the charm of a country inn but behind the ordinary exterior is a little haven. You'll get a nice welcome. The decor verges on the kitsch, but the bedrooms are comfy, well-maintained and good value. Doubles from 135F with washing facilities up to 275F with bath and satellite TV. There's a charge for use of the garage.

|●| RESTAURANT AU BOUT DE LA RUE

60 rue de la Gare (Southwest).
☎ 02.33.65.31.53 ➡ 02.33.65.46.81
lebouleux@wanadoo.fr
Closed Sun and public holidays except Christmas and Mother's Day.

Service noon–2pm and 7.30–10pm. The jazzy retro decor works well in this excellent place. The attentive staff make you feel welcome. The cooking is as imaginative as the decor, with dishes such as salad of warm *andouille*, pan-fried fresh prawns with star anise, salmon fillet with Camembert cream sauce and steak *tartare* sliced with a knife not a grinder. *Formule bistrot* 82F and menus 108–135F. Good selection of wines at reasonable prices, and interesting coffees from Costa Rica, Ethiopia and Colombia.

|●| AUBERGE DES VIEILLES PIERRES

Le Buisson Corblin; take the Argentan road and it's 3km from the centre.
☎ 02.33.65.06.96 ➡ 02.33.65.80.72
Closed Mon and Tues, the Feb school holidays and the first three weeks in Aug. **Disabled access**. **Car park**.

Bright, attractive restaurant, owned by a team of talented young people who give it an informal, natural feel. The cooking is superb and dishes are skilfully prepared. The brilliant 85F weekday menu lists salt cod with leeks and braised guinea fowl with cabbage. The other menus,125–215F, are equally good.

FERRIÈRE-AUX-ÉTANGS (LA) 61450 (10KM S)

|●| AUBERGE DE LA MINE

Le Gué-Plat; take the D18, then the D21 route de Domfront and turn left 1.5km further.
☎ 02.33.66.91.10 ➡ 02.33.96.73.90
Closed Tues and Wed, Tues lunchtime and Wed in July–Aug, 3–20 Jan and 17 Aug–1 Sept. **Car park**.

Apparently this large ivy-covered brick house was once a miners' canteen – the nearby slag heaps are relics from the old mining days. But times have moved on and this delightful little place with its stylish decor is now a chic, intimate restaurant. The chef is an artist and his dishes are as beautiful to look at as they are delicious to eat: *fricassée* of prawns served in a buckwheat *crêpe*, scallops, veal sweet-

breads with *andouille de Vire* braised in a hay box, guinea fowl breast with *foie gras* and Pommeau sauce, caramelised apple on a sponge base. Menus 105–240F. Cheerful, friendly staff.

GOUVETS 50420

⅔|●| RESTAURANT LES BRUYÈRES

It's on the RN175.
☎ 02.33.51.69.82
Closed Sunday. **Car park**.

A fairly new building sitting by the side of the road. It's not very attractive, but the welcome, the springtime decor and the value for money make it worth stopping here. The chef changes the dishes on the menu every week, to take account of the fresh produce or the fish that's landed: salmon escalope with fresh noodles, rabbit à la Provençale, lamb stew with spring vegetables. The array of pastries is wicked. Menus 72–140F. Free coffee.

GRANVILLE 50400

♠ LE MICHELET★★

5 rue Jules-Michelet; it's on the seashore, near the casino.
☎ 02.33.50.06.55 ➡ 02.33.50.12.25
TV. **Car park**.

Near the sea, a few steps from the casino and the sea-water therapy centre, this little hotel has an attractive white façade. It's run by a charming young couple who give you a marvellous welcome. The bedrooms are simple, bright and well maintained. Doubles 140F with basin, 220–230F with shower/wc and 285–300F with bath. Breakfast 30F.

⅔|●| L'ÉCHAUGUETTE

24 rue Saint-Jean; it's in the upper town over the Grand port and the bridge.
☎ 02.33.50.51.87
Closed Tues and Wed outside school holidays, three weeks in March and a fortnight in Nov.

Service noon–3pm and 7pm–midnight. A special little *crêperie* in the upper town among the maze of pretty little streets. The unobtrusive staff and cosy atmosphere provide a perfect setting. The very simplest *crêpe* with butter is delicious, as is the *crêpe gratinée* with scallops. A meal costs about 60F. Free house Kir.

⅔|●| RESTAURANT LE PHARE

rue du Port; it's on the harbour.

☎ 02.33.50.12.94
Closed Tues and Wed except from July–Aug, and 20 Dec–20 Jan. **Car park**.

Service noon–2pm and 7–9.30 or 10pm. The view of the fishing fleet and the sailing boats in the harbour is splendid. The fish market, just footsteps away, supplies the restaurant with seafood – winners include fillet of sea bream with *nantais* butter, pollack with white butter, monkfish and cod with chive sauce and a medley of fish with a butter sauce. The freshest of produce at reasonable prices. Weekday menu 69F and others up to 210F. If you're feeling hungry, and flush, there's a huge lobster just for you but, at the other end of the scale, they also do a cheap and cheerful *formule express* of *moules marinière* and a jug of wine. All the desserts are home-made. Children's menu 46F. Free house apéritif.

CHAMPEAUX   50530 (15KM S)

🕍 🏠 |●| HÔTEL LES HERMELLES-RESTAURANT AU MARQUIS DE TOMBELAINE

How to get there: take the D911 that runs along the Channel coast.
☎ 02.33.61.85.94 ➡ 02.33.61.21.52
Closed Tues evening and Wed except from July–Aug, Jan, and a few days in Feb and Nov.
Disabled access. **TV**. **Car park**.

You'll find this lively hotel atop the Champeaux cliffs, across from Cancale. Comfortable double rooms 280–320F. The intimate dining room is a successful marriage of stonework, panelling and beams. The chef is a disciple of Auge Escoffier, the classic French cook, so the food is good and dishes are creative: escalope of cod with warm *andouille*, sea bass in pastry, warm *foie gras* with apples and cream, frogs' legs and snails with mushroom broth. Menus 99–350F, and a children's menu 50F. Half board 280F per person. 10% discount on the room rate Nov–April.

HONFLEUR   14600

🕍 🏠 |●| LES CASCADES*

17 pl. Thiers (Centre); it's just off the old harbour.
☎ 02.31.89.05.83 ➡ 02.31.89.32.13
Closed Mon evening and Tues except in the Feb school holidays, Easter and July–Aug, and 11 Nov to Feb. **TV**.

A rather basic hotel in a good location that's been run by the energetic Mme Cogen for a good thirty years. Doubles with shower/wc

or bath 200–300F. The simple, classic cooking revolves around fresh fish and seafood. Menus 75–185F. Half board is compulsory at weekends and in season. Phone reservations not accepted. 10% discount on the room rate.

🕍 🏠 |●| HÔTEL LE BELVÉDÈRE**

36 rue Émile-Renouf (Centre).
☎ 02.31.89.08.13 ➡ 02.31.89.51.40.
Closed Sun evening and Mon from 1 Oct–30 March, and 4 Jan–7 Feb. **TV**.

This hotel is away from the summer hurly burly of the town centre and the marina; it's a lovely master craftsman's house with a lookout on the roof, set in a peaceful garden. There are about ten bedrooms, all of which have been completely refurbished, 280–320F with shower or bath. It's often fully booked at the weekend. They serve creative dishes such as seafood with vanilla, veal cutlets with Camembert, and John Dory with fruit. Menus 105F and 148F. Half board, compulsory in season, costs 320–380F. 10% discount on the room rate Oct–April.

🕍 🏠 HÔTEL DES LOGES

18 rue Brûlée (Centre).
☎ 02.31.89.38.26

A slate-fronted hotel, near the church, run by a kindly, friendly woman who renovated the building after she had a dream telling her to do so. She has a gift for interior decoration and there are lots of ideas you can pinch and use at home, like the huge candles standing in the hearth. The bedrooms are equally lovely – the colours are warm and there are good facilities. A little glimpse of luxury at a realistic price, 335F for a double with shower/wc or 410F with bath. 10% discount but only for one night over long weekends.

|●| THÉ ET TRADITION

20 pl. Hamelin.
☎ 02.31.89.17.42
Closed evenings Sun–Fri, Tues and Wed from May–Oct (Tues only in season), and Dec–Jan.

Tea-room in a splendid building dating from just after the French Revolution. They serve continental or English breakfast from 8.30am, and at lunchtime offer a good selection of dishes such as tomato and basil tart, rabbit turnover, *quiche*, apple tart flambéed with Calvados, and cider ice cream with Calvados caramel. Menus 97–118F, or 160F *à la carte*. There is a splendid dessert and pastry menu – they have an in-house pastry chef; Bourbon mousse with egg custard is the stand-out sweet. All dishes are made to order.

⅍ |●| LA TORTUE

36 rue de l'Homme-de-Bois (Centre); it's near the church of Sainte-Catherine.
☎ 02.31.89.04.93
Closed Tues out of season and Jan. **TV**.

Service from noon and 7pm. This is a friendly, welcoming place. Mouthwatering menus 100–230F, including a vegetarian menu. All of them include a *trou Normand*, a shot of Calvados served halfway through the meal to aid digestion. Excellent dishes include pork fillet with mustard, red mullet *salade paysanne*, fresh cod fillet in cider, fillet of sole *au gratin* and an excellent pan-fried escalope of *foie gras* served on spinach. They also offer a vegetarian menu. Free coffee.

HOULGATE   14510

⅍ ♠ |●| LE NORMAND

40 rue du Général-Leclerc (Centre); it's 100m from the beach.
☎ 02.31.24.81.81 ➡ 02.31.28.03.74
Closed Wed and Thurs out of season, Dec and Jan.

Service from noon and 7pm. A little restaurant that's good and simple. The copper pots and pans on the walls are polished brightly and give the place a rustic charm. The chef prepares authentic dishes using ingredients and produce that he selects from the market across the road – try the stuffed mussels, sea snails, chicken *Vallée d'Auge* with cream, fillet of duck in Pommeau sauce, or chicken supreme with apples. Menus at 79F, served in the evening until 9pm, and others up to 160F. Double rooms 210F with basin, 250–270F with shower/wc. 10% discount for a two-night stay except during the school holidays and on holiday weekends.

⅍ ♠ |●| HOSTELLERIE NORMANDE**

11 rue E.-Deschanel (Centre); it's off la rue des Bains.
☎ 02.31.28.77.77 ➡ 02.31.28.08.07
TV.

This beautiful 19th-century building, covered in Virginia creeper, is the oldest hotel in Houlgate and has been thoughtfully renovated. They've decorated it in a pseudo Baroque style and have considerably improved the rooms without pushing the prices up too

much. Doubles 250–390F with shower/wc or 350–500F with bath. You'll get a nice welcome, and there's a lovely garden where you can have a very leisurely breakfast. In the restaurant they serve simple, satisfying dishes like calf's head and *andouille* wih mustard. Weekday menu 68F and others up to 139F. Free apéritif, a shot of house Calvados, and 10% discount on the room rate excluding weekends and public holidays.

♠ SANTA CECILIA**

25 allées des Alliés; it's 100m from the beach
☎ 02.31.28.71.71 ➡ 02.31.28.51.73
TV.

A pretty villa with a time-warp atmosphere, dating from the 1880s. The 1900s dining room is decorated with finely painted murals. You'll get a wonderful welcome from the owner. The bedrooms are faultless and individually decorated – some have been furnished in period style. Doubles 330F with shower/wc or 390F with bath.

LISIEUX   14100

⅍ ♠ HÔTEL DE LOURDES**

4 rue au Char (Centre).
☎ 02.31.31.19.48 ➡ 02.31.31.08.67
Closed Sun in winter. **TV**. **Lock-up car park**.

A rather ordinary hotel, popular with pilgrims who come to the shrine. The simple bedrooms are bright and well maintained and most of them have TV. Doubles 210–230F with shower/wc and 250–269F with bath. 10% discount for a two-night stay Nov–March.

⅍ ♠ |●| LA COUPE D'OR**

49 rue Pont-Mortain (Centre).
☎ 02.31.31.16.84 ➡ 02.31.31.35.60
Closed Fri and Sun evening out of season, the first fortnight in Jan and the last fortnight in Nov. **TV**.

A classic, well-run hotel. The bedrooms are clean, and the outdated 1970s decor has a certain kitsch appeal. The bathrooms are lovely. Doubles 280F with shower/wc or bath. Half board, from 270F, is compulsory at the weekend or for stays of more than two nights. The cooking is fairly classical and reliable, with dishes such as Normandy fish soup, duck breast with apples and Pommeau, pan-fried bass fillet with sea urchin cream, tripe *à la mode de Caen* and iced nougat truffles with caramel sauce. Weekday lunch menu 68F and others up to 190F. Free house apéritif.

🏃 🛏 AZUR HÔTEL***

15 rue au Char (Centre).
☎ 02.31.62.09.14 ➡ 02.31.62.16.06
📧 resa@azur-hotel.com
TV.

A three-star hotel that's been recently refurbished. Pleasant well-equipped bedrooms; doubles 300–380F with shower/wc or 360–480F with bath. They provide welcoming little extras like a bathrobe, a hair drier and a chocolate on your pillow to make your stay more relaxing. The breakfast room is very pretty. Free breakfast, usually 55F, out of season.

🍽 RESTAURANT AUX ACACIAS

13 rue de la Résistance (Centre).
☎ 02.31.62.10.95
Closed Sun evening and Mon except for public holidays, and the last week in Nov. **Car park**.

Service noon–2pm and 7–9.30pm. An appealing, centrally located restaurant with a cosy, Laura Ashley-style decor with spring colours and red and white stripes, vases of dried flowers and little ornaments. It's fresh and pleasant, just like the cooking: pan-fried *escalope* of *foie gras* with apples and Pommeau sauce, fillets of sole *à la Normandie*, veal sweetbreads served with asparagus in bacon parcels, pigeon *à l'étouffée* with peppers and orange, and pan-fried scallops. Many dishes combine unusual flavours. Sadly the desserts are a bit heavy. Menus from 98F (not served at weekends) to 290F. Efficient service with a smile.

MONT-SAINT-MICHEL (LE)   50170

🏃 🛏 🍽 HÔTEL DU GUESCLIN**

Grande-Rue.
☎ 02.33.60.14.10 ➡ 02.33.60.45.81
Closed Tues evening, Wed and 5 Nov–31 March.
TV. Car park.

A well-maintained hotel offering reasonable value for money when you compare it to the local competition. Comfortable, very clean doubles, 320–380F. There are two dining rooms; if you want quick service and *formules express*, head for the brasserie downstairs. Upstairs, where you get a superb view of the bay, they serve classic dishes. Set menus 68–195F with a children's menu at 52F. Efficient service and pleasant staff. Free apéritif.

BEAUVOIR   50170 (4KM S)

🏃 🛏 HÔTEL LE GUÉ DE BEAUVOIR*

Route de Pontorson: it's next to the Gué de Beauvoir campsite.
☎ 02.33.60.09.23
Closed 30 Sept to Palm Sunday. **Car park**.

This place is in complete contrast to the dull hotels around here. It's a handsome house standing in flower-filled grounds. The bedrooms are simple but have great charm, 170–270F. Breakfast, 30F, is served in the pleasant conservatory. 10% discount April–May.

PONTORSON   50170 (9KM S)

🏃 🛏 🍽 HÔTEL-RESTAURANT LE BRETAGNE**

59 rue Couesnon (Centre); it's on the main street.
☎ 02.33.60.10.55 ➡ 02.33.58.20.54
📧 bretagne@destination.bretagne.com
Closed Mon out of season and 5 Jan–10 Feb.
TV. Car park.

A lovely 18th-century coaching inn where you will be warmly welcomed. The bedrooms are all very pleasant and cost 280–300F with shower/wc or bath. Half board costs 295F per person. A crowd of regulars inhabits the restaurant, where the dishes are prepared with care and the chef uses only fresh ingredients. Classical, local and simple dishes, in no particular order – oysters *gratinées* with Camembert, *rillettes* of mackerel with cucumber *coulis*, salmon *tartare* with grapefruit, ox cheek with a *foie gras* sauce and fresh noodles, rack of lamb with rosemary, duck breast with spiced pear, and nougat with two chocolates and a coffee cream. Weekday menu 90F, then others up to 260F and a children's menu at 49F. Very good value. 10% discount on the room rate 1 Oct–30 March.

SERVON   50170 (10KM SE)

🏃 🛏 🍽 AUBERGE DU TERROIR**

Centre; on the road from Pontaubault to Pontorson turn right onto the D107.
☎ 02.33.60.17.92 ➡ 02.33.60.35.26
Closed Wed except July–Sept, Sat lunchtime, 15 Nov–6 Dec and the Feb school holidays. **Disabled access. TV. Car park**.

A charming hotel with pretty grounds in a tranquil village. The friendly young owners have created a peaceful, tasteful atmosphere. All the rooms have been attractively refurbished and they're named after famous musicians and composers. In the old presbytery there are three lovely double rooms and one that sleeps four, or you can stay in the annexe; 300F with shower/wc and 320–400F with bath. They serve wonderful Périgord specialities in tthe pleasant dining room – semi-cooked *foie gras* and breast of duck with honey – along with lots of fish – seafood stew, salmon with green cabbage and monkfish with vanilla. Menus 90–250F. 10% discount on the room rate Oct–March.

CÉAUX   50220 (15KM E)

🏃 🛏 |●| HÔTEL-RESTAURANT AU P'TIT QUINQUIN**

Les Forges; take the D275 in the direction of Avranches, then the D43, it's only 2km after the village of Courtils.
☎ 02.33.70.97.20 ➔ 02.33.70.97.42
Closed Sun evening, Mon out of season and 5 Jan–15 Feb. **TV. Car park**.

This place is miles from the hurly burly, but the road can be noisy, so you'd do best to choose a room at the back of the hotel. Doubles 150F with washing facilities, 240F with shower/wc or with bath. Menus 72–180F. Specialities include fish fillet steamed with thyme, *millefeuille* of scallops with Coteau du Layon sauce, and house duck *foie gras*. 10% discount on the room rate Nov–March.

MORTAGNE-AU-PERCHE   61400

🏃 🛏 |●| HÔTEL DU TRIBUNAL**

4 pl. du Palais (Centre).
☎ 02.33.25.04.77 ➔ 02.33.83.60.83
Closed a fortnight Dec/Jan. **TV**.

The oldest parts of this handsome, traditional Percheron house date from the 13th century, though most of it is 16th century. The square and the façade have hardly changed since the end of the 19th century, when the inn was called "John who laughs, John who weeps" – the law court used to be just next door. Renovations have not diminished the character of the interior. Doubles 260–280F with shower or bath. There's a lovely annexe at the back where the rooms are even quieter and overlook a tiny flower-filled courtyard. The food is very good. Interesting cuisine and some classical dishes: *croustillant* of black pudding, *millefeuille* of sole and wild mushrooms, smoked salmon and raw marinated salmon, chicken *fricassée* with Camembert, *aumônière Normande*. Menus 90–190F. A delightful, quite stylish place where the welcome is as warm as the one you'd get in a friendly little village inn. 10% discount on the room rate for a two-night stay Oct–March.

LONGNY-AU-PERCHE   61290 (18KM E)

|●| LE MOULIN DE LA FENDERIE

Route de Bizou; from Mortagne, take the D8 through the forest of Rénovaldieu.
☎ 02.33.83.66.98
Closed Mon evening and Tues. **TV**.

A restaurant housed in a superb watermill which has been patiently restored by the two owners. You are most pleasantly welcomed and there is a terrace by the water's edge. The cuisine is delicate, perfumed and original, and the chef gives local dishes a touch of exotic spices. Weekday menu 95F, and another at 135F.

OUISTREHAM-RIVA-BELLA   14150

🏃 🛏 |●| HÔTEL-RESTAURANT LE NORMANDIE-LE CHALUT**

71 av. Michel-Cabieu; it's near the harbour
☎ 02.31.97.19.57 ➔ 02.31.97.20.07
e hotel@lenormandie.com
Closed Sun evening and Mon from Nov–March, and 20 Dec–20 Jan. **TV. Car park**.

Two classic hotels opposite each other, run by an energetic young couple. Both places have been tastefully refurbished. Doubles 250–350F with shower/wc or bath and telephone. Wonderful food in the stylish dining room. Choose from delicate, refined versions of traditional dishes such as pan-fried oysters with Perry, lobster with lentils, and duck in cider sauce with fresh noodles. The service is a tad uptight – perhaps they are are trying just a little too hard. Weekday menu 95F, and others up to 354F. 10% discount on the room rate except in high season and public holidays.

|●| LE BRITANNIA

rue des Dunes; it's opposite the ferry.
☎ 02.31.96.88.26 ➔ 02.31.96.93.10
Closed Mon and Sun except Easter to mid Oct, and Jan. **Car park**.

An unpretentious brasserie with a fading 1970s decor where you can have a tasty snack before catching the ferry home. They do only one menu, 68F, or you can choose *à la carte*. The delicious *zakouski*, the selection of fish and vegetables that they bring with your apéritif or glass of champagne, is almost as big as a starter. A very good little place.

|●| RESTAURANT LE MÉTROPOLITAIN**

1 route de Lion; it's near the post office.

☎ 02.31.97.18.61
Closed Mon evening and Tuesfrom Oct–April, and a week at the end of Nov. **Car park**.

Decorated to look like a 1930s Parisian metro, this place offers local produce and seafood cooked to perfection and attractively presented – try the smoked cod with cider, grilled turbot with hollandaise sauce, sole with chives, cod steak in cider and apple terrine. Menus 70–192F.

PONT-L'ÉVÊQUE   14130

I●I HÔTEL DE FRANCE

1 rue de Geôle (Centre).
☎ 02.31.64.30.44 ➡ 02.31.64.98.90
Closed Christmas and New Year's Day and a fortnight in the Feb school holidays. **TV**. **Car park**.

A small hotel in a quiet street, close to the town centre. The new young owners have redecorated the rooms in country style, with personality and charm. Some have a view over the fields full of grazing cows. Doubles with basin 165F or up to 260F with shower/wc or bath. The breakfast jams and preserves are home-made.

I●I RESTAURANT LA POMME D'OR

52 rue Saint-Michel (West); it's near the town hall.
☎ 02.31.64.01.98
Closed Tues except in summer, and a week in Oct. **Car park**.

Service noon–9pm. This little bar-restaurant presents a startling array of fresh, plain cooking in its old-fashioned dining room. The affable chef prepares ten different dishes – the star turns are salt pork with lentils, duck with cider, and tripe cooked in the local way – and the desserts. Set menus 60–90F.

⚂I●I AUBERGE DE LA TOUQUES

pl. de l'Église (Centre); it's 1km from the autoroute exit.
☎ 02.31.64.01.69
Closed Mon evening and Tues except in Aug, 2–26 Jan and 3–26 Dec. **Car park**.

Service noon–2.30pm and 7–9.30pm. This is a handsome Normandy building on the bank of the Touques river near the village church. The chef prepares all the classics of Normandy cooking: chicken Vallée d'Auge with apples and cream, house tripe, veal chop *Normande*, brill with apples and lobster flan and caramelised apple mousse. 90F weekday menu and others up to 190F. Attentive service. Free glass of Calvados.

DRUBEC   14130 (8KM SW)

I●I LA HAIE TONDUE

How to get there; take the D58 and it's 2km south of Beaumont-en-Auge at the N175 junction.
☎ 02.31.64.85.00
Closed Mon evening except public holidays and Aug, Tues except public holidays and a fortnight Jan–Feb. **Car park**.

This restaurant, in a beautiful old house covered in ivy, offers very good food at reasonable prices. In fact, it's the best value for money in the area. The setting is most agreeable, the service is faultless and there's a good wine list. As for the dishes, they are perfectly prepared, even on the cheapest of the menus, which range from 119F to 225F. Dishes include *compote* of rabbit with onion marmalade, chicken with balsamic vinegar, *paupiettes* of sole with lettuce *coulis*, and fillets of duck with apricots. It's popular with coach parties, and can get crowded.

SAINT-LÔ   50000

☖ ARMORIC HÔTEL*

15–17 rue de la Marne (North).
☎ 02.33.05.61.32 ➡ 02.33.05.12.68
TV.

You'll get a very warm welcome in this quiet, out of the way, good-value hotel. The comfy bedrooms are tastefully decorated and all have phone and TV; doubles 170F with basin, 230F with bath. If you've had a tiring journey, you'll love numbers 16 and 21, both of which have a whirlpool bath and cost a bit more. Even considering the rather frugal breakfast this is one of the best places in the Manche.

☖ I●I L'AUBERGE NORMANDE

20 rue de Villedieu (Centre).
☎ 02.33.05.10.89 ➡ 02.33.05.37.26
Closed Mon and 25 Dec–7 Jan.

Élisa and Sylvain Maquaire completely refurbished the inn when they took it over. They will make you feel very welcome. Sylvain is a thoughtful, creative cook with a stylish repertoire. Try his salad of duck *foie gras* in Armagnac, ravioli stuffed with sea bass, marinated salmon *à la suédoise*, crab *bisque*, mussel soup with saffron, or duck breast with honey and Pommeau. Weekday lunch menu 88F or up to 175F. Doubles 175F with basin 199F with shower and 240F with shower/wc.

🕸 |●| LE BISTROT

42 rue du Neubourg; it's halfway between the town hall and the church of Sainte-Croix.
☎ 02.33.57.19.00
Closed Sun, Mon evening and a fortnight July/Aug.

This little restaurant, the gathering place for Caen football fans, has a genuine bistro atmosphere. Food is quick and good. There's lots of home cooking, with shepherd's pie, calf's head *gribiche* and *teurgoule* (a type of rice pudding). *Menu du jour* 75F and a *formule* at 69F for a main course and a dessert. Good value. Free house Kir.

🕸 |●| LE PÉCHÉ MIGNON

84 rue du Maréchal-Juin (East); go towards Bayeux. It's well away from the town centre.
☎ 02.33.72.23.77 ➡ 02.33.72.27.58
Closed Mon, Sat lunchtime, Sun evening, the Easter school holidays and the first fortnight in Aug.

The service in this very comfortable restaurant is impeccable and the food is marvellous – top-class gourmet cuisine prepared by a talented young chef. Stellar dishes include zander with saffron and cocoa beans, veal sweetbreads with morels, and *sabayon* of apples and cinnamon. Menu at 89F or up to 260F *à la carte*, and children's menu 45F. Free house apéritif.

SAINT-PIERRE-DE-SEMILLY   50810 (9KM E)

|●| RESTAURANT LES GLYCINES

Le Calvaire; it's by the side of the D972.
☎ 02.33.05.02.40
Closed Sun evening, Mon and Feb school holidays.

Service noon–2.30pm and 7–9pm. A converted farmhouse restaurant where in summer you eat in the wonderful walled garden. Chef Philippe Fouchard has a deft hand and creates refined, often imaginative dishes using fine fish and local produce only. The 98F menu is served daily except Sunday, and there are others up to 298F

SAINT-VAAST-LA-HOUGUE   50550

🔺 |●| HÔTEL DE FRANCE-RESTAURANT LES FUCHSIAS**

20 rue du Maréchal-Foch; it's less than two minutes from the harbour.
☎ 02.33.54.42.26 ➡ 02.33.43.46.79
ℯ france_FUSCHIAS@wanadoo.fr
Closed Mon except in July–Aug, Tues lunchtime from Nov–March, and Jan–Feb.

Service noon–2pm and 7–9.15pm (7.30–9.45pm in summer). Most of the very pretty bedrooms overlook a little garden of Eden – the fuchsia that gave its name to the hotel is a hundred years old and flourished in the valley of Saire which has a particularly mild micro-climate. Double rooms 168F with basin, and 292–465F with shower/wc or bath; there's also a little suite at 500F. They prefer you to stay half board, 264–410F per person, July–Aug. This is also one of the best restaurants in the area. Ask for a table on the veranda, which is decorated with *trompe l'oeil* murals. Menus, 87–310F, list delicious dishes: very fresh *noisettes* of Saint-Vaast oysters, *croustillant* of sea trout with seaweed butter, fish *choucroute*, and apples in puff pastry with a Calvados sauce. Every year in the last ten days of August they give chamber music concerts in the garden.

SÉES   61500

🕸 🔺 THE GARDEN HÔTEL**

12 [bis] rue des Ardrillers; it's 400m from the cathedral.
☎ 02.33.27.98.27 ➡ 02.33.28.90.07
TV. Garden. Car park.

Before becoming a hotel, this ivy-covered building used to be an orphanage. The Australian who ran the hotel has since gone home, but the English name stayed. Things are remarkably quiet around here; there's a convent next door. As a mark of respect, none of the bedrooms looks into the convent. Instead, they all overlook a flower garden. The basic bedrooms with a nice retro touch are excellent value for money; doubles 160F with basin, 250F with bath. The staff are perfectly lovely. In keeping with the spiritual atmosphere, there's an amusing collection of religious knick-knacks about the place. There's no restaurant. 10% discount.

🔺 |●| HÔTEL-RESTAURANT LE DAUPHIN**

31 pl. des Halles; it's in the heart of the old town, opposite the market.
☎ 02.33.27.80.07 ➡ 02.33.28.80.33
ℯ dauphinsees@voila.fr
Closed Sun evening, Mon out of season and the second fortnight in Jan. **TV. Car park**.

A typical half-timbered Normandy house. The Dauphin of France slept in the room with the four-poster bed in the gabled turret. It can be yours for 550F. The other rooms are rustic and rather plush; doubles from 340F with shower/wc. Although there's a stylish feel to this place, it still generates a simple and genuinely homely atmosphere. It's got the best restaurant in town, without doubt. The kitchen produces great local dishes using only the freshest ingredients: *cassolette* of scallops and langoustine, fillet of local trout, escalope of brill with noodles, and fillet of duck with cider. Wondrous desserts and an interesting selection of teas and coffees. In summer you can sit out on the pretty terrace next to the imposing corn exchange. Weekday menu 100F, wine included, and others 140–270F.

⌘ 🏠 |●| L'ÎLE DE SÉES**

How to get there; via the D258. It's 5km from the town centre.
☎ 02.33.27.98.65 ➡ 02.33.28.41.22
e ile-sees@ile-sees.fr
Closed Mon lunchtime, 1 Nov–28 Feb. **TV. Garden. Car park.**

A charming country hotel in a hefty house hidden under layers of ivy. The rooms are in a modern part of the building and don't have the appeal of the original. They look onto the garden so are quiet; doubles 330F. The couple who run the place divide the cooking between them – he does the savoury courses while she does the desserts. They serve good regional dishes, not all from Normandy – Madame is Breton and Monsieur comes from Marseille. House speciality is tripe. Menus 85–195F. Free coffee.

THURY-HARCOURT   14220

🏠 |●| HÔTEL DU VAL D'ORNE

9 route d'Aunay-sur-Odon.
☎ 02.31.79.70.81 ➡ 02.31.79.16.12
Closed Sat lunchtime in season, Fri evening, Sat out of season and a week in the Feb school holidays.
Car park.

Everyone's image of a country hotel, down to the ivy clambering up the white walls. Courteous welcome. Simple, fresh-looking rooms go for 130F with basin or 200F with shower/wc or bath. In tune with the style, the rustic dining room has paintings of rural scenes on the wall. Simple, straightforward local dishes. Weekday lunch menu 56F, and others up to 96F.

TROUVILLE-SUR-MER   14360

🏠 LA MAISON NORMANDE**

4 pl. de Lattre de Tassigny (Centre).
☎ 02.31.88.12.25 ➡ 02.31.88.78.79
TV.

Two old shops that have been made into a charming hotel, in a half-timbered house fronted by carved stone columns. Cosy sitting room and fresh rooms; any modernisations are in keeping with the style of the building. Doubles 240–280F with shower up to 330–380F with en-suite bath.

⌘ 🏠 LES SABLETTES**

15 rue Paul-Besson (Centre); it's near the casino.
☎ 02.31.88.10.66 ➡ 02.31.88.59.06
e hotelsablettes@post.club-internet.fr
Closed Jan. **TV**.

The frontage of this place is perfect and the hotel itself is as pretty as can be. It has a very cosy atmosphere, almost like a guesthouse, with a comfortable lounge and a lovely old wooden staircase. The whole place is sparklingly clean and it's run by a charming woman. Quiet, stylish doubles 240F with basin/wc and TV, 340F with shower/wc, and 380F with bath. That's good value in Trouville. 10% discount except during school holidays or on public holiday weekends.

⌘ |●| RESTAURANT LES MOUETTES

11 rue des Bains (Centre).
☎ 02.31.98.06.97 ➡ 02.31.88.42.22

A fish restaurant in a busy little street. The decor is reminiscent of a Parisian bistro. Pleasant welcome and enjoyable cooking. Particularly good choices inlcude *gratin* of salmon and Chavignol (a hard goat's cheese), pan-fried whelks with Camembert, duck fillet with apples and fish *pot-au-feu*. Menus 78–145F. Free *digestif*.

|●| RESTAURANT LE CHALUTIER

3 rue de Verdun (Centre); it's opposite the fish market in a steep little street.
☎ 02.31.88.36.39
Closed Tues evening and Wed out of season, and Jan.

Cosy little restaurant with a maritime theme running through all three tiny dining rooms. They serve fish, seafood and a few good regional specialities. Set menus 90–180F. Best to book in season.

⌘ |●| LES VAPEURS

160 bd. Fernand-Moureaux (Centre); it's next to the town hall, opposite the fish market.
☎ 02.31.88.15.24 ➡ 02.31.88.20.58.

The best known brasserie in Trouville opened in 1927 but has more of a 1950s atmosphere, thanks to the original neon signs that were added back then. All the American actors who come to the Deauville film festival eat here – Jack Nicholson's a regular. The chef, Gérard Bazire, is vigilant in keeping the standards high. Try the house specialities – steamed local mussels and freshly cooked prawns. Everything is fresh as can be; the fishing boats land their catch only minutes away. The tripe's particularly good too, especially with a nice glass of Saumur. You'll get a genuine welcome, even if you're not a celebrity. There are set menus at 70F and 119F or a meal will cost about 150F *à la carte*. You'll have to book at the weekend – unless you decide to get the day off to a good start by arriving at 10am to swallow down a few oysters with a slurp of Muscadet. Free *digestif*.

🎎 |●| RESTAURANT LA PETITE AUBERGE

7 rue Carnot (Centre); it's in a little street off pl. du Maréchal-Foch, in front of the casino.
☎ 02.31.88.11.07
Closed Tues and Wed except in July–Aug.

Service noon–2.15pm and 7–10pm. There's no *à la carte* menu and the set menus, 139–199F, change with the season. Given the quality of the food, these represent good value for money, listing such dishes as fish soup, plaice fillet soufflé braised in cider, and *crêpes* with apples.They also have tasty specialities such as flash-fried salmon with sorrel, *aiguillettes* of duck with roast apples, and *andouillette* with grain mustard. Nice welcome and efficient service. Free coffee.

|●| BISTROT LES QUATRE CHATS

8 rue d'Orléans (Centre).
☎ 02.31.88.94.94
Closed Wed and Thurs out of season, and from Nov (after the arrival of the Beaujolais Nouveau) to mid-Dec.

This place is favoured by Parisians and celebrities. The dining room has little bistro tables and rose-coloured walls – it's packed with books, postcards, photos and newspapers and has a wonderful percolator sitting on the counter. The chef has spiced up a range of classical dishes by adding a few unexpected flavours – good ones include crab and avocado *pâté*, breast of duck with ginger, *carbonnade flamande* (beef braised in beer), and lamb curry. Their speciality, however, is the *gigot de 7-heures* – a leg of lamb

that's cooked for seven hours. They also bake their own bread. Expect to pay 200F *à la carte*.

VIRE   14500

🎎 🏠 |●| HÔTEL DE FRANCE**

4 rue d'Aignaux (Centre).
☎ 02.31.68.00.35 ➡ 02.31.68.22.65
Closed 20 Dec–15 Jan. **TV**.

A large hotel built of local grey granite that looks fairly plush. Comfy bedrooms are decorated in rococo style; doubles cost 250–300F with shower/wc or bath. Rooms at the back are quieter and have marvellous views of the wooded valleys. In the restaurant try the local *andouille*, made in Vire. Set menus, 58–220F, offer classic dishes such as *cassolette* of scampi with pink peppercorns, warm *andouille* in a pastry turnover, *savarin* of fish with a warm chive sauce, and veal sweetbreads. Free coffee.

BÉNY-BOCAGE (LE)   14350 (14.5KM N)

🎎 🏠 |●| LE CASTEL NORMAND**

How to get there: take the D577 Caen road for about 9km, then turn left onto the D56 for 2km.
☎ 02.31.68.76.03 ➡ 02.31.68.63.58
e Le.Castel.normand@wanadoo.fr
Closed Sun evening, Mon, and Feb. **TV**. **Car park**.

Service 12.15–1.45pm and 7.30–9.30pm. A lovely building with lots of character near the handsome covered market on the square.The owners have decorated it entirely in blue. Refined, chic decor, and cosy atmosphere. The cooking is full of flavour and the chef combines unusual ingredients to produce dishes that would flatter a grander establishment: *andouille* with Pommeau, *profiteroles* of prawns, veal sweetbreads in a pastry case, duck breasts with dried fruit, monkfish threaded with smoked bacon, *foie gras* with apples, and veal with watercress sauce. Weekday menu 125F and others up to 325F. First-class service. Doubles 350F with shower/wc or bath. 10% discount on the room rate.

HAUTE-NORMANDIE

27 Eure

76 Seine-Maritime

ANDELYS (LES) 27700

♚ |●| HÔTEL DE NORMANDIE**

1 rue Grande, Le Petit Andely.
☎ 02.32.54.10.52 ➡ 02.32.54.25.84
Closed Wed evening, Thurs and Dec.
Garden. TV. Car park.

Service noon–2.30pm and 8–9.30pm. Run by the same family for several decades, this large hotel, in a traditional Normandy building on the banks of the Seine, is the ideal place for a pleasant weekend. You'll get a warm welcome and enjoy good cooking. Menus, 105–270F, list dishes such as monkfish with Pommeau, duck with apples, veal sweetbreads with apples, soft-boiled eggs with Roquefort cheese, and a Calvados sorbet presented as a variation on the *trou Normand* (a shot of Calvados served between courses). Doubles 200F with basin and 320F with shower or bath.

🏃 ♚ |●| HÔTEL DE PARIS**-RESTAURANT LE CASTELET

10 av. de la République; from the main square follow the signs to Le Petit Andely
☎ 02.32.54.06.33 ➡ 02.32.54.65.92
ℯ thierry.augustin@libertysurf.fr
Restaurant closed Sun evening. **TV. Garden. Car park**.

A young, dynamic owner has taken over this small castle hotel with pointed roofs. Some evenings he plays his accordion or holds a poetry evening. The rooms have been redecorated and are very comfortable. Those over the garden are quieter, though even the ones at the front don't get much traffic noise at night. Doubles 210F with

basin, 260–330F with shower/wc or bath. The restaurant has a huge terrace in summer. They specialise in good regional cuisine and use fresh ingredients: duck *foie gras* cooked in a cloth, *croustillant* of duck breasts with honey, and monkfish *blanquette*. Menus 88–195F – some supplements are expensive. Free apéritif and 10% discount on the room rate Oct–April.

♚ |●| HÔTEL DE LA CHAÎNE D'OR***

27 rue Grande, Le Petit Andely.
☎ 02.32.54.00.31 ➡ 02.32.54.05.68
Closed Sun evening, Mon, Tues and Jan. **TV. Garage**.

Service noon–2pm and 7.30–9.30pm. This solidly constructed hotel has a quiet riverside location. Built in 1751, it gets its name from the chain that once stretched from the riverbank to the nearby island. Anyone wishing to pass the chain had to pay a toll; it became known as the "Chaîne d'Or" because it made a fortune. The hotel is luxurious but the easy-going staff make you feel welcome. Doubles 470–760F with all facilities. Some overlooking the Seine are tastefully decorated and classically furnished, others are more modern. You get a view of the barges on the river from the wonderful dining room and a fire is lit when it gets cold. One of the best restaurants in this part of the world. Menus 150F, 245F and 330F.

AUMALE 76390

🏃 ♚ |●| LA VILLA DES HOUX**

av. du Général-de-Gaulle; the street is opposite the station.
☎ 02.35.93.93.30 ➡ 02.35.93.03.94
Closed Sun evening 15 Oct–15 March, and a fortnight

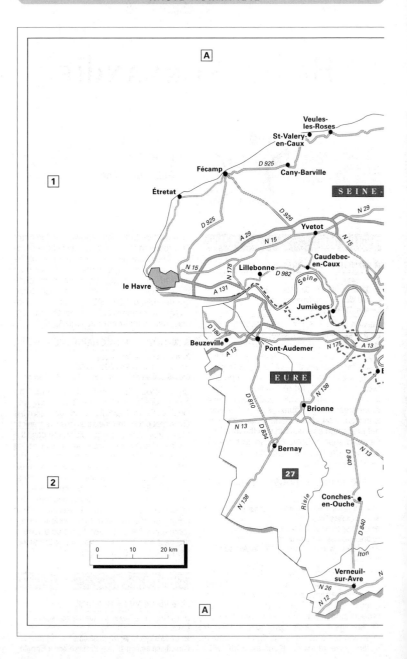

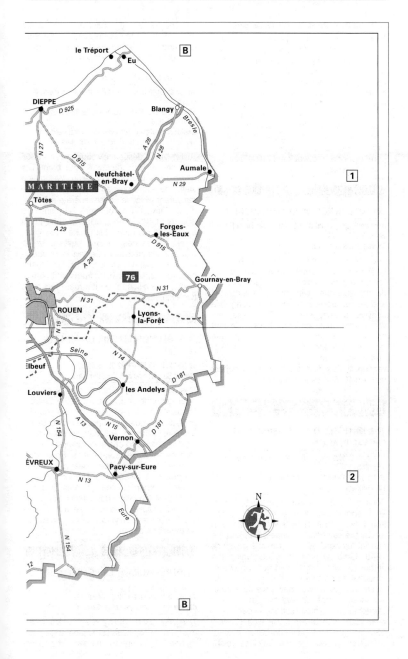

in Jan. **Disabled access**. **Garden**. **TV**. **Car park**.

This two-star hotel is run so well that it really deserves three. It's in an Anglo-Norman house with thirteen rooms. Doubles 320F with basin or shower, 340F with shower/wc or bath/wc – one has a four-poster bed and costs a little more. The stylish restaurant has a good view of the garden. The weekday 100F menu lists attractive dishes, there's a regional menu at 120F, and others at 160F and 220F which offer excellent value for money. Half board, 360F per person, is compulsory at the weekend. 10% discount in low season.

VILLERS-HAUDRICOURT   76390 (5KM SW)

🍴●❙ L'AUBERGE DE LA MARE-AUX-FÉES

route de Forges; it's on the D8 in the direction of Forges.
☎ 02.35.93.41.79
Closed Sat, Sun and Aug.

You'll need to keep an eye open for this pretty, half-timbered house on the side of the road; there are no signs. It's an authentic little inn, decorated with style and simplicity, and serves traditional, family cooking in a convivial atmosphere. The 70F menu gets you starter, main course, cheese, dessert and wine, and you'll sit round a large farm table with the regular customers. In the second dining room, where you eat more conventionally at separate tables, the cheapest menu is 100F. Free apéritif.

BERNAY   27300

🍴🛏●❙ HÔTEL D'ANGLETERRE ET DU CHEVAL BLANC*

10 rue du Général-de-Gaulle (West); it's opposite the post office.
☎ 02.32.43.12.59 ➡ 02.32.43.63.26
TV. **Lock-up car park**.

Service 11.45am–2.30pm and 7–10.30pm. They added the "Angleterre" after a visit from Edward VII in 1908. The hotel has been run by the same family since 1926, and the current owner has been in charge since 1948. Little by little he is upgrading the numerous rooms in this old building which, though it is beginning to show its age, is still lovely. The rooms with baths are the nicest, especially number 23 which is on a corner overlooking the music school garden. Doubles 130F with basin, 180F with shower, 230F with bath. Madame does the cooking, using fresh produce to prepare classic dish-

es – the sole and the roast lamb are quality. The 75F menu is served daily except Sunday, and there are others increasing in price to 180F. Free Kir or Calvados sorbet.

🍴🛏●❙ LE LION D'OR**

48 rue du Général-de-Gaulle (Centre); it's in the main street.
☎ 02.32.43.12.06; ☎ restaurant 02.32.44.23.85
➡ 02.32.46.60.58
Restaurant closed Sun evening in winter and Mon lunchtime. **TV**. **Disabled access**. **Car park**.

Tasteful, if not desperately original rooms 230F with shower/wc and 250F with bath. The whole hotel is extremely clean. Welcoming staff. They work in close conjunction with the restaurant which is under separate management. They offer a 76F weekday menu and another at 105F. The chef's love of his job is evident in how he cooks: *terrines*, *foie gras*, stocks for sauces and the pastries are all made on the premises. Specialities include fillet of trout with Camembert, pan-fried oyster mushrooms, and fresh fish from Cherbourg or Caen. 10% discount on the room rate for a two-night stay.

SAINT-AUBIN-LE-VERTUEUX   27300 (4KM S)

🍴🛏●❙ L'HOSTELLERIE DU MOULIN FOURET

☎ 02.32.43.19.95 ➡ 02.32.45.55.50
Closed Sun evening and Mon. **Car park**.

This 16th-century windmill stands in spacious grounds on the banks of the Charentonne. It's a gorgeous setting, and you can go fly-fishing nearby. François Deduit creates imaginative dishes and sauces using fresh local produce and offers very simple choices alongside more elaborate ones. Specialities include hot *foie gras,* pot-roast pigeon with carrots, or braised sea bass with pickled lemons, saffron and cumin. And for a surprise to finish with, don't miss the *grand dessert Chauvel*. Top-class service. Menus 110F (weekdays only) to 330F. 10% discount on the room rate.

SAINT-QUENTIN-DES-ISLES   27270 (4KM S)

🍴●❙ RESTAURANT LA POMMERAIE

It's on the N138.
☎ 02.32.45.28.88 ➡ 02.32.44.69.00
Closed Sun evening and Mon. **Garden**.

This long, low building, just set back from the road, has a Neoclassical façade and is surrounded by a pretty garden. The decor throughout is stylish, and the huge, bright dining room overlooks the garden where you can see the ducks splashing about in the pond. It's very relaxing. You'll be served warm appetisers as you wait for your meal. Menus, 85F (Mon–Sat lunchtimes) up to 220F, list things like pan-fried *foie gras* with redcurrants, veal braised with morel cream sauce or steamed lobster and fruit *bavarois*. Free apéritif.

BEAUMONT-LE-ROGER   27170 (17KM E)

🏃|●| LA CALÈCHE

54 rue Saint-Nicolas.
☎ 02.32.45.25.99
Closed Tues evening, Wed, the first fortnight in Jan, and a fortnight in June or July.

The chef's creativity extends beyond the kitchen – when there's a festival or a holiday, he decorates the front of the building. His cooking revels in a host of influences, and includes dishes such as *fricassée* of seafood, house *terrine* with onion preserve, chicken fritters with *pousse* spinach and house apple tart. There are a number of fish specialities, and the desserts are cooked on the premises. Smiling service and convivial welcome. Free apéritif.

BRIONNE   27800

🏃 🏠 |●| HÔTEL-RESTAURANT L'AUBERGE DU VIEUX DONJON**

pl. Fremont-des-Essarts (Centre); it's the market square.
☎ 02.32.44.80.62 ➡ 02.32.45.83.23
Closed Sun evening, Mon. **TV. Garden. Car park.**

A large half-timbered inn. Rooms overlook the garden; twin 250F with basin, 290F with shower/wc and 300F with bath. Have breakfast, an apéritif or a meal on the terrace in the courtyard. Classic menu at 83F and other, more imaginative, ones 140–210F. Regional dishes include seafood, *foie gras* with onion preserve, duck breast with peaches or apples, and beef fillet with morels. Free house apéritif.

🏃 🏠 |●| HÔTEL AQUILON**

9 route de Calleville.
☎ 02.32.44.81.49 ➡ 02.32.44.38.83
Disabled access. TV. Car park.

You'll find this large, brick-built building up by the 11th-century keep. Doubles 300–350F with shower/wc or bath. No two rooms are the same and there's a nice mini-suite with sloping ceilings. The rooms in the main building are lovely, especially number 3 which is very cheerful and

has a double aspect of the valley and the garden. Family atmosphere and attentive staff – and it's kept well heated. There's a 90F menu served in the evening, with other menus available on order. Free breakfast if you stay for a few days.

🏠 |●| LE LOGIS***

1 pl. Saint-Denis.
☎ 02.32.44.81.73 ➡ 02.32.45.10.92
Closed Sat lunchtime, Sun evening, Mon, a fortnight in the Feb school holidays and a week in Aug. **Disabled access. TV. Car park.**

This modern hotel may look as if it belongs to a chain, but it doesn't. You'll pay 340F for a double with shower/wc, 390F with bath. The cooking is fresh and full of flavour, and dishes change with the season. There's a weekday menu at 110F (160F at the weekend), then others 220–350F.

BEC-HELLOUIN (LE)   27800 (5KM N)

🏃|●| LE CANTERBURY

rue de Canterbury; it's behind the village hall.
☎ and ➡ 02.32.44.14.59
Closed Tues evening, Wed and Feb.

The big dining room has sturdy beams and fireplace, and there is a flower-filled terrace. House specialities include warm scallop *terrine*, fish *choucroute*, lamb with cumin and licorice *charlotte*. Weekday menu 89F, then 105–205F. Free coffee.

CANY-BARVILLE   76450

🏃|●| L'AUBERGE DE FRANCE

73 rue du Général-de-Gaulle; it's in the main street, beside the bridge across the river Durdent.
☎ 02.35.97.80.10
Closed Sun evening, Tues, ten days in Feb and a fortnight in Sept.

Service noon–2pm and 7–9.15pm. This large white building looks more like a café than a restaurant. The chef's creations change with the seasons – fillet of plaice with langoustines, *grenadins* of veal with morels, John Dory with creamed peas. Weekday lunch menu 88F, others from 130F up to the *menu dégustation* at 240F. Superb wines. Free coffee.

CAUDEBEC-EN-CAUX   76490

🏃 🏠 |●| LE CHEVAL BLANC*

4 pl. René-Coty; from the town hall on the banks of the Seine, go towards Saint-Arnoult-Lillebonne; pl. René-

Coty is a few metres further on.
☎ 02.35.96.21.66 ➡ 02.35.95.35.40
Closed Sun evening and Mon lunchtime except public holidays, Fri, Fri lunchtime only June–Sept, and four weeks Jan/Feb. **TV**. **Car park**.

Friendly staff, tasty cooking and attractive decor. Pretty, comfortable double rooms go for 200F with basin/wc and up to 290F with bath. Regional dishes like ox tripe *à la Normande*, the speciality of the house, are served in the restaurant. There's a lunch menu at 75F then others 110–220F. The kitchen closes at 9.30pm. 10% discount Sept–June.

SAINTE-GERTRUDE   76490 (3KM N)

|●| RESTAURANT AU RENDEZ-VOUS DES CHASSEURS

It's opposite the church
☎ 02.35.96.20.30
Closed Wed except public holidays, Sun evening, the Feb school holidays and the last fortnight in Aug.
Disabled access. **Garden**.

This is a quiet little restaurant nestling between the forest and the small village church. Hunters and travellers have been coming here for more than 150 years. Good regional dishes at prices to suit all pockets. Menus 65–148F: calf's head *sauce gribiche*, roulade of salmon with crayfish, and in winter, the chef makes a delicious game stew with pheasant, venison and hare. You can eat out on the terrace in the garden in fine weather.

SAINT-WANDRILLE-RANÇON   76490 (3KM E)

🏕 |●| RESTAURANT LES DEUX COURONNES

☎ 02.35.96.11.44 ➡ 02.35.56.56.23
Closed Sun evening, Mon and the Feb school holidays.

Service noon–2pm and 7.30–9pm. A 17th-century inn virtually in the precincts of the famous abbey. Irresistably tempting dishes include roast crayfish with *herbes de Provence*, *panaché* of kidneys and veal sweetbreads, and apple pancakes served with cinnamon ice cream. Menus 95–165F or, *à la carte*, 200–250F. Free coffee.

VILLEQUIER   76490 (4.5KM SW)

🏠 |●| HÔTEL DU GRAND SAPIN

quai de Seine; it's on the outskirts of Villequier going towards Caudebec.
☎ 02.35.56.78.73 ➡ 02.35.95.69.27
Closed Tues evening and Wed except July–Aug, 5 Feb–5 March, and the second fortnight in Nov.
TV. **Car park**.

Service noon–2pm and 7.30–9.30pm. This is a magnificent Normandy house on the banks of the Seine, with a lovely flower garden that has an enormous magnolia rather than a pine. Double rooms 260F; all of them overlook the river. This is a remarkably charming, friendly and cosy place with a new terrace. In the large rustic dining room you get menus 115–190F; there's also a short menu at 65F served during the week and at Saturday lunchtime. Excellent value for money. Booking essential.

VATTEVILLE-LA-RUE   76490 (8KM S)

|●| AUBERGE DU MOULIN

How to get there: taking the D65 from the bridge over the Brontonne, don't go into Vatteville but take the road to Aizier; it's in the hamlet of Quesnay, on the left.
☎ 02.35.96.10.88
Closed evenings, and Wed.

A multi-purpose establishment: restaurant-bar-tobacconist's-grocer's. Some villages stil have places like this but not usually as nice. The dining room offers a rustic setting with checked tablecloths, hunting trophies and wild boars' heads on the wall, and a wide, open fire. There are only a few tables and they are often full. The cuisine is just what you might expect – lots of rugged, hearty, traditional dishes at inexpensive prices: rabbit *chasseur*, snails, trout *meunière* or *andouillettes*. Menus 65–135F.

CONCHES-EN-OUCHE   27190

🏕 🏠 |●| HÔTEL-RESTAURANT LE CYGNE**

36 rue du Val.
☎ 02.32.30.20.60 ➡ 02.32.30.45.73
Restaurant closed Sun evening and Mon.

This hotel has a few comfortable rooms with classic decor. Doubles 270F with basin or 320F with bath. The traditional cooking is well seasoned, and includes dishes like oxtail in jelly, medallions of pork with cider, and pineapple with red fruit *coulis*. Lovely welcome and good-value menus from 95F to the *menu terroir* at 160F. Free apéritif.

CORMEILLES   27260

|●| LE FLORIDA

21 rue de l'Abaye.
☎ 02.32.57.80.97
Closed Mon, a fortnight in June and Dec.

The cuisine is reliable and the chef uses quality local produce. The *terrine* is excellent and specialities include rabbit in cider or veal escalope *Normande*. Weekday lunch menu 66F, others 89F and 125F – good value. Efficient service and smiling welcome.

DIEPPE 76200

♠ HÔTEL AU GRAND DUQUESNE*

15 pl. Saint-Jacques (Centre); it's in the street opposite the church of Saint-Jacques.
☎ 02.35.84.21.51 ➡ 02.35.84.29.83
TV.

Service noon–1.30pm and 7–10.15pm. This hotel has been entirely refurbished in a tasteful, modern style. Pretty, well-equipped bedrooms; 175F with basin, 245F with shower.

⅔ ♠ LES ARCADES DE LA BOURSE**

1–3 arcades de la Bourse (Centre); it's on the marina.
☎ 02.35.84.14.12 ➡ 02.35.40.22.09
TV.

Wonderful views over the marina. Modern, comfortable rooms, but nothing over the top. Doubles 280F with shower/wc or 370F with a view. Free apéritif.

I●I LE BISTROT DU POLLET

23 rue de Tête de Bœuf (Centre); it's on the quai, between Ango bridge and Colbert bridge, opposite the post office.
☎ 02.35.84.68.57
Closed Sun and Mon.

A small, friendly restaurant with a warm interior – lots of old photographs on the walls and old-fashioned music in the background. It may be wise to book, especially at lunchtime, when it fills up with faithful regulars. The owner is charming and prices are more than reasonable. They specialise in fish – the grilled bass and sea bream are wonderful – and *foie gras du pêcheur*, a typical Dieppois recipe of marinated, puréed monkfish liver. There's a lunch menu at 75F in the week, or expect to pay 130F *à la carte*.

⅔I●I À LA MARMITE DIEPPOISE

8 rue Saint-Jean (Centre); it's just by quai Duquesne.
☎ 02.35.84.24.26 ➡ 02.35.84.31.12
Closed Sun and Thurs evenings, and Mon.

Service noon–2.15pm and 7.15–9.30pm. A classic Dieppe restaurant. The brick walls are hung with copper dishes that are ever so slightly tacky but the food is tasty. Fish dishes prepared with cream are the mainstay of the menus; their superb signature dish is *marmite diéppoise*, a tasty stew of monkfish, ling, brill, sole and scallops, which costs 100F *à la carte*. Menus 105–220F. Free house apéritif.

POURVILLE-SUR-MER 76550 (4.5KM W)

I●I L'HUÎTRIÈRE

rue du 19-Août; it's west of Dieppe on the seashore.
☎ 02.35.84.36.20 ➡ 02.35.84.38.09
Closed end Sept–Easter. **Car park**.

Service 10am–approximately 8pm. A seafood restaurant specialising in oysters, clams, whelks, winkles, cockles and *crêpes*. You'll find it just opposite the place where oysters are sold direct from the oyster beds. The decor is really nice, with sea-blue walls, oyster baskets and an old diving suit in the corner. The bay windows open right onto the beach. In summer, they set up a huge terrace. Prices are steep, though not overly so.

ARQUES-LA-BATAILLE 76880 (6KM SE)

⅔ ♠ LE MANOIR D'ARCHELLES

Archelles; it's on the D1, Neuchâtel road.
☎ 02.35.85.50.16 ➡ 02.35.85.47.55
TV. **Car park**.

This is a stunning 16th-century manor house built of a mosaic of brick and flint stones. Doubles 200F with basin, 250–300F with shower/wc or bath; they also have a suite that sleeps four. The decor is more rustic than chic but that doesn't diminish its charm. The rooms in the fortified gatehouse, reached by a spiral stone staircase, are particularly attractive, giving good views of the château. Have a wander round the orchard and vegetable garden that the owner cultivates with enormous care. 5% discount.

⅔I●I L'AUBERGE D'ARCHELLES

Archelles; it's next to *Le Manoir*.
☎ 02.35.83.40.51
Closed Sun and Mon evening Sept–April. **Car park**.

This restaurant, which is owned by the same people as *Le Manoir*, is housed in beautifully converted old stables. The cuisine is equally attractive, featuring regional and gastronomic dishes. The 80F menu of the day is superb: Camembert *croquettes*, duck in cider and a home-made pastry. Other excellent menus up to 188F. Very good value. Free coffee at weekends.

ELBEUF   76500

≜ |●| LE SQUARIUM*

25 rue Pierre-Brossolette (Southeast); it's opposite the cinema.
☎ 02.35.81.10.52
Closed Sun and Aug. **Car park**.

It's advisable to book if you're planning on coming to this cosy little hotel-bar. The spacious bedrooms are well maintained; doubles 120F with basin, 160F with shower and 200F with bath. You'll get your money's worth. The restaurant operates at lunchtimes, offering two set menus at 49F and 55F or *à la carte*.

渃 ≜ |●| LE PROGRÈS**

47 rue Henry (Centre); it's almost opposite the town hall.
☎ 02.35.78.42.67 ➡ 02.35.78.42.76
Closed Sun and Fri evening. **TV**.

A quiet hotel, well situated between the Seine and the shopping streets. Good prices; doubles 160F with basin/wc, 220F with bath. There's a pleasant brasserie offering menus from 55F; if that's not your scene try the simple, regional dishes in the prettily decorated dining room. Menu at 78F or gastronomic menus 102–195F. Free breakfast if you stay or house apéritif with a meal.

|●| RESTAURANT LE JARDIN SAINT-LOUIS

24 rue Proudhon (Centre); the entrance is on pl. de la République.
☎ 02.35.77.63.22
Closed Sun evening. **Car park**.

The friendly people who run this restaurant will make you feel very welcome. Pleasant cooking of classic dishes like *tartare* of salmon with fresh herbs, roast langoustine with lemon butter and braised beef marrow with sea salt – or try the local speciality, *caille aux monstrueux d'Elbeuf*, which is quail with leeks. Weekday lunch menu 55F, others up to 130F, or around 150F *à la carte*.

SAINT-AUBIN-LÈS-ELBEUF   76410 (2KM N)

渃 ≜ HÔTEL DU CHÂTEAU BLANC**

65 rue Jean-Jaurès; cross over the bridge over the Seine and it's on the corner of the first street on the right.
☎ and ➡ 02.35.77.10.53
Closed Sun afternoon. **TV**. **Garden**.

A large house, which despite being rather noisy in the morning, on account of the nearby main road, has plenty to recommend it. There's a walled garden where you can park the car and a large, pleasant lounge where you can relax and read a paper. The spacious rooms are double glazed and very well maintained; 220F with shower/wc and 240F with bath. No restaurant, but you can have something on a tray on request. 10% discount Feb–April.

ÉTRETAT   76790

≜ HÔTEL D'ANGLETERRE

35 av. George-V (Centre); it's 100m from the sea on the Le Havre road that starts at the tourist office.
☎ 02.35.27.01.65 ➡ 02.35.28.78.44

A clean, welcoming, reasonably priced hotel away from the touristy part of town – in other words, something of a find. Doubles 260F with shower/wc, 280F with bath/wc.

≜ |●| L'ESCALE**

pl. Foch (Centre); it's opposite the old market.
☎ 02.35.27.03.69 ➡ 02.35.28.05.86
TV.

This completely refurbished hotel-brasserie is really nice. The bedrooms have wood panelling and though they are a bit small they're pleasant; doubles with shower/wc 290F. The lively ground floor restaurant-brasserie serves simple dishes – mussels and chips, omelettes, salads, pizzas and *crêpes*, and a few gourmet dishes. Menus 75F and up. From the terrace you can watch the world hurry by in the square.

≜ |●| HÔTEL LE CORSAIRE**

rue du Général-Leclerc.
☎ 02.35.10.38.90 ➡ 02.35.28.89.74
TV.

Service noon–3pm and 7–9.30pm approximately. One of the few hotels on the seafront. It's got a pretty red brick façade and a magnificent view of the famous cliffs. The modern bedrooms are all decorated in very different styles. Prices 395F with shower/wc and 445–590F with bath; the most expensive ones have a sea view. Sea view from the restaurant and of the cliffs by the beach from the terrace. Simple, ordinary cooking specialising in seafood and fish. Menus 75–195F.

|●| L'HUITRIÈRE

rue Traz-Perrier; it's on the seafront, towards the cliffs of Aval.
☎ 02.35.27.02.82

An extraordinary circular dining room with a sensational panoramic view over the beaches and cliffs. They specialise in seafood and fish and take great care over the preparation of each dish. Very good value for money on the 98F menu – also served at the weekend. Particularly delicious mussels – around 50F. The service is most attentive and they serve a complimentary *trou Normand* – a shot of Calvados between courses – to everyone. Menus 179–239F or around 150F *à la carte*. Great place to be when there's a storm.

⅔ |●| RESTAURANT LE GALION

bd. René-Coty (Centre).
☎ 02.35.29.48.74 ☞ 02.35.29.74.48
Closed Tues evening, Wed, 15 Dec–15 Jan.

Cosy restaurant with 17th-century decor, an enormous fireplace, little tinted window panes, and old beams. Service is high class, with waitresses in uniform. The menu at 120F is beautifully balanced, listing velvety smooth fish soup, escalope of salmon with Muscadet, and oysters poached in champagne. Other menus 170–245F. Free coffee.

EU   76260

⅔ 🏠 |●| HÔTEL-RESTAURANT MAINE**

av. de la Gare.
☎ 02.35.86.16.64 ☞ 02.35.50.86.25
✉ hotelmaine@aol.com
Restaurant closed Sun evening except public holiday weekends and 16 Aug–8 Sept. **TV**. **Car park**.

Bright and peaceful establishment in a master-craftsman's house opposite the old station. It was already a restaurant by 1867, and the dining room is an exceptional example of Art Nouveau decor. The rooms have modern facilities with en-suite bathrooms, TV and telephones. Some have been refurbished more recently than others. 290F for doubles with shower/wc or 310F with bath. Half-board, obligatory over holiday weekends from Easter to September, costs 320F per person, which, given the quality of the cuisine, is good value. It's worth coming just for a meal. Weekday menu 95F or 135–220F – one is a fish-lover's menu and another for carnivores. The food is modern yet firmly rooted in local and traditional cuisine. Free apéritif.

ÉVREUX   27000

⅔ 🏠 |●| HÔTEL-RESTAURANT DE LA BICHE**

9 rue Joséphine, pl. Saint-Taurin (West).
☎ 02.32.38.66.00. ☞ 02.32.33.54.05.
Hotel closed Aug. **Restaurant closed** Sun evening, Sun lunchtime also July–Aug. **Disabled access**. **TV**. **Car park**.

An amazing hotel-restaurant on the edge of an extremely pretty square. The building – where Louis Malle shot his film *Le Voleur* – started its days as the hunting lodge of François I before becoming the most sophisticated brothel in the area. It's built around an interior patio and has a gloriously retro feel. The bedrooms, which lead off a gallery, go for 150F with basin, 250F with shower/wc, and 270F with bath. You'll either get a view of place Saint-Taurin, which is very quiet in the evening, or the river. The atmosphere in the restaurant is jovial. They serve first-rate home cooking and imaginative dishes such as marrowbones with sea salt on toast, Portuguese *aïoli* with fish *pot-au-feu* or flambéed veal kidneys and sweetbreads. Menus 80F and 140F or *à la carte*. 10% discount on the room rate.

⅔ 🏠 |●| HÔTEL DE FRANCE**

29 rue Saint-Thomas (Centre); it's behind the market square.
☎ 02.32.39.09.25 ☞ 00.32.38.38.56
Restaurant closed Sat and Sun evenings, and Mon. **TV**. **Garden**. **Car park**.

A nice little two-star hotel with very comfortable, quiet, attractive rooms, 295–340F with shower/wc or bath. Staff are exceptionally hospitable and the welcoming restaurant overlooks the River Iton and the pleasant garden. The gourmet cooking is the best in town and the new chef maintains high standards: *millefeuille* of marinated raw salmon, Normandy duck *foie gras* and veal *tournedos*. The seafood platters are short of generous. Menus 150–210F, and *à la carte* 150–220F and dishes change regularly with the seasons. Free breakfast when you book quoting this guide.

|●| RESTAURANT LA CROIX D'OR

3 rue Joséphine (West).
☎ 02.32.33.06.07
Closed 24 Dec–1 Jan.

Fine food and dishes that are intelligently prepared by people who care about what they do. You get none of the pretentious mini portions typical of nouvelle cuisine here. In the large, bright dining room, waiters dressed as sailors race between tables that are often occupied by locals. The chef regularly makes the trip to the Paris food markets so the ingredients are super-fresh. The superb weekday lunch menu, 62F, offers genuine innovations like *terrine* of half-cooked salmon with a *coulis* of tomato, olives and basil, or a *clafoutis* with asparagus and langoustines, fresh shellfish and game in season, but *the* speciality has got to be the *bouillabaisse*. Other equally impressive menus 82–189F. It's a real shame that the terrace has such a noisy road going past.

GRAVIGNY   27930 (4KM N)

I●I LE SAINT-NICOLAS

38 av. Aristide-Briand (Centre); it's on the D155 towards Louviers, on the right.
☎ 02.32.38.35.15 ➡ 02.32.31.19.34
Closed the second fortnight in Aug. **Car park**.

Service noon–2pm and 7–10pm. This unobtrusive house conceals a number of lovely little dining rooms decorated in a simple, sophisticated style – intimate ones for candlelit dinners, larger ones for lively groups or there's a terrace. Chef Claude Sauvant uses only the best ingredients he can find on the market. The boned pig's trotters with truffles are delicious, as are the perch fillets with Saint-Nicolas butter and the warm oysters with cream and shallot sauce. Superb wine list. Menus from 98F.

JOUY-SUR-EURE   27120 (12KM E)

I●I LE RELAIS DU GUESCLIN

pl. de l'Église; take the N13 in the direction of Pacy-sur-Eure, then the D57.
☎ 02.32.36.62.75
Closed evenings except for reservations, Wed, and Aug. **Car park**.

A little Normandy inn with a church on one side and fields on the other. Peace and quiet are guaranteed, so you can have an undisturbed lunch outside. The daily *formule*, 95F, gets you a main course plus starter or dessert. Menus 160F and 190F; dishes include *bonhomme Normand*, *foie gras*, ox kidneys and warm tarts. Everything that's good in Normandy cuisine. Good dry cider.

CHAMBRAY   27120 (15KM NE)

🎋 I●I RESTAURANT LE VOL AU VENT

1 pl. de la Mairie (Centre); take the D63.
☎ 02.32.36.70.05
Closed Sun evening, Mon, Tues, and Aug.

Service noon–2pm and 8–9.30pm. A little village house in the Eure valley. The very stylish dining room is reached through a small lounge-smoking room where they serve apéritifs and coffee. The cooking is exquisite

and full of subtle flavours. Menus 160–240F. Specialities include *vol au vents*, fillet of beef *Saint-Amand*, veal sweetbreads with wild mushrooms in flaky pastry, fillet of roast pigeon and *millefeuille* of seasonal fruit. Free apéritif.

FÉCAMP   76400

🎋 🏠 I●I LE MARTIN

18 pl. Saint-Étienne (Centre); it's next to the church.
☎ 02.35.28.23.82 ➡ 02.35.28.61.21
Hotel closed first fortnight in March, and Sept.
Restaurant closed Sun evening and Mon except public holidays. **TV**.

Service noon–2pm and 7–9.30pm. A good little restaurant that refuses to be a slave to fashion. You'll get typical Normandy dishes and classic cuisine served in a rustic dining room with exposed beams. The 75F menu is good value, but it's not available on Saturday evening, Sunday or public holidays. The others range 90–160F. Rudimentary rooms, 150F with basin and 175F with shower – a godsend if you're on a budget. 10% discount on the room rate Sept–June.

🏠 HÔTEL DE LA MER**

89 bd. Albert-Ier; it's right on the beach.
☎ 02.35.28.24.64 ➡ 02.35.28.27.67
Closed a fortnight in the Feb school holidays. **TV**.

This modern establishment looks rather unfriendly but it's actually an excellent hotel, and one of the few right on the beach facing the sea. Comfy, well-equipped rooms, some with balcony and sea view, cost 180F with basin, 260F and 290–330F with shower/wc or 270–290F with bath. Nice homely atmosphere and pleasant owners.

🎋 🏠 HÔTEL DE LA PLAGE**

87 rue de la Plage (Centre); it's 30m from the beach.
☎ 02.35.29.76.51 ➡ 02.35.28.68.30
TV. **Disabled access**. **Garage**.

A modern well-equipped hotel very close to the beach. Doubles 230–260F with shower, 300–330F with shower/wc or 300–350F with bath. Most have been refurbished. Breakfast, 35F, is served in an attractive room, and you'll get a good-natured welcome. 10% discount Nov–April except Sat and public holidays.

🏠 HÔTEL D'ANGLETERRE**

93 rue de la Plage (Centre).
☎ 02.35.28.01.60 ➡ 02.35.28.62.95
Closed Christmas. **TV**. **Car park**.

The new owners have plans to renovate the hotel from top to bottom. The rooms they have already done are bright and colourful and particularly pleasant. Rooms of all sizes, 250–350F – the cheaper ones are those which have yet to be done up – and family rooms 320–440F. Young, friendly welcome and a bohemian spirit about the place.

|●| LE VICOMTÉ

4 rue du Président-Coty; it's 50m from the port, behind the Palais Bénédictine.
☎ 02.35.28.47.63
Closed Wed evening, Sun, public holidays, a fortnight in Aug and a fortnight end Dec/Jan.

Service noon–1.30pm and 7–9pm. A very welcoming and rather unusual, retro bistro with a refreshing atmosphere – checked tablecloths and posters from the *Petit Journal* adorning the walls. They serve just one set menu at 91F, but the dishes change every day. Regional cooking based on fresh produce. Excellent value and impeccable service.

⅔|●| LE MARITIME**

2 pl. Nicolas-Selles; it's across from the marina.
☎ 02.35.28.21.71 ➡ 02.35.27.22.08
Closed Tues evening Oct–March.

Service noon–2.30pm and dinner 7–9.30pm (10pm in season). Very good seafood restaurant near the marina. The front has been updated and painted white and blue. The place has been afloat for a number of years, though, and it's definitely found its sea legs; seafood platters, *blanquette* of salt cod, fish paella, and good meat dishes – climb aboard with confidence. Menus 95–210F. Take-away service. Free coffee.

☎ |●| AUBERGE DE LA ROUGE**

route du Havre; it's on the D925.
☎ 02.35.28.07.59. ➡ 02.35.28.70.55.
Closed Sun evening, Mon, and three weeks Jan–Feb.
Disabled access. Garden. TV. Car park.

This large, delightful inn is just over one hundred years old. The new owners are carrying on in the tradition laid down by their predecessors. This is a high-quality establishment and you can eat beside the fountain in the garden and listen to the birds. Dishes change with the seasons: grilled sole in oyster stock, duck *à la rouennaise*, frogs' legs in a pastry turnover and *crêpes soufflés*. Menus 105F (except Sun lunch), then 190–300F. They also have a few comfortable bedrooms, 350F for a double, but

they're close to the road and somewhat noisy.

☎ LE CONTINENTAL***

110 av. des Sources; it's near the casino.
☎ 02.32.89.50.50 ➡ 02.35.90.26.14
TV. Car park

An impressive, half-timbered building that's been thoroughly renovated. With its large foyer and balconies it still has the nicely old-fashioned atmosphere of old casino hotels. Well equipped bedrooms 395F. Use of the Club Med facilities by arrangement.

⅔|●| AUBERGE DE LA VARENNE

2 route de la Libération; take the D919 to Buchy, then the D41.
☎ 02.35.34.13.80
Closed Sun evening and Mon except public holidays.

A really pleasant roadside inn in a small village between Rouen and Neufchâtel. They stick firmly to traditional, local cooking – try the *cassolette* of fresh scallops with cream, the black pudding served in a pancake, or the Calvados soufflé. Weekday menu 80F then 120–210F. It's a good place to eat after visiting the old market in Buchy. Very attentive service and warm-hearted welcome. Open fire in the winter, lovely terrace in good weather. Free coffee.

SEE MAP OVERLEAF

☎ HÔTEL LE MONACO

16 rue de Paris. **MAP B4-3**
☎ 02.35.42.21.01 ➡ 02.35.42.01.01
TV. Car park.

One of the nearest hotels to the ferry, and generally well maintained. Doubles 140F with washing facilities and 205–260F with bath.

⅔ ☎ HÔTEL-CELTIC**

106 rue Voltaire. **MAP B3-1**
☎ 02.3542.39.77 ➡ 02.35.21.67.65
Closed Christmas school holidays. **TV. Car park**.

Delightfully located hotel with views of the Niemeyer theatre and the merchant port. Brightly painted doubles with modern bathrooms; with shower 195F, with shower/wc 265F, or with bath 295F. They do a weekend deal (room and dinner) for 320F, in conjunction with the *Strasbourgeoise* restaurant close by. 10% discount on the room rate.

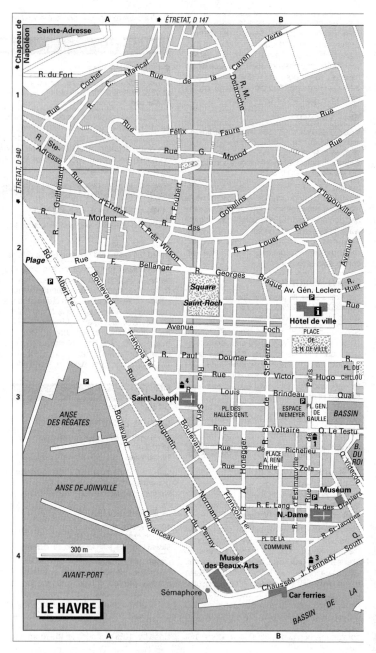

ÉTRETAT, D 147

A B

Sainte-Adresse

✦ Chapeau de Napoléon

ÉTRETAT, D 940

R. du Fort

Cochet

Maréchal

Rue de la

Caven

R. M. Delaroche

Verte

Rue

R. Ste-Adresse

Rue

Félix Faure

Rue

Rue G. Monod

R. Guillemard

Rue d'Etretat

R. Foubert

R des

Gobelins

R d'Ingouville

Rue

R. J. Morlent

R.-Prés. Wilson

R. J. Louer

Avenue

Bd Albert 1er

Rue F.

Bellanger

R. Georges

Braque

Av. Gén. Leclerc

R. Huet

Plage

Square Saint-Roch

P

Rue

Hôtel de ville

P ℹ

Avenue Foch

ANSE DES RÉGATES

Boulevard François Ter

Rue Sery

R. Paul Doumer

Rue

Louis

St-Pierre

Paris

Victor Hugo

PLACE DE L'H. DE VILLE

PL. DU CHILLOU

R.

♦ 4

R.

Quai

Saint-Joseph

PL. DES HALLES CENT.

Brindeau

ESPACE NIEMEYER

PL. GÉN. DE GAULLE

BASSIN

Boulevard Augustin

Rue

R. Honegger

de

Voltaire

R.

Q. Le Testu

♦ 1

ANSE DE JOINVILLE

Rue

PLACE A. RENÉ

Richelieu

Émile Zola

R. d'Estimauville

Rue

Q. Videcoq

B. DU ROI

Boulevard Clémenceau

François 1er

R. du Perrey

Normand

R. E. Lang

Muséum

P

R. des Drapiers

N.-Dame

R. St-Jacques

Q.

300 m

PL. DE LA COMMUNE

♦ 3

AVANT-PORT

Musée des Beaux-Arts

Chaussée J. Kennedy

South

Sémaphore

Car ferries

LE HAVRE

BASSIN DE LA

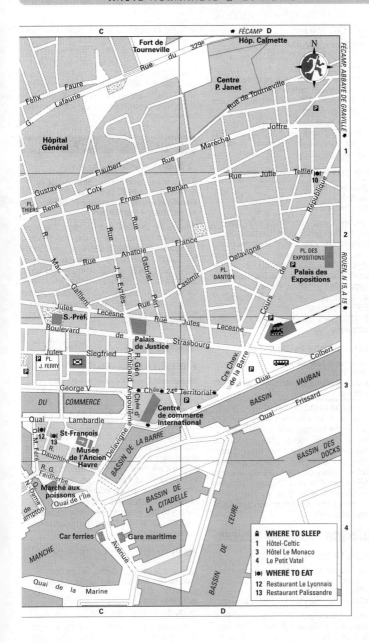

C · FÉCAMP D

Fort de
Tourneville

Hôp. Calmette

329e

Rue du

Faure

Félix

Lafaurie

G.

Centre
P. Janet

Rue de Tourneville

Joffre

N

Hôpital
Général

Maréchal

Rue

1

Flaubert

Rue

Jutte

Tellier

Gustave

Coty

Renan

Rue

10

René

Rue

Ernest

PL.
THIERS

R.

Rue

Rue

Anatole

Gabriel

France

2

Mac.

Rue

J. B. Eyriès

Casimir

Delavigne

PL. DES
EXPOSITIONS

Galliéni

Pel

PL.
DANTON

Palais des
Expositions

Jules

Lecesne

Cours

Rue

Jules

Lecesne

de

S.-Préf.

Boulevard

de

Strasbourg

Jules

Palais
de Justice

R. Gén

Colbert

PL.
J. FERRY

Siegfried

de la Barre

Quai

VAUBAN

George V

Crs Chev.

BASSIN

Frissard

COMMERCE

Archinard Angoulême

Chée

24e Territorial

Quai

DU

Chée d'

Quai

Lambardie

Centre
de commerce
international

BASSIN

Qu

St-François

Delavigne

13

R.

M. Féré

Musée
de l'Ancien
Havre

BASSIN DE LA BARRE

BASSIN DES
DOCKS

12

Dauphine

R. G.
Faidherbe

Marché aux
poissons

N.-Dame

Qu.

Quai de l'Île

BASSIN DE
LA CITADELLE

L'EURE

de
ampton

4

Car ferries

Gare maritime

Avenue

BASSIN

MANCHE

DE

Quai de la Marine

L'EURE

🛏 WHERE TO SLEEP
1 Hôtel-Celtic
3 Hôtel Le Monaco
4 Le Petit Vatel

|◉| WHERE TO EAT
12 Restaurant Le Lyonnais
13 Restaurant Palissandre

C · D

FÉCAMP ABBAYE DE GRAVILLE

ROUEN, N 15, A 15

坐 ≜ LE PETIT VATEL**

8 rue Louis Brindeau. **MAP A3-4**
☎ 02.35.41.72.07 ➡ 02.35.21.37.86
℮ hotel.celtic@wanadoo.fr

A central hotel where the gaily painted, clean rooms have modern facilities and bathrooms; 220F with shower, 250F with shower/wc and 280F with bath. Nothing special about the view but the hotel offers very good value. A 200F overnight deal on Fri, Sat and Sun nights for one, two or three persons, Sept–June.

坐 |●| RESTAURANT LE LYONNAIS

7 rue de Bretagne. **MAP C3-12**
☎ 02.35.22.07.31
Closed Sat lunchtime and Sun.

They've been very successful in recreating the atmosphere of a typical Lyonnais bistro. The copper chimney breast, checkerboard floor tiles and brick walls make a good impression and so do the typical Lyon dishes: *gâteau* of chicken livers and Lyon *andouillette* with boiled potatoes, though the warm upside-down apple tart is a more local dish. The 65F menu is served in the week, or others 78–128F. Well-selected wines. Free glass of champagne.

坐 |●| RESTAURANT PALISSANDRE

33 rue de Bretagne. **MAP C3-13**
☎ 02.35.21.69.00
Closed Wed evening, Sat lunchtime, Sun, a week in Feb and 15–30 Aug.

The dark wood interior is reminiscent of a boat – and you're in for a winning classic culinary voyage. Try the fish with cider or the mussels; if seafood doesn't tempt you, go for the *andouillette* or one of the other meat dishes. The 85F menu is excellent value for a restaurant in the touristy old town, there's also one at 118F and another at 149F, which includes drinks. People in a hurry go for the "*Oh! le pressé*" menu, 65F, served in twenty minutes. Free apéritif or coffee.

SAINTE-ADRESSE　　　76310 (2KM NW)

坐 |●| LES TROIS PICS

promenade des Régates; it's at the northernmost end of Le Havre beach.
☎ and ➡ 02.35.48.20.60.
Closed Sun and Mon evening out of season, Dec, Jan.

This place, standing on the quay, looks for all the world like a liner in dry dock. The large wooden dining room has a wonderful, panoramic view of the mouth of the Seine

and the maritime decor is imaginative and refined. From the ship's rail you can see Deauville, ten miles off in the distance. They do very decent brasserie cooking. Menus from 72F (weekdays), 115F or 182F and *à la carte* around 180F. Have a drink on the terrace in summer and when the dusk falls, you can really believe you're out at sea. Free house apéritif.

JUMIÈGES　　　76480

坐 ≜ |●| AUBERGE DES RUINES

pl. de la Mairie (Centre); it's opposite the monastery.
☎ 02.35.37.24.05 ➡ 02.35.37.87.34
Closed Tues evening, Wed lunchtime, Fri, 20 Dec–10 Jan and 16 Aug–4 Sept. **Car park**.

Service noon–2pm and 7–9pm. The best restaurant in town, where you can snuggle up in front of the fire in winter or relax under the awning in summer. Weekday menu at 92F, then 135F and 180F. If you regard yourself as a foodie, try the *émincé* of snails with garlic or courgettes *en anchoïade,* pigeon with vanilla or oyster and smoked salmon *tartare.* Four basic bedrooms with basin only, 170F. Free coffee.

DUCLAIR　　　76480 (9KM NW)

≜ |●| HÔTEL DE LA POSTE**

286 quai de La Libération (Centre); take the D982 – follow the river, and you'll see it just across from the ferry.
☎ 02.35.37.50.04 ➡ 02.35.37.39.19
Restaurant closed Sun evening.

A simple, welcoming place that deserves its excellent reputation. Comfortable doubles with shower/wc 210F, or 280F with bath; they all have a lovely view over the water. You also get wonderful views from the two dining rooms. You're in duck-rearing country here – indeed, despite Rouen's claims to the contrary, this is the place that invented the recipe for pressed duck *de Duclair*. The dish is the house speciality. Menus 80–200F.

|●| RESTAURANT AU VAL DE SEINE

380 quai de la Libération (Centre); take the D982 – follow the river, and you'll see it just across from the ferry.
☎ 02.35.37.99.88
Closed Mon evening, Tues and Oct.

The decor here is ordinary, but you'll get a smiling welcome and there's a panoramic view of the Seine and the ferries from the first-floor dining room. Very reasonable prices at this high-class *crêperie*, where you can also enjoy carefully prepared dishes, many of which feature fish: warm salad of queen scallops, mussels with raspberry vinegar, John Dory with basil and a seafood platter. Menus 60–155F. They're open all day on Sunday, when they serve cakes as well as savoury snacks.

LILLEBONNE   76170

⅍ 🏠 |●| LA P'TITE AUBERGE

20 rue du Havre (Centre); it's behind the church.
☎ 02.35.38.00.59 ➡ 02.35.38.57.33
Closed Sat lunchtime, Sun evening, a fortnight in the Feb school holidays and three weeks in Aug.
Disabled access. **TV**. **Car park opposite**.

This hotel, under new management, is in a large, half-timbered house. Most of the bright rooms have had new bathrooms fitted; doubles 170F with basin (wc along the landing), 270F for shower/wc or bath. 69F lunch menu and others 98F and 155F. Traditional cuisine served in a fresh, rustic dining room: house *foie gras*, veal sweetbreads *Rossini* and chocolate *moelleux*. Shady terrace in warm weather. Free coffee.

LOUVIERS   27400

⅍ 🏠 |●| LE PRÉ-SAINT-GERMAIN***

7 rue Saint-Germain (Centre); it's northeast of pl. Ernest-Thorel.
☎ 02.32.40.48.48 ➡ 02.32.50.75.60
Restaurant closed Sat lunchtime and Sun evening.
Disabled access. **TV**. **Car park**.

Built in the middle of an old orchard, this Neo-classical-style hotel boasts all the facilities you should expect from a three-star establishment. You can be sure of good cuisine and a delightful welcome. Menu *autour du bar* 90F, and others 125–190F. Doubles 450F with bath. Free breakfast or apéritif.

⅍ 🏠 |●| HÔTEL LA HAYE-LE-COMTE***

4 route de la Haye-le-Comte (Southwest); take the D133 towards Neubourg and it's just outside Louviers.
☎ 02.32.40.00.40 ➡ 02.32.25.03.85
📧 hotel-la-hay-le-comte@wanadoo.fr
Hotel closed Dec–March. **Restaurant closed** Mon, Fri and Sat lunchtimes except by reservation. **Disabled access**. **TV**. **Car park**.

Service noon–1.30pm and 7–9pm. This charming hotel is a little 16th-century manorhouse in its own extensive grounds.

It's a perfect base for an active weekend, and the prices are reasonable. Doubles with bath 500F. The chef's specialities are scallop and Dublin Bay prawn dishes. Menus 100–190F, around 200F *à la carte*. You can play tennis, table tennis, *pétanque* or croquet and you can hire mountain bikes. Free house apéritif.

⅍ |●| RESTAURANT LE JARDIN DE BIGARD

39–41 rue du Quai; it's on the corner of rue du Coq.
☎ 02.32.40.02.45
Closed Wed and Sun evenings.

A centrally located, unpretentious restaurant with a bright, airy dining room offering simple but carefully prepared dishes at reasonable prices. The weekday lunch menu costs 60F, and there are others 80–165F. Specialities include scallops in cider, calf's head *sauce gribiche*, fillet of trout with Camebert and thigh of duck with cider. Free house apéritif with dinner.

⅍ |●| LE CLOS NORMAND

rue de la Gare–chaussée du Vexin (Northeast); cross the Eure by rue des Anciens-Combattants d'AFN and it's right there.
☎ 02.32.40.03.56 ➡ 02.32.40.61.24
Closed Mon and four weeks July/Aug.

Rustic decor in the dining room. The cooking is traditional but imaginative. They do a number of fish specialities and lots of dishes using cream and locally grown produce – try the trout with Camembert, duck with grapes, or the salmon in cream sauce and finish off with a *charlotte* with apples and Calvados. Menu 79F during the week, with others from 98–145F. Free house apéritif before dinner.

ACQUIGNY   27400 (5KM S)

⅍ |●| LA CHAUMIÈRE

15 rue Aristide-Briand (Centre); it's opposite the town hall.
☎ 02.32.50.20.54
Closed Tues and Wed. **Car park**.

A really nice restaurant with rustic decor and a relaxed atmosphere. The chef produces new dishes every day, but typical offerings might be mushroom *galettes* with a cep *coulis*, red mullet with *beurre blanc*, veal chops *à la Normande*, game in season and seasonal fruit crumble. When it's chilly, they grill meat and fish over the fire. No menus, but the *à la carte* prices are reasonable, at 110–350F. A very good selection of wines, available by the glass. Free *digestif*.

LÉRY   27690 (7KM NE)

|●| LA FONTAINE SAINT-GABRIEL

2 pl. de l'Église.
☎ 02.32.59.09.39 **e** a.fontaine@wanadoo.fr
Closed Mon except public holidays and in summer.
Car park.

A delightful, tree-shaded square, a pretty Romanesque church, and the banks of the Eure just a stone's throw away – all this adds up to a quite charming setting for this restaurant, which serves exquisite cooking. The new owners are real professionals. Madame runs the dining room and Monsieur is the chef. He produces quality food: *foie gras* in a cloth, roast duck with thyme cream, and home-baked Vacherin pastry. Menus 130–180F or *à la carte*. Nice post-prandial walks along the riverbank.

PONT-DE-L'ARCHE   27340 (11KM N)

⅔ ♠ HÔTEL DE LA TOUR**

41 quai Foch (Centre); take the N15 over the bridge and it's on the left on the Eure riverbank.
☎ 02.35.23.00.99 **F→** 02.35.23.46.22
TV. Garden. Car park.

The preserved façade is perfectly in keeping with the pretty houses along the quay, but the interior has been completely and expertly refurbished by the charming owners, Monsieur and Mme Helouard. Everything about it – the colours, the decor, the little details that make for a comfortable stay, and the friendly welcome – gives this place a quality not normally found in a hotel in this category. If they're not full, you can tour the empty rooms and choose the one you want. Whether you opt for one overlooking the ramparts and the church of Notre-Dame-des-Arts, or one with a view of the lush riverbank, they're all equally quiet. Doubles 330F. There's a little, paved garden at the back. 10% discount.

LYONS-LA-FORÊT   27480

⅔ ♠ |●| HOSTELLERIE DU DOMAINE SAINT-PAUL**

It's 800m out of the village on the D321.
☎ 02.32.49.60.57 **F→** 02.32.49.56.05
e domaine-saint-paul@liberty.fr
Closed 2 Nov–1 April. **Swimming pool. TV. Car park.**

A substantial house, built as a hunting lodge in 1815, with various annexes around the main building. It's been in the same family since 1946. The grounds are quiet, and planted with flower beds, and there's an open-air swimming

pool. Simply decorated rooms go for 320–470F; half or full board is compulsory. Typical regional cooking with a few original touches: Camembert *croquettes*, scallop *terrine* and *fricassée* of duck. There's a 125F menu, served weekday lunchtimes, and others 150–210F, including a *menu terroir*. Best to book at the weekend. Free house apéritif.

NEUFCHÂTEL-EN-BRAY   76270

⅔ ♠ |●| HOSTELLERIE DU GRAND CERF**

9 Grande-Rue-Fausse-Porte (Centre); go down the main street and it's beyond the church.
☎ 02.35.93.00.02 **F→** 02.35.94.14.92
ark. Fri, Sat lunchtime and Dec. **TV. Car park.**

Service noon–2.30pm and 7.30–9.15pm. You'll be spoiled rotten here, and you'll have to have a good excuse ready for the waitress if you don't eat every scrap. Classic decor and traditional Normandy cooking. They do an appealing lunch *formule* for 59F (not Sun), and a variety of menus 77–166F. Well-maintained doubles cost from 240F. Half board 245F per person based on two sharing. Free coffee.

PONT-AUDEMER   27500

⅔ ♠ |●| RESTAURANT LE CAMEL-HÔTEL DU PALAIS ET DE LA POSTE

14 rue Alfred Camel; it's near the post office.
☎ 02.32.41.50.74
Closed Tues and Sun evening, last week in Feb and the first fortnight in Sept. **Car park. TV. Disabled access.**

The deliciously retro dining room is a perfect setting for the local dishes that are served with a few original touches: skate *terrine*, fillet of duck *à l'Eunoise*, *méli-mélo* of fish with tartare sauce. Weekday menu, 67F, is served lunchtime and evenings until 8pm, and there are others 97–177F. The hotel is less appealing, though the rooms are good value; doubles with basin go for 130F, 230F with shower/wc. Half board, 230–280F, is compulsory. The establishment is professionally run and you get a warm welcome. Free house apéritif.

⅔ ♠ |●| AUBERGE DU VIEUX PUITS**

6 rue Notre-Dame-du-Pré (Centre).
☎ 02.32.41.01.48 **F→** 02.32.42.37.28
Closed Mon and Tues except in summer, and 16 Dec–25 Jan. **Car park. TV. Disabled access.**

This magnificent, half-timbered 17th-century building has just twelve bedrooms, and people dining at the inn get priority. The rooms in the oldest part are cheaper and more typically Norman than those in the modern part, but the soundproofing's not as good. Doubles 180F with basin, 340F with shower/wc or 450F with bath. They serve traditional, refined Normandy cooking, which you can eat either in the cosy dining room or in an intimate sitting room. Menus change frequently; weekday lunch *menu express* 175F, and others 240–330F. Specialities include mussel and Parmesan soufflé, trout Bovary with champagne sauce, and apple tart. Half board is compulsory if you stay the night. 10% discount on the room rate Oct–March.

🏃 |●| RESTAURANT HASTING

10 rue des Cordeliers (Centre); from pl. Victor-Hugo take pl. Louis-Gillian, then rue des Cordeliers.
☎ 02.32.42.89.68
Closed Tues and Nov.

Service noon–2.30pm and 7–9.30pm. This is a little country restaurant slapped right down in the centre of town. There's a small dining room with checked tablecloths and the kitchen serves simple but tasty dishes: chop with cream and apples, duck with Madeira sauce, John Dory with sorrel sauce and couscous. Menus 60F, 75F and 85F. There's also a *formule brasserie* available on weekdays only. You'll get a friendly reception. Free apéritif.

CAMPIGNY   27500 (6KM SE)

🏃 🏠 |●| RESTAURANT L'ANDRIEN-HÔTEL LE PETIT COQ AUX CHAMPS****

La Pommeraie sud.
☎ 02.32.41.04.19 ➡ 02.32.56.06.25
e le/petit.coq.aux.champs@wanadoo.fr
Closed three weeks in Jan.**Swimming pool**. **TV**. **Car park**.

Service 12.30–2.30pm and 7.30–9.30pm. Beautifully located in glorious Normandy countryside, this welcoming restaurant has a relaxed atmosphere. That said, it's fairly sophisticated, and the food is excellent. Menus 195–390F and the one at 240F includes apéritif, wine and coffee. Chef Jean-Marie Huard is constantly inventing new dishes that delight both the palate and the eye. His speciality is a terrific *foie gras pot-au-feu* with crunchy cabbage, but it doesn't come cheap. Rooms with bath 680–865F. Half board, 650–875F per person, is compulsory May–Aug. 10% discount on the room rate.

BEUZEVILLE   27210 (12KM W)

🏠 |●| AUBERGE DU COCHON D'OR**

pl. du Général-de-Gaulle; it's opposite the town hall.
☎ 02.32.57.70.46 ➡ 02.32.42.25.70
e Auberge-du-Cochon-Dor@wanadoo.fr
Closed Mon, and Sun evening Oct–March, and 15 Dec–15 Jan. **Garden**. **TV**. **Car park**.

This inn, which has been well known for a couple of centuries, owes its continuing reputation to the chef who's been marshalling his forces in the kitchen for some twenty years. He specialises in Normandy dishes like eels stewed in cider, chicken *quenelles* with a Camembert sauce, and skate wings with cabbage, all of which you can enjoy in the large rustic dining room, There's a weekday menu at 85F, another at 115F (not served Sun lunch), and others up to 250F. Doubles 225F with shower, 240F with shower/wc and 260F with bath. There's an annexe across the road called the *Petit Castel;* all the rooms overlook the garden where you can have breakfast.

🏃 🏠 |●| HÔTEL DE LA POSTE**

60 rue Constant-Fouché; it's opposite the town hall.
☎ 02.32.20.32.32 ➡ 02.32.42.11.01
Restaurant closed Thurs and mid-Nov to April.
TV. **Garden**. **Car park**.

An authentic coaching inn dated 1844 and you drive through the gateway just like the coaches used to back then. It's in the centre of this town that suffered great destruction during the 100 Years' War. It has a garden and a terrace at the back. Bedrooms with shower or bath go for 250–290F. If you're there at the weekend, half board, 290F per person, is a good deal. Menus 79F (weekday lunchtime) and 99F (which includes cheese and dessert), with others up to 195F. The chef cooks a good number of regional speacialities such as *foie gras* and he has a weakness for *andouille*, which he prepares in several ways. 10% discount for a two-night stay Sept–June, except bank holiday weekends.

ROUEN   76000

SEE MAP OVERLEAF

🏠 HÔTEL CÉLINE**

26 rue de Campulley; off map **B1-1**
☎ 02.35.71.95.23 ➡ 02.35.89.53.71
Closed Sun 1–5pm. **TV**.

A large white building in remarkably peaceful surroundings. Clean modern bedrooms;

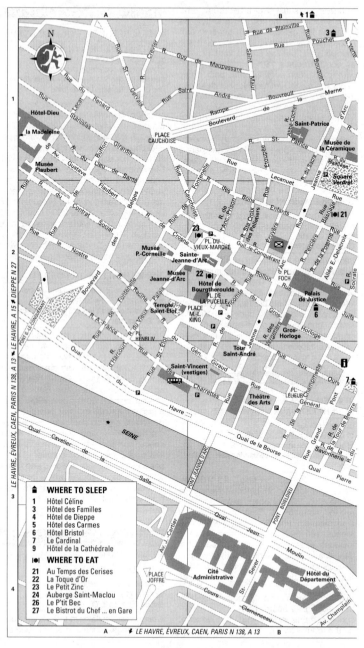

WHERE TO SLEEP

1 Hôtel Céline
3 Hôtel des Familles
4 Hôtel de Dieppe
5 Hôtel des Carmes
6 Hôtel Bristol
7 Le Cardinal
9 Hôtel de la Cathédrale

WHERE TO EAT

21 Au Temps des Cerises
22 La Toque d'Or
23 Le Petit Zinc
24 Auberge Saint-Maclou
26 Le P'tit Bec
27 Le Bistrot du Chef … en Gare

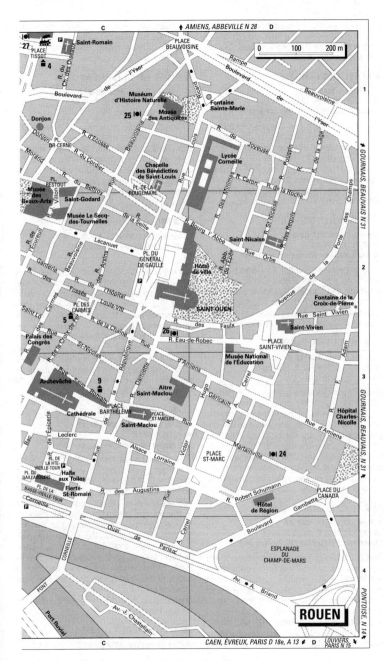

C   D

0   100   200 m

27 PLACE TISSOT
Saint-Romain
PLACE BEAUVOISINE

R. des Carmes
R. Ch. Cristau
Rampe
Boulevard
Beauvoisine

l'Yser
Boulevard
de

Muséum d'Histoire Naturelle
Donjon
Musée des Antiquités
25
Fontaine Sainte-Marie

l'Yser

PL. DR-CERNE
Morand
R. d'Écosse
R. du Cordier
Beauvoisine
Louis
R. de Joyeuse
Poussin
R. de la Cage

Lycée Corneille

PL. BESTOUT
Musée des Beaux-Arts
Saint-Godard
Chapelle des Bénédictins de Saint-Louis
PL. DE LA ROUGEMARE
R. du Beffroy
Rue
R. Caron
R. St-Nicaise
R. de la Roche
Champs

Musée Le Secq-des-Tournelles
R. de la Seille
R. des Minimes
R. Bourg l'Abbé
des Requis
de la Porte

Lecanuet
Beauvoisine
R. des Arsins
Saint-Nicaise
Rue Orbe
Ganterie
R. de l'Hôpital
PL. DU GÉNÉRAL DE GAULLE
Hôtel de ville
R. Abb. de l'Épée
Avenue
Fontaine de la Croix-de-Pierre

R. des Fossés Louis-VIII
SAINT-OUEN
Rue Saint Vivien
Saint-Vivien
PLACE SAINT-VIVIEN

5
PL. DES CARMES
R. de la Chaîne
des Faulx
Adam

Palais des Congrès
St-Nicolas
26
R. Eau-de-Robec
Musée National de l'Éducation

9
Archevêché
République
Damiette
Aître Saint-Maclou
d'Amiens
Hugo
Géricault
Carrel
Hôpital Charles Nicolle

Cathédrale
PLACE BARTHÉLEMY
PLACE ST-MACLOU
Saint-Maclou
Rue
Victor
Rue d'Amiens

R. Saint-Romain
Leclerc
R. Alsace Lorraine
Martainville
PLACE ST-MARC
24

PL. DE LA HTE-VIEILLE-TOUR
Halle aux Toiles
Fierté-St-Romain
PL. DE LA BASSE-VIEILLE-TOUR
R. des Augustins
Rue
Carrel
R. Robert Schumann
PLACE DU CANADA

Corneille
Quai
de
Paris
Hôtel de Région
Boulevard
Gambetta

PONT CORNEILLE

ESPLANADE DU CHAMP-DE-MARS

Av. A. Briand

Port fluvial
Av. J. Chastellain

ROUEN

C

some of the ones on the top floor are particularly large, but they're a little too hot at the height of summer. Reasonably priced doubles with shower 200–250F.

🛏 HÔTEL DES FAMILLES*

4 rue Pouchet. **MAP B1-3**
☎ 02.35.71.88.51 ➡ 02.35.07.54.65
Closed 22 Dec–10 Jan. **TV**. **Pay car park**.

An old house that's been turned into a lovely hotel, conveniently situated for the station. You'll be welcomed with kindness. The bright rooms are delightful, and the decor, which evokes the turn of the 18th and 19th centuries, has been put together with taste and warmth. All the bathrooms are completely modern. Doubles 200F with basin, 280F with shower/wc.

🎄 🛏 |●| HÔTEL BRISTOL

45 rue aux Juifs. **MAP B2-6**
☎ 02.35.71.54.21
Closed Sun and the first fortnight in Aug. **TV**.

A beautifully restored half-timbered building with nine bedrooms, 220–250F for a double with bath and phone. They serve a weekday lunch menu at 57F. House specialities are rabbit with mustard, and apple tart. Brilliant welcome. 5% discount on the room rate.

🎄 🛏 HÔTEL DES CARMES*

33 pl. des Carmes. **MAP C2-5**
☎ 02.35.71.92.31 ➡ 02.35.71.76.96
TV.

A very attractive place on one of the liveliest squares in the middle of town. The decor is bright and new, full of circus imagery, and the young team welcomes you with a smile. The pleasant rooms are full of colour; doubles 250F with shower/wc and 270F with bath. Breakfast 34F – the butter and yoghurt come direct from the farm and the jams are made by small companies using old methods. Excellent value. 10% discount Jan–March.

🎄 🛏 LE CARDINAL**

1 pl. de la Cathédrale. **MAP B3-7**
☎ 02.35.70.24.42 ➡ 02.35.89.75.14
Closed a fortnight Dec/Jan. **TV**. **Pay car park**.

This place has got the best location in town. Almost every room overlooks the cathedral – a splendid sight, particularly when floodlit at night. The owner is perfectly charming and rooms are extremely well maintained – three of them have a terrace which are very tempting for breakfast. Doubles 310F with shower/wc and 340–400F with a brand new bathroom. When it's sunny you can have

breakfast on the terrace. Very good value. They have a deal with the Parc Vieille Tour car park for 31F per night. 10% discount for a two-night stay Sept–June.

🛏 HÔTEL DE LA CATHÉDRALE**

12 rue Saint-Romain. **MAP C3-9**
☎ 02.35.71.57.95 ➡ 02.35.70.15.54
Closed Christmas–1 Jan. **TV**.

In a good, quiet location, on a pedestrianised street that runs alongside the cathedral. This is a delightful little hotel with an internal courtyard. Doubles range from 330F with shower/wc up to 390F with bath; the rooms with shower are prettiest. There's also a tearoom, and breakfast is served on the terrace.

🎄 🛏 |●| HÔTEL DE DIEPPE***

pl. Bernard-Tissot. **MAP C1-4**
☎ 02.35.71.96.00. ➡ 02.35.89.65.21.
TV.

Service noon–2.30pm and 7.30–10pm. A large hotel run with style by a family who've been in the business longer than anyone else in town. The rooms, comfortable but a little impersonal, cost 510–610F, or you can get a special weekend rate of 430F. The restaurant is famed for the pressed Rouen duck and good grills. Set menus at 98F and 128F are served all week, and there's a gastronomic menu at 118F. If you like prefer to eat late, try the hotel bar, which is open until 1am. Free apéritif and space in the public car park nearby.

🎄 |●| LA TOQUE D'OR

11 pl. du Vieux-Marché. **MAP B2-22**
☎ 02.35.71.46.29
Grill closed Sat evening and Sun lunchtime.

This attractive Normandy building is on the very square where Joan of Arc was burned at the stake. The stylish dining room on the ground floor is dignified and peaceful, while upstairs there's an informal room more geared to the younger generation. The 56F menu is not served on Saturday evening or Sunday lunchtime. A couple of other cheap ones 58F and 68F or around 100F à la carte. Dishes such as grilled salmon *escalope* with *beurre blanc* or lemon sole with sorrel and cream sauce. The style and range of dishes in the grill upstairs are less sophisticated than on the ground floor, but they are good value for money. Free coffee.

|●| AU TEMPS DES CERISES

4–6 rue des Basnage. **MAP B2-21**

☎ 02.35.89.98.00
Closed Sat and Mon lunchtimes, and Sun.

No other restaurant in Rouen offers such a wide range of cheese dishes. Cheerful decor with a kitsch dairy theme. Don't miss the coddled eggs, veal escalope with *Pont l'Évèque* cheese or Normandy *fondue*. 60F lunch menu, others 90–125F. The cheap prices and good food draw the local youths.

🎋 |●| AUBERGE SAINT-MACLOU

224–226 rue Martainville. **MAP D3-24**
☎ 02.35.71.06.67
Closed Sun evening and Mon except public holidays.

Housed in a timber-clad building, with a genuine rustic decor and a little terrace open in summer, this restaurant serves the kind of cooking that revives you after an exhausting day trailing around the sights: mussels *à la Normande*, veal chop with cream sauce. Lunch menu 67F then 83–153F. Free coffee.

🎋 |●| LE P'TIT BEC

182 rue Eau-de-Robec. **MAP C2-26**
☎ 02.35.07.63.33
Closed Mon–Thurs evenings, Fri and Sat.

Lovely, bright tea room that also does delicious home-made lunches, including *gratins*, coddled eggs and pastries. Delightful service from the waitresses who race about to keep the regulars happy. There's just one set menu, at 75F, but it's very well put together and satisfying, or you can eat *à la carte* for around 110F. In fine weather, sit out on the terrace, which is on one of the prettiest streets in Rouen. Free apéritif.

🎋 |●| LE BISTROT DU CHEF… EN GARE

pl. Bernard-Tissot (North). **MAP C1-27**
☎ 02.35.71.41.15 ▐➔ 02.35.15.14.43
✉ media-restauration@wanadoo.fr
Closed Sat lunchtime, Sun, Mon evening and Aug.

Chef Gilles Tournadre decided it was time to revive the tradition of being able to get a good meal in a station restaurant. There's a beautiful Art Deco dining room on the ground floor, and a large, hushed one upstairs that's always full of regulars. Dishes such as duck *terrine*, veal escalope with cream and apples, *andouillette* and rice pudding, on a menu at 89F or around 130F *à la carte*. Free coffee.

|●| LE PETIT ZINC

20 pl. du Vieux Marché. **MAP B2–23**
☎ 02.35.89.39.69
Closed Sun and the middle fortnight in Aug.

Service until 10.30pm. This wine bar has a bistro setting and a buzzy atmosphere, and has won a devoted clientele of regulars. The decor, with its magnificent zinc bar and old publicity posters, gives the place a warm, attractive feel. Menus, 130–200F, are listed on a huge blackboard, and feature good classic dishes such as fresh cod or tripe served in a small pan. Other dishes vary according to what fresh produce is available in the market. *À la carte* you'll pay about 165F for a complete meal. Wine by the glass starts at 14F.

CLÈRES   76690 (18.5KM N)

🎋 |●| LE FLAMANT ROSE

pl. de la Halle (Centre); take the D27 and turn off onto the D6 at Boulay.
☎ 02.35.33.22.47
Closed Tues and evenings except by reservation, and 15 Nov–15 Dec.

Service noon–2pm. This simple place serves regional dishes and a few brasserie classics such as calf's head *sauce ravitoge*, home-smoked salmon, perch fillets, duck breasts with cider and tripe in Calvados. 53F lunch menu, with others 72–95F. Reservations essential for dinner. Free house Kir.

RY   76116 (20KM E)

|●| RESTAURANT LE BOVARY

Grande-Rue.
☎ 02.35.23.61.46.
Closed Mon and Tues evenings, and the Feb school holidays.

Flaubert went into raptures over the church and the covered market at Ry. He was also enraptured by this restaurant, which has a cosy atmosphere and wonderful timber façade. They do a weekday lunch menu for 60F, and others up to 170F. Staff are welcoming and the service is hard to fault, which is pretty amazing at these prices. In the evening, the 115F menu is sheer delight, listing dishes such as oysters and smoked salmon or snails in puff pastry. The main courses change with the seasons, but expect something along the lines of duck breast, *coq au vin* or scallops.

SAINT-VALÉRY-EN-CAUX   76460

🎋 🏠 HÔTEL HENRI IV**

16 route du Havre (Southwest); from the centre take the Fécamp–Cany-Barville road; it's several hundred metres along on the left.

☎ 02.35.97.19.62 ➦ 02.35.57.10.01
TV.

Owner Michèle loves taking care of her guests, and she creates a cheerful atmosphere in this large, ivy-covered, brick-built hotel. Comfortable bedrooms from 185F with basin to 295F with bath. The ones at the back are the quietest and there's a patio where you can relax. Michèle also loves flying; if you'd like a trip along the coast, she can arrange it with her friends at the flying club. Free apéritif.

⊜ |O| HÔTEL-RESTAURANT LA MARINE

113 rue Saint-Léger (Southwest); from the bridge go past the Maison Henri IV, the tourist office, it's in the first road on the left.
☎ 02.35.97.05.09 ➦ 02.35.97.05.09
Closed Fri in winter. **TV.**

You'll be made to feel very welcome in this quiet family-run hotel and restaurant. Bedrooms 200F with shower/wc or 240F with bath and TV. There are no fancy trimmings but facilities are perfectly adequate. They serve a weekday menu at 65F, and others 97–167F, in two charming, old-fashioned dining rooms. Regional specialities include skate in cider and apple tart with a Calvados custard. Half board from 195F.

|O| LE RESTAURANT DU PORT

18 quai d'Amont (Centre).
☎ 02.35.97.08.93 ➦ 02.35.97.28.32
Closed Sun and Mon out of season.

As you can guess from the name, this seafood restaurant stands right by the harbour. It's the most refined establishment in town, and the prices reflect that. The 118F menu is simple and classic, while the more interesting one at 198F features *bouill-abaisse*, mackerel tart and smoked salmon *terrine*. They also do a seafood platter and a few meat dishes. The service can't be faulted. Ask for a table by the wide window with a view over the port.

🎄 ⊜ HÔTEL DES ROCHERS**

pl. de l'Église.
☎ 02.35.97.07.06
Closed 1 Feb–5 March. **Disabled access. Garden.**

A big building, which used to be a presbytery, with a delightful walled garden. They have ten or so quiet, comfortable rooms with shower or bath 250–290F. The reception is excellent, and you'll have a pleasant stay. Free coffee.

|O| RESTAURANT LES EMBRUNS

pl. de l'Église; go towards Dieppe and turn left onto the D68 at Veules-les-Roses.
☎ 02.35.97.77.99
Closed Sun evening, Mon out of season, 20 Jan–10 Feb and a few weeks after the end of the season. **Disabled access.**

This used to be a bar and tobacconist's, but has since been transformed into a gourmet restaurant. The weekday lunch menu, 75F, includes starter, main course, and dessert or coffee, and there are others up to 180F. Specialities, drawn from far beyond the local region, include *noisettes* of lamb *à la provençale*, lobster with fresh basil, chicken with morels, and duck breast with mango and preserved ginger.

🎄 ⊜ |O| HÔTEL-RESTAURANT DE LA PLAGE

92 rue Joseph-Heuzé; take the D925 towards Fécamp and it's in the main street 50m from the beach.
☎ 02.35.27.40.77
Closed Sun and Mon evenings and Wed out of season, and for a period during the Feb, Easter and Christmas school holidays.

Monsieur and Mme Pierre will welcome you warmly to this handsome brick establishment with its wooden balconies and delightful turrets. It's very quiet, and the cosy rooms are inexpensive: doubles with shower/wc 220F or 240F with bath. It's rare to find such a reasonably priced hotel of such quality on the coast. The little dining room, a mixture of traditional and modern styles, has been tastefully and lovingly decorated. The fine, quality cooking is as evident in the starters as in the house speciality of warm oysters wrapped in lettuce – try *civet* of winkles and oysters with cider and *coulis* of beetroot with apples. Menus 91–190F. 5% discount if you stay half board.

|O| RESTAURANT L'ESPÉRANCE

76 rue Joseph-Heuzé (Centre).
☎ 02.35.27.42.77

Irène runs this place entirely on her own, so you have to be patient. You eat at her dining table, where she'll sit with you while you decide what you want to order. It may take as much as half an hour before she serves your first course but you can enjoy a glass of Pommeau while you're waiting, and what she cooks is worth waiting for. She offers several menus – if you say what you want to pay, she'll tell you the dishes you're going to eat. Prices start at 35F, believe it or not,then others menus 50–130F: home-made *pâté*, a substantial *crêpe* with cheese or salmon, and home-made pastries. Madame will be delighted with whatever choice you make. Unsurprisingly, the place is full of young people who appreciate her style.

TRÉPORT (LE) 76470

👫 🏠 HÔTEL DE CALAIS

1-5-11 rue de Paris; from the quay, head up towards the church.
☎ 02.35.86.07.46 ➡ 02.27.28.09.00
Car park.

This former coaching inn, perched above the harbour, was built almost two centuries ago. Previous guests have included Victor Hugo. It's lost a little of its character through the most recent refurbishments but the rooms are nice and bright and the bathrooms have been re-fitted. Only some of the rooms overlook the harbour, and they're not all the same size, so it's worth asking for what you want. Doubles 160–200F with basin, 290–420F with bath. They also have furnished rooms and apartments. One free breakfast per room per night, except public holidays and July–Aug.

🍴 MON P'TIT BAR

3–5 rue de la Rade (Centre); it's on the port.
☎ 02.35.86.28.78

A nice, authentic, unstuffy little place that's less a conventional restaurant than a bar which serves food all day until late. Dishes are cooked using fresh market produce, prices are low, and you get a friendly reception. Good seafood platters. Menus 65–98F.

👫🍴 LA MATELOTE

34 quai François-1er (Centre); it's on the harbour.
☎ 02.35.86.01.13 ➡ 02.35.86.17.02
Closed Christmas/New Year holidays. **Disabled access**.

The reason for coming here is the wonderfully fresh fish and seafood. From the first-floor dining room you can watch the boats plying the harbour and the waves breaking on the jetty. Star dishes include fish stew *tréportaise*, fish *choucroute*, grilled sea bream, mussels *au gratin* and seafood platters. There's a 79F menu (not weekends or public holidays), and others 125–270F. Service may be rather affected, but there's a wide choice and no nasty surprises. Free coffee.

CRIEL-SUR-MER 76910 (8.5KM SW)

👫 🏠 🍴 HOSTELLERIE DE LA VIEILLE FERME**

Mesnil-Val-Plage; take the cliff road, and it's in the main street, 300m from the beach.
☎ 02.35.86.72.18 ➡ 02.35.86.12.67
Closed Sun evening and Mon out of season, and 2Dec–7 Jan. **TV**. **Garden**. **Car park**.

An enormous, traditional Normandy building with a terrace, manicured lawn, a large garden with twittering birds and an old cider press. Very comfortable, quiet bedrooms 320F with shower/wc and 380F with bath. The dining room is decorated in a beautiful, traditional style and the menus, 109–239F, feature dishes like seafood *pot-au-feu*, crayfish and Dublin Bay prawns with sherry vinegar, veal sweetbreads with mushroom sauce and Grand Marnier soufflé. Half board, compulsory in season, starts at 345F per person. Free coffee.

VERNEUIL-SUR-AVRE 27130

👫 🏠 🍴 HÔTEL LE SAUMON**

89 pl. de la Madeleine; it's on the church square.
☎ 02.32.32.02.36 ➡ 02.32.37.55.80
Closed Sun evening Nov to Easter, and 18 Dec–5 Jan.
Disabled access. **TV**.

Service noon–2pm and 7.15–9pm. A good, reliable provincial hotel that's well run. Rooms have a view of the old city walls of the square and the magnificent church tower – they're all quiet. Doubles 230–245F with shower/wc and 275–305F with bath. The restaurant is very good, and serves dishes typical of this particular part of Normandy, such as salmon, scallops with orange, lobster, seafood, veal sweetbreads and leg of duck *à la Normande*. Menus 65F, weekdays only, and others up to 159F, 220F *à la carte*. There's also a substantial self-service buffet breakfast for 40F. Free coffee.

VERNON 27200

👫 🏠 🍴 HÔTEL D'ÉVREUX-RESTAURANT LE RELAIS NORMAND***

11 pl. d'Évreux (Centre); it's opposite the post office.
☎ 02.32.21.16.12 ➡ 02.32.21.32.73
✉ hotel/dévreux@libertysurf.fr
Restaurant closed Sun evening except Easter and Whitsun. **TV**. **Car park**.

Service noon–2pm and 7–9.30pm. It's best to book. This place looks like a typical Normandy house from the outside but inside it's been decorated by the Austrian owner to remind her of home. The chef is passionate about good food. Try one of his specialities – fresh duck *foie gras*, *saucisson* of pig's trotters with truffle *jus*, pan-fried *foie gras* with apples, and a thin-crusted apple tart with an iced Pommeau soufflé. Menus 130–165F. Good, clean, quiet rooms 210F with shower/wc, 350F with bath. In the summer there's a conservatory open. 10% discount on the room rate for a two-night stay Nov–March.

🎿|◉| LA HALLE AUX GRAINS

31 rue de Gamilly; it's near the pl. de la République.
☎ 02.32.21.31.99
Closed Sun evening, Mon, a fortnight in Aug and the New Year holiday.

This restaurant is packed year round. The welcome is warm, the setting is attractive, and service is diligent. Everything – including the pizza dough – is prepared from the freshest produce, on the premises. The grilled meat is first rate, or try the snails in pastry cases, the flan soufflé with scallops, the fisherman's platter, finishing with the orange and Grand Marnier soup. Dishes of the day around 42F, or 80–100F for a complete meal. The wine list is interesting and varied, and they offer some by the glass. Free apéritif.

VERNONNET   27200 (1KM N)

|◉| LE RELAIS DES TOURELLES

Vernonnet–rue de la Chaussée (Northeast); it's opposite Vernon on the other side of the Seine.
☎ 02.32.51.54.52 ➡ 02.32.21.63.66
Closed Mon and Sun evening. **Car park**.

This charming restaurant serves a range of regional specialities, including sweetbreads with morels, veal kidneys in mustard and warm oysters on a leek *fondue*. The 99F menu is a bit special; serve yourself from the *hors d'œuvre* buffet as many times as you like, then proceed with a main course, cheese and dessert. There are other menus from 120–169F and good choices *à la carte*.

GIVERNY   27620 (5KM E)

🎿 🏠 |◉| HÔTEL LA MUSARDIÈRE**

123 rue Claude-Monet (Centre); it's just after the museum.
☎ 02.32.21.03.18 ➡ 02.32.21.60.00
Closed Dec. **TV**. **Garden**. **Car park**.

A large house with a veranda and a huge garden, not far from Monet's house. The restau-

rant can get very full, so you may have to wait a long time to be served. They offer menus at 150F and 230F, and there's a *crêperie*, too. For most of the year, the spacious double rooms go for 310–420F with shower/wc or bath. Breakfast 40F. Free apéritif. 10% discount in summer.

|◉| RESTAURANT LES NYMPHÉAS

rue Claude-Monet (Centre); it's across from the Monet museum.
☎ 02.32.21.20.31
Closed Mon except public holidays and 31 Oct–1 April. **Car park**.

Service 11am–6pm. An ideal place for a snack after visiting Monet's house and garden and the American museum. The marble tables give this place a bistro atmosphere and there are two terraces: one opposite the car park and a covered one on the other side of the building. Substantial salads and the dishes on the menus, 89–149F, change daily. You can order a plate of cheese, a simple dish or just an ice cream. Courteous welcome except when it gets very crowded.

🎿|◉| LES JARDINS DE GIVERNY

1 rue du Milieu (chemin du Roy); take the D5 from Vernon and it's on the left 1km after the petrol station.
☎ 02.32.21.60.80 ➡ 02.32.51.93.77
Closed Mon, Sun evening, and Feb. **Car park**.

Lunch noon–3.30pm, brunch until 6pm. This typical Normandy building isn't quite as idyllic as the name suggests, but it's not lacking in charm – and Monet did eat here, as did a host of other famous people including Clémenceau and Aristide Briand. Here you can get classic Normandy dishes served in a Louis XVI dining room. Menus, 130F, 170F and 230F, all feature an unusual *trou Normand* – this is usually a shot of Calvados served to aid digestion, but here you get a cider and Calvados sorbet. Excellent local specialities and fish dishes, some flavoured with seaweed. They're happy to advise on which wine to choose. Free coffee.

FOURGES   27630 (15KM NE)

🎿|◉| LE MOULIN DE FOURGES

38 rue du Moulin; take the D5 towards Magny-en-Vexin and follow the signposts in Fourges.
☎ 02.32.52.12.12 ➡ 02.32.52.92.56
Closed Sun evening and Mon April–Oct, and 1 Nov–25 March.

It's worth coming to this splendid mill on the banks of the fast-flowing Epte for the romantic setting alone. Menus, 180–270F, list finely cooked dishes such as frogs' legs, veal sweetbreads with cream, John Dory *gratiné* with mushrooms, and chocolate *profiteroles*. The shaded terrace is enjoyable in summer, but try to avoid coming at the weekend when the tour buses and cars fight over the parking spaces. Free house apéritif.

VEULES-LES-ROSES   76980

🍴 🏠 |●| RÉSIDENCE DOUCE FRANCE***

13 rue du Docteur Girard (Centre).
☎ 02.35.57.85.30 ➡ 02.35.57.85.31
Closed Tues evening, 15–30 Nov and 5–30 Jan.
Disabled access. Garden. TV.

This exceptional place is an absolute winner. It's become a hotel only recently after considerable refurbishment of the original 17th-century coaching inn. An immense fortified building built of brick and pale-coloured wood, with the coach yard in the middle, it's a quiet, restful and romantic place. The extremely spacious and comfy rooms, more like mini-suites, go for 420–590F. Their *campagnard* breakfast, 55F, includes all sorts of *charcuterie*, breads and sweet buns, or there's a classic breakfast at 45F. If the weather is good, you can eat in the garden, which is sheer bliss. Food is fresh and delicate and the cooking is high-quality traditional. Whatever you do, leave room for a dessert, particularly the iced soufflé with Benedictine. *À la carte* dishes are affordable at 150F, there's a weekday menu at 95F or other set menus 165–280F The tea room is open in the afternoon. Bike hire available. 10% discount on the room rate Mon–Thurs 16 Sept–14 June.

YVETOT   76190

🍴 |●| LE SAINT-BERNARD

1 av. Foch; it's on the N15 in the direction of Le Havre.
☎ 02.35.95.06.75
Closed Mon and Tues evenings, Wed and Feb school holidays.

Well-known gastronomic restaurant with Provençal bistro decor. They serve original cuisine, and offer a *table d'hôte* with an amazing *formule* at 60F. The chef's team pull out all the stops – start by helping yourself from the *hors d'œuvre* buffet, follow with a tasty dish of the day such as sautéed lamb, and finish with *millefeuille*. Wine and coffee are included in the price. Other menus 75–160F. Free *digestif*.

🍴 |●| LA MAISON NORMANDE

18 av. Clémenceau (Northeast).
☎ 02.35.56.50.38
Car park.

This coaching inn is situated, unsurprisingly, on the edge of the N15, just a few minutes off the motorway. It's a particularly attractive 17th-century Normandy building, built round a huge stable yard. The decor is gorgeous – little seem to have changed since Napoleon III stayed here. The cuisine is refined, producing delicious, beautifully presented dishes; home-made *foie gras terrine*, veal kidneys and sweetbreads with Pommeau, duck stuffed with ceps, and chocolate cake with caramel sauce. Menus 95–165F, and a 65F *formule* with starter, main course and dessert. Free coffee.

CROIX MARE   76190 (5KM SE)

🏠 |●| AUBERGE DU VAL AU CESNE

How to get there: it's 3km beyond Yvetot, on the D5.
☎ 02.35.56.63.06 ➡ 02.35.56.92.78
📧 valcesne@chateauxhotels.com
Disabled access. TV. Car park.

Service noon–2pm and 7–9pm. The mandarin ducks and beautiful doves outside this cosy old Normandy inn create a perfect pastoral setting. You can eat outside in summer, and the bantams will come and peck up the crumbs. The food is excellent; try the sole stuffed with prawn mousse, the escalope of turkey made to a peasant recipe, or the juicy steak. They offer a 150F menu with starter, main course and dessert, or you'll pay at least 220F *à la carte*. The delicious food and the unusual setting make the prices a bit easier to swallow. There are a few new rooms with en-suite bathrooms at 480F.

🍴 |●| AUBERGE DE LA FORGE

How to get there: it's on the N15 towards Rouen.
☎ 02.35.91.25.94
Closed Tues evening and Wed except when they fall on public holidays or the day before public holidays.
Disabled access. Car park.

Service noon–2pm and 7–9pm. A discreetly decorated country restaurant serving traditional regional dishes. The service is friendly and professional, and the owner directs his dining room staff like a ringmaster from the kitchens. Menus 99.50–250F; wine is included in the ones at 170F and 250F. Lots of tasty treats, including *fondant* of two salmons with lemon, sliced braised shoulder of beef, guinea-fowl *confit* and broccoli *bavarois*. Free Calvados sorbet.

ALLOUVILLE-BELLEFOSSE   76190 (6KM W)

🏃 |●| AU VIEUX NORMAND

How to get there: take the N15 or the D34.
☎ 02.35.96.00.00

You'll find this country inn next to a grand old oak tree on the village square. Most of the local population eat here, and there's a great atmosphere around the fire. The setting is rustic with nice table linen, and they offer a huge choice of dishes which change constantly: black pudding *gâteau*, skate with cream, steak, *marmite dieppoise* (fish stew), seafood platters, and house tripe, which is a must. Substantial menus 60–105F. They serve red wine by the jug and cider on tap. Free apéritif.

Pays-de-la-Loire

44 Loire-Atlantique

49 Maine-et-Loire

53 Mayenne

72 Sarthe

85 Vendée

ANGERS 49000

SEE MAP ON P.578

♠ HÔTEL DES LICES

25 rue des Lices. **MAP B3-3**
☎ 02.41.87.44.10

A pleasant hotel with thirteen rooms in a city-centre road that couldn't be more attractive. It's an old private residence that's been renovated and offers pretty little rooms decorated in fresh colours. Double glazing is fitted in the ones that overlook the road and they're all very well maintained. Doubles 120F with basin, 170F with shower/wc. Warm, natural welcome. Best to book.

♠ HÔTEL MARGUERITE D'ANJOU

13 pl. Kennedy. **MAP B3-4**
☎ 02.41.88.11.61 ➡ 02.41.87.37.61
TV.

Brilliantly located opposite the impressive Château of Angers. It's essential to book and they ask for a deposit. There are only eight rooms which are spotlessly clean and they all have double glazing and en-suite bathrooms – singles 190F, doubles 230F. Breakfast, served in the bar, is the real thing, with as much bread as you like.

⅍ ♠ CONTINENTAL HÔTEL**

12-14 rue Louis-de-Romain. **MAP B2-8**
☎ 02.41.86.94.94 ➡ 02.41.86.96.60
Closed Sun 12.30–5pm. **Disabled access**. **TV**. **Car park**.

The pretty frontage has an old-style sign outside. The communal areas are warm and bright and the whole place has been completely redecorated. Comfortable rooms cost 280F with shower/wc, 320F with bath. Friendly welcome by the proud owners. Very pleasant little lounge and breakfast room. 15% discount Fri–Sun.

⅍ ♠ HÔTEL DU PROGRÈS**

26 rue Denis-Papin. **MAP B2-10**
☎ 02.41.88.10.14 ➡ 02.41.87.82.93
Closed Christmas Day and New Year's Day. **TV**.

This comfy hotel offers good value for money in a district which is a bit dreary but handy for the train station. The rooms are decorated in tones of blue with identical furnishings, though they're of varying size; doubles 280–290F with shower/wc, 330F for a twin. Excellent facilities and very friendly reception. 10% discount at weekends July–Aug.

⅍ ♠ HÔTEL SAINT-JULIEN**

9 pl. du Ralliement. **MAP C2-9**
☎ 02.41.88.41.62 ➡ 02.41.20.95.19
TV.

You'd be hard pushed to find anything more central, and you'll get a nice welcome. The thirty comfortable, air-conditioned rooms are individually decorated – most have been nicely refurbished in comfy, bourgeois style. Doubles 285–315F with bath. The rooms overlooking the square are the most expensive, while those on the second floor are smaller. The small interior courtyard is ideal for breakfast on a fine day. When you book, you might ask them to reserve a table at the *Provence Caffé* next door (☎ 02.41.87.44.15) which specialises in tasty cooking from the south. It's often booked up a fortnight in advance. 10% discount March, July–Aug and Nov.

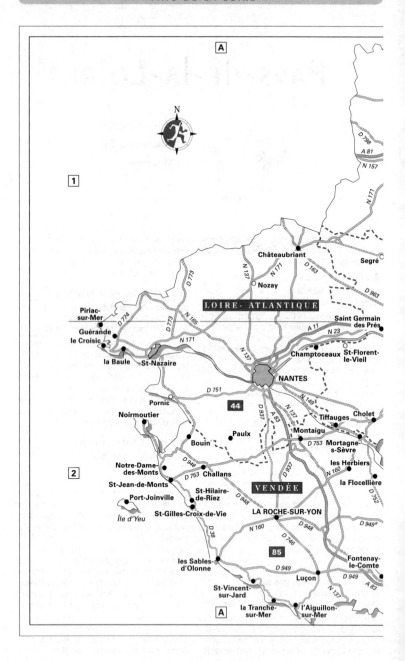

A

N

1

Châteaubriant

Segré

D 798

A 81

N 157

N 171

Nozay

N 137

N 171

D 163

D 963

LOIRE-ATLANTIQUE

Piriac-
sur-Mer

D 774

D 773

N 165

Saint Germain
des Prés

A 11

N 23

Guérande
le Croisic

N 171

D 773

la Baule

St-Nazaire

N 137

Champtoceaux

St-Florent-
le-Vieil

NANTES

Pornic

D 751

N 149

Noirmoutier

44

D 937

A 83

N 137

Tiffauges

Cholet

Paulx

Montaigu

Mortagne-
s-Sèvre

Bouin

D 753

Notre-Dame-
des-Monts

D 948

St-Jean-de-Monts

D 753

Challans

les Herbiers

N 160

la Flocellière

D 752

2

Port-Joinville

St-Hilaire-
de-Riez

VENDÉE

D 948

D 837

Île d'Yeu

St-Gilles-Croix-de-Vie

LA ROCHE-SUR-YON

D 38

N 160

D 948

D 949ᵇ

les Sables-
d'Olonne

85

D 746

Fontenay-
le-Comte

D 949

Luçon

D 949

A 83

St-Vincent-
sur-Jard

N 137

A

la Tranche-
sur-Mer

l'Aiguillon-
sur-Mer

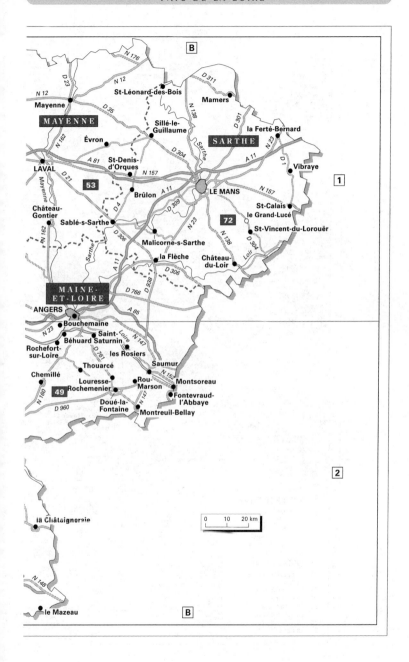

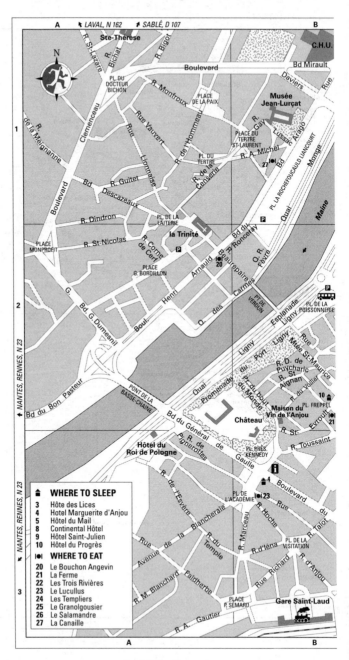

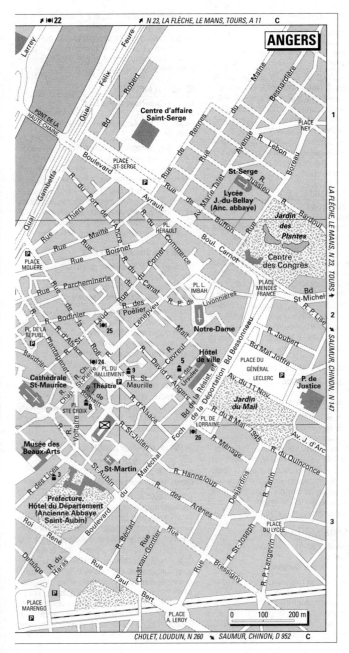

☎ HÔTEL DU MAIL**

8 rue des Ursules. **MAP C2-5**
☎ 02.41.88.56.22 ➡ 02.41.86.91.20
Closed Sun noon–6.30pm and public holidays.
TV. Pay car park.

There isn't another hotel like this one in Angers – it's a 17th-century townhouse in a very quiet street with a definite touch of *Vieille France*. The atmosphere is sophisticated and pleasingly conventional. Refurbished bedrooms furnished and decorated with lots of taste, 295–315F with shower/wc or bath. In fine weather, a buffet breakfast is served on the terrace in the shade of an ancient lime tree. Essential to book.

⍟ ❙●❙ LA CANAILLE

8 bd. Arago. **MAP B1-27**
☎ 02.41.88.56.11
Closed Sat lunchtime, Sun, public holidays and the first three weeks in Aug. **Disabled access. Car park**.

This run-down district is benefiting from a second wind and the young owners opened this restaurant to add some sun and life to the scene. The cooking style is simple, tasty and appealing – even to kids: steak kebabs, simple grilled fish and puddings with childish names. The cheapest menu is 60F (weekday lunch), rising to 85F weeknights, then 98F; you'll pay 120–150F *à la carte*. Free glass of Crémant de Loire after your meal.

❙●❙ LE BOUCHON ANGEVIN

44 rue Beaurepaire. **MAP A2-20**
☎ 02.41.24.77.97
Closed Sun, Mon, one week in Feb, and Aug.

A wine cellar with a restaurant at the back, in the heart of the Doutre district. Two small, characterful dining rooms and a big fireplace. Menus 61F weekday lunchtimes, 79F weeknights, and 98F weekend evenings. An interesting selection of dishes *à la carte* – deep-fried Camembert, salad with hot *rillauds* and Angers' speciality of potted, shredded pork, grilled *andouillette*, duck thigh *confit* and home-made pastries. You'll pay about 140F.

⍟ ❙●❙ RESTAURANT LA FERME

2–4 pl. Freppel. **MAP B2-21**
☎ 02.41.87.09.90
Closed Sun evening, Wed. **Car park**.

One of the most popular restaurants in town, with a terrace in the quiet shadow of the cathedral and a stunning dining room. It's stayed successful over the years by offering reliable cooking and generously flavoured dishes. When it's crowded the service can get slapdash. Weekday lunch menu 68F, then 92–177F. They specialise in poultry – *poule-au-pot*, escalope of *foie gras*, and breast of duck with apples. *À la carte* you can have warm *rillauds d'Anjou*, duck *choucroute* or calf's head. Main courses 60–70F. Free coffee.

❙●❙ LES TEMPLIERS

5 rue des Deux-Haies. **MAP B2-24**
☎ 02.41.88.33.11
Closed Sun, Mon lunchtime and a fortnight at Christmas.

A bright dining room with medieval decor. Lances, old swords and flags ornament the stone walls, illuminated by torch lights. It's best to book, because the tasty, traditional cooking has a lot of fans locally. Dishes are classics and well prepared using fresh produce. Weekday lunch menu 74F, *menu du templier* at 110F and *menu du Roy* at 148F. There's not a dress code exactly, but they're not keen on jeans.

⍟ ❙●❙ LES TROIS RIVIÈRES

62 promenade de Reculée. Off map **B1-22**
☎ 02.41.73.31.88
Closed Mon and Tues evenings and Wed except May–Aug. **Disabled access. Car park**.

You'll need some form of transport to get to this famous riverside fish restaurant which has a panoramic dining room. It's always full, even on weekdays, so it's best to book. The welcome and service are efficient but not formal. They specialise in fish and the cooking is excellent: surf and turf salad, salmon tournedos with red Anjou wine, fillet of perch in butter sauce. Weekday lunch menu 85F then 102–185F. Lots of good dry white wines – try the Domaine de Brizé or take the owner's advice. Free apéritif.

⍟ ❙●❙ LE GRANDGOUSIER

7 rue Saint-Laud. **MAP B2-25**
☎ 02.41.87.81.47
Closed Sat and Wed lunchtimes, Sun, and Christmas.

The beautiful dining room dates from the 16th century and has walls made of tuff, a local stone, and sturdy beams. Local cuisine with literary references: *Pantagruel* or *Gargantua* salads and *Maître Alcofribas terrine* (chicken livers and grapes macerated in Coteaux de l'Aubance). The 89F menu, available lunchtimes and dinner up to 10pm, includes an apéritif and Anjou wine. The huge 149F menu, which includes a glass of different wine with each dish, offers *andouillette* and potato *salade de mémé Gargamelle* followed by duck tournedos. There's a terrace. Free coffee.

●I LE LUCULLUS

5 rue Hoche. **MAP B3-23**
☎ 02.41.87.00.44
Closed Sun evening, Sun lunchtime in season, Mon, the
Feb school holidays and end July to end Aug.

A very good restaurant in 17th-century tuff
cellars. Faultless service and carefully prepared dishes: eggs with morels, veal sweetbreads with Savennières wine sauce, ox
cheek, fillet of zander and chocolate *millefeuille*. The 130F weekday *formule* is a good
way of investigating the region's specialities
and the dishes are accompanied by local
wines. Weekday lunch menu 90F and gastronomic menus 170–300.

●I LA SALAMANDRE

1 bd. du Maréchal Foch. **MAP B3-26**
☎ 02.41.88.99.55
Closed Sun, and Mon also in Aug.

This restaurant, on the premises of the *Hôtel
d'Anjou*, has a reputation for consistently
good cuisine. The well-proportioned dining
room has an elegant, classic decor, with a
portrait of François I on a wooden medallion.
Smart clientele and perfect service. The dishes speak for themselves: *sabayon* of pan-
fried oysters with Layon wine, grilled sea
bass with basil and cream sauce and a *tian* of
vegetables. Lunch menu 140F or 175F and
240F. Excellent wine list.

BOUCHEMAINE   49080 (11KM SW)

●I RESTAURANT LA TERRASSE

la Pointe de Bouchemaine and pl. Ruzebouc.
☎ 02.41.77.11.96
Closed Sun evening out of season.

The dining room offers one of the most wonderful panoramic views of the Maine. It's well
known for its cooking and the sauces are
heavenly. Menus start at 98F (weekday
lunchtime), then 135F and 320F. Dishes like
salmon *rillettes*, *mignon* of pork with ginger,
and salmon fillet with sorrel. The quality of
service sometimes slips. Best to book.

SAINT-SATURNIN-SUR-LOIRE   49320 (17KM SE)

●I AUBERGE DE LA CAILLOTTE

2 rue de la Loire (Centre).
☎ 02.41.54.63.74
Closed Mon and Tues in winter.

In autumn and winter you eat in the ravishing,
rustic dining room and there's a spacious,
shady terrace where you eat in summer.
Hospitable welcome with a touch of humour.

Best of all, though, is the cooking and the
appealing wine list. Menus, 115F, 158F and
175F, list an ever-changing selection of dishes: zander with *beurre blanc*, crayfish, pan-
fried eels and river fish. À *la carte* you'll pay
180F – and it's worth every centime. You'll
feel very relaxed here.

BÉHUARD   49170 (18KM SW)

●I RESTAURANT LE NOTRE-DAME

12 pl. de l'Église; follow the south bank of the Loire.
☎ 02.41.72.20.17
Closed evenings and Wed.

A nice little restaurant in one of the most captivating villages in the Angers area. Inside the
decor may be pretty ordinary but the terrace
on the square is very pleasant on a fine day.
The restaurant is known particularly for its fish.
There's a 92F lunch menu, while for 135F you
get one main course, for 175F two courses –
choose from dishes like *friture* of eels or rack of
veal à *l'angevine*. Pleasant and attentive staff.

⅀I RESTAURANT LES TONNELLES

rue Principale.
☎ 02.41.72.21.50
Closed Sun evening and Mon March–June and
Sept–Oct, Sun evening–Thurs evening Nov–Dec, and
Jan. **Car park**.

The terrace is delightful in summer when you
sit under the arbour and enjoy the wonderful
food. Weekday *formule* 140F, menus
190–360. The specialities are principally fish
dishes – roast zander with *beurre blanc*, eel,
pike and *cotriade* (stew of white fish with
mussels) – but also try their roast pigeon or
rabbit *confit*. Very tasty. Free apéritif.

SAINT-GERMAIN-DES-PRÉS   49170 (23KM W)

●I LA CHAUFFETERIE

How to get there: take the D15 between Saint-Germain-
des-Prés and Saint-Augin-des-Bois or the A11,
Beaufreau-Chalonnes exit.
☎ 02.41.39.92.92
Closed Mon–Wed. **Car park**. **Disabled access**.

This little farmhouse, deep in the country,
was taken over by a Parisian couple a few
years ago. There are two gorgeous dining
rooms with fireplaces and the chairs are
dressed in the style of the Middle Ages. They
offer good, simple cooking: pike *mousseline*,
zander with *beurre blanc*, and blancmange
perfumed with orange-blossom water.
Menus 105–160F. You'll get attentive service
from the owner – who is a trained astrologer
– while his wife runs the kitchen.

BAUGÉ 49150

🎄 🏠 🍽 HOSTELLERIE DE LA BOULE D'OR**

4 rue du Cygne (Centre).
☎ 02.41.89.82.12
Closed Sun evening, Mon and Christmas. **TV**. **Car park**.

A friendly little hotel with ten attractively decorated rooms overlooking an internal courtyard. Doubles with shower/wc and TV, 310–410F. Half board, available at weekends July–Aug, costs 410F. The restaurant specialises in regional, conventional cooking. Menus 90–190F. Best to book. Free apéritif.

BAULE (LA) 44500

🎄 🏠 HÔTEL MARINI**

22 av. Clémenceau (Centre); it's between the tourist office and the railway station.
☎ 02.40.60.23.29 ➡ 02.40.11.16.98
TV. **Charge garage**.

Recent renovation work has given this little hotel a pleasantly fresh, youthful appearance. The comfortable, tastefully furnished rooms are particularly good value for money. Doubles with shower/wc 230–400F, or 372–420F with bath. Hospitable owners. 10% discount Sept–June.

🎄 🏠 🍽 HÔTEL LUTÉTIA-RESTAURANT LE ROSSINI**

13 av. des Evens (South); it's near the town hall.
☎ 02.40.60.25.81 ➡ 02.40.42.73.52
Closed Sun evening and Mon out of season and Jan. **TV**. **Car park**.

An elegant gastronomic restaurant that's a real classic, with a dining room decorated in 1930s style. You'll get a welcoming smile from *la patronne*, while her husband, the chef, creates stylish, fresh dishes – try fillet of beef Rossini with goose *foie gras*, fish cooked in a salt crust or roast salmon in *beurre rouge*. The desserts are delicate and unusual – fig *au gratin* with almond cream. 120F weekday menu, others 170–245F. Double rooms 320–450F. Half board is compulsory July–Aug, at 300–400F. Free coffee.

🎄 🏠 🍽 HOSTELLERIE DU BOIS**

65 av. Lajarrige (Centre).
☎ 02.40.60.24.78 ➡ 02.40.42.05.88
✉ hostellerie-du-bois@wanadoo.fr
Closed Nov–March. **Garden**. **TV**. **Car park**.

Set back from a very lively street, this hotel is shaded by pine trees and has a flower garden. There are fifteen bedrooms, 360–380F with shower/wc. Half board, 380–420F, is compulsory July–Aug. Menus 95–195F. A delightful, pleasantly cool place that's full of flowers and souvenirs of Southeast Asia. 10% discount on the room rate Sept–June.

🍽 RESTAURANT CHEZ L'ÉCAILLEUR

av. des Ibis; it's near the market.
☎ 02.40.60.87.94
Closed evenings, Mon out of season, a fortnight in the Feb school holidays and a fortnight in Nov.

Undiluted pleasure here: treat yourself to a dozen plump Brittany oysters or clams with a $1/2$ litre of Gros-Plant wine. Menu at 42F and around 100F for a meal. Enjoy it all at the relaxed bar. Bliss.

🎄🍽 LA FERME DU GRAND CLOS

52 av. de Lattre-de-Tassigny; opposite the riding school.
☎ 02.40.60.03.30
Closed Tues and Wed out of season, 15 Nov–15 Dec.

The poshest *crêperie* in town – it's delightful and not at all stuffy. The wheat and buckwheat *crêpes* are equally delicious and the little farm is really attractive. They also produce delicious, home-cooked dishes – *cassoulet* with duck *confit* or calf's head *sauce gribiche* – with *formules* from 80F. Free coffee.

POULIGUEN (LE) 44510 (3KM W)

🍽 RESTAURANT L'OPÉRA DE LA MER

promenade du Port; it's by the jetty.
☎ 02.40.62.31.03
Closed Wed, Thurs out of season, and 15 Nov–15 Dec. **Car park**.

Families strolling by the harbour stop under the trees to watch the smiling, relaxed people and pirouetting staff at this popular restaurant. The terrace is chock-a-block in summer. They serve fresh salads, nice fish soup and good oysters. Menus 100–180F. There's a charge for the car park July–Aug.

PORNICHET 44380 (6KM E)

🎄 🏠 🍽 HÔTEL-RESTAURANT LE RÉGENT**

150 bd. des Océanides.
☎ 02.40.61.05.68 ➡ 02.40.61.25.53
Closed Mon in winter and 15 Dec–15 Jan. **TV**. **Car park**.

A family hotel facing the sea. It's bright and colourful, if a little bland. Doubles 305–385F with shower/wc, 385–425F with bath. Half board, 280–340F, is compulsory July–Aug. The restaurant specialises in fish and seafood: the yellow ling charlotte with shellfish *coulis* and duo of zander and pike with a reduction of Saumur red wine are particularly good. Menus 110–198F. Free apéritif.

🎋 🏠 |●| VILLA FLORNOY

7 av. Flornoy.
☎ 02.40.11.60.00 ➡ 02.40.61.86.47
Closed Nov–March. **Garden**. **TV**.

A charming hotel in a quiet street just 300m from the beach. It feels like a family house and has been decorated with taste. The sitting room is pleasant and comfortable and attractively furnished with period furniture, and there's a perfect garden where you can relax with a book. Doubles 325–430F with shower/wc or 390–540F with bath. They serve meals in the evening only, for 120F. Free apéritif.

🎋 |●| RESTAURANT LA BRIGANTINE

How to get there: it's on the harbour.
☎ 02.40.61.03.58
Closed Tues evening and Wed except school holidays, and mid-Nov to mid-Feb. **Car park**.

Though surrounded by dour, grey concrete, this is the only *crêperie* in town with a terrace on the harbour. Pleasant decor and a log fire in the dining room. They do good *crêpes*, a range of grills over the open fire – rib of beef, duck breast, or baron of lamb– and some more exotic dishes such as chicken satay or Creole black pudding from the Antilles. Menus 90–130F but *à la carte* is the better option. Free apéritif.

BATZ-SUR-MER   44740 (8KM W)

🎋 |●| RESTAURANT LE DERWIN

rue du Golf; it's on the seafront between Batz and Le Pouliguen.
Closed Tues, Wed and Thurs except during the school holidays, and Oct–April. **Car park**.

This place is popular with the sailing fraternity. It has no telephone or electronic till – cash or cheque only – but it's always full. It's the ideal place for a plate of mussels, seafood and *crêpes* while you gaze out to sea. Expect to pay 80–120F per person. Free coffee.

BOUIN   85230

🎋 🏠 |●| HÔTEL LE MARTINET**

1 pl. de la Croix-Blanche; it's beside the church.
☎ 02.51.49.08.94 ➡ 02.51.49.83.08
Restaurant closed Jan–Feb. **Garden**. **Swimming**

pool. **TV**. **Car park**.

This large, beautiful 18th-century house offers a choice of bedrooms – old-fashioned ones overlooking the square, or newer ones at ground level that give direct access to the garden and swimming pool. Doubles 290–350F. Françoise has redecorated the place and also takes care of reception. Her sons also have a role; Emmanuel looks after the kitchen garden and does the cooking while Jean-François supplies the fish and seafood. Breakfast is served in the old dining room which smells delightfully of beeswax. In the evening, typical choices include a dozen oysters, *panaché* of eel and frogs' legs, and grilled sea bass. Menus 100–125F. 10% discount on the room rate Sept–June.

🎋 |●| RESTAURANT LE COURLIS

15 rue du Pays-de-Monts; it's on the edge of town.
☎ 02.51.68.64.65
Closed Mon, Wed evening except July–Aug and the school holidays.

A white, rather squat building that's typical of the area. The spruce, flower-filled dining room is a nice place to enjoy the mouthwatering cuisine and a range of specialities that change with the seasons – zander with *beurre blanc*, turbot with bacon, and oyster and *foie gras* turnover. Weekday menu 83F and others 118–450F. Free apéritif or coffee.

BRULÔN   72350

🎋 🏠 |●| HÔTEL-RESTAURANT LA BOULE D'OR

How to get there: it's in the main square.
☎ 02.43.95.60.40 ➡ 02.43.95.07.78
Closed Sat and Sun evenings, a fortnight in Jan. **TV**.

Nothing – the owner, the customers or the atmosphere – seems to have changed in this sturdy village house over the past three decades. The aromas wafting from the plates as they're carried into the dining room are still wonderful. The cuisine is traditional and uses only fresh produce. You can feast without breaking the bank – the weekday menu costs 58F. You get half a dozen oysters, scorpion fish served with sorrel sauce, a delicious *noix* of rib steak, a cheese platter and dessert. Try the chef's specialities: *suprême* of chicken with pineapple or fillet of zander with cream and mussels. Clean, comfortable bedrooms, 120F with basin or 175F with shower/wc. 10% discount on the room rate depending on length of stay. Free coffee.

CHALLANS   85300

☆ ☎ HÔTEL DE L'ANTIQUITÉ

14 rue Gallieni.
☎ 02.51.68.02.84 ➡ 02.51.35.55.74
Swimming pool. TV. Car park.

Very ordinary from the outside but inside it's charmingly bourgeois. Refined, period furniture that's shown off to best advantage. The rooms are spacious and most of them have been tastefully renovated. The rooms, 300–400F, are all set around the swimming pool which is where you have breakfast. It's a blissful place run by a nice, energetic couple. 10% discount Sept–June.

☆ |●| RESTAURANT LA GITE DU TOURNE PIERRE

Route de Saint-Gilles; it's 3km by the D69, between Challans and Soullans.
☎ 02.51.68.14.78
Closed Sat lunchtime, Sun evening, a fortnight in March and Oct. **Disabled access. Car park.**

Time seems to have stopped at this beautiful low house, and you will discover new flavours in the dishes. Lobster has pride of place alongside home-made *foie gras*, duck *Rossini* with truffles and *foie gras*, and *fricassée* of sole with mushrooms and *foie gras*. Menus 195–370F. Faultless, unpretentious service. A good place if you're feeling flush. Free apéritif.

SALLERTAINE   85300 (8.54KM NW)

☆ |●| RESTAURANT LA COURONNE

Route de Beauvoir/Mer; take the Beauvoir road and turn left after 2km.
☎ 02.51.49.11.33
Closed Sun evening and Mon out of season.

Good food at affordable prices. You eat either in the panelled dining room with its old cartwheel or at the large counter with its impressive model boat. Menus, 68–168F, list dishes like fillet of duck, fish wrapped in crisp pancakes, and pear caramel with raspberry juice. You'll get smiling service, well-presented food and excellent value. Free apéritif.

SAINT-GERVAIS   85230 (12KM NW)

|●| RESTAURANT LA PITCHOUNETTE

48 rue Bonne-Brise (West); it's on the D948 in the direction of Beauvoir and Noirmoutier.
☎ 02.51.68.68.88
Closed Mon out of season and mid-Sept to mid-Aug.
Disabled access. Car park.

A really welcoming, pretty house with flowers everywhere, but Gérard Thoumoux's cooking outshines the decor. There are many tempting dishes: duck *foie gras* with a hot *brioche*, *cassolette* of calf's sweetbreads with a *foie gras* and mushroom sauce, fresh catch of the day and snails according to Grandma Marguerite's recipe. Weekday lunch *formule* 60F and menus 108–168F

CHAMPTOCEAUX   49270

☆ ☎ |●| HÔTEL-RESTAURANT LE CHAMPALUD**

promenade du Champalud; it's in the centre of town.
☎ 02.40.83.50.09 ➡ 02.40.83.53.81
Restaurant closed Sun evening out of season and three weeks in Jan. **TV. Disabled access. Car park.**

The hotel is in a charming village on the banks of the Loire and it's been completely overhauled. There are a dozen comfortable rooms 280–300F. The restaurant has a good reputation. Set *menu du jour* 67F (including wine), or 87–220F. À la carte, try *terrine*, zander fillet with *beurre blanc* or frogs' legs. They offer various sports facilities – tennis courts nearby, a gym and mountain bikes – and a sitting room filled with board games. Friendly, very energetic owner and good value for money. 10% discount on the room rate, Sept–June and free use of the gym.

CHÂTAIGNERAIE (LA)   85120

☎ |●| L'AUBERGE DE LA TERRASSE**

7 rue de Beauregard (Centre).
☎ 02.51.69.68.68 ➡ 02.51.52.67.96
Closed Fri evening, Sat lunchtime and Sun evening Sept to mid-June. **TV. Car park.**

This hotel, in a well-restored, substantial house in a quiet road, has a family atmosphere and a quality restaurant. Double rooms 200–250F with shower/wc. The owner, Monsieur Leroy, provides a culinary voyage of discovery through the Vendée marshes and the sea. Specialities include eel with butter and bacon and snails prepared in different ways. Menus 60–180F. There's a shady terrace which has a lovely view.

VOUVANT   85120 (12.5KM S)

☆ ☎ |●| HÔTEL-RESTAURANT L'AUBERGE DE MAÎTRE PANNETIER**

pl. du Corps-de-Garde (Centre); take the D938 in the

direction of Fontenay-le-Comte, turn onto the D30 at Alouette; it's on the square, next to the church.
☎ 02.51.00.80.12 ➡ 02.51.87.89.37
Closed Sun evening and Mon out of season, 15 Feb–6 March and 15–30 Nov. **TV**.

This inn, in the centre of one of France's most beautiful villages, near the forest of Mervent, offers a cheery welcome and good accommodation. Pleasant bedrooms with light wood furniture go for 230F with shower/wc, 280F with bath. Most important of all, the restaurant is good. You eat in a superb vaulted dining room with stone walls, oil lamps on the tables and a fireplace. The food is of the "rustic-chic" variety and chef David Prand works wonders in the kitchen: foie gras with figs, king prawns in a pastry pouch, pavé of turbot with asparagus, bass with morels, or veal sweetbreads with crayfish. Weekday menu 75F, and 100–350F. 10% discount on the room rate June–Sept.

CHÂTEAUBRIANT   44110

I●I LE POÊLON D'OR

30 [bis] rue du 11-Novembre; it's close to the post office and the town hall.
☎ 02.40.81.43.33
Closed Sun evening, Mon, a fortnight in Jan and the last three weeks in Aug.

The service is nicely formal and the rustic decor has a very French feel. Gourmet dishes like tender, succulent Châteaubriand with marrow bone, John Dory sauce mousseline, fillet of bass en écailles and a sensational apple tart with lavender. Menus 102–300F.

CHÂTEAU-DU-LOIR   72500

🏄 🏠 I●I HÔTEL-RESTAURANT LE GRAND HÔTEL**

59 av. Aristide-Briand (Centre).
☎ 02.43.44.00.17 ➡ 02.43.44.37.58
Closed mid-Nov to mid-Dec. **TV. Car park**.

This old coaching inn offers doubles with bath for 250F. The superb cuisine adds to the establishment's reputation. Meals are served in a charming, old-style dining room with a painted ceiling. Dishes such as calf's head ravigotte, duck foie gras, terrine of young rabbit in aspic, and marmite sarthoise (a stew of chicken, rabbit, ham and mushrooms). Menus 99–210F. Free coffee.

VOUVRAY-SUR-LOIR   72500 (5KM E)

🏠 I●I HÔTEL DU PORT GAUTIER-RESTAURANT LES PAS PERDUS

Le Port Gauthier; take the D61 from Marçon to Port Gauthier, then the D64.
☎ 02.43.79.44.62 ➡ 02.43.44.66.03
Closed Sun evening, Mon out of season and mid-Jan to mid-Feb. **TV. Car park**.

The owners of this modern little hotel built it alongside their home, a converted railway station. Doubles with shower/wc or bath 230–260F. The restaurant offers delicious menus 90–215F. The cheapest lists tartare of tomatoes and leg of rabbit with cloves of garlic baked whole. Enjoyable and original.

VAAS   72420 (8KM SW)

🏄 🏠 I●I HÔTEL-RESTAURANT LE VÉDAQUAIS**

Centre; take the D305 or the D30.
☎ 02.43.46.01.41 ➡ 02.43.46.37.60
Closed Fri and Sun evenings, Mon and the Feb school holidays. **TV. Car park**.

This cheery, old-fashioned village hotel occupies the old schoolhouse. Daniel Beauvais is a very good chef who doesn't talk much, while his wife, Sylvie, is a very good hostess who chats away quite happily. They offer a menu du marché, 60F, and others 85–220F. Each is a real treat – fresh-tasting, straightforward and brimming with creativity: rillette of zander with marinated eel, freshwater fish soup or leg of duck with pears, and a few little treats such as apple tart with rosemary honey for dessert. The rooms, with shower/wc 250F, are just as pleasant. 10% discount on the room rate.

MARÇON   72340 (8.5KM NE)

🏄 I●I RESTAURANT DU BŒUF

21 pl. de l'Église (Centre); take the N138, then fork onto the D305.
☎ 02.43.44.13.12
Closed Sun evening, Mon, Mon lunchtime July–Aug, and end Jan to beginning of March.

Creole dishes take pride of place on the menus here; they start at 75F (weekdays) and go up to 200F. Dishes include chicken with crayfish, prawn fricassée with coconut milk and lamb colombo. Have some punch and a few fritters to start with and round things off with a house liqueur. Free coffee.

RUILLÉ-SUR-LOIR 72340 (16KM NE)

♠ I●I HÔTEL-RESTAURANT SAINT PIERRE

42 rue Nationale (Centre); take the D305, it's 6km from
La Chartre-sur-le-Loir.
☎ 02.43.44.44.36
Closed Sun evening and the last fortnight in Dec.

This appealing little village hotel, with unassuming façade and cosy, friendly atmosphere, is one of a dying breed. The nice proprietress fusses over all her customers and
nobody around these parts can rival her 53F
menu ouvrier – the dozens of plates of *hors-
d'œuvres* are served out ahead of time to
deal with the rush. A bottle of red wine is
included in the price. On Sunday there is a
choice of leg of lamb, duck leg with pepper or
sirloin, salad, cheese platter and dessert.
They offer a few plain, simple, adequate doubles with basin for 110F.

CHÂTEAU-GONTIER 53200

♠ I●I HÔTEL DU CERF**

31 rue Garnier (South).
☎ 02.43.07.25.13 ➡ 02.43.07.02.90
Garden. TV. Disabled access. Secure parking

This hotel, next to the cattle market, has had a
facelift. As you would expect, the rooms overlooking the garden are quieter than the others:
220F for a double with shower/wc or bath.
They do meals in the evenings, Mon–Thurs.

⅔ ♠ I●I HOSTELLERIE DE MIRVAULT**

rue du Val-de-Mayenne; it's signposted, about 2km from
the town centre.
☎ 02.43.07.13.17 ➡ 02.43.07.66.90
Closed Mon and Wed lunchtime in summer, and
Jan–Feb. **TV**.

Way out in the countryside on the banks of
the Mayenne, this relaxing place is run by an
English couple. There are eleven rooms with
full facilities and river views. Doubles with
bath or shower cost 250F, which is remarkable value given the quality of the establishment. They've even set aside a reading room.
The cooking is also high quality: guinea-fowl
terrine with Pommeau and chicken *à
l'angevine*. Weekday menu 78F then others
88–178F. Free *digestif*.

I●I RESTAURANT L'AQUARELLE

Pendu-en-Saint-Fort, route de Ménil (South); it's 400m
from the centre; follow the road that runs along the
north bank of the Mayenne, towards Sablé, and at the
roundabout take the Ménil road.

☎ 02.43.70.15.44
Closed Sun evening out of season, Mon, 15–31 Jan and
the last week in Sept. **Car park**.

Situated outside town on the banks of the
Mayenne, this place will set you dreaming.
The terrace is beautiful on summer days, and
the panoramic dining room, air-conditioned
in summer, offers a magnificent view of the
river. The light, creative cooking includes
dishes like grilled freshwater fish served with
lime butter, a medley of lamb, and langoustine with thyme. Menus 82–199F.

COUDRAY 53200 (5KM SE)

I●I RESTAURANT L'AMPHITRYON

2 route de Daon (Centre); take the D22 and it's opposite
the church.
☎ 02.43.70.46.46
Closed Tues evening, Wed, Sun evening Nov–March, the
Feb school holidays, 1 May, the first fortnight in July,
and 24 and 25 Dec. **Disabled access**.

This place may look just like just any other
inn, but it's gained a reputation as one of
the most delightful places in the *département*. There's something invigorating
about both the cooking and the decor. Set
menus 95–140F. Dishes are light and
colourful: *terrine* of sardines and shrimps
with cardamon, fillet of trout with potatoes,
millefeuille of Camembert and *crêpe* with
apples. If you have a big appetite, try the
regional menu.

DAON 53200 (11.5KM SE)

⅔ ♠ I●I HÔTEL-RESTAURANT À L'AUBERGE

10 rue Dominique-Godivier; take the D22.
☎ 02.43.06.91.14
Closed Sat out of season, a week in Feb, a week in Oct.

A good country inn specialising in fish and
seafood dishes. It's popular with fishermen
because the menus are good and cheap,
50F (Mon–Sat) then 90–130F. Basic bedrooms if you're stuck for somewhere to stay.
Doubles 150–170F. Free apéritif.

BALLOTS 53350 (30KM NW)

⅔ I●I RESTAURANT L'AUBERGE DU MOUILLOTIN

9 pl. de l'Église (Centre); take the D22, and 9.5km beyond
Craon turn onto the D25 towards La Guerche-de-Bretagne.
☎ 02.43.06.61.81
Closed Tues evening, Wed, ten days in Feb and a
fortnight in Aug. **Disabled access. Garden**.

This restaurant serves delicious omelettes with all sorts of tasty fillings – bone marrow, foie gras or snails – along with mouthwatering dishes like *mousseline* of perch with *beurre blanc* or freshwater fish in cider. Weekday menu 60F, others 75–130F. As a change from the rich gourmet dishes they also serve savoury or sweet *crêpes*. The pretty dining room overlooks the garden. Free apéritif.

CHEMILLÉ   49120

🎣 🏠 |●| L'AUBERGE DE L'ARRIVÉE

15 rue de la Gare.
☎ 02.41.30.60.31 ➡ 02.41.30.78.45
Restaurant closed Sun evening out of season and the first week in Jan. **TV**. **Car park**.

A private mansion offering perfectly adequate doubles with shower/wc or bath from 250F. Half board is compulsory at high-summer weekends (190F per person) but that's no hardship, because the food, served in a plush dining room, is very good. Menus 69F (noon–1.30pm and evenings up to 8.30pm), then 89–169F. *À la carte* there's *ballotine* of duck with *foie gras*, escalope of zander with wild nettle shoots, braised swordfish with herbs, prawn kebabs with lime and wild rice, and pork fillet with spices. Pleasant terrace filled with pot plants. Excellent reception. Free coffee and breakfast if you have an evening meal and stay overnight.

CHEMILLÉ-CHANGÉ   49220

🎣 🏠 |●| AUBERGE LA TABLE DU MEUNIER

How to get there: take the N162 north from Lion-d'Angers, then the D78.
☎ 02.41.95.10.98 ➡ 02.41.95.10.52
Closed Mon evening, Tues and Wed except July–Aug, Sun evening Nov–March, and 29 Feb–9 March.
Disabled access. **Car park**.

Set in a village full of flowers, with a gentle river running by and a huge statue in the entrance, this dreamy place offers guaranteed peace and quiet. There are six different, charmingly decorated dining rooms and a huge panoramic terrace. Really tasty local cuisine with a good reputation: house *foie gras*, zander with *beurre blanc*, duck breast with apples and *beurre blanc*, and *nougat glacé* with a raspberry *coulis*. Menus

105–255F. They have a few rooms on a boat tied up nearby and you'll be lulled to sleep by the sound of the flowing water. Free apéritif.

CHOLET   49300

|●| LE PASSÉ SIMPLE

181 rue Nationale.
☎ 02.41.75.90.061
Closed Sun and Mon except public holidays, and a fortnight in Aug.

Fish dishes are the speciality in this bright, modern gastronomic restaurant. Weekday lunch *formule* 60F, a menu at 80F and others 125–185F. Specialities include zander with *beurre blanc*; for dessert try the *sabayon* of caramelised apples with acacia honey, served on a heavy slate square – not as easy as it sounds. They do a blind-tasting of wines for every table.

DOUÉ-LA-FONTAINE   49700

🏠 |●| HÔTEL-RESTAURANT DE FRANCE**

pl. du Champ-de-Foire (Centre).
☎ 02.41.59.12.27 ➡ 02.41.59.76.00
Closed Sun evening and Mon except July–Aug, and Jan. **TV**. **Car park**.

An archetypal small-town hotel which provides reliable quality. The eighteen bedrooms are decent but have seen better days, 240–260F with shower/wc or bath. The dining room is royal blue with wide seats. Good, traditional cuisine. Menus, 120–240F, list main courses like zander *charlotte* and salmon with *beurre blanc*. Peremptory welcome.

|●| LE CAVEAU

4 [bis] pl. du Champde-Foire; it's signposted from the town centre.
☎ 02.41.59.38.28
Closed Mon–Thurs and Fri lunchtime out of season.

A warm, welcoming place in the heart of the village. It's a medieval cellar that became a famous dance hall. People come here for their *fouaces*, or hearth-cakes, a sort of unleavened bread traditionally cooked in ashes. Try them with *rillettes*, goat's cheese or smothered with sweet, local butter. Several *formules* which are generously served and easy on the pocket, a 55F lunch menu and another at 110F which includes wine and coffee. The place is run by three smiling young people who will fill you in on all manner of activities in the region. Once in a while they have a theatrical evening.

LOURESSE   49700 (6KM N)

|●| RESTAURANT LES CAVES DE LA GÉNÉVRAIE

13 rue du Musée-Rocheménier (Centre); take the D761 or the D69 north from Doué-la-Fontaine.
☎ 02.41.59.34.22
Closed Mon July–Aug, Fri and Sat evenings and Sun Sept–June. **Disabled access**. **Car park**.

This gallery, hewn out of the rock, was used as a hiding place during the religious wars. There are several small dining rooms and, when it's hot outside, the tuff keeps them cool. They offer *fouaces* (wheat cakes traditionally cooked in ashes), the local speciality, which they stuff with *rillettes*, beans or mushrooms. They're served with *hors-d'œuvres* and Layon wines. One menu only, at 120F, which includes wine and coffee. Reservations only – and smoking is not permitted.

ÉVRON   53600

🛏 |●| HÔTEL-RESTAURANT BRASSERIE DE LA GARE**

Centre; it's opposite the station.
☎ 02.43.01.60.29 ➤ 02.43.37.26.53
Restaurant closed Sun. **TV**.

It looks like something out of another age and you'd probably hesitate a long time before deciding to try it out. However, it's a good place, with quiet, comfortable bedrooms with shower or bath, 216–242F. They serve generous portions of good regional cooking – the 79F menu lists dishes like house *terrine*, rib steak *façon vallée de l'Erve* and rhubarb tart. Other menus 105–145F.

JUBLAIN   53160 (17KM NW)

|●| CRÊPERIE-GRILL L'ORGÉTORIX

9 rue Henri-Barbe.
☎ 02.43.04.31.64

Monsieur takes command of the stove while Madame rules in the dining room. It's very popular – after 12.30pm there's hardly a seat left in the place. The menus are delicious and very cheap: two-course *formule* 38F, three-course menu 55F including drink. They also serve *crêpes*. Best to have your meal before taking a look at this old Gaul village.

MEZANGERS   53600 (6KM N)

🎋 🛏 |●| RELAIS DU GUÉ DE SELLE***

Route de Mayenne; it's on the D7.
☎ 02.43.91.20.00 ➤ 02.43.91.20.10
Closed Fri and Sun evenings and Mon 16 Oct–31 May, Christmas to 10 Jan, and a fortnight in the Feb school holidays. **Garden**. **Swimming pool**. **TV**. **Car park**.

Though this farmhouse, in the depths of the country, with the forest at its back and a pond at the front, has lost nearly everything of its original atmosphere, it's been restored and converted into a welcoming inn. Great menus 112F (weekdays) to 260F. Try the *terrine* of *foie gras* and fillet of zander with cider, or the escalope of veal sweetbreads with honey. You'll get absolute peace and quiet in the pleasant, comfortable bedrooms – 360–453F – which all overlook the garden, the swimming pool or the countryside. 10% discount on the room rate.

NEAU   53150 (6KM W)

🛏 |●| HÔTEL-RESTAURANT LA CROIX VERTE**

2 rue d'Évron (Centre); from Évron, go towards Laval.
☎ 02.43.98.23.41 ➤ 02.43.98.25.39
Closed Sun evening, Fri evening Nov to end March.
TV. **Car park**.

Your heart might well sink when you clap eyes on this place. Set on an unattractive junction, it has a dreary façade and ugly parasols. But you'll be pleasantly surprised when you step inside, and might even be tempted to stay longer than you planned. Superbly refurbished bedrooms with shower/wc or bath 235F, and a nice bar. The *à la carte* menu is full of tasty specialities – duck *foie gras*, scallops in Noilly, fillet of trout with Pommeau, and delicious rib steak with girolles. Weekday menu 70F, then 110–180F.

SAINTE-SUZANNE   53270 (7KM SE)

🎋 |●| RESTAURANT L'AUBERGE DE LA CITÉ

7 pl. Hubert-II (Centre); take the D7.
☎ 02.43.01.47.66
Closed Mon, Tues evening except July–Aug, Jan and a week Sept/Oct.

This restaurant, housed in a 14th-century building, serves very good food, some of it concocted from medieval recipes. The *patronne* will prepare medieval menus to order for groups. Otherwise, people usually go for the *crêpes* and *galettes*. If those don't appeal, there are menus 65–139F. Free apéritif or coffee.

DEUX-ÉVAILLES   53150 (12KM NW)

♫|●| LA FENDERIE

Site de la Fenderie; it's on the D129 between Jublains and Montsurs, at the edge of the village.
☎ 02.43.90.00.95
Closed Mon. **Car park**.

This place stands in forty acres of grounds that are full of birds. At the weekends they're also crowded with picnickers. You can avoid the crowds on fine Sundays by relaxing on the terrace opposite the pond. Menus 98–198F, or from 60F during the week, list local dishes that change daily. Good bets include the warm chicken and apple salad with cider vinega,r and the pike with *beurre blanc*. When skies are grey, enjoy the dining room with its fireplace and exposed beams. Free "*coupette*" served with your dessert.

FERTÉ-BERNARD (LA)   72400

♫ 🏠 |●| HÔTEL-RESTAURANT DU STADE

21–23 rue Virette.
☎ 02.43.93.01.67 ➡ 02.43.93.48.26
Closed Fri and Sun evenings, a week from Christmas to New Year's Day, and Aug.

A small establishment in a little side road – you feel you've gone back twenty years. It's clean and well maintained. Doubles from 250F. Nice family-style cooking on a good -value menu at 60F. Free coffee.

♫ 🏠 |●| HÔTEL-RESTAURANT LA PERDRIX**

2 rue de Paris.
☎ 02.43.93.00.44 ➡ 02.43.93.74.95
Closed Mon evening, Tues and Feb. **TV. Pay car park**.

Serge Thibaut's establishment is as pleasing to the eye as it is to the palate. Menus, 110–230F, list masterpieces such as duck *rillettes* with *foie gras* toast, roast prawns with tagliatelle and warm pineapple with *sabayon*. The wine cellar boasts almost six hundred vintage wines. Doubles from 250F with shower/wc, and there's a duplex that sleeps five. As is often the case, the exceptional talent here goes hand in hand with great modesty and outstanding hospitality. Free coffee.

♫ |●| LE BOCAGE FLEURI

☎ 02.43.71.24.04
Closed Sun and Tues evening and three weeks in Aug. **Garden**.

A little place in the middle of town, much praised by the locals. The terrace is ideal when the weather's fine. Really professional cuisine and they don't stint on the helpings. Lovely interior garden that's only a few steps from the canals. Menus from 50F. Free coffee.

|●| LE DAUPHIN

3 rue d'Huisne (Centre); it's on a pedestrianised street.
☎ 02.43.93.00.39
Closed Sun evening, Mon and a fortnight in Aug. **Disabled access**.

This delightful restaurant, in a historic building near the porte Saint-Julien, is popular with lovers and gourmets. Menus from 98F. The dishes change as frequently as the seasons.

SAINT-ULPHACE   72320 (14KM SE)

♫|●| LE GRAND MONARQUE

Centre; it's right in the heart of the village.
☎ 02.43.93.27.27
Closed Sun evening and Tues, weeknights out of season except for reservations.

This place is a hit with the locals who enjoy long, convivial Sunday lunches here. Menus begin at 55F and offer good solid bourgeois dishes like salad of *confit* of quail with *foie gras* and chanterelles and *blanquette* of lobster with baby vegetables and fresh noodles. There's a covered terrace in summer and in winter they have theme evenings: paella, *choucroute*, seafood, etc. Free coffee.

MONTMIRAIL   72320 (15KM SE)

♫|●| CRÊPERIE L'ANCIENNE FORGE

11 [bis] pl. du Château.
☎ 02.43.71.49.14
Closed Mon, end of Jan and the last week in Sept.

A pretty little restaurant with a terrace overlooking a château. Menus start at 52F, (weekday lunch), and the good food includes wonderful salads and *galettes*, delicately flavoured *taboulé*, rib steak, and ice cream with strawberries. Soft background music and friendly smiles. Free Kir.

BONNÉTABLES   72110 (20KM W)

♫ 🏠 |●| HÔTEL-RESTAURANT LE LION D'OR

1 rue du Maréchal-Leclerc.
☎ and ➡ 02.43.29.38.55

Closed Sun except Aug, a week at the beginning of Sept and three weeks in July. **TV**. **Car park**.

This charming building, which dates back to 11th century, is situated in the centre of the town. It has about fifteen delightful rooms, from 200F with basin. There's a pub, a restaurant and a *crêperie*. The cooking is from the Sarthe and dishes are sophisticated. Weekday lunch menu 55F, others 85–150F. They make all their own pastries and you should try the *tarte Tatin*. Very warm welcome. Free apéritif.

FLÈCHE (LA)   72200

⚶ ≜ |O| RELAIS HENRY IV

It's on the Le Mans road, the RN23.
☎ 02.43.94.07.10
Closed Sun evening, Mon and the Feb school holidays. **TV**. **Car park**.

The inn is on the edge of the town and set back from the road. The rooms are bright, clean and soundproofed; doubles 195–220F. The chef is really passionate about chocolate – just try his *millefeuille* – and the walls in the dining room are plastered with 200 chocolate moulds and figurines. Menus 86–182F. Nice welcome. Free apéritif.

⚶ ≜ RELAIS CICERO***

18 bd. d'Alger (Centre); it's near pl. Thiers, close to the Prytanée.
☎ 02.43.94.14.14 ➡ 02.43.45.98.96
Closed Sun evening, Christmas to New Year. **Garden**.

A beautiful residence dating from the 16th and 18th centuries, well away from the crowds and noise of the town. There's an English bar, a reading room, a comfortable breakfast room and an open fire. Bedrooms in the main house are so stylish and comfortable that they're well worth splashing out on, but the hotel proper is actually on the other side of the flower garden. There you get cosy doubles with shower or bath for 435–675F. Great breakfast. This place oozes charm. They can provide you with a meal on a tray for 150F. 10% discount Sept–June.

⚶|O| LE MOULIN DES QUATRE SAISONS

rue Galliéni (Centre).
☎ 02.43.45.12.12
Closed Sun and Wed evenings, Mon, and three weeks in Jan.

This restaurant has a great riverside location opposite the Château des Carmes. What with the owner's accent, the country inn

decor, the apple strudel for dessert, and the syrupy background music, you could almost imagine yourself on the banks of the Danube. There's a wonderful terrace, and a great atmosphere. Tasty, good-value food on menus from 92F. Dishes change regularly but might include *pastilla* of oxtail with horseradish sauce and salmon with fresh noodles. Free coffee.

⚶|O| RESTAURANT LA FESSE D'ANGE

pl. du 8-Mai-1945 (Centre).
☎ 02.43.94.73.60
Closed Sun and Tues evenings, Mon, a week in the Feb school holidays and three weeks in Aug.

An extremely good establishment, with bold modern decor. Menus start at 107F and dishes include *foie gras* with dried apricots, *suprême* of guinea-fowl in nettle sauce, *escalopines* of warm *foie gras* with peppered pears, fillet of zander with white Jasnières and warm raspberry *soufflé*. Free coffee.

LUCHÉ-PRINGÉ   72800 (13KM E)

⚶ ≜ |O| AUBERGE DU PORT-DES-ROCHES**

Lieu-dit Le Port des Roches.
☎ 02.43.45.44.48. ➡ 02.43.45.39.61
Closed Sun evening, Mon and Feb. **TV**. **Car park**.

This inn is run by an energetic, hard-working young couple who are bringing the place back to life. Brightly coloured bedrooms from 240F for a double. In the cosy dining room they serve skilfully prepared dishes at typical country prices – set menus from 115F. There's an impressive selection of dishes: *gratin* of goat's cheese gnocchi with beetroot sauce, poached char with walnuts, veal sweetbreads braised with pig's ears or tart of fresh sardines, and *Paris-Brest* (a large choux pastry ring with almond and butter cream) served with candied pineapple. The superb flowery terrace overlooks the river, as do some of the bedrooms. Free apéritif.

FLOCELLIÈRE (LA)   85700

⚶ ≜ |O| CHÂTEAU DE LA FLOCELLIÈRE

La Flocelière; follow the signposts from Saint-Michel.
☎ 02.51.57.22.03 ➡ 02.51.57.75.21
📧 erika.vignal@wanadoo.fr
Swimming pool. **TV**. **Car park**.

A luxurious hotel occupying a neo-Gothic castle. Some years ago it was renovated by the Vignal family. Given the spaciousness of the superb rooms, it's not overly expensive: 650–1050F. Guests have access to the large park and swimming pool and can look round the ruins of the 13th-century castle. You'll have to book a long time in advance. They also rent out the dungeon, big enough for three families, and there are *gîtes*, 2,500–7,000F according to size and the length of your stay. They serve an evening meal, 250F, which you enjoy in the company of the owners. 10% discount on the room rate Sept–May.

FONTENAY-LE-COMTE   85200

🛏 |●| HÔTEL FONTARABIE-RESTAURANT LA GLYCINE**

67 rue de la République (Centre).
☎ 02.51.69.17.24 ➡ 02.51.51.02.73
e fontarabie@aol.com
Closed 15 Dec–15 Jan.
Disabled access. TV. Car park.

A long time ago, on the Feast of St John, it was traditional for Basque merchants to travel to Fontenay to trade horses. They stayed in this very coaching inn, though the handsome white stone building with a slate roof has been restored somewhat since then. The new decor is tasteful, if a touch too modern, and the bedrooms are clean with adequate facilities. Try to avoid the ones overlooking the street – they're smaller and noisier. Doubles 250F with shower/wc. The restaurant, named after the wonderful wisteria over the front door, offers good regional cooking and generous portions of dishes like grilled *andouillette*, grilled calf's liver with bacon and a mouthwatering chocolate mousse. Menus 45–150F *à la carte*. You'll get a cheerful reception from young, smiling staff.

|●| AUX CHOUANS GOURMETS

6 rue des Halles.
☎ 02.51.69.55.92
Closed Sun evening and Mon.

Service noon–2pm and 7–10pm. A solidly built, refined house with a noble façade. The dining room has splendid rough-hewn stone walls and a covered terrace that overlooks the Vendée. Perfectly pitched welcome and service. Traditional and gourmet cuisine using the freshest of ingredients purchased from the market that's on the doorstep. Dishes change with the seasons: ham *de Vendée* with *ballotine* forecemeat, pan-fried crayfish with shellfish *jus* and fried parsley. Menus 85–225F.

PISSOTTE   85200 (4KM N)

🍴 |●| CRÊPERIE LE POMMIER

9 rue des Gélinières (Centre); take the D938.
☎ 02.51.69.08.06
Closed Mon. **Disabled access. Garden. Car park**.

This serene old shuttered building is next to an ancient wine cellar. It has a garden and a conservatory, and is covered in wisteria and Virginia creeper, which is unusual in these parts. They do *crêpes* served with a generous side dish – try the *Bretonne* with *andouillette*, apples and salad, the *Caprine* with goat's cheese and thyme, or the *Syracuse* with smoked breast of duck, pan-fried apples and orange sauce. Wash it all down with a nice bottle of local rosé. Menus start cheaply at 48F. Free apéritif.

|●| AUBERGE DU POT BLEU

How to get there: take the D104 out of Pisotte in the direction of l'Orbrie, 1km further on the bend, take the left turning and follow the signs.
☎ 02.51.69.16.32
Closed Mon. **Disabled access. Car park**.

An excellent restaurant with a fine reputation, nestling in the Vendée valley though it's not right at the water's edge. Their specialities include *fricassée* of eel with garlic and herbs, grilled saddle of lamb and chocolate mousse. Menus 90–210F.

MERVENT   85200 (11KM NE)

🍴 |●| CRÊPERIE DU CHÂTEAU DE LA CITARDIÈRE

Les Ouillères; take the D99 from Mervent.
☎ 02.51.00.27.04
Closed Wed in season, Mon–Fri Oct–May.

Pretty place, in a strange, 17th-century castle. Parts of it have been converted to provide accommodation for walkers. There's a gorgeous rustic dining room that smells of wood smoke and pancake batter. You can enjoy the fresh air out on the terrace in summer. They serve the most wonderful *crêpes* filled with everything from duck breast to mushrooms or there's a sweet one that's flambéed with apples. Expect to pay about 80F for a complete meal. Free coffee.

VELLUIRE   85770 (11KM SW)

🍴 🛏 |●| L'AUBERGE DE LA RIVIÈRE**

How to get there: take the D938 as far as Nizeau, then the D68.
☎ 02.51.52.32.15 ➡ 02.51.52.37.42

Closed Sun evening and Mon out of season and Jan–Feb. **Disabled access**. **TV**. **Car park**.

This place is ideal if you're after peace and quiet, luxury and fine cooking. The attractive dining room, all yellow tablecloths, beams, pot plants and tapestries, makes a great setting to eat bass with artichokes, prawns in flaky pastry or young pigeon with morels. Weekday menu 120F, others 200–250F. The charming country-style bedrooms cost 430–520F with bath. Number 10 is the only one without a river view. 10% discount on the room rate mid-Sept to mid-June.

MAILLEZAIS   85420 (15KM SE)

☆ ♔ HÔTEL SAINT-NICOLAS**

rue du Docteur-Daroux (Centre).
☎ 02.51.00.74.45 ➡ 02.51.87.29.10
Closed 15 Nov–15 Feb. **TV**. **Car park**.

The young owner of this friendly little restored hotel is in charge of everything – from the very simple rooms with shower, 230–340F, to the terrace with its tiny gardens on different levels. He knows the area like the back of his hand and will show you his own little walks through the Poitou marshlands. A very good base to explore the area. 10% discount, except during school holidays.

FONTEVRAUD-L'ABBAYE   49590

☆ ♔ |●| HÔTEL LA CROIX BLANCHE**

7 pl. des Plantagenêts; it's beside the abbey.
☎ 02.41.51.71.11 ➡ 02.41.38.15.38
Closed 8–12 Jan and 12–23 Nov.
Disabled access. **TV**. **Car park**.

A delightful hotel in an elegant building that's typical of local architecture, right next to the abbey of Fontevraud. They have 21 bedrooms set around a quiet, flower-filled courtyard. Doubles 319–499F with shower/wc or bath and telephone. Some have a fireplace made of tuff, a local stone. The restaurant, well known for its good cooking, offers a vegetarian menu for 100F and others 119–247F. A typical list might include salad of black pudding with walnuts and apples, lamb chops with onions, cheese and dessert. On the most expensive menus, which include two main courses, you might see wild mushrooms with asparagus, *goujons* of sole, beef tournedos with truffle sauce, and duck *foie gras* with figs and Calvados sauce. Nice welcome. 10% discount on the room rate Nov–March and children under two stay free.

GUENROUET   44530

☆ |●| LE JARDIN DE L'ISAC

31 rue de l'Isac; it's 6km east of Saint-Gildes-les-Bois.
☎ 02.40.87.66.11 ℮ cuisineries-clair@wanadoo.fr
Closed Mon and Tues except June–Aug, a fortnight in Feb and ten days in March. **TV**.

Two restaurants run by the same couple – a gastronomic establishment upstairs and this one below which offers unbeatable prices. In summer you eat on the flower-filled terrace in the shade of a magnificent wisteria. Menus at 62F and 85F, or *à la carte*. You could easily be satisfied with the *hors-d'œuvre* buffet, which offers a wide selection including fish *terrine*, *charcuterie* and all sorts of *crudités*. For a main course, opt for grilled meat or fish of the day, and then head back to the buffet for dessert. There are two dining rooms, the best of which looks onto the river – the other one, where the buffets are, is somewhat gloomy. Professional service and welcome. Free coffee.

HERBIERS (LES)   85500

♔ |●| HÔTEL-RESTAURANT DU CENTRE**

6 rue de l'Église (Centre).
☎ 02.51.67.01.75 ➡ 02.51.66.82.24
Closed Fri evening, Sat out of season, 22 July–2 Aug, and the Christmas school holidays. **TV**.

Located in the middle of the town but quiet enough and warmly welcoming. Ideal as a base from which to explore the region. Doubles 270–300F. Half board is compulsory during the Puy-dy-Fou show and over the weekend. This is no hardship because the owner is a good chef and produces dishes using fresh produce and lots of fish. Menus 69–159F.

☆ ♔ |●| HÔTEL-RESTAURANT LE RELAIS**

18 rue de Saumur (Centre).
☎ 02.51.91.01.64 ➡ 02.51.67.36.50
Closed Sun evening, Mon lunchtime, 30 July–8 Aug. **TV**.

This very good hotel, with its beautiful, well-renovated façade, offers 26 luxurious bedrooms; doubles 270F with shower/wc or bath. Although it's by the roadside, the double glazing is effective. In the dining room, as swanky as the bedrooms, you can choose between traditional brasserie dishes or gourmet cuisine: medallions of hind sautéed in thyme butter or Saint-Paul snails with *foie gras* and lobster *blanquette*. Hearty menus: 68F weekdays and 90–315F. Free apéritif.

SAINT-LAURENT-SUR-SÈVRE   85290 (20KM NE)

🕏 🛏 |O| HÔTEL-RESTAURANT
L'HERMITAGE**

2 rue de la Jouvence (Centre); take the D752 and it's on the river Sèvre, by the bridge opposite the basilica.
☎ 02.51.67.83.03 ➡ 02.51.67.84.11
Closed Sat out of season, a week in Feb and a fortnight in Aug. **TV**. **Car park**.

A nice family inn with a terrace overlooking the river. The chef/proprietor gets up at the crack of dawn to pick what he needs from his kitchen garden and sometimes fishes for zander in the river below the terrace. The menus, 80–160F, list good dishes, and you get generous portions: Vendée ham, zander with sorrel or chocolate *charlotte*. The dining room has changed little since the 1960s – it's straight out of *The Avengers* – and the rooms are comfortable but are getting close to needing updating. The nicest look over the river Sèvre. Doubles 220–260F. Free coffee.

LAVAL   53000

🕏 🛏 MARIN HÔTEL**

100–102 av. Robert-Buron (Northeast); it's opposite the train station.
☎ 02.43.53.09.68 ➡ 02.43.56.95.35
TV. **Pay car park**.

This establishment, which belongs to the *Inter-Hôtel* chain, is modern, functional, and well soundproofed. It's an ideal place to stop if you've just got off the TGV. Doubles 270–300F with shower/wc or bath – the ones overlooking the road are noisy. There are lots of restaurants in the area. 10% discount Fri–Sun.

|O| L'AVENIO

38 quai de Bootz.
☎ 02.43.56.87.51
Closed Sat and Sun.

This is the haunt of local fishermen and workers on a lunch break. The place is decorated with old fishing lines, reels and hooks and conversations circle around the ones that got away. Home-cooking only, delicious and in huge portions. There's only one menu, 65F, and it includes wine and a coffee. A place with a genuine, authentic feel. No credit cards.

🕏 |O| L'ANTIQUAIRE

5 rue des Béliers (Centre); it's behind the cathedral.
☎ 02.43.53.66.76
Closed Wed, Sat lunchtime and 7–31 July.

The food here is simply magnificent. The cheapest menu is a bargain at 99F and there are others up to 220F. Dishes like salad of rabbit legs with *confit* of tomatoes and rosemary or *foie gras* with an apple and cinnamon *compote*. The house speciality is crayfish tail lasagne with local *andouille*. Free coffee.

🕏 |O| LA BRAISE

4 rue de la Trinité (Centre); it's in the old town, near the cathedral.
☎ 02.43.53.21.87
Closed Sun, Mon, and a week around 15 Aug.

A cute little place with beautiful furniture, wooden beams and hand-made, hexagonal floor tiles. You receive a wonderful welcome, which will make you feel completely relaxed. The simple authentic dishes are skilfully cooked, many of them over charcoal. Grilled fish and meat are the specialities, as you would expect, or try the scallop kebabs, knuckle of pork with Armagnac or red mullet kebab. Menus from 110F. If it's sunny, sit on the terrace. Free apéritif, coffee or *digestif*.

|O| RESTAURANT LE BISTRO DE PARIS

22 quai Jehan-Fouquet (Centre); it's on the banks of the Mayenne.
☎ 02.43.56.98.29
Closed Sat lunchtime, Sun evening, Mon, 5–20 Aug.

This is the best restaurant in town and can be the most expensive, unless you choose the *menu-carte*, 140F in the week. Lots of wonderful dishes: monkfish and crayfish with tarragon, veal sweetbreads pan-fried with morels and soft macaroon with chocolate with orange salad. Year in year out, Guy Lemercier comes up with creative ideas to delight his regulars, who get a good-natured but not overly effusive welcome. Nicely old-fashioned brasserie decor, with ranks and ranks of mirrors. *Menu dégustation* 250F. Good service and fine wines.

CHANGÉ   53810 (4KM N)

🕏 |O| LA TABLE RONDE

pl. de la Mairie (Centre).
☎ 02.43.53.43.33
Closed Sun evening and Mon. **Car park**.

The upstairs restaurant is impressive and expensive; downstairs there's an attractive bistro with 1930s decor, smiling waitresses and low prices. On a fine day, you can sit on the terrace which faces the town on one side and the park on the other. There's a weekday *menu du jour* for 85F and others 115–238F, listing dishes like zander and shrimp *ballotin*, cockerel ham with cider vinegar and pear *terrine* with caramel. Everything is skilfully prepared, rich in flavour, and colourful. It's well worth the effort of getting here. Free apéritif.

GENEST-SAINT-ISLE (LE)   53940 (12KM W)

🎿 |●| RESTAURANT LE SALVERT

Route d'Olivet.
☎ 02.43.37.14.3
Closed Sun evening and Mon. **Disabled access**. **Car park**.

Just ten minutes from Laval, beside the Olivet lake, this classy restaurant has a terrace open in summer, and an open fire when the weather is cooler. Menus 95–179F, list things like *salade gourmande*, stuffed saddle of rabbit steamed in thyme, and a wonderful selection of desserts. Their bread is home-made, just like everything else. Free coffee.

COSSÉ-LE-VIVIEN   53230 (18KM SW)

🎿 🏠 |●| HÔTEL-RESTAURANT L'ÉTOILE**

2 rue de Nantes (Centre); take the N171.
☎ 02.43.98.81.31 ➡ 02.43.98.96.64
Closed Sun evening, Mon and a fortnight in Aug. **TV**. **Car park**.

The seven bedrooms here are perfectly adequate, but the decor's pretty tacky and kitsch. Doubles 160–225F with shower/wc or bath. The restaurant serves good traditional cooking, with a weekday menu at 57F, and others, 76–140F, listing dishes like *croustillant* of pigs' ears, *fondant* of oxtails and a *craquant* of star fruit with beads of soft fruit that makes a change from *tarte Tatin*. Best to book at weekends. 10% discount on the room rate.

VAIGES   53480 (22KM E)

🎿 🏠 |●| HÔTEL DU COMMERCE***

Rue du Fief-aux-Moines (Centre); take exit 2 off the A81.
☎ 02.43.90.50.07 ➡ 02.43.90.57.40
Closed Fri and Sun evenings Oct–March, and 7–23 Jan. **Disabled access**. **TV**. **Car park**.

Since 1882, when the Oger family first started running this successful hotel, their only concern has been that their guests should sleep soundly and eat well. You can quite happily spend a night or two in one of their quiet bedrooms, 310–330F with shower or

bath, and dine in the conservatory where they serve good food based on local produce: duck *foie gras*, rabbit thigh in cider, cheeses and apple tart. There's a *formule* for 91F and menus 107–270F. Free apéritif.

ERNÉE   53500 (30KM NW)

🏠 |●| LE GRAND CERF**

17–19 rue Aristide-Briand (Centre); it's on the N12 in the direction of Mayenne.
☎ 02.43.05.13.09 ➡ 02.43.05.02.90
Closed Sun evening and Mon out of season, and a fortnight in Jan. **TV**. **Car park**.

A good hotel in northern Mayenne, a region of dolmens and standing stones. The establishment is known for its hospitality, facilities and good food. The restaurant is fairly hushed, but it's more relaxed in the bistro corner. The dishes produced are intelligently planned around seasonal produce and offered on various menus: *salade gourmande*, potted ham *en persillade*, cod, *navarin* of lamb, *blanc en neige* (a dessert something like *île flottant*), and stuffed *crêpes*. Weekday lunch menu 85F, then 108–175F. They also do a dish of the day. Beautiful bedrooms 249F with bath.

|●| LA TABLE NORMANDE

3 rue Aristide-Briand (Centre); it's on the N12 in the direction of Mayenne.
☎ 02.43.05.13.09 ➡ 02.43.05.02.90
Closed Tues–Thurs evenings, a fortnight in Feb and a fortnight in Aug.

Even if the lunch or dinner service is finished, they never refuse to serve you. You may have a limited choice but, unlike many other places, at least they won't turn you away. The owners are deeply committed to what they do. The restaurant has a nice atmosphere and is popular with local workers, travelling salesmen and passing tourists. Delicious home-made dishes. Lunch menu 55F or 75–110F – good value for money.

LUÇON   85400

🎿 🏠 |●| HÔTEL-RESTAURANT LE BŒUF COURONNÉ**

55 route de La-Roche-sur-Yon (West).
☎ 02.51.56.11.32 ➡ 02.51.56.98.25
📧 boeufcouronne@wanadoo.fr
Closed Sun evening and Mon. **TV**. **Car park**.

Though a little close to the road, this is an attractive place, with a flower-laden pergola, a delightfully cosy lounge and several dining rooms. Good cooking: duck *foie gras* in port, *grenadin* of veal with chanterelles, *paupiettes* of sole with langoustine, or duck breast with peaches. Set menus 74–166F. It's a delight to watch them preparing the flambéed dishes. Four rather plush bedrooms 260–270F with shower/wc or bath. Free coffee.

LUDE (LE)   72800

|●| LA RENAISSANCE

2 av. de la Libération.
☎ 02.43.94.63.10
Closed Sun evening and Mon.

Though this is a pretty grand place, the atmosphere is in no way formal and men don't even have to wear ties. There is a bewildering choice of dishes on the menu, but the chef is happy to help you decide. He uses the freshest produce and monitors the cooking of each dish meticulously. Service is also good and comes with a smile. Weekday menu 65F and others 84–219F.

MALICORNE-SUR-SARTHE   72270

|●| RESTAURANT LA PETITE AUBERGE

5 pl. Du-Guesclin.
☎ 02.43.94.80.52
Closed evenings out of season except Sat, Mon in season and the Christmas and Feb holidays.
Car park. Disabled access.

Set on a riverbank, this restaurant has a rather attractive terrace where you can treat yourself to pike *terrine*, fillet of sea trout, cheese and dessert for a mere 84F. Prices go up a little on Sunday and there's a choice of other menus. À la carte, dishes change according to what's in season and the fish available at the market. The elegant flower-filled dining room has a fireplace and is ideal for dull days.

MAMERS   72600

☎ |●| HÔTEL-RESTAURANT LE DAUPHIN**

54 rue du Fort.
☎ 02.43.34.24.24
Closed Fri and Sun evenings. **TV. Car park.**

Pay a visit to this unpretentious little hotel if you want to try *rillettes* – a delicacy made from shredded pork cooked in its own fat – at their best. À la carte they serve specialities such as omelette with *rillettes* and *marmite sarthoise*, and there are menus 65–170F. They also have

perfectly adequate bedrooms: 170F with basin or 200–250F with shower/wc or bath.

NEUCHÂTEL-EN-SAOSNOIS   72600 (9KM W)

☎ |●| RELAIS DES ÉTANGS DE GUIBERT

How to get there: in the village turn right by the church into the rue Louis-Ragot.
☎ 02.43.97.15.38 ➡ 02.43.97.66.42
Closed Sun evening and Mon except public holidays.
Disabled access. Car park.

Set at the edge of the Perseigne forest, near the pond, this place comes to life as soon as the sun shows its face. It's got it all – pleasant decor, wonderful welcome and good prices – and you may find it difficult to get a room at the weekend. Rooms are individually decorated with sailing or hunting themes. Doubles 270–320F. In the dining room, menus go for 85–190F.

ROUPERROUX-LE-COQUET   72110 (18KM SE)

⅍ |●| LE PETIT CAMPAGNARD

It's on the D301.
☎ 02.43.29.79.74
Closed Mon and three weeks in July.
Disabled access. Car park.

A pretty little place, especially popular on Sundays. The unbeatable 60F menu offers *rillettes* (shredded pork cooked in its own fat), chicken with cider, cheese and dessert. The 56F weekday menu is also a good deal, as are the others, 100–160F – they list unusual dishes like venison flambéed with whisky or ostrich with pepper sauce. Free coffee.

FRESNAYE-SUR-CHÉDOUET (LA)   72600 (22KM NW)

⅍ ☎ |●| L'AUBERGE SAINT-PAUL

How to get there: take the D3 and the D234.
☎ 02.43.97.82.76 ➡ 02.43.97.82.84
Closed Mon and Tues except public holidays.
Disabled access. Car park.

This former stud farm is an ideal place to come if you like to eat in peace. There are four little bedrooms for 200F with bath, although they don't have quite the same timeless charm as the inn, with its fireplace and red floor tiles. Pascal Yenk's cooking is skilfully prepared and full of flavour. He offers dishes like *suprême* of bass in a potato crust, medallions of lamb with *confit* of vegetables, and roast langoustine. Wonderful set menus 130–235F. Very professional service. 10% discount on the room rate.

MANS (LE)   72000

♨ ⛨ HÔTEL LA POMMERAIE**

314 rue de l'Éventail (East); follow signs for the N23 to Paris, turn into rue de Douce-Amie at auberge Bagatelle.
☎ 02.43.85.13.93
Garden. **Disabled access**. **TV**. **Car park**.

Though just a short car journey from the city centre, this hotel, set in a large, flower-filled garden, is wonderfully peaceful. Concentrate on the garden, the hospitality and the feeling of luxury and you might even be able to forget the bland, post-war architecture. Doubles 150F with basin, 255F with bath. The energetic young hotelier lets you choose your own room. Free apéritif or coffee.

♨ ⛨ ANJOU HOTEL

☎ 02.43.40.30.30 ➡ 02.43.40.30.00
Closed 20 Dec–2 Jan. **TV**. **Pay car park**.

A practically located hotel opposite the station. The young couple who have taken it over really care for their guests and give you a warm welcome. They have redecorated the rooms and put in double glazing: 180F with basin and 250F with shower or bath.10% discount Fri–Sun.

⛨ |●| HÔTEL GREEN 7**

447 av. Georges-Durand; it's in the south of the town on the road to Tours.
☎ 02.43.40.30.30 ➡ 02.43.40.30.00
Closed Fri and Sun evenings, and the first three weeks in Aug. **TV**. **Car park**.

A pleasant hotel less than 2km from the 24-hour Le Mans circuit. Comfortable, well-decorated rooms with shower or bath go for 295F, which includes a splendid breakfast. Though the restaurant is not brilliant, it's more than adequate if you don't want to go into town for a meal. Menus 90–130F. There's also a fitness room with a Jacuzzi and a sauna.

♨ ⛨ |●| HÔTEL CHANTECLER***

50 rue de la Pelouse (East); it's between the train station and the conference centre.
☎ 02.43.14.40.00 ➡ 02.43.77.16.28
TV. **Car park**.

Just a short distance from the station, this hotel offers peace and comfort within easy reach of the old part of Le Mans. The welcome is sincere, the parking easy and the breakfast, served in the conservatory, rather good. Decent doubles with shower or bath, 370–390F. There is a restaurant on the ground floor, but it doesn't compare to the

rest of the establishment. 10% discount on the room rate at weekends (outside festivals).

|●| AUBERGE DES 7 PLATS

79 Grande-Rue (Centre).
☎ 02.43.24.57.77
Closed Sun and Mon.

The large, half-timbered house has real style – there are several of them in the street but this is one of the most typical you'll find in the old part of Le Mans. Their claim to originality is that they offer seven hot dishes on the same menu. The very youthful, relaxed welcome adds considerably to the appeal. There's a brigade of staff in the kitchen producing *carpaccio*, *foie gras* (10F supplement), local ham or duck breast with peppercorns, duck *confit* and *paupiettes* with a great deal of care and attention. To top it all, it's good value for money: 67F for a main course and a dessert, or 87F. *Appellation* wines by the carafe and all the apéritifs cost 17F. Probably advisable to book.

|●| L'ATLAS

80 bd. de la Petite Vitesse (Southeast).
☎ 02.43.61.03.16
Closed Mon and Sat lunchtime.

Open until 11.30pm. Near the station, in an area otherwise lacking in good restaurants, this Moroccan restaurant is a real find. The proprietor has done his country proud with both the opulent decor and the cuisine – try the excellent *tajines* and very fresh Moroccan pastries. Menu at 70F or 110–150F *à la carte*. Live musical evenings at weekends.

♨ |●| RESTAURANT CHEZ JEAN

9–11 rue Dorée (West).
☎ 02.43.28.22.96
Closed Sun evening, Mon and Wed evening Oct–Feb, Tues lunchtime March–Sept, the first fortnight in Jan and end of June to 12 Sept.

A typical brasserie in old Le Mans. It's an unpretentious place and is often full when its neighbours are empty – a good sign. Simplified menus built around uncomplicated main courses based on market produce: cockle stew, mussels with lentils flavoured with truffles, seafood risotto, suckling pig with *foie gras*. Weekday menu 79F, then 156–210F. Good house wines and a pleasant terrace opening out onto pl. de l'Éperon. Free apéritif.

♨ |●| LE NEZ ROUGE

107 Grande-Rue (North-West).

☎ 02.43.24.27.26
Closed Sun and Mon lunchtime and mid-Aug to 7 Sept.

This old-town gourmet restaurant is the place to come for a *mongolfière* of mussels and cockles in a leek sauce, poached turbot in champagne, fillets of grenadier served in a butter and wine sauce, or quails with figs. Weekday menu 99F, with others 155–220F. For a more relaxed atmosphere try the same establishment's charming gourmet *crêperie*, which is nearby on pl. du Hallai. Free coffee.

🏃|●| LE FLAMBADOU

14 [bis] rue Saint-Flaceau (West); it's near the town hall.
☎ 02.43.24.88.38
Closed Sun, ten days at Easter, and a fortnight around 15 Aug.

The owner/chef of this highly recommended restaurant prepares specialities from his native region of les Landes and Périgord: casserole of snails with ceps, goose casserole *à la lotoise*, *fricassée* of duck, and succulent calf's feet *à la mode de tante Alice*. The main courses are so generous that you may not be able to manage a dessert. Allow around 180F *à la carte*. You can dine in the sweet little dining room or out on the shady terrace. Warm, hearty welcome. Free coffee.

YVRÉ-L'ÉVÊQUE   72530 (5KM E)

🏃 🏠 HÔTEL-MOTEL PAPEA**

Bener; leave Le Mans on the N23 and follow signs to Papea.
☎ 02.43.89.64.09 ➡ 02.43.89.49.81
TV. Car park.

This hotel-motel is set in lovely grounds near the abbey of Epau. Some twenty comfortable chalets, separated from each other by bushes and trees, cost 235–285F for two people. Ideal if you want to stay in the country but also be very close to the city. You can get meals on a tray, 50F, on request. Lower prices for weekends, long stays and commercial travellers. Friendly welcome. 10% discount Nov–March, except during festivals.

MULSANNE   72230 (8KM S)

🏠|●| HÔTEL-RESTAURANT ARBOR-AUBERGE DE MULSANNE**

Route de Tours; it's 10 minutes from town at the race circuit.
☎ 02.43.39.18.90 ➡ 02.43.39.18.99
Restaurant closed Sat lunchtime, Sun, and three weeks in Aug. **Swimming pool. TV. Car park**.

This hotel, used by the competing teams during the 24-hour Le Mans race, is worth visiting any time of the year. The impeccable rooms cost 310F with bath, and there's a sauna and swimming pool. Weekday menu 99F, 149F weekends, and others 189–370F.

FILLÉ-SUR-SARTHE   72210 (15.5KM SW)

🏃|●| RESTAURANT LE BARRAGE

rue du Passeur; it's the last house past the church.
☎ 02.43.87.14.40
Closed Sun evening, Wed and during the All Saints' school holidays.

This restaurant is very popular locally, so if you want a table on the terrace looking directly onto the tow path and the Sarthe river, you should reserve. It's a serene, rural setting, and a perfect place to enjoy the good food: casserole of lambs' brains, *foie gras* flan and roast cod with lemon butter. Weekday menus 58 and 85F, others 138–190F. Warm welcome. Free apéritif.

DOMFRONT-EN-CHAMPAGNE   72240 (18KM NW)

🏃|●| RESTAURANT DU MIDI**

33 rue du Mans; it's on the D304, towards Mayenne.
☎ 02.43.20.52.04
Closed Mon and Tues.

The dining room is comfortable, the surroundings are classy and the service is attentive. The cuisine has an excellent reputation – the weekday lunch menu, 78F, lists mixed meat stew braised with Chinon wine, zander with smoked bacon, cheese and dessert. Other menus, 99–200F, offer perch in champagne sauce, duck breast *à l'ancienne*, mussel stew, swordfish steak and Calvados sorbet with *tarte Tatin*. Reasonably priced wines on a generally good list. Free coffee.

BEAUMONT-SUR-SARTHE   72170 (25KM N)

🏃 🏠 |●| HÔTEL-RESTAURANT DU CHEMIN DE FER**

pl. de la Gare; turn off the N138 onto the D26 towards Vivoin; the hotel is less than 1km from the town centre.
☎ 02.43.97.00.05 ➡ 02.43.97.87.49
Closed Fri and Sun evenings, Mon Nov–April, a fortnight in the Feb school holidays and mid-Oct to mid-Nov.
Garden. TV. Car park.

Cheerful staff welcome you and mouthwatering aromas waft from the kitchens. With the garden behind the house and the pastoral atmosphere in the large dining room you could almost be in the country. Treat yourself – scallops flambéed in whisky, *mar-

mite sarthoise (local hotpot), good rib of beef, pike *terrine*, sautéed rabbit with mushrooms and fillet of pork in cider. Weekday *menu du jour*, 69F, then 89–245F. Fifteen pleasant rooms, 230F with basin to 302F with bath. Free apéritif.

THORIGNÉ-SUR-DUÉ   72160 (28KM E)

🏃 🏠 |●| HÔTEL-RESTAURANT SAINT-JACQUES**

pl. du Monument; take the N23 and D302.
☎ 02.43.89.95.50 ➡ 02.43.76.58.42
Closed Mon and Dec/Jan.
Disabled access. Garden. TV. Secure parking.

This family hotel celebrated its 150th anniversary in 2000. The comfort, courtesy and good food offered are straight out of traditional hotel keeping. Doubles 340–450F. Menus 98–325F. Specialities include salad of calves' sweetbreads with *foie gras*, scallops with vanilla butter, whole steamed ox kidney with sweet garlic cream and iced nougat with raspberry *coulis*. Free coffee.

SAINT-GERMAIN-SUR-SARTHE   72130 (29KM N)

🏃 |●| RESTAURANT LE SAINT-GERMAIN

Lieu-dit La Hutte; take the N138, it's at the crossroads.
☎ 02.43.97.53.06
Closed Sun and Tues evenings, Mon, a week at the beginning of March, and Aug.

It doesn't look promising from the outside, but in spite of the traffic flashing past on the main road this is a lovely place. Madame makes sure there are fresh flowers in the dining room and Monsieur keeps up the high standards of French sauce-making in the kitchen. Try rabbit *terrine*, a splendid *cassolette* of fish, grilled rib of beef *béarnaise*, *salade gourmande*, fresh oysters, *gratin* of lobster or *fondant* of veal with morels. Lunch menu 62F, then 105–225F. Free coffee.

MAYENNE   53100

🏠 |●| L'AUBERGE DES TROIS ÉPIS

15 rue de la Madeleine; it's on the Laval road.
☎ 02.43.04.87.34 ➡ 02.43.04.83.60
Hotel closed first fortnight in Aug. **Restaurant closed** Fri evening and Sat lunchtime. **Disabled access. TV. Car park.**

Quiet, peaceful old-fashioned hotel. Doubles have shower or bath (wc on the landing),170F. The Normandy-inspired dishes in the restaurant include *andouillette* in cider. Weekday menu 59F, then 79F and 100F.

🏠 HÔTEL LA TOUR DES ANGLAIS**

13 [bis] pl. Juhel (Centre).
☎ 02.43.04.34.56 ➡ 02.43.32.13.84
Restaurant closed lunchtimes and Sat–Sun. **Disabled access. TV. Car park.**

Very close to Château de Mayenne, this hotel has one wonderful room in a fortified tower with a dramatic view of the Mayenne river. The other rooms are comfortable but more modern; 270F with shower or bath. Weekday menus 68F and 98F. There's an English-style bar with a billiard table and impressive wooden beams. They also do meals.

🏃 🏠 |●| LE GRAND HÔTEL**

2 rue Ambroise de Loré (Centre); it faces the Mayenne river.
☎ 02.43.00.96.00 ➡ 02.43.32.08.49
Hotel closed Christmas week, and Saturday Nov–April. **Restaurant closed** Sat and Sun lunchtimes out of season, public holidays, end July to mid-Aug and Christmas week. **Car park. TV.**

If only the rest of the town could be renovated as well as this hotel. Tourists arriving by car, bike and even boat are greeted with a cheery smile. Well-appointed rooms 315–464F with shower/wc or bath. In the restaurant you get Breton or Norman cuisine in a quaint ambience, with menus 100–222F. Round off the evening with a good whisky in the bar. 10% discount on the room rate.

FONTAINE-DANIEL   53100 (4KM SW)

🏃 |●| RESTAURANT LA FORGE

Centre.
☎ 02.43.00.34.85
Closed Wed, Sun evening and the Feb school holidays.

This lovely restaurant, on the main square of the pretty village, boasts a very nice terrace where you can enjoy excellent cuisine, duck *terrine*, *foie gras* and prunes and beef with grilled *andouille*. Menus 95–210F. Best to book. Free coffee.

MOULAY   53100 (4KM S)

🏃 🏠 |●| LA MARJOLAINE**

Le Bas Mont; it's on the way out of Moulay heading towards Laval.
☎ 02.43.00.48.42 ➡ 02.43.08.10.58
Closed Sun evening, Mon lunchtime. **TV. Car park.**

A hotel with a dozen brand-new, comfortable rooms that have been soothingly decorated. Doubles 250–300F. The restaurant is up and coming and you should dress smartly. The quality of the cuisine and freshness of the ingredients is exemplary – try John Dory with a cardamon-scented sauce, sea bream with sorrel and pan-fried whelks, or pigeon with blackberry *jus*. Menus 88F, 150F and 200F. 10% discount on the room rate.

⋨ ≜ |●| HÔTEL-RESTAURANT BEAU RIVAGE

How to get there: it's on the N162 between Mayenne and Moulay.
☎ 02.43.00.49.13 ☛ 02.43.04.43.69
Closed Mon and the Feb school holidays. **TV**. **Car park**.

This lovely hotel-restaurant, set on the bank of the Mayenne river, is a sight to behold. The dining room and the terrace, which stretches right down to the water, are often full with regulars. Make sure you reserve a table. Weekday menu 70F, and others up to 172F: rabbit and prune *terrine*, calf's head *ravigotte* served with a spicy *vinaigrette*, *cassolette* of queen scallops, cassolette of pork spare ribs, cheese and *crème brûlée*. Three rooms with shower/wc, 280F. Free apéritif.

COMMER   53470 (9KM S)

⋨ ≜ CHAMBRE D'HÔTE LA CHEVRIE

How to get there: 5km south of Mayenne on the N162 towards Laval, follow the signposts to La Mayenne.
☎ 02.43.00.44.30 ☛ 06.84.17.17.29
Car park.

This farmhouse is at least a hundred years old. Natural, kind welcome. The room price hasn't increased for nine years – it's an affordable 200F, breakfast included. There's a wonderful view over the countryside and neighbouring organic farm. The tow path is close by and a good place for an outing on foot, bike or horse-back. Special price for a three-night stay.

MONTREUIL-POULAY   53640 (12KM N)

|●| L'AUBERGE CAMPAGNARDE

Le Presbytère.
☎ 02.43.32.07.11
Closed Sun evening, Wed, a week in Dec and a week in Feb.

You'll get a kind welcome in this restaurant, where the service is friendly without being over-familiar. They serve apéritifs and coffee on the terrace even when the weather is not

quite fine enough to eat a full meal outside. An astonishing selection of local dishes like grandama used to make: *terrine* of duck and Pommeau in winter or of baby vegetables in summer, pike in a wine and butter sauce, sea bream with chervil, duck in cider in summer and goose in winter. Weekday menu 59F, then others 98–130F. Best to book.

LASSAY-LES-CHÂTEAUX   53119 (16KM NE)

|●| RESTAURANT DU CHÂTEAU

37 rue Migoret-Lamberdière.
☎ 02.43.04.71.99
Closed Sun evening, Mon and a fortnight in Aug.

Béatrice and Hervé have a mixed clientele of regulars and British tourists passing through. They've set aside a special dining room for the locals who lunch on the *menu ouvrier* which costs 53F including $1/4$ litre of wine. There's a great atmosphere so try and get a table in there. The dishes are all freshly cooked in the kitchens; it's simple, tasty and prepared by a real pro. Best to book.

GORRON   53120 (25KM NW)

⋨ ≜ |●| HÔTEL-RESTAURANT LE BRETAGNE**

41 rue de Bretagne (East); take the D12 to Saint-Georges-Buttavent and then the D5.
☎ 02.43.08.63.67 ☛ 02.43.08.01.15
Closed Sun evening and Mon. **TV**. **Car park**.

A good village restaurant where you can get a hearty meal and gourmet cooking. Menus, 76–175F, offer *mousseline* of zander with crab sauce, shellfish casserole with vermouth, honey-glazed roast breast of duck with Perry, and chocolate *fondant*. The decor is spruce with pastel colours, and the dining room looks over the river Colmont. Double rooms 250F. 10% discount on the room rate.

VILLAINES-LA-JUHEL   53700 (28KM E)

⋨ ≜ |●| L'HOSTELLERIE DE LA JUHEL*

27 rue Jules-Doitteau (Centre); take the D113.
☎ 02.43.03.23.24 ☛ 02.43.03.79.87
Closed Fri and Sun evenings and three weeks in the Feb school holidays. **TV**. **Car park**.

The enthusiastic chef offers superb grilled meat dishes and guinea-fowl braised in cider. It's excellent value for money, with a weekday menu at 55F and others 85–145F. Double rooms 178F with basin and up to 245F with shower. 10% discount on the room rate.

MAZEAU (LE) 85420

IØI RESTAURANT L'AUBERGE MARAICHINE

☎ 02.51.52.90.20
Closed Wed evening except July–Aug, and 15 Dec–15 Feb. **Car park**.

Old village bistro that's typical of this marshy area. Lots of local specialities: *tourte*, cod with sorrel, *farci poitevin* (stuffed cabbage), stuffed snails with ham, eels and frogs' legs. The 59F menu offers a buffet of starters, dish of the day and dessert, and there are others 90–165F. A meal *à la carte* will cost about 160F. Welcoming, convivial owner.

MONTAIGU 85600

♠ IØI HÔTEL LES VOYAGEURS

9 av. Villebois-Mareuil.
☎ 02.51.94.00.71 ➡ 02.51.94.07.78
Disabled access. Swimming pool. Car park.

A long pink hotel with a flag flying above it, made up of three buildings around a swimming pool – each facing wall is painted in a different colour and there's a Mediterranean feel. The rooms are comfortable and of varying sizes. Doubles 220–450F. In the basement there's a fitness room. The dining room is on the ground floor and looks over the swimming pool. It's huge and bright and the cooking is very tasty. Menus 69–195F. Breakfast costs 35F. Nice staff.

⅔IØI LE CATHELINEAU

3 [bis] pl. du Champ-de-Foire.
☎ and ➡ 02.51.94.26.40
Closed Sun evening, Mon, 3–18 Feb and 1–19 Aug. **Disabled access. Car park**.

Michel Piveteau is the chef here. His cooking is original and he combines unusual mixtures of flavours. His menus change every three weeks: hot oysters in Muscadet wine, zander fillet with cider and turmeric, chocolate *Marquise*. Menus from 88F. There's a tank with fresh lobsters in it. Free coffee.

MONTREUIL-BELLAY 49260

⅔ ♠ IØI SPLENDID'HÔTEL**

139 rue du Docteur-Gaudrez (Centre); near the château.

☎ 02.41.53.10.00 ➡ 02.41.52.45.17
Closed Sun evening out of season. **Disabled access**. **Swimming pool. TV. Car park**.

This convivial establishment has everything you could ask for. The beautiful building comprises adjoining 15th- and 17th-century wings with a wide range of conventional, clean rooms – doubles with basin 240F, or 320F with shower or bath/wc and twin beds. In the mornings the only sound is the fountain, while in the evening you can join locals at the lively bar. There's a pleasant dining room where they serve freshly prepared dishes in copious portions. Menus 80F (lunch) to 210F. There's a big choice of fish dishes and the house speciality is pike black pudding. There's free use of the fitness facilities at the *Hôtel-Relais du Bellay* (below). 10% discount on the room rate.

⅔ ♠ HÔTEL-RELAIS DU BELLAY**

96 rue Nationale (Centre); it's behind the château.
☎ 02.41.53.10.10 ➡ 02.41.52.45.17
Closed Sun evening Oct to Easter. **Swimming pool. Garden. TV. Car park**.

Owned by the same people as the *Splendid'Hôtel*, and sharing its reception area, this hotel, which used to be the girls' school, has a similarly relaxed, friendly welcome. In the main building, the very comfortable spacious rooms, which have been completely renovated, go for 280F with shower, 430F with bath. Some look out onto the château and the fortifications. There's no restaurant but buffet breakfast costs 45F. There is a large, pleasant garden with swimming pool, along with a fitness room, sauna, Turkish bath and Jacuzzi. 10% discount.

IØI LA GRANGE À DÎME

rue du Château.
☎ 02.41.50.97.24 _ grange.a.dime@wanadoo.fr
Open every evening from 8pm, Sun lunchtime in season, Fri–Sun evenings out of seadson.

The setting is a 15th-century barn with a fantastic beamed ceiling, looking like the upturned hull of a boat. This was the tax office in centuries past. The single menu, 120F, includes a glass of Coteaux du Layon: stuffed mushrooms, *fillettes*, knuckle of pork, duck *confit*, salad, goat's cheese and a freshly baked pastry. Coffee is also included. You are definitely advised to arrive feeling very hungry. Nice welcome and the waiting staff are dressed in period costume.

MORTAGNE-SUR-SÈVRE   85290

𝕩 🛏 |●| HÔTEL-RESTAURANT DE FRANCE ET LA TAVERNE***

4 pl. du Docteur-Pichat; it's at the crossroads of the Nantes-Poitiers/ Paris-Les Sables roads.
☎ 02.51.65.03.37 ➡ 02.51.65.27.83
Closed evenings, Sat and Sun 15 Oct–1 April. **Disabled access. Swimming pool. TV. Secure parking.**

In 1968 there was a revolution in Morragne. The *Hôtel de France*, built in 1604, was renovated. Since then, nothing has changed. You can't miss this beautiful, noble building as you arrive in the main square – it's smothered in ivy. Endless corridors and odd little corners lead to plush, comfortable rooms. Doubles 270F with shower/wc, 350F with bath and covered terrace with garden view. *La Taverne* has a sumptuous medieval-style dining room with medieval furniture and collections of copper pans around the fireplace. The food is a festival of delicate, surprising flavours: crayfish in *verjus*, turbot with nettles, slivers of veal kidneys with green peppercorns. The prices are high, but justifiably so, with menus 165–327F. During the week, the *Petite Auberge* next door offers more affordable menus, 85F and 99.50F. There's a swimming pool in the old *curé's* garden. Impeccable service. Free coffee.

NANTES   44000

SEE MAP OVERLEAF

𝕩 🛏 HÔTEL FOURCROY*

11 rue Fourcroy. **MAP B3-3**
☎ 02.40.44.68.00
Closed 22 Dec–3 Jan. **TV. Secure parking.**

Plain but quiet and decent. Doubles 150F with shower/wc, 180F with bath. Some look onto a private courtyard. 10% discount 15 July–15 Aug.

𝕩 🛏 HÔTEL SAINT-DANIEL*

4 rue du Bouffay. **MAP C2-2**
☎ 02.40.47.41.25 ➡ 02.51.72.03.99
Garden. TV. Car park.

A remarkable little hotel that's clean and well run. Doubles 150F with basin, 170F with shower or bath. The nineteen rooms all have telephones and alarm clocks – TV is an optional extra for 20F. Some rooms face the pedestrianised street, others the garden and the charming Sainte-Croix church in the Bouffay district. The prices attract younger travellers. Essential to book. 10% discount.

𝕩 🛏 |●| HÔTEL DUCHESSE ANNE**

3–4 pl. de la Duchesse Anne. **MAP D2-8**
☎ 02.40.74.78.78 ➡ 02.40.74.60.20
Closed Sat lunchtime and Sun. **TV. Pay garage.**

One of the finest hotels in Nantes, in a magnificent, palatial building behind the château – it's got two stars but deserves many more. Around sixty rooms. Those for 310F with shower/wc are very comfortable, the ones for 480F are regal and have stone balconies looking out to the château, massive bathrooms and acres of space. Prices are more modest in the restaurant: 68–197F. 10% discount on the room rate for a two-night stay.

𝕩 🛏 HÔTEL AMIRAL**

26 [bis] rue Scribe. **MAP B2-5**
☎ 02.40.69.20.21 ➡ 02.40.73.98.13

This brand new chain hotel has everything a businessperson could want: pleasant room, double glazing, mini-bars, etc. Doubles 329F. Friendly welcome. 10% discount for a two-night stay, and a special promotional rate of 240F at weekends.

𝕩 🛏 L'HÔTEL***

6 rue Henri-IV. **MAP D2-7**
☎ 02.40.29.30.31 ➡ 02.40.29.00.95
Disabled access. TV. Pay car park.

A pleasant, easy-going business hotel that's very comfortable and perfectly located opposite the château of Anne de Bretagne. Well soundproofed doubles 380F with shower/wc, 460F with bath. A professional, cheerful welcome. Free use of the car park.

𝕩 🛏 HÔTEL LA PEROUSE***

3 allée Duquesne. **MAP B2-6**
☎ 02.40.89.75.00 ➡ 02.40.89.76.00
Disabled access. TV. Car park.

There's no maybe about this unique contemporary hotel – you either love it or loathe it. A large block of heavy, compact white granite, echoing a Nantais mansion, it has large windows looking over the cours des Cinquante-Otages and the rooftops. Inside there is lots of wood, designer furniture, space and tranquillity. Doubles 500–590F. Not a aplace for those nostalgic for the hotels of yesteryear. Free breakfast.

|●| RESTAURANT LA MANGEOIRE

16 rue des Petites-Écuries. **MAP C2-19**
☎ 02.40.48.70.83
Closed Sun, Mon, a week in Feb, a fortnight in May and a fortnight in Sept.

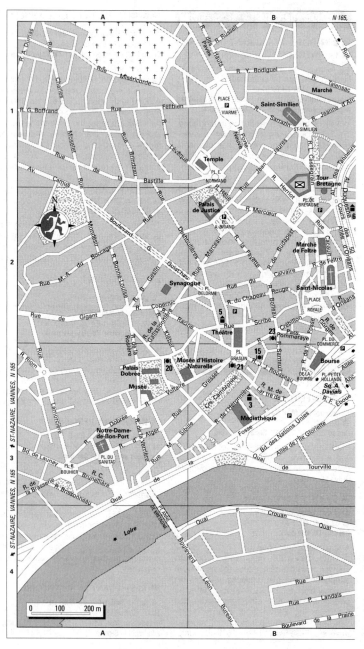

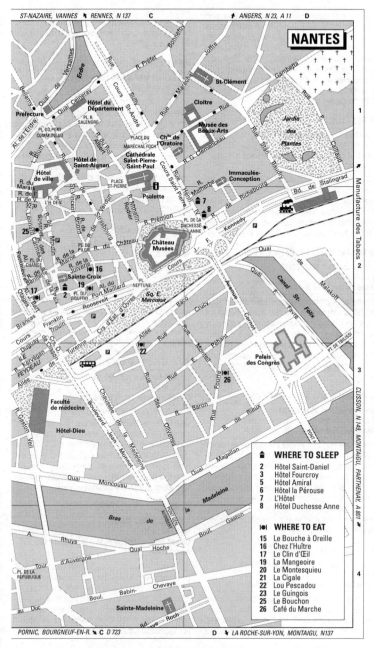

NANTES

Manufacture des Tabacs

CLISSON, N 149, MONTAIGU, PARTHENAY, A 801

⬢ WHERE TO SLEEP

2   Hôtel Saint-Daniel
3   Hôtel Fourcroy
5   Hôtel Amiral
6   Hôtel la Pérouse
7   L'Hôtel
8   Hôtel Duchesse Anne

|O| WHERE TO EAT

15   Le Bouche à Oreille
16   Chez l'Huître
17   Le Clin d'Œil
19   La Mangeoire
20   Le Montesquieu
21   La Cigale
22   Lou Pescadou
23   Le Guingois
25   Le Bouchon
26   Café du Marche

Cuisine that combines French tradition and creativity: duck *foie gras* with a compote of dried fruits, pan-fried skate wing with spices and *crème brûlée* with Cointreau. Weekday lunch menu 58F, others up to 148F. The surroundings are heavy with family photographs and souvenirs, and customers are invited to write little messages on the 400-year-old walls. You can also eat outside.

⦿ RESTAURANT LE MONTESQUIEU

1 rue Montesquieu. **MAP A3-20**
☎ 02.40.73.06.69
Closed Fri evening, Sat, Sun, public holidays and mid-July to end Aug.

A friendly local restaurant, a sort of student haunt, in a quiet spot beyond the pedestrianised Graslin area. The dining room walls are decorated with Rouen and Moustier plates and the tables covered with checked cloths. Lunch menu 65F, 79F in the evening.

⦿ RESTAURANT LE CLIN D'ŒIL

15 rue Beauregard. **MAP C2-17**
☎ 02.40.47.72.37
Closed Sat lunchtime and Sun.

Ignore the tiny, gloomy dining area downstairs, and head instead for the first floor. The bright decor and friendly atmosphere are equalled by the charming, good-hearted service. Very good food that's an imaginative blend of local and oriental favourites – try the banana *tarte Tatin*. Lunch *formule* 68F, or 78F and 98F in the evening.

⦿ RESTAURANT LE GUINGOIS

3 [bis] rue Santeuil. **MAP B2-23**
☎ 02.40.73.36.49
Closed Mon, Sun and Aug

One of the hubs of social life in Nantes, open until midnight. It offers good food, prepared from fresh market ingredients, at decent prices. The menus, 86–156F, and the lunch *formule*, 68F, list home cooking without fuss or flourish. Dishes of the day are chalked up on the blackboard: ham hock with lentils, grilled *andouillette*, veal sweetbreads *à l'ancienne*. All the classics.

⦿ LE BOUCHE À OREILLE

14 rue Jean-Jacques-Rousseau. **MAP B3-15**
☎ 02.40.73.00.25
Closed Sun, public holidays and 1–15 Aug.

Situated very close to the Nantes Opera House, this is a gathering place for theatregoers and sports fans. It's more of a place to drink than a restaurant, and the cuisine is not

fancy: caramelised black pudding, *tabliers de sapeurs* (grilled ox tripe), pike *quenelles*, and huge salads in summer. Set lunch menu 69F, *à la carte* 120F.

⦿ LA CIGALE

4 pl. Graslin. **MAP B3-21**
☎ 02.51.84.94.94

The *in* restaurant in Nantes, where visiting celebrities and local high society types come for supper after the theatre (which is just opposite). The cuisine isn't particularly brilliant and the speedy service is a little tiresome, but the decor of this 1900s brasserie – all painted ceilings, wood panelling and coloured ceramics – is undeniably superb. Jacques Demy used the place in his classic movie *Lola*. It's not too expensive to dine – weekday lunch menu 75F, or 100–150F.

⦿ CHEZ L'HUÎTRE

5 rue des Petites Écuries. **MAP C2-16**
☎ 02.51.82.02.02
Closed Sun.

A small bistro, in the Bouffay district, with rough walls covered with old metal signs. The youthful proprietor specialises in salmon and oysters, platters of seafood and smoked fish platters. Try a plate of oysters and a glass of wine at apéritif time. A meal will cost about 80F.

⦿ CAFÉ DU MARCHÉ

1 rue de Mayence. **MAP D3-26**
☎ 02.40.47.63.50
Closed evenings, Sat, Sun, and Aug.

The formula has worked for nigh on fifty years. They serve a single menu with a choice of at least three starters, a dish of the day, cheese and dessert for 95F. Add a decent bottle and you can spend a lovely afternoon. It's a super place, very popular with the business excecutives escaping from seminars at the conference centre.

⚒ ⦿ LOU PESCADOU

8 allée Baco. **MAP C3-22**
☎ 02.40.35.29.50
Closed Sat lunchtime, Sun, Mon evening, and two weeks in Aug.

It's a good idea to book, since this is one of the best seafood restaurants around and gets pretty busy. The chef is a real enthusiast and a Muscadet aficionado – anything that he prepares in a white wine and butter sauce is a surefire winner. The bass baked in a salt crust is magnificent, too, as are the skate, monkfish and, if you can afford it, lobster and crayfish from the tank. Menus 125–320F. Free apéritif.

|●| RESTAURANT LE BOUCHON

7 rue Bossuet. MAP C2-25
☎ 02.40.20.08.44
Closed Sat and Wed lunchtimes, Sun, Christmas week.

In the quiet district arount the town hall, this half-timbered house claims to be "the best restaurant in rue Bossuet". You can't argue with that – it's the only one, apart from *Les Bouchonoerie*, the trendy tapas bar that's part of the same business. You can perch on a stool and eat a tasty, cheap snack or enjoy the more classic, bourgeois setting of the dining room. There's also a shady courtyard outside. Inventive, fresh cuisine with a bias towards seafood, served in a modern, easy-going way. Specialities include shellfish *croustillant* with thyme, pan-fried smoked tuna and apple soup with mint. Menu 139F.

CARQUEFOU   44470 (10KM N)

|●| RESTAURANT L'AUBERGE DU VIEUX GACHET

Le Gachet.
☎ 02.40.25.10.92
Closed Sun evening, Mon, a fortnight at the end of Aug and during the Feb holidays. **Car park**.

An attractive country inn with a terrace on the banks of the Erdre. The inventive and delicious poultry dishes get you the best of France: quail salad with hot *foie gras* or pot-roast pigeon. The fish is good, too, and prices are very affordable. Weekday menu 95F and others up to 260F. To walk here from Nantes, simply follow the path along the Erdre – it will take about two hours. The Château de la Gacherie is just opposite.

SAINT-FIACRE   44690 (18KM SE)

|●| LE FIACRE

1 rue d'Échirens; take the D59 towards Clisson.
☎ 02.40.54.83.92
Closed evenings and weekends except for reservations, and 1–21 Aug.

Small country restaurant where you eat at unfussy, wooden tables. Very well known locally for its good wine and food, it offers a lunch menu for 60F with a choice of two starters, a main dish (veal *blanquette* or *coq-au-vin*), cheese, dessert, coffee and wine. If you have an interest in wine, corner the proprietor, who has over a hundred Muscadets in the cellar. He knows them all individually and

can talk to you about them for hours.

MESSAN   44640 (20KM W)

|●| LE TISONNIER

Centre; it's on the D723 Saint Brévin-Painbœuf road on the way into Messan.
☎ 02.40.64.29.83
Closed evenings, and Christmas to New Year's Day.

Plain restaurant-café (which is also a tobacconist's and newsagent's) where the 50F *menu ouvrier* gets you a tasty meal: sausage in Muscadet plus cheese or dessert and a $1/4$ litre of wine. Other menus, from 64F, offer dishes which are a little more elaborate: half a cockerel, scallops, frogs' legs or sirloin. It would be hard to find better value for money and swifter service.

NOIRMOUTIER-EN-L'ILE   85330

⚐ 🏠 |●| HÔTEL-RESTAURANT LES CAPUCINES**

38 av. de la Victoire (North); it's on the Bois de la Chaize road.
☎ 02.51.39.06.82 ⇢ 02.51.39.33.10
Closed Wed and Thurs out of season, and 1 Nov–15 Feb. **TV**. **Car park**.

This hotel is set between the forest and the ocean and offers peace and quiet. It's run by Anne and Jean-Luc David, whose watchwords are quality and modernity. The wholesome food and comfortable rooms make it well worth a visit. Doubles 240F with shower, 480F with bath – add another 100F in the summer. Weekday menu 69F or 79–198F; dishes include fisherman's stew or hot *andouille* with onion compote. They prefer it if you stay half board in high season or on spring public holidays, but it's not compulsory. 10% discount on the room rate Sept–June except public holiday weekends.

⚐ 🏠 |●| LE CHÂTEAU DE PÉLAVÉ**

9 allée de Chaillot; it's on the edge of the Chaize forest.
☎ 02.51.39.01.94 ⇢ 02.51.39.70.42
✉ chateau-de-pelave@wanadoo.fr
Restaurant closed 4 Jan–10 Feb and 15 Nov–25 Dec. **TV**. **Car park**.

This vast 19th-century house is set in lovely wooded grounds. It's been renovated recently but its Victorian charm is undiminished. Comfortable, spacious rooms, 280–460F with shower. Reserve well in advance. The cuisine is of good quality and mainly traditional, with a balance of meat or fish dishes. There's an excellent selection of wines that the patron purchases directly from the producers in the winter months. Half board, compulsory July–Aug, is 314–470F per person. Menus 125–220F. Free apéritif with your first meal and 10% discount on the room rate Oct–April, except weekends.

🛏 |●| HÔTEL LES DOUVES**

11 rue des Douves (Centre); it's opposite the château.
☎ 02.51.39.02.72 ➡ 02.51.39.73.09
Closed Sun evening and Mon except in school holidays, and Jan. **Swimming pool**. **TV**. **Car park**.

This plush building nestles below the château in a very peaceful spot. It's a quiet hotel with a family atmosphere. The rooms are fresh and pretty with floral decor, and all have modern facilities; 315–480F with shower/wc or bath. There's a swimming pool for people who are too lazy to make it as far as the beach. The restaurant, Le Manoir, in the same building, is run by the owners' son.

|●| HÔTEL-RESTAURANT FLEUR DE SEL***

rue des Saulniers, BP 207 (Southwest); follow the signs from the château.
☎ 02.51.39.08.68 ✉ contact@fleurdesel.fr
Swimming pool.

A magnificent place classified as a "Châteaux, demeures de tradition" hotel, built some twenty years ago by the parents of the present owner. It's set apart from the town in the middle of a huge estate with Mediterranean landscapes, and has a lovely swimming pool. The 35 rooms are well equipped; those overlooking the pool are cosy and have English pine furniture, while those with private flowery terraces have yew furniture and a maritime feel. Doubles 400–720F. The restaurant is one of the best on the island if not in the Vendée. Everything is made on the premises. Menus 138–285F. Half board, 320–535F, is available for a two-night minimum stay. You can hire bikes or go on excursions. It's ideal for a relaxing stay.

🛏 |●| HÔTEL DU GÉNÉRAL-D'ELBÉE***

Pl. d'Arme; it's at the foot of the château near the canal port.
☎ 02.51.39.10.29 ➡ 02.51.39.08.23
✉ general-delbee@wanadoo.fr
Closed Oct–March. **Swimming pool**.

A marvellous hotel in a historic 18th-century building. VIP-types stay here but it's quite unspoilt and still affordable to people who prefer more refined places with a bit of patina. Some of the rooms are in a modern part of the building and overlook the swimming

pool; doubles 490–850F depending on location and size. There's a pub-sitting room.

|●| RESTAURANT CÔTÉ JARDIN

1 [bis] rue du Grand-Four (Centre); it faces the château at the top of the old town.
☎ 02.51.39.03.02
Closed Mon–Fri from mid-Nov to end Feb, Jan and a week in Oct. **Car park**.

This elegant restaurant in a splendid creeper-covered building has a beautiful dining room with stone walls and hefty beams. It offers gourmet fish and seafood: potato tart with crayfish and prawns with celery julienne, roast sea bream with sea salt and green asparagus butter. Delicate desserts such as millefeuille of pineapple with soft fruit coulis. There's a 76F two-course formule and menus 96–206F. Friendly welcome.

NOTRE-DAME-DE-MONTS   85690

⅍ 🛏 |●| HÔTEL DE LA PLAGE

145 av. de la Mer; it's on the corner of the main street, at right angles to the beach.
☎ 02.51.58.83.09 ➡ 02.51.58.97.12
Closed Oct–March. **TV**. **Car park**.

If you're going to splash out you might just as well do it right. This is the perfect place if you want to open the curtains and see the sea – ask for a room with a sea view and you'll get the terrace thrown in. The prices aren't outrageous given the quality of the place, the nice welcome and the rooms: doubles 184–230F with basin, 336–520F with shower/wc or bath. Lots of fish served in the restaurant: savoury pancakes with local lobster, croustillant of sardines with sweet and sour sauce, or iced cherries flambéed with Poissy. Free digestif and 10% discount on the room rate except July–Aug.

PAULX   44270

⅍ |●| RESTAURANT LES VOYAGEURS

1 pl. de l'Église (Centre).
☎ 02.40.26.02.76
Closed Sun and Tues evenings, Mon, the Feb school holidays, last week in Aug and first fortnight in Sept.

The atmosphere is very Vieille France. Call up the day before and they will create carefully prepared dishes to order. At lunchtime it's the haunt of businesspeople enjoying classic cuisine, while in the evening the dishes are more unusual: warm lobster terrine with shellfish sauce, duck breasts with *beurre rouge*, iced mandarin *soufflé impériale*. The produce is selected with meticulous care – free-range chicken, locally raised meat, and exceptionally fresh fish. Menus 105–290F. Free coffee.

PIRIAC-SUR-MER 44420

⅔ ▲ |●| HÔTEL-RESTAURANT DE LA POINTE

1 quai de Verdun (North); it's by the sea wall.
☎ 02.40.23.50.04 ➡ 02.40.15.59.65
Closed Tues evening and Wed out of season, and 1 Nov–20 March. **Car park**.

A relaxed hotel. Doubles with basin 200F, with shower/wc 260F. They're not very up-to-date but some have a view of the harbour and beach. The dining room, decorated in traditional bistro style, offers substantial salads, fish and seafood. Weekday menu 55F, others 95F and 150F. Friendly welcome. Half board, 280F, is compulsory July–Aug. 10% discount on the room rate Sept–June.

⅔ |●| CRÊPERIE LACOMÈRE

18 rue de Kéroman (Centre).
☎ and ➡ 02.40.23.53.63
Closed Mon and Tues in mid season and in winter except in the school holidays.

This restaurant is a little more inventive than the standard *crêperie*, with a menu inspired by discoveries the owner made on his travels around the world. Try the fish *tajine*, the red mullet *escabèche* or fish *choucroute*. Menus at 59F and 78F. There are only ten tables so it's best to book. Free apéritif.

PORNIC 44210

|●| RESTAURANT L'ESTAMINET

8 rue Maréchal-Foch (Centre).
☎ 02.40.82.35.99
Closed Sun evening and Mon Sept–June, and 15 Dec–15 Jan.

Judging by outward appearances, this restaurant in a busy street is nothing out of the ordinary, but once you're inside, the *patronne's* delightful manner and the chef's fresh cuisine definitely are. Menus 87–180F and weekday lunch *formule* 70F. Try veal sweetbreads with Pineau des Charentes, warm skate salad or scallops *en papillote*.

|●| RESTAURANT BEAU RIVAGE

plage de la Birochère.
☎ 02.40.82.03.08

Closed Sun evening and Mon out of season, and 10–26 Dec.

Friendly, colourful restaurant in a beautiful spot looking right over the beach. Seafood is the speciality, and the chef thoughtfully crafts excellent dishes from fresh ingredients: Atlantic *bouillabaisse*, sole *meunière*, lobster salad with herbs. Good menus 125–250F.

PLAINE-SUR-MER (LA) 44770 (9KM W)

⅔ ▲ |●| HÔTEL-RESTAURANT ANNE DE BRETAGNE***

port de la Gravette.
☎ 02.40.21.54.72 ➡ 02.40.21.02.33
Closed Sun evening, Mon and Tues lunchtime 15 Sep–15 April, Mon July–Aug, Sun and Mon the rest of the year. **Disabled access. Swimming pool. TV. Car park**.

A charming hotel with lovely rooms with garden or sea view. The location is splendid and it's very quiet. Doubles with shower/wc 420–510F or 510–730F with bath. There's a fancy little bar and a gourmet restaurant with a good reputation. A large selection of menus 130–385, including themed menus based on seasonal ingredients, and a *formule* (main course and dessert) 115F. Specialities include roast monkfish with red wine and sole cooked in its skin. Superb cellar with 15,000 bottles. Excellent welcome. 10% discount on the room rate 15 Sept–15 April.

PORT-JOINVILLE 85350

▲ HÔTEL L'ESCALE

Route de la Croix du Port.
☎ 02.51.58.50.28 ➡ 02.51.59.33.55
Closed Jan. **Garden. TV. Car park**.

White with yellow shutters, this is the prettiest place on the Île d'Yeu. Despite having thirty rooms, it retains a guesthouse atmosphere, with cool marine decor and doubles 190–330F. Breakfast, 35F, is served around the old well in the middle of the bright dining room that opens onto the garden through French windows. The owner gives good advice about where to go and what to see.

⅔ ▲ ATLANTIC HÔTEL***

quai Carnot (Centre).
☎ 02.51.58.38.80 ➡ 02.51.58.35.92
Closed three weeks in Jan. **TV. Car park**.

Fifteen cute little rooms with every comfort. Half of them face the fishing harbour, the focus of local activity, while the others look out over the village – both views are pleasant. Doubles 240F out of season for a double with village view, 390F in summer with a view of the harbour. Breakfast 35F. 10% discount on the room rate except July–Aug and long weekends on spring public holidays.

🏃 🛏 |O| FLUX HÔTEL-RESTAURANT LA MARÉE**

27 rue Pierre-Henry (North).
☎ 02.51.58.36.25 ➡ 02.51.59.44.57
Closed Sun evening and mid-Nov to mid-Jan.
Disabled access. Garden. TV. Car park.

Away from the bustle of Port-Joinville, this hotel's peaceful grounds, bordering the seashore, make it a select location. Well-kept double rooms overlooking the garden cost 250–350F. Room number 15, set away from the main hotel, is especially spacious and has a fireplace. The restaurant, La Marée, is run by different people, so you pay for your meal separately from your room. The enormous dining room has a huge fireplace for winter evening and a lovely terrace for dining out beneath the shade of the trees in summer. Creamy soups are a house speciality as are the mussels *sauce poulette*. Set menus 90–195F. Smiling, friendly service. 10% discount on the room rate Sept–June excluding spring public holidays.

|O| LES BAFOUETTES

8 rue Gabriel Guist'hau (Centre); 100m from the port, past the tourist office.
☎ 02.51.59.38.38
Closed Tues Sept–June.

The small dining room is quietly decorated with pictures by local artists. The cuisine is joyfully expressive and served by really enthusiastic staff. Menus start at 85F and dishes include tasty fish soup, pan-fried crayfish and other maritime goodies.

|O| RESTAURANT DU PÈRE RABALLAND-L'ÉTAPE MARITIME

It's on the harbour on the right coming from the quay.
☎ 02.51.26.02.77
Closed Tues Sept–June.

A bar-brasserie that's decorated to look like the inside of a boat. The cuisine is refined and they serve seafood accompanied by wines bought direct from the vineyards. If you want more intimacy, go for the "gastronomic" dining room upstairs – but the food is the same. Menus 115–159F. Excellent value for money. Père Raballand is a personality in town and the atmosphere in his bistro in summer or at the weekend is unmatched.

POUZAUGES 85700

|O| RESTAURANT PATRICK

How to get there: on the D752, it's at Puzauges-Gare just after Fleury-Michon on the left.

A long modern house, painted pink. Everyone round here knows the place because the Patrick in question is a talented chef who has made a great name for himself. He gets his fish from the coast and knows how to pick it. His 115F menu lists ten oysters or salmon *tartare*, *confit* of duck or roast zander and dessert. Other menus 58–160F. It's all good.

ROCHEFORT-SUR-LOIRE 49190

🛏 |O| LE GRAND HOTEL

30 rue René-Gasnier.
☎ 02.41.78.80.46 ➡ 02.41.78.83.25
Closed Wed and Sun evening, Tues evening out of season, the Feb and All Saints' school holidays. **Garden.**

A nice old house with a garden, in the main street. It's ideal as a base for exploring the Layon area. The ground-floor dining room is decorated in shades of yellow and green. Very carefully prepared dishes with lots of local specialities: simmered frogs' legs, Anjou *rillauds*, yellow ling stewed with vegetables and a banana *bavarois*. Menus 108–210F. The rooms are fairly big but quite simple. The nicest are on the first floor overlooking the garden. Doubles from 200F. Nice welcome.

ROCHE-SUR-YON (LA) 85000

🏃 🛏 |O| MARIE STUART HÔTEL**

86 bd. Louis-Blanc (Centre); it's opposite the station.
☎ 02.51.37.02.24 ➡ 02.51.37.86.37
Restaurant closed Sat lunchtime and Sun. **TV.**

This hotel is decorated entirely with Scottish trappings, including tartans, coats of arms and a portrait of Mary, Queen of Scots. The spacious rooms are rather chic and have stylish furniture. Doubles 295F with shower/wc or bath. The restaurant serves good, simple food with some quasi-Scottish specialities: Highland steak, Scotch eggs and dumplings but also fisherman's stew. Menus 79–129F; the bar menu gives you a starter and a main course. They have a good selection of malts. Free aperitif.

⚵ 🏠 HÔTEL LE LOGIS DE LA COUPERIE***

Route de Cholet; it's five minutes from the town centre – take the main road to Cholet and then the D80.
☎ 02.51.37.21.19 ➡ 02.51.47.71.08
TV. Secure parking.

In a stately 14th-century mansion hidden away in the depths of the countryside, this is one of the most appealing hotels in the Vendée. The atmosphere is a combination of refinement and simplicity. There are just seven cosy rooms, each named after a flower, decorated in English style with canopy beds and antique furniture. Doubles 320F with shower/wc or 380F with bath. The only sounds to wake you are the ducks and the frogs in the pond. Don't miss the lovingly prepared breakfast. A cordial welcome from a charming host. Free home-made apple juice.

|●| LE CLÉMENCEAU

40 rue Georges-Clémenceau.
☎ 02.51.37.10.20

This is a genuine brasserie and it has an attractive terrace. It's well known for the freshness of the shellfish, seafood and fish. The names of the suppliers are inscribed on the menu. There's a substantial seafood platter for 80F and very tasty fish soup. Full meals from 80F. Nice staff and friendly atmosphere.

⚵|●| SAINT-CHARLES RESTAURANT

38 rue du Président-de-Gaulle (Centre).
☎ 02.51.47.71.37
✉ mail@restaurant-stcharles.com
Closed Sat lunchtime, Sun and 10–26 Aug.

Photos of jazz musicians and instruments adorn the walls, jazz plays softly in the background and even the menu features jazz references. In this good atmosphere the chef produces creations such as *carpaccio* of duck with *foie gras* and sea bream steamed over seaweed. Menus, 98–209F, offer good value for money. Free coffee.

POIRÉ-SUR-VIE (LE) 85170 (13.5KM NW)

⚵ 🏠 |●| HÔTEL-RESTAURANT LE CENTRE**

19 pl. du Marché (Centre); take the D6.
☎ 02.51.31.81.20 ➡ 02.51.31.88.21
Closed Fri and Sun evening out of season. **Disabled access. Swimming pool. TV. Car park.**

This welcoming hotel, right in the middle of the village, has clean, comfortable rooms. Doubles 185F with basin, 345F with bath. The restaurant offers simple authentic regional cooking, with dishes like fillet of zander in a butter and white wine sauce, country ham *à la crème*, and home-made *foie gras*, all for reasonable prices. Menus up to 159F. Free coffee.

MACHÉ 85190 (22KM NW)

⚵|●| AUBERGE LE FOUGERAIS

How to get there: take the D948 for 22km, after Aizenay turn left beyond the river Vie bridge and follow the signposts.
☎ 02.51.55.75.44
Closed evenings Mon–Wed except July–Aug and a fortnight in Oct. **Car park.**

A lovely converted barn covered in ivy with a shady terrace. It's a peaceful place, where unfussy, tasty food is served at simple tables. The chef adds a few vine stems to the open fire to add flavour when he grills eel, salmon, rib of beef or quail. Weekday lunch menu 65F and others up to 130F which offer good value for money. Free apéritif.

ROSIERS (LES) 49350

|●| AU P'TIT BAGNARD GOURMAND

4 rue de la Corderie (Southeast); 400m from the town centre heading towards Saumur.
☎ 02.41.51.87.76
Closed Sun evening, Mon and three weeks in Jan.
Disabled access. Car park.

The surroundings are quite exceptional, and the cuisine is superb. Menus feature very good main courses, like the *cabérillon* of duck, which is marinated in red wine for 24 hours and then cooked slowly in goose fat. To start you'll get delicious *charcuterie* or *foie gras* accompanied by fresh mushrooms and a Coteaux-de-l'Aubance. Leave room for one of the best chocolate mousses ever. The chef really knows how to make his guests feel at home. Lunchtime menu 75F (not Sun), and others from 98–160F including wine.

⚵|●| LA TOQUE BLANCHE*

2 rue Quarte: it's on the way out of the village on the Angers road, after the bridge.
☎ 02.41.51.80.75
Closed Tues evening and Wed. **Car park.**

It is becoming increasingly necessary to book a table at this up-and-coming restaurant – and it's essential for Sunday lunch. Inventive cuisine is served in an elegant, air-conditioned dining room. There's a 110F menu including wine (not served Sun), and others 148–230F. Dishes include home-smoked salmon, red mullet *mousse* and caviar sauce, liver *parfait* in port accompanied by a glass of Layon, langoustine tails sautéed with vanilla pods, poached chicken à l'*angevine*, sweet and sour duck leg and much more. Friendly welcome. Free coffee.

SABLES-D'OLONNE (LES)   85100

☎ HÔTEL DE LA TOUR

46 rue du Dr. Canteteau, La Chaume (West).
☎ 02.51.95.38.48

This nice little place is in a typical street in the Chaume district. It's run by a young couple who make guests feel like friends. Madame has decorated each room in a different theme and the furniture, which was made to order, echoes the shape of the theme: the "Tower" or the "Roofs of the District". The colours are inspired by the sea – blues and greens. Doubles 165–200F. Some rooms have a view of the port. There's also an interior garden full of flowers where you can have breakfast or you can eat in the breakfast room accompanied by Madame's singing. A very unusual place.

☎ |●| HÔTEL LES EMBRUNS

33 rue du Lieutenant-Anger, La Chaume.
☎ 02.51.95.25.99 ➡ 02.51.95.84.48
e lesembruns.hotel@wanadoo.fr
Closed Sun evening Sept–May, Nov and Feb.

It's easy to spot the yellow frontage of this building with its green shutters. The rooms are very pretty and painted in attractive colours, and they're brilliantly maintained by the welcoming young pair who run the place. Some of the rooms overlook the port while the ones looking onto a small side street are cooler in summer. Doubles 230–300F.

🎿 ☎ |●| HÔTEL ANTOINE**

60 rue Napoléon (Centre).
☎ 02.51.95.08.36 ➡ 02.51.23.92.78
Closed Oct–March. **Garden. TV. Pay car park**.

A delightful haven right in the centre of town, between the harbour and the beach. Quiet rooms, some of which look out over the garden, cost 260F with shower/wc in the annexe or 350F with bath in the main hotel. Prices are a little lower out of season. Half board, compulsory July–Aug, is 260–300F per person. The food is excellent, prepared from the freshest market produce. 10% dis-

count on the room rate Sept–June and public holiday weekends.

☎ |●| HÔTEL LES HIRONDELLES**

44 rue des Corderies (Centre).
☎ 02.51.95.10.50 ➡ 02.51.32.31.01
e leshirondelles£wanadoo.fr
Closed end Sept to end March. **TV. Car park**.

This hotel does not look very attractive from the outside but the rooms have a fresh, modern decor. Some rooms have balconies which are ideal for breakfast and others lead onto a pretty patio that's all white and planted with exotic, perfumed plants. Doubles 300–370F with shower/wc. Menus, 80–145F, list fish and seafood dishes: fish *choucroute*, prawn kebabs and mussel stew. The kindness of the hostess is completely winning.

|●| L'AFFICHE

21 quai Guiné; it's near the port, opposite the embarcation for the Île d'Yeu.
☎ 02.51.95.34.74

The outside is painted yellow and beckons you in. Inviting dishes include mussels *au gratin*, salmon fillet, sautéed lamb sweetbreads with crayfish and duck breast with cider – *gratin* of strawberries and pistachio nuts for dessert. Menus 69–158F. A flavourful treat and good value for money.

|●| LA FLEUR DES MERS

5 quai Guiné; it's on the seafront facing the harbour.
☎ 02.51.95.18.10
Closed Sun evening, Mon, Tues lunchtime and Jan.

Chic and spruce with the ambience of a luxury liner. As you go up to the top floor, you get a splendid view of the harbour. The dining room is fresh, bright and spacious, and the cuisine is delicate: *gratin* of seafood, delicious grilled sardines, fresh *moules marinière* and monkfish. Weekday lunch menu 75F and then 92–195F.

🎿 |●| RESTAURANT LE CLIPPER

19 [bis] quai Guiné.
☎ 02.51.32.03.61
Closed Tues evening and Wed, Mon July–Aug, a fortnight in Dec and a fortnight in Feb.

The setting includes wood, hurricane lamps and port-holes, and the menu features unusual fish dishes. Subtle yet astonishing combinations include sea bass with sesame seeds roasted in meat juices, monkfish *blanquette* with vegetables stewed in butter and fresh roast figs with honey and almond cream. 75F lunch menu and others up to 195F. Many local regulars. Considerate, attentive service. Free coffee.

☆|●| RESTAURANT GEORGE V

20 rue George-V–La Chaume.
☎ 02.51.95.11.52
Closed Sun evening and Mon.

The bright, elegant dining rooms on the ground or first floors look out to the harbour entrance. Chef Olivier Burban prepares excellent food – not surprisingly, fish is the main ingredient, but it is imaginatively prepared. Unexpected flavours pop up in dishes such as salad of squid fritters with walnut oil, chef's hotpot, *foie gras* cooked in a cloth with a sweet wine jelly, and *gâteau* of langoustines. Leave room for the *pain perdu* (France's answer to bread and butter pudding) or the hot apple tart. Menus 80–150F. Free coffee.

SABLÉ-SUR-SARTHE   72300

☆|●| LES PALMIERS

54 Grande-Rue (Centre).
☎ 02.43.95.03.82
Closed Tues and Sat lunchtime.

Genuine Moroccan hospitality offered by a charming couple as an antidote to *rillette* and fish stew. Abdou mans the kitchens while his French wife greets the guests. There is little passing trade in what is a pretty run-down street in the old part of town, and the owners depend on the restaurant's reputation being spread by word of mouth. The two large dining rooms are smart and very well decorated, offering comfortable surroundings in which to enjoy the best of Moroccan cuisine. They offer large helpings of aromatic stews, vegetables and excellent meat. Superb *tajines* 69–75F, *couscous* with a selection of meats 69–100F, and delicious home-made pastries. Free coffee.

|●| L'HOSTELLERIE SAINT-MARTIN

3 rue Haute-Saint-Martin (Centre); it's in a small street leading off the town hall square.
☎ 02.43.95.00.03
Closed Sun and Wed evenings, Mon, the Feb school holidays and the first fortnight in Sept.

The high-ceilinged dining room has an antiquated charm and traditional decor, with a dresser, Normandy clock, heavy red velvet curtains, copper pots and pans, and fresh flowers on every table. The parquet floor creaks underfoot. Good traditional, local food on menus 95–125F. You can also eat on the terrace.

DUREIL   72270 (16KM E)

|●| L'AUBERGE DES ACACIAS

Centre; take the D309 to Parcé-sur-Sarthe or the D23 to Malicorne, then turn down the small road that follows the Sarthe river.
☎ 02.43.95.34.03
Closed Sun evening, Mon, weeknights Nov–Feb, and three weeks in March.

It may not be smothered in Virginia creeper any more but it's still worth a visit. Dishes change seasonally – the duck breast with elderflower and the desert platter are a must. The terrace is delightful, and in winter you can eat beside the cosy fireplace. Menus from 92F during the week.

SAINT-CALAIS   72120

|●| À SAINT-ANTOINE

8 pl. St-Antoine (Northeast).
☎ 02.43.35.01.56
Closed Sun evening, Mon and Wed evening in winter, and 8–20 April. **Car park**.

The Achard brothers – who served their apprenticeships as wine waiter and chef at *Maxim's* and *Plaza Athénée* respectively – caused quite a stir when they took over an old bistro in pl. Saint-Antoine and turned it into a "real" restaurant. It's a good, unfussy place, where locals meet for lunch at the bar before returning to their occupations. The small dining room soon fills up. Superb, colourful, tasty cooking on the menus – mackerel *timbale* with tomato *confit* and *panaché* of fish and cockles. Weekday menu 65F or 120F. Good, affordable local wines.

SAINT-GERVAIS-DE-VIC   72120 (4KM S)

☆|●| LE SAINT-ÉLOI

1 rue Bertrand Guilmain; it's near the church.
☎ 02.43.35.19.56
Closed Sun evening out of season, a fortnight in Feb and Aug.

The proprietors of this restaurant were previously pork butchers – today their dining room is full every Sunday with clamouring hordes of regulars. The 58F weekday menu secures a buffet of starters, *blanquette* or *coq au vin*, cheese, tart, coffee and wine. Other menus 130–150F; the most expensive one has three dishes – a starter, a fish course and breast of duck with green peppercorns. Free apéritif.

SAINT-DENIS-D'ORQUES 72350

🎿 ❚❙❚ L'AUBERGE DE LA GRANDE CHARNIE

rue Principale (Centre); it's on the N157, halfway between Laval and Le Mans.
☎ 02.43.88.43.12
Closed Sun evening and the Feb school holidays.
Car park.

An exquisite dining room and excellent local cuisine that won't break the bank. There is always a dish of the day, such as beef stew, free-range ham on the bone in cider and wild mushroom sauce or fish stew *sarthoise*, but always take the advise of the *patronne* who will tell you what the chef has prepared using that day's fresh market produce. Menus from 89F. Free coffee.

SAINT-FLORENT-LE-VIEIL 49410

🎿 🏠 ❚❙❚ L'HOSTELLERIE DE LA GABELLE

12 quai de la Loire.
☎ 02.41.72.50.19 ➡ 02.41.72.54.38
Closed Sun evening and Mon lunchtime Oct–May.

A traditional provincial hotel well located on the banks of the Loire, a good spot to stop on between Nantes and Angers. The *Tour de la Gabelle* is on the corner which makes it look classy. The cuisine is simple but tasty: Loire eels *à la Provençale*, zander in *beurre blanc* and house *foie gras*. Menus 85F in the week, then 120–250F. The rooms are in the old style but the decoration is quite tired with a *Vieille France* feel. Doubles 290F with shower/wc or bath. Free coffee.

SAINT-GILLES-CROIX-DE-VIE 85800

COMMEQUIERS 85220 (12KM NE)

🎿 🏠 ❚❙❚ HÔTEL DE LA GARE**

rue de la Morinière; take the D754.
☎ 02.51.54.80.38
Hotel closed Oct to end March. **Restaurant closed** Mon, All Saints' and Jan. **Swimming pool. Car park**.

This pleasing station hotel was built at the turn of the 19th century. The trains have long stopped running, and the prettily decorated rooms are agreeable, even charming. Doubles 190–220F with basin or shower/wc. There are references to the history of the railways with old photographs, lanterns and ticket punchers. The chef slaves to produce good, uncomplicated food, which is served in large por-

tions. Menus 85F (not Sun) and 115F. Dishes include grilled sardines, scallops with saffron, seafood, veal kidneys with port, stuffed snails, leg of lamb with haricot beans and roast duck. Free apéritif.

SAINT-HILAIRE-DE-RIEZ 85270

🎿 ❚❙❚ RESTAURANT LA BOURRINE DE RIEZ

221 av. de la Corniche.
☎ 02.51.55.01.83
Closed Mon and Tues evening out of season, Dec, Jan.

The panelled walls are adorned with copper pots and diplomas and certificates from a whole host of culinary bodies – including the Sardine Association. You can eat well here without spending too much – set menus 70F (not Sun) and 95–195F. Dishes include salmon and scallop turnovers, *émincé* of duckling breast, *moules marinière* with bacon and balsamic vinegar, and apple tart. Free coffee.

SAINT-JEAN-DE-MONTS 85160

🎿 🏠 ❚❙❚ HÔTEL-RESTAURANT LE ROBINSON**

28 bd. Leclerc (Centre).
☎ 02.51.59.20.20 ➡ 02.51.58.88.03
📧 hotel-restaurant-le-robinson@wanadoo.fr
Closed 6 Dec–30 Jan. **TV. Car park**.

This family business has become a substantial tourist complex over the years. The original hotel has changed considerably following the many extensions and additions, but quality has been maintained. There are several types of room, all comfortable, some overlooking the leafy avenues, others overlooking the road. Doubles 210–420F. Traditional, pleasant, carefully prepared cuisine: scallop kebabs and other seafood dishes, duck breast with honey and apples. 77F menu (not Sun lunch) and others 113–192F. As usual for this part of the world, reserve well in advance. Free coffee.

🎿 🏠 ❚❙❚ HÔTEL LE RICHELIEU***

8 av. des Œillets (Southeast).
☎ and ➡ 02.51.58.06.78
Closed Tues evening and Wed, three weeks in Nov and a fortnight in Feb. **Garden. TV. Car park**.

The Norman architecture of this large comfortable house is incongruous around here. It's set back from the seafront and has its own garden. There are eight very comfortable, tastefully decorated rooms; doubles 220–450F. Menus, 99–165F, list simple food made from excellent ingredients: lobster with crumbled truffles and duck *foie gras*. They'll treat you like one of the family. 10% discount on the room rate out of season.

SAINT-LÉONARD-DES-BOIS   72590

⅍ 🏠 |●| TOURING HÔTEL***

How to get there: follow the Alpes Mancelles route.
☎ 02.43.31.44.44 ➡ 02.43.31.44.49
Swimming pool. TV. Car park.

A good place to stay, near the Sarthe river in the heart of the hills known as *les Alpes Mancelles*. Although the building is constructed from concrete, the atmosphere, hospitality, cuisine and swimming pool soon make you forget the dull architecture – it's the only branch of the *Forestdale* chain in France. Quiet, well-appointed rooms from 395F. The weekday lunch menu, 75F, offers home-smoked salmon or haddock fillet, plaice with mussels and horn of plenty mushrooms, and fresh fruit turnover, or there are other menus 95–250F. 10% discount on the room rate.

|●| LE SAINT-LÉO

pl. de l'Église.
☎ 02.43.33.81.79
Closed Wed evening and Dec/Jan.

A restaurant with lots of charm run by a man who has moved from playing the cello to orchestrating delicious menus in his kitchen. He grills cuts of meat or fish in front of you, both to be sure it's perfectly cooked and to be friendly. He uses quality produce – you'd better arrive early if you want the smoked salmon or *terrines*. Menus 70F and 98F. The view from the dining room is attractive.

SAINT-NAZAIRE   44600

🏠 HÔTEL DE TOURAINE*

4 av. de la République (Centre); it's near the town halll.
☎ 02.40.22.47.56 ➡ 02.40.22.55.05
📧 hoteltouraine.free.fr
Closed Christmas to 1 Jan.

It's hard enough to find a reasonably priced clean, pleasant hotel in Saint-Nazaire, let alone one that offers a substantial breakfast (served in the garden in good weather) for 30F, and a free ironing service to boot. This hospitable place has all those things. Doubles 135F with basin, 235F with bath.

⅍ 🏠 |●| KORALI HÔTEL**

pl. de la Gare (North).
☎ 02.40.01.89.89 ➡ 02.40.66.47.96
TV. Disabled access.

The lack of pleasant hotels in Saint-Nazaire makes you appreciate this welcoming establishment all the more. It's a modern building and the rooms have good facilities. Half board costs 338F per person. Menus 90–130F. Breakfast is served from 5am. Free coffee.

⅍|●| RESTAURANT LE MODERNE

46 rue d'Anjou (Centre).
☎ 02.40.22.55.88
Closed Sun evening, Mon and 14–31 July.

In a town not known for its cuisine, the offerings and prices of this family restaurantl should be appreciated all the more. Try the tasty traditional seafood *choucroute*, stewed scallops with morels, or duck thigh *confit*. Menus 75–240F. Service can be uptight. Free coffee.

SAINT-JOACHIM   44720 (10KM N)

⅍ 🏠 |●| L'AUBERGE DU PARC-LA MARE AUX OISEAUX

162 Ile de Fédrun.
☎ 02.40.88.53.01 ➡ 02.40.91.67.44
Closed Sun evening, Mon and March.

The inhabitants of île de Fédrun have adopted Éric Guérin as their favourite chef. This young man is full of ideas and produces inspired dishes: snails and cuttlefish with wild nettles, lacquered zander, frogs on a bed of seaweed. Menus 195F, 250F and 300F. Four rooms, under a reed-thatched roof (which is in keeping with the local *Brièronne* atmosphere) cost 380F. Free apéritif.

SAINT-BREVIN-L'OCÉAN   44250 (12KM S)

⅍ 🏠 |●| HÔTEL-RESTAURANT ROSE MARIE**

1 allée des Embruns; it's near the beach, two minutes from the centre.
☎ 02.40.27.20.45 ➡ 02.40.39.14.66

Appealing hotel run by the last member of a family that has owned the place since 1932. The food is full of the flavours of the sea – zander on vegetable caviar, fish *choucroute*, seafood platters, stuffed clams, scallop with oyster mushrooms, sole *paupiettes* and grilled lobster with truffle fragments. Menus 78F and 150F. There's a new *brasserie-bar* serving good traditional brasserie fare: steak *tartare*, Troye *andouille*, roast spare ribs and chips. Lovely doubles 250F. Full board is compulsory in summer, 250F per person. There's jazz on the terrace at the weekends. Free apéritif.

SAINT-VINCENT-DU-LOROUËR   72150

ℑ |●| L'AUBERGE DE L'HERMITIÈRE

Sources de l'Hermitière; it's 4.5 km south of Saint-Vincent-du-Lorouër.
☎ 02.43.44.84.45
Closed Mon evening. **Disabled access**.

The setting for this wood and brick house is splendid, in a wood, just by the river where there's a terrace. Even the Queen Mother has been here. It's one of the great tables in the Sarthe yet it still serves a menu for 100F – others 145–265F. Free apéritif.

SAINT-VINCENT-SUR-JARD   85520

ℑ ☎ |●| HÔTEL-RESTAURANT L'OCÉAN**

rue Georges-Clémenceau (West); it's next to musée Clémenceau.
☎ 02.51.33.40.45 ➡ 02.51.33.98.15
Closed Wed out of season and mid-Nov to end Feb. **Disabled access**. **Swimming pool**. **Garden**. **TV**. **Car park**.

This pre-war hotel continues to grow in reputation and hospitality. The rooms, which look onto a quiet garden, cost 260–450F with shower or bath. The six set menus, 85–250F, should satisfy seafood-lovers. Half board, compulsory June–Sept, is 235–405F per person. Friendly welcome; they'll let you use the pool even if you've just dropped in for a drink. Free house apéritif Oct–May.

SAULGES   53340

ℑ ☎ |●| HÔTEL-RESTAURANT L'ERMITAGE***

pl. Saint-Pierre.
☎ 02.43.64.66.00 ➡ 02.43.64.66.20
Closed Sun evening and Mon Oct to mid-April, All Saints' and Feb. **Swimming pool**. **TV**. **Car park**.

A modern hotel with bright, spacious, comfortable rooms, overlooking the park, swimming pool and countryside, 330–560F with shower/wc or bath. The restaurant serves traditional dishes with a modern twist: fresh crab *soufflé* with lobster cream, duck *terrine* with *foie gras*, beef in Chinon, rabbit and kid-

neys with Pommeau, apple tart with gingerbread ice cream. A wide selection of menus, 100–250F. Free house apéritif.

SAUMUR   49400

ℑ ☎ HÔTEL LE CENTER

pl. de la Sénatorie at Saint-Hilaire-Saint-Florent; it's 2km from the centre on the D751 in the direction of Chênehutte.
☎ 02.41.50.37.88
Car park.

A friendly, good-value little hotel just outside the town. You feel as if you're in a village but you can get into the centre very quickly. The whole place is very clean and well maintained. Doubles from 160F. The owner is on hand for any information you might need. Credit cards not accepted.

ℑ ☎ HÔTEL LE VOLNEY

1 rue Volney; it's near the post office.
☎ 02.41.51.25.41 ➡ 02.41.38.11.04
TV. **Car park**.

The rooms are spotless, homely and comforting and will calm you down if you're stressed out. The prices are remarkably stable – 160F for a double with basin, 220F with shower/wc and 265F with bath. Excellent welcome from the mistress of the house. 10% discount Nov–March.

ℑ ☎ HÔTEL DE LONDRES**

48 rue d'Orléans (Centre).
☎ 02.41.51.23.98 ➡ 02.41.51.12.63
TV. **Car park**.

Friendly hotel in a good location – the soundproofing blocks out the noise of the street. It's been redecorated in a charming, English style and is well maintained. Room numbers 25 and 28 have particularly lovely new decor, and there are a few family rooms, too. Doubles 260–280F with shower/wc. Very warm welcome from the ladies of the house. Copious buffet breakfast 37F. 10% discount.

ℑ ☎ CENTRAL HÔTEL**

23 rue Daillé (Centre); from quai Carnot take rue Fidélité and it's the first on the left after rue Saint-Nicolas.
☎ 02.41.51.05.78 ➡ 02.41.67.82.35
TV. **Pay car park**.

A modern building, entirely renovated inside and out, with a pleasant, rather refined decor and exposed beams. The 27 rooms are spacious and all different – and there's a large room that sleeps four, which is excellent value for money. Doubles with shower/wc or bath 295–395F. Affable, welcoming host. 10% discount in low season.

🏃 🏠 |O| HÔTEL ANNE D'ANJOU***

32–33 quai Mayaud (Centre); it's below the château, beside the Loire.
☎ 02.41.67.30.30 ➡ 02.41.67.51.00
e anneanjou@saumur.net
Disabled access. TV. Car park.

An elegant 18th-century building, full of charm, with a flower-filled internal courtyard and a superb listed staircase. Comfortable rooms with antique furniture 450–790F with shower/wc or bath. Some rooms are under the eaves, and there's also an opulent, Empire-style room ideal for a special treat or a honeymoon, and suites up to 980F. Professional welcome. Breakfast 55F. 10% discount mid-Oct to mid-April.

|O| AUBERGE SAINT-PIERRE

6 pl. Saint-Pierre and 33 rue de la Tonnelle.
☎ 02.41.51.26.25
Closed Sun except July–Aug, Mon, a fortnight in March and a fortnight in Oct.

The 15th-century house is panelled with wood and hung with flowers. There are several dining rooms but they're often full to bursting. Lots of shades of yellow and nice wainscotting inside with a few handsome stones in the walls. Simple, appetizing cuisine. *Formule brasserie* 59F or menus 89–150F. You can eat outside in sunny weather. It's very reasonably priced and shouldn't be missed.

🏃 |O| LA PIERRE CHAUDE

41 av. du Général-de-Gaulle; it's on l'île d'Offard, between the two bridges, going towards the station.
☎ 02.41.67.18.83
Closed Sat lunchtime and Sun, a week in Feb, the first fortnight in Nov and a week at Christmas.

The dining room has been decorated in Wild West style and they play country music. You cook your chosen meats yourself on a hot stone which is brought to your table, 90F for the dish. It's great for keeping the kids quiet. You can choose all sorts of delicious sauces to accompany your meat. They also do traditional dishes. Weekday lunch menu 65F, the "*Saloon*" at 85F and the "*Diligence*" at 118F. Free apéritif.

🏃 |O| LES MÉNESTRELS

11–13 rue Raspail; it's next to the law courts.
☎ 02.41.67.71.10
Closed Sun, Sun evening only in the mid-season.

The best restaurant in the area, with a rustic setting, original beams and exposed stonework. The set menus, 100F (lunchtimes Mon–Sat) and others up to 350F, offer fine combinations of complex flavours. Specialities change frequently, but typically you might be offered joint of zander with *Guémené andouille* or pigeon breast wrapped in cabbage with *foie gras* and truffle *jus*. Excellent welcome. Free coffee.

🏃 |O| L'AUBERGE REINE DE SICILE**

71 rue Waldeck-Rousseau (Northeast); it's on île d'Offard, between the two bridges.
☎ 02.41.67.30.48
Closed Sun evening, Mon and Aug. **Car park**.

This welcoming, quiet restaurant, situated beside a charming medieval building, is away from the usual tourist circuit. They specialise in meat grilled over the wood fire and fish dishes – try fish *terrine*, *moules marinière*, grilled salmon, eels stewed in a wine sauce, zander in a white wine and butter sauce, home-made *foie gras*, rib of Charolais beef, *andouillette*, duck *confit* or leg of lamb. Menus 110–200F. It's important to book. Free apéritif.

ROU-MARSON   49400 (6KM W)

🏃 |O| RESTAURANT LES CAVES DE MARSON

1 rue Henri Fricotelle; leaving Saumur on the N147 head for Cholet, take the D960, and it's signposted after 6km.
☎ 02.41.50.50.05.
Closed 25 Dec–15 Jan. **Open** Tues–Sat evening and Sun lunchtime 15 June–15 Sept, Fri and Sat evening and Sun lunch 16 Sept–14 June. **Car park**.

The best-known troglodyte restaurant in Saumur. A labyrinth of dining rooms in a cave, lit by candles and with a unique charm. The food is fantastic, too – they serve mouthwatering *fouées* (a kind of *galette*) filled with beans, *rillettes*, goat's cheese or *foie gras*. As a starter you could try a flambéed tart with a glass of Coteaux-du-Layon, and to finish, a salad and a delicious *gratin* of seasonal fruit. Accompany it with an excellent bottle of red Anjou. Menus 120–170F, children's menu 60F. It's not at all expensive given the quality. You have to book a table several days in advance in high season. Free glass of sparkling wine with dessert.

MONTSOREAU   49730 (11KM SE)

🏃 |O| RESTAURANT LE SAUT-AUX-LOUPS

Route de Saumur; coming from Saumur on the D947, it's at the beginning of the village.
☎ 02.41.51.70.30
Open lunchtimes, Sun only June and Sept, Tues–Sun July–Aug. **Disabled access.**

This was the first troglodyte restaurant in the region to relaunch the almost forgotten local speciality, the *galipette*: take three big mushrooms and stuff them with *rillette* or *andouille* and *crème fraîche*, snails or goat's cheese. Brown them gently in a bread oven fuelled by vine cuttings and serve with a light, fruity Gamay. Around 70F for the mushrooms including a drink or around 100F for a full meal. Excellent welcome delivered by the young owner and you'll enjoy the setting. In summer he puts tables outside. Free coffee.

SILLÉ-LE-GUILLAUME   72140

🏄 🏠 |●| LE BRETAGNE**

1 pl. de la Croix d'Or (Centre); it's near the station.
☎ 02.43.20.10.10
Closed Fri–Sun evening April–Sept, Fri evening, Sat lunchtime and Sun evening Oct–March, the Feb school holidays and the first fortnight in Aug. **TV. Car park**.

Inside this crumbling family hotel there's a superb restaurant offering fresh-tasting and exciting dishes that change with the seasons: leek *terrine*, *foie gras* salad with walnut oil, lightly smoked salmon, green lentils, *fondant* of oxtail, scorpion fish with lemongrass, and a delicious *Paris-Brest* filled with butter icing. Weekday menu 79F, and others 179F and 260F. Decent rooms 190–240F. 10% discount on the room rate.

THOUARCÉ   49380

|●| LE RELAIS DE BONNEZEAUX

Bonnezeaux; take the D24 for about 2km from Thouarcé heading towards Angers, and it's in the old train station.
☎ 02.41.54.08.33
Closed evenings Sun–Tues, and three weeks in Jan. **Car park**.

Though this restaurant is housed in a 19th-century station, there's little of the old atmosphere left. The dining room, with its panoramic view, is an elegant setting for the refined cuisine. Menus 75F or 100F (weekday lunchtime) and 140–265F. They specialise in delicious, original fish dishes. À la *carte* try milk-fed lamb, zander *suprême* in red Anjou wine, and *nougat glacé* with Cointreau. The wine list includes some amazing

old vintages. There's a shady terrace and playground for the children.

TRANCHE-SUR-MER (LA)   85360

|●| RESTAURANT LE MILOUIN

99 av. Maurice-Samson; it's between the town centre and the lighthouse.
☎ 02.51.27.49.49
Closed Mon and Tues out of season. **Car park**.

A small, relaxed dining room with exposed beams and a terrace out front that's open in summer. Tasty regional cuisine: mussel stew in Pinot, roast zander in chicken *jus*, calves' sweetbreads with oyster mushrooms, and, for dessert, a *millefeuille* with seasonal fruit. Weekday menu 75F, others up to 195F.

|●| RESTAURANT LE NAUTILE

103 rue du Phare.
☎ 02.51.30.32.18
Closed Sun evening and Mon out of season, and Jan.

Anonymous-looking restaurant with a terrace, hidden away in the residential part of La Tranche. The setting is characterless, but this is one of the region's most fashionable venues. Cyril Godard's fine, flavoursome cuisine makes it worth a visit and so do the grounds and the veranda. Try the salmon *aumônière* with saltwort, the fisherman's casserole and the flambéed prawn *cassolette*. Menus 98–185F.

VIBRAYE   72320

🏄 🏠 |●| L'AUBERGE DE LA FORÊT**

rue Gabriel Goussault (Centre).
☎ 02.43.93.60.07 ➡ 02.43.71.20.36
Closed Sun evening and Mon except for public holidays, 15 Jan–15 Feb and July–Aug. **TV. Car park**.

Peaceful, central hotel with comfortable rooms for 280F with shower/wc or bath. There's a weekday menu for 95F, a *menu du terroir* for 110F and others 170–275F. They list mainly lcal dishes, including *marmite sarthoise* with Jasnière, the local white wine. Start with *rillettes* tart and finish with the house dessert. You can also get more elaborate dishes like hot oysters on a bed of leeks, roast duck in cream and cider, etc. Free apéritif or coffee.

🏠 |●| HÔTEL-RESTAURANT LE CHAPEAU ROUGE**

pl. de l'Hôtel-de-Ville.

☎ 02.43.93.60.02 ➡ 02.43.71.52.18
Closed Sun evening except by reservation. **Disabled access**. **TV**. **Car park**.

Reliable, appealing hotel covered in Virginia creeper. The chef prepares good traditional and classic dishes – authentic *tournedos Rossini*, good local meat, fish fresh from La Rochelle and classic *crème caramel* – which are served in a dining room full of hunting trophies. Weekday menu 90F and others at 120F and 190F. Everything they serve is made in their own kitchens from the bread to the desserts. There's a good atmosphere guaranteed in the bar on market days. The sixteen bedrooms, five of them with mini-bar, are very quiet. They cost 280–330F with shower/wc or bath.

Picardie

02 Aisne

60 Oise

80 Somme

ALBERT   80300

🏃 🏠 |●| HÔTEL DE LA BASILIQUE**

3–5 rue Gambetta (Centre).
☎ 03.22.75.04.71 ➡ 03.22.75.10.47
Closed Sat evenings and Sun out of season, three weeks in Aug, and Christmas. **TV**.

You'll get a friendly welcome, comfortable rooms and good regional cooking in this attractive hotel. Doubles 290F. Menus 65–190F; try the home-made duck *pâté en croûte*, home-soaked eel and salmon duo, or the fillet of beef with green peppercorns or *béarnaise* sauce. Free coffee.

AMIENS   80000

SEE MAP ON P.622

🏠 HÔTEL VICTOR HUGO*

2 rue de l'Oratoire. **MAP C2-3**
☎ 03.22.91.57.91 ➡ 03.22.92.74.02
TV.

This very old establishment has retained some of its original charm despite extensive renovations. The double glazing keeps out the traffic noise from the crossroads. Some rooms are more comfortable than others, and each one is different. Those on the first floor have high ceilings, while the smaller attic rooms have a romantic view over the roof tops. Doubles 215F with shower/wc or 245F with bath. Breakfast 30F.

🏃 🏠 HÔTEL CENTRAL ET ANZAC**

17 rue Alexandre-Fatton. **MAP C2-1**
☎ 03.22.91.34.08 ➡ 03.22.91.36.02

e hotel-central2@wanadoo.fr
TV.

Ideally situated if you don't want to struggle too far from the station. You'll get a very friendly welcome, but you need to choose your room with care. If you're up to the task of climbing several flights of stairs, take one of the recently renovated attic rooms. The rooms on the first floor are more basic. Double with shower/wc 250F. 10% discount 17 July– 31 Aug and 15 Nov–31 Jan.

🏠 |●| LE PRIEURÉ**

17 rue Porion. **MAP B1-4**
☎ 03.22.92.27.67 ➡ 03.22.92.46.16
Restaurant closed Sun evenings and Mon. **TV**.

Situated in a quiet, picturesque street, *Le Prieuré* has kept all the old charm of the original residence. The rooms vary in quality and range from 250–350F with shower or bath. In the stark white dining room you can enjoy simple but good regional cooking. Menus 100F, 140F and 200F.

🏃 🏠 HOTEL ALSACE-LORRAINE**

18 rue de la Morlière. **MAP C1-6**
☎ 03.22.91.35.71

Open the enormous green door to reveal a delightful little hotel with thirteen rooms painted green and white. The welcome is as charming as the decor. Doubles 380–450F. Free breakfast.

|●| RESTAURANT STEAK EASY

18 rue Metz-l'Évêque. **MAP C1-11**
☎ 03.22.91.48.38 ➡ 03.22.92.90.61

Service noon–1am. The parish community

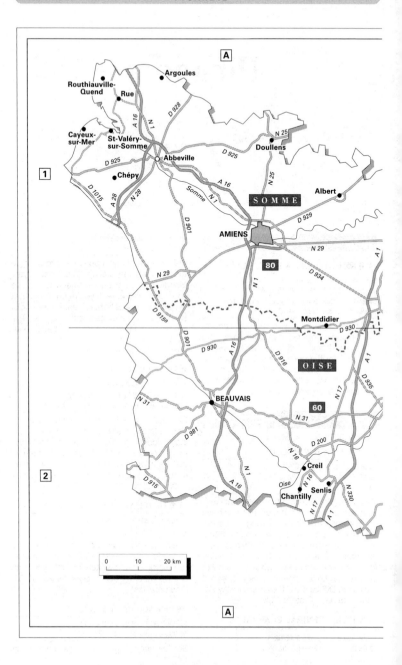

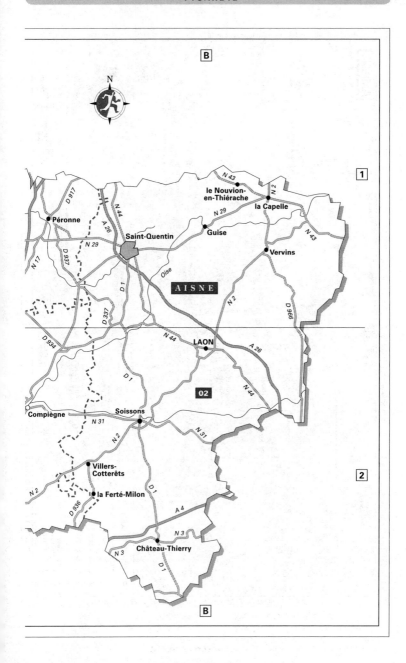

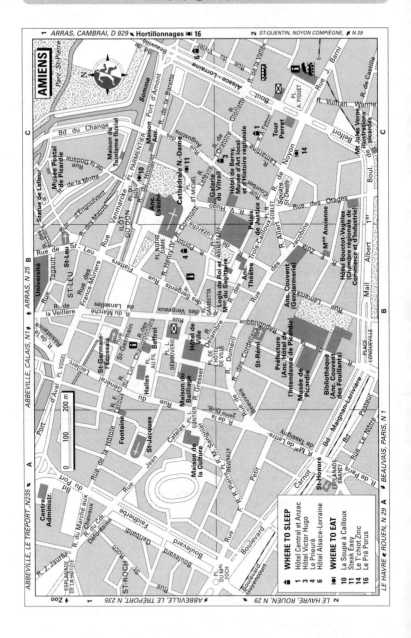

Amiens ⊗ **PICARDIE**

ARRAS, CAMBRAI, D 929 — Hortillonnages ▐●▌ 16   ST-QUENTIN, NOYON COMPIÈGNE, ✈ N 29

AMIENS

WHERE TO SLEEP
1 Hôtel Central et Anzac
3 Hôtel Victor Hugo
4 Le Prieuré
6 Hôtel Alsace-Lorraine

WHERE TO EAT
10 La Soupe à Cailloux
11 Steak Easy
14 Le T'chiot Zinc
16 Le Pré Porus

centre has undergone a total transformation into a Tex-Mex restaurant that's the haven of a younger crowd. It's worth a visit just for the decor; there's a genuine 1960s fridge hung on the wall and a full-size aeroplane strung up as if in flight. It's a temple to American cuisine served against a background of rock and blues. Quick, youthful staff.

I●I LE T'CHIOT ZINC

18 rue de Noyon. **MAP C2-14**
☎ 03.22.91.43.79
Closed Sun, and Mon lunchtime.

The cooking is first-rate at this Art Deco-style bistro – try the ham and cheese pancakes or the duck *terrine* made to a traditional Amiens recipe. Another delicious house speciality is the rabbit in aspic with oven-browned potatoes. They do a 68F *formule express* at lunchtimes and in the evenings, and a 98F *menu complet* which includes a drink. It's a local favourite.

I●I LA SOUPE À CAILLOUX

16 rue des Bondes. **MAP C1-10**
☎ 03.22.91.92.70
Closed Mon except in season, and the first week in Jan.

This popular restaurant is ideally situated in the Saint-Leu district near the cathedral. The terrace is a big draw in summer, when it fills very quickly. The cook, who buys all his produce at the nearby riverside market, prepares tasty regional dishes such as ham and cheese pancake, chicken with a Maroilles cheese sauce, salad of gizzard *confits*, salmon with bacon, and mutton with prunes, almonds and sesame seeds. Weekday lunch menu 72F and another at 112F. Expect to pay a bit more *à la carte*.

I●I RESTAURANT LE PRÉ PORUS

95 rue Voyelle; it's on the edge of Camon just before the bridge. Off map **C1-16**
☎ 03.22.46.25.03
Closed Mon and Tues evenings, and Feb.
Disabled access. Car park.

One of the lovliest settings for lunch on the banks of the Somme, just a couple of steps from the vegetable fields. Menus list lots of fish dishes – there's a weekday menu at 95F and others 165–210F. The quality of the cooking is not always high enough to justify the price of the more expensive menus.

DREUIL LES AMIENS   80730 (6KM NW)

I●I LE COTTAGE

385 bd. Pasteur; it's on the N235 in the direction of

Picquigny.
☎ 03.22.54.10.98
Closed Sun and Mon evenings, and Aug.

A good little roadside restaurant, where they serve sophisticated cuisine in an unpretentious dining room with exposed beams. The 120F menu, which is the best value, lists snail ravioli in a garlic-flavoured stock, a choice of *gratin* of scallops with leeks or veal kidneys in a grain mustard sauce, and dessert. Other menus 75F, 150F and 215F.

BELLOY-SUR-SOMME   80310 (8KM NW)

I●I HOSTELLERIE DE BELLOY*

29 route Nationale; it's ten minutes from Amiens on the N1 or the D191.
☎ 03.22.51.41.05
Closed Sunday evening, Mon, and a fortnight July/Aug.

Extraordinarily warm greeting, generous portions and service that's as down-to-earth as the decor. There's a short menu at 90F, and another at 160F, which includes *terrine* of goose *confit* with onion marmalade and home-made fruit tart. To judge by the happy faces, they've got it right.

ARGOULES   80120

♠ I●I AUBERGE DU GROS TILLEUL***

pl. du Château; it's in the village square opposite the 18th-century château.
☎ 03.22.29.91.00 ➡ 03.22.23.91.64
Closed Mon except public holidays, and Jan.
TV. Disabled access. Car park.

Because of its history – Sully is said to have planted the lime tree the restaurant's named after and it served as a branch of a Sienese bank – not to mention its delightful surroundings, this inn is listed in all the guide books. There's a weekday *formule express* at 70F and a 195F gourmet menu. *À la carte* specialities include duck flambéed with mandarin liqueur and orange sauce, poached turbot with hollandaise sauce, fresh scallops, Alsace or Normandy tart, chocolate charlotte and home-made profiteroles. Refurbished rooms with a view of the grounds, 380F for a double.

BEAUVAIS   60000

♠ I●I HÔTEL DE LA POSTE

19–21 rue Gambetta (Centre).
☎ 03.44.45.14.97 ➡ 03.44.45.02.31
Closed Sun. **TV. Pay car park.**

The small, bright bedrooms are very comfortable and well equipped. Doubles with basin cost 145F, or 205F with shower/wc. They don't serve breakfast on Sunday. The restaurant offers a good *formule brasserie* at 60F; it's a very popular choice, especially at lunchtimes. The daily special is nicely presented and changes frequently.

🎵 🛏 HÔTEL LA RÉSIDENCE**

24 rue Louis-Borel (Northeast); it's on the N1.
☎ 03.44.48.30.98 ➡ 03.44.45.09.42
TV. **Garden**. **Lock-up car park**.

This hotel is on a very quiet street in a residential area fifteen minutes' walk from the town centre, where the odd passing bicycle is the only thing to shatter the silence. You'll get a jokey, good-natured welcome, a modern, well-equipped room, and good value for money. Doubles with shower 220F, or 280F with bath. 10% discount Fri, Sat or Sun nights from Oct–May.

🎵 |❶| RESTAURANT LE MARIGNAN

1 rue de Malherbe (Centre).
☎ 03.44.48.15.15
Closed Sun evening and Mon except on public holidays, and 20 July–2 Aug.

On the ground floor there's a typical bar–brasserie where they serve a decent weekday menu for 65F. But if you want to get the most out of this place, head instead for the plush first-floor dining room. Here you can sample well-prepared Picardie specialities, including fish dishes, veal *fricassée*, scallops *Dieppois* and *crème brulée*. Menus 99.90F and 175F or about 250F *à la carte*. Free house apéritif.

CRILLON   60112 (15KM NW)

|❶| BAR-RESTAURANT LA PETITE FRANCE

7 rue du Moulin; at Troissereux, on the Beauvais-Abbeville road, fork left onto the D133 to Crillon.
☎ 03.44.81.01.13
Closed Sun and Mon evenings, Tues and mid-Aug to mid-Sept.

A rustic inn with hunting trophies on the walls. The food is very good, made with only fresh ingredients – even the dishes on the 68F menu, served at lunch and dinner, are delicious and generously served. Other menus 135F and 170F. The chef's specialities include beef *estouffade* and *foie gras escalope* deglazed with Sauternes, fish dishes and game.

AGNETZ   60600 (20KM S)

🎵 🛏 |❶| HÔTEL-RESTAURANT LE CLERMOTEL**

60 rue des Buttes; it's in the Agnetz hotel zone.
☎ 03.44.50.09.90 ➡ 03.44.50.13.00
e clermotel@dial.oleane.com
TV. **Disabled access**. **Garden**. **Car park**.

This is a modern motel-type establishment close to the beautiful Hez forest. Very comfortable bedrooms, 320F for a double with shower or bath. The ones at the back have direct access to the grounds. There's a garden and a tennis court. They serve good, modern cooking in the large dining room, and there's a buffet option, too. Menus 98–154F. 10% discount for stays of two nights or more.

|❶| AUBERGE DE GICOUR

Forêt de Hez-Gicourt; head for Gicourt and take the Gicourt Zone Hôtelière turning.
☎ 03.44.50.00.31
Closed Sun and Wed evenings, Mon, Tues, a fortnight in Feb and three weeks in Aug. **Disabled access**.

It's wise to book if you plan to eat at this popular, pleasant inn at the weekend. There is a large variety of tasty, hearty dishes on the 112F menu, and the *menu gourmand* at 158F is equally good. Staff are very attentive, and the owner/chef, Jean-Marie, always makes a point of chatting to you before you leave. The most attractive top-of-the-range restaurant in the region.

CHANTILLY   60500

🎵 🛏 |❶| AUBERGE LE VERTUGADIN

44 rue du Connétable (Centre); it's near the château.
☎ 03.44.57.03.19 ➡ 03.44.57.92.31
Closed Sun evening.

This is one of the few hotels in town that still has reasonable prices, and as there are only six rooms, it's best to book in advance. They are comfortable, though not luxurious; doubles with shower start at 230F. Toilets are on the landing. They serve classical cooking in the restaurant, but the tasty grills are even better. There's a 98F menu, served only at lunchtimes during the week, and another at 150F, which lists *foie gras* and local dishes. Free aperitif.

|❶| RESTAURANT LE GOUTILLON

61 rue du Connétable (Centre); it's near the château.
☎ 03.44.58.01.00

This restaurant has an old-fashioned decor with exposed beams and stone walls covered with vintage advertisements. All dishes are listed on a blackboard, which the waiter brings to your table. Tasty starters and house specialities include snails, duck breast, chicken *fricassée* in a curry sauce, *andouillette,* and the chef's special steak *au poivre à l'ancienne.* There's a three-course lunch *formule* for 90F but a cheaper menu at 60F. The atmosphere's relaxed, the welcome's friendly and the owner keeps a close watch on everything.

⅍ I●I RÔTISSERIE DU CONNÉTABLE*

75 rue du Connétable (Centre); it's near the château.
☎ 03.44.57.02.91
Closed Tues evenings, Wed and a fortnight in mid-June.

This is a nice restaurant with an enormous rustic dining room with the spit from the château in the open fireplace. It offers dishes such as lobster omelette, sweetbreads with morels and fresh game in season. Menus change weekly; the cheapest one, 100F, is served on weekdays only. There is another at 145F, a gastronomic one at 230F, and a range of choices *à la carte.* Free aperitif.

VINEUIL-SAINT-FIRMIN   60500 (4KM NE)

I●I RESTAURANT LES GRANDS PRÉS

route d'Avilly.
☎ 03.44.57.71.97
Closed Sun evening and Mon. **Garden. Car park**.

This place is out in the country, a five-minute drive from Chantilly. The straightforward, traditional cuisine includes dishes like marbled *foie gras* and duck *confit,* poached scallops and mussels with *anise,* and sweetbreads with oyster mushrooms. Menus at 98F (not weekends) and 152F. There's a terrace, where you can enjoy the fresh country air.

GOUVIEUX   60270 (5KM W)

🏠 I●I HÔSTELLERIE DU PAVILLION SAINT-HUBERT

chemin de Marisy, lieu-dit Toutevoie.
☎ 03.44.57.07.04 ➡ 03.44.57.75.42
Closed three weeks in Jan. **TV**. **Car park**.

This old fisherman's house is set in a charming spot on a bend in the Oise river. From the terrace you can watch the barges slipping by or simply listen to the birds. The cooking is traditional, with a 150F menu (180F at weekends) that lists a choice of nine starters, and *à la carte* dishes such as snail *profiteroles* with Roquefort and the house speciality, veal kidneys with mustard. The attractive hotel rooms cost 295–420F with

shower/wc. Those overlooking the river are the most popular, especially at the weekend.

SAINT-LEU-D'ESSERENT   60340 (5.5KM NW)

⅍ 🏠 I●I HÔTEL DE L'OISE*

25 quai d'Amont (East); take the N16 then follow the D44.
☎ 03.44.56.60.24 ➡ 03.44.56.05.11
Restaurant closed Fri and Sun evenings, Sat, and the first three weeks in Aug. **TV**. **Car park**.

A dream of a riverside hotel that's quiet and peaceful, and offers friendly hospitality. Double rooms at 300F with shower/wc or bath. The restaurant has a rustic decor and boasts a superb painting of Claude Monet's garden at Giverny. The three-course menu, 75F, is served to guests at lunchtimes (not Sun); other menus 130–210F. Excellent specialities *à la carte* and the pastries are home-made. 10% discount on Fri, Sat and Sun nights.

CHÂTEAU-THIERRY   02400

⅍ 🏠 I●I HÔTEL-RESTAURANT HEXAGONE**

50 av. d'Essômes; take the Paris road from the centre of town then follow the signs for Charly-sur-Marne.
☎ 03.23.83.69.69 ➡ 03.23.83.64.17
Closed Sun except for groups and 22–29 Dec. **TV**. **Disabled access. Car park**.

You'll get a warm welcome in this modern hotel, and you will be well looked after. Comfortable doubles with shower or bath 260F. There is a hearty buffet-style breakfast – cereals, cheese, *charcuterie* and so on – at 32F. The restaurant's cheapest menu, 78F, is perfectly adequate, and there are four others from 98–170F. Good traditional home cooking and a notable *tarte Tatin.* The River Marne flows past the bottom of the garden. 10% discount on the room rate.

CHÉPY   80210

🏠 I●I L'AUBERGE PICARDE**

pl. de la Gare; it's opposite Chépy-Valines train station.
☎ 03.22.26.20.78 ➡ 03.22.26.33.34
Restaurant closed Sat lunchtime and Sun evening. **TV**. **Disabled access. Car park**.

The large building is more of a motel than a charming inn, but it has one of the best restaurants in the region, with menus 90–205F. Their seafood and fish specialities are good – try the *paupiette* of zander with shrimps, scallops *vinaigrette* or oysters with shallots. It's best to book at weekends. Doubles with shower/wc 265F.

COMPIÈGNE   60200

🏃 🛏 |O| HÔTEL DE FRANCE-RÔTISSERIE DU CHAT QUI TOURNE**

17 rue Eugène-Floquet (Centre).
☎ 03.44.40.02.74 ➡ 03.44.40.48.37
TV.

The unusual name derives from a story about a street entertainer who taught his cat to turn a spit. Nowadays, this delightful two-star hotel provides three-star comfort and cuisine. The bedrooms are all different and very tastefully decorated. Doubles 180F with basin and 350–400F with bath. Splendid buffet breakfast at 48F. Specialities in the restaurant include leek tart with creamed *foie gras*, fresh *foie gras* marinated in Loupiac and duck breast with caramelised pears. Menus 138–225F. Friendly, courteous welcome. 10% discount on the room rate.

🏃 🛏 HÔTEL DE FLANDRE**

16 quai de la République (Centre).
☎ 03.44.83.24.40 ➡ 03.44.90.02.75
TV. Lock-up car park.

An enormous, very classical building on the banks of the Oise. The hotel offers good facilities at reasonable prices; 280–300F for a double with shower/wc or bath. Rooms are spacious and the double glazing guarantees peace and quiet. Pleasant welcome. 10% discount.

🏃 |O| RESTAURANT LE BOUCHON

5 rue Saint-Martin (Centre).
☎ 03.44.40.05.32

This restaurant is situated in a charming little pedestrianised street in the old quarter, lined with half-timbered houses. Inside, you get good regional cooking in a pleasant atmosphere created by the jovial owner. For 69F you can have the dish of the day, *pot-au-feu*, say, or a meat dish with sauce, and a glass of first-rate wine – there are more than seventy to choose from. Other menus 120–170F. They host regular wine-tasting evenings, when you get to sample six diifferent wines with your meal. Free coffee or *digestif*.

🏃 |O| BISTROT DE FLANDRE**

2 rue d'Amiens (Centre).
☎ 03.44.83.26.35

This bistro, on the banks of the river Oise, has all the features of a traditional brasserie –

spacious dining room, waiters in black aprons and speedy service. There are two menus; one at 96F, served during the week, and another at 134F, served on weekends and public holidays. *À la carte* the specialities change constantly; veal sweetbreads with morels, house tournedos and duck *foie gras*. It's a friendly, lively place. Free coffee.

|O| LA FERME DU CARANDEAU

Route de l'Armistice; take the N31 in the direction of Soissons.
☎ 03.44.85.89.89
Closed Sun evening and Mon, except for groups.

This half-timbered inn, near the clearing where the Armistice was signed, has come up with a very attractive formula. For the single price of 150F you are served an apéritif, a huge choice of *hors d'œuvre* from the buffet, spit-roast meat, cheese, dessert, as much wine as you like and coffee. There's lamb on Friday, and pork on Saturday evening and Sunday lunch. It's become so successful that you'd do well to book. Good food, generous helpings and a convivial atmosphere.

MEUX (LE)   60880 (10KM S)

🏃 |O| LA MAISON DU GOURMET

1 rue de la République; it's on the D13
☎ 03.44.91.10.10
Closed Sat lunchtime, Sun and Mon evenings, the first fortnight in January and three weeks mid-July to Aug.
Car park in the courtyard.

The owner-chef isn't new to this game – seven years at *Maxim's* in Paris and a few at the Château de Raray. The 98F menu alone makes it worth a visit; a typical selection might be *fondant* of *foie gras* with a truffle sauce, duck breast with Morelo cherries, *filet mignon* with cider sauce and a warm soufflé with soft fruit. There's more choice on the 150F menu and a wide range of dishes *à la carte*. The chef strives to give you value for money and succeeds. You'll be greeted and served in a friendly, efficient manner. It's worth booking. Free coffee.

SAINT-JEAN-AUX-BOIS   60350 (20KM SE)

🏃 🛏 |O| AUBERGE DE LA BONNE IDÉE***

3 rue des Meuniers (Southeast); take the D332 then turn left onto the D85.
☎ 03.44.42.84.09 ➡ 03.44.42.80.45
℮ a.la.bonne.idee.augerge@wanadoo.fr
Closed mid-Jan to mid-Feb.
TV. Disabled access. Private car park.

This is a picture-postcard inn with wooden shutters in the middle of Compiègne forest. The 130F menu is served daily. Try the unusual fillet of mostelle, a delicately flavoured fish served with mushrooms and wild asparagus. Other menus 190–360F and *à la carte*. You can eat on the terrace in fine weather. The pretty rooms, 380F, feature a number of personal touches along with en-suite bath/wc and direct-dial telephone. 10% discount on the room rate Nov–Jan, and free aperitif or coffee.

CREIL   60100

|●| LA PETITE ALSACE

8 pl. Charles-Brobeil (Centre); it's beside the train station.
☎ 03.44.55.28.89
Closed Sat lunchtime, Sun evening, Mon, and mid-July to mid-Aug. **Car park**.

The food is not exactly typical of Picardie but it's very good. Try the fish *choucroute* with a glass of Alsace wine or a cool beer. Weekday menu at 89F and others 120–192F. They have seafood evenings twice a month.

DOULLENS   80600

⅍ ♜ |●| LE SULLY**

45 rue Jacques-Mossion (Centre); it's beside the train station.
☎ 03.22.77.10.87
Closed Mon, a fortnight in Jan and the last fortnight of June. **TV**.

A fairly modern building, with seven modest rooms at 205F. They're very clean and well equipped but they don't have much character. The restaurant has good menus at 69F, 89F and 135F; they list regional specialities such as scallops with whisky or guinea fowl with cider. Free coffee with a meal.

FERTÉ-MILON (LA)   02460

⅍ ♜ HÔTEL RACINE**

pl. du Port-au-Blé (Centre).
☎ 03.23.96.72.02 ➡ 03.23.96.72.37
e iap@club-internet.fr
TV. **Garden**. **Car park**.

A superb little hotel in a 17th-century building. The eight rooms have been tastefully decorated and they're reasonably priced: double with shower/wc 290F, 320F with bath. Outside there's a garden with a paved courtyard

and a pretty corner tower overlooking the bank of the Ourcq. The owners organise art courses. Pleasant welcome. Free aperitif.

|●| RESTAURANT LES RUINES

2 pl. du Vieux-Château (South).
☎ 03.23.96.71.56
Closed Mon, evenings except Sat, and Aug.
Garden. **Car park**.

Good inn, owned by a landscape gardener. You dine outside in a lovely garden, next to the ruined château. Traditional, good-value cooking; the 75F *formule rapide*, served during the week, lists rabbit *terrine*, lamb with olives, rabbit and girolle stew. Other menus 110–165F.

GUISE   02120

⅍ ♜ |●| HÔTEL-RESTAURANT CHAM-PAGNE-PICARDIE**

41 rue André-Godin (Centre).
☎ 03.23.60.43.44 ➡ 03.23.61.37.85
Closed Sun evening, Mon and Christmas to 2 Jan. **TV**.
Lock-up car park.

This is a beautiful residence, encircled by a little park, in the shadow of the château belonging to the duc de Guise. The twelve comfortable bedrooms are spacious and bright. Doubles cost 240F. Service in the restaurant is pleasant, as is the food – hearty regional dishes that are not too expensive. The 60F *menu du jour* is simple but delicious, and there's a more elaborate one at 84F. The most expensive menu, 135F, lists *foie gras*, sole *meunière*, and a choice of cheese and desserts. Courteous welcome. Free coffee.

LAON   02000

⅍ ♜ HÔTEL LES CHEVALIERS**

3–5 rue Sérurier (Centre); it's in the middle of the medieval town.
☎ 03.23.27.17.50 ➡ 03.23.23.40.71
Closed 15 Dec–15 Jan. **TV**.

Fourteen functional bedrooms with low ceilings and exposed beams in a stylish old building. Doubles 290F with shower, 350F with bath, including breakfast. The welcome from the owner could be friendlier. 10% discount 15 May–30 June and 15 Sept–15 Oct.

|●| BAR-RESTAURANT LE RÉTRO

18 bd. de Lyon; it's the main street in the lower town.
☎ 03.23.23.04.49
Closed Sun lunchtime (unless you book). **Disabled**

access. **Car park**.

A friendly, busy place that is particularly popular at lunchtimes when it's full of local workers. Marie-Thérèse, the owner, has a loyal following. The 76F menu has superb traditional dishes: *onglet* and *entrecôte* steak delivered from the local abattoirs, Maroilles cheese tart, homemade *terrine*, and calf's head *ravigote*. There's also a list of freshly made salads. Menus start at 76F. The slightly kitsch dining room is festooned with green plants and artificial flowers.

⚜|●| RESTAURANT LA PETITE AUBERGE

45 bd. Brossolette (Centre); it's near the train station.
☎ 03.23.23.02.38
Closed Sat lunchtime, Sun and Mon evening except on public holidays and a fortnight in Aug. **Car park**.

Laon's gourmet restaurant. The cooking is modern and the owner's son, Willy Marc Zorn, introduces a touch of originality to tasty dishes such as sea bass with pumpkin *coulis*, *crème au lard*, and pan-fried veal sweetbreads in pale ale with a chicory *fondue*. Menus, at 129F, 150F and 220F, are appropriately priced. The same poeple run *Le Saint-Amour* (☎03.23.23.31.01), next door, which offers home-style Lyonnais cooking and an excellent Beaujolais. Free aperitif at *La Petite Auberge* only.

MAREUIL-SUR-OURCQ   60890 (7KM SW)

|●| AUBERGE DE L'OURCQ**

7 rue de Thury (Centre); take the D936 from La Ferté-Milon.
☎ 03.44.87.24.14
Closed Mon, Fri and Sat lunchtimes, 27 July–11 Aug, Jan.

The skilful chef in this high-class restaurant makes good use of local produce. *Menu du jour* at 75F, and others 133–210F. There's a wide choice of meat dishes, including *tournedos Rossini*. Specialities include breast of guinea fowl with *foie gras* and marjoram sauce. The wines are affordable.Smiling welcome and efficient service.

MONTDIDIER   80500

⚜ ♟ |●| HÔTEL DE DIJON**

1 pl. du 10-Août; it's on the Beauvais road.
☎ 03.22.78.01.35 ➡ 03.22.78.27.24
Restaurant closed Sat, Sun evening, the Feb school holidays and two weeks in Aug. **TV**. **Lock-up car park**.

This hotel has been completely renovated, with comfortable, colourful rooms at 300F for a double with shower/wc and TV. The restaurant

specialises in meat dishes, either grilled or more elaborately prepared, and offers menus at 92F and 146F. Free coffee.

⚜|●| RESTAURANT LE PARMENTIER

11 rue Albert-1er; it's opposite the post office.
☎ 03.22.78.15.10
Closed evenings, Aug and a week Christmas–New Year.

Very popular restaurant, where you can get generous portions of reasonably priced home cooking. Most dishes are prepared from fresh local produce. The menus, 70–135F, offer dishes such as seafood salad and medallions of monkfish in a whisky sauce. Cheerful staff. Free coffee.

NOUVION-EN THIÉRACHE (LE)   02170

⚜ ♟ |●| HÔTEL DE LA PAIX**

37 rue Mont-Vicary (Northwest).
☎ 03.23.97.04.55 ➡ 03.23.98.98.39
ℯ la.pierre.pierrart@wanadoo.fr
Closed Sun evening, Mon lunchtime, the Feb school holidays and the last fortnight in Aug.
TV. **Lock-up car park**.

This is a good country hotel with friendly staff. The restaurant is a delight and the cooking out of the ordinary. They offer regional dishes such as steak with Maroilles cheese sauce, seafood specialities including prawn ravioli with a shellfish *coulis* and turbot soufflé with basil and saffron, and tasty desserts to satisfy even the most demanding palate. Weekday menu at 92F, then two more at 130F and 165F. The comfortable, large bedrooms cost 250F with shower/wc and 320F with bath. Number 1 faces south and has a private terrace. Free aperitif.

ÉTRÉAUPONT   02580 (19KM SE)

⚜ ♟ |●| LE CLOS DU MONTVINAGE ET L'AUBERGE DU VAL DE L'OISE

8 rue Albert-Ledent; it's on the N2.
☎ 03.23.97.91.10 ➡ 03.23.97.48.92
ℯ contrat@clos-du-montvinage.com
Hotel closed a week in Feb and a week in Aug.
Restaurant closed Sun evening and Mon lunchtime.
TV. **Disabled access**. **Car park**.

A huge 19th-century, bourgeois residence in relaxing grounds with tennis courts. The rooms are spacious and comfortable. The ones on the second floor have exposed beams. Doubles 352F with shower/wc and 422F with bath. The charming welcome is very natural. In the *Auberge du Val de l'Oise* restaurant, run by the same family, you can enjoy very tasty cooking:

veal sweetbreads with plum brandy, beef with Maroilles cheese sauce and iced *nougatine* with soft fruit. Menus 95–125F. There's a new restaurant in the hotel whose delights are yet to be experienced. Free aperitif and 10% discount on the room rate on Fridays, except during public holidays.

PÉRONNE   80200

⅍ ⚑ |●| HOSTELLERIE DES REMPARTS**
23 rue Beaubois; it's 100m off the main street.
☎ 03.22.84.01.22 ➡ 03.22.84.31.96
TV. Lock-up car park.

This country inn, with a nostalgic, post-war feel, is in peaceful grounds on a quiet street. Comfortable, elegant bedrooms cost 250–350F. They serve traditional local dishes in the pleasant dining room. Menus 60F, 75F and 90F in the week, then others up to 215F. 10% discount on the room rate Nov–March.

ROUTHIAUVILLE-QUEND   80120

⚑ |●| AUBERGE DU FIACRE***
Hameau de Routhiauville.
☎ 03.22.23.47.30 ➡ 03.22.27.19.80
Closed Wed and 15 Jan–15 Feb.
TV. Garden. Disabled access. Car park.

The inn, in a pleasant half-timbered building, is well known locally for its very good cooking. The menu, which changes with the seasons, features fish and regional specialities. Menus start at 115F. They also offer ten or so comfortable rooms, all of which overlook the garden, from 380F a double.

RUE   80120

⚑ |●| LE LION D'OR**
5 rue de la Barrière (Centre).
☎ 03.22.25.74.18 ➡ 03.22.25.66.63
Hotel closed Jan. **Restaurant closed** Sun evening out of season. **TV. Car park.**

Comfortable, practical rooms at 300–320F. The restaurant is from a bygone age. Menus, 90–190F, list *mouclade* (mussel stew), oyster *gratiné* in vermouth, braised pork in cider and house *foie gras*.

FAVIÈRES   80120 (6KM S)

⅍ |●| RESTAURANT LA CLÉ DES CHAMPS

pl. des Frères-Caudron (Centre); take the D140.
☎ 03.22.27.88.00
Closed Sun evening, Mon, Jan and the first week in Sept. **Disabled access. Car park.**

If you want to get away from it all, come to this well-known inn set among the salt-meadows. The specialities are fish, landed at the local harbour, and dishes based around fresh produce from the market. Menus 90–240F. Free coffee.

SAINT-QUENTIN   02100

⅍ ⚑ |●| HÔTEL-RESTAURANT DE GUISE*
93 rue de Guise (Southeast); it's some distance from the town centre, on the way to La Capelle.
☎ 03.23.68.27.69 ➡ 03.23.68.05.13
TV. Disabled access. Secure parking.

The rooms are clean, comfortable, and very reasonably priced. Doubles with shower cost 110F. They offer a filling 55F *menu express* at lunchtime, but they really specialise in *couscous*, and paella. Free coffee.

⅍ ⚑ |●| LE FLORENCE**
42 rue Émile-Zola (Centre).
☎ 03.23.64.22.22 ➡ 03.23.62.52.85
✉ leflorence@wanadoo.fr
Restaurant closed Sun and Mon lunchtimes.
TV. Car park.

This hotel offers simple, clean doubles for 145F with basin, 215F with shower/wc and 235F with bath. Ask for a room overlooking the courtyard; Émile-Zola is a busy street. The restaurant has two dining rooms, one for non-smokers. It specialises in good Italian dishes such as *osso bucco*, pizza, lasagne and fresh pasta. Menus at 75F and 95F, or about 100F *à la carte*. There's a shady terrace and an Italianate fountain. Free apéritif.

⚑ |●| HÔTEL DES CANONNIERS***
15 rue des Canonniers (Centre).
☎ 03.23.62.87.87 ➡ 03.23.62.87.86
Closed Sun except for reservations and the second fortnight in Aug. **TV. Garden. Car park.**

Originally a private residence built in the 18th and 19th centuries, this hotel is located in the quiet, central area of Saint-Quentin. The spacious rooms are extremely comfortable, and feature many personal touches. The cheapest rooms at 280F have shower only, others, 380–560F, have bath. Breakfast is served in the pretty internal garden. The female owner will greet you very kindly.

⅍ ⚑ |●| HÔTEL DE LA PAIX**

3 pl. du 8-Octobre (Centre); it's near the train station.
☎ 03.23.62.77.62 ➡ 03.23.62.66.03
TV. Car park.

An impressive 1914 building which has been pleasantly modernised. Doubles cost 290F with shower/wc (240F Fri–Sun), 320F with bath (300F Fri–Sun). There are two restaurants on the ground floor. *Le Brésilien* serves traditional specialities and a gourmet menu, while *Le Carnotzet*, open only in the evenings until midnight, serves Savoy specialities. There's a two-course menu at 78F and another at 170F or, if you want to spend less, both restaurants offer inexpensive pizzas. 10% discount on the room rate.

I●I RESTAURANT LE GLACIER

28 pl. de l'Hôtel-de-Ville (Centre).
☎ 03.23.62.27.09
Closed Mon, Sun evening and a week Christmas–New Year. **Car park.**

Service until 11pm. This small, nicely decorated restaurant has a fresco on the wall, jaunty checked tablecloths and opalescent glass lamps. It opens onto the pretty, pedestrian l'Hôtel-de-Ville square, and in summer you can sit on the terrace. They serve ice cream, of course, along with house specialities such as mussels *en cocotte* with chips, steak *tartare* and *choucroute* with ham hock or fish. Dishes of the day 42F, and menus at 79F, 99F, 115F and 135F. Good value.

SAINT-VALÉRY-SUR-SOMME   80230

🏠 I●I HÔTEL DU PORT ET DES BAINS***

1 quai Blavet; it's in the lower town, on the river mouth.
☎ 03.22.60.80.09 📧 hotel-apo@wanadoo.fr
Closed Wed, Oct–May, the first fortnight in Jan and a week in Nov.

A nice little place with a freshly painted façade, situated in a town with lots of different architectural styles and surrounded by varied landscapes. The establishment has been remodelled and upgraded to a three-star. The seafood is good and both dining rooms get very busy. Menus 90–200F. Doubles with shower/wc 350F or 400–500F with bath.

🏃 🏠 I●I LE RELAIS GUILLAUME DE NORMANDIE***

46 quai Romerel.
☎ 03.22.60.82.36 ➡ 03.22.60.81.82
📧 relais_guillaume@dyadel.net
Closed Tues and 15 Dec–15 Jan. **TV. Garden. Lock-up car park.**

This tall, narrow manor house, set in a superb garden by the water's edge, is a bit of an architectural mish-mash. All the bedrooms have been refurbished and are remarkably comfortable. Doubles 355F with shower/wc, 330F with bath. Ask for a room with a sea view, or go for number 1, which has a delightful little terrace. Menus, 88–210F, list delicious regional specialities and meals are served in a beautiful dining room. 10% discount on the room rate on Sundays.

CROTOY (LE)   80550 (6KM N)

🏃 🏠 I●I LES TOURELLES*

2–4 rue Pierre Guerlain; take the A16; it's by the beach.
☎ 03.22.27.16.33 ➡ 03.22.27.11.45.
Closed three weeks in Jan. **TV.**

This red-brick, turreted building, standing by the Somme estuary, was once the home of perfumier Pierre Guerlain. Everything is meticulous, from the charming bedrooms, with their wonderful views of the estuary, to the relaxing lounge-bar and the children's playroom so you need to book well in advance. Doubles 290F with basin or 395F with bath; room number 33 is in the keep. Local specialities are served in the smart new dining room – star dishes include the fresh fish, the fish *matelotte* and the seafood platter. Menus 120–160F. Free apéritif.

AULT   80460 (21KM SE)

🏃 🏠 I●I HÔTEL-RESTAURANT VICTOR HUGO

25 rue de la Pêche; it's 100m from the centre of town.
☎ 03.22.60.40.40 ➡ 03.22.6040.00
TV. Car park.

You can't miss this place. It's in the upper part of the village overlooking Onival beach and painted a startling blue. Although it is a bit of a blot on the landscape, the hotel is attractively decorated inside with light wallpaper and cane chairs. The 35 rooms are painted in bright colours. Double rooms 310F with shower or bath. Engaging welcome. They serve a few Russian specialities in the restaurant alongside the turbot with morels, shrimps with flambéed vodka and beef strogonoff. There's a menu at 125F but you'll pay 190F for the one with caviar and champagne. Pets welcome. Free *digestif* and 10% discount on the room rate 15 Nov–15 April, except at weekends and on public holidays.

|●| RESTAURANT L'HORIZON

31 rue de Saint-Valéry; in upper Ault-Onival on top of the cliffs.
☎ 03.22.60.43.21

A little restaurant with a fishing theme, a few vaguely post-impressionist watercolours and a collection of coffee mills. There's a fabulous view looking down on the beach from the tables in the bay window. Fisherman's stew and fish *choucroute* on the menus, 78–146F, and all dishes are freshly made at affordable prices.

SENLIS   60300

🌿 🏠 |●| HOSTELLERIE DE LA PORTE BEL-LON

51 rue Bellon; it's a turning off rue de la République.
☎ 03.44.53.03.05 ➡ 03.44.53.29.94
Closed 20 Dec–10 Jan. **TV.**

A superb old house, set back from the road, with 18 comfortable and spacious rooms, 320F with shower/wc and 400 with bath. The restaurant is attractively decorated or you can eat in the shady garden in good weather. Menus 125–150F, and the chef's speciality is duck breast with honey and cider vinegar. Just ask to visit their 13th-century cellar where you have your free apéritif.

FONTAINE-CHAALIS   60300 (8KM SE)

🌿 🏠 |●| L'AUBERGE DE FONTAINE**

22 Grande-Rue (Centre); take the D330 towards Nanteuil-le-Haudouin.
☎ 03.44.54.20.22 ➡ 03.44.60.25.38
Closed Mon and Tues from Nov to end Feb, and 4–24 Jan. **Disabled access. TV.**

This well-known inn has a justifiably fine reputation. Dominique, the chef, trained with the great Bocuse and he'll captivate you with his enthusiasm. He offers several *formules* and a range of menus from 150F. His specialities include *foie gras* with pickled garlic and prunes, smooth pea sauce with roast shrimps and warm *foie gras*. Eight attractive, comfortable double rooms, 275F with shower/wc, 305F with bath. Free apéritif.

SOISSONS   02200

🏠 LE CLOVIS*

7 rue Ernest-Ringuier (Centre); it's near the town hall gardens.
☎ 03.23.59.26.57
Disabled access. Lock-up car park.

This hotel has a certain style. The very friendly owner will happily advise his guests on places to go and things to see. There are just eight bedrooms; some have a view of the Aisne river while others look onto a private courtyard where parts of the walls are the old, ruined city ramparts. Doubles cost 120–135F with washing facilities (wc is on the landing), 148–175F with bath.

🌿 |●| LE POT D'ÉTAIN

7 rue de Saint-Quentin (Centre).
☎ 03.23.53.27.39
Closed Mon.

A centrally located, no-frills restaurant where they serve family dishes, home-made *terrines* and desserts on menus priced 75–130F. Efficient, friendly service. Free coffee or *digestif*.

FONTENOY   02290 (10KM W)

🌿 🏠 |●| AUBERGE DU BORD DE L'EAU

1 rue Bout du Port.
☎ 03.23.74.25.76
Closed Wed, 23 Sept–7 Oct and 14–31 Jan. **TV.**

A charming hotel on the banks of the Aisne. Weekday lunch menu at 95F, and others from 125–195F. They bake their own bread, smoke their own salmon and make their own *foie gras* – everything is absolutely fresh. All seven rooms have bathrooms, 250F, and some have a lovely river view. Free coffee.

VILLERS-COTTERÊTS   02600

🏠 HÔTEL LE RÉGENT***

26 rue du Général-Mangin (Centre).
☎ 03.23.96.01.46 ➡ 03.23.96.37.57
Closed Sun evenings Nov–March, except public holidays. **TV. Disabled access. Lock-up car park.**

There's an authentic 16th-century coaching inn behind the 18th-century façade. The seventeen bedrooms are all different – some of them have been classifed as historic monuments. The cheapest double with shower costs 175F and there are others up to 422F, the costliest with a whirlpool bath. A charming little hotel that is value for money.

|●| L'ORTHOGRAPHE

63 rue du Général-Leclerc.
☎ 03.23.96.30.84
Closed Sun evening and Mon.

A restaurant that sets the local standard, with

friendly service. The chef prepares mouth-watering dishes; *foie gras terrine* with Sauternes jelly or glazed shrimps with tomato and basil *vinaigrette*, grilled brill with Guérande salt and *fondant* with three chocolates. Menus 89–120F. All the fish is fresh and landed nearby.

LONGPONT   02600 (11.5KM NE)

🏃 🏠 |●| HÔTEL DE L'ABBAYE**

rue des Tourelles (Centre); turn off the N2 onto the D2.

☎ and 📠 03.23.96.02.44
TV. **Lock-up car park**.

Gorgeous, ivy-covered inn in a romantic setting on the edge of the Retz forest. Rooms cost 280F for a double with bath; the substantial breakfast costs 45F. Number 111 has a view over the fortified port. Excellent, fresh local produce is served in the restaurant, and there is game in season. Menus 110–190FF. In the afternoons they serve delicious pancakes. Free Kir.

Poitou-Charentes

16 Charente

17 Charente-Maritime

79 Deux-Sèvres

86 Vienne

AIX (ILE D')   17123

⚑ |●| HÔTEL-RESTAURANT LE NAPOLÉON ET DES BAINS RÉUNIS**

rue Gourgaud (Centre).
☎ 05.46.84.66.02 ➡ 05.46.84.69.70
Closed Sun evening and Mon Oct–March, and Nov–Jan.
Swimming Pool. **TV**. **Car Park**.

This comfortable establishment with fifteen attractive rooms is the only hotel on the island. Doubles 230–340F with shower/wc and 330–390F with bath. Half board, 300F per person, is compulsory July–Aug. There's a pleasant sitting room where you can have a drink, and the restaurant serves fish dishes like salmon *tartare* or roast cod stew in red wine. Menus 91–140F, and a children's menu at 48F. The welcome and service are somewhat erratic.

ANGOULÊME   16000

⚘ ⚑ |●| LE GASTÉ

381 route de Bordeaux (South).
☎ 05.45.91.89.98 ➡ 05.45.25.24.67
Closed Sat and Sun and the first three weeks in Aug.
TV. **Car park**.

Unobtrusive roadside hotel known for its hospitality and good food. Menu at 72F. The clean, simple bedrooms cost 160F with washing facilities and 170F with shower/wc. Pleasant terrace. Free apéritif.

⚑ |●| LE PALMA

4 rampe d'Aguesseau (Centre).
☎ 05.45.95.22.89 ➡ 05.45.94.26.66.
Closed Sat lunchtime and Sun.

Service 11.45am–2pm and 7.30–9.45pm. Just on the edge of old Angoulême in a more built-up but older-feeling area and the quality of the good local dishes makes it worth finding. Try the scallop kebabs with Pineau or duck breast with almond and honeyed vinegar. Prices are attractive, with the cheapest menu at 70F, and others up to 180F. Pleasant bedrooms cost 160F for a double with basin or 210F with shower – the best ones are at the back. Warm, friendly welcome.

⚘ ⚑ |●| LE CRAB**

27 rue Kléber-La-Grand-Font (East); it's near the station.
☎ 05.45.95.51.80 ➡ 05.45.95.38.52
Closed Sat and Sun evening. **TV**. **Car park**.

A quiet, family inn with a quiet bar. In the large dining room they serve good regional dishes such as breast of duck or braised crab with Pineau. There's a weekday menu at 65F and others from 83–160F. Spruce doubles with washing facilities cost 180F, or 230F with bath. 10% discount on the room rate Fri–Sun unless there's a festival.

⚑ |●| LE FLORE**

414 route de Bordeaux (Southwest).
☎ 05.45.25.35.35 ➡ 05.45.25.34.69
Closed Sat and Sun and the middle fortnight in Aug. **TV**.
Car park.

Double rooms 200F with shower/wc or bath. Menus 80F, 125F and 175F; *à la carte* expect to pay around 200F. Good choices include the *papillotte* of salmon with baby vegetables or the braised guinea fowl with tarragon.

⚘ ⚑ |●| LE SAINT-ANTOINE**

31 rue Saint-Antoine (Northwest).

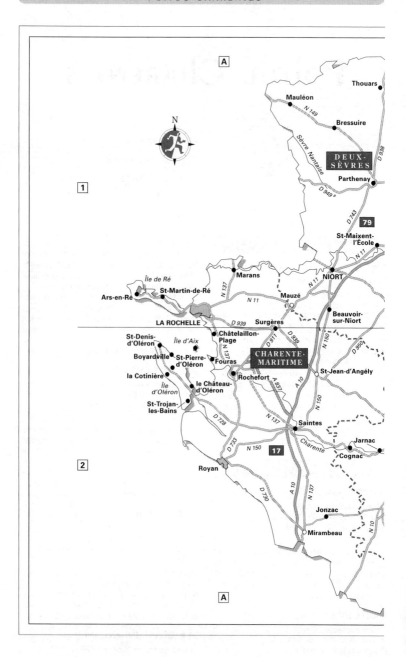

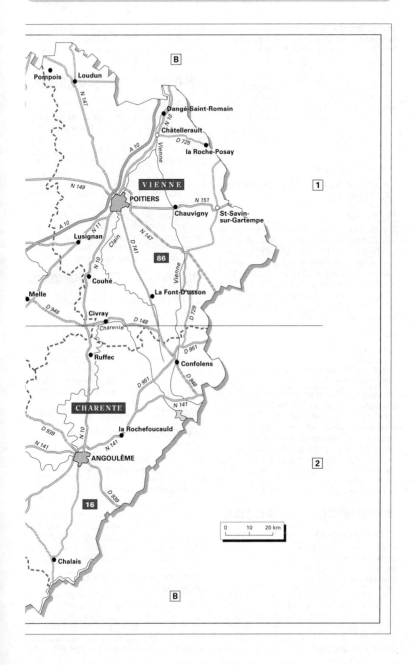

☎ 05.45.68.38.21 ➡ 05.45.69.10.31
Restaurant closed Sat lunchtime, Sun evening and 24 Dec–1 Jan. **TV**. **Disabled access**. **Car park**.

Newish place with a pleasant terrace and a cosy dining room with a fireplace. Specialities include escalope of warm duck *foie gras* with Pineau and melon, breast of young pigeon, and duck legs with buttered cabbage. Menus 82–180F, and a number of choices *à la carte*. Bedrooms are soundproofed and double rooms go for 210–340F. 10% discount on the room rate.

⚘ ⌂ HÔTEL DU PALAIS**

4 pl. Francis-Louvel (Centre); it's near the cathedral and next to the law courts.
☎ 05.45.92.54.11 ➡ 05.45.92.01.83
TV. **Pay garage**.

The façade of this 17th-century building is one of the most beautiful of its kind in the southwest. The hotel is old-fashioned, but the rustic, provincial decor has a certain charm, and it deserves its good reputation. You'll get a courteous welcome. Doubles 250F with basin and 290F with shower or bath. Some have big balconies with views of the old town. 10% discount.

|●| RESTAURANT LA CITÉ

28 rue Saint-Roch (Centre).
☎ 05.45.92.42.69
Closed Sun, Mon evening, Feb school holidays, and three weeks in Aug.

The smiling owner is very efficient, the tables are attractively set and all the fish is exceptionally fresh. Try the seafood platter, shellfish, home-made fish soup, home-made squid fritters, *fricassée* of mussels, or the house speciality, *brochette La Cité*, a kebab of mussels, prawns and scallops. There's a meat menu, too. The 72F menu is served at lunch and dinner (except Sat evening), and there are others at 120F and 160F.

GOND-PONTOUVRE (LE)   16160 (2KM N)

⚘ |●| L'ENTRECÔTE

45 route de Paris; it's on the N10.
☎ 05.45.68.04.52
Closed Sat lunchtime and Sun.
Disabled access. **Car park**.

Service noon–2pm and 8–9.30pm. This cosy tavern houses the best meat restaurant in the area. The steaks grilled over a wood fire are as good as any you would get in Argentina. They'll show you your slab of meat before it's cooked, in case you think it's too big, and will

cook it exactly as you request. The mega-rib of beef is superb for families. Menus 100––160F. Smiling owners and perfect service. Free coffee after dinner.

SOYAUX   16800 (2KM SE)

⚘ |●| LA CIGOGNE

Cabane Bambou; turn off the Périgueux road after the tunnel, on rue Aristide-Briand, it's 1.3km further on.
☎ 05.45.95.89.23
Closed Sun evening and Mon. **Car park**.

Superb restaurant with a shady terrace and a lovely view. Relaxed, courteous welcome. The owners, who spent some years overseas, have introduced a few exotic influences into their refined cuisine. Classic dishes like local snails, medallion of monkfish with orange butter and duck with sour cherries are interpreted in original ways. Dishes change with the seasons. Menus at 75F, 105F and 155F. Good value. Free coffee.

PUYMOYEN   16400 (7KM S)

⚘ ⌂ |●| L'AUBERGE DES ROCHERS

It's opposite the church.
☎ 05.45.61.25.77 ➡ 05.45.61.25.77
Car park.

Country house hotel next to a deer farm. It's modest, peaceful and quite cheap. Generous-portions on menus from 60–110F. Doubles 100F with basin, 130F with shower. Half board is 170F. Friendly staff. Free coffee or *digestif*.

CHAMPNIERS   16430 (9KM NE)

⚘ ⌂ |●| RESTAURANT LE FEU DE BOIS**

It's on the N10 in the direction of Poitiers.
☎ 05.45.68.69.96 ➡ 05.45.69.73.10
Closed Sun evening.
Disabled access. **TV**. **Car park**.

Service noon–2pm and 7.30–10.15pm. Large octagonal dining room where they grill meat over a fire fuelled by vine cuttings. Regional specialities include grilled ham. Menus 88F, 110F, 150F and 190F. They have a few rooms with bath, 300F. Free Kir or Pineau.

⚘ |●| RESTAURANT LE LOGIS D'ARGENCE

La Chignolle; it's on the N10.
☎ 05.45.69.99.93
Closed Sun evening, Mon, Tues and Wed evenings Oct–April. **Car park**.

A typical little Charentais inn with a terrace

overlooking a small garden. Pleasant decor and imaginative, tasty dishes based on local produce. Try the scallops with *foie gras*. There's a 70F lunch menu, served in the week, and others 100–200F, and several children's menus 50–70F. Free apéritif.

MOUTHIERS-SUR-BOËME   16440 (13KM S)

IOI CAFÉ-RESTAURANT DE LA GARE

pl. de la Gare; take the N10 in the direction of Bordeaux then take the fork to Blanzac.
☎ 05.45.67.94.24
Closed Sun evening. **Disabled access. Car park.**

Service 11.15am–3pm and 7–10pm. Beautiful dining room, hospitable, easy-going staff and good cooking. The 65F menu gives you a substantial meal that would be difficult to beat. Other menus 85–140F, and specialities include *foie gras* with Cognac.

CHAZELLES   16380 (20KM E)

⅔ IOI RESTAURANT LES GROTTES DU QUEROY

How to get there; take the D699, at Queroy, follow the signs to Grottes du Queroy.
☎ 05.45.23.53.85
Closed Wed except from Easter to 1 Nov, and the Feb school holidays. **Disabled access. Car park.**

Large, blissfully tranquil terrace 50m away from the prehistoric caves. Have the *gratin* of prawns with Pineau or the *foie gras* with port. Menus 75–170F. Free coffee.

VIBRAC   16120 (22KM W)

⅔ ⚐ IOI LES OMBRAGES**

Route Claude-Bonnier; take the N141, and 3.5km from Hiersac, turn left to Vibrac.
☎ 05.45.97.32.33 ➡ 05.45.97.32.05
Closed Sun evening, Mon and 20 Dec–15 Jan. **TV. Garden. Swimming pool. Car park.**

Service noon–2pm and 7.30–9.30pm. Very near Bassac abbey, which is on the pilgrim route to Santiago de Compostela, and close to a delightful beach. This hotel-restaurant is in a pleasant shady garden. Bedrooms 270F with shower/wc and 295F with bath. There's an outdoor pool, tennis courts and table tennis facilities. One of the two dining rooms is a conservatory that overlooks the shady garden. Try the scallop salad or escalope of monkfish with fruit. There's a 70F weekday lunch menu and others 105–195F, or a range of choices *à la carte*. Free apéritif.

VILLEBOIS-LAVALETTE   16320 (28KM SE)

⚐ IOI HÔTEL-RESTAURANT DU COMMERCE

How to get there: take the D939.
☎ 05.45.64.90.30
Closed Tues afternoon, ten days in June and Christmas to 1 Jan. **Car park.**

Attractive hotel in a nice hillside village. Doubles 110F with wash basin, 180F with shower/wc. The menus are straightforward: you'll get a starter, main course, cheese, dessert, coffee and $1/4$ litre of wine for all of 55F (65F in the evening). Other menus 100–140F.

SAINT-GROUX   16230 (30KM N)

⅔ ⚐ IOI HÔTEL-RESTAURANT LES TROIS SAULES**

How to get there: take the N10 to Mansle then the D739 towards Aigre; it's 3km further, on the right.
☎ 05.45.20.31.40 ➡ 05.45.22.73.81
e lestroissauleshotelrest@minitel.net
Closed Sun evening, Mon lunchtime, 19 Feb–5 March and 28 Oct–12 Nov. **Disabled access. TV. Car park.**

The village, on a bend in the River Charente, was named after a hermit who lived in Angoumois in the 16th century. This is a cosy attractive inn with attentive staff. In the restaurant there's a 62F menu (not served Sun), others 90–170F, and *à la carte*.Try their scallops in Pineau. Doubles 205F with shower/wc and 245F with bath. Half board costs 220F per person. Free apéritif.

ARS-EN-RÉ   17590

⚐ IOI LE PARASOL**

Route de Saint-Clément; it's on the left-hand side of the road.
☎ 05.46.29.46.17 ➡ 05.46.29.05.09
Closed 1 Oct to mid-March.
Disabled access. TV. Car park.

This modern house, built in traditional style, is in a good spot surrounded by pine trees well away from the road. Good, classic bedrooms, all with en-suite bath, cost 330–390F. The annexes houses studios with kitchens; these cost 465F for two half-board and 280F per extra person. Menus 135–185F. The welcome is a little off-hand.

IOI RESTAURANT LE CAFÉ DU COMMERCE

6 quai de la Prée.

☎ 05.46.29.41.57
Disabled access.

This bistro has been here the train service to Ré started over a century ago. Everyone comes here on their way to the island. The present owners spent some time in the States and brought back a counter from a Boston drugstore, along with some saloon mirrors. The menu features a variety of Tex-Mex specialities such as chilli con carne at 45.50F, BBQ ribs at 75F and cheeseburgers at 49.50F, alongside a 99F menu listing six oysters, skate wings with mustard sauce and profiteroles. À la carte, there are crêpes, salads and toasted sandwiches. It may not be the finest cuisine, and the quality has a tendency to slip in high season, but the prices are more than reasonable for the island. Children's menu at 39.50F. Wine by the glass. In the evening you can sit on the terrace and watch the boats.

I●I LE BISTROT DE BERNARD

1 quai de la Criée; it's on the harbour.
☎ 05.46.29.40.26 ➡ 05.46.29.28.99
Closed Mon evening and Tues out of season, and 15 Jan–15 Feb. **Garden**.

The terrace gives you a wonderful view of the harbour, and the dining room has large windows overlooking a garden. The dishes, which change regularly, are cooked using fresh produce bought in the superb local market. Fish and seafood feature highly, and there are a few classic dishes à la carte: tuna with foie gras, fricassée of tiger prawns and the like. Expect to pay about 200F for a meal. There are also menus at 130F and 175F, and some wines sold by the glass – the bill needn't get out of control. Children's menu 50F.

SAINT-CLÉMENT-DES-BALEINES
17590 (4KM NW)

🛏 HÔTEL LE CHAT BOTTÉ**

pl. de l'Église.
☎ 05.46.29.21.93 ➡ 05.46.29.29.97
Closed 30 Jan–12 Feb. **Disabled access. Garden. TV. Car park**.

A quiet, charming hotel on the church square. The bright rooms feature lots of natural wood – rooms 5 or 6 are panelled throughout. A traditional breakfast, served on the flowery patio, costs 47F. There's a health complex, which offers mineral baths and various treatments, a couple of tennis courts, and a number of sun-loungers dotted around the vast, beautiful grounds. Double rooms with shower 340–460F, 400–640F with bath. Book well in advance.

🍴 I●I RESTAURANT LE CHAT BOTTÉ

2 rue de la Mairie; it's 30m from the church.
☎ 05.46.29.42.09 ➡ 05.46.29.29.77
Closed Mon out of season, 10 Jan–14 Feb, and 22 Nov–18 Dec. **Car park**.

A huge dining room decorated with lots of natural wood and model boats. They light a fire in the open hearth in winter, or there's a south-facing terrace to enjoy in summer. The high-quality cuisine is based around fresh fish dishes such as mouclade, sea bass in pastry with beurre blanc, and the like. They're classical, but prepared with flair. Beyond a doubt, it's one of the best restaurants on the island and the prices are more than reasonable, given the location. The cheapest menu costs 130F, and there are others at 190F and 370F. Children's menu 70F. Free coffee.

PORTES-EN-RÉ (LES)   17880 (10KM N)

🍴 I●I RESTAURANT LE CHASSE-MARÉE

1 rue Jules-David.
☎ 05.46.29.52.03 ➡ 05.46.29.62.10
e restaurant.chasse.maree@wanado.fr
Closed Tues and Wed except during school holidays, and 15 Nov–1 April.

Service 12.30–2pm and 7.30–10pm. A delightful, elegant restaurant on the square of the island's most chic village. The walls are hung with paintings, there's an old piano and a trombone in a corner, and an intriguing collection of second-hand objects creates an attractive setting. Menus at 140F, 175F and 260F, full of delicious flavours and beautifully presented. The chef is particularly proud of his marinated sardine fillets with green peppercorns, lacquered bream with spices and sweet and sour sauce, fillet of beef with warm oysters, and caramelised pears with stem ginger. Free house apéritif.

BEAUVOIR-SUR-NIORT   79360

🍴 I●I L'AUBERGE DES VOYAGEURS

41 pl. de l'Hôtel-de-Ville.
☎ 05.49.09.70.16 ➡ 05.49.09.65.78
Closed Wed and Sun evening from Oct to Easter, Wed only from Easter to Oct, and a fortnight in Jan.

Jean-Claude Batiot, the owner of this charming stone-walled village inn, is dedicated to maintaining the reputation of local regional cuisine. Try his fresh foie gras fricassée, sautéed with potatoes, mushrooms, garlic, parsley and slivers of country ham, *fricassée* of eel, or ravioli with prawns. Menus 100–250F. Free apéritif.

VILLIERS-EN-BOIS   79360 (10KM SE)

🕴 🛏 |●| L'AUBERGE DES CÈDRES

How to get there: take the Zoorama road in Chizée.
☎ 05.49.76.79.53 ➡ 05.49.76.79.81
Closed Sun evening, Mon and Feb.
Disabled access. Car park.

An unpretentious little restaurant on the edge of the forest of Chizé. It's a favourite place for Sunday lunch, when the owner is keen to let everyone know he does all the cooking himself. Weekday menu 64F and others up to 218F. *À la carte* try the semi-cooked fresh duck *foie gras*, *fricassée* of eels with young garlic, or salmon escalope with fresh sorrel from the garden. There are also a few quiet rooms, 170F for shower, 180F with shower/wc and 210F for bath. Half board compulsory July–Aug, 250F per person. Free coffee.

BOIS-PLAGE-EN-RÉ (LE)   17580

🛏 |●| HÔTEL LES GOLLANDIÈRES**

av. de la Plage (Centre).
☎ 05.46.09.23.99 ➡ 05.46.09.09.84
Closed Nov to mid-March. **Disabled access.**
Swimming pool. TV. Car park.

A well-designed hotel complex in substantial grounds of more than a hectare, just 100m from the island's most popular beach. It's ideal if you like the holiday club concept and the owner makes sure everything runs smoothly. Impeccable doubles from 370F with shower/wc and 450F with bath. Half board, 420F per person, is compulsory in season and at holiday weekends. They serve a good buffet breakfast for 45F. In the restaurant the cheapest menu costs 125F.

🛏 |●| HÔTEL-RESTAURANT L'OCÉAN**

172 rue Saint-Martin; it's 50m from the church.
☎ 05.46.09.23.07 ➡ 05.46.09.05.40
Restaurant closed Wed except in school holidays, and 13 Jan–13 Feb. **TV. Car park.**

This wonderful hotel is in a typical island house, on a quiet street away from passing traffic. Very relaxed welcome. There's a string of delightful little sitting rooms furnished with antiques, and the charmingly decorated rooms are set round a huge flower-filled patio with an ancient pine tree growing in the middle. Doubles 380–600F with shower/wc or bath. Half board costs 370–500F per person.

The dining room is equally delightful, and there's a terrace on the patio. Dishes are made from fresh market produce and change with the seasons. Try the *chaudrée charentaise* (the local fish soup), and the cod with thyme butter for their finely balanced flavours. Menus 130F and 180F, and a children's menu at 55F. There's a bike shed.

|●| RESTAURANT AU PETIT BOIS

23 rue de l'Église (Centre).
☎ 05.46.09.37.21
Closed Sun and Mon evening out of season.

The fish served here couldn't be fresher. The good-value 92F menu lists *moules marinière* or six oysters, fish of the day – sole or plaice – and dessert. There's a cheaper menu at 65F or another at 130F, and a children's menu at 43.50F. *À la carte* you'll find prawns on skewers, sole stuffed with crab, clams with garlic butter and so on. The potatoes are grown on the island, which is becoming rarer and rarer. Also unique to the island is Le Royal, a fresh, light white wine that's well worth a taste. Just one little niggle — service can be slow.

🕴|●| LA BOUVETTE GRILL DE MER

Moulin de Morinand (North); take the Saint-Martin-de-Ré bypass, then the road to Le Bois-Plage, and it's about 1km further.
☎ 05.46.09.29.87 ➡ 05.46.09.96.05
Closed Sun evening, Mon lunchtime, Wed out of season, Dec and Jan.

One of the island's most interesting restaurants, partly because it's in an old garage in magnificent surroundings but also because the seafood is wonderfully fresh. Suggestions are chalked up on the board – *salade terre-mer*, oysters, langoustine *fricassée*, monkfish on skewers, grilled bass and, for afters, warm goat's cheese, fruit tarts, fresh pineapple or meringue. Star choices include the mouthwatering *salade Bouvette*, with salmon, scallops and cuttlefish, the *éclade* of mussels served on pine needles with a dash of raspberry vinegar, and the blissful stuffed crab. There's a short menu at 90F, or you'll spend around 180F *à la carte*. Good food in a good atmosphere. It seats just forty people, so you have to book several days in advance in season. There's a terrace with a barbecue outside. Free coffee.

COUARDE-SUR-MER (LA)   17670 (3KM N)

🕴 🛏 |●| HÔTEL-RESTAURANT LA SALICORNE

16 rue de l'Olivette (East); it's near the main street.
☎ and ➡ 05.46.29.82.37
Closed Thurs lunchtime July–Aug.

Long dining room with a terrace that runs the full length of the establishment. There's a 100F weekday menu and another at 140F, but these give only a glimpse of the chef's great talent. To experience the quality of Luc Dumond's gifts, order *à la carte*: *clafoutis* of prawns with mushrooms, lobster stew with shellfish, crayfish with *foie gras* and so on. You'll end up paying about 220F a head, which isn't bad for pricey l'île de Ré. The modest rooms, which are overdue for decoration, cost 200F for a double with washing facilities. Free coffee after a meal.

⬧ |●| HÔTEL LE VIEUX GRÉEMENT-RESTAURANT LE BANC DES PÊCHEURS

13 pl. Carnot; it's on a square behind the church.
☎ 05.46.29.82.19 ➡ 05.46.29.50.79
Closed Wed and Nov to Easter.
Disabled access. **TV**.

This hotel has been tastefully restored, drawing inspiration from the colours of the sea. Very pleasant welcome. Well-appointed rooms and bathrooms cost 240–700F; those overlooking the square are charming. You must book in advance. In the restaurant, try the 55F *formule*, which gets you nine oysters and a glass of white wine. There's another menu at 165F or a selection of sandwiches or cooked dishes. You can enjoy a glass of wine on the terrace or in the bistro inside.

⬧ |●| HÔTEL-RESTAURANT LES MOU-ETTES

28 Grande-Rue (Centre).
☎ 05.46.29.90.30 ➡ 05.46.29.05.41
Closed Sun afternoon Oct–March. **TV**.

One of the most charming places on the island, yet one of the least expensive. Fourteen rooms look over the interior terrace, with twelve others in an annexe on a very quiet street. Book early if you want to stay in summer, as there are regulars who come every year. Double with shower/wc 290–370F. Half board, 210–480F, is compulsory July–Aug. The terrace is open all day, with affordable menus at 57F, then 78–135F. They also serve single dishes, like a plate of local oysters with a glass of Muscadet or mussels with chips. Try the *mouclade* or any of the fish which is freshly landed.

|●| RESTAURANT LA CABINE DE BAIN

Grande-Rue (Centre).

☎ 05.46.29.84.26
Closed Sun evening and Mon except Easter and July–Aug.

The owner here also runs the fishmonger's next door and a fish stall at the covered market. He has an excellent reputation. The cooking is simple but very tasty, ranging from regional dishes such as mussels in Pineau to more exotic choices such as salmon sashimi. There's a good, if rather limited, 95F *menu du jour* served at lunchtimes, and lots of good choices *à la carte*: grilled salmon with olives or fillet of meagre (which is something like sea bass) served with orange butter. Reckon on paying 250F per person for a full meal.

FLOTTE (LA)   17630 (6KM E)

|●| RESTAURANT L'ÉCAILLER

3 quai de Sénac (Centre); it's on the quay.
☎ 05.46.09.56.40 **e** ecaukker@yahoo.fr
Closed Mon and 1 Nov to Easter.

Service from noon and 8pm. *L'Écailler* is one of the most reliable restaurants on the island – you could order a meal blindfold here and rely on getting something delicious. It's a 17th-century house situated across from the port, with a pocket-sized terrace in the courtyard. They serve the freshest fish and seafood only. Try the raw salmon with oysters and cream or the monkfish with honey and spices. Nothing comes cheap: expect to pay 300F per person. There are no set menus. The service is erratic.

SAINTE-MARIE-DE-RÉ   17740 (6KM SE)

⬧ HÔTEL DU PEU-BRETON**

31 rue de la Cailletière; it's on the road from Sainte-Marie to La Noue.
☎ 05.46.30.23.55 ➡ 05.46.37.15.35
e hotel.Peu.Breton@wanadoo.fr
Closed Oct. **Disabled access**. **Swimming pool**. **TV**.
Car park.

This modern hotel doesn't have the charm of the traditional buildings on the island, but it is comfortable and you will be very well taken care of. Doubles 310–360F with shower/wc, 330–380F with bath. There are some family rooms sleeping three or four. Breakfast, a self-service buffet, costs 40F.

BOYARDVILLE   17190

⬧|●| LA ROUE TOURNE

It's on the left of the road from Boyardville to Sauzelle,

practically opposite the fish ponds of the Surine.
☎ 05.46.47.21.47

An unusual, out-of-the-way place that's a pleasure to discover. Run by the same family for more than thirty years, it's a stone house with beams and a huge open fireplace. The big communal tables with benches make it friendly and they've taken the trouble to provide cushions. Fish directly from the fish ponds across the road and seafood are the specialities, washed down with a glass of crisp white Bordeaux. It won't set you back much either. Menus at 175F or 185F and children's menu at 80F, *à la carte* around 180F. Around 11pm, when you've struggled your way through a vast seafood platter, the atmosphere hots up as the owner gets out his guitar and leads the gathering in a burst of *Viva España* and other classics. There's no other place like it on the island. It's quieter at lunchtime and you won't have to book. Free coffee.

BRESSUIRE   79300

🏠 ⊜ |●| HÔTEL-RESTAURANT LA BOULE D'OR**

15 pl. Émile-Zola (Southwest); it's near the station.
☎ 05.49.65.02.18 ➡ 05.49.74.11.19
Closed Sun evening, Mon lunchtime.
TV. Lock-up car park.

This establishment serves good, if not particularly original, cooking in a plush, comfortable dining room. Cheapest menu 70F, then 89–200F. Double rooms 235–290F with shower/wc or bath. Four people can share for 300F. Warm welcome. Free coffee.

CHALAIS   16210

|●| LE RELAIS DU CHÂTEAU

Château des Talleyrand.
☎ 05.45.98.23.58
Closed Mon evening except in summer, and Wed.
Car park.

The restaurant occupies a wing of the enormous 14th-century château which dominates the valley of the Tude and the Vivonne rivers. You reach it across a working drawbridge. Period interior, and a vaulted ceiling that gives the dining room real style. Give in to temptation and order any one of the various kinds of *foie gras* listed on the *à la carte* menu. There's a 95F menu (not served Sun lunch or on public holidays) and others 130–210F. Children's menu 50F.

CHARROUX   86250

⊜ |●| HOSTELLERIE CHARLEMAGNE**

7 rue de Rochemeaux (Centre); it's next to the ruined abbey, opposite the covered market.
☎ 05.49.87.50.37
Closed Sun evening and Mon out of season.
TV. Car park.

The decor of this inn, built from stone from the ruined abbey, takes you back to a romantic past. Tasty dishes include *fricassée* of snails with honey and pine nuts and Poitou lamb with garlic. Menus 90–200F. The rooms are comfortable – number 8, with its bathroom of dressed stone, is very special. Doubles 200F with shower/wc or bath.

CHÂTEAU-D'OLÉRON (LE)   17480

⊜ |●| HÔTEL DE FRANCE-RESTAURANT LA FLEUR DE SEL**

11 rue du Maréchal-Foch (Centre); it's very near the main square.
☎ 05.46.47.60.07 ➡ 05.46.75.21.55
Restaurant closed Sun evening and Mon out of season and six weeks Dec/Jan. **TV.**

Service noon–1.30pm and 7–9pm. This typical town-centre hotel in a historic village is comfortable and welcoming. Doubles 280–360F with bath, though none with views of the sea. Half board is optional. The chef has bags of imagination – try his mussel soup, crayfish gâteau with pearls of vegetables, pan-fried skate wings with capers, or roast sea bass served with meat juices. Good-value menus at 78f and 158F.

RONCE-LES-BAINS   17390 (18.5KM S)

🏠 ⊜ |●| HÔTEL LE GRAND CHALET-RESTAURANT LE BRISE-LAMES**

2 av. de la Cèpe (Centre).
☎ 05.46.36.06.41 ➡ 05.46.36.38.87
Closed Mon lunchtime, Tues and begining of Nov to Feb. **Garden. Car park.**

An attractive, classic seaside hotel on the edge of the ocean, near the fine sandy beaches that run all the way to Royan. The nicest rooms, with sea views, lead onto the garden and cost 350F. The rooms with no view, 280F, have shower/wc or bath. The superb chef adapts the menus according to season and the fresh produce available. Lots of fish and seafood. There's an 89F lunch menu (not served Sun) and others at 120, 190F and 250F. The bread and pastries are home-made. Professional welcome and service. Free house apéritif.

CHÂTELAILLON-PLAGE   17340

⅄ ☎ HÔTEL D'ORBIGNY**

47 bd. de la République (North); it's between the town hall and Fort Saint-Jean.
☎ 05.46.56.24.68 ➡ 05.46.30.04.82
Closed Dec–Feb. **Swimming pool. TV. Car park.**

This reliable hotel began life as a holiday home at the start of the 20th century. It's a large, seaside building just 100m from the beach – and there's a swimming pool for when the tide goes out (it can recede a good kilometre hereabouts). The rooms are decorated simply but attractively and prove excellent value. Doubles 200F with shower, 250F with shower/wc or bath. Though the rooms over the street have good double glazing, those on the swimming pool side are quietest. 10% discount except July–Aug and public holiday weekends.

⅄ ☎ |O| HÔTEL VICTORIA**

13 av. du Général Leclerc (Centre).
☎ 05.46.30.01.10 ➡ 05.46.56.10.09
Closed mid-Dec to end Jan. **Car park.**

Typical late 19th-century seaside building that has been vigorously brought back to life by the welcoming owners. The pleasant rooms have been refurbished in good taste. Doubles 200F with washing facilities, 270F with shower/wc. The restaurant is reserved for residents: half board starts at 360F per person. The station is just across the road but there are very few trains at night and the place is big enough for you to find a quiet room. The welcome is not always warm enough. Free apéritif.

CHÂTELLERAULT   86100

DANGÉ-SAINT-ROMAIN   86220 (14KM N)

⅄ ☎ |O| LE DAMIUS**

16 rue de la Gare.
☎ 05.49.86.40.28 ➡ 05.49.93.13.69
Closed Sun evening, Mon and the second fortnight in Sept. **TV. Garden. Car park.**

Service noon–2pm and 8–10pm. A little hotel, lovingly run by Michel and Martine Malbrant. The restaurant overlooks the terrace and there's a garden especially designed for kids. Good cooking with menus 85–190F. Try the zander in *beurre blanc* or the braised ham with Pineau des Charentes. Doubles

with shower/wc 260F, 290F with bath. They also have rooms sleeping four. The hotel is soundproofed but light sleepers should note that the TGV line runs past the hotel. 10% discount on the room rate.

LEIGNÉ-LES-BOIS   86450 (19KM SE)

☎ |O| HÔTEL-RESTAURANT BERNARD GAUTIER

pl. de la Mairie (Centre); take the D14 and the D15.
☎ 05.49.86.53.82 ➡ 05.49.86.58.05
Closed Sun evening and Mon. **Car park.**

Extremely secluded spot, in the remotest part of northern Vienne. Apart from the freshness of the new frontage, the establishment is not too noticeable. Chef Bernard Gautier combines subtle flavours to delight the palate. There's fresh cod with spices and herbs, *gâteau* of young rabbit with tartare sauce, *tartare* of fresh salmon, zander with a light *beurre blanc*, and tournedos. If you like *andouillette à la ficelle* you're in for a real treat, and the *crème brûlée* is the best in the region. Menus at125F, 195F and 250F, with portions on the last extremely generous. They have a few clean, simple bedrooms where you'll get a good night's rest. Doubles 155F with washing facilities. Good food, good hotel and a cheerful owner — you'd be hard pushed to find better.

CHAUVIGNY   86300

⅄ ☎ |O| HÔTEL-RESTAURANT LE LION D'OR**

8 rue du Marché (Centre).
☎ 05.49.46.30.28 ➡ 05.49.47.74.28
Closed 24 Dec–2 Jan. **Disabled access. TV. Car park.**

Service noon–2pm and 7–9pm. A traditional hotel in the heart of town next to the church. The bedrooms, which are being done up in turn – ten so far out of 26 – are situated in an annexe that overlooks the quiet car park at the back. There's one family room. Doubles with shower/wc 270F, with bath 280F. In the large, attractive dining room, you'll eat dishes like zander with poppy seeds, *gâteau de crêpe soufflées* and lamb with warm goat's cheese. Menus at 95–200F. Free coffee.

⅄ ☎ |O| LE CHALET FLEURI**

31 av. Aristide Briand; take the Poitiers road out of Chavigny then first left after the bridge over the Vienne.
☎ 05.49.46.31.12 ➡ 05.49.56.48.31
Restaurant closed Mon lunchtime. **Disabled access. TV. Car park.**

This hotel, just outside the village on the banks of the River Vienne, is surrounded by gardens and trees. The spacious interior is bright and the rooms are impeccable. Doubles with en-suite bathroom 280F. You can see the river and the medieval town from the dining room, where they serve traditional cuisine. Weekday menu at 78F and others 98–178F. Cheerful welcome. Free apéritif or coffee.

🏃 I●I LES CHOUCAS

21 rue des Puys, Ville Haute; it's in the medieval town.
☎ 05.49.46.36.42
Closed Wed Dec–March, and Nov.

As you go up the splendid medieval staircase to the first floor you'll smell glorious aromas emanating from the kitchens. The setting is welcoming and has lots of character. Natural and attentive service. Try perch with tarragon sauce, *blanquette* of kid, king scallop sallad with citrus fruit or the Poitou speciality, *farci poitevin* (green vegetables and herbs mixed with pork fat, cream and eggs, wrapped in cabbage leaves and poached in ham and pork stock). Menus 69–138F. Good local wines sold by the jug. Truffle tastings Nov–March. Free apéritif.

COGNAC · 16100

🏃 🏠 HÔTEL LA RÉSIDENCE**

25 av. Victor-Hugo (Centre); 100m from pl. François 1er.
☎ 05.45.36.62.40 ➡ 05.45.36.62.49
📧 la.residence@free.fr
TV. Pay car park.

This charming little hotel, just steps from the pedestrian precinct, has smart, well-sound-proofed bedrooms. Very pleasant welcome and helpful staff. Bedrooms 200F with washing facilities, 240F with shower, 290F with shower/wc and 320F with bath. If you really want a quiet night, ask for room 109; if you like a lot of space ask for number 201, which has a sitting room and sleeps three. 10% discount except July–Aug. Free parking for motorcycles and bikes.

🏃 🏠 I●I L'ÉTAPE**

2 av. d'Angoulême.
☎ 05.45.32.16.15 ➡ 05.45.36.20.03
Closed Sat lunchtime and Sun evening. **TV. Car park**.

An ideal base if you want to visit the Hennessy or Martel Cognac houses. Informal welcome and homely atmosphere. There are two dining rooms here; the one on the ground floor oper-

ates like a brasserie and has a 62F *menu rapide*, while there's a more traditional dining room in the basement. The latter offers a range of sophisticated menus, 73–145F, listing dishes such as chicken *confit* with Pineau or steak with Cognac. Comfy doubles with basin and shower at 210F, or 270F with shower/wc or bath. Free house apéritif.

🏃 I●I RESTAURANT LA BONNE GOULE

42 allée de la Corderie (Centre).
☎ 05.45.82.06.37 ➡ 05.45.36.00.76
Closed Sun and a fortnight in May. **Car park**.

Service noon–2pm and 7.30–10pm. All the attractions of Charente can be found here – a quiet cosy atmosphere, characterful country-style decor, and good home-made food. Portions are generous – try the rib of beef in Cognac. The cheapest menu is 70F and there are others 90–150F – all include a carafe of Bordeaux. You can also choose *à la carte*. A good list of local wines. Musical evenings Fri and Sat. Free apéritif or coffee.

🏃 I●I LE COQ D'OR

pl. François 1er (Centre).
☎ 05.45.82.02.56

This is a Parisian-style brasserie right in the middle of town. Quick service, friendly welcome, a good range of prices and lots to choose from *à la carte*: salads, *choucroutes*, platters of shellfish, grills, calf's head, snails and so on. There are also some very delicious specialities such as veal chops with ceps, deglazed with Cognac. Go for the Charentais desserts: *jonchet* (cream cheese, drained on rush mats) or *caillebotte* (soured milk, more delicate than yoghurt, served with sugar and a Cognac chaser). Menus 79–249F. Very generous helpings. Free coffee or *digestif*.

🏃 I●I RESTAURANT LA BOÎTE À SEL

68 av. Victor-Hugo (Southeast).
☎ 05.45.32.07.68 ➡ 05.45.32.37.20
Closed Mon and 20 Dec–5 Jan.

Service noon–2.30pm and 7–10pm. The chef in this converted grocer's store is committed to promoting regional produce and he changes his menus with the season. Two walls are lined with wine racks, showing off a range of excellent vintages, but they can all be served by the glass. Excellent cooking; monkfish fillet with grapes steeped in Pineau des Charentes, pork *confit* with sweet spices. Menus 80–220F, or *à la carte*. Whatever you eat, start with a glass of iced Cognac. Free house apéritif.

SEGONZAC   16130 (14KM SE)

|●| LA CAGOUILLARDE*

How to get there: take the D24 towards Barbezieux.
☎ 05.45.83.40.51
Closed Sat lunchtime and Sun evening. **Garden.**

The unusual decor here combines rustic and modern styles. The first dining room has marble garden tables and leads to a second with a large fireplace fuelled with vine cuttings for the grills. Relaxed atmosphere, with jazz playing in the background. Try the stuffed snails, the pan-fried eel or the grilled cutlets with walnut oil. Good selection of Pineau wines. Lunch menu at 78F, with others at 120F and 150F, and choices *à la carte*. There's a terrace overlooking the garden.

CONFOLENS   16500

⚑ ☎ |●| LA MÈRE MICHELET*

19 allées de Blossac.
☎ 05.45.84.04.11 ➦ 05.45.84.00.92
Closed Mon from Nov to end April. **TV.**

A dynamic family-run business. In the restaurant try the Saint-Barthélemy veal sweetbreads or the lamb cutlets *confolentaise*. Menus 72–230F and *à la carte*. The recently modernised bedrooms go for 130F with washing facilities, upwards of 230F with shower/wc, and 260F with bath. Half board from 225F per person. Free coffee.

⚑ ☎ |●| HÔTEL-RESTAURANT DE LA VIENNE*

rue de la Ferrandie.
☎ and ➦ 05.45.84.09.24
Closed Sun evening, Mon, 2–15 Nov and three weeks from 15 Jan. **TV. Car park.**

This beautiful hotel with a large waterfront terrace is in one of the narrow alleys in the old neighbourhood around the church of Sainte-Maxime. It has spacious rustic bedrooms and good, inexpensive food. Try the *terrine* of chicken livers with Pineau and any of the home-made pastries. Menus 60–140F. Doubles 190F with washing facilities, 240F with shower/wc and 310F with bath. Formal welcome. Free coffee.

COUHÉ   86700

⚑ ☎ |●| HÔTEL-RESTAURANT LA PROMENADE

Lieu-dit Valence; it's 1km outside Couhé coming from

Poitiers.
☎ 05.49.59.20.88
Closed Sun evening, Mon and 1–12 Jan. **Disabled access. TV. Car park.**

Service noon–2pm and 7–9pm. You'll get a cheery welcome and a hearty meal in this friendly place that's a little like a roadside café. Good value menus at 54F (not served Sun), 82F and 115F. Specialities include *cassolette* of snails, veal *blanquette*, rabbit *civet* (a rich stew) and skate wings with black butter. The well-equipped rooms, spacious enough for families, cost 160F with shower/wc and 170F with bath. 10% discount on the room rate for a minimum three-night stay.

FONT-D'USSON (LA)   86350

⚑ ☎ |●| AUBERGE DE L'ÉCURIE*

How to get there: it's on the D727 3.5km before Usson-du-Poitou.
☎ 05.49.59.53.84
Closed Sun evening except public holidays and a fortnight in Oct. **Disabled access. TV. Car park.**

Completely lost in the fields in the country, this place is in a beautifully converted stable that's been decorated in rustic style. You'll be greeted in a kindly way. The simple dishes, cooked using quality ingredients, include eel stew, lamb sweetbreads with cream, parsley snails or *civet* of kid with wild garlic. Menus at 75F, 135F and 195F. In summer there's a tea room where home-made pastries and cakes are served. Ten comfortable double rooms with shower/wc 250F. Free apéritif or coffee. Credit or debit cards are not accepted.

FOURAS   17450

☎ HÔTEL LA ROSERAIE*

2 av. du Port-Nord (Northwest); follow the signs for port de la Fumée.
☎ 05.46.84.64.89
TV. Garden. Disabled access.

Monsieur and Mme Lacroix lavish lots of attention on their little hotel, a detached house with an unlikely-looking entrance hall done up like a 1950s Paris nightclub. The prices are very reasonable for the area. Doubles 220–330F with shower/wc or 230–350F with bath. The bright, clean bedrooms overlook the sea or the garden. Dogs welcome. Friendly, if cursory, welcome.

⚑ ☎ GRAND HÔTEL DES BAINS*

15 rue du Général-Brüncher (Centre); it's 50m from the

Vauban fort and the beach
☎ 05.46.8403.44 ➡ 05.46.84.58.26
✉ hoteldebains@wanadoo.fr
Closed Nov–Jan. **TV. Garden. Pay lock-up car park**.

Attractive old coaching inn right in the middle of Fouras which is halfway between a fishing village and an old-fashioned seaside resort. The classic rooms have some style; most of them look out onto the pretty garden where you eat breakfast in the summer. Doubles with shower but no wc cost 220–280F, or 290–350F with bath. The beach is a short walk away. Car park 30F per night. Free breakfast if you stay three nights or more.

JARNAC   16200

𝔸 |●| RESTAURANT DU CHÂTEAU

15 pl. du Château (Centre).
☎ 05.45.81.07.17 ➡ 05.45.35.35.71
Closed Sun and Wed evenings, Mon, 1–15 Jan and 15–21 Aug.

Service noon–2pm and 7.15–9pm. This is one of the best restaurants in the area, and the dishes change with the seasons and what's fresh at the market. Cosy setting. Specialities include pan-fried langoustine tails with orange, duck *foie gras*, *tournedos Rossini* and iced *soufflé* with Cognac. Weekday lunchtime menu at 101F then others at 160F and 238F, and options *à la carte*. The wine list is as impresive as the cooking and includes more than a hundred Bordeaux. Free apéritif.

ROUILLAC   16170 (16KM NE)

𝔸 ⌂ |●| AUBERGE DES FINS BOIS

19 rue de Jarnac (West); take the D736.
☎ 05.45.96.85.15 ➡ 05.45.96.82.97
Closed Mon and evenings in winter except by reservation. **TV**.

This refurbished little hotel offers good value for money. In the restaurant, choose from a 50F *formule,* set menus 92–160F, or *à la carte*; good dishes include *gratin* of snails with Pineau, eel *matelote* and iced *nougat*. Bedrooms from 180F with washing facilities and 240F with shower/wc. Free apéritif.

JONZAC   17500

𝔸 ⌂ |●| LE CLUB**

8 pl. de l'Église (Centre).

☎ 05.46.48.02.27 ➡ 05.46.48.17.15
Closed Sun evening from mid-March to end Nov, weekends from Dec to mid-Nov, and 25 Dec–10 Dec.
TV. Car park.

This little hotel, which stands on the church square, offers large, clean, well-equipped bedrooms. Numbers 1, 2, 3 and 4 are the biggest. Doubles with shower/wc at 230F and 280F with bath – excellent value for the location. They serve good-quality brasserie and bistro food, with a weekday lunch menu at 50F then others 65–145F. It's popular locally and best to book. Free coffee.

CLAM   17500 (6KM N)

⌂ |●| HÔTEL–RESTAURANT LE VIEUX-LOGIS**

How to get there: take the D142 in the direction of Pons.
☎ 05,46,70.20.13 ➡ 05.46.70.20.64
Closed Sat lunchtime and Sun evening out of season, and 14 Dec–11 Feb. **Disabled access. Swimming pool. TV**.

You'll feel as you've been invited to a friend's house when you walk into this country inn. The owner's welcoming smile has something to do with it. He used to be a photographer and prints of his pictures decorate the walls. His wife's cooking is first rate. She prepares lots of traditional family dishes and regional specialities, too. Try the pan-fried veal sweetbreads flambéed in Cognac, the gratinéed oysters with *foie gras*, or the braised monkfish with pickled vegetables. There's a 90F menu (not served Sun), and others at 130–300F. Rooms in a separate, modern building; doubles 230F with shower and 250–290F with bath. They all overlook a small garden. There's a small swimming pool and you can borrow mountain bikes. Best to book.

LOUDUN   86200

⌂ |●| HOSTELLERIE DE LA ROUE D'OR**

1 av. d'Anjou (North).
☎ 05.49.98.01.23 ➡ 05.49.22.31.05
Closed Sun evening Oct to Easter. **Disabled access. TV. Car park**.

A former coaching inn at a quiet crossroads, its faded pink walls swathed in Virginia creeper. You'll find yourself in cosy surroundings. Simple regional dishes include salad of Brittany lobster with spiced *sabayon, marbré* of Poitou rabbit with *foie gras* and strawberries *au gratin* with kirsch – imaginative enough and really good. There's an 85F menu served during the week, then others 115–220F. The bedrooms are in the same provincial vein; the more characterful ones have beamed ceilings, while the ones on the side of the building are quietest. All doubles 280F.

LUSIGNAN   86600

⅍ ♨ |●| LE CHAPEAU ROUGE**

1 rue de Chypre.
☎ 05.49.43.31.10 ➡ 05.49.43.31.20
Closed Sun evening, Mon and public holidays, the second fortnight in Oct, a week at Christmas/New Year and a week in Feb. **TV**. **Car park**.

Service noon–2pm and 7.30–9.30pm. This former coaching inn, built in 1643, has a large fireplace dominating the beautiful dining room. Good cooking, with an emphasis on fish dishes like risotto of sea trout *degleré* and trout with almonds, or try the veal sweetbreads with asparagus and local snails in a Sauvignon sauce. The 80F menu is served during the week, and there are others 120–170F. Pleasant bedrooms with good facilities cost 240F with shower/wc and 260F with bath. Numbers 4 and 10, which overlook the courtyard, are the quietest. The bar has suffered at the hands of a reckless decorator who didn't appreciate the building's original character. Free coffee.

COULOMBIERS   86600 (8KM NE)

♨ |●| LE CENTRE POITOU**

39 route Nationale; take the N11 towards Poitiers.
☎ 05.49.60.90.15 ➡ 05.49.50.05.89
Closed Sun evening and Mon Oct–June. **TV**. **Car park**.

Service noon–2.30pm and 7.30–9.30pm. This large, charming house is a gourmet's dream. Subtle, refined cuisine and sophisticated dishes – duckling with spiced caramel, poached chicken, warm *foie gras tartelettes* with sautéed truffles, and autumn fruit tart flavoured with vanilla. The menus, 110–200F, are named after queens – "Clothilde", "Diana" and "Aliénoir" – and you eat like a king. Doubles 260F with shower/wc, 300F with bath. There's a 68F lunch *formule* served on the terrace.

MARANS   17230

|●| ♨ LA PORTE VERTE

20 quai Foch (Centre).
☎ 05.46.01.09.45

Closed Wed, Sun evening 15 Sept –15 June, and the Feb and Nov school holidays. **Garden**.

Service noon–2pm and 7–9pm. This place, in the most attractive part of Marans, has a pocket-handkerchief garden where you dine in the evening, overlooking the Pomère canal. There are two charming, cosy dining rooms; the larger one has a magnificent fireplace where there's a roaring fire in winter. The cuisine is of a high standard, with a number of regional dishes including the rabbit *terrine* with Muscadet or the eel with parsley. All the dishes are very inventive and show off the flavours of the quality ingredients. Menus 85F and 130F. The rooms are magnificent and the bathrooms enormous. Unbeatable value at 290F, including breakfast.

MAULÉON   79700

⅍ ♨ |●| HÔTEL-RESTAURANT L'EUROPE**

15 rue de l'Hôpital (Centre); it's the continuation of la Grand-Rue.
☎ 05.49.81.40.33 ➡ 05.49.81.62.47
Closed Fri and Sun evenings Sept–April, Sun evening and Mon May–Aug, and mid-Dec to mid-Jan. **Disabled access**. **TV**. **Car park**.

This former coaching inn has been operating for more than a hundred years. The combination of modern decor and Jacques Durand's generous portions of elaborate dishes has given it a new lease of life. Menus, 75–180F, list house *foie gras* with honeyed carrot cake, scallops with truffled artichokes, sautéed farm chicken with crayfish and the house dessert, *délice Geneviève*. Elegant bedrooms, 280F with shower/wc, 300F with bath. Free coffee.

MELLE   79500

⅍ ♨ |●| HÔTEL-RESTAURANT LES GLYCINES**

5 pl. René-Groussard (Centre).
☎ 05.49.27.01.11 ➡ 05.49.27.93.45
Closed Sun evening except July–Aug, Mon and two weeks in Jan. **TV**.

Service 12.15–2.30pm and 7.30–9.30pm. Housed in an impressive 19th-century building, this hotel takes its name from the wisteria that smothers it. Expect to pay 245F for a double with shower/wc or 300F with bath. The cooking is just a touch refined, with dishes like eel stew, roast rabbit with wild garlic, shortcake with caramelised apples and rosemary ice cream. There's an 82F menu served during the week only, then others from 95–175F. Informal, relaxed welcome and service. Free apéritif.

MONTMORILLON 86500

♠ |●| HÔTEL-RESTUARANT LE LUCULLUS**

4 bd. de Strasbourg; it's opposite the Sous-Préfecture.
☎ 05.49.84.09.99 ⊨ 05.49.84.58.68
Restaurant closed Sat, Sun evening and Mon.
Disabled access. TV.

Ten air-conditioned doubles with shower/wc at 260F or bath at 330F. In the bistro, they serve a three-course lunch *formule*,85F including wine and coffee, and a brasserie menu. In the main restaurant, which will appeal to foodies, there are four menus starting at 115F. The chef takes great care in the preparation of his dishes, and everything is made in his kitchens, even the bread: deer with thyme, braised turbot with cream and paprika, zander fillet with watercress. In spring, plump for the suckling lamb *Montmorillonnais*. Free coffee.

NIORT 79000

♠ HÔTEL SAINT-JEAN*

21 av. Saint-Jean-d'Angély (Centre).
☎ 05.49.79.20.76 ⊨ 05.49.35.03.27
Closed Sun afternoon. **Car park.**

A basic, well-run family hotel just a stone's throw from the centre of town. Doubles range from 126F with washing facilities to 175F with bath and telephone. Delightful welcome. There's a TV lounge. A few carved birds, the work of the owner, keep you company at breakfast.

♠ HÔTEL DU MOULIN**

27 rue de l'Espingole; it's close to the main square on the Nantes road.
☎ 05.49.09.07.07 ⊨ 05.49.09.19.40
Disabled access. TV. Car park.

This recently built hotel overlooks the River Sèvre. Very comfortable bedrooms, with bath, telephone and radio, cost 270F for a double. Two are designed especially for the disabled and nine have a balcony overlooking the neighbouring gardens. Friendly welcome. This is where performers stay when they're appearing at the cultural centre across the river. If you want to know if anybody famous has stayed in your room, there's a list pinned up at reception.

♠ LE GRAND HÔTEL-BEST WESTERN***

32 av. de Paris (Centre); it's near pl. de la Brèche and well signposted.
☎ 05.49.24.22.21 ⊨ 05.49.24.42.41
Garden. TV. Pay garage.

This hotel has been refurbished and returned to its former glory by a couple who go to a great deal of trouble for their guests. The prices are good; doubles 375–435F with bath. Rooms with numbers ending in a 5, 6 or 7 overlook the internal garden, where you can have breakfast, 45F.

|●| RESTAURANT LES QUATRE SAISONS

247 av. de La Rochelle (South).
☎ 05.49.79.41.06
Closed Sun and Aug. **Disabled access.**

A restaurant offering sound, traditional, and often regional, cooking – the 130F menu typically lists dishes like stuffed snails, eel stew with wine from the Haut-Poitou, pork *filet mignon* with Pineau des Charentes, goat's cheeses and angelica *soufflé*. The cheapest menu is 59F, there's a good *menu du marché* at 69F, and others 88–158F. Free coffee.

⅔|●| RESTAURANT LA CRÉOLE

54 av. du 24-Février; it's near the tourist office.
☎ 05.49.28.00.26
Closed Sun and Mon, Tues and Wed evenings, Thurs–Sat lunchtimes.

Exotic restaurant – the 95F Caribbean menu gets you rum with *accras* (spicy appetizers), followed by Creole black pudding or *massalé* of pork from Réunion. They do a 65F menu at lunchtime, a dinner *menu-carte* at 145F, and a *snack-créole* at 40F. Free *accras* cocktail.

BESSINES 79000 (4KM SW)

♠ REIX HÔTEL

av. de La Rochelle; it's on the right after the Macif building.
☎05.49.09.15.15 ⊨ 05.49.09.14.13
Garden. Swimming pool.

An ideal place for an overnight stay on the way to your holiday destination. You can relax in the garden after the drive or cool down in the pool. Doubles with bath 330F, breakfast 35F. A decent place.

MAGNÉ 79460 (7KM W)

⅔|●| L'AUBERGE DU SEVREAU

24 rue du Marais-Poitevin; it's halfway between Niort and Coulon.

☎ 05.49.35.71.02
Closed Sun evening and Mon.

Take a swift glance at the menu, which lists dishes such as *œufs en meurette* and *fricassée* of snails, and you'd be forgiven for thinking you're in Burgundy. On the other hand, while you're enjoying your eel stew on the terrace overlooking the river you couldn't be anywhere else but the marshes of the Poitou. Weekday menu 65F or 98F. Free coffee.

COULON   79510 (13KM W)

🏃 🛆 |●| HÔTEL-RESTAURANT LE CENTRAL

4 rue d'Autremont; it's opposite the church.
☎ 05.49.35.90.20 ➦ 05.49.35.81.07
Closed Sun evening, Mon, 15–31 Jan and 1–17 Oct.
Disabled access. Car park.

Service noon–1pm and 7.45–9pm. Typically French establishment, where they serve snail *cassolette forestière*, eel *fricassée*, roast zander in Anjou wine and desserts such as *crème brûlée* with angelica or Pineau sorbet. Good, tasty menu at 99F, while the others, 135–205F, are very substantial. The small rooms, 245–255F with shower/wc or bath, will do fine if you're stuck for somewhere to stay. Free breakfast for overnight guests who book in advance and mention this guide. 10% discount on the room rate.

🛆 HÔTEL AU MARAIS***

46–48 quai Louis-Tardy; it's on the tow path.
☎ 05.49.35.90.43 ➦ 05.49.35.81.98
Closed Jan. **Disabled access. TV. Car park.**

A typical riverside hotel where you can really relax. Bright cheerful doubles 390–450F with shower/wc or 300–390F with bath; some have river views. The owners organise enjoyable walks through this intriguing area of lakes and marshes.

PARTHENAY   79200

🏃 🛆 |●| HÔTEL RENOTEL-RESTAURANT ROSALIA**

bd. de l'Europe (East); it's on the Poitiers road, on the edge of town
☎ 05.49.94.06.44 ➦ 05.49.64.01.94 ℮ hotel-le-Renotel@district-parthenay.fr
Closed Sun mid-Oct to end-March. **TV. Disabled access. Car park.**

Service noon–2pm and 7–9pm. A functional, if rather soulless, hotel surrounded by greenery. Bright doubles with shower/wc 295F or

315F with bath. The restaurant is handy if you're not in the mood to head back into Poitiers. Menus 78–210F. 10% discount on the room rate Nov–Feb.

POITIERS   86000

🏃 🛆 |●| HÔTEL DE PARIS*

123 bd. du Grand-Cerf (West).
☎ 05.49.58.39.37
Restaurant closed Sun. **TV.**

Service noon–2pm and 7–10pm. The 1960s architecture may be somewhat dated, but it's one of the better examples of old-school hotel-keeping. You'll be pampered by the owner and her staff, who know the area well. The location is a touch noisy but you can eat well at reasonable prices. Try the *fricassée* of small eels caught in the marsh, duck fillet with pears or the local lamb. Menus 69–125F. Doubles 148F with washing facillities and 192F with shower/wc. Half board 270F. 10% discount on the room rate.

🏃 🛆 HÔTEL DU CHAPON FIN**

pl. du Maréchal-Leclerc (Centre); it's near the town hall.
☎ 05.49.88.02.97 ➦ 05.49.88.91.63
℮ hotel.chaponfin-Poitiers@wanadoo.fr
Closed Fri evening in winter and 22 Dec–13 Jan. **TV. Car park.**

Warm welcome. The quiet bedrooms are spacious and are all decorated differently. Doubles from 210F with shower, 270F with shower/wc, and 290F with bath. The car park is free except in summer. 10% discount Oct–June for a minimum two-night stay.

🏃 🛆 CITOTEL LE TERMINUS**

3 bd. Pont-Achard (West).
☎ 05.49.62.92.30. ➦ 05.49.62.92.40.
TV. Pay garage.

A large hotel, lovingly run by a charming couple. The quiet bedrooms, some of them rustic, with sloping ceilings, and others more modern, have all been soundproofed to keep out the noise of the station opposite. Doubles 250F with shower, 280F with shower/wc and 305F with bath.There's a bar for guests. 10% discount.

🏃 🛆 INTER-HÔTEL CONTINENTAL**

2 bd. Solférino (West); it's opposite the station.
☎ 05.49.37.93.93 ➦ 05.49.53.01.16
℮ hotel-continental@wanadoo.fr
Disabled access. TV.

Classic hotel with clean, well-planned bedrooms. Doubles with shower/wc or bath, 260–320F; rates are lower at the weekend. 10% discount.

☎ LE PLAT D'ÉTAIN**

7–9 rue du Plat-d'Étain; it's next to the town hall.
☎ 05.49.41.04.80 ➡ 05.49.52.89.04
TV. Car park.

An old coaching inn that's hidden away in a narrow side street in the centre. The rooms are comfortable and very individual because they're given names not numbers – "Cannelle", "Valériane" or "Melon". They're quiet and spick and span. Doubles with shower/wc 260F or 300F with bath. Some look into the interior courtyard.

⅍ ☎ LE GRAND HÔTEL***

28 rue Carnot (Centre); it's near the Carnot car park.
☎ 05.49.60.90.60 ➡ 05.49.62.81.69
e grandhotelpoitiers@wanadoo.fr
Disabled access. TV. Car park.

A quiet, decent hotel in the heart of the city. Art Deco-style interior and spacious, well-equipped rooms. Doubles with shower/wc or bath, 450–499F. Friendly welcome. Free breakfast.

⅍ |○| RESTAURANT LES BONS ENFANTS

11 [bis] rue Cloche-Perse (Centre).
☎ 05.49.41.49.82
Closed Sun evening, Mon, 1–15 Aug and Christmas to 1 Jan. **Disabled access**.

Service noon–2pm and 7–10pm. This place, in Poitiers' delightful 16th-century walled city, is straight out of a fairy tale. The walls are decorated with a large fresco of Alice in Wonderland, and there are stars and angels dotted around the place. The food's good too; 57F *formule* for dish and dessert, 67F for three courses and 112–145F. Try the house semi-cooked *foie gras*, calf's head with chive sauce, and fish stew, and round it off with a chocolate soufflé. Absolute bliss. At lunchtime, you can have the dish of the day plus dessert for 57F. Free coffee.

⅍ |○| LE POITEVIN

76 rue Carnot (Centre); it's near the Carnot car park.
☎ 05.49.88.35.04 ➡ 05.49.52.88.05
Closed Sun, Easter school holidays and a fortnight in July. **Disabled access**.

Service noon–2pm and 7–10pm. This intimate restaurant has a pleasing decor with criss-crossing beams. It's popular with businesspeople at lunchtime and with lovers who want some quiet, intimate time together in the evening. There's a choice of five different dining rooms, all lit by candles. Classic regional cooking, and dishes such as eel *rillettes*, roast kid with wild garlic, lamb with three cheeses, Dublin Bay prawns with *foie gras* or fillet of beef with *foie gras*. 60F menu at lunchtimes, and others 100–230F. Free house apéritif.

|○| RESTAURANT CHEZ CUL DE PAILLE

3 rue Théophraste-Renaudot (Centre).
☎ 05.49.41.07.35
Closed Sun, public holidays and Aug.

The walls are yellowed with age and have scrawled messages from famous people all over them. Strings of garlic and chilli peppers hang from the beams. You eat at long wooden tables, where they serve authentic regional cooking and pork dishes ranging from brains *meunière* to the local *farci poitevin*, a tasty variation of stuffed cabbage. Weekday menu at 115F, or 160F *à la carte*. Open till late, but order before 11pm when prices shoot up.

CROUTELLE   86240 (2KM S)

⅍ ☎ MONDIAL HÔTEL**

La Berlanderie; take the N10.
☎ 05.49.55.44.00 ➡ 05.49.55.33.49
Disabled access. Swimming pool. TV. Car park.

The architecture of this horsehoe-shaped hotel combines the styles of Poitou and Louisiana – unusual, but pleasing. It is laid out round a glittering swimming pool that tempts you to leap in. Self-contained bedrooms with full facilities, from 298F with bath. Pleasant welcome. Breakfast 38F. 10% discount Sept–June.

SAINT-BENOÎT   86280 (2KM S)

⅍ ☎ |○| LE CHALET DE VENISE***

6 rue du Square (Centre); it's not far from the ruins of the Roman aqueduct.
☎ 05.49.88.45.07 ➡ 05.49.52.95.44
Restaurant closed Sun evening, Mon, and the Feb school holidays. **Disabled access. TV. Garden. Car park**.

Wonderful, chic hotel with modern bedrooms; 350F with terrace and shower/wc or bath. The garden at the back features riverside fountains and vast, spreading trees. The bright, uncluttered restaurant has a large bay window, and the food is skilfully prepared by Serge Mautret, a talented chef who's always searching for new flavours and combinations. Try the sweet cod with spiced skin, the farm-raised guinea-fowl with lemon, the casseroled veal chops with cocoa pods and cinnamon, or fish in an aniseed-flavoured stock. Menus 125–295F. Free apéritif.

VIVONNE   86370 (14KM SW)

🏃 🏠 LE SAINT-GEORGES**

12 Grand-Rue; it's just beside the church.
☎ 05.49.89.01.89 ➡ 05.49.89.00. 22
Disabled access. TV. Car park.

A very old hotel in the centre of Vivonne. It's slightly lacking in character since being entirely refurbished, but time will do its job. There are 26 modern rooms with trouser press, hair-drier and TV. Doubles 250F with shower/wc, 280F with bath. Buffet breakfast 35F. The owner is extremely friendly and welcoming. Since it's so close to Futuroscope, reservations are essential. There are plans for the restaurant to become a gastronomic one, so although the menus are priced 65–150F for now, this might change. 10% discount on the room rate Oct–May and free coffee.

🏃 |●| RESTAURANT HÉLIANTHE

59 Grand-Rue (Centre).
☎ 05.49.43.40.49 ➡ 05.49.89.01.74
Closed Mon, Tues – but open Tues evening during school summer holidays – and Jan. **Garden.**

There's a hint of the exotic here, and the decor points to a mix of cultures. The owners have Cambodian connections and there are souvenirs from their travels everywhere – statues of Buddha, musical instruments, pottery. The good cooking is as varied as the decor and full of unusual, even disconcerting combinations of flavours. There's a *terrine* ox tongue with honey, salmon pancake with garlic and cream sauce, sweet and sour haddock, and duckling with cherries and lime. Menus 55F, 60F and 65F served at lunchtime during the week, and there are others 99–169F. They'll serve you a glass of sparkling wine with your dessert and you can take your coffee in the beautiful garden where you'll be surrounded by banana trees and exotic fragrances. Free house apéritif.

🏃 |●| RESTAURANT LA TREILLE

10 av. de Bordeaux (South); it's opposite the park de Vonnant.
☎ 05.49.43.41.13 ➡ 05.49.89.00.72
Closed Wed evening and the Feb school holidays. **Car park.**

Service noon–3pm and 7–9pm. Napoleon paused long enough on his long march south to Spain to dine in this inn. Panic broke out as staff tried to prepare a dinner fit for the emperor. They served *farci poitevin*, a local variation on stuffed cabbage, and he loved it. Today the inn is as welcoming and well run as ever. Staff are friendly and attentive, though service can be slow. Good cooking rich in traditional flavours. The 78F menu, which includes wine, is served during the week only; if you want to try the famous *farci poitevin*, you'll have to go for the 120F *saveurs régionales* menu. At 165F there's the *Festival de Vivonne* for giant appetites – it lists lamb stew with baby onions, *mouclade*, zander with Borgueil, *compote* of duck *à l'ancienne* and a pear flan with apricot *coulis*. Free apéritif.

DISSAY   86130 (15KM NW)

🏃 🏠 |●| HÔTEL-RESTAURANT BIN-JAMIN**

It's on the N10.
☎ 05.49.52.42.37 ➡ 05.49.62.59.06
Closed Sat lunchtime, Sun evening and Mon out of season. **Open** daily 1 June–30 Sept. **Swimming pool. TV. Car park.**

Unusual architecture – a slightly uneasy marriage between a cube and the round building housing the restaurant. Appealing, subtle cuisine is served in a pretty dining room with aquamarine furniture. Try the pan-fried *foie gras* with apples deglazed with beetroot juice, the zander with sliced potato and juices of a veal knuckle, or red mullet with *foie gras* butter. There's an impressive wine list with a good selection of clarets, Burgundies and Loire wines. Weekday menu at 80F, others at 165F, 220F and 280F, and around 280F *à la carte*. Doubles with shower/wc 280F; some overlook the pool. 10% discount on the room rate.

🏃 |●| RESTAURANT LE CLOS FLEURI

474 rue de l'église (North); it's on the road to Saint-Cyr.
☎ 05.49.52.40.27
Closed Sun and Wed evenings. **Car park.**

Across the road from the fairytale château de Dissay, this restaurant has been run by Jean-Jack Berteau for more than 25 years. He scours the region for genuine Poitou produce. His calf's head *gribiche* has a well-earned reputation, as do his eel stewed in Chinon wine and lamb stew with vegetables. Weekday menu at 89F, then 132–182F. The wine list has a careful selection of local vintages. Free apéritif.

NEUVILLE-DE-POITOU   86170 (15KM NW)

🏃 🏠 |●| L'OASIS**

2 rue Daniel-Ouvrard (Centre).

☎ 05.49.54.50.06 ➦ 05.49.51.03.46
Hotel closed Sun out of season and Feb school holidays.
Restaurant closed lunchtimes, Sun. **TV**. **Car park**.

A good place, not too far from Futuroscope, with bright, spring-like rooms. Those looking onto the street are soundproofed – in any case, the street is quiet at night. Doubles 295F with shower/wc including breakfast. The restaurant, open in the evenings only, offers simple, unpretentious dishes: *colombo* of frogs' legs or steak with *foie gras*. Menus 70F, 85F and 100F. 10% discount on the room rate 11 Nov–31 March.

🍴 ●| RESTAURANT SAINT-FORTUNAT

4 rue Bangoura-Moridé (Centre).
☎ 05.49.54.56.74
Closed Sun evening, Mon, 16–30 Aug, and Jan.

A rustic building with exposed stonework, a veranda and a well laid-out courtyard. Faultess service, though the atmosphere can be a bit solemn. The cooking is excellent, combining both simplicity and sophisticated flavours. Try the *andouillette* of pig's trotters with *foie gras*, or the veal kidneys with fresh herbs and spices. There's a 98F menu, served daily, and others at 125F, 180F and 230F. The saint after whom the inn is named was an epicurean – surely he would have approved of the good food and excellent regional wines here. Free apéritif.

VOUILLÉ   86190 (17KM NW)

🍴 🏠 ●| HÔTEL-RESTAURANT LE CHEVAL BLANC**

3 rue de la Barre (Centre); take the N149 towards Parthenay.
☎ 05.49.51.81.46 ➦ 05.49.51.96.31
ℯ LeChevalBlancClovis@wanadoo.fr
TV. **Car park**.

Service noon–2pm and 7.30–9.30pm. A family-run waterside hotel overlooking the river with a terrace on the bank. The restaurant specialises in regional dishes and has a fine list of Loire, Burgundy and Bordeaux wines. Specialities include eel stewed in wine, kid cooked Poitou style, and monkfish *à la vouglaisienne*. Weekday menu at 80F, others 105–240F, and *à la carte*. Good value, but the service is a bit slow. Doubles with basin 170F, or 250F with shower/wc. 10% discount on the room rate Sept–June.

🍴 🏠 ●| LE CLOVIS**

pl. François-Albert (Centre).
☎ 05.46.51.81.46 ➦ 05.49.51.96.31
ℯ LeChevalBlancClovis@wanadoo.fr
Disabled access. **TV**.

Owned by the same people who run the *Cheval Blanc*, 50m up the street, and sharing the same restaurant. This place offers modern rooms with good facilities; doubles 270F with shower/wc or bath. 10% discount on the room rate Sept–June.

ROCHEFORT   17300

🍴 🏠 HÔTEL ROCA FORTIS**

14 rue de la République (Centre).
☎ 05.46.99.26.32 ➦ 05.46.99.26.62
Closed 27 Dec–5 Jan. **Garden**. **TV**. **Car park**.

Roca Fortis is Latin for Rochefort. The hotel, an old town house, is in a street full of beautiful buildings. Most of the rooms look onto the internal courtyard, while others overlook the flower garden where you can relax with a book. The whole place has a slightly old-fashioned charm and is very comfortable. Doubles with basin 180F, 255F with shower/wc, 275F with bath. The young owner will welcome you effusively. 10% discount Sept–June.

🏠 ●| HÔTEL LE PARIS**

27–29 rue La Fayette (Centre).
☎ 05.46.99.33.11 ➦ 05.46.99.77.34
Hotel closed 15 Dec–5 Jan. **Restaurant closed** Sun.
TV.

Service noon–2pm and 7.30–10pm. Functional, comfortable doubles with shower/wc 280–315F, 335F with bath. Traditional cooking is served in a dining room with an uninspiring modern decor – dishes include local snails with garlic butter, duck *confit parmentier* with cream and ceps, and apple tart with caramel ice cream. Menus 128F, 180F and 230F. Weekend rate 210F Oct–March.

●| RESTAURANT LE TOURNE-BROCHE

56 av. Charles-de-Gaulle (Centre).
☎ 05.46.99.20.19 ➦ 05.46.99.72.06
Closed Sun evening, Mon, Tues lunchtime and the first three weeks in Jan.

Service noon–2pm and 7–10pm. The dining room is wonderfully elegant and the service of the quality you'd expect in the finest restaurants. Though the inn-keeper is originally from Luxembourg, the cooking is principally Charentais. Try the eel with garlic and parsley, the *pots de cagouille* (little dishes of local snails), grilled leg of lamb with *mojettes* (a type of haricot bean), and various grills. Menus 160–220F and a children's menu 45F.

ROCHEFOUCAULD (LA)   16110

🏃 🏠 |●| LA VIEILLE AUBERGE DE LA CARPE D'OR***

1 route de Vitrac (Centre).
☎ 05.45.62.02.72 ➡ 05.45.63.01.88
Disabled access. TV. Car park.

Apparently you can rent rooms in the 11th-century Rochefoucauld castle for a trifling 1000F a night. This quiet old inn is more affordable. It's an attractively converted 16th-century coaching inn in the centre of town. Bright bedrooms 220–295F. Hearty local dishes are listed on the menus, which start at 68F (not available on weekends); there are others at 155F and 195F. Good fish dishes, like sea bass with morels, turbot with red-endive butter, *fricassée* of monkfish and king scallops *à la provençale*. Free coffee.

CHASSENEUIL-SUR-BONNIEURE
16260 (11 KM NE)

🏠 |●| HÔTEL DE LA GARE*

9 rue de la Gare (Centre); take the D141.
☎ 05.45.39.50.36 ➡ 05.45.39.64.03
Closed Mon, Sun evening, three weeks in Jan and three weeks in July. **TV. Car park.**

A good-value place. In the restaurant, go for the specialities — *noisette* of lamb *à la charentaise*, fillet of trout with Pineau or fillet of beef with a shallot *fondue*. There are five menus, starting at 65F. Doubles 160F with washing facilities and up to 260F with bath.

ROCHELLE (LA)   17000

SEE MAP OVERLEAF

🏠 |●| HÔTEL LE TRANSATLANTIQUE-LYCÉE HÔTELIER

av. des Minimes (South). Off map **B4-2**
☎ 05.46.44.90.42 ➡ 05.46.44.95.43
Closed Sat, Sun and school holidays. **Restaurant closed** Mon. **Disabled access. TV. Car park.**

The district, near Minimes port, is not particularly appealing but the hotel-restaurant is extremely attractive and beats all competition hands down. It's run by La Rochelle's hotel school and is staffed by eager trainees. Prices are unbeatable; doubles 150F with shower/wc and 180F with bath. Menus in the restaurant start at 90F; you'll pay around 140F *à la carte*. The restaurant seats sixty but it's so good and such good value that it

gets very busy, so arrive early or be prepared to wait for a table.

🏠 |●| HÔTEL DU COMMERCE**

6–12 pl. de Verdun. **MAP B1-4**
☎ 05.46.41.08.22 ➡ 05.46.41.74.85
Restaurant closed Fri evening and Sat from Oct to end Feb, and 3–31 Jan. **TV.**

This beautiful 18th-century mansion, on a very elegant square, became a hotel a hundred years later. The entrance hall is amazing – like something straight out of a spa. There are about sixty bedrooms, catering for all tastes and all pockets. Doubles 165F with basin but no TV up to 325F with bath. Occasionally breakfast, which is extra, gets charged automatically, so it's best to check your bill. Reduced rates end-Sept to end-April. Menus 61.77–105F.

🏃 🏠 HÔTEL LE BORDEAUX*

43 rue Saint-Nicolas (Centre). **MAP C4-3**
☎ 05.46.41.31.22 ➡ 05.46.41.24.43
e hbordeaux@Free.Fr
Closed Dec. **TV.**

This small hotel is in the Saint-Nicolas area, the fisherman's district of the old town. It is like a quiet village during the day but gets very lively at night. The hotel has been totally refurbished and the rooms are bright and well maintained. The ones in the attic get a lot of light, and some even have a balcony. Doubles with basin 180–220F, 205–260F with shower/wc or 230–290F with bath. Very friendly welcome. 10% discount Nov–March.

🏃 🏠 HÔTEL DE L'OCÉAN**

36 cours des Dames (Centre). **MAP B3-7**
☎ 05.46.41.31.97 ➡ 05.46.41.51.12
TV.

This place is wonderfully situated on the old harbour with a view of the towers, but it can be very noisy at night, even with the efficient double glazing. Quieter rooms at the back offer a better chance of a good night's sleep. Doubles 190–370F, all with shower/wc. 10% discount 1 Nov–30 March.

🏠 HÔTEL DE LA MARINE**

30 quai Duperré. **MAP B3-6**
☎ 05.46.50.51.63 ➡ 05.46.46.44.02.69
e Hotel.marine@wanadoo.fr
TV.

The hotel is squeezed between the terraces of two different establishments so it's easy to miss. A pleasant place with thirteen spruce rooms, some with a really lovely view of the old port and the sea in the distance. However, the double glazing doesn't keep out all the noise in the evening when the quay gets busy. Doubles with shower 230–300F or 250–400F with shower/wc. There's no dining room, so breakfast is served in the rooms.

🍴 🏠 HÔTEL LA TOUR DE NESLE**

2 quai Louis-Durand (South). **MAP C3-8**
☎ 05.46.41.05.86 ➡ 05.46.41.95.17
e tourdenesle@wanadoo.fr
TV.

Very well situated on a corner in the old town. Some bedrooms look onto the old port, others onto the canal and the Saint-Sauveur church. You're right in the lively, touristy part of La Rochelle here, and just seven minutes from the station, so there's inevitably a good deal of noise. In summer they open the splendid roof terrace, which affords a beautiful view of the town. Doubles with shower/wc 260–430F, 300–430F with bath. 10% discount for two nights Sept–June except Easter, weekends and public holidays.

🍴 🏠 HÔTEL LE ROCHELOIS**

66 bd. Winston-Churchill (South); Off map **A4-10**
☎ 05.46.43.34.34 ➡ 05.46.42.10.37
Disabled access. **Swimming pool**. **TV**. **Pay car park**.

Modern hotel in a good position, facing the Atlantic. Guests have free use of the sports facilities – the gym, Jacuzzi, sauna, Turkish bath and tennis courts. Or you could take it easy and lounge around by the pool. The rooms have good facilities, and those on the first floor have a terrace. Rooms with shower/wc but no sea view cost 310F; you'll pay 400–550F for a room with bath and sea view. Free breakfast, except during the major holidays and July–Aug. Free apéritif.

🍴 🏠 TERMINUS HÔTEL

pl. du Commandant-De-La-Motte-Rouge. **MAP C4-11**
☎ 05.46.50.69.69 ➡ 05.46.41.73.12
TV.

There are some personal touches in the decor here, and the ambience is rustic. Prices are more than reasonable. Rooms at the back of the hotel are quiet and those overlooking the road have been soundproofed recently – doubles with shower/wc 350F, 379F with bath. 10% discount 15 Oct–1 April.

🍴 🍴 RESTAURANT LA TERRASSE

26 rue des Templiers (Centre). **MAP B3-15**
☎ 05.46.41.79.79

The main attraction here is the terrace, which is on a very pretty little square well away from the crowds. It's an American-style place, with a thumping atmosphere and the TV permanently tuned to MTV; none of the customers seems to be over 40. Service is pretty informal, but they take great care over the food. The fried eggplant with fresh tomato sauce makes an excellent starter, which you can follow with a tasty chilli con carne or a Madison Burger made from good beef. Out of deference to the region they do some fish dishes and seafood platters. There's a weekday lunch *formule* at 45F, menus 69F and 89F, and expect to pay 130F *à la carte*. They do a brunch special on Sunday. Free apéritif.

🍴 LE SOLEIL BRILLE POUR TOUS

13 rue des Cloutiers. **MAP C2-16**
☎ 05.46.41.11.42
Closed Sun and Mon.

Small dining room with mosaic-encrusted walls and tables tightly packed around the open kitchen.Everything is made in-house with fresh, organic ingredients and subtle mixtures of herbs and spices flavour the dishes. Generous portions. The *formule* — starter and dish of the day accompanied by fresh vegetables — is very good value. The small *à la carte* menu offers sweet and savoury *crêpes*, *galettes*, tarts and salads which make a meal in themselves. The crumbles and the *tiramisù* are perfect puddings. Menus from 65F. They put two or three tables out on the pavement when the sun shines. No credit or debit cards.

🍴 🍴 LA MARIE-GALANTE

35 av. des Minimes (Southwest). Off map **B4-19**
☎ 05.46.44.05.54
Closed Mon–Thurs evenings out of season.

The cuisine here is simple, and they prepare classic fish dishes: oysters, fish soup, *moules marinière*, whelks with mayonnais, and an attractively priced fish dish of the day. The 68F *formule express* gets you salad, dish of the day and coffee; it's not served on weekends or public holidays. There are menus 85–120F. Free house apéritif.

🍴 🍴 RESTAURANT TEATRO BETTINI

3 rue Thiers (Centre). **MAP C2-18**
☎ 05.46.41.07.03
Closed Sun, Mon, 25 Sept–1 Oct and 2 Dec–2 Jan.

Service noon–2pm and 7.30–11pm. You might not instantly think of eating pizza in La Rochelle but here they're cooked in a real

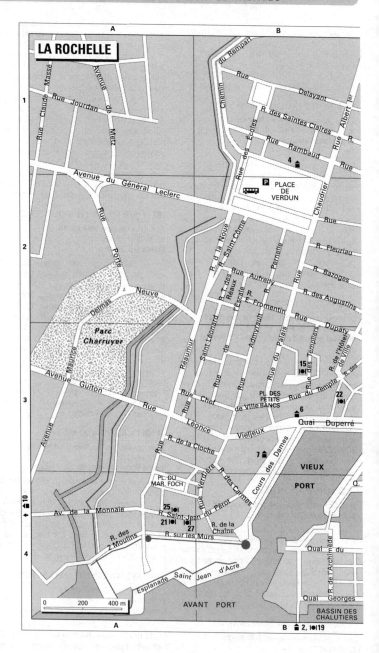

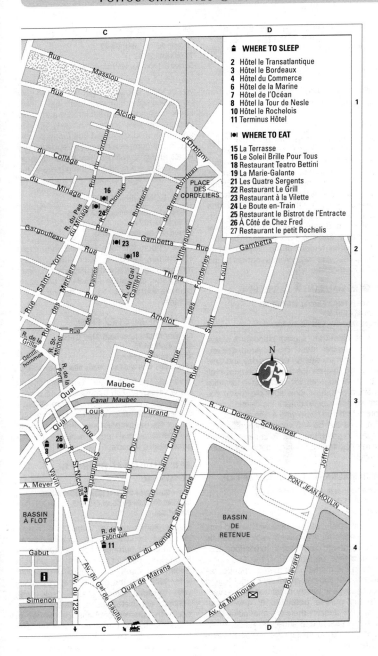

⌂ WHERE TO SLEEP

2 Hôtel le Transatlantique
3 Hôtel le Bordeaux
4 Hôtel du Commerce
6 Hôtel de la Marine
7 Hôtel de l'Océan
8 Hôtel la Tour de Nesle
10 Hôtel le Rochelois
11 Terminus Hôtel

|●| WHERE TO EAT

15 La Terrasse
16 Le Soleil Brille Pour Tous
18 Restaurant Teatro Bettini
19 La Marie-Galante
21 Les Quatre Sergents
22 Restaurant Le Grill
23 Restaurant à la Vilette
24 Le Boute en-Train
25 Restaurant le Bistrot de l'Entracte
26 À Côté de Chez Fred
27 Restaurant le petit Rochelis

wood-fuelled oven and are well above average. So is the pasta; try the *tortellini escoffier* and the *escalope corrado*. A large choice of Italian wines. Menus at 69F and 85F and a children's menu at 38F. Free house apéritif.

🎄|●| LES QUATRE SERGENTS

49 rue Saint-Jean-du-Pérot. **MAP A4-21**
☎ 05.46.41.35.80 ➡ 05.46.41.95.64
Closed Sun evening and Mon.

In a town house dating from 1842, this dining room is in a wonderful winter garden with a glass roof. The setting is superb and the formal service perfectly in keeping. The chef doesn't limit himself to classic brasserie food, and enjoys adding contemporary twists to some dishes. Try the trout with Calvados and apples or the *blanquette* of hake with pistachios and orange zest. The 80F menu is good value, and there are others 115–190F, with a children's menu at 39F. Expect to pay around 180F *à la carte*. Wine is served by the glass. Free coffee.

🎄|●| RESTAURANT À LA VILLETTE

4 rue de la Forme (Centre). **MAP C2-23**
☎ 05.46.41.27.03
Closed Sun, except for reservations.

Service 7am–3pm. A great place for a snack after a wander round the covered market, which is a must-see on Wednesday and Saturday. After a generous portion of herrings in oil with potatoes, opt for the ham hock with lentils, a *cassoulet*, or a splendid mixed grill that's guaranteed to delight the diehard carnivore. Wash it all down with a nice drop of red. Simple as can be and very nicely presented. Expect to pay about 110F *à la carte*. Dishes of the day from 55F. Free coffee or house apéritif.

|●| RESTAURANT LE PETIT ROCHELAIS

25 rue Saint-Jean-du-Pérot. **MAP A4-27**
☎ 05.46.41.28.43
Closed Sun.

A friendly bistro atmosphere with waxed cotton tablecloths and cuisine with a Lyonnais flavour, though care is taken to produce seasonal dishes dependent on the fresh produce in the market. The menus change frequently but you can generally expect to find hot sausage in pastry, roast cod with a meat *jus* and puréed potatoes, or seven-hour lamb. For dessert there's a chocolate soup with banana and orange, or vanilla *millefeuille* with a caramel sauce. Excellent value for money.

|●| RESTAURANT LE GRILL

10 route du Port **MAP B3-22**
☎ 05.46.41.95.90
Closed Sat and Mon lunchtimes, and Sun.

You sit at the bar (only ten places) unless you're lucky enough to get one of the very few tables here. Sink your teeth into a thick steak, fresh from the grill. Monique and Jacky Dupouy produce a range of tasty Basque and Spanish dishes, and you'll pay around 120F for a complete meal. It's frequented by locals and girls with passing male companions. Wines are served by the glass and the desserts are scrumptious.

|●| LE BOUTE-EN-TRAIN

7 rue des Bonnes Femmes. **MAP C2-24**
☎ 05.46.41.73.74
Closed Sun and Mon lunchtime.

Service noon–2pm and 7.15–9.30pm, 10pm in summer. Good home cooking includes monkfish *au gratin* with saffron, calf's head *vinaigrette*, *cassolette* of prawns, and apple crumble. *Menu-carte* 130F or around 150F *à la carte*.

|●| À CÔTÉ DE CHEZ FRED

rue Saint-Nicolas (Southeast). **MAP C3-26**
☎ 05.46.41.65.76
📧 chezfred@rivages.net
Closed Sun, Mon and three weeks after All Saints' Day.

Fred runs the fishmonger's next door so you know where the fish that features so prominently on the menu comes from. What's available depends on what has been caught, so opt for the simplest seasonal dishes. No set menus – you'll pay around 150F for a good meal *à la carte*.

|●| RESTAURANT LE BISTROT DE L'ENTRACTE

22 rue Saint-Jean-du-Pérot (South). **MAP A4-25**
☎ 05.46.50.62.60 ➡ 05.46.41.99.45
Closed Sun.

Service from noon and 7.30pm. The restaurant is run by Didier Cadio, an experienced chef who was number two at *Coutances*, La Rochelle's grandest restaurant. He offers a single *menu-carte* – main course and dessert – for 160F. Try the *gâteau* of langoustines with tarragon cream sauce, sole with almonds and pistachios, tournedos of roast cod with buttered cabbage, *parmentier* of young duck, and bread and butter pudding with vanilla ice. There's lots of choice. Good desserts and an impressive wine list.

AYTRÉ   17440 (3KM S)

⅍ 🏠 |●| HÔTEL-RESTAURANT LES PLATANES*

29 av. du Commandant-Lysiak; from La Rochelle take the bypass towards Aytré.
☎ 05.46.44.29.91 ➡ 05.46.31.06.90
Closed Sun. **Disabled access**. **TV**. **Car park**.

Service noon–2pm and 7–9.30pm. Simple, exceptionally good value food served in a large country-style dining room run by Mme Lechat and her smiling staff. The 62F menu changes daily and is very popular. These feasts sometimes start with skate wing with capers, followed by lamb stew with haricot beans, cheese or dessert and a $1/_4$ litre of red wine. The top price menu costs 160F but the one at 130F is particularly hearty – six oysters, cheek of monkfish with parsley, lamb stew with vegetables, cheese platter and dessert. A few simple, affordable rooms, 160F for a double with basin, 170F with shower and 180F with shower/wc Half board costs 280F per person. 10% discount on the room rate out of season.

LAUZIÈRES   17137 (7KM N)

⅍|●| BAR PORT LAUZIÈRES

port du Plomb; it's at the seafront facing the île de Ré.
☎ 05.46.37.45.44
Closed Tues except July, and Sept–March. **Car park**.

This old fisherman's hut has been converted into a shellfish bar. Local oyster farmers gather at the old-fashioned zinc-topped bar; on the other side, the dining room has a sea view and a cosy fireplace ideal for wintry evenings. Mussels at 35F or 50F, six grilled sardines at 30F, and fish platters with oysters, langoustine, prawns and sardines. Add a little wine and you're looking at not much more than 100F for a meal. Free apéritif.

CHARRON   17230 (16KM N)

⅍|●| RESTAURANT THEDDY-MOULES

72 rue du 14-Juillet; on the port road known as le Pave.
☎ 05.46.01.51.29 ➡ 05.46.01.57.31
Closed Oct–April.

People come to the quiet little village of Charron for one reason alone —to eat mussels at *Theddy-Moules*. Theddy, a mussel farmer, came up with the bright idea of arranging a few tables in a kind of large shed, putting a terrace out front, and serving the freshest seafood you can imagine. It's right on the edge of the road

and the setting is rudimentary, but customers flock here for the quality seafood at affordable prices. Try the mussels *spécial Theddy* with Pineau and cream, an *assiette dégustation* of langoustine, oysters, whelks, winkles and prawns at 68F, or a generous seafood platter at 110F. They serve fish *à la carte*, too: sole or sea bass or grilled sardines. A full meal will set you back around 120F. Free apéritif.

ROCHE-POSAY (LA)   86270

⅍ 🏠 |●| HOSTELLERIE DU VAL DE CREUSE**

9 pl. de Notre-Dame.
☎ 05.49.86.20.71
Closed Nov to end March. **Disabled access**. **TV**. **Car park**.

Service noon–2pm and 7–9.30pm. This establishment, on the banks of the Creuse, serves flavoursome dishes such as sweetbreads and morels in pastry cases, duck breast with sherry and acacia honey, and guinea-fowl *terrine* with apricots. Menus 100F, 160F and 180F. Mme Lussier-Sabourin is a charming woman who keeps the place running like clockwork. Ask for a bedroom overlooking the river. Doubles with basin 150F, 250F with shower/wc or bath. 10% discount on the room rate.

ROYAN   17200

⅍ 🏠 VILLA TRIDENT THYRSÉ

66 bd. Frédéric Garnier (Southeast).
☎ 05.46.0512.83
Closed Sun afternoon out of season. **TV**. **Car park**.

There have been a few alterations since this place was built, but little seems to have changed since 1954. As you walk into the hall, the colours really hit you between the eyes. There's a set of bongo drums next to the Formica bar, and salsa music wafts out onto the terrace that looks out to sea. All the rooms are simple and pleasant, with vintage 1950s decor. Doubles 170–220F with basin, 220–270F with shower or 270–320F with bath. They also have a few self-contained studios that you can rent by the week or for an out-of-season weekend. You only have to wander across the road to walk on the sandy beach. 10% discount.

⅍ 🏠 |●| HÔTEL ABYSSE-RESTAURANT L'ANJOU**

17 rue Font-de-Cherves (Centre); near the market, 200m from the beach.

☎ 05.46.05.30.79 x05.46.05.30.16
Closed Mon out of season, last week in Jan and last week in Sept. **TV**.

The restaurant serves generous portions of good traditional food, and naturally they do lots of fish. The dining room is decorated rather fussily but the owner welcomes you enthusiastically and the service is efficient and unpretentious. There's a 65F menu served at weekday lunchtimes and others at 98–212F, with a children's menu at 44F. Doubles 255–320F with shower/wc, 285F with bath. There are also a few apartments, perfect for families: 340–380F for three or 400–425F for four. Free apéritif and 10% discount on the room rate for a two-night stay.

⌂ HÔTEL BELLE-VUE**

122 av. de Pontaillac (Southwest); it's on the D25 from Saint-Palais.
☎ 05.46.39.06.75 ➡ 05.46.39.44.92
Closed Nov–March. **TV**. **Garden**. **Car park**.

Starting out as a family guest house in the 1950s, this place has grown into a cosy hotel. You'll get a polite, smiling welcome. There are antiques in the comfortable rooms and, as the name suggests, there's a lovely view over Pontaillac bay. Some rooms have a balcony while others look onto the garden. Doubles with shower/wc 290–375 with sea view, 315F with bath.

SAINT-GEORGES-DE-DIDONNE   17110 (4KM S)

⚹ ⌂ |●| HÔTEL-RESTAURANT COLINETTE ET COSTABÉLA*

16 av. de la Grande-Plage (Northeast).
☎ 05.46.05.15.75 ➡ 05.46.06.54.17
✉ info@colinette.not
Hotel closed Jan. **Restaurant closed** evenings except Sat, and 1 Oct–30 March.

Colinette looks like a 1950s guesthouse, while the *Costabéla* is more like a 1970s villa with flowery wallpaper and chenille bedspreads. Doubles 220–300F with shower/wc, 320–420F with bath. The menus, 89–151F, list safe, family favourites: *terrine*, *mouclade*, seafood stew in white sauce and Dublin Bay prawns with Cognac. Children's menu 39F. 10% discount on the room rate for a two-night stay Sept–June except long weekends.

SAINT-PALAIS-SUR-MER   17420 (6KM W)

|●| LE PETIT POUCET

La Grande Côte; it's on the coast road to La Palmyre.
☎ and ➡ 05.46.23.20.48

Closed Wed Oct–March, and Jan.

This concrete 1950s block used to be a real eyesore, but it's been camouflaged by Virginia creeper and ivy, and the trees and shrubs planted around it make it much more attractive. You get a magnificent view of the Grande Côte beach and the ocean beyond from the bright spacious dining room. The terrace is perfectly placed. Mostly seafood – pan-fried scallops with cider, Dublin Bay prawns with Pineau, asparagus in pastry and hot oysters with leek fondue. The decent cooking is good value, if not always tip-top quality. Menus 79F, 118F and 198F, and a children's menu at 45F. Attentive service.

MESCHERS-SUR-GIRONDE   17132 (12KM S)

⚹ ⌂ |●| LES GROTTES DE MATATA**

bd. de la Falaise.
☎ 05.46.02.70.02 ➡ 05.46.02.78.00

There are just a few rooms in this modern clifftop building. A double with shower/wc costs 300F, 350F with bath. There's a terrace where you can eat breakfast, and a breathtaking view of the turbulent grey-blue waters of the Gironde estuary. You get the same view from the *crêperie*, which is set up in one of the troglodyte dwellings in the cliffs, and the walls are made of compacted rock that's full of fossils. Around 80F for a meal. Lots of celebrities have visited the place. 10% discount on the room rate Sept–June.

MORNAC-SUR-SEUDRE   17113 (13KM N)

⚹ |●| LE TAHITI

1 route de Seudre; it's opposite the harbour.
☎ 05.46.22.76.53
✉ letahiti@libertysurf.fr
Closed Mon and Jan–March.

A simple dining room, a popular bar and a terrace on the harbour of this picturesque and charming village. The cooking is very straightforward and there's only one menu at 70F; half a dozen oysters, grilled mullet with tarragon butter, whitebait or grilled sardines, and dessert. Free coffee.

PALMYRE (LA)   17570 (18KM NW)

⌂ HÔTEL LA CÔTE D'ARGENT**

4 av. de l'Océan; take the D25.
☎ 05.46.22.40.07 ➡ 05.46.23.66.04
Closed Nov–March. **Disabled access**. **TV**. **Car park**.

A rather unattractive hotel in this odd seaside

resort that's a bit of a hotch-potch. However, the rooms are comfortable and most have a balcony. Doubles with shower/wc 239–35F, 269–345F with bath. There's a sauna for guests to use.

♪ ♠ |●| PALMYROTEL**

2 allée des Passereaux (Centre).
☎ 05.46.23.65.65 ➡ 05.46.22.44.13
Closed Nov–March. **Disabled access. Garden. TV. Car park.**

This vast hotel offers good value for money for the region. Built on the edge of the pine forest, near the Palmyre zoo, it is contemporary, with a Mediterranean-style garden. There are 46 identical, functional rooms, all with en-suite shower/wc or bath; doubles 250–510F depending on the season. Professional staff. Although half board is not compulsory, they do advise you to take that option. In the restaurant there are menus 110–220F, and children's menus 38–70F. 10% discount on the room rate for stays of two nights or 5% for one night Sept–June.

BOUTENAC-TOUVENT   17120 (28KM SE)

♪ ♠ |●| LE RELAIS DE TOUVENT**

4 rue de Saintonge (Centre); it's on the D730.
☎ 05.46.94.13.06 ➡ 05.46.94.10.40
Closed Sun evening and Mon except in summer and 15–31 Dec. **Disabled access. Garden. TV. Car park.**

Service from noon and 8pm. This dreary building, located on a roundabout, doesn't immediately appeal, but it has an absolutely enormous garden and nice, newly decorated rooms. Better still, the prices are attractive for the region – 250F for a double with shower/wc and 280F with bath. Also, they serve good, honest cooking and lots of regional dishes. Try the *mouclade* or the lamprey. Cheapest menu at 89F, others 140–280F, and an interesting wine list. Free coffee.

RUFFEC   16700

♪ |●| LE MOULIN DE CONDAC

Condac; take the Confolens road.
☎ 05.45.31.04.97 ➡ 05.45.31.29.74
Closed Mon and Tues evenings in winter, Mon lunchtime in summer. **Disabled access.**

This welcoming restaurant, in an attractively restored 18th-century mill on the banks of the Charente, offers good, traditional local cooking. The cheapest menu, 78F, is served during the week only; their gourmet menus, 100–185F, include apéritif, wine and coffee.

Try the grilled lamb with goat's cheese, medallions of trout stuffed with oyster mushrooms and Sauvignon *beurre blanc*, *gratin* of calf's head, or, in winter, the pig's trotters. There's a children's menu with regional dishes for 65F. Beautiful shaded terrace, pedalos, mini-golf and a disco at the weekends. Free apéritif.

SAINT-DENIS-D'OLÉRON   17650

♪ ♠ |●| HÔTEL-RESTAURANT LE MOULIN DE LA GALETTE*

8 rue Ernest-Morisset (Centre); it's on the town square, near the church.
☎ 05.46.47.88.04 ➡ 05.46.47.69.05
Closed 30 Sept–1 April. **Disabled access.**

Service from 12.30pm and 7.30pm. This florid seaside villa houses a nice old guesthouse. The large rooms are decorated with odd pieces of different furniture. Behind, there's a modern annexe with more rooms and a ground-floor terrace. Doubles 220–290F with shower/wc. Half board, compulsory July–Aug, costs 230–260F per person. You'll find the same old charm in the dining room, and there are a few tables on the terrace facing the market square. Menus 95–175F. The exacting owner-chef won't use anything but the freshest ingredients. Friendly welcome and a family atmosphere. No credit cards. 10% discount on the room rate Sept–June.

SAINT-MAIXENT-L'ÉCOLE   79400

♪ ♠ |●| HÔTEL-RESTAURANT LE LOGIS SAINT-MARTIN***

chemin de Pissot (Southeast); head for Niort, turn left at the last set of lights in the town and follow the signs.
☎ 05.49.05.58.68. ➡ 05.49.76.19.93.
Closed Sun evening and Mon lunchtime Nov–May, Wed and Sat lunchtimes May–Oct, and Jan. **TV. Car park.**

Huge 17th-century riverside residence set in its own grounds. Peace and quiet are guaranteed, even though you're just a few hundred metres from the town centre. It's been decorated with fine fabrics and furniture, in keeping with the style and charm of the building. Doubles 520–680F with shower/wc, 680–795F with bath. They use Bohemian crystal in the classy dining room, where they serve a lunch menu at 175F or 250–395F. Most of the dishes involve fish or seafood. 10% discount on the room rate Nov–March except public holidays.

AIRIPT   79260 (10KM S)

🍴 🏨 |●| L'AUBERGE DU PORT D'AIRIPT

How to get there: take the Niort road from Saint-Maixent, and at La Crèche follow the signs to Aiript.
☎ 05.49.25.58.81 ➡ 05.49.05.33.49
Restaurant closed Sun evening and Mon. **Swimming pool. Car park.**

Service noon–2pm and 8–10pm. Old farm converted into an inn with lots of quiet corners and a warm atmosphere. There are two large rooms for wedding receptions, and a Hollywood-style swimming pool in magnificent surroundings for everyone. Menus from 89F, or expect to pay 150F *à la carte*. Enjoy *crêpes* and grills by the pool in summer. Five bedrooms, 230F with shower/wc or bath. They don't accept credit cards. 10% discount if you stay five nights or more.

MOTHE-SAINT-HÉRAY (LA)   79800 (11KM SE)

🍴 🏨 |●| HÔTEL-RESTAURANT LE CORNEILLE**

13 rue du Maréchal-Joffre (Centre).
☎ 05.49.05.17.08 ➡ 05.49.05.19.56
📧 corneille@wanadoo.fr
Hotel closed 20 Dec–10 Jan. **Restaurant closed** Fri evening, and Sun evening out of season. **TV. Car park.**

Service noon–2pm and 7.30–9pm. A charming old family hotel, with bedrooms 230–260F. Good regional cooking: snails with garlic, scallops with asparagus tips and locally raised meat. A weekday menu at 65F and others 100–140F. Free coffee.

SAINT-PIERRE-D'OLÉRON   17310

🍴 🏨 LE SQUARE**

pl. des Anciens-Combattants (Centre).
☎ 05.46.47.00.35 ➡ 05.46.75.04.90
Closed 30 Nov–1 April. **Swimming pool. TV. Car park.**

An unpretentious little hotel with a certain style. It's far enough away from the centre to be peaceful, and it has some real attractions, among them the pretty courtyard, good swimming pool and sauna. Conventional rooms; the best are in the renovated part of the hotel. Doubles with shower/wc or bath 260–400F. 10% discount April and May.

🍴 |●| LE MILLE PÂTES

pl. Gambetta (Centre).
☎ 05.46.47.33.44.
Closed Tues evening and Wed except during school

holidays and in season, and the last two weeks in Jan.

Service until midnight. A good, inexpensive pizzeria with a terrace. The pasta is homemade, and all the pizzas are baked in a wood-fired oven. The 49F *formule*, which gets you dish of the day, $1/4$ litre of wine and coffee, hits the spot. In summer, the *à la carte* menu lists unusual specialities including seaweed ravioli, and a meal will cost about 70F. Quick, friendly service. Free apéritif.

🍴 |●| FRANÇOIS

55 rue de la République (Centre).
☎ 05.46.47.29.44 ➡ 05.46.47.02.33
Closed Sun evening and Mon out of season, and Dec.

Classical dining room, service that's beyond reproach and quite simply the best food in town. Traditional, attentively prepared cuisine: hare *terrine* with ceps, artichoke *pâté* with smoked bacon, cuttlefish stew and so on. Extremely reasonable prices; try the wonderful 79F menu. Other menus 97–168F, and *à la carte*. Free coffee.

COTINIÈRE (LA)   17310 (3KM S)

🏨 |●| HÔTEL FACE AUX FLOTS**

24 rue du Four (Centre); it's 300m from the port.
☎ 05.46.47.10.05 ➡ 05.46.47.45.95.
Closed mid-Nov to mid–Feb, except Christmas holidays. **Disabled access. Garden. Swimming pool. TV.**

A haven of peace, just away from the exhausting throng jostling around the little fishing harbour. Some rooms have a clear view of the silvery sea. The place is run by a smiling, efficient woman who takes the job of looking after her customers seriously. Double rooms with shower/wc or bath 260–460F. The restaurant has a panoramic view and a bar; other facilities include a small corner garden and a swimming pool. Specialities include seafood platters, sole fillet with morels, roast sea bream with truffles, and chocolate delights for dessert. Menus 99F, 150F and 195F, and a 69F children's menu.

CHÉRAY 17190 (5KM NW)

|●| RESTAURANT LE BREUIL

It's on the RN 675.
☎ 05.46.76.60.79 ➡ 05.46.76.60.79
Closed Tues–Thurs out of season, except during school holidays.

Robust, tasty dishes served in the rustic dining room of this old farmhouse. The owners create a warm and welcoming atmosphere. There's a 68F *formule* with a self-service starter buffet, dish of the day and dessert. Menus, 88–118F, are likely to include oysters, a meat or fish dish, cheese and dessert. Specialities include avocado with prawns, eel stewed in wine or meat, and fish grilled over the open fire.

SAINT-TROJAN-LES-BAINS 17370

⌂ |●| HÔTEL-RESTAURANT L'ALBATROS**

11 bd. du Docteur-Pineau (Southeast); it's on the outskirts of town.
☎ 05.46.76.00.08 ➡ 05.46.76.03.58
Closed mid-Nov to mid-Feb. **Disabled access**. **TV**. **Car park**.

You've got the beach on your doorstep and a magnificent view of the sea from the terrace. *Menu-cartes* 69–159F, and a children's menu at 65F. The rooms, which have been renovated, are all very comfortable. Some are at the back in a single-storey building. Doubles 340–390F with shower/wc or bath.

GRAND-VILLAGE 17370 (3KM NW)

⌇ |●| LE RELAIS DES SALINES

port des Salines.
☎ 05.46.75.82.42 ➡ 05.46.75.16.70
Closed Mon and Wed evening, Mon only out of season, and 15 Oct–20 March.

You'll find this attractive restaurant in one of a cluster of brightly painted wooden huts beside the canals in the marshes. There are a few tables inside and others on a boat tied up on the quay. The fish and shellfish dishes are full of flavour and very attractively priced. The 68F weekday lunch menu lists half a dozen oysters, pan-fried *céteaux* (which resembles sole), and a delicious *crème brûlée*. Brilliant specialities like warm oysters with *fondue* of leeks and langoustines with Pineau. Children's menu 45F. Free coffee.

SAINTES 17100

⌇ ⌂ HÔTEL BLEU NUIT**

1 rue Pasteur (West); go along cours National towards the A10.
☎ 05.46.93.01.72 ➡ 05.46.74.43.80
Closed Sun evening 1 Oct–15 April. **Disabled access**. **TV**. **Pay car park**.

The well-run hotel is located on a busy crossroads, but they've installed excellent double glazing and there are some quieter rooms at the back if you sleep lightly. The simple, tasteful rooms offer good value for money. Doubles with basin 190F, with shower/wc 240F, and 250F with bath. Family atmosphere. 10% discount.

⌂ HÔTEL DES MESSAGERIES**

rue des Messageries (Centre).
☎ 05.46.93.64.99 ➡ 05.46.92.14.34
Closed 22 Dec–5 Jan. **TV**. **Pay garage**.

Very comfortable, classic hotel in a quiet street in the old town. It started its days as a coaching inn, but there are only a few of the stones from the original building visible in the very old staircase. It has two wings, which enclose a pretty paved courtyard, and the rooms are very quiet. Doubles 290–320F with shower/wc or 310–360F with bath. They are all air-conditioned. Friendly welcome.

⌇ ⌂ HÔTEL LES BOSQUETS-CLARINE***

107 cours du Maréchal-Leclerc (West); it's on the N137, between exit 25 on the A10 and the town centre.
☎ 05.46.74.04.47 ➡ 05.46.74.27.89
Closed Sun evening out of season and 23 Dec–9 Jan. **Disabled access**. **Garden**. **TV**. **Car park**.

A comfortable hotel, which feels a bit like one of a chain, but has a little something extra. Bedrooms are spacious and well equipped; some look onto a pretty little garden. Expect to pay 310–330F with shower/wc or bath depending on the position. English, German, Spanish and Italian spoken. Free coffee.

|●| LA CARAVELLE

5 quai de la République; it's on the left bank of the Charente.
☎ and ➡ 05.46.93.45.65
Closed Sun and Christmas

Service noon–2pm and 7–10pm. Two little dining rooms, in pastel shades, facing the river. Pleasant service and decent traditional food. There's a weekday lunchtime *formule* at 61F, and menus 74–124F.

⌇ |●| RESTAURANT LA CIBOULETTE

36 rue Pérat (Centre); go down cours National and cross the Charente, follow av. Gambetta and turn into the third street on the left after the bridge.
☎ 05.46.74.07.36 ➡ 05.46.94.14.54
Closed Sat lunchtime and Sun.

The restaurant has a pretty dining room that's recently been redecorated and had air conditioning installed. The young chef, who comes from Brest, prepares lots of fish and shellfish – his successes include plaice *en papillote* with Roscoff seaweed and a shellfish *jus*, a tasty mixed "fisherman's platter", and fish smoked over beech chippings. He also pays culinary homage to the Charente with dishes such as *jaud* (chicken marinated in Cognac), *fricassée* of eel *à la charentaise*, and *mouclade*. He makes all the bread and the desserts, too. The 98F menu is served daily except Sunday and public holidays, and there are others 150–179F and a children's menu at 58F. Reasonably priced wine list – try the regional ones. Free apéritif or coffee.

I●I LE PISTOU

3 pl. du Théâtre (Centre);
☎ 05.46.74.47.53 ➡ 05.46.91.13.52
Closed Sat lunchtime and Sun in winter.

A centrally located restaurant where prices won't break the bank. The cooking goes back to basics, and some of the dishes have a Mediterranean flavour: mussels with *pistou* (the French version of Italian pesto), sea bass flambéed in *pastis*, and *paella*. There's always a fish dish of the day and lots of salads in summer. A meal will cost about 110F. Simple, friendly service.

TAILLEBOURG   17350 (12KM N)

I●I AUBERGE DES GLYCINES

How to get there: it's by the riverside on the Saint-Savinien road coming from Saintes.
☎ 05.46.91.81.40
Closed Wed, Feb and Oct. **Garden. Car park.**

This inn stands on the banks of the Charente, in an unknown but absolutely delightful riverside town. On warm days you eat in the old flower garden or on the shady first-floor terrace. It gets busy at weekends but during the week you're disturbed only by the splash of the carp jumping in the river. The place has been overhauled by the new owner and has a new style of cooking: snails, zander, cockerel in Cognac and seasonal specialities. Menus 100–138F, or about 160F *à la carte*.

PONS   17800 (22.5KM S)

🎐 ➡ I●I HÔTEL-RESTAURANT DE BORDEAUX**

1 av. Gambetta; from Saintes, take the N137 in the direction of Bordeaux or exit 36 from the A10, signposted to Pons.
☎ 05.46.91.31.12 ➡ 05.46.91.22.25
📧 hotel.de.bx@hotel.de.bordeaux.com
Closed Sat lunchtime, Sun evening and Mon lunchtime Oct–April, and the last fortnight in Feb. **TV. Car park.**

Service noon–2pm and 7.30–9.30pm (10pm in summer). The austere façade doesn't make this place look too promising, but appearances are misleading. The large dining room has a certain class, and in good weather you can dine out on the rose-bordered patio. The young owner has finally returned to his home town after working in some of the great kitchens of France. The 90F lunch menu will give you a very clear idea of what this talented man can create with simple, fresh ingredients. The cuisine changes with the seasons and dishes are always inventive; menus from 124–240F. There's an English-style bar where you can extend your evening. The rooms are simple but elegant, and some look onto the patio. Doubles with shower/wc or bath 250F. Service is extremely efficient, and the welcome very natural. Everything about this place is what you'd expect to find in a luxury establishment – except for the prices. 10% discount on the room rate Oct–April.

SURGÈRES   17700

🎐 ➡ I●I HÔTEL-RESTAURANT GAMBETTA*

49 rue Gambetta (North); its on the Niort road.
☎ 05.46.07.03.64 ➡ 05.46.07.37.32
Closed Sun lunchtime, and Christmas to 1 Jan. **TV. Garden. Car park.**

This place, popular with sales reps and travelling businesspeople, offers clean, standard doubles for 170F with basin and up to 240F with shower/wc. Those on the garden side are quietest. There is a simple menu at 70F and another at 110F, while choices *à la carte* list Burgundy specialities as well as local dishes. The proprietress comes from Beaujolais country and the wine list features good wines from her region, all at very decent prices. Half board 240F per person. Free apéritif.

THOUARS   79100

POMPOIS   79100 (4KM NW)

I●I RESTAURANT DU LOGIS DE POMPOIS

Sainte-Verge (Centre).
☎ 05.49.96.27.84 ➡ 05.49.96.13.97
Closed Sun evening, Mon, Tues, a fortnight in Jan and a week in July. **Disabled access. Car park.**

Service noon–1.30pm and 7.30–9pm. A remarkable restaurant housed in a magnificent old wine house. You dine in a huge room with beams and unadorned stone that's very typical of the Poitou. The cuisine is top of the range and the welcome is outstanding. Lunch menu 85F, and others up to 240F – try the *marbré* of duck *foie gras*, the rabbit with ginger and lime, the asparagus charlotte or the caramelised crab and lobster.

PROVENCE-ALPES-CÔTE d'AZUR

04 Alpes-de-Haute-Provence

05 Hautes-Alpes

06 Alpes-Maritimes

13 Bouches-du-Rhône

83 Var

84 Vaucluse

AIX-EN-PROVENCE 13100

SEE MAP ON P.668

♠ HÔTEL LE PRIEURÉ**

It's on the RN96. Off map **B1-5**
☎ 04.42.21.05.23 ➡ 04.42.21.60.56
Car park.

Some time ago, this old priory was converted into a lovely hotel with 23 cosy rooms. All of them look out onto the ornate Pavillon Lanfant park designed by Le Nzôtre, which is not open to the public. Doubles with basin 190F or 400F with bath. Breakfast, 40F, is served in your room or on the terrace. The proprietress welcomes you with a smile.

♠ HÔTEL CARDINAL

24 Rue du Cardinal.
☎ 04.42.38.32.30 ➡ 04.42.26.39.05
TV.

An appealing atmosphere in this quiet, comfortable hotel. Some of the rooms have been refurbished and they're much in demand, 260–350F, though people who know the place opt for the bigger rooms in the annexe, 400–450F. Relaxed, friendly welcome.

⅔ ♠ LES QUATRE DAUPHINS**

54 rue Roux-Alphéran. **MAP B2-6**
☎ 04.42.38.16.39 ➡ 04.42.38.60.19
TV.

A quiet, charming hotel named after the nearby fountain, which features four astonishing dolphins, the only ones in the world with scales. The small, tastefully furnished rooms, spaced across three floors, all have telephone and mini-bar. Double with shower 375F, 395F with bath. The place is full of Provençal prints and charming painted wooden furniture. 10% discount Dec–Jan.

♠ I●I HÔTEL SAINT-CHRISTOPHE-BRASSERIE LÉOPOLD

2 av. Victor Hugo. **MAP A2-8**
☎ 04.42.26.01.24 ➡ 04.42.38.53.17
Restaurant closed Mon. **TV**.

Slap-bang in the centre of town. It's one of *the* places in Aix because of its Art Deco design. Doubles, 420–460F, are air-conditioned and have full en-suite bathrooms; some even have small terraces. A few suites at 600F. The trump card is the *brasserie* on the ground floor, a real institution crammed with tables laid with gleaming tablecloths and with waiters in long aprons. Try the steak *tartare* or the stuffed Provençal vegetables. Menus 120F and 180F. A pleasurable place.

I●I RESTAURANT LE CARILLON

10 rue Portalis. **MAP B1-11**
Closed Sat evening, Sun, a week in Feb, and Aug. **Disabled access**.

They don't have a telephone here, so you can't reserve. You have to turn up early and take a seat with the regulars, many of them pensioners, who appreciate the home cooking. A completely unpretentious place that's ideal for lunch. Menus 60F and 80F.

I●I LE POIVRE D'ÂNE

7 rue de la Couronne. **MAP A2-13**
☎ 04.42.93.45.56

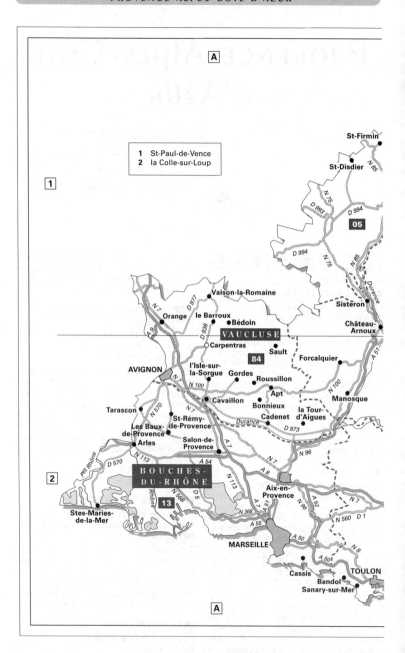

A

1 St-Paul-de-Vence
2 la Colle-sur-Loup

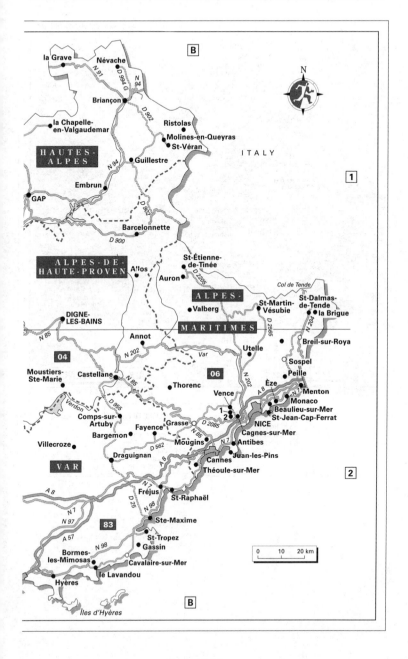

AIX-EN-PROVENCE

🛏	**WHERE TO SLEEP**	|◉|	**WHERE TO EAT**
5	Hôtel Le Prieuré	11	Le Carillon
6	Les Quatre Dauphins	12	Chez Féraud
7	Hotel Candinale	13	Le Poivre d'Ane
8	Hotel Saint Chaistgale	14	La Brocherie
		17	Lausane et sa maison
		18	L'Amphytrion

Closed Sun, Mon, and first three weeks in Aug.

The decor is as colourful as the food in this warm, welcoming place. They serve original, attractive dishes in generous portions, and the prices are pretty good. Menus change every two months. The prices are really good value: weekday lunch menu 95F or you will pay an average of 145F *à la carte*. As a guide, starters include raviolis or *caillettes* (a preparation reminiscent of haggis). For main courses try the fish *tian* or the upside-town tart of squab with apples, and don't miss the orange-scented *crème brûlée* – they bring it to your table and use a red-hot brand to caramelise the sugar, in front of you. Take a look at the grocer's at number 10 across the road. It's run by the same people. Free coffee.

⅄ |●| L'AMPHYTRION

2 rue Paul Doumer. **MAP A2-18**
☎ 04.42.26.54.10

The chef, Bruno Ungar, enjoys a love affair with Provençal cuisine – and you experience the fruits of his love in his cooking. Very local dishes which are highly coloured and richly flavoured. Lunch menu 100F, or 175F. There's plenty of space to be comfortable on the terrace and the *menu du marché* is an ideal option. You don't come here for the laughs but it's enjoyable all the same. A fine example of Aix cooking. Free apéritif.

|●| RESTAURANT LA BROCHERIE

5 rue Fernand-Dol. **MAP B2-14**
☎ 04.42.38.33.21
Closed Sat lunchtime, Sun and Aug.

Pleasant, rustic atmosphere, with a huge open, Renaissance fireplace where they cook whole chickens on the original spit. There's an excellent choice of meat dishes though, oddly enough, people come here mainly for the grilled fish. There's an original *menu brocherie* with a self-service *hors d'œuvre* buffet, main course from the spit and dessert of the day. *Formule* 75F at lunchtime or 92F, or menus 119F and a good Provençal menu at 148F.

⅄ |●| CHEZ FÉRAUD

8 rue du Puits-Juif. **MAP A1–12**
☎ 04.42.63.07.27
Closed Sun, Mon lunchtime and Aug.

Right in the centre of old Aix, where you get a real feel of old Provence. The home cooking is prepared attentively by the father and served by the son under the watchful eye of the mother – try the *soupe au pistou* or *pieds et paquets* which is lamb's tripe and trotters,

or slowly cooked *daube*, braised beef in wine sauce. Ask to be shown the secret cellars. There's a terrace. Free house apéritif.

|●| LAURANE ET SA MAISON

16 rue Victor-Leydet. **MAP A2-17**
☎ 04.42.93.02.03
Closed Sun, a fortnight in Jan and a fortnight in Feb.

An enticing-looking, friendly place in a lovely setting that's very sunny. Fresh, inventive cooking, showing off the flavours of the south: stuffed vegetables, tart with duck *confit* and ceps and a *tajine* with figs and apricots. About 150F *à la carte*.

BEAURECUEIL   13100 (10KM E)

⅄ � |●| RELAIS SAINTE-VICTOIRE★★★

☎ 04.42.66.94.98 ➡ 04.42.66.85.96
e relais-ste-victoire@wanadoo.fr
Closed Fri lunchtime, Sun evening, Mon and the first week in Jan. **Swimming pool. TV. Car park**.

This establishment, at the foot of Mont Sainte-Victoire, is one of the best restaurants in the region, run by a family of real characters. The decor is brightly coloured and there's a collection of unusual paddles on the walls. René Berges' cooking is full of strong sun-drenched, southern flavours: poached eggs with truffle cream, preserved tomato tart served with grilled sardine fillets, or rack of lamb glazed with local honey. *Formule-cartes* 160–400F. Rooms, 450–800F with bath, overlook the grounds or the countryside. Free house apéritif.

PUYLOUBIER   13144 (15KM NE)

⅄ |●| LES SARMENTS

4 rue Qui Monte.
☎ 04.42.66.31.58
Open Sat, Sun lunchtime and public holidays, and Fri evening to Sun evening June–Aug

The walk from Mont Sainte-Victoire to this tiny hillside village is wonderful. People flock here from Aix on Friday and Saturday to enjoy good cooking served by a hard-working family. The solitary menu, 160F, lists dishes like *pieds et paquets* (lamb tripe and trotters), lamb shank *confit* and authentic fish soup. Local wine included in the price. Free apéritif.

ALLOS   04260

⅄ ☆ |●| HÔTEL-RESTAURANT LES GENTIANES★★

Grand-Rue.

☎ 04.92.83.03.50 ➡ 04.92.83.02.71
Closed Tues out of season, 17 April–10 May and 12 Nov–4 Dec.

Small inn, popular with skiers in winter and walkers in summer. It's run by a mother and daughter team who create a friendly atmosphere. Really pretty rooms with doubles 350F with shower/wc, breakfast 35F. The menus, 75–160F, list honest, hearty dishes including rib steak with ceps, *daube* with polenta, and salmon fillet on a bed of ravioli They also serve *crêpes* during the school holidays. Free *digestif*.

BEAUVEZER 04370 (13KM S)

🏕 🍴 HÔTEL LE BELLEVUE**

pl. du Village; it's on the D908 towards St André des Alpes.
☎ 04.92.83.51.60 x04.92.83.51.60
e bellevue@alpes.net.fr
Closed 1 Nov–23 Dec. **Car park**.

A charming place to stop between Provence and the Alps – it's a haven of peace and tranquillity behind an ochre façade. The comfortable double rooms, tastefully decorated in warm colours and Provençal prints, go for 240–265F with basin and 285–310F with bath. Six rooms have views of the mountains, and there's a suite that sleeps four to six for 490F. You eat heartily in the restaurant – lunch menu 85F, others 115–160F. Delicious regional dishes: aubergine and garlic flan, bass *en papillote*, cep ravioli, duck with olives. 10% discount on the room rate 5 March–1 April and Oct. Free apéritif.

ANTIBES 06600

🏕 🛎 HÔTEL DE L'ÉTOILE**

2 av. Gambetta (Centre); it's 5 minutes from the station.
☎ 04.93.34.26.30 ➡ 04.93.34.41.48
e omfp@hotel-etoile.com
TV. **Pay car park**.

The only hotel of this category in the centre of Antibes. Although modern and comfortable, it's better for an overnight stop than as a place to spend a holiday. Spacious rooms with good sound insulation. Doubles 280–310F with shower/wc or 320–350F with bath. It's a friendly place, but the requirement to pay for your room in advance is a little tiresome. 10% discount Sept–June.

🏕 🛎 LE MAS DJOLIBA***

29 av. de Provence (Centre).
☎ 04.93.34.02.48 ➡ 04.93.34.05.81
e info@pcastel-djoliba.com

Closed Nov–Jan. **Swimming pool**. **TV**. **Car park**.

A pretty Provençal house surrounded by greenery. The delightful rooms, decorated in the local style, are 450–490F with shower/wc or 540–640F with bath. They prefer you to stay half board in season but it's not compulsory; it costs 400–505F per person. There's a relaxing swimming pool so you don't have to fight your way to the crowded beach. It's the only hotel in its category to offer such good facilities at these prices. Friendly, professional welcome. Free coffee.

🍴 RESTAURANT LE SAFRANIER

1 pl. du Safranier.
☎ 04.93.34.80.50
Closed Sun evening and Mon in winter, Mon and Wed lunchtime in season, and 15 Dec–15 Jan.

It's astonishing that places like this still exist on the Côte d'Azur. You feel as if you're in an authentic, small Provençal village in this haven of tranquillity with its lovely terrace covered in greenery. Friendly welcome and good service. There's a menu at 62F, or you'll pay 120–160F *à la carte*. Excellent fish soup and a superb *bouillabaisse*, which you have to order in advance. Grilled fish always available. Credit cards not accepted.

JUAN-LES-PINS 06160 (1KM W)

🏕 🛎 LA JABOTTE*

13 av. Max-Maurey: it's off bd. James-Wyllie which borders Cap d'Antibes.
☎ 04.93.61.45.89 ➡ 04.93.61.07.04
Closed Sun afternoon and 15 Nov–15 Dec. **Disabled access**. **Car park**.

This hotel offers good value for money. Spotless rooms with shower or bath at 290–410F. The bungalows looking onto the terrace are particularly nice. Half board is competitively priced at 250–370F per person. There's a suite with two double rooms – good for families or groups of four – and it has a view of the mountain. Friendly welcome, but you should avoid arriving between 1pm and 6pm on a Sunday, when they take a break. Relaxing atmosphere and a gentle pace. 10% discount for a minimum three-night stay Nov–March, excluding school holidays.

🏕 🛎 HÔTEL SAINTE-VALÉRIE***

rue de l'Oratoire.
☎ 04.93.61.07.15 ➡ 04.93.61.47.52
e sainte-valerie@juanlespins.net
Closed 30 Sept–15 April. **Garden**. **Swimming pool**. **TV**. **Car park**.

A stylish hotel that's ideal for a romantic holiday. Set in a quiet part of Juan-les-Pins just a short distance from the Gould pine woods and the sea, it has a pool and a pretty, shady garden where you can take refuge from the heat. Meals are served in the garden – menu 135F. Modern, tastefully decorated double rooms 580–700F with shower/wc and 640–960F with bath. 10% discount on the room rate out of season.

APT   84400

🎰 🏠 ♨️ HÔTEL-RESTAURANT LE PALAIS**

24 pl. Gabriel-Péri (Centre); it's opposite the town hall.
☎ and ➡ 04.90.04.89.32
Restaurant closed Mon.

A relatively characterless hotel that is best described as modest, in an old house in the centre of town. Hotels are not Apt's strong point, so this will do well enough for an overnight. Doubles 180F with basin, 230–280F with shower/wc or bath. Straightforward Provençal cooking, such as soup with pesto and aubergine *tian aïoli*, on menus 69–129F. Free coffee.

ARLES   13200

🏠 HÔTEL LE CLOÎTRE**

16 rue du Cloître (Centre); it's between the amphitheatre and Saint-Trophime.
☎ 04.90.96.29.50 ➡ 04.90.96.02.88
📧 Hôtel.cloitre@hotmail.com
Closed 1 Nov–15 March. **Car park.**

A charming, really tranquil hotel that's supported by 13th-century vaulted arcades, in a narrow, climbing street. The largest rooms, which date from the 12th and 17th centuries, have big beams and are decorated with gleaming tiles. Simple doubles 250F with basin/wc to 295F with bath, and the big ones go for 360–390F. Remarkably kind owner.

🏠 HÔTEL CALENDAL**

22 pl. Pomme (Centre); it's between the arena and Roman theatre.
☎ 04.90.96.11.89 ➡ 04.90.96.05.84
📧 contact@lecalendal.com
Disabled access. Garden. TV. Pay garage.

This hotel, in the middle of the town, is decorated with local fabrics and dotted with huge vases of stunningly coloured flowers. Arles is famous for photography and the stairwell is hung with lots of unusual photographs. There's a cool patio where you can shelter from the sun. The arena where they still hold bull-fights is close by. Air-conditioned rooms 280–320F with shower/wc, 380–480F with bath. Three of the rooms have a terrace. They've enlarged the reception and built a private garage which is a rare luxury (30F per night). Snacks and salads are served in the garden, and there is a tea-room. A lovely place. 10% discount.

🎰 🏠 HÔTEL DE L'AMPHITHÉÂTRE**

5 rue Diderot (Centre); it's near the Roman theatre.
☎ 04.90.96.10.30 ➡ 04.90.93.98.69
📧 contact@hotelamphitheatre.fr
TV.

Previously known as *Hôtel Diderot*, this place has been totally renovated and has a charming new look. All the bedrooms have been decorated in Provençal style; doubles cost 290–350F with shower/wc, 345–420F with bath. The charming owner serves an unusually good breakfast. 10% discount Nov–March.

♨️ HÔTEL MIREILLE

2 pl. Saint-Pierre; it's the other side of the Rhône in the Trinquetaille district.
☎ 04.90.93.70.74 ➡ 04.90.93.87.28
Closed Nov–March. **Garden. Swimming pool. Car park. Garage.**

A curtain of trees closes off the swimming pool, which is presided over by a watchful old statue. Doubles overlooking the garden and pool cost 399–650F. Half board is compulsory during the Fiera and at Easter. There's a huge and pleasant dining room. Lovely seafood (including *bouillabaisse provençale*) and quality meat dishes on menus 110–130F. Good welcome. 10% discount if you stay a week half-board, and free house apéritif.

♨️ L'ESCALADOU

23 rue Porte-de-Laure (Centre).
☎ 04.90.96.70.43

If you want a taste of authentic Arles, this is the place. It's patronised by locals, and Jean-Charles Signoret, who runs it, also makes traditional costumes for local festivals and garlands the ladies with traditional ribbons. The waitresses wear his costumes. Menus 85–140F. Real fish soup and *bouillabaisse*.

🎰 ♨️ LA CHARCUTERIE

51 rue des Arènes (Centre).
☎ 04.90.93.44.44

A genuine Lyon-style bistro right in the centre of Arles. The owner, François, drives all the way to Lyon to supply the kitchen with the authentic produce like the *andouillette de Bobosse* – a must. The restaurant is on the premises of an old *charcuterie* dating back to the 1940s – the marble slab and butcher's hooks have survived. Regouya cooks very tasty dishes in front of you on an old marble counter. François is also a painter: his canvasses are all over the walls. In summer, the menu lists salads, grills and *tapas* and there's a welcoming terrace that seats about a dozen customers. About 90F for lunch and 130F for dinner. Free house apéritif.

I●I LE JARDIN DE MANON

14 av. des Alyscamps; it's a little way from the town centre, at the bottom end of bd. des Lices, beyond the police station.
☎ 04.90.93.38.68
Closed Wed, Sun evening Nov–March, and the Feb and All Saints' school holidays. **Garden**.

A friendly restaurant with a small garden at the back (watch out for the mosquitoes in the evening). Excellent, creative cuisine; 85F lunch menu, then 98–200F, and all the dishes change with the seasons. The extensive wine list offers good value for money.

I●I CÔTÉ COUR

65 rue Amédée-Pichot.
☎ 04.90.49.77.76
Closed Wed and ten days in Jan.

A superb dining room with walls of chiselled stone, hand-made floor tiles, sturdy beams and air conditioning. The tables are laid with Provençal tablecloths. The dishes come in huge portions but are resolutely classical: aubergine *charlotte*, leg of lamb *à la provençale*, or *fricassée* of fish with rosemary butter. Menus 105–198F (all include cheese and dessert). *À la carte* dishes include veal sweetbreads with saffron or Bresse chicken ballotine with rice. Nice dessert menu. Charming, if slightly diffident, welcome from the young team.

I●I LA GUEULE DU LOUP

39 rue des Arènes (Centre).
☎ 04.90.96.96.69

You're practically in the kitchen when you walk into this place from the street door – you go upstairs into the dining room. There are magic charts and documents about sorcery on the wall – the owner used to be a magician

but decided to become a restaurateur and gave it all up (well, almost; he still does a gourmet dinner show on a Friday night). Delicious dishes such as Roquefort flan with dried figs, veal sweetbreads with cream and garlic sauce or joint of lamb Provençale. The dining room is so small, it's best to book. Gastronomic menu from 140F.

ARVIEUX · 05350

光 ♠ I●I LA FERME D'IZOARD***

Hameau de la Chalp; it's 30km northwest of Saint-Véran in the direction of Brançion over the col de l'Izoard or via Guillestre in winter when the col is closed.
☎ 04.92.46.89.00 📠 04.92.46.82.37
e j.fryehet@wanadoo.fr
Disabled access. Swimming pool. TV. Car park.

Family-run establishment with good facilities including a heated pool. The building is rustic, but the decor is elegant and stylish. Prices are fair considering the high standards: 365–810F for a double, or they have studios or self-contained two-roomed apartments with kitchenette and bathroom. Simple but tasty cooking, with lots of grills on the open fire, and menus 98–198F. It's a lovely place to relax in superb countryside. 25% discount for a fortnight's stay Jan, June and Sept.

ASPRES-SUR-BUËCH · 04150

光 ♠ I●I HÔTEL DU PARC**

Route de Grenoble (Centre).
☎ 04.92.58.60.01 📠 04.92.58.67.84.
e marodriguez@wanadoo.fr
Closed Sun evening and Wed out of season, and 6 Dec–6 Jan. **Garden. Car park**.

It's very pleasant to lunch on the terrace near the rose garden. The *menu du jour*, 90F, and others up to 180F list substantial mixed salads, good chicken *basquaise*, strawberry *bavarois* and more. Doubles with basin 185F and up to 285F with bath. All the rooms are clean and have good facilities. 5% discount for a three-night stay.

AURON · 06660

光 ♠ I●I HÔTEL LAS DONNAS**

Grande-Place (Centre); it's next to the ice-rink.
☎ 04.93.23.00.03 📠 04.93.23.07.37
Closed end April to mid-July, end Aug to mid-Dec. **TV**.

A pleasant, peaceful hotel with some forty sunny rooms, 270–500F, half of which have balconies overlooking the ski runs. The restaurant serves good wholesome food – menus, 110–140F, offer beef *fondue* and *raclette, mousseline* of fish, *rillettes* of young rabbit and so on. Around 140F *à la carte*. Half board, 220–400F, is compulsory during school holidays. Lovely glassed-in terrace. Free apéritif or coffee.

AVIGNON   84000

SEE MAP OVERLEAF

🎿 🛏 HÔTEL MIGNON*

12 rue Joseph-Vernet. **MAP B2-4**
☎ 04.90.82.17.30 ➡ 04.90.85.78.46
e hotel.mignon@wanadoo.fr
TV.

Though the decor in this well-kept and welcoming place is a little busy, it's not unattractive. The rooms are tastefully furnished, and have double glazing and efficient insulation. Doubles 230F with shower/wc. Each room has a telephone, cable TV and a whole host of services you wouldn't expect in a one-star hotel. Breakfast 25F. There's three flights of stairs and no lift. 10% discount Nov–Feb.

🎿 🛏 |●| HÔTEL-RESTAURANT LE MAGNAN**

63 rue du Portail-Magnanen. **MAP C3-6**
☎ 04.90.86.36.51 ➡ 04.90.85.48.90
e magnan@wanadoo.fr
Garden. TV. Car park.

Though not particularly attractive, this hotel is conveniently situated very close to the station and the city walls. There are positive points inside, too, like the quiet, relaxing patio with a cool garden and the clean rooms with modern facilities. Doubles with shower/wc 245–375F. Breakfast 35F. Children under twelve stay free. The restaurant is adequate if you don't want to to eat in town. Menus 85F and 115F. Free bottle of Côte du Rhône.

🎿 🛏 HÔTEL DE BLAUVAC**

11 rue de la Bancasse. **MAP B2-8**
☎ 04.90.86.34.11 ➡ 04.90.86.27.41
TV.

A very good hotel in an elegant 17th-century mansion, ideally located in a narrow street in the historic centre close to place de l'Horloge. It has kept some of the original features of the house which was the residence of the Marquis de Blauvac – the elegant wrought-iron staircase, and some arched stone doorways. The decor is a happy combination of

old stones and modern design. Well-appointed doubles, 300–350F with shower/wc or 385–425F with bath. Attentive service. 10% discount for a two-night stay.

🎿 🛏 HÔTEL DE GARLANDE-CITOTEL**

20 rue Galante. **MAP B2-9**
☎ 04.90.85.08.85 ➡ 04.90.27.16.58
e hotel.carlande@avignon-et-provence.com
Closed Sun out of season. **TV.**

An old house, beautifully situated near the Saint-Didiert bell tower. A delightful place feeling more like a guesthouse than a hotel. Michèle Michelotte has gone to great lengths to make her establishment comfortable and welcoming. Attractive, well-maintained rooms cost 330–350F with shower/wc and 380–450F with bath. 10% discount for a two-night stay, except during the festival.

🎿 🛏 HÔTEL BRISTOL***

44 cours Jean-Jaurès. **MAP B3-7**
☎ 04.90.16.48.48 ➡ 04.90.86.22.72
e bristol.avignon.best.western@wanadoo.fr
Disabled access. TV. Pay garage.

A modern, rather stylish, and very welcoming hotel. All the rooms have air conditioning and efficient double glazing. Doubles with shower or bath 380–560F. There's a charge for the garage and you need to book in advance. 10% discount Aug–June.

🎿 |●| LE WOOLLOOMOOLOO

16 [bis] rue des Teinturiers. **MAP C3-21**
☎ 04.90.85.28.44

Striking, very trendy restaurant in a converted printworks. The only light comes from a central hanging chandelier with quantities of real candles. It's a fusion of a colonial eatery in Sumatra and an arty New York loft and is infused by the disconcerting atmosphere of a Peter Greenaway film – the old printing press is still there and petals are strewn over the tables and floor. They serve tasty world cuisine: *taramasalata*, chicken *yassa*, red mullet *ceviche* with cardamon, beef *maffe* and sea bream *à la brésilienne*. Menus 69F and 89F or around 150F *à la carte*. Free punch with spice syrup.

🎿 |●| LE JUJUBIER

24 rue des Lices. **MAP C3-20**
☎ 04.90.86.64.08
Closed evenings except festival time, Sat, Sun and Aug.

Fresh Provençal cuisine served in a dining room that's delightfully decorated to resemble a local farmhouse. The menus are written by

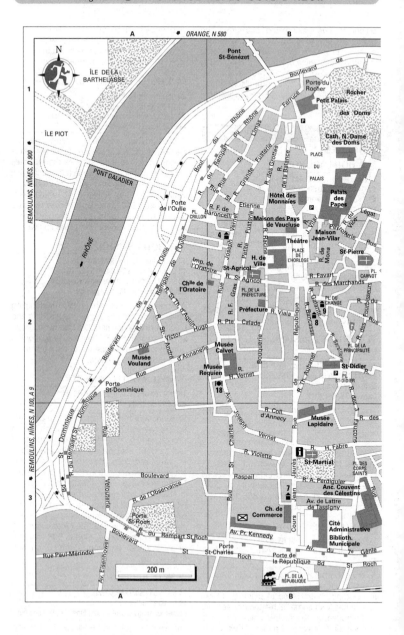

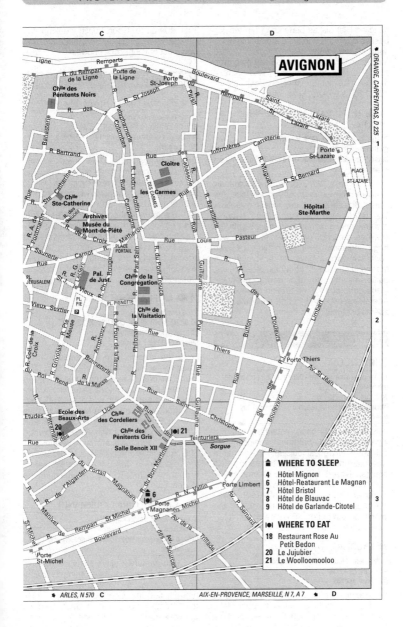

AVIGNON

WHERE TO SLEEP

4 Hôtel Mignon
6 Hôtel-Reataurant Le Magnan
7 Hôtel Bristol
8 Hôtel de Blauvac
9 Hôtel de Garlande-Citotel

WHERE TO EAT

18 Restaurant Rose Au
    Petit Bedon
20 Le Jujubier
21 Le Woolloomooloo

◆ ARLES, N 570 C

AIX-EN-PROVENCE, MARSEILLE, N 7, A 7 ◆ D

hand and list dishes perfected from recipes passed down through the generations: nettle soup, tuna with *sauce verte*, stuffed aubergines, rabbit *bouillabaisse*, lamb with spelt, preserved octopus, and lambs' tongues. The list of dishes changes weekly. 100–120F *à la carte*. Free coffee.

🕿 |● | RESTAURANT ROSE AU PETIT BEDON

70 rue Joseph-Vernet. **MAP B2-18**
☎ 04.90.82.33.98
Closed Sun, Mon lunchtime, 6–14 Aug and a fortnight in winter.

The welcoming atmosphere in this friendly restaurant is due in good part to Rose, the owner. She's turned it into a local institution. The resolutely Provençal cuisine features mouthwatering dishes that change with the seasons: *crespéou vauclusien* (pancake with frogs' legs and chives), shoulder of lamb *confit* with whole cloves of garlic, and *pain Martegau* (bread with potatoes, green beans, garlic mayonnaise and cod). Lunchtime *menu-carte* at 110F or 165F in the evening. Attentive service and friendly welcome. Free apéritif or *digestif*.

BANDOL   83150

🕿 |● | L'OULIVO

19 rue des Tonneliers; it's 100m from the port beside the church.
☎ 04.94.29.81.79
Closed Sun lunchtime in summer, and weekday evenings in winter.

Very simple, very good restaurant, where a wonderfully kind *patronne* serves fresh, authentic Provençal cuisine. They offer a weekday lunch menu at 75F for starter, main course, dessert and coffee, or others100F and 120F. There's a remarkable evening menu which includes a notable dish called *alouettes sans tête*, aubergine turnovers and lamb tripe and trotters. There's a pleasant terrace in summer. Free coffee.

|● | L'AUBERGE DU PORT

9 allée Jean-Moulin; it's on the seafront.
☎ 04.94.29.42.63
Disabled access.

You couldn't dream of a better spot. They've fixed up an old fishing boat at the back of the terrace, and it rather sets the tone; you'll get fish soup with shellfish, artichokes with baby squid, aïoli, *bouillabaisse*, fish stew, octopus and so on. Menus 128–260F, and at least

300F *à la carte*. Good-quality cooking and substantial helpings that will help you part with most of your holiday budget.

BARCELONNETTE   04400

🕿 🏠 |● | HÔTEL DU CHEVAL BLANC**

12 rue Grenette (Centre).
☎ 04.92.81.00.19 ➡ 04.92.81.15.39
Closed Sun out of season and 1 Oct–20 Dec.
TV. Car park.

This hotel-restaurant has been in the Barneaud family for three generations, and the fourth is waiting eagerly in the wings. Double rooms with shower/wc and TV 290F. Dish of the day 70F and a single menu at 90F. The traditional cooking features game, fresh noodles and spinach pie. It's a very popular place with cycle tourists; you can store bikes in the stables, and they prepare special "sporty" breakfasts, (normal breakfast 35F), and packed lunches on request. Free coffee.

🕿 |● | AZTÉCA HÔTEL***

3 rue François-Arnaud.
☎ 04.92.81.46.36 ➡ 04.92.81.43.92
✉ hotel-azteca@wanadoo.fr
Closed 5–30 Nov. **Garden**.

From the outside, you could mistake this place for a rather chic private clinic. The rooms are prettily decorated, three of them in an unusual Mexican-Alpine style – the people who built the villa at the end of the 19th century made their fortune in Mexico. Doubles 330–380F with shower/wc, 360–500F with bath. It's a quiet place with a peaceful garden where you can have a buffet breakfast for 50F. In summer the breakfast is laid out on the dresser in the Mexican-style salon. Friendly welcome. There's a shuttle up to the slopes. Free gift.

|● | LA MANGEOIRE GOURMANDE

pl. des 4-Vents; it's near the church.
☎ 04.92.81.01.61
Closed Sun evening and Wed out of season, and 15 Nov–30 Dec.

The 17th-century vaulted dining room of this restaurant is genuinely welcoming. Loïc Balanec, a young chef bristling with talent, has brought new life to the restaurant, and his really tasty food strikes a good balance between tradition and innovation. Delightful dishes: skate *provençale* with mint, salted chicken, or a Potence with beef, flambéed in whisky (for two). This is a restaurant with a reputation, so you should book. Weekday lunch menu 98F, others 160–210F.

UVERNET-FOURS 04400 (4.5KM SW)

🖈 |●| RESTAURANT LE PASSE MONTAGNE

How to get there: take the D902 towards Pra-Loup, and turn before the junction for col d'Allos.
☎ 04.92.81.08.58
Closed Tues evening, Wed, 15–30 June and 15 Nov–15 Dec. **Car park**.

This place has the warm atmosphere of a wooden chalet, and you can admire the peaks of Pain de Sucre and Chapeau de Gendarme from the terrace. It's a relaxed place: the menu looks as if it has been written by a schoolchild on a sheet from an exercise book, and there are snatches of poems pasted on the walls. The peaceful atmosphere is heightened in winter when they light a roaring fire in the huge fireplace. The chef has rediscovered Provençal cooking from his grandmother's era but used his talent to adapt it to the present day – dishes include fresh ewe's milk cheese with *cébettes* (tiny Provençal onions), stuffed baby vegetables, lasagne with snails, *tarte aux sanguins* (a type of mushroom), and roast capon with cream and morels in pastry. Set menus 97–169F. Free coffee.

SUPER-SAUZE 04400 (5KM SE)

🏠 LE PYJAMA

It's at the foot of the ski runs.
☎ 04.92.81.12.00 📠 04.92.81.03.16
Closed six weeks May/June and mid-Sept to 20 Dec. **TV. Car park**.

The rooms are furnished with old pieces of furniture and ornaments, and they look out onto a peaceful panorama of larches. They all have wide terraces, and some have mezzanines. Doubles 260F in low season, 290F in mid-season and 320F in high season. There are places where you can curl up with a book in winter and tables outside where you can have a cool drink in summer. There's an interesting junk shop on the ground floor. Pets welcome.

PRA-LOUP 04400 (6KM SW)

🖈 🏠 |●| LE PRIEURÉ

Les Molanes
☎ 04.92.84.11.43 📠 04.92.84.01.88
Closed May and Oct–Nov. **Swimming pool. TV. Car park**.

An 18th-century priory that's been converted into a very warm, rustic hotel with breathtaking views of the Pain de Sucre and Chapeau de Gendarme mountains. Doubles 280–480F. Appetizing cooking – trout with Génépy butter, *charbonnade* and the like. Menus from 52F or around 150F *à la carte*. Free coffee.

🖈 🏠 |●| AUBERGE DU CLOS SOREL**

Les Molanes; it's next to the train station entrance.
☎ 04.92.84.10.74 📠 04.92.84.09.14
Closed 15 April–15 June and 1 Sept–15 Dec. **Swimming pool. TV. Car park**.

A charming mountainside inn in a very old farmhouse. It's very close to the ski slopes and, in summer, there's a lovely pool. Cosy rooms with beams and stone walls 420–900F. You can have tea by the fireside, and they serve honest dishes in the candlelit restaurant, where there's a *menu-carte* for 160F. Friendly welcome. Free house apéritif.

BARGEMON 83830

🖈 |●| RESTAURANT LA TAVERNE

pl. Philippe-Chauvier (Centre); it's on the village square.
☎ 04.94.76.62.19
Closed Mon and Tues lunchtime out of season, and 15 Nov–1 March.

Charming, old-fashioned inn in an amazing village, clinging tenaciously to the hillside. Fine, Provençal cooking infused with a few fresh ideas: snail stew in pastry, lamb *confit* with dried tomatoes, fan of red mullet and scorpion fish with *sauce bigarrade*, local *caillette* from the Haut Var. It's where the locals come for Sunday lunch. Menus 110–160F. Shaded terrace. Free coffee.

BARROUX (LE) 84330

🏠 |●| HÔTEL-RESTAURANT LES GÉRANIUMS**

pl. de la Croix.
☎ 04.90.62.41.08 📠 04.90.62.56.48
Closed 15 Nov–24 March. **Car park**.

A village hotel in a handsome white stone building that has been beautifully renovated. The terrace and some rooms have sweeping views of the plains. It's a quiet spot where only the chafing cicadas disturb the silence. Traditional comfort without fuss. Doubles 260F with shower/wc, 290F with bath. Menus, 95–185F, list simple, traditional Provençal cooking with no frills. Specialities include quail *pâté* with onion marmalade, rabbit with savoury, pigeon with apples and *crème brûlée* with liquorice.

BAUDUEN   83630

☎ |●| L'AUBERGE DU LAC**

rue Grande (Centre).
☎ 04.94.70.08.04
e auberge.lac@wanadoo.fr
Closed Jan–Feb and 15 Nov–31 Dec.

This rustic inn is located in a charming little village on the banks of lake Sainte-Croix. The owner has been cosseting his guests here for more than twenty years. The rooms are attractive and pleasant, particularly those which look onto the lake; 380F with bath. The restaurant serves delicious menus 120–200F; half board, 370F per person, is compulsory June–Sept. In summer, you can eat on a little terrace tangled with vines, while in the winter the warm dining room is very welcoming. Good local cuisine, game in season, fish and local wine.

BAUX-DE-PROVENCE (LES)   13520

☎ |●| HOSTELLERIE DE LA REINE-JEANNE

It's in the village.
☎ 04.90.54.32.06 ➡ 04.9-.54.32.33

When the main street is heaving with tourists in the summer, all you want to do is get out fast but this is a charming refuge when they've all gone. The old house has been lovingly and astutely renovated. The rooms are pleasant and individual. Doubles 280–550F and the most expensive one is more like an apartment with an amazing view and incredible terrace. In the restaurant they serve quality local dishes. Menus 115F and 165F.

BEAULIEU-SUR-MER   06310

🏃 ☎ HÔTEL SELECT*

1 pl. du Général-de-Gaulle (Centre); it's 100m from the station.
☎ 04.93.01.05.42 ➡ 04.93.01.34.30
Closed Nov. **TV**.

This very cosy hotel is as friendly as a family guesthouse. It's the best value for money in the town, though rooms facing the square are slightly noisy. Doubles 280–320F with shower/wc or bath. The proprietor is friendly and genuinely helpful – he can tell you anything you need to know about the region. Stay six nights (including breakfast) and get the seventh night free.

🏃 ☎ HÔTEL LE HAVRE BLEU**

29 bd. Maréchal-Joffre (North).
☎ 04.93.01.01.40 ➡ 04.93.01.29.92
e hotel.lehavrebleu@wanadoo.fr
Disabled access. TV. Car park.

A Victorian hotel with a quiet family atmosphere. The clean, simple decor, white paintwork and bright blue shutters are very Mediterranean. Doubles 300–320F with shower/wc or bath; some have a terrace. 10% discount.

🏃 ☎ HÔTEL COMTÉ DE NICE***

25 bd. Marinoni; coming from Nice, don't follow the road down to the sea but turn off towards the market square.
☎ 04.93.01.19.70 ➡ 04.93.01.23.09
TV. Pay garage.

You immediately feel good when you walk into this hotel. The family will greet you warmly and the rooms are well appointed, with air-conditioning, telephone, mini-safe, and hair drier; doubles 395–580F with bath. Good breakfasts for 48F. You pay 48F for the garage.There's a sauna and fitness centre. The beach and the harbour are five minutes away. 10% discount except during holiday time and the Monaco Grand Prix.

BÉDOIN   84410

🏃 ☎ HÔTEL LA GARANCE**

Sainte-Colombe; it's 3km from the village on the Mont Ventoux road.
☎ 04.90.12.81.00 ➡ 04.90.65.93.05
Disabled access. Swimming pool. TV. Car park.

Garance is the French word for madder, which used to be grown in the area. It was used to dye the trousers of the French soldiers in the 1870 wars, and brought prosperity to the region for many years. You'll love the decor and the tranquility of this captivating hotel. Clean, stylish doubles 260F and 290F with shower/wc or bath. The pleasant terrace, which overlooks Mont Ventoux, is the ideal place for an invigorating outdoor breakfast (39F). Low-key welcome, but efficient, attentive service. There's no restaurant, but if you go half board you can take meals at *La Colombe* (see below), which is directly opposite. 10% discount Sept–June.

🏃 |●| RESTAURANT LA COLOMBE

Sainte-Colombe.
☎ and ➡ 04.90.65.61.20
Closed Sun evening and Wed, and end Nov to end March. **Car park**.

Bustling yet relaxed restaurant in an enchanting location. It's decorated in bright Provençal colours, and there's a congenial, sunny terrace. The proprietress settles you down with a broad smile and the proprietor prepares fresh, tasty food. Menus 115–280F. In summer they do pesto soup and kid stew, and in autumn, there's venison steak with truffles, spit-roasted game and stews. The red wines come from the Côte du Ventoux. You'll get an enthusiastic welcome from the owner. Free coffee.

BONNIEUX   84480

|●| RESTAURANT DE LA GARE

chemin de la Gare (Northwest); it's on the D145 in the direction of Goult.
☎ 04.90.7582.00
Closed Sun evening, Mon and Jan. **Disabled access**.

The old station was turned into an art gallery by the grandmother of the owner of this restaurant. The huge dining room has an old-fashioned charm and there's a gorgeous terrace overlooking the garden and beyond to a ruined château. The lunch menu, 65F, which includes $^1/_4$ litre of wine, lists hors d'œuvres from the buffet and a freshly cooked dish of the day. Dishes on the other menus, 120–165F, are distinctly Provençal in flavour: good fresh fish, a bouillabaisse that you have to order three days in advance, fresh fish, Lubéron lamb, and so on. Easy-going welcome, and a chef who takes time to chat with his guests.

|●| LE FOURNIL

5 pl. Carnot (Centre).
☎ 04.90.75.83.62
Closed Mon, Tues evening Oct–March, and Dec–Jan.

This establishment, with a pleasant terrace, stands right in the heart of the village next to the fountain. It's building a solid reputation, so you might need to book. Good traditional cooking: galette of pig's trotters, ravioli with a filling of lamb's brains, twice-cooked kid, roast milk-fed lamb, and pot-au-feu of new vegetables with basil. There's a very decent 105F lunch menu served during the week and others at 145F and 205F.

BORMES-LES-MIMOSAS   83230

⚐ 🏠 HÔTEL PARADIS**

62 impasse de Castellan (South); it's on the right as you go down from the village.
☎ 04.94.01.32.62 📠 04.94.01.32.60

Closed Jan–March and 30 Sept–31 Dec. **Garden. Car park**.

This peaceful hotel is well off the tourist track. The very nice owner is justifiably proud of his lush garden. Clean, simple, pleasantly decorated doubles, 260F with shower/wc and 350–420F with bath. They also have a separate building, which looks onto the paradisal garden – perfect for families or groups. 10% discount Sept and April–June except weekends and public holidays.

⚐ 🏠 |●| L'HÔTEL DE LA PLAGE**

rond-point de la Bienvenue-La Favière; take the road in the direction of the port, then turn off to La Favière.
☎ 04.94.71.02.74 📠 04.94.71.77.22
📧 hotel.sarl@wanadoo.fr
Closed Oct–March. **TV. Car park**.

Other than a few concessions to fashion and some improved comforts, this place has barely changed since opening in 1960, and it still has the same regular guests. There are games of pétanque in the evening, after the guests have dined. Rooms 270–300F with shower/wc or 290–320F with bath. Half board, 350F, is compulsory July–Aug. Good selection of menus 80–140F. The only blot on the landscape is the concrete blocks on the way to the beach. Free apéritif.

BRIANÇON   05100

⚐ 🏠 |●| L'AUBERGE DE L'IMPOSSIBLE**

43 av. de Savoie (Nord).
☎ 04.92.21.02.98 📠 04.92.21.13.75
📧 rerousseau@wanadoo.fr
Closed Mon out of season, lunchtimes in winter, and Nov. **Car park**.

An unpretentious hotel-restaurant with fifteen or so decent rooms. Doubles 190F with basin and 290F with shower/wc – these are reasonable prices for the area. Simple, nourishing family cooking is served in the restaurant, like fish fondue and tartiflette. Lunch menu 68F and others 89–110F. In summer you dine on the terrace. They offer half board, 240–290F per person, weekly rates and ski-packages. There's a good atmosphere, and in the winter they sometimes host crêpe parties or karaoke evenings for the residents. 10% discount on the room rate May–June and Sept–Oct.

⚐ |●| L'AUBERGE DU MONT PROREL**

5 rue René Froger (East).
☎ 04.92.20.22.88 📠 04.92.21.27.76
Closed May, Oct and Nov. **TV. Car park**.

At the lower end of Vauban fortress, this chalet is at the foot of the Prorel ski lift that leads up to the Serre-Chevalier area. Rooms are clean and cosily comfortable, and about half of them have a balcony. Doubles 220F with basin, up to 320F with bath. Half board from 280F and they offer weekly rates. The restaurant serves classic regional cooking on menus 85–135F. Free house apéritif.

🍴 🏠 |●| LE CRISTOL**

6 route d'Italie (Northeast); on the N94, it's north of the upper town, 200m from the gate in the town walls.
☎ 04.92.20.20.11 ➡ 04.92.21.02.58
TV. Car park.

A traditional hotel where you get a warm welcome. The bright dining room is decorated with reproductions of Aubusson tapestries, stitched by the proprietress' mother-in-law. Doubles with shower/wc 220–360F. The rooms at the rear have balconies and you can enjoy the sun in the morning and the view over Vauban fortress. Half board, 235–305F, compulsory July–Aug. Menus 70–155F. 10% discount on the room rate.

🍴 🏠 AUBERGE EDELWEISS**

32 av. de la République (Centre).
☎ 04.92.21.02.94 ➡ 04.92.21.22.55
Closed Nov. **TV**.

A small hotel, well located very near Vauban's magnificent fortress, opposite the cultural centre and the conference centre. The east-facing rooms have a lovely view of the local woods, while, facing west, they overlook the town. It's clean and quiet, though the decor is dull. Doubles 290–330F with bath. 10% discount out of season.

🍴 |●| LE PÉCHÉ GOURMAND

2 route de Gap.
☎ 04.92.21.33.21
Closed Christmas and a week at the end of April.
Disabled access. **Car park**.

Though it's set on a corner of a huge junction, this restaurant also has a flowery, shaded terrace well away from the streams of cars, and two elegant dining rooms. The excellent menus list goat's cheese ravioli with green pea *purée* and roast guinea-fowl breast with rosemary *jus* – both are quite delicious. There's a respectable selection of cheeses, good desserts and an extensive list of coffees – try the *Papouaisie*. Weekday lunch menu 80F, then 130–245F. Service is a bit stiff, but amiable enough. Free apéritif.

🍴 |●| RESTAURANT LE RUSTIQUE

rue du Pont-d'Asfeld (Centre); coming down from the Grande Gargouille take the first left after the fountain and it's 300m further on.
☎ 04.92.21.00.10
Closed Mon out of season,Tues lunchtime except public holidays, 20–30 June and 20 Nov–10 Dec.

Country decor, good quality country cooking and a warm welcome – just what you want. The speciality is fresh trout served with all manner of sauces – try it with apples flambéed in Calvados, with leek *coulis*, with garlic and cream, or with Roquefort cheese. The very generous salads are good, too, and they do a tasty *fondue savoyarde* with morels. Menus 99F and 150F, and *à la carte* around 150F. Slow service. Free apéritif.

🍴 |●| LE PIED DE LA GARGOUILLE

64 Grande-Rue; it's in the old town opposite the municipal library.
☎ 04.92.20.12.95
Closed except for Fri–Sun evenings out of season, lunchtimes in season, and Nov.

This restaurant centres on an open fire where the host keeps an expert eye on the delicious grilled dishes. The walls are adorned with antique skis and snow shoes. Excellent sweet and savoury *tourtons*, or pancakes, but specialities include mountain dishes and steak grilled over the embers. Menu 115F, *à la carte* around 145F. Enthusiastic welcome. Free apéritif or coffee.

LA VACHETTE   05100 (4KM NE)

🍴 |●| LE NANO

Route d'Italie; it's on the N94, in the direction of Montgenèvre and Italy.
☎ 04.92.21.06.09
Closed Sun and Mon except July–Aug.

The warm, pleasant setting, the quietly efficient service and, above all, the quality of the cooking make this one of the best places to eat in the area and it's popular with gourmets. The fine, classical dishes are skillfully seasoned: *roulade* of rabbit with basil, boned cockerel with spiced sauce, and very good desserts. Menus 140F, a seafood menu at 200F (three courses, cheese and dessert), and the one at 270F is a small feast. Free coffee.

CHANTEMERLE   05330 (7KM N)

🍴 🏠 |●| LA BOULE DE NEIGE***

Route de Grenoble; it's in the centre of the village.
☎ 04.92.24.00.16 ➡ 04.92.24.00.25

Closed 22 April–16 June and 9 Sept–15 Dec. **TV**.

Prices aren't the cheapest, but this is a wonderfully comfortable establishment, and you won't want to leave. Doubles with shower/wc or bath 460–860F, and half board 360–510F. The restaurant is very pleasant and the cooking is delicate – fillet of pork *mignon* with endive sauce and rack of lamb with garlic cream sauce. Menus 130–180F. The *patronne's* welcome is quiet and charming.The ski-lift for the Serre-Chevalier slopes is 100m away. Free coffee.

SALLE-LÈS-ALPES (LA)   05240 (8KM N)

|●| LA MAROTTE

36 rue de la Guisane; it's in the main street.
☎ 04.92.24.77.23
Closed lunchtimes, Sun, Oct–Nov and May–June.

A really nice restaurant that's been here for years. The boss prepares delicious dishes to the taste of his guests who seem rarely to be disappointed. One menu only, 95F, or *à la carte*. Try the vegetable *terrine*, the house speciality. The herring and shallot bread and the apple *tarte Tatin* deserve a round of applause, as does the whole place. It's best to book.

CAGNES SUR MER   06800

☗ LE VAL DUCHESSE**

11 rue de Paris; it's 50m from the beach.
☎ 04.92.13.40.00 ➡ 04.92.13.40.29
Garden. Swimming pool. TV. Car park.

Set in a quiet street, away from the traffic and the impersonal high-rises down by the sea, this place has a pretty garden planted with palm trees, a swimming pool, ping-pong table and games for the children. The decor is full of southern colour and you can rent studios from 250–370F. Apartments that sleep four, with bathrooms and south-facing terraces, go for 350–510F. Prices go down if you stay a week or more. Warm reception.

☗ LE MAS D'AZUR

42 av. de Nice, Cros-de-Cagnes.
☎ 04.93.20.19.19
Garden. TV. Car park.

At first sight this hotel, set on the edge of the main road, doesn't look very promising. But inside you travel back in time about 25 years. It's a charming old Provençal house with a courtyard, where you're welcomed warmly by the kindly owners. On top of that, it's just three minutes' walk from the beach. Fifteen

quiet rooms and a most appealing garden. Doubles with shower/wc 310–335F.

|●| LE RENOIR

10 rue J.-R.-Giacosa; it's opposite les Halles.
☎ 04.93.22.59.58
Closed Sun and Thurs evenings, Mon, 15 Dec–15 Jan, and July.

The outside of the restaurant, across from the covered market, looks dreary, but the sumptuous first-floor dining room is cheerily decorated in shades of yellow. The food is equally appealing: rabbit with *tapenade*, *sanguins* (mushrooms that grow in pine woods) cooked with red peppers, *daube* with ceps and *fricassée* of fish. The *patronne*, who is kindness itself, will help you choose. Menus 85F and 145F.

|●| LA TABLE D'YVES

85 Montée de la Bourgade, Vieux Cagnes
☎ 04.93.20.33.33
Closed Tues and Thurs lunchtimes, Wed, and the Feb and All Saints' school holidays.

Yves Merville has twenty years of experience in the finest kitchens behind him, and today, although he's working in a pocket-sized kitchen, he and his wife run their place with professionalism and charm. The decor – blue and ochre walls with bleached beams – is welcoming. Two menus only, 135F and 170F. Dishes change frequently, allowing the chef to give full flight to his imagination: *cappuccino* of little crabs, chicken risotto with curry, mould of lamb with Provençal courgettes, and bread and butter pudding with pan-fried fruit.

CANNES   06400

☗ LE CHANTECLAIR

12 rue Forville; it's near the Palais des Festivals and the Midi beach.
☎ and ➡ 04.93.39.68.88
Closed mid-Nov to around 21 Dec.

Though it's ideally located 100m from the liveliest part of town, this hotel is nonetheless perfectly quiet. Functional rooms with white walls and simple pine furniture cost 220–260F – sometimes they're not as clean as a real stickler might hope. There's a charming patio where you can have breakfast. You'll get a warm welcome from the chatty host who will explain where you can park for free in the town.

☗ HÔTEL MOLIÈRE**

5–7 rue Molière (East); it's 100m from La Croisette.

☎ 04.93.38.16.16 ➡ 04.93.68.29.57
Closed 15 Nov–25 Dec. **Disabled access**. **Garden**. **TV**.

This hotel is housed in two adjoining buildings; one of them 19th-century, with a pretty façade, and the other modern. Each is furnished in the appropriate style. Lovely rooms with shower or bath 450–700F. Although the hotel is very close to the town centre, the location is quiet and there is a large garden in which to enjoy breakfast. Friendly welcome. 10% discount.

🕭 🛊 HÔTEL DE FRANCE***

85 rue d'Antibes (Centre).
☎ 04.93.06.54.54 ➡ 04.93.68.53.43
📧 infos@h-de-France.com
Closed 22 Nov–26 Dec. **TV**. **Lock-up car park**.

This place has been completely refurbished without entirely losing its Art Deco style. It's in the busiest part of town right on the main thoroughfare and has thirty rooms with modern facilities – air conditioning, safe, hairdrier and the rest – for 470–670F. Rooms 501–508 have a view of the sea. 10% discount Sept–July excluding 31 Dec.

🕭 🛊 LE SPLENDID***

4–6 rue Félix Faure.
☎ 04.97.06.22.22 ➡ 04.93.99.55.02
Disabled access. **TV**.

It's not a palace such as you find on La Croisette but it's pretty close. Behind the majestic turn-of-the-century façade, there's one of the town's loveliest hotels, wonderfully run by Annick Cagnat and her family. The beautiful rooms have antique furniture and all sorts of little extras to make your stay feel really luxurious. The prices – 640–900F for a double – are well justified. Free breakfast.

🕭 ❙●❙ LE JARDIN

15 av. Isola.
☎ 04.93.38.17.85
Closed Sun evening and Mon.

This is one of the most popular restaurants in town among locals. It's a simple little place far from the tourist areas and the boisterous crowds of the Croisette. The district is a little depressing, as is the bar, where a TV mumbles and flickers in the corner. But walk through it to arrive at the hidden garden where you can dine in peace on simple, tasty food: *daube provençale*, grilled sole, breast of duck with green peppercorns or sardines, bass or sea bream grilled over embers. Prices are gratifyingly low, menus 75–115F, and the welcome is pleasant. Free apéritif.

🕭 ❙●❙ LE COMPTOIR DES VINS

13 bd. de la République (Centre).
☎ 04.93.68.13.26
Closed Mon–Tues evenings, Wed, Sun, and Feb.

You enter via the cellar, selecting your wine first, then choose your food to suit. It took the owner some time to get the local Cannois used to the idea of a bistro-cellar and he succeeded. It's busy and buzzy, especially in the evening. Good, wholesome dishes: sausage with pistachios or *blanquette* of veal, a huge range of sandwiches and some Savoyard specialities. Weekday lunch menu 89F, 145F in the evening, or 120F *à la carte*. Wine, by the glass or the bottle, is good value. Free house apéritif.

🕭 ❙●❙ LE BOUCHON D'OBJECTIF

10 rue Constantine (East).
☎ 04.93.99.21.76
Closed Sun evening and Mon out of season except when there are conferences.

Each month this friendly restaurant stages an exhibition of a different photographer's work. The simple, original food includes snails with dill in flaky pastry, rabbit *terrine* with grapes and pistachios, and suckling pig with honey. Menus 92F and 145F. There's a pretty terrace facing onto a modern pedestrianised area. Free apéritif.

❙●❙ RESTAURANT AUX BONS ENFANTS

80 rue Meynadier (Centre); it's opposite Forville market.
Closed Sat evening except in season, Sun, Aug and New Year.

There's no telephone, so the regulars, often of a certain age, pop in during the morning to reserve a table while the staff, seated at the tables in the dining room, are peeling the vegetables bought in the Forville market. Home cooking and regional dishes: goat's cheese *terrine* with tomato *confit*, sole *meunière*, aubergine and sardine fritters, *aïoli*, tarts and home-made iced *nougat*. Menu 96F. Good-natured greeting and service.

❙●❙ RESTAURANT AU BEC FIN

12 rue du 24-Août (Centre); it's between the train station and the rue d'Antibes.
☎ 04.93.38.35.86
Closed Sun, the first week in July and the first fortnight in Nov. **Disabled access**.

This restaurant gets very full, so don't arrive too late. The menus, 105F and 125F, offers a staggering choice with nearly twenty starters and almost as many main courses. Mostly local cuisine: *daube provençale* (a slowly braised beef stew), vegetable *soupe au pis-*

tou, scorpion fish *à la pêcheur*, etc. Good daily specials, and you won't even notice the bland decor. Free apéritif.

|●| CÔTÉ JARDIN

12 av. Saint-Louis (Northwest); it's behind the Palais de Justice.
☎ 04.93.39.98.38
Closed Sun, Mon, and Feb.

A very good restaurant outside the touristy part of Cannes, beyond the railway line in a discreet cul-de-sac. It's a charming Provençal villa in a perfumed garden. The cooking is wonderfully fragrant: ginger soup, chicken with coconut, duck *confit* topped with celeriac purée and orange zest, caramel *croustillant*, and pan-fried apples with sesame seeds. Imaginative and really tasty. Menus 125F (lunch) and 205F. Free apéritif.

⅍ |●| RESTAURANT LOU SOULEOU

16 bd. Jean-Hibert (Southwest); it's on the road to Mandelieu.
☎ 04.93.39.85.55
Closed Mon out of season, Mon–Wed lunchtimes in summer, and Nov.

This restaurant is behind the old harbour in a district where few tourists go. The menus are excellent value for money, listing dishes such as *blanquette* of monkfish with mussels, fillet of sea bass with watercress, and *bourride du pêcheur*, a fish soup full of monkfish, lobster, mussels, garlic *croûtons* and *rouille*. Dishes of the day 128F, menus from 148F. Sip a Kir as you admire the view of the Estérel hills. Free apéritif.

GOLFE-JUAN   06220 (4KM NE)

⅍ 🏠 HÔTEL CALIFORNIA*

222 av. de la Liberté (East); it's on the N7, 800m from the station, close to the seashore.
☎ 04.93.63.78.63
Closed 1 Nov. **TV. Car park.**

This 1930s house, set back from the main road, has been converted into a hotel with pretty double rooms 150–200F in low season, 250–280F in high season. Studio apartments also available. 10% discount except July–Aug.

🏠 |●| LE PALM-HÔTEL

17 av. de la Palmeraie.
☎ 04.93.63.72.24 ➡ 04.93.63.18.45
Restaurant closed 15 Oct–1 March. **Car park.**

Unfortunately, the N7 passes close by, which is a minus, but this beautiful old house has lots of charm and the owners have a real

sense of hospitality. Spruce rooms which have been done up in style; 380–480F for a double. There's a terrace where you can eat reliable local dishes. Menus 100F and 149F, and half board from 290F. Free apéritif.

VALLAURIS   06220 (6KM NE)

⅍ |●| LE MANUSCRIT

224 chemin Lintier (Centre); it's in the centre of town off the bd. du Tapis-Vert.
☎ 04.93.64.56.56
Closed Mon and Sun evening in season, Mon and Tues out of season, and 15 Nov to early Dec.

The interior of this fine grey-stone building, which used to be a perfume factory, is exceptional, and the food is pretty good. You can eat in the dining room, where there's a wonderful display of prints and canvases, in the conservatory, which is full of subtropical flowers, or on the terrace beneath the hundred-year-old magnolia tree. The weekday lunch menu, 105F, and others, 140–185F, all offer a wide range of dishes: seafood *terrine*, pan-fried *andouillette* in champagne, fish stew, veal sweetbreads and kidneys, and other such delights. Affordable wines. Free apéritif.

VALBONNE   06560 (11KM N)

⅍ |●| LA FONTAINE AUX VINS

3 rue Grande; it's in the old down.
☎ 04.93.12.93.20
Closed Wed except in season.

Predominantly a wine bar, this place also serves "Provençal *tapas*" – little dishes of tasty morsels – along with original sandwiches and attentively prepared dishes. Around 80F *à la carte*. Wines are carefully selected and affordable, and they also offer a good pale ale. If you want to buy some of the products they serve, you can get them at *Olivier and Co* next door. Free coffee.

|●| L'AUBERGE FLEURIE

1016 route de Cannes (South); it's on the right, 1km before you get to Valbonne, coming from Cannes.
☎ 04.93.12.02.80
Closed Sun evening and Mon, Mon only July–Aug, and Dec. **Disabled access**.

A very good restaurant in a pretty, wisteria-covered building with huge mirrors in the dining rooms. Inventive, sunny dishes are made from the best ingredients with the simplest flavours: *croustillant* of fish with *ratatouille*, rolled quail with ceps and girolles, John Dory with salt, and *crème brûlée*. Menus 128–165F. Lots of regular patrons, and service with a smile.

CARPENTRAS 84200

🎿 🛎 HÔTEL LE FIACRE**

153 rue Vigne (Centre).
☎ 04.90.63.03.15 📠 04.90.60.49.73
TV. Pay car park.

This 18th-century convent, located in a quiet street in the centre of town, was converted into a town house and then, some forty years ago, into a hotel. You go up a monumental staircase to the rooms, which are all individually decorated and look out onto a delightful courtyard. 290F for a double with shower/wc and 390F with bath. Breakfast 40F. 10% discount for two nights Sept–June.

MONTEUX 84170 (5KM SW)

🎿 🛎 |●| LE SELECT HÔTEL***

24 bd. de Carpentras.
☎ 04.90.66.27.91 📠 04.90.66.33.05
Closed Sat and Sun evening out of season, and 18 Dec–10 Jan. **Swimming pool. TV. Car park.**

You'll get a really friendly welcome from the Dutch couple who own this characterful old famhouse. Doubles with bath 340F. The simple, original food is fine, light and of excellent quality – menus 95–170F. In summer, eat on the terrace in the shade of the plane trees beside the swimming pool. Try the delicious Côtes-du-Ventoux rosé. Free apéritif.

PERNES-LES-FONTAINES 84210 (5.5KM S)

🎿 |●| DAME L'OIE

56 rue Troubadour; it's on the D938.
☎ 04.90.61.62.43

There's a fountain in the middle of the dining room, where the decor is English country style – sort of Beatrix Potter. Kindly welcome and service. The cuisine is typically southern – simple but nicely prepared, with stunning flavours. Try salad Landaise with *foie gras*, sardines, roast lamb with Provençal herbs, or duck breast with seasonal fruits. It's good value, with a weekday lunch menu 70F and others 105–150F. Dishes change regularly with seasonal produce. Good local wines. Free apéritif or coffee.

CASSIS 13260

🛎 |●| LE CLOS DES ARÔMES**

10 rue Paul-Mouton; it's a two-minute walk from the town centre.
☎ 04.42.01.71.84 📠 04.42.01.31.76

Closed Mon–Wed lunchtimes except on public holidays. **Car park.**

An elegant restaurant, just ouside the centre of town, looking like a Provençal dolls' house. Enjoy sophisticated dishes in the large, shady, flower-filled courtyard. Menus 120F and 160F. Specialities include beef *daube à l'ancienne*, baked sea bream, stuffed sardines and *bouillabaisse*. There are fourteen peaceful rooms: doubles 400F with shower/wc, 500F with bath. Free apéritif.

🛎 |●| LE JARDIN D'EMILE

plage du Bestouan.
☎ 04.42.01.80.55 ✉ provence@lejardindemile.fr
Closed a fortnight in early Jan and a fortnight at the end of Nov. **Garden. TV. Car park.**

A charming, enjoyable place with a great view. Seven ravishing rooms – including a honeymoon suite and two attic rooms – go for 400–650F with shower/wc or bath. The chic but relaxed restaurant serves creative Mediterranean cooking; *pieds et paquets* (lambs tripe and trotters), flaked fresh cod with potatoes and garlic. There's a weekday lunch menu at 98F, *bouillabaisse* menu at 150F, and others up to 245F. Dine in the garden if at all possible, under ancient pines, olives, figs and cypresses.

CASTELLANE 04120

🛎 |●| MA PETITE AUBERGE

pl. Centrale (Centre); at the foot of Notre-Dame-du-Roc.
☎ 04.92.83.62.06 📠 04.92.83.68.49
Closed Wed out of season. **Garden. TV. Car park.**

A old-style hotel which has been sensitively renovated. Comfortable, appealing doubles for 280F with shower/wc or bath. Good traditional, unfussy food: starling *pâté*, simply grilled red mullet, lamb chops with herbs, and a splendid *crème caramel*. There's a veranda and a garden with huge, ancient, shady lime trees. Menus 90–210F.

GARDE (LA) 04120 (3KM SE)

🎿 🛎 |●| AUBERGE DU TEILLON**

Route Napoléon; it's on the N85 towards Grasse.
☎ 04.92.83.60.88 📠 04.92.83.74.08
Closed Mon except July–Aug, and Sun evening Oct to Easter. **TV.**

People come here from all along the coast at the weekend. You feel cocooned in the rustic little dining room, where chef Yves Lépine uses Provençal ingredients to produce flavoursome dishes: snails in *brioche* with vermouth and *foie gras*, smoked lamb ham, veal kidneys with morels, roast, boned pigeon with ceps and rack of lamb *à la Provençale*. Menus, 110–240F. Prolong the pleasure by staying the night; doubles cost 200F with basin, 230F with shower, 290F with shower/wc. Half board, 300F, is compulsory July–Aug. Rooms facing the main road can be noisy, so ask for ones at the back if you want a lie-in. A simple, cordial welcome. 10% discount on the room rate.

ROUGON   04120 (17KM SW)

⚹ ☎ |●| AUBERGE DU POINT-SUBLIME**

How to get there: it's on the D952 at the entrance to the Verdon Gorges.
☎ 04.92.83.60.35 ➡ 04.92.83.74.31
📧 point.sublime@wanadoo.fr
Closed Oct to 8 April, and Nov. **TV**. **Car park**.

There are two small dining rooms here, one non-smoking. Whichever you choose, there is quite a treat in store: checked tablecloths, tiled floors, green plants and photographs of the Verdon around the rooms. *Formule* with dish of the day 76F, menus 115–210F. Fresh local dishes perfumed by countryside herbs: hot goat's cheese salad, rabbit *caillette*, *civet* of lamb, and regional dishes like trout and scrambled eggs with truffles. The desserts alone are worth a visit – particularly the fig *crème brûlée* – and there are some wonderful local apéritifs flavoured with oranges, walnuts, honey, blackberry or herbs. Doubles 220F with basin, 265F with shower, 290–310F shower/wc and 290–310F with bath, are blissfully peaceful. Half board, 270–290F, is compulsory in summer, and you'll need to reserve for July and August. 10% discount on the room rate except weekends and school holidays.

PALUD-SUR-VERDON (LA)   04120 (25KM SW)

⚹ ☎ |●| HÔTEL-RESTAURANT LE PROVENCE**

route La Maline; take the D23, it's 50m from the village.
☎ 04.92.77.38.88 ➡ 04.92.77.31.05
📧 hotelleprovence@aol.com
Closed Nov to Palm Sunday.
Disabled access. **TV**. **Car park**.

This hotel has wide views of the route des Crêtes. Doubles with shower/wc or bath 240–270F. Half board costs around 265F per person. Menus 70–130F. Specialities include cockerel with shrimps, rabbit *à la provençale*, salmon with sorrel and lamb tripe and trotters.

There's a relaxing lounge with a billiard table, or you can sip a cool drink on the terrace and savour the peace and quiet. Baby-sitting service. Half-price breakfast (full price 45F), which is just like a complete meal.

⚹ ☎ HÔTEL DES GORGES DU VERDON***

How to get there: take the D952, the road north of the gorges.
☎ 04.92.77.38.26 ➡ 04.92.77.35.00
Closed Nov to Easter. **Swimming pool**. **TV**. **Car park**.

This hotel is in the heart of the Verdon Gorges, on a hillside facing the village and the surrounding countryside. The spectacular, wide-screen scenery helps you forget the hotel's somewhat gloomy, modern architecture. The rooms are similarly uninspiring, but they're well equipped, clean and comfortable and decorated in Provençal style. Doubles with shower/wc or bath 450–800F. They serve very decent food, mostly traditional Provençal dishes: *anchoïade*, artichokes *en barigoule* (stuffed with mushrooms and herbs), lamb chops with tarragon, fillet of salmon with olive oil and savoury, or scrambled eggs with truffles. Menus 120F and 160F. Half board, compulsory in season and at weekends, costs 420–550F. Free apéritif.

CAVAILLON   84300

☎ HÔTEL BEL-AIR

62 rue Bel-Air (Centre).
☎ 04.90.78.11.75

An archetypal hotel for travellers on a budget who like an old-fashioned atmosphere and value friendliness and good company more than comfort. The seven pleasant rooms are simply decorated. Doubles with basin/wc 190F, or 270F with shower/wc. Each room has a bowl of sweets and an information pack about Cavaillon and its environs. Breakfast, with fresh fruit and home-made jam, is served at a big communal table, for 38F.

☎ HÔTEL DU PARC**

183 pl. François-Tourel (West); it's near the tourist office.
☎ 04.90.71.57.78 ➡ 04.90.76.10.35
📧 hotel-du-parc.fr
TV. **Pay car park**.

A huge old house opposite the Roman arch. Good hospitality and family atmosphere. The rooms are classically decorated and fit in well with the architecture. If you choose one facing the park at the side of the hotel you'll be woken by birdsong. Doubles 270F with shower/wc, 290F with bath. Breakfast 38F. There's a sun lounge on the large, colonnaded terrace.

❤️ LA CUISINE DU MARCHÉ

pl. Gambetta (Centre).
☎ 04.90.71.56.00
Closed Tues evening and Wed.

It's quite a job to find this place. It's on a square that's like a roundabout, and you have to look up to see the sign at first-floor level of a soulless building. But climb the stairs to the first floor and you will find an attractive, unfussy dining room with a view over the main square. Chef Olivier Mahieu prepares excellent fresh dishes with a strong southern French accent: *émincé* of scorpion fish with artichoke, aubergine *millefeuille*, *brousse* (unsalted goat's cheese) with ceps, and lamb tripe and trotters *à la Provençale*. Weekday lunch menu 80F, then 100–190F.

CHAPELLE-EN-VALGAUDEMAR (LA) 05800

🏕 🏠 ❤️ HÔTEL-RESTAURANT DU MONT-OLAN**

☎ 04.92.55.23.03 ➡ 04.92.55.34.58
Closed 15 Sept–1 April. **TV**. **Car park**.

Chalet-style hotel where all the well-kept rooms look out to the soaring peaks that dominate the village. Owners Monsieur and Mme Voltan serve up huge quantities of ravioli with honey and potato pie in a large dining room with a panoramic view of the fast-flowing Navette river. Menus 70–130F. An ideal place to build up your strength for an assault on the mountains. Doubles 245–265F with shower/wc. Free coffee.

CHÂTEAU-ARNOUX 04160

❤️ AU GOÛT DU JOUR

It's on the N85, opposite the château.
☎ 04.92.64.48.48
Closed Mon and Tues lunchtime out of season, 3 Jan–12 Feb and 26 Nov–12 Dec.

This relaxed bistro is the cheaper sibling of the upmarket *Bonne Étape* next door. The sunny decor creates an elegant, refined atmosphere, but the food is very reasonably priced. Menus 85F and 130F. The main courses, written up on a slate, change with the seasons and what's freshest in the market. Try the mussel and saffron soup, fresh

anchovies marinated in fennel, duck leg with olives or delicious *tarte alsacienne* with strawberries.

❤️ L'OUSTAOU DE LA FOUN

How to get there: it's 1.5km north on the N85.
☎ 04.92.62.65.30
Closed Sun evening and Mon, a week at the end of Nov.

This restaurant, which occupies a Provençal hacienda, manages to be chic yet relaxed at the same time. The chef, who comes from a family of farmers and *charcutiers*, really knows his stuff, and he organizes cookery courses where he passes on some of his knowledge. His dishes balance fine ingredients and create delightful flavour combinations: braised and pan-fried calf's head served on potatoes and goat's cheese, sardine and herb fritters, rabbit and artichoke casserole with rosemary and juniper, pigeon *croustillé* with ceps, and upside-down lamb tart with herbs and fresh goat's cheese. If you have any room for dessert, try the *crème brûlée* with thyme or strawberry salad with liquorice ice cream. The accompaniments are unusual while remaining simple. Weekday lunch menu 95F and others 120–208F.

COLLOBRIÈRES 83610

🏕 ❤️ LA PETITE FONTAINE

pl. de la République.
☎ 04.94.48.00.12
Closed Mon, the Feb school holidays and 15–30 Sept.

One of the best places for miles around, in a peaceful village in the Maures mountains famous for its *marrons glacés*. The rustic restaurant is decorated with old implements and the cooking is delicious: *fricassée* of chicken with garlic, rabbit in white wine, beef *daube à la provençale*, and duck breast with ceps. Weekday menu 130F or 160F. They serve wine from the local co-operative by the glass. Free *digestif*.

COMPS-SUR-ARTUBY 83840

🏠 ❤️ GRAND HÔTEL BAIN**

How to get there: it's between Draguignan and Castellane.
☎ 04.94.76.90.06 ➡ 04.94.76.92.24
Closed 12 Nov–26 Dec. **TV**. **Car park**.

The Bain family has owned this hotel since 1737. Today it is frequented by local hunters, who relish the hearty local dishes: *pâté* studded with local truffles, omelettes served with truffles, trout with basil in pastry, rabbit with tomato and basil, *daube à la provençale*, roast rack of lamb, and goat's cheese. Menus 82–198F. Pleasant rooms make for a pleasant country stay in this local institution; 275F with shower/wc or 295F with bath.

CROIX-VALMER (LA)   06480

🎋 🏠 PARC HÔTEL***

av. Georges Selliez; after the traffic lights in the centre of town, take the Ramatuelle road and it's 2km further.
☎ 04.94.79.64.04 ➡ 04.94.54.38.91
Closed Oct to early May.
Garden. Swimming pool. Pay garage.

A wonderfully maintained Belle Époque hotel with private grounds. The spacious, sunny rooms with burnished antiques, have splendid views of the islands and the sea, and the prices aren't a shock. The owners have kept their commitment to avoid falling into the price-traps of Saint-Tropez. They cost 380F with shower, 570F with bath. Very cordial welcome. The swimming pool is in a palm grove. 10% discount May, June and Sept.

DIGNE-LES-BAINS   04000

🎋 🏠 ◉ HÔTEL DU PETIT SAINT-JEAN*

14 cours des Arès (Centre); it's on the corner of pl. Charles-de-Gaulle.
☎ 04.92.31.30.04 ➡ 04.92.36.05.80
Closed 24 Dec–6 Jan. **Garage**.

Cosy, small and welcoming hotel with a nostalgic feel of times past. It offers all the warmth of Provence. Double rooms 150F with basin, 280F with shower/wc. The cheerful host serves decent food in the first-floor restaurant: rabbit with onions, stew of suckling pig, *aïoli*, *bœuf en daube* or *blanquette* of veal. Menus 60–140F. Free use of garage.

🎋 🏠 ◉ HÔTEL DU GRAND PARIS****

19 bd. Thiers.
☎ 04.92.31.11.15 ➡ 04.32.32.82
e GrandParis@wanadoo.fr
Closed Sun evening and Mon out of season, and 1 Dec–1 March. **TV. Car park**.

Stylish hotel that has been converted from a 17th-century convent. The welcome is slightly formal but the place oozes discreet charm. The chef prepares very classical dishes using good ingredients to create delicious flavours: *foie gras* and lentil *terrine*, *émincé* of lamb with Châteauneuf du Pape vinegar, roast zander fillet with seasonal baby vegetables.

Menus from 150F or around 210F *à la carte*. Lovely, comfortable double rooms 420–600F. Breakfast 65F. Free apéritif.

🎋 🏠 ◉ HÔTEL VILLA GAÏA***

Route de Nice; it's 4km from the centre on the Castellane road.
☎ 04.92.31.21.60 ➡ 04.92.31.20.12
Closed Nov–March. **Disabled access. Car park**.

This quiet hotel, an impressive building set in shady, green grounds, was converted from an old clinic and still runs on some of the old rules. Dinner is served at the same time every night, and there's a single menu, 150F, featuring superb regional dishes. They use vegetables from the garden, local cheeses, and meat and fish direct from the market. You dine on the terrace, in the library or the salon, depending on the whim of the moment. Excellent breakfast, 55F. This is essentially a luxury guest house. Rooms 490–510F or 440F half board which is compulsory July–Aug. Free apéritif.

◉ L'ORIGAN

6 rue Pied-de-Ville (Centre); in the pedestrianised area.
☎ 04.92.31.62.13 **e** rest-origan@wanadoo.fr
Closed Sun and a fortnight in Feb.

A restaurant in the heart of the old quarter of the spa town. Chef Philippe Cochet prepares delicious food such as John Dory fillets with basil, a cold *aïoli* of cod and vegetables, *pieds et paquets* (lamb tripe and trotters), stuffed veal fillet and red mullet with chives. Menus 118–215F.

DRAGUIGNAN   83300

◉ RESTAURANT LE BARON

42 Grand-Rue (Centre).
☎ 04.94.67.31.76
Closed Mon except public holidays and for groups.

Though the white stone frontage of this building looks rather grand, inside it feels more like a doctor's surgery than a restaurant. The food is good, however, and the classics from the Mediterranean and the Franche Comté are listed on the menus 67–145F: monkfish *bourride* (stew), cockerel in *vin jaune* or with morels. Free house apéritif, coffee or *digestif*.

◉ LE DOMINO

28 av. Carnot (Centre); it's on the main street.
☎ 04.94.67.15.33
Closed Sun, Mon and Nov.

This building has a lot of character and so does the stylish Tex-Mex restaurant inside. Kindly welcome and attentive service. *À la carte* you'll pay around 150F per person for salads, spiced-up meat dishes and typical Mexican dishes such as chicken or beef *fajitas* and spare ribs. You can dine on the veranda or out under the palm trees.

EMBRUN 05200

⚑ 🏠 |●| HÔTEL DE LA MAIRIE**

pl. de la Mairie or pl. Barthelon (Centre).
☎ 04.92.43.20.65 ➡ 04.92.43.47.02
Closed Sun evening and Mon in winter, 8–25 May and Oct–Nov. **Disabled access. TV**.

This hotel is a model of its type, with a superb, convivial brasserie, high-quality food and competent, charming staff. It's a favourite with locals for an evening drink or Sunday lunch. Specialities include ravioli with morel sauce, sautéed prawns *à la Provençale* and excellent duck *confit*. Menus 98–130F. Best to book. Clean, bright rooms 290–310F for a double – choose one which looks out onto the square. Free coffee.

⚑ 🏠 |●| HÔTEL NOTRE-DAME**

av. Général-Nicolas – route de Chalvet; coming from Guillestre, turn right before the post office then right again.
☎ 04.92.43.08.36 ➡ 04.92.43.58.41
Closed Sun evening and Mon, except for school holidays, and Jan. **Garden. TV. Car park**.

Just five minutes' walk from the centre of town, this family hotel is a peaceful haven set at the far end of a large garden. After receiving a warm welcome you will be shown to extremely clean rooms with excellent beds. Doubles with shower/wc 290F. Good quality cuisine using only local produce – duck breast, or lamb tripe and trotters – is served on the menus, 85–149F. Half board, compulsory in summer, starts at 280F. Free coffee.

|●| RESTAURANT PASCAL

Hameau de Caléyère.
☎ 04.92.43.00.69
Closed Sept.

It's not the place for a romantic tête-à-tête, but the family atmosphere is convivial and infectious – you'll leave in a good mood. The *patronne* greets all her customers by shaking their hand. There's only one menu, 65F, and it's substantial. The vegetables, eggs and meats all come from local farms. The local heart-starter *digestif* is called *vipérine* – it bites like a snake. Not for the squeamish.

SAINT-ANDRÉ-D'EMBRUN 05200 (6KM NE)

⚑ |●| RESTAURANT LA GRANDE FERME

Les Rauffes; it's on the Crévoux road.
☎ 04.92.43.09.99 ✉ lagrandeferme@wanadoo.fr
Closed evenings, Wed and Oct–Nov.

Owners Nicole and Thierry will welcome you into the magnificent vaulted dining room that they have restored themselves. This restaurant has a well-deserved reputation in the region and it serves excellent traditional cuisine – try the baked eggs with Queyras blue cheese and the pear *gratin* with brandy from the Hautes-Alpes. Menus 80–110F. Good selection of wines. *Gîtes* available for rent – 10% discount on the price.

SAINT-SAUVEUR 05200 (10KM S)

|●| RESTAURANT LES MANINS

Bourg Saint-Sauvin; take the road to Les Orres and look for the signposts off to the left.
☎ 04.92.43.09.27
Open July to mid-Sept noon–9pm, reservations only the rest of the year.

Fantastic restaurant with breathtaking views from the terrace looking down at Lac de Serre-Ponçon and Embrun. Architect Eric Boissel built this elegant wooden building with his own hands, and designed all the furniture. The dishes are devised by Nicole, who's an attentive hostess. Try the *grand mézé*, a complete Middle Eastern meal with individual dishes of red peppers, *tzatziki, hummus, köfte*, feta cheese, fresh onions, *tapenade* and the like. They also do mixed salads, substantial pizzas and good *crêpes*, and there's a splendid crumble for dessert. Pizzas at 60F, expect to pay 125F *à la carte*.

ENTRECASTEAUX 83570

⚑ |●| LA FOURCHETTE

Le Courtil (Centre); it's next to the church.
☎ 04.94.04.42.78 ✉ pierrelenicolas@lemel.fr
Closed Sun evening, Mon, and Jan–Feb.

In the shadow of the famous château, this place attracts gourmet travellers who enjoy delicious food while admiring the wonderful view from the terrace. Chef Pierre Nicolas runs the kitchens while his American wife greets you. Simple, quality cooking and honest prices; 90F for the two-course lunch menu (weekdays), and a range of others up to 200F. Dishes include *foie gras*, truffles and sautéed king scallops. Free coffee.

ÈZE   06360

🎿 🏠 ❘●❘ HERMITAGE DU COL D'ÈZE**

Grande Corniche (North); from Èze, take the D46 and then the Grande Corniche; it's 500m on the left.
☎ 04.93.41.00.68 ➡ 04.93.41.25.05
Restaurant closed Mon, Thurs and Fri lunchtimes and 15 Oct–15 Feb. **Garden. Swimming pool. TV. Car park.**

Monsieur and Mme Bérardi's hotel is the place to relax in peace and quiet. The swimming pool will ease your aching limbs after a mountain walk – the location is at the start of a lot of trails. There is a splendid view of the southern Alps and the cooler air at this altitude provides relief from the heat of the coast. Doubles 170–310F with shower/wc or bath. The chef personalises his recipes, working with only fresh produce and, in some seasons, fruit and vegetables from the garden. Menus 95F, weekdays only, and 190F. Half board 230–275F. Free coffee.

🏠 AUBERGE DES DEUX CORNICHES**

It's 1km along the D46 in the direction of Col d'Èze.
☎ 04.93.41.19.54 ➡ 04.92.10.86.26
Closed Thurs lunchtime and 10 Nov–1 Feb.
TV. Car park.

This hotel is in a quiet spot above the village of Èze, high enough up for you to get a view of the sea from your room. It's often full in summer. Charming welcome from the owner. Pleasant double rooms, some with balcony, 340F. Carefully prepared food.

FAYENCE   83440

🎿 🏠 HÔTEL LA SOUSTO

4 rue du Paty.
☎ 04.94.76.02.16 📧 guy.corteccia@wanadoo.fr

You'll get the best of Provence in this attractive little hotel in the centre of the old village above the valley. The simply furnished rooms have a hotplate, fridge and basin; some also have a shower. Each room has its own personality – number 5 has a sunny little terrace overlooking the valley. Doubles with shower/wc 270F. 10% discount.

FONTVIEILLE   13990

🎿 🏠 HÔTEL LE DAUDET***

7 av. de Montmajour; it's on the way out of the village on the road to Arles.
☎ 04.90.54.76.06 ➡ 04.90.54.76.95
Closed Oct–March. **Swimming pool. Car park.**

This new hotel is named after the writer, Alphonse Daudet, whose mill is nearby. Built around a patio, it has about fourteen straightforward rooms with their own terrace. There's a swimming pool among the pine trees. Doubles 310–370F with shower or bath. Free apéritif or coffee.

🎿 ❘●❘ LA CUISINE AU PLANET

144 Grand Rue; it's in the old village.
☎ 04.90.54.63.97
Closed Mon, Tues lunchtime out of season, Mon and Tues lunchtimes in season, a fortnight in Feb and a fortnight in Nov.

This charming, creeper-covered restaurant is run by a couple who are crazy about the area and prepare local dishes with a light touch all their own. Menus 145–190F. Impressive wine list. Free coffee.

FORCALQUIER   04300

🎿 🏠 ❘●❘ HOSTELLERIE DES DEUX LIONS***

11 pl. Bourguet.
☎ 04.92.75.25.30 ➡ 04.92.75.06.41
📧 hoteldeuxlions@aol.com
Closed Mon evening and Tues out of season.
TV. Car park.

A rather stylish, comfortable hotel-restaurant which changed hands in the course of the year. Unusually, they've put the prices down! Menus 87–158F. There are a few lovely rooms from 300F with shower/wc or 330F with bath. Free coffee.

🏠 LE CHARAMBEAU

Route de Niozelles (Southeast).
☎ 04.92.70.91.70 ➡ 04.92.70.81.83
Closed 15 Nov–15 Feb.
Disabled access. Swimming pool. TV. Car park.

This hotel occupies a converted 18th-century farm in the middle of a seven-hectare expanse of hills and meadows. It's a lovely place to stay, looking down over the valley. Ten freshly decorated, attractive rooms. Some have balconies, others wide terraces and all have good facilities; one room has been converted for disabled use.

Doubles 305–430F with shower/wc or bath.

LARDIERS   04230 (18KM N)

|●| LE CAFÉ DE LA LAVANDE

How to get there: take the D950 towards Banon, and at Notre Dame turn right onto the D12 towards Saumane.
☎ 04.92.73.31.52
Closed Sun and Mon out of season, a fortnight in the Nov and Feb school holidays.

Old-fashioned country café in a village that looks out to the Lure mountains. Regulars drop in for a morning glass of white wine or a *pastis* in the evening, but its worth taking the time for a meal. It's simple food, all fresh and good: duck with cherries, lamb stew, creamed salt cod. Menus from 100F.

FRÉJUS   83600

🛏 HÔTEL OASIS

Impasse J.B. Charcot – Fréjus Plage.
☎ 04.94.51.50.44 ➡ 04.94.53.01.04
Closed mid–Oct to mid–March. **TV. Car park.**

A small, quiet 1950s building in a cul-de-sac five minutes from the beach. It's run by a young couple who welcome you like regulars or family friends. The rooms are varied – old-fashioned wallpaper in some, pretty Provençal decor in others – and though not big, they're more than adequate. Doubles with shower or shower/wc 200–450F. Breakfast on the terrace under an awning.

🍴 🛏 |●| HÔTEL ARENA***

139 rue du Général-de-Gaulle (Centre); it's next to pl. Agricola.
☎ 04.94.17.09.40 ➡ 04.94.52.01.52
✉ info@arena-hotel.com
Closed Jan. **Disabled access. Garden. Swimming pool. TV. Car park.**

A lovely place if you want to spend a little more. It's an old establishment – they claim that Napoleon slept here – but it's been attractively and tastefully renovated. The decor is pure Provence: warm colours on the walls, mosaic floors and painted furniture. The rooms aren't huge but they're very pretty, air-conditioned and efficiently sound-proofed (you don't hear the trains on the lines nearby): 450–580F with shower/wc, 480–750F with bath. There's a lush garden with luxuriant greenery and a swimming pool. The flavoursome cuisine consists of mainly Mediterranean dishes with a pinch of individuality. Menus 145–265F. Free coffee.

GAP   05000

🍴 🛏 |●| HÔTEL-RESTAURANT LA FERME BLANCHE***

Route des Romettes (Northwest); from the station take the col Bayard road, turn right onto the Romettes road then turn left, and it's at the end of the road.
☎ 04.92.51.03.41 ➡ 04.92.51.35.39
Closed Sun evening in winter and 2–10 Jan. **TV.**

This charming hotel, away from the main road, has a nice sunny terrace. In the public areas, lovely furniture complements the vaulted rooms and they've used an old bank counter as the bar. Rooms are bright and comfortable, though the decoration is looking a little tired; doubles with shower 180F, or 310F with bath. Breakfast, 45F, is served until noon. Meals can be taken in the restaurant, *La Roseraie*, which the hotel has recently acquired. Menus start at 130F: kid stew and potatoes *Dauphinois* with ceps, crayfish stew or *marbré* of rabbit with prunes. There is a half-board option, 260F per person. The welcoming owner is a mine of information about walks and cultural events. 10% discount on the room rate.

🍴 🛏 |●| HÔTEL-RESTAURANT PORTE-COLOMBE**

4 pl. Frédéric-Euzières (West).
☎ 04.92.51.04.13 ➡ 04.92.52.42.50
Restaurant closed Fri evening and Sat, 30 April–19 May and 4–25 Jan. **TV. Car park.**

Don't let the electric shutters and cable TV distract you from the beautiful view of Gap and its cathedral. This hotel is in a modern, unappealing building but the rooms are individual and comfortable, and some have serving hatches so you don't have to get up for breakfast. Fine cuisine includes salmon *mousseline* with crab *coulis*, ravioli *en tourtons* and succulent desserts. Menus 85–160F. Doubles 270F with shower/wc and 290F with bath. 10% discount Oct–June.

🍴 🛏 |●| LA GRILLE***

2 pl. Frédéric-Euzière (Centre).
☎ 04.92.53.84.84 ➡ 04.92.52.42.38

Though the building itself is pretty dreary, the welcome at this hotel is most affable and the rooms are spacious, quiet and comfortable. As in a lot of other hotels in Gap, the furnishings and decor are looking tired. Air-conditioned doubles with shower/wc 270F, 350F with bath and mini-bar. Menus 90–145F. 10% discount on the room rate.

⚘ |●| AU 2ÈME SOUFFLE

pl. de la Cathédrale (Centre).
☎ 04.92.53.57.87
Closed Sun and Mon evening.

This unusual multi-purpose establishment next to the cathedral is a restaurant, tea-room, gallery and second-hand clothes store all in one. Lasagne is the house speciality, and they serve excellent savoury and sweet tarts and mixed salads. Original, tasty dishes of the day, 42–65F, include roast pork with peaches, coconut chicken. Menu 80F. Attractive, typical local decor in the dining room and on the terrace. Free coffee.

⚘ |●| LE TOURTON DES ALPES

1 rue des Cordiers (Northeast).
☎ 04.92.53.90.91

A well-established, successful restaurant which serves the region's best *tourtons* (potato fritters) with green salad and raw ham. They're included in the menus at 85F and 115F, or you can order them *à la carte*. Free coffee.

|●| LA MUSARDIÈRE

3 pl. du Revelly (Centre)
☎ 04.92.51.56.15
Closed Tues evening, Wed, 17–21 April and 1–15 July.

Many of the dishes at this spruce, pretty restaurant are traditional Alsatian specialities, because the owners come from that part of the world. The generous *Menu Alsacien*,135F, includes knuckle of pork braised in beer, fish *choucroute* and zander in Riesling. Other menus 110–160F. They do some delicious salads. Courteous service.

⚘ |●| RESTAURANT LE PASTURIER

18 rue Pérolière (Centre); it's in the pedestrian area.
☎ 04.92.53.69.29
Closed Sun, and Mon lunchtime July–Aug except public holidays.

The elegant, intimate atmosphere at this restaurant makes it ideal for a romantic dinner. The owners are lively and welcoming, and chef Pascal Dorche changes his menus frequently, sometimes producing unusual dishes. His honest cooking is more than satisfying – goat's cheese *nougat* with pistachios and lavender flower, a *madeleine* with pike and prawns, artichoke bottoms and Banyuls wine vinegar, ravioli stuffed with leeks and morels, and unmissable white chocolate and coconut dessert. Menus 120–350F, *à la carte* 250–280F. There's a small terrace open in summer. Free apéritif.

LAYE   05500 (11.5KM N)

|●| RESTAURANT LA LAITERIE DU COL BAYARD

How to get there: take the N85 from Gap and follow the signs.
☎ 04.92.50.50.06
Closed Mon except school holidays and public holidays, and 15 Nov–15 Dec. **Car park**.

The farmer, the farmer's son and the farmer's grandson run this place, which is a must for cheese-lovers. They serve *fondues*, a *Plateau Champsaurin*, which offers a selection of ten different cheeses, and a variety of generous salads which you can choose with blue cheese dressing or smoked ham sauce. Menus 85–195F or 110F *à la carte*.

MONTGARDIN   05230 (12KM E)

⚘ |●| L'AUBERGE DU MOULIN

How to get there: take the N94 in the direction of Embrun and it's on the right in the village.
☎ 04.92.50.32.98
Closed Sun evening and Mon, and by reservation only during the rest of the week.

Known locally as the Three Sisters, this place is run by three women who are wonderful cooks. Many of the superb local dishes feature duck or goose. The single menu, 140F, is satisfying and skilfully prepared; it lists *gâteau* of spleen and duck liver, *fricassée* of whole duckling done like a *coq au vin*, fresh cheese with honey, and a good *bavarois*. There's a family atmosphere, and you will have a most enjoyable meal. Free apéritif.

SAINT-JULIEN-EN-CHAMPSAUR 05500 (20KM N)

⚘ ▦ |●| LES CHÊNETS

How to get there: take the Grenoble road to Fare, then turn right towards Saint-Bonnet and Saint-Julien.
☎ 04.92.50.03.15.
Closed Wed and Sun evening out of season, 3–21 April and 13 Nov–27 Dec.

A mountain chalet with a warm family feeling. Simple double rooms go for 230–279F with shower/wc or bath. The cuisine is better than good and majors on regional dishes. At the simpler end of the scale are *tourtons* (potato fritters with ham and salad) or *crème brûlée* for dessert, or, more pricey, duck *carpaccio* with grapefruit *vinaigrette* and braised lambs' tongues and cheeks. Perfectly ripened cheeses and excellent home-made desserts. Menus 100–200F. Free apéritif.

GASSIN   83580

🖀 |●| HÔTEL BELLO-VISTO**

pl. des Barrys (East).
☎ 04.94.56.17.30 ➡ 04.94.43.45.36
Restaurant closed Tues.

This excellently situated little hotel, on the edge of the village, has a terrace with a superb view of the bay of Saint-Tropez. Rooms are spruce, clean and well priced for the area – doubles with shower/wc 280–420F. You'll need to book in July and August. Provençal cuisine dominates in the restaurant – roast rabbit with garlic or truffle galette. Menu 140F.

GORDES   84220

🖀 |●| LE PROVENÇAL

pl. du Château (Centre).
☎ 04.90.72.10.01 ➡ 04.90.72.04.20
Closed 15 Nov–15 Dec. **TV**. **Car park**.

A straightforward hotel with gratifyingly low prices – rooms in the Lubéron area are generally expensive. Eight very clean rooms with new bathroom fittings go for 280–330F with bath. Rooms 1 and 2 have lovely views of the château. Breakfast 35F. The restaurant, on the other hand, serves reliable, good, Provençal, dishes without any great surprises but, with menus starting at 125F, it's pricey. Several dishes of the day, and a good choice of pizzas.

🖀 |●| AUBERGE DE CARCARILLE**

Les Gervais (South); it's 3km below Gordes on the D2.
☎ 04.90.72.02.63 ➡ 04.90.72.05.74
e cacaril@club-internet.fr
Closed Fri out of season and 15 Nov–28 Dec. **Disabled access**. **Swimming pool**. **TV**. **Car park**.

A welcoming inn that's modern but not obviously so. The dining room is quite elegant and creates the right atmosphere for the traditional Provençal cuisine: rabbit brawn with herbs, crayfish *quenelles*, *tripou* (mutton tripe and sheep's trotters), *bouillabaisse*, etc. Menus 98–220F. The pleasant rooms are not cheap, but that's not surprising in the heart of Lubéron. Doubles 370–420F with bath. Breakfast 48F.

🕅 🖀 LE MAS DE LA SÉNANCOLE***

Imberts; 5km outside Gordes on the D2.
☎ 04.90.76.76.55 ➡ 04.90.76.70.44
e gordes@mas-de-la-senancole.com
Closed Nov–March. **Disabled access**. **Garden**. **Swimming pool**. **TV**. **Car park**.

Though this is a completely new building, it has been built in the old Provençal style and fits well into the surroundings. The exceptionally comfortable doubles with shower/wc go for 600–700F or 900–1000F with bath. There are also two superb apartments with an enclosed balcony and outsize bathrooms. The swimming pool is surrounded by greenery. Quality place, quality welcome, quality service. Free apéritif.

GOULT   84220 (8KM SE)

🕅 |●| LE CAFÉ DE LA POSTE

pl. de la Libération; it's on the village square.
☎ 04.90.72.23.23
Closed Wed and Nov–March; on evenings and Sun the restaurant is closed but the bar is open.

In this pretty village, in the shade of the trees, you can dine in a friendly atmosphere. Good-value house specialities include rabbit *à la pebrade*, vegetable *terrine*, *crespéou*, *aïoli* and *anchoïade*. *Menu du jour* 70F, or 75F *à la carte*. Children's menu 50F. Free coffee.

|●| AUBERGE LE FIACRE

quartier Pied-Rousset; it's 5km out of the village on the N100 in the direction of Apt.
☎ 04.90.72.26.31
Closed Sun evening out of season, Thurs lunchtime in season, and 12 Nov–10 Dec. **Car park**.

An excellent restaurant serving light, inventive Provençal cooking using local produce. The owners will give you a kind, cheerful welcome. Mother and daughter wait at table while father is in charge of the cooking. The vegetable soup with basil and the lamb *tian* alone make a visit worthwhile, and they do game in season. In summer you can dine outside under the lime trees where you are serenaded by a chorus of cicadas. Menus, 110F and 140F, offer good value for money.

MURS   84220 (8.5KM NE)

🕅 🖀 |●| LE CRILLON

Centre.
☎ 04.90.72.60.31 ➡ 04.90.72.63.12
e crillon.murs@wanadoo.fr
Closed Thurs out of season, 10–25 Jan. **TV**. **Car park**.

This country hotel, in a characterful village in the Lubéron wilds, offers stylish doubles, some with terraces or mezzanines, for 280–285F with shower/wc or bath. Weekday menu 75F, then 110–130F and a children's menu 50F.

There are some lovely dishes which are made using wild mushrooms or truffles: *tournedos* with morels, truffle omelette, stewed hare and local game. 5% discount for a minimum six-night stay half- or full board.

BEAUMETTES 84220 (9KM SE)

⅍ |●| RESTAURANT LA REMISE

It's in the middle of the village.
☎ 04.90.72.23.05
Closed Wed, Tues evening out of season, and mid-Jan to mid-Feb. **Disabled access**.

The unpretentious 90F menu is one of the most reasonably priced in the Lubéron. The others, 140–180F, are significantly more elaborate, listing dishes such as fish soup, sea bass with tarragon, *émincé* of beef with ceps, scallops *à la Provençale*, and *fricassée* of lamb with garlic. Meals served on the shady terrace. Free coffee.

GOURDON 06620

⅍ |●| AU VIEUX FOUR

rue Basse; it's a turning off the main street.
☎ 04.93.09.68.60
Closed evenings, Sat, 1–15 June, mid-Nov to mid-Dec.

A pleasant place for a spot of lunch. Good family dishes. Start with a plate of local *char-cuterie* or shepherd's salad, then follow it with rabbit with thyme or meat grilled over the coals. Finish off with *clafoutis*. Menu 98F, or *à la carte* around 120F. Free *digestif* – but you have to ask nicely.

GRAVE (LA) 05320

⅍ ≜ |●| AUBERGE EDELWEISS**

Centre.
☎ 04.76.79.90.93 ➡ 04.76.79.92.64
Closed 10 May–15 June and 25 Sept–22 Dec. **TV**.

This enjoyable hotel is owned by the orga-nizers of the annual Mieje ski race, a slip-sliding race that's known worldwide. The modern hotel stands well away from the noise of the road. The clientele is interna-tional and sporty and there's always a riotous atmosphere late into the evening. You can relax on the terrace and gaze upon the summits of the 4000m Écrins, or enjoy the sauna and Jacuzzi. The place has been renovated recently but rooms are on the small side; 290–330F. Menus 90–140F. 10% discount on the room rate.

GRÉOUX-LES-BAINS 05320

⅍ ≜ |●| HÔTEL-RESTAURANT DES ALPES**

19 av. des Alpes; it's in the middle of the village.
☎ 04.94.74.24.24 ➡ 04.94.74.24.26
Closed Dec–Feb. **Swimming pool**. **TV**. **Car park**.

A bright, fresh house where the simple, tastefully decorated rooms have views over the village, the park or the pool. Doubles with shower/wc 275–315F, 315–355F with bath. The restaurant serves a good range of inter-esting dishes: aubergine and sardine *mille-feuille*, fresh salmon with drizzled olive oil, roast rabbit haunch with honey, or sea bass baked with finely sliced potatoes. Menus 90–175F. Warm welcome. Free coffee.

GRIMAUD 83310

⅍ ≜ LE GINESTEL

Chemin des Blaquières; it's 3km from Grimaud village and 1.5km from Port-Grimaud on the D61.
☎ or ➡ 04.94.43.48.45
Closed Oct–March. **Disabled access**. **Swimming pool**. **Garden**. **Car park**.

When the dust has settled from the dirt track you drive along to get here, you'll find yourself looking at an unpretentious hotel with eigh-teen rooms, each with a private terrace over-looking the park and swimming pool. There's a pontoon on the River Giscle where boats tie up. Doubles with shower/wc 250–550F depending on the season. Free Kir.

⅍ ≜ |●| HÔTEL LA PIERRERIE***

Quartier du Grand Pont; it's 2km from Port-Grimaud on the D61.
☎ 04.94.43.22.55 ➡ 04.94.43.24.78
Closed Nov–March. **Garden**. **Swimming pool**. **TV**.

An attractive little hotel out in the country-side, above the gulf of Saint-Tropez. It's built like a typical Provençal *mas*, with lots of small stone buildings in the greenery and among the flowers. Rooms with shower/wc or bath, 380–640F. It's wonderfully quiet. Stay six nights, get the seventh free.

≜ ATHÉNOPOLIS***

Quartier Mouretti; it's 3km outside Grimaud on the road to la Garde-Freinet.
☎ 04.94.43.24.24 ➡ 04.94.43.37.05
℮ athenopolis@var-provence.com
Closed Nov–March. **Disabled access**. **Swimming pool**. **Garden**. **TV**. **Car park**.

Attractively decorated rooms with balconies

or terraces. The swimming pool is inviting and the atmosphere is peaceful – ideal if you want to relax and sleep. Doubles with shower/wc or bath 510–680F. Very generous breakfast and the provide dinner for residents for 120F. The garden and the surroundings are delightful.

GUILLESTRE   05600

🕺 🛎 |●| LE CHALET ALPIN**

Route du Queyras; as you leave Guillestre, turn left onto the Queyras road.
☎ 04.92.45.00.35 ➡ 04.92.45.43.41
Closed 20 April–5 May and 15 Nov–20 Dec. **Car park**.

A family-run establishment with decent rooms at honest prices; doubles 230–270F with shower/wc or bath. The ones facing south over the park have a splendid view. Traditional, well-prepared cooking in the restaurant, on menus 75–170F; scallops with fresh fruit, *terrine* of duck *foie gras*, *crépinettes* of salmon with a saffron infusion, duck breast with sour cherries and Génépi wine. Half board from 260F. Free *digestif*.

SAINT-CRÉPIN   05600 (9KM N)

|●| L'AMISTOUS

Centre.
☎ 04.92.45.25.30
Closed Mon and Tues out of season, 15 Nov–15 Dec.

This restaurant is popular with locals and tourists alike. Their pizzas are particularly good, and they serve a smoky *cassolette* of veal sweetbreads and an absolutely delicious trout *au bleu*. You must try the chef's *potence* ("gallows") – meat or shellfish flambéed in whisky or *anis*, and served with special home-made sauces. Weekday lunch menu 55F, others up to 120F, and *à la carte* at about 120F. There's an extensive wine list, with at least one wine from each region at an affordable price.

HYÈRES   83400

🕺 🛎 HÔTEL DU SOLEIL**

rue du Rempart (Northeast).
☎ 04.94.65.16.26 ➡ 04.94.35.40.40
e soleil@hotel-du-soleil.fr
TV.

A hotel absolutely engulfed by ivy in a very peaceful, dreamy spot next to the medieval town. The rooms of this old building are haphazardly furnished and smell of lavender.

Doubles 220–340F with shower/wc, 250–390F with bath. 10% discount except in school holidays and summer.

🕺 🛎 HOSTELLERIE PROVENÇALE LA QUÉBÉCOISE**

20 chemin de l'Amiral-Costebelle (Southwest); coming off the motorway, turn right at the roundabout to Costebelle, then go straight on and follow the signs.
☎ 04.94.57.69.24 ➡ 04.94.38.78.27
Swimming pool.

The Quebecois owner left the freezing Canadian winters behind some years ago for this Provençal hotel in the woods on a sunny hillside. You can understand why. Each room is different and all are attractive. Doubles with basin 248F, 288F with shower, or 330F and 408F with shower/wc and bath. Half board, compulsory July–Aug, costs 322–392F. A very likeable hotel with fair prices. 10% discount Sept–June.

🕺 🛎 |●| HÔTEL-RESTAURANT LES PINS D'ARGENT***

bd. de la Marine; it's next to Saint-Pierre harbour.
☎ 04.94.57.63.60 ➡ 04.94.38.33.65
e pins.dargent@wanadoo.fr
Closed Sun (except public holidays) April–Sept, Sun evening and Mon May–June, and Oct–March.
Swimming pool. TV.

Attractive hotel in a 1900s building sheltered by palm trees and umbrella pines. The genuine warmth of the welcome is something special in such a touristy town. Pleasantly furnished, pretty rooms with bath 430F. Rooms 205 and 309 are especially nice. The dining room is right next to the swimming pool and makes a pleasant place to eat the fine cuisine. Highlights include fish soup with *rouille*, sardines with *tapenade* and courgette *confit*, and local lamb chops. Menus 110–190F. Half board, 400F, is compulsory July–Aug. Free house apéritif, and 10% discount on the room rate except at Easter, Whitsun, Ascension and July–Aug.

ISLE-SUR-LA-SORGUE (L')   84800

|●| LE CARRÉ D'HERBES

13 av. des 4-Otages (Centre).
☎ 04.90.38.62.95
Closed Tues, Wed and Jan.

An idyllic spot in a town which is swamped by visitors as soon as the weather gets good. Dine in a pretty room full of antique furniture and bric-à-brac, on the terrace or in a converted aviary. Menu 160F or 195F *à la carte*, children's menu 650F. The fresh food is full of original aromas – try *tartine de la bergère*, rabbit and olive stew, or pan-fried polenta and roast chicken with thyme, and finish with fruit crumble. Attentive, helpful service.

LARAGNE-MONTÉGLIN 05300

🎿 ✿ HÔTEL CHRISMA**

25 route de Grenoble (North).
☎ 04.92.65.09.36 ➡ 04.92.65.08.12
Closed 15 Nov–1 March.
Swimming pool. Garden. Car park.

If you're simply looking for somewhere to stop for one night, this is a good place. Neat rooms with shower/wc or bath 220–290F. The rooms overlooking the garden – where they do frequent barbecues – are lovely. You'll get a warm welcome. Free apéritif and 10% discount Sept–June excluding holiday weekends.

🎿 |●| L'ARAIGNÉE GOURMANDE

8 rue de la Paix (Centre).
☎ 04.92.65.13.39
Closed Tues evening, Wed and 15 Oct–15 Nov.

Located in the centre of the town, this unpretentious place is pleasant and clean. Good traditional cooking and a range of set menus: *formule rapide* 60F, weekday lunch 75F then others 120–180F. Dishes include *terrine* with juniper, lamb's tongue with *sauce gribiche*, and fillet of red mullet on leek *fondue*. Attentive service. Free coffee.

SAINTE COLOMBE 05700 (17KM W)

✿ |●| LE CÉANS**

Les Bégües; take the N75 in the direction of Serres, then the D30 towards Orpierre, then take the Laborel road out of the village to Bégües.
☎ 04.92.66.24.22 ➡ 04.92.28.29
📧 le.ceans@infonie.fr
Closed Nov–March. **Garden. Swimming pool**.

A family-run establishment halfway up the mountains in the Buech area, surrounded by orchards and lavender fields. Madame runs the place while Monsieur and their son produce reliable, tasty regional dishes. *Menu du jour* 85F, and others 120–190F. Specialities include snail profiteroles, lamb chops with honey and *fricassée* of chicken with morels. The rooms are small but quiet; doubles with shower/wc 230F. A garden, swimming pool, sauna, Jacuzzi – everything for a pleasant stay.

SAVOURNON 05700 (18KM N)

🎿 ✿ |●| L'AUBERGE DES RASTEL*

How to get there; take the D21 towards col de Laye.
☎ 04.92.67.13.05 ➡ 04.92.67.13.05
Closed Wed out of season, a week at Christmas and a week in early June.

A cheap, friendly inn away from everything, in a village midway up the mountains. It's a favourite with walkers and paragliders. Simple, functional double rooms 180F with shower/wc. The young owner/chef prepares delicious, no-frills dishes using only the freshest local produce. Menus 76–110F. There's a terrace and a bright, large dining room. You'll get a slobbering 70kg welcome from Mao, the dog. Free coffee.

LARCHE 04530

✿ |●| AUBERGE DU LAUZANIER

It's on the D900, just before the Larche pass.
☎ 04.94.84.35.93
Car park.

An enticing hideaway in Haute Ubaye, between Barcelonnette and the Italian border, run by a trio who have made it very comfortable. The substantial, tasty cooking is ideal for skiers and walkers – they offer platters of *charcuterie*, *tourtons*, omelettes, roast lamb with a morel crust and fruit tarts with raspberries or bilberries. Weekday menu 55F, and others for a bit more. There's a *gîte* with spotless rooms for 100F a night.

LAVANDOU (LE) 83980

✿ HÔTEL LE RABELAIS**

2 rue Rabelais (Southeast); it's opposite the old port.
☎ 04.94.71.00.56 ➡ 04.94.71.82.55
📧 hotel.lerabelais@wanadoo.fr
Closed 11 Nov–20 Jan.
Disabled access. TV. Car park.

A small hotel with salmon-coloured walls and green shutters that's very close to the centre and not far from the beaches either. Comfortable, pretty rooms cost 230F with basin, 380F with shower/wc and a balcony overlooking the fishing harbour for breakfast.

🎿 ✿ HÔTEL CALIFORNIA**

av. de Provence (Centre).
☎ 04.94.01.59.99 ➡ 04.94.01.59.28
📧 hotel.california@wanadoo.fr
Garden. TV. Car park.

The young couple who own the hotel, which is just eight minutes from the beach, have completely refurbished it. The husband is an architect who has put his talents to good use in the new design, while the wife has a wonderfully welcoming way with her guests. You will feel at ease immediately, and you can spend hours gazing out at the bay and the islands. The rooms aren't huge, but they have been thoughtfully arranged. Doubles with shower/wc 240–390F. The cheaper rooms look over the garden. Free breakfast.

⌂ |●| HÔTEL-RESTAURANT BEAU SOLEIL**

Aiguebelle-plage; it's 5km from the centre as you head towards Fréjus.
☎ 04.94.05.84.55 ➡ 04.94.05.70.89
Closed Oct to Easter. **Disabled access. TV. Car park.**

A quiet little hotel, which on summer nights makes a peaceful respite from the cacophony in Lavandou. The dynamic young owners, Monsieur and Mme Podda, offer a kind and considerate welcome to tourists. Simple, but very pleasant, well-maintained rooms all with sea view and air conditioning, cost 250F with shower/wc, 300F with bath. Half board, compulsory in high season, is 310–400F per person. Menus, 98–165F, list a wide choice of local specialities, including stuffed capon, *bouillabaisse*, and a very special *bourride* or fish stew.

ÎLE DU LEVANT 83400

⌂ |●| HÔTEL LE PONANT

It's on the island that's 30min by boat off Le Lavandou.
☎ 04.94.05.90.41 ➡ 04.94.05.90.41
e ponant@club-internet.fr
Closed 21 Sept–1 June.

A wonderful place – as long as you're a naturist. The 1950s building stands out like the prow of a boat on a crest of coastal cliffs. There are huge, wide terraces leading out from the rooms, with nothing between them and the sea. Each room is personally decorated by Frets, the unusual boss of this unusual place. They're all different and seductive in their own way – a chunk of rock emerges in one bathroom while another might be all wood. Rooms have shower/wc. Half-board only, 300–450F per person. Simple but tasty cuisine.

RAYOL-CANADEL 83820 (13KM E)

⅍ |●| MAURIN DES MAURES

av. du Touring-Club (Centre); it's on the main street in the centre of the village.
☎ 04.94.05.60.11
Closed evening 11 Nov–20 Dec.

The owner, Dédé Del Monte, paces up and down behind his bar like a croupier behind a gaming table. The locals, perched on their stools, exchange gossip over a *pastis* that's drunk straight-up and undiluted in these parts. Dishes in the restaurant include *bouillabaisse*, *millefeuille* of aubergines, a trio of grilled vegetables, mixed grill or grilled fish. Reserve a table by the window so you can admire the view of the bay. An authentic restaurant in an area that tends to lose its soul as the weather gets warmer. Weekday lunch menu at 70F, then others at 120F and 144F. Children's menu 60F. Free apéritif.

MANOSQUE 04100

⅍ |●| RESTAURANT LE LUBÉRON

21 [bis] pl. Terreau (Centre).
☎ 04.92.72.03.09
Closed Sun evening, Mon except in July, and ten days Aug/Sept.

The intense flavours of Provence are found in the food here, even though the chef is from the north of France. He's got a creative imagination, and offers dishes such as artichoke and truffle salad, grilled pigeon with rosemary, and lamb stew with lots of olive oil and basil. Weekday menu 60F, and others 100–185F. Tasteful rustic decor, and a terrace with a pergola. Free glass of Bon de Muscats from the Lure distillery.

⅍ |●| RESTAURANT DOMINIQUE BUCAILLE

43 bd. des Tilleuls (Centre).
☎ 04.92.72.32.28
Closed Wed evening and Sun. **Disabled access**.

This classy, bright, modern dining room is a big new success. The chef adds his own touches to classic, precisely cooked dishes with appetising, unusual flavours: poached egg with *foie gras* and coarsely mashed potato, roast John Dory with pepper served in a casserole of pickled tomatoes and *gnocchi*, vegetables pickled in olive oil in a pastry case. Menus 100–260F. The wine list has a selection of excellent local wines, particularly the Coteaux-de-Pierrevert from the Blaque domain. Decent prices. Free *digestif*.

MARSEILLE   13000

SEE MAP OVERLEAF

1st arrondissement
🏚 HÔTEL BEAULIEU-GLARIS*

1 pl. des Marseillaises; M° Arles. **MAP D1-15**
☎ 04.91.90.70.59 ➡ 04.91.56.14.04
e hotel-beaulieu@wanadoo.fr
Closed Christmas to 1 Jan. **TV**.

A stone's throw from the monumental steps of Saint-Charles station, where you get a great view of the city. It's handy if you're travelling by train and while not the height of luxury, it's clean and well maintained. The rooms at the back are huge and quiet, and get lots of sun. Doubles 160F with basin, 250F with shower/wc.

🍴 🏚 HÔTEL DU COQ*

26 rue du Coq. **MAP D1-6**
☎ 04.91.62.61.29 ➡ 04.91.64.02.05

Unpretentious hotel just five minutes from Saint-Charles station; if you telephone, they'll come and collect you by car. You get an excellent welcome. Prices are reasonable; 165F for a room without shower, 195F with shower. The street is quiet, and nearly all the rooms are at the back. 10% discount and free breakfast.

🏚 HÔTEL AZUR**

24 cours Franklin-Roosevelt; M° Réformés-Canebière.
Off map **D1-2**
☎ 04.91.42.74.38 ➡ 04.91.47.27.91
TV.

A pleasant hotel with friendly owners on a steep, quiet street lined with handsome buildings. The rooms have been renovated and have air conditioning; doubles with shower/wc or bath 290–450F. The nicest rooms look out onto little gardens at the back where there's a Christmas tree that's grown tall. Lovely breakfast with home-made pastries.

🍴 🏚 SAINT-FERRÉOL'S HÔTEL***

19 rue Pisançon; M° Noailles-Estrangin-Préfecture.
MAP C2-5
☎ 04.91.33.12.21 ➡ 04.91.54.29.97
e st.ferreol@wanadoo.fr
TV.

This hotel is in a good location, close to the old port. The glitzy rooms are named after famous painters – Van Gogh, Picasso, Monet and Cézanne – and decorated with appropriate prints. Doubles with good facilities, 440–580F. No charge for children under four. Breakfast 45F with fresh orange juice. Excellent welcome. 10% discount.

|●| LA PART DES ANGES

33 rue Sainte. **MAP C2/3-40**
☎ 04.91.33.55.70

Service 9am until 2am the following morning, Sun 1–6pm. A friendly wine bar where you come to buy wine from the barrel when you're doing the shopping or for a good bottle after the opera.There's a little dining room at the back, where you can eat salads, meat kebabs with rice, a green vegetable and a glass of wine – for 45F. Great atmosphere.

🍴|●| LES MENUS PLAISIRS

1 rue Haxo; M° Vieux-Port–Hôtel-de-Ville. **MAP C2-32**
☎ 04.91.54.94.38
Closed evenings and weekends.

Lunch only. A nice little place with lots of old clocks on the wall. The boss has become a proud Marseillais who champions his town while taking orders and serving dishes. A really warm atmosphere and hordes of customers who appreciate the good value you get here.The menu changes daily and dishes are appetizing: a small salad with chickpeas or feta, skate wing with *beurre blanc*, lasagne, sautéed pork with red kidney beans, and some good little desserts like fig tart with custard. *Formules* 50–65F. Terrace. Free coffee.

|●| PIZZERIA AU FEU DE BOIS

10 rue d'Aubagne; M° Noailles. **MAP C2-33**
☎ 04.91.54.33.96
Closed Sun.

This place is well-known for its outstanding pizzas cooked in a wood-fired oven. They cost 55–70F, with a range of toppings including *royale* (mushrooms, garlic, sausage and cheese) and *orientale* (meat, cream cheese, egg and tomatoes). *À la carte* you can get *pieds et paquets* (mutton tripe cooked with sheep's trotters), and lasagne for 60F. Inconsequential decor, regular customers, and friendly service. If you're in a rush, get a portion of pizza to take away from the counter outside.

|●| LES COLONIES

26 rue Lulli. **MAP C2-41**
☎ 04.91.54.11.17
Closed Sun.

Service 8am–7pm. A warm, welcoming, original place where they don't allow smoking because it's too small. This is where you buy tea, chocolates, jams and biscuits baked by "Le Petit Duc" from Saint-Rémy. It occupies an old bank building that's been decorated to within an inch of its life. Voluminous curtains,

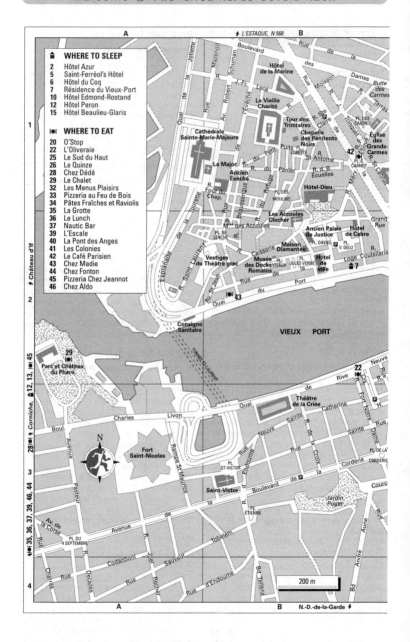

WHERE TO SLEEP

2 Hôtel Azur
5 Saint-Ferréol's Hôtel
6 Hôtel du Coq
7 Résidence du Vieux-Port
10 Hôtel Edmond-Rostand
12 Hôtel Peron
15 Hôtel Beaulieu-Glaris

WHERE TO EAT

20 O'Stop
22 L'Oliveraie
25 Le Sud du Haut
26 Le Quinze
28 Chez Dédé
29 Le Chalet
32 Les Menus Plaisirs
33 Pizzeria au Feu de Bois
34 Pâtes Fraîches et Raviolis
35 La Grotte
36 Le Lunch
37 Nautic Bar
39 L'Escale
40 La Pont des Anges
41 Les Colonies
42 Le Café Parisien
43 Chez Madie
44 Chez Fonton
45 Pizzeria Chez Jeannot
46 Chez Aldo

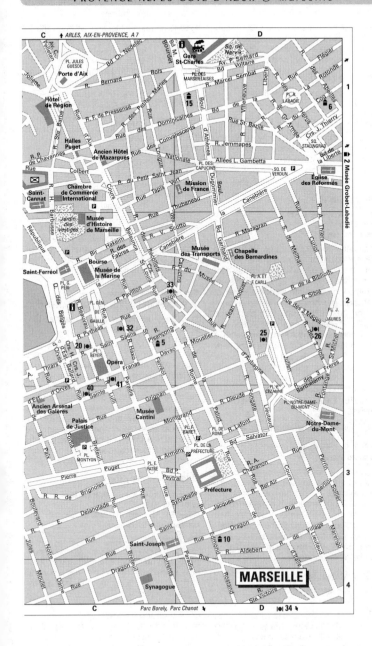

elaborate chandeliers. Good for lunch: cannelloni with *brousse* (a local cheese), stuffed vegetables, or cream cheese with honey and spiced bread. A meal will cost around 100F.

⅔ |●| L'OLIVERAIE

10 pl. aux Huiles; M° Vieux-Port–Hôtel de Ville.
MAP B2-22
☎ 04.91.33.34.41
Closed Sat lunchtime, Sun, and Aug. **Pay car park**.

A typical local bistro with a sunny welcoming owner, good service and superb Provençal cooking. There's a good lunch menu at 100F, 140F in the evening, including wine. You'll pay around 220F *à la carte*. Free coffee.

⅔ |●| O'STOP

16 rue Saint-Saens. **MAP C2-20**
☎ 04.91.33.85.34
Closed 7–8am only.

Service 8am–7am (23 hours out of 24). The snack bar opposite the opera is an institution; it attracts everyone from bourgeois gentleman to ladies of easy virtue, and it's not uncommon to bump into an opera singer or stagehand. The house specialities – *alouettes* (or meatballs), pasta with pesto and *daube à la Provençale* – are very decent. The sandwiches have good fillings and should not be ignored. Great atmosphere in the early hours. Dishes of the day 55F. Average price *à la carte* about 100F. Free aperitif.

2nd arrondissement
⅔ 🛎 HÔTEL LA RÉSIDENCE DU VIEUX PORT***

18 quai du Port; M° Vieux-Port–Hôtel-de-Ville. **MAP B2-7**
☎ 04.91.91.91.22 ➡ 04.91.56.60.88
TV. Disabled access.

This great family hotel , on the town hall side of the Vieux Port (the old port), has a good view of Notre-Dame. Rooms are large, light, air-conditioned and pleasantly furnished – though the bathrooms are a bit small – and you can sit on your balcony and watch the boats. Doubles 590F, and they've got a suite sleeping four or five for 750F. Friendly service and good breakfast. 10% discount.

|●| CHEZ MADIE-LES-GALINETTES

138 quai du Port. **MAP B2-43**
☎ 04.91.90.40.87 or 04.91.53.48.48
Closed Sun.

Way out at the end of the quay you'll find this restaurant that's the place to come for robust, authentic Provençal cooking. It's now run by

Madie's granddaughter and, although she still serves the chicken in Meunière sauce, her real speciality is meat. Her father was a wholesale butcher. Authentic *pieds et paquets* – lamb tripe and trotters. The clams with thyme are also good. Simple, fragrant cooking. Lunch menu 80F with starter and main course, or 110F and 150F. Around 180F *à la carte*.

|●| LE CAFÉ PARISIEN

1 pl. Sadi-Carnot. **MAP B1-42**
☎ 04.91.90.05.77

Service 4am–10pm. The last Marseille café to have retained its early 20th-century decor and atmosphere to match. At breakfast time, this is where locals come to read the paper quietly, on their way home with their *baguette*. At lunchtime, people swarm here, as there's always a substantial dish of the day and a dessert trolley. In the evening, especially at the weekend, *tapas* is the draw. There's always a hubbub of voices and lively discussion. You'll pay 100–120F *à la carte*.

6th arrondissement
⅔ 🛎 |●| HÔTEL EDMOND ROSTAND**

31 rue Dragon; M° Estrangin-Préfecture. **MAP D3-10**
☎ 04.91.37.74.95 ➡ 04.91.57.19.04
Garden. TV.

A well-kept family hotel in a quiet little street. It is named after the dramatist who wrote *Cyrano de Bergerac* and was born in a house close by. The bright, modern rooms all have bathrooms and direct-dial phone. Doubles 290F, and rooms sleeping four 450F. Ask for a room with a view of the garden. Breakfast, 36F, includes excellent home-made jam, and there's a nice lunchtime menu for 80F, listing grills and Provençal specialities. 10% discount on the room rate for long stays.

⅔ |●| LE SUD DU HAUT

80 cours Julien; M° Noailles. **MAP D2-25**
☎ 04.91.92.66.64
Closed Sun, Mon, Thurs–Sat evenings, Tues–Sat lunchtimes and 15 Aug–6 Sept.

The setting is like a bric-à-brac shop with its assorted holiday souvenirs and bits and pieces picked up in junk shops. Outside, there's a terrace where you can admire the wonderful fountain in cours Julien, and the good atmosphere is enhanced by the Afro-Cuban-Carribbean music that plays in the background. Old recipes are revamped here, and a touch of finesse added to dishes – stuffed vegetables, roast goat's cheese with herbs, rib of beef with a Roquefort pancake, duck *confit* with a walnut crust, and rack of lamb with herbs. Prices are reasonable; 70–90F *à la carte* at lunchtime, 150–180F for dinner. The service manages to be both attentive and relaxed. Free apéritif.

✖ |●| LE QUINZE

15 rue des 3-Rois; M° Cours-Julien-Notre-Dame-du-Mont. **MAP D2-26**
☎ 04.91.92.81.81
Closed lunchtimes and 24 Dec.

Service from 7.30pm. This street, which runs parallel to the famous cours Julien, acts as a kind of overflow for it – and nowadays has just as many restaurants. This particular one is lively, laid-back and has a great atmosphere. Despite its name, it's not the local rugby fifteen that everyone raves about here, but the football team, Olympique Marseille. Simple home cooking: *daube*, good barbecued meats and suckling pig in cider. Substantial menus 89F and 109F. Free apéritif.

7th arrondissement
✖ ♠ HÔTEL PERON**

119 corniche Kennedy (West). Off map **A3-12**
How to get there: take bus no. 83 from the Vieux Port and get off at the Corniche-Frégier stop.
☎ 04.91.31.01.41 ➡ 04.91.59.42.01
e marseillehotelperon@mintel.net
TV. Car park.

Irresistibly kitsch 1950s hotel, where each room is decorated in the style of a different French region, with moulded plaster murals and dolls in traditional dress. The bathrooms teem in ceramic fish and sea creatures. It's homely and very appealing. Doubles with bath 320–350F. As it's right beside the sea, you get a great view from the balconies at the front. Rooms at the back, though lacking the view, are quieter. Cheerful welcome and attentive service. 10% discount.

|●| LE CHALET

Jardin du Pharo (West). **MAP A2-29**
☎ 04.91.52.80.11
Closed Nov–Feb.

Service noon–6pm. Outdoor café in the gardens of the palace built by Napoléon III for the Empress Eugénie. They practically cook out of doors, and the unpretentious dishes cost 68–78F: grilled swordfish, cuttlefish *à l'armoricaine* (with onions and tomatoes) or tuna *provençale*. Salads around 50F, dishes of the day 74F and 84F, and 90–150F for a complete meal. In summer, when the centre of town can be unbearably hot, the shaded terrace gets a light, refreshing sea breeze. A

lovely place for a quiet afternoon drink, with a very beautiful view of the old port.

✖ |●| PIZZERIA CHEZ JEANNOT

Vallon des Auffes. Off map **A2/3-45**
☎ 04.91.52.11.28
Closed Mon and New Year holidays.

Nestling in the bottom of the picturesque Vallon des Auffes, this big pizzeria has a significant reputation built up over years of success. Tasty, soft pizzas, fresh pasta, lamb tripe and trotters (not in summer), or breaded mussel kebab. Everything is incredibly fresh so don't let the idea of frozen ingredients enter your head. Around 120F *à la carte*. There are several terraces at the water's edge. It's in a friendly fishing port which has been a little spoilt by the ravages of the 1960s building craze. Free coffee or apéritif.

|●| CHEZ FONFON

140 rue du Vallon-des-Auffes. Off map **A3-44**
No phone.
Closed Sun evening and three weeks in Jan.

Service noon–2pm and 7–10pm. The glory days were twenty years back in Fonfon's time. At that time the tourists flooded in. Now, under its new management, the Marseillais have come back. It's in a superb location with an unbelievable view – you can watch the boats as they manœuvre into port. The fresh fish is a feast. Choose the one you want and they cook it as you wish. Excellent *bouillabaisse* for 250F – an authentic one is never cheap – and around 300F for a meal.

8th arrondissement
✖ |●| PÂTES FRAÎCHES ET RAVIOLIS

150 rue Jean-Mermoz, on the corner of rue Émile Sicard (South); M° Rond-Point-du-Prado. Off map **D4-34**
☎ 04.91.76.18.85
Closed evenings, Sun, public holidays and Aug.

You have to go through the kitchens of this Italian deli to get to the veranda, where all windows open out onto a gravel courtyard. Start with San Daniele ham or a mozzarella kebab before devouring one of the great pasta or ravioli dishes. Expect to pay 100F for a meal. It's in a very quiet, middle-class area. Free coffee.

|●| LA GROTTE

Calanque de Callelongue (South); M° Castellane. Off map **A3-35**
How to get there: take a no. 20 bus from the metro station to Callelongue, the starting point for the Cassis to Calanques walk.
☎ 04.91.73.17.79

There's nothing here but are a few cabins, a tiny port with the occasional boat and *La Grotte*. The terrace, shaded by an awning, is very popular with Marseille locals at lunchtimes, when the superb flower-filled patio gets too much sun – they reserve that for dinner. It's advisable to book a table. Truly excellent pizzas, and more expensive grilled fish. It's a large place and feels a bit like a factory (electronic orders, 200 covers) but it's still friendly. 120–250F *à la carte* but they don't accept credit cards. Don't forget mosquito repellent – there are quite a few at night.

|●| CHEZ ALDO

28 rue Audemar-Tibido. Off map **A3-46**
☎ 04.91.73.31.55
Closed Feb.

An insignificant-looking place, you might think, but it's packed day and night. The pizza and the fresh fish landed at the port of La Madrague draw the crowd. The simply grilled fish is brilliant, or try the fresh prawns, mussels or squid cooked over the embers. Around 150–180F *à la carte*. Friendly welcome and a lovely terrace.

𝄞|●| CHEZ DÉDÉ

32 bd. Bonne Brise. Off map **A3-28**
☎ 04.91.73.01.03
Closed Sun evening, Mon, Tues and Wed lunchtime in winter.

The restaurant's terrace juts out over the water, while the dining room is decorated with unsophisticated and amusing model boats. The menu is simple, listing oven-baked pizzas, pasta, mussel kebabs and grilled fish. The grilled sardines are delicious. Around 150F *à la carte*. Free apéritif.

𝄞|●| L'ESCALE

2 bd. Alexandre Delabre – Les Goudes. Off map **A3-39**
☎ 04.91.73.16.78
Closed Sun evening, Mon, 15 Jan–15 Feb.

This restaurant is on the edge of the fishing village. It's run by a man who used to be a fishmonger, so the quality and freshness of the fish could not be bettered. The setting is lovely, with a big terrace overlooking the sea and the fishing port, and a beautiful dining room with a big wooden bar. They offer excellent *bouillabaisse* and seafood *paella*. À la carte around 200F, and children's menu 45F. Free apéritif.

9th arrondissement
𝄞|●| LE NAUTIC BAR

Calanque de Morgiou; M° Rond-Point-du-Prado. Off map **A3-37**

How to get there: at the metro stop, take a 23 bus and get off at the Morgiou-Beauvallon stop; it's a bit of a walk.
☎ 04.91.40.06.37
Closed Jan, but best to phone at any time.

This place, known as "chez Sylvie" to the locals, has a nice terrace that makes an ideal place to feast on seafood or whitebait, fish soup (60F) or fried *girella*, a brilliantly coloured local fish, (85F). There's a set menu at 140F. Sip some chilled wine and enjoy the cool sea breeze in wonderful surroundings. It's got everything you could want after a morning's swimming and diving, but note that the roads to the creeks are closed to unauthorised vehicles June–Sept, to avoid forest fires. Free *digestif*.

|●| LE LUNCH

Calanque de Sormiou (West); M° Rond-Point-du-Prado. Off map **A3-36**
How to get there: at the metro take a no. 23 bus to the La Cayolle stop and then hop on the free shuttle (7.30am–7pm).
☎ 04.91.25.05.37
Closed end Oct to mid-March.

In summer, when the road is closed to cars and motorbikes, you book a table by phone and use the shuttle. Going down towards the creek you get a magnificent view of the blue sea dotted with little spots of turquoise. All you have to do then is to sit on the terrace with a glass of chilled local Cassis white and order a plate of sea bream or red mullet from the menu. Fish are sold by weight; expect to pay about 200F. Good *bouillabaisse* – order it one day in advance.

CIOTAT (LA)   13600 (7KM E)

𝄞|●| LA FLEUR DE THYM

17 av. Franklin-Roosevelt.
☎ 04.42.08.32.44
Closed Sun evening and Wed out of season.

A restaurant that's totally charming and, after a change of premises, has come into its own. The terrace by the sea is an ideal place for a light meal of salads or grilled meat. Inside they serve sturdy, strongly flavoured regional dishes from Provence and the Landes. Menus 155F and 198F in the dining room, or a short menu for 100F served on the terrace. Free welcome cocktail.

MENTON   06500

♜ |●| HÔTEL NAPOLÉON***

29 porte de France, baie de Garavan.

☎ 04.93.35.89.50 ➡ 04.93.35.49.22
Closed mid-Nov to mid-Dec. **Swimming pool**. **TV**.

This large hotel, a typically dreary 1960s/1970s building, doesn't look much from the outside, but inside it's a different story. The spacious rooms are comfortable and most have a terrace with a sea view; doubles 680F, or 400F with a mountain view. Breakfast is served in your room or by the pool. Attentive, efficient service.The private beach is open April–Oct and there's a small restaurant offering simple dishes. Around 180–200F *à la carte*.

⋇ ☗ HÔTEL CHAMBORD***

6 av. Boyer; it's next to the tourist office and the casino.
☎ 04.93.35.94.19 ➡ 04.93.35.30.55
TV. **Car park**.

A friendly family hotel on the main street in the centre of Menton. It's not unusual to meet people who've been coming here since it opened in 1976. The spacious, really comfortable rooms go for 500–680F, breakfast included. The rooms with double bed are at the rear of the building, the twin rooms have a view of the gardens. All just a stone's throw from the sea. Free breakfast.

⋇ |●| LE MIDI

103 av. de Sospel.
☎ 04.93.57.55.96
Closed Sun and Wed evenings and July.

This unusual restaurant is well away from the racket of the centre. It's run by people who love traditional Menton dishes, and the menu lists them all in the local dialect – the easiest way to try the local delicacies is to order the *Assiette du Midi*. Alternatively, opt for the *formule-maison* which gets you a panoply of dishes to dip into, followed by a home-made fruit tart. All the produce is fresh and on Friday they offer home-made ravioli. Weekday lunch menu 75F, then others up to 140F or *à la carte* around 200F. Free apéritif.

⋇ |●| A BRAÏJADE MÉRIDIOUNALE

66 rue Longue.
☎ 04.93.35.65.65
Closed lunchtimes in summer, Wed and 15 Nov–15 Dec.

The rustic dining room has exposed stonework and behind the bar there's a big wood-fired oven that gives a good flavour to the meat dishes. You know exactly what you're getting here – the range of set menus include everything from apéritif to coffee, and possibly even a liqueur after dinner. Weekdays lunch menu 115F, others

up to 265F. Lots of marinated and grilled meats, including garlic chicken kebabs and Provençal favourites such as beef stew *niçoise* with ravioli or fish *aïoli*. Everything is served in generous portions by nice, friendly staff. Free *digestif*.

ROQUEBRUNE-CAP-MARTIN   06190 (3KM S)

☗ |●| LES DEUX FRÈRES

pl. des Deux Frères.
☎ 04.93.28.99.00 ➡ 04.93.28.99.10
e 2freres@webstore.fr
Closed Mon and mid-Nov to mid-Dec. **TV**. **Car park**.

This special place, which stands on the outskirts of the old village, is housed in a belvedere that gives a marvellous view of the whole area. The young Dutch owner has entirely restored the house and redecorated it charmingly; 595F for a double with either a sea or, more commonly, mountain view. The lovely dining room is the perfect setting to savour dishes that are full of flavour and prepared with imagination from high-quality produce: chilled mussel soup, *fricassée* of Bresse chicken with citrus fruit, lamb steaks in a herb crust and grilled fish. Lunch menu 120F and others up to 245F.

BEAUSOLEIL   06240 (8KM S)

☗ HÔTEL BOERI**

29 bd. du Général-Leclerc (Centre).
☎ 04.93.78.38.10 ➡ 04.93.41.90.95
TV.

A pretty hotel with geraniums in window boxes, surrounded by palm trees. It's tucked away among the high-rises in the suburbs of Monte Carlo. Very large, air-conditioned, doubles, decorated in a restrained fashion, from 250F with shower/wc and 325F with bath. You can just glimpse the sea from rooms 201, 202, 301 and 302.

⋇ ☗ HÔTEL DIANA**

17 bd. du Général-Leclerc (Centre).
☎ 04.93.78.47.58 ➡ 04.93.41.88.94
TV. **Pay car park**.

This hotel has an amazing Belle Époque façade, and is less expensive than a hotel on the other side of the street – this side is France, the other is Monte Carlo. The view is stunning if you like huge, concrete towers. All rooms are air-conditioned. Doubles 290F with shower and 340F with bath. Good welcome. 10% discount.

MOLINES-EN-QUEYRAS   05350

🎿 🏠 |O| LA MAISON GAUDISSARD**

Gaudissard (North); as you come into town, turn left after the post office, and the hotel is 600m further on.
☎ 04.92.45.83.29 ➡ 04.92.45.80.57
✉ maison-gaudissard@wanadoo.fr
Closed 15 April–15 June and 15 Sept–20 Dec.
Car park.

This establishment has been a tourist centre since 1969 when Bernard Gentil transformed his home into France's first cross-country ski centre. He's constantly introducing new services and facilities. In winter, they offer courses in cross-country skiing and other ski-related activities, including a trek to Queyras. In summer, hiking and paragliding bring the crowds in. After your exertions, you can relax on the terrace high above the village, where you get a wonderful view of the mountains. There's also a sitting room and a Finnish sauna. Doubles with shower 300F, with shower/wc 360F or with bath 380F. Breakfast 38F. The dining room offers a single menu at 95F. Half board starts at 290F per person. *Gîtes* are available for 90F a night. 10% discount on the room rate except during school holidays.

AIGUILLES   05470 (10KM N)

🎿 |O| LA TÊTE DE L'ART

How to get there: take the D5 in the direction of Château-Ville-Vieille, then the D947 to Aiguilles.
☎ 04.92.46.823.49
Closed Sun evening and Mon out of season, a fortnight in April and three weeks in Nov.

This restaurant, run by a Parisian, is right in the middle of the village. The owner worked in the capital for twenty years or so before deciding to leave the rat race and settle here. He collects pigs, and you'll spot model pigs, drawings, photos, oils, ornaments and statuettes all over the place. They serve pizzas, *pierrades* – where you cook your main dish yourself over a hot stone – *fondues* and mixed platters of sausage or cheese. Menus 79F, 89F and 120F, or *à la carte*. It's best to book in high season when they also hold two concerts a month – jazz, rock and so on – though prices stay the same. Free apéritif.

MOUGINS   06250

🎿 🏠 |O| LE MANOIR DE L'ÉTANG***

Les Bois de Fontmerle, route d'Antibes – it's not signposted.
☎ 04.92.28.36.00 ➡ 04.92.28.36.10
Hotel closed Nov–Feb. **Restaurant closed** Mon out of season. **Garden. Swimming pool**.

Jean Cocteau dreamed of turning this magnificent site, on the road from Antibes to Mougins, into a "cinema city". The project fell apart, and the remarkable building was put to different use as a unique hotel. The huge rooms look onto the vast garden and the lazy lake. Doubles 600–900F. You can lounge around on a deckchair by the pool. The restaurant serves sophisticated, delicate cuisine which you can eat indoors or out on the terrace. 150F weekday lunch menu and another at 190F. 10% discount on the room rate Oct, March and April.

|O| RESTO DES ARTS

rue du Maréchal-Foch.
☎ 04.93.75.60.03
Closed Tues lunchtime out of season. **Disabled access**.

An appealing, homey place in a town full of glitzy establishments catering to celebrities and millionaires. Denise prepares traditional, tasty, simple dishes made to recipes handed down from her mother and her mother's mother; there have been six generations of cooks in the family. She goes off every morning looking for the best ingredients, which she uses to prepare dishes such as *daube provençale*, *aïoli* (salt cod with garlic mayonnaise), fish *pot-au-feu*, *stouffi* of lamb with *polenta*, and stuffed baby vegetables. Gregory, lately hairstylist to the stars, now waits at table, having decided to settle in Mougins. He's easy-going and very relaxing. The lunch menu at 65F is a steal and the other one costs only 100F. Friendly, laid-back service.

🎿 |O| LES PINS DE MOUGINS

2308 av. Maréchal Juin, quartier Val de Mougins.
☎ 04.93.45.25.96
Closed Sun evening except July–Aug, and Mon. **Garden**.

You can escape the tourist masses in the centre and spend some quiet time in this attractive restaurant. Fresh, tasty dishes; the 100F menu lists scallop salad with avocado and fresh tomatos, *aïoli* and *crème brûlée*, and there are others at 135F and 160F. The dining room is brightly decorated in yellows and green and there's a terrace in the garden, under the pine trees. Free coffee or *digestif*.

MOUSTIERS-SAINTE-MARIE   04360

🖍 🛖 LE RELAIS

pl. du Couvert.
☎ 04.92.74.66.10 ➡ 04.92.74.60.47
ℓ Le.Relais@wanadoo.fr
Closed Fri out of season and Jan to 20 Feb. **TV**.

On the bank of the stream in the centre of the village, this inn is really popular in summer, when it's best to book. Very pretty rooms 280F with basin, 350 with shower/wc or 480F with bath. If you're a light sleeper, avoid the ones that look out onto the pounding waterfall. The restaurant deserves special mention for its traditional dishes like *foie gras* cooked in a cloth, *millefeuille* of aubergine, local lamb, red mullet *en chartreuse* (braised with cabbage), and trout poached in walnut wine. There are some vegetarian dishes too. *Formule* 90F, menus 140F or around 220F *à la carte*. Slightly curt welcome. 10% discount on the room rate March–June and Nov.

🛖 AUBERGE DE LA FERME ROSE***

chemin Embourgues; it's at the foot of the town.
☎ 04.92.74.69.47 ➡ 04.92.74.60.76
Closed 15 Nov–15 Dec and mid-Jan to end Feb.
Disabled access. **TV**. **Car park**.

This is a little gem, a typical Provençal farmhouse deep in the country. You'd expect a traditional rustic decor, but not a bit of it. The owner, a real fan of the 1950s and 1960s, has decorated the bar and the bedrooms with a jukebox, bistro tables, coatstands, and lots of bric-à-brac dating from that era. Even the kitchen, where they prepare breakfast, contiinues the theme. It could all so easily look a bit tacky, but everything fits in perfectly. The rooms are really quiet and the ones on the ground floor have a pretty terrace. Doubles 480F with shower/wc. An ideal place for a romantic stay. The copious breakfast is a meal in itself.

NICE   06000

SEE MAP OVERLEAF

🛖 HÔTEL DU DANEMARK*

3 av. des Baumettes. **MAP A3-4**
☎ 04.93.44.12.04 ➡ 04.93.44.56.75

Lovely, quiet, ochre house, hidden behind a few pines and pretty trees in the old part of Nice. The area is full of residential blocks of flats but it's conveniently near the Promenade des Anglais and the owners are so nice that you won't mind the unprepossessing aspect. The rooms are simple, tastefully decorated and

clean. Doubles 220F with shower/wc or bath.

🖍 🛖 HÔTEL LOCARNO***

4 av. des Baumettes. **MAP A3-7**
☎ 04.93.96.28.00 ➡ 04.93.86.18.81
TV. **Garage**.

Just minutes from the Promenade des Anglais, this comfortable modern hotel has fifty air-conditioned rooms, some with particularly good facilities. Doubles 280–420F with shower/wc and 380–580F with bath. It's a place executives use when they're in Nice on business. There's a sitting room and snooker room. You have to book space in the garage. Formal but friendly welcome. 10% discount except during the Monaco Grand Prix.

🛖 |●| HÔTEL LES CAMÉLIAS**

3 rue Spitalieri. **MAP C3-5**
☎ 04.93.62.15.54 ➡ 04.93.80.42.96
Closed Nov. **Garden**. **Disabled access**. **Pay car park**.

It's a haven of tranquillity with a little garden full of exotic plants right in the heart of Nice. The regulars all have their own favourite room; 300F with shower/wc and 400F with bath, breakfast included. There's a bar in the foyer for pre-dinner drinks, a TV room and a small selection of books. Half board 250F and the guest's menu costs 70F.

🛖 HÔTEL DE LA BUFFA

56 rue de la Buffa. **MAP B3-14**
☎ 04.93.88.77.35 ➡ 04.93.88.83.39
ℓ buffa.3soleils@informa.fr

A sweet little hotel with simple rooms at modest prices. Doubles 320–400F, all of them air-conditioned. Warm welcome and efficient service. There's virtually a mini-tourist office in reception.

🖍 🛖 HÔTEL AMARYLLIS

3 rue Alsace-Lorraine. **MAP B2-6**
☎ 04.93.88.20.24 ➡ 04.93.87.13/25
Closed 20 Nov–20 Dec and 10–24 Jan. **TV**.

It's hard to tell whether you're in Nice or Manhattan because the decor is just like so many of the simple hotels you find in New York. Fortunately the prices are from this side of the pond – 360F for a double with shower/wc and TV. Some rooms give onto the quiet courtyard. Accommodating, friendly welcome. 10% discount out of season.

🖍 🛖 HÔTEL L'OASIS***

23 rue Gounod. **MAP B3-9**
☎ 04.93.88.12.29 ➡ 04.93.16.14.40
Garden. **TV**. **Car park**.

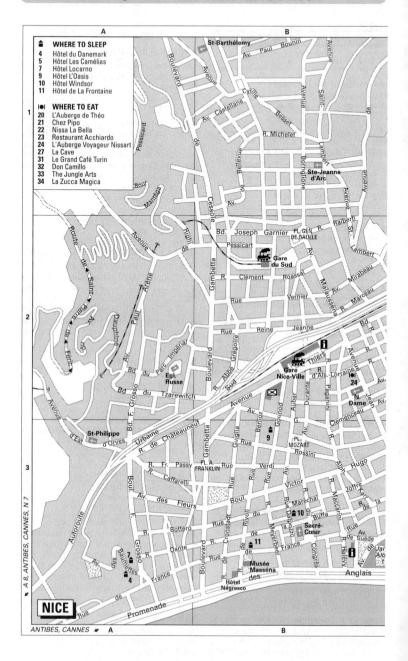

WHERE TO SLEEP
4 Hôtel du Danemark
5 Hôtel Les Camélias
7 Hôtel Locarno
9 Hôtel L'Oasis
10 Hôtel Windsor
11 Hôtel de La Frontaine

WHERE TO EAT
20 L'Auberge de Théo
21 Chez Pipo
22 Nissa La Bella
23 Restaurant Acchiardo
24 L'Auberge Voyageur Nissart
27 La Cave
31 Le Grand Café Turin
32 Don Camillo
33 The Jungle Arts
34 La Zucca Magica

NICE

ANTIBES, CANNES ⬋ A

A 8, ANTIBES, CANNES, N 7

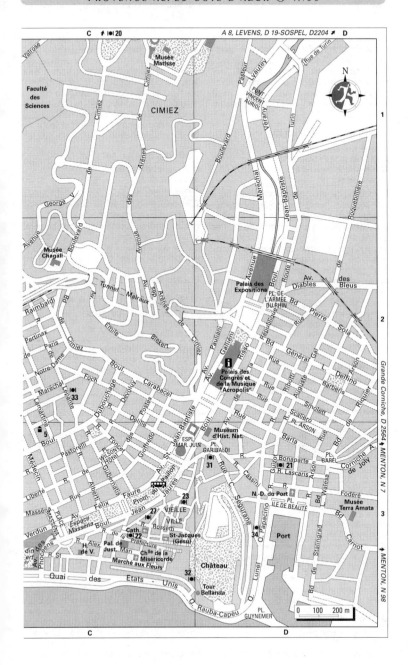

Set back a little, on a road near the Promenade des Anglais, this hotel is in a peaceful, shady garden – a real oasis in the centre of town. Comfortable double rooms 410–470F. This hotel once entertained Chekhov and his compatriot, a certain Vladimir Ilyich Ulianov – more commonly known as Lenin. 10% discount Sept–June.

⅍ ☎ HÔTEL DE LA FONTAINE***

49 rue de France. **MAP B3-11**
☎ 04.93.88.30.38 ➡ 04.93.88.98.11
ℯ hotel-fontaine@webstore.fr
Disabled access. **TV**.

Right in the centre of Nice, a short walk from the sea and the pedestrianised streets. Though it looks unremarkable from the outside, stay here and it's a different story. The good-looking rooms are clean and pleasant, and you can breakfast on the patio accompanied by the rushing noise of the fountain. You'll get a warm welcome from the friendly-owner who does everything to make sure you enjoy your stay. He and his staff are all polite, friendly and totally natural. Double rooms with shower/wc 550–590F; ask for one overlooking the courtyard. Three stars for the buffet breakfast, 50F. Unspecified discount on the room rate.

⅍ ☎ |●| HÔTEL WINDSOR***

11 rue Dalpozzo. **MAP B3-10**
☎ 04.93.88.59.35 ➡ 04.93.88.94.57
ℯ windsor@webstore.fr
Restaurant closed Sun. **Swimming pool**. **TV**. **Car park**.

WIth its marvellous Oriental-looking foyer, its tropical garden planted with brilliantly coloured bougainvillea, palms and bamboos, and its little swimming pool, this place is something special. Guests can use the sauna, Turkish baths and massage rooms, and there's a relaxation room decorated with plants and Thai statuettes. The owners are keen on contemporary art and each room has been decorated by a different artist. Double rooms 550F with shower/wc or 750F with bath. À la carte only in the restaurant – you'll pay about 150F for a good meal that is primarily southern in flavour. Afterwards, listen to the bird-song – some of it real, some of it recorded – and enjoy the art. Free apéritif.

|●| CHEZ PIPO

13 rue Bavastro. **MAP D3-21**
☎ 04.93.55.88.82
Closed lunchtimes, Mon Jan–May, and 15–25 March.

An extraordinary place. You can glimpse the long wooden tables through the door and customers sit side by side. They serve *socca*, a thin, flat cake made from chickpea flour which is a Nice speciality. Those who know say that this place has the best *socca* in town; it's definitely worth trying, as is the *pissaladière* (onion tart), or the sweet Swiss chard pie. You won't spend much more than 50F on a full meal, including a drink.

⅍ |●| THE JUNGLE ARTS

6 rue Lepante. **MAP C2-33**
☎ 04.93.92.00.18
Closed Sun and Aug.

Fashionable world cuisine restaurant offering traditional French food, African dishes, kangaroo steaks, horse-meat hamburgers, spare ribs, or goose breast. Lunch *formule* 65F or evening menu 95F. The funky red and orange decor evokes the savannah, with lots of animal skins in frames, and waitresses dressed as panthers. Free apéritif.

⅍ |●| RESTAURANT VOYAGEUR NISSART

19 rue Alsace-Lorraine. **MAP B2-24**
☎ 04.93.82.19.60
Closed Mon and 1–15 July.

Service 11.30am–2pm and 6.30–10pm. Good regional cuisine served "properly" in a rustic setting. It's almost a curiosity because restaurants like this are vanishing. Menus 67F and 109F and one with well-prepared Nice specialities for 89F. The house specialities are *osso bucco*, wild mushrooms in oil, ravioli, courgette tart, baby vegetables, peppers *à la Provençale*, and *soupe au pistou* (vegetable soup with pesto). Different menus daily. Free apéritif.

⅍ |●| LA ZUCCA MAGICA

4 [bis] quai Papacino.
☎ 04.93.56.25.27
Closed Sun and Mon.

A quirky place run by Marco, the vegetarian cousin of Luciano Pavarotti. When it opened, everything predicted failure. They were proved wrong, however, and today Marco has to turn people away. The dining room is decorated with Halloween pumpkins and illuminated by a small forest of candles. There's no menu, so you eat what you're given – lasagne, red peppers stuffed with pasta, pumpkin and gorgonzola tart and the like. The dining room is so dark that it is sometimes hard to see what's on your plate, but you can depend upon it being tasty and inventive, and all of it is prepared from only the freshest market produce. He uses a lot of chickpeas, lentils and beans, and many seasonings that pay homage to his Roman heritage. 90F at lunchtime and around 130F for dinner. Free coffee.

🕏 |●| L'AUBERGE DE THÉO

52 av. Cap-de-Croix. Off map **C1-20**
☎ 04.93.81.26.19
Closed Mon and 20 Aug–10 Sept.

Service until 11pm. An inn with a delightful patio up in the hills of the Cimiez area. The dishes have a strong Italian/Tuscan influence: fresh pasta with prawns, char-grilled meat or fish, and a good choice of tasty pizzas that hardly fit on the plates. A good place. 95F weekday lunch menu, then others 160F and 250F. Free *digestif*.

|●| RESTAURANT ACCHIARDO

38 rue Droite. **MAP C3-23**
☎ 04.93.85.51.16
Closed Sat evening, Sun, and Aug.

This very popular restaurant caters more for local people than for the tourist trade. It's in the old town, and the surroundings are very informal. The big tables are covered with red oilcloths and the atmosphere is cheery. Dishes of the day are always good – typically tripe *à la Niçoise*, *soupe au pistou* (vegetable soup with basil sauce), *daube*, *ratatouille*, or ravioli with bolognaise sauce, pesto or Gorgonzola. 120–150F *à la carte*. Wine from the barrel. Cash only.

🕏 |●| LA CAVE

rue Francis Gallo. **MAP C3-27**
☎ 04.93.62.48.46.
Closed lunchtimes and Mon.

The decor in the little dining room is chocolate-box cosy, and despite its name, there's no cellar in sight. You can also eat on the little terrace overlooked by old apartment buildings. The young chef turns out flavourful cooking using fresh Provençal produce: red mullet fillets with olive paste, fillet of sea bream with a citrus sauce, fish *pot-au-feu*. He'll finish off the seduction with a chocolate and orange tart, a creamy chocolate pudding or a wonderful lemon tart. Menus 130F and 220F. Free house apéritif.

|●| NISSA LA BELLA

6 rue Sainte-Reparate. **MAP C3-22**
☎ 04.93.62.10.20
Closed Tues, Wed (Wed lunchtime only in season), and a fortnight in June.

This restaurant serves typical dishes from Nice that are full of the intense flavours and aromas of Provence. Portions are so enormous that you'll only need to order one course, whether you choose baked rabbit with polenta, beef stew *provençal*, homemade ravioli, or stuffed baby vegetables. The handsome ochre dining room has a relaxed atmosphere – most of it is open to the street – and there's a second dining room at the back which is cool in summer. You'll leave feeling satisfied and generally well disposed towards the world. Around 130F *à la carte*.

|●| LE GRAND CAFÉ TURIN

5 pl. Garibaldi. **MAP D3-31**
☎ 04.93.62.29.52
Closed June.

Service 8am–10pm out of season, 5pm–11pm July–Aug. This seafood restaurant is an institution in Nice, serving fresh oysters daily, copious platters of oysters, prawns and whelks, and sea urchins in season. The two dining rooms and the terrace are always full but you can simply stop by for a drink if you want. They don't accept cheques but they do accept credit cards. 150–200F *à la carte*.

🕏 |●| DON CAMILLO

5 rue des Ponchettes. **MAP C3-32**
☎ 04.93.85.67.95
Closed Sun and Mon lunchtime.

In an attempt to steer clear of the crowds while remaining central, Stéphane Viano chose a quiet spot between the cours Saleya and the seafront to open his restaurant. The large dining room is attractively decorated in light colours, and the food is very high quality: risotto with courgette flowers, roast sea bream with anchovy *jus* and lemon zest, escalope of *foie gras* with sweet and sour summer fruits and onion conserve. The desserts are prepared by a talented pastry chef. *Menu du marché* 185F, or 250F *à la carte*. The professional service is very affable. Free house apéritif.

VILLEFRANCHE-SUR-MER   06230 (7KM E)

🕏 🏠 |●| HÔTEL RESTAURANT LE PROVENÇAL**

4 av. du Maréchal-Joffre.
☎ 04.93.76/53/53 ➡ 04.93.76.96.00
Closed 1 Nov–23 Dec. **Garden.**

A pretty house with blue shutters and three towers. The rooms are clean and pleasant, particularly those on the second and third floors, which have views of the garden and the sea. Doubles 380–590F with shower or bath – all are air-conditioned. They're very popular, so you need to book well in advance. There's a delightful patio for breakfast or dinner – the delicious food includes fish soup, ravioli with pesto, stew of dried cod *en stoffi-cada* (with garlic, tomatoes, potatoes and olives), and rabbit *provençal* flambéed in *marc de Bandol*. Menus 112–125F. 10% discount on the room rate Sept–June.

⅔ |●| RESTAURANT MICHEL'S

pl. Amélie-Pollonnais; it's on the port.
☎ 04.93.76.73.24
Closed Tues.

This is the "in" place at the moment, and the atmosphere's pretty laid-back. The large terrace comes into its own on summer evenings. There are no set menus, but the *à la carte* menu is full of wonderful dishes – fish and seafood, mostly, prepared with seasonal produce. There's a salmon *chausson*, *terrine* of starling with juniper berries, monkfish and scampi kebab with a sweet and sour sauce, veal chop with apple and Calvados purée, and strawberry cheesecake with egg custard. About 160F *à la carte*; dishes of the day 78F. Friendly attentive service. Free apéritif.

⅔ |●| LA MÈRE GERMAINE

quai Courbet (South); it's on the port.
☎ 04.93.01.71.39

This restaurant is in a perfect situation on the port and is undoubtedly one of the best places between Nice and Monaco. It has a magnificent view of Villefranche's natural harbour, a lovely dining room, and a terrace. There's an army of smart waiters. Dishes are prepared using only the freshest ingredients and the fish and seafood are brilliantly fresh: *escabèche* of sardines and fillets of sole cooked to perfection. Like everything else, the desserts are prepared in-house. Menu 225F. *À la carte*, prices climb steeply – expect to pay 300–400F. Free coffee.

ORANGE   84100

⅔ 🏠 HÔTEL LE GLACIER**

46 cours Aristide-Briand (Centre).
☎ 04.90.34.02.01 ➡ 04.90.51.13.80
Closed Sun Nov to Easter, and 23 Dec–1 Feb. **TV. Car park. Lock-up garage.**

This very comfortable hotel has been well run by three generations of the Cunha family. All the rooms are decorated differently; some in Provençal style while others look more English. Doubles with shower/wc 285F, or 340F with bath. There's a charming breakfast room. Musicians performing in the festival often stay here. 10% discount Sept–June.

⅔ 🏠 HÔTEL ARÈNE***

pl. de Langes (Centre); it's near the town hall.
☎ 04.90.11.40.40 ➡ 04.90.11.40.45
Closed 8–30 Nov. **TV. Pay garage.**

A quiet, delightful hotel in the pedestrianised area. The air-conditioned rooms are decorated in a pretty, typically Provençal style. A few of them have a terrace, where you can eat breakfast (49F, with Provençal pastries and home-made jam). Doubles 440–600F with shower/wc or bath. It really is a pity there's no restaurant. 10% discount Nov–March.

⅔ |●| RESTAURANT LE YACA

24 pl. Silvain (Centre).
☎ 04.90.34.70.03
Closed Tues evening except in summer, and Wed.

The exposed beams and stonework create an intimate and pleasant setting, and there are pretty pictures on the walls and fresh flowers on the tables. The classic dishes are thoughtfully prepared: seafood stew, home-made chicken liver *terrine* with onion marmalade, gratinéed leg of lamb with olive purée, and *fillet mignon* with shallots. Menus 70–130F. Free coffee.

|●| RESTAURANT LA ROSELIÈRE

4 rue du Renoyer (Centre); to the right of the town hall.
☎ 04.90.34.50.42
Closed Wed and Nov.

The decor is a mish-mash of enamel advertising signs from the 1950s and 1960s, cartoon characters, teddy bears and bits and pieces picked up in second-hand shops. If the weather's not good enough to eat outside, come inside and listen to the music, which ranges from Jacques Brel to Mahler. The sole menu, 110F, gives you a choice of four starters, four main courses, and a few desserts. The banana tart is out of this world. Fred changes the menu each week depending on the seasonal produce that's freshest in the market; choices may include pig's trotters, herrings in oil, or veal kidneys *à la Provençale*. The cellar is full of good inexpensive wines. Credit cards are not accepted.

PIOLENC   84420 (4KM N)

🛏 🍽 AUBERGE L'ORANGERIE

4 rue de l'Ormeau; take the N7.
☎ 04.90.29.59.88 ➡ 04.90.29.67.74
✉ orangerie@orangerie.net
Closed Mon out of season and ten days in Nov.
Disabled access. TV. Car park.

A beautiful inn surrounded by trees. After working in various hotels around the world, Gérard
and his wife decided to set up their own place,
and have been here now for more than ten
years. The six cosy rooms with rustic-style furniture go for 380–400F with shower/wc or bath.
The one with a secluded private terrace is particularly lovely. The whole house is decorated
with copies of masters painted by Gérard himself. In the restaurant you'll find a lunch menu at
100F then 150F and 200F – stuffed crab,
colombo of fish, thin slices of kangaroo meat
with ginger and orange, and some good traditional Provençal dishes, too. Gérard's cellar,
which has more than 350 different vintages, is
unbelievable, as is his selection of whiskies.
Half board, compulsory Easter to 30 Sept, is
340–430F. Free coffee.

PEILLE   06440

🛏 🍽 BELVÉDÈRE HÔTEL

3 pl. Jean-Miol.
☎ 04.93.79.90.45
Closed Mon, and 20 Nov–25 Dec.

You have to book in writing to get a room at
this hotel. The very friendly Mme Beau-
seigneur has five clean, simple rooms that
each have a splendid view of the mountain.
Doubles 250F with washing facilities, half
board 250F per person. You get a bird's eye
view of the valley from the very good restaurant, offering appealing menus 100–170F.
Specialities include lemon chicken, gnocchi
and ravioli stuffed with ricotta cheese. Free
cherries steeped in brandy for dessert.

🛏 🍽 L'AUBERGE DE LA MADONE

☎ 04.93.79.91.17 ➡ 04.93.49.99.36
✉ cmillo@clubinternet.fr
Closed Wed, 3–21 Jan and 20 Oct–20 Dec.

The Millo family have run this typically
Provençal place for fifty years. The comfortable double rooms have been freshly refurbished – all with balconies and magical views
over the Peillon valley – and cost 480–960F.
The terrace is attractively decorated with
flowers and you dine under olive or mimosa

trees. Half board 580–880F. Weekday lunch
menu 150F, then 220–260F. They serve traditional, intensely flavoured dishes with a
touch of genius – try the suckling lamb with
potatoes and olive purée. Free coffee.

PELVOUX   05340

🛏 🍽 LE SAINT-ANTOINE**

How to get there: on the Briançon–Embrun road, turn off
onto the D994 into the Vallouise valley and it's 11km on.
☎ 04.92.23.36.99 ➡ 04.92.23.45.20
✉ hotel.st.antoine@wanadoo.fr
Closed Sun evening, 1 May–5 June and 30 Sept–1 Dec.

The valley is still wild and it's on the edge of
the Écrins national park. The hotel is a reliable, efficiently run establishment with a
friendly atmosphere. The rooms are simple
and clean and some have balconies overlooking the stream. Doubles with basin
180–220, 220–270 with shower/wc. Honest,
tasty traditional dishes – including Savoy
favourites like *fondue*. Menus 85–140F. Free
coffee and 10% discount on the room rate if
you stay at least ten days.

PLAN-DE-LA-TOUR   83120

🛏 MAS DES BRUGASSIÈRES**

☎ 04.94.55.50.55 ➡ 04.94.55.50.51
Closed 10 Oct–20 March.
Swimming pool. TV. Car park.

A charming hotel in a pleasant village at the
heart of the Massif des Maures, just 5km from
the sea and 12km from Saint-Tropez. It's run
by a couple of travellers who have decorated
the place with oddments that they've picked
up on their travels. Relaxing welcome, rooms
(450–560F), and swimming pool. They do a
special pool-side breakfast, served from 10am
to 1pm. Easy-going welcome and ambience.
Free apéritif, and if you stay more than three
nights, you get two breakfasts free.

PONTEVÈS   83670

🛏 🍽 LE ROUGE GORGE**

Quartier les Costs; take the D560 2km east of Barjols,
go over the bridge and drive up the hill to the village.
☎ 04.94.77.03.97 ➡ 04.94.77.22.17
Closed Dec–March. **Swimming pool. TV. Car park.**

Lively inn in a village that is typical of many in
the Var between the Gorges du Verdon and
the Côte. The welcome is as warm as the climate. In the evening, you dine by the pool on

good local dishes like soup with beans, stuffed vegetables, *aiguillettes* of lamb with rosemary, *daube* of beef *à la Provençale* and salmon marinated with herbs and olive oil. Menus 100–145F. Comfortable, unpretentious rooms with shower/wc or bath, 300–340F. Dozens of walks to do in the sweet-smelling countryside. Free apéritif.

RISTOLAS   05460

⅍ 🏠 |●| LE CHALET DE SÉGURE**

How to get there: take the road that goes up behind the church, then follow the signposts.
☎ 04.92.46.71.30 ➡ 04.92.46.79.54
Closed Mon, 10 April–25 May and 20 Sept– 20 Dec. **Car park**.

This chalet, in the tree-covered mountains of Haut Queyras, is the ideal place to recharge your batteries. The owner, Jean-Marie, organises outings in snow-shoes in winter and up tracks into the wilds of the mountains in summer. His hobby is carpentry and he's made a lot of the furniture for the hotel. Pascale, his wife, likes to embroider samplers and she has hung many of them on the walls. In the dining room a mannequin will greet you wearing traditional costume in winter or a turn-of-the-century school uniform in summer. Menus 75–125F. Specialities include duck breast with honey and spices and apples with caramel. Bright double rooms 270F, half board 285F per person. 10% discount on the room rate July–Aug.

ROUSSILLON   84220

⅍ |●| RESTAURANT MINCKA'S

pl. de la Mairie (Centre).
☎ 04.90.05.66.22
Closed Thurs except May, July–Aug, and 2 Nov to end Feb.

Very prettily decorated little restaurant in a mountainous region of rich, rust-red rock. The good menus, 90F and 105F, offer a selection of imaginative dishes with powerful flavours: beef *daube* with cardomom, pork stew with fresh ginger and honey, and couscous. Service is easy-going – sometimes too much so. It's best to book. Free apéritif.

SAINT-DALMAS-DE-TENDE   06430

⅍ 🏠 |●| LE TERMINUS**

rue des Martyrs-de-la-Résistance; it's opposite the station.

☎ 04.93.04.96.96 ➡ 04.93.04.96.97
Closed 24 Oct to mid-Nov. **Garden**. **Car park**.

The friendly welcome makes you immediately feel at ease in this old family home. The nights are cool and restful in the mountains, and it will probably be the birds that wake you. Very pretty, simple double rooms 248–314F. There's a pleasant garden at the front and an attractive dining room with a fireplace and a wood-fired oven. Menus, 95–170F, list dishes all prepared on the spot by the *patronne* – her ravioli is unforgettable. Half board 255F. Free house apéritif.

|●| LA CASSOLETTE

20 rue du Général-de-Gaulle; it's on the riverbank.
☎ 04.93.04.63.82
Closed Sun evening and Mon except public holidays, and March.

This tiny, pretty, family-run restaurant serves good home cooking. If they run out of things, the boss will go next door to the butcher to fetch an extra *tournedos* or duck breast. Wholesome leek, potato and courgette tart, rabbit *à la provençale*, ravioli, and grilled duck breast with *foie gras*. Dish of the day 55F, menus 80–160F.

SAINT-DISDIER   05250

⅍ 🏠 |●| AUBERGE LA NEYRETTE**

How to get there: it's where the Saint-Étienne-en-Dévoluy road crosses the road to Veynes.
☎ 04.92.58.81.17 ➡ 04.92.58.89.95
🄴 lameyrette@devoluy.com
Closed 15 Nov–15 Dec. **TV**. **Car park**.

Impeccable rooms in an old water mill standing in solitary splendour at the bottom of a little valley. There are only twelve rooms, which fill quickly; it's best to book. Doubles with shower/wc or bath 345F. The restaurant is very good, offering trout fished in the lake nearby, house *terrine* or *tourtons* (which are something like pancakes). Menus 98–189F or 160F *à la carte*. Free apéritif.

SAINT-FIRMIN   05700

⅍ 🏠 |●| HÔTEL-RESTAURANT LE VAL DES SOURCES**

Saint-Maurice-en-Valgaudemar; before Le Roux, turn right over the bridge then right again; it's on the left 300m on.
☎ 04.92.55.23.75 ➡ 04.92.55.23.75
🄴 le.val.des.sources@wanadoo.fr

Comfortable hotel located in a wild, austere valley. Claude and his wife took it over from the family but have improved the facilities in the rooms which are simple but have good beds. Doubles 180F with basin, 240F with shower, and 300F with shower/wc. The tasty food is nourishing and many of the dishes are local specialities: *oreilles d'âne* (a pastry case made in the shape of donkey's ears, filled with spinach and chard), ravioli with honey, and *flozon* (potato tart with smoked bacon and shallots). Menus 75–150F – it's best to book a table. In summer, half board, which costs 220–300F, is compulsory. There are *gîtes* in the grounds. Free apéritif.

CHAUFFAYER   05800 (4KM S)

🛏 |●| LE BERCAIL**

It's on the N85, the route de Napoléon, on the right on the road to Gap.
☎ 04.92.55.22.21 ➡ 04.92.55.31.55
Closed Sun evening.

The hotel-restaurant offers good value for money, with prettily decorated, comfortable rooms – doubles with basin 170F, with shower/wc or bath 200–250F. The large dining room has a lovely feel and there's a shaded terrace for summer meals. The cuisine is regional and classic; with menus 80–200F. *Noisette* of lamb, trout *meunière* and raviolis are the specialities.

🍴🛏 |●| LE CHÂTEAU DES HERBEYS***

It's on the N85, the route de Napoléon.
☎ 04.92.55.26.83
Closed Tues except in school holidays, and Nov–March.
Garden. Swimming pool. TV. Car park.

Looking down on the route Napoleon took on his return from Elba from its vantage point on a hill, stands a noble and beautiful old house surrounded by substantial grounds. The rooms are high-ceilinged – some have coffered ceilings – and luxurious, with herring bone parquet floors, plush and tasteful fabrics and curtains, and splendid bathrooms. The "Roy" room is a truly royal suite with a canopied bed, TV sitting room and a Jacuzzi. It's also the most expensive. Doubles with bath 450–700F, breakfast 50–55F. In the park there is a tennis court and a swimming pool. The restaurant (not tested) offers *foie gras* and goose. Menus 125–230F. Free coffee or *digestif*.

SAINT-JEAN-CAP-FERRAT   06230

🍴🛏 HÔTEL LE CLAIR LOGIS**

12 av. Centrale (Centre); it's in the centre of the peninsula, on the corner of allée des Brises.

☎ 04.93.76.04.57 ➡ 04.93.76.11.85
Disabled access. Garden. TV. Car park.

In a quiet residential area, this haven of peace and tranquillity has an exotic garden. All eighteen rooms have a balcony or a little terrace. General de Gaulle came here to relax back in 1952. The prices are quite high, but reasonable for a peninsula which is a millionaires' haunt. Doubles 450F with shower/wc, 650F with bath in peak season. It's a good hotel, ideal for a romantic weekend on the Côte d'Azur. 10% discount Oct–May.

|●| LE SLOOP

It's on the new harbour.
☎ 04.93.01.48.63
Closed Tues evening and Wed out of season, Tues and Wed lunchtimes in season, and 15 Nov–15 Dec.

This is by far the nicest of a whole string of fancy restaurants by the harbour. You'll receive a warm welcome. The chef, who used to work in a top restaurant, produces sophisticated cooking – the single menu, 160F, offers good choices and excellent value. Try fresh salmon *tartare* and *aïoli*, minestrone with saffron and fresh thyme, grilled sea bream, whole roast sea bass *à la Niçoise*, and veal chop studded with truffles and served with its own juices. There's a pleasant terrace facing the harbour.

SAINT-MARTIN-VÉSUBIE   06450

🍴🛏 |●| HÔTEL-RESTAURANT LA BONNE AUBERGE**

allée de Verdun; turn left as you leave Saint-Martin and head for Colmiane and Boreon.
☎ 04.93.03.20.49 ➡ 04.93.03.20.69
Closed mid-Nov to mid-Feb. **TV.**

This beautiful stone hotel is comfortable and well run. Well-maintained doubles go for 270F with shower/wc and 300F with bath. Try to avoid the ones that look out onto the avenue, which gets particularly busy at the weekend. Menus, 98F and 150F, list traditional, delicious food: *terrine* of grouper *confit*, trout *meunière*, lamb stew, duckling with olives, quail casserole and so on. Pleasant terrace, surrounded by a hedge. Half board 280F. Free house apéritif.

SAINT-PAUL-DE-VENCE   06570

🛏 AUBERGE LE HAMEAU***

528 route de la Colle; 1km from the village on the D7.
☎ 04.93.32.80.24 ➡ 04.93.32.55.75
Closed 6 Jan–16 Feb and 16 Nov–22 Dec. **Garden. Swimming pool. Car park.**

Set in the deep countryside, this place has a superb view of the village of Saint-Paul. There's a pleasant terraced garden and a swimming pool. Comfortable air-conditioned rooms with nice furniture go for 580–830F. Ask for a room in the main building rather than the annexe, which has less character.

SAINT-RÉMY-DE-PROVENCE   13210

♠ I●I HÔTEL VILLE VERTE**

pl. de la République (Centre).
☎ 04.90.92.06.14 ➡ 04.90.92.56.54
Restaurant closed Jan. **Disabled access.**
Swimming pool. TV. Car park.

It is claimed that Charles Gounod, the composer of *Faust*, wrote the opera *Mireille* in this hotel. It is just minutes from the centre and has prices to suit everybody. Doubles with shower 220F, 280F with bath – some have balconies. They also have studios with kitchenette for two people, rented by the week. There's a swimming pool, courtyard and pleasant terraces. The restaurant, which dates from the 17th century, is popular with families. Menus at 80F and 100F.

🏃 ♠ I●I LE CHALET FLEURI**

15 av. Frédéric-Mistral, route de Maillane.
☎ 04.90.92.03.62 ➡ 04.90.92.60.28
Closed end Nov to early March. **Garden. Car park.**

An old-style family guesthouse with a little garden where you can take a pre-prandial stroll among the bays, laurels, and topiaried peacocks. Good, wholesome family cooking; rabbit with olive paste or cuttlefish with parsley follow a traditional soup. Half board 600F. The rooms, 250–290F for a double, are practical and stuffed with ornaments. You can look out of the window and check on your car at the end of the garden. It's wonderfully quiet. In the morning over breakfast, you can chat to the owner about the bull races.

🏃 ♠ LE CHEVAL BLANC**

6 av. Fauconnet (Centre).
☎ 04.90.92.09.28 ➡ 04.90.92.69.05
Closed Nov–May. **Disabled access. TV. Pay car park.**

Refurbished rooms with shower/wc or bath and direct-dial telephone for 280–310F. There's a lovely terrace and a veranda. The private car park is a considerable asset in the centre of Saint-Rémy, but there's a charge of 30F for a space. 10% discount for a minimum three-night stay.

♠ HÔTEL L'AMANDIÈRE**

av. Théodore Aubanel; it's 700m from the town centre, in the direction of Noves.
☎ 04.90.92.41.00 ➡ 04.90.92.48.38
Closed Jan to mid-March and 30 Oct–15 Dec.
Disabled access. Swimming pool. TV. Car park.

A young, vibrant hotel just outside Saint-Rémy where it's quiet and green. Comfortable, spacious rooms 300F with shower/wc and 330F with bath. With its wonderful breakfast and warm welcome, this place is one of the best of its type.

♠ HÔTEL DU SOLEIL**

35 av. Pasteur (South).
☎ 04.90.92.00.63 ➡ 04.90.92.61.07
Closed 5 Nov–20 March. **Swimming pool. Garden.**
TV. Garage. Lock-up car park.

The hotel is set around a large courtyard with space enough for cars to park. It also has a swimming pool, terrace and garden. All rooms have TV. Doubles 305–395F with shower/wc or bath – the ones with bath are bigger. There's a garage for bikes, motorbikes and a lock-up for the cars.

♠ L'HÔTEL DES ATELIERS DE L'IMAGE***

traverse de Borry, 5 av. Pasteur (Centre).
☎ 04.90.92.51.50 ➡ 04.90.92.43.52.
Disabled access. TV. Car park.

Located in the old Saint-Rémy music hall, this place has sixteen rooms for 660F with shower/wc and 750F with bath. They're all decorated in a contemporary fashion, with stylish photos all over the walls. Photography is *the* topic of conversation in the bar and they hold conventions on the subject. Though it's right in the heart of the old town, this is a remarkably relaxing place. They offer a reduced rate for a long stay in winter. Breakfast 70F.

I●I RESTAURANT LA GOUSSE D'AIL

25 rue Carnot (Centre).
☎ 04.90.92.16.87
Closed winter.

Service until 11pm. Intimate atmosphere and food that offers value for money. Lunch menu 90F, others 175–215F, with different dishes each day. House specialities include *pavé* of beef with creamy garlic sauce, snails *à la Provençale* and a few vegetarian dishes. Tuesday is *bouillabaisse* day and on Friday it's *aïoli*. Great wine list. Jazz on Thursdays.

I●I L'ORANGERIE CHABERT

16 bd. Victor-Hugo.
☎ 04.90.92.05.95

Closed Sun evening and Mon out of season, Mon and Tues lunchtimes July–Aug, three weeks in Nov and three weeks in March. **Garden**.

The clientele here includes some of the great and good, the odd general's widow and well-to-do wine-growers. You can dine in the sizeable garden. There's a classy but relaxed atmosphere but there's nothing slap-dash about the cuisine. Even the short menu is balanced and perfectly prepared: *marbré* of *brousse* cheese in olive oil, goujons of whiting with green apples and a calorie-free, diet dessert. Menus 114F, 162F and 218F.

|●| LA MAISON JAUNE

15 rue Carnot (Centre).
☎ 04.90.92.56.14
Closed Mon, Sun evening in winter, Tues lunchtime in summer, and Jan–Feb.

Stylish place where you'll be served imaginative dishes at realistic prices. There's a light weekday lunch menu for 120F (not on public holidays), and gourmet menus 175–295F. House specialities include stuffed artichokes, roast fillet of lamb with olive paste, roast pigeon in Baux wine and hot walnut tart. There's a superb terrace.

|●| XA

24 bd. Mirabeau (Centre).
☎ 04.90.92.41.23
Closed Wed and Oct–March.

This place is like a prettily decorated flat with its bistro chairs, mirrors and spotlights, and its appealing terrace. *Menu-carte* 140F, or *à la carte* starters cost 60F, main courses 85F and desserts 35F. The food is good and imaginative – *parfait* of aubergine, grilled sardines *à la Sicilienne* (served with pasta, cheese and pistachios), *mousseline* of scorpion fish, and *pannacotta* for dessert. They must be doing something right – they've been going more than fifteen years.

|●| LA SOURCE

13 av. de la Libération.
☎ 04.90.92.44.71
Closed Wed and Jan.

A serene, quiet place – just like the couple who run it. It's best to book if you want a table on the terrace by the garden. Monsieur produces tasty, traditional Provençal dishes; red mullet fillets with a black olive *coulis* or *noisette* of lamb stuffed with truffles. Menus 160F and 230F. There's a tempting swimming pool, but you're not allowed in it.

GRAVESON   13690 (9KM NW)

≜ LE CADRAN SOLAIRE

It's in the village.
☎ 04.90.95.71.79 ➡ 04.90.90.55.04
Garden.

An enchanting old post house in a quiet place that's been converted into a beguiling little hotel. The rooms are comfortable and painted in contemporary colours. Doubles 310–330F. There's a shady garden and a terrace where you can have a snack. Breakfast is served until noon.

≜ |●| HÔTEL DU MOULIN D'AURE**

quartier Cassoulen; it's just outside the village on the Tarascon road.
☎ 04.90.95.84.05 ➡ 04.90.95.73.84
✉ hotel.moulin.d.aure@wanadoo.fr
Swimming pool. Car park.

A little haven surrounded by vast grounds with pines and olive trees. The cicadas sing, the swimming pool awaits, and the proprietress has a friendly smile. Pleasant rooms with bath 320–450F. Nice, lazy atmosphere; in summer you can eat the Provençal or Italian dishes they serve by the pool if you really can't be bothered moving. Menu for 130F. Ideal for families.

≜ |●| LE MAS DES AMANDIERS**

route d'Avignon.
☎ 04.90.95.81.76
Closed lunchtimes, and 15 Oct–15 March.
Disabled access. Swimming pool. TV. Car park.

In spite of the rather unappealing surroundings this hotel gets booked up in summer. It offers attractive, reasonably priced rooms for 330–340F with bath, and a little restaurant where you can have dinner – menus 95F and 145F. Out of season, when they have more time, the owners might take you to market with them or to visit the perfume museum. They know how to look after their guests.

SAINT-TROPEZ   83990

≜ LOU CAGNARD**

18 av. Paul-Roussel (North); it's on the edge of town.
☎ 04.94.97.04.24 ➡ 04.94.97.09.44
Closed 2 Nov–27 Dec. **Garden. TV. Car park**.

A large, typically Provençal house with nicely renovated rooms for 280–310F with shower/wc and 340–550F with bath. Pleasant terrace and flower garden. If you want a good night's sleep on summer nights you should reserve a room that looks onto the garden.

为 🏠 HÔTEL LOU TROUPELEN***

Chemin des Vendanges (Centre).
☎ 04.94.97.44 88 ➡ 04.94.97.41.76
TV. **Car park**.

This place doesn't pretend to be the most fashionable hotel in town but it has a lovely family atmosphere and the prices are good value for St-Tropez. Doubles 430–550F with shower/wc or bath. The free car park is a great advantage, and you're just 400m from the centre of the village and five minutes' drive from the beaches. There's no restaurant and the ones in the village are hugely expensive, so if you're on a budget, make the most of the breakfast that's served outside under the trees. 10% discount 20 April–20 May and 20 Sept–14 Oct.

为 ❘●❘ CANTINA EL MEXICANO

16 rue des Remparts (Centre); go up rue de la Mairie, under the gateway and it's 100m further, on the right.
☎ 04.94.97.40.96
Closed lunchtimes

One of the few fashionable places in St-Tropez where the prices won't send a shiver down your spine. Out front there's a little mosaic-lined pond, a statue of the Virgin and a variety of kitsch models. They serve real Mexican dishes: tacos, quesadillas, tortillas, and fantastic margaritas. It's delicious, generously served and the place has real atmosphere. Lots of local people come here regularly. You'll pay about 160F. Free *digestif*.

为 ❘●❘ CHEZ FUCHS

7 rue des Commerçants (Centre); it's near the port.
☎ 04.94.97.01.25
Closed lunchtimes in season, Tues out of season and Nov. **Car park**.

Summer evenings are very busy, but out of season you'll find no-one but locals in the dining room upstairs. Lovely artichokes *barigoules* (filled with diced mushrooms and bacon), stuffed vegetables or squid à *la provençale*, and a good range of local wines. 200–250F for a meal. Authentic cuisine in a genuine setting. Free coffee.

SAINT-VALLIER-DE-THIEY   06460

为 🏠 ❘●❘ HOSTELLERIE LE PRÉJOLY**

route Napoléon, pl. Rouguière (Centre); coming from Grasse it's at the beginning of the village on the right.
☎ 04.93.42.60.86 ➡ 04.93.42.67.80

Closed Sun evening and Mon except July–Aug, and Dec–Jan. **Disabled access. Garden. TV**.

A chic establishment with reasonable prices. The charming hotel is set in a large, quiet garden, and it has a sauna and solarium. Most of the rooms have a terrace; doubles 250–350F with shower/wc or bath. The restaurant is the real draw; weekday menu 100F, or 195F, listing scampi omelette, pan-fried scallops with crayfish butter, honeyed breast of duck, rib steak with a truffle-scented *jus*, rabbit stew, mutton tripe and sheep's trotters à *la Provençale*, calf's tongue, and so on. Good, classical cuisine which sets greater store in quality ingredients than in originality. Half board compulsory in summer, 340–380F. Free apéritif.

SAINT-VÉRAN   05350

为 🏠 ❘●❘ AUBERGE-GÎTE D'ÉTAPE LE MONCHU

La Chalp-Sainte-Agathe.
☎ 04.92.45.83.96 ➡ 04.92.45.80.09
📧 info@lemonchu.fr
Closed 15 April–15 June and 15 Sept–20 Dec. **Car park**.

In the highest village in France, at an altitude of 2040m, Nathalie and Philippe Babinet have converted their big farmhouse into a welcoming *gîte* with the comforts of a more than decent hotel. The cooking is traditional, and meals are served in a very handsome dining room with a vaulted ceiling. Specialities include *fondue*, *tartiflette*, and *raclette* (which you have to order in advance). Menu 95F or 125F à *la carte*. All the rooms are very bright and comfortable; half board, 180–300F, is compulsory. Facilities include sauna, billiard room and table tennis. 10% discount Jan, June and Sept.

为 🏠 ❘●❘ LES CHALETS DU VILLARD***

Quartier Le Villard.
☎ 04.92.45.82.08 ➡ 04.92.45.86.22
📧 info@leschaletsduvillard.fr
Closed Tues lunchtime, 20 April–20 June and 20 Sept–20 Dec. **TV**.

Exceptional place with super-comfortable, spacious studios and two-roomed apartments that all have a balcony and look full south onto the valley. Each has a music centre, dishwasher and luxury bathroom, and some have whirlpool baths. There are even some studios adapted for people with allergies. Doubles 240F, and 370–640F according to facilities and season. Half board is

130F extra per person, per day. You dine in the restaurant-grill *La Gratinée* on the ground floor; menus 95–140F. 10% discount on the room rate Jan and June.

🎿|●| LA MAISON D'ÉLISA

Le Raux; it's in lower Saint-Véran.
☎ 04.92.45.82.48
Closed April–May, and 15 Sept– 20 Dec.

The dining room here is built from larch wood, with substantial beams, panelled walls and wooden floors. There's also a terrace with a view over the valley and, in the distance, the majestic peak of Roche Brune. Marie is an excellent cook, and her spicy *fricassée* of veal with courgettes and potatoes is astonishingly good. It's sometimes listed on the *menu du randonneur*, which is served at lunchtime and costs 80F. Very good home-made desserts, cakes and tarts. Other menus 100F, 150F and 200F or about 150F *à la carte*. It's best to book, because the dining room is small and the place has a loyal local following. Free house apéritif.

SAINTE-MAXIME   83120

🎿 🏠 |●| L'ENSOLLEILLÉE**

29 av. Jean-Jaurès (Centre); it's on the corner of rue F-Martin, 50m from the beach.
☎ 04.94.96.02.27
Closed Oct–April. **TV. Car park**.

Lovely welcome and decor in this old-fashioned hotel – you'll be treated with genuine kindness here, and the rooms are simple, comfortable and clean. Rooms 250–290F with shower or 300–350F with shower/wc. Half board, compulsory July–Aug, costs 260–340F. The restaurant is full of surprises. Menus 99–138F. 10% discount on the room rate April–15 June and after 15 Sept except Easter, Whitsun and Ascension. Free coffee.

|●| HÔTEL-RESTAURANT-MONTFLEURI

3 av. Montfleuri (Northeast).
☎ 04.94.96.18.26
📧 montfleuri.ste.maxime@wanadoo.fr
Swimming pool.

You imagine from the outside that this is a classic, deeply traditional seaside hotel. Inside, it's full of energy, driven by a young couple who create a terrific atmosphere. They're thorough professionals who are super-confident, and therefore relaxed, about what they do. All the rooms are different, all are equally pleasant. Doubles with

shower/wc or bath, 250–950F, depending on season and facilities. Good, family cooking served at tables set out around a Hollywood-esque swimming pool.

🎿|●| AUBERGE SANS SOUCI

34 rue Paul-Bert (Centre).
☎ 04.94.96.18.26
Closed Mon out of season and 30 Oct–14 Feb.

This inn is a great place to eat – the food is typical of Provence, simple, tasty, and full of the flavours of the *garrigue*, the local heathland. In summer you can dine on the pleasant terrace in the town's "gourmet" street or, if there's a nip in the air, in the cosy dining room. The menus, 98F and 140F, feature sautéed veal *Provençal*, tripe *à la Niçoise* with white wine, marinated sardine fillets, red mullet glazed with saffron with a fennel and lemon sauce, and *mérou* (a somewhat tasteless Mediterranean fish) fillet with vermouth sauce. Free apéritif.

|●| RESTAURANT LA MAISON BLEUE

24 [bis] rue Paul-Bert (Centre); it's in the pedestrianised area on the seafront.
☎ 04.94.96.51.92 📧 maisonbl@aol.com
Closed Tues in Oct, 3 Jan–24 March, 4 Nov–28 Dec.

A little house decorated in blue, ochre and yellow. The decoration has been very tastefully done in a sort of Provençal "Thousand and One Nights" style. The terrace, with its comfortable bench seats, is a lovely spot for a good meal: fresh fish soup, ravioli with a sardine filling, stuffed mussels, sea bream with fennel *en papillote*. Menus 99F and 140F. This is a very good place, but the service could be more attentive.

ISSAMBRES (LES)   83389 (4KM NE)

🎿 🏠 |●| LE PROVENÇAL***

How to get there; take the N98 towards Saint-Raphaël.
☎ 04.94.96.90.49 📠 04.94.49.62.48
📧 info@hotel.le.provencal.com
Closed Tues lunchtime,weekday lunchtimes 8 July–19 Aug except for public holidays, 6 Jan–6 Feb, and 1 Nov–21 Dec. **TV**.

A dream of a place for an old-fashioned holiday, this charming hotel has a view over the gulf of Saint-Tropez and the beach. They're all smiles when you arrive and their cooking is superb. *Menu-cartes* 148F or 230F, or if you wish you can order a simple grilled fish with no hassle. Rooms cost 341–610F. There's a pretty terrace and a lovely beach with fine sand. Free apéritif.

SAINTES-MARIES-DE-LA-MER 13460

⌂ HÔTEL MÉDITÉRRANÉE

4 rue Frédéric-Mistral; it's in the middle of town near the arena.
☎ 04.90.97.82.09 ➡ 04.90.97.76.31

A tiny little hotel that's as clean as you like and well run. There are flowers and plants everywhere. Doubles 230–280F – three of them overlook the little courtyard.

⌂ |●| MAS DES SALICORNES**

rue d'Arles; at the beginning of the village on the D570.
☎ 04.90.97.83.41 ➡ 04.90.97.85.70
e lessalicornes@wanadoo.fr
Closed mid-Nov to end of March. **Swimming pool**. **TV**. **Car park**.

Some evening, the Merlins and their friend Jojo, a teller of Provençal stories, entertain you after you've dined on delicious, traditional dishes and drunk their invigorating local wine. They organise flamenco evenings on the beach for only 150F, which you reach by horse-drawn carriage, and run cookery classes. Comfortable double rooms with whitewashed walls 250–300F. Menu at 90F.

⌂ |●| LE MIRAGE**

14 rue Camille-Pelletan (Northeast); it's 200m from the beach.
☎ 04.90.97.80.43 ➡ 04.90.97.72.22
Closed lunchtimes except Sun, and end Oct to March. **Garden**. **Disabled access**. **Car park**.

This modern, comfortable hotel with a white façade was a cinema from 1953–63. Today it has a pretty sitting room on the first floor, and offers doubles with shower/wc or bath for 280–320F. The terrace opens onto a little garden where you can sometimes have a quiet picnic.

⌂ HÔTEL LE BLEU MARINE**

av. du Docteur-Cambon.
☎ 04.90.97.77.00 ➡ 04.90.97.76.00
Closed Nov–April, except Christmas and New Year holidays. **Disabled access**. **Swimming pool**. **TV**.

As you might have guessed from the name, the sea isn't far away. Tasteful decor, friendly welcome, and all 26 rooms face the swimming pool. Doubles 280–400F. In summer, light snacks and salads are served by the pool.

SALON-DE-PROVENCE 13300

⌘ ⌂ GRAND HÔTEL DE LA POSTE**

1 rue des Frères-Kennedy (Centre); it's at the end of the cours Carnot.
☎ 04.90.56.01.9 4 ➡ 04.90.56.20.77
Closed Sun end Oct to end Feb, and 15 Jan– 5 Feb. **TV**. **Pay car park**.

A good place to stay in the centre of town, with well soundproofed rooms at 190F with shower or 260F with bath. The owners, keen to provide all sorts of services to their guests, act as an unofficial tourist information centre. 10% discount Nov–March.

⌂ HÔTEL VENDÔME**

34 rue du Maréchal-Joffre (Centre).
☎ 04.90.56.01.96 ➡ 04.90.56.48.78
e hotelvendome@ifrance.com
TV.

The rooms in this hotel, decorated in intense Provençal colours, go for 255–300F. They all have huge bathrooms that are a little retro. Ask for one overlooking the cool, delightful patio. Attentive, slightly formal staff.

|●| LA SALLE À MANGER

6 rue du Maréchal-Joffre (Centre); it's next to the Fontaine Moussue.
☎ 04.90.56.28.01
Closed Sun evening and Mon.

The Miège family took over this 19th-century residence and transformed it into a vibrant, lively place which is renowned for gourmet cuisine. It's a real pleasure to sit on the terrace under the chestnut trees or in the Rococo salons. A weekday lunchtime *formules* at 89F (two courses) and 135F (three courses). Have a plate of Bouzigues oysters, a casserole of stuffed cuttlefish or lamb with *tapenade*. A good choice of desserts for around 45F each. Good local wines. Best to book.

|●| RESTAURANT REGAIN

13 pl. Neuve; it's at the foot of the château.
☎ 04.90.56.11.04
Closed Sun evening and Mon.

A small, unobtrusive restaurant with a terrace for fine weather. The owner and his wife are characters and the cooking has personality. Good menus 100F and 175F. The specialities are typically Provençal, including the saddle of young rabbit with artichoke *coulis* and the lavender honey *nougatine*, which is a small iced cake. On Friday you can have aïoli (salt cod with garlic mayonnaise), dessert, wine and coffee for 130F – order this in advance.

SANARY-SUR-MER 83110

⌘ ⌂ |●| HÔTEL-RESTAURANT BON ABRI**

94 av. des Poilus; 200m from the harbour and beaches.
☎ 04.94.74.02.81 ➡ 04.94.74.30.01
Closed Mon and 15 Nov–15 Dec. **Disabled access**.
Garden. **Pay ar park**.

A very simple but quite delightful hotel behind a lush garden full of greenery and bushes. The nine large rooms have been fully re-designed and brightly redecorated. Doubles 210–265F with shower/wc, 250–325F with bath. Half board, compulsory during the school holidays, costs 225–255F. The cuisine has had a make-over as well; try the veal sweetbreads in a pastry case or *émincé* of duck with caramel. Lunch menu 68F, or 110F and 140F. It's an even lovelier place now than it was before. Free apéritif and free use of the car park – out of season only.

|●| L'OCÉAN JAZZ

74 route de la Gare.
☎ 04.94.07.36.11 ➡ 04.94.34.68.62
Closed Sat lunchtime, and Sun evening Nov–March.
Disabled access. **Car park**.

An excellent little restaurant with a weekday lunch menu at 80F including $1/4$ litre of wine, and others 99F and 150F. They put a dish of olive paste and hunks of bread on the table to start you off. Carefully prepared regional dishes made with fresh local produce and presentation worthy of a much grander place. Efficient, easy-going service and a truly friendly welcome. The dining room is charming and the terrace is splendid. You eat to an accompaniment of gentle swing, and there are live duos and trios on Friday evenings.

SAULT   84390

☆ |●| HOSTELLERIE DU VAL DE SAULT***

Ancien chemin d'Aurel; it's 1.5km from the centre of the village – follow the signs.
☎ 04.90.64.01.41 ➡ 04.90.64.12.74
e valdesault@aol.com
Closed Nov–March. **Disabled access**. **Swimming pool**. **TV**. **Car park**.

This fairly new hotel-restaurant is a haven of peace in a gorgeous landscape of lavender and forests. It faces Mont Ventoux and has eleven spacious rooms each with a little sitting area and a terrace. Doubles with bath 510–790F. In the kitchen, Yves Gattechaut skilfully combines traditional ingredients to create innovative flavours. His *galette* made from spelt, a kind of wheat, with lamb offal and *compote* of shallots is a real treat, as is his fish soup with pesto and saffron, and his leg of lamb with bacon. Week-

day lunch menu 132F and 190F in the evening. Children's menu 69F. If you love truffles and feel like splashing out a bit, there's a wonderful "*diamant noir*" menu. As good as anything you'll eat in a top restaurant.

SEYNE-LES-ALPES   04140

☆ ☆ |●| LE VIEUX TILLEUL

Les Auches; it's a ten-minute walk from the centre of the village
☎ 04.92.35.00.04 ➡ 04.92.35.26.81
Closed Sat lunchtime, Sun evening Nov–March. **Car park**.

Near-perfect hotel near the ski slopes in a sweet village in the Vallée de la Blanche. In summer you can lounge around in the shade of the huge trees in the grounds. The rooms, in the old farmhouse, have been attractively and originally renovated; doubles 240–280F. Honest mountain cuisine: sheep's cheese salad, pork with Roquefort and the like. Weekday lunch menu 80F, or 95–140F. 10% discount on the room rate.

SISTERON   04200

☆ ☆ |●| GRAND HÔTEL DU COURS***

allée de Verdun (Centre).
☎ 04.92.61.04.51 ➡ 04.92.61.41.73
e hotelducours@wanadoo.fr
Closed Nov–March. **TV**. **Car park**.

A chic hotel with fifty rooms. Provincial atmosphere, courteous welcome and attentive service. The rooms are all very clean but some are noisier than others. Avoid those that look out onto the main road, and plump instead for one with a view of the château or the cathedral. Doubles 330–470F with shower/wc or bath. The lively, attractive restaurant serves sound local specialities: red peppers with salt cod, aubergine with anchovy butter, *foie gras* on spiced bread and lamb *daube à la Provençale*. Menus 90F, 120 and 150F. Free apéritif.

|●| LES BECS FINS

16 rue Saunerie; it's in the centre of the lower town, parallel to the tunnel.
☎ 04.92.61.12.04 **e** becsfins@aol.com
Closed Wed and Sun out of season, 12–26 June and 4–20 Dec.

A gourmet restaurant in a town that has a reputation for rearing excellent lamb. They're pretty serious about their cooking, but the atmosphere is relaxed, warm and friendly. The menus are well judged and in the purest traditions of Provence – *terrine* of *foie gras*, snail stew in white wine, sautéed lamb, duck breast prepared nine different ways and Châteaubriand prepared eight different ways. As you would expect lamb chops feature in many dishes. Menus 126–290F.

TARASCON   13150

⌂ |●| HOSTELLERIE SAINT-MICHEL

Abbaye de Frigolet; it's 12km from the centre of town.
☎ 04.90.90.52.70 ► 04.90.05.75.22
✉ abayedefrigolet@frigolet.com
Garden.

A former abbey offering rooms with a variety of facilities; spacious doubles 250F or others 182–320F. The meals are served in the old refectory that's more like a museum – it's got a fantastic entrance – or in the garden. Appetizing *aïoli* with rabbit or sautéed veal with honey. And you have to try the ice cream served with Frigolet liqueur. Menus 90–150F.

|●| LE BISTROT DES ANGES

pl. du Marché.
☎ 04.90.91.05.11
Closed evenings, Sun and a fortnight at Christmas.

A heavenly surprise right in the middle of the town. You can watch the owner peeling her carrots in the morning as she chats to the postman or the first clients who come for a coffee. The dining room is light, airy and spacious and the terrace is lively. Handsome cooking; dish of the day 65F, and salads for the same price that are a meal in themselves. *Formule* at 85F or a menu at 100F.

THORENC   06750

⌂ |●| HÔTEL DES VOYAGEURS**

av. Belvédère (East).
☎ 04.93.60.00.18 ► 04.93.60.03.51
Closed Thurs out of season. **Garden**. **TV**. **Car park**.

Twelve faultlessly clean rooms, 280–300F. Half board, compulsory in season, costs 280F per person. The good restaurant offers a weekday menu at 95F and another at 155F; they list dishes such as calf's head *sauce ravigote* and sautéed rabbit *chasseur*. There's a pleasant terrace and garden with a view of the village.

|●| LE CHRISTIANA

L'Audibergue.
☎ 04.93.60.45.41
Closed evenings, and 1–20 Dec.

Set at the foot of the Audibergue ski runs, this restaurant sees a lot of regulars from Cannes. The menus are substantial, and you can help yourself to the five starters – country ham, fried garlic bread, crudités, *terrines* and calf's head – as often as you like, following them with tripe *à la Niçoise*, roast lamb, wild boar or hare stew, cheese and dessert. All that for 120F. Dish of the day 65F. Booking essential at weekends and public holidays.

TOULON   83000

⅔ ⌂ HÔTEL MOLIÈRE*

12 rue Molière (Centre); it's in the pedestrian area next to the theatre.
☎ 04.94.92.78.35 ► 04.94.62.85.82
Closed Jan. **TV**. **Car park**.

A very simple family hotel with unbeatable prices. The owners really know how to make you feel welcome and do their best to make sure you have a pleasant stay. Comfortable, clean, soundproofed doubles 115F with basin but no TV, 185F with shower/wc. Room numbers 18, 19 and 20 have a great view of the harbour. An excellent place of its kind. 10% discount for a two-night stay, Sept–June.

⅔ ⌂ HÔTEL LE JAURÈS*

11 rue Jean-Jaurès (Centre).
☎ 04.94.92.83.04 ► 04.94.62.16.74
TV.

A long-standing favourite which really should have two stars. It's friendly, clean and offers some of the best value for money in town. 160F for a double with shower/wc, 180F with bath. The rooms overlooking the courtyard are quiet. Covered storage for bikes. 10% discount Sept–June for a two-night stay.

|●| RESTAURANT LE CELLIER

52 rue Jean-Jaurès (Centre).
☎ 04.94.92.64.35
Closed Sat lunchtime, Sun, and weekends and public holidays July–Aug.

Warm, friendly restaurant where you get a choice of menus, 85–160F, listing dishes like mussels with shallots, red mullet in Côtes-de-Provence wine, and monkfish in cider. The decor is not exactly tasteful, but that's half the appeal of this quiet little place.

|●| LE JARDIN DU SOMMELIER

20 allée Courbet; beside pl. d'Armes, behind the arsenal.
☎ 04.94.62.03.27 ✉ jsommelier@infonie.fr
Closed Sat lunchtime and Sun.

The *sommelier* and chef who run the place believe that what's on your plate and what's in your glass are equally important. Their sunny restaurant is full of wonderful aromas and pretty colours. Mouthwatering smells waft from the kitchens, where they prepare fabulous dishes such as fresh tomato and aubergine tart, crayfish *tartare*, fillet of Aberdeen Angus and hot chocolate *moelleux* with vanilla cream. Menus 120–220F, and around 220F *à la carte*. Needless to say, you'll get a friendly welcome.

TOUR-D'AIGUES (LA)   84240

♨ I●I AUBERGE DE LA TOUR

51 rue Antoine-de-Très (Centre); it's opposite the church.
☎ 04.90.07.34.64
Closed Mon, and Nov.

This good, friendly restaurant has a handsome, tastefully decorated dining room with a vaulted, white stone ceiling and a shaded terrace that's open in good weather. Menus, 67F (weekday lunchtime) and 99–180F, feature fish and traditional Provençal dishes like lamb tripe, meatballs *à la Provençale*, kid *blanquette* and crayfish *fricassée*. Free apéritif.

UTELLE   06450

♠ I●I LE BELLEVUE*

route la Madonel; it's on the edge of the village.
☎ 04.93.03.17.19 ➡ 04.93.03.19.17
Hotel open July–Aug only. **Restaurant closed** Wed out of season, and Jan–Feb. **Car park**.

Very simple but very good hotel with a splendid view. Clean, comfortable rooms go for 300F with shower/wc, while half board, 290F, is compulsory in August. The restaurant has a good reputation. Reserve a table with a view in the rustic dining room. The chef's specialities are *pissaladière* (onion tart), rabbit with herbs, home-made ravioli and *daube provençale*. Lunch menu 80F and others up to 160F.

I●I AUBERGERIE DEL CAMPO

route d'Utelle.
☎ 04.93.03.13.12

As the road climbs steadily up towards Utelle, you'll see a few cars parked under a tree at the side of the road. Just below, there's an old, lovingly restored shepherd's house dating from 1785. In the rustic dining room, with its handsome fireplace and olive wood floors, you are served classic dishes like ravioli with

duck and cep filling, king scallop *fricassée* with raspberry vinegar, trout braised with tarragon and splendid desserts. Lunchtime *formule* 80F and set menus 115–190F. The beautiful terrace looks over the Gorges de la Vésubie. Friendly atmosphere. Dinner by reservation only. Free apéritif.

VAISON-LA-ROMAINE   84110

♠ HÔTEL BURRHUS**

1 pl. Montfort (Centre); take the Bollène exit off the A7.
☎ 04.90.36.00.11 ➡ 04.90.36.39.05
e info@burrhus.com
Closed Sun Jan–Feb, and 15 Nov–20 Dec.
TV. Car park.

Attractive hotel, all ochre walls and wrought iron, with a billiard room. The bedrooms are distributed here and there in the rabbit warren of corridors and they're all different. Some are decorated in Provençal style, others are more basic. Doubles with shower/wc 240–290F, with bath 280–320F. There's a shaded terrace on the main square where you can enjoy a snack. Faultless welcome. The owners are into contemporary art and hold regular exhibitions.

♠ I●I L'HOSTELLERIE DU BEFFROI***

rue de l'Évêché (South).
☎ 04.90.36.04.71 ➡ 04.90.36.24.78
e lebeffroi@wanadoo.fr
Hotel closed Feb–March. **Restaurant closed** weekday lunchtimes and end Oct to 1 April. **TV. Car park**.

This exceptional hotel is housed in two residences from the 16th and 17th centuries. The salon has been magnificently furnished, and the bedrooms have good facilities. Doubles with shower/wc or bath from 480F. Lunch menu 98F, 145F in the evening. The food is good: lamb *daube à l'avignonnaise*, *aïgo-boulido* and there's a salad bar on the terrace in summer.

VALBERG   06710

♠ I●I HÔTEL LE CHASTELLAN**

rue Saint-Jean; it's behind the tourist office off the main square, up the road to the left.
☎ 04.93.02.57.41 ➡ 04.93.02.61.65

This is a family-run hotel for families to stay in. It boasts 37 lovely rooms, a large, airy dining room and a games room for the children. Doubles 380F and five suites for 580F. They all have shower/wc or bath and direct-dial telephone, and prices include buffet breakfast. There's only one menu, 110F, and half board is 335F per person.

|●| CÔTÉ JARDIN

It's behind the main square.
☎ 04.93.02.64.70
Closed Wed out of season. **Garden**.

You rarely think of gourmet food when you think about ski resorts, but here's the exception to the rule. True, you can get *tartiflette*, *raclette* and *fondue*, but it would be a pity to opt for dishes that are more typical of Savoy than of Provence. The dishes on the menus, 85–185F, show off the talents of the chef: *croustillant* of scallops with oyster mushrooms, home-made *terrine* with *foie gras*, duck breast with spiced orange. Not only does the food taste good, but the presentation is exceptional. The dining room faces the garden. Friendly service.

VENCE   06140

🏠 |●| AUBERGE DES SEIGNEURS**

pl. Frêne (Centre).
☎ 04.93.58.04.24 ➡ 04.93.24.08.01
Hotel closed 15 Nov–15 March. **Restaurant** closed Mon and Tues lunchtime.

This beautiful 15th-century building is situated on the ramparts at the entrance to the old town. The rooms, which are more like suites, are named after painters; some have mountain views. Prices are more than reasonable – 374–394F. The restaurant offers sophisticated, imaginative cooking on menus from 170F. Warm welcome.

|●| LE P'TIT PROVENÇAL

4 pl. Clémenceau.
☎ 04.93.58.50.64
Closed Sun evening and Mon out of season.

A new restaurant, with a relaxed informal atmosphere, in the centre of the old town.The food is extremely imaginative and typically Provençal. Dishes change frequently, but typically would include stew of cheek of suckling

pig, ravioli *à la bouillabaisse*, leg and shoulder of rabbit with *tapenade*, and stuffed baby vegetables. Weekday lunch menu 75F and up to 155F. If you eat on the terrace you can admire the lively, historic town.

|●| LA FARIGOULE

15 av. Henri-Isnard.
☎ 04.93.58.01.27
Closed Tues and Wed in winter, Wed and Thurs lunchtime in season.

You come here for the authentic atmosphere and the tasty Provençal cooking which has a touch of the exotic – sardine tart with coriander and pickled lime, sautéed rabbit with olives, suckling lamb roast with cardomom. Menus 135–160F or 250F *à la carte*. The chef trained with the great Alain Ducasse when he had his restaurant in Juan-les-Pins. Try his speciality dessert – a heroic dish of roast figs.

VILLECROZE   83690

🎋 🏠 |●| AUBERGE DES LAVANDES*

pl. du Général-de-Gaulle (Centre).
☎ 04.94.70.76.00 ➡ 04.94.70.10.31
Closed Tues evening and Wed except July–Aug, and 6 Jan–1 March. **Car park**.

A very pleasant little place with a lighthearted, informal atmosphere. The restaurant is just as good as the hotel, with a pretty, lavender-coloured dining room and a terrace on the square shaded by plane trees. There are a lot of regulars, which isn't surprising as the food is good, inexpensive and served in generous portions. Star dishes include scallops *à la Provençale, daube à la Provençale* (a slowly braised, rich beef stew), rabbit *à l'anchoïade*, *estouffade* of beef with olives, and the delicious local goat's cheese. Menus 90–180F. Doubles 280F with shower/wc, and 310F with bath. Free apéritif and breakfast.

Rhône-Alpes

01 Ain

07 Ardèche

26 Drôme

38 Isère

42 Loire

69 Rhône

73 Savoie

74 Haute-Savoie

AIX-LES-BAINS — 73100

🕏 🏠 |●| HÔTEL BROISIN*

10 ruelle du Revet (Centre).
☎ 04.79.35.06.15 ➡ 04.79.88.10.10
Closed 1 Dec to end Feb. **TV.**

A little hotel in a quiet side street in the centre of town, just a short walk from the spa. It's a very typical spa town hotel with the atmosphere of a family guesthouse. Many of the elderly guests have been coming here for years. The rooms have been freshened up and prices are modest; 157F for a double with basin, 208F with shower/wc. The restaurant doesn't merit a visit unless you're staying. Menus from 55F. 10% discount on the room rate Sept–June.

🏠 |●| HÔTEL-RESTAURANT LES PLATANES**

173 av. du Petit-Port (West); it's near the lake.
☎ 04.79.61.40.54 ➡ 04.79.35.00.41
Closed 15 Nov–15 March. **TV. Car park.**

Set in a residential area of comfortable detached houses near the lake, this hotel has a lovely, shaded terrace. At weekends, the owner organises musical evenings – New Orleans jazz to Django on a Friday, French *chansons* from Brel to Brassens on a Saturday. The cuisine, firmly in the classical mould, features many Savoy specialities: deep-fried Reblochon cheese and *fricassée* of quail *à la*

mondeuse. The chef also has a deft touch with fish dishes. Menus 105–240F. The decor in the bedrooms has seen better days, but the facilities are good, and they're very quiet. Doubles with shower/wc 200–260F.

🏠 |●| HÔTEL-RESTAURANT AU PETIT VATEL**

11 rue du Temple (Centre).
☎ 04.79.35.04.80 ➡ 04.79.34.01.51
Closed Jan. **TV. Garden. Car park.**

In a quiet street in the centre of town, just next to the Anglican church of St Swithin, this charmingly old-fashioned establishment has an elegant air. The rooms at the back, complete with balcony, overlook a little garden with walls swathed in ivy. Doubles 270F with shower/wc. The dining room has a pleasant atmosphere and there's a delightful terrace in the garden. Tasty, classical cooking – the freshwater fish, particularly the trout, are good, as are the *fondues* and *raclettes*. 65F weekday lunch menu, then 110–180F.

🏠 |●| HÔTEL-RESTAURANT LE MANOIR***

37 rue Georges-1er; it's behind the spa.
☎ 04.79.61.44.00 ➡ 04.79.35.67.67
📧 info@hotel-lemanoir.com
Swimming pool. Garden. TV. Car park.

A reliable hotel, set among the trees, that's full of character though not quite top of the

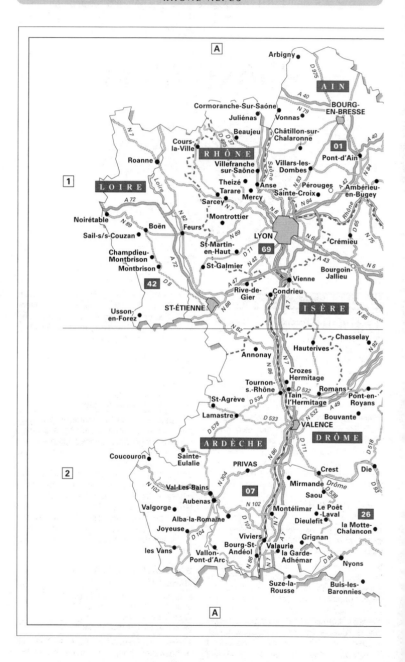

A

Arbigny

AIN

D 975

A 40

N 79

BOURG-
EN-BRESSE

Cormoranche-Sur-Saône

Juliénas   Vonnas

Châtillon-sur-
Chalaronne

Beaujeu

N 7

Cours-
la-Ville

01

Pont-d'Ain

D 37

D 485

RHÔNE

Roanne

Villefranche-
sur-Saône

Villars-les-
Dombes

A 40

A 42

N 83

Ambérieu-
en-Bugey

N 84

Theizé

Anse

Pérouges

LOIRE

Tarare

Mercy

Sainte-Croix

Saône

N 84

Rhône

D 65

1

Sarcey

N 7

N 6

N 75

Noirétable

Montrottier

A 72

N 89

Boën

Feurs

LYON

Crémieu

N 89

N 6

N 6

Sail-s/s-Couzan

N 82

St-Martin-
en-Haut

69

D 11

Champdieu-
Montbrison

D 42

A 43

Bourgoin-
Jallieu

Montbrison

St-Galmier

42

D 8

D 8

A 47

Rive-de-
Gier

Vienne

N 6

ST-ÉTIENNE

Condrieu

ISÈRE

N 85

Usson-
en-Forez

N 88

A 7

N 82

Chasselay

N 92

Hauterives

Annonay

N 86

Crozes
Hermitage

N 7

Tournon-
s.-Rhône

Romans

Tain
l'Hermitage

D 532

Pont-en-
Royans

St-Agrève

D 534

A 49

Lamastre

D 533

Bouvante

N 532

VALENCE

D 518

ARDÈCHE

N 86

DRÔME

D 111

Coucouron

Sainte-
Eulalie

PRIVAS

Crest

Die

2

N 102

Val-Les-Bains

D 304

07

Mirmande

Drôme

D 93

Valgorge

Aubenas

N 102

Saou

D 538

Alba-la-Romaine

Montélimar

Le Poët
-Laval

26

Joyeuse

D 104

D 107

Dieulefit

la Motte-
Chalancon

les Vans

Viviers

N 7

Grignan

Vallon-
Pont-d'Arc

Bourg-St-
Andéol

A 7

Valaurie
la Garde-
Adhémar

D 94

Nyons

N 86

Suze-la-
Rousse

Buis-les-
Baronnies

A

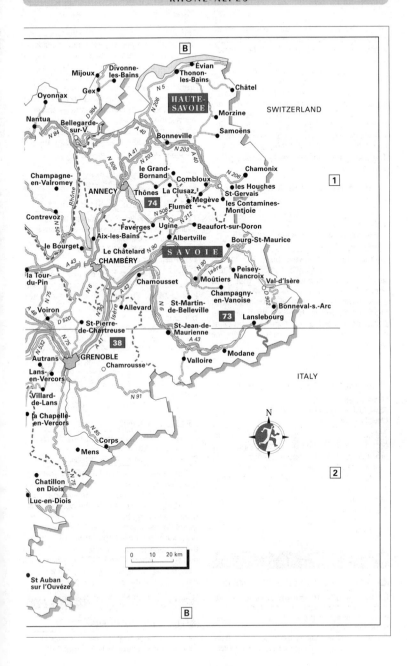

range. The "*manoir*" is actually a series of out-buildings belonging to two Belle Époque mansions, the "Splendide" and the "Royal". The cosy, well-equipped rooms are decorated in a style that's in keeping with the building. Doubles 395–695F with shower/wc or bath. The sitting rooms are comfortable, the garden pleasant and the indoor swimming pool very 1930s Hollywood; there's also a Jacuzzi and fitness room. Excellent regional cuisine – try the suckling pig *à la savoyarde* or any of the delicate freshwater fish. Menus 145–295F. The young, relaxed staff create an easy-going atmosphere.

IOI RESTAURANT L'AUBERGE DU PONT ROUGE

151 av. du Grand-Port (Northwest).
☎ 04.79.63.43.90
Closed Sun, Mon and Tues evenings, Thurs and 15 Dec–20 Jan.

This restaurant is always busy. The dining room is not particularly beautiful and the terrace in the gravel courtyard isn't that great either. But the owners are friendly, and the cooking brings out the maximum flavour from ingredients the chef chooses with meticulous care. The fish dishes are dependent on what is landed from the lake – trout or perch, for example – and there are specialities from Périgord. Weekday lunch menu 68F, others 98–195F.

IOI RESTAURANT LA POULE-AU-POT

20 rue des Bains (Centre).
☎ 04.79.35.01.19 ➡ 04.79.61.25.96
Closed Wed lunchtime.

Traditional cooking, using quality ingredients to produce well-prepared dishes that are full of flavour: *poule-au-pot fondue*, Savoy standards like *tartiflette*, and a few classics like a good steak with Roquefort sauce. You eat in the relaxed surroundings of an authentic bistro. In summer make for the pleasant terrace on the pedestrian street. Weekday lunch menu 75F, then 80–135F.

ALBA-LA-ROMAINE   07400

IOI RESTAURANT LA PETITE CHAUMIÈRE

Quartier de la Roche; it's signposted on the main square in Vieil Alba, take the road at the bottom to the preserved hamlet of La Roche.
☎ 04.45.52.43.50
Closed Tues and Wed lunchtime in summer; Mon–Thurs and Sun evenings, and Fri and Sat lunchtimes in winter.

The setting is very unusual and the welcome is delightful. There are only a few tables inside, as most are on a dreamy terrace overlooking an imposing, sheer tower of crumbling rocks – you wonder how on earth it's still standing. Traditional, old-fashioned, family cuisine – cream of carrot soup, sautéed lamb with spices and a real crème caramel – served in handsome portions. You eat to the distant accompaniment of jazz and Latin rythms. The 80F menu includes cheese or dessert, the 90F includes both. Booking advisable.

ALBERTVILLE   73200

🌣 ⬆ IOI AUBERGE COSTAROCHE**

1 chemin Pierre-du-Roy (South); take the pont du Mirantin – it's near the medieval town of Conflans and the château in Costaroche.
☎ 04.79.32.02.02 ➡ 04.79.31.37.59
TV. **Garden**. **Car park**.

A large, rather dull building in a residential area surrounded by a garden planted with lots of trees. The young couple who have recently taken it over are trying to give it more personality. For a start they give you a charming welcome. The rooms have been gently renovated. Doubles with bath 220–300F. The dining room is not very intimate but the cooking, mainly classic dishes, is decent: raviolis gratinéed with cheese or flambéed king prawns *à la Provençale*. Weekday lunch menu 75F, others 95–185F. 10% discount on the room rate.

IOI LE LIGISMOND

How to get there: it's in the medieval town of Conflans.
☎ and ➡ 04.79.37.71.29
Closed Sun evening and Wed in summer.

In the winter, you'll need to book by phone. Conflans is closed to traffic, so leave your car and climb up to the village from Albertville. You can eat on the delightful terrace overlooking the lovely little square in the middle of the medieval town. The restaurant produces wonderful traditional dishes: try the zander fillet, for example. Weekday lunch menu 72F, others 100–170F. The welcome is sincere, service is with a smile, portions are generous and the prices are affordable.

MONTHION   73200 (8KM SW)

IOI LES SEIZE CLOCHERS

How to get there: on the D925, between Grignon and Notre-Dame-des-Millières, turn left onto the D64.

☎ 04.79.31.30.39
Closed Mon evening and Wed except July–Aug.
Car park.

There's a view of sixteen bell towers from the restaurant's bay window or the terrace, and you can see the comb of Savoy. Good, classic dishes, such as *diots* (vegetable and pork sausages in white wine), *tartiflette* and *fondue*, and a few more traditional ones like *fricassée* of snails *à la Savoyarde* (with cheese and potatoes) and chanterelles in puff pastry. The large, old-style dining room looks over the Combe de Savoie. 88F lunch menu (except Sun), then 115–165F.

PLANCHERINE   73200 (11KM W)

🏕 IOI CHALET DES TRAPPEURS

Col de Tamié; from Albertville, follow the signs for Gilly-sur-Isère and then col de Tamié.
☎ 04.79.32.21.44
Closed Mon. **TV**. **Garden**.

The characterful, attractive chalet is sturdily built of wood, and, as you might expect in a trapper's chalet, great logs burn in the hearth, hunting trophies line the walls and animal skins are draped on the benches. They serve Savoy specialities like *tartiflette* and *fondue*, substantial omelettes, and some remarkable local dishes: *fricassée* of rabbit with *trompette de la mort* mushrooms or country-style fillet of *féra*, which is a kind of salmon. Weekday lunch menu 72F and others 94–160F. There's a large terrace and deckchairs in the garden. While you're in the area, buy some of the cheese made by the monks in the nearby abbey of Tamié. Free apéritif.

ALLEVARD   38580

🏕 🏠 IOI LA BONNE AUBERGE*

10 rue Laurent-Chataing.
☎ 04.76.97.53.04 ➡ 04.76.45.84.62
Closed Sun and Mon evenings out of season, and Oct.
TV.

The welcome you get here couldn't be bettered. Bedrooms have a view of Brame-Farine; doubles 195F with shower/wc, TV and direct-dial phone. Half board 240F per person. The specialities in the rustic restaurant include snail flan with wild garlic, fillet of pork with *sassenage* cheese, chestnut charlotte, salad of pork cheeks *confit*, duck with bilberries and *tartiflette* of goat's cheese. Weekday lunch menu 52F, then others 68–170F. Free *digestif*.

🏕 IOI LA TOUR DU TREUIL

chemin de la Tour du Treuil (East); turn left at the post office on the road to Glapigneux.
☎ 04.76.97.58.91
Closed Mon and Jan.

This restaurant, in an impressive, remarkably well restored 14th-century tower, is one of the most original places in the region. On the ground floor there's a vast dining room with dry stone walls and an imposing fireplace. The esoteric food, much of it prepared from medieval recipes, is wonderful – try the *pâté* of roast leg of lamb and the amazing broth. 85F weekday lunch menu, or 120–165F; prices are reasonable, considering the setting and the quality of the cooking. There is no terrace – even in summer there's a chill north wind. As an. Free apéritif, which here is Hypocras wine, made from an ancient recipe.

GONCELIN   38570 (10KM S)

IOI RESTAURANT LE CLOS DU CHÂTEAU

How to get there: on the D525 from Allevard.
☎ and ➡ 04.76.71.72.04
📧 closchateau@netsysteme.net
Open Fri, Sat, weekday lunchtimes except Wed.
Disabled access. **Car park**.

This 13th-century house, in the mountains of Chartreuse and Belledonne, is run by an extremely nice English pair who've given it a new lease of life. It's easy to pass it by, because it's set back from the road in very extensive grounds. You dine in the shade of the hazels and ancient ceders with a view over the mountains, or in the restaurant which has a French-style ceiling. Bag a table by the fire in winter. Suzie Glayser is in charge of the service while her husband creates wonderful flavours in the kitchen: specialities include crayfish ravioli in a creamy broth, and beef "Wellington" with *foie gras*. There's a lunch *formule* at 95F and menus 125–250F.

FERRIÈRE (LA)   38580 (17KM SE)

🏠 IOI AUBERGE NEMOZ

Hameau La Martinette; take the D525 in the direction of Fond-de-France.
☎ 04.76.45.03.10 ➡ 04.76.45.88.75
Closed Mon– Wed during term-time and mid-Nov to mid-Dec. **Car park**.

The chalet is at the end of a forest track in the little-known valley of Haut-Breda. It's a relaxed place full of young people with stone walls and a wide fireplace. If you're not a big fan of real *raclette* cooked on a wood fire, or *tartiflette* either, go for the menus at 125F or 160F, where you'll find a few specialities including Breda salad with smoked fillet of trout, fresh trout with almonds, *en papillotte* or *au bleu*, fresh salmon, mutton *terrine* with *tapenade* or chicken with shrimps. There are a couple of charming rooms, 350F including breakfast. Best to book.

AMBÉRIEU-EN-BUGEY   01500

☎ HÔTEL TERMINUS ET DE LA GARE**

80 rue Roger-Salengro (South).
☎ 04.74.38.00.02 ➽ 04.74.46.89.47
TV. Car park.

There are eighteen clean, inexpensive, slightly old-fashioned rooms in this hotel, which is named for the town's lovely old station: doubles with shower cost 150–190F. If you have a room on the station side, you will hear the noise from the trains as soon as you open the windows. There's a family atmosphere and a popular bar where, from early morning, the locals come to put the world to rights with the owner.

MEXIMIEUX   01800 (15KM SW)

☆ ☎ HÔTEL-BAR DU LION D'OR**

16 pl. Vaugelas (Centre); take the N84 in the direction of Pérouges.
☎ 04.74.61.00.89 ➽ 04.74.61.43.80
Closed Nov. **TV. Garage**.

The hotel was rebuilt after the war – a German tank ran it over – and it's been refurbished since. The rooms are big and pleasant and the quietest ones are at the back. Doubles with shower/wc 220F, with bath 250F. There's no restaurant, but the bar on the ground floor offers simple, cheap food. You can get a meal for 65F. Excellent welcome. Free house apéritif.

ÉVOSGES   01230 (23KM NE)

☆ ☎ |●| L'AUBERGE CAMPAGNARDE**

How to get there: as you leave Saint-Rambert, head for Belley; 1km from town, take the D34.
☎ 04.74.38.55.55 ➽ 04.74.38.55.62
Closed Tues evening and Wed, and Jan. **Swimming pool. TV. Lock-up car park**.

The winding road up is gorgeous, threading through steep vineyards and past huge white rocks that erupt from the broom bushes. The inn is like a holiday complex offering games for the children and mini-golf. Most rooms

have been renovated and they're comfortable and quiet; 180F with basin, 282F with shower/wc, 312F with bath. The dining room is cosy but they could really do with offering a more modest menu – the cheapest costs 100F, but it shows that the produce and ingredients they use are top quality. Other menus 135–180F. The cuisine is full of flavour and some of the dishes are very subtle.

PEZIÈRES-RESINAND (LES)   01110 (25KM NE)

☆ |●| LE BOOMERANG

How to get there: take the N504 to Saint-Rambert and then turn left onto the D34; it's signposted from the village of Oncieu.
☎ 04.74.35.58.60 ➽ 04.74.38.58.32
Closed Mon, 14 Oct–16 Nov.

Just one of a few scattered houses huddled in one of Bugey's superb isolated valleys, this astonishing inn is owned by Brent Perkins, originally from Adelaide, who settled here with his kangaroo, Skippy, after marrying a French woman. You'll get a genuine "barbie" – a vegetarian barbecue costs 105F – along with steak with British and Australian sauces, ostrich fillets, and roast emu with bush herbs. Menus up to 158F. The wine list divides its favours between Australia and Bugey. Free *digestif*.

ANNECY   74000

SEE MAP OVERLEAF

☎ CRYSTAL HÔTEL**

20 rue Louis-Chaumontet. **MAP A1-4**
☎ 04.50.57.33.90 ➽ 04.50.67.86.43
℮ annecycrystal@aol.com
TV. Free car park or pay lock-up garage.

This concrete building is away from the town centre – a good fifteen minutes on foot – in a charmless district behind the station. But you don't hear the trains, you'll be made really welcome and the modern rooms, despite the 1970s decor, have good facilities. Doubles with shower/wc 209–306F. It's more a place for an overnight stop than a longer stay.

☆ ☎ ALÉRY HÔTEL**

5 av. d'Aléry. **MAP A2-6**
☎ 04.50.45.24.75. ➽ 04.50.51.26.90
℮ hotel.alery@wanadoo.fr
TV. Car park.

Characterful, traditional hotel in a good – if dull – spot between the station and the old town. Doubles 240–370F with shower/wc or bath. The owners welcome you charmingly, the facilities are perfect and you'll have a quiet night in the rooms at the back. Good breakfast. 10% discount out of season.

☎ |●| HÔTEL LES TERRASSES

15 rue Louis Chaumontel. Off map **A1-9**
☎ 04.50.57.08.98 ➡ 04.50.57.05.28
Restaurant closed Sun except July–Aug, and mid-Dec to mid-Jan. **TV. Car park**.

A stunning old house that's been transformed into a spruce, modern little hotel. The rooms are plain (white walls, pale wood furniture), quiet and comfortable, and offer good value for money, from 250F for a double. The area is dull, however. There's a restaurant with menus starting at 85F, which is adequate if you don't feel going back into town. Excellent welcome.

🏖 ☎ HÔTEL DU NORD**

24 rue Sommeiller. **MAP A2-7**
☎ 04.50.45.08.78 ➡ 04.50.51.22.04
e annecy.hotel.du.nord@wanadoo.fr
TV. Car park.

This hotel is in a plum situation in one of the shopping streets in the centre of town, near the station, the lake and the old town. You'll get a warmhearted welcome. The place has a certain charm with its panelled reception and loggia. The rooms are pastel-pretty, with lovely bathrooms, and half of them have air-conditioning. Doubles with shower/wc 268F and 338F. Free parking 6pm–10am. 10% discount for a two-night stay Sept–June.

☎ HÔTEL DU PALAIS DE L'ISLE***

13 rue Perrière. **MAP B3-2**
☎ 04.50.45.86.87 ➡ 04.50.51.87.15
e palaisle@aol.com
TV.

An imposing 18th-century residence, superbly lcated in the narrow, winding old streets, with the River Thiou running beneath it. A few rooms overlook the palace, while others look towards the château and the old town. Soundproofing and air conditioning are gradually being introduced so you can sleep well on hot, noisy summer nights. The resolutely modern rooms are superb, with furniture designed by Philippe Starck. Doubles with bath 340–495F.

🏖 ☎ HÔTEL DE BONLIEU***

5 rue de Bonlieu; it's beside the Palais de Justice.
MAP B1-3
☎ 04.50.45.17.16 ➡ 04.50.45.11.48
TV. Car park.

A good, dependable little hotel near the lake and the old town that's ideal if you're looking

for peace and quiet and all mod cons. It's targeted more at young business execs than carefree travellers, but you'll get a friendly welcome and prices are sensible: double rooms 390–490F with shower or bath. There's a charge for the car park July–Aug. 10% discount.

🏖 |●| FRICH'TI DUDU

9 rue Louis-Armand (North); it's in the pedestrianised precinct. Off map **B1-10**
☎ 04.50.09.97.65
Closed evening, except reservations, weekends and 1–15 Aug.

Service 11.30am–3pm. A popular restaurant in an area that's seriously short of good places to eat. This bizzarely named place fills that gap and is well worth a visit. It's chocka at lunchtime, prices are incredibly cheap and you eat like a king. The cooking is simple, with various *formules* 38–60F. Free coffee.

🏖 |●| WISHBONE GARDEN

29 [bis] rue Vaugelas. **MAP A2-13**
☎ 04.50.45.25.96
Closed Sun and Mon.

An unusual place, where chicken is king. The speciality is free-range chicken served with a battery of sauces: Mexican, mushroom, honey, raspberry vinegar, and wonderful potatoes. You order your chicken by the chunk: quarter, half, or whole. Excellent desserts, particularly the crumble and the *fondant au chocolat*. In the evening it's *à la carte* only: chicken with *tartiflette* or grilled duck breast. The dining room is on two floors, and the terrace is well away from the hurly-burly of the tourists. The jovial British owner creates a relaxed atmosphere and really knows his stuff. Weekday lunch *formule* 55F, including drink, or around 100F *à la carte*. Free house apéritif.

|●| TAVERNE DU FRÉTI

12 rue Sainte-Claire. **MAP A3-11**
☎ 04.50.51.29.52
Closed lunchtimes and Mon except school holidays.

The *Fréti* is one of the few places on this touristy street that still offers quality and reasonable prices. It's a cheese shop, and naturally they specialise in cheese dishes: sixteen types of *fondue*, 64–98F, *raclette* at 65F, *tartiflette*, 68F, and potatoes with blue cheese or goat's cheese. There's a pretty dining room upstairs – a 1970s version of rustic – where you can eat if the weather's not good enough to sit outside under the arcade.

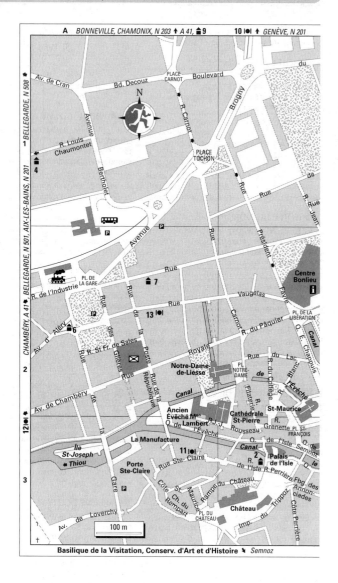

Basilique de la Visitation, Conserv. d'Art et d'Histoire ↘ *Semnoz*

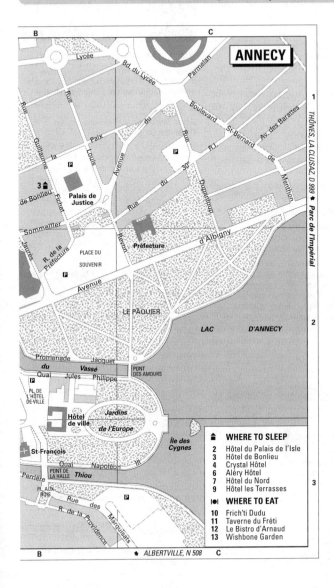

ANNECY

WHERE TO SLEEP

2 Hôtel du Palais de l'Isle
3 Hôtel de Bonlieu
4 Crystal Hôtel
6 Aléry Hôtel
7 Hôtel du Nord
9 Hôtel les Terrasses

WHERE TO EAT

10 Frich'ti Dudu
11 Taverne du Fréti
12 Le Bistro d'Arnaud
13 Wishbone Garden

|●| LE BISTRO D'ARNAUD

36 av. de Chambéry; it's at the entrance to town, near pont Neuf. Off map **A3-12**
☎ 04.50.45.51.42
Closed Sun and Mon.

This warm, friendly place lists dishes of the day on a blackboard. Specialities from Lyon feature strongly: *pot-au-feu*, calf's head, pike *quenelles* (like fish balls) and *andouillette*, for instance. Realistic prices – weekday lunch menu 78F, and another at 120F. There are a few good wines served by the jug which won't turn the bill into a crisis.

SEVRIER   74320 (5KM S)

🕮|●| AUBERGE DU BESSARD

525 route d'Albertville; on the N508.
☎ 04.50.52.40.45
Closed 21 Oct–19 March. **Car park**.

If you dream of eating on the banks of the lake, the water lapping at the terrace while you dine on fine fresh fish, here's just the place. It's something of a local institution and has been run by the same family for the last fifty years. The atmosphere is warm and friendly. You'll pay about 150F *à la carte*; there's also a 97F weekday menu, 130F at the weekend. It could well list fish *terrine*, perch or *féra*, a kind of salmon, with sorrel, and a choice of cheese or dessert. Free *digestif*.

SAINT-JORIOZ   74410 (9KM S)

🕮 ☗ |●| HÔTEL AUBERGE DE LA COCHETTE*

Lieu-dit "La Magne" à Saint-Eustache; go to St-Jorioz and follow the signs.
☎ 04.50.32.03.53 ➡ 04.50.32.02.70
✉ info@hotel-la-cochette.com
Hotel closed 15 Dec–15 March. **Restaurant closed** weekdays Sept to end April. **Car park**.

All you have to do is climb – straight up from Sant-Jorioz, following the arrows. The magnificent view over the lake of Annecy, 6km away as the crow flies, is breathtaking. The owner loves paragliding – you can go up with him and land just behind the hotel. He has nice rooms, 170–190F with basin, 220–260F with shower/wc or bath. The food is delicious, with great menus from 98–158F listing such delights as snails in flaky pastry with garlic cream and salad with chicken and crayfish. It's wonderful to eat on the terrace. Free *digestif* and 10% discount on the room rate Sept–June.

CHAPEIRY   74540 (11KM SW)

☗ |●| AUBERGE LA GRANGE À JULES

Le Pélevoz; leave the A41 motorway at the Rumilly exit and take the N201 in the direction of Annecy. After Alby, turn left towards Chapeiry and you'll find it after the bridge on the right.
☎ 04.50.68.15.07
Closed Sun, Mon and Tues evenings, and Wed.
TV. Garden. Car park.

This is a lovely, rustic little place at the back of beyond. In summer, you can have lunch or dinner in the garden under the trees and among the flowers. In winter, the open fire takes the chill off the air. They produce good dishes using fresh ingredients: potato tart with *foie gras* or frogs' legs with parsley. Weekday menu 98F and others up to 245F. The *navarin* of lamb in pastry is memorable. Large double rooms with flowery wallpaper, 200–270F with shower or bath.

DOUSSARD   74210 (12KM SE)

🕮 ☗ |●| À L'AUBERGE

Route de Chevaline.
☎ 04.50.44.86.28 ➡ 04.50.44.86.28
Closed Nov. **Car park**.

This old house is full of activity from dawn to dusk. It can seem a bit chaotic but the friendly owner actually runs the place well – the liveliness is part of the charm. The regulars hang around the bar before going to eat in one of the two warm dining rooms or on the terrace. The straightforward regional cuisine is good and really affordable. A single-menu at 75F or around 85F *à la carte*. There's a little *crêperie* next door, run by the owner's husband. Attractive rooms, 250F with shower/wc. For cyclists and walkers, there's a dormitory in a converted stable, which costs 55F per person per night. 10% discount on the room rate 15 Feb–15 June and free *digestif*.

DUINGT   74410 (12KM SE)

🕮 ☗ |●| HÔTEL-RESTAURANT DU LAC**

☎ 04.50.68.90.90 ➡ 04.50.68.50.18
✉ info@hoteldulac.com
Hotel closed 16 Oct–9 Feb. **Restaurant closed** Sun evening and Mon out of season, and 1 Oct–27 April.
TV. Car park.

The lovely hotel is far enough away from the road that you see only the lake and hear only the birds. The rooms have all been completely refurbished; doubles with shower/wc 280–410F, 330–460F with bath. Half board is compulsory July–Aug, 330–385F per person. The place is full of young people, the owners among them. You're served with a smile in the bright, fresh restaurant, and the chef creates interesting, inventive dishes. You'll enjoy a skilful blend of colours, flavours and textures – try *féra* (a type of salmon from the lake) with sesame *vinaigrette*, or *confit* of rabbit with mixed spices. Weekday lunch menu 98F, others 135–385F. Gorgeous terrace for sunny days and a private beach. 10% discount on the room rate out of season and free apéritif.

GRUFFY   74540 (17.5KM SW)

⚲ 🏠 I●I AUX GORGES DU CHÉRAN**

Pont de l'Abîme; take the N210 and 1km after Chaux turn onto the D5 – once you've passed Gruffy, it's a further 1.5km.
☎ 04.50.52.51.13 ➡ 04.50.52.57.33
Closed 11 Nov–25 March. **TV. Car park**.

This nice chalet practically clings to the cliff above the Chéran near the bridge over the abyss. Rooms 1, 4, 5 and 6 have balconies overlooking the gorge. Newly refurbished rooms 250–370F with shower/wc or bath. The restaurant has the usual local specialities on menus 85–150F. The cooking isn't trying to win any awards but you'll eat well – try the trout with almonds, fillet of beef with morels, and the bilberry tart. You can eat on the terrace or inside. Perfect, attentive welcome. 10% discount on the room rate Sept–June.

SEMNOZ (LE)   74320 (18KM S)

⚲ 🏠 I●I HÔTEL SEMNOZ-ALPES 1704 MÈTRES**

How to get there: by the D41.
☎ 04.50.01.23.17 ➡ 04.50.64.53.05
Closed Easter to Whit and 30 Sept–25 Dec. **Car park**.

This isolated hotel, in the middle of the Alpine meadows at 1704m, was built by an Annecy architect in 1876. You get a Cinemascope view over the Alps, and a very warmhearted welcome. The rooms are typically decorated and are being renovated one by one – numbers 1 to 5 are really lovely. Double with basin 170F, with shower/wc 260F and with bath 290F. Menus, 85–138F, list classic, regional dishes: *croûte au fromage*, strips of duck with bilberries, *féra* with orange, and *tournedos* with chanterelle mushrooms. 10% discount on the room rate.

LESCHAUX   74320 (18KM S)

⚲ I●I LES QUATRE VENTS

Col de Leschaux; by the N508 which skirts lac d'Annecy and then the D912 in the direction of Col de Leschaux.
☎ 04.50.32.03.58
Closed Tues except during school holidays, and 12 Nov–9 Dec.

The restaurant is on the route over the peak, on the edge of the wild Bauges country. It's a nice little place which pretty ordinary, something between a roadside caff and a country inn. Inside you'll get a bright, friendly welcome and you'll eat in a warm dining room with an open fire. The menus are substantial; a weekday menu at 85F, and others up to 145F. Good home cooking and regional dishes: *crudités*, steak and chips, *escalope bornandine*, goat's cheese with walnuts, or frog's legs *à la savoyarde*. Free coffee.

ANNONAY   07100

⚲ 🏠 HÔTEL DU MIDI**

17 pl. des Cordeliers (Centre); it's in the lower town.
☎ 04.75.33.23.77 ➡ 04.75.33.02.43
TV. Car park.

Set in a good location on a very lively square, this hotel is a sturdy building of quite remarkable dimensions, with wide corridors, large rooms (especially the ones overlooking the square), and thick, plush carpets. There are pictures and engravings of hot air balloons all over the place – the Montgolfier brothers, who invented and ascended in the first hot air balloon, were born in Annonay. Doubles with basin 170F, 230F with shower/wc and 270F with bath. 10% discount for a three-night stay.

I●I RESTAURANT MARC ET CHRISTINE

29 av. Marc-Seguin; it's opposite the old station.
☎ 04.75.33.46.97
Closed Sun evening, Mon, the Feb school holidays and 15 Aug–1 Sept. **Disabled access. Garden**.

Service noon–2pm and 7.15–9.30pm. The inventive cooking here is appreciated by an essentially local clientele. Christine gives her guests a warm welcome and ushers them into a sitting room decorated in peachy tones. Marc does the cooking, and prepares dishes that combine classic and local ingredients, though sometimes he could go easy on the butter and cream: crayfish and sweet onion soup, Burgundy snails with pig's trotters, sea bream *royale* and grilled tenderloin of beef. Main courses about 70F *à la carte*, and menus from 100F. A large selection of wines available by the glass. In summer you can eat outside in the pleasant garden.

SATILLIEU   07290 (14KM S)

🕏 🏠 |●| HÔTEL-RESTAURANT SAPET**

pl. de la Faurie; from Annonay, follow the signs first for the centre of town and then for Lalouvesc D578A.
☎ 04.75.34.95.42 ➡ 04.75.69.91.13
Closed a week from Christmas to New Year's Day. **Swimming pool**. **TV**. **Lock-up car park**.

Service noon–2pm and 7–9.30pm, 8pm in winter. This place, in the centre of the village, has an excellent reputation. The welcome is really nice and the cooking first-rate. One of the specialities is *crique ardéchoise*, made with grated potatoes sprinkled with garlic, onions and parsley. 60F weekday menu and others 84–148F. The recently renovated bedrooms are clean and comfortable; doubles with shower/wc 240F. Half board starts at 210F. Arrangements can be made for mountain biking or hiking, and there's an open-air pool. Free house apéritif.

ANSE   69480

🕏 🏠 |●| HÔTEL-RESTAURANT LE SAINT-ROMAIN**

Route de Graves; it's signposted, 200m off the main road.
☎ 04.74.60.24.46 ➡ 04.74.76.12.85
📧 hotel-saint-romain@wanadoo.fr
Closed 26 Nov–6 Dec. **TV**. **Car park**.

Traditional, classic *Logis de France* hotel. Honest cooking: chicken *chartreuse*, game stew, numerous ripe cheeses and home-made desserts. The dining room has sturdy, tree-trunk beams and there's a pleasant terrace for the summer. Menus 100–310F. Rooms are sizeable and they all have bathrooms; doubles 310F. Free coffee.

🕏 |●| LE COLOMBIER

Pont de Saint-Bernard; it's 2km from the centre of town, in the direction of Trévoux, on the banks of the Saône.
☎ 04.74.67.04.68 ➡ 04.74.67.20.30
Closed Sun evening and Mon except April–Sept, and Nov to end Feb. **Car park**.

Service from noon and 7pm. Cross the bridge and it's almost as if you've passed into a different time zone. Boats glide up and down the Saône and busy waiters thread their way through tables of cheerful people tucking into plates of whitebait or frogs' legs,

on the terrace or in the dining room. This waterside restaurant, which looks like a river-side café or *guinguette* from a hundred years ago, has been providing good food at reasonable prices for more than twenty years – delicious grilled pig's trotters and carp goujons. Menus from 90F – *hors d'œuvre* buffet, whitebait and tart – up to 220F. Free apéritif, *digestif* or coffee.

MARCY-SUR-ANSE   69480 (7KM SW)

|●| LE TÉLÉGRAPHE

How to get there; take the D79 for Lachassagne and turn left onto the D70.
☎ and ➡ 4.74.60.24.73
Closed Sun evening, Mon, a fortnight in June and a fortnight in Nov. **Car park**.

You can order any of the menus with confidence – 105F (not Sun) and 125–250F. The house *terrine* and *andouillette* with mustard sauce are delicious, while the *croustille* of St Marcellin goat's cheese has a real tang. Great desserts and flavourful Beaujolais. The pleasant terrace is well away from the road, so it's relaxing.

ALIX   69380 (10KM SW)

🕏 |●| LE VIEUX MOULIN

How to get there: take the D39 in the direction of Lachassagne, turn left for Marcy, and it's a turn off to the right.
☎ 04.78.43.91.66 ➡ 04.78.47.98.46
Closed Mon, Tues (except public holidays) and 13 Aug–9 Sept. **Car park**.

Service until 1.15pm, then until 9.15pm. This mill, built of pale gold stones, has been converted into a completely charming restaurant with three cosy dining rooms and a barn for families or large groups. Menus, 120–280F, list good, reliable dishes: frogs' legs, *andouillette*, monkfish with leek *fondue*. Portions are huge. Afterwards you could have a game of *boules* or relax on the terrace. Free coffee.

THEIZÉ   69620 (13KM W)

🕏 🏠 |●| HÔTEL-RESTAURANT LE THEIZEROT*

Centre; take the D39 Lachassagne road and it's signposted to the right.
☎ 04.74.71.22.26
Hotel closed Dec. **Restaurant closed** Sun and Mon evenings, and Tues. **Car park**.

An old village café with a few cheap, simple rooms from 110F with basin, 130F with shower. It's not the height of luxury but ideal if you've done too many miles on your bike or walked through too many vineyards. Weekday menu 68F or 78–128F. Filling regional dishes: *lyonnais* salad, *andouillette*, pike *quenelles* and *choucroute* in winter. Free house apéritif.

🚶 🏠 |●| HÔTEL-RESTAURANT LA FEUILLÉE

How to get there: take the D39 Lachassagne road and turn right to Theizé.
☎ and ➡ 04.74.71.22.19.
Closed first week in Oct. **TV**.

The large café-restaurant serves honest home cooking – in summer there's a 65F menu which includes wine and coffee. Meals to order in the evenings and on Sunday. The five rooms have been attractively arranged, all with shower (wc along the landing), at 150F for a double. Good value. Free house apéritif.

ANTRAIGUES-SUR-VOLANE   075F30

|●| LO PODELLO

It's on the village square.
☎ 04.75.38.71.48
Closed Jan–Feb.

The welcoming terrace is set on the typical village square while the dining room is warmly welcoming with stone walls and old wood that gleams gorgeously. The jovial owner is happiness personified and he dispenses decent regional cuisine; try the excellent *caillette*, *mignon* of veal with goat's cheese and parsleyed potatoes, and finish off with a light cream cheese. Menus 85–165F.

|●| RESTAURANT LA REMISE

Pont de l'Huile.
☎ 04.75.38.74
Closed Fri, Sun evening and 10 Dec–6 Jan.

An inviting dining room in country-rustic style and one of the best tables in the Volane valley. It's as busy in the week as it is on a Sunday. Seasonal dishes, fresh produce – all very pukka! Menus 120F and 200F, both including apéritif and *digestif*. Sadly, the welcome is sometimes approximate.

BURZET   07450 (18KM W)

🏠 |●| HÔTEL-AUBERGE LES MYRTILLES

pl. de la Confrerie (Centre); it's on the D245.
☎ 04.75.94.45.39 ➡ 04.73.94.48.77

Closed Sun evening and Mon except July–Aug, and mid-Nov to mid-Dec. **Garden**. **TV**. **Car park**.

There's a sense of quiet confidence about this place. The rooms are quite simple but the facilities are regularly improved, though up to now, there's only one with an en-suite bathroom. Two of them look over the quiet, charming little garden that gets lots of sun. Doubles 189–289F, half board from 230F. Pleasant dining room and the terrace is on the square. The kitchen concocts tasty, sometimes imaginative, dishes using fresh produce: *caillette* or duck breast with ginger. *Formule* at 79F (main course with either starter or dessert), menus 98–125F. Service and welcome by a young, efficient team.

ARBIGNY   01190

🚶 🏠 |●| LE MOULIN DE LA BREVETTE**

How to get there: take the D37, then the D933, and turn right off the road from Arbigny to Pont-de-Vaux.
☎ 03.85.36.49.27 ➡ 03.85.30.66.91
e moulin.brevete@wanadoo.fr
Closed 15 Nov–15 Feb except for reservations.
Disabled access. **Car park**.

This old mill – minus its wheel – stands deep in the countryside. The bedrooms, in a converted farmhouse, are large, bright, comfortable and quiet. Doubles with shower/wc 350F, 450F with bath. Numbers 15–19 and 29–32 have the best views. Nice welcome. They do simple meals in the restaurant – Bresse chicken, *coq au vin*, snails and the like. Menus 120–208F. A genuine place and honest food. Free coffee.

AUBENAS   07200

🏠 |●| HÔTEL DES NÉGOCIANTS*

pl. de l'Hôtel-de-Ville (Centre); it's in the old part of town opposite the château.
☎ 04.75.35.18.74
Closed Sun, a fortnight end of March and a fortnight end of Oct. **TV**. **Car park**.

The advantage is the central location and the cheap prices for the clean rooms, most with TV, and all with decent beds. Doubles with basin 120F, 210F with shower/wc. The restaurant serves fairly ordinary but filling dishes from various regions: fish soup, Ardèche *caillette* (a bit like haggis), duck with olives, beef Ardèche-style. Menus 60–110F.

🏠 |●| AUBERGE DES PINS

95 route de Vals.
☎ 04.75.35.29.36 ➡ 04.75.89.00.15

Hotel closed ten days in Feb, ten days in Oct.
Restaurant closed Sun. **TV. Garden. Car park**.

A charming, sprawling building in a pleasant setting with lots of pine trees in the garden. The rooms are big enough, clean and good value for money, and most have air-conditioning; doubles with shower/wc 220–240F. The restaurant is sunset yellow, and serves dishes including *caillette*, omelette with ceps and the house speciality – Lyonnais dishes. *Menu du jour* 65F, then 90–120F. A good few reasonable wines that are fairly priced and don't send the bill rocketing sky high.

🎿 🏠 |●| LA PINÈDE**

Route du camping Les Pins (Northwest); it's on the road to Lentillère, the D235, 1.5km from the town centre.
☎ 04.75.35.25.88 ➡ 04.75.93.06.42
✉ la/pinede@wanadoo.fr
Closed 10 Dec–1 Feb. **Swimming pool. TV**.

A traditional holiday hotel in a very peaceful location, in shady grounds so it's probably best to book in summer. Doubles 260–320F with shower/wc or bath. Half board, compulsory July–Aug, costs 290F per person. The restaurant offers decent value for money, with a 70F menu (not served Sun), and others up to 190F. There's a swimming pool with a panoramic view, a tennis court, and a climbing wall. Free coffee and 10% discount on the room rate.

|●| LES COLONQUINTES

rue du quai de l'Ardèche; it's on the RN104 in the direction of Privas.
☎ 04.75.93.88.33
Closed Sat lunchtime and Mon in season, Sun evening and Mon out of season, and a fortnight in Jan.
Disabled access. **Garden**.

An appealing garden-terrace offers inviting shade and quiet and there's a charming dining room with a vaulted ceiling. People murmur in Provençal accents. The cooking is wonderfully fresh, thoughtfully prepared and attractively presented. The menu lists shoals of fish dishes – sea bream, salmon, squid or whiting. There's a 70F *formule rapide* served at lunch during the week, then several others from 98F to 298F.

|●| LE CHAT QUI PÊCHE

6 pl. de la Grenette; it's near Saint-Benoît cathedral.
☎ 04.75.93.87.49
Closed Tues and Wed, end Oct to beginning Nov, and 20 Dec to April.

This restaurant is in a really lovely 17th-century Ardèche house. They serve strictly local, regional dishes that are generously served

and very good: chestnut flan with chicken *jus*, fresh duck *foie gras*, *fricassée* of snails, *caillettes* and *andouillettes ardéchoises* and *fondant ardéchois*, a delicious mixture of chocolate, chestnut and vanilla cream. Menus 98–180F or *à la carte*. Polite, charming welcome.

|●| RESTAURANT LE FOURNIL

34 rue du 4-Septembre (Centre); it's near Saint-Benoît cathedral.
☎ and ➡ 04.75.93.58.68
Closed Sun, Mon, the Christmas, Feb and Nov school holidays, and second fortnight in June.

This handsome 15th-century building with its patio and vaults is the ideal setting to try the exquisite dishes prepared by Michel Leynaud. It's altogether a very stylish affair, from the welcome to the gourmet food: rabbit with herbs and olive paste or lobster stew with morels. Menus 98–190F, and *à la carte* about 150F. Extensive wine list. Occasionally the service can be slow

VALS-LES-BAINS   07600 (5KM N)

🏠 |●| HÔTEL SAINT-JEAN

112 [bis] rue Jean-Jaurès (Centre); it's just set back from the road, on the banks of the river Vatour.
☎ 04.75.37.42.50 ➡ 04.75.37.54.77
Closed 1 Nov to early April. **TV**.

A tall, 19th-century building with a slightly sad outside but an exuberant welcome and comfortable rooms. They have all been renovated and are beyond reproach, though they're very small. Doubles 235–270F. Neutral decor but the overall effect is faultless. There's a big dining room with wide bay windows – menus from 235F. It's a classic-style place that offers peace and quiet.

🏠 |●| GRAND HOTEL DE L'EUROPE

86 rue Jean-Jaurès.
☎ 04.75.37.43.94 ➡ 04.75.94.66
Closed 15 Dec–15 Jan.

A friendly welcome and the sweet life await you in this ochre-fronted hotel. The dining room is equally colourful, painted in blue and yellow. There's a terrace under the pine trees. Doubles 260–280F with shower/wc or bath. And the cooking is tasty and reliable which is an added bonus. Menus 90–190F. The kind of place that's ideal for a stay that won't break the bank.

🏠 |●| GRAND HÔTEL DE LYON

11 av. Paul Ribeyre (Centre).
☎ 04.75.37.43.70 ➡ 04.75.37.59.11
Closed Oct–April. **Swimming pool. TV**.

A solid, serious hotel built at the beginning of the 20th century – a place that won't let you down. The rooms are big, painted in pastel shades and well maintained. The bedding is cosy and smells of roses. Doubles 330–390F. The swimming pool has a wave machine and a mini-Niagara falls – plus it's heated. There's a TV room, a billard saloon and a pretty little dining room. You can stay half board if you wish. Honest, fortifying dishes of quality food. Here you can really realx.

♠ |●| HÔTEL-RESTAURANT LE VIVARAIS

5 rue Claude Expilly (Centre).
☎ 04.75.94.65.85 ➡ 04.75.37.65.47
Closed Feb. **Swimming pool**. **TV**. **Car park**.

Easy to find: it's the most beautiful building in town and it's painted pink. Since 1930, they have been perfecting the art of providing good beds and good food for their guests. The current mistress maintains her realm to perfection. The decor is Art Deco, from the wallpaper and the colours to the furniture and even some of the baths. High degree of comfort and luxury, with excellent service. Doubles 350–600F – depending on size – with shower/wc or bath. The standard at table is just as high and Madame is the best ambassadress of her region's cuisine. There's a three-course *formule* at 100F including a glass of wine and a coffee, a *menu ardéchois* at 178F, and one using chestnuts in every course at 198F.

|●| RESTAURANT CHEZ MIREILLE

3 rue Jean-Jaurès, (Centre); it's at the end of the main road.
☎ 04.75.37.49.06
Closed Tues evening and Wed out of season.

Mireille is run by Colette, whose cuisine is highly recommended. Everything is cooked in her kitchen – it seems odd to have to say this, but it's not always the case. The filling *menu ardéchois* has two starters, and is simply superb. While the cooking is certainly respectful of tradition, there's something individual about it, too: white pudding with cep *coulis*, *terrine* with three different meats, sautéed kid with wild mushrooms. Menus 90–160F.

SANILHAC 07110 (25KM SW)

☼ ♠ |●| AUBERGE DE LA TOUR DE BRISON**

How to get there: take the D104, then the D103 in the direction of Largentière then follow the road to Montréal.
☎ 04.75.39.19.56

Closed Tues evening, Wed except July–Aug, and 10 Jan–20 March. **Disabled access**.**Swimming pool**. **TV**. **Car park**.

This pleasant hotel, run by a nice couple, has twelve air-conditioned rooms, some with a whirlpool bath and, on a clear day, a view of the Alps. Doubles 220F with basin/wc, 270F with shower/wc and 330F with bath. There are some family rooms with fireplaces. The cheapest menu, 145F, is very generously served. Dishes include chicken liver mousse with chestnuts or a traditional *caillette*. There are tennis courts and a swimming pool on the spot and lots of other activities in the area. Free apéritif and garage for motorbikes. 10% discount on the room rate.

SAINT-PONS 07580 (26KM E)

♠ |●| HOSTELLERIE GOURMANDE MÈRE BIQUETTE**

Les Allignols (North); turn left off the N102 onto the D293, at Saint-Pons you should start to see signs for the inn – it's 4km along.
☎ 04.75.36.72.61 ➡ 04.75.36.76.25
Closed Nov–31 March but reservations accepted. **Swimming pool**. **TV**. **Lock-up car park**.

The natural setting for this old farmhouse is quite spectacular. The grounds are extensive, and there are breathtaking views of the mountains and the valley. No sound breaks the silence. The country-style bedrooms are very handsome with lots of wood panelling. Prices reflect the quality – doubles 310–450F with shower/wc or bath. A welcoming, refined restaurant serving good, basic classics: *foie gras* in a pastry case, frogs' legs and local dishes as well. Menus 100–250F, half board is available for a minimum of two or four days, depending on the season. They can lend you a mountain bike.

AUTRANS 38880

☼ ♠ LE MONTBRAND**

How to get there: take the Gève road 500m from the centre of the village and turn left onto the first road after the cemetery. The hotel is 200m along.
☎ 04.76.95.34.58 ➡ 04.76.95.72.71
Open Christmas to Easter and July–Aug; other times of the year by reservation only. **TV**. **Car park**.

This huge chalet is a little way outside the village in the quiet of the countryside – there's nothing behind it but fields and woods, and in winter, the cross-country ski trails start practically at the front door. It's an intimate place with eight rooms, 300–320F with shower/wc or bath. There are two communicating rooms. Relax in the cosy wood-panelled lounge. Breakfast can be eaten there or brought up to your room. Friendly welcome. 10% discount 4–20 Jan.

MÉAUDRE   38112 (6KM S)

☎ |●| AUBERGE DU FURON**

How to get there: by the D106.
☎ 04.76.95.21.47 ➡ 04.76.95.24.71
Closed Sun evening and Mon out of season, and mid-Oct to 10 Dec. **TV**. **Car park**.

Service noon–2pm and 7–9pm. On the edge of the forest and very close to the ski trails, the inn is wonderfully situated for both summer and winter activities. The proprietress gives her guests a warm welcome, the regional dishes are attentively prepared and prices are reasonable. They have just a few rustic, comfortable bedrooms, all with bath, for 255F. There's an 80F menu (not served Sun) and others up to 170F, with an excellent 105F regional menu. Dishes include *gâteau* of liver with crayfish, rabbit *terrine* with hazelnuts, ravioli with trout fillet, or *gratin à la crème du Vercors*. Nice local wines – Châtillon-en-Diois or a Gamay de Savoie.

BEAUFORT-SUR-DORON   73270

☆ ☎ |●| HÔTEL-RESTAURANT LE GRAND MONT**

pl. de l'Église (Centre); take the Albert-Beaufort road.
☎ 04.79.38.33.36 ➡ 04.79.38.39.07
Closed 25 April–8 May and Oct. **TV**.

A delightful hotel on the outskirts of the ancient village. The rooms are looking just a little tired but they're comfortable. Doubles with shower/wc 280–300F. In the restaurant, a traditional bistro with an old-style dining room, they serve primarily regional dishes: *diots* with *crozets* (local vegetable and pork sausages cooked in white wine and served with square-shaped noodles), and tart or omelette with Beaufort cheese. Menus 60–165F. Free coffee.

BEAUJEU   69430

☆ ☎ |●| HÔTEL-RESTAURANT ANNE DE BEAUJEU**

28 rue de la République (Centre).
☎ 04.74.04.87.58 ➡ 04.74.69.22.13
Closed Sun evening, Mon, and mid-Dec to mid-Jan. **TV**. **Garden**. **Car park**.

Service noon–2pm and 7.30–9pm. Though the hotel is named after the daughter of Louis XI, who lived in the late 15th century, the building is not of that era. It has a garden, a plush foyer and an impressive dining room. Doubles 315–365F. The cooking has lost some of its creativity, but they still serve classic dishes such as *chartreuse* of pigeon braised with cabbage, and monkfish with apples and vinegar. Menus 113–282F. Free house apéritif and 10% discount on the room rate Nov–March.

BELLEVILLE   69220

☆ |●| LE BUFFET DE LA GARE

pl. de la Gare.
☎ 04.74.66.07.36 ➡ 04.74.69.69.49
Closed evenings except for reservations, weekends, 25 Dec and three weeks in Aug. **Car park**.

As a rule, French train stations and their surroundings aren't as appealing as they once were. This restaurant is an exception. A cute little house full of flowers and plants, it's decorated with old posters, Art Deco light fixtures, and quirky old mirrors. Hélène Bessy, the owner, always has a smile and a kind word for her customers. The 89F menu, which is chalked up on the blackboard, might include leeks *vinaigrette*, stuffed tomatoes and courgettes, cheese and dessert; you'll pay around 120F *à la carte*. Her husband supplies the wine. Reservations necessary in the evening for groups. During the grape harvest, the place is still pretty busy at one o'clock in the morning. Free *digestif*.

BOËN   42130

☆ |●| LE CUVAGE

La Goutte des Bois; it's 1km out of Boën in the direction of Leigneux, on a narrow road overlooking the D8.
☎ 04.77.24.15.08
Closed Mon and Tues Oct–April.

Wherever you sit for your meal – on the veranda or the terrace in summer – feast your eyes on the superb panoramic view. The menus are built for big appetites. For 95F you get as much *charcuterie*, house *terrine* or house *foie gras* as you can manage, followed by meats grilled over the embers or spit-roast suckling pig. An inn that's generous with its welcome. Free apéritif.

SAIL-SOUS-COUZAN 42890 (6KM W)

♠ |●| LES SIRES DE SEMUR*

Les Promenades (Centre); take the N89.
☎ 04.77.24.52.40 ➡ 04.77.24.57.14
Closed Fri and Sun evenings, Sat lunchtime, and a
week in Aug. **TV. Car park**.

On a village square dominated by the ruins
of a medieval castle, the hotel is run by a
very nice Burgundian man and his wife. The
cooking is absolutely authentic and prepared by a chef who is always on the lookout for new ideas. One of his sources of
inspiration is ancient cookbooks – try his
guinea-fowl in flaky pastry with a sauce from
a recipe by Apicius, the Roman gourmet.
Menus 65–225F. The wine cellar is well
stocked. The hotel is a decent one-star with
showers and wc on the landing, but it's
being updated. Rooms 155F with basin,
205F with bath. You'll get a very nice welcome and enjoy the homely atmosphere.

BONNEVAL-SUR-ARC 73480

♠ |●| AUBERGE LE PRÉ CATIN

☎ 04.79.05.95.07 ➡ 04.79.05.88.07
Closed Sun evening, Mon, 5 May–25 June and 1
Oct–20 Dec. **TV**.

Service noon–2pm and 7–9pm. A lovely
stone house with a roof made of *lauzes*, flat
stones each weighing an average of 70kg. It
was built only recently but it's in the style typical of the village and blends in well with the
other buildings. You'll get a relaxed, stylish
welcome. The chef is self-taught and very
talented, so while the cuisine is genuinely
local it's very different from the standard *tartiflette* and *raclette*. He creates dishes based
entirely around the best produce he can find;
he cooks his *diots* in Cignin wine and does
good ravioli. While the portions are adequate,
the prices can be a bit crazy. Menus
100–160F. There's one huge bedroom with
shower/wc at 350F for two people.

BONNEVILLE 74130

⚜ ♠ |●| HÔTEL DE L'ARVE**

70 rue du Pont (Centre).
☎ 04.50.97.01.28 ➡ 04.50.25.78.39
Closed Fri evening, Sat except in Feb and Aug, and
Sept. **TV. Lock-up car park**.

A conventional provincial hotel where the
owner plays cards with his friends. The

rooms are classic, with good facilities – the
ones at the back look onto the garden courtyard with its picturesque entrance and the
medieval rue Brune. Doubles with shower/wc
or bath 250F. Menus start at 78F (weekdays
only) and others 80–210F. Good simple traditional dishes: *fricassée* of scallops with
ceps, veal kidneys with girolle mushrooms,
pan-fried scallops caramelised in orange
juice, langoustines with bacon, and breast of
duck with quinces. Fast service with a smile.
10% discount on the room rate Sept–July.

BOURG-D'OISANS (LE) 38520

⚜ ♠ |●| LE FLORENTIN**

Rue Thiers (Centre).
☎ 04.76.80.01.61 ➡ 04.76.80.05.49
Closed Tues in May and June, 1 Oct–15 Dec and 15
April–15 May. **TV. Car park**.

The Nevros have created a very homely
atmosphere in their hotel. They know the area
well and are able to give you all sorts of
advice on things to do and see. Clean, comfortable doubles, 175–250F with basin,
50–310F with shower/wc or bath. Tasty
cooking: roast lamb with garlic, cheese pastries, chicken with crayfish. Menus 105–195F.
Half board, compulsory July–Aug, costs
245–295F. Free house apéritif.

GARDE (LA) 38520 (4KM N)

⚜ |●| LES GORGES DE SARENNE

Centre; take the N91 then the D211.
☎ 04.76.80.07.85
Closed Sun evening out of season, Mon, a fortnight in
June and a fortnight Sept/Oct. **TV. Car park**.

Service from noon and 7pm. There are 21
bends in the road up to Alpe-d'Huez and this
restaurant is the perfect rest stop, with a wonderful view of the gorges and the forest. Rose-
Marie and Jacky greet you warmly. Service is
swift, the atmosphere friendly, and the place
is sparklingly clean. Weekday lunch menu
69F, with others 70–130F. Their specialities
are crab *au gratin*, salmon escalope with
queen scallops and sorrel sauce, and scallop
salad. They also do delicious *raclette*, *fondue*
and *gardette*, their own style of *fondue*.
There's a little terrace for sunny days. They
have a few guest rooms at 220F a night but
you must stay for a minimum of two nights.
Half board 385F. They offer a good weekend
deal – two days' skiing, dinner, bed and
breakfast for 550F per person. Free coffee.

ORNON   38520 (7KM S)

🕭 |●| RESTAURANT LE POTIRON

La Palud; take the D526 in the direction of La Mure.
☎ 04.76.80.63.27.
Closed Sun evening out of season. **Disabled access**.
Car park.

You'll find this restaurant on a bend in the road.
It has a warm decor and is always pretty busy.
Good snacks are served all day: *casse-croûte
campagnard*, raw ham, bacon omelette, fresh
cream cheese, soup, salad and *terrine*. The
95F menu gets you a plate of raw ham and the
meat dish of the day served with vegetables
prepared in Dany's own special way – in the
form of celery flan, say, or courgette fritters
with coriander, or "donkey's ears" (vegetable
turnovers). Try the homemade walnut or gentian wine. Menus 65–155F. In winter, it's best
to call in advance or you might find it's closed.
Free apéritif.

VENOSC   38520 (15.5KM SE)

🕭 🏠 |●| HÔTEL-RESTAURANT LES AMIS DE LA MONTAGNE*

Le Courtil; take the N91 then the D530.
☎ 04.76.11.10.00 ➡ 04.76.80.20.56
Closed 29 Sept–22 Dec and 21 April–16 June.
Swimming pool.

What the Durdan clan don't know about
Venosc, a little mountain village 1000m up,
isn't worth knowing. They run hotels, *gîtes*
restaurants, shops and boutiques, give skiing lessons and rent out rooms. Most of their
efforts, however, are focused on this hotel,
which is sheer delight if you're after peace
and quiet. Rooms 250–320F with shower/wc
or bath; half board 270–290F per person.
Great breakfasts, 40F. You dine in the grill
room, which has lots of atmosphere. Menus,
62–140F, list regional food; the speciality is
grenaillade (potatoes with Saint-Marcellin, a
mild goat's cheese), scrambled eggs with
morels, trout with walnuts, duck thigh with
bilberries and so on. There are at least a
dozen sorts of salads, grills, *fondues* and
raclette. The desserts look good and taste
better. The hotel has a pool, a Turkish bath
and a sauna. 10% discount on the room rate.

MIZOEN   38520 (18KM E)

🏠 |●| LE PANORAMIQUE**

Le bourg; take the N91 then the D25.
☎ 04.76.80.06.25 ➡ 04.76.80.25.12
TV. **Car park**.

In a charming old mountain village, set in wild
country with splendid views of the deep valley,
this huge chalet is a lovely place for a break.
Comfortable rooms, 285–335F; some have
balconies which are planted with luxuriant
flowers in summer. Half board 265–285F, is
compulsory June–Sept and 14 Dec–1 May. In
good weather, the well-prepared classic cuisine is served on a sunny terrace from where
you can enjoy the panoramic view. Menus,
110F and 140F, list *fondue*, *raclette* and *tartiflette*.

BESSE-EN-OISANS   38142 (20KM E)

🕭 🏠 |●| HÔTEL ALPIN

How to get there: take the N91, then the D25.
☎ 04.76.80.06.55 ➡ 04.76.80.12.45
Sheds for bikes and motorbikes.

In one of the most beautiful villages in the
Oisan area, this chalet hotel offers genuine
mountain hospitality. The simple, no-frills
rooms are beautifully maintained, and cost
220–270F for a double. It's well worth going
half board, which costs 230–250F. The
pleasant dining room has huge beams hewn
from pine trunks and walls built from local
stone. The good family cooking is generously served, but they eat early, and there's no
dinner menu – you get what the *patronne*
feels like cooking. There's always a hearty
soup, good *hors d'œuvres* and a tasty,
homely main dish. They can prepare specialities to order, including *fondue*, *farcis* and
*crozets*Menus 70–120F. À *la carte*, available
for lunch or dinner, lists snacks such as
omelettes or *tartiflette*. *Gîtes,* studios or small
apartments for rent. Free coffee and 10%
discount on the room rate in low season.

BOURG-EN-BRESSE   01000

🕭 🏠 |●| HÔTEL-RESTAURANT DU MAIL**

46 av. du Mail (West); from the centre of town, follow
the signs for Villefranche-sur-Saône.
☎ 04.74.21.00.26 ➡ 04.74.21.29.55
Closed Sun evening, Mon, 14–31 July and 22 Dec–6
Jan. **TV**. **Lock-up car park**.

The pretty, comfortable rooms in this hotel
are decorated in contemporary style, and
you'll appreciate the air conditioning in
summer. Those overlooking the garden are
quietest – even the double glazing in the
others can't cut out all the noise from the
station. Good value doubles 110F with

shower/wc and 220F with bath. The rather plush restaurant is popular with the locals. Set menus, 150–300F, list traditional local cooking such as frogs' legs and *poulet de Bresse*, and an impressive dessert trolley. Nice terrace. Free *digestif*.

☎ HÔTEL DE FRANCE***

19 pl. Bernard (Centre).
☎ 04.74.23.30.24 ➡ 04.74.23.69.90
TV. Car park.

Mid-19th-century hotel in the centre of town, on a charming little square with a village atmosphere. The entrance is very grand, and you almost hesitate to walk on the beautiful mosaic floors. Stylish doubles with basin but no TV 195F, and up to 420F with bath. Some have been refurbished. The whole place has a chic feel, but the welcome is relaxed and friendly. There's a plush bar that stays open late.

☎ LES NÉGOCIANTS**

9 rue Charles-Robin (Centre); it's at the corner of 10 rue du 4-Septembre.
☎ 04.74.23.13.24 ➡ 04.74.23.71.61
Closed Sat and Sun out of season. **TV. Pay car park.**

A charming 17th-century coaching inn that has aged beautifully. There's a monumental wooden staircase, panelled walls and old-fashioned lanterns. The welcome is quietly polite, as if the staff didn't want to spoil the serenity of the place. If you have a room overlooking the flowery inner courtyard you will forget you're in the town centre. Doubles 200F with shower, with shower/wc 265F or 300F with bath. Free use of car park and 10% discount in Oct.

☎ LE LOGIS DE BROU**

132 bd. de Brou (South); it's near Brou museum.
☎ 04.74.22.11.55 ➡ 04.74.22.37.30
TV. Lock-up car park.

A blank, 1960s building that's hardly brightened up by the blue balconies. However, inside it is a comfortable, attractive hotel. The hall is full of flowers and the owner greets you with a winning smile. The bright, clean rooms in soft colours are well soundproofed. Doubles with shower/wc 320F or 350–400F with bath.

🎤 ☎ LE TERMINUS***

19 rue Alphonse-Baudin (Centre); it's 50m from the train station.
☎ 04.74.21.01.21 ➡ 04.74.21.36.47
TV.

This classic terminus hotel has a grand Napoleon III hall and a wonderful antique lift.

It is set in superb grounds with a rose garden and ornamental ponds, so all the rooms are quiet. They vary in style – some have period furniture, while others are modern. Doubles with shower/wc and TV 380F or 450F with bath. Breakfast 50F. Free apéritif.

◖◗ CHEZ TRICHARD

4 cours de Verdun (Centre); it's opposite the cinema.
☎ 04.74.23.11.24
Closed Sun, Mon and three weeks in July.

This bistro is a local favourite. The short menu lists local specialities: pike *quenelles*, Bresse chicken with cream and morels, and steak with Roquefort or mustard sauce. Swift, experienced staff. Menus 78–90F.

◖◗ LA TABLE RONDE

126 bd. de Brou (Southwest); head for Brou church.
☎ 04.74.23.71.17
Closed Sat lunchtime, Sun and a fortnight in Aug.

Service noon–2.30pm and 7.15–11pm. In the space of just a few years, this restaurant has become *the* place. The cosy dining room is small so you should consider booking. You may well see a celeb or two, and photographs of stars who have eaten here line the walls. The fairly rich cooking is a mixture of modern and classical – chicken, frogs' legs, calf's head *gribiche*, and the like – and is full of interesting tastes and flavours. At 78–98F, the menus are well within the reach of mere mortals and the dishes change weekly. À la carte is a bit more pricey, but duck breast with creamed *foie gras* isn't something you eat every day. Courteous service.

◖◗ LA BRASSERIE DU FRANÇAISE

7 av. Alsace-Lorraine (Centre); it's near the tourist office.
☎ 04.74.22.55.14
Closed Sat evening, Sun, Aug and 24 Dec–2 Jan.

This splendid Second Empire dining room attracts a clientele of lawyers, journalists and Bourg notables. The ceiling mouldings and bevelled mirrors are lovely, and the service is as classy as the cooking. Excellent, honest regional cuisine and traditional brasserie dishes; *choucroute*, chicken in cream sauce, seafood platter, and steak and chips. Dish of the day 70F, menus 135–295F. Terrace in summer.

CEYZÉRIAT   01250 (8KM SE)

☎ ◖◗ HÔTEL-RESTAURANT RELAIS DE LA TOUR**

1 rue Joseph-Bernier (Centre); it's on the D979.
☎ 04.74.30.01.87 ➡ 04.74.25.03.36

Closed Wed and Sun evening out of season and 15 Oct–10 Nov. **TV**.

This is a typical, classic country hotel that's always full of regulars. The reception desk and lounge look like they date from the 1970s, which is a stark contrast with the rustic bedrooms. 220F for a double with bath. In the dining room, which has deep, comfortable chairs and an impressive antique dresser, you can eat decent, traditional regional cooking with menus starting at 75F for weekday lunch.

MEILLONNAS   01370 (15KM NE)

⚸ |●| AUBERGE AU VIEUX MEILLONNAS

How to get there: take the N83 in the direction of Lons-le-Saunier, then the A40 to Meillonnas.
☎ and ➡ 04.74.51.34.46
Closed Tues evening, Wed and Sun evening from Easter to 1 Nov. **Car park**.

Service noon–2pm and 7–10pm. This little village inn in a pretty ochre-coloured stone house is typical of this peaceful part of the world. Monsieur does the cooking while Madame looks after the front of house. In fine weather, you can eat in the delightful garden with its weeping willows, pine trees and banana plants. Dishes include raw ham from the Tarn, veal escalopes in lime juice, rabbit with rosemary in flaky pastry, medallions of monkfish with saffron, chicken with cream and morels, and frogs' legs with a parsley garnish. Weekday lunch menu 68F, then others 98–210F. Free coffee.

BOURGET-DU-LAC (LE)   73370

🏠 |●| HÔTEL-RESTAURANT LA CERISAIE**

618 route des Tournelles (North); 2.5km from Bourget, on the D42 in the direction of Les Catons.
☎ 04.79.25.01.29 ➡ 04.79.25.26.19
Closed Sun evening, Wed out of season, 1–8 Jan, and Nov. **TV**. **Car park**.

Service 12.15–2pm and 7.15–9pm. The hotel stands at the foot of the Dent du Chat mountain, surrounded by fields planted with cherry trees. The proprietors are from Chamonix – Brigitte looks after the hotel while husband Philippe does the cooking. Some rooms have a splendid view of the lake which inspired Lamartine, one of France's great Romantic poets. Doubles 165F with basin, 230–280F with shower/wc. Half board, 270F, is compulsory July–Aug. The chef produces a lot of fish dishes – the 98F menu (not served

Sun) lists *lavaret* (a salmon-like fish) roasted with morels, zander with crayfish tails and Saint-Marcellin (a mild cheese) *en chemise*. Other menus 135–225F.

🏠 |●| HÔTEL DU LAC

bd. du Lac (Centre).
☎ 04.79.25.00.10
Closed Wed and 15 Nov–15 March.
Disabled access. **Car park**.

This hotel, a pretty stone building standing close to the water, has recently been taken over by a new team. Simple doubles with basin 190F, up to 300F with shower/wc. In summer, sit on the flower-filled terrace and watch the comings and goings at the lakeshore. Fish, including fried freshwater fish and *lavaret*, is much in evidence *à la carte* and on the set menus, 115–170F.

VIVIERS-DU-LAC   73420 (3KM E)

|●| RESTAURANT LA MAISON DES PÊCHEURS

611 rive du Lac (East); follow the lakeshore in the direction of Aix-les-Bains.
☎ and ➡ 04.79.54.41.29
Closed Mon evening and Tues. **Garden**.

If you wander into the garden of this waterside restaurant, you'll see all the bright fishing boats that have been hauled out of the water to dry. In the bar, fishermen compare the size of their catch over a drink. Fish dishes are the mainstay of the kitchen's reputation: fillets of perch or *lavaret*, frogs' legs, trout, and fried freshwater fish. Weekday menu 68F, with others 118–198F.

BOURG-SAINT-ANDÉOL   07700

⚸ 🏠 |●| HÔTEL-RESTAURANT LE PRIEURÉ**

quais du Rhône.
☎ 04.75.54.62.99 ➡ 04.75.54.63.73
Closed Sat lunchtime and Sun evening out of season, Sun in summer, the last fortnight in Sept and Christmas. **TV**.

The oldest part of this imposing building on the banks of the Rhône dates from the 12th century. Each bedroom is individually furnished and the lounges and terrace overlook the Rhône. Doubles 350–380F. The main road can be disturbing so ask for one on the side. Summer platter for 54F, a weekday lunch menu 68F, and others up to 145F. Specialities include red mullet sautéed with sorrel and veal sweetbreads with apple and Calvados. Free apéritif.

BOURG-SAINT-MAURICE   73700

⅄ ♠ |●| HÔTEL-RESTAURANT LA PETITE AUBERGE*

Le Reverset; it's 1km from the centre of town on the N90 in the direction of Moûtiers.
☎ 04.79.07.05.86. **Restaurant** ☎ 04.79.07.37.11
➥ 04.79.07.26.51
Hotel closed May and 15 Oct–15 Nov. **Restaurant closed** Sun evening and Mon. **Car park**.

Service noon–2pm and 7.30–9pm. This quiet little inn is away from the main road. Unpretentious, but ageing rooms go for 220F with shower or 270F with bath. The restaurant, separate from the hotel, offers simple, pleasant food of consistent quality, and fast and friendly service. You can eat in the low-ceilinged dining room in winter, or the tree-shaded terrace in summer. Set weekday menu 80F, and others 118–128F. Free apéritif and 10% discount on the room rate Sept–June.

⅄ ♠ HÔTEL ATLANTIC***

69 route d'Hauteville (Southwest): it's 2km from the centre of town; take the N90 in the direction of Moûtiers, then turn left onto the small road to Hauteville.
☎ 04.79.07.01.70 ➥ 04.70.07.51.55
Disabled access. TV.

This hotel is well enough out of town to be peaceful, and the garden trails out into the surrounding fields. It's a fairly recent building but it's hard to believe that the stone walls haven't been there for ever. Though it's a chic little place, you receive a genuinely warm welcome from the two sisters who own it. They split their time between running this hotel and a hut up in the mountains. The feeling in the hotel is spacious and bright, from the reception area to the rooms. Doubles with shower/wc 260F, 390F with bath, 440F for the nicest ones with balconies and a mountain view. Free use of sauna.

SÉEZ   73700 (4KM [)

⅄ ♠ |●| RELAIS DES VILLARDS**

Villard-Dessus; it's 4km from the centre – take the N90 that goes up to the Petit-Saint-Bernard pass.
☎ 04.79.41.00.66 ➥ 04.79.41.08.13
Closed Mon in winter, May and 1 Oct–20 Dec. **TV. Car park**.

You're just 20km from Italy here, and this typical chalet provides the last stop before the border for many travellers. Ten pleasant,

attractive rooms with shower 260–320F or 300–380F with bath. Half board 250–340F. You'll get a warm welcome and service with a smile. Cooking is traditional, with a few Savoy specialities: *matafan* (a coarse pancake), *tartiflette*, *fondue* made with Beaufort cheese, and so on. Menus 78F, 130F or *à la carte*. The hotel arranges sporting activities and courses in paragliding, riding, white-water rafting and mountain-biking. They also offer a ski package at Les Arcs. Free apéritif.

|●| RESTAURANT L'OLYMPIQUE

rue de la Libération; take the N90 in the direction of Tignes-Val d'Isère for the Col du Pont Saint-Bernard.
☎ 04.79.41.01.52
Closed Wed and 11–28 June. **Disabled access**.

Service noon–2pm and 7.30–8.45pm. A very simple restaurant owned by a local man with an infectious good humour. Menus at 88F (lunchtime) and 120F, or *à la carte*. The choice is long and varied: fillets of sole in lemon sauce, veal kidneys in Madeira and chicken with crayfish. At 62F their *fondue* is one of the cheapest around. You can eat here almost all year, which is unusual in this neck of the mountains.

BOUVANTE   26190

⅄ ♠ |●| AUBERGE DU PIONNIER

col du Pionnier
☎ 04.75.48.57.12 ➥ 04.75.48.58.26
Closed Tues out of season and 1 Nov to Christmas.

There's a "hôtel au naturel" classification in French hotels, and this one, on the edge of a forest and by the GR9 walking trail, qualifies. Its nine simple rooms look over the mountains, the pine forest and the meadows where wild animals come to feed. Doubles with basin 170F, 265F with shower/wc. In the restaurant, over plates of steaming dishes, conversations turn to the woods, the wild and hunting. The amazing lady owner is both waitress and cook – menus, 85–180F, feature solid slices of *pâté*, chicken with cream sauce and potatoes, and a slice of homemade tart. Her speciality is chicken with crayfish tails. Half board, compulsory in summer, costs 250F. Free coffee.

BUIS-LES-BARONNIES   26170

♠ LES ARCADES-LE LION D'OR

pl. du Marché (Centre).
☎ 04.75.28.81.13 ➥ 04.75.28.12.07
Closed Jan. **TV. Lock-up garage**.

Well-located in the centre of town on a ravishing arcaded square. There's a family atmosphere and you get an excellent welcome. The furnishings in the hall are higgledy-piggledy but the rooms are spruce with modern bathrooms and good beds. Doubles from 190F, 320F for a room sleeping four. In summer, they open the garden to guests.

⚘ ESCAPADE CLOÎTRE DES DOMINICAINS

rue de la Cour du Roi Dauphin (Centre).
☎ 04.75.28.06.77 ➡ 04.75.28.13.20

Reception staffed 9am–noon and 5–7pm. Housed in a restored, 16th-century Dominican convent in the centre of town, this is a good option if you want to be centrally located without paying a fortune. It's very well run. Ask for a room looking out onto the cloisters. A studio costs 290F a night for two, and apartments for two to five people can be rented by the week, 2150–2,950F. There's no restaurant but you can order a meal for 75F. Bikes can be parked in the courtyard.

❙●❙ LE GRILL DU FOUR À PAIN

24 av. Boissis d'Anglas (Southwest); coming into town, it's before you reach the Mensonges bridge.
☎ 04.75.28.10.34
Closed Sun evening, Mon Sept–June, Mon lunchtime July–Aug, and 15 Nov–15 Feb. **Car park**.

A nice little restaurant where the service is pleasant and the sophisticated food is good and inexpensive. Menus 88–148F. Specialities include asparagus and artichoke *ratatouille*, scallop *cassolette* and lamb with creamed thyme sauce. They do a *plat du terroir* for 68F including a glass of wine, and the wines are very reasonably priced. There's a shaded terrace in the garden.

❙●❙ LA FOURCHETTE

Les Arcades, pl. du Marché; (Centre).
☎ 04.75.28.03.31
Closed Sun evening and Mon.

The chef started over twenty years ago, and still approaches his work with the same serious professionalism as he did then. Delicious regional cuisine and a smiling, friendly welcome. Pleasant dining room with sponged walls hung with watercolours. The specialities include ravioli *de Royans au gratin*, lamb shank with herbs, *croustade* with morels and very tender meat. If you're lucky enough to find crayfish with cream and tarragon sauce on the menu, go for it.

Menus 130F and 190F. A good selection of local wines at honest prices, 39–57F.

PLAISIANS　　　　26170 (8.5KM SE)

🜲 ❙●❙ AUBERGE DE LA CLUE

How to get there: take the D72 then the D526.
☎ 04.75.28.01.17
Closed Mon–Fri and Sun evening out of season, Mon April–Sept, and Oct. **Disabled access. Car park**.

Hordes of gourmets stream up the mountain to this place, especially at the weekend. The restaurant serves hefty portions of good, cheap food concocted by two brothers. Their mother, who's got a terrific laugh and a great line in patter, looks after the dining room. She'll set a *terrine* on your table for you to help yourself until your meal arrives – you could do worse than to start with *caillette*, a delicious haggis-like preparation of baked pork and vegetables with herbs, and follow it with home-made mutton tripe and sheep's trotters or kid stew, rabbit with olive paste, fresh monkfish or lamb's sweetbreads. For dessert, try the quince sorbet with quince liqueur – it's out of this world. Menus 145–165F. You can see the Ventoux from the window. Free coffee.

MÉRINDOL-LES-OLIVIERS　　26170 (9KM W)

🜲 ⚘ ❙●❙ AUBERGE DE LA GLORIETTE

How to get there: on the D147.
☎ 04.75.28.71.08 ➡ 04.75.28.71.08
Closed Sun evening and Thurs out of season, and 5 Jan–1 Feb. **Car park**.

On the left there's a baker's where people come to bake their own bread and cakes, on the right an old-style restaurant, and in between the two a wonderful terrace. Sit in the shade of the old plane tree for breakfast, relax to the gurgling of the nearby spring, and gaze at the hillsides with their olive groves and apricot orchards. Doubles 250F with shower/wc, 300F with bath. The rooms at the back are particularly quiet. In the restaurant, snacks include good savoury tarts, sausage with olives and a fruit tart straight from the oven. À la carte you'll pay around 150F, and in the evening, there's a single menu at 100F. Free apéritif.

CHALAMONT　　　　01320

❙●❙ RESTAURANT CLERC

Grande-Rue.
☎ 04.74.61.70.30 ➡ 04.74.61.75.00

Closed Mon, Tues, 28 June–7 July, 15 Nov–1 Dec and 3–20 Jan. **Car park**.

Service noon–2pm and 7.30–9.30pm. The menu tells you that the restaurant has specialised in frogs' legs for three generations and the cooking is traditional. The chef is gradually trying to introduce some changes but doing so slowly so as not to upset the local people who've been coming here since the first generation opened the place. There's a "traditional" menu at 150F and others up to 330F that read like guides to local cooking: frogs' legs sautéed in butter with herbs, salad of *goujons* of fried carp, chicken with morels. Weekday lunch menu 90F.

SAINTE-CROIX   01120 (16KM SW)

🛏 |●| CHEZ NOUS

It's in the village; take the D22 as far as Pizay, then turn right onto the D61.
☎ 04.78.06.60.60 ➡ 04.78.06.63.26
Closed Sun evening, Mon, and Dec.

Set well back from the road, in the bucolic countryside, this comfortable establishment offers very quiet rooms in a modern annexe. Doubles with bath 295F. Menus start at 88F (not served Sun), with others 112–295F. Though you can get traditional cuisine, they also list interesting variations on the regional theme: fresh frogs' legs, chicken with cream sauce, and fish.

CHAMBÉRY   73000

🛏 |●| HÔTEL-RESTAURANT AUX PERVENCHES**

Les Charmettes (Southeast); from the centre of town head for vallon des Charmettes and the Jean-Jacques Rousseau museum.
☎ 04.79.33.34.26 ➡ 04.79.60.02.52
📧 info@pervenches.net
TV. Car park.

Service noon–2pm and 7–9pm (later by reservation). In the late summer of 1736, Jean-Jacques Rousseau brought Mme de Warens to live in a country house in Les Charmettes. Thanks to his reputation, the delightful little valley has been spared the worst excesses of the developers and has retained its country feel – the hotel is certainly like a country inn. In summer, you eat on the terrace in the shade of the trees with only the sound of birdsong to intrude on your enjoyment. Really traditional dishes form the basis of this cuisine; the 95F menu, called "*tradi-*

tion", lists house *foie gras* with sea salt, duck breast with honey and spices and so on. Other menus up to 195F. Double rooms with basin 170F, 210F with bath. They're cool in summer but in need of a bit of modernising.

🛏 |●| HÔTEL DE LA BANCHE*

pl. de l'Hôtel-de-Ville (Centre); it's near the old town.
☎ 04.79.33.15.62
Closed 1–10 May and 1–15 Sept.

A popular place, well located on a pedestrianised square, near the old town centre. The rooms are from another era and prices are attractive; double 200F with shower, 220F with shower/wc. Numbers 18, 19 and 20 look onto an extraordinary colonnaded alleyway. The restaurant is good and cheap, too: menus, 65–120F, list *tartiflette*, frogs' legs and cod *Lyonnaise* with potatoes. Free coffee.

🛏 |●| HÔTEL LE REVARD**

41 av. de la Gare (Centre); it's opposite the train station.
☎ 04.79.62.04.64 ➡ 04.79.96.37.26
TV. Garage.

Very welcoming professional staff at your service in reception. The rooms are rather cold and almost aggressively functional – they resemble ones you'd expect to find in a chain. Some, happily, look onto a lovely little garden. Doubles with shower/wc from 260F. The restaurant serves traditional dishes and is good for a quick meal. Menus from 62F.

🛏 |●| HÔTEL-RESTAURANT SAVOYARD**

35 pl. Monge (Southeast); it's on the square next to the carré Curial.
☎ 04.79.33.36.55 ➡ 04.79.85.25.70
Closed Sun except public holidays or for groups.
TV. Car park.

Service noon–2pm and 7–10.30pm. This is a big, friendly establishment with ten or so soundproofed rooms with geranium-filled window-boxes. Doubles with shower/wc 270F. Half board is compulsory at the weekend in Feb. The owner is descended from a long line of restaurateurs. Menus, 80–138F, feature Savoy specialities and regional dishes. This place has been on the right track for years. Free coffee.

🛏 CITY HÔTEL**

9 rue Denfert-Rochereau (Centre); it's between carré Curial and Saint-François cathedral.
☎ 04.79.85.76.79 ➡ 04.79.85.86.11
TV. Car park.

The hotel is right in the centre of town, so the rooms overlooking the street are noisy. Even though the street has been pedestrianised the bars get lively, especially on Friday and Saturday nights. The rooms are functional and decorated in very contemporary style – which is a bit of a surprise in an 18th-century building. You'll get a friendly welcome and at least the room prices are decent. Doubles 270F with shower/wc and 300F with bath. 10% discount on the room rate.

▮●▮ L'HYPOTÉNUSE

141 carré Curial (Centre).
☎ 04.79.85.80.15 ➡ 04.79.85.80.18
Closed Sun, Mon, a week in winter, 14 July–14 Aug.

This restaurant, situated on the peaceful old barracks square, boasts a modern, stylish decor that provides an appropriate setting for the chef's sophisticated, flavourful cooking. Weekday lunch menu 89F, and 98–250F – good value for money. Try the leek and Reblochon cheese turnover, rabbit *confit* with pine honey, steamed bass with hazelnut oil, or the sole *gratinée*. In the summer, they open up a terrace on the square.

▮●▮ EL MOSQUITO

153 carré Curial (Centre).
☎ 04.79.75.28.00
Closed Sun.

Where most Tex–Mex joints put all the effort into creating the right decor, this one puts all its effort into preparing the right food. The menu lists chilli and tacos, of course, along with some Inca and Aztec dishes that are quite remarkable. The desserts are just as good, beautifully presented and served with wide smiles. 100–120F for a complete meal.

▮●▮ RESTAURANT LA VANOISE

44 av. Pierre-Lanfrey; it's near the main post office.
☎ 04.79.69.02.78
closed Sun evening.

The decor is bright, young and modern and the restaurant has a clientele of loyal regulars. In contrast, the cooking is traditional, but it does display brilliant, inventive touches. The menus change every two weeks and the dishes on the à *la carte* menu change even more frequently. The chef likes to cook all kinds of fish such as char *meunière* or red mullet with basi and *bouillabaisse*. Menus 120–240F, or 200F à *la carte*. The wine list is as long as your arm, listing prestigious Burgundies or little-known Savoy wines. Best to book.

APREMONT   73190 (8KM SE)

▮●▮ RESTAURANT LE DEVIN

Lieu-dit Au Devin; take the D201, and once you get to Apremont, follow the signs.
☎ 04.79.28.33.43
Closed Sun evening, Mon, a week in Jan and a week Aug/Sept.

Service noon–3.30pm and 7pm–midnight. This is a country restaurant of the first degree, somewhat lost among the hills of the Apremont wine country. The dining room is rustic and pretty, and the menu features honest and interesting Savoy dishes that stray well beyond the standard tourist fare of *fondue* and *tartiflette*. The house speciality is *farçon savoyard*, potatoes baked with bacon, prunes, pears, raisins and eggs. You can choose à *la carte* or from the 75F weekday lunch menu or others up to 110F.

SAINT-JEAN-D'ARVEY   73230 (8KM NE)

⚕ 🏠 ▮●▮ HÔTEL-RESTAURANT THERME*

How to get there: take the N512 and then the D912 in the direction of La Feclaz; it's outside the village on the road to Bauges.
☎ 04.79.28.40.33 ➡ 04.79.28.46.63
Closed Wed except July–Aug. **TV. Car park**.

This used to be a conventional place but it's now run by a young woman who does everything herself. It's her home as well as a hotel – take a look at her welcome message on the menu. The rooms are modest, with basin only, 160F, but they're quiet and well maintained. The dining room is charming; the view from the vast terrace takes in the entire Savoy valley. Good, simple cooking – weekday lunch menu 90F, then others 130–170F. Occasional theatrical or musical evenings. Free coffee.

CHAMONIX   74400

⚕ 🏠 LA BOULE DE NEIGE*

362 rue Joseph-Vallot (Centre).
☎ 04.50.53.04.48 ➡ 04.50.55.91.09
📧 laboule@claranet.fr
Closed Nov. **Car park.**

Very close to the centre, but off the tourist beat. They have a few, really nice rooms done up in traditional style; doubles with basin at 205F or 285F with shower, depending on the season. You can help yourself to as much breakfast as you like from the buffet, and there are hearty breakfast dishes à *la carte*. The clientèle is young and international, and everyone gets a great welcome: the young owners are happy to give you any information you need. Free coffee.

🕴🏠 HÔTEL DES LACS**

992 route des Gaillands (Southwest); it's five minutes from the centre of town in the Gaillands area.
☎ 04.50.53.02.08 ➡ 04.50.53.66.64
Closed end Sept to beginning of June.

This hotel, which faces Mont Blanc, is an old house with an old-fashioned bar – but it's a different story in the rooms, which have been entirely refurbished. They're tasteful, functional and good value for money. Some even have a balcony and a view of Mont Blanc. Doubles with shower or bath 280–310F. Polite, friendly welcome. Free apéritif.

🏠 HÔTEL DU FAUCIGNY**

118 pl. de l'Église (Centre); it's opposite the tourist office.
☎ 04.50.53.01.17 ➡ 04.50.53.01.17
Closed June and Nov. **TV**. **Garden**. **Car park**.

An unpretentious little hotel with a homely atmosphere in a quiet street. It's a family-run place and though the rooms aren't particularly attractive, the facilities are perfectly adequate. 350F for a double with shower/wc. There's a small, interior courtyard and a pleasant garden.

🕴🏠 |●| HÔTEL LA SAVOYARDE***

28 rue des Moussoux (North); it's beside the Brévent cable car station.
☎ 04.50.53.00.77 ➡ 04.50.55.86.82
€ lasavoyarde@wanadoo.fr
Closed Tues lunchtime, 9–23 May and 26 Nov–20 Dec. **TV**. **Car park**.

The little chalet, facing Mont Blanc, has been renovated and extended. There are fourteen charming rooms with all mod cons, which justifies the price, 580–738F. The restaurant serves very good food and the service is great. Menus 88–185F, and even the cheapest one is superb: Reblochon (a mild local cheese) in flaky pastry or chicory salad for starters, escalope of sea trout with a creamed parsley sauce or the local version of cabbage soup as main courses, and cheese or pastry of the day to finish. If you'd rather just have a dish, try the jacket potatoes or raclette. Free apéritif.

🕴 |●| LE BERLUCOQUET

79 Galerie Alpina (Centre).
☎ 04.50.53.98.41
Closed Sun and Mon out of season.

This wine bar is in a lovely little wooden room – sitting here, you forget that you're on the ground floor of the *Alpina* hotel, which is one of the town's architectural monstrosities. The wine list changes constantly, because the boss searches out wonderful vintages and makes all sorts of interesting discoveries which he sells at honest prices. There's an easy-going family atmosphere. Mum's in the kitchen, where she prepares lots of slow-cook dishes like *daube à la provençale*, *pot-au-feu* and so on. There's a short lunch menu, 79F, and others 125–140F. They offer a few cheese specialities not commonly found in the region: *fondue* made from Comté cheese, and *boîte chaude*, which is Vacherin cheese melted in the oven. Lots of wines by the glass, of course, beers from specialist breweries and *pastis* made to an old recipe. There's a small cellar set aside for cigar-smokers. Free *digestif*.

🕴|●| LE PANIER DES QUATRE SAISONS

24 galerie Blanc-Neige.
☎ 04.50.53.98.77 € lepanierdes4saisons@cham.org
Closed Wed, a fortnight in mid-June and a fortnight in mid-Nov.

A flight of stairs off la rue Paccard leads to this small, really charming restaurant offering excellent cooking. For freshness and inventiveness, it's unmatched by any of the touristy places – and it's good value for money. The 85F (weekday lunch) menu gives you a good meal and includes a glass of wine; other menus 110–190F. The friendly, personal welcome is refreshing in a town where so many restaurants herd you in and out as fast as possible. Free *génépi*.

ARGENTIÈRE   74400 (6KM NE)

🕴|●| LA CRÈMERIE DU GLACIER

766 route de la Glacière; in summer, take the dirt road after the Lognan cable car; in winter take the chemin de la Rosière.
☎ 04.50.54.07.52 € claudyraunel@wanadoo.fr
Closed Tues evening and Wed in winter excluding school holidays, 15 May–15 June, 20 Sept–20 Dec. **Car park**.

This restaurant, way out in the forest, is where the people from Chamonix come to get back to nature and breathe some real fresh air. They serve snacks and substantial plates of local dishes: *farçon* (potatoes with milk, eggs, bacon, raisins and prunes), which traditionally accompanies smoked ham or cured meat, simple omelettes, huge salads, *fondues* and cheese *croûtes*. In winter, there's a lunch menu at 60F and a children's menu at 40F, and expect to pay 100F *à la carte*. Free house aperitif.

LES HOUCHES   74310 (8KM W)

🎿 🏠 AUBERGE LE MONTAGNY

Lieu-dit Le Pont; as you come into the village from Chamonix, it's 450m further along on the left.
☎ 04.50.54.57.37 ➡ 04.50.54.52.97
Closed Nov and Jan. **TV. Car park**.

This farm was built in 1876 in the centre of a tranquil mountain hamlet. You'd hardly recognise it now because of all the changes that have been made, but it still has a cosy charm and the wood panelling hasn't been tampered with. The rooms are huge and pretty, and all have superb, bright bathrooms; doubles 410F. Warm welcome. The ski slopes are nearby. 10% discount except during school holidays.

CHAMOUSSET   73390

🏠 |●| HÔTEL-RESTAURANT CHRISTIN**

La Lilette (centre); take the N90 from Albertville in the direction of Chambéry, and when you reach Pont-Royal, follow the signs for Chamousset.
☎ 04.79.36.42.06 ➡ 04.79.36.45.43
Closed Sun evening, Mon, and 15 Sept–10 Oct. **TV. Car park**.

The perfect country inn, on a tiny square shaded by chestnut trees. You can hear a little brook flowing somewhere nearby, but you can't see it through the thick vegetation. The pleasant dining room has huge bay windows. The very classic cuisine uses excellent ingredients and, given the huge portions, proves good value. There's a 68F menu (not served Sun), and others 87–180F. The rooms are in the annexe and, though somewhat lacking in charm, they're spacious and comfortable; doubles 200F with shower/wc, 220F with bath. If you're a light sleeper, you may be disturbed by the trains going by at night. The staff are solicitous.

CHAMPAGNE-EN-VALROMEY   01260

🎿 🏠 |●| AUBERGE DU COL DE LA LÈBE*

How to get there: take the D8 and follow the signs for Col de la Lèbe.
☎ 04.79.87.64.54 ➡ 04.79.87.54.26
Closed Mon (Mon evening July–Aug), Tues, 1 Jan–14 April, ten days at the end of June and 15 Nov–15 Dec. **Swimming pool. TV. Car park**.

Right out in the country, on the way up to the pass, this restaurant has a cosy dining room

with lots of wood and house plants. The service is stylish but not in the least pretentious, and the sophisticated cooking includes dishes like *pâté* of ox cheek with *foie gras*, fillet of beef *gourmandine*, zander with chive cream and *terrine* of pears and summer fruits. Menus 98–212F; half board starts at 275F. They also do grills over the coals. Rooms are fairly modest but their old-fashioned air gives them a degree of style and you're guaranteed lots of peace and quiet up here. Doubles 195F with shower, 275F with bath. You get a wonderful view of the Valromey valley from the swimming pool. A free glass of local wine with each dessert.

PETIT-ABERGEMENT (LE)   01260 (15KM N)

🏠 |●| LA SOUPIÈRE A DES OREILLES

How to get there: on the D31.
☎ 04.79.87.65.81 ➡ 04.79.87.54.46
Closed Sun evening and Mon excluding school holidays, and 1 Nov–15 Dec. **Car park**.

A substantial stone building in a quiet village 800m up. Claude Masclet left the French railways and moved here with his wife Colette some ten years ago. The move was encouraged by a TV personality friend, so the Masclets decided to name the place after his TV show – it translates as "The Soup Tureen Has Ears". Most customers have become friends and you quickly feel at home. The rooms are simple but pleasant and the only sound you'll hear is the bells from the Romanesque church next door. Doubles with shower/wc 190F. The rustic dining room is a great place to eat good home cooking: excellent raw ham, *diots* (pork and vegetable sausages), hot sausage, *fondues*, and chicken in cream and morel sauce. Menus 75–145F. The terrace gets the full force of the sun; it's off the bar, where there's always an exhibition of paintings. Claude has set up an annual painting festival, held at the beginning of August. If you're here in winter and enjoy cross-country skiing, you'll be in your element.

CHAMPAGNY-EN-VANOISE   73350

🏠 |●| LES CHALETS DU BOUQUETIN****

Le Planay; head in the direction of Champagny-le-Haut.
☎ 04.79.55.01.13 ➡ 04.79.55.04.76
e info@bouquetin.com
Closed 15 Oct–15 Dec. **TV. Disabled access. Car park**.

The menus here change every day and you eat good, wholesome, local dishes. *À la carte*, around 150F, you can get *raclette*, *pierrade* (where your food is cooked on a hot stone), *fondue*, *pela* (potatoes, onions and Reblochon cheese), or *croûte savoyarde* (ham on a base of flaky pastry with cheese sauce). The large terrace under the birch trees affords a panoramic view of Courchevel. They have rooms and flats for two to twenty people, let on a daily or weekly basis. Doubles 350–420F with bath.

CHAPELLE-EN-VERCORS (LA) 26420

☆ ☎ I●I HÔTEL DU NORD

av. de Provence (Centre).
☎ 04.75.48.22.13
Closed Sun lunchtime Oct–April, and a fortnight in Nov.

A brilliant, understated, unpretentious hotel with seven rooms. Doubles 185F with shower and 250F with shower/wc. Rooms have views over the Vercors rather than of the mountains. Family and regional cooking, including dishes like mushroom ravioli, roast lamb and cep omelette. There's a dish of the day for 50F including wine, a menu at 75F, and *à la carte* for around 100F. Half board 195–230F. Free apéritif.

CHASSELAY 38470

☆ ☎ I●I L'AUBERGE DE LA BOURRELIÈRE**

au bourg (Centre); it's on the D518 between Saint-Étienne-de-Geoirs and Saint-Marcellin.
☎ 04.76.64.21.03 ➡ 04.76.54.25.97
TV. Car park.

This inn, run by a nice couple, is typical of a new generation of country hotels that combine dynamism and tradition. Comfortable bedrooms for 190F with bath. The pleasant dining room has a good open fire and stone walls, and it leads on to a well-sheltered terrace. Excellent regional cuisine, executed with passion and served in absolutely huge portions. The weekday lunch menu, 60F, includes $\frac{1}{4}$ litre of wine, and there are others 95–148F. Good local specialities include pancakes *dauphinois* served with fresh tomato *coulis*, ravioli with St Marcellin cheese, frogs' legs with cream, *croustillant* with girolles, and snails. Every evening except Saturday they cook frogs' legs in ten different ways – you can eat as many as you like if you order a starter from the *à la carte* menu. Free *digestif*.

CHÂTEL 74390

☆ ☎ I●I HÔTEL-RESTAURANT LES FOUGÈRES**

route du Petit-Châtel (Centre).
☎ 04.50.73.21.06 ➡ 04.50.73.38.34
Closed 20 April–5 July and 24 Aug–18 Dec. **Car park**.

This authentic old farm was restored without losing its original style. It's a cheerful establishment run by a dynamic young couple. In summer it's a perfect place to unwind for a bit, while in winter everyone gets to know each other over *fondue* or *croûte savoyarde*. The bathrooms in the panelled bedrooms have been updated; rooms with shower/wc cost 240–280F for a double. Half board, 250–320F per person, is compulsory in winter. The restaurant's not open in summer, though a good buffet breakfast is served until 11am. They don't take credit cards. Free apéritif.

☆ ☎ I●I HÔTEL-RESTAURANT LA PERDRIX BLANCHE**

Pré-de-la-Joux (Centre); it's 2.5km from the centre in the direction of le Linga, at the bottom of the cable lifts.
☎ 04.50.73.22.76 ➡ 04.50.73.35.21
Closed 1 May to mid-June and mid-Sept to 1 Nov. **TV. Car park**.

This really delightful Savoy chalet stands well away from the resort in the fir trees at the foot of the ski runs. The rooms are clean, simple and cosy – some have a balcony. The soundproofing isn't totally adequate, though. Doubles 350F with shower/wc or bath. Half board, compulsory in the winter holidays, costs 300F per person. The typical local cooking – *tartiflette, berthoud* (marinated cheese that has been baked in the oven) and *fondue* – is just the thing after a day's skiing or hiking, and the menus, 80F and 120F, satisfy big appetites. Free apéritif.

I●I RESTAURANT LA BONNE MÉNAGÈRE

How to get there: it's one street north of the tourist office.
☎ 04.50.73.24.45
Closed lunchtimes in summer, May and June, mid-Sept to 20 Dec.

You'll get a delightful welcome here. The two dining rooms, decorated with old enamel plaques and little bunches of dried flowers, are popular with the local ski crowd. They serve starters like *charcuterie*, or large salads and main dishes like *berthoud, fondue*, and *croûte aux champignons* (mushrooms on a layer of flaky pastry covered with cheese and then grilled). For dessert, try the pear sorbet with pear liqueur. The prices are fair; the weekday menus at 70F and 75F include coffee and wine, or *à la carte* you'll spend 100–130F.

I●I RESTAURANT L'ABREUVOIR-CHEZ GINETTE**

hameau de Vonnes; head for Switzerland and you'll find the restaurant 1km out of town, very near lac de Vonnes.
☎ 04.50.73.24.89
Garden. Car park.

Berthoud de la vallée d'Abondance, the local speciality, is prepared very well at this authentic, country place. It's an absolutely delicious dish made from cheese, diced and marinated in white wine vinegar, Madeira and garlic before being put into the oven. They do other Savoy specialities and on holiday nights Louky gets his accordion out and everyone has a good time. Menus 80–160F or *à la carte*. From the garden, you get a great view of the mountain and the lake, which is lit up at night. Free house aperitif.

CHAPELLE D'ABONDANCE (LA) 74360 (5.5KM W)

⅍ 🏠 I●I L'ENSOLEILLÉE**

rue Principale (Centre).
☎ 04.50.73.50.42 ➡ 04.50.73.52.96
🅔 info@hotel-ensoleille.com
Closed 15 April–31 May and 30 Sept–15 Dec.
TV. Swimming pool. Car park.

The hotel, in a huge family house, thoroughly deserves its reputation. The rooms have traditional decor, but modern facilities – they've added a heated swimming pool and a Jacuzzi. Doubles with bath cost 350F. Half board, from 300F per person, is compulsory during the school holidays. Madame and her husband look after the dining room and the guests, one son runs the bar and the *Carnotzet* – where the *fondue* lovers gather – and the other is the chef. He uses only the finest ingredients, from the selection of various meats cooked on a hot stone – a local speciality – to the *cassolette* of calf's sweetbreads with cream and mushroom sauce. The dining rooms are welcoming and full of people enjoying themselves. There's a weekday menu at 115F, and others 130–180F. Free house apéritif.

⅍ 🏠 I●I LES GENTIANETTES**

Centre.
☎ 04.50.73.56.46 ➡ 04.50.73.56.39
🅔 gentianettes@wanadoo.fr
Swimming pool. TV.

A lively new place that's run by professionals. It's in the centre of the village, away from the noisy road and just footsteps from the cross-country ski trails. Bright, comfortable rooms cost 350–500F with shower/wc or bath. Half board, 260–415F per person, is compulsory in season. The restaurant, decorated like a mountain chalet, serves sophisticated cuisine that's unusually inventive for the region: mixed fish with wild chives, duck breast with bilberry vinegar, or escalope of veal with cheese and potatoes. Lunch menu 110F (not Sun), or around 150F *à la carte*. There are lovely walks in the surrounding area and a pretty little indoor swimming pool. Free apéritif or coffee.

CHÂTELARD (LE)　73630

⅍ I●I LE ROSSANE-CHEZ EVELYNE

Centre.
☎ 04.79.52.11.23 ➡ 04.79.54.83.44
Closed Wed, Thurs and Sun evenings.
TV. Garden. Car park.

On the edge of a somewhat charmless town, this is a good place from which to explore the wild Bauges region. Évelyne, the owner, will give you a firm handshake as she welcomes you to her well-run establishment. The rooms have been well refurbished with excellent facilities but for modest prices – doubles with shower/wc go for 195F. Most of them have fantastic views over the countryside. The restaurant is invaded at lunchtime; they offer a lunch menu for 70F and others 100–150F. You can have a postprandial snooze in a deck-chair in the garden, which is hardly distinguishable from the surrounding countryside. Free apéritif.

CHÂTILLON-EN-DIOIS　26410

🏠 I●I HÔTEL-RESTAURANT DU DAUPHINÉ

pl. Pierre Dévoluy (Centre).
☎ 04.75.21.13.13
Closed Tues evening, Wed, the All Saints' and Christmas holidays, and Jan–Feb.

An old hotel-café-restaurant right in the heart of the village. Its eight rooms are nicely old-fashioned but painted in fresh colours. The old furniture adds lots of charm and the floorboards creak. Room no. 7 has an iron bedstead and the bathroom is discreetly hidden in an alcove. Doubles 170F with washing facilities and 220F with shower/wc. There's a shaded terrace overlooking the road and an attractively decorated dining room (old mirror, bistro tables and friezes on the walls). The seasons and the whim of the chef are responsible for the frequent changes to the menu: fresh goat's chees with pesto and pickled tomatoes, *bouillabaisse* Provençale, *aiguillette* of guinea-fowl with blackcurrants. The *menu du jour*, 78F, includes a glass of wine. You can choose with your eyes closed because everything is freshly cooked and the chef has real originality. He also cooks for the local school – lucky kids! Even if you're not eating, you should try the home-made plant syrups – thyme, sage and lime, and the unusual "*café du barman*". Very friendly welcome from the dynamic young team.

CHÂTILLON-SUR-CHALARONNE 01400

🎋 🏠 |●| HÔTEL-RESTAURANT DE LA TOUR**

pl. de la République (Centre).
☎ 04.74.55.05.12 ➥ 04.74.55.09.19
Closed Sun evening, Wed and 11–25 Dec.
Disabled access. TV. Lock-up garage.

A delightful establishment in a beautifully preserved medieval town, this hotel has exposed white stonework, half-timbering and a pepper-pot turret in pink brick. It was built in the 16th century and turned into a hotel three centuries later. The place has been renovated with great sensitivity and style, and is run by a young, welcoming team. In the restaurant the prices start a little high with the 115F menu (not served Sun); there are others 135–325F. Dishes include *gâteau* of chicken livers, stuffed chicken, chicken with cream and morel sauce, crayfish ravioli, pan-fried butterfly prawns and frogs *meunière*. Classic, spacious rooms, all recently redecorated. Doubles with shower or bath 380F. Free "*coupe du Routard*" with dessert.

ABERGEMENT-CLÉMENCIAT (L') 01400 (8KM S)

|●| RESTAURANT LE SAINT-LAZARE

How to get there: take the D2 as far as Châtillon-sur-Chalaronne and go on another 5km.
☎ 04.74.24.00.23 ➥ 04.74.24.00.62
Closed Wed and Thurs.

Even though the premises are on the ground floor of a substantial, fairly modern house in the centre of the village, the business has been going for ages. Christian Bidard, the young owner-chef, took over from his great-grandparents who opened a baker's-cum-grocer's-cum-café-cum restaurant in 1899. This is one of the best tables in the region and the setting in a

large, bright dining room, painted in soft shades is ideal. Attentive service. Inventive and delicate dishes with a good number of imaginative fish dishes; zander in season or sardines stuffed with minced chard, crayfish tails with grapefruit flesh and avocado *sabayon*. Also on offers are dishes using local, farm-raised chickens and meat. For dessert, try the pear *orientale*. Menus start at 120F, then 140–380F. The wines are selected from local growers but there are some from further afield, like the sweet wines.

CLUSAZ (LA) 74220

🎋 🏠 |●| LES AIRELLES**

Centre.
☎ 04.50.02.40.51 ➥ 04.50.32.35.33
📧 info@clusaz.com
TV.

A dream of a hotel in the centre of the village. It's been carefully renovated; bright, colourful doubles with all mod cons and shower/wc, 350–450. Half board, 300–470F, is compulsory over the winter school holidays. Guests can use the Jacuzzi, sauna and swimming pool in the hotel *Les Sapins*, a bit further up, which belongs to relatives. Genuine, simple welcome, just like the food. Weekday lunch menu, 80F, and others up to 160F list all the regional specialities. Free apéritif.

|●| LE CHALET DU LAC

Lac des Confins; just before you get to the lake, take the dirt road on the right.
☎ 04.50.02.53.26 📧 chalac@club-internet.fr
Car park.

This is a family business, and everybody is involved in running it smoothly. Everything's simple and genuine. The menus, 73–93F, feature Savoy specialities such as old-style *fricassée* of suckling pig, *tartiflette*, and sautéed chicken with three types of vinegar. Try the platters of home-made *charcuterie*, fritters or *tomme blanche*. Around 120F *à la carte*. There's a sunny terrace with lake views. The atmosphere is informal – even a bit crazy some evenings.

|●| RESTAURANT L'OURSON

pl. de l'Église (Centre).
☎ 04.50.02.49.80
Closed Sun evening, Mon and 25 April–10 June.

A pretty place on the first floor of a building right in the centre of the resort. The cooking is good enough to tempt any gourmet traveller and prices are attractive. The weekday lunch menu, 105F, and others, 135–280F, list

Savoy dishes like warm goat's cheese salad, chicken supreme with herb mustard,and *mousse glacée* with a herb-flavoured liqueur. The chef's speciality is bass, unusually flavoured with vanilla and *crème brûlée*.

COMBLOUX 74920

⚑ ⚐ |●| LES GRANITS**

1409 route de Sallanches; it's 1.5km from the centre on the Sallanches road.
☎ 04.50.58.64.46 ➡ 04.50.58.61.63
Closed mid-April to mid-June and mid-Sept to Christmas. **Disabled access**. **TV**. **Car park**.

Double rooms with basin 270F, or 330F with shower/wc or bath. Half board 275F per person. The hotel's quite close to a road – it's not very busy, but if you want to ensure a quiet night, ask for a room in the annexe. In the attractive dining room you can choose from the menus, 86–99F, or *à la carte*, around 125F. Typical Savoy dishes: *matafan*, *diotz*, *tartiflette* and *fondue*. Free coffee.

⚐ |●| HÔTEL-RESTAURANT LE COIN SAVOYARD**

300 route de la Cry; it's opposite the church.
☎ 04.50.58.60.27 ➡ 04.50.58.64.44
Closed Mon out of season, 15 April–1 June, and 20 Sept–8 Dec. **Swimming pool**. **TV**. **Car park**.

Lots of people come here year after year, so it's best to book well in advance. The cheerful, informal doubles, with shower/wc or bath, cost 430F. You can have a drink or something light for dinner – a good omelette and salad, a steak with morels or a *fondue* – in a traditional Savoy setting. There are no set menus, so expect to pay about 150F *à la carte*. There's a sunny terrace facing Mont Blanc and the pool is great in the summer.

CONDRIEU 69420

⚑ ⚐ |●| HÔTEL-RESTAURANT LA RÉCLUSIÈRE

14 route Nationale (Centre).
☎ 04.74.56.67.27 ➡ 04.74.56.80.05
Closed Mon evening, Tues and Feb.

Chef Martin Fleischmann enlarged this restaurant and added a few rooms, which are very comfortable and stylish. Doubles with shower or bath 300–400F. In the restaurant, menus, 140–320F, list minestrone with shellfish and saffron, duck breast with apples fried with smoked bacon and spiced *jus*, and Armagnac ice cream. Good wine list and attentive service. Free house aperitif.

CONTAMINES-MONTJOIE (LES) 74170

⚐ |●| LE MONT-JOLY*

La Chapelle.
☎ 04.50.47.00.17
Closed Oct–Nov. **Car park**.

This pretty gingerbread hotel on the outskirts of town is friendly and quiet and just 2km from the ski slopes. It offers simple, freshly decorated rooms and a few chalets next to the main building. Doubles cost 210F with basin, 245F with bath. Half board, 210–260F, is compulsory in winter. The restaurant is pretty ordinary but offers set menus at 65F or 90F, or *fondue* and *raclette* for around 100F *à la carte*. There's a nice terrace surrounded by trees with a view of the mountains.

⚑ ⚐ LA CLEF DES CHAMPS*

route de la Frasse; it's above the village, in the street opposite the tourist office.
☎ 04.50.47.06.09 ➡ 04.50.47.09.49
Closed 22 April–20 June and 10 Sept–20 Dec. **Garden**. **Car park**.

An old restored farmhouse up the slopes in the resort. Reservations are essential in winter and advisable in summer. Doubles with shower/wc 230F – numbers 2, 3, 4 and 9 have balconies with views over the valley. Half board, compulsory during the winter and summer seasons, is 210–230F per person. They offer special rates for children under eight. The restaurant is open to residents only. 8% discount Jan, April, June and Sept for full or half board.

⚑ ⚐ |●| HÔTEL-RESTAURANT LE GAI SOLEIL**

288 chemin des Layers; it's above the church.
☎ 04.50.47.02.94 ➡ 04.50.47.18.43
📧 gaisoleil@wanadoo.fr
Closed 15 April–14 June and 14 Sept–19 Dec. **Car park**.

In an old wooden farmhouse, built in 1823, this is a beautifully decorated hotel that's maintained with great care. You'll get a tremendous welcome. Handsome rooms, some with a mezzanine floor, and all with direct-dial telephones and en-suite bathrooms, for 300–430F. Half board, 285–375F, is compulsory during the school holidays. There's a set menu at 99F, and another, 149F, which is for residents only. 10% discount in Jan, April, June and Sept. Free house apéritif.

CONTREVOZ   01300

犬 |●| LA PLUMARDIÈRE

How to get there: on the N504.
☎ 04.79.81.82.54 ➡ 04.79.81.80.17
Closed Sun evening and Mon in winter, Jan. **Garden.**

A charming inn in a village lost in the country-side. This huge farmhouse has retained some of its original features, including the big fire-place and an enormous pair of blacksmith's bellows. There's a wonderful garden that's full of fruit trees, where you can eat in good weather. Excellent regional cuisine is featured on the 90F weekday lunch menu – country salad, roast chicken with thyme and potatoes *dauphinoise*. But the cooking is so good that you might be tempted by the other menus, 130–220F. Try the *foie gras*, and the home-smoked salmon and duck fillets. Free coffee.

CORMORANCHE-SUR-SAÔNE   01290

犬 ♠ |●| HÔTEL-RESTAURANT CHEZ LA MÈRE MARTINET

How to get there: take the N6 in the direction of Villefranche as far as Crêches-sur-Saône and then the D51;
alternatively, take the D51 from Saint-Laurent-sur-Saône.
☎ 03.85.36.20.40 ➡ 03.85.31.77.19
Closed Mon and Feb. **TV. Garden. Car park.**

A nice little village inn where you'll receive a very warm welcome. Menus, 70–220F, list delicious local cuisine: chicken breast with cream, fresh frogs' legs with parsley and gar-lic, zander and carp with leek *fondue*, fried Saône fish in season, shrimp salad, and farm-house chicken with cream sauce. In fine weather, you can sit out on the little terrace in the garden. A few double rooms with bath for 250F. Free apéritif. 10% on the room rate.

CORPS   38970

犬 ♠ |●| LA MARMOTTE

rue Principale.
☎ ➡ 04.76.30.01.02
Closed Wed out of season and the last fortnight in Dec.

An unpretentious little inn on the village's main street. Regional cuisine with a personal touch at very reasonable prices. It's a comfortable setting and there's a small terrace in summer. Substantial dishes on menus 68–95F: *pot-au-feu* with ravioli, home-made *caillette*, pastry parcels stuffed with vegetables, *andouillette* with shallots, and *fondue* with goat's cheese

with walnuts. There are also some rooms, 170F with shower, 190F with shower/wc. An overnight deal for room, dinner from the *menu du terroir* and breakfast, all for 185F per person. Free coffee

犬 ♠ |●| HÔTEL DE LA POSTE**

pl. de la Mairie (Centre).
☎ 04.76.30.00.03 ➡ 04.76.30.02.73
Closed 2 Jan–15 Feb.

This hotel, in the centre of the village on the "route Napoléon", is one of the best-known places in the region. The heavy, fussy, old-fashioned interior decoration may not be to all tastes, but the rooms are comfortable; 235F with shower, 250F with shower/wc and 300–450F with bath. The cooking has an excellent reputation. There's a weekday menu for 110F, 125F at weekends, and oth-ers 150–250F. You get a wide choice *à la carte*: queen scallops with morels, joint of lamb cooked on a spit, wild boar stew, calf's sweetbreads with cream, trout braised with crayfish and wild duck *grand-mère*. There's a fight for tables on the terrace in good weath-er, even though the road goes past right in front. Free coffee or apéritif.

犬 ♠ |●| BOUSTIGUE HÔTEL**

route de la Salette.
☎ 04.76.30.01.03 ➡ 04.76.30.04.40
Closed 15 Oct–1 May. **Swimming pool. TV. Car park.**

Signs on the road leading to Notre-Dame-de-la-Salette, which is a place of pilgrimage, tell you "C'est par là" (This way) and "Vous approchez" (You're getting close), as they lead you to this rather large hotel. You would be hard pushed to find a better place to relax than this, with its pool, its sauna and its putting green. It's on a plateau 1200m up, and it has a panoramic view of the village of Corps and lac du Sautet. The rooms are not very big but they're pleasant; 260F with shower/wc and 266–342F with bath. Bernard Dumas, the chef, prepares modestly priced local dishes: ravioli with snails, calf's sweetbreads with mushrooms, pork cheek, wild mush-rooms, and chicken from Beaumont. Menus 92–140F. Free *digestif*. 10% discount on the room rate in May, June and Sept.

COUCOURON   07470

♠ |●| HÔTEL-RESTAURANT AU CARREFOUR DES LACS**

☎ 04.66.46.12.70 ➡ 04.66.46.16.42
Closed Dec–Feb. **TV. Car park.**

An attractive mountain inn near a lake in the middle of the Ardèche plateau. Clean rooms 130F with shower, 275F with bath. Half board, compulsory in season, costs 200F per person. The handsome dining room offers good food prepared from fresh ingredients, including fine *charcuterie*, delicious local cheeses and home-made desserts. Set menus 70–140F.

COURS-LA-VILLE   69470

🏃 🏠 I◉I LE NOUVEL HÔTEL**

5 rue Georges-Clémenceau (Centre).
☎ 04.74.89.70.21 ➔ 04.74.89.84.41
Closed 25 Dec–3 Jan and a week in Aug. **TV**.

Good regional food at reasonable prices, served in a friendly dining room. Menus from 90F (except Sun) to 178F. They also offer pretty rooms with direct-dial telephone – 170F with basin, 270F with bath. Free house apéritif.

🏃 🏠 I◉I LE PAVILLON**

Col du Pavillon; it's 3km from Cours-la-Ville on the D64 heading in the direction of Écharmeaux.
☎ 04.74.89.83.55 ➔ 04.74.64.70.26
✉ hotel-le-pavillon@wanadoo.fr
Closed Sat and Sun evening Nov–March, Sat only July–Aug, and Feb. **TV. Disabled access. Car park**.

Service noon–2pm and 7–9pm. This hotel, surrounded by fir trees, stands absolutely alone at an altitude of 755m. The owners are keen travellers, and photographs of their expeditions to Morocco, India and the Arctic line the walls. The modern, comfortable rooms cost 340F with shower or bath, and the ground-floor ones have a private terrace and a view over the grounds. The pleasant restaurant offers a lunch *formule* for 78F then menus 99–220F: asparagus and prawn flan, poached halibut and salmon in vermouth. Free house apéritif, coffee or *digestif*.

MARNAND   69240 (10KM S)

🏃 🏠 I◉I HÔTEL-RESTAURANT LA TERRASSE

How to get there: from the centre of Thizy turn left for Marnand.
☎ 04.74.64.19.22 ➔ 04.74.64.25.95
Closed Sun evening, Mon, and the Feb and All Saints' school holiday. **Disabled access. TV. Car park**.

Occupying a converted industrial building, this well-designed hotel looks great, and it's in a good location, with lovely views over the Beau-

jolais hills from each room. Brightly decorated doubles with bath go for 260F. The restaurant is just as attractive, and features unusual dishes alongside more traditional choices: pan-fried scallops with puréed leeks, fish fillets with chorizo, and fresh fruit ice cream with chocolate sauce. Menus 75–210F. Easy-going welcome. 10% discount on the room rate Sept–June.

CRÉMIEU   38460

🏃 🏠 I◉I L'AUBERGE DE LA CHAITE**

cours Baron-Raverat.
☎ 04.74.90.76.63 ➔ 04.74.90.88.08
Closed Sun evening, Mon, 2–31 Jan and three weeks in April. **TV. Garden. Car park**.

Service noon–2pm and 7.30–9pm. This hotel has a beautiful setting, in a medieval village with ruined fortifications. Doubles 240F with shower, 260F with shower/wc, 300F with bath – those overlooking the garden are lovely. You'll be treated like a king in the restaurant or on the terrace. Menus start at 80F (weekdays), with others 130–190F: *terrine* of duck with orange, salmon *quenelles*, fried chicken with rum and ginger, or roast duck with two kinds of peach. 10% discount on the room rate for a two-night stay Sept–June.

I◉I HÔTEL DE LA POSTE

21 rue Porcherie; it's opposite the covered market.
☎ 04.74.90.71.41
Closed Wed out of season, a fortnight in Feb and three weeks in Sept.

This wasn't a post office and it's not a hotel either – or rather, it's not a hotel any more. Rather, it's a typical, old-fashioned bistro, with flowers at every window, old ads on the walls, and banquette seating. At lunchtime it attracts a young business crowd, who enjoy well-priced dishes of the day or set menus 108–158F. Fish and shellfish feature highly: mussels *poularde* (in cream sauce), fried smelt, fish *pot-au-feu*, and fillet of beef Madagascar.

SAINT-HILAIRE-DE-BRENS   38460 (6KM SE)

🏃 I◉I AU BOIS JOLI

La Gare; coming from Crémieu, it's at the junction of the Morestel and Bourgoin-Jallieu roads.
☎ 04.74.92.81.82 ➔ 04.74.92.93.27
Closed evenings, Mon, the first week in Jan and 20 Aug–20 Sept. **Garden. Car park**.

Service noon–1.30pm. This renowned restaurant has been run for generations by the Vistalli family. It has two large dining rooms that can accommodate about a hundred people and it's decorated with pine cones and cowbells. Try frog's legs *provençale*, chicken with crayfish, zander fillet with sorrel, or game, including wild boar, in season. Weekday lunch menu, 70F, then 100–165F. Delicious wines. Free coffee.

CREST 26400

⚔ 🏠 |●| LE KLÉBER**

6 rue Aristide-Dumont (Centre).
☎ 04.75.25.11.69 ➡ 04.75.76.82.82
Closed Sun and Tues evenings, Mon, first three weeks in Jan and the second fortnight in Aug. **TV**. **Car park**.

Service noon–1.30pm and 8–9.30pm. This smart-looking little restaurant is decorated in ochre-yellow shades. It's known for its gourmet food and specialises in fish and regional dishes. There's a weekday menu at 98F and others up to 260F. Try the lobster stew with a verbena infusion or the *aiguillette* of beef with *bordelaise* sauce. A few prettily decorated rooms at affordable prices: doubles cost 180F with shower, 260F with shower/wc. This is the most attractive place in town. Free apéritif.

⚔ |●| LA TARTINE

10 rue Peysson (centre); it's near the church of Saint-Sauveur.
☎ 04.75.25.11.53
Closed Sat lunchtime, Sun and Wed evenings, the All Saints' and Feb school holidays and end of June.

The restaurant occupies the whole of the first floor of a very old house that's typical of the ones you find in old Crest. There's a piano in the large, lofty dining room – this place is popular with musicians, and your visit may coincide with an impromptu jazz jam. Véronique, the owner, makes imaginative snacks and serves simple food – there's a dish of the day and various grills. *Menu du jour* 60F then others 98–123F. It's very busy at lunchtime and at the weekend so it's advisable to book. Free coffee.

SAOU 26400 (14KM SE)

⚔ |●| L'OISEAU SUR SA BRANCHE

La Placette (Centre).
☎ 04.75.76.02.03
Closed Mon and Tues evenings out of season, Dec–Jan.

Converted by a restaurateur-poet who settled here after years of travelling, this red and yellow bistro has an old packing case and a map of the world in the hall. Dishes are an array of colours and flavours, and your choice arrives

at the table labelled with its name. In the week, you can eat a main course for 55F, the *menu du bistro* at 80F or select your own dishes from the *menu-carte* for 150F. Not surprisingly, it attracts a lot of regular customers. To cap it all, there's a lovely terrace in the shade of the plane trees – very romantic in the moonlight. Free house apéritif.

|●| L'AUBERGE DE L'ESTANG

Lieu-dit le Pas de l'Estang; take the road for Bourdeaux then, at the sign, turn left into the small lane.
☎ 04.75.76.05.70
Closed weekday evenings in season, Mon–Thurs out of season.

The modern building is a bit of a shock in the quiet countryside but don't be put off. Relax at a table on the grass in the shade of a weeping willow and you can enjoy the peace and quiet of the superb countryside stretched out before you. The cuisine is strongly flavoured and full of sunshine, using local farm produce and vegetables from the garden enlivened by the flavours of Provence. Dish of the day 45F and a menu at 85F. Charming service. You can continue on foot along the small path that leads to the foot of the Synclinal de Saou.

OMBLÈZE 26400 (29.5KM NE)

⚔ 🏠 |●| AUBERGE DU MOULIN DE LA PIPE

How to get there: from Crest follow the road to Die, at Mirabel et Blacons, turn onto the D70 as far as Plan-de-Baix, then take the D578 for a further 5km.
☎ 04.75.76.42.05 ➡ 04.75.76.42.60
Closed mid-Nov to end Jan. **Disabled access**. **Car park**.

This restored old mill lies at the far end of a valley with views of the gorges, a river and the waterfalls. It attracts outdoorsy people of all ages who come to Omblèze for the climbing school, flying trapeze and circus courses, and the rock, blues and reggae concerts. The various *formules*, based on meat or fish, are traditional or exotic, depending on the mood of the chef. Menus 79–149F. Doubles 245–270F with shower. There are three *gîtes* for groups and three furnished apartments to rent. 10% discount on the room rate Sept–April.

DIE 26150

🏠 HÔTEL DES ALPES

87 rue Camille Buffardel (Centre).
☎ 04.75.22.15.83 ➡ 04.75.22.09.38
TV. **Car park**.

The wide staircase is all that remains from this former (14th-century) coaching inn. The hotel, nonetheless, offers a couple of dozen comfortable rooms with good facilities – the second-floor rooms have a splendid view of the Glandasse mountains and are very quiet. Doubles 220–250F. Some might find that the pink everywhere in the house is too much. Madame's second passion for puzzles adds to the kitsch in the place. That said, the welcome is pleasant and it's a good base for exploring the town and the countryside.

🏃|●| LA FERME DES BATETS

quartier des Batets; it's 3km from the centre of town on the D518 road to Crest.
☎ 04.75.22.11.45
Closed Sun evening, Wed and 15–31 Oct. **Car park**.

If you're footsore and weary from walking in the Vercors ,this old farmhouse – the dining room is a converted 17th-century stable – will come as a welcome sight. Try the guinea-fowl with thyme or boned quail with juniper and a glass of local wine like a Châtillon-Champassias from Cornillon. Menus 108–164F. It can get very busy. Free glass of Clairette – a local sparkling wine – with dessert.

BARNAVE   26310 (13KM SE)

🏃 🏠 |●| L'AUBERGERIE

Grande-Rue.
☎ 04.75.21.82.13 ➡ 04.75.21.84.31
Restaurant closed Tues in season, Mon–Fri in winter. **TV**.

You know you're here when you see the sheep. The large dining room occupies a converted stable, and upstairs there's an informal café where villagers come to play cards. They serve dishes such as savoury pie, goat's cheese pastries, guinea-fowl in a cream sauce and rabbit in Clairette de Die, a local sparkling wine. Menus 85–130F. The oldest house in the village has been converted to provide five tasteful, simply decorated rooms with kitchenettes; 200–220F. You can also rent them for the weekend or by the week. 10% discount on the room rate for a two-night stay Sept–April.

LUC-EN-DIOIS   26310 (19KM SE)

🏃 🏠 |●| HÔTEL DU LEVANT**

route de Gap (Centre); take the N93.
☎ 04.75.21.33.30 ➡ 04.75.21.31.42
Closed Sun and Mon evenings (except for residents), and 1 Nov–31 March. **Swimming pool. Car park**.

This 17th-century coaching inn offers comfortable rooms for 160F with shower, 250F with bath. Those at the back have a stunning view of rooftops and mountains. You eat in a rustic, delightfully decorated dining room. The cuisine is traditional but with a touch of the Mediterranean. Lunch menu 65F, then 99–130F. Half board is compulsory at the weekend in summer. There's an enormous garden with a pool on the other side of the road. Free coffee. 10% discount on the rom rate for a two-night stay Sept–June.

DIEULEFIT   26220

🏃 |●| AUBERGE LES BRISES

Route de Nyons; it's 1.5km from the centre of town.
☎ 04.75.46.41.49
Closed Tues and Wed out of season, and Jan–Feb.

This restaurant has quickly made a name for itself for its good food and friendly reception. Chef Didier le Doujet and his wife have created a little corner of their native Brittany in the Drôme, though they've swapped the flavours of the Atlantic for local ones – try the duck ham salad or the egg custard with *picodon* cheese. Very appealing menus, 95–190F, list dishes such *croustillant* of stuffed whiting with garlic, fish *blanquette*, and veal kidneys with morels. There's also a *plat du terroir* at 60F. Eat on the shady terrace in summer or in the rustic dining room. Free apéritif.

LE POÊT-LAVAL   26160 (8KM NW)

🏠 |●| LES HOSPITALIERS

It's halfway between La Bégude and Dieulefit.
☎ 04.75.46.22.32 ➡ 04.75.56.49.99
Closed Mon and Tues (except for residents), and mid-Nov to mid-March. **Car park**.

The hotel looks down over one of the most lovely villages in the Drôme. It's an idyllic place for a romantic weekend or a honeymoon. There are some twenty rooms, 350–1100F, which offer sophisticated luxury. The salon and dining room are superb; pale wood, ancient beams and cosy furnishings. Vases of flowers everywhere. The superb terrace looks over marvellous countryside and is the place for dinner as the sun goes down. It's advisable to stick to the menus, 160–340F, because *à la carte* can be pricey. Wines start at 95F. After your meal take a wander along the windy roads or visit one of the local Protestant museums.

FÉLINES-SUR-RIMANDOULE 26160 (12KM NW)

⅍ |●| RESTAURANT CHEZ DENIS

How to get there: take the D540 then the D179.
☎ 04.75.90.16.73
Closed Mon and Tues evenings, Wed out of season, and Jan–Feb. **Car park**.

Denis is actually the present chef's father, but there haven't been any drastic changes since he retired, and the whole place quietly carries on just as it ever did. On Sunday and sunny days people flock to this handsome restaurant up in the hills, where you'll eat on a cool terrace in a relaxed atmosphere to the sound of a running stream. Set menus 99–230F. The 115F menu offers good value for money and specialities include ravioli with dill butter, a fish duo with sorrel cream, snails *au gratin* with noodles and duck with olives. It's best to book at weekends. Free coffee.

DIVONNE-LES-BAINS 01220

⅍ ♠ |●| LA TERRASSE FLEURIE**

315 rue Fontaine (Centre); it's very near the casino.
☎ 04.50.20.06.32 ➡ 04.50.20.40.34
Closed 31 Oct–1 March. **TV**.

A very quiet and aptly named hotel with a flowery terrace and balcony. It's remarkably peaceful, despite being so close to the centre of town. The modern rooms have charm – doubles with shower/wc or bath 280–340F – while the restaurant offers simple, inexpensive home cooking; menus 71–93F and a *menu terroir* at 130F. Excellent value for Divonne. 10% discount on the room rate Oct–May.

ÉVIAN 74500

⅍ ♠ HÔTEL CONTINENTAL**

65 rue Nationale (Centre).
☎ 04.50.75.37.54 ➡ 04.50.75.31.11

The new owners of this hotel spend a lot of time in the USA, and they've turned this place into somewhere that's full of life. Each room has its own personality and the atmosphere is genuinely friendly. Courteous welcome and great prices, considering the charm of the place and the size of the rooms. Doubles with shower/wc or bath 230–340F. 10% discount on the room rate Sept–June.

PUBLIER 74500 (3.5KM W)

⅍ ♠ |●| HÔTEL-RESTAURANT LE CHABLAIS**

rue du Chablais; it's on the D11.
☎ 04.50.75.28.06 ➡ 04.50.74.67.32
Closed Sun in winter, 20 Dec–31 Jan, and 1 May. **TV**. **Car park**.

A clean, tidy, efficient place with a Swiss feel. The hotel's right on the lake and half of the rooms have a superb view of it. They're really attractive, though facilities are standard; doubles 165–185F with basin, 210–235F with shower, 240–300F with shower/wc or bath. Brasserie menu 92F at lunchtime, others 105–166F. Free house apéritif or 10% discount on the room rate Sept–June.

BERNEX 74500 (10KM SE)

⅍ ♠ |●| L'ÉCHELLE

How to get there: it's beside the church.
☎ 04.50.73.60.42 ➡ 04.50.73.69.21
Closed Mon and Tues except school holidays and 25 Nov–18 Dec. **Car park**.

A restaurant where everyone takes time out to enjoy the finer things in life. Chef Pierre Mercier follows the methods of his mother, "la Félicie", who used to cook for the mountain walkers at Saint-Michel. Try the snail *brochettes*, duck *aiguillettes à la mondeuse*, or grilled meats. Weekday lunch menu 68F, or 147–195F. Wine from local vineyards. They have a few rooms for 270–320F per person. Free *digestif*.

|●| RESTAURANT LE RELAIS DE LA CHEVRETTE

Trossy; get there on the D21 and the D52 – go through Bernex and head for Dent-d'Oche.
☎ 04.50.73.60.27
Closed Wed except in school holidays and 6 Nov–20 Dec. **Garden**. **Disabled access**. **Car park**.

This picture-perfect chalet, with red and white wooden shutters, has a menu featuring typical Alpine produce: dried meat and ham, omelettes, and bilberry tart. In winter you can sit by the open fire, while in summer you can enjoy the garden, which has a stream running through it. You'll pay 100F for a substantial meal *à la carte*. There's a good wine list, with Savoy wines. Warm welcome.

THOLLON-LES-MÉMISES 74500 (10KM E)

⅍ ♠ HÔTEL BON SÉJOUR**

Centre.
☎ 04.50.70.92.65 ➡ 04.50.70.95.72

Closed 15 Nov–20 Dec. **Garden. TV. Garage.**

This is a family hotel where everyone chips in. The younger Duponts are refurbishing the bedrooms one by one; in all of them you'll sleep like a baby. Doubles with shower/wc or bath cost 280–320F. The good mountain cuisine is prepared with care and served generously. Prices are attractive, too, with menus 90–130F. There's a terrace and a garden. Free apéritif.

VACHERESSE 74360 (20KM SE)

☎ |●| AU PETIT CHEZ SOI

☎ and ➡ 04.50.73.10.11
Car park.

You'll find this old house at the head of the Abondance valley, between Lake Geneva and the ski resorts. It's a very traditional, friendly place, where you eat whatever has been prepared that day on menus at 70F or 90F. The daughters come in to lend a hand, as, occasionally, do the guests. The rooms look as if they're from another era, but you'll get as good a night's sleep here as anywhere. Doubles 200F with shower/wc. Free apéritif.

FAVERGES 74210

⅔ |●| LA CARTE D'AUTREFOIS

25 rue Gambetta (Centre).
☎ 04.50.32.49.98
Closed Sun evening, Mon, and the last week in Jan, last week in June and last week in Aug.

A little restaurant in a delightful spot not far from the lake of Annecy, with a small ski resort nearby. It has a nice retro dining room and honest, flavourful cooking – it's about as far as you can get from the standard fare dished up in the local tourist traps. Try the home-made ravioli or *fricassée* of veal kidneys and even the kangaroo and ostrich. Menus 85F, 90F and 125F. Free apéritif.

FEURS 42110

|●| CHALET DE LA BOULE D'OR

42 route de Lyon (East); it's near the Feurs east exit.
☎ 04.77.26.20.68
Closed Sun evening, Mon, second fortnight in Jan, and the first three weeks in Aug.

A gourmet restaurant that's not too expensive – on weekdays, at any rate. The staff are attentive without being intrusive. The food is

delicate, and the wines have been carefully selected (though prices are quite high). All the dishes are good: duck *foie gras*, scallops with morels, *marbré* of rabbit, and roast monkfish. The appetisers are full of subtle flavours and the desserts are out of this world. Menu at 98F (weekdays), the others, 155–310F, seem a bit overpriced.

MARCLOPT 42210 (11KM S)

☎ |●| LE KHAN

☎ 04.77.54.58.40
How to get there: leave the A72 at the Montbrison-Montrond exit and take the D115 to Marclopt.
Closed Thurs evening except in season, the second week in Jan and a fortnight in Oct. **Car park.**

This modern inn, with a misleading name, prides itself on serving authentic French food: home-made *foie gras*, wine from local vineyards, home-made jam for breakfast. The decor features stone walls built by the owner's son and murals painted by local artists. The welcome you'll get from the proprietress couldn't be warmer, and her cooking is fresh and original; you're given a dish of food so you serve yourself. Menus 110F –190F; the *foie gras* menu, which you have to order in advance, serves the delicacy in a variety of preparations. The spacious guestrooms, decorated in charming rustic style, cost 185F. The breakfast, 30F, is superb.

PANISSIÈRES 42360 (12KM NE)

☎ |●| HÔTEL-RESTAURANT DE LA POSTE

95 rue J-B Guerpillon; take the D89 then the D60 in the direction of Tarare (Centre).
☎ 04.77.28.64.00 ➡ 04.77.28.69.94
Restaurant closed Sat lunchtime. **TV.**

A popular hotel that the owners have completely restored. The rooms are simple but good value; doubles 220F and 250F. Superb views over the Forez mountains, and an elegant dining room serving decent, good cooking. Weekday lunch menu 65F, others 85–175F. Excellent welcome.

VIOLAY 42780 (22KM NE)

⅔ ☎ |●| HÔTEL-RESTAURANT PERRIER**

pl. de l'Église; from Feurs, head for Balbigny then take the D1 in the direction of Tarare.
☎ 04.74.63.91.01 ➡ 04.74.63.91.77
Closed Sat and Sun evening, and Jan–Feb.
TV. Disabled access. Lock-up car park.

Jean-Luc Clot and his wife will make you feel very welcome when you arrive. The village is a popular centre for cross-country skiing and there's a pretty church over the road from the hotel. It's well run and prices are affordable – 150F for a double with basin or 220F for a sumptuous, romantic double with bath. Much of the cooking in the restaurant is inspired by the cuisine of southwest France. Prices are reasonable – there's a weekday menu at 85F, others 95–185F and, for 99F the *menu terroir* includes wine and coffee. Try the *confits* of duck or chicken, cockerel with tarragon, veal sweetbreads flambéed with Madeira, or the scallops *Normande*. Free apéritif and 10% discount on the room rate.

FLUMET 73590

⅍ 🏠 |●| HÔTEL-RESTAURANT LE PARC DES CÈDRES***

Centre.
☎ 04.79.31.72.37 ➡ 04.79.31.61.66
Closed April–May and Oct to 20 Dec. **TV**. **Car park**.

The family who have run this establishment for a century belong to the old school of hotel-keeping. The building is surrounded by substantial grounds planted with cedar trees, there are club chairs in the sitting room and a snooker table in the bar. Some of the rooms were redecorated in the 1970s while others are more traditionally rustic. Doubles 250F with basin, 275–350F with shower/wc or bath – some have terraces or balconies. In the restaurant, good-quality produce makes for good cooking: truffled *terrine*, stewed kidneys flambéed with Cognac, and calf's liver with Apremont wine. Menus 92–178F. The terrace under the cedar trees is wonderful in summer. 10% discount on the room rate or free *digestif* with your meal.

NOTRE-DAME-DE-BELLECOMBE 73590 (5KM S)

🏠 |●| LA FERME DE VICTORINE

Le Mont-Rond; take the N218 in the direction of Les Saisies and 3km before Notre-Dame-de-Bellecombe, take the left towards Le Planay.
☎ 04.79.31.63.46 ➡ 04.79.31.79.91
Closed Sun evening and Mon in spring and autumn, 25 June–5 July, and 14 Nov–20 Dec.

The dining room has a huge fireplace for cold winter days and, in the summer, they open a bright, sunny terrace with a great view of the mountain. Menus, 110F at lunchtime in the week, or 135–220F, list nicely prepared traditional Savoy dishes. Try mushroom *fondue*, *tartiflette* made with

tamié (a local cheese), chicken with morels, or *reblochonnade*. Even the biggest appetites will be satisfied with the *farcement* (potatoes baked with eggs, milk, raisins and prunes). Good Savoy wines also available.

SAISIES (LES) 73620 (14KM S)

⅍ 🏠 |●| LE MÉTÉOR*

How to get there: in the village, follow the signs to the Village Vacances.
☎ 04.79.38.90.79 ➡ 04.79.38.97.00
Closed 28 April–7 July and 2 Sept–1 Dec.

This typical, wooden chalet built in a forest clearing is quietly set apart from the ski resort but just 100m from the slopes. The rooms, nothing special but perfectly acceptable, cost 250F with shower/wc; in winter half board is compulsory and costs 250–300F. Lunch menu 70F, 98F in the evening. They serve Savoy specialities such as *fondue*, *raclette* and *tartiflette*. Warm welcome and atmosphere. Free house apéritif.

⅍ |●| RESTAURANT LE CHAUDRON

Centre; take the D218, and it's beside the police station.
☎ 04.79.38.92.76
Closed May to mid-June and mid-Sept to mid-Dec.

Service from noon and from 7pm. Though the decoration at this restaurant is typical of hundreds of places in the mountains, the food is fine. The good regional dishes are amply served and fortifying after a day's skiing: *diots*, *fondue*, *reblochonnade*, fillets of *féra* (a type of salmon), and beef topped with cheese. Menus from 75F, at lunchtime, up to 170F or around 175F *à la carte*. There's a nice terrace where you can get a good view of Mont Blanc on a clear day. Warm ambience and friendly service. Free *digestif*.

GARDE-ADHÉMAR (LA) 26700

🏠 |●| LOGIS DE L'ESCALIN

Northwest; take the Montélimar-Sud exit off the A7 then go 1.5km along the road to Donzère.
☎ 04.75.04.41.32 ➡ 04.75.04.40.05
Closed Sun evening, Mon and the first fortnight in Jan. **TV**. **Garden**. **Car park**.

A little hotel on the side of a hill overlooking the Rhône Valley. The motorway is a couple of kilometres away as the crow flies, but seems much, much further. The hotel, a handsome building in local style painted white with blue shutters, provides seven fresh, refurbished rooms; doubles 350F with shower/wc. There's a weekday menu at

110F and others up to 260F. Dishes include frogs' legs with sorrel in pastry, fresh fish and curried shrimp. The cheapest wines on the list are reasonably priced – Vinsobres, Croze Hermitage or Saint-Joseph – and they also serve wine by the glass. The very pleasant garden provides shade. A good place for a relaxing weekend or a stop on the road south.

GEX   01170

🏃 🏠 HÔTEL-RESTAURANT DU PARC**

av. des Alpes (Centre).
☎ 04.50.41.50.18 ➡ 04.50.42.37.29
Closed Sun evening, Mon and Jan. **TV. Car park**.

Service 12.30–2pm and 7.30–9pm. This traditional, characterful hotel has been run by the same family for over seventy years. The park it is named after is across the road and the hotel itself has a huge, prize-winning garden full of geraniums, roses, begonias and all sorts of colourful flowers. Rooms 280F with shower/wc, 350F with bath. There used to be a restaurant which was due to close in winter 2000. 10% discount.

CESSY   01170 (2KM SE)

🏠 🍽 MOTEL LA BERGERIE

805 route Plaine (South); it's on the N5, Geneva–Paris road.
☎ 04.50.41.41.75 ➡ 04.50.41.71.82
TV. Car park.

This place is surrounded by fields, so peace and quiet are the order of the day. The rooms are large and have en-suite bath and good facilities; doubles 200F. It's far from luxurious but it offers value for money. They do a substantial breakfast for 30F, served until noon. There's also a modestly priced restaurant with menus at 70F and 120F.

SEGNY   01170 (6KM SE)

🏠 LA BONNE AUBERGE**

rue du Vieux-Bourg (Centre); take the N5.
☎ 04.50.41.60.42 ➡ 04.50.41.71.79
Closed Christmas to 15 March. **Garden. TV. Lock-up car park**.

An authentic country inn hidden from the road by the trees in the garden. There are flowers everywhere, even on the murals by the stairs. Attractive rooms go for 200F for a double with shower/wc or 225F with bath – very good value for a hotel near Gex. Warm

welcome and family atmosphere. There's no restaurant, though they serve breakfast complete with home-made jam.

CROZET   01170 (8KM SW)

🏠 🍽 LE BOIS JOLY*

route du Télécabine (South); take the D984 in the direction of Bellegarde and turn right onto the D89 as far as Crozet; it's 500m from the cable car.
☎ 04.50.41.01.96 ➡ 04.50.42.48.47
Closed Fri, and Easter school holidays. **TV**.

This is a big establishment on the lower slopes of the Jura. There is a splendid view of the Alps from the terrace, where you can eat in fine weather. The simple rooms have good facilities – some of them have balconies – and are reasonably priced for the area: 190F with basin and 280F with bath. The restaurant provides generous portions of regional dishes such as frogs' legs or guinea-fowl with morel sauce. Menus 85–180F. Half board and full board available.

COL DE LA FAUCILLE   01170 (11.5KM NW)

🏃 🏠 🍽 HÔTEL DE LA COURONNE**

How to get there: take the N5.
☎ 04.50.41.32.65 ➡ 04.50.41.32.47
Closed 15 April–15 May and 15 Sept–15 Dec.
Swimming pool. Garden. TV. Car park.

A vast chalet 1300m up, just at the Faucille pass on the way to the Jura. It's one of the tourist centres in the region (like Mijoux and Lélex) and where skiiers from Geneva come. Big, comfortable rooms with charming wooden balconies overlook the forest or Mont Rond, which is 1550m high. Doubles with bath 300F. In the cosy restaurant, menus (100–120F) list dishes like *foie gras* with yellow wine, snails with hazelnuts in a pastry case and *blanquette* of shellfish and lobster. In winter there's a huge open fire to welcome you after skiing. In summer they open the swimming pool. Free apéritif.

GRAND-BORNAND (LE)   74450

🏃 🏠 🍽 HÔTEL-RESTAURANT LA CROIX SAINT-MAURICE**

Centre.
☎ 04.50.02.20.05 ➡ 04.50.02.35.37
Closed Easter to 20 June and 15 Sept–15 Dec.
Disabled access. TV. Pay car park.

This hotel, run by the same family for some thirty years, strikes the right tone in this family resort, and every year, regulars come back for what amounts to a family reunion. The south-facing rooms look over the Aravis mountains; some have a balcony or terrace. All rooms are en-suite, with either shower/wc or bath. They cost 200–250F in summer, 260–320F in winter. Half board is obligatory in high season and costs 235–355F per person. The restaurant, open only in winter, offers an 88F weekday menu and others up to 175F. Lots of regional specialities *à la carte*, including rissoles of *reblochon* cheese with salad, *fricassée savoyarde* with *polenta* or potatoes *au gratin*. 10% discount on the room rate except during school holidays.

🏃 🏠 |●| HÔTEL-RESTAURANT LES GLAÏEULS**

Centre; it's at the foot of the slopes, where the cable cars start from.
☎ 04.50.02.20.23 ➡ 04.50.02.25.00
Closed mid-April to mid-June and mid-Sept to mid-Dec.
TV. Car park.

A very well-run hotel. Though the façade is pretty ordinary, in summer the flowers at every window and on the terrace make it look lovely. It's a very traditional place, with cosy sitting rooms and classic decor. The owners are polite and friendly. Rooms have good facilities and cost 260–360F with shower/wc or bath. Good cooking in the restaurant, with unusual yet classic dishes: *foie gras* escalope with citrus fruit, snails *marinière* with nettles. Menus 90–240F. There's a sunny terrace. Free coffee.

🏠 HÔTEL LES CIMES***

Le Chinaillon (Centre).
☎ 04.50.27.00.38 ➡ 04.50.27.08.46
e info@hotel-les-cimes.com
Closed 1 May–15 June and 10 Sept–20 Nov.

A stone's throw from the old village of Chinaillon and 100m from the pistes, this is a traveller's dream come true. The couple who run the place converted an ordinary place above a chic boutique into a friendly inn that is full of the fragrance of wood and polish. Bedrooms are wonderfully quiet, with comfortable feather beds. Doubles cost 490–750F with shower/wc or bath; the price includes a superb breakfast. Half-board can be arranged with a restaurant nearby. The owners look after their guests very well.

🏃|●| LA FERME DE LORMAY

Vallée du Bouchet; it's 7km from the village, in the direction of the col des Annes – turn right when you get

to the little chapel.
Closed Tues in summer, weekday lunchtimes in winter, 1 May–20 June and 10 Sept–20 Dec.

There's an authentic atmosphere in this old farmhouse-inn; for ages, in an attempt to keep the place for local people, there was no sign outside the door. In summer, when they serve food on the terrace, try the chicken with crayfish, the trout or the house *quenelles*. When the weather gets cold the tables are put close together round the fireplace, and there is more *charcuterie* and pork on the menu – the roast pork and bacon soup are both delicious. It's cooking you want to linger over. There's just one snag: if the owners don't like the look of you, they'll send you elsewhere. About 150–220F *à la carte*. Free house apéritif.

GRENOBLE   38000

SEE MAP OVERLEAF

🏃 🏠 HÔTEL DE L'EUROPE**

22 pl. Grenette. **MAP C3-1**
☎ and ➡ 04.76.46.16.94
e hotel.europe.gre@wanadoo.fr
TV.

The hotel is in a lively pedestrianised area right in the centre of Grenoble, but the rooms are well soundproofed and noise isn't a problem. It's a comfortable place, the welcome is genuine, and the prices are unusually modest for the town: 160F for a double with basin, 220F with shower, 260F with shower/wc and 260–330F with bath. Rooms are all regularly upgraded. There's also a gym and a sauna. 10% discount 15 July–15 Aug.

🏃 🏠 HÔTEL DES PATINOIRES**

12 rue Marie-Chamoux; it's 500m south of the Palais des Sports, off the av. Jeanne-d'Arc. Off map **D4-2**
☎ 04.76.44.43.65 ➡ 04.76.44.44.77
e infor@hotel-patinoire.com
TV. Pay garage.

It may not be the easiest place in the world to find, but this is one of the best hotels in town and is good value for money. The owners are genial, attentive and full of information about where to go and what to do. Warm atmosphere and decor – many of the pictures on the walls are painted by the owner. It's superbly well maintained and extremely quiet. Comfortable rooms cost 275F with shower/wc, 300F with bath. They provide a few inexpensive dishes in the evening, if you don't want to go out. 10% discount on the room rate July–Aug.

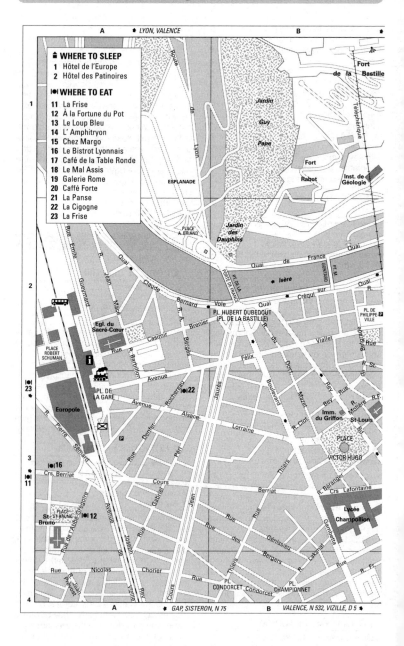

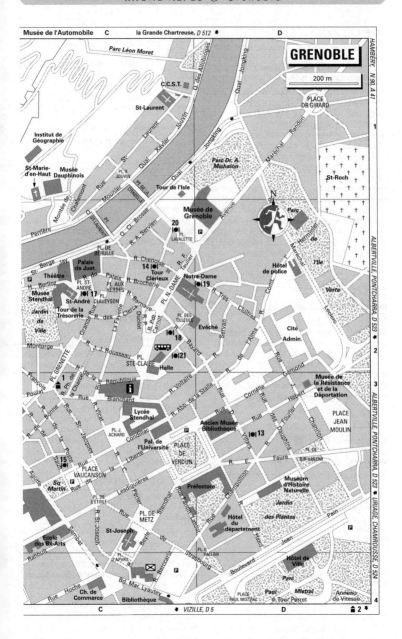

Musée de l'Automobile   C   la Grande Chartreuse, *D 512* ✦   D

GRENOBLE

200 m

Parc Léon Moret

CHAMBÉRY, N 90, A 41

C.C.S.T.

St-Laurent

PLACE
DR GIRARD

Institut de
Géographie

Parc Dr. A.
Michalon

St-Roch

St-Marie-
d'en-Haut   Musée
Dauphinois

PL. X
JOUVIN

Tour de l'Isle

Parc

ALBERTVILLE, PONTCHARRA, D 523 ✦

Musée de
Grenoble

20

PL.
LAVALETTE

de

N

l'Île

PL. DE
BÉRULLE

R. Chenoise

Palais
de Just.

14

Tour
Clérieux

Hôtel
de police

Verte

St-
Berge

Théâtre

PL. AUX
HERBES

Palais

R. Brocherie

Notre-Dame

19

PL. ST-
ANDRÉ

17

St-André CLAVEYSON

PL.

PL. N.-DAME

Musée
Stendhal

Tour de la
Trésorerie

PL. DES
TILLEULS

Evêché

Cité
Admin.

ALBERTVILLE, PONTCHARRA, D 523 ✦ URIAGE, CHAMROUSSE, D 524

Jardin

de

Ville

Montorge

R. J. J. Rousseau

18

PL.
STE-CLAIRE

21

Halle

1

PL. GRENETTE

République

Musée de
la Résistance
et de la
Déportation

Poulat

Rue   Blanchard

PLACE
JEAN
MOULIN

Lycée
Stendhal

PL. J.
ACHARD

Ancien Musée
Bibliothèque

13

Pal. de
l'Université

PLACE
DE
VERDUN

PL. DE
BIR-HAKEIM

15

Sq.
Martin

PLACE
VAUCANSON

PL. DE
L'ÉTOILE

Préfecture

Muséum
d'Histoire
Naturelle

Jardin

des Plantes

PL. DE
METZ

St-Joseph

Hôtel
du
département

École
des Bx-Arts

PL.
D'APVRIL

PL. F.
VALLIER

Hôtel de
Ville

Ch. de
Commerce

Bibliothèque

Bd. Mar. Lyautey

PLACE
PAUL MISTRAL

Parc

Paul   Mistral
Tour Perret

Anneau
de Vitesse

C   ✦ VIZILLE, D 5   D   🏠 2 ✦   4

⅄|●| LA CIGOGNE

11 rue Denfert-Rochereau; it's next to the station. **MAP A3-22**
☎ 04.76.17.16.88 **@** bodelors@wanadoo.fr
Closed Sat lunchtime, Sun, Mon–Wed evenings, Aug.

A quirkily decorated little restaurant which quietly makes its presence felt. It's popular as a lunch place for local workers. The decor is random, with a pretend roof to the bar, an old typewriter, a bread paddle and old radio sets stuck on the walls. The chef produces remarkable regional dishes and substantial portions – try the marvellous steak cooked "blue", which is almost crisp on the outside but still red in the middle. There are also a number of delicious cheese dishes like *racleton*, which is potatoes, country ham, *crème fraîche* and Raclette cheese, all cooked on an open fire. Lunchtime menu 48F, with others 95–120F. They serve very early – by 1.30pm, the dining room is practically empty. Free *digestif*.

⅄|●| LE MAL ASSIS

9 rue Bayard. **MAP C2-18**
☎ 04.76.54.75.93
Closed Mon, Sun and 15 July–15 Aug.

Service noon–2pm and 7.30–10pm. This place, a local favourite, has wood panelling and a fireplace and the service is charming. There's a single menu at 138F, lunch dishes for 57F, and *à la carte* choices in the evening for 65–90F. Dishes include *fondant* of vegetables, saddle of rabbit with *aïoli*, Provençal fish stew and plain chocolate *marquise*. Free apéritif.

⅄|●| LA FRISE

150 cours Berriat. Off map **A3-11**
☎ 04.76.96.58.22
Closed evenings, Sun and 15–31 Aug.

Near the Magasin, the contemporary art centre, this place has a bright, colourful interior with pictures by local artists on the walls. Tasty dishes, around 70F, are prepared using fresh ingredients and served in big portions, and the delicious desserts are home-made. Friendly welcome. Free coffee.

⅄|●| LE LOUP BLEU

7 rue Dominique-Villars. **MAP D3-13**
☎ 04.76.51.22.70
Closed Sat lunchtime, Sun, public holidays and three weeks in Aug. **Disabled access**.

Service noon–2pm and dinner 8–10.15pm. This unobtrusive restaurant, with the old shutters still in place, is quiet and atmospheric, and the cooking and the service are both first-rate. Dishes on the 70F lunch menu change with the seasons. If you want a slightly more refined meal, go for the other menus, 110–190F, which offer traditional dishes and excellent meat and fish. Some are worth a mention: sea bass with walnut wine, duck breast stuffed with *foie gras*, and scallops with roasted ceps. Free apéritif.

|●| À LA FORTUNE DU POT

34 rue de l'Abbé-Grégoire. **MAP A3-12**
☎ 04.76.96.20.05
Closed Sun, Mon and Aug.

This place is on the corner of the Marché Saint-Bruno, the most lively and popular market in Grenoble. The decor is a bit of a hotch-potch, with dry stone walls hung with pictures, a Formica bar and an old clock that doesn't work any more, but the atmosphere is great, aided by the genial host. It's always full of people telling stories and having a good time. There's a single menu at 75F at lunchtime which goes up to 85F in the evening.

|●| LA PANSE

7 rue de la Paix. **MAP C2-21**
☎ 04.76.54.09.54
Closed Sun and mid-July to mid-Aug.

The minimalist decor at this fashionable, vaguely intellectual place is a bit cool for some tastes, though it's brightened up by colourful pictures. The welcome's a bit cool, too. The cooking is highly distinctive, with a touch of sophistication: hot oysters, quail with fresh *foie gras* and Madeira, veal with chanterelles, and escalope with morels. Menus 77F at lunchtime, 89F in the evening, and 107–158F. Apremont or Cahors at 60F. Relaxed atmosphere.

⅄|●| CAFÉ DE LA TABLE RONDE

7 pl. Saint-André. **MAP C2-17**
☎ 04.76.44.51.41
Closed Sun.

Service until midnight. About as central as you can get, this café is an institution in Grenoble. Established in 1793, it's the second oldest café in France after *Le Procope* in Paris, and tradition, hospitality and conviviality are its watchwords. The terrace is a great vantage point from which to watch the world go by on the square, and the decor in the dining room is splendid. There are lots of good dishes *à la carte*: *choucroute*, pig's trotters cooked to the house recipe, grilled beef, *diot* with shallots, calf's head, and so on. Menus 80–180F and affordable wines: Gamay de Savoie at 76F, Crozes-Hermitage at 103F, and others served by the glass or jug. Free apéritif.

🎄 |●| L'AMPHITRYON

9 rue Chenoise. **MAP C2-14**
☎ 04.76.51.38.07
Closed Sun lunchtime and three weeks in Aug.

An unusual place on a street lined with nothing but restaurants. The decor is minimalist, with an unexpected Roman wall at one end. There's an eclectic range of dishes – Italian ravioli with spinach or salmon, say, or lamb delicately spiced with home-made *harissa* – for 52–72F. Portions are substantial; the "*Brick*" couscous, a mixture of different types of couscous, is a meal in itself. Menu 90F. You can get a Côtes-du-Rhône or Balaouane at 69F a bottle, or a $1/2$ litre of red at 34F. The welcome is very warm which is in deep contrast to the coolest of cool atmospheres. Free *digestif*.

🎄 |●| CHEZ MARGO

5 rue Millet (Centre). **MAP C3-15**
☎ 04.76.46.27.87
Closed Sat lunchtime and Sun.

This restaurant, in a quiet little street, is often busy. Even on weekday evenings there's a reliable stream of regulars who drop in. The dining room is split-level, decorated in a smartly rustic style, and the atmosphere is very informal. The cooking is traditional, prepared with care, and the regional dishes are quite substantial. There's a 99F lunch menu, and others 112–161F. You get lots of choice: *fricassée* of scampi with ravioli, sliced veal sweetbreads with ginger and lime, *caillette* served on a potato cake, monkfish medallions with wild mushrooms, *confit* duck thigh. Dishes of the day use fresh market produce – *fricassée* of kid with fresh tarragon, for example. A short, well-selected wine list with Bordeaux starting at 76F, Réserve Chez Margo at 48F, and a good Crozes-Hermitage at 108F. Free apéritif.

🎄 |●| CAFFÈ FORTÉ

4 pl. Lavalette. **MAP C2-20**
☎ 04.76.03.25.30 ➡ 04.76.03.25.55
Closed Sun lunchtime.

This delightful place stands opposite the Grenoble museum in a quiet, wide road. The lofty dining room is vaguely baroque in style, and in summer the terrace is always full. The atmosphere is pretty easy-going but on the

ball. The boss makes no bones about being a Johnny Hallyday fan and not being able to stand the *Front National* party. As for the food, the steak *tartare* is huge, the chips are real, and the salads and pasta are excellent. *À la carte* around 120F. Pleasant welcome. Free house apéritif.

🎄 |●| LE BISTROT LYONNAIS

168 cours Berriat. **MAP A3-16**
☎ 04.76.21.95.33
Closed Sat lunchtime, 24 Dec–1 Jan.

Opposite the Magasin, the contemporary art centre, this restaurant has a warm interior charmingly decorated in period style. In summer, there's a little terrace that's well protected from the road by a fragrant wisteria and lots of greenery. Good Lyonnais dishes on the menus, 125–185F. If you've got time for an extended lunch, try the Roquefort and scallop *terrine*, the fresh sardines marinated in lemon, the fillet of beef with a morel crust, the *sauté* of veal sweetbreads with port, or the scambled eggs with truffles. Wine prices are reasonable; jugs of Côtes-du-Rhône or Beaujolais cost around 58F. Free apéritif.

🎄 |●| GALERIE ROME

1 rue Très-Cloîtres. **MAP D2-19**
☎ 04.76.42.82.01
Closed Sun, Mon and three weeks in Aug.

The decor of this restaurant is colourful and original, with numerous paintings and brilliantly lit sculptures. There's also a quiet, charming patio. The *à la carte* menu is quite short, listing good *terrines*, tasty meat dishes, light sauces and interesting salads all at reasonable prices – about 150F for a meal. The dish of the day, 60F, is written up on the blackboard. In the evening, if business is slow, they stop serving at 9.15pm. Free *digestif*.

MEYLAN   38249 (4KM NE)

🎄 |●| LA CERISAIE CLUB

18 chemin de Saint-Martin; leave Grenoble on bd. Jean-Paris, then follow av. de Verdun and av. des Sept-Laux. Before arriving in Montbonnot, turn right into le chemin de Saint-Martin.
☎ 04.76.41.91.29 @ lacerisaieclub@club.internet.fr
Closed Sat lunchtime, Sun evening. **Swimming pool**.

A lovely private mansion in a big garden just minutes from Grenoble. The dining room has a high ceiling and the decor is luxurious. On sunny days you get a fabulous view from the superb terrace, which is surrounded by flowers. The place well deserves its good reputation, which has largely spread by word of mouth. A lunchtime *formule* at 95F, and menus, 130–260F, of sophisticated dishes. *À la carte*, try *millefeuille* of pan-fried *foie gras*, salmon with citrus butter or rack of lamb with violet mustard. Best to book. The pool is for customers only. Free coffee or *digestif*.

CORENC   38700 (10KM N)

|●| CAFÉ-RESTAURANT DE LA CHAPELLE

12 route de Chartreuse; it's 3km after Corenc-Village – take the D512 in the direction of Saint-Pierre-de-Chartreuse.
☎ 04.76.88.05.40
Closed Mon unless it's a public holiday, and Sun evening. **Disabled access**. **Car park**.

If you're here in summer, do what the locals do and head for the hills instead of sweltering in the centre of town. This unpretentious café-restaurant has a long-established reputation for its home cooking, friendly atmosphere and, best of all, its shady terrace. Menus 70–118F. If you don't like local specialities like *gratin dauphinois*, *fondue* or bilberry tart, you could try their salads, trout with almond, *civet* stews or grills.

|●| LA CORNE D'OR

159 route de Chartreuse (Northeast).
☎ 04.76.88.00.02
Closed Sun evening in season and a fortnight in Jan.

This substantial house, dominating the valley, is a lovely cool place to come when Grenoble is blistering in the sun. You get superb, panoramic views from the bay windows in the colourful dining room and from the terrace, which is surrounded by greenery. The reputation of the inspirational cuisine is growing and it's affordable. The appeal of the place is the *rôtisserie* but they also offer fried mozzarella and aubergines, pickled red peppers, house *terrine*, lasagne with salmon, and ravioli. Menus 85F and 120F, and a jug of Lyonnais costs 42F. Friendly welcome.

URIAGE-LES-BAINS   38410 (10KM SE)

🛏 🏠 |●| AUBERGE DU VERNON

Les Davids; follow the signs for Chamrousse via col du Luitel.
☎ 04.76.89.10.56
Closed Sun evening and 1 Oct–20 March.

Service until 9pm. This country inn looks like something from a fairy story; it's a little farm with a pond, a huge tree, flowers all over the place and a phenomenal view of the mountains. The Girouds, who have run the place for thirty years, serve good home cooking in

generous portions – this is real country food – *charcuteries* or omelette *paysanne*. 80F weekday lunch menu, others from 110F and a small selection of specialities to order, including veal sweetbreads with ceps or chicken with morels. Six very pretty, tiny doubles; 185F with basin, 270F with shower/wc. Peace and quiet guaranteed. Free coffee.

🛏 🏠 |●| HÔTEL-RESTAURANT LES MÉSANGES**

How to get there: 1km along the Saint-Martin-d'Uriage road, turn right onto the Bouloud road.
☎ 04.76.89.70.69 ➡ 04.76.89.56.97
Hotel closed 25 Oct–30 Jan, and April. **Restaurant closed** Tues, except to residents. **Swimming pool**. **TV**. **Car park**.

Service 12.30–2pm and 7.30–9pm. The Prince family, who have owned this place since 1946, have established a solid reputation. All the rooms have been refurbished; the loveliest ones have big balconies from which you can see down the valley as far as Vizille, while the lesser ones look across the fields. Doubles 290F with shower/wc, 350F with balcony and TV, too. In the restaurant, there's a 90F menu (not served Sun), and others 115–260F including a *menu terroir* of local dishes. Specialities include pigeon in a caul with caramelised spices, pig's trotters, duo of lamb with pickled garlic and ice cream with Chartreuse. It's all very rich. 10% discount on the room rate Sept–June.

GRIGNAN   26230

|●| LE CLAIR DE LA PLUME

pl. du Mail, (Centre); it's below the château, close to the town hall.
☎ 04.75.46.59.20 ➡ 04.75.91.81.31
e plume2@wanadoo.fr
Garden.

Super situation in the old town across from one of the most beautiful wash-houses in the Midi. It's a very elegant 18th-century house with a serene atmosphere and a small, relaxing garden. The whole place reeks of good taste, comfort and refinement. Urbane, polite welcome. All the rooms, priced from 490F, are different. You have breakfast in the old kitchen which is full of original character. Bread and jams are made in-house.

|●| LA PICCOLINA

How to get there: it's below the château, close to the town hall.
☎ 04.75.46.59.20

Closed Mon and Tues out of season, Tues only June–Sept, and 10 Dec–20 Jan.

This pizza place rivals many a gourmet restaurant. They serve good salads and tasty pizzas cooked in a proper wood-fired oven. There's also a choice of excellent grills, rib of beef or rack of lamb. The dining room is small and, because it's good, it gets full quickly. There's a *formule rapide* at 60F (not available Sun or public holidays) and menus at 85F and 115F. Modestly priced wines – 52F for a jug, 68F for a litre of Vinsobres.

|●| LE POÈME

Montée du Tricot; it's 50m from the town hall.
☎ 04.75.91.10.90
Closed Mon.

A new place that's making a name for itself. The cuisine is very elaborate and has lots of creative verve. There are only four dishes on the menus, from 145F, but they change all the time: bream *en papillotte*, hare tart, snails in a pastry case and so on. *À la carte* can get expensive. The decor has a certain unobtrusive distinction so as not to distract diners from their meal. Faultless service. On the wine front, Côteaux du Tricastin starts at 80F. At the weekend, it's best to book.

VALAURIE   26230 (8KM SE)

🎐 🏠 |●| DOMAINE LES MÉJEONNES***

How to get there: take the RN7, then the D133 in the direction of Grignan-Noyons; it's 1km from the village.
☎ 04.75.98.60.60 ➡ 04.75.98.63.44
Closed Sun evening out of season. **Swimming pool. TV. Car park.**

If you want to see this old farmhouse at its best then arrive in the mellow glow of late afternoon or in the evening when the floodlights illuminate the trellised vines and the old stones. You can see it on a hill, far from the road. It's been recently re-inhabited and renovated; the lovely spacious, comfortable rooms go for 345F for a double with shower or bath. Menus, 98–180F, list good, appetising food and a glance reveals a few constants: lamb shank braised in wine, roast supreme of goose, ravioli, and duck *foie gras* in Muscat de Beaume-de-Venise. You'll get a courteous welcome – and the swimming pool is superb. 10% discount on the room rate Sept–June.

🏠 |●| LA TABLE DE NICOLE

Route de Grignan.
☎ 04.75.98.52.03 ➡ 04.75.98.58.45
Swimming pool. Car park.

A favourite spot for visiting Americans, way out in the country. It has everything you hope to find in the Midi – a charming dining room with dry stone walls, a wide fireplace, bright pictures, soft lights and Provençal tablecloths – in a rich, relaxed atmosphere that suits its clientele. The *patron* is chatty and at ease. The food is delicious. The cheapest menu, 145F, lets you choose from at least fifteen different *hors d'œuvre* dishes, laid out on a table; the main course changes daily, but will be a local dish with tasty vegetables *au gratin*. *Foie gras* is listed on the 195F menu and there's a truffle menu at 290F. There's an impressive selection of regional cheeses, but the menus are so generously served that there's hardly space for a dessert. Lots of Côtes du Rhône wines on the remarkable wine list, with *vins de pays* – rich Cornas, Saint-Péray and Saint-Joseph – Crozes Hermitage, and many others. If you're really celebrating there's a Château-Pétrus 1992 for 4100F. About ten rooms with excellent facilities, from 380F.

HAUTERIVES   26390

🏠 |●| LE RELAIS**

pl. de l'Église (West); it's opposite the church.
☎ 04.75.68.81.12 ➡ 04.75.68.92.42
Hotel closed Sun evening and Mon out of season and mid-Jan to mid-Feb. **Restaurant closed** Mon in summer. **Car park.**

The thick, sturdy walls of this handsome 19th-century building are lined with photos and engravings of Ferdinand Cheval – the local postman who constructed an extraordinary sculpture from stones he collected on his rounds. The large, rustic bedrooms cost 180–250F with washing facilities, 310F with shower/wc or bath, and the restaurant offers regional menus 85–160F.

JOYEUSE   07260

🎐 🏠 |●| HÔTEL DE L'EUROPE**

Centre; it's on the D104.
☎ 04.75.39.51.26 ➡ 04.75.39.59.00
Disabled access. Swimming pool. TV. Car park.

Overall, you get fair value here for a place that's on the way to the gorges of the Ardèche and the Cévennes. The small refurbished bedrooms cost 160F with basin and from 220F with shower/wc or bath. They serve tasty, simple dishes such as omelettes with ceps and *charcuterie*, chestnut custard and pizzas of impressive size. Menus from 58F. The large heated indoor pool has a great view over the Cévennes. There's also a *boules* area. 10% discount on the room rate Oct –April.

❘●❘ RESTAURANT VALENTINA

pl. de la Peyre (Centre).
☎ 04.75.39.90.65
Closed Mon out of season, Jan–March and Oct–Dec.

Service noon–2pm and 7–11pm. This is the only restaurant in the old town, and since it's well away from traffic, the terrace overlooking the nice little square is a pleasant place to sit. The owners are a nice Italian couple who are keen travellers. Authentic Italian cooking – pasta with pine nuts, tortellini with ceps, and tagliatelli with smoked salmon and vodka sauce. The home-made desserts are seriously good. Menus from 125F, or you'll pay 50F or so for a single dish. Good Italian wines.

SAINT-ALBAN-AURIOLLES 07120 (10KM SE)

⅔ 🏠 ❘●❘ HÔTEL DOUCE FRANCE**

It's on the D208.
☎ 04.75.39.37.08 ➡ 04.75.39.04.93
Closed Mon except in summer, and Jan.
Disabled access. Swimming pool. Car park.

It's best to book in summer if you want to stay in this reasonably priced hotel in the midst of the vineyards. In the main building, which lacks real character, doubles with shower cost 230F; a room in the bungalows by the swimming pool, which are better situated, is 280F. Menus, 70–200F, list the likes of pan-fried *foie gras*, oysters *gratinée* with leek *purée* and grilled sea bass. Free apéritif.

JULIÉNAS 69840

⅔ 🏠 ❘●❘ CHEZ LA ROSE**

Centre.
☎ 04.74.04.41.20 ➡ 04.74.04.49.29
e chez-la-rose@wanadoo.fr
Hotel closed Feb school holidays and 1–15 Dec.
Restaurant closed Mon, Tues and Thurs lunchtimes (except on public holidays), three weeks in Feb and a week in Dec. **TV. Car park.**

Service noon–2pm and 7.15–9.30pm. With its elegant façade, this building has the look of an old post-house. Two buildings house comfortable, rustic bedrooms; doubles with shower/wc or bath cost 570F, and there are a few little suites, one with a private garden. The magnificent dining room is a perfect setting for the famously tasty regional cooking, produced by a seriously good chef. 20% discount if you dine in the restaurant.

LAMASTRE 07270

🏠 ❘●❘ HÔTEL DU MIDI-RESTAURANT BARATTÉRO

How to get there: from Lamastre, head for Le Puy; it's 2km further, on the right.
☎ 04.75.06.41.50 ➡ 04.75.06.49.75
Closed Fri and Sun evenings, Mon, and Christmas to end-Feb. **TV. Car park.**

A gourmet restaurant that has enjoyed a good reputation for several decades. The dining room is classy and cosy. You get the measure of the cooking from the cheapest menu, 188F, though the more you spend, other menus 278–422F, the more unusual and luxurious the ingredients; Bresse chicken cooked in a bladder or a divine iced chestnut soufflé. The service is meticulous and old-style French. You feel you have to sit straight at your table and not clatter your cutlery. Rooms in the hotel are equally cosy and perfectly maintained; doubles from 470F.

CRESTET (LE) 07270 (8KM NE)

⅔ 🏠 ❘●❘ LA TERRASSE**

Centre; take the D534 in the direction of Tournon; Crestet is on the left.
☎ 04.75.06.24.44 ➡ 04.75.06.23.25
Closed Sat in winter and 25 Dec–3 Jan. **Disabled access. TV. Swimming pool. Car park.**

There's an air of serenity about this classic establishment – you get the feeling that the people here know how to live. Acceptable rooms, from 210F for a double with basin. Menus, 65–138F, list a good selection of regional dishes; it's worth trying *picodon*, the local goat's cheese, which has a slightly piquant flavour. The dining room has a lovely view of the Doux valley and, in summer, when the swimming pool area is ablaze with flowers, a rampant vine provides shade for the terrace. Free house apéritif.

SAINT-BARTHÉLMY-GROZON 07270 (8KM S)

🏠 ❘●❘ LA TERRASSE**

It's in the village.
☎ 04.75.06.58.92
Closed All Saints' to Easter. **Car park.**

The lady owner always takes time to chat with her clients and to make sure they're properly looked after. She has an equally straightforward approach to her cooking – it's honest and generously flavoured. Traditional dishes – menus start at 60F – served inside or out on the shady terrace in summer.

The simple rooms are old-fashioned, clean and cheap at 170F for a double. There's a pleasant family atmosphere.

LANS-EN-VERCORS 38250

🏃 🛏 |O| AUBERGE DE LA CROIX-PERRIN**

col de la Croix-Perrin; from Lans-en-Vercors, head in the direction of Autrans, col de la Croix-Perrin is 3.5km further on.
☎ 04.76.95.40.02 ➡ 04.76.94.33.10
Closed Mon out of season and 12 Nov–20 Dec. **Car park**.

This old mountain hut, deep in the forest 1200m up, has been modernised without losing any of its charm. The handsome wood-panelled dining room has panoramic views, and the traditional mountain cooking and the hearty welcome make the city seem far, far away. Menus, 89–149F, list a fish dish of the day, ravioli from Royans or duck breast with peaches. You have to order *fondue* in advance. Doubles with shower/wc cost 270F, half board 280F per person. There's a pleasant veranda with views over forest and mountains, and a huge terrace. Free apéritif.

LANSLEBOURG 73480

🏃 🛏 |O| HÔTEL DE LA VIEILLE POSTE**

Centre.
☎ 04.79.05.93.47 ➡ 04.79.05.86.85
Closed 15 April–4 June, 28 Oct–26 Dec. **TV**. **Car park**.

This oversized chalet stands right in the centre of the resort, so you can hear the traffic noise from the main road. However, you get a friendly welcome and, in spite of its size, there's a family atmosphere. The son of the house is quite a skiier, and members of the French national team are regulars here – the bar and the dining room overflow with medals and cups. Menus, 75–110F, feature home cooking and traditional dishes. Bedrooms are modern and pleasant and have been refurbished – some have a terrace. Doubles with shower/wc or bath 260–200F. Free apéritif.

LÉLEX 01410

🏃 🛏 |O| HÔTEL-RESTAURANT MONT JURA**

ancienne route de Mijoux (Centre); take the D991.
☎ 04.50.20.90.53 ➡ 04.50.20.95.20

Closed Tues out of season and a fortnight in Nov. **TV**. **Car park**.

This place is in the middle of a ski resort which has retained its village atmosphere. The building itself doesn't have much character and the interior is pretty ordinary, but you'll get a good-natured welcome. The rustic rooms are spacious and comfortable, with doubles 185F with basin and 280F with shower or bath. The regional cooking is lavishly served and prices are affordable – try *fricassée* of suckling pig, *foie gras*, *gratin* of crayfish, and game in autumn. Menus 98–149F. Free apéritif.

LYON 69000

SEE MAP OVERLEAF

1st arrondissement
🏃 🛏 HÔTEL SAINT-VINCENT**

9 rue Pareille; M° Hôtel-de-Ville. **MAP B1-1**
☎ 04.78.27.22.56 ➡ 04.78.30.92.87
Closed Aug. **TV**.

This hotel is freshly painted and not lacking in charm. All the rooms are very well equipped, and a few have beautiful fireplaces. They cost 230F with shower, 270F with shower/wc and 290F with bath. There are also a few triples. An excellent welcome is guaranteed. Free breakfast. 10% discount.

🏃 |O| LA RANDONNÉE

4 rue Terme; M° Hôtel-de-Ville. **MAP C1-31**
☎ and ➡ 04.78.27.86.81
Closed Sun lunchtime, Mon, the last fortnight in Aug.

At the foot of a steep road going up to Croix Rousse, this restaurant, one of the least expensive in Lyons, is very popular with its penniless young customers. The nice owners prepare simple, home cooking and typical Lyonnais dishes at very reasonable prices. *Formules* and menus 49–90F; they've even got one for vegetarians. Wines are very cheap, too. It can be hard to find a table among all the youngsters who pile into the two little dining rooms. Free parking in the Terreaux car park at night. Free *digestif*.

🏃 |O| ALYSSAAR

rue du Bât-d'Argent (Centre). **MAP D2-19**
☎ 04.78.29.57.66
Closed lunchtimes, Sun, Mon and Christmas holidays.

Alyssaar is a Syrian whose genuine kindness makes his customers feel special. He will happily explain the various specialities served on the *assiette du Calife*, a selection of Syri-

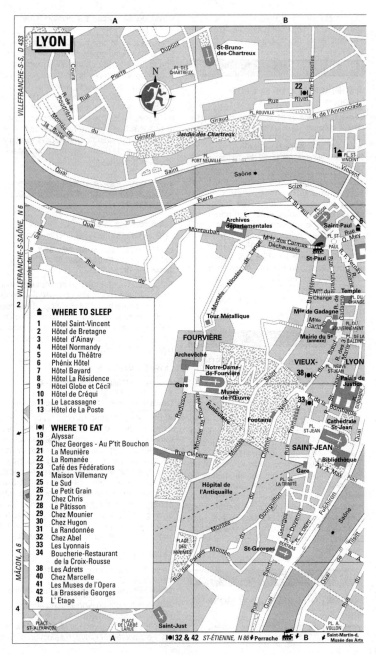

LYON

WHERE TO SLEEP

1 Hôtel Saint-Vincent
2 Hôtel de Bretagne
3 Hôtel d'Ainay
4 Hôtel Normandy
5 Hôtel du Théâtre
6 Phénix Hôtel
7 Hôtel Bayard
8 Hôtel La Résidence
9 Hôtel Globe et Cécil
10 Hôtel de Créqui
11 Le Lacassagne
13 Hôtel de La Poste

WHERE TO EAT

19 Alyssar
20 Chez Georges - Au P'tit Bouchon
21 La Meunière
22 La Romanée
23 Café des Fédérations
24 Maison Villemanzy
25 Le Sud
26 Le Petit Grain
27 Chez Chris
28 Le Pâtisson
29 Chez Mounier
30 Chez Hugon
31 La Randonnée
32 Chez Abel
33 Les Lyonnais
34 Boucherie-Restaurant
   de la Croix-Rousse
38 Les Adrets
40 Chez Marcelle
41 Les Muses de l'Opera
42 La Brasserie Georges
43 L' Etage

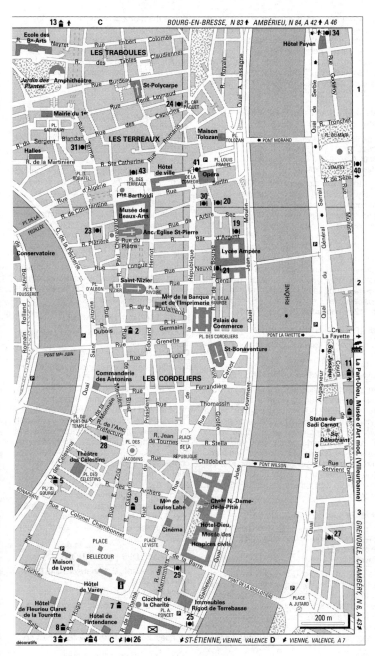

an delicacies, and in which order you should eat them – it's a gastronomic journey on a fly-ing carpet that will take your palate places it's never been before. The beef with cherries is amazing, as is the lamb kebab with aubergines. The "Thousand-and-one-nights" dessert is a revelation. Menus 78F, 87F and 105F. Free *digestif*.

|O| RESTAURANT CHEZ GEORGES-AU P'TIT BOUCHON

8 rue du Garet; M° Hôtel-de-Ville or Louis-Pradel. **MAP D1-20**
☎ 04.78.28.30.46
Closed Sat, Sun and Aug.

Set this down alongside an old Paris bistro and you wouldn't be able to tell them apart – it's got the checked tablecloths, imitation leather banquettes, the mirror-lined walls and the original, zinc-topped bar. The attentive but unobtrusive owner serves at table while his wife is busy in the handkerchief-sized kitchen. Well-balanced Lyonnais menus list sausage with lentils, grilled veal sausage, an astonishingly good Saint-Marcellin (a mild cheese from the Dauphiné), and a great upside-down apple tart. Set menus, 90–125F and around 160F *à la carte*.

|O| RESTAURANT LA MEUNIÈRE

11 rue Neuve; M° Cordeliers or Hôtel-de-Ville. **MAP D2-21**
☎ 04.78.28.62.91
Closed Sun, Mon, and mid-July to mid-Aug.

An exuberant place where you'll get a won-derful welcome, an abundance of good local dishes, a buffet of enticing starters, and a friendly atmosphere. They serve traditional Lyons food: *cochonnaille* (sausage made from various parts of the pig), *tablier de sapeur* (ox tripe egged, crumbed and fried), and *andouillette* – perfect with a Beaujolais or Côtes-du-Rhône to wash it down. Lunch menu 98F, with others 120–160F. Best to book for dinner.

⅍ |O| LES MUSES DE L'OPÉRA

pl. de la Comédie; take the lift beside the entrance to the opera house to the 7th floor. **MAP D1-41**
☎ 04.72.00.45.58
Closed Sun.

Service until midnight. This long, narrow sev-enth-floor dining room gives you great views of the street way down below. The decor is fashionably black, which means your eye is drawn outside to the large terrace which overlooks the square. Inside, you'll dine on the colourful, original, skilfully prepared food

that is the hallmark of chef Philippe Chavent. The *menu du jour* offers typical Lyons dishes, while *à la carte* there's an astonishingly good *croustillant* of lamb with dried apricots and a *terrine* of lentils and chicken livers. Lunch menu at 105F, and evening menus 139F and 169F. Free house apéritif.

⅍ |O| L'ÉTAGE

4 pl. des Terreaux; M° Hôtel-de-Ville. **MAP C1-43**
☎ 04.78.28.19.59
Closed Sun, Mon, bank holidays, a few days in Feb, the last week in July and the first three weeks in Aug.

Push open the heavy door and you find your-self in a wood-panelled salon draped in red. From the tables by the windows you get a good view of the fountain. The cooking is ele-gant, fine, and precise, and though the dish-es change frequently the quality remains the same: *marbré* of chicken with pickled onions and apple chutney, roast salmon with papri-ka, semolina and hazelnut oil, and Saint-Mar-cellin goat's cheese. Dish of the day 68F, menus 110–280F and, if you want a change from Lyonnais dishes, there's a lobster menu for 270F to order two days in advance. Lots of regulars. Free coffee.

|O| RESTAURANT LA ROMANÉE

19 rue Rivet; 800m from M° Croix-Paquet. **MAP B1-22**
☎ 04.72.00.80.87
Closed Sat lunchtime, Sun evening, Mon and Aug.

This place has a long-standing reputation for good cooking; Élisabeth Denis is a fine chef who's inspired by the flavours of the south. She changes her menus every couple of months, and produces dishes of boundless invention – mushroom *terrine*, red mullet with garlic, breast of duck with mushrooms and truffle-scented sauce, and a variety of home-made desserts, though there's a small choice. The impressive wine list runs to a total of four hundred wines, all of them selected by Daniel Denis, the chef's hus-band. Prices run from cheap to very expen-sive. The restaurant can only seat 25, and is often fully booked days in advance. The din-ing room is a smoke-free zone. Menus 110–215F.

⅍ |O| CAFÉ DES FÉDÉRATIONS

8 rue du Major-Martin; M° Hôtel-de-Ville. **MAP C2-23**
☎ 04.78.28.26.00
Closed Sat lunchtime, Sun and Aug.

Scenes from the classic Tavernier movie, *L'Horloger de Saint-Paul*, were filmed in this local institution that hasn't changed in decades. It is one of the best Lyonnais *bou-*

chons – the name given to the city's popular brasserie-bar-restaurants – and the perfect place to taste really good Lyonnais cuisine. The dishes are traditional: *gras-double* (marinated for two days in white wine and mustard), *tablier de sapeur* (ox tripe egged, crumbed and grilled), calf's head *ravigote*. Splendid *hors d'œuvres* include *charcuterie*, bowls of lentils, beetroot, brawn and calf's feet, mixed seasonal salads, and sausage cooked in red wine. Lunch menu 120F, and an evening *formule* with more choice at 148F. Service is swift and friendly. Free Kir.

⅍ |●| CHEZ HUGON

12 rue Pizay; M° Hôtel-de-Ville. **MAP D1-30**
☎ 04.78.28.10.94
Closed Sat, Sun and Aug.

As you wander around the town hall area, you'll find this authentic Lyonnais *bouchon* in a little alley. It's unchanged over the years. The dining room has only a few tables, covered with checked tablecloths, where you can eat excellent Lyons specialities like sheep's trotters, *tablier de sapeur* (ox tripe egged, crumbed and grilled), and *gâteau de foies de volaille* (chicken livers mixed with *foie gras*, eggs and cream). Menu 120F or *à la carte* , around 160F. Free coffee.

|●| MAISON VILLEMANZY

25 montée Saint-Sébastien; M° Croix-Pâquet.
MAP C1-24
☎ 04.78.39.37.00
Closed Sun, Mon lunchtime and 1–14 Jan.

This unspoilt house, once the residence of a doctor-colonel, sits high above the city on the slopes of La Croix-Rousse. There's a magnificent terrace from where you can survey the town – the view's very popular, so it's best to book. Guillaume Mouchel, in charge in the kitchens, was a pupil of Jean-Paul Lacombe, one of Lyon's great chefs. You get lots of choice on the well-devised 126F *menu carte*, which changes every two days. To eat lightly, go for the dish of the day plus green salad for 70F. A reasonably priced wine list.

2nd arrondissement
⅍ ☗ HÔTEL NORMANDIE**

3 rue du Bélier (South); M° Perrache. Off map **C4-4**
☎ 04.78.37.31.36 ➡ 04.78.40.98.56
TV.

This hotel, named after the great French liner, is in a quiet street. It has about forty small rooms, for 164F with basin, 295F with bath. The double glazing keeps out most of the noise from the railway station. Some rooms have been spruced up, and more are due the same treatment. Pleasant staff can tell you where to go and what to see. 10% discount except at weekends and in school holidays.

☗ HÔTEL D'AINAY*

14 rue des Remparts-d'Ainay (South); M° Ampère-Victor-Hugo. Off map **C4-3**
☎ 04.78.42.43.42 ➡ 04.72.77.51.90
TV.

If you're on a budget, this very simple hotel will suit you down to the ground; it's in a quiet, rather delightful pedestrianised neighbourhood not far from the magnificent basilica. The friendly young couple who run it put a good deal of effort into creating a restful atmosphere. The rooms have good double glazing and look onto the road, the courtyard or the pl. Ampère. Doubles 180F with basin, 240F with bath.

⅍ ☗ HÔTEL DE BRETAGNE*

10 rue Dubois (Centre); M° Cordeliers. **MAP C2-2**
☎ 04.78.37.79.33 ➡ 04.72.77.99.92
TV.

This hotel, halfway between the Saône and place des Cordeliers, is run by people from the Auvergne and offers good value for money. The rooms are clean, smart, and soundproofed – good for the ones overlooking the street which are big and bright. The ones over the courtyard are very gloomy. Doubles with shower/wc cost 245–290F, while rooms that sleep three or four go for 275F. 10% discount.

⅍ ☗ HÔTEL DU THÉÂTRE**

10 rue de Savoie; M° Bellecour. **MAP C3-5**
☎ 04.78.42.33.32 ➡ 04.72.40.00.61
TV.

The show starts as you walk through the door: a staircase, dressed like a stage set, leads up to reception on the second floor and sets the tone for the rest of the hotel. If you're lucky, you'll get one of the rooms overlooking the place des Célestins and the theatre – the view is stunning. It's best to book well ahead of time and ask for one of those rooms. There's a nice little breakfast room and the atmosphere is relaxed. Rooms 300F with shower/wc and 360F with bath. One free breakfast per double room.

⅍ ☗ HÔTEL LA RÉSIDENCE***

18 rue Victor-Hugo; M° Bellecour or Ampère-Victor-Hugo. **MAP C4-8**
☎ 04.78.42.63.28 ➡ 04.78.42.85.76
TV. **Disabled access**.

Halfway between Perrache and Bellecour in a lively pedestrianised street with lots of shops. They practise old-style hotel-keeping here – the kind that is handed down from father to son, keeping all the good traditions – plus it's one of the cheapest three-star places in town. The rooms have all had a make-over, and are cosy and air-conditioned; 325F with shower/wc, 355F with bath. Professional welcome. 10% discount July–Aug.

♠ HÔTEL BAYARD**

23 pl. Bellecour; M° Bellecour. **MAP C4-7**
☎ 04.78.37.39.64 ➡ 04.72.40.95.51
TV.

Though they're all newly decorated, no two rooms are alike in this hotel, and some have lots of personality: several have canopied bed, polished parquet floor, and a great view of the place Bellecour; number 5 has an enormous bathroom; and number 15, which overlooks the courtyard, can sleep four. Doubles 357–377F. The little breakfast nook has a very countrified feel. Follow the signs up the stairs to the reception on the first floor.

🎎 ♠ HÔTEL GLOBE ET CÉCIL***

21 rue Gasparin; M° Bellecour. **MAP C3-9**
☎ 04.78.42.58.95 ➡ 04.72.41.99.06
TV.

A top-notch three-star in the city centre. Each room has been decorated in a style appropriate to its size and has its own character – some have handsome marble fireplaces, balconies and air conditioning. The rooms that overlook the street are brighter than the others. The service can't be faulted, and it comes with a smile. Doubles 720–760F with shower/wc or bath, including breakfast. 10% discount on weekdays.

🎎 |●| LE PETIT GRAIN

19 rue de la Charité (South); M° Ampère or Bellecour. off map **C4-26**
☎ 04.72.41.77.85
Closed Sun, evenings after 8pm, Mon and 15–25 Aug.

A simple little snack bar in an old milliner's shop near rue Auge-Comte, the street with all the antique shops. It's prettily decorated with a scattering of objects picked up from street markets by the cheerful Vietnamese owner. You can have a substantial *bo bun* (stir-fried beef and noodles), a huge, delicious salad, or a dish of the day, which is usually Vietnamese or Chinese. Terrific pear and chocolate or apple and cinammon tarts. *Formules* and menus 43–66F. Make a visit to the fabric

museum or the decorative arts museum across the street after lunch. Free apéritif.

|●| RESTAURANT CHEZ MOUNIER

3 rue des Marronniers; M° Bellecour. **MAP C3/4-29**
☎ 04.78.37.79.26
Closed Sun evening, Mon, the last week in Aug and first fortnight in Sept, and the first week in Jan.

Lyon is famous for its puppets; the one in this restaurant window, smiling at passers-by and inviting them in, is the comic character Guignol. This is the most authentic of the *bouchons* in this touristy street, with two bare, stark little dining rooms. There's a good atmosphere created by Christine Moinier, and the regional cooking retains all of its character: *gnafrons* (little sausages), *tablier de sapeur* (ox tripe egged, crumbed and grilled). For 48F (weekday lunchtimes), you can have a main course and dessert – a give-away. For 61F you get three courses and there are another two menus under 100F.

🎎 |●| LE PÂTISSON

17 rue du Port-du-Temple (Centre); M° Bellecour.
MAP C3-28
☎ 04.72.41.81.71
Closed Fri evening, Sat April–Sept, Sat lunchtime Oct–March, Sun, and the third week in Aug.

Yves Perrin, owner of the only vegetarian restaurant in the city, has worked in some very good restaurants in France and Belgium. His diplomas are proudly displayed on the walls. He became a vegetarian for health reasons, and his dishes show the same skill and flair as they ever did – try his medallions of tofu with a *julienne* of saffron-flavoured vegetables or the millet and aubergine *provençale*. Dish of the day 55F, menus 68–110F. No smoking. Free house apéritif.

|●| LA BRASSERIE GEORGES

30 cours de Verdun; it's next to Perrache station.
Off map **B4-42**
☎ 04.72.56.54.54
Closed 1 May.

Service 11.30am–11.15pm, but to 00.15am on Fri and Sat. This cosmopolitan Art Deco brasserie, which has been open since 1836, is a great barn of a place, seating 1000 diners served by 200 staff. The cuisine is in the grand tradition: sausage in *brioche*, *quenelle* of pike and, inevitably, *choucroute*. Weekday lunch menu 89F, then 102–153F – ham with mashed potatoes is served free to children under three. They serve good beer, and the atmosphere is cheery, with a lively jazz evening on Saturday. Sadly, the horrible

Perrache car park makes the view really ugly.

🎿 |●| CHEZ ABEL

25 rue Guynemer (South); M° Ampère. off map **B4-32**
☎ 04.78.37.46.18
Closed Sat lunchtime, Sun, and Aug.

This place, just a stone's throw from the Saône and 200m from the basilica, has very old wainscotting and a creaky parquet floor. It looks like a folk museum, full of oddments, hefty wooden tables and a beer pump from 1925. House specialities include liver, calf's head, *andouillette*, chicken with rice and *quenelles* of pike. Menus 90F and 140–185F; *à la carte*, prices soar. Free *digestif*.

3rd arrondissement
🟦 LE LACASSAGNE***

245 av. Lacassagne (East); M° Grange-Blanche; it's a fair distance from the centre, near the hospitals and the town of Bron. Off map **D2-11**
☎ 04.78.54.09.12 ➡ 04.72.36.99.23
TV. Disabled access. Car park.

You need a car to get to this pleasant hotel on the edge of town. It has big rooms – some overlook a garden. Nice welcome and reasonable prices. Doubles 220F with shower/wc and 310F with bath. Light meals – salad, *croque-monsieur*, cream cheese and so on – provided for 74F or 84F on request.

🎿 🟦 HÔTEL DE CRÉQUI**

158 rue de Créqui (East); M° Guichard; it's not far from the TGV station. Off map **D3-10**
☎ 04.78.60.20.47 ➡ 04.78.62.21.12
Closed Easter, Aug and Christmas holidays. **TV.**

A spruce new hotel near the law courts, a ten-minute walk from the town centre. The bedrooms are comfortable, with cheerful yellow walls and blue carpets, but they're a bit of a squeeze. All rooms cost 387F, with bath. Smiling, professional staff. They do simple meals – 60F for the dish of the day – and there's a wine bar (not at weekends). 10% discount on the room rate.

|●| CHEZ CHRIS

1 rue de la Victoire; M° Guichard. **MAP D3-27**
☎ 04.78.60.86.33
Closed Sat lunchtime, Sun, public holidays and a week around 14 July.

Chris, an ex-Miss France, has certainly made a name for herself with her restaurant. Her generous cooking is based upon good, reliable Lyonnais dishes: tripe *roulade*, veal with garlic, and classic desserts like *crème*

caramel tart, bread and butter pudding and prunes in wine. The dining room is run by Daniel, whose distress if you don't finish everything on your plate can be a bit off-putting. Lunch *formules* 52F and 68F, menus 95–110F.

4th arrondissement
🎿 🟦 HÔTEL DE LA POSTE

1 rue Victor Fort (North); M° Croix-Rousse. Off map **C1-13**
☎ and ➡ 04.78.28.62.67

One of the least expensive hotels in town and certainly one of the nicest, located in the heart of the marvellous Croix-Rousse neighbourhood. It's housed in a working-class block of flats and though the building is not exactly oozing with charm, it's very well maintained. The lovely proprietress has a friendly smile for everybody, but reserves half of her twenty rooms for regulars. Rooms 100F and 155F with basin, 190F with shower. 10% discount July–Aug.

|●| BOUCHERIE-RESTAURANT DE LA CROIX-ROUSSE

3 pl. des Tapis; M° Croix-Rousse. Off map **D1-34**
☎ and ➡ 04.78.28.48.82
Closed Sun evening, Mon, Wed evening and May.

Proprietor Yves Daguin is first and foremost a butcher, and to get to the restaurant you have to go through his shop. He doesn't pretend to be a chef, and though he can turn his hand to a tasty *andouillette beaujolaise* (a type of sausage cooked in Beaujolais wine), his best dishes are simple and unadorned, without sauce. For starters, share a platter of lamb kidneys, testicles and sweetbreads or the selection of *saucissons de Lyon*, before moving onto the meat of your choice. There's a very good selection of reasonably priced wines from tiny vineyards in Beaujolais and Côtes-du-Rhône. Dish of the day 48F, menus 67F and 84F. Dinner *à la carte* will cost 120–200F depending on your appetite and how many courses you order. There's a big terrace in front of the shop.

5th arrondissement
🎿 🟦 PHÉNIX HÔTEL***

7 quai de Bondy; M° Hôtel-de-Ville. **MAP B2-6**
☎ 04.78.28.24.24 ➡ 04.78.28.62.86
Disabled access. TV. Car park.

The hotel, in a splendid 17th-century building, offers big, tastefully decorated rooms. It's the only hotel in town to have rooms with a view of the Saône; others look over the Croix-Rousse hill. They're beautifully appointed and impeccably maintained. Very professional welcome and an international clientele. Doubles 980–1080F, including breakfast. Free coffee.

🏿 |●| LES LYONNAIS

1 rue Tramassac; M° Vieux-Lyon. **MAP B3-33**
☎ 04.78.37.64.82
Closed Sun evening, Mon and three weeks in Aug.

An imitation Lyon *bouchon* that just about works. There are portraits of the illustrious unknown of Lyon on the wall in the big, yellow-painted dining room. Since it opened this friendly place has drawn regular crowds for its efficient service, good food and affordable prices. The typical Lyon dishes include *tabliers de sapeur*, hot sausages, calf's head with sauce *gribiche*, and pike balls with shellfish sauce. Weekday lunch *formules* 58F and 68F, and in the evening, a *menu du marché*, which changes with the seasons, at 103F and a *menu Lyonnais* at 110F. Free coffee.

🏿 |●| LES ADRETS

30 rue du Bœuf; M° Vieux-Lyon. MAP **B2-38**
☎ 04.78.38.24.30
Closed Sat, Sun and Aug.

This typically Lyonnais place isn't at the forefront of fashion but it's always full of people of all ages. The excellent lunch menu, 80F, offers three generously served courses: as good a fish soup as you'll eat in Marseilles, venison *sauté* with fresh noodles, and calf's brains. It's perfectly accompanied by a jug of wine which, like the coffee, is included in the price. Other menus 115–195F. Free apéritif.

6th arrondissement
🏿 ⬛ HÔTEL FOCH***

59 av. Foch; M° Foch. Off map **D1-17**
☎ 04.78.89.15.01 ↦ 04.78.93.71.69

It's right in the middle of the *arrondissement* but only a five-minute walk from the peninsula. It's a charming, discreet hotel on the second floor of an old building. The reception has a salon with leather sofas, and the breakfast room has a parquet floor. It's a quiet place with spacious, well-appointed rooms, and it feels luxurious but not ostentatious. Friendly, personal welcome. Doubles 460F with shower/wc or 550F with bath. 10% discount.

🏿 |●| CHEZ MARCELLE

71 cours Vitton (East); M° Masséna. Off map **D1-40**
☎ 04.78.89.51.07
Closed Sat, Sun and Aug.

The scores of regulars come here not for the decor but for the marvellous food. Marcelle is one of the last genuine *"mères"* – the name given to the old-fashioned style of female cook – in the city. First comes the selection of *hors d'œuvres* – a series of salad bowls full of lentils, fresh green beans (in season), wonderful *cervelas* (a delicious pork sausage), bacon, cooked peppers and so on. Next, you can have an amazing *tablier de sapeur* (ox tripe egged and crumbed before being grilled), calf's liver, or thick slabs of succulent meat. End the feast with a terrific *crème caramel* – a house rule insists customers should never claim to be full. Make sure you have no plans for the afternoon. Lunch menu 150F, *à la carte* only at dinner, which gets very expensive. Free apéritif.

7th arrondissement

🏿 |●| L'AROMATE

94 Grande-Rue-de-la-Guillotière (right bank); M° Saxe-Gambetta. Off map **A4-49**
☎ 04.78.58.94.56
Closed Wed evening, Sun, the first Mon in the month, end July to 20 Aug, and the New Year holidays.

The "La Guillotière" area is known for its range of foreign restaurants but here is a tiny place producing Camargue cuisine. It's run by a brilliant couple who fuss over their clients like crazy. *Taureau* – which means bull – prepared in all ways imaginable: *andouillette*, haunch, grilled, pan-fried, *tartare* and so on. There's also a good range of carefully prepared fish and squid dishes. Start with an *"améthyste"* – the house apéritif that's as good as it is surprising – and finish with a heavenly dessert. Presentation, size of portions, seasonings and the service all make this an excellent place. When the bill comes, you pay as you have eaten – with pleasure. Menus 85F and 130F and around 180F *à la carte*. Free house apéritif.

|●| EN METS, FAIS CE QU'IL TE PLAÎT

rue Chevreul; M° Jean-Macé.
☎ 04.78.72.46.58
Closed Mon and Tues evenings, Sat, Sun and Aug.

A really good restaurant with two dining rooms; you can see into the kitchen from the first one, which has a bar, while the second one has metal grills at the windows and tables brightened up by modern, colourful lamps. It's a relaxing place, with easy-going, attentive service. The menu lists dishes like fresh vegetables with olive oil, meltingly good duck thigh with prunes, and sea trout *meunière* on a bed of spinach. The produce and ingredients are the freshest, and the attention paid to precise cooking is impressive. You'll pay 140F and 200F *à la carte* depending on your choice of dishes and wine. There's a selection of good wines served by the glass.

CHAPONOST   69630 (10KM SW)

🎿🏠|O| RESTAURANT LE CROÛTON

27 [bis] av. Paul-Doumer (Centre); take the D50.
☎ 04.78.45.06.47
Closed Wed and Aug.

This lovely little restaurant has the makings of a real favourite for foodies. The tasteful, restful dining rooms are spread across two floors. The clientele, mostly businesspeople and families, come here for home cooking prepared with imagination. There's a weekday menu at 66F, then others up to 190F, and *à la carte*. Free apéritif.

CHASSELAY   69630 (10KM SW)

|O| GUY LAUSSAUSAIE

Le bourg; take the A6, then the N6 and the D16.
☎ 04.78.47.62.59
Closed Tues evening, Wed, Feb school holidays and 5–25 Aug. **Car park.**

Guy Lassausaie studied with some of the great chefs before taking over the family business, determined to give it a new lease of life and to add an attraction to this somewhat ordinary village. The dining room is very, very chic since being even more sumptuously decorated. His cooking is of the classic school, with a subtle touch of modernity which takes it out of the ordinary; *cappuccino* of pickled chicory, roast quail with pistachio nuts, celery pie, and oxtail braised with rosemary. The cheeses are ripened to perfection and there is a sumptuous dessert trolley. Menus 190–400F. There's also an interesting wine list with wines from round the world. Attentive service and decent prices for this quality of restaurant.

MEGÈVE   74120

🎿🏠|O| HÔTEL CHALET DES OURS*

Chemin des Roseaux (Centre).
☎ 04.50.21.57.40 📠 04.50.93.05.73
✉ kellowjill@aol.com
Closed Thurs evening, May and Nov. **Car park.**

It's a big surprise to find such a little gem in the opulent surroundings of Megève. Owned by an English woman, this lovely place is a haven of refinement, simplicity and kindness. The panelled rooms are decorated simply with vases of flowers and soft feather beds. Doubles with shower/wc 320–450F; half board, 320–390F per person, is compulsory in winter. There's a reading room with a beautiful fireplace and a TV, and a small dining room in the basement. They offer a menu at 95F, or a rather exotic Thai menu to order for dinner. It's sheer pleasure to have five different kinds of tea to choose from at breakfast! 10% discount on the room rate except in high season.

PRAZ-SUR-ARLY   74120 (5KM SW)

🎿🏠|O| LA GRIYOTIRE***

Route de la Tonnaz; take the N212.
☎ 04.50.21.86.36 📠 04.50.21.86.34
✉ griyotire@wanadoo.fr
Hotel closed Mid-April to mid-June and mid-Sept to mid-Dec. **Restaurant closed** lunchtimes. **Swimming pool. Garden.TV. Car park.**

A dream of an Alpine chalet, in the middle of a family resort not far from Megève, set well away from the main road that runs through the middle of the village. The rooms have been decorated in exquisite taste and every one is different. There's lots of wood everywhere and the feather beds are as soft as can be; doubles with shower/wc 370–450F. Half-board, compulsory during the winter school holidays, 340–390F. Charming welcome and a family atmosphere – there's even a games room for the children. *Fondue* and *raclette* are served on winter evenings. Menus 80–145F. There's a lovely garden, a sauna and a swimming pool open in summer. Free *digestif*.

MENS   38710

🏠|O| AUBERGE DE MENS***

pl. du Breuil (Centre).
☎ 04.76.34.81.00 📠 04.76.34.80.90
Disabled access. TV. Car park.

This huge, renovated house offers comfortable rooms at 275F for a double with shower/wc or bath. The decor is fresh and colourful and there's a lovely garden where you can relax on quiet evenings. They serve traditional home cooking, with a menu at 90F.

🎿|O| CAFÉ DES ARTS

rue Principale (Centre); from Grenoble take the N85 then the D526.
☎ 04.76.34.68.16
Restaurant closed Sun evening, Mon–Sat evenings except for reservations, Wed, and Sept–May. **TV.**

This charming place is the most famous café in the Trièves and it's listed as a historic monument. In 1896, Gustave Riquet, a painter from Picardy, decorated the ceilings and walls with beautiful allegorical frescoes and views of the countryside. The self-taught chef-owner prepares superb dishes dependent upon what's good in the market. The choice is limited, but you can be sure that whatever is on offer will be inspired. Try the house *terrine* of *foie gras* and the fresh fish. Lunch menu 75F and 110F in the evening. Dinner by reservation only. Free coffee.

TRÉMNIS   38710 (15KM S)

沿 🏠 |●| HÔTEL DES ALPES

hameau de Château-Bas: take the D66 from Mens then the D216.
☎ 04.76.34.72.94
Closed Sun evening and Mon out of season, and Nov–Feb.

This is the type of hotel you'd expect to see on an old sepia postcard of the mountains. Set in marvellous countryside, it's been wonderfully run for generations. There's a vaulted café-bar and a grandfather clock ticking away in the dining room next to the buffet. In these comforting surroundings you can eat good family cooking from a series of menus at very low prices, 70–135F. Doubles cost 200F with basin and 280F with shower – some of the beds are a little soft. Free coffee.

CHICHILIANNE   38930 (20KM W)

沿 🏠 |●| AU GAI SOLEIL DU MONT-AIGUILLE**

La Richardière; take the N75 then the D7, it's 2.5km from the village, where all the walking trails start.
☎ 04.76.34.41.71 ➡ 04.76.34.40.63
Closed 1 Nov–20 Dec.

Surrounded by a fantastic ring of mountains, this hotel is at the foot of Mont Aiguille, among the woods, copses and wheat fields. The house, built in 1720, has its original stone staircase, and there has been a hotel here for fifty years. The *patronne* is warm-hearted and welcoming. Rooms are super-clean and reasonably priced; 200F with basin, 275F with shower/wc and 285F with bath. Good, classic dishes are served in the restaurant: chicken liver *soufflé*, pork stew, chicken with crayfish and various grilled meats. Menus 85F (not Sun), and 100–200F. Cheaply priced wines with a Cuvée at 50F and a Châtillon-en-Diois at 55F. It's lively in high season. Free house apéritif.

🏠 |●| CHÂTEAU DE PASSIÈRES**

How to get there: take the D526 from Mens to Clelles, then the D7 to the foot of Mont Aiguille.
☎ 04.76.34.45.48 ➡ 04.76.34.46.25
Closed Sun evening and Mon except July–Aug, and Dec–Jan. **Swiming pool**. **TV**. **Car park**.

A 15th-century château, owned by the mayor, in a magnificent location. All the rooms are bang up to date in terms of facilities, and the prices, 300–420F, are attractive. Numbers 1, 4 and 5 are the most expensive, because they have original wood panelling. You can sit and chat in the charming sitting room – a veritable picture gallery – well into the small hours. There's a good bar, and imaginative cooking served in a large dining room. Menus, 120–220F, list specialities such as *compote* of duck or trout with walnuts, turnovers studded with truffles on a creamed leek *fondue*, salmon steak with dandelion honey, *fricassée* of ceps, and snails on a bed of ravioli. There's a nice swimming pool in the grounds.

MIRMANDE   26270

沿|●| RESTAURANT MARGOT

Centre; it's near the post office.
☎ 04.75.63.08.05 ✉ perso@wanadoo.fr/margot
Closed Wed, and Dec–Jan.

This restaurant, like the listed village, is a mixture of stylishness and rustic simplicity. It's a place for people who love old-style cooking. In summer you can go inside to cool off in the tastefully decorated dining room, or sit out on a bench on the terrace in the shade of the climbing vines. There's a weekday lunch menu at 75F, and others up to 140F. You get a good choice of regional specialities *à la carte*: braised veal *à la provençale*, lamb *Tonton Firmin* and chocolate *fondant*. On a Thursday, they hold jazz evenings. Free apéritif.

CLIOUSCLAT   26270 (2KM N)

沿 🏠 |●| LA TREILLE MUSCATE**

How to get there: it's 1km from Mirmande on the D57.
☎ 04.75.63.13.10 ➡ 04.75.63.10.79
Closed Wed and 15 Dec–1 March.
Disabled access. **Garden**. **TV**. **Car park**.

A large, pretty house with green shutters and walls part-covered in ivy. Inside, the rooms have a sophisticated charm and some have a terrace with a view over the countryside; 350F with shower/wc, 550F with bath. There's a lovely enclosed garden and the dining room is bright and roomy, with a corner fireplace and a few stylish tables. The cuisine, which uses local produce, is typical of this sunny region: pressed chicken in a *pot-au-feu* with mustard, and preserved lamb with garlic. The weekday lunch menu, 90F, and others up to145F offer great value. Excellent welcome. Free coffee.

MODANE 73500

🛪 🏠 |●| HÔTEL-RESTAURANT LE PERCE-NEIGE**

14 av. Jean-Jaurès (Centre); it's opposite the station.
☎ 04.79.05.00.50 ➡ 04.79.05.12.92
Closed Sun out of season, 1–19 May, 1 Oct–6 Nov. **TV**.

This is an ideal place for an overnight stop in a town that is not sufficiently appealing for a longer stay. The rooms are simple and the welcome slightly offhand. Doubles 250F with shower/wc up to 385F with bath. All the rooms are well soundproofed, which is just as well since the hotel is on the road and opposite the railway track. The traditional cooking is good, though. Menus 76–119F. 10% discount outside the summer and winter seasons.

AUSSOIS 73500 (15KM NE)

🛪 |●| FORT MARIE-CHRISTINE

How to get there: take the D215, and turn right before getting to Aussois.
☎ 04.79.20.36.44 📧 fort.m.c@wanadoo.fr
Closed Sun evening and Mon for the periods 15 Sept–15 Dec and 23 May–15 June, then 22 April–22 May and 4 Nov–22 Dec. **TV**. **Car park**.

This sturdy fortress, on an outcrop of rock, is part of a string of fortresses built by the crown of Piedmont and Sardinia to protect their kingdom from French invasion. The lofty halls and vaults have been extensively restored, though the interior retains the severe atmosphere of a garrison. The restaurant is renowned for its splendid local cooking: pork *fricassée*, cockerel with bilberries, *agnelot* (home-made ravioli) with sage, *civet* of rabbit with Gamay wine served with polenta, and *diots* (herb sausages cooked in wine). The prices won't have you up in arms, either, with menus 88–165F and good local wines by the jug. The small terrace in the interior courtyard is roasting in summer. Free apéritif.

MONTBRISON 42600

🛪 🏠 |●| HÔTEL-RESTAURANT DES VOYAGEURS

16 rue Simon-Boyer (Centre).
☎ 04.77.96.17.64 ➡ 04.77.58.95.02
Closed Sat and Sun evenings, and a fortnight end Dec.
TV. **Car park**.

This hotel, in a little street in the centre of town, has got a bit of old-fashioned charm. The spacious rooms, furnished in the 1930s and 40s, go for 140F with shower, 200F with bath. You'll get traditional cooking in the restaurant, where they offer menus for 62F (not Sun), 80F and 120F. 10% discount for a two-night stay and a free coffee.

🛪 🏠 |●| LE GIL DE FRANCE

18 [bis] bd. Lachèze; it's just beyond the centre.
☎ 04.77.58.06.16 ➡ 04.77.58.73.78
Disabled access. **TV**. **Car park**.

A modern hotel on the outskirts of town, situated in front of a big park. The rooms and bright and fresh with modern facilities, 290F with shower/wc. The friendly young team bring a personal touch to the place, and it's better than many of the hotels in the centre. Don't expect miracles in the restaurant – 59F lunch menu or 69F and 169F. Free coffee.

🛪 |●| LE GOURMANDIN

4 [bis] rue des Pénitents (Centre).
☎ 04.77.58.58.72
Closed Sun evening, Mon, a fortnight in Jan and a fortnight in July.

Christian Bellot decided to open his restaurant in an old, disused crockery warehouse in the town that was the capital of the counts of Forez. The modern decor feels very comfortable but the black ceiling won't be to everyone's taste. The restaurant undoubtedly deserves its two stars and the well-heeled customers certainly enjoy the cuisine. The chef prepares seasonal game particularly skilfully, and his meat and fish dishes are finely judged. Try the house *foie gras*, the *foie gras gâteau*, the lobster *fricassée* with vanilla, or game in season. Weekday menu 98F then 135–310F. Attentive, professional service. Free coffee.

🛪 |●| RESTAURANT YVES THOLLOT

93 route de Lyon; take the D496.
☎ 04.77.96.10.40
Closed Sun evening, Mon, Feb school holidays and three weeks in Aug.

On the outskirts of Savigneux in a craft zone, near a chain hotel and looking not dissimilar. This is where Yves Thollot decided to open his restaurant. He welcomes you with a wide smile and his delicious cooking is very good: frogs' legs and apple salad, pan-fried *foie gras* with green apples and raspberry *coulis*, grilled bream, zander with *beurre blanc* and house butterscotch ice cream with hot chocolate sauce. Menus 110–155F. Free apéritif.

CHAMPDIEU   42600 (5KM)

|●| HOSTELLERIE DU PRIEURÉ

Route de Boën; it's on the D8, away from the centre.
☎ 04.77.58.31.21
Closed Thurs except public holidays, and three weeks in Aug. **Car park**.

This good place, on the border of the *département*, is run by a chef who's absolutely on top of traditional cooking techniques. He offers a simple option for 80F – a main course with a starter or dessert – and gourmet choices on the others, 106–240F. You might find it a bit pretentious given its roadside location (though it's not that close to the traffic), but you won't criticize the food. Affordable wine.

SAINT-ROMAIN-LE-PUY   42610 (8KM S)

▲ |●| AUBERGE LES TRABUCHES**

How to get there: take the D8 from Sury-le-Comtal to Montbrison, turn left before the Parot spring and follow the signs to the right.
☎ 04.77.97.79.70 ➡ 04.77.97.79.74
Closed Mon, Feb and Nov. **TV**.

Six simple rooms with basin, 230F, share common bathing and toilet facilities; the five others at ground level in the annexe have en-suite shower/wc and TV and cost 280F. Cheery welcome. They offer simple menus – 75F in the week, then up to 150F.

MONTÉLIMAR   26200

▲ HÔTEL PIERRE**

7 pl. des Clercs (Centre); it's near the church of Sainte-Croix in the old town, next to a little square.
☎ 04.75.01.33.16
Closed Feb. **TV**.

This prettily renovated, 16th-century town house looks like a little convent in the middle of old Montelimar. Its pretty porch, candelabra-studded corridor, paved courtyard, ivy-covered terrace and dressed stone staircase create a striking atmosphere. The twelve rooms – 160F with basin, 250F with bath – are fairly ordinary compared to the rest of the place, though some have been refurbished. The best is number 2, which has a balcony swamped in Virginia creeper where you can have breakfast. There's space to park bikes.

▲ HÔTEL BEAUSOLEIL

pl. d'Armes-Allées Provencales (Northwest).
☎ 04.75.01.19.80 ➡ 04.75.01.08.17
Garden. Car park.

A characterful hotel offering sixteen pleasant rooms, 180F with washing facilities along the landing, or 280F with shower/wc or bath. It's well away from the traffic but close to the centre of the town. Breakfast is served in a lovely garden. Nice welcome.

▲ SPHINX HÔTEL

19 bd. Marre-Desmarais (Centre).
☎ 04.75.01.86.64 ➡ 04.75.52.34.21
TV. Pay lock-up car park.

Exceedingly well located out of ear-shot of the traffic jams and the noise. The front of the building is covered with ivy. It's a lovely 17th-century private mansion with wood panelling inside, antique furniture and sophisticated taste. The superb salon has a tranquil atmosphere so it's a perfect place to relax. You get an appropriately stylish welcome. The rooms are personalised and have very good facilities: air conditioning, direct dial phone, and mini-bar. Doubles 275–330F. When it's sunny, breakfast is served on the terrace. There's a charge of 20F for the car park.

▲ HÔTEL DU PARC

27 bd. Charles-de-Gaulle (West).
☎ 04.75.01.00.73 ➡ 04.75.51.27.93
TV. Pay garage.

A classic hotel without real character but it's across from the park. The owners keep it spotless and welcome you most civilly. Bright, comfortable rooms with shower or bath, 280–380F. A 30F charge for the garage.

|●| LA PETITE FRANCE

34 impasse Raymond-Daujat (Centre).
☎ 04.75.46.07.94
Closed Sat lunchtime, Sun and public holidays.

You have to be quite determined to find this restaurant in a small cul-de-sac, or just lucky. It's worth making the effort because it's a nice little place with a fresh, friendly dining room. It has a vaulted ceiling, murals, pale wood, green plants and quiet music in the background. It's frequented by locals. Well worked dishes and a good-value short menu, 85F. A taster of dishes includes pan-fried monkfish with paprika and cream, *paupiette* of salmon and scallops, a duo of veal sweetbreads and hot *foie gras* with raspberry vinegar. Decent wines, starting at around 70F for a *Côteau de Tricastin*.

|O| LE CHALET DU PARC

bd. Marre Desmarais, Allées Provençales (Northwest); it's next to the tourist office.
☎ 04.75.98.60.60 ➡ 04.75.98.63.44

A dynamic young couple took over this place with the express aim of turning it into a top-class gourmet restaurant – an excellent idea. The cooking is a revelation of inspiration, produced by a chef who's bursting with ideas and enthusiasm. He puts together remarkable liaisons of flavours and uses only fresh produce: scallops rolled in smoked ham, rabbit thigh in lemon caramel, grilled supreme of guinea-fowl with fresh herbs and perfectly-judged salmon *unilatérale* (cooked from one side only). The luscious *dôme de chocolat* with iced vanilla is a fix for any chocoholic. Menus from 96F. The downstairs dining room is still a little bare but they've put all the effort into what really counts – the cooking.

MONTROTTIER   69770

🏔 🛏 |O| L'AUBERGE DES BLÉS D'OR**

La Curtillat – route de Saint-Julien-sur-Bibost; take the N89, then the D7; after Saint-Bel, head for Bibost, then take the D246 and keep going until 2km before Montrottier.
☎ and ➡ 04.74.70.13.56
Closed Tues, evenings reservations only. **TV**. **Car park**.

It's best to book in season – to be sure of a room or a table. Out of season, check that they're serving meals. This country inn, standing alone among the fields and surrounded by flowers, has been superbly restored. The rooms, 300F, are in an annexe and look over the valley. They boast all mod cons and total silence. The lovely, rustic dining room has a creaking parquet floor and vast beams. Flavoursome cuisine with a regional slant, on menus 120–200F. If you're there on a Saturday, the place is often taken for wedding breakfasts or family celebrations. You can sit on your terrace watching the sun go down behind the hills, with the church of Montrottier illuminated in the distance. 10% discount on the room rate or a pot of local honey.

MORZINE   74110

🏔 🛏 |O| HÔTEL LES LANS***

quartier des Prodains; it's 300m from the cable car that goes to Avoriaz.
☎ 04.50.79.00.90 ➡ 04.50.79.15.22
Closed 1May–15 June and 15 Sept –12 Dec. **TV**.

He was a ski instructor, she's mad about local history and culture. Today, with their two daughters, they put life into this huge chalet that's newly built but in harmony with the surrounding mountains and woods. The prices are unbeatable considering what you get. Half board is compulsory, 240–260F in summer, 300–450F in winter. Monsieur Mallurez happily takes care of the cooking but escapes from the kitchen once a week to take people on wildlife discovery trips, while Madame conducts guided tours. During some periods of the summer, trips are free for children under ten. A most unusual place that frequently hangs out the "no vacancies" sign when its competitors are still empty. Christmas and New Year are celebrated – at no extra charge for residents.The welcome is aloof. 10% discount on the half-board rate.

🛏 |O| LES PRODAINS**

Village des Prodains; it's at the foot of the Avoriaz ski-lift.
☎ 04.50.79.25.26 ➡ 04.50.75.76.17
e hotellesprodains@aol.com
Closed 25 April–25 June, 5 Sept–15 Dec. **Swimming pool**. **TV**. **Car park**.

You'll get a very warm welcome at this friendly family establishment at the foot of the ski runs. The chalet has pretty rooms with balconies, all with a fantastic view of the slopes. Doubles with shower/wc 300–320F. The huge terrace gets swamped by skiers as soon as the sun comes out. Menus 48–128F; although you can get a tasty *tartiflette*, the inventive cooking is not limited to mountain dishes. Try the *émincé* of duck with pineapple, the pan-fried scallops served in a crusty case, or desserts such as iced drops of sour cherry with vanilla cream. Swimming pool for the summer, when the boss also takes guests up to the mountain hut where he serves tasty mountain dishes.

🏔 |O| RESTAURANT LA GRANGETTE

How to get there: it's near the Nyon cable car.
☎ 04.50.79.05.76
Closed Mon evening, 16 April–9 July, 1 Sept–18 Dec.

A little family business at the foot of the ski slopes where you can enjoy a tasty meal in a friendly atmosphere. The good lunch menu, 61F, gets you dish of the day – beef *bourguignon* with mashed potato, say – and home-made tart for dessert. Other menus up to 148F. The house speciality is frog's legs in cream sauce. Lots of walking trails start (or finish) here. Free coffee.

🏃🏽|●| LA CHAMADE

Centre; it's near the tourist office.
☎ 04.50.79.13.91 **e** lachamade@aol.com
Closed Tues and Wed out of season, June and Nov.

This is a local institution with a menu that flies off in all gastronomic directions, from pizzas cooked in a wood-fired oven to regional specialities. It's recently been put on a slightly different track now that son Thierry, who's a chef, has taken over in the kitchen and his wife runs the dining room. Thierry likes pork in all its guises, and offers *pâté* of pig's head, *atriaux* (a type of patty), and grilled suckling pig. The two dining rooms are a bit over the top. There's a menu at 270F or expect to pay 200F *à la carte*. The terrace is really great in summer. Free *digestif*.

MONTRIOND 74110 (6KM NE)
|●| AUBERGE LA CHALANDE

Lieu-dit Ardent.
☎ 04.50.79.19.69
Closed Mon evening in winter, Mon–Thurs and Fri lunchtime Sept–Oct, and 20 April–20 May, and 20 Oct–20 Dec.

Gilles Lanvers runs this old chalet that's feels like it's way out in a lost mountain hamlet – though it's at the foot of the ski lifts going up to Avoriaz. It used to belong to his mother, and he hasn't changed the warm, rustic surroundings a bit. He turns out delicious dishes, whether you choose from the menus, 90–175F, or *à la carte*, around 200F. On the cheapest menu, you'll get cheese *croûte*, braised sausage with leeks and potato fritters, and bilberry tart. The more expensive menus feature salmon and crayfish. Wonderful welcome. It's best to book.

MOÙTIERS 73600
🏃🏽 🏠 |●| HÔTEL WELCOME'S**

33 av. Greyffié-de-Bellecombe; it's near the station.
☎ 04.79.24.00.48 **➡** 04.79.22.99.96
e hotel.welcome@wanadoo.fr
Closed 15 April–10 July and 30 Aug–20 Dec.
Disabled access. TV. Car park.

A comfortable station hotel where they pride

themselves on giving a nice welcome. The pleasant comfortable rooms cost 280–330F for a double – the ones at the rear are very quiet. You get traditional cooking in the restaurant, where they serve a few brasserie dishes and some good fish dishes. Menus 65F (weekday lunch) and 90–140F. Free parking for motorcycles and bikes. Free coffee.

FEISSONS-SUR-SALINS 73350 (12KM SE)
🏠|●| LE BALCON DES TROIS VALLÉES**

How to get there: take the D915 to Bozel then the D89.
☎ 04.79.24.24.34 **➡** 04.79.24.24.79
e b3v@club-internet.fr
Closed Wed Dec–April and June–Sept, end of May and 1 Nov. **Car park.**

The population of this tiny, isolated village grew to 154 with the arrival of the four people who run this hotel. They renovated the squat chalet, taking great care to respect its style and proportions. It looks a bit functional from the outside, but that's largely made up for by the warm decor inside. Double rooms with basin go for 190–220F, 210–250F with shower/wc. It's a very friendly place and they serve lots of good Belgian beers – you'll drink four for the price you'll pay for one in places like Courchevel. They also serve local dishes like mountain ham and *génépi*, and standard dishes given an imaginative twist. Menus 75–132F. You can hire all sorts of equipment including cross-country skis, mountain bikes and tennis racquets. Free apéritif and 10% discount on the room rate 1 May–15 June and Oct–Nov.

LÉCHÈRE (LA) 73260 (12KM N)
🏃🏽|●| RESTAURANT LA VIEILLE FORGE

Bellecombe; take exit 37, signposted Valmorel
☎ 04.79.24.17.97
Closed lunchtimes, Tues, Jan and Feb. **Car park.**

You won't find the usual stultified spa town atmosphere in this restaurant. It used to be a blacksmith's, and the decor features some of the old smithy equipment and a jumble of musical instruments including a piano and a balafon (an African instrument something like a xylophone), which customers are free to use. Tasty, traditional cooking, with lots of meat dishes in sauce, on the set menus 65–150F. There's live music every Friday and they're open very late – until 4am in summer. Free apéritif or coffee.

VALMOREL 73260 (14KM W)
🏃🏽 🏠 |●| CHÂTEAU DU CREY

Les Avanchers, hameau du Crey; take the D95 and it's at the lower end of the resort.
☎ 04.79.09.87.00 ➡ 04.79.09.89.51
Closed Nov. **Swimming pool**.

A classic, family-run chalet in an absolutely authentic mountain hamlet. Everyone, even the bear of a dog, knows how to give you a warm welcome. Rooms are well-appointed; there are family rooms sleeping four or five, and doubles with shower/wc or bath 250–300F. In the restaurant, menus cost 70–120F. They list mountain specialities and a few other dishes, including scallops with prawns, steak with morels and monkfish with oyster mushrooms. À la carte, you choose from a range of Savoy specialities. The vast swimming pool, open in summer, is rather unusual – it's inflatable. Free coffee and 10% discount if you stay half board.

|●| RESTAURANT LE SKI ROC

Centre; it's in a pedestrianised street off the main street.
☎ 04.79.09.83.17
Closed 20 April–20 June and mid-Sept to mid-Dec.

This place looks pretty ordinary, but it is actually *the* place to eat in Valmorel. There's a great ambience in the trendy bar, where the crowd often spills out into the restaurant. Young, efficient staff, and good-value menus, 85F on weekdays, then 98–130F. It's decent, straightforward cooking without frills; *à la carte*, you can get mountain dishes like *fondue* and *braserade* and excellent *raclette* made with Reblochon, a mild local cheese. Relax in a deck-chair on the terrace when the sun shines. Free *digestif*.

NANTUA   01130

|●| RESTAURANT BELLE RIVE

23 route de la Cluse (Northwest); take the N84 from Cluse and it's just before you get to Nantua.
☎ 04.74.75.16.60
Closed Tues evening and Wed out of season. **Car park**.

This place, right by the lake, is very popular with families for big get-togethers and with local workers for lunch. You'll need to book or get there early if you want a table on the pleasant veranda overlooking the lake. The 66F lunch menu is pretty decent, the 95F one includes the famous *quenelles de Nantua*, and there are others up to 185F. You have to wait a full fifteen minutes for them; they're freshly cooked and when they arrive they're well worth it.

CHARIX   01130 (10KM S)

▲ |●| AUBERGE DU LAC GENIN

How to get there: take the N84 in the direction of Bellegarde, then turn left at Le Martinet onto the D95.
☎ 04.74.75.52.50 ➡ 04.74.75.51.15
Closed Sun evening, Mon, and 15 Oct–1 Dec. **TV**. **Car park**.

The magnificent lake and the setting in the beautiful, dark Jura forests makes the trip up here worthwhile. In summer, it's a corner of paradise for fishermen and walkers, but be sure to have the right equipment and chains on your car tyres in winter, when the weather can be really severe. Unsurprisingly, the best rooms have windows onto the lake. They aren't exactly luxurious, and prices are average: 130F with basin, 200F with shower, 250F with bath. The 69F menu is unimaginative, but there are others, 95–115F, which list mountain ham, meats grilled on the open fire, wine sausage, and veal cutlet with mustard. It's substantial rather than gourmet cooking and there's a real family atmosphere.

CHÂTILLON-EN-MICHAILLE   01200 (12KM SE)

🌲 ▲ |●| AUBERGE DE LA FONTAINE**

Ochiaz (East); take the N206, then the N84, turn off at the Ochiaz exit and take the D101 to Châtillon.
☎ 04.50.56.57.23 ➡ 04.50.56.56.55
Closed Sun evening and Mon, Tues also out of season, 2–25 Jan and 5–14 June. **Lock-up car park**.

This pretty stone inn, festooned with flowers in summer, is just next to the gently trickling fountain in a delightful village. It is a smart little place, without being formal. The rooms are comfortable and quiet and you'll get a restorative night's sleep at reasonable prices – doubles 180F with basin, 220–240F with shower/wc or bath. You can eat very well – pike *quenelles* or gratin of crayfish tails– though dishes could do with a little more imagination. Menus start at 98F (weekdays only) then 125–350F. Free coffee and 10% discount on the room rate.

LALLEYRIAT   01130 (14KM E)

🌲 |●| LES GENTIANES

How to get there: take the N84 in the direction of Bellegarde as far as Neyrolles and then the D55.
☎ 04.74.75.31.80
Closed Wed, Sun evening, and the end of Jan.

Given that it is named after a mountain flower, you'd expect to find that this lovely stone-walled village inn specialises in traditional mountain food. The Parisian chef does serve regional cuisine, but also offers novel dishes such as warm *foie gras* with three fruits in Armagnac, veal sweetbreads with morels in flaky pastry and *millefeuille* of scallops with nettle butter. Prices are fair. Weekday lunch menu 75F, and others 105–210F. Free coffee.

LANCRANS 01200 (17KM SE)

🏃 🛏 |●| LE SORGIA**

Grande-Rue; take the D991 to Lélex and Mijoux.
☎ 04.50.48.15.81 ➽ 04.50.48.44.72
Closed Sun evening, Mon, 20 Aug–15 Sept and 22–31 Dec. **TV. Car park**.

An old village bar-restaurant which, over a century, has grown to become a hotel-restaurant with a balcony and veranda overlooking the valley. The rooms, filled with period furniture, are comfortable and pleasant, particularly those with the valley view. Doubles 225F with shower/wc or 245F with bath. They serve simple, local dishes in generous portions: *féra*, which is a freshwater salmon, cooked in Savoy wine, and snails and baby mushrooms in flaky pastry. 80F weekday menu and others 110–195F. Pleasant welcome. Free house apéritif.

NOIRÉTABLE 42440

🏃 🛏 |●| HÔTEL-RESTAURANT AU RENDEZ-VOUS DES CHASSEURS**

Route de l'Hermitage (Southwest); it's about 2km from the centre of the village on the D53.
☎ 04.77.24.72.51 ➽ 04.77.24.93.40
Closed Sun evening and Mon out of season, the Feb school holidays and mid-Sept to mid-Oct. **TV. Car park**.

Though the thundering motorway is just 6km away, all you can see from the dining room of this hotel are the Forez mountains that go on for miles around. The inn has fourteen rooms, 160F with basin and 225F with shower/wc or bath. The cheapest menu in the week is 60F, and there are others 100–200F. All the scents and flavours of Forez can be found in the dishes here, which include leek *terrine* with *Bleu d'Auvergne* cheese, *parfait* of chicken liver with bilberries, pigeon *pot-au-feu* and game in season. 10% discount on the room rate for a two-night stay Sept–June.

JURÉ 42430 (20KM NE)

🏃 |●| AUBERGE LE MOULIN

How to get there: take the D53, and turn right onto the D86 before you get to Saint-Just-en-Chevalet.
☎ 04.77.62.55.24
Open Sat, Sun, public holidays March–Nov, and Tues–Sun July–Aug. **Closed** 15 Nov–7 March. **Car park**.

Service 11.30am–8.30pm. This little inn, in an old mill, has an idyllic setting. Its electricity is supplied by the stream running under the mill. It's a shame it's not open more. Apparently, the Lumière brothers made their first moving pictures here. The country menus, 65–110F, are delicious, and offer excellent *terrines*, *rissoles*, free-range poultry, and home-made pastries that go down a treat with cider. They prefer you to order in advance. Very affordable wines. Free house apéritif or *digestif*.

NYONS 26110

🛏 |●| LA PICHOLINE***

Promenade de la Perrière; it's on the hilltop as you come into the town.
☎ 04.75.26.06.21 ➽ 04.75.26.40.72
Restaurant closed Mon evening and Tues out of season, 18–31 Oct and Feb.
Swimming pool. TV. Car park.

The decor in the foyer and the restaurant is a bit chi-chi, but the owners make a real fuss of their guests, most of whom are elderly couples. Big, light and pleasant rooms 325–410F; numbers 1–10 have breathtaking views looking south. Half board is compulsory July–Aug. Decent food, and the regional menu, 130F, is extremely satisfying. The swimming pool is surrounded by olive trees.

🛏 |●| HÔTEL LA CARAVELLE

8 rue des Antignans (South); from the pont de l'Europe, you go along the Promenade de la Digue.
☎ 04.75.26.07.44 ➽ 04.75.26.23.79
Closed mid-Nov to mid-Dec. **Garden. TV. Lock-up car park**.

Just away from the centre, this hotel is surrounded by a huge, pleasant garden full of perfumes. It's an old *bastide*, a substantial private residence, with nine very comfortable rooms and a pair of small apartments (bedroom and a little sitting room with a child's bed). Really opulent atmosphere, polite welcome. The place for peace and quiet. Most of the rooms have a view over the garden, some have balconies. Prices start at 350F. There's a shady terrace for a drink.

|●| RESTO DES ARTS

rue des Déportés (Centre).
☎ 04.75.26.31.49
Closed Wed, Tues also in low season, and Nov.

Right in the heart of old Nyons. It's a rendezvous for local artists and gourmet winemakers – it belongs to Claude and Monique Bonfils who are wine-growers in the Drôme and real food-lovers as well. There's a relaxed yet fashionable atmosphere and the place is nearly always full. The cooking is tasty and generously served and while traditional, it has a personal touch – dishes such as red mullet with *foie gras*, duck *confit* with wild mushrooms, slivers of duck with apricot honey, pan-fried *foie gras* with apples, and a duo of king prawn and scallops. There's a dish of the day and a *menu du jour* for 70F. As you would expect, the wine list has a host of good Côtes du Rhônes.

|●| LE PETIT CAVEAU

9 rue Victor Hugo; it's in the street at right angles to the Pavillon du Tourisme.
☎ 04.75.26.20.21
Closed Sun evening, Mon and 15 Nov–15 Dec.

Muriel Cormont is a graduate of the Suze-La-Rousse wine university and her husband used to work for the great chef, Robuchon. It was Muriel's bright idea to offer three different glasses of wine (75F) that she selects to perfectly suit the dishes you have chosen. Her husband is a seriously good chef – try the roast saddle of rabbit with hazelnuts, roast lamb, *confit* of lamb chops, sweetbread and kidney kebabs, or red pepper risotto. Good wine and excellent cuisine – you get the best of both worlds at reasonable prices. Weekday menu 110F, others 160F and 180F. The menus change nearly every week.

SAINT-FERRÉOL-TRENTEPAS   26110 (12KM N)

♠ |●| AUBERGE DE TRENTE PAS

It's in the village; from Nyons, take the D94, then the D70 in the direction of Bourdeaux.
☎ 04.75.27.71.39 ➡ 04.75.27.71.39
Closed Nov–March.

The village is typical of those found in the mountains of the Drôme. This straightforward establishment has very simple, clean rooms and family cuisine prepared with soul. You're served in the convivial dining room where the beams are painted blue. Dish of the day 68F, menu 88F, and rich Syrah from the Pays de Grignan for 65F. The style is more for cyclists and hikers than romantic weekenders. Véronique makes you feel welcome; she's enjoying her country retreat after years in polluted Paris. Rooms start at 200F and you can stay half board if you wish.

CONDORCET   26110 (7KM E)

|●| LA CHARRETTE BLEUE

route de Gap.
☎ 04.75.27.72.33

Closed Tues evening and Wed, Sun evening also Oct–March, and 3 Jan–8 Feb.

Word of mouth is always the best publicity – just follow the trail and you'll get here. Very professional, honest cooking – tradition with an individual twist. The fresh herbs from the hills and the heath are deliciously combined: pressed *pot-au-feu*, rack of lamb with a garlic crust and guinea-fowl hams with pickled lemons. Menus start at 98F and end with the one at 182F, which includes *foie gras*. Wine by the glass from 15F and bottles from 44F. The dining room is prettily arranged but there's a terrace for sunny days – the best tables are under the olive tree. Delectable cuisine, warm welcome and efficient service.

MIRABEL-AUX-BARONNIES   26110 (7KM S)

⅍ |●| LA COLOQUINTE

av. de la Résistance; take the D538 in the direction of Vaison-la-Romaine.
☎ 04.75.27.19.89
Closed Wed, Thurs lunchtime, Sun evening Nov–March, and the Feb, All Saints' and Christmas school holidays.

When the sun's out it's nice to sit on the lovely, shaded patio, otherwise you dine in the colourful dining room with hefty beams and well-spaced tables. The food is good and only fresh seasonal produce is used. Menu 160F, *à la carte* 205F. The colourful dishes are full of flavour, very carefully prepared and seasoned, the fish is cooked to perfection: tasty *terrines*, pan-fried *foie gras* with clarified butter, roast kid with thyme, bream with *sauce vierge*, oyster mushroom *gâteau*, duck breast and wild mushrooms. A fine choice of perfectly ripe cheeses and various desserts. The wine list has a good selection of Côtes-du-Rhones starting at around 75F. Free Myro (the local version of Kir).

OYONNAX   01100

⅍ ♠ NOUVEL HÔTEL**

31 rue René-Nicod (Centre); 150m from the train station.
☎ 04.74.77.28.11 ➡ 04.74.77.03.71
TV. Pay car park.

Despite its name, this place is getting on a bit – but it is not without individuality, as you'll see when you get to reception where there's a display of the plastics for which Oyonnax is famous. The refurbished rooms are good value. Doubles cost 180F with basin, 200F with shower, while larger rooms with shower/wc or bath go for 250F. It's the little things they do that make all the difference. You can have breakfast brought to your room for no extra charge. Free use of the car park.

👫 🏠 |O| HÔTEL-RESTAURANT BUFFARD**

pl. de l'Église; it's in the middle of town, 100m from the train station.
☎ 04.74.77.86.01 ➡ 04.74.73.77.68
Restaurant closed Fri and Sun evenings, Sat, and 25 July–15 Aug. **TV. Car park.**

Service noon–2.30pm and 7.15pm–9.30pm. This hotel-restaurant has maintained its excellent reputation for a hundred years – it celebrated its centenary in 1998. Rooms with period furniture 180F with basin, 230F with shower, and 260–320F with bath. In the restaurant they serve rich home cooking in generous portions. There's a dish of the day for 50F and menus, 75–190F. Some include regional specialities such as *quenelles Nantua*, *gratin* of crayfish tails, frog's legs, chicken with morels and *délice* of duck liver. Free apéritif, coffee or house *digestif*, and 10% discount on the room rate.

PEISEY-NANCROIX   73210

|O| L'ORMELUNE

☎ 04.79.07.93.32
Closed 30 April–15 June and 1 Nov–15 Dec.

A small, traditional restaurant in the heart of a charming old village. Warm welcome, convivial atmosphere and well-priced menus, 88F and 148F, giving good value for money. In winter there's a dish of the day around 55F, and several *formules*. À la carte, you'll pay about 150F. They offer classic Savoy specialities like *fondue*, *tartiflette* (potatoes with onions, bacon and Reblochon cheese), and good *raclette*; the house speciality is *entrecôte* steak served on a *lauze*, or stone.

|O| RESTAURANT CHEZ FÉLIX

Plan-Peisey; it's between Les Mélèzes and Val Landry.
☎ 04.79.07.92.41
Closed 1 Sept–20 Dec and 21 April–1 July. **Car park.**

In a 19th-century Alpine chalet on the edge of the Vanoise park, this place serves *crêpes*, which you sprinkle with fresh, home-made raspberry juice. There are no set menus, but they offer all sorts of regional specialities *à la carte*. If you opt for crêpes, a meal will cost about 70F or more like 150F for a Savoyard meal. There's a bird's-eye view of the Ponturin gorge from the terrace.

|O| RESTAURANT L'ANCOLIE

How to get there: make for Landry and then Peisey-Nancroix.

☎ 04.79.07.93.20 ➡ 04.79.07.91.65
Closed Mon in winter.

Service 12.30–1.30pm and 7.30–9pm. The building, tucked away behind a curtain of greenery, dates back to 1760, and is a classified historic monument. In the tasteful dining room, decorated with old farm implements, you can eat classy, tasty food using old recipes reworked to satisfy today's tastes. Menus, 145–208F, list inventive dishes such as *blanquette* of kid with morel sauce, snail casserole, pork *sauté*, *entrecôte* steak with the lees of Mondeuse wine, house *terrines*, and *galettes* with Reblochon cheese and walnuts.

PONT-D'AIN   01160

👫 |O| RESTAURANT LE TERMINUS

71 rue Saint-Exupéry (North); take exit 9 off the A42, then take the N75 in the direction of Bourg-en-Bresse.
☎ 04.74.39.07.17
Closed Sun evening, Mon and public holiday evenings. **Car park.**

Though this restaurant has two pretty little dining rooms and a terrace for warm weather, the real effort goes into the cooking rather than the decor; you get generous portions of regional food at decent prices. Menus start at 65F, with others from 79–160F. Friendly welcome and efficient service. Free coffee.

PONT-EN-ROYANS   38680

|O| RESTAURANT LE GOURNIER

Grottes de Choranche (North); 2km beyond the village, there's a road on the left that leads up to the caves and the restaurant.
☎ 04.76.36.09.88 ➡ 04.76.36.11.91
Closed evenings and Nov–March.

Lunchtime only. This restaurant has a wonderful panoramic view over the superb Cirque de Choranche with its remarkable caves. The cooking is tasty and well judged: chicken with crayfish, good tarts and regional dishes such as *caillette*, a sort of haggis, served with salad. Menus 68–145F, children's menu 50F.

PRESLES   38680 (10KM NE)

👫 🏠 |O| AUBERGE DE PRESLES

au Bourg (Centre); take the D292 from Pont-au-Royans.
☎ 04.76.36.04.75
Closed Tues and 15 Nov–20 Dec.

A hugely romantic place in the Coulmes mountains out in the wilds of Vercors. Reached by a wonderful road that climbs the cliff, this charming village inn is run by Ginette and Jean-Marie who make you feel most welcome. You'll also enjoy their good regional cooking. Menus, 79–95F, list *tartiflette*, raviolis *au gratin* and delicious home-made tarts with walnuts or hazelnuts. They also offer snacks, like omelettes and sandwiches, and grills on the open fire. Vercors specialities are available to order only. It's probably best to book. They also run a mountain hut, opposite the restaurant, where you can get a room with bath. Half board is compulsory and costs 195F per person. Free coffee.

PRIVAS 07000

❙●❙ LE GOURMANDIN

cours de l'Esplanade (Centre); it's on the corner of rue Pierre-Fillat.
☎ 04.75.64.51.52
Closed Sun evening, Wed, a week in Feb and the second fortnight in Aug.

This is the best place to eat in Privas – you could genuinely call it a fine table. Philippe Bourjas has a way of modernising the local dishes and refining old recipes with delicate and creative adjustments. And he doesn't stint on the portions. Try the cassolette of cheese ravioli in a cep sauce, or the kidneys which are tasty and good. Menus 98–238F. The setting is sober, the service conscientious and pleasant but without fuss. There's a good wine list.

ALISSAS 07210 (4KM SE)

❧ ❙●❙ RESTAURANT LOUS ESCLOS

Quartier Rabagnol (Southeast); it's beside the D2, which bypasses Alissas.
☎ 04.75.65.12.73
Closed Sun evening, Mon, a fortnight in Jan and a fortnight in Aug. **Car park**.

A rather stylish place in a lane off the main road, though you can hear the traffic when you eat on the terrace. The air-conditioned dining room is quieter and the bay windows look out over the arid hills. Menus, 99–160F, include pan-fried snails with s*auce Esclos* and *mignon* of pork with Madeira sauce. Nicely prepared and you can appreciate the quality of the seasonal produce. Incidentally, *esclos* is local dialect for "clogs". Free coffee.

BAIX 07210 (24KM E)

♠ ❙●❙ L'AUBERGE DES QUATRE VENTS

Route de Chomérac; it's on the D2.
☎ 04.75.85.84.49 ➡ 04.75.85.84.49

Closed Sat lunchtime and Sun evening out of season, and the Feb school holidays. **TV. Car park**.

There's a soothing provincial atmosphere in the large, light but soberly decorated dining room. The strange ceiling rises like a pyramid, filling the place with the sound of voices. Tablecloths and chandeliers but it's not fussy. Good, local dishes: duck thighs with girolles or fresh cream cheese with soft fruit and a fruit *coulis*. *Menu du jour* 70F, or 127–190F, and fairly priced wines. Natty, quiet rooms 175F–250F depending on the facilities which are clean and modern.

QUINCIÉ-EN-BEAUJOLAIS 69430

❧ ❙●❙ RESTAURANT AU RAISIN BEAUJOLAIS

How to get there: take the D37 from Beaujeu in the direction of Saint-Vincent and it's on the right about 4km along the road.
☎ 04.74.04.32.79 ➡ 04.74.69.02.12
Closed evenings, Sat, three weeks in Aug and the last week in Jan.

Service noon–3pm. This unpretentious bistro is just the kind of place you hope to happen on for lunch in the wine country. The chatty proprietor looks after the dining room while his wife runs the kitchen, preparing the tasty, slowly cooked dishes. There's a weekday menu at 75F, and others up to 138F; dishes include frog's legs *persillade*, snails in garlic butter and *andouillette Bobosse* (a type of sausage) in Mâcon-Villages. When it comes to the wine, you have a huge choice of Beaujolais *appellations*. There's an enclosed, air-conditioned terrace, which is great in summer. Free Kir.

❧ ❙●❙ AUBERGE DU PONT DES SAMSONS

Le-Pont-des-Samsons; take the D37 in the direction of Beaujeu.
☎ 04.74.04.32.09
Closed Wed evening and Thurs. **Car park**.

Service until 2pm at lunchtime and 9pm in the evening. The crossroads is hardly an ideal location, and the restaurant doesn't look much from the outside. But the decor is nice and it's spotlessly clean. Better still, the excellent dishes are served in huge portions: *foie gras*, scallop sallad, zander in *beurre blanc*, red mullet with *anis*, duck breast with red fruits, and steak with green peppercorns. Four menus 98–208F. Attentive service from start to finish. Free coffee.

CHIROUBLES   69115 (11KM NW)

|●| LA TERRASSE DU BEAUJOLAIS

How to get there: take the D9 to Villié-Morgon, then turn left onto the D86.
☎ 04.74.69.90.79 ➡ 04.74.69.93.26
Closed Mon evening, Mon–Fri from mid-Dec to 1 March, and the Feb school holidays. **Car park**.

Service 11.30am–2pm and 6.30–8.30pm. Gorgeous place on the winding road that leads you to the major Beaujolais vineyards. Blessed by a cool breeze year round, it also has a playground for children, and attracts lots of famililes at weekends. À la carte they do good mixed salads, great *terrines*, pastry cases filled with all manner of tasty things and the local *andouillette*. Menus 125–285F.

RIVE-DE-GIER   42800

⅍ |●| RESTAURANT GEORGES PAQUET

Combeplaine; take the La Madeleine exit off the A47.
☎ 04.77.75.02.18
Closed Mon lunchtime, Tues–Thurs and Sun evenings, Feb school holidays and mid-July to mid-Aug. **Car park**.

Set in a desolate area of factories and industrial wasteland, between the motorway and the main road, this restaurant serves good food. It's got a hushed atmosphere and is decorated in bright warm colours. The speciality is seafood and all sorts of fish served with tasty sauces. There are two weekday lunch menus, 70F and 85F; the latter offers a choice of three starters and three main courses, followed by cheese or dessert. It also includes a drink, so it's very good value for money. The other menus, up to 230F, are a bit overpriced. On Friday evening, by reservation only, they can do a menu that offers nothing but desserts – perfect if you've got a sweet tooth. Free coffee.

SAINT-MARTIN-LA-PLAINE   42800 (8KM W)

|●| LE FLAMANT ROSE

How to get there: take the D37, and follow the signs to the Parc Zoologique.
☎ 04.77.75.91.13.
Closed Sun and Mon evening.

The beautiful terrace is the only lovely thing about this big building, which stands in front of a stretch of water opposite the zoo. Inside, however, the two dining rooms get lots of light – though admittedly the one reserved for the excellent, substantial 60F lunchtime menu isn't as attractive as the one where the 110–235F

menus are served. The chef takes some risks, successfully combining sweet and savoury flavours, and prepares delicious desserts and home-made bread. They can also pack you a picnic for about 55F. Very warm welcome.

SAINTE-CROIX-EN-JAREZ   42800 (10KM E)

🏠 |●| LE PRIEURÉ*

How to get there: take the D30.
☎ 04.77.20.20.09 ➡ 04.77.20.20.80
Closed Mon, Jan and Feb. **TV**.

The road that leads up to this delightful, beautiful place runs along the Couzon and past the dam. Here you get bed and board in the former guest quarters of a 12th-century monastery, most of which was dismantled during the Revolution, its stones used to build the village. The four rooms, 260F with bath, are simple but very well equipped and wonderfully quiet. The restaurant is on the first floor and has a beamed ceiling *à la Francaise*. Unpretentious, traditional cuisine and regional dishes: home-made *terrine* or tripe with tomato, for example. Menus 100–165F. The bar has a vaulted ceiling and in summer, there's a terrace on the village square – you'll appreciate the freshness of the air up here. Kindly welcome.

ROANNE   42300

🏠 |●| HÔTEL DE L'ANCRE

24 pl. du Maréchal-de-Lattre-de-Tassigny (Centre).
☎ 04.77.71.22.70
Closed Sun and 1–15 Aug.

This modest hotel, in a lovely building of the kind you'd find in a 1930s seaside resort, doesn't seem to have changed much since that era. Even the ashtrays advertise brands that no longer exist. If you're of a nostalgic bent and looking for cheap accommodation, then this is the place for you. Rooms 180F with bath. Home cooking is served in a magnificent dining room with a parquet floor. Menus 50F (weekday lunch) and 85F.

🏠 HÔTEL DE LA GRENETTE

12 pl. Maréchal-de Lattre-de-Tassigny (Centre).
☎ 04.77.71.25.59 ➡ 04.77.71.29.69
TV.

A little hotel recently taken over by a lovely couple who've started to refurbish it. Rooms are basic but well maintained; 220F with shower, 240F with shower/wc. The reception may be shut on Friday, Saturday or Sunday afternoons, so it's best to phone in advance.

2₺ 🏠 HÔTEL TERMINUS**

15 cours de la République (pl. de la Gare) (West); it's opposite the train station.
☎ 04.77.71.79.69 ➡ 04.77.72.90.26
TV. Car park.

A good hotel of its kind, that's well located. It has about fifty rooms with bath, 220–260F, which are pretty standard. Ask for one over-looking the courtyard, where it's quieter. The terrace is nice in summer. 10% discount at weekends Dec–April.

🍽 LE CENTRAL

20 cours de la République; it's opposite the train station.
☎ 04.77.67.72.72
Closed Sun and Mon, three weeks in Aug and a week between Christmas and New Year's Day.

The Troisgros family – renowned nationally and internationally as chefs – have opened up this less expensive, but still trendy, restaurant next door to their gourmet, starred flagship, *Troisgros*. Rigged up to look like an old-fashioned grocery store, it sells smartly packaged pots of goodies, mustard with wine, duck *rillettes* and balsamic vinegar. There are photographs of the suppliers on the walls of the two dining rooms. A menu at 100F and one at 155F that's a treasure trove of invention, while the *à la carte* menu gives a glimpse of the imagination that goes into the cooking next door. The wine is affordable and served bistro-style, with the bottle uncorked.

2₺ 🍽 L'AVENTURE

24 rue Pierre-Despierre.
☎ 04.77.68.01.15
Closed Sun, Mon, ten days in May, three weeks in Aug.

Jean-Luc Trambouze is a young chef from Roanne who's on the way up. You'll find his restaurant in a small street near the Loire. The frontage is bistro-blue but inside there's a cosy dining room decorated in pale colours. The kitchen opens out into the dining room, not to be showy but to add to the friendly atmos-phere of the place. The chef's dishes are full of imagination and fresh ideas. There are no par-ticular specialities: it's the dynamism of the cooking and the audaciousness of the sea-sonings that make his dishes so distinctive. He offers an excellent lunch menu for 105F which includes wine and others 128–205F. Affordable wine list. Free apéritif.

POUILLY-SOUS-CHARLIEU   42720 (14KM N)

🍽 AUBERGE DU CHÂTEAU DE TIGNY

How to get there: take the D487, it's east of the village

and is signposted.
☎ 04.77.60.09.55
Closed Mon, Tues, Jan and the last fortnight in Sept.

This is undoubtedly a favourite spot in the Roanne region. Marie Blin and Jacques Riv-ière were at one time market gardeners who supplied the region's top restaurants. They both loved old buildings and good food so one day, they decided to give it all up to restore a magnificent little manor house and turn it into this delightful inn. The menus are exceptional, both for the wide choice offered and for the freshness of the innovative cook-ing, including the fish. It's also the best value for money in the region. There's a *menu rapide* at 77F, served weekday lunchtimes, that consists of dish of the day, salad and dessert. Gourmet menus 125–210F. When the weath-er's nice, you can dine on the very pleasant terrace or in the cool interior. Marie will give you a charming welcome. The river and lake add to the wonderful setting.

NOAILLY   42640 (15KM NW)

2₺ 🏠 🍽 CHÂTEAU DE LA MOTTE***

La Motte; take the N7 to Saint-Germain-Lespinasse, then the D4 towards Charlieu. It's between Noailly and La Benisson-Dieu.
☎ 04.77.66.64.60 ➡ 04.77.66.64.38
Closed Sun evening and Mon except July–Aug, and 1 Nov to Palm Sunday. **Swimming pool**. **TV**. **Car park**.

This romantic château is in the upper price bracket but it's very special. The absolutely charming rooms are decorated and furnished with imagination and taste. Doubles 450–800F. Traditional local cuisine is listed on the weekday lunch menu, which at 95F is excellent value, and there are others 140–295F. You can go horse riding with owner Sylvie Fayolle, there's a swimming pool in the grounds, and a pergola down by the ornamental lake that's perfect for a few quiet hours with a book. If you stay four nights, the prices go down. 10% discount on the room rate Sept–June.

ROMANS-SUR-ISÈRE   26100

🏠 HÔTEL MAGDELEINE**

31 av. Pierre Sémard (Centre); the road runs at right angles to the station.
☎ 04.75.02.33.53 ➡ 04.06.81.09.03.37
Closed Sun, except for reservations. **TV**.

A strategically placed hotel right near the sta-tion, the historic centre and the factory shops. The owner originates from the Vosges and he runs the place expertly. He does everything himself – reception, cleaning, breakfasts and even the ironing. The rooms are being renovated one after the other, they're quite big and have new bedding and efficient double glazing. Doubles with shower or bath 225F. It's spotlessly clean and you get a genuinely warm welcome. There aren't enough places like this.

🏕 🛏 |●| HÔTEL DES BALMES**

Hameau des Balmes; it's about 4km from the centre; take the D532, Tain road for 2km, then turn right in the direction of Les Balmes.
☎ 04.75.02.29.52 ➡ 04.75.02.75.47
Hotel closed Sun evening out of season. **Restaurant closed** Mon. **Swimming pool. TV. Pay car park**.

This hotel, in a sleepy little village, has twelve pretty rooms with bath and balcony for 280F. In the restaurant, *Au Tahiti*, the owners have created an exotic decor with glass beads and shells – somehow you can sense that they've never actually visited that part of the world, but it's still fun. The cooking is strictly regional French – ravioli, Drôme guinea-fowl, lamb from the Préalpes. Menus 85–120F. Free *digestif*.

🏕 |●| RESTAURANT LA CASSOLETTE

16 rue Rebatte (Centre); it's in a pedestrianised street near tour Jacquemart.
☎ 04.75.02.55.71
Closed Sun, Mon, and 25 July–17 Aug.

An intimate restaurant in a charming, 13th-century building, where the three dining rooms have vaulted ceilings. There's a range of menus, 75–205F, listing *fricassée* of sole and lobster, tournedos steak with morels, beef with red Crozes-Hermitage wine sauce, fillet of quail with Vieux Marc and scallop ravioli. Good wine list. Free coffee.

|●| LE CAFÉ DES ARTS

49 cours Pierre Didier (Centre).
☎ 04.75.02.77.23
Closed Sun.

The round dining room is encircled by a veranda. It's a bit smart but not formal because it's softened by lots of green plants. You can watch the ballet of the chefs behind the glass. The dishes are substantial with lots of fresh fish dishes – try tuna and salmon *tartare*, roast sea bream with dill *jus*, or pan-fried king prawns on a bed of red peppers. Local dishes figure on the menus too, and carnivores are well catered for – duck breast with orange or steak *tartare*. *Menu-cartes* (giving choices for each course) and *formules* (with choices of two out of three courses) 80–150F. The service is efficient and friendly. They open the terrace under the plane trees when the sun shines; it's cut off from the

road (which can be noisy in the daytime), by a thick green hedge.

GRANGES-LÈS-BEAUMONT   26600 (4KM W)

🏕 🛏 |●| LES VIEILLES GRANGES**

Granges-lès-Beaumont; take the D53 Tain road for 3km then turn left at the sign.
☎ 04.75.71.50.43 ➡ 04.75.71.59.79
Closed Sun evening, Mon, and Tues lunchtime.
TV. Car park.

This collection of old buildings overlooking the Isère, surrounded by fruit trees, has been renovated and turned into a romantic hotel-restaurant with a terrace shaded by lime trees. Comfortable double rooms go for 240–320F – the more expensive ones have a river view. In the dining room you can eat tasty food, with menus 100–130F. It's easy to decide on the main course – try the delicious *caillette* (pork and vegetable faggot) – but more difficult to choose a wine. Luckily, the staff are patient and helpful. 10% discount on the room rate Oct–April.

SAINT-AGRÈVE   07320

🛏 |●| DOMAINE DE RILHAC**

Lieu-dit Rilhac; from Saint-Agrève, follow the road to Le Cheylard for about 1km; take the D21 fork off the D120, and follow the arrows.
☎ 04.75.30.20.20 ➡ 04.75.30.20.00
Closed Tues evening and Wed, and Jan–Feb.
TV. Car park.

A 16th-century farm that has been tastefully restored and converted into a delightful hotel-restaurant. It's a luxury hotel at affordable prices, set deep in the countryside in a stunning spot facing monts Mézenc and Gerbier. It has a dressed-stone façade, blue shutters and finely engraved wrought ironwork inside that goes well with the ochre plaster and the exposed beams. Six double rooms from 400F. Breakfast is served until 10.30am. Half board can be compulsory July–Aug, so it's best to check. A three-course weekday lunch menu at 135F, and others 160–380F. The *à la carte* menu changes with the seasons but the price can spiral out of control; specialities include duck breast with chestnut flower honey and home-made *terrine de foie gras*.

SAINT-AUBAN-SUR-L'OUVEZE   26170

🛏 |●| AUBERGE DE LA CLAVELIÈRE

It's in the main street of the village; on the D546, halfway between Buis-les-Baronnies and Séderon.
☎ 04.75.28.61.07 ➡ 04.75.28.60.30
Closed Sat lunchtime and a fortnight over New Year.

A great mariner, François-Hector d'Albert, who fought for the Americans in the War of Independence hailed from this charming village way off the beaten track. At the middle of the village is this simple, warm and welcoming hotel in a solid stone house. The simplest of rooms but they're well maintained and have good beds; doubles 240F. In winter not all the rooms are open, so it's best to telephone in advance. The cooking offers family dishes and regional cuisine. Local workers and travelling salesmen hole up here at lunchtime to make the most of the 70F menu. The menus at 105F and 140F are more elaborate: red mullet *millefeuille bohémienne*, lamb sweetbreads in a pastry case and smoked salmon ravioli with salad.

SAINT-ÉTIENNE   42000

⅔ ♠ HÔTEL LE CHEVAL NOIR**

11 rue François-Gillet (Centre).
☎ 04.77.33.41.72 ➡ 04.77.37.79.19
TV. **Car park**.

This old hotel, which had lost its original splendour, was bought by a couple of former bankers who completely renovated the place to give it, and themselves, a new lease of life. Most of the numerous rooms have good, modern facilities. The prices are very modest considering its central location; doubles go for 190F with shower or 280F with bath, with cheaper deals during the week. 10% discount.

♠ |●| HÔTEL LE BALADIN**

12 rue de la Ville (Centre); it's in a busy pedestrianised street.
☎ 04.77.37.17.97 ➡ 04.77.37.17.17
Closed Aug. **TV**.

This place fills up very quickly, especially during the theatre season when the actors appearing at the Comédie de Saint-Étienne stay here. It's a pleasant little hotel with fourteen small rooms, all with shower or bath; 240F. They serve food in the snack bar on the ground floor, but it's closed on Sunday and for lunch on Monday.

⅔ ♠ HÔTEL DES ARTS**

11 rue Gambetta (Centre).
☎ 04.77.32.42.11 ➡ 04.77.34.06.72
TV. **Pay car park**.

Not far from the museum of old Saint-Étienne, in a small square off the Grand-Rue where the trams run, this two-star hotel is good value for money. Doubles 300F with shower/wc or bath. Very friendly welcome and English spoken. 10% discount or free breakfast.

⅔ ♠ HÔTEL TERMINUS DU FOREZ***

31 av. Denfert-Rochereau; it's opposite the Châteaucrux station, five minutes from the centre.
☎ 04.77.32.48.47 ➡ 04.77.34.03.30
℮ hotel.forez@wanadoo.fr
Closed 6–27 Aug. **TV**. **Car park**.

This is a big, classic three-star hotel, with stylish decor and pleasant, modern facilities. It's a family place, which makes a nice change from the chain hotels on the outskirts. Doubles 345F with shower/wc and 395F with bath. Friendly welcome and helpful, smiling staff. The restaurant, *La Loco*, is on the ground floor – cheapest menu 69F. 10% discount on the room rate Thurs–Mon.

♠ |●| L'ALBATROS

67 rue Saint-Simon; turn left after the arms factory, opposite the golf course.
☎ 04.77.41.41.00 ➡ 04.77.38.28.16
Closed a fortnight in Aug, and a fortnight Dec/Jan.
Disabled access. **Swimming pool**. **TV**. **Car park**.

A place to enjoy peace and greenery, overlooking the golf course, in the higher part of the town. The rooms here are modern and functional and cost 450F. Good welcome.

⅔ |●| LA FOURCHETTE GOURMANDE

10 rue Francis Garnier (Centre).
☎ 04.77.41.76.86
Closed Sat lunchtime and Sun evening.

This place is a real favourite. It used to be *Le Petit Coq*, where the Saint-Étienne football team came to celebrate their victories back in the glory days of the 1970s. The place went downhill, along with the team, until the new owner took over. He's friendly and professional, and has completely refurbished the dining room and revolutionised the menu; seafood pot with king prawns, crayfish, *Marmiton Champenois* (scallops and shrimp), shrimp *clafoutis* with asparagus tips, roast saddle of lamb with rosemary – refined, luscious dishes. Lunch *menu du jour* 58F, others 89–159F. Free apéritif.

⅔ |●| CORNES D'AUROCHS!

18 rue Michel-Servet; it's 150m from the town hall.
☎ 04.77.32.27.27

Closed Sat lunchtime and Sun, and end-July to end-Aug.

A fun bistro offering Lyonnais cooking and typical specials: *andouillette*, *tablier de sapeur*, brains and a "Gargantua" platter which gives you a bit of everything. Lots offish dishes. The 80F lunch menu is a good deal, including a glass of wine and coffee. Other menus 110–200F. The owner is bald and jovial, his wife is smiling and welcoming. They don't like you to smoke in the restaurant, but don't seem to worry about loading your cholesterol level. Free pear liqueur or Marc du Pays at the end of your meal.

🏠 |●| RESTAURANT LA RISSOLÉE

23 rue Pointe-Cadet (Centre); it's on the edge of the pedestrianised area.
☎ 04.77.33.58.47
Closed Sat lunchtime, Sun and Aug.

The distinction of this restaurant, which is in a district that boasts lots of them, is its Belgian specialities. The menus are written on recycled *Tintin* albums. They do huge plates of food with a mound of rissoled potatoes for about 59F, and substantial helpings of mussels cooked in various ways and served with chips. In the evening they offer superb *carbonade*. Menus 89–139F, beer included. You have to try an "SB", the house cocktail – it'll blow your socks off. Free house *digestif*.

🏠 |●| LE CERCLE

15 pl. de l'Hôtel-de-Ville (Centre).
☎ 04.77.25.27.27
Closed Sun and Mon evening.

This restaurant occupies part of the former premises of the Saint-Étienne bridge club, in a superb building opposite the town hall. The owners have kept the panelling and the gilding in one of the most beautiful rooms, the style of which is pure Napoleon III. The restaurant attracts local worthies but prices are nevertheless very reasonable, with a weekday lunch *formule* (main course and dessert) and menus 98–320F. Decent food, pleasantly presented, and friendly service. Free apéritif.

|●| CARPE DIEM

6 rue Léon Nautin.
☎ 04.77.38.65.36
Closed Sun and Mon evenings.

You go along a small pedestrian street in the old town to get to this restaurant where the dining room is a pleasant mixture of old stone, ochre and blue. The cooking is a

delight: for 135F you get a plate of *foie gras* cooked in three ways, a *croustillant* of salmon and scallops followed by soft fruit *au gratin*. There are other menus at 98F and up to 225F. The service is executed with great care and finesse. Superb wine list and another with Kirs, whiskies and even cigars. Excellent, smiling service to complete the picture.

|●| NOUVELLE

30 rue St-Jean (Centre).
☎ 04.77.32.32.60
Closed Sun evening, Mon, a week in winter and three weeks in summer.

The fashionable place to eat in Saint-Étienne, right in the centre of town. It's got everything a gourmet restaurant should have – subtle decor, young, very elegant staff and the kind of menu you dream about – but it doesn't charge the prices you might expect. Menus 98F (weekday lunch) then 150–305F. The young chef loves to revamp "poor man's food" like *brandade de morue* (salt cod pounded with garlic, olive oil and cream), and does creative things with pasta – ravioli stuffed with lamb or salmon lasagne. Portions are generous, and it's all very imaginative, even if some sauces are not as light as they could be. It's best to book.

🏠 |●| RESTAURANT À LA BOUCHE PLEINE

8 pl. Chavanelle; it's near the fire station.
☎ 04.77.33.92.47
Closed lunchtimes, Sun, Mon, and Aug.

Photos of the regulars cover the walls of the cosy little dining room, where you'll bump into actors and sundry night-owls congregating in the small hours. Like them, when you've finished a meal lovingly prepared by Henriette, you'll want to be told the recipe for the *diable au corps*, the explosive house cocktail that they set light to. You get a really nice welcome from Marco. Menus 119–180F. The cooking is the sort you get in a classic Lyonnais bistro. Best to book. Free apéritif.

SAINT-PRIES-EN-JAREZ   42270 (2KM N)

|●| RESTAURANT DU MUSÉE

Lieu-dit La Terrasse; follow the signs to the museum of modern art.
☎ 04.77.59.24.52
Closed Sun evening.

Stéphane Laurier (who runs the *Nouvelle* restaurant in town – see above), has taken over this restaurant inside the museum. The decor is exactly in line with that of the museum itself. His cooking is very inventive, skillfully using spices and mixing unusual flavours – try the *croustillant* of fish with spice for size. Lunch menus 65F and 85F and a *menu-carte* at 120F. Even the cheapest menu changes daily and you get excellent value for money. Efficient service. And there's a lovely terrace that opens in the warm weather.

SAINT-GENEST-MALIFAUX   42660 (12KM S)

🌲 I●I AUBERGE DE CAMPAGNE LA DILIGENCE

Le Château du Bois; take the N82 to Bicêtre then the D501; it's 3km from the village.
☎ 04.77.39.04.99
Closed Mon and Tues except July–Aug, and Jan.

This was orignially the farmhouse of the 13th-century castle, which is still inhabited. Now it's a really nice restaurant that belongs to the agricultural college of Saint-Genest. Good food and pleasant service with seasonal menus, 65F on weekdays then 95–145F. The handsome dining room has a fireplace and there's a terrace in the farm courtyard. You can camp in the grounds for next to nothing. Breakfast is not included. The farm has got horses, and you can go riding. It's advisable to book. Free apéritif.

🌲 I●I RESTAURANT MONTMARTIN

18 rue du Velay; take the N82, then the D501 to Plafony.
☎ 04.77.51.21.25
Closed evenings except for reservations, Wed, a week in Jan, and a week in July.

Located in one of the less attractive villages in this part of the world, this place was established post-war by the grandmother of the present owners, who have kept the warm atmosphere and the creaking parquet. No nouvelle cuisine here; this is the place for generous portions of rich food including morels, frog's legs and *quenelles*. Weekday menu 79F, then 102–185F. It's very popular with families for Sunday lunch. Free *digestif*.

SAINT-VICTOR-SUR-LOIRE   42230 (15KM W)

I●I LE CROQUE CERISE

Base Nautique de Saint-Victor; take the D3A.
☎ 04.77.90.07.54
Closed Sun and Wed evenings, Mon, and Jan–Feb.

The big building is not particularly elegant, but the dining rooms with their large windows and the terrace by the harbour are really pleasant. Meticulously prepared dishes include whitebait, pizza cooked in a wood-fired oven, and grapefruit *terrine*. Weekday menu 75F or 120–180F. The food, service and welcome are spot on.

SAINT-PAUL-EN-CORNILLON   42240 (17KM SW)

🌲 I●I LA CASCADE*

How to get there: go in the direction of Firminy, take the D3, and turn left onto the D46 before the bridge.
☎ 04.77.35.70.02
Closed Mon in winter, and first week in Sept. **Car park**.

No views of cascades here, but you can see the Loire instead. The classic dining room gets lots of light, and there's a very pleasant terrace shaded by plane trees and an impressive sequoia. It's a pity that the car park is so badly placed between the terrace and the river. The chef's speciality is king prawns grilled with saffron, and the menus provide dishes such as salad of Fourme de Montbrison cheese and trout *meunière*. Thoughtfully prepared, simple food that's served with care. Free apéritif.

BESSAT (LE)   42660 (18KM SE)

🏠 I●I HÔTEL LA FONDUE-RESTAURANT CHEZ LE PÈRE CHARLES**

Grande-Rue (Centre).
☎ 04.77.20.40.09 ➡ 04.77.20.45.20
Closed Sun evening 1 March–3 Nov. **TV. Car park**.

A good restaurant way up at 1170m in the middle of the Pilat regional park, where the people of Lyon and Saint-Étienne come to pump a bit of oxygen into their lungs. Splendid gourmet dishes: goose *foie gras*, *tournedos* with paprika cream, veal chops with girolles, trout stuffed with ceps and a selection of sweets and home-made chocolate desserts. Dish of the day 52F, and lots of menus 76–255F. Warm atmosphere. Doubles 210F with shower/wc and 280F with bath. The bathrooms are big but the rooms with shower have a strange arrangement like a revolving cupboard which hides the toilet and the shower.

🌲 🏠 I●I AUBERGE DE LA JASSERIE

La Jasserie; it's 6km after Le Bessat – follow the arrows from the village.
☎ 04.77.20.40.16 ➡ 04.77.20.45.43
Closed Thurs in winter, except during school holidays.

This old farmhouse, with its little bell tower, is a bit of an institution. It's one of those simple country inns that hasn't changed for generations, where you sit at wooden tables and chairs in a huge old dining room. It's at the bottom of the ski runs so it's an ideal place to warm up over a hot chocolate and a slice of bilberry tart. The only drawback is that it's too crowded and noisy at the weekend. Snacks 55F and menus 82–145F. If you want to stay, you can sleep on a bunk-bed in their basic dormitory for 60F. You have to share facilities and go half board. Free house apéritif.

SAINT-JUST-SAINT-RAMBERT 42170 (20KM NW)

I●I RESTAURANT DU REMPART

2 rue de la Loire; take the turning westward off the D8, when you're going in the direction of St-Genest-Lerpt.
☎ 04.77.52.13.19
Closed Sun evening, Mon, a week in Feb and three weeks in Aug.

A couple of rustic dining rooms up on the first floor of a very old house built in the town walls. There's a gifted, inventive chef at work – excellent *foie gras*. Menus 90–200F. Smiling, pleasant service. In summer, meals are served on the flowery terrace at the foot of the town walls.

SAINT-CHRISTO-EN-JAREZ 42320 (23KM NE)

🏠 I●I HÔTEL-RESTAURANT BESSON-LES TOURISTES*

Route de la Combe; go to Saint-Chamond, then take the D2 in the direction of Valfleury and col de la Gachet.
☎ 04.77.20.85.01
Closed Wed and 1–15 Sept.

Far away from the hurly-burly of Saint-Étienne and Saint-Chamond, at an altitude of 800m on the south side of the Monts du Lyonnais, this quiet, old-fashioned hotel offers rooms with a view of the Pilat mountain range. Doubles 190F with bath (wc along the landing). It's pretty standard food in the restaurant, but they do have good *charcuteries*. You can get a country snack or choose from menus 70–160F. Disabled access to the restaurant.

SAINT-MARCELLIN-EN-FOREZ 42680 (25KM NW)

I●I MANOIR DU COLOMBIER

9 rue Carles-de-Mazenod; on the A72, take the Andrézieux-Bouthéon exit, the D8 to Bouson and the D498 to the village.
☎ 04.77.52.90.37
Closed Tues evening and Wed.

In a little village at the foot of the Forez mountains this beautiful 16th-century manor house is a rare vestige of the past. There are three dining rooms, all decorated differently, and a wonderful courtyard where you can eat. The food is pleasant, if not particularly sophisticated, and portions are generous. The cheapest menu, 95F, is good and there are others

140–270F. If you can stretch to it, treat yourself to the tasty roast pigeon. Friendly welcome.

SAINT-SAUVEUR-EN-RUE 42220 (25KM S)

🏄 🏠 I●I CHÂTEAU DE BOBIGNEUX

Bobigneux; take the N82 south to col du Grand-Bois, then the D22 for 11km; it's 2.5km from the village.
☎ 04.77.39.24.33 ☛ 04.77.39.25.74
Closed Wed and Nov–Feb. **Car park**.

After eighteen years in Greenland the owners took over this 16th-century stone manor house, which is right next to a farm belonging to Madame's brother. They've created a delightful, romantic place to stay, and prices are reasonable. The farm provides them with all the fresh produce they need, and Monsieur, who is a talented chef, creates great dishes. There's a *menu campagnard* served in the week for 70F, and others up to 200F. Try the oyster mushrooms in flaky pastry. The dining rooms have been pleasantly renovated, and the terrace and garden are both lovely. There are six pretty, bright, spacious country-style rooms, with neither TV nor phone, 215–230F. Lovely welcome. Free apéritif.

SAINT-GALMIER 42330

I●I LA CHARPINIÈRE

Lieu-dit la Carpinière.
☎ 04.77.52.75.00 ☛ 04.77.54.18.79
Swimming pool. **TV**. **Car park**.

A splendid establishment in substantial grounds so you're guaranteed quiet. Pleasant and functional rooms 450F. They have a range of facilities including a fitness centre, Turkish bath, sauna, tennis courts and a swimming pool. The restaurant is in a conservatory and offers high-quality cooking that's both original and refined. Menus 98–235F. The service is particularly attentive. It's not the cheapest place but you won't be let down.

I●I LE BOUGAINVILLIER

Pré Château; it's signposted from the Badoit source on the banks of the Coise.
☎ 04.77.54.03.31
Closed Sun evening and Mon, the Feb school holidays, and three weeks in Aug. **Car park**.

A pretty building swathed in Virginia creeper in the rather stylish little town which is the source of Badoit mineral water. The restaurant has three dining rooms, one of them a veranda overlooking a walled garden by the water's edge. Gérard Charbonnier is one of the most interesting young chefs in the area.

He spent two years in Gagnaire's well-known restaurant, where he was encouraged to be creative. He's retained his inventiveness, but has had to restrain his creative urges to a more traditional style that's also more affordable. His fish dishes are delicate and skilfully prepared. The 130F menu isn't available at weekends, when there are others up to 305F. Charming, low-key welcome. Well worth the fifteen-minute drive from Saint-Étienne.

VEAUCHE   42340 (6KM S)

🏊 🏠 ◉ HÔTEL-RESTAURANT DE LA GARE

55 av. H.-Planchet; take the D12 – it's next to the train station and a huge factory.
☎ 04.77.54.60.10 ➡ 04.77.94.30.53
Closed evenings Sun and public holidays. **Car park**.

A reliable neighbourhood restaurant providing good food at sensible prices. There's a weekday menu at 49F and others 69–260F. The 105F menu lists fine, delicately prepared dishes: *compotée* of pig's trotters or salmon flan, cheese, and a good selection of desserts. Pleasant, conventional decor and a warm friendly welcome. The hotel has ten basic rooms, which you should bear in mind if you're stuck for somewhere to stay – under general circumstances, however, the view of the station and the factory is probably not quite what you're looking for. Free coffee.

ANDREZIEUX-BOUTHÉON   42160 (8KM S)

🏠 ◉ LES IRIS***

32 rue Jean-Martouret; take the D12.
☎ 04.77.36.09.09 ➡ 04.77.36.09.00
Closed Sun evening, Mon, a week in the Feb school holidays, a fortnight in Aug and a week at All Saints'.
Disabled access. Garden. Swimming pool. TV. Car park.

This handsome residence, reached by two elegant flights of steps, stands on the outskirts of a rather industrial town near Saint-Étienne airport. The ten functional but pleasant bedrooms, named after flowers, are in the annexe. On two levels, they overlook the swimming pool and the garden with its gigantic cedar trees; 450F with bath. The restaurant serves conventional cuisine and has a decor to match. An 85F weekday lunch menu, and others 110–215F; your meal is served with zeal and professionalism.

CHAZELLES-SUR-LYON   42140 (10KM NE)

🏊 🏠 ◉ CHÂTEAU BLANCHARD**

36 route de Saint-Galmier; very near the hat museum.
☎ 04.77.54.28.88 ➡ 04.77.54.36.03
Closed Sun evening, Mon and a fortnight in Jan.
Disabled access. TV. Car park.

This "castle", in France's millinery capital, is actually a 1930s folly that was once the home of a hat-maker. It lay neglected for forty years but has since been restored to its original splendour. The garish frontage is decorated with friezes, while inside, the decor is a glorious confusion of neo-greco-classical-kitsch. Very well-equipped doubles from 310F with bath; number 6, which has its original decor, costs 400F. The restaurant fits into its surroundings very nicely. You'll get a warm welcome and classic, well-presented menus starting at 115F on weekdays with others 165–265F. It specialises in fresh fish. You can eat on the terrace. Free *digestif*.

SAINT-JEAN-DE-MAURIENNE   73300

🏊 🏠 ◉ HÔTEL-RESTAURANT DU NORD**

pl. du Champ-de-Foire.
☎ 04.79.64.02.08 ➡ 04.79.59.91.31
Closed Sun evening and Mon lunchtime except Feb and July–Aug, and Oct. **TV. Car park**.

A former coaching inn with a little tower. The restaurant, which has a vaulted ceiling and stone walls, is in the old stables. The cooking is well judged and reliable, and although it's classical, the chef has some original ideas – try the home-made *foie gras*, calf's sweetbreads in pastry or beef steak with morels. There's an 80F weekday menu, and others up to 230F. The rooms are identical, with the same soothing decor. Doubles 275F with shower/wc. 10% discount on the room rate Sept–June and free house apéritif.

SAINT-MARTIN-DE-BELLEVILLE   73440

🏠 ◉ LE LACHENAL**

Centre; 50m from the ski-lifts.
☎ 04.79.08.96.29 ➡ 04.79.08.94.23
Closed mid-April to end June, and 1 Sept–20 Dec.

A lovely doll's house of a place, with cosy rooms with flower-painted shutters and panelled walls. Doubles 300F with shower/wc. Simple, flavourful dishes: fillet of Salers beef with mushrooms, *fondue* flavoured with Kirsch, frogs' legs in cream sauce. Menus 100–190F. The Lemattre family are wonderful hosts. It's often full, so it's best to book.

🏃 I●I CHEZ BIDOU

Quartier des Granges; it's 4km from the centre on the D117 going towards Ménuires.
☎ 04.79.08.97.12
Closed May–June and Sept–Nov.

In a battered old chalet, far away from the tourist traps that abound here, the tiny vaulted dining room serves Savoyard specialities such as *diots* (vegetable and pork sausages in white wine) with *crozet* and polenta cooked with butter and grated cheese, fish stew with pike, trout, perch, crayfish and vegetables, *matafan*, *raclette* and *tartiflette*. Menus 98–130F. À la carte, the bill will come to around the same. It's best to book. Free apéritif, coffee or *digestif*.

🏃 I●I LA BOUITTE

Quartier Saint-Marcel; take the D117 towards Les Ménuires (about 2km).
☎ 04.79.08.96.77
Closed May–June and 1 Sept–15 Dec. **Car park**.

Without doubt, this is the best restaurant in the valley. They combine simple ingredients in astonishing ways to create excellent dishes that are full of flavour; try the salad of lean bacon and *croutons*, warm *foie gras* escalope on a corn *galette*, calf's liver with spinach, or rabbit tart with shallot conserve. The desserts are out of this world, as are the *petits fours* they serve with coffee. You'll have a first-class meal in the stylish country dining room. Attentive, faultless service. Menus 145–295F – well worth it for René Meilleur's wonderful cooking. Free coffee.

SAINT-MARTIN-EN-HAUT 69850

🏃 I●I RESTAURANT LES QUATRE SAISONS

pl. de l'Église (Centre).
☎ 04.78.48.69.12
Closed Tues and 1–15 Sept.

A surprising restaurant on the pretty square of a hilltop village at the edge of the Monts du Lyonnais. Generous portions of home cooking are served in the fresco-lined dining room. Lunch menu 60F, then others 95–168F. The welcoming owners know how to take care of their customers. Free apéritif.

AVEIZE 69610 (9KM NW)

🏃 🏠 I●I HÔTEL-RESTAURANT RIVOLLIER

Le bourg; take the D34.
☎ 04.74.26.01.08 ➡ 04.74.26.01.90
Closed Mon.

It's a wonder how a place this size can survive in such a small village. However, once you've experienced the sheer professionalism, first-class welcome and service, and eaten a superb meal in the pleasant airy dining room, you'll be less surprised. They offer delectable menus at 62F (weekdays), 95F and 162F and a wide selection of dishes of the day such as *ballotine* of duck with figs and pike soufflé with shrimps. If you're stuck for accommodation, they also have eight very basic rooms at 160F with shower or 220F with bath. Free apéritif.

SAINT-PAUL-LÈS-MONESTIER 38650

🏃 🏠 I●I HÔTEL-RESTAURANT AU SANS SOUCI**

How to get there: at Monestier-de-Clermont, take the D8 Gresse-en-Vercors road.
☎ 04.76.34.03.60 ➡ 04.76.34.17.38
Closed Sun evening and Mon out of season, and Jan.
Swimming pool. TV. Car park.

Service noon–1.30pm and 7–8.30pm. This family-run hotel, surrounded by greenery at the foot of the Vercors regional park, has been running smoothly for three generations. It's a pleasure to be here, and you'll feel even better after a meal in the welcoming restaurant. They offer a 92F weekday menu, and others from 105–140F. Excellent specialities include snail ravioli in a nettle stock, suckling pig cooked in a game sauce, duck breasts in honey and balsamic vinegar, saddle of rabbit in walnut wine, char with shrimps, and beef with morels. You can play *boules* or pool, or have a swim. Double rooms 280F with shower/wc, 350F with bath. Free coffee.

SAINT-PIERRE-DE-CHARTREUSE 38380

🏃 🏠 I●I L'AUBERGE DU CUCHERON*

Col du Cucheron (north); it's 3km north of the town centre, on the D512.
☎ 04.76.88.62.06 ➡ 04.76.88.65.43
Closed Sun evening and Mon except during school holidays, and 15 Oct–25 Dec. **Car park**.

This nice old inn, surrounded by trees, is one of a dying breed. The views are magnificent, and the *patronne* is charming. There are seven rooms, 162F with basin, 205F with shower/wc, and 215F with bath. They prefer you to stay half board, 210–240F, but it's not compulsory. Menus 96–160F, or *à la carte* with specialities such as salmon and pike *terrine*, veal with morels and iced nougat. You're just 20m from the ski runs in winter, and peace reigns in summer. 10% discount on the room rate except in school holidays.

SAINTE-EULALIE 07510

↟ ≙ |●| HÔTEL DU NORD**

Le bourg; it's opposite the church.
☎ 04.75.38.80.09 ➡ 04.75.38.85.50
Closed Wed except July– Aug, and 11 Nov–11 Feb.
Disabled access. Car park.

This hotel has had a face-lift. Half the rooms have been refurbished, and there are two new sitting rooms, one with a veranda; both have magnificent views over the Loire plain. Double rooms 235F with shower/wc; half board, for a minimum three-night stay, costs upwards of 244F. Menus, 98–155F, list interesting specialities such as duck thigh *confit* with bilberry sauce, trout *soufflé* with *beurre blanc*, and pork *estouffade* in Ardèche wine. For dessert you absolutely must try the *crème brûlée* with bilberries and raspberries. It's a magnet for fly-fishermen – the chef is smitten by the sport. Free apéritif.

SAGNES ET GOUDOULET 07450 (8KM SW)

|●| HOSTELLERIE CHANEAL

It's in the village.
☎ 04.75.38.80.88 ➡ 04.75.38.80.54
Closed Mon–Fri Oct to Easter, Wed the rest of the year except July–Aug. **Car park.**

Instead of leaving the country for the town, the young chef decided to stay and take over the family business – he's the fourth generation to run the place. The climate is harsh and the winters are long which doesn't make things easy, so the business is seasonal – sometimes when the snow is deep, it's hard to get deliveries up here. Inside the thick walls, the rooms are comfortable and the walls are built of stone and wood. Doubles 240F, and half board from 250F. The chef uses carefully selected local produce in cooking which shows off the flavours to their best advantage. He makes the *charcuterie* and bread himself, and there are *terrines* of wild plants and local trout. Menus 100–140F. Fantastically warm welcome. The young man needs all the support he can get – and he's worth it.

SAMOËNS 74340

↟ ≙ |●| LE MOULIN DU BATHIEU**

Verclan: take the D4 in the direction of Morillon, then turn left to Samoëns 1600.
☎ 04.50.34.48.07 ➡ 04.50.34.43.25
@ moulin-du-bathieu@wanadoo.fr
Closed May and 5 Nov–22 Dec. **TV. Car park.**

The only thing to break the silence here is the babbling brook that used to turn the mill wheel. The bedrooms, with their wood-clad walls, have a warm, soothing feel. Several of them are on split levels, making them ideal for families. Doubles with shower/wc 320–600F. You have to book to eat in the restaurant. Menus 110–180F, one featuring Savoyard specialities: *fondue*, *pela*, *féra*, meats cooked on a stone. Free coffee and free use of the gym.

|●| LA FANDOLIEUSE

Centre.
☎ 04.50.34.98.28
Closed spring and autumn but it's worth telephoning.

Service noon–2pm and 4.30–11pm. In the 15th century the people of this valley spoke a poetic, sing-song dialect called *Mourmé*; *Fandolieuse* is their word for dancer. This pleasant little *crêperie*, in a 16th-century house with wainscotted walls, has given all its *crêpes* a *Mourmé* name. *Tapotu* means drum, *violurin* means musician, *crépioti* describes the crackling winter water and *souffluche*, the whining wind. They also do *fondues* and a very substantial *soupe châtrée*, made with bread, Tomme cheese and onions – it's a local speciality that was traditionally eaten on the feast of Saint Christopher. À *la carte* only – around 100F.

SUZE-LA-ROUSSE 26790

≙ |●| HÔTEL LE COMTE**

route de Bollène (West); as you leave town on the Bollène road, it's on the right.
☎ 04.75.04.85.38 ➡ 04.75.04.85.37
Swimming pool. Disabled access. TV. Car park.

A big Provençal farmhouse that's been wonderfully converted. It's got shady grounds and a swimming pool. Doubles with luxurious bathrooms and polished wood panelling cost 270–350F with shower or bath; the nicest rooms are in the tiny keep, and a few have a terrace overlooking the neighbouring vineyards. Excellent menu for 95F: *caillette* which is a local kind of haggis, tart with smoked cod mousse, braised beef à *la Provençale*, courgette *au gratin*, and *gratin* of warm fruit.

SAINT-RESTITUT 26130 (8KM NW)

|●| RESTAURANT LES BUISSES

Southeast; leave Saint-Restitut by the Suze-la Rousse road, go past the statue of the Virgin Mary, and follow the D218.
☎ 04.75.04.96.50
Closed Sat lunchtime and Mon out of season. **Car park**.

A beautiful country house way out in the truffle-oak forests with a Provençal garden. In summer the crickets sing, and you sit out on the terrace to enjoy robustly flavoured cooking from the south. There's also a spacious, newly decorated dining room with a working fireplace. Lovely welcome and a nice relaxed atmosphere. Lunch menu at 100F and another at 150F, with a choice of five flavoursome starters and main courses. Specialities include lamb fondue, *assiette des Buisses* (a platter of aubergine, peppers, pickled tomatoes and courgettes with a drizzle of local olive oil), deep-fried courgette flowers and so on. Remarkable wine list.

TAIN L'HERMITAGE   26600

🛏 HÔTEL LES 2 COTEAUX**

19 rue Joseph Pála.
☎ 04.75.08.33.01 ➡ 04.75.08.44.20
Closed mid-Jan to mid-Feb and Christmas to New Year's Day.

A family hotel in a superb location on the banks of the Rhône just by a bridge to the Ardèche. Though a little the worse for wear, the ones looking west have a magnificent view of the river and the Château de Tournon. One room even has a small terrace. That said, the rooms at the back also have a lovely view over the Hermitage hills. Well maintained doubles with shower 190F, 250–310F with shower/wc or bath. The breakfast terrace also has a gorgeous view of the Rhône flowing by. Nice welcome.

CROZES-HERMITAGE   26600 (3KM N)

|●| LE BISTROT DES VINS

How to get there: take the D153 and it's in the village.
☎ 04.75.07.18.03
Closed Mon–Wed.

This is serious wine-country and this charming village is in the Crozes-Hermitage vineyards. It's a bistro-style dining room with a small terrace, run by a very welcoming young couple. Tasty cuisine using fresh market produce and, naturally enough, you accompany your meal with a jug of the local vintage at knock-down prices. There's one menu only, 85F, offering a choice of starters, dish of the day, cheese and dessert. It's

doing well and has established a regular clientele. It may be best to book.

TARARE   69170

🍴|●| RESTAURANT JEAN BROUILLY

3 ter route de Paris.
☎ 04.74.63.24.56
Closed Sun, Mon, Feb school holidays, and three weeks in Aug.

The Brouillys have been running things here for a good twenty years. The house, built by an industrialist, is pretty typical of the region, with beautiful grounds. Jean Brouilly is a considerable chef and a welcoming man. Whether you choose pan-fried *foie gras* with rhubarb, quartet of scallops with caviar on salt cod mousse, veal fillet with a magnolia flower, red mullet with olives, or zander fillet with watercress sauce, you will appreciate his skilful handling of fresh produce and delicate balancing of flavours. He combines herbs, spices and wild produce to most original effect. Menus 160–380F. On warm days you can eat on the veranda and admire the grounds. Free glass of Beaujolais.

SARCEY   69490 (12KM E)

🍴 🛏 |●| LE CHATARD**

1 allée du Mas; take the N7 in the direction of Lyon, turn left onto the D118.
☎ 04.74.26.85.85 ➡ 04.74.26.89.99
Closed Sun evening Oct–April and early Jan.
Disabled access. **Swimming pool**. **TV**. **Car park**.

A reliable, peaceful hotel-restaurant with a nice swimming pool. The restaurant attracts businesspeople and local families because of the prices and the top-quality menus, 90F for lunch during the week, then others up to 260F. Doubles 260–340F; they don't have huge charm but they've got all mod cons. 10% discount July–Aug except on Sat.

THÔNES   74230

🍴 🛏 |●| HÔTEL DU COMMERCE**

5 rue des Clefs (Centre).
☎ 04.50.02.13.66 ➡ 04.50.32.16.24
Closed Sun evening, Wed out of season, a week in April and a fortnight in Nov. **TV**. **Car park**.

The big attraction here is the food. The chef, Robert Bastard-Rosset, really knows his business, and runs to a few inspired surprises –pike *quenelles* (a sort of light fish ball), with a crayfish *coulis* and the best *farcements* in the region. A good range of menus; 80F (weekday lunchtime) and 125–350F. Perfect service in a cosy dining room with wood everywhere. The rooms have great views of the forest, even though the place is in the middle of the town. They're very colourful, sometimes a bit too much so, but can't be beaten for value. Doubles 235–435F with shower/wc or bath. The *patronne* has been taking care of her guests for over thirty years. Free *génépy*.

MANIGOD · 74230 (8KM SE)

⅔ ☎ |●| HÔTEL-RESTAURANT DE LA VIEILLE FERME**

col de Merdassier; from Thônes, take the D12 then the D16 towards Manigod, go through La Croix-Fry and head for the resort of L'Étale.
☎ 04.50.02.41.49 ➡ 04.50.32.65.53
Closed Wed except during school holidays, May and 1 Nov–15 Dec. **TV. Car park**.

An archetypal Alpine chalet at the foot of the Étale ski slopes. They have five pretty rooms, 300–350F with shower or bath. The menus, 90–140F, list food that's as typical and authentic as the place – try the *farcement* and leeks *au gratin*. Half board, compulsory during the school holidays, costs 300F. Charming service. Free coffee. 10% discount out of season.

THONON-LES-BAINS · 74200

⅔ |●| RESTAURANT LE VICTORIA

5 pl. des Arts (Centre).
☎ 04.50.71.02.82
Closed Christmas to 1 Jan.

The lovely Belle Époque glass frontage is overrun by greenery, which makes the dining room pleasantly private. They serve good, traditional cooking, using fine ingredients, and prepare tasty dishes of both freshwater and sea fish – try the sea bass in a salt crust. In summer they offer huge crispy salads. Menus 72F, (not Sun), and 115–165F. Free apéritif.

MARGENCEL · 74200 (5KM SW)

⅔ ☎ |●| HÔTEL-RESTAURANT LES CYGNES**

port de Séchex; when you get to Margencel, head for the port of Séchex on the D33.
☎ 04.50.72.63.10 ➡ 04.50.72.68.22
Closed Tues out of season, Dec and Jan. **TV. Car park**.

Known simply as *Chez Jules*, this is a local institution in a small port by the side of Lake Geneva. It's been going since the 1930s. The restaurant is famous for fresh fish – try the small fry, soup of freshwater fish, fillets of perch, *féra* (a type of salmon) *à l'ancienne*, or fish *pot-au-feu*. Menus 100–220F. The rooms are delightful; some have been freshened up and numbers 7, 8 and 9 have a lake view; 290F with shower/wc. Free coffee, and 10% discount in spring and autumn.

ARMOY · 74200 (6.5KM SE)

⅔ ☎ |●| HÔTEL-RESTAURANT LE CHALET**

L'Ermitage; it's on the D26.
☎ 04.50.71.08.11 ➡ 04.50.71.33.88
Closed out of season except for reservations.
Swimming pool. Garden. Car park.

This building, which resembles a Swiss chalet, stands at the top of a wooded slope high above the village and Lake Geneva. You get lots of peace and quiet and a superb view from most of the rooms, some of which have their own terrace. If you're here in summer, ask for one of the wooden chalets around the swimming pool. Doubles 170–190F with basin, 250–280F with shower/wc. Menus 90F (except Sun lunch), and 95–180F. The cuisine is carefuly prepared – home-made *charcuteries*, salmon with tarragon. There's a big garden and a fine view of the lake – you won't want to leave. Free house apéritif.

TOUR-DU-PIN (LA) · 38110

⅔ ☎ |●| HÔTEL DE FRANCE-RESTAURANT LE BEC FIN**

pl. du Champ-de-Mars (Centre).
☎ 04.74.97.00.08 ➡ 04.74.97.36.47
Closed Sun evening. **TV. Pay car park**.

The owner here is keen to maintain quality and service. The rooms, across the road from the restaurant, are really decent; 150F with shower/wc, or 240F with bath. The old-style restaurant is equally good, offering excellent dishes that change with the seasons. Specialities include warm snail salad, ravioli with shrimps, and the classic *gratin dauphinois*, which is potatoes baked with cream and topped with cheese. There are also some good fish dishes. Menus 98–160F. Free coffee.

SAINT-DIDIER-DE-LA-TOUR · 38110 (4KM SE)

⅔ |●| AUX BERGES DU LAC

58 route du Lac.
☎ 04.74.97.32.82

Closed weeknights in winter, and the Christmas school holidays. **Car park**.

This place has simply got it right. You can have a nice meal and enjoy yourself in an atmosphere so good that you hardly notice the occasional noise from passing trains. Menus are cheap – 60–165F – and the chef prepares excellent fish dishes. It's perfect for Sunday lunch. Free apéritif.

VIGNIEU   38890 (10KM NW)

🎄 🏠 I●I CHÂTEAU DE CHAPEAU CORNU***

How to get there: take the D16 in the direction of Saint-Chef-Morestel.
☎ 04.74.27.79.00 ➡ 04.74.92.49.31
📧 chapeau.cornu@wanadoo.fr
Restaurant closed Sun evening. **Swimming pool**. **TV**. **Car park**.

An odd name for a special place, which occupies a 13th-century castle. It's now a charming hotel-restaurant, which offers bright, comfortable double rooms furnished with antiques and contemporary art, from 420F and suites 790–900F. There are also a few simple doubles in an annexe, with basin only, which cost 200F. The restaurant has vaulted dining rooms and a terrace; all dishes are prepared using only local produce. Menus from 105F. Specialities include goat's cheese with spinach and poppy seeds, Royan ravioli stuffed with snails, trout stuffed with oyster mushrooms, sweetbreads braised with morels, and delicious fresh fruit *au gratin*. Free apéritif.

SAINT-SAVIN   38300 (16.5KM NW)

I●I RESTAURANT LE DEMPTÉZIEU

pl. du Château (Northwest); take the N6 in the direction of Bourgoin-Jallieu, then the D143 on the right.
☎ 04.74.28.90.49
Closed Mon evening, Tues and 1–15 Jan. **Car park**.

Yves and Corinne Bello have turned this old village café into a wonderful gourmet restaurant. They'll give you a very natural welcome and unpretentious service with a smile. Dishes are fancy and well tuned to today's tastes: warm scallop salad with hazelnut oil, *fricassée* of fresh frogs' legs with cream sauce and half a pigeon with a shrimp *coulis*. Weekday lunch menu 70F, and 90–186F. You're guaranteed a delicious meal.

TOURNON-SUR-RHÔNE   07300

🎄 🏠 I●I HÔTEL AZALÉES**

6 av. de la Gare (Southwest).
☎ 04.75.08.05.23 ➡ 04.75.08.18.27
Closed 25 Dec–5 Jan.
Disabled access. **TV**. **Car park**.

Service noon–2pm and 7–9.30pm. You can sit on the terrace and watch the steam train puffing its way through Haut-Vivarais en route to Lamastre. Comfortable, modern doubles 240F with shower or bath. Menus, from 93F, list mainly regional cooking with a good goat's cheese flan and, for dessert, iced chestnut soufflé. 10% discount on the room rate.

🎄 I●I RESTAURANT AUX SABLETTES

187 route de Lamastre (West); go 3km along the Lamastre road, turn left, and it's opposite the Acacias campsite.
☎ 04.75.08.44.34
Closed Wed except July–Aug. **Car park**.

This restaurant and bar, which specialises in beer, is a bit out of the way, but it's popular with young locals and people from the nearby campsite. The decor doesn't have much character, but the menu lists a few original specialities: fish *choucroute* and meats cooked with beer – they even put beer in the mousses and tarts. The less adventurous will be well satisfied with the ravioli, a delicious regional speciality, or any of the pizzas and grills. Menus 62–130F. Free house apéritif.

I●I RESTAURANT L'ESTRAGON

6 pl. Saint-Julien; it's opposite the church.
☎ 04.75.08.87.66
Closed Wed except in summer, and beginning of Feb to mid-March.

In a great location, in the middle of a pedestrianised area very close to the Rhône, this place offers good, simple food at reasonable prices. Menus 64–100F. There's a "*pierre chaude*" (hot stone), menu, comprising a salad, veal or steak, cheese and dessert. The salads are huge and the zander with red wine and pickled shallots is very tasty. Efficient, attentive service.

USSON-EN-FOREZ   42550

🎄 🏠 I●I HÔTEL RIVAL*

rue Centrale (Centre).
☎ 04.77.50.63.65 ➡ 04.77.50.67.62
Closed Mon Oct–June and the Feb school holidays.
TV. **Car park**.

A typical family hotel in a little mountain village up in the Forez. The restaurant serves large portions of traditional dishes, with a weekday menu for 68F and others

110–140F. Try the warm *galantine* with snails or the *génoise* with veal and morels. You can eat on the terrace. The rooms are clean and affordable, if lacking in character. Doubles 140F with basin and 250F with bath. Very friendly proprietress. Free apéritif, and 10% discount on the room rate.

SAINT-BONNET-LE-CHÂTEAU 42380 (14KM NE)

♠ I●I LE BEFRANC

7 rue d'Augel; it's on the edge of town on the road from Usso-en-Forez.
☎ 04.77.50.54.54 ➡ 04.77.50.73.17
TV. Car park.

This beautiful town with a medieval centre is the capital of *pétanque*. The hotel is a short distance from the centre and offers spruce rooms that have been attractively decorated. Doubles 210F. Regional dishes are the order of the day in the restaurant and menus are priced 75–165F. Charming welcome.

I●I LA CALÈCHE

7 rue François-Valette.
☎ 04.77.50.15.58
Closed Tues evening and Wed.

A ravishing little inn that's pretty in pink. The dining room has a warm, welcoming atmosphere. The owner does the cooking, which shows lots of variety and originality, and he uses good quality produce. Menus from 89F. A popular place where it's advisable to book.

VALENCE 26000

⚔ ♠ HÔTEL DE L'EUROPE**

15 av. Félix-Faure (Centre); it's near the tourist office and the station.
☎ 04.75.82.62.65 ➡ 04.75.82.62.66
Closed Sun 2–6pm. **TV. Car park**.

A conveniently located hotel with quiet, air-conditioned rooms that have been complete-ly refurbished. The double glazing is very effi-cient at keeping out the noise from the street below. Doubles with good facilities, 215F with shower and 260–295F with bath. One free breakfast when two stay.

⚔ I●I RESTAURANT L'ÉPICERIE

18 pl. Saint-Jean (Centre); it's next to Saint-Jean church.
☎ 04.75.42.74.46
Closed Sat lunchtime, Sun, three weeks in Aug and Christmas to New Year's Day. **Disabled access**.

It's some time since the grocer's shop closed. The premises became a restaurant which has since established a repuation that's as solid as the walls. Good, regional dishes to be appreciated; salad of grilled ravioli, roast mountain lamb with morels, monkfish with watercress, red mullet with Syrah wine sauce or Roseval potatoes with dried ham. Menus 115–330F. When the weather's nice, you can sit on the terrace on a little square opposite an old covered market and be at peace with the world. Free coffee.

I●I RESTAURANT ONE TWO...TEA

37 Grande Rue (Centre).
☎ 04.75.55.96.31
Closed Sun, public holidays and three weeks in Aug.

The interior is a combination of brick and wood, there are pictures on the walls and vases full of flowers, in a sort of quasi "British look". It's crammed at lunchtime and for din-ner, though a small terrace takes the overflow in summer. You'll get a substantial meal for a modest 120F; pie with *crudités*, salmon fillet with anchovy butter, huge complicated sal-ads, steak with shallots or a *gâteau* of chick-en livers with tomato *coulis*. It's tasty and fill-ing, but leave room for a portion of the good apple pie, crumble or *tarte Tatin*. Good value for money. Welcoming staff.

I●I AUBERGE DU PIN

285 [bis] av. Victor Hugo (East); it's not far from the train station.
☎ 04.75.44.53.86
Closed Aug.

The *Pic* is a four-star deluxe establishment with a two-star restaurant, a Relais & Châteaux sign and prices to match. The *Auberge du Pin*, next door, is much more affordable. There's a *menu-carte* at 155F – the dishes are prepared in the same kitchen as in the fabulous restaurant next door. It would be unrealistic to quote any particular dishes because they change so frequently. but the cooking is full of flavour and the dish-es are a combination of local and more tradi-tional choices. The bright yellow dining room is small, so you ought to reserve in autumn and winter when the terrace isn't open.

VALGORGE 07110

♠ I●I HÔTEL LE TANARGUE**

chez Coste (Centre).
☎ 04.75.88.98.98 ➡ 04.75.88.96.09
Closed end Dec to beginning of March. **TV. Car park**.

Huddling at an altitude of 500m, at the foot of

Mont Tanargue on the edge of the Ardèche, this cosy hotel offers large pretty doubles for 260F. Ask for one with a view of the valley. Menus start at 90F and specialities include mountain *charcuterie*, *caillette*, and salmon *terrine* with Puy lentils. Portions are generous and particular care is paid to preparing the vegetable dishes. The dining room is vast and there's an impressive pair of giant bellows hanging above the fireplace.

VALLOIRE 73450

☆ ♨ |●| HÔTEL CHRISTIANIA**

Centre.
☎ 04.79.59.00.57 ➡ 04.79.59.00.06
✉ info@christiania.hotel.com
Closed 20 April to mid-June and 10 Sept–10 Dec.
TV. Car park.

Everyone in Valloire seems to drop in for a drink at the lively bar at some time during the day. They're all sports fans and express forthright views on stories in *L'Équipe*, the French daily sports paper. A relaxed, friendly, family atmosphere. The rooms are stylish, with good facilities; 200F with basin, 280F with shower/wc, and 300–320F with bath. Half board, compulsory in winter, costs upwards of 290F per person. The big dining room next to the bar offers home cooking and great traditional dishes including *diots* (pork sausages in white wine with vegetables) and *biscuit de Savoie* with pears and chocolate. Menus 85–180F. Free coffee.

☆ ♨ |●| HÔTEL LA SETAZ-RESTAURANT LE GASTILLEUR***

Centre.
☎ 04.79.59.01.03 ➡ 04.79.59.00.63
Closed 20 April to beginning of June, 20 Sept–15 Dec.
Garden. Swimming pool. TV. Car park.

Despite its unprepossessing exterior, this is a very classy place, admirably well run by Monique Villard. Chef Jacques Villard prepares the kind of dishes that take his French customers back to their childhood and adapts them to suit modern tastes: *cassolette* of snails, braised pigeon with pickled garlic, and so on. You will find some of his specialities on the menus, 130F on weekdays, and 170–220F. Service is flawless, and you'll get a pleasant welcome. In the summer, they open the heated swimming pool and often have barbecues in the garden. The hotel rooms are starkly contemporary, but they face due south and some have balconies or terraces. Doubles with

shower/wc or bath 460–520F. Half board is compulsory at Christmas and Feb–March. Free *digestif*.

|●| L'ASILE DES FONDUES

rue des Grandes Alpes; it's near the church and the tourist office.
☎ 04.79.59.04.71
Closed May–June and Sept–Nov.

The restaurant, in an old house, has a charming country dining room with lots of style. It's possibly not as old as it's trying to appear, but the welcome you get is so lovely that you'll be tempted to come back time and time again. They offer at least ten types of *fondue*, as much *raclette* as you can eat, and *diots*, the local pork and vegetable sausages in white wine. You can eat for 100–150F *à la carte*.

VALLON-PONT-D'ARC 07150

♨ |●| HÔTEL-RESTAURANT LE BELVEDÈRE

route des Gorges; it's 6km outside Vallon.
☎ 04.75.88.00.02 ➡ 04.75.88.12.22
Closed end Nov to end March.

The trees hide the gorge so you can't see it from the hotel which is also set back a bit. It's a traditional establishment with neat, functional rooms that are a bit small, though some have balconies. Doubles with shower or bath 270–370F. The long, bright dining room is painted pink and has a bay window. Appetising, healthy, uncomplicated cooking, professionally served. Tasty, classic dishes: house *terrine*, meat dishes in sauce and a platter of local cheeses. Honestly priced menus, 95–120F. There's a patio in summer.

♨ |●| HÔTEL CLOS DES BRUYÈRES-RESTAURANT L'OLIVETTE

route des Gorges; it's just on the outskirts of Vallon, by the roundabout.
☎ 04.75.37.18.85 ➡ 04.75.37.14.89
Closed Oct to end of March.
Garden. Swimming pools. TV. Car park.

A modern-looking, standardised type of building by the side of the road but the hotel offers good facilities and behind it, there are nice green spaces with trees. Though the rooms are functional they have a touch of individuality. Doubles 290–360F, depending on facilities and season. The most expensive ones have a view of the garden and the two swimming pools; avoid those that overlook the *route des Gorges*. The dining room is airy but lacks character. Menus 65–150F.

⚥ |●| RESTAURANT LE CHELSEA

bd. Peschère-Alizon (Centre); it's on the main street.
☎ 04.75.88.01.40
Closed Oct–April.

An Ardèche version of a trendy, young restaurant. The little dining room, which leads out onto the garden, is decorated with pictures of cartoon characters. The salads and pastas are obviously the *Chelsea*'s trump card, but they've added a few cooked dishes to their repertoire: try duck breast with honey and mint or *croustillant* of salmon with curry. Weekday menu at 89F, good salads 40–55F, and dishes of the day 60–100F. A reliable place. Free coffee.

ORGNAC-L'AVEN   07150 (23KM S)

|●| HÔTEL DE L'AVEN

pl. de la Mairie (Centre).
☎ 04.75.38.61.80 ➡ 04.75.38.66.69
Hotel closed end Nov to mid-March (except for groups). **Restaurant open** Sun lunchtime out of season. **TV**.

The affable, attentive owner welcomes you to his simple establishment, which he runs very well. The corridors and rooms smell fresh. Doubles with shower or shower/wc 200–270F. The regional cooking is straightforward and unaffected and served in a rustic-style dining room or on the terrace. Menus 90–155F. A nice place.

VANS (LES)   07140

⚥ ♠ |●| HÔTEL LES CÉVENNES

pl. Ollier (Centre); it's in the main square.
☎ 04.75.37.23.09
Closed Mon, the first fortnight in May and the first fortnight in Oct. **Car park**.

From the minute you walk in here, you're aware of a very special atmosphere, a sort of gentle madness that's infected the whole place for some thirty years. The highly individual decor is a real jumble, with flowers, paintings, photos and old documents all jostling for space. The restaurant serves generous portions – try the *crêpe* from the Cévennes, the *coq au vin*, or any of the regional dishes. Set menus from 95F. It is undoubtedly better known for its cooking than as a hotel; its double rooms, with average facilities, go for 160F with shower/wc on the landing. Free coffee and 10% discount on the room rate.

♠ |●| HÔTEL-RESTAURANT LE MAS DE L'ESPAÎRE

Bois de Païolive
☎ 04.75.94.95.01 ➡ 04.75.37.21.00
ⓔ espaire@wanadoo.fr
Swimming pool. **TV**.**Car park**.

There's a sense of calm in this sturdy, imposing building. And you are put at your ease by the excellent welcome. All the facilities you need for a good stay: a splendid setting, lots of space inside and out, a swimming pool and the chafing of the cicadas. Doubles with en-suite bathrooms from 310F. The cuisine offers a variety of traditional specialities from the Cévennes, the Ardèche and Lyons. The 90F menu offers a main course plus starter or dessert, and there are other menus 130–250F. You can go on wonderful walks through the magic Païolive forest which adjoins the property.

♠ |●| LE CARMEL-ANCIEN COUVENT**

How to get there: it's next to the post office.
☎ 04.75.94.99.60 ➡ 04.75.94.34.29
ⓔ lecarmel@wanadoo.fr
Restaurant closed lunchtimes. **Swimming pool**. **TV**.
Car park.

There's an air of serenity and peacefulness about this charming old convent. It's not hard to imagine how the nuns used to live. Keep an eye out for the confessional, which has been converted into a telephone box. The rooms are as clean as can be, spacious and full of light. Some are beginning to show their age. Doubles 350–400F with shower/wc or bath. Breakfast, 45F, or free for under 10s, is served until noon. The restaurant is only open in the evening, when it offers set menus for 95–140F.

|●| RESTAURANT LE GRANGOUSIER

rue Courte; it's opposite the church.
☎ 04.75.94.90.86
Closed Wed and Sun evening except July–Aug.

This stylish restaurant serves both simple menus and gourmet ones to delight to the ardent foodie. The cooking is imaginative – try stuffed rabbit with fresh noodles or the *foie gras* with cream and nettle sauce. The dining room, with its vaulted ceiling and dressed stone walls, is the perfect setting for these wonderful delicacies. Menus start at 110F, and the wine list includes a number of very affordable bottles.

VIENNE   38200

|●| RESTAURANT L'ESTANCOT

4 rue de la Table-Ronde (North).

☎ 04.74.85.12.09
Closed Sun and Mon.

In a quiet side street in the old town near the Saint-André-le-Bas church, *L'Estancot* has a pretty façade with windowboxes laden with flowers and a long, beautiful dining room. Menus 67–108F. The house specialities are *criques* (made with potatoes, chopped parsley and eggs; only served Sat), and *paillassons* (plain, unadorned potatoes) accompanied by all sorts of delicious things. Other delights include roast lamb with Provençal herbs, liver *gâteau*, sea-urchin flan with shellfish sauce, veal kidneys with walnut wine, and warm *foie gras escalope* with port. Reservations only.

ESTRABLIN   38780 (8KM SE)

⚐ ≜ LA GABETIÈRE***

How to get there: take the D502 and it's on the left after the crossroads that lead you to Estrablin.
☎ 04.74.58.01.31 ➡ 04.74.58.08.98
Garden. Swimming pool. TV. Car park.

You'll want to hide away forever in this lovely, luxurious 16th-century stone manor house – especially if you get a room with a view of the grounds. The decor is exquisitely tasteful, and the welcome is simple, warm and attentive. Rooms 290F with shower/wc, 320–380F with bath; there's also a suite in the tower that sleeps four. There's a welcoming bar, a TV room, a heated pool, and picnic tables in the garden. This really is an unusually lovely place and the charming *patronne* will give you all sorts of information about what to see. 10% discount Oct–May.

⚐ ❙●❙ FRANTONY

ZA Le Rocher; take the D41 in the direction of Grenoble and it's by the huge roundabout.
☎ 04.74.57.24.70
Closed Mon and Tues except feast days and public holidays.

Though it is oddly located, in a business park surrounded by roads and concrete buildings, the dining room is attractive and the dishes are interesting and sometimes unusual. The chef used to work for an Emir, so his cuisine has got a touch of sophistication and elegance: he sometimes offers ethnic menus or gypsy dishes. Try the Barbary duck with onions and coriander, frogs' legs and spinach lasagne, quail stuffed with olives and polenta, or *marbré* of *foie gras* with aubergine. Menus 79F, 99F and 165F, or *à la carte*. Free house apéritif.

VILLARD-DE-LANS   38250

≜ VILLA PRIMEROSE**

147 av. des Bains.
☎ 04.76.95.13.17
Closed 1 Nov–20 Dec. **Car park**.

Here's a place where they really make you feel welcome. The quiet rooms in this beautiful building look out onto the Gerbier mountain range. Expect to pay 140–250F for a room for one to three people; they have some communicating rooms that are very good for families. There's no longer a restaurant, but the owner lets residents use the kitchens to cook meals which they are invited to eat in the dining room. Breakfast 25F.

⚐ ≜ ❙●❙ À LA FERME DU BOIS BARBU**

How to get there: it's 3km from the centre in the direction of Bois-Barbu.
☎ 04.76.95.13.09 ➡ 04.76.94.10.65
Hotel closed three weeks in June and 15 Nov–1 Dec. **Restaurant closed** Wed and Sun evening 30 March–30 June and Sept–Dec except in school holidays. **TV. Car park**.

A real mountain inn on the edge of a forest, next to a quiet road. You can sit on the flowery terrace, shaded by a lime tree, or relax in a nice comfy armchair while Nadine, your hostess, plays the piano. Rooms 250–280F with shower/wc – most have been refurbished. It's ideal for cross-country skiers, since the trails are just nearby, or for mountain bikers. Menus, 95–130F, list delicious local dishes: stuffed breast of veal with walnuts, house *caillettes*, frog's legs in Diois wine sauce, steak with morels, Bleu du Vercors cheese croquettes, and iced soufflé with Chartreuse. 10% discount on the room rate in low season.

⚐ ≜ HÔTEL LE DAUPHIN***

220 av. du Général-de-Gaulle; opposite the tourist office.
☎ 04.76.95.95.25 ➡ 04.76.95.56.33
ℯ hoteldau@aol.com
TV. Car park.

This is a nice hotel with a homely atmosphere set a little back from the square. The whole place has been refurbished. The *patronne* makes a real fuss of her guests who are of all ages. The rooms are all quiet, and some have a view of the pine trees. Doubles 350–380F. Arrangements can be made for half board with the restaurant which is separate from the hotel. 10% discount for two nights or more.

⚐ ❙●❙ MALATERRE

Lieu-dit Malaterre; from Villars, take the D215C, shortly

after Bois-Barbu turn onto the forest road signposted to Malaterre.
☎ 04.76.95.94.34
Open daily noon–6pm July–Aug and Dec–March; Fri evening July–Aug; Sun Sept–Oct and April–June.
Closed Feb, March and Nov. **Car park**.

This is an excellent restaurant in an old wooden house in the forest. The building, once the home of a forester, dates from the 1900s; there's no electricity, and water is brought up by tanker. Lydia and Bernard, who run a farm nearby, decided to revive this place by providing good food and drink for cross-country skiers and walkers. There's a fantastic variety of foresters' implements ornamenting the walls, and the atmosphere is genuinely warm. When the weather's fine it's wonderful to sit out on the terrace, and when it's cold you can warm your hands around a bowl of good vegetable soup and dunk a hunk of home-made bread that's been baked in the wood-fired oven. Menus, 60–100F, list genuine regional cuisine that relies on fresh produce from the farm – try the Vercors platter, Royans ravioli, *caillette*, blue Vercors cheese, mushroom omelette, *charcuterie*, *gratiné* of ravioli with cream, or fillet of smoked trout. And leave space for pudding – there's home-made spice cake with honey, upside-down apple tart and *tarte du chef*. At tea time they offer delicious ice creams. To drink, you can choose between the local *rataplane*, wine sold by the litre jug at 60F, cider, or local apple juice. On summer Friday evenings, your hosts recount the legends of the Vercors around the fire. Free *digestif*.

CORRENÇON-EN-VERCORS 38250 (5.5KM S)

🏠 |●| HÔTEL LES CLARINES**
Centre.
☎ 04.76.95.81.81 ➡ 04.76.95.84.98
Closed Tues except school holidays, 15 April–15 May and 15 Oct–15 Dec. **Swimming pool. TV. Car park**.

This family hotel has been going since the 1950s, and is showing signs of wear and tear, but the atmosphere is still great. There's a pretty good choice when it comes to the food. *À la carte* you can get dishes like spiced duck breast with honey, salmon turnover and prawns, and rabbit *provençale*. Menus 110–185F. There's a beautiful terrace and swimming pool in pleasant surroundings. Very comfortable rooms go for 300F or 480F.

BALME-DE-RENCUREL (LA) 38680 (12KM W)

⚂|●| CAFÉ-RESTAURANT DE LA BOURNE (CHEZ CAROLINE)

How to get there: it's at the D531-D35 crossroads.
☎ 04.76.38.97.03

A classic little village restaurant that hasn't changed in centuries, and has a stalwart clientele of regulars. There's a very substantial menu at 68F, and others 95–155F. Wonderful family dishes include *raviolis de Royans*, frogs' legs with cream, chicken with crayfish and a wonderfully aromatic beef *daube*. They plonk a litre of red on the table. Free apéritif.

VILLARS-LES-DOMBES 01330

|●| AUBERGE LES BICHONNIÈRES**
Ambérieux-en-Dombes; take the D904
☎ 04.74.00.82.07 ➡ 04.74.00.89.61
Closed Mon and Tues lunchtimes in season, Sun evening and Mon Oct–June, and Christmas–New Year.

As the rooms look out onto a courtyard full of trees and flowers, you're guaranteed a bit of peace and quiet here – and as a bonus, you'll be woken by birdsong. Doubles cost 320F with shower/wc; the decor is tasteful, with furniture that comes from the region. When the weather's nice, you can dine on the patio – the menus, 98–185F, list tempting dishes such as *cassolette* of frogs' legs with parsley and duck *foie gras* with walnuts. The welcome could be a tad warmer.

|●| RESTAURANT L'ÉCU DE FRANCE
rue du Commerce (Centre); it's on the main street, near to the church.
☎ 04.74.98.01.79 ➡ 04.74.98.27.77
Closed Tues evening, Wed and Jan.

An affordable place to eat in this somewhat touristy town. The rustic dining room offers regional specialities including frogs' legs, of course, chicken in cream sauce and duck breast. Menus 90–215F. Low-key but friendly welcome.

BOULIGNEUX 01130 (4KM NW)

|●| LE THOU
How to get there: take the D2 Chatillon-sur-Chalaronne road.
☎ 04.74.98.15.25
Closed Mon and Tues. **Garden**.

A pleasant restaurant that appeals to everyone. The dining-room walls are hung with a variety of pictures, and there's a mature garden with a terrace. The chef's speciality is carp served in many delicious guises: salad of warm carp with mustard, *goujons* of carp, and *profiteroles* of carp mousse. The cheeses and the desserts are perfect, and the wine list is splendid. Menus from 175F, or around 300F *à la carte*.

ARS-SUR-FORMANS   01480 (19KM W)

🎿 🏠 |●| HÔTEL-RESTAURANT LA BONNE ÉTOILE

It's on the D904.
☎ 04.74.00.77.38 ➡ 04.74.08.10.10
Closed Mon evening, Tues and Jan.

The village is where the relics of Saint Curé are to be found and it attracts many pilgrims. The Pope went there and had a meal in the restaurant. The plate he used has become a relic, too, and is hung up outside the door. This is a friendly, welcoming establishment and the clean rooms smell of the countryside. Doubles 220F with shower/wc. The owner collects all sorts of nick-nacks to ornament her establishment – lots of dolls and coffee pots in particular. Simple, unpretentious dishes that won't make you swoon nor leave you hungry. Menus 110–155F. 10% discount on the room rate.

VILLEFRANCHE-SUR-SAÔNE   69400

|●| LE JULIENAS

236 rue d'Anse; it's in the main street, near the edge of town going in the direction of Lyons.
☎ 04.74.09.16.55
Closed Sat lunchtime and Sun, 1–20 Aug and Christmas to New Year's Day.

A delightful, classic dining room with old wood panelling, mirrors, paintings on the walls and classical music playig quietly in the background. It has a rather sad feel to it but it's brightened up by the smile and kindness of the radiant hostess. Classical cuisine offering authentic, traditional dishes: marinated salmon, snails, veal *grenadin* with green peppercorns, Charolais steak with shallots, or zander with mustard sauce. Dish of the day 50F, menus 85F (not Sat evening), 120F and 160F. Best to book.

LIERGUES   69400 (5KM SW)

🎿|●| AUBERGE DE LIERGUES

Centre; take the D35 in the direction of Tarare.
☎ and ➡ 04.74.68.07.02
Closed Tues evening, Wed and 10–30 Aug.

The welcome you get here makes a nice change. The owner likes to have a good laugh and will practically insist on your having a glass of Beaujolais – hard to resist in a place like this, where there are more local wine-growers about than tourists. There's a pair of *formules* at lunchtime for 58F and 68F, and three menus 90–125F. There are lots of specialities from Lyon, and game in season. Eat in the bistro with its wooden tables rather than in the dining room. Free apéritif.

VAUX-EN-BEAUJOLAIS   69460 (17KM NW)

🎿 🏠 |●| AUBERGE DE CLOCHEMERLE**

rue Gabriel-Chevallier; take the D43 in the direction of Odenas, and at Saint-Étienne-des-Oullières, turn left in the direction of Vaux.
☎ 04.74.03.20.16 ➡ 04.74.03.28.48
Closed Tues evening and Wed in summer, Tues and Wed in winter, and early Jan. **TV. Disabled access.**

This village, which inspired Gabriel Chevallier's novel *Clochemerle*, is the only one in France where people come from far and wide to see the street urinal. The restaurant serves excellent food which is in evidence on all the menus, 100–330F, and the prices are justified. As time goes on, the cuisine is favouring more and more gourmet dishes yet still offers good value for money. Lovely shaded terrace for the summer. All the rooms have been freshly refurbished though they have kept their charm because of the period furniture. Doubles 270–320F with shower or bath. 10% discount on the room rate.

VIVIERS   07220

|●| RESTAURANT DE L'HORLOGE

Faubourg le Cire; it's on the RN86.
☎ 04.75.52.62.43
Closed Sun evening and Mon.

When you see the neon signs, it's hard to believe what awaits inside. The dining room is vast and decorated by huge murals from the 19th century, painted by a passing artist. The robust, tasty cooking is prepared using fresh market produce. You eat well and cheaply: dish of the day 40F, and three menus 58F (a steal), and up to 105F.

VOIRON   38500

|●| RESTAURANT LE BOIS JOLI

la Tivollière; take the Chambéry road for about 2km, and turn left.
☎ 04.76.05.22.25 ➡ 04.76.66.10.79
Closed Sun evening and 1–22 Jan. **Disabled access. Car park.**

Service noon–2pm and 7–9pm (10pm in summer). The tasty, hearty cooking ranges from quails with morels to liver gâteau, kidneys in Madiera sauce, kid with morels and chicken with crayfish. There is a lovely veranda where you can sit and relax while you survey the countryside. Weekday lunch menu 58F, then others 75–130F.

CHARAVINES-LES-BAINS 38850 (13KM NW)

⌂ |●| HÔTEL-RESTAURANT BEAU RIVAGE**

15 rue Principale (West); it's on the D50 by the lake.
☎ 04.76.06.61.08 ➡ 04.76.06.66.58
Closed Sun evening, Mon out of season, and 20 Dec–1 Feb. **TV. Car park.**

A classic, family lakeside hotel. In winter you get a panoramic view from the dining room, and in summer a magnificent view of the lake from the terrace. The rooms are very pleasant and the hearty, no-frills food is good value. Menus 88F (not Sun), with others 125–220F. Specialities include deep-fried perch fry, sea bass *bonne femme*, *foie gras*, pork fillets with chanterelles and lots of freshwater fish. Doubles 210F with shower/wc and 290F with bath. Free access to the beach.

MONTFERRAT 38620 (13KM N)

|●| AUBERGE FÉFETTE

Le Vernay (North); follow the lake road from Montfrerat.
☎ 04.76.32.40.46
Closed Mon evening, Tues, 15–30 April and 15–30 Oct. **Car park**.

A nice little house way out in the countryside up from the lake. The chef cooks lots of dishes from her native southwest, while her unruffled husband runs the dining room. Good menus, 125–165F, with dishes that

change with the seasons: *papillote* of *foie gras* with raspberries, scallop salad with pan-fried girolles, roast monkfish with sea salt, potted lamb with apricots, *fricassée* of lobster in Banyuls wine, and so on. Dine on the terrace in good weather. Best to book.

VONNAS 01540

|●| L'ANCIENNE AUBERGE

pl. du Marché.
☎ 04.74.50.90.50 ➡ 04.74.50.08.80
Closed Jan.

Service until 2.30pm, then until 10pm. Because of its associations with the famous chef, Vonnas is known as Blanc-city. This old family inn, where, apparently, Georges Blanc first developed his passion for cooking, stands opposite a romantic little wooden bridge over the Veyle. It dates back to 1872, but has been respectfully restored so it looks virtually unchanged. You can still see a beautifully written inscription painted on the façade, from the days when it was *Café-Restaurant Blanc Aîné*. Georges may not be in the kitchen any more, but he's supervises the smooth running of the house, which is now the responsibility of Isabelle Blanc. The recipes and produce used remain true to the region: country *terrine*, sautéed frog's legs, chicken livers with *foie gras*, eggs and cream, and *poulet de Bresse* cooked to grandmother Blanc's recipe. And the prices are reasonable; the cheapest menu, served on weekdays only, still costs only 98F, and the others, 170–230F, are simply amazing. Charming welcome and friendly service.

Index

A

M

W

X

Y

Z

Stay in touch with us!

ROUGHNEWS is Rough Guides' free newsletter. In three issues a year we give you news, travel issues, music reviews, readers' letters and the latest dispatches from authors on the road.

I would like to receive ROUGHNEWS: please put me on your free mailing list

NAME ....

ADDRESS ....

Please clip or photocopy and send to: Rough Guides, 62–70 Shorts Gardens, London WC2H 9AH, England or Rough Guides, 375 Hudson Street, New York, NY 10014, USA.

ROUGH GUIDES: Travel

Alaska
Amsterdam
Andalucia
Argentina
Australia
Austria

Bali & Lombok
Barcelona
Belgium &
 Luxembourg
Belize
Berlin
Brazil
Britain
Brittany &
 Normandy
Bulgaria
California
Canada
Central America
Chile
China
Corsica
Costa Rica
Crete
Croatia
Cuba
Cyprus
Czech & Slovak
 Republics

Dodecanese &
 the East Aegean
Devon &
 Cornwall
Dominican
 Republic
Dordogne & the
 Lot
Ecuador
Egypt
England
Europe
Florida
France
French Hotels &
 Restaurants
 1999
Germany
Goa
Greece
Greek Islands
Guatemala
Hawaii
Holland
Hong Kong &
 Macau
Hungary

Iceland
India
Indonesia
Ionian Islands
Ireland

Israel & the
 Palestinian
 Territories
Italy
Jamaica
Japan
Jordan
Kenya
Lake District
Languedoc &
 Roussillon
Laos
London
Los Angeles
Malaysia,
 Singapore &
 Brunei
Mallorca &
 Menorca
Maya World
Mexico
Morocco
Moscow
Nepal
New England
New York
New Zealand
Norway
Pacific
 Northwest
Paris
Peru
Poland
Portugal
Prague
Provence & the
 Côte d'Azur
The Pyrenees
Romania
St Petersburg
San Francisco

Sardinia
Scandinavia
Scotland
Scottish
 highlands and
 Islands
Sicily
Singapore
South Africa
South India
Southeast Asia
Southwest USA
Spain
Sweden
Switzerland
Syria

Thailand
Trinidad &
 Tobago
Tunisia
Turkey
Tuscany &
 Umbria
USA
Venice
Vienna
Vietnam
Wales
Washington DC
West Africa
Zimbabwe &
 Botswana

AVAILABLE AT ALL GOOD BOOKSHOPS

ROUGH GUIDES: Mini Guides, Travel Specials and Phrasebooks

MINI GUIDES

Antigua
Bangkok
Barbados
Beijing
Big Island of Hawaii
Boston
Brussels
Budapest
Cape Town
Copenhagen
Dublin
Edinburgh

Florence
Honolulu
Ibiza & Formentera
Jerusalem
Las Vegas
Lisbon
London Restaurants
Madeira
Madrid
Malta & Gozo
Maui
Melbourne
Menorca

Montreal
New Orleans

Paris
Rome
Seattle
St Lucia
Sydney
Tenerife
Tokyo
Toronto
Vancouver

TRAVEL SPECIALS

First-Time Asia
First-Time Europe
Women Travel

PHRASEBOOKS

Czech
Dutch
Egyptian Arabic
European
French
German
Greek

Hindi & Urdu
Hungarian
Indonesian
Italian
Japanese
Mandarin
  Chinese
Mexican
  Spanish
Polish
Portuguese
Russian
Spanish
Swahili
Thai
Turkish
Vietnamese

AVAILABLE AT ALL GOOD BOOKSHOPS

ROUGH GUIDES:
Reference and Music CDs

REFERENCE

Blues:
  100 Essential CDs
Classical Music
Classical:
  100 Essential CDs
Country Music
Country:
  100 Essential CDs
Drum'n'bass
House Music
Hip Hop
Irish Music
Jazz

Music USA
Opera
Opera:
  100 Essential CDs
Reggae
Reggae:
  100 Essential CDs
Rock
Rock:
  100 Essential CDs

Soul:
  100 Essential CDs
Techno
World Music

World Music:
  100 Essential CDs
English Football
European Football
Internet
Money Online
Shopping Online
Travel Health

ROUGH GUIDE MUSIC CDs

Music of the Andes
Australian Aboriginal
Bluegrass
Brazilian Music
Cajun & Zydeco
Music of Cape Verde
Classic Jazz
Music of
  Colombia
Cuban Music
Eastern Europe

Music of Egypt
English Roots Music
Flamenco
Music of Greece
Hip Hop
India & Pakistan
Irish Music
Music of Jamaica
Music of Japan
Kenya & Tanzania
Marrabenta
  Mozambique
Native American
North African
Music of Portugal
Reggae
Salsa
Samba
Scottish Music
South African Music
Music of Spain
Sufi Music
Tango

Tex-Mex
West African Music
World Music
World Music Vol 2
Music of Zimbabwe

Will you have enough stories to tell your grandchildren?

©2000 Yahoo! Inc.

Yahoo! Travel